P9-DGW-053

Wine

André Dominé

Wine

Photographs
Armin Faber
Thomas Pothmann

Authors
Eckhard Supp
David Schwarzwälder
Anthony Rose
Dunja Ulbricht
Hélène Jaeger
Ulrich Sautter
Joachim Krieger
Patrick Fiévez
Sabine Rumrich
Wolfgang Faßbender
Steffen Maus
Beate Berkelmann-Löhnertz
Michael Ben-Joseph
Klaus Feiten
Hartwig Holst

KÖNEMANN

Endpaper:
Detail from a Roman mosaic
Vine in a crater
Archeological Museum, El Djem, Tunisia
© A.K.G./Photo: Erich Lessing

Frontispiece:
Juan de Espinosa, *Still life with grapes,*
Oil on canvas, 83 × 62 cm,
Musée du Louvre, Paris
© A.K.G., Berlin/Photo: Gilles Mermet

**Notes on abbreviations used in the entries on
Select Producers**

→ = Specially recommended
*–**** = Grading system for wines

The standard unit of volume in this book is the U.S. gallon
which is the equivalent of 128 fl. oz.

© 2004 KÖNEMANN*, an imprint of Tandem Verlag GmbH, Königswinter

Creative and Publishing Director: Peter Feierabend
Art Direction: Sabine Vonderstein
Project Management: Sabine Baumgartner
Editorial Team: Uta Büxel, Kordula Esser, Ulla Wöhrle
Specialist Advisor: Dr. Christa Hanten
Indexes: Christoph Eiden
Cartography: Studio für Landkartentechnik, Detlef Maiwald

Original Title: Wein

For the English edition:
Translation from German: Paul Aston, Helen Atkins, Peter Barton, Anthea Bell, Susan Cox, Richard Elliott, Harriet Horsfield,
Susan James, Eithne McCarthy, Michele McMeekin, Martin Pearce, Michael Scuffil, Christine Smith, and Anthony Vivis in asso-
ciation with Cambridge Publishing Management, Cambridge, U.K.
Editorial Team: Catherine Hurley, Annie Jackson, and Emma Johnson-Gilbert in association with Cambridge Publishing Management
Typesetting: Sheila Kirby for Cambridge Publishing Management
Project Management: Jackie Dobbyne and Sheila Hardie for Cambridge Publishing Management
Project Coordinator: Nadja Bremse-Koob

For the new, updated edition:
Translation from German: Susan James, Eileen Martin in association with Cambridge Publishing Management
Proofreading: Tammi Reichel for A-P-E International; Alison Kelt and Kevin Parnell for Cambridge Publishing Management
Typesetting: Paul Queripel for Cambridge Publishing Management
Project Management: Karen Beaulah and Mine Ali for Cambridge Publishing Management

*KÖNEMANN is a registered trademark of Tandem Verlag GmbH

Printed in Germany

ISBN 3-8331-1032-5

10 9 8 7 6 5 4 3 2
X IX VIII VII VI V IV III II I

CONTENTS

André Dominé, Eckhard Supp, Dunja Ulbricht

A HISTORY OF
ENJOYING WINE

THE MANY PLEASURES OF WINE

As increasing numbers of people in an ever-growing number of countries are becoming interested in wine, the drink has taken on a new role. Sharing a bottle with friends, colleagues or relatives is no longer simply a pleasant way of creating a congenial and relaxed atmosphere: wine itself is becoming a source of encounters with new people and new experiences.

Today, wine is part of enjoying life – for women and men, and all classes of society.

The times when good wine was the preserve of a social elite are, thankfully, well and truly past. Nowadays, all wines are accessible to everyone, at least in principle, as even the most exclusive vintages can be sampled by anyone who is so inclined, either at one of the increasingly common tasting events, in one of the many tasting clubs that have been set up, or by buying a bottle with like-minded friends to discover together what the quality and character of a famous wine is all about.

Wine—both a cult and a cultural drink—has also become more egalitarian in that never before in its history has such a huge, high-quality range been available to so many people. The sheer number of different wines from which to choose offers consumers an interesting point for comparison. A semi-luxury item, wine differs from all other agricultural products in that its infinite varieties far outnumber even those of cheese.

Whether you simply follow your nose or are guided by information and advice received, you may well find that you have questions about wine and would like to know more. This book deals in detail with all aspects of the subject, including the best way to drink a particular bottle, its potential for cellaring, grape varieties and vineyards, harvesting and fermentation, methods of production and maturation, and the origins of wine, as well as individual countries and regions.

Knowing what you are drinking enhances the pleasure, and every wine has its own story. With simple table wines, this is usually limited to the grape variety and region of origin. In the case of a great wine, however, it leads us to a specific vineyard and a tradition that often will have been followed for generations. With manually produced wines from regions whose potential has only been demonstrated in recent years or decades, the story may lie with the wine producer personally. Wine is increasingly cited as a reason for visiting a specific location, be it a traditional vine-growing area with historic estates or a region that is only just beginning to achieve recognition, giving rise to personal encounters with other peoples, landscapes, and cultures.

THE NEW AGE OF WINE

The euphoria that has gripped the world of wine is the result of developments that began in the 1950s. Until then, wine, whether a glorious

The strictest hygiene in the winery is essential for the development of wine as a popular consumer product.

Many wine producers in the famous village of Hautvillers near Épernay adorn their houses with signs reflecting an aspect of their work.

yields and concentrating on the optimal ripeness of the grape—an endeavor in which modern technology would play only an incidental role. Aided by favorable economic conditions, this brought about a fundamental change in the entire world of wine. In the classic wine-producing regions it was most readily evident in completely renovated and redesigned cellars, whereas in the countries of the New World, it led to a rise in new estates and cellars being established. This dynamism continued during the 1980s and 1990s. As a result, increasingly convincing wines gradually began to appear on the market, where they were greeted ever more enthusiastically by the consumer. Not only did demand for top-quality wines rise, but the quality of the simpler wines also continued to improve. A new genre of publishing sprang up, providing an ever-growing number of interested consumers with increasingly detailed information.

In a parallel development, the trend spread to what had been less well known or little recognized winemaking countries and regions, whose native growers or foreign investors were keen to show that great wines could be produced there.

Even though the results are frequently as disappointing as ever, more and more of today's wines are being tailored to the general market, industrially produced using all the technological, enological and economic means available. This often gives rise to perfectly pleasant bulk-productions, which are enhanced using all sorts of tricks, both permitted and otherwise. Here we see the dividing line running through the world of wine, although the boundary is somewhat fluid: on one side are the industrially produced wines, and on the other those produced by manual methods which, increasingly, are based on an awareness of environmental issues. Only the latter guarantee the diversity and richness of enjoyment and experience that an interest in wine has to offer. It is to these wines and their producers, and to the wine lovers that seek them out, that this book is dedicated.

vintage or a crude, low-quality variety, was seen simply as an intoxicant or as one more part of the diet, depending on social circumstance.

The wine producers' situation became particularly desperate from the end of the 19th century to the middle of the 20th century. A series of infections, culminating in the catastrophic phylloxera epidemic, decimated almost every vineyard. Then, just when the replanted vines were producing their first good yields, economic crises and war brought about a serious slump in sales. Against such a background, the desire for a secure income and an effective means of protection against pests and diseases was entirely understandable. Indeed, these became the recurring themes of agriculture in general after 1945, and are scarcely less influential today. Once the use of artificial fertilizers, chemical agents and productive clones had enabled growers to achieve the necessary yields, attention turned primarily to the cellars where the wine was produced, and undoubted progress was made in terms of hygiene and temperature control.

Nevertheless, the wines from the famous estates and younger wines from a select few producers who followed their own tradition and philosophy continued to serve as a yardstick. In the 1970s, however, a new way of thinking began to gain acceptance, recognizing that high quality could only be achieved by reducing

WINE AND HEALTH

Wine is made up of more than a thousand substances, not all of which have been analyzed in detail. The majority of these components, such as vitamins and minerals, come from the grapes, the raw material of wine, while others, like ethanol and glycerin, are products of the winemaking process. Others still, such as sugar and vitamin C, are either partially or completely removed.

The most significant constituent of wine, 75–90 percent, is water. The 15 percent variance is accounted for by the amounts of tannic acid, organic acids, mineral salts and pectins which form the wine's extract, and which differ from wine to wine.

The second largest constituent of wine is ethyl alcohol. Alcohol content also varies according to the type of wine, and is given on the label as a percentage by volume (% vol). This information is compulsory and therefore not an indication of quality. A wine with an alcohol content of 11% vol can be light and very pleasant, while another with 13% vol can

Wine is as much a part of our diet as bread and cheese. Moreover, it has certain qualities that have a positive effect on health, provided it is consumed in moderation.

go straight to your head. The decisive factor is always the structure of the wine and the balance of its various components, such as acids, residual sugar, alcohol, tannins, and color compounds. The other constituents are present in much smaller quantities. The sugar content of dry wines is generally less than 0.25 ounces per gallon (2 grams per liter), while in a botrytized sweet wine it can reach almost 67 ounces per gallon (500 grams per liter).

Over the centuries, wine came to be seen not just as a luxury item, but a medicine as well. For a long time it was also a basic foodstuff, usually mixed with water to quench thirst. Many publications described wine as the "most hygienic drink," and it was indeed safer to drink diluted wine than water alone.

The early 20th century was very much the era of the temperance movement, which campaigned against the direct and indirect consequences of alcohol consumption. Pressure from these groups led to prohibition, most famously in the U.S.A. The sale of alcohol remains strictly regulated in North America and Scandinavia to

The proportion of phenolics in each part of the grape

Stalk · Seed · Flesh · Skin

When eating grapes both the fruit and its skin should be consumed to maximize the intake of phenolics. Looking at the proportions contained in the individual parts of the grape, it is easy to see why red wine is higher in phenolics than white. During the production of red wine, more specifically during fermentation of the must, skins and pulp are in contact with the grape juice, and it is in this phase that the phenolics bond with the must. With white wines, however, pressing takes place more quickly and skin contact time is shorter.

Regular, moderate consumption

"Not too much and not too little" should be your motto if you wish to benefit from the positive effects wine can have on health. Moderate consumption is considered to be two to four glasses of wine a day, depending on an individual's body weight, and there is a definite difference between the sexes. After drinking the same amount of alcohol, a woman weighing 124 pounds (55 kg) will have a higher concentration of alcohol in her blood than a man weighing 180 pounds (80 kg). Regular intake is also very important: the recommended level of two to four glasses a day is not intended to be averaged out across a number of days. In other words, drinking no alcohol at all during the week and then consuming large quantities at the weekend is not advisable if you want to enjoy the health benefits of wine. In addition, wine should be drunk with food and not on an empty stomach.

this day, and labels on bottles sold in the U.S.A. must include a warning about the possible damage to health. In the 1990s, attention was increasingly drawn to the positive effects of moderate alcohol consumption, without glossing over the dangers of excessive drinking. Indeed, wine is a traditional and daily accompaniment to meals in Mediterranean countries. The Saturday night "binge," by contrast, tends to involve beer and spirits.

The revisionist argument was first put forward by the French scientist Serge Renaud in a *60 Minutes* program for the American C.B.S. channel entitled *The French Paradox*. The program presented the results of a worldwide epidemiological study which had shown that, although the French ate as much fat as Americans, the number of deaths from coronary heart disease in France was 2.5 times lower than in the U.S.A. The study also indicated that the higher a country's wine consumption, the lower its mortality rate due to heart disease. Vascular disease is comparatively rare in France, Portugal, and Italy, but is encountered most frequently in the Scandinavian countries and the U.K. Alcohol helps blood flow more easily around the body, and a regular intake of wine reduces the level of harmful cholesterol (low-density lipoprotein or L.D.L.) in the blood. The health benefits of wine are not solely due to alcohol, however. Scientific studies have shown that not all alcoholic drinks have the same positive effects, and so other constituents of wine, such as the phenolics, must also be taken into account. These compounds have a protective effect on capillaries and on the collagen in the walls of blood vessels. They hinder the aggregation of platelets and thus prevent the formation of clots. Phenolics also have powerful antioxidant properties, which inhibit degradation of the cell walls both in coronary arteries and in the brain. In addition to its protective effects with regard to heart disease, therefore, wine is also thought to be beneficial in the treatment of cancer and Alzheimer's disease.

Nevertheless, wine alone is not responsible for the results of the studies. A dietary comparison of the Mediterranean and the U.S.A. shows that the peoples of southern Europe eat more fresh fruit and vegetables, less red meat, more cheese and less full-cream milk, more olive oil, but less butter and bacon fat. Mediterranean cuisine involves exactly the kind of diet that today's experts recommend.

It would appear, therefore, that enjoying wine regularly, responsibly, and in moderation can contribute to a long and healthy life.

Mineral content (in g/l)

	Must	Wine
Potassium	1–2.50	0.7–1.50
Calcium	0.04–0.25	0.01–0.20
Magnesium	0.05–0.20	0.05–0.20
Sodium	0.002–0.25	0.002–0.25
Iron	0.002–0.005	0.002–0.02
Phosphorus	0.08–0.50	0.03–0.90
Manganese	0–0.05	0–0.05

Some of the potassium and calcium is lost because it is precipitated along with the tartaric acid, forming crystals which are sometimes seen on the part of the cork which comes into contact with the wine.

Vitamin content (in mg/l)

	Must	Wine
Ascorbic acid (Vitamin C)	38.0–95.0	0
Thiamin (Vitamin B1)	0.10–0.50	0.04–0.05
Riboflavin (Vitamin B2)	0.003–0.08	0.008–0.30
Pantothenic acid (Vitamin B5)	0.5–1.00	0.4–1.20
Pyridoxine (Vitamin B6)	0.3–0.50	0.2–0.50

Wine contains minute amounts of vitamins. Vitamin C, for example, is present in the must, but not in wine. It should also be noted that the effects of certain vitamins appear to be neutralized if sulfites are present in the wine, even in very small quantities.

Phenolics in g/l

	Must	Wine
Anthocyanins	0.004–0.90	0–0.50
Flavones	Trace amounts	0–0.05
Tannins	0.1–1.50	0.1–5.00

Anthocyanins are red and blue pigments found in the skins of dark grape varieties. Flavones are yellow pigments and there are small amounts in all pale and dark skinned grape varieties. Tannin is present in various forms, depending on whether it is in the skin, the flesh, or the stalk of the grape. Moreover, the tannic compounds in a wine can increase while it is being aged in barrels.

A Long History: Wine in Antiquity

Egyptians began to extract the precious grape juice using pressing methods that remained unchanged for thousands of years.

From Egypt to Greece

The Nile Delta also witnessed the first flowering of the wine trade. Long caravans and fast ships brought their liquid cargo to the most important trading centers of the Mediterranean. There is a (not uncommon) view among historians that the foundations of our modern economy—its money, contracts, payment systems, courts, accounting procedures and commercial professions, even our way of counting and measuring time—were developed as a result of the wine trade from Pharaonic Egypt.

Ancient Greece was the next stage in the vine's conquest of the ancient world. The Minoans on Crete had close cultural and economic ties with the Egyptians, and probably forged the first link between Egypt and Greece. It is also possible, however, that viticultural knowledge reached Greece via Asia Minor or Thrace. Whatever the case, we know that wine became an important part of Greek culture in the second half of the 2nd millennium BC. Vines were planted throughout ancient Greece, and the islands of the Aegean were famous for the resulting produce both within the country and beyond. Chios, the Bordeaux of the ancient

The development of viticulture is inextricably linked with the birth of European civilization and culture, particularly in the Mediterranean region. It is likely that nomadic peoples were fermenting wild grapes and berries into wine as early as 6,000–7,000 years ago. With the transition to a settled existence, grapevines, along with olives and figs, became the first wild fruits to be cultivated by man. Although the existence of vinifera plantations can be conclusively proved only from the 4th millennium BC in Egypt and Mesopotamia and from around 2500 BC in the Aegean, there are indications that there were rudimentary vineyards in the Near East as early as the 6th millennium BC. The oldest known tools and vessels which may have been used for producing wine were made in the 5th and 6th millennia BC in the region north of the Caucasus (present-day Georgia and Armenia), and in the 4th millennium BC in Persia.

The origin of the word "wine" is not absolutely clear. Its derivation can be traced back to the Latin *vinum*, which itself comes from the Greek *oinos* or *woinos*, but that is the extent of linguistic evidence. What is certain, however, is that the cradle of viticulture was the eastern Mediterranean or the Caucasus, and that it first began to flourish in Pharaonic Egypt. Under the Pharaohs, knowledge of viticulture and wine-making was meticulously expanded, and the

Egyptian mural from the tomb of Nakht at Thebes. 15th century BC.

Ancient Egyptian depictions of grapes and viticulture reveal the importance of wine during the age of the Pharaohs. Relief fragment, Amarna period, about 1350 BC (found at Hermopolis)

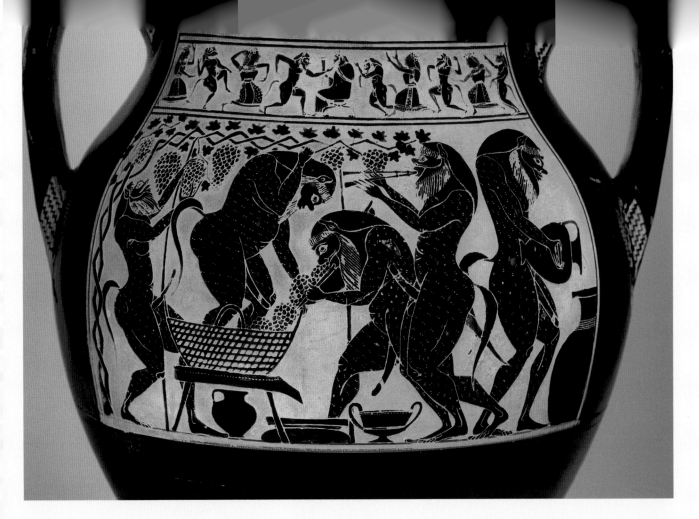

world, sent exports as far as Egypt and present-day Russia, and the wines of Thasos, Lesbos, and Rhodes also enjoyed a good reputation. Wines from Lesbos were matured under a thin layer of FLOR YEAST, in a similar fashion to sherry, but in other parts of the country it was usual to improve the smell and taste of wine with spices, honey, resin, and other fragrant substances. The Greek philosopher and scientist Theophrastus (4th century BC) recognized the important interrelation between grape variety, mesoclimate, and soil quality, and even the Romans, centuries later, were aware that Greek grape varieties were synonymous with low yields and thus higher quality wines.

Wine was so important to the Greeks that they declared it a divine gift: Dionysus, or Bakchos (the Roman Bacchus), a popular deity from Asia Minor, was supposed to have created the vine and used his divine power to make wine, milk, and honey flow from the ground. It was said that he freed man from his day-to-day worries with this lush vegetation—thanks in no small part to the intoxicating effects of wine.

THE EARLY WINE TRADE SHAPES THE ECONOMY

Following their decisive conquest of territories throughout the Mediterranean region during the first half of the 1st millennium BC, the Greeks

Amphora by the Amasis painter from Athens. Around 530 BC. Antiquities collection of the University of Würzburg Martin von Wagner Museum.

introduced viticulture to their new colonies: Sicily, southern Italy and the south of France saw the development of new European vines. Southern Italy rose to the status of OINOTRIA or "wine land" for the Greeks, a designation that became *Enotria* under the Romans, who planted vines throughout Italy as early as the 3rd century BC. The Romans not only turned viticulture into a fully developed branch of trade managed according to economic criteria, but also brought it to central Europe.

The most important center of the wine trade in Italy had long been Pompeii, from where wines were exported even to the far-off Bordeaux region. When the city was destroyed by the volcanic eruption of 79 BC, the Romans made great efforts to develop viticulture in all parts of the Empire, to such an extent that in the Roman heartland, modern day Lazio, almost all cultivable land was stocked with vines. This prompted the Emperor Domitian to forbid the planting of any further vineyards—an edict that remained in force for almost two hundred years.

From the Roman Wine Empire to Plutocratic Florence

Marcus Aurelius Probus was the first to lift Domitian's ban in order to ensure his troops in the northern and eastern provinces were supplied with wine. He ordered intensive viticulture along the Mosel and the Danube, paving the way for the modern vine-growing regions of Germany and Austria. Trier and Bordeaux, already important export centers for the Empire's more northerly colonies, now became centers of viticulture in their own right, which made the task of supplying Imperial outposts with wine significantly easier, both in financial and logistical terms.

In Spain, the south of France, and along the Rhône, the Romans were able to build on the work already done by the Phocaeans, a Greek people who founded the city of Marseille (Massilia). As they consolidated their Empire, repelling or subjugating Gauls, Celts, and Teutons, the Romans planted large areas with vines almost everywhere they went. They imported new varieties of vine or improved what was already in place, spreading their knowledge of winemaking and its associated paraphernalia, such as the press, the amphora, and even the wooden barrel. However, neither the wines from Marseille, nor the majority of

Left
Fresco from Herculaneum depicting a banquet. National Museum, Naples

Right
This fresco of Bacchus, covered with grapes, standing in front of Vesuvius, and also showing a snake in front of an altar, is from the House of the Centenary in Pompeii, 1st century AD (in the National Museum in Naples).

the Spanish wines, had a particularly good reputation, and only Rhône wines, plus a few from Andalusia and other provinces of the Iberian peninsula, were traded in Rome, the center of power.

Toward the end of the Roman era, the Wachau, Mosel Valley, Rheingau, Pfalz, Burgundy, Bordeaux (although not the present-day Gironde area, but rather the regions lying further inland, such as Bergerac), Rhône Valley, and La Rioja wine regions all became centers of the European wine industry, and largely remain so today. However, this coincided with the "migration of the peoples," a troubled period of social and military upheaval in most of the colonies during which the decadent pleasures of the declining Roman Empire no longer seemed to have their place.

The disintegration of Roman power brought stagnation to almost all of Europe's wine-producing regions. Viticulture, too, survived some difficult times of its own: the long Arab rule in Spain, which proved surprisingly tolerant regarding the ban on alcohol that is one of the most important tenets of the Islamic faith; and the sacking and pillaging of Bordeaux in 870, the climax of a series of conquests by Gascons, Saracens, Ostrogoths, Visigoths, and eventually even Vikings. Nevertheless, it was not until the 7th and 8th centuries, in the north—in Germany, and above all France—that the continent really began to see an upturn in the wine trade. In the south—Italy and Spain—it took a little longer.

Decay and High Finance

The consequences of the fall of the Roman Empire were demonstrated most dramatically in Italy itself. The collapse of centralized political control, only gradually replaced by the Catholic Church, created a power vacuum in the country. Time and again, foreign peoples were able to invade: Rome was conquered by the Ostrogoths, the Visigoths, and in 455 by the Vandals, and large areas of the country were devastated and plundered. Moreover, the established economic and social mechanisms lost their status and their role. Although viticulture did not disappear completely from the lives of the Italians, it went from being a flourishing branch of the national economy to a purely subsistence farming activity for people living in rural areas.

Not until the development of the coastal cities of Genoa and Venice, which profited from the Crusades, and the emergence of Florence as

a European capital of finance in the 13th and 14th centuries, did the wine trade began to revive. It was in Florence of this period that some of today's most renowned Italian wine producers first began making a name for themselves, including the Antinoris and the Frescobaldis. These families had both made their fortunes in other fields or in the financial trade between the Vatican and England, but their experience and contacts convinced them that there was money to be made from wine.

Their trade was not primarily concerned with Tuscan wines, however, but rather, and particularly in the case of the Frescobaldis, with the wines from the dynamically evolving French Bordeaux region, which found great favor at the royal court in England.

Even so, viticulture in the financiers' Tuscan homeland was not entirely unaffected. Although it was to be centuries before the Italian wine industry recovered and subsequently surpassed its former glory, wine, both for everyday drinking and for trade, gradually became a more profitable agricultural commodity again, aided by the practice of sharecropping.

Silenus giving drink to two satyrs, with a drunken Dionysius in Ariadne's lap; a detail from a fresco in the Villa dei Misteri in Pompeii, about 50 BC.

THE RISE OF FRANCE

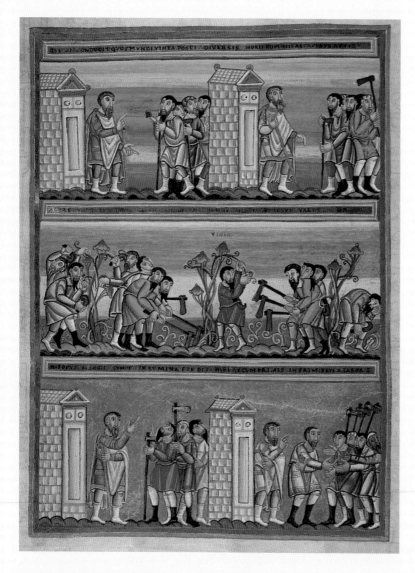

In France, things developed very differently. Following the final disintegration of the Roman Empire, Visigoths, Burgundians, and Franks took possession of the land. The Merovingians, Carolingians, and especially Charlemagne all promoted viticulture, particularly in the Burgundy region, where one of the most famous groups of vineyards in the world, the Grand Cru Corton-Charlemagne, is still named after him.

The most important role in the development of viticulture in Burgundy, however, can be ascribed to the medieval monasteries. Bernard de Fontaines entered the monastery at Cîteaux near Nuits-Saint-Georges in 1113, where he preached a new, ascetic doctrine directed against the extravagances of the Benedictine Abbey at Cluny. His followers in both church and political circles grew quickly in number, and becoming Abbot of Clairvaux enabled him to acquire some land on

This miniature from the 11th-century *Golden Gospels of Echternach* shows workers in a vineyard.

which he planted vines. His successors nurtured the beginnings of wine production in Chablis and the Côte d'Or, and chose Chardonnay and Pinot Noir as the most suitable grape varieties. They also created the basic structure of the hierarchical classification of the region's vineyard plots—a system that is still in use today.

The foundations for the current high status of the Bordeaux region were also laid in the medieval era. Wine became France's most important export during this period at a time when viticulture was still a subsistence farming activity in the other wine-producing nations of Europe, and the trade was generally in cheaper, mass-produced wine.

RED WINE REACHES GERMANY

In Germany, it was Charlemagne who was chiefly responsible for furthering the development of viticulture. From his Palatinate (Pfalz) on the Rhine, so the story goes, he noted that the snow melted early on the most promising Rheingau locations, and so had vines planted there. He issued rules concerning the making of wine, and made sure that only the best grape varieties were chosen. He also established the *Straußwirtschaft* or *Buschenschenke*, a tradition still very much alive in southern Germany and Austria in which premises display a bunch of twigs or broom (*Strauß*) or a bush (*Busch*) outside to signify that homegrown wine is on sale. Charlemagne's vision of the economic importance of vine growing, and the conclusions he drew from this regarding the need for regulation, indicated the way forward for Germany's viticultural development.

Charlemagne may have initiated the revival, but, just as in Burgundy, it was the Benedictine and Cistercian monasteries that furthered the cause and were the actual protagonists in winemaking. In 1136, the Cistercians founded a monastery at Eberbach, in the Rheingau. In the 12th and 13th centuries, this monastery became Europe's largest wine producer, and in its heyday had as many as two hundred trading outlets across the entire continent. The walled Steinberg vineyard, still one of the most famous vineyards in the world, was laid out following the Burgundian model and primarily planted with red grape varieties, which the Cistercians had brought with them from their French homeland. There are solid economic reasons why the

Church and the monasteries devoted themselves so intensively to viticulture. In granting the right to collect tithes (one-tenth of a landowner's annual produce or income), Charlemagne gave the Church the opportunity to sell its wares in the markets of Europe and increase not just its financial resources, but consequently its political and military power as well.

Under the influence of the monasteries, not only the Rheingau, but the whole of Germany became a veritable sea of vines. Between the 12th and the 17th century, 750,000 acres (300,000 ha) were used for viticulture—three times more than today. The wine trade was concentrated in the cities of Cologne and Frankfurt, where the Eberbach monastery had its largest outlets. Cologne alone handled 2.67 million gallons (100,000 hectoliters) of wine every year, trading with England, Scandinavia, and the Baltic countries.

Spain and Portugal Become World Powers

In the Iberian Peninsula, the development of an independent wine industry no longer controlled and organized by Rome occurred later than in France and Germany. Although the consumption of alcohol was forbidden during the centuries of Moorish rule, the making and exporting of wine was a welcome source of tax revenue. It can cause little surprise, then, that following the Christian reconquest of Spain (which was fully reunited at the end of the 15th century) and the admission of Spanish traders to the London market, exports to England quickly became an important factor in the country's economy. Very few people were aware that Spain had been producing outstanding wines in the regions around modern day Toro, La Rioja and Navarra since the 13th century, because these were drunk in Spain itself and not exported.

The Iberian peninsula profited immensely from the developments occurring in other parts of Europe. The collapse of the monopoly on dessert wine held by the maritime power Venice, and the end of English control in Bordeaux, created a new demand in various sections of the market. Andalusia, in particular, successfully attracted English traders with tax concessions and other privileges, a state of affairs which continued virtually unchanged even during the years of military conflict. The wines of the Málaga and Jerez regions, moreover, while not the finest in Europe, were popular for blending with poorer vintages.

Spain's efforts to become a world power in the 15th and 16th centuries, for which the circumnavigators of the globe and Columbus' discovery of America had paved the way, brought European vines to the American continent for the first time. The conquistador Hernán Cortés brought seedlings to Mexico during the early years of the colonization, and in the middle of the 16th century the first vineyards were established in what is now Chile. South America was cultivating vinifera long before North America and present-day California. On occasion, the resulting wines were even exported back to Europe—before viticulture in Chile, Argentina, Peru and Brazil fell into a kind of long hibernation, from which it has only awoken in the last couple of decades.

These wood carvings from Petrus de Crescentiis' *Treatise on Agriculture* (Ruralium Commodorum), completed around 1303, depict winemaking tasks that are still carried out today, using the same methods or with the aid of modern technology. Here we see grapes being trampled and the barrels being cleaned.

DEVELOPMENT OF THE WINE TRADE

Between 1600 and 1800, England became not only a political and military world power, but also the driving force behind the global wine trade and its continued development, particularly in what were historically its main arenas, namely France, Spain and Portugal. They inherited much from the Dutch who, during the first half of the 17th century, originally played this role. The Dutch were the first to recognize the potential of global trade when coupled with significant financial investment, and established colonies around the world. As a result, they were able to partially inherit the mantle of Spain (with whom they had been at war for almost 80 years) and Portugal, possessing a trading fleet several times larger than that of France and England put together.

It was the Dutch who first loaded ships with wine in Oporto. They introduced distilling in the Armagnac and Cognac regions, and at the beginning of the 17th century drained the marshes of Médoc, where small vineyards were placed amid huge areas of forest. As wine merchants, they filled the gap left when the English lost control of Gascony, and their efforts benefited local families, such as the Pontacs and Lestonnacs, who established the châteaux which laid the foundations for all the 19th- and 20th-century *premier cru* sites.

It was not until the second half of the 17th century that the combined military efforts of the English and the French ended the supremacy of the Dutch trading fleet, fully exploiting the pirates and buccaneers who made the seas a dangerous place to help them in their task. The War of the Spanish Succession then ensured that England gained the ascendancy. London became one of the world's most important centers of commerce and the wine trade, while Anglo-Irish families evolved as the new bourgeoisie in Bordeaux, where they not only established *négoces*, a form of business which still exists today, but also put their stamp on the landscape with numerous new vineyards.

ENGLISH CAPITAL CONQUERS THE WORLD

Thanks to its privileged relationship with the country, and following pioneering work by the Dutch, England had also begun to develop the wine industry in Portugal; port wine became the most fashionable drink in London society. However, the Portuguese vintners paid a high price for access to what at that time was the most important market in the world. Traders' rights to the wine frequently extended to the vintners' daughters as well, and at times, the proud nation was even at risk of becoming a

Historical barques on the River Douro at Oporto. These ships were once used to carry young wine down from the terraced vineyards in the upper part of the valley to the lodges at Vila Nova de Gaia, where it was matured for sale as port wine.

Crown colony. Indeed, the history of the wine trade was not short of such unpleasant phenomena.

The period from the 16th to the 18th century was a time of profound social and economic change in Europe that saw the birth of a world economy dominated by Europe and based on capitalist principles. Increasing urbanization led to the creation of large new markets. Paris dominated the French domestic market as firmly as London controlled the world market. The progressive removal of internal customs duties, the building of new transport links, and the ability to obtain wine from all over Europe made consumers more demanding and more discriminating.

The burgeoning wine trade spread to the South American colonies and then to the rest of the recently discovered New World. In North America, Tuscan noblemen and English settlers were laying out vineyards as early as the 17th century, making use of the numerous native varieties of *labrusca* vine. In South Africa, which was still a Dutch possession, the Groot Constantia estate was established, which by the 18th century was renowned for its very sweet Muscat wines, but then quickly disappeared back into the fog of history. New names also made their appearance on the European wine scene: the Madeira, the Hungarian Tokaji, and later the Sicilian Marsala regions became famous, primarily for producing the dessert and liqueur wines which were so popular at that time.

GROWTH AND DECLINE AGAINST A MILITARY BACKGROUND

The wine industry was caught in a spiral of development that could no longer be arrested. In France at the start of the 18th century, where the upturn was already leading to over-production, sales problems, and low prices, the government tried to ban the planting of any new vineyards, but failed miserably in their efforts. Almost all the world's wine-producing nations profited from this situation, with the exception of Germany. There too, the close of the 15th century had seen the wine industry flourishing, aided by the general level of prosperity, population growth and the development of large cities. In addition, temperatures remained unusually warm for a period of almost 200 years. Wine production rose to record levels, but consumption kept pace: 32 gallons (120 liters) per head per year put Germany on a par with Italy and France, where it remained into the first half of the 20th century.

However, the rapid cooling of the climate, and the military conflicts that had regularly turned much of Germany into a battlefield since the beginning of the 17th century, brought about a swift decline in the wine industry. Although the crisis point came during the Thirty Years War, the problem originated much earlier, and was largely homegrown. The expansionist tendencies of viticulture had been too extreme, and the economic crisis that marked the disintegration of the medieval feudal system was not caused by the War, having itself triggered the Peasant Wars of 1524–1526.

Recovery was much slower in Germany than elsewhere. The devastation that resulted from the War was too severe, and massive emigration, including that of winegrowers, depopulated the ravaged country even further. Not until the late 17th century did the world upturn in the wine industry reach Germany, where, in the same way that Cabernet Sauvignon became the most prestigious grape variety in 20th-century Bordeaux, Riesling now had its finest hour.

Jan Vermeer, *Woman with Wine Glass.* 1659/60. Herzog Anton Ulrich Museum, Braunschweig.

Wine Improves its Character

Riesling was the first grape variety to deliver the categories of wine that still make up the basic structure of the German wine industry and its regulations: the first official SPÄTLESE was recorded in the Rheingau in 1775, and toward the beginning of the 19th century the practice of leaving grapes on the vine to become overripe, in order to achieve very sweet or botrytized wines, became common. The designation KABINETT also came into being in the 18th century. The word was derived from the *Cabinett-Keller* (cellar room) where the estates would store their best wines. The Eberbach monastery and Schloss Vollrads both had such rooms, but the first authenticated use of the term was at the Schloss Johannisberg in 1779.

As in Germany, where the movement toward Riesling—which replaced the prevailing red grape varieties in many regions—took place over a long period of time, the style of wines in other European wine regions was also evolving. The changes were particularly drastic in the Bordeaux region, whose red wines originally had little in common with the dark, tannic wines produced there today. Not for nothing did the English call their prized Bordeaux reds CLARET (from *clair*), for they were indeed pale in color, light, and not very alcoholic. In order to satisfy the market's increasingly sophisticated demands, they were blended with more powerful, mostly Spanish base wines, but this could never be anything but a temporary solution. Ever larger zones were taken over by Cabernet Sauvignon, and the introduction of longer maceration times during fermentation meant that fuller, more concentrated wines could be produced by the estates themselves, without having to resort to blending.

The revolution in the vineyard and the cellar reached its climax during the 18th century. The first attempts were made at an ampelographic categorization of the different grape varieties, the use of sulfur as a stabilizer became widespread, and Napoleon's minister of the interior, Chaptal, saw to it that adding beet sugar to the must was authorized and put into practice. In the Champagne region, the invention of the modern glass bottle and stoppers made of natural cork enabled wines to be systematically fermented in the bottle, turning previously still wine into something approaching the sparkling wine we know today.

The development of transport links made wine an important commodity, and all manner of advertising began to appear.

The general development of the wine industry eventually affected the Rheingau as well, and in addition to its role as the champion of Riesling and the *Spätlese/Auslese* wine categories, the region also distinguished itself with the first filters and the first pipe-systems for pumping wine. In Italy, however, the evolution of the modern Chianti and Barolo wines took until the middle of the 19th century. Nevertheless, all this new knowledge and technology did not prevent the catastrophe that arrived in Europe from overseas and almost destroyed its wine industry within a few years.

The Golden Age

Prior to the devastating catastrophe caused by the tiny PHYLLOXERA louse, the development of the European wine industry had reached astounding proportions. One of the most important events of the 19th century was the official classification of the wines of Bordeaux, more specifically those from the Médoc and Sauternes regions, according to a system that is still in use today. Bordeaux reds had been much sought after since the end of the 18th century, and the region's estates were technically advanced, although the relationship between the producers and the wine trade was not always perfect. Wine merchants tried to use their financial power to impose conditions on the owners of the estates, but many were successful in resisting the dictates of market forces. Then, at the World Fair in 1855, the classification of the Médoc *domaines* into first, second, third, fourth, and fifth growths—a system borrowed from the *courtiers* (brokers)—was a triumph. The golden age of wine had begun.

Since the beginning of the 19th century, ever more magnificent buildings had been springing up in the wine regions around Bordeaux, frequently earning themselves the designation *Château*—a term that began to be applied to the whole estate. Production across the area as a whole rose from 53 to more than 133 million gallons (two to five million hectoliters) in little more than two years. Burgundy also began to regain some recognition. Its wine industry was mostly in the hands of the Church, and had been destabilized by the French Revolution. In addition, the *domaines* had become progressively smaller as ownership passed to successive generations, and they no longer had much power in the marketplace. The revival of Burgundy's fortunes lasted until the construction of the railway line to Paris in 1851: the extension of the line into the south of France soon brought strong competition from the more powerful and full bodied wines of the Midi.

In comparison with the central European countries, Italy's entry into the modern era was very delayed. Wine production had fallen into a deep crisis in terms of quality and sales, resulting in the wines being sold almost exclusively on draft. Bottles and corks were not common in Italy until late on, and the wines with which we are familiar today did not exist before the middle of the 19th century, including Chianti, Brunello and Barolo. The men and women to whom Italy owed its unification were also responsible for helping the country's wine industry to regain its standing: Garibaldi convinced the wine producers of the usefulness of sulfur; Cavour and the Marchesa Falletti, with the help of the French enologist Oudart, provided a modern identity for Nebbiolo; and in Tuscany, Baron Ricasoli concocted his recipe for Chianti. Wine merchants such as the Gancia, Martini, Coppo, and Cinzano firms were established in Piedmont, the first cooperatives came into being in Tuscany, and a viticultural institute was founded at San Michele in the Trentino.

As a luxury product, Champagne was an early beneficiary of advertising campaigns, which often made use of titillating erotic images.

In Germany, the Prussian Customs Union proved to be the biggest blessing for the wine industry, which, as elsewhere, was churning out ever greater quantities. Schools of viticulture, state-owned *domaines*, and research institutions appeared in both Prussia and Bavaria, and these had a decisive influence on the qualitative development of the wines. The Institute at Geisenheim dates from 1870, and ten years before that, Baron August Wilhelm von Babo, inventor of the Austrian must weight scales, founded the viticultural school at Klosterneuburg. The wine producers also made great progress: in 1855, the year of the Bordeaux classification, the first cooperatives were established in Neckarsulm, Fellbach, and Mayschoß. From the middle of the century German sparkling wine (*Sekt*) became increasingly popular, and this helped even the smaller, more acidic vintages find market success.

In the 18th century, Riesling growers in the Rheingau began to encourage over-ripeness and noble rot, developing a style of wine that remains influential to this day.

Disaster and a New Beginning

The 19th-century obsession with collecting and classifying botanic species and then introducing them into new environments led to American *labrusca* vines being planted in Europe, even though it was already known that they were not particularly suited to the production of top-quality wines. Therefore it was in this way that the fungal disease powdery mildew (*Oïdium*) was brought to France in 1847, subsequently spreading throughout Europe. Downy mildew (*Plasmopara*) followed in 1878, and black rot in 1880. Nonetheless, the biggest disaster was caused by the phylloxera louse, (now known as *Viteus vitifolii*), which first appeared in the southern Rhône region in 1863. This tiny, yellow pest came from the east coast of America, where the native *labrusca* vines had become resistant to its attack. Within the space of a few years, however, it caused such extensive damage to the roots of the European *vinifera* varieties that almost all the vines were irretrievably lost.

It quickly became clear to the European wine industry that phylloxera threatened to become a major catastrophe. As early as the 1870s, the idea was being postulated of grafting the precious European vines onto American rootstocks, whose immunity to phylloxera had

Selection on the vine was practiced as early as the 1950s.

The shallow baskets were typical of the grape harvest in the Champagne region.

since been discovered. The first grafted vines were being planted by 1880, but the scale of the damage was already immense: 6.25 million acres (2.5 million ha) of vineyard were destroyed in France alone, and production fell by more than two thirds in just under 15 years. Between 1873 and 1885, phylloxera spread throughout Portugal, Italy, Germany, Australia, South Africa, and California. In the years that followed, only a very few areas remained free of the pest: a few coastal strips in the south of France, some areas of the Mosel region, parts of Australia, China and South America, and a few Mediterranean islands. Today, it is estimated that around 85 percent of the world's vines are grafted onto American rootstocks.

The Triumph of Vinifera

Following the introduction of systematic grafting, North America and the New World became one of the most interesting areas into which the European *vinifera* vine spread, little by little replacing the *labrusca* vines and inter-species hybrids in the region's vineyards—a process which is still continuing. In contrast to South America, experiments with *vinifera* vines had not begun in the north until the 17th century, when French, German and Italian wine merchants helped set up plantations in Virginia, Pennsylvania and Florida. These attempts were a total failure, however, because the European vine varieties had no resistance to the native diseases and pests. The first hybrids—crosses of

The wars and economic crises of the early part of the 20th century left the wine industry severely shaken. By the 1920s, the most important *appellations* were once again being coveted throughout the world, and even German Riesling wines fetched prices on a par with the great Bordeaux and Champagne vintages. In the wake of the Second World War, however, the wine industry became entirely geared toward bulk production.

The More, the Better

In the wine industry, as elsewhere, the move into the modern era following the Second World War largely involved mechanization, industrialization, and mass production. The traditional small business structure of the wine trade persisted in the majority of European countries, but at the same time there was a drive for ever more efficient, labor-saving methods that would raise output. Germany, in particular, specialized in cultivating ever more productive varieties of grapevine, although the resulting wines seldom reached a level of quality that enabled them to compete with the classics. Moreover, misapprehensions concerning the consolidation of arable land, and the increasing use of chemicals in the vineyard, contributed to the wines gradually becoming thinner and weaker.

Italy also began to restock large areas of vineyard during the 1960s, but with disappointing results, as a "vertical" tasting makes clear: the 1940 to 1960 vintages are generally much fresher, livelier, and more concentrated than younger wines from the 1960s and 1970s.

During the 1970s, even the producers in Burgundy succumbed to the demands of bulk production, with the result that there, too, wines became increasingly thin and lacking in character. This situation did not improve until the end of the 1980s and the start of the 1990s, when more concentrated Pinot Noir and Chardonnay wines again came to the fore.

The trend reversed during the last quarter of the 20th century, and many of Europe's vineyards were no longer cultivated. Between 1980 and 2000, the area used for viticulture throughout the world fell from 24.5 to 20.5 million acres (9.8 to 8.2 million ha), and although this was principally at the expense of the European estates, they still formed 65 percent of the total. The Old World also continued to account for 75 percent of the annual output of wine, which had been reduced to 7,000 million gallons (266 million hectoliters) by the beginning of the 1990s, compared with 8,700 million gallons (330 million hectoliters) a decade earlier.

European and American vines—were discovered accidentally. *Vinifera* vines had reached Mexico in the early part of the 17th century, but did not arrive in California until the 1880 Gold Rush. The state quickly became the country's leading wine region, and by the end of the century was already producing a million gallons (37,500 hectoliters) a year. With Prohibition, from 1920–1923, production fell significantly again, but this proved only a temporary setback for the wine industry in California and the rest of the New World.

As the colonial armies of Europe continued to conquer new continents, the wine grape reached Australia around the end of the 18th and the beginning of the 19th century. The first vineyards were planted only a few years after the first settlements were established, and it was not very long before Australian wines were finding success at wine fairs in London. At first, the wine industry was primarily concentrated in the state of Victoria, but the arrival of phylloxera forced growers to switch to the sandy soils of the country's hot interior, and the focus of production shifted to powerful dessert and liqueur wines. South Australia and New South Wales became the country's most important wine regions, as they still are today.

In earlier times, all the equipment used for harvesting grapes and producing wine was made of wood. It was difficult to clean and heavy to carry and the harvested grapes often oxidized before they reached the winery. Not until the 1960s were modern and lighter materials gradually introduced.

MODERN TIMES

The revival during the 1960s of California's Napa Valley wine industry, which had been in stagnation since Prohibition, ushered in a new era in the history of wine. A few pioneers, among them the Mondavi family, had recognized the Valley's suitability for the top French grape varieties, particularly Chardonnay and Cabernet Sauvignon, and they were quickly copied by other producers. Ten to fifteen years

Stainless steel tanks were first used in the New World. Today they are found everywhere, even in pioneering Old World wineries.

after their successful beginnings, these wineries were offering stiff competition to the great figures of the Bordeaux wine industry. Because the designations of origin that previously had been so readily seized upon—"Chablis" was produced in the U.S.A., while "Hermitage," "Beaujolais" and "Champagne" were produced in Australia—were protected in the European countries who were their customers, the only possibility left open to producers in the New

World, if they wanted wines the consumers would recognize, was to name them according to the varieties of grape that were used.

The New World was also in the vanguard of technological developments in the vineyard and the wine cellar. Australia, with its hot climate, introduced steel tanks and temperature controls for the fermentation process during the 1950s and 1960s. A significant proportion of new vineyards were planted on level ground and were mechanically cultivated from the start. They possessed irrigation systems, and could be managed in an efficient, cost-effective manner. Nevertheless, it would be wrong to imagine that competition between the Old and New Worlds can be measured by the degree of industrialization in the wine industry.

In fact, the wine-producing countries of Europe also made extensive use of technological and chemical aids: cultured yeasts, computerized temperature control, various types of FERMENTATION vessel, the most modern wine presses, and last but not least, vacuum evaporators, reverse osmosis, and ceramic membranes for filtering the fermented wine. Not only did the Old World play a part in developing some of these technologies, it also uses them in even its most renowned estates.

The divisions which are often portrayed as a conflict between the Old and New Worlds are actually apparent within every wine-producing country, and separate the small winemaking operations, which to a certain extent continue to favor manual methods of production, from the large-scale industrial wineries, which produce millions of gallons (hectoliters) a year and use efficient marketing techniques to sell their wines throughout the world. This does not mean that "hand-made" wines are automatically better. All too often, the opposite is the case, and some of the world's most renowned and highly-prized wines come from industrial plants. Nevertheless, the top wines from the smaller producers remain attractive, for they always bear the mark of the individual and have an inimitable style that cannot be equaled by the large wineries.

ORGANIC WINE AND THE QUALITY REVOLUTION

In response to the progressive industrialization of the wine industry and the increasing use of chemicals and technology in both the vineyard and the cellar, estates have been established since the 1970s that are managed according to "natural," ecological, or biodynamic principles. Motivated by concern about the traditional wine producers' often irresponsible use of pesticides, fungicides, and herbicides, some "organic" operators appeared more concerned with using methods that would not harm the environment than with the quality of their products. Since then, however, much progress has been made. In France and Germany, in particular, a sizeable proportion of total production now comes from the organic wine industry, and the majority of Europe's wine-producing nations have top estates that produce wines of excellent quality, despite, or perhaps even because of the fact that their practices are ecologically sound.

The most significant change experienced by the world's wine industry in recent decades has been a general improvement in quality. In Europe, the trend started in Italy, which, encouraged by the astonishing wines coming out of California and Australia in the 1970s, began a complete shake-up of its own wine industry, which at that time was geared to bulk production. The methanol scandal that rocked the country in the mid-1980s did nothing to slow the upward momentum. In little more than a decade, Italy managed to secure a place among the elite of the world's wine industry with new wines, tailored to suit international tastes, and a return to traditional wines such as Chianti and Barolo.

Austria, too, survived a huge scandal—that of wines adulterated with glycol—and went on to carve out quite a name for itself. Germany, meanwhile, managed to put its history of extremes (its wines were first very sweet, then dry, and often just acidic) firmly behind it, and remembered its tradition of quality wines, characterized by their body and complexity. The Spanish wine industry, which was ancient by European standards, also showed that it could produce the finest vintages.

WE'VE NEVER HAD IT SO GOOD

Although the average quality of the wine filling European glasses reached an all-time high, the different styles and types of wine became increasingly uniform. The very fashionable Chardonnay, Cabernet Sauvignon, Merlot and Sauvignon Blanc grape varieties were planted everywhere, even in places where the climate meant that their chances were slim from the outset. The use of cultured yeasts, steel tanks, and casks made of French oak, together with

the international exchange of viticultural and winemaking knowledge by the so-called "flying winemakers," further increased the tendency toward greater uniformity.

Only in recent years has the trend slowed to some extent. In the U.S.A., the tables have turned completely and it has now become fashionable to drink almost "anything but Chardonnay and Cabernet." Interest is growing in outstanding, distinctive wines with regional character— particularly in Europe, whose grape varieties provide a huge pool of genetic resources. At the same time, the winemakers of the New World are increasingly returning to wines which reflect

the individuality of a particular *terroir*, and their products are becoming more delicate and elegant, lighter in terms of EXTRACTIONS, and less marked by the flavors of wood. In the coming years and decades, therefore, the wide and multi-faceted range on offer should make the world of wine that little bit more varied and interesting.

Like cathedrals full of barrels: maturation in small, new oak *barriques* is essential nowadays for all the better red wines.

THE RIGHT CHOICE

Everyone has their own taste in wine—we can accept that. But where quality is concerned, it is not a question of preference. Wine is perhaps the most varied and innovative consumable item we can buy ready-made—but it is not easy to know what we are buying. We cannot tell from the label whether the winemaker has exploited the full potential of a particular location and grape variety. We cannot tell whether he or she has used the most "natural" methods in the vineyard and the winery, and translated them into wine of the quality that is a prerequisite for real enjoyment. Even so-called "organic" wine offers no real guarantee in this respect.

Nowhere in the world has legislation caught up with the use of chemicals and technology in the wine industry. Indeed, it lags further behind than ever before. So far, law-making bodies have reacted slowly, if at all, to new developments, with the result that in many wineries worldwide, anything goes. Wine producers experiment with anything that is not expressly forbidden—and sometimes even if it is. In most countries, none of this needs to be declared on the label.

More so than with many other items of food or drink, therefore, we as consumers need to acquire some knowledge, sharpen our senses, and be fully aware of the wine we are drinking. An important aspect of this is the effect a wine has on the body. If only moderate consumption of a particular wine causes stomach problems and headaches, then it has probably been manipulated by some chemical and/or technological means. To deserve the designation "quality wine," it should not only taste good, but contribute to a person's physical wellbeing as well.

THE DIVERSITY OF WINE

Traditional views as to what wine is all about have their origins in the 19th century, and are based on assumptions that are fundamentally different than those facing the 21st-century consumer. In the first place, the range of wines offered then was much more limited. The wine trade was basically confined to the large châteaux and merchant-houses of Bordeaux and Burgundy, a few German vintners, and the odd specialty wine such as Tokay or port. Wines sold by the makers themselves were largely destined for the local and regional market, and thus easier to overlook than their equivalent today.

Nowadays, however, the world of wine is significantly larger and rather more diverse. Professional wine industries now operate in countries where, even a few decades ago, vineyards were primarily a source of table grapes. Improved transport has made it easier to import specialty wines from all over the world. Never before, moreover, have such large numbers of consumers been prepared to risk trying something new, thereby creating a market for wines that is very different than the traditional wine trade, not only because it is so varied, but also because of the speed at which it changes.

The globalized world of the third millennium is no longer a place for the romanticized notions of previous centuries with regard to wine—the appeal of which was, in any case, reserved for a social elite. Wine's appeal now encompasses all sections of the population. It has become a mass-produced article across much of the world, and thus increasingly an industrial product as well. The range of wines offered is almost incomprehensibly vast, even for a connoisseur. In very general terms, the current wine market can be divided into four main categories.

PART INDUSTRY, PART CRAFT

The biggest group on the market by far continues to be the wines that reach, at best, a minimum technical standard, have probably been produced industrially, and are sold at the lowest prices in the shops. They generally come from a commercial bottling line, and their origins are obscured with an imaginative brand name or by identifying on the label only the larger zone of vineyards from which the grapes came. These simple wines, which have disproportionately high sums spent on packaging and advertising, are estimated to form three-quarters of the present world market for wine.

A second, rapidly growing group of modern wines are now being produced, which are squarely aimed at the more sophisticated, brand-conscious consumer, but necessarily follow a standardized, international model that is subject to the fast-moving dictates of fashion. These wines justify their prestige factor and by no means low prices with their method of production, which makes use of every technological, physical, and chemical means available.

The third category, "traditional" wines in the best sense of the term, is experiencing a real renaissance with an increasingly knowledgeable section of consumers. These estate-bottled wines are produced with a craftsman's care and a sense of responsibility, using "natural" methods in both vineyard and winery. They reflect the regional grape varieties from which they are made, and are thus the real representatives of variety within the world of wine. Their main advantages are that they are "easy drinking," and that the price/enjoyment ratio is readily understood by the consumer.

The fourth category comprises the truly great wines—vintages that do not simply give the illusion of fine quality. This group is naturally small, and their production demands the highest levels of skill, enthusiasm, and boldness. Wines in this category are distinguished by a complexity and intensity of AROMA and flavor, and are balanced, without excessive TANNIN or fruit. They reflect not only the grape variety, but also the soil and the particular vintage, that is to say the *terroir*. Their multi-layered bouquet is demanding and can be enigmatic, meaning that these wines are sometimes "difficult." In principle, all of the world's wine regions are capable of producing such wines, and the traditional, prestige regions and their renowned winemakers do not, on average, provide any more of them than some of the newer regions. Prices range from moderate, for wines that are not of great value to collectors, to completely over inflated prices for bottles that the market has found to be a very good investment commodity.

Anybody who is healthy and whose senses of taste and smell are not impaired, has all the basic equipment necessary not only for drinking wine, but for appreciating its quality as well. This is what separates the consumer from the connoisseur; for the latter, wine is not simply a means to an end. A connoisseur wishes to understand the wine he or she is drinking, so as to experience its aromas and flavors in all their dimensions. To this end, it is hoped that the following pages dealing with the smell, taste and color of wine will enhance your enjoyment of drinking it.

Variety is the key to the range of wines available today. The classic regions may still be dominant, but wines from all countries are finding a place in the wine racks.

Wine Tasting

To a certain extent, tasting a wine is the opposite of drinking it. When casually consuming a wine, you are primarily concerned with its overall aromatic impact; the point of a critical tasting, however, is to identify all those components of the wine that affect the senses. Only when you have decoded as many of its facets as possible, by considering its sweetness, acidity, and bitterness, and picking out the aromas that characterize it, can you really understand a wine. When we drink a wine, we are aware of its flavor and aroma; only when we taste a wine do we consciously experience it.

Right page, below
It is best to take notes of your impressions of a wine. People now often use laptops or organizers for this purpose.

It makes sense to cover up the labels, and not just for professional wine tastings. You can make a more objective judgment if you are not influenced by famous names.

Wine as we know it today has a greater variety of styles and levels of quality than any other agricultural product. Accordingly, wine tasting is one of the most demanding food-testing activities. The basic requirement, whether for the objective judgement of the professional or the largely subjective view of the layman, is the sharpening of all the relevant senses. If we are to identify as precisely as possible what is good or bad about a wine, and why, we must know how to use our senses of sight, smell, and taste selectively.

A good starting point is to learn the right tasting technique. Full sensory perception of a wine requires four steps: smelling, tasting on the tongue, considering the aftertaste at the back of the mouth, and finally, observing the wine's color.

In the past, tasters would usually judge the color of the wine first. Nowadays, however, color can no longer reliably provide any meaningful information. Just looking at a dark, almost black wine, for example, will not tell you whether the color has been manufactured to give the drink a fashionable, pleasing appearance, or whether it does indeed reflect the extraction of substances from the grapes. Similarly, a violet-blue tinge in the glass does not necessarily indicate a young, fresh wine. Those qualities can only be revealed by a combination of smell and taste. As a result, the traditional tasting sequence "color, smell, taste" is now outdated.

In any tasting that takes into account the technological and chemical processes available to the modern wine industry, the most meaningful information will always be provided by the sense of smell, with taste in second place, and color last.

Organizing a Wine Tasting

The most suitable set-up for a wine tasting is a room free of other smells, a table with a white paper tablecloth, odorless glasses, a moderate room temperature (so as not to impair the volatile aromas of the wines), and an atmosphere that is as relaxed as possible.

The most interesting results are produced by "blind" tastings where the bottles are covered so as to remove the influence that a "big" or an unknown name, a good or a bad reputation can have, and to which even a professional taster is not fully immune.

The best training for the palate is a thematic tasting. As well as demonstrating the differences between the various bottles, these tastings really bring out a wine's individual nuances. Such a tasting might concentrate, for example, on one grape variety from different regions or vineyard sites, the same type of wine from different producers, the same wine across a number of vintages, or the same wine drunk from different styles of glass or at varying temperatures. Nothing much can be learned from tasting a Riesling alongside a Cabernet, for example, unless the taster already has so many previous impressions of both grape varieties stored in the memory, that comparisons are made more in the head than on the tongue.

To organize a successful wine tasting, you must first be clear as to what you are hoping to achieve. If the object is to classify wines according to their quality, then it is vital to compare like with like—the chosen wines must share a common basis in terms of taste. Consequently, wines of either the same grape variety, or roughly the same CUVÉE (blend) and the same vintage are most suitable for such tastings. If the idea is to identify a bottle by assigning it to a particular region, grape variety, vintage or winemaker, then you should choose wines which do, in fact, reflect their origins, having been cultivated and produced using the most natural methods possible. If tastings are not carried out "blind" (those which take place at the cellars of a particular producer, for example), only experienced tasters can hope to arrive at any halfway objective conclusions; everyone else runs the risk of being influenced by the estate's reputation, or by the eloquence of the winemaker.

A Methodical Approach

If you are tasting a number of wines, it is a good idea to make a written note of your impressions. The blank forms often used at professional tastings are only partially helpful for this, since they generally put the visual inspection of a wine first, and use a points system for ranking wines that tends to be incomprehensible for the lay person. Understanding a wine and assessing its quality require a sensory rather than a mathematical approach. In an age when technology is used to manipulate wines at will, they can no longer solely be judged on each of their individual characteristics, but only as an overall package.

The most eloquent part of a wine is its smell. Start your tasting with a sniff, and you can already tell a great deal. Faults that have developed in the vineyard, in manufacture or in storage are easily detected, such as when the wine smells musty, vinegary or of SULFUR. The smell also gives an indication of whether the wine has undergone protective (i.e. not exposed to air) or oxidative handling, whether it was stored in wooden barrels or in stainless steel tanks, and, very importantly, whether its aromas are due solely to the grape variety or also encompass the soil and position of the vineyard.

Using taste next, you can judge the quality of a wine from its balance of sweetness and acidity, and, in a red wine, from the maturity of its tannins. The "length" of a wine, its alcoholic strength, and its texture are also decisive factors.

Finally, depending on the grape variety, the intensity and tone of the color can give you a good indication of the quality of the vintage and the age of the wine.

For a wine to be pronounced "good," the smell, taste, and color must go well together. Most of the failings of modern-day wine criticism are the result of excessive importance being attached to only one of the sensory impressions offered by a wine: white wines, for example, are often judged solely on their BOUQUET, red wines are judged primarily by their color. A really great wine, however, defies a standardized tasting completely. Its complex bouquet is so multifaceted that a great deal of concentration and experience is needed to unravel it. The wine may be so far outside the norm in color, aroma, and taste that only an open-minded wine taster could recognize its quality.

A question mark will always remain over the conclusions of even the most experienced wine expert, however, since they are always the product of subjective abilities. Tasters, as well as consumers who rely on the opinions of serious wine critics, should always bear that fact in mind.

First smell the wine,

then take a mouthful,

consider the aftertaste on the soft palate,

and look at the color.

A HISTORY OF ENJOYING WINE   33

The Smell of Wine

The range of aromas presented by a wine is most clearly detected using the sense of smell. Around two-thirds of an attentive taster's perceptions of a wine will be gained via his or her nose. This organ can perceive the variety of volatile compounds that constitute the aroma of a young wine or the bouquet of a mature one. There are several hundred components responsible for the bouquet of a bottle-matured red wine of average complexity. Analyzing the aroma of even a simple, young white is a sensory feat requiring precision work.

The human nose is designed to distinguish between thousands of different smells. It is the brain, however, that has to filter, identify, and evaluate our sensory perceptions. To be aware of what you are tasting, therefore, you must have previous wine-drinking experiences stored in your memory, a basic understanding of the composition of a wine and of the workings of the sense of smell, and last, but not least, you must have the ability to describe your sensory perceptions in order to communicate and make a mental note of them.

Anatomy of the Sense of Smell

The olfactory center in humans is located at the top of the nasal cavity, in the uppermost of the three nasal conchae. Around ten million nerve cells are packed into the olfactory mucosa (mucous membrane), which is roughly 2 inches (5 cm) square. Each nerve cell has between ten and twenty branching filaments to which the aroma molecules can attach themselves. Most of these molecules arrive through the nose in the air we breathe in, but some also reach the olfactory center from the oral cavity via the retro-nasal passage.

For us to perceive the bouquet of a wine, the volatile aroma molecules, which can stimulate our sense of smell even in concentrations of one ten-millionth of a gram, must get to the olfactory mucosa. This is why it is best to take a long, deep breath when smelling a wine, so that the air has a chance to spread out and fill the nasal cavity. If you breathe in too hastily, most of the aroma molecules may be propelled straight past the olfactory center.

1 Olfactory epithelium
2 Nasal conchae
3 Air flow, breathing in
4 Mouth cavity

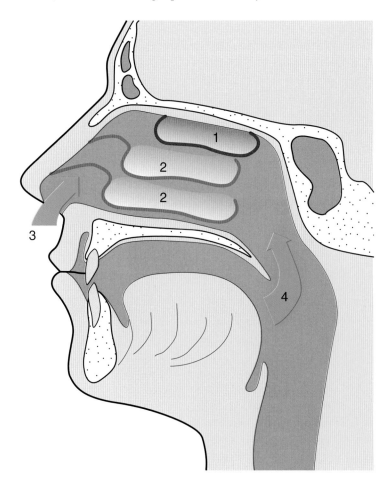

Cross-section of the olfactory epithelium: under the mucous coating, the actual olfactory cells (shown here in yellow) lie between the supporting and basal cells. They extend their cilia out from the olfactory epithelium, searching for aroma molecules. The layer underneath is connective tissue.

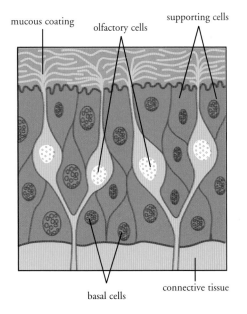

mucous coating   olfactory cells   supporting cells

basal cells   connective tissue

A mature red wine is frequently characterized by aromas such as cedar resin or cinnamon sticks.

Citrus smells will often be encountered in young whites.

Red berries and cherries are the typical aromas found in young reds.

The volatile chemical compounds responsible for the smell of a wine are present in much smaller concentrations than the non-volatile flavor compounds. To release as many of the aroma molecules from the liquid as possible, first swirl the glass (roughly a third full) around in a circle. Then dip your nose into the glass and breathe in the vapor above the surface of the wine. Behind every nuance of an aroma lies a chemical compound. The broad spectrum of smells in a wine provides the experienced taster with a great deal of information, giving clues as to grape variety, vineyard location, methods of fermentation and maturation, and age. Because there are so many different aromas in red and white wines, however, they can be difficult to identify and decode.

The Aromas of Simpler Wines

To avoid perceiving simply a diffuse jumble of smells, it helps to concentrate on individual groups of similar aromas. Basic chemical compounds are the first to reveal themselves: fruity aromas in white wine can range from banana, melon, and pineapple, through apple and peach to lemon; in red wines they are usually "darker," and can be reminiscent of berries, cherries, or plums. Second, there are the VEGETAL aromas: flowers, leaves, grasses, and vegetables. The aromas of simpler wine usually fall into these two categories, and generally reflect nothing more than the smell of a particular grape variety. A distinction should be made, however, between the basic, but nonethe-

less appealing, wines produced for the mass market, and industrially produced wines specifically tailored to have a particular aroma. Modern fermentation technology and enzymes enable wines to be "constructed" with certain aromatic nuances, for example banana in Chardonnay, to suit an imagined "public taste." The smell of such wines is beguiling at first, but when compared with the taste and finish is often revealed to be an illusion.

The Bouquet of a Great Wine

Professionals usually use the term "bouquet" only when the aromas are not merely fruity or vegetal, but also reflect the *terroir*, vintage, method of maturation, and age of a wine. With white wines, this extended spectrum of aromas can reveal overtones of honey, straw, butter cookies, vanilla, cedar wood, and minerals. The more complex range of aromas in a great red wine can include various spices, chocolate, coffee, smoke, and several types of wood. There are also a number of fairly unattractive smells, which often differ only slightly from the more pleasant ones, at least as far as their chemical composition is concerned. These unpleasant aromas include pickled cabbage, soap, acetic acid, wet wool, and petrol. If one of these smells dominates the bouquet, then it is a fault, and the wine will be undrinkable. However, a small trace of one of these "taints" embedded within the broad sweep of aromas in a really great wine can add to the complexity of its bouquet.

THE TASTE OF WINE

Regions of taste reception on the tongue

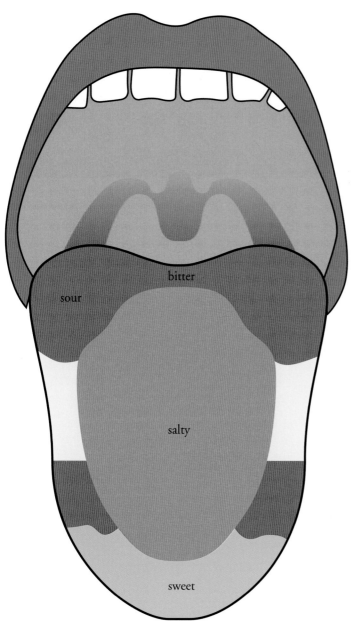

The papilla, which have taste buds embedded in their epithelium (top layer of skin), receive taste signals particularly strongly in the area around the base of the tongue.

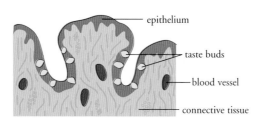

Papilla of the tongue

The flavor of a wine is revealed in various ways: we taste it on our tongue, but still perceive its aroma in the throat. The taste buds on the tongue can only detect a few basic tastes. Apart from sweet, sour, bitter, and salty, we can also distinguish *umami*—the savory note of glutamate—and no doubt further tastes will follow. Research has also found that the taste zones are not as clearly separated as the traditional taste diagram shows. Current research is devising a new classification of taste zones. Within the mouth, we can also detect the texture of foods: whether they are runny or viscous, dry or creamy. The subtleties of a taste, however—the complexity of its aromas—are detected by the olfactory center by way of the back of the throat.

Only aroma molecules that escape from the liquid and reach the olfactory center along with the air we breathe can contribute to our impression of how a wine tastes. Thus it is not bad manners to slurp and gurgle when tasting a wine, but an absolute necessity to allow optimal disclosure of a wine to the senses.

WHITE WINE

When wine flows over the tongue, depending on its temperature, the taste buds will perceive its sweetness first, closely followed by its acidity (sourness)—the two components that characterize the basic structure of a white wine. The impression of sweetness is not created purely by

The traditional diagram of the tongue shows the four basic flavors of sweet, salty, sour, or bitter. Texture can also be detected in the mouth area, i.e. whether a substance is viscous or runny, creamy or dry. In addition, all aromas are captured by the olfactory epithelium, which they reach via the retronasal channel. This is why experienced tasters often draw air into the mouth together with the wine when tasting.

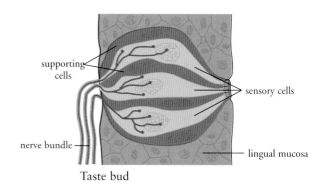

Taste bud

unfermented RESIDUAL SUGAR, however, but also by the alcohol. Both sweet and dry white wines have a sweet-sour structure, and the balance of this structure is an important indicator of the production method and quality of a white wine. It is a simplification to say that a first impression of sharpness and acidity denotes a wine of simpler or lesser quality, but true nonetheless. All too often, such products are the result of unripe grapes, yields that are too high, and technological and/or chemical manipulation. A high level of acidity, however, needs to be embedded within a correspondingly lavish overall structure.

Sweetness, too, must be counterbalanced by something else in the structure and aromatic spectrum of a wine. If it is not encased in fruit, or the delicately bitter overtones produced by a wooden barrel or NOBLE ROT, sweetness makes a wine seem one-dimensional and flabby. Excessive bitterness, on the other hand, indicates that the producer has made an error of some sort, such as fermenting rotten grapes, over-pressing the MUST, or using too much chalk in the de-acidification process.

The sensory impressions of a white wine gained in the mouth can be very diverse. Texture and flavor should be well matched: if a wine is relatively viscous as it flows over the tongue, for example, we would expect it to stimulate correspondingly sumptuous taste sensations there. Nevertheless, only the complexity of its aromas, which is most readily appreciated at the moment when you start to swallow, gives us an indication as to the true greatness of a wine. Modest wines for the mass market limit themselves to only a small fraction of the range of possible aromas: they are either purely fruity, purely vegetal, or simply excessively woody. A really fine white wine, however, will always have a long-lasting, multi-layered bouquet, in which fruity aromas can be complemented by spicy overtones and the delicate fragrances of wood, along with underlying hints of minerals which reflect the *terroir* of the vineyard.

RED WINE

The main difference between red wine and white wine is the presence of tannins. These substances are derived from the seeds, stems, and skins of the grapes, as well as from the wooden barrels sometimes used in the maturation process. Consequently the quality of the tannins is the most important indicator as to whether the grapes were ripe when they were harvested, and thus whether the basic require-

ment for a great wine has been fulfilled. Tannins cannot be detected by the nose, however, and must be examined with particular care when the wine is tasted in the mouth.

Unpleasantly bitter tannins that are very astringent and leave a distinctly grainy texture in the mouth point to a bad vintage, unripe grapes, diseases or faults in the vineyard (yields that are too high or too low), and/or defects in the production process (too much press wine). Mature tannins, on the other hand, seem silky, transparent, and smooth. Despite the astringency, they give a hint of sweetness, and carry the fruitiness of the wine through into the aftertaste. Mature tannins are produced by harvesting grapes at their optimal ripeness, and by exploiting this potential to the full with production methods that are as gentle as possible. A striving for soft tannins even in young wines has fundamentally altered perceptions about the taste of great reds.

The balance of sweetness, acidity, and bitterness is also crucial to the taste of red wine. Since red wine is usually matured without any residual sugar, the sweetness factor is determined largely by its alcohol content, along with any woody aromas that may be present. The more acids and bitter tannins in the wine, the greater the level of alcohol needs to be, because bitterness and acidity will reinforce each other's impact on the tongue.

As a wine matures, not only do its aromas change, but also other components, such as alcohol, acids, and tannins. In a great wine, these lend the finish greater complexity and finesse.

THE FINISH

Just as with white wine, the true quality of a red is revealed only as you start to swallow. If at that moment the wine comes alive and fills the whole mouth and throat with its opulence, releasing aromas that range from dark, fruity blackberries, blackcurrants or plums, through spicy notes of clove or pepper, to the caramelized, woody aromas of tobacco, cedar or coffee, and if these aromas linger a while in the mouth and throat after swallowing, then you are dealing with a really superb wine. After several years' maturing in the bottle, the structure of such a wine will be a complex combination of fruit flavors, aromatic overtones resulting from the production process, and influences from the *terroir*. If the finish is merely a repetition of the same simple fruit flavors, obvious grape aromas and one-dimensional tannins that have already been experienced, without adding any new revelations, then it is a more basic wine. Appropriately termed "short" in the jargon, wines that have little or no impact after they have been swallowed are, ultimately, a disappointment to the taster.

THE COLOR OF WINE

The color of a wine plays a less significant role in our enjoyment because, objectively, it has no influence on the flavor. At a tasting, however, it is an important and underestimated indicator of quality, because the development, extraction, and maturation of a wine's aroma compounds and its pigments are closely linked. The color can give clues as to how good the vintage was, the grape variety, intensity of flavor, method of production, and maturity. This assumes, however, that the color is natural, i.e. that it has not been artificially boosted with additives or enzymes. Using such practices, even a medium quality red wine can now be given a very dark, if not almost black, color relatively cheaply.

When winemaking only involved chemicals that were already naturally present in the grapes, color was an entirely reliable indicator of quality. Generally speaking, the deeper and darker a wine's red coloring was, the greater the amount of tannins and other substances in its extractions. The acidity and maturity of a wine could also be accurately estimated from the presence of blue or brown tinges respectively.

Assessing the color on anything other than aesthetic principles, however, requires extensive knowledge of the chemistry of wine. For a long time, therefore, although color continued to be judged at tastings, it was seldom regarded as a reflection of quality. It was not until very dark, almost black, red wines became fashionable, that more serious attention was again given to how a wine looked. Since dark reds achieved greater market success, some winemakers started to give nature a helping hand. Consumer ignorance of the technological and chemical methods of manipulation that had become available meant that color was overestimated as a sign of quality.

All red wine grapes, and to a limited degree all white wine grapes, contain natural pigments. Depending on the grape variety, these can be paler, darker, or more concentrated in the skins of the fruit. Consequently, a wine's potential color is decided in the vineyard, and starts with the genetic code of the particular grape variety. This does not mean, however, that all Pinot Noir or all Cabernet is the same, since the most

commonly cultivated grape varieties exist in numerous versions. Selective cloning of plants that produce small or large fruits, or low or high yields, has laid the foundations for improvements in terms of quality and quantity. Beyond this, pruning, canopy management, and the application of fertilizer affect the quality of a wine in general, and its color in particular. Then the winemaking process itself must make full use of the grapes' potential for producing a good color (and with it a good aroma). Finally, the duration and method of maturation will leave their mark on a wine's appearance, and here again, changes in color are bound up with the evolution of its taste and smell.

The Subtle Palette of White Wines

White wine is often described as colorless, since the grape juice usually has no SKIN CONTACT during VINIFICATION. This perception is not entirely accurate, however. The colors found in white wine range from pale green through to golden yellow, but are more difficult for the human eye to perceive, simply because they largely occupy the ultraviolet region of the spectrum. A mixture of green and yellow plant pigments (PHENOLICS) are present in the flesh as

well as the skins of pale-colored grapes, which is why even white wine, which is not fermented along with the skins, contains a certain amount of pigment.

Grapes with a slight purple or grayish-pink tinge have the most potential for producing a good color. In other varieties, anomalies in the chemical structure of the pigments can lead to greenish tinges in the wine or a tendency to turn into a brownish color.

Dark, Mysterious Wines

Red wine contains on average ten times more color compounds than white wine. These anthocyanins are only found in the skins of the grapes, and are produced by the action of direct sunlight as the fruits ripen. The thicker and riper the skins, therefore, and the less juice the grapes contain, the greater the potential for producing wine of a good color. In addition, tannins have a stabilizing effect on the pigments, which is why wines that are rich in tannins have a deeper color. Thick-skinned grape varieties such as Cabernet Sauvignon and Syrah naturally deliver dark red wines, while the color from thin-skinned varieties will not be as intense. Nevertheless, assuming optimal conditions in the vineyard, even a thin-skinned grape variety can produce wines with a deep color, if the yield is kept low and the canopy is adequately managed. In the winery, the extraction of color will largely depend on how long and at what temperature the grape juice remains in contact with the skins. When fermentation starts, the color compounds are subjected to physical, chemical and biological influences which leave greater or lesser traces in the wine. It is easy to overdo this, however, and rob the wine of any elegance. Consequently, the most intensely-colored wines are not always the best. Even so, only in exceptionally rare cases will a pale, watery appearance be concealing a great wine.

Every wine has its own particular color, which can provide information about type and age.

From the left: young, fresh white; older, possibly *barrique*-aged white; the ruby color of a mature, relatively light-bodied red; the blackish red of a concentrated red wine; the delicate effervescence of a young champagne; the fascinating golden color of a mature dessert wine.

Handling Wine: A Question of Age

Even for the poet Horace, who was enjoying wine with discretion and moderation in Roman times and wrote 16 poems on the subject, great wine was always old wine—provided that the fermented grape juice had sufficient substance to withstand years of storage in earthenware amphorae. Less sophisticated wine, by contrast, was simply the produce of the most recent harvest. The position has altered little since that time. Today, 2,000 years after Horace, connoisseurs still find old wine irresistibly attractive. Every year, record sums are paid at auction for aged rarities. Whether the contents of such finds are worth the price is entirely questionable, of course. First, very few wines actually have the capacity to be kept for several decades, and second, the maturation process is terribly susceptible to a wide variety of hazards.

Aging Potential

When laying down a wine, it is important to differentiate between the length of time a wine can be cellared before it "dies," and the time it needs to reach its peak. Although scientists from different disciplines have repeatedly studied wine from their respective angles, there are no technical standards from which to gauge the aging potential of fermented grape must—we can only give a rough prediction.

Few wines have the capacity to last for centuries, as this legendary bottle from 1787, once owned by the American President Thomas Jefferson, has done.

The life expectancy of most wines is only a few years. Even if a wine is suitable for aging, however, a lot will also depend on the external storage conditions. Generally speaking, sweet wines will keep for longer than dry ones.

If anything, it has become even more difficult to estimate how long a wine will keep, given that advances in the modern wine industry have brought a rapid increase in the number of methods of physical and chemical manipulation. With many of today's wines, whose basic structure may have been altered, we have absolutely no experience to inform our assessment.

The practice of buying a significant stock of expensive bottles, possibly *en primeur* (i.e. long before the wine is delivered and can be tasted), is never advisable, therefore, unless you have reliable information regarding the development of the wine in question. Even a famous name and a cult status are no longer any guarantee that the contents will have a long life.

Red Wine

The backbone of a red wine, and the factor that largely determines its capacity for aging, is tannin—a chemical substance with preservative properties. It dissolves into the wine from the skins, seeds, and sometimes also the stems of the grapes during the winemaking process, and also from the wooden barrel during maturation. The quality and quantity of tannins in red wine vary. Quantity depends partly on the grape: thicker-skinned varieties such as Cabernet Sauvignon and Syrah contain more of these preservatives, and thus have a greater capacity for aging. The vintage (a dry summer produces thicker skins and correspondingly more tannins) and the work of the winemaker also play a role, however, because low yields, long skin-contact times and barrel-aging enable larger amounts of the compounds to be extracted. At least as important for the development of a wine's flavor is the quality of the tannins. Only tannins that were fully ripe when the grapes were harvested will integrate harmoniously into the overall taste of a wine after years in the bottle. What is often described as the maturation of the tannins during bottle-aging is in essence a gradual reduction in the number of such compounds in the wine: polymerization alters the structure of the tannins, which form bigger and more complex molecules and eventually precipitate as SEDIMENT. Wines that taste excessively raw, ASTRINGENT, and bitter in their youth will still do so when they have been aged; indeed, they may seem even less harmonious, since older tannins of this sort often make the mouth seem dry.

The widespread belief among wine collectors that a harsh, unbalanced red need only be kept for long enough to become a great wine is, therefore, a fallacy. Similarly erroneous is the assumption that a young wine that is already pleasantly drinkable is not a good candidate for aging.

The constituents of a great red wine generally begin to weave themselves into a harmonious whole around three to four years after bottling. Reacting with the little oxygen it contains, a wine with a suitable extract will gradually start to develop a bouquet—its originally fruity fragrance will be enriched with spicy, leathery, and earthy nuances. The interactions of alcohols, aldehydes, and acids initially produce a beneficial change, but eventually lead to the impoverishment of both the taste and the smell of the wine. Tartaric acid, which is the most stable component of the wine, scarcely decreases at all, and will become the dominant aroma.

Visually, the progress of the aging process can be gauged from the color of the wine. In a young red (and depending on grape variety), it should be as intense, dark, and purple-tinted as possible. As the pigments oxidize, they are precipitated along with the tannins. As a consequence, the color of the wine loses its blue tinge and becomes first a glowing red, then gradually brownish. The chemical deterioration that occurs in wine at the end of the aging process is reflected in a parallel loss of color. Depending on the grape variety, method of production, and storage conditions, this can occur after anything from a few years to (ideally) several decades, and leaves the wine looking extremely faded—a sure sign that its aroma has reached the end of the road.

WHITE WINE

Long-term cellaring of white wines is a considerably more risky venture than laying down reds. Except for dessert wines, their aging potential is far smaller, because they are largely lacking in antioxidant tannins. The role played by the various acids in determining the lifespan of white wine has yet to be sufficiently explained by science to allow us to make reliable predictions. In the end, any such forecasts can only rely on past experience, and experience tells us that, irrespective of grape variety, the greater the amount of tartaric acid and extract in a white wine, the longer it can be kept in the bottle. As a general rule, wines that had significant contact with oxygen before being bottled, such as those matured in wooden barrels, are considerably more stable than those

The color of a wine is a clear indicator of its age.

that were largely protected from the air during the production process. The likely importance of "good" oxidation in relation to longevity is also indicated by the fact that white wines that are made from botrytized grapes invariably age well in the bottle.

DESSERT WINES

Wines containing residual sugar tend to be better suited to long-term cellaring than dry ones. The longer you wish to keep a wine, the higher the amount of sugar should be. Whites with only a little residual sugar can be allowed to develop for up to a decade, provided that they have sufficient extract capable of the task. Really great dessert wines, such as certain Sauternes, Tokaji Aszú, and those made from the Chenin Blanc grape variety (which has particularly good aging potential), can last for generations. Even after decades in the bottle, they are usually still bursting with fragrances and aromas.

The Private Wine Cellar

Many wine lovers dream of having their own cellar, a storage room in which the wines they have collected over the years can be left to attain perfection in the cool, damp darkness. Since prices went virtually through the roof in the 1990s, particularly for famous Bordeaux vintages and then for high-status wines from other regions, many wines have become prohibitively expensive even after just a few years in the bottle. A wine lover on an average income, therefore, must buy wines that need ageing while they are still quite young, and store them him- or herself.

Modern apartments and houses rarely have adequate space for this purpose, however, and even those that do are generally too warm for long-term wine storage. Alternatives do exist: "artificial cellars," for example, are a kind of fridge for wine that come in a variety of expensive sizes. If you simply want to store a couple of dozen bottles for immediate drinking, then any spare corner will do—such as under the stairs. Wine should never be stored next to a boiler or cooker, however, even for a few weeks.

If you have a large number of bottles to be kept over a period of years or even decades, they should be stored in a room that can meet

The owner and his good friends enjoy tasting sessions in this comfortable cellar, which is decorated with the lids of wine cases.

certain basic criteria in terms of temperature, humidity, level of light, and lack of odors. It is worth remembering, however, that even the best cellar cannot turn a poor wine into nectar of the Gods, no matter how long it stays there.

Temperature

The temperature of the room is important because biochemical reaction rates in wine double with each increase of 18°F (10°C). If you want to store bottles over a period of decades, you should choose a storage area that never gets warmer than 59°F (15°C). If, on the other hand, your main concern is to develop the wine's potential, regardless of when this is achieved, then your collection will be quite all right at up to 68° F (20°C). Long-term exposure to temperatures above this level can produce "boiled," jammy aromas in the wine.

A wine cellar can be too cold, however. Although wine has a lower freezing point than water (the exact temperature being determined by alcohol content), even a full-bodied wine will force open its bottle at between 25° and 17°F (−4° and −8°C). Before this point, and depending on the duration of the exposure, very cold temperatures will precipitate tartrates from the wine. These crystals do not affect the taste of the wine in the slightest. If anything, they merely indicate that a wine was not stabilized prior to bottling.

Temperature Fluctuations

The standard temperature of the cellar has less effect on the wine than fluctuations between hot and cold. If the temperature rises and falls sharply and swiftly with the seasons, the bottles begin to "breathe": the liquid and air inside expand rapidly with a sudden rise in temperature, and contract if the temperature drops. This creates a positive or negative pressure in the bottle respectively, which is equalized either by wine being forced out between the cork and the neck of a horizontal bottle, or by air being drawn in. This allows oxygen to come into contact with the wine which can initiate undesirable reactions. Consequently, a "weeping" bottle is not merely aesthetically displeasing, but it can also be an indication of problems during storage.

Humidity

The importance of the humidity in a wine cellar is frequently underestimated. It should be between 75% and 85%. If there is insufficient water vapor in the atmosphere, moisture will evaporate from the corks; they become dry, then start to deteriorate, and may no longer be able to prevent harmful oxygen getting into the wine. For this reason, wines stored in a very dry atmosphere generally mature much faster, and not always particularly well. High humidity conserves the corks, but can cause mold to develop on their exposed surface. As long as no wine has escaped between the cork and the rim of the bottle, however, the mold should not have any negative effects on the wine. Damp cellars used to be a hazard for wine labels, which often came away from the bottle, decomposed or became illegible. Modern labels are printed on special paper, however, and are rarely affected by dampness.

Light

Wine, in common with most food and drink, is altered by light. After a few weeks of being stored in a brightly lit room, its color, taste, and smell can all be impaired, principally by ultraviolet rays. Most wines are sold in colored bottles, which filter out some of the light, but a certain amount will always penetrate even very dark bottles, encouraging the absorption of oxygen into the wine. Consequently, storage areas should not have any kind of opening that allows a constant stream of daylight to enter. Artificial lighting should only be switched on when really necessary, and you should avoid using fluorescent tubes. Wines will also be better protected if stored in their original cases rather than on open shelves.

Odors

Although under normal conditions corks do not allow any liquid to seep out of the bottle, they do permit tiny amounts of gas to pass through. If the air in the storage room contains strong odors, therefore, particularly solvents (such as may escape from cans of paint or sealant), scented additives in cleaning agents or detergents, and perfumes used in room sprays, they may get into the bottle and taint the smell and taste of the wine. Another danger for wine is chlorine. This chemical element is contained in many cleaning and disinfecting materials, and can combine with phenol that may be hidden in the cork to form trichloranisole, creating the feared cork taste in wine.

Storage Position

Wine bottles should always be stored on their side, so that the cork is kept moist. Whether you lay them in wooden cases, on shelves, or in clay or cement pipes does not significantly affect the ageing process. The chosen method will have more to do with the amount of space available and the number of bottles to be stored. To avoid tiresome searches, single bottles should be kept in a shelving system. Original wooden cases, on the other hand, can simply be stacked on top of one another, and do not need to be emptied or even opened.

Record-keeping

Every bottle of wine is labeled with a "drink-by" date, which depends on a number of factors. If your collection is relatively small, a little label affixed to each case or shelf, giving the name of the wine, its vintage, and number of bottles should suffice. A small sign can be hung around the neck of single bottles. If you have a large number of bottles from a variety of origins, however, they should be logged in a cellar book. This can also be used to make a note of tasting impressions, allowing you to track the progress of a wine as it matures, provided you have several bottles of the same vintage. In addition, a number of companies now offer special computer software for managing a wine collection.

Old cellar vaults with a natural earth or stone floor, high humidity, and a temperature that hardly changes throughout the year provide the ideal conditions for storing and aging wine.

SERVING TEMPERATURE

The serving temperature of a wine has a crucial effect on how it will smell and taste. Chilling or warming an unopened bottle does not alter the composition of the contents, it is true, but a great wine will not reveal its full complexity if it is too cool, and a fizzy white will seem rather insipid at room temperature. The main reason for these variations is the complexity of wine: its vital ingredients react differently to the cold and warmth.

How Smell is Affected

The volatile compounds that make up the smell of a young wine and the bouquet of a mature one are released more quickly as the liquid gets warmer. To a certain extent, therefore, the correct serving temperature for a particular wine is determined by its aroma. The general rule of thumb is that the cooler the wine, the less its bouquet will be revealed.

The smell of most wines will barely be detectable even at 46°F (8°C). Consequently, the serving temperature of both red and white wines should be neither too cold, nor too warm, if you wish to experience the maximum number of pleasant—or even

An ice bucket looks reassuringly cold, and is the classic choice, especially for white and sparkling wines. Champagne should not be enjoyed in any other way.

unpleasant—aromatic nuances. High-quality reds can be served up to 64°F (18°C), while a complex white will be fine up to 61°F (16°C). There are no hard and fast rules, however, and you must always take into account the temperature to which the wine will be exposed after it has been poured: the first mouthful should not be the only one that tastes perfect. If you want to enjoy a mature Bordeaux over the course of a long evening around the fireplace, for example, it would be better to keep the bottle somewhat cool. Once in the glass, the wine will quickly match the external temperature of the room. In addition, dry heat accelerates the volatilization of the delicate aroma compounds.

If the serving temperature is too high, the alcohol in the wine can become volatile and leave an unpleasantly sharp sensation in the nasal cavity. Faults in the wine also become more obvious at higher temperatures. In the end, however, it is the quality of the wine that determines its ideal serving temperature: simpler products need lower temperatures, whilst more complex, higher quality wines benefit from greater warmth.

How Taste is Affected

The papillae on the tongue react differently to cold and warmth, and their perception of the various dimensions of wine—sugar, acidity, tannins, carbonic acid, and alcohol—is temperature dependent. A few degrees too warm or too cold, therefore, and a perfectly balanced wine can be completely ruined. The ease with which we can detect the various constituents of wine (apart from aroma) does not run parallel to the temperature curve: warmth reinforces our impression of sweetness and acidity, while cooler temperatures emphasize bitterness and tannic astringency.

In the case of simple white wines, therefore, which contain no tannins, the less sugar and acid are incorporated in their body and extract, the more they need to be chilled. Only at relatively low temperatures can their fruitiness be fully appreciated. This is especially true for whites that have been made from high-yield vines or have been pressed in air-tight tanks without undergoing biological de-acidification. These wines, in which a hint of carbonic acid normally acts as a guarantee of freshness, require chilling so as not to appear simply stale.

Carbon dioxide in solution not only makes a sparkling wine bubble, but is also the reason why such wines—whether Asti Spumante, Sekt, Prosecco or Champagne—are best chilled. Even here, however, there is a clear relationship between quality and temperature, at least to a limited degree: only sparkling wines whose charm lies principally in their fizziness should be served well chilled; those that are made with an excellent base wine, such as vintage champagne, can be treated like white wine in terms of temperature.

Full-bodied, superior whites that have generally been matured in wooden casks and have thus absorbed a certain amount of tannins should arrive at the table not far short of the temperature range for reds. Besides the fact that fridge temperatures would make the tannins taste bitter, the quality of wines such as white Burgundy or Californian Chardonnay can only be truly appreciated when they are able to reveal the full extent of their aromatic complexity.

The correct temperature for red wines is always determined by their tannins. The more they contain, the warmer they should be when served. The finesse of an old red is shown to best advantage at around 64°F (18°C). Great reds with a lower tannin content should be served a few degrees cooler, however, so as to give suitable prominence to their fruit.

Red wines should only be served cool if they contain hardly any tannins. In such cases, rosé wines are invariably a better alternative.

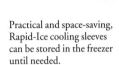

water for 15 to 30 minutes (the process takes considerably longer in a fridge). If stored in a wine cellar at around 57°F (14°C), more complex whites can be brought directly to the table, where their aromas will be fully developed after about ten minutes in the glass.

Red wines can be transferred into a decanter that has been rinsed in warm water. They will warm more evenly and more gently, however, in a wine glass at room temperature. Rapid heating next to a radiator or other heat source is not advisable, since only the wine nearest the heat will be warmed, which may adversely affect the overall impression of harmony.

Practical and space-saving, Rapid-Ice cooling sleeves can be stored in the freezer until needed.

Acrylic wine coolers keep the wine at the desired temperature for a long time. A further advantage of this type of cooler is that the label on the bottle remains clearly visible.

Earthenware wine coolers are placed in cold water before use till the porous material is saturated. The temperature reduction brought about by condensation then helps to keep the bottle cool. These coolers are also suitable for red wines.

BRINGING WINE TO THE CORRECT TEMPERATURE

Superior wines that are the result of gentle pressing can be very sensitive to large fluctuations in temperature, and may seem closed or lacking in balance if suddenly subjected to extremes of heat or cold. Consequently, the best way to bring a bottle of wine to the correct temperature is to gently warm or cool it over a period of time.

With a great red, this is best achieved by leaving it in a relatively cool room, then transferring it to the living room shortly before serving. The temperature here tends to be around 68°F (20°C), which will quickly warm the wine in the glass by a degree or two, bringing it to the ideal drinking temperature.

White wines can generally be cooled ahead of time in the fridge, but should be removed a little while before you wish to drink them (how long before depends on their quality), so that they are not overly cold when served. If you do need to cool a bottle rapidly, however, stand it in iced

Serving temperatures		
Wine	Description	Temperature
Sparkling wines		
dry, fruity	very well chilled	39–43°F (4–6°C)
Champagnes		
non-vintage cuvée	well chilled	43–48°F (6–9°C)
vintage	cellar temperature	54–57°F (12–14°C)
White wines		
light, acidic	well chilled	43–48°F (6–9°C)
exotically aromatic	chilled	46–50°F (8–10°C)
full-bodied, woody	cool	57–61°F (14–16°C)
Rosé	well chilled	43–48°F (6–9°C)
Red wines		
light, fruity	cellar temperature	54–57°F (12–14°C)
medium bodied	moderately warm	61°F (16°C)
full-bodied, tannic, mature	room temperature	64°F (18°C)
Dessert wines	chilled to moderately warm	54–61°F (12–16°C)

DECANTING WINE

A decanting funnel makes the task of transferring wine into a carafe much easier. The fine sieve inside holds back any sediment and guides the wine into the carafe.

Right page, large picture
White wines can also be much improved by decanting, because they also need more oxygen. This is particularly true of aged, noble sweet wines.

Transferring a wine from the bottle to a carafe is much more than simply a way of displaying your knowledge of etiquette. Indeed, there are two important reasons for recommending that a wine should be decanted.

• Old wines—principally red wines—should be separated from the sediment that will have formed in the bottle over the years.

• Young wines should deliberately be brought into contact with the oxygen in the air, in order to let their tannins mature.

Although decanting in its proper sense—that is, separating the wine from the sediment—is a long-established custom among wine lovers, the need to aerate wine that has not yet formed any sediment is more controversial. While those in favor of the practice argue that the wine really opens up in the carafe, its opponents express concern that overly generous contact with the air may result in a loss of freshness and especially fruitiness.

The chemical reactions that take place in the wine after it has been poured from the bottle have yet to be researched in detail. Consequently, we can only explain in very general terms why it is that some wines that have hardly any smell when the cork is first removed can be bursting with aromas after a short time in a decanter; why others open up for a short time,

Cleaning decanters

Decanters should be rinsed out in hot water, dried on the outside, and then left to drain—special stands can be bought for this purpose. Traces of red wine pigment and fine streaks of scale that build up gradually on the inside of the decanter are best removed with activated oxygen. This is available in tablet form, such as those used to clean dentures.

but then become closed once again; why some develop an unpleasant smell; or why some varieties of wine may hardly evolve at all, while another variety "dies" within a few minutes.

In practice, therefore, all we have to help us decide whether or not to decant—a question that arises anew every time we open a bottle—is a basic understanding of the stability of wines (based on a knowledge of winemaking technology), past experience, and, last but not least, our drinking habits and personal preference.

Over the months or years that it lies in storage, wine gradually absorbs the oxygen in the bottle. At the moment it is uncorked, therefore, the wine is often particularly reactive, and oxidizes in a relatively short space of time. At the same time, acids and alcohols react to form esters, which alter the smell and taste of the wine. Generally speaking, the fewer stabilizing tannins there are in the wine, the quicker these changes take place. In the case of very old red wines, whose tannins have largely polymerized and fallen to the bottom of the bottle to form sediment, these should be carefully decanted directly before being served, if at all, and never several hours in advance. Ideally, you should use a vessel that has a capacity not much greater than that of the bottle. In good light, preferably shining from underneath, pour the wine slowly into the decanter. As soon as the first cloudy material becomes visible in the neck of the bottle, stop pouring, and serve the wine immediately.

Decanting a wine

Bring the bottle from the cellar without shaking it up, and proceed with great care. A good light shining from beneath is essential so that you can see when the sediment on the bottom starts to move toward the neck of the bottle. Whether you use a candle, torch, or elaborate technical construction is a matter of personal preference.

Decanting Young Wine

Young red wines should always be deliberately aerated if they contain a lot of tannin. The carafe should be around half full when the wine has been poured in. After as little as half an hour, the smell and taste will usually be perceptibly different: the undesirable smells that can sometimes develop in unfiltered wines dissipate, the aroma becomes more complex, and the taste becomes softer and less bitter.

Fragile reds, on the other hand, should always be poured straight into the glass from the bottle. Served via a decanter, such wines can taste metallic and sharp.

Contrary to usual practice, it is often a good idea to aerate white wines, too, due to recent changes in vinification methods. Chardonnay that has been fermented and matured in wooden casks, in particular, should always be left to breathe in a carafe for an hour or more before serving. This allows any undesirable yeast smells in these often unfiltered wines to break down, and develops their floral and fruity aromas, which otherwise tend to be eclipsed by the smell of the wood.

The History and Shape of the Decanter

Glass carafes for serving wine existed as early as the 18th century, although the shape of these early vessels was designed simply to be aesthetically pleasing, and they were often elaborately decorated. The most important criterion for a decanter is that it is made from clear glass, so that the color of the wine can be assessed and also displayed to best advantage. Modern decanters are designed with their function in mind, and so simple forms are preferred. The ideal vessel in which to let wine breathe is a wide-bellied carafe with a narrow neck. It should have around twice the volume of the bottle to be decanted, to allow even absorption of oxygen at the surface and concentrate the developing aromas directly above the wine.

From top to bottom
The popular duck decanter with silver lid, containing a medium-aged red wine.

This modern, big-bellied carafe was designed to allow young wines to breathe. The large surface area allows aromas to develop quickly in red and white wines.

The classic cut-glass carafe with a low body and large diameter is mainly used for serving older, tannin-rich red wines that need to breathe.

WHICH GLASS FOR WHICH WINE?

SPARKLING WINE AND CHAMPAGNE

Think of sparkling wine or champagne as a wine rather than as a carbonated drink when choosing a suitable glass. Its delicate scent, developed over years in the bottle, can only be detected if it is concentrated in the glass above the surface of the liquid. The ideal glass for sparkling wine, therefore, has a slim, tulip-shaped silhouette that turns in towards the rim.

LIGHT, ACIDIC WHITES

The glass does not need to be very wide, because only the fruity aspect of these wines should be emphasized. Glasses with particularly tall funnels are not suitable since these wines do not contain enough alcohol to act as a carrier for the aroma compounds. To reduce the impact of the acidity, it is best to choose glasses that curve slightly outwards at the rim. This channels the wine onto the tip of the tongue, the area that responds to sweetness.

FULL-BODIED, WOOD-AGED WHITES

The recommended glass for whites that have been aged in wood is one with a relatively large volume, because the wine needs sufficient contact with air in order to reveal its complex aromas. The funnel should be taller than with light whites, since the high alcohol content would otherwise assault the nose rather unpleasantly. In addition, the mix of aromas only becomes harmonious a little way above the surface of the wine.

INTENSELY AROMATIC, LUXURIOUS WHITES

These wines need a glass that is somewhat larger and more open than is the case with more acidic whites. The funnel should not be too tall, however, so that the complex and fragile aromas are not lost before time. The wide mouth of the glass directs the liquid to the edge of the tongue, thereby giving more emphasis to the acidity. A glass of this shape enables these wines to display their many layers and really do justice to their deservedly excellent reputation.

Cleaning wine glasses

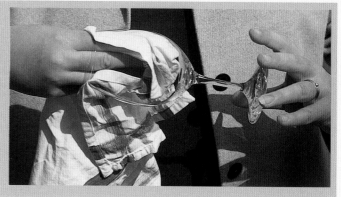

Most modern wine glasses are dishwasher safe. Alternatively, wash them in hot water using very little detergent, rinse in clean water, then dry and polish them with a lint-free cloth. The seemingly smooth surface of the glass actually has a degree of roughness at molecular level, which can trap not only the aromas of wine, but also odors from detergents, towels, and cupboards. For this reason, wine glasses must never come into contact with perfumed detergents or towels that have been treated with fabric softener. Traces of grease and lipstick are best removed with a little unperfumed soap.

LIGHT, FRUITY, YOUNG REDS

Young, light reds (especially the *primeur* wines) are best served in a glass that is similar to the one for exotically aromatic whites, but slightly smaller in volume so as to concentrate the delicate fruit fragrances. Again, the funnel should not be overly tall. Very smooth reds, in particular, become even better when drunk lightly chilled from a glass of this type.

ELEGANT, SPICY, SILKY REDS

The multi-layered, delicately fruity aroma of a wine such as Pinot Noir requires a large surface area to develop fully. A balloon-shaped glass gives optimal support to the spicy notes that are a particular characteristic of these wines, and a slight outward curve at the rim emphasizes fruitiness on the tongue whilst reducing the often prominent impression of acidity.

LUXURIOUS, VELVETY REDS

Dark, velvety red wines tend to have a well-structured, luxurious aroma which they will only release if given sufficient surface area. The ideal glass, therefore, is a tulip shape with a wide bulge to about a third of its height. Depending on how concentrated and alcoholic the wine is, a bigger or smaller glass can be chosen. A Merlot from Pomerol or Saint-Émilion, for example, can be served in a very large glass.

TANNIC, EXTRACT-RICH REDS

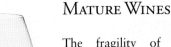

These very dark wines need a great deal of contact with oxygen to develop their bouquet fully. Glasses with a wide diameter and large volume are important, therefore, to do justice to their complexity. At the same time, the funnel needs to be fairly tall (meaning the glass looks visibly elongated) so that the fumes from the alcohol are not too pronounced by the time they reach the nose.

MATURE WINES

The fragility of mature wines demands a glass that can concentrate the aromas. Since the ratio of liquid to air is important for the intensity of the bouquet, the ideal glass is a relatively large balloon shape which narrows considerably at the rim. This allows the wine sufficient space in which to blossom. Mature wines should not be swirled too vigorously, since too much movement rapidly makes them seem metallic.

DESSERT WINES

The wide variety of dessert wines cannot really be catered for with a single glass. For Sauternes, however, or wines with a full, almost viscous texture and intense aroma, the glass should be funnel-shaped toward the bottom, giving the small serving the largest possible surface area over which to develop its complex aromas fully. The glass should become narrower towards the rim to concentrate the bouquet.

Serving Wine

The decanting operation requires a steady hand. It is essential not to subject the bottle to any shaking that could stir up the sediment, especially when there is a lot of it. A vintage port, for example, may contain a great many tannins—not least because of the added brandy. The sediment that builds up as it matures over the decades can easily comprise a sixth or more of the bottle contents. To decant such a wine perfectly, ingenious minds have developed the decanting machine. This consists of a metal cradle in which the bottle is laid several hours before serving, to let the deposits sink to the bottom. After uncorking it at an angle, a crank allows the user to tip the bottle very slowly and without any jolts, so that clear wine can be poured into the decanter without the sediment being disturbed.

In the case of old wines, where there is a concern that increased contact with air in a decanter could be damaging, a serving basket may be useful. These ensure that the bottle is

All wines can benefit from careful serving. This includes choosing the right kind of glasses.

always kept at an angle, preventing the sediment from being stirred up as would otherwise be the case every time the bottle is returned to the vertical position after pouring. Again, the bottle should be placed in the basket ahead of time, uncorked very carefully, and the wine allowed a further, brief standing time before being served.

Baskets are particularly helpful for serving old red wines that have a sediment, but might deteriorate if aerated by decanting.

How to Open and Serve Sparkling Wines

Sparkling wine in general, and champagne in particular, is very much the drink for festive occasions. At the same time, however, it is a very sophisticated wine that will always have spent a few years maturing in the bottle. To ensure that the delicate mix of aromas that has developed over time is still intact when the wine reaches the glass, the bottle must be opened very carefully. Nothing is more detrimental to the overall impression of elegance and harmony than the cork exploding from the bottle. In the pictures below, the SOMMELIER at the Ritz in Paris demonstrates the perfect way to open and serve champagne.

Champagne is best served in a bucket of iced water and chilled to 46–50°F (8–10°C).

Remove the foil covering cleanly by cutting around the bottle neck.

Pull the foil away, then untwist and remove the wire muzzle.

With your hand around the neck of the bottle, keep the cork in place with your thumb.

Gripping the cork with one hand, carefully twist the whole bottle with the other.

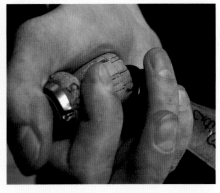

Champagne lovers never let the cork off with a bang, because this allows too much carbon dioxide and aroma to escape.

Support the bottle on outstretched fingers, with your thumb in the hollow at the bottom.

Hold the bottle level over the glass and the champagne will flow out gently, without too much foam.

A tulip-shaped, clear crystal glass enhances both bouquet and sparkle.

Corkscrews

Ever since the early 17th century, when corks became the most common way of sealing wine bottles, inventors and engineers have puzzled over ways to remove them. The forerunners of the modern corkscrew were special pliers for gripping the corks, which originally protruded above the rim of the bottle neck. Almost a century went by after the invention of the cork plug before metal spirals came into use. The inspiration for these came from the twisted tools used in England to remove gun-cotton from the barrels of rifles. Corkscrews are generally considered to be an English invention, therefore, and the best have always come from Great Britain, right up to the present day.

The simplest type of corkscrew consists of a metal helix, a shaft, and a handle. The most crucial element, though, as far as effectiveness is concerned, is the helix, which must be easy to twist into the cork, but should not break it up as it is being extracted. The most reliable corkscrews, therefore, are generally those with a spiral about 2$\frac{1}{2}$ inches (6 cm) long that is open in the middle. Even corks that have become porous over a long period of storage can be removed without any problems using this type of corkscrew. A helix with a solid core, by contrast, may cut right through the cork or simply pull out its center. Consequently, they are only suitable for removing corks that are relatively short and very hard. The problem of cutting right through the cork can be avoided using a two-pronged extractor, whose blades are inserted between the cork and the neck of the bottle. Called a "Butler's Friend," it works something like a pair of pliers, but needs considerable care when used.

The effort that can sometimes be required to pull the cork from the bottle has also inspired inventive types to come up with new devices. In the end, two models have achieved success: the "Waiter's Friend," which has a folding lever that is positioned on the rim of the bottle and allows the cork to be prised out; and a device that sits over the neck of the bottle and uses a counter-screwing action to extract the helix complete with cork.

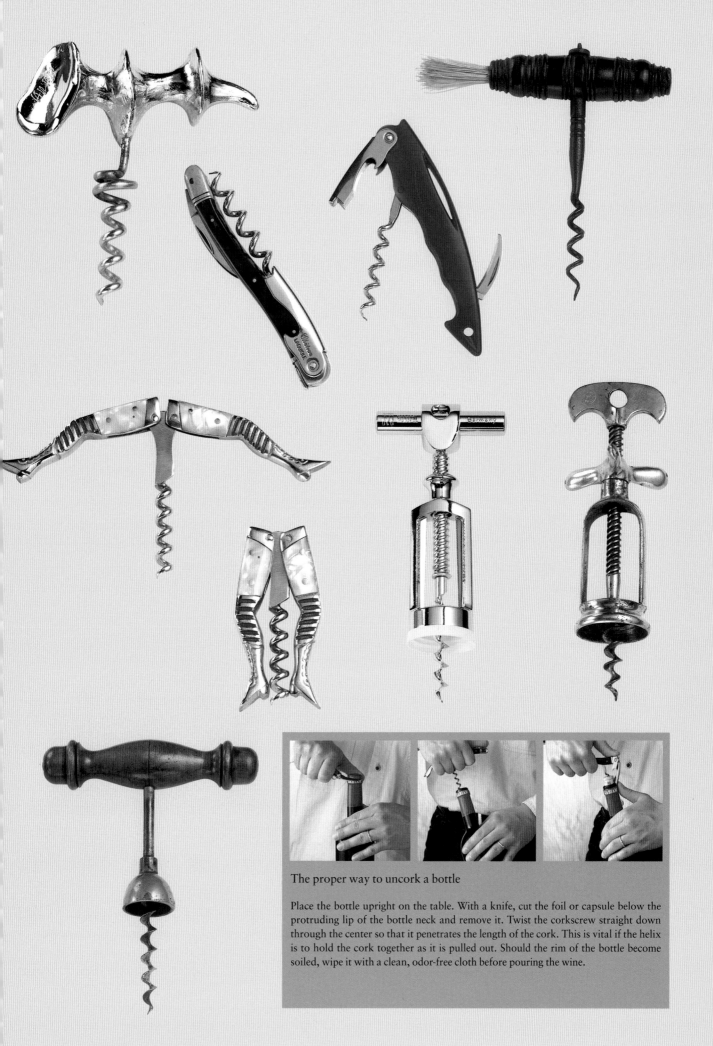

The proper way to uncork a bottle

Place the bottle upright on the table. With a knife, cut the foil or capsule below the protruding lip of the bottle neck and remove it. Twist the corkscrew straight down through the center so that it penetrates the length of the cork. This is vital if the helix is to hold the cork together as it is pulled out. Should the rim of the bottle become soiled, wipe it with a clean, odor-free cloth before pouring the wine.

Wine and Entertainment

According to received wisdom, there is a strict set of rules for drinking wine with food: whites go with fish, reds with meat, dry wines should be served before sweet, young before old, no wine with salad, champagne with caviar, and so on. In no other area of life are rules passed on to successive generations as unquestioningly as with food and drink, even though the type of food we eat, and the ways we cook and serve it, have seen a number of fundamental changes in the past 50 years, as has the wine industry.

Progress in enology and a number of improved techniques, machines, and chemical agents triggered a revolution in the wine industry from around the middle of the 20th century. We began to intervene in, and increasingly tighten our control over, the winemaking process using stainless steel tanks, temperature control systems, fermentation enzymes, cultured yeasts, and aroma additives, and thus it is no longer the vagaries of nature that decide what the alcohol content, levels of tannin and acidity, and aromas in a wine will be. Almost every aspect of the taste of a wine can now be manipulated. Moreover, wine has become subject to the dictates of fashion, and this has fundamentally altered our long-established perceptions of how wine should taste. There is a wealth of luxurious, full-bodied, wood-flavored whites on the market today, for example, which have nothing in common with the classic acidic "fish wine"

except color—and often not even that. Many of the world's great reds, moreover, can be soft and mellow even when they are young, and no longer have to be matured for years before they are ready to drink.

The only rule which is valid today is that there really are no rules any more. Modern wines are aromatically too complex to have overly simple dictums applied to them. Not only are there hundreds of different grape varieties worldwide, which are bottled in an infinite number of blends, but also carefully produced hand-made wines which reflect the part played by the soil and climate of their respective vineyards, and by the individual winemaker.

If wine and food are to be matched so that they do not interfere with, but instead complement or even emphasize each other's flavors, then the most suitable place for a particular wine within a menu must really be assessed on an individual basis.

Which Wine for Which Guests?

There are a number of aspects to consider when planning a menu comprising a series of courses and wines. The first thing to bear in mind is the occasion. Are you planning a light-hearted garden party in high, midsummer temperatures, or a contemplative evening with other wine lovers? If you provide an unsuitable bottle at

Left
A light bistro wine with jumbo shrimp (prawns).

Right
The ideal combination: game with red wine.

the wrong time, there is a risk that both a good wine, and also the event itself, will be badly served. It is not a sign of meanness, therefore, to refrain from offering a great Bordeaux at an afternoon barbecue; its astringent, bitter heaviness would not go at all well with a highly seasoned sausage. A fruity red with a fresh acidity would be much more enjoyable, especially since the complex aromas of the Bordeaux would quickly evaporate with the high air temperature.

You should not ask too much or too little of your guests. People who rarely drink wine find an elegant, top-quality white just too demanding—it often seems rather thin. Similarly, a great red comes across as unpleasantly astringent and heavy. A wine that is well-made and easy to drink, on the other hand, would be enjoyed by all. As a rule, novices prefer light-colored (i.e. white and rosé) wines, and find inky, super-concentrated reds largely inaccessible.

At a garden party, a wine buff is likely to find a luscious, fruity Californian Zinfandel more of a pleasant surprise than any rosé wine. Committed Burgundy drinkers will be put off by a powerful Australian Shiraz, but a good Pinot Noir from a different country may gently lead them to explore new territory. It is easy to impress (and possibly even convert) fans of Bordeaux with an excellent New World Cabernet or Merlot. If you have an open-minded wine

lover as a guest, he or she will hardly be overjoyed if you proffer a simple, albeit perfectly creditable *vin de pays* and rave about its value for money, when a quality wine from an unknown region would always be a pleasure, and need not cost a fortune.

Unique fine wines should always be reserved for a special occasion, not merely out of respect for their high quality, their origins, and the knowledge of the winemaker who produced them, but also in order that they can be enjoyed with deliberate awareness of the unusual pleasures they afford. Wines like these are satisfying in their own right, and so it is not vital that they accompany and complement good food.

If your cellar houses any such rare, character-laden bottles, then a visit from friends who know something about wine is an opportunity not to be missed. For it is only when these liquid treasures are shared in like-minded company that they will fulfil their real purpose and provide some unforgettable moments.

Bottles should be matched not only to the food, but also to the occasion. A relaxed gathering of friends would enjoy a cheerful, uncomplicated wine, for example, while a stylish party requires stylish wines.

The Art of Enjoying Wine

Our next task is to develop some kind of theory concerning the art of enjoying wine. Its principles are dictated by the human sense organs, which will perform to the best of their capabilities if carefully nurtured. The most important principle is to avoid any sort of culinary boredom. The nerves involved in both smelling and tasting quickly become dulled, but will remain sharp and alert if they continue to be subjected to new stimuli. Thus, the food and wine on a menu should include as many of the different basic taste sensations as possible. An aperitif of dry champagne, for example, should not necessarily be followed by an equally dry white wine, just as a Barolo following a Chianti will not surprise the taste buds.

Of course, this is not to say that there should be arbitrary changes of direction within a menu. Our olfactory and taste organs also become progressively overloaded, and so a delicate Pinot Noir will scarcely be experienced to full advantage when following a luscious dessert wine, for example. Consequently, the flavors in a wine should become more, rather than less intense as a menu progresses. From this we can derive a few useful rules.

• Light, fresh wines, whether red or white, should generally be served before luxurious, alcohol-rich ones.

• Wines with attractive, woody overtones are best drunk after fruity wines that have been matured in a tank.

- The sweeter a wine is, the further toward the end of the meal it should be offered. If you really must have *foie gras* with Sauternes as a starter, you should plan to follow it with a course which will refresh the palate before you serve any delicate wine.
- The finesse of a great, bottle-matured wine is more readily appreciated if it is drunk before an equally good younger wine, because the latter contains considerably more tannins, and thus is more intense in terms of taste.

MATCHING WINE AND FOOD

The features of a wine you should consider when planning to match it with food can be divided into three basic categories.
- The first and most important aspect is a wine's impact in terms of the tastes that can be detected on the tongue, such as sweetness, acidity, and bitterness.
- Secondly, the texture of the wine should be assessed—the lasting impressions that are left in the mouth such as cold, warm, creamy, silky, watery, dry or rough.
- Finally, the aromas that are detected in the nasopharynx should be taken into account.

The food you are intending to serve should be analyzed using the same system.

CONTRASTING EFFECTS

The taste characteristics of wine and food persist for longest, and thus possibly cause most interference when they combine on the tongue. This does not mean, however, that the food on your plate must always taste the same as the wine in your glass. Indeed, that can be unpleasant, particularly in the case of bitter substances. Instead, it is much better to plan appealing contrasts, with the aid of the following list.

Wine	Food	Remarks
Sweet	Sweet	Take the intense sweetness into account
Sweet	Salty	A high alcohol content results in bitterness
Acid	Sour	Use caution with vinegar
Acid	Salty	
Bitter	Sweet	Sweetness derived from fat, not from sugar

Impressive starters: Far Eastern-inspired tapas accompany a fresh, intensive white wine. Curiosity is aroused, the palate tickled and the taste nerves are prepared for further enjoyment.

TEXTURE

The textures of a wine, i.e. the physically perceptible attributes that characterize it, are detected throughout the oral cavity, and are almost as important as the basic tastes (sweet, sour, salty, and bitter) with regard to possible combinations of food and wine. It is advisable to offer comparable textures in the glass and on the plate, particularly when, in a menu of several courses, a balance of tastes is important. A luxuriant wine goes better with rich foods, therefore, and the interplay of aromas in a light wine is properly revealed only when accompanying an equally light meal. A delicate wine might make an excessively greasy roast palatable, but will have no other function than that of a refreshing drink.

The same is true for creamy wines and creamy foods, which need that reciprocal textural harmony so as not to seem too thin, insipid, acidic, or even bitter. The only impact that cannot be matched with a comparable texture in food is the feeling of roughness in the mouth due to an excess of young, immature tannins. Their dryness can best be integrated into a meal in conjunction with the syrupy consistency of a gravy made from the reduced juices of roast meat, in which there will be a delicate mix of sweet and bitter aromas.

AROMAS

When planning appropriate combinations of food and wine, this is the one area that permits a certain degree of creativity. Provided that the basic tastes and textures are well matched, you can experiment to your heart's content without any real danger. The aromas of wines and food are detected in the nasopharynx, and are their most varied and at the same time most volatile components. Unlike the basic tastes and textures, aromas cannot distort one another; in the worst case scenario, one aroma can eclipse another. Similar aromas in wine and food almost always produce successful combinations. Nevertheless, caution is called for, because spiciness or fruitiness in a wine can be fundamentally different than the aromas in food that are described with the same vocabulary. The more concretely you try to define the smells you want to match, the more convincing the result will be.

A contrast between aromas will often produce the most thrilling sensory experience, particularly since many food smells, such as fish or cheese, are not found in any wine. In such cases, the method of preparing the food, and especially the seasoning, is the crucial factor. Beyond this, whether you serve fish accompanied by the aroma of herbs (as found in Sancerre, for example) or smoke (Pouilly-Fumé) is ultimately up to you.

Sparkling Wine and Champagne

The classic sparkling wine exists in nearly as many variations as still wine. It can be dry or sweet, full-bodied or light, and aged by protective or oxidative methods. The only thing common to them all is the presence of a certain amount of carbon dioxide, which is what creates the bubbles in your glass and the tingling in your mouth. Most high quality sparkling wines (except sweet ones) are excellent as an aperitif, because the carbonic acid in them pleasantly refreshes and sensitizes the papillae on the tongue.

The world's most famous sparkling wine is champagne, of which there are a great number of styles on the market. Two factors in particular determine its suitability as an accompaniment to food, namely sweetness and acidity. The majority of champagnes have the designation *brut* (dry), but can still contain up to $1/4$ ounce of residual sugar per pint (15 grams per liter). In inappropriate combinations, this high level of potential sweetness can make even a great champagne seem flabby and sticky. The classic combination of caviar and champagne, for example, only works if the wine is bone dry (*extra brut*). Other than this, champagne always works well accompanying appetizers that tone down the interplay of sweetness and acidity in the drink without drowning its freshness and elegance.

As well as all the characteristics that stimulate the senses, there is a psychological dimension to the enjoyment of sparkling wines, particularly champagne. More so than a still wine, these wines impart a celebratory atmosphere to any gathering. Champagne's reputation as a festive drink has become part of western culture. To get the most out of champagne and other quality sparkling wines, therefore, the occasion and the company must be taken into account, otherwise the guests may be somewhat bewildered or the host considered snobbish.

Champagne is traditionally served as an aperitif, and is well suited to the role—it does indeed stimulate the appetite. If you are not going to serve appetizers as well, you should choose a mature, creamy, well-balanced sparkling wine, to avoid empty stomachs being irritated by aggressive acids. Sparkling wine works much better as an aperitif, however, when accompanied by some choice nibbles. These can range from green olives (not too salty), through fancy canapés, to exotic little fish or meat kebabs. The only important factor is to ensure that the sophistication of the company, drink, appetizers, and subsequent menu are appropriately matched.

Bubbles throughout the Meal

Dry sparkling wines can be a worthy accompaniment to a meal. In a similar fashion to light, tangy whites, their high acidity (boosted further by the carbonic acid) makes them an ideal choice to go with fish dishes. Raw seafood, in particular, be it fresh oysters or Japanese sushi, is perfect with a bone dry sparkling wine. A mouthful of Spumante will remove any trace of oiliness from smoked fish. Even moderately spicy Asian cuisine can go well with a glass of sparkling wine; highly seasoned foods usually work best with stronger, acidic wines whose sweetness derives from fruit, whereas richer wines that have a high sugar content should be avoided.

A common mistake is not to be selective when choosing a sparkling wine to accompany dessert, for most will almost always be far too dry to stand up against sweet foods. If need be, a medium dry sparkling wine could be served with a light, fruity, but not overly sweet dessert. The Italian dessert wine Moscato d'Asti would also be a good choice: its low alcohol content and gentle effervescence, combined with the grape variety's fruitiness, sweetness, and wealth of aromas, not only make it the perfect accompaniment to a light fruit tart, but also mean that it could be served with a starter of *foie gras* as an alternative to Sauternes. More so than a luxurious still wine, which quickly deadens the taste buds, a good Moscato cleans the palate and prepares it for further pleasures.

Typical grape varieties: Chardonnay, Pinot Noir, Pinot Meunier, Chenin Blanc, Mauzac Blanc, Xarel·lo, Parellada, Macabeo, Riesling, Muscat.

Typical wines: Champagne, Crémant, Cava, Franciacorta, Sekt, Spumante.

Sparkling wine makes a good aperitif. Plenty of nibbles form a good accompaniment, including canapés and olives.

Left page, large picture
Champagne is a symbol of celebration and enjoyment. Depending on age and grape variety, it can form the perfect accompaniment for a whole menu.

Left page, small picture
Fresh oysters with lemon, appetizingly arranged on ice, accompanied by a sharp and sparkling young Champagne Extra Brut.

LIGHT, ACIDIC WHITES

Wines in this group are characterized by a pronounced sharpness, and seem fresh, fruity, and relatively light to both the nose and the mouth. Their alcohol content is often less than 12% vol, and even the stronger wines always have a stimulating effect. Most of them are aged protectively in stainless-steel tanks, which gives them an almost steely nature. Depending on their quality, these wines make do with fruitiness alone or reveal additional mineral overtones specific to their vineyard site.

When matching this type of wine to food, the first thing to take into account is its acidity, which under no circumstances should be accentuated any further. Generally speaking, these wines will not have been softened by MALOLACTIC FERMENTATION, and their high concentration of malic acid can occasionally seem very aggressive. Wine waiters have traditionally recommended these wines as the ideal accompaniment to fish, since their acidity—in addition to or instead of lemon—can bring a lightness of flavor even to relatively oily fish (or those prepared with a lot of oil). Moreover, a young, very dry wine from this group would not overpower a more delicate fish dish.

The clearly accentuated flavors of these wines do not overload the taste buds. In addition to their traditional role with fish, therefore, they are a good choice to accompany a variety of starters. All white meat and poultry dishes are suitable, as well as creamy soups and salads, if their seasoning is not too sweet.

Because of their refreshing nature, these acidic wines also work well as a deliberate counterbalance to the sumptuousness of some regional specialties such as a *choucroute* from Alsace (sauerkraut cooked with pork and sausages) or the Austrian *Tafelspitz* (boiled fillet of beef).

For maximum impact, the aromas must be precisely matched with those of the food. Although many wines in this group are similar in their basic, acid-dominated flavor and generally smooth texture, the aromas that determine fragrance and finish vary widely. Fresh hay, grass, green pepper, apple, citrus fruits, peach, apricot, quince, gooseberry, flowers—depending on the grape variety, the entire green and yellow range can be found here. Riesling tends to have floral nuances, Sauvignon Blanc is often grassy, Grüner Veltliner tastes peppery, and Albariño of minerals.

The subtlety of these aromas means that a degree of harmony with those in the food is advisable. Sauvignon, therefore, can be supported aromatically with fresh herbs like mint, basil, tarragon, and cilantro (coriander) leaves, while Riesling is better served with fruity side dishes, such as slices of baked apple. If well chilled, their fresh, lively taste and moderate alcohol content make these wines a good choice for pleasant drinks at an outside party or picnic, where they are an excellent complement to broiled fish, small poultry kebabs, barbecued vegetables, or a salad buffet.

Left page
Light, fresh white wines are the classic accompaniment to fish and seafood.

Typical grape varieties: Albariño, Melon, Chenin, Sauvignon, Riesling, Silvaner, Grüner Veltliner.

Typical wines: Vinho Verde, Rías Baixas, Muscadet, Anjou, Sancerre, Entre-Deux-Mers, Marlborough Sauvignon, Alsace, Mosel.

Asparagus demands a wine that can tackle its well developed aroma, such as a dry Riesling or Sancerre.

FULL-BODIED, WOOD-AGED WHITES

White wines that have been matured in wooden barrels are frequently reminiscent of great reds, both in their alcohol content, which is often as high as 13 or 14% vol, and their opulence. The distinct tannic dimension to their structure is a further link with red wine, although in this case the tannins come from the wood of the barrels rather than from the grapes themselves.

The acidity of such wines is generally reduced to moderate levels by malolactic fermentation, and is further masked by the inherent sweetness of the alcohol. They tend to seem astonishingly full-bodied, even when young, and have good potential for bottle aging. Their aromas can be vaguely reminiscent of exotic fruits like papaya, guava, and mango. Wines made from the Chardonnay grape frequently have distinct hints of pineapple.

TEMPERAMENTAL STARS

Although very popular, the combination of "white" taste and "red" texture makes this group the wine waiter's biggest headache, for they do not take at all well to being accompanied by unsuitable foods.

The first consideration when looking for the right match should be the full-bodied nature of these wines. Alcohol is largely perceived as texture in the mouth: the wine seems more viscous and leaves behind a sensation of warmth. Contrary to established practice, therefore, these wines are not generally suitable accompaniments for fish dishes. Their high alcohol content makes the fish taste oily and old. Conversely, the slightly sour sauce often served with poached fish makes the wine seem a little sweet and flabby. Moreover, the tannins resulting from barrel maturation produce a fairly unpleasant taste when combined with fish oil. Only shellfish, which are naturally slightly sweet, can adequately counter the heaviness of wood-matured whites.

The alcohol content of these wines means that they are an unsuitable accompaniment to salty foods, because salt combined with alcohol produces a bitter taste. Particular care needs to be taken with cheese, therefore, especially blue varieties. Very spicy foods are also best avoided, as they intensify the effect of the alcohol, and vice versa.

Despite these restrictions, Meursault and similar wines can accompany food in a number of excellent combinations.

BETTER WITH CREAM

Dishes prepared with reasonable amounts of cream and butter are almost always the perfect

choice, because they can hold their own against the wine's creamy texture and the initial impression of subtle sweetness it produces in the mouth. In addition, the fat content of the food will lessen the astringency of the tannins in the wine, while the tannins, for their part, prevent the dishes from seeming overly rich. Stylish combinations of food and wine can be created, therefore, if the basic tastes work well together, the textures are similar, and consideration is given to the aromas. Whether the wine has the sumptuous pineapple fragrance of wood-matured Californian Chardonnay, the exotic aromas of Australian or New Zealand Sauvignon, the powerful elegance of a German, Italian, or Austrian Grauburgunder, or the highly individual hints of smoked bacon fat and

honey in the best wood-matured Bergerac Sec, it can be integrated into the meal with success if you ensure that the aromas in the food are, as far as possible, an identical match. A simple trick is to include roasted nuts in the meal, because their smell carries the wine's finish through into the food. Tarragon, honey, or a touch of vanilla acts in a similar way: a sauce flavored with any of these, accompanying white meat or poultry, sets off perfectly the aromas of nuts, cream, and often freshly-made toast in these wines.

A great oak-fermented Chardonnay really comes into its own alongside delicate poultry with a cream sauce and walnuts.

Typical grape varieties: Chardonnay, Sauvignon Blanc, Semillon, Pinot Blanc, Pinot Gris, Grenache Blanc.

Typical wines: Corton Charlemagne, Meursault, Puligny-Montrachet, Graves, Limoux, and numerous New World wines.

Luxurious, Highly Aromatic Whites

Exotic cuisine often experiments with a wide range of ingredients and spices. Highly aromatic, full-bodied white wines make an excellent accompaniment.

This group of wines surprise the nose and palate with a whole range of luxurious, exotic, almost perfume-like aromas. The scent of apricots, peaches, lychees, and mangoes can waft up from the glass as distinctly as the fragrance of jasmine, honeysuckle, and rose, or the smell of honey, cinnamon, cloves, and nutmeg. Gewürztraminer and its fellows owe their impressive bouquet to the derivatives of special proteins in the cells of the grape flesh. They completely overwhelm the olfactory nerves, and the impression of extreme opulence is reinforced by their impact on the tongue. The combination of high alcohol content and low acidity, however, can make these wines seem rather eccentric.

The Dominant Partner

The aromatic distinctiveness of these wines imposes clear limits on the types of food they can accompany: delicate flavors will simply be drowned. Oysters, white fish, tender kid or veal, and subtle sauces will not stand a chance against the onslaught of a wine from this category.

The first impression that such wines make on the tongue is one of sweetness, which may be caused by a very little unfermented sugar, but is primarily the result of lavish fruit and a high alcohol content. The low acidity of the wine increases the sensation that your mouth is completely coated.

For a successful combination of these wines with a meal, the food should always have a certain richness to it. Choose dishes that are a little sweet or have a fairly high fat content. Foods that are mildly spicy, somewhat salty or have a definite smoky taste will also hold up well. Distinctly sour food, however, will make full-bodied wines such as Gewürztraminer, Muscat, or Viognier seem heavy-handed, and should be avoided.

Working on the basis that the texture of the food must fill the mouth as much as that of the wine, we can then begin to play with the aromas—a particularly exciting task with this group. Depending on the grape variety, the fruity fragrances seem to offer the best chance for successful matches of food and wine.

Exotic fruits such as mango, papaya or guava tend to go well with Gewürztraminer. They can be used to flavor a sauce or added, finely diced, to a salad or strewn over braised meat. Viognier often benefits from the aromas of dried fruits such as apricots or raisins. Shreds of orange peel and the oily extract of citrus fruit suit almost all highly aromatic wines.

If matured for a few years, these wines also develop an exotic spiciness, which offers other interesting possibilities. Curries and chutneys will not harm these wines in the slightest, provided that they are not excessively sharp or sweet. Thai dishes prepared with coconut milk

and subtle amounts of chili can also make a convincing accompaniment for exotically aromatic wines. Viognier, for example, is excellent with broiled shrimp (prawns) flavored with orange oil.

In addition, the daring combination of fruity-spicy aromatic wines and ethnic, fusion, or Tex-Mex cooking may open up new horizons for the connoisseur who is always on the lookout for an unusual taste experience. Their creamy texture and range of intense aromas make these wines the ideal partner for cheese. Gewürztraminer and similar wines really come into their own here, especially with cheeses that are rich and creamy, very salty, or particularly pungent, whereas most red wines, contrary to popular belief, seem dull and bland, if not tasteless. The only rule here is to match textures: the more luxurious the wine, the creamier the cheese should be. A hint of residual sugar is always a good idea, too, and helps the flavor of these wines withstand even a mature blue cheese.

Red wines are not up to the job when faced with strongly flavored cheeses. However, aromatic whites are excellent.

Typical grape varieties: Gewürztraminer, Muscat, and Viognier.

Typical wines: Gewürztraminer from anywhere in the world, Muscat d'Alsace, Condrieu.

Young, Light, Fruity Reds

Red wines that were allowed only a short skin contact time, and thus have not absorbed much in the way of color, tannins, and extract compounds, are accompaniments to a meal in the truest sense of the term: their fruitiness, slight acidity, and relatively low alcohol content stimulate the appetite, refresh the palate, and quench thirst. In principle, every red wine grape variety that has pale flesh can produce a wine of this type, either using the Beaujolais method (fermentation by CARBONIC MACERATION) or through a short skin contact time at low temperature. In practice, however, producers prefer to use grape varieties whose extravagant fruitiness makes them particularly suitable for the task.

PRIMEUR wines form part of this group. Always in demand, they are brought onto the market with astonishing rapidity by numerous producers in every vine-growing country, year after year. Whether Beaujolais Nouveau or Vino Joven, this category always goes well with regional dishes.

The straightforwardness and accessibility of flavor and aroma in this group of wines make them ideal partners for simple dishes, including many well-known favorites from Mediterranean cuisine, but seem inappropriate with more sophisticated and lavish creations. Care must be taken to choose the right occasion for serving these wines: a group of connoisseurs, for example, may not feel sufficiently challenged. A more appropriate setting might be a relaxed lunch, where the goal is not sublime pleasure so much as simply to satisfy one's hunger and thirst.

Undemanding All-rounders

The acidity (emphasized by the lack of tannins), lightness of texture, and powerful fruitiness of these wines are accentuated by the relatively cool temperature at which they are served, and therefore require a counterbalance on the plate. Particularly suited to the task are foods with a relatively high fat content, such as braised meat, sausages, ragouts, stews, and dishes accompanied by butter or cream sauces rather than gravy made from the reduced juices of a roast. These wines also tend to go very well with dishes from their respective regions of origin, and with substantial foods such as pizza or spaghetti Bolognese, in which the sweetness

and acidity of ripe tomatoes create a similar balance of the basic tastes.

Contrary to received wisdom, this type of red wine also makes a very good accompaniment for fish. Fried or broiled (grilled) seafood, in particular, whose taste becomes more rounded with subtle roasting aromas, goes particularly well with lightly chilled Beaujolais or Lemberger, whose high acidity makes the fish seem especially fresh. It is important that the wine is relatively low in alcohol and tannins, because these can create an unpleasant blubbery or metallic taste when combined with fish oil.

Acidic red wines can also come to the rescue if artichokes are being served. A chemical substance in this vegetable alters perception in the taste buds, making everything consumed at the same time seem sweet, including water. Only wines with a degree of acidity, therefore, can hold their own.

Rosé: More Than an Alibi

Rosé wines, whose pale color is produced by the fermenting juice having only very short contact with the grape skins, can be combined with meals in a similar way to the reds of this group, although care is required regarding the level of acidity. Some rosé wines are made from grape varieties that have very little natural acidity, and, like Grenache, for example, have a subtle sweetness even when processed as dry wines. Consequently, they cannot always be employed in exactly the same circumstances as the reds. Nevertheless, fresh tasting, fruity members of this category, such as Weißherbst, Schilcher, or the charming Spanish and Portuguese rosado wines, are often an attractive alternative, and not simply an easy option for those unable to choose between red and white.

The advice is often given not to drink wine with artichokes or tomatoes, but a fresh red will take on the challenge.

Right page
A cool, fruity red wine is an excellent accompaniment to char-grilled scampi with their smoky aroma.

Typical grape varieties: Gamay, Dolcetto, Corvina, Lemberger (Blaufränkisch), Trollinger (Schiava, Vernatsch).

Typical wines: Beaujolais, Dolcetto, Bardolino, Valpolicella, *primeur* wines.

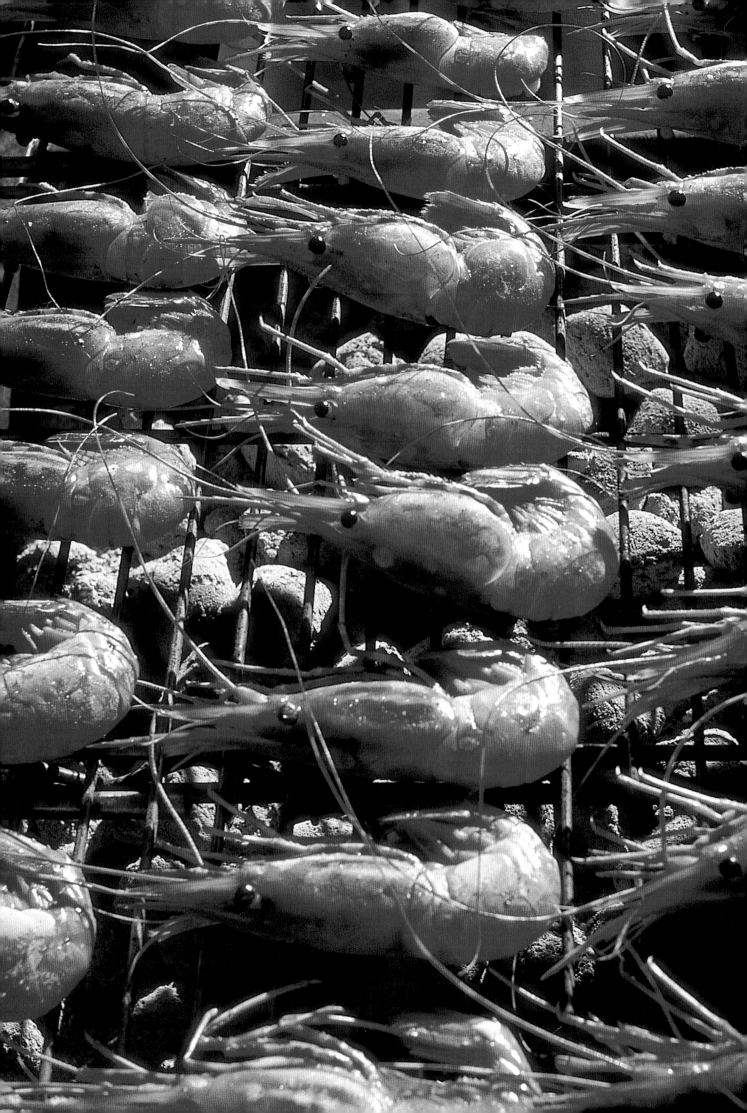

Elegant, Spicy, Silky Reds

Red wines made from grape varieties with relatively thin skins are naturally pale in color. Thus, their tannin content is lower than in thick-skinned varieties such as Cabernet Sauvignon or Syrah. In the right location, however, Pinot Noir, Sangiovese and the like can produce wines that rank among the greatest in the world. Although heavy and concentrated, such wines are also characterized by finesse: the transparency of their color matches their silky texture, and their soft tannins should not be too obtrusive. In addition, delicate acidity is perfectly balanced by an equally delicate sweetness. The particular appeal of these wines is their bouquet which, depending on grape variety and maturation method, can include aromas ranging from raspberries, violets, wild cherries, plums, blackberries, and numerous spices, to smoke, soil, oak, and liquorice.

The finely-tuned balance of acidity, sweetness, and tannins in these wines is the essence of their charm, and requires special consideration when choosing food to accompany them. It is all too easy to ruin the taste of a Gevrey-Chambertin or Brunello. Their delicate taste, which in some cases can seem almost fragile, should not be paired with very sumptuous dishes. The nature of the sauce is the deciding factor here. If it is excessively concentrated, creamy in texture, and has a very full flavor, it will make an elegant wine appear thin and bland. Sauces made with butter, cream, or egg yolks also pose a danger: the coating they give the tongue is so long-lasting that the papillae can hardly detect a delicate wine at all. The ideal partner for younger wines in this group are dishes with the fine, distinct aromas of young spring vegetables and fresh herbs, accompanying preferably lean meat, and underscored with a light sauce. Silkier, more mature wines, on the other hand, are better suited to autumnal dishes and the earthy, smoky aromas of freshly picked wild mushrooms. Aggressively fruity Pinot Noir wines are among the few reds that can cope with Asian-inspired cuisine, provided the spices in the food are not too strong. Pinot Noir and ginger, in particular, can make an amazingly harmonious combination.

Straightforward Sangiovese wines often work best with a rustic style of cooking, which favors fresh herbs rather than finicky seasonings. Concentrated Chianti and Brunello wines, which are often improved with a touch of Cabernet Sauvignon and matured in small wooden barrels, smell strongly of cherries. They frequently reveal a delicate scent of orange peel as well, however, which makes them the perfect choice with mildly orange-flavored sauces.

Grape varieties such as Grenache and Pinotage can also be included in this category, even though they can seem rather powerful in their youth—as is the case, for example, with Châteauneuf-du-Pape and other Grenache-based wines from the southern Rhône region. The fruity sweetness present even in dry wines of this type makes them the ideal accompaniment for dishes that taste of dark fruits such as prunes.

Left page, large picture
This kind of wine has a particular affinity with mushrooms. The newest of reds are especially suited to champignons.

Left page, center
More mature reds are served with boletus mushrooms—Sangiovese wines are preferred in particular.

Left page, bottom
The earthy note of chanterelles combines exceptionally well with Pinot Noir.

Typical grape varieties: Pinot Noir, Sangiovese, Grenache, Pinotage.

Typical wines: red Bourgogne, Brunello di Montalcino, Chianti Classico.

This piquant, fruity mix requires a sweeter wine, such as a spicy Pinotage.

LUXURIOUS VELVETY REDS

The plump wines made from grape varieties such as Merlot or Zinfandel make particularly pleasant accompaniments to a meal. There are relatively few problems combining them with food; they can be served within a succession of other wines, and are appropriate for almost every occasion and time of year. In their youth, such wines are characterized by a luxurious fruitiness that covers the entire palette of reddish-black berries, from blackberries, through black-currants, to cranberries. They normally mature more quickly than tannic reds; with every year they remain in the bottle, their intense fruitiness gives way a little more to the aromas of chocolate, cocoa, coffee, cedar, toast, and smoke. In the mouth, these wines feel full, velvety, and soft. Since they are made from grape varieties with skins of medium thickness, the tannin content is usually less than in wines made from Cabernet Sauvignon or Syrah, for example, and generally integrates to good effect in the overall package. In addition, the level of acidity tends to be low, except in bad vintages or where the yield has been too high. If the grapes are ripe when harvested, these wines have a good alcohol content, which

The taste of charbroiled meat is robust enough to cope with an equally inten-se wine, such as a smoky, mouth-filling Zinfandel.

also makes them glossy and lends a certain sweetness. They make for agreeable, easy drinking.

The sweet fruitiness of these wines, alongside their soft, sleek texture and opulent range of aromas, always goes well with similarly structured dishes that are not overly heavy. Our first impression is that sweetness, bitterness, and acidity are well balanced, and this harmony should be reflected in the food. Merlot, for example, makes a good partner for braised meat dishes, which if cooked carefully, develop a strong, full, slightly bitter-sweet flavor. A touch of acidity can always be provided by the sauce, perhaps using fruit, tomatoes, or balsamic vinegar.

Zinfandel wines are frequently reminiscent of jam, and can cope with a fair degree of seaso-

ning in the accompanying food. Even salty or somewhat spicy foods—rarely a good idea with other wines—are permissible, thanks to Zinfandel's lavish fruitiness. It is advisable to be careful, however, with chilies or cayenne pepper if the wine, however fruity, has a high alcohol content. Hot spices together with a high percentage of alcohol by volume will really set your tongue on fire.

The compatible nature of soft, velvety reds makes devising combinations with food a largely straightforward affair. We therefore have a great deal of room for maneuver with regard to matching the more volatile aromas. Herbs such as rosemary, thyme, mint and bayleaf, and seasonings such as cinnamon,

cloves, black pepper, juniper berries, and fennel seeds are the best way of linking the flavors on the plate with those in the glass.

Wines on which the wooden barrel has left its mark are good with well seared or broiled fish, poultry, and vegetables: the caramelized proteins and sugar on the food bear an astonishing resemblance to the aromas that toasted barrels impart to the wine.

Typical grape varieties: Merlot, Zinfandel, Blauer Zweigelt, St. Laurent.

Typical wines: Pomerol, Saint-Émilion, and numerous New World wines.

The ideal accompaniment to char-grilled meats is a full bodied, *barrique*-matured red wine.

Tannic, Extract-rich Reds

Right page, below left
Shallots give entrecôte steak the subtle sweetness that demands a great Bordeaux.

Right page, below center
Garlic, a natural medicine and a favorite flavoring, will tame even the most fully developed tannins.

Right page, below right
Fresh, lightly roasted garlic will harmonize beautifully with full-bodied reds.

Red wines made from particularly thick-skinned grape varieties not only have a dense, dark color, but also an extravagant tannin and extract structure that make them seem almost solid. Their fruity components call to mind blackberries, plums, and black cherries, but they are also characterized by a range of darker aromas, from herbs, chocolate, and coffee, through to tobacco, leather, and smoke. Some have a high alcohol content which, combined with maturation in (frequently new) wooden barrels, gives them a certain sweetness and smoothness, while the impression the tannins create on the tongue is, to a greater or lesser degree, one of bitterness. These wines really seem to fill the mouth, because their three basic tastes—bitterness (tannins), sweetness (alcohol and glycerin), and sourness (tartaric acid)—affect nearly all the taste zones, each of which is sensitive to different stimuli.

The tannins leave a distinct tang in the mouth, and so the utmost care must be taken when matching these wines with food. The younger a tannic wine is, the greater the danger that it will seem unpleasantly bitter and astringent on the tongue. Older reds can also have this effect, if they are from poor or mediocre vintages when there was insufficient sun to ripen the grapes fully; their tannins still seem "green," even after years of bottle-aging. Overly long barrel-aging can also leave these wines tasting dried out and harsh. Combined with proteins, immature or excessive tannins make the tongue and inside of your cheeks feel leathery, much as very strong tea does. Choosing appropriate food will mitigate any such unwelcome effects; moreover, the right dish can really encourage a wine with mature tannins and a good balance of body and fruit to reveal its full flavor.

The astringent, almost grainy texture of immature tannins needs something to balance it in the mouth. For roundness of taste, therefore, the food must provide what the wine lacks, namely delicate sweetness and a certain glossiness. The easiest way to integrate aggressive tannins is to combine them with the aromas of braised meat cooked with mild, roasted, slightly sweet vegetables such as onions, garlic, or carrots. Of course, this type of dish would also suit wine containing mature tannins. In such cases, however, you should be slightly more restrained with the sweetness of the gravy and add a subtle note of spices and herbs. Tannins are part of the group of compounds known as phenolics, and it is the large number of these in luxurious red wine that makes it a particularly healthy drink in combination with meat dishes.

A Balancing Act

These wines tend to have a high alcohol content, which needs to be borne in mind when planning combinations of food and drink. Milk fat, i.e. butter and cream, makes alcohol taste particularly strong, so before choosing a dish with a cream or butter-based sauce, you should, if possible, check the alcohol level on the wine label. If it is above 13 percent by volume there is the risk that the fat will unbalance the wine and make it taste burnt.

Care is also required with very salty dishes, because alcohol combined with salt creates an impression of bitterness. If you wish to serve a tannic red wine, therefore, the food should never taste overtly salty; at most, salt should be used to support the aromas of the herbs and other seasonings. Both the sweet and the more acidic elements in these wines are usually too discreet to need to be taken into account in the choice of food. It is more important to show regard for the subtle aroma of these "dark" wines—which is, after all, the essence of its charm—by cautious seasoning of the dishes.

Typical grape varieties: Cabernet Sauvignon, Syrah, Tannat, Mourvèdre (Monastrell), Tempranillo, and Nebbiolo.

Typical wines: Bordeaux such as Médoc, Northern Rhône wines such as Hermitage, Côte-Rôtie, the best Languedoc-Roussillon wines, Madiran, Bandol, Rioja, Australian Shiraz, Barolo, Barbaresco.

The mighty structure of a great Barolo will be softened by, for example, well-marbled beef and homemade pasta.

MATURE WINES

The term "old wine" has not been clearly defined, either in terms of chemistry or in terms of its effect on the senses. There is no minimum length of time that a bottle must spend in a cellar to qualify, and nowhere does it say in black and white how such a wine should smell and taste. Every wine has a different potential for aging, depending primarily on the grape variety or *cuvée* from which it is made, followed by the vintage, method of production, factors such as the level of alcohol, sweetness, or acidity, and finally, the conditions in which the bottled wine is stored.

Taking into account the grape variety and vintage, the first clue to the maturity of a red wine is provided by the sediment that has settled out in the bottle. These reddish-brown deposits comprise polymerized phenolics, including tannins and color compounds, that have formed so many bonds that they can no longer be held in solution. The more sediment has formed, and the lighter the color of the wine has become, the softer the wine will taste. Note, however, that a great deal more sediment will precipitate from a tannic, richly-colored Cabernet Sauvignon than from a silky Pinot Noir.

White wines also change color during bottle-aging, but rather than getting lighter they become darker—that is, browner—due to gradual OXIDATION of their phenolics. Wines that were fermented and finished in wooden barrels, however, age better than those from stainless steel tanks.

The only generalization we can make, therefore, is that fine, old wines, whether red or white, are characterized by the fragility of their aroma. Consequently, they are not particularly suitable as accompaniments to a meal: subtle nuances of their bouquet or flavor are all too easily submerged.

RESPECT FOR THE AGED

If you nonetheless wish to serve a decades-old wine with food, a few ground rules should be borne in mind. The texture, basic taste, and aromas of a wine become more delicate and susceptible to interference with each year of bottle-aging, and so the primary requirement is culinary restraint. Fatty, strong-smelling, acidic, sweet, and very spicy foods are clearly out, since the taste of the wine would be not merely distorted, but completely overwhelmed.

Saltiness can also be tricky, even when relatively subtle, because it quickly creates a bitter taste when combined with alcohol that would totally upset the balance of a mature wine.

Great, mature reds usually develop aromas of soil and wet leaves. It is a good idea to pick up this theme in the food, and thus support the smell and taste of the wine. Black truffles are ideal for this purpose, incorporated into a sauce or the stuffing of a roast, or freshly sliced and scattered over the dish.

White wines from wooden barrels, particularly Chardonnay, often have a hint of fresh bread and roasted nuts when mature, aromas which can easily be incorporated into a meal. Mature Riesling is a greater challenge, since it often develops a distinct note of petrol. A subtle herb flavoring such as lovage can be extremely helpful here.

A MATURE BOUQUET DESERVES TO BE SAVORED

The most exciting thing about uncorking a very old bottle is smelling the bouquet of the mature wine. You should always give your guests the chance to taste such a wine before the meal, so that they can grasp all its subtleties without any interference or distortion. It is important to serve the wine at around 64°F (18°C), because only at this relatively high temperature can the mature bouquet really come into its own. An aged red can be carefully decanted to separate it from its sediment, but this should not be done until just before you are going to drink it, so that the bouquet loses none of its nuances.

If a wine is from a good estate and a good vintage, has been matured for a few decades, and has developed a complex mix of totally new aromas, then it deserves your undivided attention. The best way to enjoy it is after a light, unobtrusively seasoned meal that has been rounded off with a piece of mild cheese (never a sweet dessert), or, if in doubt, on its own without any culinary accompaniment. Not for nothing are very mature, botrytized vintages known as "meditation wines." To do full justice to the very complex, intertwined age notes of such exceptional wines, you should devote your full concentration to them.

Simple but classy: spaghetti with truffles with a well-aged Barolo or Barbaresco.

It is not at all unusual for mature red wines to develop truffle notes. All you need to do is enjoy!

Dessert Wines

Wines containing residual sugar lead an unjustly shadowy existence when it comes to serving them with food, for included amongst their ranks are some of the greatest wines in the world. On many menus, dessert wines either find no place at all, or are simply served alongside *foie gras* or the sweet course without any real thought. Only in exceptional cases, however, does the simple motto "sweet with sweet" lead to a satisfactory combination. Usually, neither the food nor the wine is really experienced to its best advantage.

The dominant sweetness of these wines is partly the result of unfermented grape sugar, the proportion of which varies from around $1/4$ to 2 ounces or more per pint (20 to 100 grams or more per liter). Among the other sweet substances contained in the wines is alcohol, which not only tastes sweet itself, but also reinforces the sweetness of the sugar. Acidity is the next strongest taste component, and also needs to be taken into account when deciding what food to serve. Sweetness deadens the taste buds even at a relatively low intensity, making anything that is less sweet seem dull and bland. To a certain extent, however, acidity and sweetness can neutralize each other.

In contrast to almost all other wines, the flavors and aromas of a dessert wine play only a secondary role in planning a successful meal combination. The most important consideration is that the sweetness of the wine should have a complement in the dish served with it. This certainly does not mean, however, that it must always be balanced by sugar in the food. Salt, in particular, often makes an excellent contrast to sugar, which is why most cheeses (as long as they are rich and strong smelling) work much better with sweetish whites than with reds—witness the classic combination of port and Stilton.

A medium dry, aromatic white can also go perfectly with Asian cuisine, whose spiciness should not be coupled with acidic wines. A further possibility is to counter the sweetness in the wine with fat, as in the combination of *foie gras* with Sauternes.

Almost as important as balancing the sweetness, the second factor to be considered when matching dessert wines with food is their texture. The degree of viscosity, which is largely determined by the wine's sugar, glycerin, and alcohol content, must be suited to the dish concerned. The more delicate the consistency of a wine, the lighter the food should be; oilier wines should be served with correspondingly creamier dishes. A Riesling TROCKENBEERENAUSLESE, for example, is excellent with a warm apple tart made with shortcrust pastry, while a Sauternes is an excellent accompaniment for puff pastries filled with confectioner's custard.

Combining dessert wines and food becomes a real challenge if you try to take the varied aromas into account as well as the basic tastes and the texture. Depending on their grape variety, method of production, and age, dessert wines release fragrances ranging from orange peel, mangoes, and apricots, through quince, figs, and raisins, to honey and caramel. A good tip with young dessert wines, which at this stage have an acidic structure, is to serve fruity sauces that create an aromatic bridge between the wine and the food. High-quality dessert wines should never be served too cold, since this can easily make them seem unbalanced. In the event that a particular wine is too sweet for the chosen dish, however, cooling the wine can restore a degree of harmony again.

Combining it with a dessert wine often adds an entire new dimension of enjoyment to a fine dessert.

Left page
Almond biscuits are a suitable base for enjoying dessert wines.

Hélène Jaeger

IN VINEYARD AND WINERY

THE GRAPEVINE AND ITS VARIETIES

The grapevine is a long-lived, perennial plant, and unlike annual plants, it can exist in one spot for a number of years—around 30, on average. Grapes are produced at the end of its yearly life-cycle, but the individual stages of development leading up to this point are not independent events: each successive stage is the result of the preceding one. Buds that develop in year N, for example, were formed in the spring and summer of the previous year (N-1). If the plant was exposed to diseases or climatic events such as hailstorms during that year, they would affect not only the crop of the N-1 vintage, but that of vintage N as well.

The vine is a woody plant with herbaceous elements. Its perennial structures (the stock, scion, and roots) store starch, carbohydrates, and other supplies. These essential energy reserves enable the plant to survive the winter and guarantee that there will be growth in the spring, producing new leaves to take over the role as energy provider.

The vine draws all the raw materials it needs for growth and grape production from the surrounding natural environment. Its root system draws water and minerals from the soil and converts them into various growth hormones that circulate around the plant as required. As soon as temperatures start to rise at the beginning of spring, sap can be seen flowing where the canes have been pruned. Winegrowers speak of the vines "crying" or "bleeding;" this signals the start of the growth cycle.

The part of the vine that grows above ground is woody, and consists of the trunk (stock and

The vines start to shoot in late spring. Soon after the first young leaves have appeared, the buds which will produce bunches of grapes also begin to form, growing straight upwards.

Vines can easily reach 60 to 100 years old—like this Grenache Gris—if the demands made of them in their youth are not excessive, and their ever decreasing yields are tolerated; the compensation is the improving quality of the wine.

scion) and biennial canes. The latter can be long or short, depending on pruning, and their buds sprout the annual shoots, some of which will bear grapes. Photosynthesis takes place in the vine leaves, as with all chlorophyll-containing plants: the chlorophyll absorbs the sunlight, which enables the leaves to extract carbon dioxide from the air and convert it into sugar. The energy obtained in this way is used to produce a variety of fundamentally different substances over the course of the vegetative process. These include hundreds of AROMA compounds, which are stored in the grapes (see diagram opposite).

Many factors influence the quality of the grape harvest, and consequently that of the wine as well. The nutrients needed for growth and fruit production are drawn from the air and the soil, which means that both the above-ground and the below-ground parts of the vine must be cultivated in order to achieve the best possible development.

The amount of foliage exposed to the sun, through which photosynthesis occurs, is of central importance. Winegrowers support the process by creating an optimal canopy surface area and thus a balanced leaf to fruit ratio. Vine density, row orientation, and the height of the trellises can all be tailored to help achieve this. If the number of vines per acre is kept low (1,200 to 1,600 per acre or 3,000 to 4,000 per hectare, for example), the rows can be planted further apart, increasing the amount of sunlight that reaches the ground. To balance this out, the height of the canopy can be raised (tall,

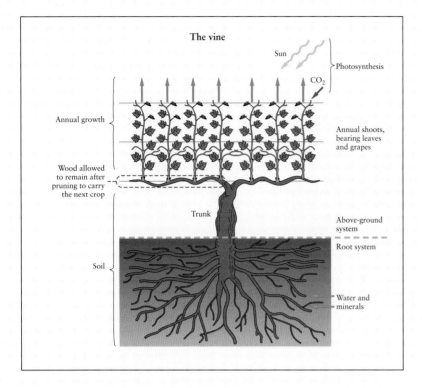

The vine

Sun

Photosynthesis

CO_2

Annual growth

Annual shoots, bearing leaves and grapes

Wood allowed to remain after pruning to carry the next crop

Trunk

Above-ground system

Root system

Soil

Water and minerals

to accumulate in the fruit. If ripening does not take place, energy supplies are principally directed toward the tips of the shoots. The end of vegetative growth is a natural process accelerated by lack of water. Hence, heavy rain during this phase can significantly disrupt the ripening process. High atmospheric humidity also brings with it the risk of diseases from molds and fungi.

A further factor affecting the quality of the crop is the yield capacity of the vine. Suppose that two almost identical vines, with the same root system and the same leaf surface area exposed to the sun's rays, have equal reserves of energy. If one vine has to share these nutrients among eight bunches of grapes, while the other only has four to supply, the berries of the first vine will have a lesser concentration not only of sugar, but also of color and flavor. Consequently, the grower must find a balance between yield size and quality that will allow the crop to ripen sufficiently, but also provide a viable level of income per acre (hectare).

If the size of the crop in a newly-planted vineyard is too high, the quality of the grapes will be lower; the process of storing reserves of nutrients in the roots and woody part of the vine suffers, and this has long-term negative consequences for the plant.

broad vines) or the tops of the trellises opened up by training each vine into a lyre shape. If the vines are planted more densely (around 3,200 to 4,000 per acre, or 8,000 to 10,000 per hectare), there will be a few casualties, but the canopy can be thicker. In such cases, the vigor of the vines must be controlled by not over-using fertilizer, and, if necessary, by removing summer shoots and side shoots to increase ventilation. In practical terms, therefore, this means that the more densely the vines are planted, the more work is required to tend them, and thus the higher the production costs will be.

The onset of VERAISON (the period when the grapes start to change color) signals the end of the vine's vegetative growth, when sugar starts

During the growth phase, nutrients are primarily sent to the tips of the canes and to the flowerheads. Under optimal conditions, growth stops during the ripening phase, and the carbohydrates are redirected to the berries and the green parts of the plant. They are stored in the grapes as sugar, and in equal measure as glucose and fructose in the green parts, and as starch in the woody part of the vine.

Vineyard with widely spaced rows in Hawkes Bay, New Zealand.

Old vines and harvest quality

The term *vieilles vignes* (old vines) is increasingly common on wine labels, usually in conjunction with a higher price. If vines are old, their yields are low, and their grapes rich in sugar and other substances that improve quality. However, there are no fixed rules defining what counts as old: depending on the opinion of the winegrower, it can mean vines of more than 40 years of age. Nevertheless, old does not necessarily equate with good. Some old vines are diseased, meaning that although the yield is low, the quality is also not optimal. It may also be the case that there are fewer vines in the plot and so what is described as a low yield is in reality simply the produce of a smaller number of vines rather than a low yield per plant.

Varieties of Grapes

There are hundreds of grape varieties worldwide, although only a few of these have real economic importance. Wine grapes are varieties of the species *Vitis vinifera*, and each has distinguishing characteristics, such as the shape of the leaves and grapes, the presence of tiny hairs, or the color of the young foliage. Different varieties also have varying degrees of susceptibility to diseases and frost.

Wine lovers are primarily interested in the produce of these *vinifera* varieties. The wines differ in appearance, smell, taste, and in the balance of alcohol and acidity. Some varieties, for example, lose a great deal of their acidity as the fruits become riper and their sugar content increases. If the grower waits too long before harvesting these grapes, the wines that are made from them tend to be rather heavy. Other varieties, such as Riesling, Mosel, the Petit Manseng of Jurançon wines, and the Chenin Blanc of Côteaux du Layon, have the ability to concentrate the sugar while at the same time retaining a good level of acidity.

Certain grape varieties can be recognized by their distinctive smell, such as the Muscat varieties or Gewürztraminer. Others are given away by their color, like the very dark Tannat or the much lighter Pinot Noir. The latter requires particularly favorable climatic conditions to achieve a color of sufficient intensity during the ripening phase, and thus cannot be grown successfully everywhere. Some grape varieties are more adaptable, however, such as Chardonnay, which is found all over the world.

Nevertheless, grape variety alone is not the deciding factor. Depending on the properties of the soil in which the vine is planted, the local climate, yield size, and methods of production, the character of wines made from a particular variety can vary considerably.

The Wine Grape

The wine grape consists of the flesh, skin, and seeds. With the exception of the colored *teinturiers* planted in some countries, even red grape varieties have white flesh. The PHENOLICS are found in the skins and seeds, as well as in the stalks of the grape (pedicel) and the bunch (peduncle). The aroma compounds are also located mainly in the skins of the berries.

The transfer of these substances into the wine takes place either before or during alcoholic

Certain grape varieties, such as Touriga Nacional in the Douro Valley, are easily identifiable even in the autumn, because their foliage turns such an intense color.

FERMENTATION, depending on the grape variety. In red grapes, it is achieved by fermenting the MUST in contact with the skins of the berries, whereas with white grapes, this kind of MACERATION is seldom employed. The size of the berries determines the ratio of juice to solids. Large berries have a lot of juice and little skin, but it is more difficult to extract the color and flavor. The size of the berries depends on the grape variety, but it is also influenced by the vigor of the individual vine and by the availability of water.

There can be qualitative differences even with a single grape variety, as a result of the crossings and mutations that can occur naturally within a site. If a winegrower decides to replant a vineyard, there are generally two ways to go about it. The first, and currently increasingly less common method, is "mass selection," which involves selecting the best vines from the grower's individual sites over the course of a number of years and taking cuttings from them to obtain new scions. The second option is to buy clones from vine nurseries. Each grape variety can have several clones, which may be more or less productive or have differing sugar-storage capabilities, depending on the characteristics of the parent vine. All the vines of a particular clone have been produced from a single original plant, and are therefore identical. Their health is guaranteed in principle, because they are required to be free of disease. Nevertheless, some growers refuse to use clones because they fear that their wines will become standardized.

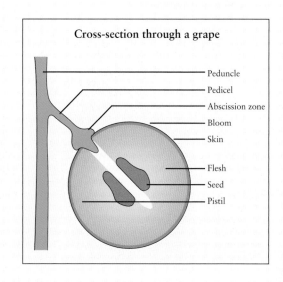

Cross-section through a grape

- Peduncle
- Pedicel
- Abscission zone
- Bloom
- Skin
- Flesh
- Seed
- Pistil

Chardonnay: Originating in Burgundy (France), where it produces such contrasting wines as the mineral-tasting Chablis and the multi-faceted, mouth-filling Montrachet, Chardonnay has conquered the world. The reason for this is its adaptability in terms of climate, soil, and methods of winemaking. All over the world, the Chardonnay grape produces, at the very least, pleasant wines, and very convincing, great wines if given the appropriate commitment. It is also better suited than any other white grape to vinification and maturation in barrels.

Sauvignon Blanc: Related to the Cabernet varieties, Sauvignon Blanc is often blended with Semillon, where it shows its class in great dessert wines, or the dry Graves Bordeaux. Wines made from Sauvignon Blanc alone first appeared in the Loire (France), in Sancerre and Pouilly-Fumé:, which reveal the aromas of blackcurrants and gooseberries, and have a fresh acidity combined with inimitable mineral overtones. If harvested early, Sauvignon Blanc develops grassy, vegetation aromas. It has become the second most popular white variety after Chardonnay.

Riesling: Also known as Rhine Riesling and Johannisberg Riesling, this is, along with Chardonnay, one of the best white wine varieties in the world. Its homeland is the Rheingau (Germany), where as a superior, fairly late-ripening grape, it produces excellent wines with mineral and fruit dimensions, and also the Mosel valley, which is the most important region for this variety. Riesling retains its acidity as it matures, making it the ideal grape for various types of SPÄTLESE and AUSLESE wines. It loses its raciness, however, if planted in too warm a climate.

Merlot: This highly productive variety is suitable both for VARIETAL wines and for blending with stronger, more tannic grapes. The best results are achieved in France, in the Bordeaux region, particularly in Saint-Émilion and Pomerol, where some long-lived wines of the highest quality are produced. It is also popular in Switzerland's Ticino, northern Italy, and southeastern Europe. Merlot is fruity, velvety, and matures faster than Cabernet, but in pure varietal form has only lately attracted international attention. It is currently being planted at a significant rate.

Cabernet Sauvignon: As the basis of the famous *crus classés* of the French Médoc, this variety has risen to become the most popular red wine grape. Good Cabernet wines are dark red, smell of cedar and blackcurrants, have considerable body and a firm structure, and age extremely well. This late-ripening, robust variety flourishes in warmer climates, delivering high-quality wines in California, Australia, South Africa, Chile, and also Italy and Spain.

Pinot Noir: Pinot Noir is responsible for the famous red wines of France's Côte d'Or, and plays an important role in the Champagne region. It was introduced to new areas by Cistercian monks, and found a place in Alsace, Germany, Austria, Switzerland, the northeast of Italy, and eastern Europe. Pinot Noir is one of the most challenging red grape varieties for a grower, since it requires a low yield and the utmost care during VINIFICATION to produce wines of convincing quality.

The Most Important White Wine Grape Varieties

Albariño

Albariño is the finest white wine variety grown in the Spanish region of Galicia, and one of the greatest white varieties in Europe. Characterized by small, densely clustered grapes with hard skins and many seeds, it delivers average-sized yields in humid climates. It is highly resistant to BOTRYTIS CINEREA, but susceptible to leaf diseases. Albariño produces the best results when planted on slate or granite. Its elegant wines have complex aromas of exotic fruits, pears and apples, with discreet vegetation notes and a hint of eucalyptus. It produces particularly fine dry whites in the Rías Baixas D.O. region.

Chenin Blanc

This great French variety from Anjou in the Loire has two distinctive characteristics: it has a high natural acidity and is susceptible to botrytis. Depending on vintage, ripeness, and the intentions of the grower, Chenin from the Loire can produce a whole spectrum of different wines, from sparkling, through bone dry, to wines which have extremely concentrated RESIDUAL SUGARS and age well. In California and South Africa, Chenin Blanc is a very versatile grape. Even in a hot climate and with high yields, its level of acidity delivers balanced, but neutral varietals, which are commonly used in blends for everyday, mass-market wines.

Gewürztraminer

Gewürztraminer is the most commonly planted variety of the Traminer vine. It has grayish-pink grapes that produce wines with a golden gleam and an unmistakable BOUQUET reminiscent of roses and Muscat. The low yielding but demanding variety is only really convincing if its grapes are harvested when very ripe. For this reason, it tends to appear as an *Auslese* or *Spätlese*, often has a high alcohol content, and is frequently oily. The most interesting wines are produced in Alsace, Germany, Switzerland, Austria, and northern Italy, but is also planted widely in the wine-producing countries of eastern Europe, and can be found in the U.S.A. and New Zealand.

Malvasia

The Malvasia family of grape varieties, including an early red variety, probably originated in Asia Minor. It was widely planted throughout Ancient Greece, particularly on the islands, where rich, oily dessert wines are still made from it today, as they are in the Lipari Islands off Sicily, and as Malmsey in Madeira. Malvasia also has a significant presence in central Italy, where, by contrast, it is usually made into dry wines. In Spain it is used in white Rioja and Navarre, where it loses a lot of its heaviness. Malvasia is highly aromatic and productive, with a delicate acidity that prefers a dry climate, but is, unfortunately, in decline.

Müller-Thurgau

Professor Hermann Müller, from Thurgau in Germany, grew this crossing of Riesling and Chasselas (Gutedel) at Geisenheim in 1882. It was previously, but erroneously, known as Riesling x Silvaner. An early-ripening variety that needs damp, deep soils, Müller-Thurgau delivers high yields, but is very susceptible to mildew and other diseases. Its low acidity produces wines that seem soft and round, and have a subtle hint of Muscat that is lost if the grapes become very ripe. Müller-Thurgau is the most widely planted grape variety in Germany, and is also very important in Austria, the Czech Republic, Slavonia, Slovenia, Hungary, and Luxembourg.

Muscat

Muscat, Moscato or Muskateller —behind the names lies one of the oldest and most ramified families of vines. Most renowned is the Muscat Blanc à Petits Grains, whose small, aromatic grapes are the basis for one of the world's most popular sweet sparkling wines, the Italian Asti, previously known as Asti Spumante. Muscats are grown in many countries, however: wines from the Greek island of Samos, and Muscat de Frontignan from France are famous examples. It is also widely planted in Spain, Austria, Eastern Europe, the U.S.A., South Africa, and Australia, producing extremely sweet, oily, but nevertheless complex dessert wines.

Pinot Blanc

Also known as Pinot Bianco, Weißburgunder, and Clevner, this grape variety is a distinct member of the Pinot family, and is descended from Pinot Noir, presumably by way of Pinot Gris as an intermediate stage. A demanding, but fairly robust variety, it needs well-ripened grapes to develop its character, which is to be found in roundness and good body, rather than in the somewhat discreet aroma. Pinot Blanc is winning increasing numbers of converts in the New World, and plays an important role in northern Italy and the Austrian province of Styria, as well as in Slavonia, Slovenia, Hungary, and Romania.

Pinot Gris

Also known as Pinot Grigio, Grauburgunder, and Ruländer, this robust relative of Pinot Noir has grayish-pink tinted grapes, and requires deep soils. In the 14th century, it arrived in the Lake Balaton area of Hungary from France. In Alsace, Austria and Germany, it produces *Spätlese* and *Auslese* wines which are frequently of the highest quality —full of EXTRACTIONS and extremely rich, with delicate spiciness but little acidity. It is currently enjoying its greatest popularity as Pinot Grigio, which is primarily grown in the northern regions of Italy, where its high yields are made into a light, neutral white wine.

Semillon

This variety has a tendency to become NOBLE ROT, and is responsible for the great sweet wines of Bordeaux. The best dry wines are produced in Pessac-Léognan, also in France. Semillon wines can age very well, developing aromas of honey, candied fruits, and chocolates, while often retaining a fresh, citrus note. Although planted widely throughout the world, Semillon only develops real and distinctive character in Hunter Valley, Australia. Various winemakers, particularly in South Africa and California, have recently achieved success with attractively creamy, full-bodied Semillon wines fermented in barrels.

Silvaner

Once the most widely planted variety in Germany, Silvaner has now been driven out by Müller-Thurgau in many areas. It is decidedly neutral if not grown on an eminently suitable site, but can produce wines that are pleasantly dry, moderately acidic, and make a strong impression on the palate. Franconia (Franken), in central Germany, is the most significant region for Silvaner, but it also delivers convincing quality in Alsace, if treated carefully in both vineyard and winery. It can still be found in Switzerland, where it is often called Johannisberger, and in the South Tyrol; and is still cultivated in eastern Europe, particularly Romania and Slovenia.

Trebbiano

The best-known version of this white wine grape is the Italian Trebbiano Toscano, which was previously one of the main ingredients in Chianti. A relatively neutral-tasting variety, its main use is in France (where it is known as Ugni Blanc) in the distilling of Cognac and Armagnac. In the south of France, it is also used for blending with largely inconsequential wines. Trebbiano's greatest asset is that it delivers extremely high yields while retaining a degree of acidity. Its most important VARIETAL expression is the D.O.C. Trebbiano d'Abruzzo, from the Abruzzi region of Italy. Trebbiano is planted widely throughout the world.

Palomino

Palomino is the main grape for manzanilla and sherry. It takes well to the hot, dry soils of Andalusia in southern Spain, particularly the *albariza* soils around Jerez, where it can easily yield 750 to 900 U.S. gallons per acre (70 to 80 hl/ha). Currently, it is also made into dry, neutral white wines, although it lacks the necessary acidity and aromas, which is added by OXIDATION and the use of FLOR YEAST. Palomino is grown in Australia for producing sherry-style wines, and is the second most widely planted grape variety in South Africa, where it is mainly used in brandy. The Portugese grape variety known as Perrum is also believed to be Palomino.

THE MOST IMPORTANT RED WINE GRAPE VARIETIES

BARBERA

Once the stuff of everyday drinking in Piedmont in northern Italy, and now the country's most cultivated grape variety after Sangiovese, Barbera has become a top-quality product in the last two decades. Thanks to the de-acidification process and fermentation in barrels, it now delivers complex, fruity reds with a firm structure and good aging potential. This is true only in Piedmont, however, and perhaps southern Italy. Elsewhere, a great deal of characterless, acidic, blending wine is made from Barbera, particularly in Argentina and California.

DOLCETTO

Along with Barbera and Nebbiolo, Dolcetto, the "little sweet one," is the third grape variety of Piedmont in northern Italy, and the quickest to ripen. As a result, it was often given the least favorable sites and fermented into wine that was ready to drink early—filling the coffers of the winemakers as quickly as possible. Dolcetto is now being accorded more attentive treatment, necessary due to its high tannin content and tendency to deposit large amounts of sediment while in the cellar. When successful, however, it has an attractive, dark ruby-red color, and wonderful aromas of sweetish berries, quince, and even a delicate hint of almonds.

CABERNET FRANC

Also known as Bouchet or Breton, this variety has long been seen as the little brother of Cabernet Sauvignon. It ripens early, making it better suited to cooler regions, which accounts for its strong presence in Saint-Émilion in France (where it is the main grape in Cheval Blanc). The Loire region also produces varietal Cabernet Francs that have an attractive taste of berry fruits, unobtrusive tannins, but often a higher acidity than the mightier Cabernet Sauvignon. Although this variety is often used in light bistro wines, particularly in the northeast of Italy, some first-class, velvety, mouth-filling wines have come out of the Loire in recent years.

GAMAY

Gamay owes its fame to Beaujolais, where it lends fruitiness and charm to the region's wines. Gamay Noir à Jus Blanc, to give it its full name, is planted there at a density of 3,600 to 4,000 vines per acre (9,000 to 10,000 per hectare). The grapes must be picked by hand, because they are usually fermented whole using CARBONIC MACERATION (which draws a lot of aroma compounds from the skins, but few tannins). If wines are produced by fermenting the must, however, they have a very interesting potential for aging. Elsewhere, Gamay has gained a permanent foothold only in the Loire and the Ardèche in France, and in Switzerland.

CARIGNAN

Carignan plays an important role as an intensely colored, tannic, blending wine. Although being a highly productive variety, it can be abused. Carignan ripens late and is susceptible to downy and powdery mildew. Consequently, it is losing ground in the south of France, as it has done in La Rioja (northern Spain). With low yields and old vines, however, it can deliver extremely characterful wines, such as in Priorat (in Catalonia) or Languedoc (southwestern France), where it is still the dominant grape variety in terms of quantity. It is also widely planted on Sardinia and in the Maghreb (north africa), California, Chile, Argentina, and Mexico.

GARNACHA TINTA

Garnacha Tinta is the most widely planted variety in Spain, where it is produced almost exclusively as young or rosé wines. This undemanding variety is not harmed by a hot and arid climate, and contributes body and alcohol to a blend, although it tends to oxidize easily. Only very occasionally does it show its class, such as in the Priorat region of Catalonia, or in France, in Châteauneuf-du-Pape, or the naturally sweet Banyuls wines. It is represented in the wine-growing regions in the south of France, as well as on Corsica, Sardinia, and Sicily. In the New World, Grenache has been introduced wherever heat and aridity are a problem.

MALBEC

Malbec was once widely planted in Bordeaux, but has been superseded there by Merlot. Its main stronghold in France is now Cahors where, as Auxerrois, it is responsible for the region's famous "black wine." Given a medium-sized yield, this dark, tannic variety can deliver characterful reds with good potential for aging. The same is true of Malbec from Argentina, where it is a very popular variety that has produced some interesting, quality wines in recent years. In Chile, on the other hand, it has so far been used as a blending wine, as has also been the case in many *appellations* of southwest France.

MOURVÈDRE

Also known as Monastrell, this is Spain's second most important grape after Garnacha, and is one of the most typical vines of the eastern Mediterranean. It usually produces soft, dry, but meaty wines, in which black berry fruits are the dominant aroma. Although in Spain it is mostly used for reds that are designed to be drunk young, Mourvèdre from the south of France has a different character. Extremely late-ripening and with noble tannins, it plays a role in fine southern Rhône blends, and finds top form in Bandol. Growers in California and Australia are also beginning to recognize its qualities.

NEBBIOLO

Probably the greatest Italian red wine variety, Nebbiolo is grown on little more than 12,500 acres (5,000 hectares) in Piedmont and Valtellina, Lombardy. Barolo, Barberesco, and a number of other D.O.C. wines owe their multi-layered bouquet (which has notes of tea leaves, roses, spices, and tar), powerful tannin structure, and enormous aging potential to this small-berried variety. Nebbiolo demands the very best sites, or it will not ripen. Its name derives from *nebbia*, the Italian word for fog, reflecting how late in the year it is picked. Experiments with this variety in other countries have so far failed to produce any convincing results.

SANGIOVESE

The most widely planted red wine variety in Italy is also one of its best. It is the grape responsible for the Tuscan Brunello, Chianti, and Vino Nobile wines, and for the wines of the Torgiano and Montefalco regions in Umbria. In Romagna, however, it is also used for rather thin bulk wines. In cool years, the late-ripening Sangiovese rarely manages to ripen fully, whereas its wines from warmer vintages are characterized by a lively acidity and delicate TANNIN structure, and always retain a charming elegance. Sangiovese has hitherto been largely unsuccessful in Argentina, but has demonstrated good potential in California.

SYRAH

This superb variety from the northern Rhône in France has found success throughout the world. It delivers full-bodied, hefty wines that have excellent tannins and complex aromas, including violets, black cherries, wild herbs, liquorice, humus and various spices—a combination that winemakers and consumers are greeting ever more enthusiastically. An early ripener, Syrah has conquered Provence and the whole of the Midi. It is also gaining ground internationally: the great Australian Shiraz wines are particularly important, and there have recently been some excellent Californian Syrahs. Good Shiraz wines are also produced in South Africa.

TEMPRANILLO

Spain's highest-quality vine is also known as Tinta del País, Tinto Fino, Cencibel and Ull de Llebre. Although the vegetative stage of its annual cycle is short, it is sensitive to heat and most diseases. Its dark wines typically have an aromatic, fruity character, and their potential for aging in wood is particularly prized. The tannins are soft and sweet, and become very smooth in the barrel. Tempranillo is the main grape variety in La Rioja and Ribera del Duero, and thus responsible for Spain's greatest wines. As Tinta Roriz, it also contributes to some of the best red wines from Portugal.

Terroir

The same variety of vine planted in different locations can produce wines that differ greatly in terms of both structure and aroma—the "*terroir* effect." A TERROIR is a defined area in which the physical and chemical conditions of the natural environment, the geographical location, and the climate give rise to specific and identifiable products. Consequently, the term denotes the interaction of a number of factors, including soil, vineyard aspect, climate, vine, and grower.

The nature of the soil depends on a number of factors, not least the geological parent material from which it was created by gradual weathering. The composition of this material (for example, granite, slate, or limestone from the Mesozoic or Tertiary periods) naturally influences the properties of the soil. Physical, chemical and biological processes all play an important role in weathering, although micro-organisms are the most industrious agents of soil formation: there are billions of fungi, algae, and bacteria in a patch of live earth, in varying proportions, depending on the conditions. These microflora also affect growth cycles and the interaction between soil and roots. Larger creatures such as worms, snails, mites, and insects are also hard at work, and make a significant contribution to loosening and aerating the soil.

The expression of *terroir* in a vine and its grapes is imparted by live soil that supplies the plant with the substances it needs for growth and fruit ripening. Nutrients from the minerals in the rock dissolve into the groundwater, and are drawn up by the vines. Of course, mineral or organic fertilizers can be used to supplement the natural supply of nutrients: nitrogen, phosphorus, potassium, calcium, and magnesium are all important, as are essential micronutrients. However, the expression of *terroir* is lost completely if mineral fertilizers are used too heavily to produce a significant increase in yield. For this reason, fertilizers should not be used solely with the vine in mind, as often happens, but primarily with regard for the soil and the micro-organisms it contains. This complex task can best be achieved by adding composted organic material, which supplies the soil with essential elements and nutrients and stimulates the activities of the living organisms.

Some experts believe that every patch of live soil contains its own specific mix of bacteria and yeasts. They are also to be found on the skins of the grapes and are responsible for fermentation. From this point of view, for optimal expression of the *terroir*, these micro-organisms should be allowed to complete the fermentation process by themselves, without the addition of cultured yeasts or bacteria.

TOPOGRAPHY AND CLIMATE

Topography also plays a role in the expression of the *terroir*, in that aspect and water supply influence the life-cycle of the vine—as does climate, in a variety of ways. The wider climatic conditions (for example Mediterranean or continental) determine the climate in the wine region, and thus the length of the active growth phase. The vines used must be suitable for the particular location. In cooler regions, for example, early-ripening vines are preferable. In a low mountain range, factors that must be taken into account include the elevation, aspect, and incline of the plot, and the presence of water courses or forests; sites higher up the slopes tend to be less prone to frost in spring than those lower down or on the valley floor. In regions with a hotter climate, by contrast, where the grapes sometimes suffer from an excess of sugar and a lack of acidity, vineyards at higher elevations produce grapes with a better balance. In the most varied ways, therefore, the interplay of topography and climate influences the character of the grapes and thus of the wine.

Left
The composition of the soil has a clear influence on the character of the wine. Soils weathered from slate bedrock, such as are found in the Mosel Riesling vineyards and in the southern French region of Banyuls, are considered extremely high quality.

Right
Even more importantly, however, a soil must be live, because the micro- and macro-organisms it contains enable the vine to take up minerals from the soil and give expression to the *terroir*.

Steep plots in Hessigheim, Württemberg, Germany.

Terraces on the Douro, Portugal.

Sloping vineyards by the sea in Collioure, France.

Boundary walls in Burgundy, France.

The combination of conditions in a particular vineyard, such as temperature, exposure to the sun, and humidity, is called the mesoclimate. These all have an effect on the vines, but the parameters can be modified by different methods of vineyard organization and by controlling the vigor of the plants.

Terroir, then, is a wide-ranging term encompassing all the factors that can influence the typical character of a wine. In the wine-producing and wine-exporting countries of the New World, marketing focuses primarily on the grape variety, whereas the fame of European wine countries largely rests on the various *terroirs*, that have long been recognized and classified. It is particularly important in this modern era that these *terroirs* are preserved and do not become standardized.

Terroirs were historically given fixed boundaries by winemakers who realized that a specific plot of land regularly produced a special wine. Their observations were often made over the course of several generations, and respect for a particular *terroir* became part of a cultural history that the winemaker helped to create.

The manner in which a grower cultivates his vineyard gives due regard to soil and choice of grape variety, and handles the grapes in the winery, influences the character of the wine, and can emphasize or obscure the *terroir*. In the absence of an aware and attentive winemaker, even the best *terroir* will not find convincing expression.

The Qualities of the Soil

The nature of the soil depends on how the geological parent material has been altered and shaped by physical, chemical, and biological processes. In general, soils suitable for viticulture are those that are not particularly fertile or deep. Vines have been, and indeed still are, planted on soils weathered from rocks of various geological periods, from the Paleozoic through to the Quaternary. In France, for example, there are vines grown on granite in Beaujolais, chalky marl in Chablis, Tertiary chalk cliffs in the Champagne region, and Mesozoic limestone in the Bordeaux region, while the naturally sweet Banyuls vines flourish in soils on slate. In other parts of the world, vines are cultivated in the soils of former volcanic regions, such as in Tokaj in Hungary.

The depth of the soil determines the spread of the root system. A deep soil with extensive water reserves can be used for bulk production. A relatively shallow, dry soil, by contrast, is generally better at delivering greater quality. Soils that are highly compacted or waterlogged, can have a negative effect on root growth.

Soil is made up of a number of constituents, in varying proportions. Silica is the dominant ingredient in the sandy vineyard plots along the coasts of the Mediterranean and in large parts of Australia. In the famous Graves region of Bordeaux, it is present in the form of gravel and fine-grained soils. Loam consists of silica (sand) and clay, and the proportion of each determines the grade. Loamy and clay soils are more compact, and hence less suitable for viticulture. A soil with a high clay content is fairly impermeable. It contracts in dry weather, becoming hard, cracked, and extremely difficult to cultivate. The organic material in the soil—plant residues, manure, added compost—binds with the clay, and this clay–humus complex is a key factor in stabilizing soils against the dangers of erosion and compaction.

Limestone can also be a component of vine-growing soils, and rootstocks for grafting are selected for their tolerance of lime. Chalky soils tend to be fairly infertile, and produce high-quality wines. Depending on the proportions of the different components (sand, clay, and lime), calcareous soils are described as chalky clay, chalky, or sandy clay soils.

Stony soils are generally good for producing quality wines, but are more difficult to cultivate. The stones help the soil retain water by aiding drainage and preventing direct evaporation. They also store heat during the day and release it at night, which helps the ripening process.

The chemical composition of a soil can include varying amounts of a number of trace and macro-elements, such as nitrogen, phosphorus, potassium, calcium, and magnesium, as well as iron, manganese, boron, and several others.

Chalk and marl in Chablis.

River gravel deposits along the Rhône.

New plots of Pinot Noir in Burgundy.

Clay soil in Nackenheim, Germany.   Uprooted vineyard, exposed to the power of erosion.   Gravel and fine-grained soil at Château Latour.

Countering the Danger of Erosion

The major problems faced by soils are erosion and the washing away of nutrients as water rushes down the slopes during heavy storms. The consolidation of agricultural land can add to the problem: as rows of vines are extended and walls and heaps of stones removed, water can run down the slopes even faster, increasing erosion. The structure of the soil may also be a factor. Soils that are loosely packed but consolidated allow rain to penetrate, whereas if there is a crust on the surface, the water forms rivulets that flow faster and faster and cut deeper and deeper, washing away the topsoil and the nutrients along with it. The earth must then be laboriously transported back up to the vineyard slopes.

One of the factors that aids the stability of the soil is the clay–humus complex. For humus to be created, decomposed organic matter must be added in the form of compost or manure. Most wine-producing countries continue to use mainly mineral fertilizers, however, which do not fulfil this structural purpose. Similarly important are the creatures living in the soil, because they ensure that the soil remains permeable.

In between the solid material in soil are pores filled with water or air, ideally constituting 50 percent of the total volume of the soil. If large agricultural machinery is driven across the ground, particularly in damp conditions, the soil is compressed and the pores disappear; the heavier the equipment, the more the earth is compacted. To maintain the structural stability of the soil, the grower should avoid driving machinery in vineyards during wet weather.

Cultivation of the soil is another means of countering erosion, but must be carried out with care, because on steep slopes it could accelerate the process rather than hinder it. In principle, cultivating the soil facilitates the penetration of water and limits the formation of rivulets. If, however, the speed of the runoff increases, erosion on a cultivated plot will be more severe than on an uncultivated one. Nevertheless, cultivation aerates the soil, which is beneficial for the creatures living in it, and thus increases stability.

The problems of erosion can also be countered by growing grass between the rows of vines, in order to stimulate the growth of micro-organisms. Here too, however, care is required. Depending on the species chosen, competition with the vines can be so intense that yields are considerably reduced, or the grapes may not get enough nitrogen, which can disrupt alcoholic fermentation. For this reason, such a COVER CROP is not appropriate in every situation, although it is undoubtedly one of the best ways of looking after the soil. In the end, it is down to the skill of the winemaker to find the best compromise between the desired outcome and the dictates of circumstance.

DESTROYED AT THE ROOT?
MECHANIZATION IN THE VINEYARD

Every day at first light he would walk to the vineyard, a heavy tool on his shoulder. He would eat lunch with his neighbors in a simple stone or wooden hut; all the hard labor was done by hand, or where feasible, with horses or oxen.

Talk to a winegrower over 60 and you might hear an account like this. Does he regret that those days are gone? A little, perhaps—village life may have been better back then. But mechanization has made his work significantly easier over the last 50 years.

Tractors first appeared in vineyards in the 1950s. Their function, and consequently their appearance, has evolved and changed with time, and from region to region. Small vineyard tractors that drive between rows are used where the vines are sufficiently spaced; they are common in Germany, the south of France, California, and Chile, for example. If the vines are planted closer together, as they are in Burgundy or Champagne, so-called straddle-tractors which span one or two rows are used, although their

One of the biggest problems in modern viticulture is compaction of the soil caused by heavy machinery. Ideally, vineyards should be worked with horses or mules, as shown here, plowing on the Los Boldos estate in Chile.

extremely high center of gravity can make the use of these machines precarious: where the slopes become steeper, they can lose their grip and tip over. Manufacturers are attempting to overcome these difficulties and improve stability by shifting or if necessary reducing the weight.

Little by little growers have been forced to adapt their vineyards for mechanization, by planting the vines in rows and as far as possible training the curtain of foliage along wire frames, so that machinery can pass in between. In vineyards that are laid out in terraces, however, such as in Portugal's Douro valley, in Germany along the Mosel and in the Wachau, in France in the north of the Côtes du Rhône, or in any mountainous wine region of the world, it is impossible to mechanize viticulture. Here, the work is done manually, just as it always has been, although helicopters are used in some areas for spraying the vines.

The difficulty of mechanizing production is often one of the reasons used to justify

In Burgundy, around 100 of the top estates jointly produce compost, which this specially designed spreader then applies in the vineyards.

In densely planted vineyards, straddle-tractors can negotiate the narrow rows to carry out tasks such as spraying and canopy pruning.

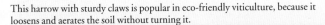

This harrow with sturdy claws is popular in eco-friendly viticulture, because it loosens and aerates the soil without turning it.

The weight of small caterpillar tractors is distributed more evenly. Consequently, they cause less soil compaction than tractors with tires.

elevated prices in industrialized nations, where it is more cost effective, once wages and employer's social security contributions are taken into account, for the work to be done mechanically rather than by hand. Elsewhere in the world—in South America, for example—labor is still very cheap, and wine producers are largely turning back to human workers.

Although many tasks are done by specialized machines nowadays, including pest control, soil cultivation, foliage trimming, and to a certain extent, grape picking, one task that has proved difficult to mechanize is the pruning of the vines.

Soil compaction

The use of ever heavier machines in vineyards compacts soil to a depth of 12 inches (30 cm), compressing the pore spaces within it. As a result, the soil is not adequately aerated. Such damage can be avoided, however, or at least reduced. The first step is to restrict the driving of machinery through vineyards to the bare minimum, only spraying crops, for example, if absolutely necessary.

The second step is to buy lighter vehicles and equipment. Inflating the tires to a lower pressure can also help, because it increases the

area of the tire in contact with the ground, thereby reducing the weight pressing down on the soil at any particular point. Caterpillar vehicles cause little soil compaction, because their weight is equally distributed over a larger contact area, and they have the advantage of being able to cope with steep slopes.

Soils that have been compacted by heavy machinery are not well aerated.

Vine Cultivation: Pruning the Vines

The grapevine is a climbing plant that originally grew up trees. Left to its own devices, it tends to grow horizontally, because the first buds to burst are generally the ones at the very end of the cane tips. The vines should therefore always be pruned to counter this tendency for rampant growth, because it weakens the structure of the plant—the vine becomes fragile, difficult to tend, and little suited to bearing high-quality fruit.

If vines are not pruned the risk of fungal diseases also rises sharply. More and more buds sprout, and so the number of shoots and bunches of grapes increases. The shoots get thinner and thinner, and the grapes ever smaller, and quality can suffer considerably as a result. Nevertheless, experiments with zero pruning and minimal pruning are on the rise.

Pruning crucially influences both the quantity and the quality of the yield, by determining how many buds are allowed to remain on the vine. Each bud puts forth a shoot, which in turn bears up to three bunches of grapes. The level of productivity depends on the vine variety and on the location of the buds on the stock.

If the crop is large, there may be too many bunches for the vine's ability to photosynthesize. This results in an unfavorable leaf to fruit ratio and a corresponding difficulty in ripening the grapes. In addition, because the grapes are given priority access to nutrients, the vine itself is weakened as it cannot build up much in the way of reserves. By contrast, if too few buds remain on the vine, the plant does not have sufficient outlet for its growth capabilities. Plant growth may be vigorous (with thick shoots), but the fruit crop will be insignificant.

Left
Guyot pruning leaves a long cane.

Right
Vines are pruned in winter.

This makes no improvement to the quality of the grapes, but simply leads to a reduction in yield and income.

The art of VINE PRUNING lies in finding the ideal compromise for an optimal crop. The general "balance" of the vine must be taken into account, to avoid an overly-dense curtain of foliage. It is also important to limit the number of cuts made to the vine, because these are the entry points for diseases affecting the wood.

The pruning method used will largely depend on the productivity of the particular variety of vine. In productive varieties, every bud will bear bunches of grapes, whereas none will develop from the lower buds of less productive ones. In the former case, "spur pruning" should

Double bow-trained vine

Simple bow-trained vine

be used to avoid over-production; in the latter, only the less severe "cane pruning" method will produce a satisfactory yield. With spur pruning, the canes are cut back to two or three buds. This method is principally employed with vines that are trained into a goblet shape (the gobelet system) or into single or double cordons. Cane pruning involves leaving at least five buds. To prevent the sideways extension of the stock, and in preparation for the following year's pruning, a two-bud spur is also left. This is called Guyot pruning, which can be simple (one spur, one cane) or double (two spurs, two canes). In the double system, the canes are trained unilaterally (on the same side of the stock) or bilaterally (on both sides of the stock) in a bow shape.

The timing of pruning influences the timing of budding. The experienced winegrower will prune as late as possible, and an old German saying holds that "the best pruning is a March pruning" (i.e. in late spring). In some regions of Europe, tradition demands that pruning is not carried out before the feast day of St. Vincent, the patron saint of winegrowers, on January 22. One thing is certain, however: it is vital to wait until all the leaves have fallen and the sap has retreated, because only then will the plant have finished storing up the reserves that will see it through the winter and start growth again in the spring. Where there is a danger of frost during spring, it is advisable to delay budding for as long as possible. Consequently, sites at risk from late frost are the last to be pruned. Cane pruning is preferred in such areas, because the buds on the ends of the canes are the first to burst, while the others do not come to life until somewhat later. If the first perish in the frost, others remain to replace them.

The height of the trunk is also determined by pruning. For mechanical harvesting, it is helpful to increase the height of the trunk. To enable it to grow straight and without cut wounds, the wild shoots growing out from the trunk should preferably be removed during the growth phase. This woody matter can be burned or shredded for compost, which can later be used as mulch for the soil.

Pruning takes a long time, and if the wood is thick, can be difficult and strenuous work. For this reason, attempts have been made to mechanize the process. The advent of pneumatic and electric secateurs was the first step forward, reducing the force needed to cut through the vine. To speed up the operation, some growers now use machines that remove and shred a portion of the vine, much like cutting a hedge. This is 20 to 30 percent faster than hand-pruning.

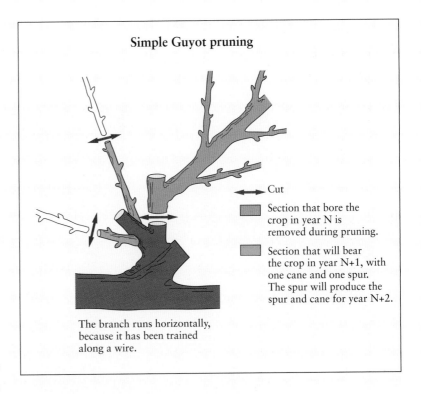

Simple Guyot pruning

← Cut

Section that bore the crop in year N is removed during pruning.

Section that will bear the crop in year N+1, with one cane and one spur. The spur will produce the spur and cane for year N+2.

The branch runs horizontally, because it has been trained along a wire.

In countries where labor is hard to come by, such as in Australia, attempts are being made to mechanize pruning as fully as possible. One of the most widely-used systems involves pre-pruning the part of the vine that will bear the following year's crop, and completely removing the rest mechanically, so that the wood cannot grow too long. The next year, the roles are reversed. Comparative studies have shown that the crops produced by this method are not as good as those delivered by traditional, manual pruning, due to the uneven distribution of bunches of grapes.

Although pruning partially determines future yield size, it is not an exact science. Numerous factors influence the fruitfulness of a particular bud, and the success of flowering and the other stages of the growth phase. If it becomes clear after flowering that the crop is too large, individual flowerheads and bunches can always be removed at that point.

Methods of Cultivation

The primary goal of a winegrower is to produce quality grapes in sufficient quantities to ensure that his business remains viable. Various methods of cultivation can be employed to achieve this, from the traditional, through the judicious use of integrated or organic practices, to BIODYNAMIC CULTIVATION. The fundamental differences between them are mainly concerned with the control of pests and diseases in the vineyard, but also with the cultivation of the soil, weed control, use of fertilizers, and finally, the winemaking process itself.

Over-exploitation of Vines and Soil

In the period from 1960 to 1980, agriculture as a whole made heavy use of newly available chemicals for controlling pests and diseases. In viticulture, the products were applied at a precisely stipulated stage of vine development, and then, depending on the length of time they remained effective, reapplied at regular intervals. The use of fertilizers was similarly indiscriminate, and could disrupt the natural balance of the soil or lead to an excess of a particular substance such as potassium or nitrates. At the time, people were probably unable—and unwilling—to appreciate the effects that some of these products would have on the environment and consumers, and alternative products and methods of monitoring did not yet exist. Consumers were also slow to

Some wine producers make measured use of natural fertilizer—as here in Beaujolais—and compost in place of artificial fertilizers.

Left
Green manuring is increasingly being practiced, as here in the Napa Valley. A variety of plants are sown, and then plowed under before they run to seed.

Right
In this vineyard, compost and straw are being spread as a mulch.

tackle such issues, although there was a clear interest in alternative and ecological lifestyles as early as the 1970s.

Integrated Production

Since the beginning of the 1990s, more and more winegrowers have been switching to what is known as the "integrated" method of cultivation, in which chemical products for pest and disease control are used in a more considered manner. Treatment is only undertaken once the severity of a disease or infestation has reached a certain level. The grower chooses the products that are least harmful to the environment and vineyard worker, and does not deploy them until circumstances are favorable, in order to achieve the best results. The right moment may be determined by the life-cycle of the pest, the stage of development reached by the vine, or by the weather.

Conscientious monitoring in the vineyard is essential if environmentally-friendly agriculture is to be successful and help reduce the use of chemical treatments. However, collecting the necessary information does take time.

What motivates winegrowers to switch to integrated cultivation is not economics, but rather the need to optimize work on the vineyard. Integrated production involves following certain principles regarding fertilizers and soil cultivation. The guidelines recommend growers limit the addition of nitrogen, and shred and

Biodynamic cultivation

The theory behind this system holds that disease in a plant (or any other living organism) is an indication that the natural equilibrium has been disturbed. The disease must, of course, be treated, but the main goal is to restore the balance between the plant and its environment. Naturally, this cannot be achieved overnight, just as growers cannot switch from their previous practices to biodynamic methods in the space of a day.

Biodynamic agriculture originated in Germany at the beginning of the 20th century, under the influence of the anthroposophist Rudolf Steiner. His concept, which is also the basis of a philosophy and system of education, can be applied to all branches of agriculture.

A winegrower practicing biodynamism is allowed to use small amounts of copper and sulfur as a treatment for the vines. They may also be dusted with preparations made from quartz crystals, nettles, or dandelions. To "dynamize" the soil, preparations made of animal horn are employed in addition to compost.

The raw material for horn-based preparations.

The cosmic influence on the vines varies with the position of the nine planets of the solar system, the twelve constellations, the sun, and the moon. The effects of the various procedures intensify if this influence is respected. Soil should be cultivated during an earth influence, which stimulates the roots. The work should preferably be done in the afternoon, to harness the energy of the setting sun. To stimulate fruit set, the vines should be tended under a fire influence, and preferably very early in the morning, so as to benefit from the power of the rising sun. The sowing calendar, which is published every year, gives detailed advice for each day.

The biodynamic viewpoint holds the use of agrochemicals responsible for a series of problems. Herbicides destroy the living organisms in the soil and hinder healthy vine growth. Plants whose balance is thus disrupted attract parasites and diseases, but the agents used to treat the condition cause further disturbances in the soil. This eliminates the influence of the *terroir*, and the wines lose their typical character.

The biodynamic route is not an easy one, as there are no universally applicable remedies; every winegrower choosing this method of cultivation must find the best solutions for his or her own vineyards.

compost the matter cut from the vines during pruning, returning it to the soil.

Organic cultivation demands that a host of more rigorous conditions are met. Disease and pest control can only be undertaken using products of natural origin—of which copper and sulfur are the most important. Growers are now advised to reduce the application of copper, however, because it is taken up by the soil and disrupts biological processes.

Naturally, all the principles of integrated production are also heeded with organic cultivation. At one end of the scale are growers' own individual practices, very few of which are regulated by any kind of association, and at the other is a set of clearly defined regulations and a system of regular checks. Just a few years ago, organic wines were likely to be squarely in the firing line as far as many wine critics were concerned, but now the position is very different.

In many countries around the world, winegrowers are increasingly prepared to accept the sometimes very lengthy transition period to organic production and the strict rules governing production.

Horn compost is energetically "dynamized" before use.

Integrated Pest Management

Hartwig Holst

The aim of pest management is of course to ensure all-round healthy vines and the production of healthy grapes for wine making or directly for the table.

Integrated pest management concerns not only direct means of control, but also a large number of indirect measures. The integrated concept involves maintaining vine diseases and infestations below the threshold where they would become economically damaging, using all the financially, ecologically, and toxicologically justifiable methods of damage control available.

Methods of Damage Control

• Viticultural methods. The aim of these methods is to increase the vine's natural resistance on the one hand, and at the same time to engineer the vineyard mesoclimate in such a way that disease pathogens and vine pests do not find the living conditions they need. This includes the choice of a vine variety suitable for the location, appropriate use of fertilizer, and timely canopy management.
• Physical and mechanical methods. In addition to mechanical weed control, this category principally includes acoustic and visual methods of scaring off birds, the use of bird nets to protect the ripening grapes, and plastic mesh sleeves to prevent damage caused by wild animals trying to eat the plants.
• Biological methods. Biological pest control involves countering harmful organisms using

The vineyard is safe for butterflies once again.

Vineyard scent dispensers continuously release sexually enticing pheromones which disorient the male grape berry moth, thereby preventing impregnation of the female. This is known as the confusion method.

other organisms. Integrated pest management in viticulture currently allows the use of two such agents: first, preparations of *Bacillus thuringiensis*, which are used to control grape berry moths, and second, the fungal pathogen *Metarhizium anisopliae*, which is harmful to the black vine weevil. Natural pest control can also be significantly aided if the grower treats vines with chemicals that do not harm beneficial insects. This is particularly true in the case of the predatory mite *Typhlodromus pyri*, which can remain unaffected if an appropriate agent is chosen, so that direct intervention to control the spider mite is seldom necessary.
• Biotechnological methods. The natural reactions of pests to chemical or physical stimuli are exploited as a means of combating them. Yellow, white or red colored disks may be used, for example, as scarers, as with the cultivation of fruit crops and ornamental plants. Currently, the method with the greatest practical significance in this category is the use of pheromones (sexual scents). In viticulture, this mainly involves the pheromones of the grape berry moths. "Pheromone traps" can be used as a reliable way of indicating when the pest reaches its flight stage, and thus when there is greatest risk of infestation. The male moths are lured into the traps by scents which mimic the pheromones secreted by female moths, and are caught on the sticky surface at the bottom. By regularly checking the traps the winegrower can determine accurately the peaks of the flight stage and hence the optimal time to treat the vines and avoid unnecessary spraying. As well as their use for prognostic purposes,

pheromones are also employed in combating grape berry moths directly by what is known as the confusion method.

This method also makes use of synthetically produced pheromones of the female grape berry moths. The male moths can detect even the tiniest concentrations of these chemicals via their antennae, and when they do, they follow the trail to the source of the pheromones. Under natural circumstances, they would find the female who is secreting the scent.

In the confusion method, the synthetic pheromones are contained in plastic dispensers, which are evenly distributed throughout the vineyard at a density of around 200 per acre (500 per hectare). The pheromones continuously diffuse from these dispensers into the surrounding environment, flooding the treated area. The male moths become disoriented and confused, because they can no longer detect a trail of pheromones. Finding a partner is no longer possible. As a result, the females are not impregnated, and can only lay unfertilized eggs. This method can be used to control both types of grape berry moth—cochylis (*Eupoecilia ambiguella*) and eudemis (*Lobesia botrana*). The dispensers need only be deployed once, before the first generation of moths takes flight. The distinguishing feature of the confusion method is that it has a specific effect, targeting only the cochylis and the eudemis moth. Consequently, it does not harm beneficial insects such as predatory mites, ichneumon wasps, lacewings, assassin bugs, and ladybirds. These are the most environmentally-friendly pest control measures currently available.

• Chemical methods. Integrated pest management will always involve chemical agents. It is important that growers aim to use insecticides, acaricides, fungicides, and herbicides only when the pests or disease pathogens exceed the damage threshold. Appropriate thresholds

Left
Once the caterpillar of the grape berry moth hatches from the egg, it eats into the buds on the vine, destroying the immature flower inside.

Right
The larva of the willow beauty (*Peribatodes rhomboidaria*) is a pest that eats vine buds. These brown caterpillars hollow out the buds, preventing normal shoot development.

have been worked out for the main pests. In the case of fungal pathogens, preventive measures are often necessary. Nevertheless, improving existing prognostic methods, and developing new ones, has a significant part to play in avoiding unnecessary prophylaxis.

Integrated pest management takes the concerns of environmental protection very much into consideration. Whilst all available means of pest control may be used, winegrowers should give preference to biological and biotechnological methods wherever possible.

Moths caught on the sticky base of a trap.

VINE PESTS AND DISEASES

Viruses, bacteria, phytoplasma, fungi, mites, insects, and nematodes—the vine has many enemies. Fortunately, they are rarely found in the same place simultaneously. Some diseases and pests are more common in some wine regions than others.

DISEASES

Of the 40 or so known vine viruses, those involved in the complex of diseases known as fanleaf degeneration occur most frequently. These viruses are spread by threadworms (nematodes), and infected vines may suffer extremely reduced yields. Fanleaf degeneration is combated by only planting healthy vines (following strategies similar to those used in tree nurseries), and by allowing cleared vineyards to lie fallow for a period before they are replanted. Care must be taken to remove as much root material as possible, so that the nematodes have nothing to live on and die of starvation. Treating the soil with agents to kill nematodes is harmful to the environment, and so the practice is banned in some countries (Germany and Switzerland, for example), whilst other countries (such as France) impose tight controls.

Two significant vine diseases are caused by phytoplasma, organisms similar to bacteria: Pierce's disease, which causes a great deal of damage in the U.S.A.; and *flavescence dorée*, which mainly occurs in the south of France.

Certain harmful fungi attack the trunk of the vine and can cause it to die, while others damage the green parts of the vine (leaves, shoots, and grapes). The first group includes the diseases eutypa dieback and esca. To limit their spread the grower must prune the vines without creating large wounds through which the fungi can enter. It is essential that dead rootstocks are burned, otherwise they can become new sources of infection.

Of the second group of fungi, three are particularly widespread: downy mildew (*Plasmopara*), powdery mildew (*Oidium*), and gray rot (*Botrytis*). Downy mildew primarily attacks the leaves, and to such an extent that the vine sheds them before time. This severely affects photosynthesis, reduces the concentration of fructose in the grapes, and alters the composition of the nutrient reserves in the roots of the vine. Copper is an important active ingredient for controlling downy mildew. Commonly used preparations are copper oxychloride and Bordeaux mixture (copper neutralized with lime).

Powdery mildew can colonize foliage and grapes, causing a reduction in quality or even the loss of the crop. Not all vine varieties are equally susceptible: some, such as Carignan, are very prone to infection; others, such as Syrah or Pinot Noir, less so. Once the fungus has taken hold, however, it is very difficult to treat, and so preventative measures are essential. *Oidium* control is generally undertaken using preparations containing sulfur. Organically-based products are also available, and should be deployed only once or twice a year, to prevent the appearance of resistant strains of fungus.

Powdery mildew: individual berries have split open.

Phomopsis infection: pycnidia (the spore receptacles) on winter wood.

The third great enemy of the vine is *Botrytis*, or gray rot, which can affect both the quantity and the quality of the yield. It is best combated through the use of preventative strategies that promote the vitality of the vine and ensure good ventilation in the canopy. This necessitates reducing the amount of nitrogen added to the soil, training the vines so that they have adequate space, and undertaking work on the canopy (removing the secondary shoots; thinning out the foliage) in good time.

Organic substances used to control fungal diseases can be divided into three categories: products that work on the contact principle, and thus only protect the organs to which they are applied (contact fungicides); products that penetrate the treated organs and stop the attack within the plant (locally systemic fungicides); and products that penetrate and spread throughout the vine (systemic fungicides).

PESTS

The two types of grape berry moth, cochylis (*Eupoecilia ambiguella*) and eudemis (*Lobesia botrana*), are significant vine pests. They produce two or three generations every summer, and their various larval stages damage the buds, the immature flowers, and the maturing grapes.

The chosen methods of control must be appropriate for the particular stage of development (eggs or larvae), and be deployed at the right time. The less harmful the products are to the environment, vineyard-workers, and beneficial insects, the more precisely an optimal treatment date must be determined; in some cases, one or two days can make a great deal of difference.

Spraying the vines with pesticide.

Eutypa dieback: cross-section through a trunk.

Methods of treatment

Treatment should be targeted specifically at the areas damaged by the pest or disease, such as the foliage (as with mildew) or the grapes (e.g. grape berry moth). Good coverage of the affected parts is vital to the success of the treatment, as is the choice of agent, time of deployment, use of the correct nozzle setting on the spraying equipment, and the speed at which the machinery is driven through the vineyard. Incorrect settings on the spraying equipment and too much speed can lead to unnecessary pollution of the environment (such as increased drift).

Serious Vine Diseases

Beate Berkelmann-Löhnertz

Downy Mildew
(*Plasmopara viticola*)

Downy mildew is one of the two most significant fungal diseases of the vine. Spring storms with heavy rain appear to be required for the initial infection of vine leaves by spores from the soil. Later, warm and humid weather conditions encourage the spreading of the fungus. The first symptom is the "oil spot," a lighter-colored, often circular area on an infected leaf. Subsequently, the undersides of these leaves will reveal the typical fungal growth. Vines subjected to severe attacks may lose a high proportion of their yield. The quality of the grapes is affected, as is the maturation of the canes. All European vines are susceptible, particularly Müller-Thurgau, Chasselas, and Portugieser.

Gray Rot or Botrytis
(*Botrytis cinerea*)

Young grapes are easily infected if the must weight is still below 62° OECHSLE (i.e. the specific gravity of the grape juice is less than 1.062), and the weather is humid. If the stalks of the grapes and the stems of the bunches are also colonized, many will fall to the ground before the harvest. Botrytis breaks down certain pigments in red wine grape varieties, and so it is particularly important to monitor the health of such vines. Gray rot also affects vine propagation, because it can impede the adhesion of the graft and disrupt young growth. Botrytis infection of ripe grapes is a desired event, however, and is known as "noble rot." These "botrytized" grapes can produce very fine wines, such as those in the German *Auslese* and BEERENAUSLESE categories.

Powdery Mildew
(*Oidium tuckeri*)

Powdery mildew is the other most significant fungal disease of the vine. All the green parts of the vine can be affected, most strikingly the young shoots at the beginning of the vegetative phase. However, the aptness of the name of the disease is most evident when the grapes are infected: in severe attacks, the majority of the berries are coated with a grayish-white growth that makes them look as if they have been dusted with flour. Periods of high pressure, with hot days and cool nights, encourage the spread of the fungus. All European vine varieties are susceptible, but particularly Portugieser, Elbling, Kerner, Trollinger, Silvaner, and Carignan. Wines from severely infected vineyards usually taste tainted.

Phomopsis (Dead Arm or Excoriose)
(*Phomopsis viticola*)

The striking symptoms of this disease usually emerge in winter, at pruning time: severely infected canes display distinct pale patches, elongated longitudinal fissures, lesions, and a large number of microscopic holes for spores. The risk of infection is particularly high during the growth period in spring, if cool weather has slowed the development of the shoots and there is a lot of rain. The disease spreads slowly, because the spores are transmitted mainly in drops of water. During dry, warm springs, the danger of infection is low, and so preventative measures are unnecessary. The Müller-Thurgau grape variety is highly prone to this infection.

Rotbrenner
(*Pseudopezicula tracheiphila*)

The name of this fungal disease in German is literally "red burner," and stems from the typical appearance of the foliage of infected red wine grape varieties. The reddish-brown edges and yellow to green middles of the partially dead leaves make the affected vine look burnt. Rotbrenner mainly affects vines in steep plots, and so is only significant in certain localities, such as the Mosel valley and parts of Franconia (Franken). Riesling is particularly susceptible, since it tends to be planted in sloping vineyards that are dry, stony, and lacking in humus—favorable locations for the fungus. Where required, measures to control this disease must be undertaken preventatively, and early: in practice, this means that vines should be sprayed when four to five leaves have developed.

Eutypa Dieback
(*Eutypa lata*)

Eutypa dieback is the result of a harmful fungus that not only affects grapevines, but is also dreaded by growers of apricots and blackcurrants, for example. The fungus causes the vines to die off, in a similar fashion to esca. Two striking symptoms are cankers and small leaves. Previously, the disease was thought only to affect vines that are more than 12 years old, but the latest research has shown this to be untrue. Direct treatment of infected wood is not possible, and so here again, preventative measures are important. Eutypa dieback has become more common in recent years and is often linked to esca infections. Special research is therefore now being carried out both into the pathogens and the spread of the disease.

Esca
(A complex of pathogens, including *Phaeoacremonium* spp.)

The incidence of this disease has increased in recent years. Esca is primarily found on older vines, and can be a chronic infection: individual vines in a plot show the typical leaf symptoms and stunted growth, before eventually dying off—usually not until the following year. The exact cause of the disease is not known, although recent research has shown that the *Phaeoacremonium* spp. fungus is part of the pathogen complex. Because no treatments have been developed, preventive measures must be undertaken to try to reduce the risk of infection. Intensive research is being carried out into the micro-organisms involved, and possible ways of combating them.

Root Fungi
(*Armillaria mellea, Roesleria hypogaea, Rosellinia necatrix*)

These three root rot pathogens cause dieback of the vines and stunted growth. The fungi colonize both old and new roots, and produce characteristic fan-shaped sheets of mycelium, rhizomorph "shoestrings," and tiny fruiting bodies on or under the epidermis of the roots. The three fungi can occur separately or in combination. The death of a vine can seldom be put down to a single cause—individual plants will often have been already weakened or stress-damaged. Unfavorable conditions in the vineyard, such as standing surface water, appear to play an important role in this regard. The presence of these fungi is difficult to detect with any certainty, because they require special conditions and grow very slowly.

Some Feared Vineyard Pests

Hartwig Holst

Grape Berry Moths (1)

The grape berry moths are the most significant of the vine pests. Cochylis moths (*Eupoecilia ambiguella*) are light yellow with a dark band on a light background, while eudemis moths (*Lobesia botrana*) have wings with a brown, marbled pattern and faint cross. The damage is caused by their larvae.

Grape Berry Moths (3)

As well as eating the flower buds, the first generation grubs also use a number of flower parts to spin their cocoons—little bundles made from fragments of flowers and the grub's own silk. Some of the fully developed grubs enter these cocoons and pupate, the pupae becoming the moths of the second generation.

Grape Berry Moths (2)

The first generation eggs are laid singly on the buds of the flowerheads. Inside the eggs, the first larval stage develops: a grub less than $1/_{10}$ inch (2 mm) long. These grubs feed on the buds, eating their way through to the immature flower, which they also destroy.

Grape Berry Moths (4)

The second generation of grubs feeds on and in the ripening grapes. Large population densities can more or less destroy the whole bunch. Often, however, the grapes attacked by the grubs also become infected with fungi. Gray rot (*Botrytis cinerea*), in particular, spreads from the eaten grapes to envelop the rest of the bunch, leading to the dreaded sour rot.

VINE LEAFHOPPERS (1)

Vine leafhoppers (*Empoasca vitis*) overwinter in the trunks of evergreen trees, the adults returning to the vineyards in spring. These green insects are mainly found on the undersides of the vine foliage, where they lay their eggs in the leaf veins. The resulting larvae do not have wings at first. Tiny wing buds become visible during the final larval stage.

WILLOW BEAUTY CATERPILLAR

The larva of the willow beauty moth (*Peribatodes rhomboidaria*) is a pest that eats vine buds. The grayish-brown caterpillars hollow out the buds, preventing normal shoot development. Damage can be severe, particularly in seasons where shoot growth is delayed. The caterpillars resemble twigs, and are therefore hard to detect.

VINE LEAFHOPPERS (2)

The larvae and adult insects suck on the leaf veins, causing the leaves to curl inwards. They also become discolored, initially at the edges: white wine varieties turn yellowy, and red varieties strikingly reddish. The discoloration spreads between the veins in the centers of the leaves. The affected leaves dry out, leading to early leaf drop in severe cases.

BLACK VINE WEEVIL

The black vine weevil (*Otiorrhyncus sulcatus*) is about $\frac{1}{2}$ inch (1 cm) long and grayish-black in color. The adult beetle feeds on the vine buds in spring, later causing a typical pattern of damage around the leaf edges. It overwinters in the soil, both as larvae and in its adult form. The damage done by the larvae feeding on the roots of the vines is particularly significant. Damage to the bark can cause serious harm to the main root stem of young vines.

PHYLLOXERA

The PHYLLOXERA louse arrived in France around 1860, in vines imported from the United States. The tiny, yellow insect appeared in England for the first time in 1863, and in the same year, growers in the southern Rhône area of France noticed a vine disease that they had never seen before. The French scientist, Jules Planchon, originally named the pest that was responsible *Phylloxera*, but nowadays it is known scientifically as *Daktulosphaira vitifoliae*. By the end of the 19th century, phylloxera had spread to almost all the wine-producing countries of Europe. Today, it is present in almost all the wine regions of the world.

Phylloxera damages vines primarily by attacking the roots. This causes sustained disruption of the plant's food supply, and even the death of the vine. There is still no really effective chemical treatment. One measure that was used successfully in the past, and is still valid today, is grafting. The scions of susceptible vine varieties (of the species *Vitis vinifera*) are grafted onto phylloxera-resistant rootstocks (hybrids of *Vitis berlandieri*, *Vitis riparia*, and *Vitis rupestris*).

Phylloxera is now rare in vineyards planted with grafted vines, but this does not mean that it has disappeared altogether: Certain rootstocks with *Vitis vinifera* ancestry are still susceptible. The hybrid AxR1 rootstock, which was mainly used in California in the 1960s, is a case in point. It adapts well to all soil conditions, and does not exhibit the symptoms of phylloxera until late on. Californian winemakers are now suffering the consequences of this carelessness, because they are having to replant all their vineyards with resistant rootstocks.

Left and center
The phylloxera louse (*Daktulosphaira vitifoliae*) produces leaf galls, mainly on American vine varieties. Inside these galls are the foliar phylloxera (*gallicola*), their eggs, and hatched "crawlers." The galls have an opening on the upper surface of the leaf through which the crawlers emerge. They feed on other areas of the leaf or leaf stalk, causing new galls to form.

Right
Root-living phylloxera (*radicola*) feed on the vine roots, causing swellings. This impedes the plant's uptake of water and nutrients and can lead to restricted growth or even the death of the vine.

LIFE CYCLE OF PHYLLOXERA
Hartwig Holst

The phylloxera louse finds a new host not by moving to a new plant, but by moving from the leaves to the roots of the vine. The winter eggs laid by the sexual form of the insects hatch at the beginning of the vine's vegetative phase. Once they are fully developed, the young fundatrix lice (stem mothers) create leaf galls, in which they lay their eggs. The "crawlers" that hatch from these eggs spread out over the shoots and create new galls on the young foliage. In late summer, the crawlers no longer head toward the tips of the shoots, but move down the vine and seek out its roots—beginning the underground phase of the cycle. The crawlers migrate first to the deeper layers of the soil, where they spend the winter. The following spring, they feed on young roots, causing swellings and growths, and complete their development as egg-laying females. Parthenogenesis produces several generations of root-living crawlers. Some of the crawlers become nymphs (lice with wing buds) and leave the soil, beginning the above-ground phase of the cycle. The nymphs become winged adults, and seek out American vines on which they lay both large and small eggs. The large eggs hatch into females, while the small eggs produce males. After mating, the female lays only one egg—called a winter egg—on the trunk of the vine. During the next vegetative phase, a new fundatrix louse will hatch from the egg, and the cycle begins again.

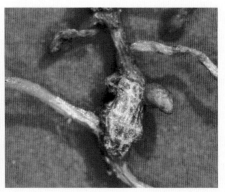

Development Cycle of the Phylloxera Louse

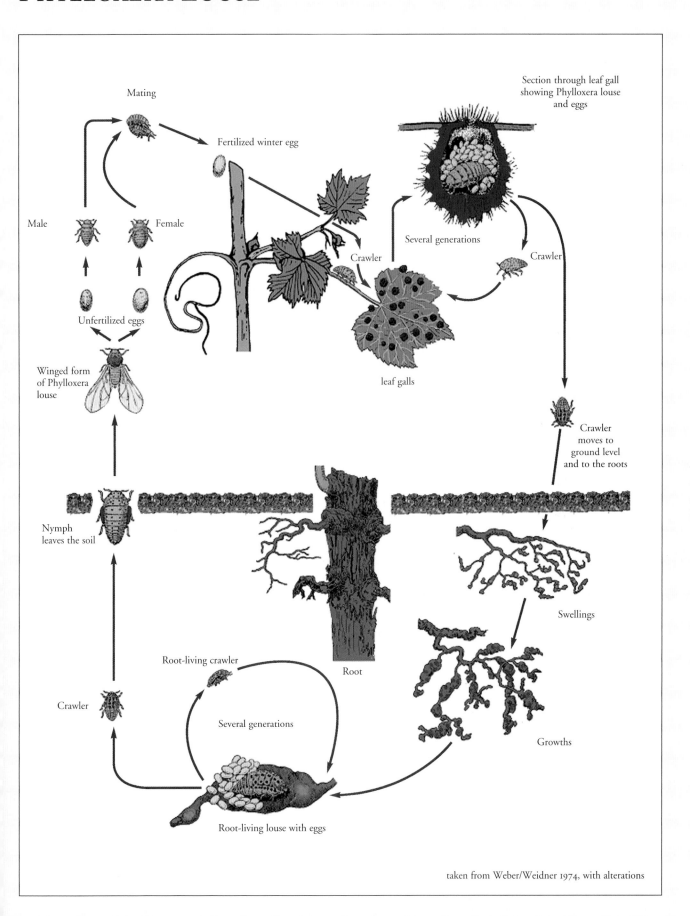

Mating

Fertilized winter egg

Section through leaf gall showing Phylloxera louse and eggs

Male

Female

Several generations

Crawler

Crawler

Unfertilized eggs

Winged form of Phylloxera louse

leaf galls

Crawler moves to ground level and to the roots

Nymph leaves the soil

Swellings

Root-living crawler

Root

Crawler

Several generations

Growths

Root-living louse with eggs

taken from Weber/Weidner 1974, with alterations

THE WORKING YEAR IN THE VINEYARD: CARE OF THE SOIL—AND MORE

Planting new vines is the most time-consuming job in the vineyard—and the most satisfying when the young plants thrive.

WEED CONTROL

Grapevines demand constant and careful attention. The work carried out on both the soil and the plants is crucial for the quality of that season's wine, but also lays the foundations for the following year. The techniques used to cultivate the soil depend on the grower's chosen methodology. Chemical weed-killing employs herbicides that reduce the need for manual or mechanical soil cultivation. However, the soil is generally cultivated once or twice a year to loosen and aerate it. This can be done in the fall, or in spring, or in both seasons. Another

The leaves of the vines grow so thickly, especially in the damper wine-growing regions, that they have to be pruned to let light and air get to the vine stocks.

possibility is to target the use of herbicides only along the rows of vines. Following this, the ground in between the rows is either cultivated or planted with a grass cover crop.

The most promising course of action combines various methods of cultivation: piling up earth around the trunks of the vines and tilling, leveling, or hoeing the soil in between, as necessary. The layer of earth around the graft zone serves to protect the vine from the effects of very cold spells in winter. The piles of earth must be removed in the spring to prevent the scion from growing under the soil and putting down unwanted roots.

The frequency of weeding will depend on the extent of the weed population. Following rain, it can sometimes be difficult to drive tractors across the plots. If the grass is to be a permanent feature, it will have to be mown several times per season. To reduce competition during the growth period, however, some growers prefer temporary coverage: the grass is destroyed at the end of the winter, either by mechanical soil cultivation or with herbicides.

Once again, however, there is no solution that can be applied in all situations. The soil's properties, access to the plot, the problems of erosion, spring frosts, competition for water, and operating costs all have to be taken into account. Sowing grasses is an interesting strategy that looks after the structure of the soil and the creatures living in it, but it is not suitable for steep slopes, because the tractor tires cannot get a grip on such a surface. Neither is it recommended in areas where there is a risk of late frosts: the cover crop raises the moisture content of the soil, thereby increasing the danger of frost damage in spring.

Maintaining and Training the Vines

There is also a series of tasks to be undertaken to look after the vine. The best time to repair trellises, stakes, and wires is during the winter, usually after pruning. If the cane pruning method has been used, the cane is fastened to the wire of the trellis. As soon as growth has begun, superfluous shoots are removed to aid ventilation in the canopy and make pruning easier the following winter. The WATER SHOOTS (i.e. shoots growing directly from the trunk)

should also be removed, either at the same time or later on.

If the vineyard uses a cordon training system, the shoots must be tied up with trellis wire as soon as they are long enough, and fastened along the wires between the stakes. This work has to be done manually, and the canopy should be trimmed at the same time.

In cooler regions, growers may decide to remove a certain number of bunches per vine around midsummer (i.e. just before veraison), to ensure a high-quality crop. This practice is mainly used with red grape varieties to increase the concentration of color compounds, and is known as "crop thinning" or *vendange verte*. If it is carried out early enough, the vine compensates for the loss with the remaining bunches.

In spectacular hillside positions such as these along the Mosel, the winegrowers use ropes to move ploughs and other equipment. The best sites cannot be maintained without using such aids.

Nowadays we know that care of the leaves is extremely important for better wine quality. If all shoots that do not support fruit are removed, the grapes are improved in flavor.

GRAPE RIPENESS

Between budbreak at the end of the winter and ripe grapes at the beginning of fall, the vine goes through a number of stages of development, some of which are particularly important. At the beginning of the process, the buds get thicker, and gradually the first leaves start to appear. By the time the first five or six have properly unfolded, the bunches of grapes can already be identified. The success of fruit set is governed by the weather and health of the plant during the previous year, and gives an indication of likely yield-size. In the northern hemisphere, flowering occurs between the middle of May and the middle of June, depending on the region. Although every flower bud blossoms, not all will produce a grape, because some will drop off either before or after pollination. The percentage of fruit remaining on the vine compared with the original number of flowers is called the pollination rate. This rate varies between 10 and 50 percent, depending on the grape variety and climatic conditions. Young berries can also drop off in the two weeks after flowering, again depending on the robustness of the particular grape variety. Cold spells and rain are decidedly unhelpful. As a rule of thumb, harvesting begins 100 days after flowering.

At fruit set, the bunches of grapes tend to grow horizontally. Once the berries become pea-sized, the bunches sag and hang downwards. Grapes can sometimes develop without pollination taking place; they are small, seedless, and have a high sugar content when ripe. This phenomenon is called PARTHENOCARPY, and if it occurs on a large scale, it can affect the quantity of the yield, although not the quality.

During the stage known as veraison, the grapes of white varieties gradually become translucent, and red varieties begin to develop their color. The shoots now stop growing and metabolic function is directed entirely toward the grapes. The process of ripening begins and sugar accumulates in the berries as they are given priority access to the products of photosynthesis. At the same time, levels of acidity drop. Although the amount of tartaric acid in the grapes remains relatively constant, it increases as a proportion of the overall ACID content, due to the sharp fall in the level of malic acid.

Physiological ripeness is reached when the grapes achieve sufficiently high sugar levels without losing too much acidity. In cooler regions, it can sometimes be difficult to achieve the minimum sugar content prescribed by the *appellation*. In hotter regions, by contrast, the problem is more likely to be too great a loss of acidity. In both cases, corrections can be made during the winemaking process.

In addition to physiological ripeness, the ripeness of the aromatic and phenolic compounds must be taken into account. Aromatic ripeness is the point at which the grapes are richest in aromas or aroma-forming compounds. To assess phenolic ripeness, the grower must monitor the development of anthocyanins and tannins, the former being responsible for the color, the latter guaranteeing the structure of the wine, and, in the long term, the stability of the color. As the grapes ripen, the concentration of anthocyanins increases until a peak is reached, after which the level drops again. Harvesting should ideally take place when this maximum is achieved, but analyzing the concentrations is expensive and tricky, and thus rarely carried out. If the grape variety is suitable for the *terroir*, aromatic and phenolic maturity will usually be achieved as soon as the grapes are physiologically ripe.

In some European wine-producing regions, the date when harvesting may begin is officially controlled, and special permission must be obtained if an earlier harvest seems advisable. The date is determined by the trade associations on the basis of tests carried out in the vineyards. There is no such regulation in the New World and even in Europe things are starting to become more flexible. In Germany, for instance, the rules have been relaxed in recent years to allow producers greater creative freedom. The object of the harvesting ban is to prevent growers picking the grapes too early—fearing bad weather, for example. They are free to harvest as late as they wish, however. Harvesting is organized on each estate sector by sector, according to which grape varieties ripen first. In some regions, as much as four to six weeks may pass between bringing in early-ripening white varieties and late-ripening red varieties, to say nothing of late-picked grapes for TROCKENBEERENAUSLESEN or EISWEIN.

A leaf bud grows from a node.

The bud opens.

Bunches of grapes will form from these flower buds.

Flowering, or inflorescence.

The grapes grow for 100 days.

Pinot Noir grapes starting to change color.

Pinot Noir grapes during veraison.

Ripe Riesling grapes.

Overripe grapes with noble rot.

Overripeness

If the grapes are not picked once they are ripe, the stage of overripeness begins. One of the most famous types of overripeness on the vine is achieved with the aid of noble rot, producing wines such as Sauternes, Tokaji, *Beerenauslesen*, and *Trockenbeerenauslesen*. The fungus responsible is the same one that causes gray rot (*Botrytis cinerea*), but the conditions are different. Noble rot requires misty, slightly humid mornings, followed by sunny afternoons. The fungus develops under the skins of the grapes, leading to a loss of moisture and an increase in the concentration of sugar. The crop is harvested in several stages, by searching out affected bunches, or even individual grapes. Overripeness can also be achieved away from the vine, by picking and storing bunches once they are ripe. In Jerez or Málaga, for example, the grapes are laid out in the sun for a few days before being pressed. In the Jura and Burgenland regions, grapes destined for VIN DE PAILLE are air-dried on straw or reeds, and not pressed before the end of the year. In certain regions of Italy, grapes are hung on racks for months and then pressed the following year during Holy Week, forming the basis for VIN SANTO.

Harvesting the Grapes

Manual Harvesting

Growers may opt to harvest their crop manually, or be forced to do so on account of the local conditions. If the slopes are steep, the plots small and fragmented, or the vines old and low, there is often no other choice. Elsewhere, harvesting machines can be used, but many winemakers still decide to pick the grapes by hand.

One of the most important reasons for choosing manual harvesting is to deliver the grapes to the winery in perfect condition. It is advisable to transport the grapes in crates, so that if they are damaged, the juice can run away before it oxidizes. If the crop is in good health,

Taking a break during a grape harvest in Brackenheim, Germany.

and arrives in the winery as unscathed as possible, the need to add sulfur can be significantly reduced, or even avoided completely.

Grapes that are crushed under their own weight in a tipper truck and are in the sun for several hours, by contrast, are plainly less interesting from the point of view of quality, even if they were picked by hand.

Manual harvesting allows the grapes to be sorted during and directly after picking, before they have even left the vineyard. In addition, this method gives the winemaker the option of only destemming a proportion of the yield. Mechanical harvesting does not allow such a choice, because the machine removes only the grapes from the vines, and not their stalks.

Economic factors are not such a crucial consideration for the top châteaux and estates, and they may decide to retain hand-picking for the sake of tradition, even though it is a costly procedure. Where small harvesting teams of not more than 10 or 20 people are used, the atmosphere during the harvest is usually very convivial, with the same pickers often returning year after year because they enjoy working together. Many growers are unwilling to sacrifice this aspect of the process, and stress that they consider it one of the high points of the viticultural year.

Reliable grape pickers will also carefully remove unripe or damaged grapes.

Carrying the grapes is a strenuous activity.

Mechanical harvesters can only be used where there is sufficient space between the rows.

The speed of the machine and the quality of the harvested grapes are closely linked.

Grapes are transferred to another vehicle moving in tandem with the harvester.

Mechanical harvesting should not cause damage to the grapes.

Whether undamaged or not, the journey to the winery should not be too long.

A mechanical harvester even takes over the laborious task of destemming the grapes.

MECHANICAL HARVESTING

Harvesting machines are used for economic and technical reasons. In France, for example, mechanical harvesting costs on average two to three times less than hand picking, once wages and employers' social security contributions are taken into account. Of course, the same is not true in countries where wages and contributions are lower. In some New World countries, for instance Australia, the lack of vineyard labor makes mechanical harvesting essential.

One of the advantages of mechanical harvesting is that it can be used as circumstances dictate. Harvesting can be done at night, while it is cool, and work can continue around the clock if the crop must be brought in urgently, perhaps because the grapes are very ripe or the weather is bad. Confirmed users of mechanical harvesting also express satisfaction at no longer having to worry about providing facilities, food, and accommodation for the pickers.

These benefits are of no use, however, if quality suffers as a result. Not all grape varieties are equal in this respect: mechanical harvesting works very well with Chardonnay, for example, but less well with Pinot Noir, if it is intended for wines with aging potential.

The quality of the work done by a mechanical harvester also depends on the shake setting and the speed with which it moves. The quicker it passes along the rows, the harder it has to shake the vines to loosen the grapes. This damages the crop, injures the vines, and breaks the stakes.

If good quality is to be achieved using mechanical harvesting, a few changes also have to be made in the winery. With white grape varieties, which are particularly susceptible to oxidation, the time between picking and pressing must be kept as short as possible. In some cases, this can mean acquiring an additional grape press.

Mechanical harvesters cannot be used where wines are made by pressing whole bunches (such as Champagne, Crémant, Beaujolais, and Sauternes wines in France), because the machines deliver only individual grapes. This is why the rules governing some *appellations* expressly forbid the use of mechanical harvesters and require the grapes to be picked by hand.

Taking Delivery of the Harvest

The first step after harvesting is to sort the grapes. This is carried out on special tables, either in the vineyard or as soon as the grapes arrive in the winery. Leaves and any grapes that are unripe or affected with gray rot are removed. Sorting is particularly important for red wine production to avoid negative consequences during MACERATION and fermentation, but can only be done effectively if the grapes are intact, i.e. have been damaged as little as possible during transportation.

Manual sorting can be dispensed with if the grapes have been harvested mechanically. A correctly set harvesting machine will not pick shrivelled up or unripe grapes, and rotten ones drop off at the slightest touch of the vine. Leaves are largely removed by fans on the machine.

The crop will arrive in the winery either loaded directly onto a trailer, or in vats, baskets, or crates. Where possible, shallow containers that can hold only a small amount should be

Set into the floor of the stainless steel troughs that receive the harvest in many wineries, is an endlessly revolving screw whose rotation propels the grapes forward, to the press in the case of white wine varieties, or to the crusher-destemmer in the case of reds.

used, to prevent the grapes from being crushed under their own weight and releasing juice which will oxidize. The longer the journey between vineyard and winery, and the higher the temperature of the air, the more important this factor becomes.

Ideally, crates should be emptied by hand; this allows the grapes to arrive in the winery almost unscathed. Small vats should be emptied with forks or derricks. Some vehicles have beds that tip; others have a continuous screw (Archimedes screw) in the floor that conveys the crop to the winery via a large hose. A self-emptying container with a slowly revolving screw of large diameter can give satisfactory results if not overfilled.

Next, the grapes are crushed and/or destemmed (separated from the stalks of the bunch). The way these stages are carried out differs, depending on the type of grape and chosen methods of pressing and fermentation.

In large wineries making mass-produced wines, the grapes are delivered in large trailers.

A tipping mechanism empties the crop from the trailer.

High-quality grapes are brought to the winery in small crates and emptied by hand.

The undamaged bunches are tipped into a destemmer.

At the Marqués de Riscal winery in La Rioja Alavesa, the grapes are not harvested until optimal ripeness has been reached.

The crop is transported to the winery in small crates.

At the winery, the crates are loaded onto a conveyor belt one by one.

At the end of the conveyor belt the boxes are emptied automatically and the bunches all fall onto the sorting table.

The workers check the health of the grapes.

Unripe or unhealthy grapes are removed by hand.

From the sorting table, the bunches are fed into a destemmer.

The stalks and bunchstems leave the winery on a conveyor belt.

Outside, they drop into a trailer to be taken away.

Oxidation

OXIDATION is the process whereby oxygen combines with the compounds in must or wine, causing discoloration and unpleasant aromas. White wines are more susceptible than reds, since the greater concentration of PHENOLICS in the reds inhibits oxidation.

Once the grapes are picked, appropriate precautions should be taken to prevent oxidation. These include:
• Avoid crushing the grapes too much and releasing the juice.
• Minimize the time the harvested grapes spend out in the vineyard.
• Always avoid picking the grapes during the hottest part of the day.

• Prevent air getting to the grapes; frozen carbon dioxide (dry ice) is used, which covers the grapes with a protective layer of gas as the ice thaws out.
• The most important antioxidant, used throughout winemaking history, is sulfur dioxide. It can be employed during the entire production process, from harvesting the grapes through to bottling the wine.

Nowadays, producers try to add as little sulfur dioxide as possible, because high concentrations can cause a distinct and unpleasant smell. All wine-producing countries have regulations setting out the maximum permitted levels of sulfur dioxide.

Many winemakers sprinkle SULFUR over the crop to prevent oxidation.

NOBLE AND MASS-PRODUCED WINES

To make a good wine, you need good grapes. This ought to be the principle guiding every winemaker. From a practical point of view, it is much easier to make wine using healthy, ripe grapes than ones that are damaged and not ripe enough. Consequently, wine production really begins in the vineyard. One of the keys to obtaining a quality crop is to ensure that the grape production, namely VINIFICATION, maturation, and bottling. Better hygiene, for example, prevents a vinegary edge developing. It is increasingly rare for wines to turn to vinegar. Another significant improvement has been the use of temperature regulation during wine production, which has made it possible to control the FERMENTATION process.

In order to emphasize the character of small estates and support the *terroir*, the appropriate small fermentation barrels are required.

variety, the rootstock, and the soil are well matched. The winemaker's preferred methods of cultivation—as regards vine density, pruning, canopy management, soil cultivation, and the age of the vines, for example—also influence the end result, as do the changing climatic conditions and the presence or absence of pests and diseases that make each vintage a new challenge.

Advances in ENOLOGY have contributed to a better understanding—and therefore greater mastery—of the three main stages of wine

Nowadays, winemakers also have the knowledge and the means to compensate for any deficiencies in the grapes. With experience, they can produce good wine even in difficult vintages. Nevertheless, all these positive developments can just as easily be a step in the wrong direction if they lead to vinification being seen as an industrial process. Each country takes a different view of such matters, and procedures that are allowed in some countries (such as aromatizing the wine with oak shavings) are prohibited in others.

Agreement also needs to be reached over what constitutes a wine, a good wine, and a great wine. According to the European Union definition, wine is a product "obtained exclusively by alcoholic fermentation, wholly or partially, of raw grapes, whether crushed or not, or of their must." In some parts of the world, however, drinks made from other fruits may also be called "wine."

Beyond this, a distinction can be made between mass-produced wines and noble wines. The former are required only to fulfil the basic criteria and industry norms—in a word, to be

speaking, we drink less, but better wine. Such wines must display all the usual qualities, but also reflect their region of origin, grape variety, and VINTAGE. Given the right climatic conditions, a good wine can sometimes become an excellent one. The goal of every good winemaker is to exploit fully all the advantages of the grapes while at the same time allowing their natural character to come through. One of the greatest dangers of modern enology is the standardization of wines as a result of overly systematic interventions and adjustments. In some cases, the methods of vinification and the

"drinkable." Consumers expect a standardized quality, and this is delivered using high-yielding vines planted in fertile soil. These everyday wines are primarily intended for sale in their country of origin, and are increasingly being rejected in favor of finer wines. As late as the 1960s, and especially in France, this type of wine was watered down and used as a thirst quencher and daily accompaniment to meals.

Today, however, consumer interest is moving toward wines of higher quality. Generally

techniques of the enologist or winemaker can be more evident in a wine than the TERROIR. Each winemaker has his or her own way of doing things, and the acceptability of the resulting wines will depend entirely on enlightened consumers choosing to buy them.

Large wineries make use of the latest technology to produce large volumes of wine, maintaining as far as possible the same quality from year to year.

Preparing the Grapes: Specific Gravity and Potential Alcohol Content

A drop of grape juice is placed on the glass of the refractometer.

The sugar content is then measured.

Oechsle hydrometer for determining must weight.

The amount of sugar in a must is determined by measuring its SPECIFIC GRAVITY (relative density). In the case of white musts, this is usually done before pressing. With red musts, a little liquid is drawn from the maceration or fermentation tank. The measurement is taken using must weight scales or a refractometer. Water, which has a density of 62.4 pounds per cubic foot at 39.2°F (1 kg per liter at 4°C), is used as a benchmark. The greater the amount of sugar in the must, the higher its specific gravity will be. The relationship between specific gravity, sugar concentration, and potential alcohol level is shown in tables. Producers work on the basis that a white must needs 0.28 ounces of sugar per pint (17 grams per liter) to achieve an alcoholic strength of 1% vol, while red musts require 0.3 ounces per pint (18 grams per liter), because they contain a greater proportion of solids. In the case of red musts, the initial

Throughout the winemaking process musts and new wines are repeatedly analyzed in the laboratory to ascertain the relative proportions of their main constituents and, in particular, to check that fermentation is proceeding properly or is fully complete.

measurement is more problematic, because it is only carried out on the must that runs off when gentle pressure is applied. Moreover, the concentration of sugar is not the same in all parts of the grape. It is important that the measurement is taken before fermentation begins, because otherwise a proportion of the sugar will already have been converted into alcohol. In addition, the results must be adjusted to take into account the temperature of the must.

Different countries use different systems of measurement and conversion, including GRAD, BRIX, BAUMÉ, and OECHSLE. These will be noted in the chapters dealing with the individual countries.

The established values of 0.28 or 0.3 ounces of sugar to a pint (17 or 18 grams to a liter) to achieve an alcoholic strength of 1% vol do not always apply. Some of the cultured yeasts available today can produce the same concentration of alcohol with only 0.27 ounces per pint (16.5 grams per liter) of sugar. This seemingly inconsequential factor is, in fact, very significant, particularly if producers want or need to enrich the must. Depending on the productivity of these yeasts, a varying amount of sugar must be added to increase the alcoholic strength.

The decision to enrich the must is made on the basis of specific gravity measurements, and again, different wine-producing regions take different views. The grapes must have a minimum sugar content when they are picked, which in regions with *appellations* is laid down in regulations. This prevents harvesting beginning too early.

If the grapes are low in natural fructose, the situation can be improved to a greater or lesser degree. Special regulations have been introduced in some wine-producing regions. In each case, the legislation dictates the required minimum natural sugar content and the extent to which it may be increased. There are three methods of enriching the must:

- Adding sugar (CHAPTALIZATION)
- Adding grape concentrate
- Concentrating the must

In Europe, these methods are mutually exclusive. This is a regulatory restriction. There are no technical or qualitative reasons to prohibit their simultaneous use.

Grape concentrates have a higher sugar content than normal must and grape sugar may be added instead of sugar beet syrup or cane sugar. However, this affects the volume of the enriched harvest. European regulations do not allow the original volume to be increased by more than 11 percent, 8 percent, or 6.5 percent, depending on the region. With a traditional grape concentrate, all the components of the must are concentrated. Rectified concentrated grape must (R.C.G.M.) can also be used, which contains only sugar, the other components having been removed, principally by demineralization. Grape concentrate is denser than fermenting must, and it is important to homogenize the two during the ENRICHMENT process.

The newest enrichment technique is concentration, which involves removing a proportion of the water in the must. There are a number of ways of achieving this, including boiling it away, freezing the must and removing the lumps of ice as they form, and REVERSE OSMOSIS. The latter is a filtering process: the must circulates along the FILTRATION membrane, but does not penetrate it; a pressure differential allows only the water to get through.

The term "enrichment" encompasses a range of very different practices, and does not harm

The balance of the wine

Before the winemaking process begins, it is important to bear in mind that it is not alcoholic strength that gives a wine a harmonious taste, but the balance of its various components. Consequently, the sugar content of a must, and hence the potential alcohol level of the resulting wine, must be coordinated with other factors.

With white wine, the balance of alcoholic strength and acidity is crucial.

Given the same level of acidity, one wine can seem lively, even with a low alcohol content, whereas another with a high alcoholic strength tastes rather flat. As a result, the level of acidity in a must will have a bearing on enrichment. With reds, the astringency imparted by the tannins is also a significant factor in the balance of the wine.

Many of the larger estates now themselves monitor levels of substances that change during the fermentation process, such as alcohol, acid, tannins and residual sugar.

the quality of the wine, provided that certain rules are followed. It is a way of correcting a small deficiency in natural sugar, but will destroy the balance of the wine if overdone. Producers should always try to respect their raw material. Even the addition of grape concentrate can alter the original balance, which is why chaptalization is preferred in areas that have classed *appellations*.

Methods of concentrating the must alter the natural balance of the various components in the wine. As the volume of the liquid reduces, the proportion of solids increases, concentrating not only sugar, but also acids and immature TANNINS. Although these hi-tech methods are now widely used even in quality wine regions, they are in fact contributing to the continued standardization of wines, which cannot be in the interests of either the conscientious winemaker or the dedicated wine lover.

Jean-Antoine Chaptal and chaptalization

Jean-Antoine Chaptal (1756–1832), Count of Chanteloup, was a trained chemist, and Minister of the Interior under Napoleon. Having published an influential article on wine in 1799, he wrote his famous work *L'Art de faire le vin* (The art of winemaking) in 1807. Although the process of chaptalization bears his name, he did not invent it. He was responsible for popularizing the method, however, which had been developed at the beginning of the 19th century, and involved adding cane sugar to compensate for any lack of ripeness in the grapes. Wine was enriched with honey in ancient times, and cane sugar was also used in the 18th century. Beet sugar did not appear on the scene until the second half of the 19th century.

Jean-Antoine Chaptal, the "inventor" of the enrichment process.

Chaptalization is carried out by stirring cane or beet sugar into the must. The sugar is not tipped directly into the tank, because it would fall to the bottom without dissolving. Instead, the sugar is added to a quantity of must in a tub

and stirred until it is completely dissolved. This mixture is then put back into the original tank.

Previously, chaptalization was usually carried out in a single procedure at the beginning of fermentation. Today, however, producers are altering their methods and spreading out the addition of sugar, especially in the case of red wine production. This enables the fermentation process (and thus the maceration time) to be extended without the risk of the wine developing a vinegary edge. The method is proving particularly interesting with grape varieties whose color is difficult to extract. The solids in the must of red grapes sometimes make it difficult to take any accurate measurements of must weight. In such cases, repeated chaptalization (usually twice) allows the producer to correct any errors in the original assessment and to control the enrichment process more accurately.

Pressing

Pressing takes place at different points in the winemaking process, depending on whether white or red wine is being produced. White wine grapes are generally pressed directly after being picked. The juice is sugary and sticky, which impedes run off and prolongs the pressing process. Fermentation takes place straight afterwards. During the production of red wine, the grapes or whole bunches are macerated and fermented before being pressed.

There are a number of pressing techniques. The choice of which one to use will depend on economics, the amount to be pressed, the type of wine to be produced, the available personnel, and possibly also the regulations in force in a particular region.

A Tried and Tested System

Wooden presses were used in ancient times, a fact proven by archeological finds and numerous accounts. The oldest surviving presses in France, Germany, Italy, and Spain are extremely impressive. Before the 19th century, only the nobility and the monasteries had their own presses. These were often imposing lever presses such as the one at Clos de Vougeot in the Côte d'Or. The growers paid a fee to have their grapes pressed. After the French Revolution, smaller presses gradually caught on in the wineries.

The old presses had a horizontal trough into which the grape material or POMACE was spread. In the case of lever or beam presses, one end of a heavy lever (formed by a long beam) squashed the grapes under a thick, heavy board. The other end of the lever was attached to a screw or spindle that raised or lowered the lever, depending on which way it was turned. Other wine presses had a central screw that pressed down on the boards forming the lid of the press. These devices did not retain the pomace at the edges, however, and so the lid had to be removed several times during the pressing operation, and the partially pressed grapes piled up again, until all the juice was extracted.

Improvements were made to this type of press over time. The grape material was held in place with baskets or grilles, the wooden screw was replaced with an iron one, and the screw-tightening system adapted to increase its efficiency and reduce the effort needed to operate it.

These hand-operated vertical presses were still in use in the 1960s, and can be seen in vine-growing villages and wineries today, where they often serve as decoration. The vertical principle continues to be employed in Champagne and other traditional regions although now, of course, the process is mechanically assisted.

Adopting the Horizontal

Most producers now use horizontal presses, in which a press head forces the juice or wine through the perforated wall of a revolving cylinder. Changing the direction of rotation

Left
Gentle, hydraulic basket presses such as this one are still used in the Champagne region.

Right
Historical table press: the grapes were spread on the table and weighted with the wooden lid, then the heavy central beam would be forced lower and lower using the two screws. This example is from La Rioja.

Pressing cycles

How pressing is carried out depends on the desired end product. It generally takes place after destemming and crushing in the case of white wines, and after fermentation with reds. The process itself involves alternately pressing the grapes or must and then breaking up the press cake. Modern pneumatic presses allow the degree of pressure, its duration, and its rate of increase to be precisely controlled and monitored.

When white grapes are being pressed, these factors vary according to the variety, ripeness, and health of the grapes. In some years, the juice is easily extracted, and pressing can proceed relatively swiftly; in others, the process takes more time, and requires greater force.

If the pressure is increased too rapidly, the juice or wine may not be able to run off

Even with a modern press, the grapes are gently spread out with the feet, just as they always have been.

quickly enough, and pockets of liquid will form. If, on the other hand, the cake is broken up too much, the resulting must can be cloudy and astringent. It is advisable to open the press in between operations to check how dry the cake is, and thus decide whether or not to continue pressing. In the case of red wine production, the winemaker can taste the already fermented wine during pressing, to determine when to stop the process. This interruption always benefits the success of the operation.

The liquid that runs off before pressing begins is called "free-run" juice or wine. It has fewer tannins, and is usually of better quality. Generally, the majority of the liquid is then released by applying a gentle pressure, before the remaining must is pressed to obtain the press juice or press wine.

The basket, placed on a movable frame, is filled with grapes and pushed under the hydraulic basket press, which squeezes out the juice.

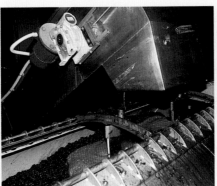

The pomace is transported from the fermentation tank to the press by conveyor belt, which means that there is no need for pumps.

The size of the press corresponds to the volume of pomace that the fermentation tank will hold. Today, pressing is mainly carried out in (usually pneumatically operated) horizontal presses.

automatically loosens the cake of debris that forms. Provided that they are operated with the necessary sensitivity—meaning that only gentle pressure should be applied and the cake not broken up too often—presses of this type achieve very satisfactory results.

GENTLY DOES IT

Pneumatic presses constitute the latest stage in the development of the horizontal press. An airbag inside the cylinder is inflated, squeezing the must against the walls. The cake is broken up by slowly rotating the cylinder once the bag has deflated again. This is a much gentler system, and produces excellent results.

A further advantage of this method is that small amounts can be pressed, whereas mechanical presses must be filled to a minimum level. This factor is very important in areas such as the Côte d'Or in Burgundy, where the large number of *appellations* means that producers are generally dealing with very small quantities.

There are also automated systems, called continuous presses, in which a continuous screw or conveyor belt transports the grapes through a cylinder, where they are subjected to increasing pressure. Belt presses squeeze the grapes between two perforated belts mounted one above the other, and are a little gentler than screw presses, which work like a large mincer. In both systems, the juice or wine runs off through the perforated walls. The free-run juice is collected at one end of the cylinder, and the press juice further to the rear.

Once pressing is complete, the remaining pomace is usually filtered. These continuous systems can produce only medium quality wine at best.

ALCOHOLIC FERMENTATION

During the fermentation process, sugar is turned into alcohol by the action of YEAST, releasing carbon dioxide and heat. Depending on the type of wine being produced, all the sugar may be fermented into alcohol to produce a dry wine, or only a portion, creating medium dry or sweet wines.

WHITE WINES

White musts obtained from pressing must be clarified before fermentation begins. The juice can be cleaned by removing suspended solids such as particles of soil and pieces of stem, grape skin, or other undesirable organic matter. The clarifying process is essential to the aromatic quality of the wine, but it must be used in moderation so as not to remove any of the vital material and thus prevent the must fermenting properly. If CLARIFICATION is excessive, fermentation slows down, and may even cease altogether. The cloudiness of a must depends on the ripeness and health of the grapes. Overripe grapes heavily affected by rot will produce the cloudiest musts. All the mechanical processes to which the grapes are subjected, from harvesting through to pressing, contribute to the formation of solids, which is why such procedures should be keptto a minimum and be carried out as gently as possible.

Clarification can be static or dynamic. In the former case, the must is left to stand in a tank for between 12 and 24 hours, to let the solids settle. The clear portion of the must, which may still contain some fine solids, is then separated from the coarse SEDIMENT. It is essential to

Cultured yeasts control fermentation. Various strains are used, depending on the type of wine.

The dried yeast powder is first mixed with a little must in a bucket.

The yeast organisms swell up and immediately begin the process of converting sugar into alcohol.

The pros and cons of cultured yeasts

Wherever grapes are grown, various types of yeast are also present. As soon as the skins of the grapes are damaged, these yeasts come into contact with the sweet juice. Some winemakers and enologists take the view that ambient yeasts are essential for a true expression of *terroir*. However, these natural yeasts are not always present in the environment in sufficient quantities to bring about adequate fermentation. The use of chemicals in the vineyard, for example, can cause a drop in the yeast population.

Increasing numbers of winemakers prefer not to take any risks, and add commercially-produced yeasts, whose properties are known in detail. This can be done before fermentation begins, or used only as an initial boost where fermentation is slow or has been interrupted.

Cultured yeasts come in the form of an industrially produced powder or granules, and are specifically chosen to fulfil a number of criteria. From a technical point of view, they must produce a significantly faster fermentation and a good output in terms of converting sugar into alcohol. If dry wines are being made, the yeasts must have a high tolerance to alcohol, so that they can survive until fermentation is complete. Otherwise, there is a risk that fermentation would cease at between 11.5 and 12% vol, even though there was still sugar remaining in the must.

The yeasts are also selected with regard to their taste and smell. Generally speaking, neutral yeasts are preferable, because they do not affect the aromas of the wine. With certain grape varieties, however, strains that contribute to the development of a variety-specific aroma are chosen.

There is a danger that use of the same cultured yeasts the world over will lead to a standardization of wines. For this reason, an increasing number of wine-producing regions are selecting their own distinct strains. Nevertheless, many scientists hold the opinion that the raw material, i.e. the grapes, have considerably more influence on the eventual taste and aroma of a wine than the yeasts.

Temperature control

Yeasts are very sensitive to the temperature of their environment. When it is too low, they cannot multiply sufficiently, and fermentation is slow to begin. If the grapes have been harvested during very cold weather, therefore, it may be necessary to warm the must. This is particularly important in the case of red grapes, because temperature also affects the extraction of color.

If the temperature gets too high, on the other hand, the activity of the yeast slows down, and may even cease altogether. This will have a negative effect on the aromas of the wine. Heat is released during alcoholic fermentation, and thus it is vital to check the temperature regularly, so that action can quickly be taken should there be any large

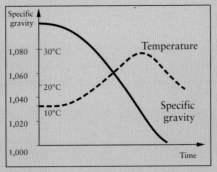

A fermentation graph.
During fermentation, the specific gravity of the must continually decreases. The temperature rises until it reaches a certain level, then drops again.

increase. It is much more difficult to reduce the temperature once it has become too high, than to maintain it at a stable level.

There are a number of ways of adjusting the temperature. Some of these are adaptations to existing tanks—installing cooling elements, for example—and do not involve pumping out the must. Some tanks can simply be cooled by spraying them with cold water; there are also fermentation tanks with a double wall through which coolant can circulate. Alternatively, the must can be pumped out of the fermentation tank and circulated through separate cooling units, before being fed back into the tank again.

---

ensure that fermentation does not begin during this period, because the bubbling would prevent the solids settling out. For this reason, the must is either kept at a low temperature or sulfur is added. The antioxidant sulfur dioxide has a further role to play, to the extent that it inhibits the growth of bacteria and wild yeasts.

Clarification can also be carried out dynamically—with the aid of a centrifuge, for example. Following clarification, the must can be fermented in a tank or in barrels.

RED WINES

The color of red wine is produced during maceration. During this process, phenolics, which include naturally occurring color compounds and tannins, and are found primarily in the skins of the grapes, are gradually extracted and begin to color the wine. The alcoholic fermentation of red grapes takes place both in the liquid, or must, and also in the solid components—the skins, seeds, and stalks. To ensure satisfactory extraction of pigments and tannins, it is important to maximize contact between the solids and the liquid, otherwise the carbon dioxide that is released carries the solids to the surface, where they form a "cap." To bring the solids back into contact with the must, the fermenting liquid can be pumped from the bottom of the tank and released over the cap, a procedure called "pumping over" or REMONTAGE. Alternatively, the cap can be manually or mechanically submerged using mixing paddles or poles, which is known as PIGEAGE, or "punching down the cap." Extra pigments and tannins can be drawn out by extending the skin contact time. If the maceration time is too long, however, and continues after the alcoholic fermentation is complete, it

Temperature control is fundamental to the modern fermentation process. The most reliable method of regulation is to supply each tank with its own, individually controlled cooling system. This stainless steel tank is cooled by means of icy water pumped through the encircling band.

can have decidedly negative consequences, because the wine is no longer protected from the oxygen in the air through the release of carbon dioxide.

Once fermentation is complete, the free-run wine is drawn off. The remaining solid matter, or whatever will not run off unaided, is pressed, and the resulting press wine can either be blended in immediately or finished off separately, depending on the desired type of wine. Press wine is considerably richer in tannins than free-run wine, and in general it is of lower quality.

Whether dealing with white or red must, and whether fermentation is carried out in tanks or wooden barrels, it is important not to fill the vessels to the brim. Alcoholic fermentation produces carbon dioxide, and the turbulent bubbling can cause the must to overflow if the containers are too full.

Traditional Red Wine Production in Burgundy

The great red wines of Burgundy are made exclusively from Pinot Noir, which is a challenging grape variety, particularly as regards extracting the color. From the harvest onwards, therefore, producers try to avoid oxidation. The grapes are picked by hand, and usually transported in crates. Unwanted matter is then removed on the sorting table, or *table de tri*. The next step is the total or partial destemming of the grapes, depending on the grade of the *appellation*, the condition of the stalks, and the style of the winemaker.

In years when ripening the grapes has been difficult and the stalks are still green, they can all be removed. Some producers would rather destem the entire crop and have longer maceration times. Others prefer to leave the stalks on a proportion of the grapes, particularly when producing wines for aging. There are advantages and disadvantages to both methods.

One of the golden rules is to minimize the use of pumps to move the grapes around, because they crush the stalks and seeds, which can give the wine a herbaceous edge and harsh, ASTRINGENT tannins. Conveyor belts have proved to be a good way of transporting the grapes to the destemming machine or filling the fermentation tank. Sulfur is usually added at this point. An initial "pumping over" takes place, for the purposes of homogenization, and the levels of sugar and acid are measured for the first time.

The alcoholic fermentation then gets under way, with *pigeage* and *remontage* operations

Opposite
Pinot grapes are crushed underfoot—the traditional method and the gentlest. Once fermentation has begun during this gentlest of all pressing methods, the cap of skins is broken up and submerged in the must—a process known as *pigeage*.

carried out every day. Once fermentation is complete, a few more days' maceration may be allowed. Carbon dioxide is no longer being produced, and so the cap gradually sinks. Caution is required if open tanks are being used, because there is a danger of a vinegary edge developing once fermentation is complete.

Emptying the tank starts with the wine being run off. The pomace is then pressed, and the free-run wine blended with some or all of the press wine. Next, the wine is clarified and transferred to barrels, where, sooner or later (depending on the vintage), MALOLACTIC FERMENTATION begins. With a particularly acidic vintage, for example, this may not begin until spring.

Once the malolactic fermentation is finished, the first RACKING is carried out. The clear wine is separated from the sediment that has settled at the bottom of the barrel. The wine is exposed to the air during this process, to allow some of the carbonic acid with which it is saturated to be given off as carbon dioxide gas.

The wine is then transferred to another barrel for a period of maturation. Further racking may become necessary during this time, using either an oxidative or protective method, depending on the results of a tasting.

Malolactic fermentation

This second fermentation converts malic acid to lactic acid with the aid of lactic bacteria, which may be naturally present in the winery or artificially added. As with alcoholic fermentation, the reaction is accompanied by the release of carbon dioxide, but in much smaller quantities. Malolactic fermentation alters the taste of the wine, and so is deliberately encouraged or specifically avoided. It reduces the wine's ACID content, improves its aromas, and sometimes leads to a slight increase in volatile acids. The wine is made more stable, because there is no longer a danger that this second fermentation will take place in the bottle.

The lactic bacteria can also cause a decrease in other components of the wine besides malic acid. If they affect the sugars, for example, the taste may develop a lactic acid edge.

Naturally present or artificially added lactic bacteria alter the taste of wine.

Consequently, it is vital that all the sugar is broken down during the alcoholic fermentation. Sulfur dioxide added after pressing or to the tanks or barrels can render the bacteria inactive, without overly impairing the yeasts.

Most red wines undergo malolactic fermentation. Its use with whites and rosés depends on the region and the style of the wine. In regions with a Mediterranean-type climate, where the wines are often lacking in acidity, this second fermentation is avoided. In cooler regions, the wines tend to contain more acid, and so malolactic fermentation is often employed, provided that dry wines are being produced. If a wine contains RESIDUAL SUGAR, chemical de-acidification is used in preference to malolactic fermentation. In countries where there is no great tradition of producing sweet wines, this tends to be the practice with dry whites as well.

Barrels and Bottles:
The Ideal Winery

"Assuming unlimited funds, describe your ideal winery." This could be a question from a viticultural exam or the title of an enologist's dissertation. Talk to any wine producer about the subject, and without exception, each one would give an answer reflecting the same priorities: the gravity principle, precise temperature control, equipment and rooms that are functional and easy to clean, and enough space for all the necessary tasks to be performed. Pleasing aesthetics

Barriques (small 60-gallon (227-l) oak barrels) have become a generally indispensable medium in which to mature high quality red wines.

should not be ignored, but rank below these on the wish list.

The ideal winery would be built against a hill, to allow ground level entrances, ideally on three floors. The cellar would be located on the lowest level of this winery—preferably underground, to make use of the cool, stable soil temperature. The floor above it, at normal ground level, would house the fermentation tanks and other areas for bottling and labeling. The top floor, opening onto the hill at the back and thus also at ground level, would receive the harvest.

In reality, of course, it is seldom possible even to get close to this ideal arrangement. Sometimes the sloping site may be all that is missing, or the site may lack the geographical and geological conditions to make it possible.

White grapes would be emptied onto a conveyor belt and gently transported to the press. The must would then flow into a tank on the floor below.

Red grapes would be tipped onto a slightly elevated *table de tri*, sorted, and then fed directly into a combined crushing and destemming machine at the end of the table. A movable sorting table and crusher-destemmer would enable workers to position the run-off point above the tank that is to be filled.

This very gentle process would transfer the white must and the red grapes to the floor below without the need for pumps. This is particularly important, because pumps crush the stalks of bunches that have not been destemmed, which can give the wine a herbaceous edge.

A fully-automated winery?

The ideal winery would not be fully automated, because winemakers like to retain control over the proceedings.

The only point on which they are almost all agreed is temperature control. The tanks are fitted with temperature probes and a double wall through which warm or cold water can circulate. The temperature in the individual tanks is displayed on an electronic control desk. Separate readings are given for each tank, because the must will not be at the same stage of fermentation in every one. The operator selects a suitable minimum and maximum temperature for each tank: the minimum temperature might be set at 68°F (20°C), for example, and the maximum at 95°F (35°C). As soon as one of these thresholds is reached,

In modern wineries, an electronic system controls and monitors the fermentation process in each individual tank.

the computer can control the release of cold or warm water into the space between the walls.

With some tanks, it is possible to automate the task of "pumping over" (*remontage*), so that, for example, it can be set to take place every eight hours for half an hour. The frequency and duration are usually decided by the winemaker after he or she has checked the tank, then the operation is set to take place automatically. Pre-set machines can also be used for *pigeage*, or punching down the cap. They are mounted on rails above the tanks. Here too, however, the winemaker will want to decide on the timing and duration. In reality, therefore, such systems can be considered a form of technical support rather than actual automation.

Once the white must had been clarified, it would run into tanks on the next floor down. Red wines would be fed into barrels, while the pomace would be removed from the tank and delivered to the press by conveyor belt. Racking would be carried out by using a pressure differential to "push" the wine from one vessel to another—a gentler method than pumping.

Hygiene in all areas of the winery is a fundamental consideration. Today's easily cleaned, stainless steel equipment and machinery are therefore a necessity.

The health and safety of the staff who work in the winery must also be taken into account. Catwalks must be installed to provide safe access to the upper parts of the tanks, floors must be easy to clean without becoming slippery, and there should be sufficient space between the tanks to facilitate cleaning.

In recent years, increasing attention has been paid to the problem of waste water removal. For each pint (50 cl) of wine produced, between one and two pints (50–100 cl) of water is needed for cleaning the equipment (harvesting crates, hoses, tanks, barrels) and premises. Depending on the procedures used, this waste water contains chemicals, in greater or smaller concentrations, that could damage the life in streams and rivers. An increasing number of wineries are trying to purify this effluent, so that only clean water drains into the environment. Unfortunately, systems to do this have so far been designed for large-scale wineries only.

The ideal winery, therefore, should be in a position to handle both the grapes and the wine as gently as possible, maintaining the highest levels of hygiene and safety, while also operating in a way that is friendly to the environment.

Left
Modern fermentation tank with integrated pumping system.

Right
Everything must be right at hand during vinification.

Below
The use of stainless steel makes it significantly easier to maintain an optimum standard of hygiene in the winery.

FRENCH OAK FORESTS

Since the 1990s, the demand for BARRIQUES—small oak barrels traditionally used in Bordeaux, usually with a 59-gallon (225-liter) capacity—has risen in leaps and bounds. In all the world's wine-producing countries, an ever-growing number of winemakers are choosing them as the vessels in which to vinify special white wines or mature their best reds. Oak from a number of countries is used to make *barriques*, but French oak is generally considered to be the finest raw material.

An oak tree takes 150 to 230 years to reach maturity and the stage when it can be used for timber. Consequently, sustainable, high-quality production can only be achieved by managing forests for the long term. Controls on logging were imposed in France as early as the middle of the 17th century, in order to end the unregulated exploitation of the forests and guarantee a high-quality supply for future generations. As a result, France's oak forests are probably the finest in Europe today. The pedunculate oak (*Quercus robur*) and the sessile oak (*Quercus petraea*) account for more than one-third of France's 34 million acres (14 million hectares) of woodland, and only a small proportion of this is allowed to be used for COOPERAGE.

For a French oak, the route from the forest to the winery is a long one. The owner of the forest generally sells his trees to a forester before they have been cut down, and the forester then sees to the felling and commercial exploitation of the entire tree. The bark-covered stemwood used in the production of barrels is usually entrusted to a specialist timber merchant, the *merrandier*, who cuts it into *merrains*, the long lengths of wood from which the staves of the barrel are fashioned.

The finest oak forests in France have been managed by the State since the time of Louis XIV. The trees used for the highly prized small wooden barrels are over 200 years old.

The timber supplied to the cooper is generally this stave wood, but sometimes the middleman is cut out and the cooper begins his task by preparing the bark-covered stemwood himself.

The production of stave wood requires a trunk that is free of defects, more than 16 inches (40 cm) in diameter, and can be divided into lengths of 43 inches (1.10 m)—the length of a stave. A forester's idea of a splendid oak, therefore, may not be the same as that of someone out for a stroll among the trees.

Of the 11 million acres (4.5 million hectares) of oak woods in France, 4.5 million acres (1.85 million hectares) are in public ownership (as national forests or communal woodland) and are administered by the National Forestry Office (*Office National des Forêts*). The rest is privately owned. Most of the finest forests are managed by the state, as it is not easy for private individuals to bear the costs involved in exploiting them, because their capital is tied up for a very long period of time.

The quality of the timber depends principally on the forestry practices employed. A stand of trees managed as a high forest can usually regenerate itself naturally with the seedlings produced when the acorns drop. Sometimes, however, plantings are needed to supplement this process. With a coppice system, regeneration is provided by the shoots growing from the stumps of the trees. In a coppice-with-standards, both forms of regeneration occur side by side. Today, most managed woodland is operated as high forest.

The trees in the overstory of a high forest stand are almost all the same age. Improvement

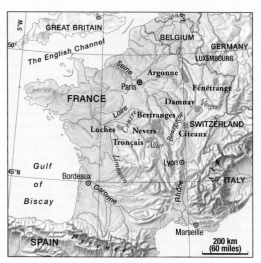

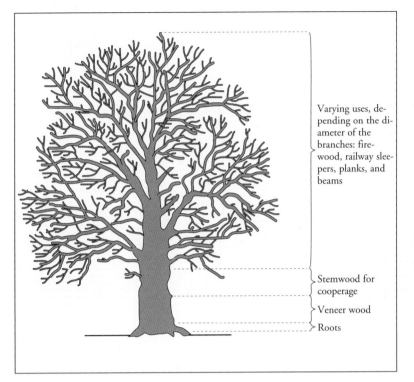

Varying uses, depending on the diameter of the branches: firewood, railway sleepers, planks, and beams

Stemwood for cooperage

Veneer wood

Roots

complete unit. The coopers or their buyers inspect the area to be felled with all due care, and discuss things with the foresters. They assess each part of the trees and indicate whether they are interested in buying. Some coopers also make the actual purchase themselves. The lots are sold in September and October at auctions with decreasing bids: a series of prices is announced, starting at a level suggested by the Forestry Office, and the first person to interrupt the bidding is awarded the lot.

If the purpose of the auction is to sell standing trees, the forester will fell them during the winter. Should a tree damage another as it falls, the forester has to pay the owner compensation. The wood is taken away as soon as it is dry enough, to avoid damaging seedlings, paths, and ditches. In the forests of eastern France, the trees are usually sold "at the wayside," meaning that they have already been felled.

The level of attendance at an auction will depend on the reputation that wood from a particular forest enjoys among winemakers. The sale in Tronçais, near Nevers in central France, is one of the more important dates on the calendar, as many coopers must have wood from this forest in stock if they wish to satisfy their customers. To secure their supply, they will often act directly as buyers.

work is carried out as they grow, which involves selecting the best trees to become the overstory and felling the remainder. When a forest plantation reaches full maturity after about 200 years, only around 40 of the original 20,000 trees per acre (100 out of the original 50,000 per hectare) will still be standing. There are a number of factors to be taken into consideration. If, for example, thinning out allows too much light to penetrate the canopy, it may stimulate the growth of the lower branches and decrease the value of the timber. Once maturity is reached, the stand is felled progressively over a period of around 15 years. The canopy is thus opened up evenly, improving the growth prospects of the seedlings and next generation of trees.

The best wood is obtained from mature high forest trees. Younger oaks in a high forest often have defects, and tend to produce shorter logs. This kind of understory tree accounts for 90 percent of French oaks. Fully mature high forest timber is still relatively rare, and commands correspondingly high prices on the market.

The oaks in the understory of high forest stands are usually complemented by hornbeam and beech trees. This understory is completely cleared during the inspections carried out every 25 years or so, and a selection process among the overstory trees removes those that are mature, dying, or in the way. Thinning out yields a large amount of hard-to-sell firewood.

Each year, the Forestry Office publishes a detailed list of the sections that have been released for sale in each forest, and marks the relevant trees. The lots are always sold as a

Fully mature oaks from high forests provide the best wood for cooperage. The timber is cut to the required dimensions *in situ*.

Stave Wood

Historically, a number of types of wood were used for wine barrels, including acacia, beech, poplar, chestnut, and cherry wood. Over the course of time, however, winemakers have discovered that only barrels made of oak or chestnut impart suitable aromas to the wines stored in them. Oak is the preferred choice, for two reasons: the aromas it contributes are far more interesting, and its properties best fulfil the cooper's technical requirements. Chestnut, however, is susceptible to woodworm, and is rarely used nowadays.

There are over 250 species belonging to the genus *Quercus*, but only three are important for cooperage. These are the sessile oak (*Quercus petraea*, synonym *Quercus sessiliflora*), the pedunculate oak (*Quercus robur*, synonym *Quercus pedunculata*), and the American white oak (*Quercus alba*). In French oak forests, sessile and pedunculate oaks usually stand side by side. The two species are easily distinguished by their acorns: the acorns of a pedunculate oak develop on long stems (peduncles), whereas on a sessile oak, they are attached directly to the twig. In the forests of Limousin, pedunculate oaks predominate. The fact that competition from the understory is not very intense and the soil is fertile means that the wood is wide-grained, i.e. the distance between the annual growth rings is relatively great, because the spring growth, which lays down larger pores in the wood than the summer growth, is much more vigorous. In central France and the Allier region, where sessile oaks are the dominant species, poor soil fertility and competition among the trees impede annual growth, and so the wood is tight-grained and has smaller pores.

Research into the composition of the wood has shown that sessile oaks are richer in aromatic substances such as vanillin and methyl octalactone, whereas pedunculate oaks primarily contain phenolic compounds such as ellagitannins or catechol tannins.

Depending on the type of wine being vinified (white or red, with medium- or long-term aging potential, etc.), oak from a particular species or origin is preferred. There are no rules, however, and it is up to each winemaker to combine his or her own experience with the advice of the cooper. For this reason, winemakers tend to use barrels from various cooperages, and also from different origins. The degree of *chauffe* (TOASTING) to which the barrels are subjected

Many traditional wineries and châteaux once had their own cooperage workshops —nowadays frequently set up as museum exhibits— but few today still produce barrels themselves.

The lengths of timber are stored outside for a time before being worked, in order to let the wind and weather remove any unpleasant flavor compounds and tannins.

also has an influence on the aromas imparted to a wine as it matures. Wood from Limousin is largely used for brandy.

Both pedunculate and sessile oaks can be found in varying concentrations throughout Europe. A number of coopers have looked to the countries of eastern Europe to try to ensure a continued supply, but many of the forests they found there had suffered years of poor management. The Séguin-Moreau cooperage in the Charente has joined forces with Russian partners to build up an enterprise there; although the results are interesting in terms of flavor, Russian oak barrels are no better than French ones. Oak from Croatia has a good reputation, but there, too, stocks of high-quality stave wood are small.

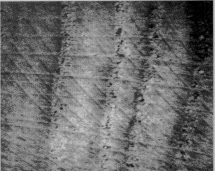

American white oak has the densest structure, and is easily made into barrels.

The wide-grained pedunculate oak is found in all French forests. Its wood is particularly rich in tannins.

The tight-grained wood of the sessile oak is also used for cooperage, and gives the wine a note of vanilla.

Calculating the cost

To produce 35 cubic feet (1 m³) of stave wood, 176½ cubic feet (5 m³) of bark-covered stem-wood is needed. The processing is done by the coopers themselves or left to specialist *merrandiers*. To ensure that the finished barrels are watertight, European oak wood must be split following the grain; therefore there is an extremely high degree of wastage. American oaks, by contrast, are denser and less porous, and can therefore be sawn without regard to the direction of the grain. This means that optimal usage is made of the wood, there is correspondingly little waste, and consequently, prices are lower.

The economic return from barrel-making using American oak is around 50 percent, while with European oak the figure is only 20 to 25 percent. As a result, 35 cubic feet (1 m³) of staves from French oaks—enough to make about ten barrels—cost the equivalent of approximately US $2,755 at the time of writing, whereas the same amount of American oak can be bought for less than US $1,380 on average. To the price of materials must be added storage, manufacturing, and transport costs.

American oak has been highly regarded for some time, not just on the American continent, but above all in Spain and Portugal, and more recently in South Africa and Australia as well. French winemakers and enologists have been more critical, complaining that its impact on the wine is too strong. Thanks to detailed research, American oak can now be employed in a more targeted fashion; its attractive price makes the decision even easier. Analyses have shown that American oak contains fewer tannins than French oak, but more aromatic compounds, particularly methyl octalactone. Barrels made from American oak need a long and heavy toasting during the production process, and are used for short periods of maturation (six to nine months at most), since their influence on the wine would otherwise become too dominant.

The choice of barrel remains an important decision for the winemaker, since it will have a considerable influence on the final quality of the wine. He or she must ensure that the aromas imparted by a particular barrel can be successfully integrated into the character of the wine.

Left
Fortunately, the stem wood no longer has to be split with an axe, since we now have electric cleavers to do the job.

Right
The barrel staves split from the stem wood are stacked up for a further period of outdoor storage. The best quality staves will be left to season for three years.

Barrel Making

The tools of the cooper's trade: hammer, adze, draw knife, plane, lever, and compasses.

The split wood is passed through a bandsaw so that the staves are equal in both length and width from the outset.

The cooper uses a metal ring to hold the tapered staves as he begins to assemble the barrel.

When the circle is complete, the cooper secures it by hammering a second and then a third hoop around the barrel.

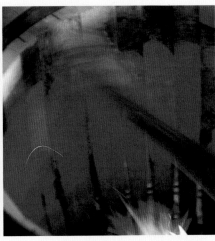

The staves are still splayed out at the other end of the barrel, and are heated over an open fire so that they can be bent to shape.

The intensity of this toasting is crucial in determining the aromas the finished barrel will impart to the wine.

The cooper places a metal cable around the barrel and uses leverage to draw it progressively tighter, whilst also dampening the outside of the staves.

The staves at the other end eventually form a perfect closed circle that can be secured with a hoop.

The barrel still has no opening in the side, and so the cooper bores a bung-hole into the oak, which he then enlarges to a prescribed size.

The outside of the barrel is given its final planing before the bottom and lid are fitted.

Barrel Maturation

There is no instant recipe for success in the art of turning grapes into wine, and the same is true of maturing the wine in barrels. The first decision each winemaker must make is the extent to which barrels should be used. In some cases, a proportion of the wine may be finished off in barrels, and the rest in tanks; the two are reintegrated directly before bottling to homogenize the blend. For wine matured in barrels, especially new *barriques*, the origin of the wood, and the degree of toasting can emphasize particular characteristics in the wine that have been determined by the grape variety, weather conditions, and soil properties.

As a rule of thumb, the more "structure" a wine has, the better it will withstand barrel aging. If a light wine is matured in a wooden barrel, all the care and effort that has been put into it up to that point can quickly be wasted. As well as adding certain aromatic compounds, barrel aging allows slow oxidation, which encourages maturation. The various components of the wine combine with each other, making the wine more harmonious. At the same time, this controlled development makes the wine less perishable and more resistant to future oxidation—in short, it gives it greater

Many influential estates have made architectural attractions of their cellars.

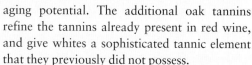

Tartrates and fine deposits are removed from the barrels using water pressure.

aging potential. The additional oak tannins refine the tannins already present in red wine, and give whites a sophisticated tannic element that they previously did not possess.

Winemakers agree that the best way to achieve an appealing but integrated note of wood and more body in a white wine is to carry out the fermentation process in the barrel and then allow a period of maturation with the wine in contact with the lees. In this case, the must is transferred to the barrels after clarification. Once the alcoholic fermentation is complete, the barrel is topped up and the bung-hole sealed. The lees—the deposit left after fermentation—are stirred up periodically, a process known as BÂTONNAGE. This ensures that the oxygen introduced into the barrel is carried right to the bottom, preventing the development of any faults in the aroma of the finished wine. How often the lees are stirred depends on the wine and the style of the winemaker. Initially, it may happen twice a week, then gradually be reduced to once every two weeks. Whatever the frequency, it is generally continued for three months. After this time, the wine is either left on the lees or racked off. In the latter case, it may be transferred directly to another barrel, or the winemaker may use the opportunity to blend the wine (the process of ASSEMBLAGE) before returning it to tanks or barrels.

Alcoholic fermentation in small barrels is out of the question with red wines, because it takes place in contact with the skins, seeds, and possibly the stalks. It would be difficult to

The pipette, used to take samples from the barrels, is the winemaker's most important tool.

Samples are taken regularly to check the progress of the wine by tasting or analysis.

Pneumatic pressure makes for especially gentle rakking of the wine.

transfer all this into a barrel, and even more difficult to get it out again. After the wine is drawn off from the tank and pressing has taken place, it can be returned to the tank or to barrels for the process of malolactic fermentation. Barrels seem to produce more convincing results in this regard, because the tannins are blended more smoothly.

All barrels "drink" the wine, particularly new ones: the loss is estimated to amount to three to five percent. This means about 3 US gallons (11 liters) will disappear from a Bordeaux *barrique* with a 59-gallon (225-liter) capacity. The barrels cannot be left with an empty space inside, because a vinegary edge may develop in the wine. Consequently, they must regularly be topped up, a procedure known in French as *ouillage*. This occurs weekly at the beginning of the maturation period, and then at increasing intervals. In the Gironde, it is common to see barrels oriented so that their bung-holes are on the side, to reduce both evaporation and the amount of air getting in—and thus minimize the need for topping up. Thanks to new, airtight stoppers made of silicon, however, barrels can continue to be positioned with the bung-holes

Oak slats can be suspended in a tank to give the wine attractive and desirable oak aromas without incurring the expense of barrel maturation. The method is principally practiced in New World countries.

facing upwards, which makes it much easier to carry out the various tasks needed to monitor the progress of the wine.

The duration of barrel aging varies from three to more than 18 months, and will depend on the type of wine being matured and the amount of volatile acid that forms in the barrel. If the level becomes too high, the period of barrel maturation is shortened. This decision is usually made by a taster, who is able to assess the general balance of the wine. A frequent mistake is to end barrel maturation too early, because the woody aromas that are often very prominent at the beginning need time to become smoother.

Barrel maturation, whether of red or white wine, is more labor intensive than aging the same volume in a tank. Add to this the cost of purchasing the barrels into the equation, and it is easy to see why it is so much more expensive. In deciding to use barrels, therefore, winemakers take into account not only the type of wine being produced, but also the final price. Only high-quality wine is worth carefully MATURING in wood, to give it a harmony and complexity that it could never attain in a more neutral container.

Truth and illusion

Although aromatic compounds are absorbed during maturation in oak barrels, this is not "aromatizing" the wine in the true sense. Adding wood chips or installing wooden slats in stainless steel tanks is a different matter, however, because they have only one purpose: to impart aromas to the wine in the same way that seasonings are used with food. The positive secondary effects of barrel maturation, deriving from beneficial oxidation or contact with the lees, are not achieved with artificial additives.

The controversial use of wooden chips or slats in tanks is officially still banned in Europe, but properly registered experiments are permitted, and laboratories are already carrying out research and tests.

Some producers try to simulate the aromas produced by barrel maturation by steeping oak shavings in the wine, teabag-style.

Elsewhere in the world, this form of additive is widely used, and wines treated in such a way have long been sold across the globe. There is a problem with this winery practice: European legislation requires that any product labeled as wine is made entirely from grapes, a regulation that emphasizes the traditional precepts of purity. In an apparent effort to tailor products to the demands of the market, however, modern winemaking practice is resorting to a wide range of additional substances and aromatic compounds, even going as far as using specially manipulated cultured yeasts and a variety of enzymes. Should the consumer not claim the right to be informed about these additives, just as they are with other food and drink products?

CLARIFYING AND BOTTLING

Fining using egg whites is a very gentle method that is traditional but still much used today.

As it matures, wine naturally becomes clearer and more limpid, but this self-clarification is seldom sufficient to guarantee the stability of the wine over a long period of time. For this reason, wineries make use of additional physical or chemical methods of purification. Such treatments must be carried out with great care, however, because if they are too harsh, they will diminish the wine and have a detrimental effect on its quality. A compromise has to be found between stability and structure. Moreover, stabilization should not prevent the further development of wines that are meant for bottle aging.

No clarifying procedure is suitable for all wines. An appropriate method must be selected, depending on the nature of the wine: red, white, or rosé, dry or with RESIDUAL SUGAR, to be drunk young or matured, produced in bulk or for a small number of consumers. Some great red wines should be bottled without any form of clarification, and the consumer suitably advised that a degree of sediment will form as the wine ages in the bottle.

Two methods of clarification that are usually used in conjunction with one another are fining and filtration. Fining is a physico-chemical process whereby an additive is poured into the wine which binds with the solids (such as proteins or tannins) that are making it cloudy, or are likely to do so later on. The flocs formed settle out as sediment, and the clear wine can then be racked off. The choice of fining agent depends on the wine. Bentonite (a clay formed by the weathering of volcanic rock) and/or gelatin are preferred for white wines. With red wines, powdered or beaten egg whites are used as well as gelatin. The dosage depends on how cloudy the wine is. To avoid over-fining, which would only increase the structural instability of the wine, the degree of clarification that can be expected is tested by adding the fining agent to a small quantity of wine and allowing it to settle for up to 30 days before separating the liquid from the sediment.

The fining process is sufficient to clarify some red wines, which can then be bottled. In most cases, however, it is carried out before filtration, in order to make the latter easier. Filtration is a mechanical process in which the wine is forced

The first stage of egg white fining is breaking the eggs and separating the whites from the yolks.

Only the whites are used, and are stirred into each individual barrel of wine—a costly procedure.

The egg white binds with the particles floating in the wine and sinks to the bottom, where it is drawn off.

under pressure through porous material and the solids are left behind. The most commonly used filters include precoat filters, sheet filters, and membrane filters.

The first type of filter generally involves repeatedly passing wine and diatomaceous earth (kieselguhr) through a series of filtering plates. The kieselguhr is deposited as a filtration bed with a continually renewing active surface. Sheet filters make use of compressed filtration material between the filtering plates, and the pore size of this material is selected according to the desired degree of clarification. If a very turbid wine is filtered too finely, the filters quickly become blocked and the procedure must be stopped, so a coarse filtration is used first. A further filtration to remove unwanted yeasts and fungi can be carried out before bottling, using membrane filters or special sterilization filters.

The finer the filtration medium, the greater the stability of the wine, but the more it is stripped of its good qualities. For this reason, some winemakers offer connoisseurs unfiltered bottlings, in which the structure of the wine remains intact. The American wine critic Robert Parker has made a great contribution toward convincing both winemakers and consumers of the benefits of bottling red wines without fining and filtration.

TARTRATES

Sometimes, particularly with white wines, small, hard crystals can be seen suspended in the wine or adhering to the cork. These look like sugar, but are, in fact, TARTRATES. Tartaric acid is naturally present in grapes, and thus also in wine. It crystallizes at low temperatures. To avoid this occurring in the bottle, winemakers can try to initiate the precipitation process whilst the wine is still in the tank or the barrel. This can happen naturally during the winter, if the temperature in the winery falls sufficiently, or can be artificially induced by chilling the wine.

At the lower end of the quality hierarchy, heat treatment or pasteurization to remove micro-organisms can also be considered. This can be undertaken either before, during, or after the bottling process.

BOTTLING

The equipment required for bottling depends on the size of the operation. Small estates often use manual bottling machines, in which the bottles are filled, one by one, and then corked using a second machine, again operated by hand. Other producers make use of commercial bottling services, whose equipment is usually technically impressive, guaranteeing the quality of the bottling process. Unfortunately, these services tend to lack flexibility, since their capacity—which can vary from 1,000 to 10,000 bottles an hour, depending on the size of the plant—must be booked in advance. In addition, the filtration carried out by bottling firms to indemnify themselves is often too harsh.

A bottling line consists of a washing unit to clean the empty bottles on the inside, a filling unit that fills the bottles to a preset level, and a corking machine. After filling, bottles can be topped with capsules straight away, labeled, packaged in cartons, and sent to a warehouse, from where they can be dispatched as required. Alternatively, they can be stored *tiré-bouché* ("filled and corked") in a wine cellar, from where they can be fetched when needed, cleaned, supplied with labels and capsules, and packed in cartons, which can then be sealed and piled on pallets for dispatch.

As modern as some of today's bottling lines may be, the boxes are often still packed by hand—and not just in South Africa.

BOTTLES

By the beginning of the 19th century, the use of bottles was already widespread. They were still blown by mouth, however, as can be seen from their irregular shapes.

The art of glass-making seems to have been mastered by the Egyptians in the 4th millennium BC. It was the Phoenicians who disseminated both glass vessels and the knowledge of how to make them throughout the Mediterranean region. According to Pliny the Elder, Phoenician soda merchants were preparing their meal on a beach, and, lacking any stones with which to make a fireplace, they used lumps of soda, which then combined in the fire with the sand, producing soda glass. That particular story may belong to the realm of fable, but the discovery of

one of the most versatile artificially manufactured materials used by man is indeed likely to have been a chance occurrence.

In addition to its decorative function, glass has always played a vital role in everyday life as a storage vessel, although in antiquity glass would certainly only have held valuable substances such as perfume oils. The fact that it could be made into almost any shape, blown, cut, bent, ground, and given almost any color, yet also melted down again at any time—recycled—led to the art of glass-making flourishing under the Romans,

Dwarves and giants

Champagne bottles come in an astonishing range of sizes. The smallest is the 7 fl oz (18.5 cl) quarter bottle or *quart-avion*, which, as its French name suggests, is mostly used by airlines. Next come the half bottle (14 fl oz/37.5 cl), the standard bottle (28 fl oz/75 cl), and the magnum (56 fl oz/1.5 liters). The largest bottle sizes all have biblical names, as the list below shows, although no one knows when this idea came into being or who was responsible for it.

• A Jeroboam contains about four standard bottles. Jeroboam was the founder and first ruler of the divided kingdom of Israel, from 931–910 BC.

• A Methuselah contains the equivalent of eight bottles. Methuselah was a patriarch before the time of the Flood, and is famous for having lived 969 years.

• A Salmanazar has a capacity of 12 bottles. This name is apparently related to the Babylonian royal name Shalmaneser.

• A Balthazar contains 16 standard bottles. Balthazar was Regent of Babylon, as well as the name of one of the Three Wise Men from the East.

• A Nebuchadnezzar has a capacity of 20 bottles. Its namesake ruled Babylon for over 40 years, during which time it became the capital of the Orient.

who popularized it throughout Europe. Glass furnaces have been found in all Roman provinces, and a few were undoubtedly still in use in the post-Roman era. For a long time, its fragility and the cost of production meant that glass remained the preserve of the wealthier sections of society (ordinary folk continued to carry and serve liquids in vessels made of clay, leather, or wood), but the triumph of glass was inevitable.

Balloon-shaped bottles appeared in the 16th century, with a wickerwork covering for protection. The use of bottles spread throughout Europe around the middle of the 17th century. Initially, they were relatively short, with a wide body and long, thin neck, but gradually evolved toward the shape we know today, principally to make it easier to store them on their side.

By the beginning of the 19th century, individual wine-producing regions were already using characteristic bottles, such as the flute bottle for Rhine wines, the BOCKSBEUTEL in Franconia (Franken), the straw-covered FIASCO for Chianti, as well as the Burgundy, Bordeaux, and Champagne bottles, among many others. Since then, the catalogs of glass factories have continued to expand. Today, some *appellations* have typical bottles, and even large producers or merchants may use their own, individual shapes.

Italian bottlers caught the attention of the market with designer bottles. These are now used on an international scale, but seldom by the top producers.

Everyday wines are bottled in standard shapes, because economic considerations are of paramount importance. Technical advances have made it possible to manufacture bottles that are lighter and more durable than before, leading to important savings in transportation and glass recycling costs.

As the habits of consumers change, so glass manufacturers are adapting and becoming more imaginative. Most wine is sold in shops, where it has to compete with thousands of other products. The wines have to draw attention to themselves on the shelf, and so some producers go for a distinctive shape, others certain colors—both for bottles and for labels. In the midst of all this innovation and creativity, however, it should not be forgotten that a wine is part of the tradition and culture of its country of origin, and this should be reflected in the design of the bottle.

We know that today's consumer is much more discerning and drinks less, but better quality wine. For some meals, particularly in restaurants, a whole 25 fl oz (75 cl) bottle may be too much, but a half bottle (12½ fl oz/ 37.5 cl) is too little. Consequently, bottles that

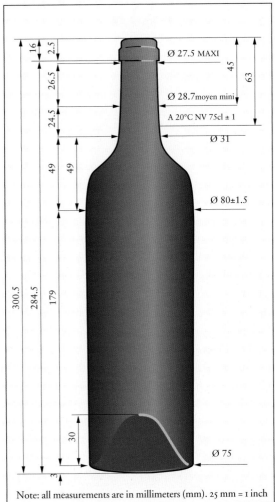

Ø 27.5 MAXI

Ø 28.7moyen mini

A 20°C NV 75cl ± 1

Ø 31

Ø 80±1.5

Ø 75

Note: all measurements are in millimeters (mm). 25 mm = 1 inch

TRADITIONAL BORDEAUX BOTTLE

STANDARD SIZE RING
The standard neck ring takes a standard capsule and guarantees perfect corking.

GENEROUS SHOULDER
The broad shoulder gives an impression of class and elegance.

SLIGHTLY TAPERING BODY
The slightly tapering shape is reminiscent of the earlier Bordeaux bottles.

DEEP INDENTATION (PUNT)
This enables the bottle to be held securely in the horizontal position, making pouring the wine more pleasurable.

contain 17 fl oz (50 cl) have been brought onto the market, but are only slowly gaining ground.

The glass bottle is still the most commonly used container for drinks of every sort, although some wines are now being sold in plastic bottles or Tetra Pak cartons. Increasingly common is the "BAG IN A BOX" container, which consists of a plastic foil bag of wine (usually about 1–1¼ gallons/3–5 liters) inside a cardboard box. The bag collapses as the wine is drawn off, thus maintaining an almost airtight seal around the remaining contents. This kind of packaging looks set gradually to replace the sale of draft wine, because the "airless tapping" mechanism preserves the wine for up to six months once the seal has been broken.

BOTTLE MANUFACTURE

The main raw material for the production of glass bottles is silicic acid (silicon dioxide, 70 percent), which occurs in nature primarily in the form of quartz sand. It is possible to make glass purely out of sand, but this requires temperatures in excess of 3,272°F (1,800°C). Consequently, an alkali is added (soda or potash, around 15 percent), which lowers the melting point to 2,732°F (1,500°C). Quicklime (10 percent) prevents the glass from crystallizing as it cools. The remaining 5 percent is mostly aluminum oxide, magnesium, or iron oxide, which primarily help to determine color and viscosity. Scrap glass (from manufacturing remnants or bottles collected for recycling) is also added. The amount of each ingredient is measured using electronic precision balances.

The mixture is melted down in a furnace at around 2,822°F (1,550°C). Bubbles of gas form in the molten glass at this stage, which rise to the surface and burst during the fining process. The now homogenous mass flows into channels which feed the molding machines. A plunger pushes the molten glass through a calibrated orifice at regular intervals. This produces a series of gobs of glass, which are cut off with automatic shears. Their weight, and hence the rhythm of the plunger, is determined by the amount of molten glass needed for the particular article being made. The temperature, now between 2,012° and 2,372°F (1,100° and 1,300°C), is constantly monitored, because a sudden sharp drop would cause the glass to lose its viscosity.

The molding process can now begin (see diagram, opposite). Each gob of molten glass drops into a parison mold. The lower part of this mold is a ring that shapes the upper part of the bottle neck. A plunger punches through the molten glass via the ring, and compressed air is blown in through the hole this creates, forming a hollow body from the gob.

This parison is transferred into a finishing mold, and compressed air is again introduced to give the bottle its final shape. This method of manufacture is known as the blow-and-blow technique. In the press-and-blow technique, the first blow molding operation is replaced by a pressing operation. Some machines can produce up to 700 bottles a minute.

Once molding is complete, the glass still has a temperature of 1,202°F (650°C). The external walls tend to cool off quickly, whilst the temperature inside the cavity drops much more slowly. If the bottles were allowed to cool naturally, the glass could develop cracks and easily break. For this reason, they are put through another furnace on a conveyor belt, so that they can cool off very gradually from around 1,022°F (550°C).

The bottles then have to undergo one final process to remove microscopic flaws on the surface of the glass. One method involves spraying the bottles with metal oxide vapors, which act on the surface of the glass, and this is carried out during the heating phase between molding and cooling. Alternatively, a protective film of polyethylene is applied to the surface of the glass once cooling is complete.

At the end of the production process, the size, shape, capacity, and technical properties of the bottle are checked. They are then piled in several layers on pallets to be dispatched. The pallets are usually tightly wrapped in plastic film so that no dust, small insects, or other pollutants can get in.

Although the true raw material for glass making is quartz sand, recycled glass has become very important for bottle manufacture.

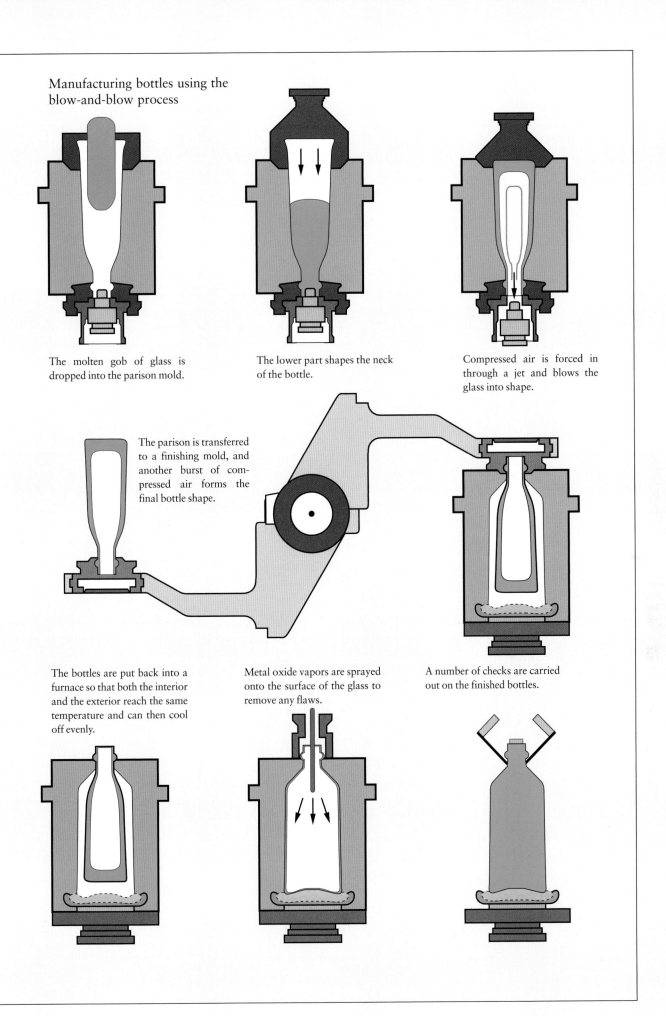

Manufacturing bottles using the blow-and-blow process

The molten gob of glass is dropped into the parison mold.

The lower part shapes the neck of the bottle.

Compressed air is forced in through a jet and blows the glass into shape.

The parison is transferred to a finishing mold, and another burst of compressed air forms the final bottle shape.

The bottles are put back into a furnace so that both the interior and the exterior reach the same temperature and can then cool off evenly.

Metal oxide vapors are sprayed onto the surface of the glass to remove any flaws.

A number of checks are carried out on the finished bottles.

André Dominé

WINES OF THE
WORLD

THE WORLD OF WINE: A SURVEY

A glance at the distribution of wine-growing regions on our planet shows at once that vines will grow only in certain conditions. The most important factor for viticulture is climate, and above all, temperature. Here there is a striking difference between the northern and southern hemispheres. In the southern hemisphere, the 59°F (15°C) line during the winter month of July describes an almost straight course, running between about 60 and 50 degrees latitude south,

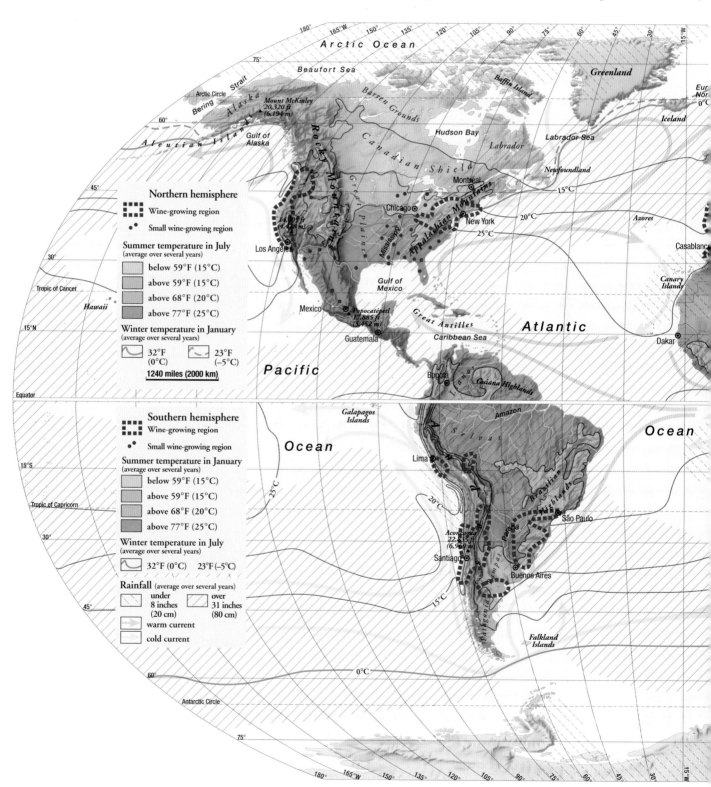

missing land entirely. Whereas in the northern hemisphere, where the considerably larger land masses receive more warmth in summer—and where warm water currents such as the Gulf Stream are a contributory factor—the 32°F (0°C) line passes through a number of major wine-growing areas. However, the map also shows that vines clearly prefer moderate conditions. They seldom thrive where temperatures rise above 77°F (25°C) in the summer months of July and January in the northern and southern hemispheres respectively. Rainfall and drought also play an important part. It is almost impossible to grow wine with less than 8 inches (200 mm) of rain a year; on the other hand, too much rain also makes it difficult to cultivate grapes. All over the world, however, wine growers have found ways of adapting to natural conditions, and they have been particularly resourceful in borderline areas.

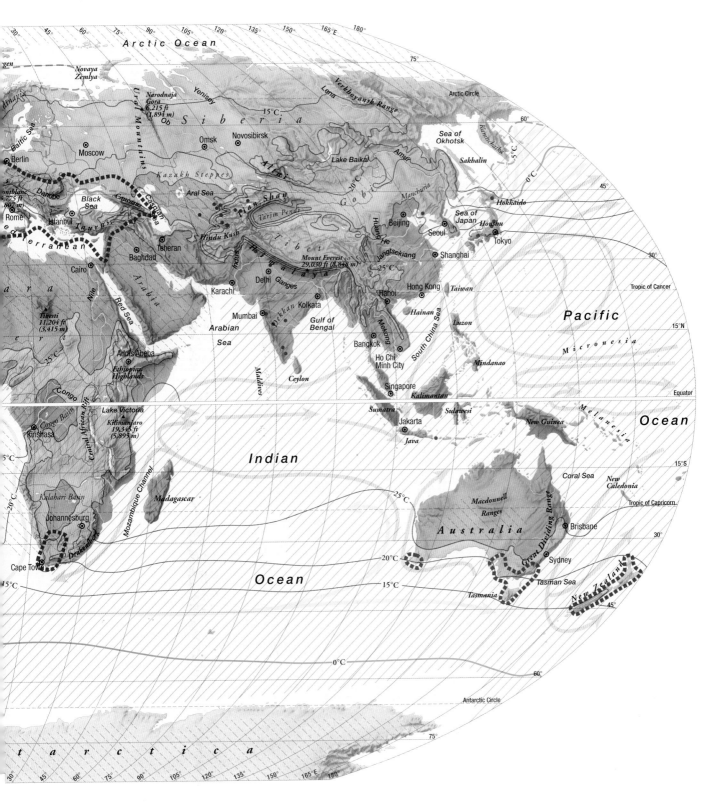

Map Legend

Wine-growing region

Vineyard

Summer temperature in July
(average over several years)

below 59°F (15°C)

above 59°F (15°C)

above 68°F (20°C)

above 77°F (25°C)

Winter temperature in January
(average over several years)

32°F (0°C)

23°F (–5°C)

Warm current
(Gulf Stream)

311 miles (500 km)

Map Labels

–5°C

Peninsula

White Sea

RUSSIA

Kazan

Volga

Nijni-Novgorod

Oka

Moscow

Don

52° latitude north is regarded as the northern limit for wine growing

20°C

Kiev

Khar'kov

Dnieper

Dnepropetrovsk

UKRAINE

Donets

Rostov

MOLDOVA

Chişinău

–5°C

Odessa

Sea of Asov

Krasnodar

Crimea

0°C

Caucasus

B l a c k   S e a

Pontic Mountains

0°C

Istanbul

Sea of Marmara

25°C

Bursa

Ankara

Kızılırmak

20°C

TURKEY

Tuz Gölü

İzmir

Konya

Adana

Gaziantep

Euphrates

Antalya

Aleppo

SYRIA

Nicosia

CYPRUS

LEBANON

Beirut

Rhodes

25°C

VITICULTURE IN EUROPE

As noted on the map, 52 degrees latitude north can usually be regarded as the northern limit for wine growing. However, several British winegrowers, in a very sportsmanlike manner, seem to have ignored this "rule." The further north viticulture extends, so the average temperatures will be cooler, and the amount of rainfall to which the vines are exposed will increase. While cool temperatures inhibit the ripening process, too much moisture can threaten the health of vines and grapes alike, and at the same time thin the MUST. The more extreme the temperatures and the rainfall, the more the vine's photosynthesis is impaired, and with it the formation of glucose; as a result, it is impossible to grow grapes for winemaking north of 54 degrees latitude.

The close connection between rivers and wine-growing areas, especially in the north, center, and east of Europe, is also obvious. The Loire and the Garonne, the Rhine and the Rhône, the Danube and the Dniester are all life-lines to important viticultural areas, where they moderate any extremes of climate.

In a large part of western Europe, average July temperatures vary between 59 and 68°F (15 and 20°C), and it is in this zone that the majority of Europe's classic viticultural regions lie. A moderate climate, with adequate to relatively high rainfall, provides ideal conditions for producing both fragrant white wines with a good structure of acidity, and well-balanced red wines with good potential for MATURING.

Even in the relatively small area of Spain, the south of France, and Italy a remarkable number of interlocking temperature zones occur. However, two elements clearly distinguish the Mediterranean south from the north of Europe: these are distinctly higher temperatures and much stronger sunshine. These factors contribute to the optimum ripening of the grapes from appropriate vine varieties, and the result is a completely different type of wine, full and velvety.

In eastern Europe, where the weather is often hot, with summer temperatures of over 68°F (20°C), hard frosts can also occur. During the course of the year these can give rise to extremes of temperature from which the rest of Europe is largely spared. Great fluctuations between day and night temperatures, however, tend to improve the quality of the wine. The supreme product of such conditions is Tokaji, in which fullness and freshness are united in timeless grandeur.

NORTH AMERICA AND SOUTH AMERICA

The U.S.A. is almost bisected by the 32°F (0°C) line. South of it—apart from the Pacific seaboard—temperatures of over 77°F (25°C) predominate, and as such the land is unsuitable for wine growing. Meso- or microclimates may offer limited opportunities, but two other extremes complicate matters: drought or almost tropical humidity. In the northeast, rain and cold restrict the chances of wine growing. Only on the west coast, thanks to the moderating influence of the Pacific, do certain areas provide ideal conditions for making outstanding red wines in particular.

- Wine-growing region
- Vineyard

Summer temperature in July
(average over several years)
- below 59°F (15°C)
- above 59°F (15°C)
- above 68°F (20°C)
- above 77°F (25°C)

Winter temperature in January
(average over several years)
- 32°F (0°C)
- 23°F (−5°C)

- Warm current
- Cold current

621 miles (1,000 km)

In the South American continent, only a few exceptional districts offer the conditions necessary for making good wine. The best of these are in the Andes where, even in the dry regions, rivers provide the irrigation without which viticulture here would be impossible.

On the Argentinian side of the Andes the altitude—and there are vineyards at up to and even above 6,500 ft (2,000 m)—often moderates the prevailing heat, and well-balanced wines can be made. In Chile, on the other hand, the influence of the Pacific Ocean provides a temperate climate, in fact one of the best in the world for wine growing. On the Atlantic coast conditions are considerably less favorable, as the wine-growing regions shown on the map suggest, although Uruguay is something of an exception. In sub-tropical climates the temperature often makes it impossible to produce wines of quality. In addition, the heat and humidity can encourage diseases to which only the hybrid vine varieties are resistant.

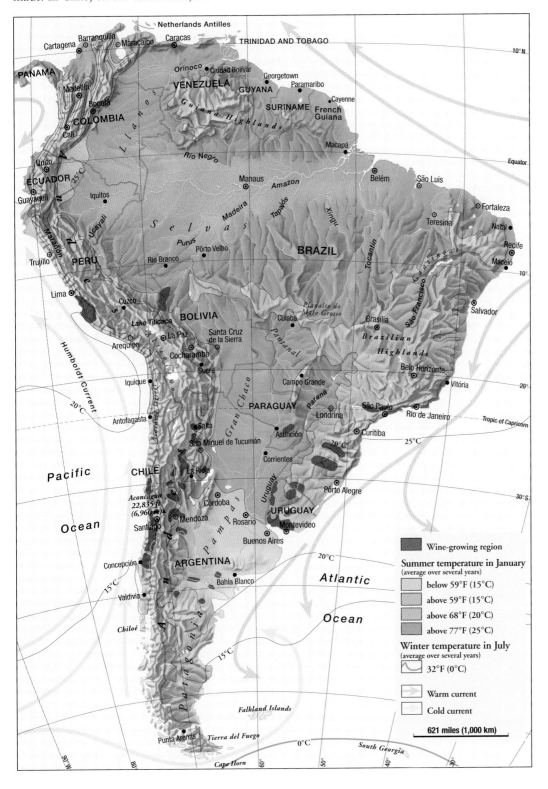

Wine-growing region

Summer temperature in January
(average over several years)
below 59°F (15°C)
above 59°F (15°C)
above 68°F (20°C)
above 77°F (25°C)

Winter temperature in July
(average over several years)
32°F (0°C)

Warm current

Cold current

621 miles (1,000 km)

GRAPE-GROWING AREAS AND WINE PRODUCTION

The vine gives us two kinds of fruits. Some taste delicious as they are, and take their place on the table as dessert grapes or raisins. The others usually have too thick a skin to be eaten as raw fruit, and are therefore used to make wine. The reason for this difference lies in a process of the selection of varieties that can be traced back over thousands of years. It is unusual to find grapes that are good both for eating as fruit and for making wine. As the statistics of grape-growing areas illustrate, some countries grow vines for dessert grapes or raisins over very large areas, far outstripping the planted areas of wine-producing countries. This is why Turkey comes fourth in the overall table, because it is the world's leading producer of dessert grapes and raisins. Although in 1998 the official statistics of the *Office International de la Vigne et du Vin*

The Spätburgunder grape, with its small berries, is used for making wine, but in many parts of the world vines are cultivated principally or exclusively for the production of dessert grapes.

(OIV)—the international wine bureau based in Paris—ranked Iran in sixth place with 270,000 hectares growing vines, and China was placed tenth, it appears that countries which mainly produce dessert grapes and raisins are no longer listed in the tables. This is probably also due to a lack of up-to-date information. The fact remains that quite a number of Asian and North African countries have extensive vine-growing areas but do not use them—or use only a small part of them—for wine production.

Little has changed at the top of the wine production table. Italy and France compete for the top listing as far as production is concerned, and often change place, depending on the climate of a particular year. Spain, which still has the largest grape-growing area of all, continues in third place for wine production. Considerably more interesting is the lower end of the list. Portugal, which was for a short time pushed out of the ten most important wine-producing countries, has been able to consolidate its production. It has today almost tripled its production compared to the end of the 1970s, when it made 96 million gallons (3.65 million hectoliters). Chile has overcome the crisis which led to a drastic slump in production between 1986 and 1990, and is now producing increasingly large amounts of wine, growing grape varieties that are in international demand in restructured vineyards. In Argentina, production has been falling for more than 25 years, and the decline continues. What the figures do not show is the increase in the production of high-quality wines.

Areas planted in 1000s of acres (hectares)		Source: O.I.V. 2000
Country	Area planted	World percentage of areas planted
Spain	2,901 (1,174)	14.9
France	2,266 (917)	11.6
Italy	2,244 (908)	11.5
Turkey	1,436 (581)	7.4
USA (California)	1,021 (413)	5.2
Portugal	645 (261)	3.3
Romania	613 (248)	3.1
Argentina	516 (209)	2.7
Chile	430 (174)	2.1
Australia	346 (140)	1.8
10 countries in total	12,462 (5,025)	63.6
The world in total	19,485 (7,885)	100

Wine production in millions of gallons (1,000 hectoliters) Source: O.I.V. 2000				
Country	Wine production 2001		1990	Percentage of change
France	1,538 (58,240)		1,730 (65,529)	−12.2
Italy	1,354 (51,300)		1,448 (54,866)	−6.5
Spain	822 (31,130)		1,021 (38,658)	−19.5
USA	628 (23,800)		419 (15,852)	+50.1
Argentina	321 (12,150)		371 (14,036)	−13.4
Australia	284 (10,770)		117 (4,446)	+142.2
Germany	255 (9,660)		225 (8,514)	+13.5
South Africa	197 (7,470)		237 (8,998)	−16.9
Portugal	185 (7,010)		300 (11,372)	−38.4
Chile	159 (6,000)		105 (3,978)	+50.8
10 countries in total	5,743 (217,530)		5,973 (226,239)	−3.8
The world in total	7,284 (275,892)		7,468 (282,897)	−2.5

WINE CONSUMPTION

France is the leader in wine consumption per country—at 1,439 million gallons (34.5 million hectoliters), beating Italy at 814 gallons (30.8 million hl) (the trend is moving downward). The U.S.A. follows with 550 million gallons (21.2 million hectoliters), then Germany at 518 million gallons (19.6 million hl), Spain at 365 million (13.8 hl) and Argentina at 327 million (12.4 hl). Other wine-growing countries consume less than 265 million gallons (10 million hectoliters) a year.

THE EXTREME REGIONS OF AFRICA

The only wine growing worth mentioning in Africa is in the extreme regions. In the North African countries of the Maghreb only mountain slopes provide conditions suitable for viticulture. In the very south—therefore below the equator—the Benguela Current from the Antarctic moderates temperatures. In practice, however, only the Cape area offers the conditions for viticulture in southern Africa.

André Dominé, Eckhard Supp, Ulrich Sautter, Wolfgang Fassbender

FRANCE

THE FRENCH WINE REGIONS

Geological and climatic diversity combine to make France one of the most richly diverse wine countries in the world. Under differing natural conditions, the vine varieties have acclimatized over the centuries, and diverse methods of cultivation have developed.

Champagne, France's northernmost wine region, borders the area where average temperatures are not sufficiently high to ripen grapes. Toward the Atlantic coast, rainfall is too high for growing vines. The acidic character of Champagne is determined by this border climate.

Alsace enjoys a particularly favorable climate, and the Vosges mountains to the west form a superb natural border to the wine-growing district. Here, on sloping sites facing the sun, the grapes become overripe, and the moisture rising from the fluvial plain encourages the development of the NOBLE ROT fungus, which is responsible for the greatest wines of the region.

In the northern part of Burgundy, which has the best-known *appellation* of Chablis, the winegrowers must take frost protection measures to prevent some of the best Chardonnay locations from freezing. The Chardonnay grape, which has spread all around the world, develops incomparable mineral expression here on the soil, which is a mix of marine limestone and

Historic estates, surrounded by vines, are a frequent sight not only in Beaujolais but all over France.

clay. Here, as in other Burgundy *appellations*, it generally rains so much that growers use a particularly high planting density to control the growth of the vines. This also applies to Beaujolais. Between the broad valley of the Saône and the Monts du Beaujolais, the Gamay grape finds its ideal *terroir* on the granitic or marl soil, but the winegrowers have to prune the vines in a completely different way to that used by their neighbors in Burgundy for the Pinot Noir vines.

The far eastern French wine regions of Jura and Savoie are characterized by their situation in the mountains. Beside the cultivation of some unique grape varieties, the Jura region is also home to *vin jaune*, a wine kept for six years under a film-forming yeast.

At its estuary, the Loire is a climatically mild and very damp area, because of the influence of the warm Gulf Stream. Thus in the Muscadet region, near the mouth of the Loire, the grapes must often be brought in early. Up river, the continental influences increase, so that great dry and sweet white wines as well as excellent reds thrive here. The Cabernet Franc grape is being increasingly propagated now, as it yields better results than Cabernet Sauvignon in the earlier cool temperatures.

The Bordeaux region, in particular the Médoc, is the stronghold between the Gironde river and the Atlantic Ocean, where a temperate climate

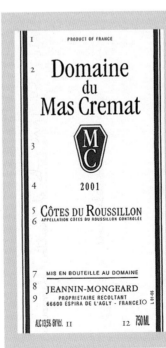

1 Details of the country of origin

2 Name of the wine estate or wine merchant

3 Coat of arms or logo of the producer

4 Vintage

5 Wine region and name of the appellation

6 Wine designation: statutory guarantee of controlled appellation

7 Here: fermented in oak barrels (*elevé en fût de chêne*), or often here, the name of the *cuvée*

8 Bottled at the property where it is made

9 Name of the winegrower or the property

10 Name of the owner-manager (or name of the firm)

11 Address of the business

12 Alcoholic strength (often rounded to the nearest 0.5%, rarely an exact figure)

13 Nominal volume of the bottle

Champagne
Alsace
Jura
Burgundy
Beaujolais
Loire Valley
Bordeaux
Southwest
Rhône Valley
Savoie and Bugey
Provence
Corsica
Languedoc
Roussillon
Wine-growing areas in neighboring countries

60 miles (100 km)

accommodates late ripening, and good, porous, gravel beds prevent frequent rainfalls from thinning the vines. In the Southwest it is often warmer and the mountains have greater influence.

WHERE THE MEDITERRANEAN RULES

The influence of the Atlantic extends amazingly far to the east and, in the cultivated areas of the Southeast, three factors above all influence vine cultivation: warmth, wind, and aridity. These are at their most temperate in the northern Rhône, where they lend superb balance to both red and white wines. Here, and throughout the Midi, is the realm of the Syrah grape, while further south—at their stronghold of Châteauneuf-du-Pape—the Grenache and Mourvèdre grape varieties dominate. In Provence—the epitome of Mediterranean life—the proximity of the Alps to the north affects the wines as much as the Mediterranean Sea does to the south. Accordingly, there is a great range of grape varieties and wine styles. Corsica, meanwhile, is not only geographically closer to the Italian coast, but its typical grape varieties are Italian and are best suited to the Mediterranean climate.

The Languedoc-Roussillon region overlooks the Golfe du Lion and is one of the largest wine regions in the world. This region receives the greatest number of sunshine hours and also shares raging northwesterly winds with Provence, which guarantee the best health for the grapes. These wines reach their optimum concentration in reduced yields.

Champagne—Home of a Noble and Historic Drink

Champagne is an invigorating and often even erotic bubbly, the legendary drink of the elite, the undisputed quality sparkling wine. From the Sun King Louis XV to the czars, from Winston Churchill to the English royal family, Formula One winners to stock market flotations—the sparkling wine from the northernmost wine region of France is always present. Unlike any other wine, it has established its *appellation* as a brand name with which the greatest prestige— and the highest prices!—are inextricably linked. Even though there is increasing competition, which must be taken seriously, from Spanish Cava and Italian Franciacorta, as well as Californian and Australian products, the world's premier *appellation*, which specializes exclusively in the production of sparkling wine fermented in the bottle, is the undisputed holder of pole position in the world, even though today it produces less than ten percent of wine in this category.

The name of the wine region which lies northeast of the French capital—in the Middle

A great champagne has tremendous aging potential.

Were it not for Dom Pérignon, champagne would not be what it is today.

Ages, it also included today's Île de France and Paris—comes from the Latin word *campus* and refers to the vineyards and countryside along the Marne valley, known as *Champagne viticole*. The region's geographical extent was strictly defined and delimited by a decree of the Institut National des Appellations d'Origine in 1927. The region is centered around the towns of Reims and Épernay and, from its earliest history, it has been at the crossroads of the major north–south and east–west trade routes. An area blessed with great prosperity, its wine history can be traced back to the 5th century, although it did not specialize in sparkling wines until considerably later.

Dom Pérignon and his Legacy

A generic *vin de Champagne*, which was predominately still and only foamed occasionally in the bottle, has existed since the 17th century, when these slightly pinkish still wines, made chiefly from the Pinot Noir grape, enjoyed a certain popularity in the salons of London café society. From the second half of the 17th century onwards, this *vin de Champagne* underwent the radical changes which made it the sparkling product, fermented in the bottle, which we know today.

The cornerstone of this development was laid by the monk, Dom Pérignon, the famous cellarmaster of the Abbey of Hautvillers. He did not, as is often believed, invent champagne in its present form, but he was revolutionary in his choice of grape varieties, his vineyard techniques, and his blending of *cuvées* from different varieties and vineyards. He was also the first to

ferment an adequate red wine, and the first to press true white wines from black grapes. He initiated the use of stronger bottles with corks tied down with string, which could withstand greater pressure, thus making it possible to supply and export sparkling wines.

Until the 19th century, production of this sparkling champagne amounted to little more than a few thousand bottles. It was the cellarmaster of the famous Veuve (widow) Clicquot who first invented the RIDDLING process called REMUAGE and the exact dose of BOTTLING LIQUOR *liqueur de tirage* for the second fermentation, which advanced production to industrial levels. Commercial success arrived in the middle of the 19th century with a group of young Germans by the names of Krug, Bollinger, Roederer, and Deutz—names which are still the elite of the champagne industry today. They quickly ousted the majority of the local merchants from the market and took up the reins in Reims and its environs.

This success outlived world wars and changes of ownership—today almost every fourth bottle of champagne comes from the cellars of the Louis Vuitton Moët Hennessy (L.V.M.H.) group which owns famous brands such as Veuve-Clicquot-Ponsardin, Krug, Pommery, Ruinart, Moët et Chandon, and Canard-Duchène—and culminated in the sale of 300 million bottles of champagne in the millennium year. That such an unprecedented development was possible is based not only on a unique combination of climate, soil, and grape varieties, but also on the champagne trade's far sightedness and discipline which, over the centuries, has helped it build up the most homogenous *appellation* in the world.

The most visible expression of this unity has been the long-established pricing system used to pay growers for the grapes supplied by them to the champagne houses, which formerly owned very few vineyards. Each year, these prices are established in negotiations and then fixed as standard for the whole region. This pricing committee was established after the collapse of the market in the 1920s and early 1930s. In addition, a number of winegrowers took the CHAMPAGNE METHOD into their own hands and until 1990 ensured relative market stability for the growers and winemakers. Since then, however, not even champagne has been exempt from the ups and downs of the market and the economy.

In damp cellars, labels may rot, but not the champagne.

Chalk is doubly important in Champagne. It not only affects the soil in which the vines grow, but it also provides endless cellars that maintain an ideal temperature and in which wines can survive for over 100 years.

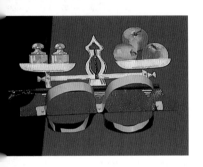

Hautvillers is worth a detour for the growers' signs alone.

ACIDITY AND SUGAR FOR GOOD CHAMPAGNE

The majority of planted vines, and all the classified vineyards of Champagne, lie on the deep, chalkly soil of the slopes of the hills. These provide both good humidity and excellent drainage and their high pH values are responsible for the high acidity levels of the grapes. The slopes also offer the essential requirement—sufficient warmth—since, in what is for vineyards a very northerly location, champagne can hardly guarantee a surfeit of warmth and light for the grapes. Furthermore, the weather, which is affected by maritime changeability, means a longer growing season, which contributes to increased acidity even in ripe grapes—one of the most important factors for sparkling wines. Big, structured white or red wines are never produced in the Champagne region. Despite the original existence of many different grape varieties, in the vineyards between Reims and Épernay only three grapes have been successful, Chardonnay, Pinot Noir, and Pinot Meunier. This may be because of their proximity to Burgundy—two of these vine varieties are also used to make great white wines in Chablis and the Côte d'Or—or because these grapes are well adapted for ripening in cooler climates.

In the region as a whole, more than 35 percent of the whole area given over to vineyards is planted with the simple base variety, Pinot Meunier. Pinot Noir occupies a good third and Chardonnay just over a quarter of the area. However, in the top communes where the base wines for *cuvées de prestige* are made, the reverse is the case, with Chardonnay in the lead at over two fifths. Although almost all champagne is white, it is no contradiction that the black grape varieties dominate in the vineyards. However, when these black grapes are picked, they must be pressed rapidly, using a specific procedure, to prevent the color running from the grape skins. This is the main reason mechanical harvesters are banned in Champagne, since they crush the grapes and the start of the MACERATION process is then inevitable.

Champagne is not exempt from another problem in post-war European wine cultivation: the trend toward attaining ever bigger yields per acre. Between 1940 and 1980, yields increased threefold in the region and, despite an increase in permitted grape quantities—from 330 to 350 pounds for $26\frac{1}{2}$ gallons (150 to 160 kg for 100 liters) of MUST—this led to thinner and thinner base wines, with the final result being that up to 3.5% vol of the actual alcohol was no longer made from the sugars in the grape juice but from CHAPTALIZATION.

Who has actually bottled your wine?

Beside technical details (see illustration), a champagne label often bears a number in very small print which is usually preceded by two letters: these refer to the type of bottler of the champagne concerned, as follows.

N.M.: *Négociant-manipulant*—these merchants or houses harvest or buy grapes, must, or base wines which they then process in their own cellars.

R.M.: *Récoltant-manipulant*—this winegrower makes his own champagne in his own cellars from his own grapes.

R.C.: *Récoltant-coopérateur*—this winegrower is a member of a cooperative, and he sells the wine made by the cooperative to his own customers.

C.M.: *Coopérative de manipulation*—wine cooperative which makes and matures champagne in its own cellars from its members' grapes.

S.R.: *Société de récoltants*—an organization of independent winegrowers which makes and bottles champagne from the harvests of its members.

N.D.: *Négociant distributeur*—wine merchant or company which buys champagne which has already been bottled and then provides the label.

R.: *Récoltant*—this winegrower allows his grapes to be made into wine by a *négociant-manipulant* and receives back the champagne in bottles.

M.A.: *Marque auxiliaire*—literally, additional brand: this is the reseller's own brand shown on the label.

Information on a champagne label:

Champagne House	MOËT et CHANDON
Place	Épernay
Year established	Fondée en 1743
Appellation	Champagne
Cuvée	Cuvée Dom Pérignon
Alcoholic strength	12.5%
Nominal volume	750 ml
Type of dosage	Brut
Registered no. and type of bottler	élaboré par
Firm, place, country	MOËT et CHANDON ÉPERNAY/FRANCE
Registered trademark and design	Muselet EPARNIX
Vintage	Millésime 1990

Champagne consumption

Champagne is always something special and it should be treated as such, so that it can meet all expectations. The level of care required begins when you buy it. Basically, there is an appropriate champagne for every occasion and every dish—it just has to be the right one. Almost no other wine has such a broad range. By mixing grape varieties, wines from different vineyards, and different vintages, as well as altering DOSAGES, each champagne producer has the opportunity to bestow each CUVÉE with its own personal character. Thus there are slim and corpulent, fruity and flowery, fresh and mature, sweet and very dry, young and mature champagnes. And of course, there are good and bad, fine and ordinary, harmonious and coarse, expensive and cheap ones. Even in the case of the most popular type of champagne—non-vintage BRUT—there are big differences. In such cases, the advice of a SOMMELIER, a specialist in the trade, an expert wine merchant, a serious wine guide, or one's own experience is helpful.

Champagne makes a wonderful aperitif, provided it is lively, fresh, and dry, as are the majority of non-vintage *bruts* and young Blanc de Blancs. Blanc de Blancs wines are a superb accompaniment to oysters and shellfish. For caviar and lobster, a more powerful *brut* is preferable. Many fish dishes are ideally accompanied by a *brut* or Blanc de Blancs. However, if the taste, consistency, or sauce of a dish are stronger, then the champagne should also have more structure and complexity, and so a vintage or rosé wine would be recommended. The rare *cuvées de prestige* require careful matching. A powerful, dry champagne can be good with cheese, while for desserts—if possible not too sweet—*sec* and *demi-sec* champagnes are recommended.

The best temperature at which to serve champagne is between 43°F and 48°F (6°C and 9°C), at which temperature the wine should be gently chilled. Ideally, once open, the bottle should be kept in a bucket filled with ice and water. You should not serve champagne in flat champagne glasses, but instead in clear, slender, tulip-shaped, crystal glasses with a stem long enough to ensure that the body heat of the hand is not transmitted to the bowl.

THE COMMUNES AND WINE VILLAGES

The unique character of Champagne and its wines lies in the fact that, over the last two centuries, its protagonists have built up a tremendously strong corporate identity from an *appellation*, a method—BOTTLE FERMENTATION—and a product conceived like a brand. There are no fluctuations between locations and vintages, and those wine-specific attributes such as origin, grape variety, producer, and VINTAGE do not apply.

Champagne is first and foremost a landscape, a geographical area, and a designated *appellation*—the only significant French wine region which has a single, albeit tremendously popular and strong *appellation*. As in all top French wine regions, Champagne has its own specific, classified *terroirs* and *crus*. Although the majority of its bottled products come from blends of different wines and different vintages, such classification details are only very rarely listed on the labels. What is relevant, however, is how prices are set for grapes from the different areas and communes in the wine region, the best prices being paid for grapes from the *grands crus* and then for those from the *premiers crus*.

This is based on the subdivision of the entire *Champagne viticole* into five natural areas with different conditions, each of which favors different grape varieties, namely: the Montagne de Reims, the Marne Valley, the Côte des Blancs, the Côte de Sézanne and the Côte des Bar in the Aube. The vineyards on the northern and eastern slopes of the Montagne de Reims are chiefly planted on sandy, clayey soil on chalk cliffs, sandstone, and

In Cuis, one of the Côte des Blancs villages, the champagnes are made exclusively from the white Chardonnay grape and are noted for their striking freshness.

The house of the champagne producer is evidence of its glorious past.

marl. Marl and sandy clay form the topsoil in the Marne Valley, while on the Côte des Blancs, sand and clay on chalk cliffs predominate. On the Côte de Sézanne, marl, clay and sand lie on chalk, while in the Aube, gravelly limestone soil is dominant.

GRANDS AND PREMIERS CRUS

The vineyards of 17 communes in total—Montagne de Reims (nine), the Côte des Blancs (four) and the Marne Valley (four)—have *grand cru* status and growers in these communes are paid 100 percent of the agreed prices for their grapes.

There are a further 38 communes, amounting to just 12,000 acres (5,000 hectares), whose vineyards have *premier cru* status and growers in these communes receive between 90 and 99 percent of the full price for their grapes. Very few of the communes are known to the consumer or even feature on the labels (for example, the Clos des Goisses of the Philipponnat house). One of the most famous examples is the Clos du Mesnil vineyard belonging to the Krug house, which produces a champagne made solely from Chardonnay grapes from the house's own vineyard in Le Mesnil-sur-Oger, which grows only this variety. In the higher areas of this location, the grapes make particularly dense, aromatic

The still wines of Champagne

The overwhelming dominance of sparkling wine in Champagne makes it easy to forget that the region also produces some still wines. Under the Coteaux Champenois *appellation*, white, red, and rosé wines are produced, but these are often reserved for weak years.

By nature, the climate is not suitable for the production of powerful, expressive wines, but in good years interesting, fruity wines with good acidity can be produced. These include wines made by renowned Champagne houses such as Bollinger, Moët et Chandon, and Ruinart. In addition to good, but often extremely expensive Chardonnay whites, the red Coteaux Champenois wines are particularly worth mentioning—drunk chilled, these are superb accompaniments to fish dishes.

A rarity is the still Rosé des Riceys from the commune of Riceys in the Aube, made purely from Pinot Noir grapes, which is surprisingly aromatic and fruity. The town of Bouzy on the Montagne de Reims is the best source for these delicate, light-colored reds, which are only of any real interest in the sunniest years. Coteaux Champenois reds are also made from Pinot Noir grapes in Ambonnay, Aÿ, and Cumières.

champagne, full of finesse. The person who discovered their qualities was Eugène-Aimé Salon, the founder of the house of the same name, which today still produces one of the best champagnes in the area from local grapes.

Similar (almost) pure Chardonnay champagne is also produced in other communes in the Côte des Blancs, where famous Champagne houses such as Veuve Clicquot-Ponsardin, Moët et Chandon, Mumm, Perrier-Jouët, Heidsieck Monopole, Pommery & Greno, Pol Roger, and Taittinger all have their own vineyards, but where the wines are seldom bottled as single-varietal or from a single village. By far the most popular are the *cuvées de prestige*, which are made almost exclusively from grapes from *grand cru* communes, but in which grapes are also used from communes where Pinot Noir is the dominant variety at over 80 percent. Examples of such *cuvées de prestige* are Bollinger's R.D., Laurent-Perrier's Cuvée Grand Siècle, Roederer's Cristal, Ruinart's Dom Ruinart, Moët et Chandon's Dom Pérignon, Deutz's Cuvée William Deutz, and Pol Roger's Winston Churchill. Made from particularly high-value wines, often fermented or stored in wooden barrels, which mature over many months on the lees, and whose structure and balance also imply great aging potential, such *cuvées de prestige* represent the very best champagnes—rare and costly, but also expensive jewels for special celebrations.

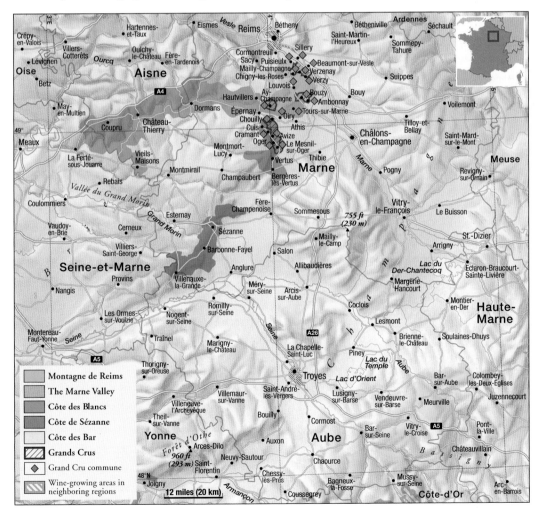

Montagne de Reims
The Marne Valley
Côte des Blancs
Côte de Sézanne
Côte des Bar
Grands Crus
Grand Cru commune
Wine-growing areas in neighboring regions

12 miles (20 km)

Chalk Cellars and Millions of Bottles

Unlike any other wine region, in Champagne the name of the product is linked with a specific production process—in this case, bottle fermentation, which is also known as the champagne method or *méthode champenoise*. With its numerous, strictly regulated procedures, the production of champagne is one of the most complex in the wine world.

The rules with which growers must comply begin in the vineyard itself. The maximum yield is 89 to 98 pounds per acre (100 to 110 kg per hectare), and this limit may be increased by the regulatory authorities in specific years—although many critics feel it is too high to be able to guarantee base wines that are both concentrated and structured. The must yield in PRESSING is also regulated, to prevent any undesired color or taste transferring from the grapes to the must by overly-strong pressing.

Grapes must be harvested by hand. Mechanical harvesters are forbidden in order to prevent

For the most famous Champagnes, the base wines are stored in wooden barrels and so some houses still employ their own coopers.

premature crushing and fermenting of the grapes, and to keep both the astringency and color of the must to a minimum. The harvested grapes are taken as quickly as possible to one of the many pressing centers belonging to the big champagne houses and cooperatives. The traditional round, very flat wicker winepresses, which still take precedence over modern pneumatic presses, can hold 8,818 pounds (4,000 kg) of grapes, (a quantity known as a MARC). The first and best must extracted from the grapes is known as the *cuvée*—this is mostly used to make the highest value wines. The rules state that a maximum of $26^1/2$ gallons (100 liters) of juice can be made from 350 pounds (160 kg) of grapes and thus, from the 8,818 pounds (4,000 kg) in a press, 660 gallons (2,500 liters) of wine may be made, the *cuvée* accounting for four-fifths of this. The next amount of the juice extracted from the *marc* is known as the *première taille*, followed by the

deuxième taille. These pressings show higher pH and TANNIN levels and are only used in ordinary champagne brands.

MÉTHODE CHAMPENOISE

After pressing, the must is purified, sulfurized, occasionally also clarified and afterwards fermented, by which time almost all base wines will have undergone MALOLACTIC FERMENTATION. FERMENTATION takes place mostly in temperature-controlled stainless steel vats. Only at the famous brands of Krug, Alfred Gratien, and Bollinger are the once-common wooden casks still used systematically. A number of wine growers who have only a limited variety of different *terroir* characteristics available, can still give their wines some complexity by aging them partly in wood. This will provide some oxygenation to the wine, which assists in harmonizing flavor, but under no circumstances does it involve imparting the vanilla or smoky notes of barrel-fermented Chardonnay.

After a certain amount of aging, there follows one of the most important stages in making champagne, the ASSEMBLAGE process, which is the true art of the cellar-master and the closely guarded secret of each champagne house or grower. The base wines from Chardonnay, Pinot Noir, and Pinot Meunier grapes are blended, and wines from different vineyards and even from different vintages are also used, unless a VINTAGE (*millésimé*) champagne is involved.

The aim is to produce, every year, a champagne which matches the brand as closely as

Left
At Ruinart in Reims, a model shows how the cellar was originally arranged.

Right
The champagnes develop their special finish in almost endless chalk cellars.

possible. It is primarily through the addition of wines from earlier vintages, the *vins de réserve* (reserve wines), that balanced, complex endproducts are achieved.

The wine which is the result of the *assemblage* process is then put into bottles with a mixture of wine, YEAST, and sugar, known as the bottling liquor or *liqueur de tirage*, and the bottles are capped with a crown cork. The sugar added at this stage is not for sweetening purposes—this comes later—but is used solely to feed the yeast, to ensure complete fermentation of the base wine. Approximately 1.5 percent vol of additional alcoholic strength may result from the second fermentation which takes place completely in the bottle, the real crux of the *méthode champenoise*, whereby the internal pressure of the bottle reaches four to six atmospheres through the carbon dioxide building up, at the same time as the alcohol.

The second fermentation ideally takes place at very cold, stable temperatures—conditions which are especially found in the chalk cellars used by some houses such as Charles Heidsieck. Some of these tunnels are occasionally open to visitors, and with their white walls, against which hundreds of thousands of bottles are stacked carefully waiting for the completion of their yeast fermentation, cellars are a spectacular sight.

In addition to the production of alcohol, the yeast also has an important function in contributing to taste. After complete fermentation, the yeast slowly begins to decompose—a process known as yeast autolysis—and forms a series of

Champagne has always had a luxurious ambience—and this also applies in its homeland.

always lie steeply in the rack. Today, machines are used for this purpose and complete the same work in a shorter time and without requiring the same level of technical input from specialists. Some houses still have at least their *cuvées de prestige* riddled by hand, although there is no conclusive evidence that machine *remuage* results in a reduction in quality.

Ordinary brand champagnes are then made ready for sale, while the better *cuvées* remain for a certain time, sometimes several years *sur pointe* while the wine matures further. The last step in creating champagne is the process known as DISGORGEMENT (*dégorgement*), which was previously done by hand (*à la volée*) but is mostly done by machine today. This removes the yeast deposits that have collected in the neck of the bottle during the riddling process. The neck of the bottle, containing the yeast deposit, is frozen in a liquid coolant (salt solution) and the bottle is then opened. The pressure in the bottle shoots out the sediment.

To top up the wine lost in the disgorgement process, a *liqueur d'expédition* or dosage is added to the wine, which also serves to balance the sweetness of the finished wine. Mostly this dosage is a mixture of the base wine and sugar syrup, the amount of additional sugar used determining the sweetness (*brut, sec, doux*, etc.) of the wine. After corking and attaching the metal cap and wire muzzle, labeling and packing, the champagne is finally ready for that special party, glittering ball, celebration of success at work, wedding, anniversary, or special birthday.

fragrant and flavorsome substances which enrich and round off the champagne. At the same time, the carbon dioxide created during the second fermentation gets better and finer in the wine, so a particularly long storage time leads to the finest and longest-lasting fizziness in the glass.

"LIQUEUR" IN WINE?

When the sparkling wine has almost reached its desired maturity, the yeast deposit, which over the months has dropped to the bottom of the bottle, is carefully moved to its neck. This process of riddling or *remuage* was once done manually, with the bottles placed head down in special riddling racks (*pupitres*) and turned slightly every two days, so that one part would

Types of champagne

Extra-brut: also known as *brut non dosé, brut nature, ultra-brut, brut zéro, brut intégral:* this is a champagne made with no dosage, which naturally has less than 0.04 ounces per pint (2 g per liter) of RESIDUAL SUGAR.

Brut: this dry champagne has a low dosage, up to a maximum permitted level of ¼ ounce per pint (15 g per liter) of additional sugar.

Sec: although the name means dry, the *liqueur d'expédition* in this case gives it a sugar content of just over ¼ to ½ ounce per pint (17–35 g per liter).

Demi-sec: primarily designed as a dessert wine, the sugar content of this sweet wine is ½ to 1 ounce per pint (35–50 g per liter).

Doux: the sugar content of this rare, very sweet champagne is anything over 1 ounce per pint (50 g per liter).

Brut sans millésime: this bone-dry, non-vintage is the signature of each brand of champagne, because it represents 80 percent of total turnover. Varies widely.

Blanc de Blancs: made exclusively from white Chardonnay grapes, as a rule this is fresh and lively and a good aperitif.

Blanc de Noirs: made exclusively from black Pinot Noir or Pinot Meunier grapes, this has stronger structure and fruitiness.

Crémant: champagne which is semi-sparkling and more winey; that from Cramant is the most sought after, not to be confused with *crémants* from other regions.

Rosé: or pink champagne is seldom made from black grapes with some skin contact, but is more often a mixture of red and white wine; often more powerful and fruitier than white, it is good with food.

Millésimé: vintage champagnes come only from years in which conditions have been particularly good. They are aged for three and often six years, have more volume and body, and mature well for several more years in the bottle.

Cuvée de Prestige, etc.: these are the deluxe wines of the champagne houses. For the most part, they are long matured wines from an outstanding vintage—some of which have legendary reputations—and naturally, prices to match.

Ruinart—light, nervy, refreshing

Deutz—lively, nervy, good with seafood

De Venoge—fruity tones, pleasant aperitif

Lanson—citrus notes, crisp

Pommery—winey, harmonious, and fresh

Veuve Clicquot Ponsardin—aromatic, fine fruit

Laurent Perrier—complex, fruity tones, lively

Pol Roger—harmony, elegance, complex aroma

Piper Heidsieck—classic, balanced

Jacquard—complex bouquet and good length

Krug Grand Cuvée—a wine full of finesse

Louis Roederer—fine fruit, balanced, and elegant

Moët et Chandon—straight, consistent

Ayala Brut—delicate bouquet, good fizz

Taittinger—fruity, good mouthfeel

BILLECART-SALMON***−*****
AŸ
27 acres (11 ha); 1,200,000 bottles • Wines: Grande Cuvée, Blanc de Blancs, →Nicolas-François Billecart Brut, Elisabeth Salmon, Brut Réserve, Brut Rosé
The vintage Nicolas-François Billecart champagnes of this family-owned house are the best.

BOLLINGER*****
AŸ
320 acres (130 ha); 1,600,000 bottles • Wines: Grande Année Brut →R.D. Extra Brut, →Cuvée Vieilles Vignes Françaises
This house, founded in 1829 by Jacques Joseph Placide Bollinger, from Württemberg, makes one of the few wines which is still fermented in barrels, with some oxidation, and matures very well. Its R.D. Extra Brut is one of the best champagnes of all.

DEUTZ****
AŸ
74 acres (30 ha) some bought-in grapes; 1,000,000 bottles • Wines: Amour de Deutz, Brut Classic, Brut Millésimé, Brut Blanc de Blancs, Brut Millésimé Demi-Sec →Cuvée William Deutz
Once known as Deutz and Geldermann, this house was founded in 1838 by two men from Aachen. After the family branch split (the Geldermann champagne winery and the château de l'Aulée went to J.-R. Lallier), Deutz, which also owns the northern Rhône Delas-Frères house, was incorporated into the Roederer champagne house.

EGLY-OURIET****
AMBONNAY
22 acres (9 ha); 68,000 bottles • Wines: Brut Tradition, Brut Rosé, Brut Cuvée Spéciale, Brut Blanc de Noirs, →Brut Millésimé, →Coteaux Champenois
One of the best champagne wine producers, which also produces an outstanding red Coteaux Champenois.

FLEURY PÈRE ET FILS***
COURTENON
32 acres (13 ha); 175,000 bottles • Wines: Brut Millésimé, →Fleur de l'Europe, →Rosé Brut, →Robert Fleury
Even in 1970 Jean-Pierre and Colette Fleury were champions of natural production methods. In 1989 they established BIODYNAMIC CULTIVATION, and with their lively Fleur de l'Europe have produced the first biodynamic champagne.

PIERRE GIMONNET****
CUIS
211 acres (26 ha); 200,000 bottles • Wines include: Brut Club Premier Cru, →Extra Brut Oenophile; →Brut Fleuron Premier Cru, →Millésimé de Collection
All the Gimmonet family's vineyards are on the Côte des Blancs; they therefore specialize in Blanc de Blancs, and their wines display great finesse.

GOSSET****
AŸ
1,000,000 bottles • Wines: →Brut Excellence, Grande Réserve, →Celebris, Grand Millésimé, Grand Rosé
Gosset champagne is pressed mostly from black grapes, which gives it a good structure and a delicate bouquet. The aroma of Celebris combines dried fruit and apricot notes. Ripe fruit and a special creaminess make this *cuvée* into a *champagne de table* par excellence.

A. GRATIEN***−****
ÉPERNAY
170,000 bottles • Wines: Brut, Cuvée Paradis, →Millésimé
One of the traditionally-run houses of Épernay, not very well known abroad, which has consistently good products.

CHARLES HEIDSIECK***−****
REIMS
120 acres (50 ha); 2,000,000 bottles • Wines: Brut Réserve, →Charlie, Blanc des Millénaires
This house in Reims has beautiful chalk cellars and belongs to the most reliable name in the luxury sector. Founded in 1785 by Florens-Louis Heidsieck, the parent company split in the 19th century into Heidsieck Monopole and Piper-Heidsieck, Charles Heidsieck coming from the latter.

JACQUESSON****
DIZY
99 acres (40 ha); 350,000 bottles • Wines: Brut Perfection, →Blanc de Blancs, Grand Vin Signature
In the 19th century, this family firm, founded in 1798, produced up to a million bottles a year. Today, though output is much lower, it produces a small but very reliable range of wines, including the well matured Signature vintage champagne, which has an excellent potential for aging.

KRUG*****
REIMS
52 acres (21 ha); 500,000 bottles • Wines: Grande Cuvée, →Clos du Mesnil, Collection, →Millésimé, →Brut Rosé
The epitome of champagne. Founded in 1843 by Johann-Joseph Krug, from Mainz, Germany, the house is now majority-owned by Louis Vuitton, but is still run by the family. Its Blanc de Blancs from the *grand cru* Clos du Mesnil commune and its Millésimé are two of the highlights of champagne.

LANSON**−****
REIMS
4,216 acres (520 ha); 7,000,000 bottles • Wines: Black Label, Blanc de Blancs Brut; Gold Label Millésimé, Grande Cuvée.
The history of this great name goes back to the year 1760. Today its extensive vineyards supply grapes for the Marne et Champagne group. Black Label is distinguished by freshness and body, while the Grande Cuvée is in the champagne top league.

LAURENT-PERRIER***−*****
TOUR-SUR-MARNE
247 acres (100 ha); 6,000,000 bottles • Wines: Brut, Ultra Brut, Grand Siècle, →Grande Siècle La Cuvée
This old family firm—one of the few names surviving from the influx of German champagne entrepreneurs in the 19th century—has had its first real success in recent decades under the management of Bertrand de Nonancourt.

MOËT & CHANDON***−*****
ÉPERNAY
1,903 acres (770 ha); 30,000,000 bottles • Wines: Brut, Brut Premier Cru, Brut Impérial, Dry Impérial, →Dom Pérignon
This giant from Épernay is one of the flagships of the L.V.M.H. Group. Its Dom Pérignon is one of the best champagnes of all.

MUMM***
REIMS
469 acres (190 ha); 8,000,000 bottles • Wines: Cordon Rouge, Cordon Rouge Millésimé, Cordon Rosé, Mumm de Cramant
This house, founded by two Germans in 1827, is part of the Allied Domecq group and now appears to be more concerned with quality. Its Cordon Rouge is probably one of the best-known champagnes.

PHILIPPONNAT***–****
AŸ
40 acres (16 ha); 600,000 bottles • Wines: Brut Royal Réserve, Royal Réserve Rosé, Royal Réserve Millésimé, Cuvée Première Blanc de Blancs, →Clos des Goisses
Good reserve wines are the secret of the Philipponnat champagnes, which are very harmonious and mature. Its top wine is its Clos des Goisses champagne made entirely from Chardonnay grapes.

POL ROGER***–****
ÉPERNAY
457 acres (185 ha); 1,600,000 bottles • Wines: Brut Réserve, Brut Millésimé, Brut Chardonnay, →Cuvée Sir Winston Churchill
Mature champagne with good aging potential is the specialty of the Pol Roger family, whose top *cuvée* was Winston Churchill's favorite wine.

POMMERY***–****
REIMS
Some bought-in grapes; 5,800,000 bottles • Wines: Brut Premier, Brut Rosé, Brut Millésimé, →Blanc de Blancs Summertime, →Louise Pommery.
This famous house, founded in 1836, once rose to prominence under the widow Louise. It is now preparing for a renaissance in the hands of Paul-François Vranken.

LOUIS ROEDERER****
REIMS
490 acres (200 ha); 2,600,000 bottles • Wines: Brut Premier, →Cristal Brut, →Brut Millésimé, Blanc de Blancs Millésimé, Brut Rosé Millésimé
The Russian Czars used to drink Cristal champagne from the Roederer house, founded in 1760. Roederer champagnes are convincing, with their almost purist character and structure.

RUINART***–****
REIMS
2,100,000 bottles • Wines: R de Ruinart Brut, R. de Ruinart Rosé, R. de Ruinart Millésimé, Brut Millésimé, Brut Millésimé Blanc de Blancs, →Dom Ruinart Blanc de Blancs, Dom Ruinart Rosé
The oldest surviving champagne house has belonged for several years now to the Louis Vuitton group.

SALON****
LE MESNIL-SUR-OGER
4 acres (1.5 ha) 80,000 bottles • Wines: →Salon Brut Millésimé
Salon's vintage wines are deemed by almost all connoisseurs to be the best Blancs de Blancs. They are only produced in outstanding years. Like the neighboring Delamotte house, Salon is part of Laurent-Perrier.

JACQUES SELOSSE****
AVIZE
16 acres (6.3 ha); 48,000 bottles • Wines: Grand Cru Blanc de Blancs Tradition, →Extra Brut, →Blanc de Noirs Brut Contraste, →Grand Cru Substance
This star among Champagne's *récoltants-manipulants* shines with its Cuvée Substance (previously known as

Origine), which it puts together from reserve wines matured using the Solera system. Using biodynamic cultivation methods and intuition, Selosse champagnes are the perfect expression of *terroir* and vintage.

DE SOUSA****
AVIZE
57 acres (7 ha); 60,000 bottles • Wines: Brut Tradition, Rosé Brut; Blanc de Blancs Millésimé, Millénaire, Caudalies and Reserve.
In only a few years, Erick de Sousa has risen to be one of the best *récoltants-manipulants* with his full bodied-wines.

TAITTINGER***–*****
REIMS
670 acres (270 ha); 5,000,000 bottles • Wines: Réserve, Taittinger Brut Millésimé, →Comtes de Champagne Blanc de Blancs
One of the last champagne houses still completely in private ownership, and with 5 million bottles, also one of the largest. Taittinger shines in particular with its Chardonnay champagne, Comtes de Champagne, which connoisseurs reckon in good years is better than Krug's famous Clos du Mesnil.

TARLANT***
ŒUILLY
32 acres (13 ha); 100,000 bottles • Wines include: Brut Tradition, Brut Blanc de Blancs, Reserve, Prestige Millésimé, Brut Zero, →Cuvée Louis Brut, Rosé
This is now the twelfth generation of this old wine family. It runs its vineyards organically and produces pure-colored fruity wines. Its Cuvée Louis, made in wooden casks, is convincing.

VEUVE CLICQUOT PONSARDIN**–*****
REIMS
710 acres (286 ha) • Wines: Brut Carte Jaune →La Grande Dame, Vintage Reserve
The Widow Clicquot really existed and one of her cellar-masters, a German by the name of Müller, contributed as much to the development and completion of the *méthode champenoise* as Dom Pérignon. This house's Carte Jaune is one of the most popular brands and Grande Dame, its top *cuvée*, is one of the finest and most complex champagnes.

Below
In the 19th century, champagne houses displayed their success in brick and marble.

ALSACE

Alsace captivates the visitor in a way that hardly any other of France's wine regions can. Between the plains of the Rhine and the Vosges mountains lie Eguisheim and Riquewihr, Ribeauvillé and Mittelbergheim—magnificent Renaissance villages which testify to the prosperity of the wine producers of the 15th and 16th centuries, when Alsace wines were exported successfully throughout Europe.

Alsace wines are not governed by the French wine laws, not least because the region was for a long time part of Germany, and has only been an undisputed part of France since 1945. There are just three designations of origin (*Appellation d'Origine Contrôlée*), each of which applies to the whole region: one for the grape variety wines, one for the *grands crus* and one for the Crémant d'Alsace sparkling wine. The grape variety structure also differs from that of other French wine-growing areas, being closer to that of the wine regions on the other side of the Rhine, in Germany.

Approximately 35,700 acres (14,450 ha) of vines are planted along the 105-mile (170-km) *Route du Vin*. The wine route winds its way past vineyard upon vineyard between Thann in the south and Marlenheim in the north, with a tiny enclave situated high in the north of Alsace, near Wissembourg. Around 32 million gallons (1.2 million hectoliters) or 160 million bottles of wine are produced each year. Only eight percent of the total is produced using red grapes, making Alsace predominantly a white wine area.

Culture, gastronomy, and wine are all interwoven in Alsace.

Alsace is a place where traditions are preserved, and this applies equally to wine.

DIVERSE SOIL TYPES PROTECTED BY THE VOSGES MOUNTAINS

When the middle part of an earlier massif began to sink 50 million years ago, the parts that survived were the Vosges on the western side of the mountain range, and the Black Forest on the eastern side. The Rhine river now flows through the middle, but the vineyards extend further west, along the lower slopes of the Vosges. The mountains provide warm, protected climatic conditions and keep precipitation at bay. Because of the rift valley that was created, different geological formations came to the surface in Alsace: sand, pebbles, marl, loess, limestone, clay, slate, granite, and even volcanic rock—the Rangen vineyard to the south of Thann is renowned for this type of subsoil. The character of the wines differs according to the type of soil in which the grapes are grown. Anyone tasting Alsace wines will quickly learn that a Gewürztraminer from a granite soil tastes different than one grown in a maritime shale and limestone base.

The diversity of soil types is also reflected in the *grands crus*, the vineyards classified as being the very best, currently numbering 50. They have been selected and delineated, following long discussions, since the 1970s. Up until now, only the Riesling, Muscat, Tokay d'Alsace, and Gewürztraminer grape varieties could be sold as *grand cru*. Theoretically, however, other grape varieties are now permitted for certain *grand cru* vineyards. While the basic maximum yield for ordinary Alsace wines is 2,113 gallons (80 hectoliters) per hectare (1,981 gallons/75 hl for Pinot Noir), it is 1,453 gallons (55 hectoliters) for *grands crus*.

Below right
Sunshine and mist, responsible for the region's late-harvested sweet wines.

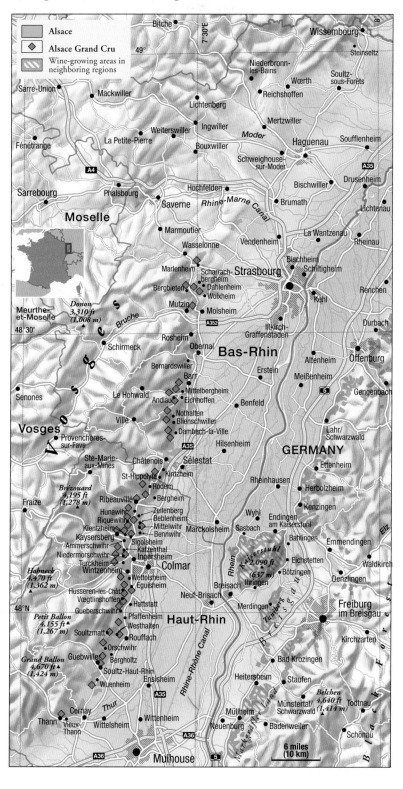

ESTABLISHED HOUSES AND COMMITTED NEWCOMERS

The traditional merchants, or NÉGOCIANTS, still play an important role in the wine production of Alsace. Many of them came into being during the 17th and 18th centuries, when politically unsettled times put an end to the upturn that had been taking place in wine growing. During this time the merchants started buying grapes, must or wine from small growers, thus making their existence secure, and took over the job of MATURING and marketing the wines themselves. Trimbach, Hugel, and Beyer are three of the best-known *négociants*, and their importance in terms of wine production in Alsace remains immense.

The cooperatives form another of the region's mainstays. The first to be formed was the Cave Vinicole de Ribeauvillé, in 1895, and soon after wine producers throughout the region formed themselves into similar groups. Today the enormous Eguisheim cooperative (using the name Wolfberger) produces a tenth of the entire output of Alsace wine from around 3,090 acres (1,250 hectares). That enormous concerns like this are unable to offer exclusively first-class growths is only to be expected. What is astonishing, though, is the level of success many of these cooperative wines achieve in terms of awards. A prime example is the Cave Vinicole de Pfaffenheim, which is now one of the region's best products.

Alongside the *négociants* and cooperatives, the 1,100 wine producers who market their own wines have been attracting increasing attention for a number of years. They often reduce their yields to a level well below the permitted upper

limits, or adopt ideas from other regions of France. Thus red wine has made its debut over the last few years. While Pinot Noir was already cultivated here, it was almost always made into a hybrid between rosé and red wine, which would be served chilled. Now a number of winegrowers are trying to produce real reds, and are experimenting with longer must fermentation and storage in barrels. Maturation in BARRIQUES, which imparts various degrees of oak flavor to the wine, has also become fashionable over the last few years. Several of the Pinot Noir wines matured in this way are a match for the great red Burgundies. Many winegrowers are also turning their attention to white wines fermented in *barriques*—here and there the visitor to Alsace is likely to come across Pinot Gris or Sylvaner wines that have spent a few months in barrels of this sort. Pinot Noir is also being commercially produced in small quantities as a white Blanc de Noirs.

Rodern, one of the most beautiful wine villages, revealing the checkerboard pattern of its vineyards.

RENAISSANCE OF THE SPARKLING WINES

The specialty sweet wines, the *vendanges tardives* (late-harvested wines) and *sélections de grains nobles* (produced from even riper grapes), have experienced an upswing over the last few years. Another innovation in wine production in Alsace, at least as successful, is the Crémant d'Alsace sparkling wine. Although it was produced in a few small areas by the end of the 19th century, official recognition only dates from 1976. *Crémants* are produced using the classic bottle fermentation process exclusively, spend at least nine months on their yeast, and consist primarily of the Pinot Blanc, Pinot Gris, and Sylvaner grape varieties, and occasionally Chardonnay (which is permitted to be used only in the production of sparkling wine in Alsace). Riesling is seldom used. Within a few

years, Crémant d'Alsace has developed into a winner both in France and as an export, and 14 percent of all Alsace wines are now sparkling.

However, another category of wines with a rich tradition is currently in free fall. The Edelzwicker which, in the early 20th century, was a high-quality *cuvée* or blend of noble grape varieties, is of little consequence now. In winemaking of the last few decades, this wine has mutated into the "garbage can" of the Alsace winegrowers. Only a few demanding producers (e.g. Hugel) offer Edelzwicker today, and those who do often use the French name Gentil, which has not yet become debased.

The Seven Grapes of Alsace

Nearly all still Alsace wines are single-varietal wines. In general, reference is made to just seven Alsace grape varieties: Riesling, Gewürztraminer, Muscat, Pinot Gris, Sylvaner, Pinot Blanc, and Pinot Noir, the sole red variety. But others, whose names can be read on labels from time to time, do exist. Chasselas used to be widespread, but today only covers a few acres. It usually produces a neutral everyday wine and can therefore be ranked alongside Sylvaner and Pinot Blanc. Very seldom do these three grape varieties attract the sort of attention given to the noble Riesling, Gewürztraminer, Muscat, and Pinot Gris varieties. The latter was once known exclusively as Tokay d'Alsace, although it is not related to its Hungarian namesake. The term Tokay may now be used only to designate Pinot Gris wines, and from 2006 on, it will have disappeared for good.

The name Muscat actually embraces two different varieties: Muscat Blanc à Petits Grains and Muscat Ottonel, which are almost always blended together. The same is true of Pinot

Blanc: true Pinot Blanc and Auxerrois are usually blended and only occasionally drawn off independently to produce single-varietal wines. Production of Klevener de Heiligenstein, a less flowery relative of Gewürztraminer, is permitted only within the limits of the Heiligenstein commune. The name Klevner, on the other hand (without the second e) is commonly used as a synonym for Pinot Blanc.

SWEET OR DRY?

Whether an Alsace wine is dry or sweet is not stated on the label. While Sylvaner and Pinot Blanc wines are almost always thoroughly fermented, and most Muscats also reach the bottle without any great degree of sweetness, this is not true of the Riesling, Pinot Gris, and Gewürztraminer varieties. A few growers (e.g. Trimbach) are known for their consistently dry style, but many *grand cru* wines have a distinct residual sweetness that balances out the alcohol levels of 13 or 14 percent.

Alsace has a long tradition of very sweet wines, made from ripe and very ripe grapes and were already produced hundreds of years ago. However, growers have been producing them on a large scale for only a few years. In 1984 the French authority in charge of the *appellation* system, the I.N.A.O., laid down official requirements for them. For the *vendange tardive* or late-harvested wines, they stipulate a specific must gravity of at least 95° on the OECHSLE scale. *Sélection de grains nobles* wines, produced from even riper grapes, can only be produced using grapes that reach a minimum of 110°. Growers with a greater commitment to quality, however, frequently exceed the official SPECIFIC GRAVITY levels by considerable amounts.

Hand-picking.

Left
Pinot Gris grapes affected by noble rot.

Right
Ripe Gewürztraminer grapes.

The addition of sugar to either class of sweet wine is forbidden, even though this is a perfectly legal and customary practice for all other Alsace wines. Compared to the world-famous German *Beerenauslese* and *Trockenbeerenauslese* wines, the sweet wines of Alsace usually have rather less residual sugar and therefore more alcohol. In this respect they have a greater resemblance to their counterparts from Sauternes.

Vin de paille (traditionally made from grapes dried on beds of straw) and *vin de glace* (made from grapes naturally frozen on the vine) are very rarely encountered in Alsace: only a handful of dedicated wine producers are bold enough to experiment with these particular sweet specialties.

GRANDS CRUS AND OTHER NAMED VINEYARD WINES

Up to now, only the four noble grape varieties (Riesling, Gewürztraminer, Muscat, and Pinot Gris), and only three percent of all the region's wines, have been permitted to use the *grand cru* designation. However, discussions over the classification of the top vineyards, which began in 1975, continue to this day. It is said that many of them have become too large, and that other vineyards widely recognized as being among the best were not even included in the classification. Thus the renowned Kaefferkopf in Ammerschwihr has still not been made a *grand cru*—the reason for this being the lack of uniformity of the vineyard, which comprises various soil types. Other vineyards have failed to win a classification because they are all owned by the same grower.

Generally speaking, however, the Alsace *grand cru* classification is a useful tool in the identification of top wines. Other named vineyard wines have managed to get established in its wake, and there are many above-average wines in the ranks of these *lieux-dits* or named locality wines that offer significantly better value than a *grand cru*.

The 50 *grands crus* of Alsace

Vineyard and locality	Geological characteristics
Altenberg de Bergbieten	clay marl containing natural gypsum
Altenberg de Bergheim	limestone marl
Altenberg de Wolxheim	limestone marl
Brand (Turckheim)	granite
Bruderthal (Molsheim)	limestone marl
Eichberg (Eguisheim)	limestone marl
Engelberg (Dahlenheim and Scharrachbergheim)	limestone marl
Florimont (Ingersheim and Katzenthal)	limestone marl
Frankstein (Dambach-la-Ville)	granite
Froehn (Zellenberg)	clay marl
Furstentum (Kientzheim and Sigolsheim)	limestone
Geisberg (Ribeauvillé)	limestone marl and sand
Gloeckelberg (Rodern and Saint-Hippolyte)	granite and clay
Goldert (Gueberschwihr)	limestone marl
Hatschbourg (Voegtlinshoffen and Hattstatt)	limestone marl and loess
Hengst (Wintzenheim)	limestone marl and sandstone
Kanzlerberg (Bergheim)	clay marl containing natural gypsum
Kastelberg (Andlau)	slate
Kessler (Guebwiller)	sand with clay
Kirchberg de Barr	limestone marl
Kirchberg de Ribeauvillé	limestone marl and sandstone
Kitterlé (Guebwiller)	volcanic sandstone
Mambourg (Sigolsheim)	limestone marl
Mandelberg (Mittelwihr and Beblenheim)	limestone marl
Marckrain (Bennwihr and Sigolsheim)	limestone marl
Moenchberg (Andlau and Eichhoffen)	limestone marl and alluvium
Muenchberg (Nothalten)	stony volcanic sandstone
Ollwiller (Wuenheim)	sand with clay
Osterberg (Ribeauvillé)	marl
Pfersigberg (Eguisheim and Wettolsheim)	chalky sandstone
Pfingstberg (Orschwihr)	limestone marl and sandstone
Praelatenberg (Kintzheim)	granite and gneiss
Rangen (Thann and Vieux-Thann)	volcanic
Rosacker (Hunawihr)	dolomite limestone
Saering (Guebwiller)	limestone marl and sandstone
Schlossberg (Kientzheim)	granite
Schoenenbourg (Riquewihr and Zellenberg)	marl containing sand and gypsum
Sommerberg (Niedermorschwihr und Katzenthal)	granite
Sonnenglanz (Beblenheim)	limestone marl
Spiegel (Bergholtz and Guebwiller)	clay marl and sandstone
Sporen (Riquewihr)	stony clay marl
Steinert (Pfaffenheim and Westhalten)	limestone
Steingrubler (Wettolsheim)	limestone marl and sandstone
Steinklotz (Marlenheim)	limestone
Vorbourg (Rouffach und Westhalten)	limestone and sandstone
Wiebelsberg (Andlau)	quartz and sandstone
Wineck-Schlossberg (Katzenthal and Ammerschwihr)	granite
Winzenberg (Blienschwiller)	granite
Zinnkoepflé (Soultzmatt and Westhalten)	limestone and sandstone
Zotzenberg (Mittelbergheim)	limestone marl

Select Producers in Alsace

Albert Boxler***–****
Niedermorschwihr
25 acres (10 ha); 55,000 bottles • Wines include:
→ *Riesling Sommerberg, Riesling Brand, Riesling Vieilles Vignes, Gewürztraminer Brand, Pinot Gris, Muscat,* → *Vendanges Tardives*
Although this estate in remote Niedermorschwihr is not in the best position, it has long outgrown its status as a hot tip. Jean-Marc Boxler's concentrated and juicy Rieslings are among the longest-lived in Alsace.

Ernest Burn***–****
Gueberschwihr
25 acres (10 ha); 60,000 bottles • Wines include: Gewürztraminer Clos Saint-Imer, Pinot Gris Clos Saint-Imer, → *Muscat Clos Saint-Imer,* → *Cuvées La Chapelle*
An unusual estate with unusual wines: opulent, concentrated, and juicy. Additionally, the top-quality *cuvées* from the Clos Saint-Imer plot (which is part of the Goldert *grand cru*) are marketed under the La Chapelle label.

Cave de Pfaffenheim*–****
Pfaffenheim
593 acres (240 ha); 2,000,000 bottles • Wines include: Gewürztraminer Zinnkoepflé, Gewürztraminer Steinert, Muscat Goldert, Pinot, Vendanges Tardives
Founded in 1957, this is the most committed of the Alsace wine cooperatives, and regularly sweeps the board in competitions. It produces elegant wines in a modern winery.

Marcel Deiss*****
Bergheim
49 acres (20 ha); 120,000 bottles • Wines include: Riesling Altenberg, → *Gewürztraminer Altenberg, Riesling Schoenenbourg,* → *Grand Vin d'Altenberg, Pinot Burlenberg Vieilles Vignes*
Jean-Michel Deiss is most at home in the vineyard, and this is the basis of his leading position among Alsace winegrowers. Yields are minimal and the wines uniquely concentrated. Even the simplest Sylvaners show finesse, and the rare and expensive Grand Vin, a *cuvée* or blend of Gewürztraminer, Riesling, and Pinot Gris, even more so.

Dirler-Cadé***
Bergholtz
138 acres (17 ha); 100,000 bottles • Wines include: Sylvaner Vieilles Vignes, Gentil, Muscat Spiegel, Gewürztraminer Kessler, Gewürztraminer Saering, Gewürztraminer Spiegel
Jean-Pierre Dirler's undisputed specialty is the Gewürztraminer. Here in the south of the Alsace wine route, it is particularly full-bodied and spicy. On this estate, cultivated according to biodynamic principles, the Sylvaner produced from old vines demonstrates this variety's potential.

Domaine Barmès-Buecher***–****
Wettolsheim
40 acres (16 ha); 90,000 bottles • Wines include: Riesling Hengst, Gewürztraminer Steingrubler, Pinot Gris Rosenberg; → *Pinot Vieilles Vignes, Vendanges Tardives, Sélections de Grains Nobles, Crémant d'Alsace*
François Barmès convinces with a style of wine that is unmistakable: natural fermentation with wild yeasts, crystal clear fruit, aging in steel tanks, and late bottling. The Vendanges Tardives always have a specific must gravity above the official minimum, and the Pinot, matured in *barriques*, is one of the region's great red wines.

Domaine Paul Blanck***–*****
Kientzheim
86 acres (35 ha); 220,000 bottles • Wines include: → *Riesling Schlossberg,* → *Riesling Furstentum, Pinot Gris Furstentum, Gewürztraminer Furstentum,* → *Vendanges Tardives, Sélections de Grains Nobles,* → *Pinot "F", Sylvaner*
The slender bottles used by this grower seldom contain anything but top-flight wine. Frédéric and Philippe Blanck age their dense Rieslings and Gewürztraminers in steel tanks. An exception is their red wine, which is matured in *barriques*.

Domaine Julien Meyer**–****
Nothalten
20 acres (8 ha); 60,000 bottles • Wines include: → *Riesling Muenchberg, Gewürztraminer Cuvée des Pucelles,* → *Sylvaner Zellberg, Pinot, Crémant*
Patrick Meyer experiments with malolactic fermentation, and storage in *barriques*, and even dispenses with filtration.

Domaine Schoffit***–*****
Colmar
37 acres (15 ha); 120,000 bottles • Wines include: → *Riesling Clos Saint-Théobald,* → *Gewürztraminer Clos Saint Théobald, Muscat,* → *Chasselas Vieilles Vignes*
Bernard Schoffit owns a parcel of land (Clos Saint-Théobald) in the Rangen vineyard, the southernmost and most famous of the *grand crus*. This winegrower benefits from the volcanic rock to make incredibly elegant and concentrated wines that are left to mature for a long time on the lees.

Domaine Weinbach****–*****
Kaysersberg
64 acres (26 ha); 130,000 bottles • Wines include: Gewürztraminer Furstentum, Riesling Schlossberg, Gewürztraminer Altenbourg, Riesling Cuvée Theo, → *Riesling Sélection de Grain Nobles,* → *Riesling Quintessence*
Colette Faller and her daughters run this imposing estate with great dedication. The Clos des Capuchins has been in the family since 1898. The name Quintessence, not officially classified, was introduced by the Fallers to denote outstanding sweet wines.

Pierre Frick***–****
Pfaffenheim
30 acres (12 ha); 80,000 bottles • Wines include: Sylvaner, Pinot Blanc, Muscat, → *Riesling Steinert,* → *Pinot Gris S.G.N.,* → *Gewürztraminer S.G.N.*
In 1981 this producer switched from organic to biodynamic methods, wholeheartedly supported by Pierre and Chantal Frick. Their wines, to which no extra sugar is added, disclose their grape variety and *terroir* with uncompromising clarity.

Hugel****
Riquewihr
61 acres (25 ha); bought-in grapes; 1,300,000 bottles • Wines include: → *Riesling Jubilée, Gewürztraminer Jubilée, Pinot Gris Jubilée, Muscat Tradition* → *Gentil,* → *Vendanges Tardives,* → *Sélections de Grains Nobles, Pinot Jubilée*
The firm of Hugel, stretching back 360 years, was one of the driving forces behind the *grand cru* system, but it no longer uses vineyard names on its wines today as it believes the classification to have been overly generous. The best wines, therefore, are called Jubilée, while the second best are known as Tradition. Gentil is the name given to one of the best Alsace Edelzwickers.

JOSMEYER**–****
WINTZENHEIM
61 acres (25 ha); bought-in grapes; 240,000 bottles
• *Wines include: Riesling Brand, 'Riesling Hengst, Riesling Le Kottabe 'Auxerrois "H", Pinot Blanc Mise du Printemps*
One of Jean Meyer's specialties is his Auxerrois, an unusually concentrated example of this grape variety, which grows in the Hengst vineyard (hence the "H").

ANDRÉ KIENTZLER***–****
RIBEAUVILLÉ
28 acres (11 ha); 80,000 bottles • *Wines include:*
→Riesling Greisberg, →Riesling Osterberg, Muscat Kirchberg, Pinot Gris Kirchberg, →Chasselas
André Kientzler produces concentrated, minerally wines in his modern winery buildings between Ribeauvillé and Bergheim. The long-lived Chasselas is one of the region's few successful wines to be made from this grape variety.

MARC KREYDENWEISS***–****
ANDLAU
30 acres (12 ha); 60,000 bottles • *Wines include:*
→Riesling Wiebelsberg, Pinot Gris Moenchberg, Gewürztraminer Kritt, →Riesling Kastelberg →Clos du Val d'Eléon, →Klevner Kritt, Pinot Blanc Kritt
Marc Kreydenweiss is completely committed to biodynamic wine production. His concentrated Rieslings, and rarities such as the Clos du Val d'Eléon (a blend of Riesling and Pinot Gris), or the mature Kritt Klevner (a pure variety of Auxerrois), are as remarkable as his modern tasting room.

SEPPI LANDMANN***–****
SOULTZMATT
21 acres (8.5 ha); 65,000 bottles • *Wines include:*
→Riesling Zinnkoepflé, →Gewürztraminer Zinnkoepflé, Pinot Gris Vallée Noble
Seppi Landmann's Vendanges Tardives and S.G.N. Zinnkoepflé Gewürztraminer are even more eloquent than he is, but even the simpler Rieslings, Pinot Gris, and Sylvaners reflect the vitality of this particular winegrower.

MEYER-FONNÉ***–*****
KATZENTHAL
25 acres (10 ha); 75,000 bottles • *Wines include:*
Gewürztraminer Kaefferkopf, Gewürztraminer Wineck-Schlossberg, Riesling Kaefferkopf, Riesling Wineck-Schlossberg, →Pinot Gris Hinterburg, →Muscat Tiré sur Lie, Pinot Noir
This estate, run by Félix Meyer, is still a well-kept secret, but his simultaneously dense and elegant Rieslings, Gewürztraminers, and Pinot Gris are extremely good value.

FRÉDÉRIC MOCHEL**–****
TRAENHEIM
81 acres (10 ha); 75,000 bottles • *Wines include Pinot Blanc, Muscat, Riesling Altenberg de Bergbieten, →Riesling Cuvée Henriette*
Frédéric Mochel and his son Guillaume have worked their way up ever so quietly to join the elite of Alsace Riesling producers. Mineral, dry, complex—all these virtues mean that the Cuvée Henriette in particular sets the standard.

RENÉ MURÉ***–****
ROUFFACH
70 acres (29 ha); 330,000 bottles • *Wines include:*
Gewürztraminer Clos Saint-Landelin, Riesling Clos Saint-Landelin, Muscat, →Pinot, Vendanges Tardives, →Sylvaner "Cuvée Oscar"
A top-flight, carefully worked vineyard (part of the Vorbourg *grand cru*) and long storage on the lees—little

Marc Kreydenweiss, biodynamic winegrower.

else is needed by René Muré for the production of elegant, dense wines that include a very fine Sylvaner.

ANDRÉ OSTERTAG***–*****
EPFIG
45 acres (18 ha); 100,000 bottles • *Wines include:*
→Riesling Muenchberg, Pinot, Pinot Gris Zellberg, Pinot Gris Muenchberg, Vendages Tardives, Sélections de Grains Nobles
Ostertag, when he took over this estate in 1985, introduced aging in *barriques*, malolactic fermentation for white wines as well as reds, and the use of wild yeasts. He has divided his wines into three very different categories: *vins de fruit* (displaying the character of the grape variety), *vins de pierre* (showing the character of the vineyard) and *vin de temps* (made from grapes that are overripe or affected by noble rot).

JEAN-PAUL SCHMITT**–***
SCHERWILLER
65 acres (8 ha); 45,000 bottles. • *Wines include:*
Riesling Rittersberg, Gewürztraminer Rittersberg, Vendanges Tardives
First of all, you have to find Jean-Paul Schmitt and his estate in the Huhnelmühle. The isolated position and the lack of *grand cru* vineyards have not discouraged this young winemaker. The Riesling, as well as the Gewürztraminer and Pinot Gris, are extremely elegant, upright wines.

TRIMBACH**–****
RIBEAUVILLÉ
80 acres (33 ha); bought-in grapes; 1,000,000 bottles
• *Wines include: Riesling Frédéric Émile, Gewürztraminer Seigneurs de Ribeaupierre, Pinot Gris, →Riesling Clos Sainte-Hune*
The wines of this merchant are almost always dry and in great demand with restaurants. The Riesling from the three-acre (1.2-ha) fully-owned vineyard Clos Sainte-Hune is a legend.

ZIND-HUMBRECHT****–*****
TURCKHEIM
99 acres (40 ha); 160,000 bottles • *Wines include:*
→Riesling Clos Saint-Urbain, →Riesling Pinot Gris Clos Jebsal, Riesling Clos Windsbuhl, Riesling Herrenweg, Muscat
Léonard Humbrecht and his son Olivier produce exceptional wines in the cellar of their modern winery. The concentrated Rieslings, Pinot Gris, and Gewürztraminers from the Clos Saint-Urbain enclave are some of the truly great wines of this region.

Jura

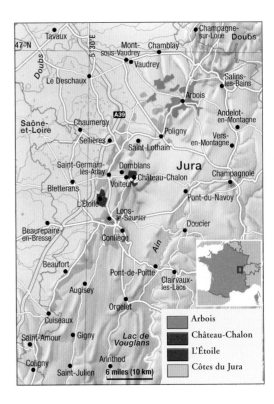

The wines of the Jura are seldom named in any discussion of France's greatest wines, with one exception: the legendary *vin jaune* that was prized at the French court as far back as the Middle Ages and is still valued as a rarity today. With only around 4,448 acres (1,800 ha) of vineyards (before the (Reblaus) catastrophe at the end of the 19th century it was almost 49,420 acres (20,000 ha)) and just 2,906,000 gallons (110,000 hl) of wine production, the Jura is one of the smaller wine-producing areas. The center of production is the small medieval town of Arbois, where the French chemist, Louis Pasteur, discovered the causes of alcoholic fermentation.

A Harsh Region

The Jura, situated between Burgundy and Switzerland, has a harsh climate, and is dominated by limestone mountains. Growing between 820 and 1,640 feet (250 and 500 m), the grapes make use of every sheltered spot they can find. The vineyards face west, southwest and to a certain extent south, and the soil consists overwhelmingly of blue, red, and black marl, and,

In the Jura, cask-aging is a quite particular skill, since it cultivates and accentuates the unmistakable character of the region's dry white wines.

to the north, partly of limestone scree and slate as well.

The climate is full of contrasts: cold winters and hot summers are followed by generally sunny autumns. The indigenous grape varieties are best adapted to these conditions. For white wines and *vin jaune* the Savagnin plays the leading role. According to many experts, this variety, also known as Naturé, is related to the Traminer; it accounts for 15% of the planting area and results in low yields of between 320 and 375 gallons per acre (30 and 35 hl/ha). Picking often continues into November and occasionally into December. Light red wines are traditionally obtained from the Poulsard grape. This variety, also known as Ploussard, was previously only capable of producing a light and sweet pale red, but there are now Poulsards that mature into proper red wines as a result of several days of must fermentation. More intensely colored reds, however, have always been made from the Trousseau grape. Chardonnay (also called Melon d'Arbois here) and Pinot Noir, both imported from Burgundy, are grown to produce single-varietal wines or *cuvées* in a blend with indigenous varieties.

Wines with their own Unique Style

Over the last few decades, more and more independent wine producers have emerged from the shadow cast by the cooperatives and the enormous company Henri Maire—who dominates a large proportion of wine production in the

Jura—to make a mark for themselves. Today's white wines are clearer in terms of fruit, and the red wines have become more elegant. Yet the region's wines have been able to retain their unmistakable style: a nutty spiciness, honey perfume, or overtones of dried fruit predominate in the Savagnin white wines or Chardonnay and Savagnin blends, while a charming blackcurrant or cherry fruit along with discreet animal notes can be detected in the red wines. The Crémant du Jura has rapidly developed into one of the region's major successes and Macvin has also become an increasingly hot tip. This *vin de liqueur* is a mixture of fermented grape juice and *marc* brandy, from which it takes its name. Whereas Macvins and *vins de paille* (made from grapes dried—traditionally on straw—after picking) are served at a maximum temperature of 50°F (10°C), Savignins and *vins jaunes* are customarily served at between 57° and 61°F (14° to 16°C) in order to bring out their richness of taste in full. Likewise, most red wines should not be served at more than 61°F (16°C).

Vin jaune, the most famous of all the yellow wines, comes from the picturesque Château-Challon.

The Jura *appellations*

ARBOIS

Arbois is not just a picturesque medieval town and the Jura's main center of wine production, but also the name of an *appellation*, which was recognized as France's first *Appellation d'Origine Contrôlée* in 1936. The vineyards, covering 2,100 acres (850 ha) are spread over 12 communes. Only one locality, Pupillin, known for its good Poulsard, is entitled to put its name on its labels. The *appellation* currently offers red and white wines, *vins de paille*, *vins jaunes*, and sparkling wines.

CHÂTEAU-CHALON

The birthplace of *vin jaune* is the only *appellation* dedicated exclusively to this type of wine and covers a total of four communes. The producers, whose vineyards total a mere 124 acres (50 ha), have banded together to form a committee that every year checks the grapes for ripeness and condition before harvesting, and sets the permitted yields. In bad years—such as 1984, for example—the Château-Chalon *appellation* is not awarded.

L'ETOILE

This tiny *appellation* with a planting area of just 198 acres (80 ha) is reserved for white wines: still, sparkling, *vin jaune*, and *vin de paille*. The vineyards are spread over three communes whose slopes have the best possible orientation. The marl soil is studded with minute, star-shaped fossils that give the village of L'Étoile and the *appellation* their name.

CÔTES DU JURA

Around 60 wine-growing communes, cultivating approximately 1,530 acres (620 ha), make up this general *appellation*, which covers the whole wine region. Among the best-known localities are Poligny, Voiteur, Arlay, Le Vernois, Grevingey, and Rotalier. Both red and white wines are recognized by the Côtes du Jura *appellation*; rosé, sparkling wine, *vin jaune*, and *vin de paille* are allowed to be sold under the designation as well.

CRÉMANT DU JURA

In 1995 the legal foundations were laid for the Crémant du Jura, and within a short while this sparkling wine became a winner. Sparkling wines had been produced in the region for two centuries, but only in the last few years have producers properly understood what lies at the heart of the Jura Crémant's charm: freshness. As is the case with champagne, the second fermentation takes place in the bottle. Both red and white grapes are used in the production of the basic wine. Frequently producers blend Pinot Noir (pressed white), Chardonnay, and also Trousseau and Savagnin, but some single-variety sparkling wines do exist. Compared to champagne, the Jura Crémant is usually more sparkling, has an aroma of green apples or pears, and is only seldom characterized by yeasty overtones. Its success has been astonishing: over a sixth of the entire production of the Jura is today sold as Crémant. And at a reasonable price, too!

MACVIN DU JURA

This *vin de liqueur* is the Jura equivalent of Pineau des Charentes (in the Cognac region) or Floc de Gascogne (in Armagnac). The *appellation* has been in existence only since 1991, but growers have been producing Macvin for centuries. Made from a combination of red or white must that has undergone its preliminary fermentation and *marc* brandy, it retains a considerable amount of residual sugar. An 18-month period of barrel-aging is stipulated for this refined specialty.

THE JURA SPECIALTIES—
VIN JAUNE AND VIN DE PAILLE

Vin de paille or "straw wine" used to be made in many different wine regions throughout the world. Before the introduction of modern cellar technology, this represented one of the few methods of producing long-lasting sweet wines in years when there was no noble rot. Apart from the Jura, the only other French regions that still produce *vin de paille*—in small quantities—are Alsace and the Rhône. At their best, the sweet "straw wines" from the Arbois, Côtes du Jura, and L'Étoile *appellations* are extremely long-lived elixirs with an AROMA of dried fruit and honey. They are usually made from Savagnin and Chardonnay grapes, but also, to a far lesser degree, red varieties, primarily the pale Poulsard. The grapes, picked when ripe, were spread out to dry on straw mats. This method has its disadvantages, however, as it can easily lead to the grapes rotting. In the Jura, therefore, the switch was made to laying the grapes out on a wire rack or wooden frame, or in a box with holes drilled into it, and setting them to dry in the warmest possible place. As soon as the grapes have lost most of their water content—which can take up to three months—they are pressed and fermented. It is not unusual for 100 pounds (45 kg) of grapes to yield a mere gallon or so (3.5 to 4 l) of wine. Through the OXIDIZATION that occurs during the drying process, the wines acquire a deep golden to amber color. The *vin de paille* of the Jura must have a potential alcohol content of at least 18 percent, a proportion of which is present as residual sugar. Because their ACID also concentrates during drying, however, good *vins de paille* have a

Vin jaune or "yellow wine" is France's most unusual white wine, maturing for six years beneath a layer of yeast before it is sold in the traditional bottle.

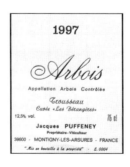

remarkable elegance. Frequently sold in half bottles (14 fl. oz/0.375 l), *vin de paille* is ideal as an aperitif and makes for an interesting taste experience as an accompaniment to either cheese or dessert.

THE YELLOW WINE

Unlike *vin de paille*, the other great specialty of the Jura, *vin jaune*, displays no noticeable sweetness. Château-Chalon is the most famous of these yellow wines—made exclusively from the Savagnin grape—although it is also produced under the Arbois, Côtes du Jura, and L'Étoile *appellations*. It is made using a technique unique in France, which is similar to that used for sherry. After fermentation the young wine is matured in old 60-gallon (228-l) barrels that are not quite filled to the top. What would result elsewhere in rapid oxidization leads here to the multiplication of special strains of yeast that are indigenous to the barrels and cellars of the winegrowers. After fermentation they form a protective cap (*voile*) over the surface of the wine which not only protects it from oxygen, but also imparts a very special aroma and taste. The yeasts also give the wine the dark yellow to bright golden hue that has made it famous. The wine needs to age for six years and three months, during which time a considerable proportion of it evaporates. The finished product is sold in bottles known as *clavelins* containing 21 fl. oz (62 cl). Because of the low yields, expensive production, and the evaporation that takes place during aging, *vin jaune* is never cheap, but it is a natural wine that is eminently capable of aging, with alcohol levels typically reaching 13 to 15 percent. Dry, with distinct nut, almond, or roast meat overtones, at its best it also displays a piquant acidity and spicy flavor and has the potential for a long life. A top wine can easily last for several decades, and some *vins jaunes* have reached the age of 100 years or more—in an enjoyable condition, needless to say. But why wait so long? *Vin jaune* is, after all, an excellent aperitif, and complements shellfish and many curry dishes perfectly. The traditional cuisine of the Jura also uses the wine in many of its dishes, the classic example being *coq au vin jaune*. *Vin jaune* with a ripe, unpasteurized Comté cheese (a specialty of the same region) is part of one of the most fascinating combinations of French wine and cheese.

SELECT PRODUCERS OF THE JURA

CHÂTEAU D'ARLAY***–****
ARLAY
74 acres (30 ha); 100,000 bottles • Wines include: Côtes du Jura Trousseau, Poulsard, Côtes du Jura Blanc, Chardonnay à la Reine, → Vin Jaune, → Vin de Paille, Macvin

The Counts of Laguiche have turned this picturesque château on the banks of the Bresse, which was cultivating vines as long ago as the 12th century, into one of the Jura's most famous wine estates. The operation is particularly strong on exports, and has every reason to be proud of its concentrated wines, which age well. One of the best wines from the château, which has a park well worth visiting, is the white Côtes du Jura, a *cuvée* of Chardonnay and Savagnin.

DOMAINE BERTHET-BONDET**–***
CHÂTEAU-CHALON
22 acres (9 ha); 40,000 bottles • Wines include: Côtes du Jura Tradition, Côtes du Jura Rouge, Crémant du Jura, Macvin, Vin de Paille, → Château-Chalon

Jean Berthet-Bondet and his wife Chantal have been producing remarkable wines at their splendid 15th-century estate since 1985. The Château-Chalon is made from low-yielding Savagnin grapes—just 320 gallons per acre (30 hl/ha). Typical of their nutty, emphatically spicy white wine is the Tradition, made from Savagnin and Chardonnay grapes.

DOMAINE DE LA PINTE**–***
ARBOIS
74 acres (30 ha); 100,000 bottles • Wines include: → Arbois Blanc, Arbois Rouge, Poulsard, Macvin, Vin Jaune, → Vin de Paille, Arbois Les Grandes Gardes

This winery was founded in the 1950s and has gradually been built up into its current position as one of the most reliable estates in the region by Roger Martin. Just 37 acres (15 ha) are planted with Savagnin, and for a short while now the estate has been run organically. The Vin de Paille and Cuvée Les Grandes Gardes reds both possess remarkable elegance.

DOMAINE ROLET***–****
ARBOIS
150 acres (61 ha); 400,000 bottles • Wines include: Arbois Chardonnay, → Trousseau, → Vieilles Vignes Poulsard, Arbois Rosé, Crémant du Jura, Vin de Paille, Macvin, → Vin Jaune

Despite its size, this firm, founded at the end of the Second World War, convinces with the even quality of its wines. Along with dry whites, *vin de paille* and *vin jaune*, the four Rolet siblings also produce a notable red Trousseau, which is aged for at least 18 months, and a powerful, fruity Poulsard from 20 year-old vines.

FRÉDÉRIC LORNET**–****
MONTIGNY-LÈS-ARSURES
37 acres (15 ha); 50,000 bottles • Wines include: Arbois Trousseau, Chardonnay, Savagnin, Vin Jaune, Vin de Paille, Macvin

From the (mostly) old vines in his vineyards, Frédéric Lornet obtains minerally and long-lived white wines (Savagnin) but also remarkable reds (powerful Trousseau).

JEAN MACLE****
CHÂTEAU-CHALON
30 acres (12 ha); 40,000 bottles • Wines include: → Château-Chalon, Côtes du Jura Blanc, Côtes du Jura Rosé, Crémant du Jura, Macvin

This company, founded in 1850, is now run by its sixth and seventh generations. Its Château-Chalon *vin*

jaune—a lean, spicy, and elegant example of its type—is made from just 10 acres (4 ha) of vines.

PIERRE OVERNOY***–****
PUPILLIN
10 acres (4 ha); 15,000 bottles • Wines include: Vin Jaune, Arbois Savagnin, Chardonnay, → Poulsard

Pierre Overnoy took the estate over from his parents in 1968. He and his comrade-in-arms Emmanuel Houillon work as naturally as possible. Wild yeasts are used to ferment the must, and the finished wines are not filtered.

JACQUES PUFFENEY**–***
MONTIGNY-LÈS-ARSURES
17 acres (7 ha); 30,000 bottles • Wines include: Arbois Blanc, → Arbois Trousseau, Poulsard, → Savagnin Vieilles Vignes, → Vin Jaune

A traditional winegrower who makes very little fuss about the concentrated white wines (Savagnin), fruity reds and spicy *vin jaune* to be found in his wooden-barreled cellar.

ANDRÉ AND MIREILLE TISSOT****
MONTIGNY-LÈS-ARSURES
79 acres (32 ha); 120,000 bottles • Wines include: Vin Jaune, Arbois Blanc, Chardonnay, Vin de Paille, → Pinot, Crémant du Jura Brut, Savagnin

The Tissots have developed this estate into a leading operation over the last few years. One of their specialties is the wooden-barrel-aged Pinot, an astonishingly elegant red wine. Organic cultivation methods are used.

JACQUES TISSOT**–***
ARBOIS
72 acres (29 ha); 120,000 bottles • Wines include: Arbois Tradition, Vin Jaune, Vin de Paille, Trousseau, → Poulsard, Crémant du Jura, Macvin, Poulsard Rosé, Château-Chalon, Savagnin Vendanges de Novembre

It is not really possible to visit Arbois without going past Jacques Tissot's inviting cellar. It is located in the center of the small town and serves as both storage depot and tasting room for his better than average *vin jaune* and wide range of red and white wines.

An appealing sense of tradition at Château Berthet in Chalon.

BURGUNDY

Burgundy and its wines are legendary in the wine world. Many a connoisseur will confidently declare that no other red wine in the world can beat the complexity, fullness, and style of a great Pinot Noir from the Côte de Nuits. The great Chardonnays from Chablis and the Côte de Beaune have also retained their originality and perfection, despite the worldwide love affair with Chardonnay. Yet, wherever there is light, there are shadows too. The region is highly fragmented and standards of quality can be extremely erratic, even in the higher price categories. Those purchasing at random run the risk of disappointment even more than in other regions.

HISTORY

The earliest evidence of wine growing in Burgundy dates back to the 2nd century AD. However, it is possible that the Celts were cultivating vines and pressing wine even before the Romans arrived. The history of Burgundian wine growing during the Middle Ages is of great importance to the whole of Europe.

The tradition of wine growing in the monasteries began with donations to the abbey of St. Benignus in 587 and the monastery at Bèze near Gevrey in 630. In 910 Cluny was founded in the Mâconnais. In the centuries that followed,

La Tâche, monopoly of the *domaine* of the Romanée-Conti and their most powerful *grand cru*.

the abbey not only grew into a center of clerical power, but it also procured important real estate in the wine-growing communities of the Côte d'Or.

The Cistercian Order founded in 1098 in Citeaux near Nuits-St.-Georges systematically promoted the culture of wine growing in the monasteries. The Clos de Vougeot was used by the monks to explore different aspects of wine growing, which then quickly spread throughout Europe as the Order grew in size.

Two events that took place in the late Middle Ages have a bearing on the wine industry today. A decree issued by Philip the Bold in 1395 was to drive the Gamay variety out of Burgundy, paving the way for Pinot Noir's domination of quality wine production. In 1443 the Chancellor of Philip the Good, Nicolas Rolin, donated the Hospices de Beaune, whose annual wine auction is still regarded today as the most important measure of the wine market in Burgundy.

Following the French Revolution, the Napoleonic law of inheritance provided the basis for the social and land ownership structure that still prevails in Burgundy today. Since that time, property has been divided equally between all the children of a family, which has meant that the parcels held by individual landowners have tended to get smaller and smaller. In 1851 came the opening of the rail link

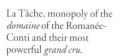

between Dijon and Paris, which provided access to a vast market and increased the demand for cheap wines, usually produced from the Gamay variety. However, the first attempt to classify superior wines dates back to the same period, coming in 1861. Following the PHYLLOXERA attack of the 1870s, resistance to grafted vines was greater in Burgundy than anywhere else. Nevertheless, the crisis had generally eased by the start of the 20th century. The creation of the A.O.C. system in the 1930s, along with gradual moves toward bottling wines at the property where they are made, prepared the ground for present-day Burgundy.

GEOLOGY, TOPOGRAPHY, AND CLIMATE

Burgundy's leitmotif is the *terroir*. What this signifies is the whole of the natural environment in which a vineyard is located, in other words, the combination of soil, topographical, and climatic features. In Burgundy the famous *terroirs* are, without exception, characterized by limestone. Chablis, with its limy, chalky soil, offers ideal conditions for Chardonnay. The limy, loamy, and marly soils of the Côte d'Or were created by the erosion of the high plateau of Jura limestone rising above the Côte d'Or, as strata broke off and fell into the valley. This explains why, within a very small area, a variety of *terroirs* are to be found with characteristic properties that are reflected in the flavor of the wines. In the Côte Chalonnaise and the Mâconnais limestone deposits are more sporadic and mixed with more loamy, sandy soils. Of great importance to all Burgundy's *terroirs* is the interaction between good drainage in rocky areas and the water retention of the loamy, clay, or marly substrata.

The topography of Burgundy's vineyards is far less spectacular than elsewhere. The steepness of the land and its south-facing orientation are less dominant factors here, with most of the *grands crus* in the Côte d'Or, for instance, facing due east on only a slight incline. The elevations vary between around 650 and 1,300 feet (200 and 400 m), with lighter wines tending to come from higher vineyards.

The climate is neither particularly warm nor especially dry. Winters are cold and can return with late frosts well into spring, particularly in Chablis. High summer temperatures reflect the continental influence, but are far less consistent than in the more southerly wine-growing areas. Precipitation is a particular threat, and the risk-taking yield discipline of the winegrower,

The château belonging to Bouchard Père et Fils is situated in the old part of the town of Beaune.

resulting from hard pruning, takes on the greatest importance. Seasonal fluctuations are greater here than in regions with a more moderate climate. On the other hand, in the Burgundian climate, the Pinot Noir can take on a mixture of finesse and robustness, elegance and strength almost unparalleled anywhere in the world.

OUTLOOK

Apart from the legendary wine-producing areas of Chablis and the Côte d'Or, recent years have seen the arrival of an ever-increasing number of supposedly secondary areas too. In the Mâconnais, on the Côte Chalonnaise and the Hautes Côtes enthusiastic winegrowers are producing wines well above the average. In the meantime, however, they have become just as rare and almost as expensive as their big brothers next door. When one considers that the total wine-growing area of Burgundy is just over 61,500 acres (25,000 ha), it is clear that at present the region as a whole is far from exhausting its potential for producing top-quality wines.

The Geography of the Wines of Burgundy

The northerly outposts of Burgundy are the wine-growing enclaves around Chablis and Auxerre in the department of Yonne (13,100 acres/5,300 ha). Chablis has become a symbol of quality thanks to its vigorous, elegant Chardonnay and has top-quality *grand cru* and *premier cru* locations. From the Côtes d'Auxerre come light, white and red wines, among which the fragrant, dry reds from Irancy, in particular, have acquired a degree of prominence. On the same degree of latitude, but some 25 miles (40 km) to the east, is the small wine-growing area of

Châtillonais, which belongs to the department of the Côte d'Or, yet only produces simple wines with the A.O.C. Bourgogne, except for a few interesting *crémants*. About 60 miles (100 km) southeast of Chablis begins the Côte d'Or itself (23,000 acres/9,300 ha), the heart of Burgundy. Almost all of Burgundy's *grands crus* and *premiers crus* are found within the confines of this wine-growing area that stretches for some 30 miles (50 km). Its northern part, the Côtes de Nuits, produces complex Pinot Noir wines with plenty of finesse, but virtually no white wines. The Pinot Noir produced on the Côte de Beaune is more solid and robust. The great wines come from Chardonnay. Above all, the combination of mellowness, fruit, and mineral characteristics make it unique. In the hinterland of the Côte d'Or communes is the Hautes Côtes region. These wines are referred to as Hautes Côtes de Nuits or Hautes Côtes de Beaune, depending on their geographical location. They generally tend to be somewhat lighter, and above all, harder structured than wines from the lower regions.

The southern end of the Côte de Beaune forms the boundary with the department of Saône-et-Loire (25,450 acres/10,300 ha). The best wines (both reds and whites), from the Côte Chalonnaise, which abuts the Côte de Beaune are extremely reasonably-priced alternatives to those from the Côte d'Or. Although there are no *grands crus* here, a number of truly noteworthy *premiers crus* are evidence of the region's pretensions. One of the area's curiosities is the town of Bouzeron, which focuses solely on Aligoté. A small region to the west of the Côte Chalonnaise, the Couchois, produces mainly simple wines. A few miles to the east begins the Mâconnais, a district that occasionally produces somewhat rustic Chardonnays, although the good examples are pleasant and absolutely typical of this variety. Wines of above-average character and aspiration come from the village of Pouilly-Fuissé and its surrounding area. The red wines are usually light blends of Pinot Noir and Gamay. The Mâconnais extends southward into the Rhône department and with it the Beaujolais region.

The A.O.C. System and the Quality Pyramid in Burgundy

The reputation of Burgundy's classification system vies with that of Bordelais for being exemplary in the French understanding of wine.

Map legend

- Châtillonnais
- Tonnerrois
- Chablis
- Auxerrois
- Bourgogne Irancy
- Vézelay
- Côte de Nuits
- Hautes Côtes de Nuits
- Côte de Beaune
- Hautes Côtes de Beaune
- Côte Chalonnaise
- Mâcon
- Mâcon Villages
- Saint-Véran
- Pouilly-Fuissé, Pouilly-Loché and Pouilly-Vinzelles
- Wine-growing areas in neighboring regions

16 miles (25 km)

Immediately following the foundation of the I.N.A.O. (*Institut National des Appellations d'Origine*) in 1935, the legislators defined all the important indications of origin for Burgundy in the years that followed, incorporating the classifications that had already been established in the mid-19th century. The *Appellation d'Origine Contrôlée* (A.O.C.) covers the following elements: the variety of grape(s), traditional wine-growing techniques, the wine's minimum and maximum alcohol content and its typical style.

THE GEOGRAPHICAL ORIGIN

The A.O.C.s are structured according to quality grades like the layers of an onion. Regional, communal, and *grand cru appellations* are graded according to the regard in which they are held and, within the regional and communal A.O.C.s, there are in turn more refined classifications. The simplest regional A.O.C. is Bourgogne. Any white or red wines produced from grapes harvested in Burgundy are entitled to use this *appellation*, as are Gamay reds from the ten cru communes in Beaujolais, for the sake of honor to some extent. The Bourgogne A.O.C. may be supplemented by other *appellations* associated with additional official requirements. For example, Bourgogne Aligoté is a white wine that must be produced purely from the Aligoté grape variety. "Bourgogne passe-tout-grains" is a wine produced from no more than two-thirds Gamay and no less than one-third Pinot Noir, which have been pressed together. Other additions restrict the regional origin. Around 54 percent of all Burgundian wines carry a regional A.O.C. on the

This is Burgundy—three adjacent plots with widely divergent natural conditions in relation to aspect, slope, and height. With the same grape variety but separate production processes, the result is three wines with a completely different bouquet.

There are hundreds of small winegrowers in Burgundy who welcome visitors and who sell their wines to them direct.

label. Apart from the different A.O.C.s beginning with "Bourgogne," the "Mâcon" and "Mâcon supérieur" *appellations* also belong in this group.

Communal (*villages*) A.O.C.s stand for a type of wine introduced and associated with a particular wine-producing commune. If the name of an individual location is also mentioned, the wine concerned must come from there. *Villages* wines account for some 34 percent of Burgundy's wine production, *premiers crus* for around 10 percent. The *grand cru* A.O.C. is still reserved for the 32 best locations on the Côte d'Or and seven in Chablis. In 1861 Dr Jules Lavalle devised the first systematic classification, which was officially sanctioned by the agricultural authorities in Beaune. The *grands crus* incorporated in the A.O.C. statute in the 1930s largely reflect the classification at the time. The most rigid upper yield limits apply to *grands crus* and they tend to assume primary responsibility for upholding Burgundy's reputation. They account for barely two percent of the total amount of Burgundy produced.

THE UPPER YIELD LIMITS

This is the foremost quality criterion in Burgundy. The climatic conditions and capriciousness of the Pinot Noir, in particular, require modesty if great wines are to be made. The regulations laid down by the A.O.C. system do, however, leave scope for casual interpretations, which do nothing to promote the reputation of Burgundy. In reality, an ever increasing number of *premier* and *grand cru* wines are appearing on the market, which really are quite thin.

THE GRAPE VARIETIES

Burgundy is a region *par excellence* when it comes to single-grape wines. The Burgundian palate strives to achieve the greatest complexity by probing the full diversity of a grape variety. Ideally, the *terroir* should be reflected in the wine. Burgundy's two leading grape varieties, in particular, are especially sensitive not only to the soil and microclimate, but also to man's cultural achievements.

PINOT NOIR

The Pinot Noir variety is hard to cultivate, difficult to press, and maturing the wine calls for real flair and sensitivity. Pinot Noir wines could certainly not be described as straightforward. The origin of the variety is uncertain; in Burgundy it can be traced back as far as 4 BC. The large number of sub-varieties is evidence that man has worked intensively with this family of grapes for many centuries.

The vines put out shoots early in the spring, making them susceptible to late frosts. If they are to ripen evenly and develop an intensive aroma, the grapes requires a long, equable growing season, during which heat can be just as damaging as moisture.

The small, compact grapes are not only at great risk from BOTRYTIS, but also from viruses: genuine and bogus mildew give the winegrower cause for concern. Although vine cultivation has created a number of less sensitive Pinot Noir clones, it is often the more sensitive varieties that produce the highest-quality wines. In

In autumn the Pinot Noir displays its magical colors.

Left and right
The Chardonnay vine is easy to cultivate, but only produces outstanding wines when grown on a particular type of terrain.

Burgundy approximately 50 highly selected clones are approved. Producers with a strong sense of tradition rely on what is known as *sélection massale* either entirely or as an addition to these "official" clones. This procedure involves reproducing certain vines that have proved themselves in terms of health and ripening characteristics.

The Pinot Noir requires extreme care from the vineyard staff. Many of the Burgundian winegrowers attempt to limit the vigorous growth and high yields of the individual vines. Cutting back the fruit cane hard is intended to achieve this goal. The foliage also requires a good deal of care and attention. This is important because there must be enough healthy foliage for photosynthesis, but at the same time foliage must be deliberately removed to allow air to reach the grapes.

Old vines *(vieilles vignes)* promise particularly high-quality wine, because their roots are deep and well spread out, and they have an inherently lower yield. The Pinot is also no easy partner during winemaking, even in the best vintage years. Virtually no other variety of grape makes it so difficult to achieve the desired color and tannin content. At the lower end of the scale, the grape produces light-colored wines low on structure, while excessively long and intensive maceration, extremely low fermenting temperatures, or the exaggerated use of pressed wine may produce more color, but can also bring green fermenting substances and hints of bitterness to the wine. Little wonder that the waves of contradictory winemaking philosophies are so powerful when it comes to Pinot Noir. While some vineyards use automatic rotofermenters, others stick to the manual immersion of the cap of skins. Some producers swear by cold-maceration prior to the start of alcoholic fermentation, to obtain color and particularly elegant tannins; some let maceration take place in the wine at the end of fermentation in warm temperatures. Others, however, use a combination of the two techniques. The least controversial issue remains the use of wooden casks. The traditional Burgundian *pièce*, capable of holding 60 gallons (228 l), is the barrel of choice for any serious Pinot. There is plenty of scope for individuality here too, ranging from the correct type of wood to be used and the degree of roasting to the proportion of new wood. The types of wine produced from the Pinot Noir are as numerous as the *terroirs* and the people who work them.

CHARDONNAY

It is debatable whether Burgundy is the home of Chardonnay. There is a village of the same name in the Mâconnais, yet it would appear that the village was named after the grape, rather than the other way round. Although the Austrian enologist, Ferdinand Regner, identified a certain genetic similarity between Chardonnay and the Burgundy family, there is no evidence of a direct affiliation. It may be that Chardonnay did not reach Burgundy until the 16th century; what is certain, however, is that it did not take over from the Aligoté in terms of large-scale cultivation until the mid-19th century.

Unlike Burgundy's main red grape variety, the Chardonnay is very easy to cultivate. In contrast to the Pinot Noir, it is less susceptible to viruses and fungus, but its early shoot development can leave it vulnerable to late frosts. It can tolerate relatively high yields without a complete breakdown in quality, it ripens uniformly and delivers constantly high volumes of must. A very important element is choosing the right time to harvest. If allowed to overripen, Chardonnay will tend to lose its acidity, producing excessively broad, plump wines.

Enologists enthuse over the versatility of Chardonnay. Relatively simple provenances can produce fresh, fruity whites with the help of modern, reductive wine processing.

Traditional types of wine, whether aged in wooden casks or not, are golden, fruity, and expansive. Almost all top-quality wines are fermented in the *pièce*, where after the first RACKING they are molded through repeated, week-long agitation of the fine yeast (so-called *tonnage*), into sparkling, full, strong wines that combine fruit and nerve, wood, and yeast influences in a complex yet multifaceted unit.

GAMAY

In Burgundy the rivalry between Gamay and Pinot Noir dates back to the 14th century. Because Gamay produces high yields, its grapes are bigger than those of the Pinot, their flesh juicy, and skins thin, it usually goes to produce mass-consumption wines with little structure. In the *cru* communes of Beaujolais, however, where there are low yields, it is still able to demonstrate the potential of the *terroir* type. In the rest of Burgundy, it is now only used in the Mâconnais and on the Côte Chalonnaise for blending with Pinot Noir.

ALIGOTÉ

In centuries gone by, the Aligoté—probably an indigenous Burgundian variety—was an important ingredient in the blend of white grapes used to produce white Burgundy. This high-yield variety has a tendency to dry acidity, but can develop a remarkable fruitiness in good locations and ripe years. Simpler, somewhat lean Aligoté wines are ideal for the production of *crémant* and the typical Kir (an aperitif made with *crème de cassis*). The town of Bouzeron on the Côte Chalonnaise has the only communal A.O.C. for Aligoté.

Whenever a vineyard in Burgundy is surrounded by a wall, it is entitled to call itself a *clos*.

CHABLIS—THE CHARDONNAY THAT CAME IN OUT OF THE COLD

The history of Chablis over the last fifty years has been a didactic drama on the relationships between vineyard technology and publicity. From roughly 1,250 acres (500 ha) of vines in the mid-1950s and 1,850 acres (750 ha) at the start of the 1970s, the vineyard area of Chablis and its neighboring communes have since exploded to reach the present level of 10,625 acres (4,300 ha). The media have had a crucial part to play in this development. At the start of the 1980s they made Chablis the embodiment of the pretentious, dry white wine imbued with the French way of life.

The risk of frost in Chablis is greater than in virtually any other major wine region in the world. Winegrowers face the possibility of late frosts well into May, which can inflict serious damage on young shoots. The extreme years of 1957 and 1961 brought winegrowers to their knees, particularly since even the *grands crus* were only able to command very low prices at that time. Since then two methods of combating frost have become established. The obvious method involves heating the vineyard, which means placing oil heaters in the rows of vines. The second method uses what would appear to be a somewhat paradoxical effect. When temperatures drop to freezing, the vines are sprayed with water. This produces a film of ice on them, which acts like a miniature igloo, protecting the young shoots. Since both methods have specific advantages and disadvantages, their use provokes heated debate, although they have evidently both worked well enough to date to sustain Chablis' vine cultivation and even introduce a recent period of prosperity.

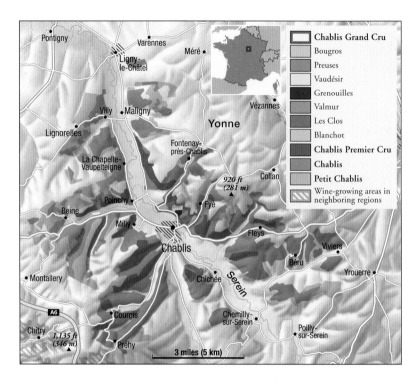

Left and right
The wine fraternity of Les Piliers Chablisiens at the ceremony of the "Ban de Vendanges," the prelude to the grape harvest.

The question of frost protection illustrates why Chablis was able to make such a great career as a media theme. In the first place, it is the precarious nature of this good fortune that arouses the interest of wine connoisseurs worldwide. Second, there is the tendency of winegrowers to take polarized stances that adds spice to the stories.

The geology of Chablis and its neighboring communes is of the greatest importance to its typology and classification. The region lies at the edge of the Parisian basin on a stone formation from the upper Jura. The other end of this basin emerges in southern England close to the

town of Kimmeridge, which gives its name to this soil mixture of chalk, clay, and oyster fossils. All Chablis' *grand* and *premier cru* locations have this sort of soil. Until a few years ago the next youngest limestone stratum, known as Portland limestone, also found in the region, was regarded as inferior. Portland soils were only granted the A.O.C. "Petit Chablis" classification. Opinion is now divided over this classification criterion. There is no doubt, however, that the flint clay characteristic of good Chablis is directly related to Kimmeridge limestone. It is equally certain that, particularly in Chablis with its marginal climate, the quality of a location depends not only on the soil type but also on the microclimatic features.

Finally, there are disputes surrounding the aging of Chablis wines. The so-called *feuillette*, a wooden cask holding 35 gallons (132 l), is of historical importance. In past decades, however, discoloration caused by old wood during fermentation and aging were probably also traditional. The introduction of stainless steel vats and a controlled fermentation temperature are among the most important technical innovations contributing to Chablis' new reputation. Under the effects of the worldwide trend in the 1980s, the *barrique* also came back into fashion. Fermentation in wood and agitation of the yeast *(tonnage)* are less controversial as vinification techniques than in the Côte de Beaune. Many producers ferment their wines in vats and siphon them off into oak barrels of varying ages only when the malolactic fermentation is complete. While advocates stress that aging the wine in wooden casks moderates the occasionally quite sharp acid of the Chablis and enriches the range of aromas, advocates of the steel vat miss out on the mineral core of *barrique* Chablis, which defines the regional type.

Over the last twenty years wine growing in Chablis has in many respects acquired a new quality. Technical aids (including machine harvesting) have improved profitability, while the worldwide increase in wine awareness has raised demand. Although it is unlikely that the region's ups and downs have been overcome once and for all—climatic risks alone are too imponderable—the Chablis winegrowers have laid the foundations for ensuring that possible extreme fluctuations can be subdued. A region in which wine growing was promoted by the Cistercians as early as the 12th century, a region that supplied Paris with its decanter wine for centuries; a region, finally, that aroused the interest of English wine connoisseurs as early as the 16th century, and in 1770, achieved the first auction success of a white Burgundy at

The old gate of Chablis, a quiet little town with 2,500 inhabitants in the north of Burgundy, which has won world renown through its wine.

Christie's in London, will stand its ground in future too. Least of all will the "Chablis copies," for some time very widespread abroad, succeed in driving the original out of the market. Chablis winegrowers have even gone to the highest court in Bermuda to protect the name of their genuine wines.

A good Chablis is a pleasure to drink—from the greenish-yellow sparkle, through the delightful flinty bouquet, to the interplay of body and acid, a nerviness that defines the type. The concentration of its minerals must make a young Chablis seem almost meager in comparison. Ideally, these proportions are found in different quality classifications. Wines in the *grand cru* category display every characteristic most intensively, yet they always retain a coolness of style compared with the Côte de Beaune Chardonnays. The *premiers crus*, with their elegance and mineral element, may represent the most typical Chablis wines, but unfortunately also the most disappointing, due to their neutrality and leanness. Over the last twenty years the *premier cru* zones have undergone a particularly marked expansion. Young vines are responsible for some mediocre results, but the relatively high yields per acre are undoubtedly also damaging. There were years in which the Petit Chablis locations had lower yields per acre than the *premiers crus*. Even with the simple Chablis, there is a wide variation in quality. Where the idea of producing the prototype of Chablis as a simple table wine intended to be drunk young is still being genuinely implemented, the Petit Chablis is a very estimable specialty.

Select Producers in Chablis

Jean-Marc Brocard***–****
Prehy

*237 acres (96 ha); bought-in grapes; 1,000,000 bottles •
Wines include: Bourgogne blancs; Kimmeridgien,
Portlandien; Sauvignon de Saint-Bris, Petit Chablis,
Chablis: →Domaine Sainte-Claire Viellies Vignes, Chablis
Premier Cru: Beauregard, Côte de Jouan, Montée de
Tonnerre; Chablis Grand Cru: Bougros, Les Clos*
Only wines matured in stainless steel, which above
all display the mineral qualities of their *terroir*. The
Brocards have now begun converting to biodynamic
cultivation methods, which means that the wines are
gaining in density.

La Chablisienne**–****
Chablis

*3,000 acres (1,200 ha); bought-in grapes; 5,600,000
bottles • Wines include: Chablis; → Vieilles Vignes,
Chablis Premier Cru: Beauroy, Fourchaume, Les Lys;
Chablis Grand Crus: Les Clos, →Grenouilles,
Bourgogne rouge Epineuil; Crémant de Bourgogne*
One of the best cooperatives in Europe. The wines are
clean, typical and of good caliber—from the fresh Petit
Chablis to the superb, oak-aged Grand-Cru-Cuvée of
the Château Grenouilles.

Vincent Dauvissat*****
Chablis

*27 acres (11 ha); 70,000 bottles • Wines include: Petit
Chablis, Chablis, Chablis Premier Cru: → La Forest,
Sechet, Vaillons, Chablis Grand Cru: Les Clos, →Les
Preuses*
Dense, well-proportioned, long-lasting wines whose
complexity is enriched by a stylishly small proportion of
batches fermented in *barriques*.

Daniel-Etienne Defaix***–****
Milly

*62 acres (25 ha); 180,000 bottles • Wines include:
Chablis, Chablis Premier Cru: Côte de Lechet, →Les Lys,
Vaillon; Chablis Grand Cru Blanchot, Bourgogne rouge*
Daniel Defaix swears by another style of Chablis that has
more body and is allowed more time to develop, which is
why he is particularly keen on old vines.

Domaine Barat***
Milly

*42 acres (17 ha); 90,000 bottles • Wines include:
Chablis, Chablis Premier Cru →Côte de Lechet, Les
Fourneaux, Mont de Milieu*
Michel Barat's wines are often rather reserved when
young, but they have plenty of structure and character
that begin to develop after two years' aging in the bottle.

Domaine Billaud-Simon****
Chablis

*49 acres (20 ha); 140,000 bottles • Wines include: Petit
Chablis, Chablis, Chablis Tête d'Or; Chablis Premier
Cru: Fourchaume →Mont de Milieu, Montée de
Tonnerre; Chablis Grand Cru: Blanchots, →Les Clos,
Les Preuses, Vaudésir*
The yield of old vines from Mont de Milieu and
Blanchot is aged in wood, while the rest of the range
underlines the nervy, crystalline side of the Chablis.
Not least the Petit Chablis offers genuine value.

Domaine Bernard Defaix***–***
Milly

*202 acres (25 ha); 190,000 bottles. • Wines include: Petit
Chablis, →Chablis Vieilles Vignes; Chablis Premiers
Crus: Les Vaillons, Les Lys, →Côte de Lechet Réserve*

Sylvain and Didier Defaix produce very lively, mineral,
typical Chablis wines and know how to add complexity
to their Vieilles Vignes and Réserve by using finely
calculated barrel maturation.

Domain William Fèvre****–*****
Chablis

*381 acres (47 ha); 300,000 bottles. • Wines include:
Chablis Grand Cru: → Les Clos, → Preuses, Bougros,
Vaudésir, Valmur; Premiers Crus: →Montée de
Tonnerre, →Fourchaume, Vaillons, Montmains;
→Chablis*
One of the most important estates in Chablis, with
plentiful *grand cru* and *premier cru* vineyards. After
being taken over by Joseph Henriot and becoming part
of the Beaune Bouchard Père et Fils company, the wines
have risen spectacularly in quality. The vineyards are
now clearly differentiated, and the excessive influence
of wood in William Fèvres' day has made way for an
admirable delicacy of touch in maturation.

Domaine Long-Depaquit**–****
Chablis

*161 acres (65 ha); 300,000 bottles • Wines include:
→Chablis; Chablis Premier Cru: La Forêt, Les Lys,
Montée de Tonnèrre, Les Vaillons, Vaucoupin, Chablis
Grand Crus: Blanchot, Bougros, Les Clos, →La
Moutonne Monopole, Les Preuses, Vaudésir*
Gérard Vullien is the driving force behind the high-class
estate owned by the Beaune house of Bichot. The wines
often need time to develop their class. This applies in
particular to the monopoly wine, the *grand cru* La
Moutonne, an unofficially assembled location in the
climats Vaudésir and Les Preuses with a particularly
favorable microclimate and a powerful result.

Domaine Raveneau*****
Chablis

*19 acres (7.5 ha); 40,000 bottles • Wines include:
Chablis Premier Cru: Butteaux, Chapelot, →Montée
de Tonnerre, Vaillons; Chablis Grand Cru: Blanchot,
→Les Clos, Valmur*
From vineyard to bottle, Jean-Marie and Bernard
Raveneau put everything into ensuring that each
climat gives its full expression. With low yields,
natural yeasts, and aging in old *pièces*, they
obtain wines of breathtaking character and depth
that age wonderfully.

Jean-Paul Droin****
Chablis

*49 acres (20 ha); 140,000 bottles • Wines include:
Chablis, Chablis Premier Cru: Fourchaumes,
Montmains, Vaillons, → Vosgros, Chablis Grand Cru:
Blanchot, Les Clos, →Grenouilles*
Experience has made Jean-Paul Droin a master with the
barrique. Today his wines possess a clear balance, retain
their mineral qualities, and grow in variety.

Jean Durup**–***
Maligny

*420 acres (170 ha); 1,500,000 bottles • Wines include:
Chablis, Chablis Premier Cru: Fourchaume, Montée de
Tonnerre, Montmains, Vau de Vey*
Jean Durup, a Parisian lawyer, has successfully fought to
extend the Chablis growing area and has himself built
up the largest estate of the *appellation*. His consistently
reliable wines are aged in stainless steel and are sold as
Domaine de l'Eglantière, Château de Mailigny and
Domaine de Valèrie, among others. Most of his wines
are exported.

ALAIN GEOFFROY**–****
BEINES

104 acres (42 ha); bought-in grapes; 450,000 bottles
• *Wines include: Chablis, →Chablis Vieilles Vignes;*
Chablis Premier Cru: →Beauroy, Fourchaume, Chablis
Grand Cru: Les Clos, Vaudésirs
Alain Geoffroy, one of the leading figures in Chablis,
has in recent years considerably improved the quality of
his fresh, harmonious, age-worthy wines.

CORINNE & JEAN-PIERRE GROSSOT****
FLEYS

45 acres (18 ha); 95,000 bottles • *Wines include: →Chablis;*
Chablis Premier Cru: Côte de Troems, Fourchaume, →Les
Fourneaux, Mont de Milieu, Vaucoupin
Corinne and Jean-Pierre Grossot number among the
most serious winegrowers in Chablis, producing wines
typical of the *terroir* with well-ripened grapes and
reasonable yields.

THIERRY HAMELIN**–***
LIGNORELLES

91 acres (37 ha); bought-in grapes; 240,000 bottles
• *Wines include: Petit Chablis; Chablis, →Chablis Vieilles*
Vignes; Chablis Premier Cru: Vau Ligneau, Beauroy
With courage and commitment Thierry Hamelin has
built up his functional cellar in the main Petit Chablis
area and expanded his vineyard holdings. His wines,
vinified in tanks, are clean, nervy and mineral.

MICHEL LAROCHE**–****
CHABLIS

247 acres (100 ha); bought-in grapes; 2,000,000 bottles
• *Wines include: Chablis, Chablis Premier Cru:*
Fourchaume, Vaillons, Vau de Vey, Chablis Grand Cru:
Blanchots, →Les Clos, →Réserve de l'Obédiencerie
Thanks to the foresight and dynamism of Michel
Laroche, the tiny estate founded 150 years ago has
grown into a unique *domaine* and international trading
house, producing clean wines within the standard range
and reduced-yield quality wines. Some of the *grands*
crus are aged in wooden casks.

SYLVAIN MOSNIER***
BEINE

122 acres (15 ha); 70,000 bottles. • *Wines: Petit*
Chablis, Chablis, Chablis Vieilles Vignes, Chablis
Premier Crus: Beauroy, Côtes de Lechet

The little town of Chablis is
surrounded by vineyards.
The soil consists of
kimmeridge, the deposits
of fossil shell beds.

Once a teacher of mechanics, this winegrower has made
a solid reputation for himself. His well structured wines,
often reticent when young, mature outstandingly and
show plenty of character—just like their producer.

GILBERT PICQ***–****
CHICHÉE

32 acres (13 ha); 80,000 bottles • *Wines include:*
Chablis, →Chablis Vieilles Vignes, Chablis
Premier Cru: →Vaucoupin, Vosgros
In just a few years Didier Picq and his brother Pascal
have taken the family business to the top. Their wines
are well-structured and aromatic, displaying after a few
years the typical aromas of moss, mushrooms, and
honey that connoisseurs love.

OLIVIER SAVARY***
MALIGNY

42 acres (17 ha); 120,000 bottles • *Wines include: Petit*
Chablis, Chablis, Chablis Premier Cru Fourchaume
Olivier and Francine Savary have managed to attract
attention with the quality of their wines. Their Chablis
and particularly their *premier cru* are well-structured
white wines with a volume that gives them a special
charm, but also good aging potential.

The Auxerrois

The area of Auxerre was an important source
of wine for Paris well into the 19th century. It
was only when the Yonne and Seine water-
ways met with rivalry from the railways that
the heady days of the auxerrois came to an
end. Today the area, covering a total of some
3,200 acres (1,300 ha), has a limited but underestimated wine presence. Most of the light,
fine Chardonnays and Pinots are stacked high
under the label of A.O.C.s Bourgogne
or Bourgogne Côtes d'Auxerre. Bourgogne
Aligoté is also successfully produced in
Auxerre. The winegrowers of the Auxerre
region have continued to raise their profile in
recent times, as the *terroirs* are their capital.
This evidently leads to those Bourgognes with
the right to include the name of their
commune after the regional *appellation*
gaining more business. Apart from the general
term of origin "Bourgognes Côtes d'Auxerre,"
we therefore often see the names of the
communities of Chitry, Coulanges-la-Vineuse,
Epineuil, Joigny, Tonnerre, and Vézelay on the
labels. There is also the Bourgogne Côte-Saint-
Jacques, the name of a famous location to
the north of Auxerre. All these efforts are
obviously intended to acquire an independent
appellation one day.

The Irancy community has succeeded in this.
Its 309 acres (125 ha) have been classified as
a communal *appellation*. Irancy is a richly
colored, delicately perfumed red wine growing
in kimmeridge chalk. It is usually made purely
from Pinot Noir grapes, but the indigenous
César variety is also permitted as an addition.
The ripe César is rich in tannin, giving the Irancy
a notable age-worthy structure. The Sauvignon
de Saint-Bris, a specialty of the large wine-
growing community and their direct neighbors,
originating in the chalk plateaus, was separately
classified for many years as V.D.Q.S. Now,
however, this single-variety, aromatic, and
rounded white wine has also received the accolade of *Appellation d'Origine Contrôlée*.

DOMAINE COLINOT***
IRANCY

25 acres (10 ha); 55,000 bottles • *Wines include:*
Bourgogne Irancy (Palottes, Les Mazelots, Côte
du Moutier, Cuvée Vieilles Vignes)
A pioneering operation in Irancy. Many
cuvées are enriched with the yield of 70-year-
old César vines.

DOMAINE GOISOT****
SAINT-BRIS-LE-VINEUX

59 acres (24 ha); 150,000 bottles • *Wines*
include: Sauvignon des Saint-Bris, Bourgogne:
Aligoté; Côtes d'Auxerre "Corps de Garde"
Typical regional white wines of great elegance
from one of the best Burgundian Aligotés.
The red wines are especially stylishly aged
in wooden casks, which mature in medieval
vaulted cellars.

KINGS OF STYLE:
WINES OF THE CÔTE DE NUITS

The Côte de Nuits combines the sort of conditions found in few other places in the wine-producing world. First, there is the variety of high-grade soil created by the outcrop of Jura limestone. In addition, there is the ideally critical climate, which does not make life too easy for vines and winegrowers and at the same time produces the best possible aroma in the plant physiology, and this in a variety that stands for originality, the greatest distinction and pretension in every respect. Last but not least, the

people who work here seem to have wine growing and cellar management in their blood. The wine of the Côte de Nuits is red in color. It is not that the small number of white wines pressed are less good, but simply that the winegrower begrudges every acre of land not used for the greatest expression this region can provide, namely, the Pinot Noir.

Geographically speaking, everything takes place within the space of a half-hour car journey. On the outer edges are the less privileged towns, comparatively speaking, of Marsannay and Fixin in the north, the peaceful little towns of Nuits, Comblanchien and Corgoloin in the south. The heart of the region comprises the great names that have the pride of having a *grand cru* named after their respective towns: Gevrey-Chambertin, Morey-St-Denis, Chambolle-Musigny, Flagey-Échezeaux, Vosne-Romanée. Villages and vineyards come together here to create an especially harmonious ensemble, radiating the unity of life and work.

The series of villages and vineyards is interrupted by small side valleys, so-called *combes*, where the orientation of the vineyards turns from east to south. These locations include a number of outstanding *premiers crus*, for example, Lavaux St-Jacques in Gevrey and La Combe d'Orveau in Chambolle. The rule of thumb that applies to the Côte de Nuits is that *grands crus* run eastward and lie half-way up the mountain, usually on only a slight incline but with particularly meager soils, while locations below the *grands crus* produce communal A.O.C. wines on lower land and in slightly deeper soil. A few *premiers crus* are higher up the mountain than the *grands crus*, while others are also sited between the single communal locations and the *grands crus*, depending on the soil conditions. On the other side of the Route Nationale there are locations classified as regional A.O.C. Bourgogne. Communal locations in communes less closely related to the wine than in better known places are classified as "Côte de Nuits Villages."

The special fascination of the Côte de Nuits lies in the wealth of variety among its wines. Detecting the *terroir* characteristics of the wines from individual villages or even individual *crus* is a particularly pleasurable challenge. However, the stylistic differences that come into play due to the vine cultivation and cellar technology are also significant. However accepted the concept

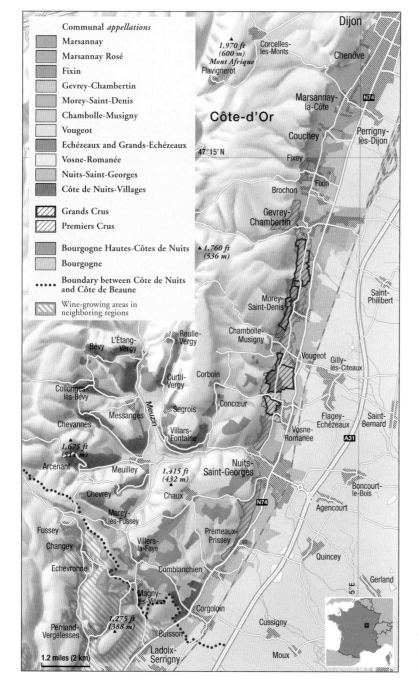

of *terroir* may be, the winegrower's own philosophy on aging will equally influence his product. On the other hand, a winegrower can emphasize still further the structure given to a wine by the *terroir* through pressing and aging. In Burgundy a productive rivalry exists between conservatism and sophistication. Innovations such as the *macération préfermentaire au froid* (cold maceration of the grapes before the start of alcoholic fermentation) proclaimed by the star enologist, Guy Accad, in the 1980s are being successfully

Both Fixin (left) and Nuits-Saint-Georges (right) are strongholds of solid, long-aging red wines.

adapted by many winegrowers to suit their own style. Other winegrowers oppose such innovations and their wines are no less good. Many paths lead to the same goal in the Côte de Nuits, but not all of them by far, as is demonstrated time and again by the region's remoteness from the consumer. The most important prerequisites for the emergence of great Pinot Noir wines are the mental application and economic resources necessary in order to take on important extra work to achieve lower yields.

APPELLATIONS

COMMUNAL A.O.C.s:
Maximum basic yields of 10.5 gallons/120 sq. yds (40 l/100 sq. m) for red wine, 12 gallons/ 120 sq. yds (45 l/100 sq. m) for white wine
MARSANNAY: 465 acres (188 ha) in Marsannay, Couchey and Chenôve, roughly 10 percent white wine, classical A.O.C. for fruity rosé wines (to which the upper yield limit on white wines applies).
FIXIN: 240 acres (97 ha) in Fixin and Brochon, almost exclusively red wines that are deeply colored and rich in tannin.
GEVREY-CHAMBERTIN: 983 acres (398 ha) in Gevrey and Brochon, 100 percent red wine, 26 *premier cru* locations (213 acres/86 ha), full-bodied, aromatic, age well.
MOREY-SAINT-DENIS: 222 acres (90 ha); almost only red wine, 20 *premiers crus* (109 acres/44ha), more delicate wines than Gevrey, more robust than Chambolle.
CHAMBOLLE-MUSIGNY: 378 acres (153 ha); exclusively red wine that is particularly fragrant, smooth and elegant, 24 *premiers crus* (151 acres/61 ha).
VOUGEOT: 44 acres (18 ha); 7.5 acres (3 ha) of this white wine, 4 *premiers crus* (29 acres/ 11.5 ha), wines similar in type to the Clos de Vougeot.
VOSNE-ROMANÉE: 368 acres (149 ha) in Vosne and Flagey, exclusively red wine, 15 *premiers crus* (142 acres/57.5 ha), distinctly spicy, balanced, elegant wines.
NUITS-SAINT-GEORGES: 724 acres (293 ha) in Nuits-Saint-Georges and Premeaux,

almost only red wine, 41 *premier crus* (353 acres/143 ha), compact, substantial wines.
CÔTE DE NUITS-VILLAGES: 398 acres (161 ha) in Fixin, Brochon, Remeaux, Comblanchein, Corgoloin, almost exclusively red wine, generally better than Bourgogne rouge but surpassed by the A.O.C.s with place names.

GRANDS CRUS:
Maximum basic yield of 9 gallons/120 sq. yds (35 l/100 sq. m)
CHAMBERTIN: 35 acres (14 ha) in Gevrey
CHAMBERTIN-CLOS DE BÈZE: 34 acres (13.9 ha) in Gevrey, may also be referred as Clos de Bèze (without additions).

Maximum basic yield of 9.5 gallons/ 120 sq. yds (37 l/100 sq. m):
CHAPELLE-CHAMBERTIN: 12 acres (4.8 ha) in Gevrey
CHARMES-CHAMBERTIN/MAZOYÈRES-CHAMBERTIN: 72 acres (29.1 ha) in Gevrey
GRIOTTE-CHAMBERTIN: 7 acres (2.7 ha) in Gevrey
LATRICIÈRES-CHAMBERTIN: 18 acres (7.1 ha) in Gevrey
MAZIS-CHAMBERTIN: 21 acres (8.4 ha) in Gevrey
RUCHOTTES-CHAMBERTIN: 8 acres (3.3 ha) in Gevrey. Chambertin wines have weight, fire and structure. They develop an opulent bouquet.

Maximum basic yield of 9 gallons/120 sq. yds (35 l/100 sq. m)

CLOS SAINT-DENIS: 15 acres (6.2 ha) in Morey
CLOS DE LA ROCHE: 40 acres (16 ha) in Morey
CLOS DES LAMBRAYS: 20 acres (8.2 ha) in Morey
CLOS DE TART: 19 acres (7.5 ha) in Morey

Wines that occasionally give the impression of meagerness while young, but develop a fruity, perfumed silkiness with maturity.
BONNES-MARES:
37 acres (15 ha) in Chambolle and Morey, spicy, soft wines with a rich bouquet.
MUSIGNY: 24 acres (9.9 ha) in Chambolle, of which 1.5 acres (0.6 ha) are white wine, finely structured yet deep red wine.
CLOS DE VOUGEOT: 125 acres (50 ha) in Vougeot.
ECHÉZEAUX: 79 acres (31.8 ha) in Flagey
GRANDS-ÉCHEZEAUX: 21 acres (8.6 ha) in Flagey, soft, full wine that develops an aromatic fruit.
RICHEBOURG: 17 acres (7.06 ha) in Vosne, rich Burgundy, bursting with fruit and fullness.
ROMANÉE-CONTI: 4 acres (1.65 ha) in Vosne
LA ROMANÉE: 2 acres (.75 ha) in Vosne
ROMANÉE-SAINT-VIVANT: 23 acres (9.27 ha) in Vosne. Opulence, depth, complexity, strength and charm: ideal examples of Pinot Noir.
LA GRANDE RUE: 4 acres (1.65 ha) in Vosne, harmonious, elegant wine.
LA TÂCHE: 14 acres (5.5 ha) in Vosne, can number among those Burgundies strongest in minerals, captivating in intensity and spice.

A National Shrine:
The Domaine de la Romanée-Conti

The Domaine de la Romanée-Conti, referred to simply as D.R.C., enjoys a cult status even greater than that of Pétrus or Mouton in the Bordeaux region. No other estate in one of the traditional wine regions so symbolizes its commitment to quality as does the D.R.C. to Bourgogne. It is the only *domaine* in Burgundy with more than one vineyard that manages exclusively to produce *grands crus*. The D.R.C. does not rack grapes harvested from its less illustrious parcels of land.

Historically, the D.R.C. had its origins with the monks from the monastery of Saint-Vivant, who claimed for their own five outstanding locations in Vosne and Flagey. In 1584 the monks sold this estate under the name of Le Cros de Cloux. It was only in 1651, after Roman ruins were found close by, that Burgundy's most prestigious vineyard was renamed Romanée. In 1760 the *domaine* finally fell into the ownership of Prince von Conti. However, the name Romanée-Conti only became established following the French Revolution, when the expropriated estate was first referred to by this name at auction in 1794.

The estate's present structure was essentially created by Jacques-Marie Duvault-Blochet during the last thirty years of the 19th century, when he bought additional parcels of land in Richebourg, Echézeaux, Grand Echézeaux and part of La Tâche. He bequeathed the *domaine* to the Villaine family, who have run it since 1911.

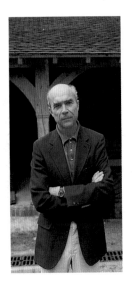

Aubert de Villaine is fully aware of the cultural and historical importance of the Domaine de la Romanée-Conti

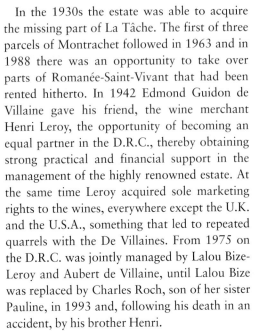

The Clos de Vougeot is at the root of Burgundy's wine hierarchy. Today the historic buildings under the management of the La Confrèrie des Tastevins wine fraternity are used to hold many events.

In the 1930s the estate was able to acquire the missing part of La Tâche. The first of three parcels of Montrachet followed in 1963 and in 1988 there was an opportunity to take over parts of Romanée-Saint-Vivant that had been rented hitherto. In 1942 Edmond Guidon de Villaine gave his friend, the wine merchant Henri Leroy, the opportunity of becoming an equal partner in the D.R.C., thereby obtaining strong practical and financial support in the management of the highly renowned estate. At the same time Leroy acquired sole marketing rights to the wines, everywhere except the U.K. and the U.S.A., something that led to repeated quarrels with the De Villaines. From 1975 on the D.R.C. was jointly managed by Lalou Bize-Leroy and Aubert de Villaine, until Lalou Bize was replaced by Charles Roch, son of her sister Pauline, in 1993 and, following his death in an accident, by his brother Henri.

The soil at Romanée-Conti is only about 24 inches (60 cm) deep and is interspersed with a good deal of limestone and 45 to 50 percent clay. What is particularly unique about the soil is its ability to provide the right amount of drainage, thanks to the limestone; and water retention, thanks to the clay. However, in the upper part of Romanée-Conti there is a severe risk of erosion, as there is also in the lower parcels of La Tâche. Prince Conti had fresh loam brought to the estate from the meadows of the Saône valley as early as 1886/87. No fewer than 800 wagon loads were deposited.

Soil management is one of the central themes of the *domaine*. In the final analysis, perfectionist vine cultivation, the lowest yields (roughly 6.5 gallons/120 sq. yds, 25 liters/100 sq. m as a long-term average), and attention to detail in vinification are treated as a matter of course in a *domaine* of this size. The crux remains the retention of the irreplaceable natural conditions. For this reason, organic cultivation methods were introduced as early as the 1980s, and these have been consistently developed to the present day.

The cultural and historical heritage is treated with the greatest reverence and respect. This consistently conservative approach was exemplified by the fact that only when the battle against phylloxera finally proved hopeless in 1945 were the own-rooted vines of the Romanée-Conti uprooted, and La Tâche restocked with the grafted scions.

The Clos de Vougeot:
A Microcosm of Catholic Burgundy

125 acres (50 ha) within a half-mile long wall make the Clos de Vougeot the largest *grand cru* in Burgundy and a wine of special symbolic significance. It reflects both the history and present of Burgundy in all its facets. The Cistercians received some land near Vougeot in 1110 and created this *cru* as the first of their major feats in wine growing. Parcel by parcel, donation by donation, they added to the land, uprooted and planted, set up a cellar right in the middle of the vineyard and around 1330 they built the wall.

The Clos de Vougeot became the first experimental vineyard known to man. The monks studied the microclimate and growth conditions, varieties of Pinot, and soil types. If the origin of the concept of *terroir* can be in any way pinned down, then it must be to here. According to legend, the monks are said to have quite literally tasted the soil to learn as much as possible about the differences.

The Clos de Vougeot is unique in its variety. Every few yards the ground changes. The ratio of clay to limestone, the depth, local climatic conditions, all these factors that are largely uniform within most other *grand cru* locations are subject to great diversity here. The only definable trend is that in the upper section, particularly where the château has been standing since 1551, the soil is particularly scant and rich in limestone. Lower down, alongside the main highway, the less valued loamy, heavy soils susceptible to waterlogging predominate. But there too are veins of limestone that make it impossible to generalize.

This mosaic of locations was helpful to the Cistercians in their research. Even their wine, which must have been a blend of grapes from all the different parcels, does not seem to have come to any harm from it.

Secularization cast a new light on the patchwork quilt of the Clos de Vougeot.

Today between 65 and 82 owners share the vineyard's parcels of land. Accurate records of ownership are hard to keep due to the notorious disputes on inheritance. It is clear that in view of this widely dispersed ownership, it is now virtually impossible to produce a Clos de Vougeot in the manner envisaged by the founders of this vineyard—a wine that acquires its complexity from the blending of all or at least some clearly distinct *climats*. (*Climat* in Burgundy refers to a vineyard's mesoclimate

In area, the Clos de Vougeot is the largest *grand cru*, but between 65 and 82 owners divide up the area among them, which is typical of the way in which vineyard ownership in Burgundy has been split up into ever smaller properties.

Richebourg is one of the leading *grands crus* of the Vosne-Romanée commune, producing wonderfully rich, powerful, long-lasting reds.

and its soil.) Most pressings today come from individual parcels of varying size. Each year roughly 40 different wines come onto the market with "Clos de Vougeot" on their label. Little wonder that many of these wines do not merit the *grand cru* classification. Today the Clos de Vougeot is not only a microcosm of natural growth conditions, as it has always been, but it also offers a social and economic image of Burgundy in all its variety—both good and bad.

A good Clos de Vougeot, however, is a *grand cru* through and through. Although it does not develop the exotic spice of the neighboring Grands-Echézeaux and does not sparkle through the fineness of nearby Musigny, it has a special stature and density, which gives the Pinot Noir variety with all its complexity its own expression.

What is typical of the *terroir* of the Clos de Vougeot is not the marked refinement of an individual outstanding feature, but the fact that this wine depicts the entire image on an exceptional level. This also explains why the vineyard continues to merit its special status, even nine hundred years after its foundation.

Select Producers in the Côte de Nuits

Château de La Tour****
Vougeot
14 acres (5.5 ha); 28,000 bottles • Wines: Clos de Vougeot
The largest holding within the famous *clos* and the only *domaine* and cellar based there has been meeting the challenge with its masculine, concentrated, age-worthy Clos. It is supplemented by the Domaine Pierre Labet of the Côte de Beaune.

Clos de Tart****–*****
Morey-Saint-Denis
19 acres (7.5 ha); 25,000 bottles • Wines: →Grand Cru Clos de Tart
The only Burgundian *clos* still with only one owner, the Mommessin family, has under the management of Sylvain Pitiot finally rediscovered the sort of reliability associated with its status, demonstrating elegance and complexity year after year.

Domaine Alain Burguet****
Gevrey-Chambertin
15 acres (6 ha); 25,000 bottles • Wines: Bourgogne Rouge, Gevrey-Chambertin and →Vieilles Vignes, En Champeaux →En Reniard
Robust wines, sometimes with a tendency to be slightly coarse when young, though produced with great care, enabling this producer to keep pace with many *premiers crus*.

Domaine Charlopin****
Gevrey Chambertin
37 acres (15 ha); 75,000 bottles • Wines include: Marsannay; Fixin; Gevrey Chambertin: Clos de la Justice, →Vieilles Vignes; Morey-Saint-Denis; Chambolle-Musigny; Vosne-Romanée; Grand Cru: Bonnes Mares, Charmes-Chambertin, Clos Saint-Denis, Clos de Vougeot, →Echézeaux, Mazis-Chambertin
Philippe Charlopin makes wines in his own image—powerful and enigmatic—and has for years been one of the protagonists of the new Bourgogne. He has doggedly expanded his estate through the addition of special treasures which include, most recently, the elegant and complex Echézeaux.

Domaine Bruno Clair****
Marsannay
57 acres (23 ha); 110,000 bottles • Wines include: Marsannay Blanc, Rosé, Rouge; Morey-Saint-Denis En la Rue de Vergy →Blanc; Rouge, →Savigny-lès-Beaune Les Dominode; Gevrey Chambertin Premier Cru: Cazetiers, Clos du Fonteny, Clos Saint-Jacques; Grand Cru: Corton-Charlemagne, Chambertin Clos de Bèze
Stately, robust red wines that need a long time to breath, while young Marsannay Blanc—made from Chardonnay and Pinot Gris—and the original Marsannay Rosé are charming.

Domaine Confuron-Cotétidot*****–*****
Vosne-Romanée
27 acres (11 ha); 35,000 bottles • Wines include: Gevrey-Chambertin: Champs-Chenys, Premier Cru: →Lavaux Saint-Jacques, Les Petites Chapelles; Chambolle-Musigny; Vosne-Romanée and Premier Cru →Les Suchots; Nuits-Saint-Georges and Premier Cru; Grand Cru: Clos de Vougeot, Echézeaux
A pioneer of cold maceration before fermentation. Otherwise somewhat conservative production methods, wines rich in extracts. The small proportion of new wood used in aging allows the wine itself to take center stage.

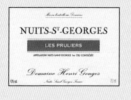

Domaine Dugat-Py*****
Gevrey-Chambertin
17 acres (7 ha); 25,000 bottles • Wines include: Gevrey-Chambertin: Les Evocelles, Couer du Roy Vieilles Vignes; Premier Cru: Corbeau, Fonteny, Perrière, Lavaux Saint-Jacques, →Petite Chapelle; Grand Cru: Chambertin, Charmes-Chambertin, →Mazis-Chambertin
A rising star of the last decade, now producing very deep-colored, beefy wines that combine density and a solid structure with elegance.

Domaine Dujac***–****
Morey-Saint-Denis
31 acres (12.7 ha); 70,000 bottles • Wines include: Morey-Saint-Denis: Blanc, Rouge, Premier Cru Les Monts Luisants; Chambolle Musigny Grand Cru: Bonnes Mares, →Clos de la Roche, Clos Saint-Denis, Echézeaux
The red wines combine floral aromas, delicate fruit, and now also a clearly finer wood note and mild tannins. The grapes are fermented as whole fruit. Recently, the *terroir* has increased its expression in the wine.

Domaine René Engel****
Vosne-Romanée
17 acres (7 ha); 40,000 bottles • Wines: Vosne Romanée and Premier Cru Aux Brûlées; Grand Cru: →Clos de Vougeot, Echézeaux, Grands Echézeaux
Philippe and Frédéric Engel themselves oversee every detail of their estate and produce spicy, elegant, age-worthy wines.

Domaine Henri Gouges****
Nuits-Saint-Georges
36 acres (14.5 ha); 50,000 bottles • Wines include: Bourgogne Blanc, Rouge; Nuits-Saint-Georges blanc Premier Cru Les Perrières; Nuits-Saint-Georges and Premier Cru: Les Chaignots, Les Vaucrains, →Les Saint-Georges
Robust, beefy reds with only a hint of wood that require long aging—and a white wine rarity made from a Pinot Noir mutation using white grapes.

Domaine Jean Grivot****
Vosne-Romanée
36 acres (14.5 ha); 60,000 bottles • Wines include: Vosne-Romanée and Premier Cru: Les Beaumonts, Les Brûlées, Les Chaumes, Les Suchots, Les Reignots; Nuits-Saint-Georges and Premiers Crus Les Boudots, Les Pruliers, Les Roncières; Grand Cru: →Richebourg, Clos de Vougeot, Echézeaux
Exquisitely extracted red wines with an even density and subtlety that give the greatest expression to their *terroirs* after adequate aging in the bottle.

Domaine Anne Gros****–*****
Vosne-Romanée
16 acres (6.5 ha); 30,000 bottles • Wines include: Bourgogne Hautes-Côtes de Nuits blanc, Vosne-Romanée Les Barreaux, Chambolle-Musigny Premier Cru La Combe d'Orveau, Grand Cru: Clos de Vougeot (climat Le Grand Maupertui), Richebourg
Great wines that concentrate the variety, define the *terroir* and have a clear expressive force and an immense potential.

Domaine des Lambrays****
Morey-Saint-Denis
26 acres (10.5 ha); 45,000 bottles • Wines: Puligny-Montrachet; Morey-Saint-Denis and Premier Cru; Grand Cru →Clos des Lambrays (Monopole)

The new owners, the Freund family, have at last provided the excellent estate manager Thierry Brouin with the means for better exploitation of the potential of this long-neglected *grand cru*.

DOMAINE LEROY*****
VOSNE-ROMANÉE
54 acres (22 ha); 40,000 bottles • Wines include: Vosne Romanée Les Genevrières and Premier Cru Beaumonts, Aux Brûlées; Nuits-St-Georges Premier Cru Boudots, → Volnay Premier Cru Santenots; Grand Cru: Chambertin, Musigny, Clos de la Roche, Richebourg, Clos de Vougeot
A legend! The personality of Lalou Bize-Leroy plays as much a part in this as biodynamic cultivation, minimal yields and archaic wine production techniques.

DOMAINE MÉO-CAMUZET****–*****
VOSNE-ROMANÉE
37 acres (15 ha); bought-in grapes; 65,000 bottles • Wines include: Hautes-Côtes de Nuits Blanc; Vosne-Romanée and Premier Cru: Aux Brûlées → Les Chaumes, Au Cros Parantoux; Nuits-Saint-Georges and Premiers Crus Aux Boudots, Aux Murgers; Grand Cru; Richebourg, → Clos de Vougeot, Echézeaux, Corton
Wines exhibiting large quantities of silky tannin and developing opulent fruit while still quite young. Stylishly modern without denying its origins.

DOMAINE DENIS MORTET*****
GEVREY-CHAMBERTIN
27 acres (11 ha); 55,000 bottles • Wines include: Bourgogne Rouge; → Marsannay Les Longeroies; Gevrey-Chambertin: Combe-du-dessus, → En Motrot, Au Vellé, En Champs Vieilles Vignes and Premier Cru: → Les Champeaux, Lavaux Saint-Jacques; Chambolle-Musigny Premier Cru Aux Beaux Bruns; Grand Cru: Chambertin, Clos de Vougeot
With Denis Mortet, each *climat* has its own profile. In his tireless search for perfection, he puts everything into vine cultivation and wine production to represent the *terroir* in finely woven, meaty, spicy, remarkably complex Pinots.

DOMAINE DE LA ROMANÉE-CONTI*****
VOSNE-ROMANÉE
62 acres (25 ha); 95,000 bottles • Wines: Grand Cru: Echézeaux, Grands-Echézeaux, Richebourg, Romanée-Conti (Monopole), Romanée-St-Vivant, La Tache (Monopole), Montrachet
Wines that come very close to the perfect equilibrium of fruit and wood, structure and softness and are faithful images of their *terroirs*. The cult status of these wines is merited.

DOMAINE JOSEPH ROTY****
GEVREY-CHAMBERTIN
23 acres (9.5 ha); 50,000 bottles • Wines include: Bourgogne; Marsannay; Gevrey-Chambertin and Premier Cru Les Fonteneys; Grand Cru: Charmes-Chambertin, → Griottes-Chambertin, → Mazis-Chambertin
Delicately fruity red wines fermented exceptionally slowly and aged in the *domaine*. Many *cuvées* stay in the barrel for up to 30 months.

DOMAINE GEORGES ROUMIER****–*****
CHAMBOLLE MUSIGNY
30 acres (12 ha); 35,000 bottles • Wines include: Chambolle-Musigny and Chambolle-Musigny Premier Cru: → Les Amoureuses, Les Cras; Grand Cru: Ruchottes-Chambertin, Bonnes Mares, → Musigny
Christophe Roumier gives a new dimension to this famous *domaine*, in which elegance is achieved through a particularly successful combination of body, fruit, and wood.

DOMAINE ARMAND ROUSSEAU****
GEVREY-CHAMBERTIN
35 acres (14 ha); 65,000 bottles • Wines: Gevrey-Chambertin and Premier Cru Les Cazetiers, → Clos Saint-Jacques, Lavaux Saint-Jacques; Grand Cru: Chambertin, Chambertin Clos de Bèze, → Ruchottes Chambertin, Charmes-Chambertin, Mazis-Chambertin, Clos de la Roche
Traditional, clean, powerful wines from the best locations in Gevrey. They are often accessible even when young, but have lasting depth and class.

DOMAINE JEAN TRAPET***–*****
GEVREY-CHAMBERTIN
32 acres (13 ha); 60,000 bottles • Wines include: Bourgogne; Marsannay; Gevrey-Chambertin and Premiers Crus Clos Prieur, Petite Chapelle; Grand Cru: Chambertin, → Chapelle-Chambertin, → Latricières-Chambertin
Jean-Louis Trapet has rescued this famous estate from decline and returned it to the top. His *grands crus* are outstanding, juicy, fruitily elegant and enchanting wines. He has been using biodynamic cultivation since 1998, and the other wines have also gained in density.

DOMAINE COMTE DE VOGÜÉ*****
CHAMBOLLE-MUSIGNY
31 acres (12.5 ha); 35,000 bottles • Wines: Bourgogne Blanc (from the Musigny location), Chambolle-Musigny and Premier Cru Les Amoureuses; Grand Cru: Bonnes Mares, → Musigny
Heavily laden with tannin while young but maturing into wines with an opulent bouquet, glow, and play, exclusively from locations in Chambolle-Musigny. Back on top after a weak period in the 1970s and 1980s.

DOMAINE DE LA VOUGERAIE***–*****
PREMEAUX
300 acres (37 ha); 150,000 bottles. • Wines include → Clos Vougeot, Vougeot; → Les Evocelles; Premier Cru Les Cras; → Clos Prieuré, → Clos Blanc de Vougeot; Musigny
The Boissets, famous for playing a leading part in the Burgundian wine business, brought together all the numerous vineyards they owned and then appointed Pascal Marchand, giving him a free hand. A splendid rise to eminence.

JOSEPH FAIVELEY***–*****
NUITS-SAINT-GEORGES
297 acres (120 ha); bought-in grapes; 900,000 bottles • Wines include: Mercurey: Premier Cru Clos du Roy; Gevrey-Chambertin Premier Cru Les Cazetiers; Chambolle-Musigny Premier Cru La Combe d'Orveau; Nuits-Saint-Georges Premier Cru: → Les Damodes, Les Porets; Grand Cru: Chambertin Clos de Bèze, Mazis-Chambertin, Latrizières-Chambertin, Musigny, Clos de Vougeot, Echézeaux, Corton Clos de Faively
The house of Faively is an exquisite *domaine* that only produces small amounts from bought-in grapes and has itself a remarkable portfolio of top-quality locations. François Faively guarantees a classical style with robust, aromatic reds that need aging.

NICOLAS POTEL***–****
NUITS-SAINT-GEORGES
12 acres (1.5 ha); some bought-in grapes; 150,000 bottles. • Wines include: Nuits-Saint-Georges Premiers Crus: Damodes, Vaucrains, Pruliers; Grands Crus: Charmes-Chambertin, Chambertin Clos de Bèze, Clos Vougeot; Pommard Premiers Crus: Rugiens, Jarolliéres; Volnay Premiers Crus: Champans, Pitures; Beaune Premier Cru Grèves
The young Nicolas Potel founded his company in 1997. As he has friendly relations with numerous top winegrowers and uses time-consuming natural vinification methods, he succeeds in producing excellent wines.

CÔTE DE BEAUNE: WHERE CHARDONNAY HOLDS COURT

The area cultivated with vines in the Côte de Beaune is almost twice as large as that in the Côte de Nuits, standing at over 7,400 acres (3,000 ha). Unlike the latter region, though, it is only in the simpler locations of the Côte de Beaune that red wines dominate; the greatest wines here are Chardonnays. Although Corton is the most important *grand cru* in the Côte de Beaune (and throughout Burgundy) in terms of area, having some 242 acres (98 ha) of Pinot Noir, the most prestigious wine comes from Montrachet, which is located well to the south. The white Corton-Charlemagne and the *premiers crus* and Villages wines from Puligny, Chassagne, and Meursault are also highly rated by wine connoisseurs worldwide. The Pinot

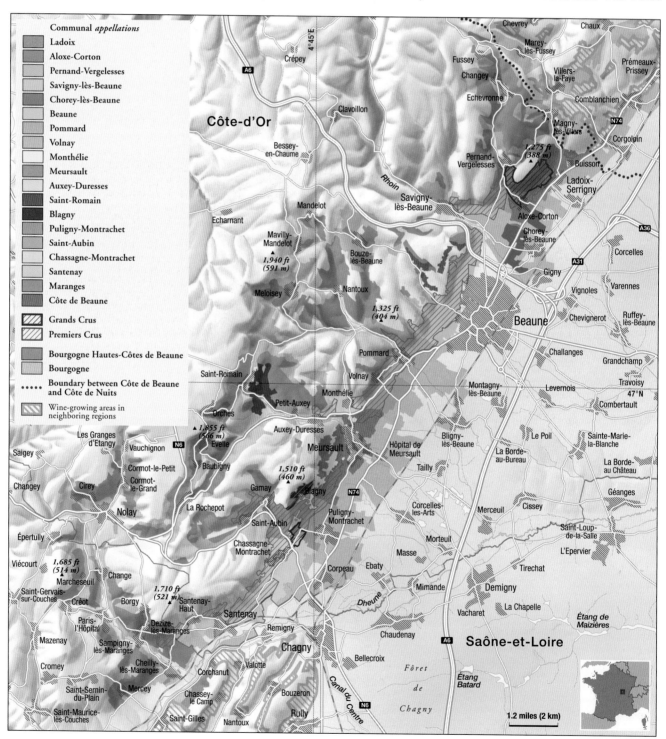

Communal *appellations*

- Ladoix
- Aloxe-Corton
- Pernand-Vergelesses
- Savigny-lès-Beaune
- Chorey-lès-Beaune
- Beaune
- Pommard
- Volnay
- Monthélie
- Meursault
- Auxey-Duresses
- Saint-Romain
- Blagny
- Puligny-Montrachet
- Saint-Aubin
- Chassagne-Montrachet
- Santenay
- Maranges
- Côte de Beaune

Grands Crus

Premiers Crus

Bourgogne Hautes-Côtes de Beaune

Bourgogne

Boundary between Côte de Beaune and Côte de Nuits

Wine-growing areas in neighboring regions

Appellations

COMMUNAL A.O.C.s:

Maximum basic yields of 10.5 gallons/ 120 sq. yds. (40 l/100 sq. m) for red wine, 12 gallons/120 sq. yds (45 l/100 sq. m) for white wine.

LADOIX: 220 acres (89 ha) in Ladoix-Serrigny, 85 percent red wine, 7 *premiers crus* (35 acres/14 ha), lush red wines heavy in fruit; robust whites for maturation.

ALOXE-CORTON: 314 acres (127 ha) in Aloxe-Corton and Ladoix-Serrigny, almost exclusively red wines, 15 *premiers crus* (91 acres/37 ha), deep-colored, robust, age-worthy red wines.

PERNAND-VERGELESSES: 314 acres (127 ha) in Pernand-Vergelesses, 75 percent red wine, 5 *premiers crus* (141 acres/57 ha), powerful, dry red wines; spicy, soft white wines.

SAVIGNY-LÈS-BEAUNE: 870 acres (352 ha) in Savigny-lès-Beaune, over 90 percent red wine, 22 *premiers crus* (356 acres/144 ha), red wines with a rich bouquet and mild fruitiness and striking, delicately nervy white wines.

CHOREY-LÈS-BEAUNE: 331 acres (134 ha) in Chorey-lès-Beaune, 95 percent red wine, fruity, elegant reds.

BEAUNE: 1023 acres (414 ha) in Beaune, over 90 percent red wine, 41 *premiers crus* (796 acres/332 ha), powerfully structured red wines and whites that are smooth and elegant.

POMMARD: 773 acres (313 ha) in Pommard, exclusively red wine, 28 *premiers crus* (309 acres/125 ha), aromatic, robust reds that need time to mature and are not always reliable.

VOLNAY: 558 acres (226 ha) in Volnay and Meursault (*premier cru* "Santenots"), exclusively red wine, 35 *premiers crus* (356 acres/144 ha), fragrant, elegant red wines rich in finesse that number among the best of the Côte-de-Beaune.

MONTHÉLIE: 297 acres (120 ha) in Monthélie, over 90 percent red wine, 11 *premiers crus* (77 acres/31 ha), frequently a slightly rustic version of the Volnay.

MEURSAULT: 899 acres (364 ha) in Meursault, almost exclusively white wine, 17 *premiers crus* (326 acres/132 ha), rich, smooth Chardonnays, mainly with strong wood.

AUXEY-DURESSES: 334 acres (135 ha) in Auxey-Duresses, 75 percent red wine, 9 *premiers crus* (79 acres/32 ha), slightly softer, generally well-proportioned red wines; white wines in the style of a simpler Meursault.

SAINT-ROMAIN: 205 acres (83 ha) in Saint-Romain, 55 percent white wine, relatively high vineyards, somewhat light wines.

BLAGNY: Scarcely used A.O.C. with only 17 acres (7 ha) under cultivation in Meursault and Puligny-Montrachet, exclusively red wine, 6 *premiers crus*, fruity, light reds.

PULIGNY-MONTRACHET: 514 acres (208 ha) in Puligny-Montrachet, almost exclusively white wine, 16 *premiers crus* (247 acres/ 100 ha), mineral, elegant white wines with nerve and style.

SAINT-AUBIN: 358 acres (145 ha) in Saint-Aubin, 55 percent white wine, 29 *premiers crus* (242 acres/98 ha), fruity, elegant, nervy whites; mild, harmonious red wines.

CHASSAGNE-MONTRACHET: 754 acres (305 ha) in Puligny-Montrachet, 60 percent white wine, 54 *premiers crus* (393 acres/159 ha), slightly broader whites than Puligny-Montrachet; robust red wines that can offer great harmony when matured.

SANTENAY: 803 acres (325 ha) in Santenay and Remigny, over 90 percent red wine, 12 *premiers crus* (306 acres/124 ha), beefy red wines with a good framework of tannin.

MARANGES: 445 acres (180 ha) in Cheilly-lès-Maranges, Dezize-lès-Maranges, Sampigny-lès-Maranges, almost exclusively red wine, 7 *premiers crus* (247 acres/100 ha), honest wines rich in tannin.

CÔTE DE BEAUNE: Sub-A.O.C. for "Beaune" + 62 acres (25 ha) in Beaune, 60 percent red wine, not to be confused with Côte de Beaune-Villages.

CÔTE DE BEAUNE-VILLAGES: 109 acres (44 ha) in 14 communes, exclusively red wines, typical, fairly simple wines with a strong structure.

GRANDS CRUS:

Maximum basic yields of 9 gallons/120 sq. yds for red wine (35 l/100 sq. m), 10.5 gallons/120 sq. yds. (40 l/100 sq. m) for white wine.

CORTON: 248 acres (100.4 ha) in Aloxe-Cortin, Ladoix-Serrigny and Pernand-Vergelesses, almost exclusively red wine, 6 acres (2.4 ha) of white wine. The red Corton is a deeply colored, muscular wine tightly packed with fruit, tannin and acid that can be aged for a long time.

CORTON-CHARLEMAGNE: 126 acres (51 ha) in Aloxe-Corton, Ladoix-Serrigny and Pernand-Vergelesses, exclusively white wine. The higher southwest locations of the Corton produce concentrated, mineral white wines with a rigid structure.

MONTRACHET: 15 acres (6.2 ha) in Puligny-Montrachet and Chassagne-Montrachet.

CHEVALIER-MONTRACHET: 18 acres (7.2 ha) in Puligny-Montrachet. Mineral, aromatically complex white wines that develop a luxuriously opulent bouquet with age. Its great concentration and vigor raises the Montrachet above all other Burgundian whites.

BÂTARD-MONTRACHET: 28 acres (11.4 ha) in Puligny-Montrachet and Chassagne-Montrachet. Somewhat broader and weightier than Montrachet, although almost of equal rank in terms of size.

BIENVENUES-BÂTARD-MONTRACHET: 9 acres (3.69 ha) in Puligny-Montrachet. An enclave in Bâtard-Montrachet with an east-southeasterly slope, slightly more elegant than Bâtard-Montrachet, divided among 15 owners.

CRIOTS-BÂTARD-MONTRACHET: 2.5 acres (1 ha) in Chassagne-Montrachet.

Noir wines are perhaps unjustifiably eclipsed by the uniqueness of their white counterparts. The Pinot Noir from the Côte de Beaune usually tends to have a more solid structure, without the characteristic subtlety of wines from the Côte de Nuits.

The climate in the Côte de Beaune is less variable than in the Côte de Nuits. Compared with the Côte de Nuits, the areas planted with vines in the Côte de Beaune are more spread out, with the wine-growing area extending across the width and height of the mountains. Side valleys (*combes*) fracture the band of vineyards further and break the prevailing eastward aspect of the vineyards in a southerly direction. The two *grands crus* are not neighbors, but rather the north and south poles of the region. The Corton has particularly meager soils on a substratum of volcanic origin. On the southwest flank, reserved for Chardonnay especially in the higher locations, the soil is particularly rich in chalk.

The name Charlemagne, usually used to refer to this area of 124 acres (50 ha) or more, is reminiscent of Charles the Great, who had wine made for his own consumption from the best parcels to be found there. Corton *rouge* grows in reddish soils containing limestone and iron. Since almost 250 acres (100 ha) are under cultivation, it has become usual to attach the name of the *climats* to the name "Corton." The magic of Montrachet, the "bare mountain," lies in the unique combination of the meager soil with a hard limestone substratum and an ideal micro-climate. The southerly and southeasterly locations in Montrachet are so thoroughly flooded with light and heat that the Chardonnay ripens fully even in those years when it has difficulties in reaching its optimum ripeness in other locations.

THE AUCTION OF THE HOSPICES DE BEAUNE

On August 4, 1443 Nicolas Rolin, the Chancellor of the Philip the Good, and his wife, Guigone de Salin, left the hospital now known as the Hôtel-Dieu in perpetuity to the town of Beaune. Since the 13th century, hospitals like this one had grown up in many parts of Europe to fulfill two main social functions. They took in the destitute sick and gave them medical help, and also provided accommodation for travelers, such as young people on study trips. Like many others, the Hôtel-Dieu de Beaune earned its keep (and that of its residents) from wine. Over the course of time, penitent believers who were worried about their salvation bequeathed to the hospital vineyards in almost all communes of the Côte de Beaune.

From the Côte de Nuits, the two parcels Clos de la Roche and part of Mazis-Chambertin also found their way into the foundation's portfolio. Today the Hospices de Beaune (Hôtel-Dieu and Hospice de la Charité) own 151 acres (61 ha) of vines, from which they produce 37 different wines. Each *cuvée* is named after the donor of the parcel concerned. Except for two Villages locations, these are exclusively *premiers* and *grands crus*. The Beaune merchants seek to maintain this tradition today, when the young wines of the Hospices de Beaune are auctioned each year on the third Sunday in November—the auction has been held on this day since 1859. The three-day round of festivities begins on Saturday evening in the Clos de Vougeot and ends on Monday morning in Meursault. The highlight is the festive ceremony in the Hôtel-Dieu. On this occasion, the individual *cuvées* are auctioned off for prices usually well in excess of their market value.

The early 15th-century architecture of the Hospices de Beaune buildings is among the few well preserved examples of secular structures from that time period.

On the Saturday before the auction, visiting experts price the wines in the cellars of the Hospice.

Consequently, the surcharges paid are regarded as an important and precise measure of the economic situation in Burgundy and also of the esteem in which it is held internationally. Although the only people allowed to attend the auction are merchants from Beaune, they frequently bid on behalf of clients from elsewhere.

The money raised by the auction (3.5 million euro in 2002, for example), still goes to the hospital, which moved into a new building in 1971. The wines of the Hospices de Beaune are principally of good to very good quality. The Hospice itself lays the foundation for a good primary product with its careful work in the

vineyards. Over 20 winegrowers take care of the vines, and their standard practice includes cutting them back hard and dressing them with dried manure to reduce yields. The first completion phase is also monitored by the Hospice. The red wines are usually well extracted and gain additional structure by blending back with pressed wine, without exhibiting too much drying tannin. The white wines are fermented in wood and often still have a residual sweetness on the day of the auction. The further completion, which plays a major role in the final wine quality, takes place in the cellars of the merchant who auctioned the lot. For this

The bids at the auction held in the market hall in Beaune far and away exceed the market value of the *appellations.*

reason, the foundation's coat of arms, which shows all wines included in the holdings, is no guarantee of a great wine. The crucial element is the name of the bottler, which can be found in the bottom right-hand corner of the label. Some trading houses try to polish up their image by bottling Hospice de Beaune.

There is also a Hospice in Nuits-Saints-Georges with vineyards, which has 30 acres (12 ha) of *premier cru* locations and today supports a home for the elderly. The auction of young wines takes place on the Sunday before Palm Sunday and is essentially a local event, though the wines enjoy a thoroughly good reputation.

The *cuvées* of the Hospices de Beaune

The name of the *appellation* comes first, followed by the name of the donor, then the number of barrels, which can vary from year to year. In 2002 a total of 696 barrels were auctioned, 576 reds and 120 whites. The sequence of the most important *appellations* listed here corresponds to the value of the individual 50-gallon (228-l) *pièces.*

RED WINES:
Clos de la Roche: Cyrot-Chaudron, 2 *pièces*
Clos de la Roche: Georges Kriter, 2 *pièces*
Mazis-Chambertin: Madeleine Collignon, 17 *pièces*
Corton: Docteur Peste, 30 *pièces*
Corton: Charlotte Dumay, 30 *pièces*

Volnay-Santenots: Gauvain, 13 *pièces*
Volnay-Santenots: Jéhan de Massol, 30 *pièces*
Pommard, Raymond Cyrot, 22 *pièces*
Beaune: Dames hospitalières, 30 *pièces*
Beaune: Guigone de Salins, 30 *pièces*
Pommard: Billardet, 30 *pièces*
Pommard: Suzanne Chaudron, 19 *pièces*
Beaune: Rousseau Deslandes, 30 *pièces*
Beaune: Nicolas Rolin, 30 *pièces*
Beaune: Brunet, 19 *pièces*
Volnay: Muteau, 12 *pièces*
Auxey-Duresses: Boillot, 9 *pièces*
Beaune: Clos des Avaux, 25 *pièces*
Beaune: Cyrot-Chaudron, 21 *pièces*
Beaune: Hugues et Louis Bétault, 25 *pièces*

WHITE WINES:
Batard-Montrachet: Dames de Flandres, 4 *pièces*
Corton Charlemagne: Francois de Salins, 6 *pièces*
Corton Vergennes: Paul Chanson, 4 *pièces*
Meursault-Genevrières: Philippe le Bon, 7 *pièces*
Meursault Charmes: Grivault, 9 *pièces*
Meursault-Genevrières: Baudot, 24 *pièces*
Meursault Charmes: Bahèzre de Lanlay, 15 *pièces*
Meursault: Humblot, 10 *pièces*
Meursault: Goureau, 9 *pièces*
Meursault: Loppin, 11 *pièces*
Pouilly-Fuissé: Françabe Poisard, 21 *pièces*

THE CÔTE DE BEAUNE AND "ECO" WINES

For many years the "eco" prefix had a rather esoteric ring about it, particularly when used with wine, and rarely inspired confidence. The 1990s saw a remarkable change in Burgundy and particularly in the Côte de Beaune. The main elements of this ecological movement were no longer general ideological principles, but rather the simple acknowledgment that there had to be a change in direction in the interests of quality. Anne-Claude Leflaive, co-owner of one of the most famous white wine *domaines* in Burgundy, ventured an alarming prognosis at the beginning of the 1990s: "If we don't look after the soil, within ten years there'll be no soil, no vineyards and no wine left in Burgundy."

This may sound like an exaggeration, but the essence of the message was even more serious than it may have appeared initially. Under the auspices of all-round chemical and hi-tech supervision, drinkable wines are now being produced throughout the world. Burgundy, on the other hand, lives off its authenticity, off its small structures, off the *terroir*. But even a soil with *terroir* properties quickly sinks into an industrially standardized substratum if it is over-fertilized, if ill-considered chemical and physical measures destroy its soil life, and if it erodes.

This point marked the start of the new ecological movement in Burgundy. The application of natural cultivation or even biodynamic culture is seen as a means of producing wines more typical of the *terroir* and preserving the uniqueness of Burgundy. Wherever the resulting

The Canadian, Pascal Marchand, took the Domaine des Épenaux into the top group of Pommards using traditional, and ecological methods.

No question about it— nothing beats harvesting by hand!

perspective involves maintaining or even increasing quality, the economic risks associated with the ecological transformation can be calculated and managed. The Domaine Leflaive, for example, spent several years trying out conventional and biodynamic cultivation techniques in parallel in each of its parcels. Conventional techniques have now been abandoned.

This trend is particularly remarkable since it is being initiated from the tip of the quality pyramid. One of the pioneering *domaines*, that of Lalou Bize-Leroy, is competing with Romanée-Conti for first place. Following in the tracks of the Domaine Leflaive, Dominique Lafon, the young owner of the Domaine des Comtes Lafon and another of Burgundy's top enologists, has joined the ecologists. The Domaine des Grands Épenaux des Comte Armand in Pommard has even managed to improve its reputation following the changeover.

The success of the Burgundian "eco" wine-grower is based on a willingness to go the limit in every respect within the vineyard. Limiting yields to a minimum is generally accepted as a guiding principle when it comes to high quality in conventional cultivation too.

However, measures aimed at controlling yield also improve the vine's natural defenses against fungal infection. Furthermore, ecological cultivation calls for the harvested grapes to be rigorously selected. Soil management is also crucially important. A balanced soil life makes for stronger plants, directs root growth, and optimizes the metabolic process. Only if the soil biology is intact can nutrients and minerals be

In the Back Country

The wine-growing areas referred to as the "Hautes Côtes" lie in the mountains above the Côte d'Or. At a height of some 1,640 feet (500 m), the ripening conditions for Chardonnay and Pinot Noir are considerably less favorable than in the valley, where vines grow at a height of 820 to 985 feet (250 to 300 m). The difference in altitude generates a temperature variation of between one and one-and-a-half degrees Celsius on average, which means that harvesting begins a week later than usual, too. The villages of the Hautes-Côtes are mainly known for their aromatic raspberries and blueberries.

In parallel to the valley locations, a distinction is made between the Hautes-Côtes de Nuits and the Hautes-Côtes de Beaune. In 1961 regional sub-A.O.C.s of the A.O.C. Bourgogne were set up for both areas. The vines grow in easterly sites protected from the wind in quite deep, chalky soils. Unfortunately, the qualitative potential is still not being adequately exploited. Moderate rackings benefit primarily from the name "Hautes-Côtes" on the export markets, which suggests a prestigious analogy to the "Haut-Médoc."

Above the Côte d'Or lies another charming wine region.

broken up and made accessible to the root system. Only under these conditions does the *terroir* concept really makes sense.

To provide the soil with the best possible supply of nutrients, a producer cooperative for compost has even grown up on the Côte de Beaune, going by the name of the "Groupement d'Étude et de Suivi des Terroirs" (G.E.S.T.). According to the soil scientist, Claude Bourguignon, a compost is prepared from 20 percent horse manure, 20 percent cow manure, and 40 percent chopped up pieces of tree foliage and MARC, in which the fermentation is monitored with the same scrupulous care as with a wine. The aim is to achieve a humus,

Anne-Claude Leflaive uses biodynamics to guarantee the *terroir* character of her superb white wines.

loose, fragrant compost that is not too rich in nutrients (yields should remain low), but above all promotes the micro-organic life of the soil.

This compost will probably also have a favorable effect on the subsequent alcoholic fermentation with spontaneous yeasts, since the soil's healthy micro-flora also promotes the desired yeast strains. Over 80 *domaines* have joined the G.E.S.T. to date, including giants such as the Beaune merchant Louis Jadot.

SELECT PRODUCERS IN THE HAUTE CÔTES DE NUITS ET DE BEAUNE

LES CAVES DES HAUTES-CÔTES*–***
BEAUNE
1,433 acres (580 ha); 2,000,000 bottles • Wines include: Bourgogne Blanc, Aligoté; Bourgogne Rouge, Passetoutgrains; Hautes-Côtes de Nuits, Hautes-Côtes de Beaune, Gevrey-Chambertin, Beaune, Pommard; Crémant, Château de Bligny
Technically well-equipped, the cooperative cellar located to the south of Beaune produces clean wines at fair prices.

DOMAINE FRANÇOIS CHARLES**–***
NANTOUX
27 acres (11 ha); 60,000 bottles • Wines include: Hautes-Côtes de Beaune: Blanc, Rosé; Aligoté, Meursault; Beaune Premier Cru Les Epenots, Pommard, Volnay
The *domaine* now managed by Pascal Charles became known for its balanced, aromatic red wine; however it needs to be aged in the bottle for a few years.

DOMAINE FRIBOURG**–***
VILLERS-LA-FAYE
47 acres (19 ha); 35,000 bottles • Wines include: Bourgogne: Blanc, Aligoté Hautes-Côtes de Nuits and Rouge
In good years the *domaine* supplies very good Chardonnay; the red wines combine substance and fruit.

DOMAINE LUCIEN JACOB***
ECHVERONNE
35 acres (14 ha); 70,000 bottles • Wines include: Bourgogne Aligoté; Hautes-Côtes de Beaune Rouge, Savigny and Premier Cru, Beaune; Crémant de Bourgogne
Lucien Jacob has done a lot for the Hautes-Côtes, thanks not least to the good quality of his wines.

DOMAINE HENRI NAUDIN-FERRAND***–****
MAGNY-LÈS-VILLERS
54 acres (22 ha); 135,000 bottles • Wines include: Bourgogne: Aligoté, Vieilles Vignes, Hautes-Côtes de Beaune Blanc, Rosé; Rouge Côte de Nuits Villages Vieilles Vignes, Crémant
Henri Naudin has for some time been one of the driving forces behind the Hautes-Côtes. His two daughters, Anne and Claire, have raised the standard further still.

DOMAINE CLAUDE NOUVEAU**–****
CHANGE
32 acres (13 ha); 40,000 bottles • Wines: Bourgogne Aligoté, Santenay; Hautes-Côtes de Beaune Rouge, Maranges and PremierCru La Fussière, Santenay and Premier Cru Grand Clos Rousseau
Right in the south of the Hautes-Côtes, Claude Nouveau's white wines are characteristically fresh, while he produces reduced yields of beefy, attractive reds.

Select Producers in the Côte de Beaune

Comte Senard* – ****
Beaune**
22 acres (9 ha); bought-in grapes; 40,000 bottles
• Wines include: Grand Cru Corton Blanc Cos de
Meix, Corton-Charlemagne; Chorey-lès-Beaune,
Aloxe-Corton and Premier Cru Les Valozières
Conservative, substantial wines with a very rigid structure.

Domaine Marquis d'Angerville**
Volnay**
32 acres (13 ha); 55,000 bottles • Wines include:
Pommard; Meursault Premier Cru Santenots: Volnay
Premier Cru: →Clos des Ducs, Frémiets
Finely woven, yet uncommonly concentrated Volnays
that develop their aromatic complexity late and are
intended to be left to mature.

Domaine du Comte Armand* – *****
Pommard**
18 acres (7.5 ha); 32,000 bottles • Wines include:
Auxey-Duresses; Volnay; →Pommard Premier Cru
Clos des Épeneaux, Volney Premier Crus Les Fremiers
Admirably deep, complex reds. The grapes harvested for
the Clos des Épeneaux are pressed separately according
to the age of the vine, so that they can be assembled later
from ideal basic wines. Natural cultivation.

Domaine d'Auvenay***
Meursault**
10 acres (4 ha); 7,000 bottles • Wines include: Auxey-
Duresses Blanc, Meursault Les Narvaux, Puligny
Montrachet Premier Cru Les Folatières, Grand Cru:
Chevalier-Montrachet, Bonnes Mares, Mazis-Chambertin
Lalou Bize-Leroy's private domaine produces wines that
are models of concentration and clarity.

Domaine Simon Bize**
Savigny-lès-Beaune**
178 acres (22 ha); 80,000 bottles. • Wines include:
Savigny-lès-Beaune, →Grands Liars and Premiers Crus
Marconnets and →Vergelesses, Corton-Charlemagne
Patrick Bize has succeeded in bringing out the elegance
so typical of Savigny in his wines, both red and white.

Domaine Jean-Marc Boillot**
Pommard**
27 acres (11 ha); 45,000 bottles • Wines include:
Meursault, Puligny-Montrachet, Grand Cru Bâtard-
Montrachet; Pommard Premier Cru: →Jarollières,
Rugiens, Volnay and Volnay Premier Cru
Jean-Marc Boillot has a unique collection of premiers
crus and concentrated wines.

Domaine Bonneau du Martray***
Pernand-Vergelesses**
27 acres (11 ha); 55,000 bottles • Wines: Grand Cru:
Corton-Charlemagne, Corton Rouge
The coherent estate lies entirely on the famous
Montagne de Corton and its enormously well-aging
Corton-Charlemagne is at its peak. The rare red Corton
has almost caught up.

Domaine Chandon de Briailles**
Savigny-lès-Beaune**
32 acres (13 ha); 50,000 bottles • Wines include:
Pernand-Vergelesses Premier Cru, Savigny-lès-Beaune,
Grand Cru: Corton Blanc, Corton Clos du Roi
Under feminine management, the estate is adding more
and more depth and finesse to the style of its wines.

Domaine du Château de Pommard*
Pommard**
49 acres (20 ha); 60,000 bottles • Wines: Pommard

Jean-Louis Laplanche, France's foremost expert on
Freud, manages this historical estate with passion
and has made it into a magnet for visitors.

Domaine Coche-Dury** – *****
Meursault**
26 acres (10.5 ha); 45,000 bottles • Wines: Bourgogne
Aligoté, Meursault and Meursault Premier Cru:
Perrières, Rougeots; Volnay Premier Cru
There are few in Burgundy with such mastery of white
wine production as Jean-François Coche-Dury, who
usually gives them two years in pièces and racks them
unfiltered. His red wines are also of a high standard.

Domaine Marc Colin**
Saint-Aubin**
49 acres (20 ha); 130,000 bottles • Wines include:
Saint-Aubin Premier Cru Les Combes, Chassagne-
Montrachet and →Premier Cru Les Caillerets, Grand
Cru Montrachet; Saint-Aubin Premier Cru →Santenay
Vieille Vigne
Marc Colin's wines, both reds and whites, have a clear,
pure line and great finesse.

Domaine Germain Père & Fils**
Chorey-lès-Beaune**
42 acres (17 ha); 85,000 bottles • Wines include:
Pernand-Vergelesses Blanc, Meursault; Chorey-lès-
Beaune; Beaune Premier Cru; Les Cent Vignes, Les
Cras, Les Teurons
Jacques Germain has made a name for the beautiful
Château of Chorey thanks to its Beaune premiers crus;
partly robust, partly filigree-like, aromatic, intensive,
classical reds that age superbly.

Domaine Guyon* – ****
Savigny-lès-Beaune**
116 acres (47 ha); 220,000 bottles • Wines include:
Meursault Premier Cru Les Charmes Dessus,
Chambolle-Musigny →Aloxe-Corton →Volnay, Grand
Cru Corton: Bressandes, Clos du Roi
This large estate spread over the Côte is well-known for
reliable wines with clear fruit.

Domaine Michel Lafarge**
Volnay**
25 acres (10 ha); 50,000 bottles • Wines include:
Meursault; Beaune Premier Cru: →Les Grèves, Les
Teurons; Pommard Premier Cru Les Pézerolles Volnay
vendages sélectionées and Premier Cru: →Clos du
Château des Ducs
Balanced, stylish wines numbering among the best
Volnays and Beaunes. The premiers crus have a
considerable maturing potential.

Domaine de Comte Lafon***
Meursault**
35 acres (14 ha); 60,000 bottles • Wines include:
Meursault and Meursault Premier Cru: Les Charmes,
Les Perrières, Les Genevrières; Grand Cru Montrachet;
Volnay Premier Cru: Champans, Santenots du Milieu
With a perfectly ripened harvest, thanks to biological
cultivation, and meticulous cellar work, Dominique
Lafon achieves magnificent white wines and fragrant,
concentrated Pinots year after year. There has been a
sister estate in Mâconnais since 1999.

Domaine Leflaive***
Puligny-Montrachet**
54 acres (22 ha); 110,000 bottles • Wines include:
Puligny-Montrachet and Premier Cru: Les Combettes,
Les Folatières, Les Pucelles; Grand Cru: Chevalier-
Montrachet, Montrachet

By switching over to biodynamic cultivation, Anne-Claude Leflaive has ensured that the wines from her world-famous *domaine* express their *terroir* masterfully.

Domaine de Montille****
Volnay
18.5 acres (7.5 ha); 30,000 bottles • Wines include: Puligny-Montrachet Premier Cru Les Caillerets; Pommard Premier Cru: Les Grands Épenots, Pézerolles, Rugiens; Volnay Premier Cru: Les Mitans, → Taillepieds
Remarkable Pommards and Volnays with little chaptalization. Often delicate when young, they develop a great opulence as the years go by.

Pierre Morey****
Meursault
23 acres (9 ha); 45,000 bottles • Wines include: Meursault and → Premier Cru Perrières, Grand Cru Bâtard-Montrachet; Pommard and Premier Cru Les Grands Épenots
Opulently fruity white wines finished with great attention to detail. Biodynamic cultivation.

Domaine Jacques Prieur****–*****
Meursault
52 acres (21 ha); 90,000 bottles • Wines include: Meursault Premier Cru Les Perrières; Grand Cru: Chevalier-Montrachet, Montrachet; Volnay Premier Cru: Clos des Santenots; Beaune Premier Cru
Since the merchant house of Antonin Rodet acquired a share in this exquisite estate, Martin Prieur and the enologist Nadine Gublin have truly worked wonders.

Domaine Rapet***–****
Pernand-Vergelesses
146 acres (18 ha); 80,000 bottles. • Wines include Aloxe-Corton, Beaune, Pernand-Vergelesses and Premiers Crus Île de Vergelesses, → Clos Villages, Caradeux, Grand Cru: Corton, Corton-Charlemagne
The wines of the family domains, especially the Chardonnays, have gained recently in definition and reputation.

Domaine Roulot****
Meursault
81 acres (10 ha); 55,000 bottles. • Wines include: Bourgogne Blanc, Mersault and Premiers Crus Perrières and Charmes
Jean-Marc Roulot bottles wine from several delightful Villages vineyards; the two *premiers crus* are his masterpieces.

Domaine Sauzet****
Puligny-Montrachet
20 acres (8 ha); bought-in grapes; 120,000 bottles • Wines include: Puligny-Montrachet and Premier Cru: → Les Combettes, Grand Cru: Bâtard-Montrachet, Bienvenues-Bâtard-Montrachet
Very clean, elegant wines with accentuated fruit that clearly express the character of the *terroir* with unobtrusive hints of wood.

Domaine Tollot-Beaut****
Chorey-lès-Beaune
59 acres (24 ha); 130,000 bottles • Wines: Grand Cru Corton-Charlemagne; Chorey-lès-Beaune, Savigny-lès-Beaune and Premier Cru, Beaune and Premier Cru: Clos du Roi, Grèves, Aloxe-Corton
The young generation of Tollots has raised this well-known estate to a high and consistent standard.

Maison Bouchard Père & Fils**–*****
Beaune
321 acres (130 ha); bought-in grapes; 600,000 bottles • Wines include: Meursault Premier Cru: Pommard Premier Cru Rugiens; Beaune Premier Cru: Grèves,

Vigne de l'Enfant Jésus; Grand Cru: Montrachet, Chevalier-Montrachet, Corton, La Romanée
Joseph Henriot has brought qualitative consistency to this famous trading house with its important *domaine* (since 1995?).

Maison Champy**–****
Beaune
101 acres (12.5 ha); some bought-in grapes; 450,000 bottles. • Wines include: Bourgogne Signature, Beaune and Premier Cru, Auxey-Duresse, Chorey-es-Beaune, Savigny and Premier Cru, Penand-Vergelesses, Pommard, Meursault Saint-Roamin, Chambolle-Musigny, Nuits-Saint-Georges,; Grand Cru: Clos de Vougeot, Corton, Corton-Charlemagne, Échezeaux; Chablis, Premier Cru, Grand Cru.
Founded in 1720, the first wine business in Beaune, Champy has undergone an impressive renaissance since 1990 at the hands of Henri and Pierre Meurgey and Pierre Beuchet. Particularly noteworthy characteristics are the expression of the *terroir* in question and the quality of their brand wine Bourgogne Signature.

Maison Chartron et Trébuchet**–****
Puligny-Montrachet
22 acres (9 ha); bought-in grapes • Wines include: Saint-Romain, Rully, Meursault, Puligny-Montrachet and Premiers Crus: Clos de Cailleret, Folatières; Grand Cru: Chevalier-Montrachet, Bâtard-Chevalier-Montrachet; Volnay, Monthélie, Chassagne-Montrachet
Jean-René Chartron has expanded his top-quality *domaine* with the addition of a company that he founded with his friend, Louis Trébuchet. Concentrating primarily on white wine, there is a broad and extremely reliable range on offer, supplemented by a few reds.

Maison Joseph Drouhin***–*****
Beaune
151 acres (61 ha); 240,000 bottles • Wines include: Chablis, Beaune Blanc Premier Cru; Grand Cru: Montrachet Marquis de Laguiche, Corton-Charlemagne; Beaune and Premiers Crus; → Volnay Premier Cru Grand Cru: Musigny, Bonnes Mares, Clos de Vougeot, Grands Echézeaux
Extremely elegant and profound style of white wine. Breathtakingly fruity reds.

Maison Louis Jadot***–*****
Beaune
360 acres (144 ha); bought-in grapes; 8,000,000 bottles • Wines include: → Meursault Premier Cru Perrières, Puligny-Montrachet Premier Cru; Grand Cru: Chevalier-Montrachet Les Demoiselles, Corton-Charlemagne; Gevrey-Chambertin; Nuits-Saint-Georges, Beaune, Santenay; Grand Cru: Chapelle-Chambertin, Musigny, Bonnes Mares, Clos de la Roche
This highly consistent company owned by three Americans has an admirable range of top-quality locations. The typical Jadot Pinot is soft and dense, but still ages very well.

Maison Olivier Leflaive***–****
Puligny-Montrachet
30 acres (12 ha); bought-in grapes; 800,000 bottles • Wines include: Saint-Aubin, Saint-Romain, Santenay, Rully, Puligny-Montrachet Premier Cru Champ Gain, Meursault Premiers Crus Les Charmes; Grand Cru: Criots-Bâtard-Montrachet; Pommard Premier Cru, Volnay Premier Cru Champans
Since 1994 Olivier Leflaive has been running his wine business entirely independently of the famous *domaine*. The emphasis is on similarly clearly defined white wines, but the red *premiers crus* are also of a high standard.

NOT JUST JUNIOR PARTNERS: WINES OF THE CÔTE CHALONNAISE

Chalon was an important Celtic trading post in Gaul. Its harbor also served as a transhipment point for wine. Well over 20,000 Roman amphorae have been found in graves in the Sâone. Geologically, the Côte Chalonnaise is not a continuous outcrop like the Côte d'Or. As a result, the vineyards here no longer stretch across the region in a single band. There are no *grands crus*, but five communal A.O.C.s, four of which also have *premier cru* locations. The A.O.C. locations of the communes of Bouzeron, Rully, and Mercurey in the north are almost a complete continuation of the Côte de Beaune. Towards the south, vineyards appear wherever the geology has left behind limestone. The isolated vineyards of Givry in the center and Montagny in the south of the region also have a communal A.O.C. Since most vines on the Côte Chalonnaise grow at heights of between 985 and 1,150 feet (300 and 350 m), the micro-climate in the different locations plays a crucial role here and harvesting usually begins a few days later than on the Côte d'Or. In bad years, Chardonnay and Pinot Noir have difficulties in ripening, while in good years wines can be produced that are the equal of their big brothers from the north in all but price. For this reason the region has been held in high regard over the last ten years—particularly in view of the notorious shortage of good Burgundies.

NICHE MARKETING

Historically, however, the Côte Chalonnaise has occupied two niches on account of the lower seasonal constancy of its wines. First, the Gamay zone begins in the Côte Chalonnaise. Today it covers roughly one-eighth of the area and is usually pressed with lower-quality batches of Pinot Noir into Bourgogne Passetoutgrains. Second, the area is a center of sparkling wine production. Harvested Chardonnay and Pinot Noir grapes that are rich in acid are ideal for the production of Crémant de Bourgogne.

At present there seems to be a polarization of quality on the Côte Chalonnaise. While in the lower- and medium-price brackets, the trend is toward full harvests and therefore a standard-ization of wines, better estates are in the same situation as their colleagues in the Côte d'Or, who have to set aside their wines for regular customers leaving nothing for new customers, despite rising prices. The fatalistic reference made by many producers to the territorial hier-archy of Burgundy also seems to serve as an alibi. The higher susceptibility to oxidation of the Côte Chalonnaise's Pinot Noir, for instance, which is often used as an excuse, also has something to do with a lower yield discipline and not only the *terroir*. The A.O.C. regulations of all communal A.O.C.s, with the exception of Mercureys, antici-pate yields of around 1 to 2.5 gallons per 120 sq. yds (5 to 10 liters per 100 sq. m).

CHALONNAISE
Bouzeron
Rully
Mercurey
Givry
Montagny
Côte Chalonnaise
MÂCONNAIS
Mâcon
Mâcon Villages
Viré-Clessé
Saint-Véran
Pouilly-Fuissé
Pouilly-Loché and Pouilly-Vinzelles
Wine-growing areas in neighboring regions

Left
The wine-growing villages around Chalon-sur-Saône grow Bourgognes with their own profile.

THE APPELLATIONS OF THE CÔTE CHALONNAISE

BOUZERON ALIGOTÉ: 151 acres (61 ha) on particularly meager soils, the only communal A.O.C. for Aligoté.
RULLY: 756 acres (306 ha) on light soils, early ripening wines, 65 percent white wines.
MERCUREY: 1,604 acres (649 ha); 90 percent earthy Pinot Noir, upper yield limits as in the Côte d'Or (as a basic yield: 10.5 gal-lons/120 sq. yds (40 l/100 sq. m) for red wine, 12 gallons/120 sq. yds (45 l/100 sq. m) for white wine).

GIVRY: 541 acres (219 ha); red wines (85 percent) are compared to Volnay, the Chardonnay (15 percent) is famous for its highly unusual licorice bouquet.
MONTAGNY: 638 acres (258 ha) (all current sites are *premiers crus*, 100 percent Chardonnay, very popular in England. For Pierre Poupon it is a white wine "that keeps the mouth cool and the head clear."
BOURGOGNE CÔTE CHALONNAISE: 1,058 acres (428 ha) 75 percent white wines.

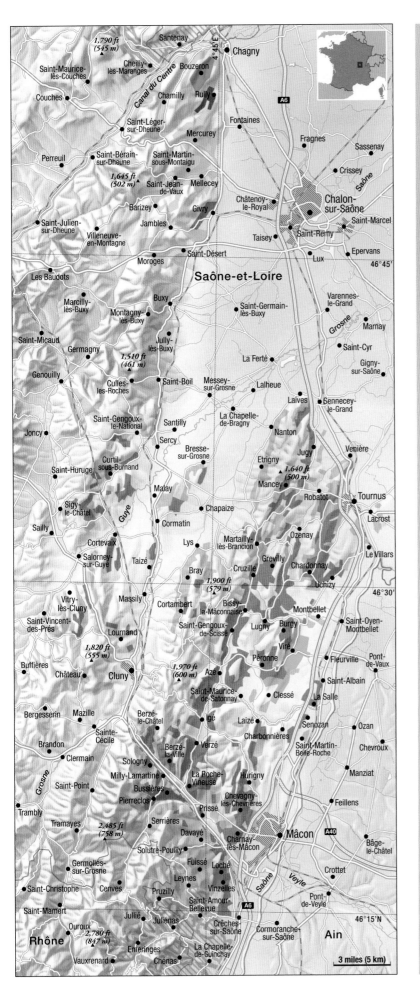

Cremant de Bourgogne

Nadine Masson supplies good crémant and fine Sautenay.

The A.O.C. Crémant de Bourgogne came into being in 1975. For a long time, however, this sparkling Burgundy remained something of an outcast. Sparkling wine, it was felt, belongs in Champagne.

It was only the boom in the champagne market that led to a certain degree of introspection. Many parts of Burgundy have ideal conditions for the production of basic *crémant* wines, particularly the slightly higher acid level of wines from the Côte Chalonnaise and from the Hautes-Côtes, but also wines from the north. The Côte Chalonnaise is the historical center of crémant. Here, they were quick to recognize that Chardonnay and Pinot always had enough class to support the *cuvées*, in addition to which, Aligoté can contribute a delicate spice. Consequently, the department of Saône-et-Loire has the best conditions for crémant production anywhere in Burgundy.

This development was also not without consequences in the department of the Côte d'Or. In the Hautes-Côtes itself, there are plenty of wines that develop their greatest charm as crémants. In addition to this is the fact that the Châtillonais, that northerly enclave belonging to the Côte d'Or for administrative purposes, is a mini-El Dorado for crémant, and there is a very active community of producers in the department of Yonne too, who have devoted themselves to crémant production.

After a distinct setback in the mid-90s, the demand for crémant has increased sharply. Today's production is just under 10 million bottles.

The statutory provisions are aimed at setting the value of the A.O.C. very high right from the start, although the upper yield limits of 17 gallons per 120 sq. yds (65 liters per 100 sq. m) are too high for this. Selective hand-picking is the prescribed method. Only 26 gallons of must may be made from 331 lbs of grapes (100 liters per 150 kg). After the initial fermentation, the basic wine begins a secondary fermentation in the bottle with a minimum period of nine months in yeast according to traditional methods. However, good crémants remain in contact with the yeast for significantly longer.

In the case of crémant, removal of the sediment is also followed by racking, traditionally with a low sugar content in Burgundy.

Not Just Poor Relations: Wines of the Mâconnais

Barrels of different sizes and ages are used to fine-tune the character of the wine.

It is in the Mâconnais that Burgundy begins its transition into southern French culture. In an area measuring 30 × 9 miles (50 × 15 km), the vineyards lie between meadows and arable land, spread across limestone hills. Climatically, the Mâconnais has more sun and fewer worries over frost and hail than most other parts of Burgundy. Consequently, historically speaking, vine cultivation has had a rural orientation and been rather lacking in ambition.

The north of the region, in particular, is dominated by mixed agriculture and organization into cooperatives (some 70 percent of all wines in the Mâconnais are produced by cooperatives), while in the south there are a greater number of professional winegrowers and private estates. The spectacular rock formations of Solutré and Vergisson are made from the same Jura limestone that characterizes the Côte d'Or and have become the symbol of wine growing in the Mâconnais. Not far from these particularly privileged Chardonnay locations, there is also granite soil like that in Beaujolais. The transition between the two is in many respects smooth. The Chardonnays from Saint-Amour, a Beaujolais-Cru commune, for instance, have a claim to the communal Mâconnais A.O.C. St-Véran. Red Mâcon, on the other hand, is mainly Gamay or with the emphasis on Gamay, although it is rarely of good caliber. Roughly two-thirds of the Mâconnais vine-cultivation area is stocked with Chardonnay. There are no *premiers* or *grands crus*, the quality pyramid being limited to regional and communal A.O.C.s. There is no doubt that a few producers from certain

Right page
The rock of Solutré dominates the Pouilly-Fuisse region—the underground prehistoric museum is worth a visit. It has exhibits from the Old Stone Age period—the Solutrean—from which the rock derives its name.

communes have been consistently producing outstanding Chardonnays that are being sold below-value in view of the current regulations, at least in terms of their classification.

The region suffers from a misrepresentation of its producing capability. Due to a lack of prestige, up to three-quarters of Mâconnais whites have in recent years been sold under the A.O.C. Bourgogne. An important reason for this is that the cooperatives themselves have largely left the marketing of their wines to the wine trade, who, unlike the cooperatives, have no interest in consumers linking these reliable Chardonnays to the name Mâcon. Even today, only about half the wines from the Mâconnais carry the name of their own area. Nevertheless, in recent years a few cooperatives have started to market relatively large quantities of their wines themselves.

The Mâconnais is about to enter a period of expansion—not so much in terms of quantity, but rather quality and attitude. The wines of the A.O.C. Pouilly-Fuissé have rapidly won international prestige and appreciation. Even Saint-Véran, until recently the only other communal A.O.C. of any importance, has benefited from the boom on the Burgundy market. The 1999 vintage saw the establishment of the third communal A.O.C. of "Viré-Clessé."

There are gratifying signs that producers are becoming bolder when it comes to working to improve the quality of their wines, for example, in the conflict over the sweet wines of Jean Thévenets (which were finally denied the A.O.C.). It is to be hoped, therefore, that in addition to the highly mechanized production of balanced, value-for-money Chardonnays, the regional A.O.C.s of Mâcon and Mâcon-Villages will find a suitable place on the market for more demanding types of Mâconnais wine.

APPELLATIONS

MÂCON/PINOT-CHARDONNAY MÂCON: 171 acres (69 ha); Only Mâcon is now used as a declassification A.O.C.
MÂCON SUPÉRIEUR: 2,175 acres (880 ha); higher alcohol potential required than for Mâcon.
MÂCON VILLAGES OR MÂCON followed by the name of the commune: 7,532 acres (3,048 ha) in 43 locations. The name "Villages" can be used only with white wines. Upper yield limits (basic): 14 gallons/120 sq. yds (55 l/100 sq. m) for rosé and red wines,

16 gallons/120 sq. yds (60 l/100 sq. m) for Chardonnay.
VIRÉ-CLESSÉ: For the first time with sales of the 1999 vintage.
POUILLY-FUISSÉ 1843 acres (746 ha), **POUILLY-LOUCHÉ** 72 acres (29 ha), **PUILLY-VINZELLES** 124 acres (50 ha): Chardonnay with nutty overtones and a lovely smoothness, maximum yield 11 gallons/120 sq. yds (50 l/100 sq. m).
ST-VÉRAN: 1,379 acres (558 ha); maximum yield (basic) 12 gallons/120 sq. yds (55 l/100 sq. m).

Select Producers in the Côte Chalonnaise

Stéphane Aladame***–****
Montagny

*15 acres (6 ha); 20,000 bottles • Wines: →Bourgogne
Aligoté, Montagny Premier Cru: Les Coères, → Les
Burnins; Crémant*
Since 1992, this young winemaker has gained a solid
reputation with his well-structured white wines.

Clos Salomon***–***
Givry

*17.3 acres (7 ha); 35,000 bottles • Wine: Givry
Premier Cru*
Wine from Givry was appreciated at the Papal Court in
Avignon as early as 1375. Under Ludovic du Gardin,
this historic location has regained its former glory. Its
red wine proves it—with style and structure.

Domaine René Bourgeon***–****
Givry

*22 acres (9 ha); 40,000 bottles • Wines: Givry Blanc Clos
de la Brûlée; Bourgogne, Givry Villages, Givry La Baraude*
René Bourgeon has now transferred his biodynamic
operation to his son Jean-François and son-in-law
Christophe Zaninot. The wines continue to be excellent.

Domaine Jean-Claude Brelière***–****
Rully

*19 acres (7.5 ha); 40,000 bottles • Wines: Rully Blanc
La Barre and Premier Cru Les Margotés; Rully Premier
Cru: Les Préaux, Les Montpalais, Les Champs Cloux*
When he began pruning his vines, people thought he
was mad. Now the balance and elegance of his wines
speak for themselves.

Domaine Brintet***
Mercurey

*32 acres (13 ha); 70,000 bottles • Wines include: Mercurey
Blanc: Vieilles Vignes; Premier Cru: Les Crêts; Mercurey:
La Charmée, La Perrière, Les Crêts, La Levrière, Rully*
The Brintets number among the up-and-coming
producers of the Côte Chalonnaise; within a few years
they have developed a remarkably dense style of wine.

Domain Vincent Dureuil-Janthial***–****
Rully

*33.4 acres (13.5 ha); 78,000 bottles • Wines include:
Rully: Blanc, Rouge, Premiers Crus; Nuits Saint-
Georges, Bourgogne*
Raymond, a representative of the best tradition, has now
transferred the family estate to his son Vincent, who
quickly became acquainted with more modern wines.

Domaine Jacqueson****
Rully

*22 acres (9 ha); 60,000 bottles • Wines include: Rully
Premier Cru: →La Pucelle, Grésigny; Rully →Les
Chaponnières Mercurey Les Vaux and Premier Cru
Naugues*
Henri and Paul Jacqueson have demonstrated for many
years that Rully is as suitable for red wines as for whites;
these are remarkably structured, spicy wines.

Domaine Joblot****
Givry

*32 acres (13 ha); 65,000 bottles • Wines: Givry Blanc
and Premier Cru Servoisine; Givry Rouge and Premier
Cru: →Servoisine, Cellier aux Moines*
The brothers Jean-Marc and Vincent Joblot have
conjured up concentrated reds with distinct fruit and
overtones of wood, which provide an elegant stage for
the *terroir* of Givry.

Domaine Emile Juillot***
Mercurey

*28 acres (11.5 ha); 45,000 bottles • Wines include:
Bourgogne Côte Chalonnaise blanc, Mercurey and
Premier Cru La Cailloute; Mercurey Château Mipont,
Mercurey Premier Cru: Champs Martins, Les Combins,
Les Croichots*
Jean-Claude Theulot is renowned for his solid, well-
structured, carefully finished red wines.

Domaine Michel Juillot***
Mercurey

*74 acres (30 ha); 180,000 bottles • Wines include:
Mercurey Blanc, Grand Cru Corton-Charlemagne;
Mercurey and Premier Cru: →Les Champs Martins,
Grand Cru Corton-Perrières*
As an apostle of the Mercurey *appellation*, Michel
Juillot has made a significant contribution to its
renaissance. His reds are substantial, packed with fruit
and with wood overtones.

Domaine François Lumpp****
Givry

*16 acres (6.5 ha); 35,000 bottles • Wines include: Givry
Blanc Premier Cru Crausot and Petit Marole; Givry and
Premier Cru: →Clos du Cras Long, →Clos Jus, Crausot*
Isabelle and François Lumpp draw attention to white
and red wines with finesse.

Domaine du Meix-Foulot***
Mercurey

*49 acres (20 ha); 55,000 bottles • Wines: Bourgogne
Aligoté, Mercurey Blanc and Rouge; Mercurey Premier
Cru: Les Biots, →Clos du Château de Montaigu, Les Velys*
Low yields and conservative vinification techniques lead
to complex, traditional wines in the finest sense.

Domaine de Villaine****
Bouzeron

*49 acres (20 ha); 110,000 bottles • Wines include:
→Bouzeron, Rully Les Saint-Jacques; Mercurey Les
Montots, Bourgogne*
Well-aging Aligoté in *cru* quality from a competent
producer. Aubert de Villaine is a co-owner and one of
the two directors of the Domaine de la Romanée-Conti.
His vineyards use bio-cultivation techniques. Excellent
other *crus*.

Maison André Delorme**–***
Rully

*161 acres (65 ha); bought-in grapes; 450,000 bottles
• Wines include: Bouzeron, Rully, Montagny Premier
Cru; Rully Premier Cru: Grésigny, Les Cloux, La Fosse,
Marissou; Givry Premier Cru Clos du Cellier aux
Moines; Crémant de Bourgogne*
André Delorme founded his house in 1942 for the
production of crémant. Still a specialist in this sector, the
focus has for some time been on the still wines of the
Domaine de la Renarde, with which Jean-François
Delorme gained much prestige.

Maison Antonin Rodet**–****
Mercurey

*309 acres (125 ha); bought-in grapes; 7,000,000 bottles
• Wines include: Série Cave Privée with communal
A.O.C.s of the Côte d'Or, Rully Château de Rully, Givry
Château de la Ferté, →Mercurey Château de Chamirey*
The increasingly reliable merchant on the main street of
Mercurey is on the up and up. Provenances outside the
Côte Chalonnaise are appearing more and more
frequently on foreign markets.

Select Producers in the Mâconnais

Cave de Mancey**—***
TOURNUS

371 acres (150 ha); 600,000 bottles • Wines: various Mâcon-Villages, → Vieilles Vignes; red domaine wines like → Mâcon Mancey: Domaine Jean Chapuis Domaine André Dupuis

The small cooperative in the north of the Mâconnais is moving more and more toward pressing and racking the grapes of its cooperative members separately.

Château Fuissé***—****
FUISSÉ

74 acres (30 ha); 200,000 bottles • Wines include: Pouilly-Fuissé: Les Clos, Les Combettes, Vieilles Vignes

At Jean-Jacques Vincent's estate, freshness and the spicy aspects of the Chardonnay are at the fore. Depending on the vintage, he represses some or all of the malolactic acid conversion, to achieve optimum balance in his wines.

Domaine Barraud***—****
VERGISSON

17 acres (7 ha); 40,000 bottles • Wines: Mâcon-Vergisson, Saint-Véran Pouilly-Fuissé: → La Verchère, Vieilles Vignes

Very good, cask-fermented Pouilly-Fuissés, the Cuvée Vieilles Vignes is a particular success.

Domaine de la Bongran****—*****
CLESSÉ

37 acres (15 ha); 80,000 bottles • Wines include: Viré-Clessé, Mâcon Viré Domaine Gillet, Cuvée Levroutée, Cuvée Botrytis

Jean Thévenet produces wines in Clessé's special microclimate, partly with late harvests and their residual sweetness and even highly sweet Botrytis Chardonnays.

Domaine Cordier Pére & Fils****
FUISSÉ

27 acres (11 ha); 60,000 bottles • Wines include: Saint-Véran, Pouilly-Fuissé, Métertière, → Vignes Blanches, → Vers Cras

Roger and Christophe Cordier are well known for their opulent Chardonnays, sometimes rounded off with a breath of residual sweetness.

Domaine des Deux Roches***
DAVAYÉ

84 acres (34 ha); bought-in grapes; 330,000 bottles • Wines include: Saint-Véran, Les Cras, Les Terres Noires, Pouilly Fuissé; Mâcon, Mâcon Villages, Mâcon Pierreclos

Jean-Luc Terrier and Christophe Collovray produce dense, mineral Chardonnays that combine wood and fruit a wonderful complexity. The red wines are also impressive.

Domaine J.A. Ferret****
FUISSÉ

37 acres (15 ha); 40,000 bottles • Wines: Pouilly-Fuissé: Tête de Cru Les Perrières, Tête de Cru Le Clos, → Hors-Classe "Les Ménétières," → Hors-Classe Tournant de Pouilly

This is the stronghold of traditional Pouilly-Fuissé, where honey-scented wines with discreet hints of wood are produced from the grapes of old vines.

Domaine Guffens-Heynen*****
VERGISSON

7 acres (3 ha); 17,000 bottles • Wines: Mâcon Pierreclos and Le Chavigne, Pouilly Fuissé: Premier Jus, Clos de Petit Croux

Using archaic instruments (the press dates back to the 17th century), perfectionist wines are pressed, offering aromas of wood, fruit, acid, and late harvest.

Domaine Guillot-Broux**—***
CRUZILLE

40 acres (16 ha); 90,000 bottles • Wines: Mâcon Chardonnay Les Combettes, Mâcon Grévilly Les Genièvrières; Mâcon Cruzilly, Mâcon Grévilly Rouge

In good vineyards, Jean-Gérard Guillot-Broux uses bio-cultivation to produce substantial reds, and ripe, golden-colored Chardonnays with a delicate hint of hazelnut.

Domaine René Michel et ses Fils***—****
CLESSÉ

37 acres (15 ha); 80,000 bottles • Wines: Viré-Clessé: Cuvée traditionelle, Vieilles Vignes Blanc; Mâcon Rouge

René Michel and his three sons bring in hand-picked late harvests from old vines, which in most years are fermented without chaptalization.

Domaine Saint-Denis
LUGNY

12.3 acres (5 ha); 30,000 bottles • Wines include: Bourgogne Rouge, Mâcon Chardonnay, Mâcon Lugny, Passerillés de Novembre

Hubert Laferrère is passionate about keeping close to nature in cultivating vines and relies on natural yeasts for fermentation. This results in wines of outstanding structure with a marked character, and in fine sweet specialty wines.

Domaine Jacques and Nathalie Saumaize***—****
VERGISSON

17 acres (7 ha); 35,000 bottles • Wines include: Saint-Véran: En Crèches, also Vieilles Vignes, Poncelys; Pouilly-Fuissé: La Roche, → Vieilles Vignes

A young operation showing that mineral characteristics and the use of wood do not represent a contradiction for the good wines of the Crus des Mâconnais.

Domaine Saumaize-Michelin***
VERGISSON

22 acres (9 ha); 50,000 bottles • Wines include: Saint-Véran: En Crèches → Vieilles Vignes, Pouilly-Fuissé: Vignes Blanches, → Clos de la Roche, → Les Ronchevats; Mâcon rouge Les Bruyères Tradition

Roger Saumaize numbers among the best winegrowers in Vergisson. His white wines are both nervy and mineral and display skillfully balanced spice and hints of roasting from the barrels.

Domaine du Vieux Saint-Sorlin****
LA ROCHE-VINEUSE

18 acres (7.5 ha); bought-in grapes; 90,000 bottles • Wines include: → Viré-Clessé, → Saint-Véran, Pouilly-Fuissé: Bourgogne Rouge

Oliver Merlin makes tremendous wines that respond superbly to the use of wood.

Maison Auvigne**—****
CHARNAY-LÈS-MÂCON

12 acres (5 ha); bought-in grapes; 270,000 bottles • Wines include: Mâcon Solutré; Saint-Véran, Pouilly-Fuissé: Les Chailloux, Vieilles Vignes, Hors Classes

Jean-Pierre Auvigne has specialized in wines from the immediate vicinity.

Maison Verget****
SOLOGNY

Bought-in grapes • Wines include: Mâcon Vergisson La Roche, Saint-Véran; Pouilly-Fuissé, Ladoix, Meursault, Corton Charlemagne, Bâtard Montrachet

The commercial sector of Guffens Heynen specializes exclusively in white wines for which grapes are bought in and vinified in-house.

BEAUJOLAIS

Beaujolais Nouveau is perhaps the best-known of all French wines. Each year on the third Thursday in November its arrival is welcomed across the globe, from Tokyo to Los Angeles. What used to be no more than a local custom—the sale of *Beaujolais nouveau* in the bars of Lyons (the *bouchons*) has now become a worldwide cult.

There is no doubt that Beaujolais has profited from this boom, but the variety of its products is often suppressed by the popularity of the *nouveau* (or *primeur*). In the narrow strip of land between Lyons and Mâcon, wines are produced that can hold their own against the famous Burgundies produced further north. It may be regrettable that these top-class Beaujolais were for many years less famous than other French growths; on the other hand, though, this factor has influenced prices so that first-class Beaujolais are significantly cheaper than comparable Burgundian wines.

From a historical perspective, Beaujolais was never part of the region of Burgundy. However, when the northern section was annexed to the department of Saône-et-Loire, it became part of Burgundy, at least for administrative purposes. By contrast, the majority of Beaujolais and its capital city Villefranche-sur-Saône belong to the department of Rhône, whose administrative center is Lyons. Nonetheless, for the purposes of wine law, the entire Beaujolais region belongs to Bourgogne.

The Beaujolais is a delightful region to the northwest of Lyon. The Wine Route runs through its most beautiful villages and hamlets.

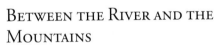

This old mill has given its name to the most well known Beaujolais *cru*: Moulin-à-Vent.

In the 14th century, the most important grape variety in Beaujolais, the Gamay, had even taken over the best sites in the Côte d'Or, something that enraged Philip the Bold, Duke of Burgundy. In 1395 he ordered that the Gamay vines should be ripped out. Pinot Noir was, therefore, planted further to the north. However, Gamay survived in Beaujolais and in the Mâconnais. Its finest expression is achieved in the crystalline soils of northern Beaujolais, the *crus*. Nine or ten *crus*—the exception being the recently selected Régnié—were also granted the right to label their Gamay as Bourgogne. Elsewhere in Beaujolais, the *appellation* Bourgogne is bestowed only on the rarely cultivated varieties of Chardonnay and Pinot Noir.

BETWEEN THE RIVER AND THE MOUNTAINS

The Beaujolais region stretches from Lyons to Mâcon and is roughly 34 miles (55 km) long and up to 9 1/2 miles (15 km) wide. Around 3 1/2 million gallons (1.4 million hl) of wine are produced from a total of 57,000 acres (23,000 ha), almost half of which are marketed as Beaujolais Primeur or Nouveau. Apart from the vineyard and merchants, cooperatives traditionally also play a large part. The 19 *caves* produce around one-third of the total harvest. The areas under cultivation cover the lower slopes rising from the Saône plane of the Monts du Beaujolais, up to 1,475 feet (450 m). In the south the soils, consisting mainly of marl and a limestone substratum, date back to the Mesozoic age. Yet toward the Saône, there are

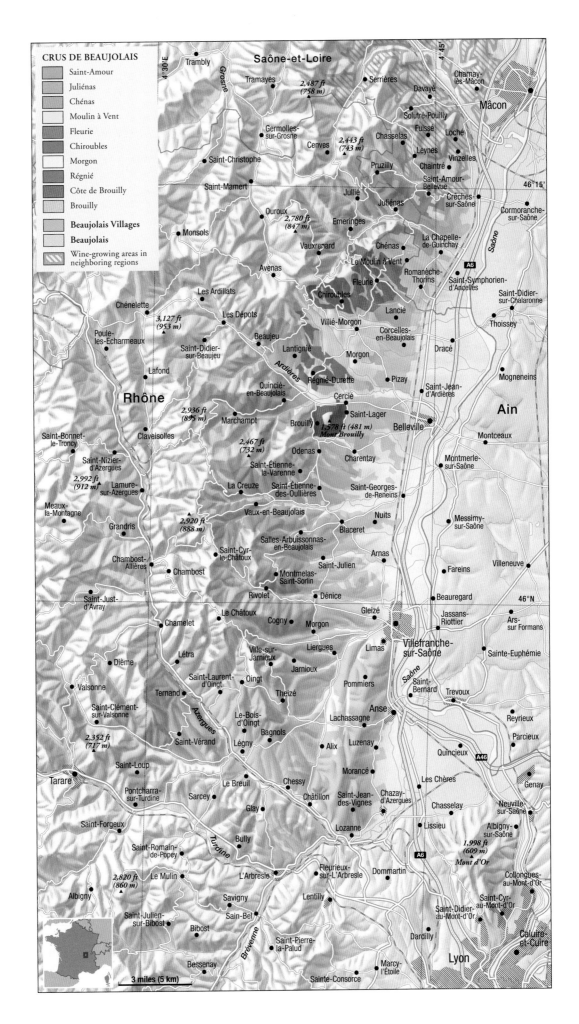

CRUS DE BEAUJOLAIS

- Saint-Amour
- Juliénas
- Chénas
- Moulin à Vent
- Fleurie
- Chiroubles
- Morgon
- Régnié
- Côte de Brouilly
- Brouilly
- **Beaujolais Villages**
- **Beaujolais**
- Wine-growing areas in neighboring regions

Trambly

Saône-et-Loire

Tramayes

2,487 ft (758 m)

Serrières

Charnay-lès-Mâcon

Davayé

Mâcon

Germolles-sur-Grosne

2,443 ft (743 m)

Cenves

Chasselas

Solutré-Pouilly

Fuissé

Loché

Leynes

Vinzelles

Saint-Christophe

Pruzilly

Chaintré

Saint-Mamert

Jullié

Saint-Amour-Bellevue

Crèches-sur-Saône

46°15'

Cormoranche-sur-Saône

Ouroux

2,780 ft (847 m)

Emeringes

Juliénas

Monsols

Vauxrenard

Chénas

La Chapelle-de-Guinchay

Avenas

Le Moulin à Vent

Romanèche-Thorins

Saint-Symphorien-d'Ancelles

A6

Saint-Didier-sur-Chalaronne

Les Ardillats

Fleurie

Chénelette

Les Dépots

Chiroubles

Lancié

Thoissey

3,127 ft (953 m)

Poule-les-Echarmeaux

Beaujeu

Villié-Morgon

Corcelles-en-Beaujolais

Dracé

Saint-Didier-sur-Beaujeu

Lantignié

Morgon

Pizay

Lafond

Ardières

Régnié-Durette

Saint-Jean-d'Ardières

Mogneneins

Quincié-en-Beaujolais

Cercié

Rhône

2,936 ft (895 m)

Marchampt

Brouilly

Saint-Lager

1,578 ft (481 m)
Mont Brouilly

Belleville

Ain

Saint-Bonnet-le-Troncy

Claveisolles

2,467 ft (732 m)

Odenas

Charentay

Montceaux

Saint-Nizier-d'Azergues

2,992 ft (912 m)

Lamure-sur-Azergues

Saint-Étienne-la-Varenne

Montmerle-sur-Saône

Meaux-la-Montagne

La Creuze

Saint-Étienne-des-Oullières

Saint-Georges-de-Reneins

Messimy-sur-Saône

Grandris

2,920 ft (888 m)

Vaux-en-Beaujolais

Nuits

Blaceret

Chambost-Allières

Salles-Arbuissonnas-en-Beaujolais

Arnas

Fareins

Villeneuve

Chambost

Saint-Cyr-le-Châtoux

Saint-Julien

Montmelas-Saint-Sorlin

Saint-Just-d'Avray

Rivolet

Dénice

Beauregard

46°N

Le Châtoux

Gleizé

Jassans-Riottier

Ars-sur-Formans

Chamelet

Cogny

Morgon

Limas

Villefranche-sur-Saône

Sainte-Euphémie

Dième

Létra

Ville-sur-Jarnioux

Liergues

Valsonne

Saint-Laurent-d'Oingt

Oingt

Jarnioux

Pommiers

Saône

Saint-Bernard

Trevoux

Reyrieux

Ternand

Theizé

Anse

Lachassagne

Saint-Clément-sur-Valsonne

Le-Bois-d'Oingt

Bagnols

Luzenay

Parcieux

2,352 ft (717 m)

Saint-Vérand

Légny

Alix

Quincieux

A46

Saint-Loup

Morancé

Les Chères

Genay

Tarare

Pontcharra-sur-Turdine

Le Breuil

Chessy

Saint-Jean-des-Vignes

Chazay-d'Azergues

Chasselay

Neuville-sur-Saône

Sarcey

Châtillon

Albigny-sur-Saône

Saint-Forgeux

Glay

Lozanne

Lissieu

1,998 ft (609 m)
Mont d'Or

Azergues

Bully

Saint-Romain-de-Popey

Turdine

A6

Collonges-au-Mont-d'Or

2,820 ft (860 m)

Le Mulin

L'Arbresle

Fleurieux-sur-L'Arbresle

Dommartin

Saint-Cyr-au-Mont-d'Or

Albigny

Savigny

Lentilly

Saint-Didier-au-Mont-d'Or

Saint-Julien-sur-Bibost

Sain-Bel

Caluire-et-Cuire

Bibost

Brévenne

Saint-Pierre-la-Palud

Dardilly

Bessenay

Marcy-l'Étoile

Lyon

Sainte-Consorce

3 miles (5 km)

generally alluvial soils in the most easterly sites, which date to early times. The best vineyards, to the north of Villefranche, are crystalline in nature and date back to the Paleozoic age. They contain granite and slate, with the latter releasing minerals upon decomposition, which influence the aroma developed by the wines.

Beaujolais extends as far as the Saône in the east. Vineyard locations spread across the slopes facing it, the wooded Monts du Beaujolais meet it above and behind these. In the north, the hills of Beaujolais almost reach the famous rocks of Solutré, while in the south they run seamlessly into the Monts du Lyonnais and the slopes blend into the neighboring department of the Loire in the west.

A Culinary Region

Beaujolais can boast neither spectacular natural beauty nor cultural monuments of world importance. The favorite dishes are borrowed from Burgundy or Lyons, and although the region's gastronomy cannot be described as great, save for a few exceptions, it offers good, native dishes. Terrines and sausages—principally the *andouillette*—*boeuf bourgignon*, and eggs in red wine sauce are typical. Sausages are often part of a hearty breakfast. In the wine region of Beaujolais, a tradition grew among the vine workers of something called the *mâchon*, or second breakfast, particularly at harvest time. It

The *vignerons* of Beaujolais still value their *mâchon*, or second breakfast, in the vineyard.

Père Bréchard, one of the fathers of today's Beaujolais.

has become rather less substantial these days and is now regarded as a snack for winegrowers who work in the vineyards early in the morning. At such times there are dried sausages and smoked ham in the basket, farmhouse bread, naturally a bottle of Beaujolais and, not least, cheeses from the Monts du Beaujolais. These cheeses, made by the farmers themselves from goat's or cow's milk, are highly rated in Beaujolais itself and in Lyons. A Beaujolais is an ideal accompaniment for all these specialties and the spicier the food, the simpler and younger the wine can be. The great, matured *crus* of Beaujolais, on the other hand, can also be drunk with expensive meat and game dishes. However, these should be served warmer than a young Beaujolais, Beaujolais Villages, or even Beaujolais Primeurs (at around 60°F/16°C). For these fruity, low-tannin wines 53–57°F (12–14°C) is an ideal temperature, otherwise they lose what characterizes a good Beaujolais—the fruit.

Based on soil conditions, Beaujolais is classified according to three different *appellations*.

A.O.C. Beaujolais and Beaujolais Supérieur

The largest *appellation* by area takes in the entire southern half of the growing area, but also includes the lower, easterly locations, so that it is produced in 72 communes. Some

25,945 acres (10,500 ha) are under cultivation with a maximum permitted yield of 706 gallons per acre (66 hl/ha), the minimum alcohol content at 9.5 percent by volume, and 10 percent by volume for the Supérieur. Each year an average of 1,656,000 acres (670,000 ha) produce a yield. Only one hundredth of the entire production is classified as Beaujolais Supérieur, and the white wines made from Chardonnay account for only 184,210 gallons (7,000 hl).

A.O.C. Beaujolais Villages

The center of the region, northwest of Villefranche, close to the small town of Beaujeu and on the northwest border of Beaujolais, is divided into 38 communes, most of which are entitled to replace the label "Villages" with their own name. On an area of just under 15,000 acres (6,100 ha) with a maximum yield of 640 gallons per acre (60 hl/ha) and at least 10 percent by volume potential alcohol, roughly 9,247,000 gallons (350,000 hl) are vinified. Here, too, it is Chardonnay that produces the rare white wine, representing one hundredth of the production.

A.O.C. Cru du Beaujolais

On a narrow strip of land between Mont-Brouilly and the Mâconnais are the slopes of granite and slate where the grapes used for the top wines ripen. The maximum yield is limited to 31½ gallons per acre (58 hl/ha) and the wines must have a minimum alcohol content of 10 to 10.5 percent. These wines include, running from south to north, Brouilly (3,262 acres/ 1,320 ha), Côte de Brouilly (741 acres/ 300 ha), Régnié (1,186 acres/480 ha), Morgon (2,817 acres/1,140 ha), Chiroubles (939 acres/ 380 ha), Fleurie (2,174 acres/880 ha), Moulin-à-Vent (1,680 acres/680 ha), Chénas (692 acres/ 280 ha), Juliénas (1,483, acres/600 ha) and Saint-Amour (766 acres/310 ha), totaling some 15,800 acres (6,400 ha), which yield 9,511,200 gallons (360,000 hl) of wine on average.

Gamay and Whole Grape Maceration

Beaujolais is indisputably dominated by the grape variety *Gamay noir à jus blanc*, the black Gamay with the white juice. Except for a small amount of Chardonnay and Aligoté for Beaujolais Blanc and even less Pinot Noir, which together account for just one percent, the vineyards are exclusively stocked with Gamay. Therefore Beaujolais is by far the most important Gamay area of France—and the world.

Gamay is an early ripening, high-yield variety. Winegrowers wishing to produce a high-quality wine keep the Gamay's growth in check. This is done first by increasing the plant density, thereby promoting competitive pressure between the vines; in Beaujolais there are between 22,000 and 32,000 plants per acre. Second, the yield is reduced by rigorous pruning of the vines. For the Villages and Crus it is tradi-

Winegrower Marcel Lapierre in Morgon has a mind of his own. He places his trust in the old table press that presses the grapes so gently, not fancying the use of sulfur in his wine preparation. The resulting wines are unconstrained, first-class Beaujolais.

A precise record of the wines' development is kept on blackboards.

Coteaux du Lyonnais

From the 16th century, vine growing flourished in the hills that abut Beaujolais and extend westward from Lyons to the start of the northerly Rhône locations. However, following the phylloxera crisis of the late 19th century, the vine-growing Renaissance remained modest. Barely 865 acres (350 ha) are stocked with this *appellation* today, producing some 578,947 gallons (22,000 hl) of wine. The area produces almost exclusively red wine from the Gamay grape with small propor-

tions of white growths from Aligoté and Chardonnay. Red wines must have a minimum alcohol content of 10 percent by volume, white wines of 9.5 percent by volume. After the *appellation* was acknowledged in 1984, the area was energized. Nowadays the best wines can hold their own with their neighbors in Beaujolais. The Saint-Bel cooperative is currently at the top of the quality ladder, but the dozen or so independent winegrowers are not resting on their laurels.

finally fermented. The shorter the maceration time, the less tannin is absorbed into the wine. Temperature plays an important part in the fermentation process. The fruit of a *vin nouveau* is better at around 68°F (20°C), the structure of a *cru* at 86°F (30°C). But as with almost every red wine, Beaujolais also undergoes a biological acid conversion, which reduces the often high acid content and stabilizes the wine.

To Age or Not to Age—that is Sometimes the Question

Although the summers in Beaujolais are often hot and dry, the must may only be concentrated by a maximum of two percent alcohol by volume. In addition, the Gamay creates little natural sugar, and none at all if the yields are too high. A small number of winegrowers dispense with chaptalization. The particular charm of Beaujolais lies in its intensive, enticing aromas. They range from flowers, such as violets, roses, and lily of the valley to fruits such as cherries, raspberries, redcurrants, or blackberries. Although these aromas have their purest expression in young wines, many of the region's wines have sufficient structure to be allowed to age for a few years. Famous for their long-lasting potential are Morgon, Chénas, and Moulin-à-Vent. Surprisingly, well-aged Beaujolais Crus often resemble Burgundies in taste and bouquet.

tional for the training method of *Gobelet* to be followed, in which the shape of the vine is similar to that of a goblet. In the Appellation Beaujolais, the Guyot method may also be used; the vine is trained along a wire frame; otherwise each vine is tied to a stake. Pruning and VINIFICATION require hand-picking, which usually starts in mid-September and lasts for around three weeks.

The Juliénas brotherhood resides in the castle at the foot of the village.

Juliénas has become the embodiment of the Beaujolais-Cru.

The Secret of the Fruit

Beaujolais grapes must reach the cellar undamaged and the winegrowers use crates that hold no more than 175 pounds (80 kg) of grapes. This is a requirement for the full grape or carbon dioxide maceration customary in Beaujolais. There are many variants, but the principle is always the same. The grapes are tipped into tanks or wooden containers whole. The grapes lying on the bottom become partially crushed, so that must collects around them that begins to ferment. Carbon dioxide is produced and this saturates the atmosphere. Starved of oxygen, the other grapes are forced to use intracellular fermentation, which means that the must draws a particularly high level of aromas from the skins.

Depending on the desired character of the wine, the must is drained off after four to ten days, the residue pressed and, once the drained-off must and pressed must have been assembled,

Select Producers in Beaujolais

Château des Jacques***
Romanèche-Thorins
89 acres (36 ha); 250,000 bottles • Wines: Beaujolais Villages Blanc, Moulin-à-Vent
In this pretty little château, belonging to the Burgundian house of Louis Jadot, one of the most interesting white Beaujolais is produced, while the Moulin-à-Vent is finished along Burgundian lines.

Château du Moulin-à-Vent**—****
Romanèche-Thorins
77 acres (31 ha); 160,000 bottles • Wines include: →Moulin-à-Vent Cuvée Exceptionelle
This 17th century château produces remarkably concentrated wines.

Château de Pizay**—***
Pizay-en-Beaujolais
143 acres (58 ha); 500,000 bottles • Wines include: Beaujolais Rouge, Morgon, Régnié, Brouilly →Beaujolais Blanc
Its origins lie in the 11th century. A specialty is white Beaujolais made from Chardonnay.

Château Thivin***—****
Odenas
64 acres (26 ha); 140,000 bottles • Wines include: Beaujolais Villages, Brouilly, →Côte de Brouilly, Cuvée Zaccharie Geoffray
The top-quality Cuvée Zaccharie wines spend nine months maturing in small wooden casks.

Collin-Bourisset**—***
Crèches-sur-Saône
30 acres (12 ha); 1,600,000 bottles • Wines: →include Moulin-à-Vent, Brouilly, Fleurie, Mâcon
The company came into existence in 1821; its own Moulin-à-Vent is partly aged in small wooden casks. In addition, the wine of the Hospices de Moulin-à-Vent is vinified and exclusively marketed.

Coudert Père et Fils***
Fleurie
25 acres (10 ha); 45,000 bottles • Wines: Fleurie Clos de la Roilette
The Fleuries produced on this estate comes from 40-year-old vines. Eight to twelve days of temperature-controlled fermentation are followed by six months in the barrel.

Domaine Emile Cheysson**—****
Chiroubles
64 acres (26 ha); 100,000 bottles • Wines: Chiroubles, →Chiroubles Cuvée Prestige
Emile Cheysson founded the estate in 1870. Seven to eight days' full grape maceration are the norm; the wines are text-book Beaujolais.

Domaine Michel Chignard***—*****
Fleurie
20 acres (8 ha); 35,000 bottles • Wines include: Fleurie, Fleurie Cuvée les Moriers
Michel Chignard's Fleurie, produced from old and ancient vines, is among the most acknowledged in Beaujolais.

Domaine du Clos du Fief***—****
Juliénas
32 acres (13 ha); 80,000 bottles • Wines: Beaujolais Villages, Saint-Amour, Juliénas →Juliénas Cuvée Prestige
Already into the third generation (the committed Michel Tête is on the estate), demonstrating the aging capability

of Beaujolais. The *cuvée de prestige* from the Juliénas *appellation* is exemplary.

Domaine Dominique Piron**—****
Villié-Morgon
42 acres (17 ha); bought-in grapes; 400,000 bottles • Wines include: Morgon, Moulin-à-Vent, Brouilly, Régnié, Beaujolais-Villages, →Morgon Côte du Py
The full grape fermentation process takes up to 15 days for top-quality wines. Combined with the high average age of the vines (40 years), this produces remarkably concentrated Beaujolais.

Domaine Jean-Charles Pivot**—***
Quincié-en-Beaujolais
30 acres (12 ha); 90,000 bottles • Wines include: Beaujolais-Villages
The estate produces a fruity, vigorous Beaujolais-Villages from old vines.

Domaine Ruet****
Cercié-en-Beaujolais
30 acres (12 ha); 60,000 bottles • Wines include: →Régnié, →Brouilly, Beaujolais-Villages, Morgon
Jean-Paul Ruet produces wines bubbling over with fruit on this estate that has been family-owned since 1926.

Domaine des Terres Dorées****
Charnay-en-Beaujolais
49 acres (20 ha); 100,000 bottles • Wines: →include Beaujolais Cuvée à l'Ancienne, Beaujolais Blanc
Red Beaujolais made the old-fashioned way by Jean-Paul Brun is not chaptalized, an exception in Beaujolais.

Georges Duboeuf**—****
Romanèche-Thorins
25 acres (10 ha); bought-in grapes; 18,000,000 bottles • Wines include: Fleurie Clos des Quatre Vents, Brouilly Château de Pierreux, Beaujolais-Villages, Régnié Sélection Georges Duboeuf
Georges Duboeuf is the king of Beaujolais. No one else has helped to raise the profile of Beaujolais since the 1960s to the extent this dynamic wine merchant has. His best *cuvées* number among the most impressive Beaujolais anywhere.

Denise und Hubert Lapierre**—****
La Chapelle-de-Guinchay
18.5 acres (7.5 ha); 40,000 bottles • Wines: Chenas, Moulin-à-Vent, Moulin-à-Vent Vieilles Vignes →Chenas Vieilles Vignes, Chenas Fût de Chêne
The Chenas Fût de Chêne comes from vines over 80 years old, the top *cuvée* of the estate founded in 1970.

Marcel Lapierre****
Villié-Morgon
• Wines: Morgon, Beaujolais
Marcel Lapierre caused a sensation when he began to harvest grapes when they had reached a perfect ripeness and turn them into wine without sulfur. Suddenly the unimagined potential of the Gamay was there to taste.

Laurent Martray****
Odenas
22 acres (9 ha); 12,000 bottles • Wines: Brouilly Cuvée Vieilles Vignes, Brouilly Cuvée Corentin
On this estate founded in 1987 Laurent Martray only produces two *cuvées*; he presses Cuvée Corentin from the oldest vines. From harvesting to racking, all stages are performed manually.

Along the Loire: Châteaux and Vines

The long, wide valley of the Loire constitutes the most far-flung wine region in France. It ranges from the Massif Central and the Auvergne via the expansive central course of the river with its countless majestic châteaux—a popular destination for visitors to France—down to the Atlantic, where it also forms the southern border of Brittany. At the source, where the river leaves the uplands of the Massif Central and sets out on its long journey, vineyards are to be seen, though they bear no *appellations contrôlées*. Along the entire course of the Loire and the banks of its tributaries, the vines occupy slopes facing the sun that offer conditions favorable to ripening. The region has around 125,000 acres (50,000 ha) under vines, which makes it half the size of the Bordeaux wine-growing region and marginally larger than the Rhône Valley.

It is assumed that wine was grown along the river even in the first decades of our era, but there is documentary evidence only for the upper stretches, more precisely the Auvergne, from the 5th century. The Dutch had already discovered the wines of the Loire in the 11th century, which they could easily ship down the river and by sea to the Lowlands. In England, too, the wines of Poitou and Anjou were uncommonly popular at the time, but once Bordeaux got into its stride, the market for the Loire product virtually disappeared for a long time.

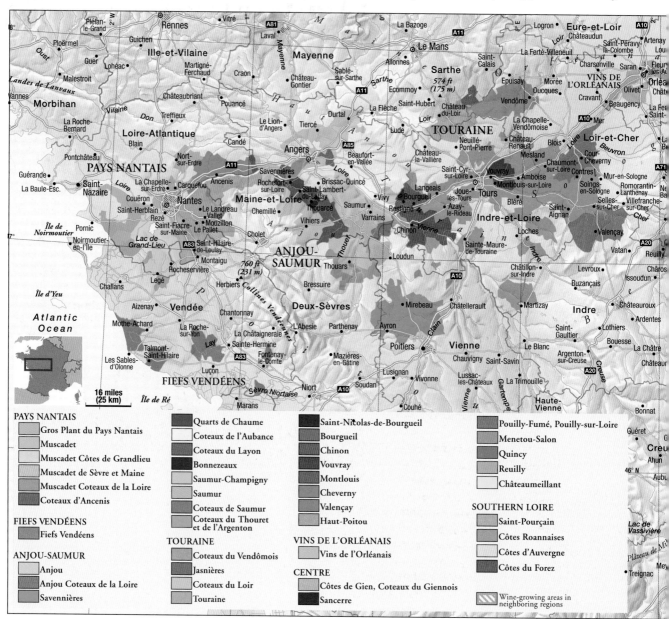

PAYS NANTAIS
- Gros Plant du Pays Nantais
- Muscadet
- Muscadet Côtes de Grandlieu
- Muscadet de Sèvre et Maine
- Muscadet Coteaux de la Loire
- Coteaux d'Ancenis

FIEFS VENDÉENS
- Fiefs Vendéens

ANJOU-SAUMUR
- Anjou
- Anjou Coteaux de la Loire
- Savennières
- Quarts de Chaume
- Coteaux de l'Aubance
- Coteaux du Layon
- Bonnezeaux
- Saumur-Champigny
- Saumur
- Coteaux de Saumur
- Coteaux du Thouet et de l'Argenton

TOURAINE
- Coteaux du Vendômois
- Jasnières
- Coteaux du Loir
- Touraine
- Saint-Nicolas-de-Bourgueil
- Bourgueil
- Chinon
- Vouvray
- Montlouis
- Cheverny
- Valençay
- Haut-Poitou

VINS DE L'ORLÉANAIS
- Vins de l'Orléanais

CENTRE
- Côtes de Gien, Coteaux du Giennois
- Sancerre
- Pouilly-Fumé, Pouilly-sur-Loire
- Menetou-Salon
- Quincy
- Reuilly
- Châteaumeillant

SOUTHERN LOIRE
- Saint-Pourçain
- Côtes Roannaises
- Côtes d'Auvergne
- Côtes du Forez

- Wine-growing areas in neighboring regions

Saumur, on the Loire, the center of sparkling wine production and home of very elegant red wines.

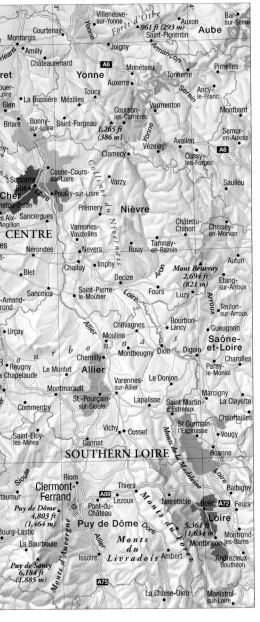

The geographical extent of the region means that the *terroirs* and consequently the wines themselves turn out very differently. The continental climate of the Massif Central or the Sancerre region has virtually nothing in common with the temperate Atlantic climate of Muscadet country near the Loire estuary except the river they share. Although Champagne, Alsace, and, of course, the German wine-growing areas are quite a bit further north, the Loire marks the northern limit of Atlantic France. For the same reason, climatic conditions are overall much more unstable than in more southerly regions, and the variations between vintages are much more pronounced than in the Rhône Valley or Languedoc.

SEVEN AT A STROKE

In terms of winemaking, the Loire region can be subdivided into seven areas. Directly by the mouth of the river, with vineyards right up to the Atlantic, is Muscadet and Gros Plant country, the Pays Nantais, whose vineyards lie largely to the south of the Loire. The second area, the beginning of the "Garden of France," includes Anjou and Saumur, home of the white quick-change artist Chenin Blanc. Adjacent to this is Touraine, the realm of Cabernet Franc, which extends from Bourgueil and Chinon to Blois. The country around the city of Orléans forms a small, isolated V.D.Q.S., before it crosses into the stronghold of Sauvignon Blanc beyond Gien, i.e. Sancerre and Pouilly. Along the upper Loire there are only V.D.Q.S. areas (Saint-Pourçain, Côte Roannaise, Côtes de Forez and Côtes d'Auvergne), while in the middle

the once famous Poitou has managed to salvage a small wine industry over the centuries.

As varied as the wines of the Loire are, freshness and finesse are their common denominators. They owe these to the natural acidity that remains preserved in the grapes on the northern climatic limit even when they are completely ripe physiologically. Yet the Loire has the right wine for every occasion: white, rosé, and red wines are produced here as well as sparkling wines and *pétillants*. The rosé palette ranges from the simple to the elegant, the reds from the light and fruity to multifaceted wines with aging ability, the whites from the superficial to the easy-drinking or opulent and sometimes incredibly complex sweet wines, the fizz from uncomplicated *pétillants* to quite exquisite sparkling wines.

If no Loire vineyard can compete with the famous labels of Burgundy, Champagne, or Bordeaux, we can confidently blame the Parisians. There is scarcely a bistro, brasserie, or restaurant in the capital that does not have one of the agreeable, inexpensive Loire tipples on its wine list—a Muscadet or Sauvignon, Cabernet or Gamay. The wines are easy to sell, and as is always the case in the wine world everywhere, this does not encourage growers to go for quality. Even so, the region has unique wines to offer us today, and three grape varieties are principally responsible for this.

The *caves* of Vouvray served as accommodation and perfect wine cellars.

Opposite
Although the Loire has its venerable *crus*, it has never in its history produced as many outstanding wines as it does today.

THREE UNRECOGNIZED GENIUSES

The top variety is the highly versatile Chenin or Chenin Blanc, which is also called Pineau de la Loire here. Almost every conceivable variety of wine is made from it, ranging from light dry wines to heavy dessert wines or even fortified liqueur wines. In France, Chenin is not very common outside the Loire region, but it is intensively cultivated in South Africa (where it is called Steen), California, and South America. The Loire dessert wines made from Chenin are notable for their capacity to improve with age. Vintage 1874 or 1893 Vouvray or Coteaux du Layon still arouse enthusiasm.

Cabernet Franc—often mocked in the Bordeaux region as Cabernet Sauvignon's little brother—provides single-variety Loire red wines that are multifaceted, elegant, and that will keep. Though lighter than in Bordeaux, they can be as good.

It would be unforgivable not to mention the Sauvignon Blanc, which occupies a special position. Particularly in the Sancerre and Pouilly area, wines of enormous spirit and finesse are made, which stand out most agreeably from the often very superficial Sauvignon-based Bordeaux white wines.

BETWEEN THE RIVER AND THE SEA: WHITE WINE WITH FISH?

The name Muscadet has nothing to do with Muscat or Muscatel. It describes the old Burgundian white wine variety Melon de Bourgogne, introduced by the Dutch to the Loire which later almost completely disappeared from Burgundy. It is nowadays cultivated on about 27,000 acres (11,000 ha) between the lower reaches of the river and the Atlantic coast and produces light, fruity, and tangy white wines that go excellently with sea food. This flat, occasionally gently undulating area is climatically affected by the ocean, resulting in mild winters and the very damp summers. Basically a neutral variety, Muscadet has one critical advantage: compared with many others, it is relatively frost-resistant and ripens early. Generally, the harvest in the Pays Nantais can be completed by September 20, before the onset of the autumn rains common to these latitudes.

THE SUR LIE SPECIALTY

To give the wines a touch more complexity, the best are left to mature on the yeast in the tank or barrel until bottled. This gives them a discreet aroma of yeast, a depth, and a certain sparkle deriving from the fizz of the fermentation that cannot escape from the wine because it is not racked or in contact with the air. Wines cultivated in this way, which have to be bottled in the Muscadet districts themselves, are labeled SUR LIE, i.e. on the yeast or lees.

No one can demonstrate the potential of the Fiefs Vendéens as impressively as Thierry Michon on the family estate of Domaine Saint-Nicolas.

Opposite
The Château de la Preuille produces one of the longest lasting Muscadets.

Close to the Atlantic there is rarely ideal weather during harvesting, although it would be welcomed by the winegrowers.

Sur lie wines are not of course permitted in the generic *appellation*, whose wines are bottled under the plain Muscadet label. The name can be used only for wines from one of the three higher-quality areas set up in 1995 after the reclassification of the Muscadet area. They are the Coteaux de la Loire, Sèvre-et-Maine, and Côtes de Grandlieu. Muscadet of the Coteaux de la Loire is produced in the eastern part of the Pays Nantais, on both sides of the river in the area around the town of Ancénis. Sèvres-et-Maine Muscadet, which comes from the area of the two rivers of these names (south and east of Nantes), is the largest *appellation*. In these parts, vines dominate what is virtually a monoculture area. The most recent designation of origin, the Muscadet Côtes de Grandlieu, is used for wines produced around the Lac de Grandlieu, which is also an interesting bird sanctuary.

In the Pays Nantais, another fresh white wine is produced from the Gros Plant variety, known as Folle Blanche in the south-west. The region's few reds come from the Coteaux d'Ancenis and the Fiefs Vendéens—these are mostly plain, fruity wines produced from Gamay and Cabernet. However, at Brem-sur-Mer, the Domaine Saint-Nicolas has been proving since 1998 that this region bordering the Atlantic is certainly suited to providing wines with body, structure and character, especially if they are cultivated in a natural manner and with reduced yield.

SELECT PRODUCERS OF THE PAYS NANTAIS

CHÂTEAU DE LA PREUILLE***
SAINT-HILAIRE-DE-LOULAY
99 acres (40 ha); 250,000 bottles • Wines: Muscadet sur lie : → Château de la Preuille, Château de Saint Hilaire, Moulin de Saint Hilaire; Gros Plant sur lie, Gamay de Loire
As two of the few producers of Muscadet-Landes, Philippe and Christian Dumortier also produce very drinkable red wines as well. However, their best wines are the Muscadets they produce from various *domaines*.

CHÂTEAU LA RAGOTIÈRE***–****
VALLET-LA-REGRIPPIÈRE
152 acres (61.5 ha); 420,000 bottles • Wines include: Muscadet de Sèvre et Maine sur lie: → Château Ragotière, → Petit Château, La Morinière, → Collection Privé 'M'; V.D.P. Domaine Couilland
The Couillaud brothers can offer an impressive range of A.C. and *vins de pays*. Their whole output consists of white wines, with the Chardonnay Vin de Pays surpassing even the Muscadets.

DOMAINE DE BEAUREGARD***
MOUZILLON
62 acres (25 ha); 100,000 bottles • Wines: Gros Plant sur lie, Muscadet de Sèvre et Maine sur lie; Fief du Clairy, Domaine de Beauregard
The wines of Henri Grégoire come from one of the best Muscadet *terroirs*, and with their light mineral character go excellently with oysters. In addition, they are unbeatable value for money.

DOMAINE CHÉREAU-CARRÉ***–****
SAINT-FIACRE-SUR-MAINE
148 acres (60 ha); 250,000 bottles • Wines include: Muscadet Sèvre et Maine sur lie; Château du Coing de Saint Fiacre: Comte de Saint-Hubert, → Grande Cuvée, → Tradition Millénaire; Château Oise-linerie de la Ramée, Château de la Gravelle Grande Cuvée
The most celebrated business of the Pays Nantais belongs to Véronique Günther-Chéreau, who produces an extraordinarily diverse range of excellent Muscadets.

DOMAINE DE L'ÉCU***–****
LE LANDREAU
52 acres (21 ha); 120,000 bottles • Wines include: Muscadet Sèvre et Maine Sur Lie Expressions: de Gneiss, → d'Orthogneiss, → Granite; Brut Ludwig Hahn, Gros Plant du Pays Nantais
Guy Bossard is a supporter of biodynamic viticulture, whose benefits are backed up by careful work in the winery. His Muscadet-Cuvées are among the best in the region.

DOMAINE SAINT-NICOLAS**–****
BREM-SUR-MER
79.1 acres (32 ha); 110,000 bottles • Wines include: VDQS Fiefs Vendéens; Les Clous, Maria, → Hauts des Clous, → Plante Gâte, Grande Pièce, → Poiré, → VdT Soleil de Chine
After changing over to biodynamic cultivation in 1998, Thierry Michon has created a fascinating range of wines in his vineyard by the Atlantic. These wines demonstrate, for the first time, the potential of the Fiefs Vendéens.

BIODYNAMIC WINE ON MONASTIC SLOPES

Growers in the Loire have gone in for biological—more specifically, biodynamic—viticulture more wholeheartedly than in other regions of France. Their spokesman is Nicolas Joly, owner of the entire single-site Coulée de Serrant, a *clos* in Savennières. Cistercian monks planted this 17-acre (7-ha) vineyard, on a steep slope overlooking the Loire, to vines in the 12th century. During the past 800 years, it became so celebrated that it was visited by two French kings and the Empress Josephine, who adored its wines.

The Coulée de Serrant is among the most characterful dry white wines in the world. When Nicolas Joly took over responsibility for the site at the end of the 1970s, he initially fell in entirely with the advice of the local agricultural chamber. Progress in vineyards hitherto run on conventional lines meant introducing chemical fertilizers and sprays. But after only two years Joly noticed a rapid decline in soil quality and the local flora and fauna. By chance, he came across Rudolf Steiner's writings about biodynamics. The first experiments were encouraging, and so from 1984 Joly turned his entire 30-acre (12-ha) wine-growing estate over to biodynamic cultivation. The results were incalculable. Gradually the biological balance of the vines was restored. Joly's wines gained increasingly in character and

Ex-banker Nicolas Joly is the most prominent advocate of biodynamic vine cultivation in France and shows how his integral process can be used to increase the quality and expression of the wine.

strength, which they had previously lacked. In 1997, now publicly committed as a spokesman for biodynamic viticulture, Joly published his findings in an easy-to-follow guide based on his own experiences.

Underlying the biodynamic approach is an exchange between the cosmos and the earth, familiar to previous centuries but only recently restated and made comprehensible by Steiner, the founder of anthroposophy. According to Joly's theory, only a living soil with all its micro-organisms can be the basis of healthy, high-quality viticulture. He distinguishes four states of aggregation, which he links with parts of the vine: minerals and root, liquid and leaves, light and flowers, and warmth and fruit. Vegetation contains a polarity between gravity, which tends downward, and lightness, which strives upward. A grower who knows how to interpret such tendencies can distinguish a remarkably strong gravity in a vine, which is capable of driving its roots several yards down, as well as the effort to develop upward. With its short flowering, the plant holds back until the sun has become effective and warm enough so its entire effort can be focused on the fruit.

By studying climate and locality, biodynamic proponents are able to promote the life of the vine, but also reinforce its individual characteristics. "A biodynamically produced wine is not necessarily good, but it is always genuine," says Joly. Whereas the things that really make the character of a site or a whole *appellation* fall by the wayside when chemical fertilizers and pesticides are used in the vineyard and artificial yeasts and enzymes appear in the winery, the biodynamic approach goes for a subtle interaction with all the parameters that make a *terroir*. To counter the creeping dilution of the *terroir* concept and wines, Joly uses various preparations produced by homeopathic methods intended to promote the health of the vine and create a natural balance in the vineyard.

Sparkling pleasures of the Loire

The Loire is one of the most important sparkling wine regions. Production developed particularly in the Saumur, Vouvray, and Montlouis regions, partly due to the tuff caves there, which offer ideal conditions for fermentation in the bottle. For winegrowers, producing sparkling wine is an effective way of making good use of their grapes when bad weather precludes proper ripening. These days 14 million bottles are produced in the region. In the Saumur area, the *mousseux* constitutes the major production volume of any type, and even in Vouvray it is 40%. Since 1975, there has been a Crémant de Loire *appellation*, whose production methods are borrowed from those of Champagne.

Wine-growing areas of the Massif Central

In the upper Loire, there are five areas of cultivation with V.D.Q.S. status whose wines are, of course, only of regional importance and almost never appear anywhere else in France or in foreign markets.

Châteaumeillant, a wine-growing area 37 miles (60 km) north of Montluçon, has a very long tradition of viticulture. Nowadays only about 247 acres (100 ha) are planted with vines—besides Pinot Noir and Pinot Gris, mainly Gamay—from which a pale, nervous Vin Gris is made. In addition, perfumed, round red wines are made. Saint-Pourçain lies southeast of Moulins on the Sioule. Gamay and Pinot Noir are cultivated on 1,240 acres (500 ha) from which pleasant reds with complex fruit are made. The white wines of the region are made from Sauvignon Blanc, Chardonnay, Aligoté, and the indigenous Tressalier variety. The Côte Roannaise is an area scattered over two dozen villages on both sides of the Loire around Roanne, whose 371 acres (150 ha) are planted with Gamay. The best, fruity, and charming red wines come from Renaison, Saint-André d'Apchon, and Villemontais.

Côtes d'Auvergne is a 1,240-acres (500-ha) region on the edge of the Massif Central running north and south of the city of Clermont Ferrand and divided into five areas. Gamay is used to make dry rosés and fruity, sometimes very full-bodied reds. The best of these come from Chanturgue, Châteaugay, and Boudès. The 494 acres (200 ha) of vineyard of the last of the five, the Côtes du Forez, are scattered over the slopes on the edge of the Loire Valley northwest of Saint-Étienne. The driving force of the region is the local cooperative Les Vignerons Foréziens in Trelins.

These treatments are optimized by taking the constellations of the moon and the important planets into account, whose effects have been studied by Maria Thun in experiments over many years. The results, the wines of the Coulée de Serrant, the Vouvray of the Domaine Huet, the Pouilly-Fumé of Daguenau, the Burgundy of the Domaine Leroy in Burgundy and the Rieslings and Gewürztraminers of Marc Kreydenweiss in Alsace, to mention only the best known, present personalities of their own, regardless of fashion. And they are so good and so successful that happily more and more growers in France are becoming receptive to the arguments of the biodynamic school.

The Château de la Roche-aux-Moines owns the famous Coulée de Serrant site, on which grows one of the greatest white wines cultivated on biodynamic principles.

V.D.Q.S.

The term *Vin Délimité de Qualité Supérieure* (V.D.Q.S.) is a category established between *vins de pays* and the coveted *Appellations Contrôlées* (A.C.s) to designate quality wines. Wines of this category are generally always upgraded after a time to A.C.s, so that today only 23 of these V.D.Q.S.s remain. As permitted grape varieties, origins, maximum yields, and vinification are strictly regulated, as with A.C. wines, and yet the wines lack the prestige of A.C. wines, growers have an interest in being upgraded into the higher category. For consumers, these wines are very interesting because the quality is often good and the price low.

PEARLS OF SWEET WINE IN ROSÉ COUNTRY

When you travel upriver from the Pays Nantais, you reach the Anjou and Saumur region, whose 37,100 acres (15,000 hectares) planted to vines produce a wide range of wines. Anjou, the western part of this region around the city of Angers, is a well-established concept, especially in the French market, with its cheap, medium-dry rosés, though they are markedly losing ground these days. Until the phylloxera disaster, the region was planted almost exclusively with white wine varieties. Afterward, they returned to a mere 20 percent of the area planted, and have only recently become more common again.

Rosé d'Anjou is an unpretentious-to-weak wine produced from the native Grolleau or Groslot variety that is still cultivated on about 9,880 acres (4,000 ha) but is increasingly being ousted by Cabernet Franc or Gamay. The Cabernet Franc especially, which now covers almost a third of the red wine areas in Anjou, has made a lot of friends, with its Cabernet d'Anjou, a rosé with a more decidedly acidic quality that is rarely sweet. But the grape also

The wine region of the Loire provides endless fascination, with its ancient walls and Romantic scenery.

produces some of the best reds of the region, and under the Anjou-Villages label, an *appellation* allocated the *terroirs* southeast of Angers, achieves remarkable strength and structure.

The real specialty of Anjou are of course the whites made from Chenin Blanc. The vines grow mainly on the south-facing schist slopes near Angers, which once produced mainly sweet Savennières but are now developed mostly as dry wines. Its two single-site labels Coulée de Serrant—a 17-acre (7-ha) monopoly—and La Roche-aux-Moines, which have separate *appellation* statuses, are the outstanding bases for wonderfully intense, complex growths that improve with age and are reckoned among the best white wines in the world. However, Chenin is most suited to the production of sweet wines, to which four Anjou *appellations* are dedicated. In the same district on the left bank of the Loire where Anjou-Villages is made, mellow dessert wines are produced under the Coteaux de l'Aubance label, with a dry counterpart bottled as Anjou Blanc. But the most important and largest sweet-wine area is the Coteaux du Layon, on the steep slopes of the Loire tributary of the same name, running 30 miles (50 km) southward from Rochefort-sur-Loire. In recent years, talented growers have invested enormously to create wines under the Chaume and Villages *appellations*, which can bear comparison with the more famous growths of the *grand cru* areas of Bonnezeaux and Quarts de Chaume, which in turn are embedded in the Coteaux du Layon.

Things are quite different in the Saumurois, the eastern part of the region. Instead of schist, the character of the wines is determined by the white chalky tuff. Here, red and white grapes are in balance, though the red wines, especially the Saumur-Champigny Rouge *appellation* made from Cabernet Franc, are not only the best known but, with their aromas of red fruits, harmony, and elegance, are also are the best. The whites—the dry wines are marketed as Saumur Blanc or Saumur Champigny, the sweet ones as Coteaux de Saumur—are made mainly from Chenin Blanc, and display a fine touch of acidity and very good aging ability. In marketing terms, of course, the leading role in the region is played neither by white nor red but by sparkling wines called Saumur Mousseux, made from Chenin, Chardonnay, and occasionally Sauvignon Blanc.

HEAVENLY TIPPLE

Some of the best sweet wines in the world come from Anjou-Saumur. Although celebrated since the 15th century and further developed by the Dutch in the 16th and 17th centuries, in recent decades they were unrecognized classics and largely ignored. This is changing due partly to the re-awakened interest in sweet wines and partly to the re-awakened quality consciousness of the growers, who are now ready to take the risks always associated with producing sweet wines. The basic material of the sweet Loire wines is the Chenin Blanc, which despite its alternative name Pineau de la Loire is not related to the Pinot varieties of Burgundy. It is native to the Loire itself and was already cultivated in Anjou in the 9th century. Chenin can be

turned into a wide range of different wines depending on the degree of ripeness. In worse years, the grapes cannot produce more than 6 oz (170 g) of sugar or about 10 percent abv (alcohol by volume), in which case they are suitable only for dry whites and sparkling wines. If weather conditions are more favorable and help the grapes reach a sugar content of 7 oz–9 oz (190–260 g), at least some finish up as medium-dry or sweet wines.

In exceptional years, however, when the sugar content can reach 17.5 oz (500g), almost exclusively sweet wines are made from the grapes. Their potential alcohol content is then up to

In almost no other region is the architecture as sophisticated as it is along the Loire, where even the wine cellars have often been designed and built with great creativity and skill.

Haut Poitou

In the Middle Ages, the wines of Poitou, the region around the city of Poitiers, were better known than the growths of Bordeaux. They were shipped via the port of La Rochelle mainly to England, until in the 13th century the city fell into French hands and English merchant ships could no longer enter the port. These days Haut-Poitou, a 1,730-acre (700-ha) area south of Saumur, is a V.D.Q.S. label found on bottles of all kinds of grape—Sauvignon Blanc, Gamay, Cabernet and others. The renaissance the region has seen in recent years is founded above all on the quality of its white wines made from Sauvignon Blanc. The best and most dynamic producer in the district is the cooperative in Neuville.

30 percent abv, such as is often found in the Vouvray, Montlouis, Coteaux de l'Aubance *appellations*, or the Bonnezeaux and Quarts de Chaume *grands crus* of Coteaux du Layon. There the microclimate of the slopes of the Loire and its tributaries provides ideal conditions. The very high sugar concentration in the grapes can be attained in two ways; either by the *passerillé* process (turning the grapes into raisins) on hot, dry autumn days, or botrytization. The former is rare in the Loire region, happening only in outstanding years such as 1947 or 1989. Botrytization is much more common. It requires a morning autumn mist that is dispelled by the sun during the morning to make way for a clear day, which—in favorable circumstances—is followed by a clear, cold night. The *Botrytis cinerea* penetrates the skin of the berries, perforating them so that the fruit fluid evaporates and sugars are strongly concentrated in the berry as extract substances. The harvest is generally carried out in several phases, with only the ripest grapes being picked. Whereas some growers vinify, remove, and bottle each batch separately, others seek the maximum harmony and balance, for which they blend the wines brought in at different times. Generally the must

ferments at relatively low temperatures, with the transformation of sugar into alcohol taking up to two months. Once the wine reaches the desired alcohol content—in the case of medium-sweet wines 12–13 abv, or 13–14 abv for sweet wines—the fermentation process is stopped. Despite the enormous sugar residue thus left in the wines, the *moelleux* (a label for mellow non-botrytized wines) made from Chenin Blanc, never seem big and sticky because the marked acidity of the grape gives them incomparable rigor. In the first two years, the wines manifest an intense, fresh fruitiness, after which they close up until, five to eight years later, they develop a rich bouquet, with overtones of apricot and honey. Wines of good vintages can be left to age for decades, whereby they develop more and more complexity and harmony. Unfortunately the temptation to open them much too early can rarely be resisted.

Select Producers in Anjou-Saumur and Haut-Poitou

Pierre Aguilas★★★★
Chaudefonds-sur-Layon
59 acres (24 ha); 90,000 bottles • Wines include:
→*Coteaux du Layon Les Varennes, Anjou Les Paragères, Cabernet d'Anjou Domaine Gaudard, Coteaux du Layon Domaine Gaudard*
Apart from a rosé, the Cabernet d'Anjou of the Domaine Gaudard, Pierre Aguilas produces exclusively Coteaux du Layon whites. Despite the enormous risk, he always aims for perfect, complete ripeness and strong botrytization with his grapes. The quality of the wines is his reward.

Château Bellerive★★★–★★★★
Rochefort-sur-Loire
30 acres (12 ha); 30,000 bottles • Wines: →*Quarts de Chaume Clos de Chaume, Quarts de Chaume Quintessence*
The vineyards of Serge and Michel Malinge lie in the heart of the Quarts de Chaume and offer optimum conditions for the development of noble rot. The wines are harmonious and balanced.

Château Pierre Bise★★★★–★★★★★
Beaulieu-sur-Layon
131 acres (53 ha); 150,000 bottles • Wines: →*Coteaux du Layon Beaulieu, Chaume, Quarts de Chaume, Savennières*
In good years, the great sweet wines of Claude Papin can compete with the most celebrated sweet wines of all France—though at much more acceptable prices, of course. Papin is a doughty champion of the *terroir* philosophy.

Château d'Épiré★★★★
Savennières
22 acres (9 ha); 45,000 bottles • Wines: →*Savennières; Cuvée spéciale, Moelleux*
The wines of the *domaine* have rediscovered the legendary qualities (especially their aging ability) that once made the château famous.

Château de Fesles★★★★
Thouarcé
86 acres (35 ha); 180,000 bottles • Wines: →*Bonnezeaux, Coteaux du Layon; Anjou, Savennières*
In the space of a few years, Bernard Germain has put Château Fesles back at the top, but also creates excellent sweet wines at La Guimonière and La Roulerie.

Château du Hureau★★★★
Saumur
52 acres (21 ha); 110,000 bottles • Wines: →*Saumur-Champigny Grande Cuvée, Lisagathe, Saumur Blanc*
Reds with intense color and good structure prosper on the clay and chalky soils of Philippe Vatan's vineyards, but there is also a splendid Chenin Blanc.

Château La Roche-aux-Moines – Coulée de Serrant★★★★★
Savennières
36 acres (14.5 ha); 55,000 bottles • Wines: →*Savennières: Coulée de Serrant, Becherelle, Roche aux Moines*
The absolute star of Savennières, Nicolas Joly, is France's leading champion of biodynamics. His wines speak for themselves.

Château de Villeneuve****
Sousay-Champigny
69 acres(28 ha); 140,000 bottles • Wines: Saumur Cormiers, Saumur-Champigny Vieilles Vignes such as Grand Clos
Jean-Pierre Chevalier is a qualified enologist and one of the first to achieve a new density, fruit, velvetiness and character for Cabernet Franc.

Château Yvonne****
Parnay
17.3 acres (7 ha); 20,000 bottles • Wines: Saumur, Saumur-Champigny
Françoise Foucault has proved herself a talented wine-maker and conjures up some high quality Chenins.

Clos Rougeard****−*****
Chacé
25 acres (10 ha); 20,000 bottles • Wines: Saumur-Champigny: →Les Poyeaux, →Bourg; →Saumur Blanc Brezé
The Foucault brothers' wines are among the top reds of Anjou. There is also a small output of sweet wine, which is among the best in the Loire region.

Philippe Delesvaux***−****
Saint-Aubin-de-Luigne
36 acres (14.5 ha); 50,000 bottles • Wines include: →Anjou Rouge, Anjou Villages, Coteaux du Layon: Sélection de Grains Nobles, Le 20
Few other Anjou winegrowers can match Philippe Delesvaux's versatility with dry whites and reds as well as sweet wines. This is especially evident in his outstanding Sélection.

Domaine de Bablut***
Brissac
185 acres (75 ha); 320,000 bottles • Wines include: →Coteaux de l'Aubance: Bablut, Grandpierre, Vin Noble, Anjou Villages, Château de Brissac
This large estate is run by Christophe Daviau with bravura. His red Anjou Villages are convincing, but his strength is the whites, especially the medium dry.

Domaine des Baumard****
Rochefort-sur-Loire
91 acres (37 ha); 140,000 bottles • Wines: →Coteaux du Layon Le Paon, Savennières Clos du Papillon, Trie Spéciale, Quarts de Chaume
Florent Baumard is a specialist in mellow Coteaux-du-Layon wines, but the clean freshness of his dry Savennières cuvées is very convincing.

Domaine du Closel***−****
Savennières
37 acres (15 ha); 70,000 bottles • Wines include: →Savennières: Cuvée Spéciale, Clos du Papillon
Dry and medium-dry, late-picked Savennières are the specialty of this estate, whose top site is the Clos du Papillon.

Domaine du Collier****
Chacé
10 acres (4 ha); 17,000 bottles • Wines: Saumur, Saumur-Champigny
A great beginning by Antoine Foucault after his apprenticeship in Clos Rougeard. Classy whites and the finest reds.

Domaine René-Noël Legrand**−****
Varrains
37 acres (15 ha); 60,000 bottles • Wines: →Saumur, Saumur-Champigny: Les Terrages, Les Lizières, →Les Rogelins
In recent years, the son of one of the founders of the *appellation* has convinced with his steadily improving wines.

Domaine de Montgilet**−****
Juigné-sur-Loire
91.4 acres (37 ha); 150,000 bottles • Wines include: Anjou, Anjou-Villages, Coteaux de l'Aubance, Vin de Pays
Fine sweet Chenins are the mark of the Lebreton brothers, but they also produce fresh, dry whites and solid reds, some with a very fine wood note.

Domaine Ogereau****
Saint-Lambert-du-Lattay
59 acres (24 ha); 70,000 bottles • Wines include: →Anjou-Villages, Anjou Sec Prestige, Coteaux du Layon: Saint Lambert, Saint Lambert Prestige
Vincent Ogereau vinifies his whites and reds with remarkable perfection. The wines are partly aged in the barrel, though without losing any fruitiness or elegance.

Domaine Jo Pithon****
Saint-Lambert-du-Lattay
30 acres (12 ha); 30,000 bottles • Wines: Anjou, Savennières, Coteaux du Layon, Quart de Chaume
Jo Pithon is a master of Chenin. After the delicate and richly sweet wines, he has now distinguished himself with dry wines.

Domaine des Roches Neuves****
Varrains
49.5 acres (20 ha); 120,000 bottles • Wines include: →Saumur Blanc Insolite, Saumur-Champigny, Terres Chaudes, Vieilles Vignes, Marignale
Fully ripe grapes, which Thierry Germain harvests at great risk, and aging the best *cuvées* in new wood gives the red wines enormous fruit, depth and velvetiness. Outstanding Insolite.

Domaine des Sablonettes***−****
Rablay-sur-Layon
32 acres (13 ha); 35,000 bottles • Wines include: →Anjou, Anjou Villages; Coteaux du Layon Coteaux du Layon Rablay
Joel and Christine Menard are virtuosi in all areas—rosés, reds and dry white wines. But the elite are their sweet wines, particularly their Champ du Cygne—the finest fruits of organic cultivation.

Domaine de la Sansonnière****
Thouarcé
20 acres (8 ha); 20,000 bottles • Wines include: →Rosé d'Anjou, Anjou Blanc, Coteaux du Layon Les Blanderies, Anjou Blanc Vignes Françaises, Rouges les Gélinettes
Using biodynamic cultivation and really putting his heart into it, Marc Angeli achieves a clean tone, an enormous volume of fruit and the highest degree of complexity.

Maison Bouvet-Ladoubay**−****
Saumur
Some bought-in grapes; 2,700,000 bottles • Wines include: Saumur brut: Saphir, Trésor, →Instinct; Nonpareils: →Anjou Cabernet Sauvignon, Cabernet Franc, Vin de Pays du Jardin de France Cot
The sparkling wine company, founded in 1851, has caused a sensation with its fascinating dense and aromatic red wines, but with Instinct it has now proved that it still remains at the top for Brut.

Pierre Soulez***−*****
Savennières
62 acres (25 ha); 120,000 bottles • Wines include: Anjou Villages; Savennières: Château de Chamboureau Roche-aux-Moines Cuvée d'Avant Sec and Doux, Château de la Bizolière, Clos de Papillon Moelleux
Some of the best sweet wines of Savennières and the Roche-aux-Moines single-site come from Pierre Soulez, who runs the paternal estates after parting company with his brother Yves.

THE GARDEN OF FRANCE

Touraine is the land of the famous Loire châteaux and the Garden of France. Of the 24,700 acres (10,000 hectares) under vine, about half the production is bottled under the Touraine label, with red and white being about equal. A large part of the output, especially the Gamay, goes on sale shortly after the harvest as *primeur*. Characteristic of the geology of the area is the whitish tuff, which was also used to build the finest Loire châteaux. Most of the vines are planted in the immediate vicinity of the great river, though also along its tributary, the Cher, east of Tours. The manifold ecoclimatic influences of Touraine enable a wide range of grapes to be cultivated. Among the whites there is not only the customary Chenin but also Arbois, Sauvignon Blanc—the most widely cultivated white variety—Pinot Gris and increasingly Chardonnay. The reds include Cabernet Franc, Cabernet Sauvignon, Malbec, Pinot Noir, Gamay, Pineau d'Aunis, and Grolleau. However, the best wines come from the Cabernet Franc grape. The variety called Breton, a Bordeaux grape that arrived via Brittany, has proved thoroughly at home and produces a pure single-variety wine such as is found virtually nowhere else in the world.

If we disregard the Saumur area, the territory begins around Bourgeuil, facing upriver. A wide range of different *terroirs* gives it a highly individual character. If Cabernet Franc is planted in alluvial soil, the end product is an easy-drinking light bistro wine. In higher localities, where clay and chalk prevail, it gains greater structure and a marked tannin content. Where it enjoys a lot of sun and poor soils, it shows real class. In good years, the round, ripe tannins then combine with a lively *nervosité* that lend the wine finesse and complexity even after decades.

BOURGEUIL AND CHINON

The *appellations* that reflect Cabernet Franc at its best are Bourgeuil, Chinon, and Saint-Nicolas-de-Bourgeuil. The last-named is the most westerly, and with 1,980 acres (800 ha) the smallest of the three. Its lighter soils produce fruity and in France highly popular reds and rosés that are ready to drink very young. Immediately east of Saint-Nicolas is the Bourgeuil region, the best-known *appellation* of Touraine. Its vineyards occupy 2,970 acres (1,200 ha) on the north bank of the Loire, every

A wine renaissance is under way at many Loire châteaux.

If Bacchus had a choice today, it might be for Vouvray.

last square yard being stocked with Cabernet Franc. Sand and gravels over an excellent chalky substratum prove ideal for the most solidly structured Loire reds with the strongest tannin content.

On the other Loire bank, along its tributary the Vienne, is the Chinon district, whose 4,450 acres (1,800 ha) make it the largest of the three. The wines here are very varied depending on the kind of soil they grow on. Here too the denser, stronger wines come from the higher, chalk-bearing tuff formations like those near Cravant, for example, while the lighter wines come from vineyards close to the river.

WHITE IN RED COUNTRY

Even though red Cabernet dominates, Touraine is not just red wine country. Chenin is also cultivated here, and on both sides of the Loire provides the whole range of wines it is capable of, ranging from dry, through sweet to sparkling. Beside the small Jasnières label, where the wines are emphatically dry, the *appellations* Vouvray and Montlouis stand out. With about 4,450 acres (1,800 ha) under vine, Vouvray is the most important white area in Touraine and the largest Chenin *appellation* overall. The grape finishes up about 60 percent as still wine and 40 percent sparkling. Unique are the numerous tuffstone cellars of the region, whose cool climate in earlier times, when wine presses and cellaring knew fewer technological tricks, first made the second fermentation possible.

Select Producers in Touraine

DOMAINE PHILIPPE ALLIET***
CRAVANT-LES-COTEAUX
22 acres (9 ha); 35,000 bottles • Wines: →Chinon Vieilles Vignes, Chinon Coteau de Noiré
Absolutely top reds at this price level are available nowhere else in France. That Chinon can be more than a rather flabby red is proven by Philippe Alliet not only with his site wine Coteau de Noiré but also with his generic Chinon. A model business for the whole *appellation*.

DOMAINE YANNICK AMIRAULT**—*****
BOURGUEIL
42 acres (17 ha); 80,000 bottles • Wines: Bourgueil: →Les Quartiers, La Petite Cave; Saint-Nicolas-de-Bourgueil: →Les Graviers and Vieilles Vignes, Les Malgagnes
Yannick Amirault uses the grapes from his vineyards—which grow only Cabernet—like a Bourgignon. Time-consuming care of the soil and optimum maturity enables him to give each of his locations its own individual character. The height of skill.

DOMAINE DES AUBUSIÈRES**
VOUVRAY
54 acres (22 ha); 110,000 bottles • Wines: →Vouvray: tendre Cuvée Silex, Demi-sec Les Giradières, Sec Le Marigny, Moelleux Le Plan de Jean, Moelleux Cuvée Alexandre, Demi-sec Le Bouchet
A solid business that supplies outstanding products in both the dry and mellow and sweet ranges. The range of various *cuvées* and site wines is relatively large.

DOMAINE BERNARD BAUDRY**
CHINON
62 acres (25 ha); 110,000 bottles • Wines: →Chinon: Les Granges, Crois Boissée, Les Grézeaux, Clos Guillot
A further top grower of the Chinon district who also makes an unusual white Chinon from Chenin, even if in small quantities.

DOMAINE FRANÇOIS CHIDAINE**
MONTLOUIS
39.5 acres (16 ha); 70,000 bottles • Wines: Montlouis: Choiselles, Demi-sec Les Tuffeaux, Clos Habert, Brut Méthode Traditionelle
François Chidaine devotes himself to his vineyards with endless care and love. This is bringing in results. His wines have remarkably clean lines, and Les Tuffeaux is a mineral marvel.

DOMAINE COULY-DUTHEIL*
CHINON
222 acres (90 ha); 600,000 bottles • Wines: Chinon: →Clos de l'Écho and Crescendo, →Clos de l'Olive, La Coulée Automnale; Chinon Blanc: Les Chanteaux; Saumur-Champigny Les Moulins de Turquant
Pierre and Jacques Couly-Dutheil are among the better known Chinon producers. Their cellar, which is sunk into the slope and in which the carriage of grapes takes place only by means of gravity, is among the show businesses of the region.

DOMAINE DRUET*—****
BENAIS
54.5 acres (22 ha); 105,000 bottles • Wines: →Bourgueil Grand Mont, Bourgueil 100 Boisselées
Pierre-Jacques Druet provides his reds with a good portion of tannins to ensure long life. They give a correspondingly reserved impression when young, but after some years maturing in the bottle they gain great complexity.

DOMAINE HUET**—*****
VOUVRAY
86.5 acres (35 ha); 150,000 bottles • Wines: →Vouvray: Le Haut-Lieu Sec, Le Mont Moelleux, Clos du Bourg Moelleux, Le Mont Sec, Clos du Bourg Demi-sec
Top-class Vouvray, both dry and sweet. All the wines produced by the business are distinguished by their uncommonly well-defined fruit aromas.

DOMAINE CHARLES JOGUET—****
SAZILLY
99 acres (40 ha); 200,000 bottles • Wines: →Chinon: Terroir, Jeunes Vignes, Clos de la Cure, Les Varennes du Grand Clos, Clos du Chêne Vert, Clos de la Dioterie
For many years Charles Joguet was the driving force of the Chinon appellation. Since his successor Alain Delauney took over, the wines have lost a little of their depth. Only the very top *cuvées* of the Clos de la Dioterie and du Chêne Vert continue the old tradition.

DOMAINE HENRI MARIONNET*—*****
SOINGS
148 acres (60 ha); 370,000 bottles • Wines: →Touraine: Domaine de la Charmoise Sauvignon, Rosé, Gamay, →M, →Premiére Vendange; Vinifera: Sauvignon, Chenin, →Provignage, Gamay, Cot
Henri Marionnet has had international successes with his clean, very aromatic and attractive wines made from Sauvignon and Gamay grapes. After acquiring a plot first planted in 1851 which produces the Provinage, he has been experimenting with authentic root stocks and producing some of the most original wines in France.

DOMAINE DU CLOS NAUDIN**—*****
VOUVRAY
30 acres (12 ha); 60,000 bottles • Wines: →Vouvray: Sec, Demi-sec, Moelleux, Brut Réserve, Méthode traditionnelle, Réserve
No one in the Vouvray region can match Philippe Foreau in creating dry, incomparably classy sparkling wines from outstanding still wines by maturing them in the bottle. But his extremely durable and long-lived semi-sweet and sweet Vouvrays are amongst the best that this appellation can produce.

DOMAINE DE LA TAILLE-AUX-LOUPS**
MONTLOUIS-SUR-LOIRE
39 acres (16 ha); 75,000 bottles • Wines: Montlouis: Sec Dix Arpents, Demi-sec, Moelleux Cuvée des Loups, Brut Tradition, Pétillant Non Dosé; Vouvray Sec Clos de Venise
Jacky Blot has proved—and continues to prove—to the wine world that Montlouis can match anything produced by Vouvray on the other side of the Loire. Now he needs to show that his own newly acquired Vouvrays can come up to the standards of his outstanding Montlouis.

DOMAINE TALUAU—FOLTZENLOGEL*
SAINT-NICOLAS-DE-BOURGEUIL
54.5 acres (22 ha); 120,000 bottles • Wines: Saint-Nicolas-de-Bourgeuil: Jeunes Vignes, Cuvée du Domaine, Vieilles Vignes, Le Vau Jaumier; Bourgueil Cuvée du Domaine
Joël Taluau has made a specialty of Cabernet Franc. His wines are the quintessence of a fruity, soft, and well-rounded style that is typical for the *appellation*.

FLINT AND GOOSEBERRIES

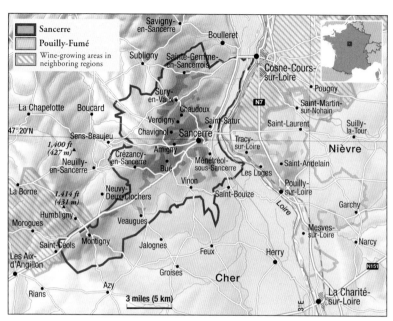

The upper Loire is a stronghold of Sauvignon, in fact the true, genuine thing—Sauvignon Blanc. Not the Sauvignon Gris, or the Sauvignon Violet, or the Sauvignon Jaune or even the Sauvignonasse or Sauvignon Vert, a relative of the Tocai Friulano, which is still sold in South America under the name of Sauvignon. As most members of this extensive family of grape varieties are of little or no importance, the *blanc* is often omitted. In the 1970s and 1980s Sauvignon in the form of Sancerre—the major *appellation* in this area—was one of the most popular white wines in almost the whole world, comparable with the Pinot Grigio, which was also fashionable at the time. Not much of this craze for white Sancerre is left now, but the grape itself continued its triumphal march across the wine-growing countries of the world. In terms of white wines, it is a march outshone only by that of the Chardonnay grape. Sauvignon Blanc is now found not only in the Loire and Bordeaux but also in Styria (Austria), Friuli (Italy), California, Australia, South America (though with the above caveat!), and South Africa.

Sauvignon has an uncommonly intense aroma. When young or harvested too soon, it manifests its typical grassy vegetational character.

In the upper Loire, in the vineyards around Sancerre and Pouilly-Fumé, Menetou-Salon and Reuilly, Sauvignon can unfurl a complex intensity and finesse—even without being blended with other varieties—such as is rarely found elsewhere.

SANCERRE AND POUILLY

Sancerre, a charming old wine-growing area, whose houses straddle a hilltop above the Loire, is the best known of the four names. The town itself and 14 of its neighboring villages constitute the 4,940-acre (2,000-ha) Sancerre cultivation area. Until the phylloxera disaster in the late 19th century, Pinot Noir and Gamay were the principal grapes. Afterwards, whites were given preference, and the light, fruity red wines made from Pinot fell out of favor, and today make only a third of the output.

Sancerre provides Sauvignon with three separate *terroirs*, though most wines are blended from grapes of different localities. In the extreme west, clay soils and chalk marls are predominant, and produce the strongest wines. Around the town itself you find the famous flint, the aroma of which is reminiscent of newly struck matches. Between the two zones the most delicate wines of the *appellation* thrive on gravel and limestone. Aging is usually done in steel tanks, as best suits the fruity, direct character of Sauvignon, and barrels are rarely used. Not so well known as its popular neighbor but more highly regarded by connoisseurs are the Sauvignon wines from Pouilly-sur-Loire, on the other bank of the Loire.

Pouilly-Fumé is the *appellation*, applied solely to white wines made from Sauvignon Blanc. The name is the source of some confusion with the

Few top localities are so easily overviewed as Clos de la Poussie near Sancerre.

village of Pouilly-Fuissé in the Mâconnais in Burgundy, where the wines are of course made from Chardonnay. In Pouilly, not only are the hills softer than in Sancerre, the wines too are more rounded, softer and somewhat less emphatically aromatic. The best Pouillys, which are occasionally aged in wood, are, however, more complex and longer-lived than the Sancerre drinker will be used to.

The western neighbors of Sancerre have also specialized in Sauvignon. Menetou-Salon, and even more Quincy and Reuilly, lie in the great arc of the Loire so far from the river that one often ascribes them to another unspecified center. About half-way between Sancerre and Bourges is the Menetou-Salon district which, like Sancerre, produces red and white wines. Here the Sauvignon Blanc is often just as good as the more famous district directly on the Loire, only much cheaper.

Somewhat more rustic are the wines of the twin *appellations* Quincy and Reuilly, which are produced beyond Bourges along the central reach of the Cher. Sauvignon is cultivated on

Wine for Parisian palates

North of Sancerre are two other wine-growing areas directly on the Loire. One is the Coteaux du Giennois, a V.D.Q.S. area where the typical upper Loire grapes—Sauvignon Blanc, Pinot Noir, and some Gamay—are cultivated. The other is Orléans, once an important wine center, but one whose wine has for centuries been sold only in Paris. The cultivated area is now down to 247 acres (100 ha). Unlike other areas of this part of the Loire, it produces mainly Burgundian varieties: a lot of Pinot Meunier (otherwise found in France mainly in Champagne), Cabernet, Chardonnay, and Pinot Gris.

about 247 acres (100 ha) of Quincy. In Reuilly, vines are planted in almost equal measure in red and white varieties. The Gamay harvested here is not an *appellation* wine but instead is sold as *vin de pays*.

SELECT PRODUCERS ON THE UPPER LOIRE

CHÂTEAU DU NOZET – LADOUCETTE***–****
POUILLY-SUR-LOIRE
257 acres (104 ha); 1,200,000 bottles • Wines include: Pouilly-Fumé: Baron de L, Sancerre Comte Lafon Grand Cuvée
Ladoucette is symbolic of Pouilly and Sancerre in general. Whenever Sauvignon is discussed worldwide, you hear this name mentioned.

DOMAINE HENRI BOURGEOIS**–****
CHAVIGNOL
148 acres (60 ha); 500,000 bottles • Wines include: Pouilly-Fumé Sancerre: Grande Réserve, Les Baronnes, La Chapelle des Augustins, Jadis
A family-run estate producing clean, clearly defined Sancerres and Pouillys with the latest winery technology.

DOMAINE PASCAL COTAT****
SANCERRE
4.5 acres (1.9 ha); 14,000 bottles • Wines: Sancerre: Chavignol La Grand Côte, Cuvée Spéciale, Les Mont Damnés
Pascal Cotat's wines are among the best Sancerre has to offer; sold in advance.

DOMAINE DIDIER DAGUENEAU*****
SAINT-ANDELAN
27 acres (11 ha); 50,000 bottles • Wines: Pouilly-Fumé: Silex, En Chailloux, Pur-Sang
Dagueneau's reputation is based on the extraordinary Sauvignon-Cuvées Silex and Pur Sang, which are known throughout the world as model wines of this grape variety.

DOMAINE MASSON-BLONDELET***
POUILLY-SUR-LOIRE
44.5 acres (18 ha); 100,000 bottles • Wines: Pouilly-Fumé: Les Angelots, Villa Paulus, Tradition Cullus, Sancerre
Jean-Michel Masson's wines manifest clear Sauvignon fruit and solid qualities.

DOMAINE LA MOUSSIÈRE***–*****
SANCERRE
119 acres (48 ha); 275,000 bottles • Wines include: Sancerre: Blanc, Rouge: La Moussière, → Ceneration XIX; → Edmond
Alphonse Mellot and his son Alphonse have gone back to the best of craftsmanship, and use only their own grapes. With new inspiration and modern technology, they create outstanding wines.

DOMAINE HENRY PELLÉ**–****
MOROGUES
131 acres (53 ha); 500,000 bottles • Wines include: Menetou-Salon: Morogues, Clos des Blanchais; Sancerre La Croix au Garde
Henry Pellé's Clos des Blanchais has proved for years that Sauvignon Blanc from Menetou is no poor relative of a Sancerre.

DOMAINE VINCENT PINARD***–****
BUÉ
37.1 acres (15 ha); 100,000 bottles • Wines: Sancerre Blanc: Florès, Nuance, Harmonie; Sancerre Rouge and Charlouise
Whether fermented in tanks or barrels, Vincent Pinard's white and red wines possess great intensity and splendid ripe fruit. The Cuvée Charlouise has proved itself one of the best red wines of this *appellation*.

SILICES DE QUINCY***–****
QUINCY
17.3 acres (7 ha); 12,000 bottles • Wines: → Silice de Quincy, VdT: Silice Millénium, Silicette Millénium
Jacques Sallé, the wine journalist and former "Vintage International" publisher, has been involved as a winegrower in his home region since 1995. Using biodynamic cultivation methods and barrel fermentation, he gets a great deal of character and body out of his Sauvignon vines, some of which are very old indeed.

Bordeaux: Making a Career of an Emporium

Bordeaux is more than just a famous wine-growing area. It is a symbol for great wine in general, a model for the whole world of wine. Bordeaux is the largest and most successful *appellation* in France and the world, producing over 100 million gallons (four million hectoliters (660 million bottles) of wine a year from more than 247,000 acres (100,000 ha) of vines, or as much as the whole of Germany. The elite wines, which have established the fame of the region in modern times, constitute a modest five percent of this, of course, but their aura is so strong that it is not just the local wine industry that benefits. The whole wine industry from Italy to California, Australia to Austria, and Chile to Germany is orientated to Bordeaux style and quality and takes it as a benchmark.

Viticulture is documented in the Dordogne by the Roman poet Ausonius, who settled in what is now the Saint-Émilion region in the 4th century AD and made his own wine. It is not clear whether there had been vine cultivation in the Landes around Burdigala, now Bordeaux, even earlier. At any rate, as neither Pliny the Elder nor Strabo mention it, historians assume that the vine arrived much later, after it had already become established in Provence and the Rhône Valley. The Romans treated Bordeaux as

just a trading center for exporting their wines to England.

Even the assumption that Roman legionaries brought the main grape variety of the region from what is now Albania seems questionable in the light of recent research. As we now know that Cabernet Sauvignon contains genetic material from Cabernet Franc and Sauvignon Blanc, it is more likely that it came about much later as a cross or spontaneous mutation of these two varieties. Another untenable theory is that it is the old Biturica grape, named for the Gaulish tribe of Bituricans, a name that mutated over time by folk etymology to Vidure (*vigne dure*) meaning "hard vine wood" and is still current in the Graves region.

Early medieval sources relating to the history of regional viticulture are likewise meager. A series of successive conquests of Bordeaux by various peoples—Gascons, Saracens, Vandals, and Visigoths—is documented, as is the total destruction of the city by Vikings in 870, but wine growing never succumbed. However, the true success story of the vine began only in 1152, when Eleanor of Aquitaine married the duke of Normandy, Henry Plantagenet, who later became King Henry II of England. With the aid of generous excise privileges, Gascony became the most important supplier of the English court and London society, so that when the rival exporting port of La Rochelle was taken over by the French, Bordeaux retained its pre-eminent position in the English wine trade.

The expanse of the Gironde seen from Château Latour in Pauillac.

THE DEVELOPMENT OF
MODERN BORDEAUX

Bordeaux's reputation is based on the aging potential of its wines.

At that time, the wines did not come from the Médoc, the modern heart of the region—it was fenland until the 17th century and at best suitable for plowing—but from the gravelly soils of Graves and the upriver territories of Gaillac and Bergerac. They were not in the least comparable with the vigorous, dark, and ageable reds of our day, but light and thin (hence "claret" as they became known in England, from the Latin *vinum clarum*). Until the 14th century, almost all wine drunk in England came from Gascony. The end of the Hundred Years' War in 1453 put an end to this export splendor, when Gascony was annexed by France. Although trading links with England were not severed entirely, other markets gained in importance until Holland became a world power during the 17th century, and took over England's place in Bordeaux's trading affections.

With their huge fleet, the Dutch controlled the greater part of world trade and imported wine from all areas under cultivation, but especially Portugal and Bordeaux. At the beginning of the 17th century they also drained the marshes of the Médoc with an ingenious canal system, and introduced sulfurization as a way of conserving wine. This created the basis for the great wines of later centuries. It was also the time when the great châteaux such as Haut-Brion, Latour, Lafite, and Margaux were first established.

But Dutch control of the seas did not last long. By the 18th century the English were back in Bordeaux, founding trading companies such as Barton & Guestier, which until very recently controlled the fate of the wine industry in the region. Soon after, this successful approach was taken up by a series of German immigrants.

The trading firms and their traveling buyers, the *courtiers*, made the first attempts to classify individual châteaux in the early 19th century. This was intended to bring stability to a very unstable market, which always tended to fluctuate between overheating and crisis. The result of these endeavors, which focused solely on the Médoc region and Sauternes, was the classification of 1855 and triumphal presentation of the châteaux at the Paris Exposition in the same year. The golden age of Bordeaux had begun.

TURBULENCE IN THE
20TH CENTURY

Despite the enormous prestige that Bordeaux wines have enjoyed since then and have managed to further enhance, the 20th century was a period of crisis. It began with the phylloxera catastrophe, which wiped out virtually the entire stock of vines. After a brief period of recovery, during which exports to Germany, England, and Belgium picked up again, and laws for the protection of labels of origins were worked out, the First World War and economic crisis led to the collapse of important foreign markets such as Russia and the U.S.A.

Only in the 1950s did the sales graphs begin to point steadily upwards. It was the heyday of the Médoc's neighboring regions. In 1953 and 1955 respectively the wines of Graves and Saint-Émilion were classified—only Pomerol still has no official hierarchy even today—and the best wines of the region reached a dizzying price level as a result of sharply increased demand. The ensuing shortage of wine was to some extent compensated for by one or two shippers adding wines from other areas. The fraud was discovered in 1973, to great scandal, and prices tumbled again.

At the same time, the Bordeaux region was increasingly exposed to competition from the New World. Californian or Australian growths triumphed over Bordeaux's best in top-ranking competitions. They included wines such as the Australian Grange Hermitage or those of California's Clos du Val estate, run by natives of Bordeaux. The international competitors trumped Bordeaux with wines that had the same strength and density as the great

The vine varieties of Bordeaux

For all the differences between the *terroirs* in the various areas of Bordeaux, the wines have a common basis: a small number of grape varieties used in proportions that vary according to the *terroir* or fashion. Red has priority, and occupies a good 85 percent of the area under cultivation, and this proportion has risen in the last 15 years.

RED WINE VARIETIES

Cabernet Sauvignon—one of the best red wine grapes in the world and the star of the Bordeaux region, it probably developed from Cabernet Franc and Sauvignon Blanc. Its special qualities reside in its concentration of PHENOLICS, without the fruit being wholly masked by the tannins thereby. Cabernet wines are dark red, smell of cedar and blackcurrant, and manifest much strength and structure on the palate. When immature or with excessive yields, the aroma changes in the direction of green paprika pods.

Cabernet Franc/Bouchet/Breton—the grape was long considered the junior brother of Cabernet Sauvignon, but recent discoveries show Franc as the parent. Its wines have a fine berry fruitiness, and are slimmer than Cabernet Sauvignon and have more discreet tannins, but may therefore also be more acidic.

Merlot (Noir)—the grape ripens early and has a high yield, and is therefore well-suited to both aging on its own and blending with stronger wines of greater tannin content. In the Bordeaux region, its best results are in the Saint-Émilion and Pomerol *appellations*. Its wines are fruity and velvety, and it matures more quickly than Cabernet.

Petit Verdot—a late-ripening variety and therefore difficult in the aging, it produces wines that have intense color and high tannin content. Small quantities of the grape go into Médoc wines.

Malbec/Cot/Auxerrois/Pressac—a red wine variety that was once very widespread in the Bordeaux region. It was replaced there by Merlot, but is still cultivated in Cahors. The wines have a rustic character, but are very well suited to blending with other varieties.

WHITE WINE VARIETIES

Sémillon—with a tendency to noble rot, the grape is the basis for the great sweet wines of the Bordeaux region. The best dry growths are found in Pessac-Léognan. Sémillon wines have good aging ability, and then develop aromas of honey, candied fruits, and chocolates while often retaining a fresh lemony tang.

Sauvignon Blanc—when young or harvested too soon, the grapes manifest their typical grassy-vegetal aromas. Good Sauvignon wines develop an aroma of blackcurrants or gooseberries and are fruity with good acidity. When fully ripe or over-ripe, they become more complex, developing ripe fruit, and can even come to resemble highly ripe Rieslings. In the last century the French considered Riesling as just a variety of Sauvignon. The Sauvignon family also has rare red varieties.

---

growths of the Gironde region but were much more accessible.

This new style of wine was so successfully promoted and insisted upon by the American specialist in Bordeaux, Robert Parker Jr., the wine king of the 1980 and 1990s, that it became a standard for the whole international market. To keep pace with the new requirements, the estates of Médoc, Graves, Saint-Émilion, or Pomerol looked primarily to re-equipping their wineries. Vinification had changed both in respect of tannin structure and the make-up of grape varieties, in which Merlot became increasingly prominent. Bordeaux became a hotbed of technical innovation. Such modern techniques as concentrators—appliances for REVERSE OSMOSIS —and vacuum evaporizers are now used in the wineries of the most celebrated châteaux. Many estate managers even resorted to methods for which they had long criticized the New World, such as using wood chips instead of aging in expensive wooden casks.

Left
Typical gravelly soil in the Médoc area.

Right
Château Mouton-Rothschild, one of the most famous wine-growing estates in the world.

IDEAL TERROIR

Not only does the Gironde make the Médoc climate more temperate and favor wine growing, it also offers splendid opportunities for relaxation along its banks.

Even though the Dutch had to drain a large part of the territory—later the most successful part—before vines could be planted, Bordeaux had nonetheless the best possible natural conditions for great wines. Lying exactly half-way between the Equator and the North Pole, it enjoys a particularly balanced climate that is ideal for wines with strength and structure on the one hand and finesse and elegance on the other. The proximity of the Atlantic with the warm Gulf Stream ensures mild conditions and prevents extreme variations of temperature. The extensive forests of the coast of Aquitaine offer additional protection against storms from the sea. Frost risk—the grower's great enemy in Champagne or Burgundy—hardly exists here, if we disregard the exceptional year of 1991. However, June can be very unstable, which causes problems when the vines flower. Long, dry hot summers and an often variable autumn make the harvest a lottery in bad years.

In respect of soil conditions, three zones should be distinguished within the huge Bordeaux area, each of which forms an independent entity. Bordeaux is not a wine-growing area with a single, homogeneous *appellation* but a complicated, hierarchically subdivided network of 54 *appellations* in all, some of which date back to the first days of A.C. legislation, others to recent decades. A law passed in 1911 protecting French *appellations* specified that only wines from the Gironde department

could be sold as Bordeaux wines—a regulation intended to put a stop to the hitherto frequent blending with other more stronger provenances, although this could still occur, as the scandal of 1973 showed.

A large proportion of the wines—40 percent of the total output, and up to 70 percent of the whites—are marketed under the regional *appellations* Bordeaux, Bordeaux Supérieur, or Bordeaux Crémant. These labels indicate wines from areas for which no higher grade or more closely defined indication of origin is provided, or those grown in *appellation* vineyards that do not come under the *appellation*.

TWO SEAS AND THEIR VINEYARDS

The remaining A.C.s are generally divided into three zones. The first lies on the left bank of the Garonne and Gironde, and is a strip of sandy, gravelly soils (*graves*) north and south of the city of Bordeaux washed down from the Pyrenees, Limousin, and the western Massif Central. This zone is subdivided into the Médoc *appellation* north of Bordeaux, on whose thin, well-drained sand and gravel soils virtually only red grapes are grown, and Graves proper in the west and south, which incorporates the sweet wine areas of Sauternes. The latter's alluvial soils are well suited to both delicate, aromatic reds and dry whites, as well as sweet specialties.

Between the Garonne and Dordogne rivers is the Entre-Deux-Mers district, the area "between two rivers," a plateau of the Tertiary period with heavy clay and gravel soils. Its wines range from aromatic, lively, and even mellow wines to sometimes very full-bodied reds in which Merlot dominates. Lastly, on the right bank of the Dordogne, we find a number of wholly independent areas of very varying quality. The soils are similar to those of Entre-deux-Mers. Different wines grow on the gravel soils of Pomerol to those growing on the clayey chalk of the Fronsadais or in Saint-Émilion.

The three zones mentioned are heavily subdivided, with the subdivision system varying considerably from zone to zone. The best arranged is that of the Médoc, which is divided into Haut-Médoc and Médoc proper. The former, closer to Bordeaux, contains the highly prestigious communal *appellations* Margaux, Listrac, Moulis, Saint-Julien, Pauillac, and Saint-Estèphe. The Graves area has no such

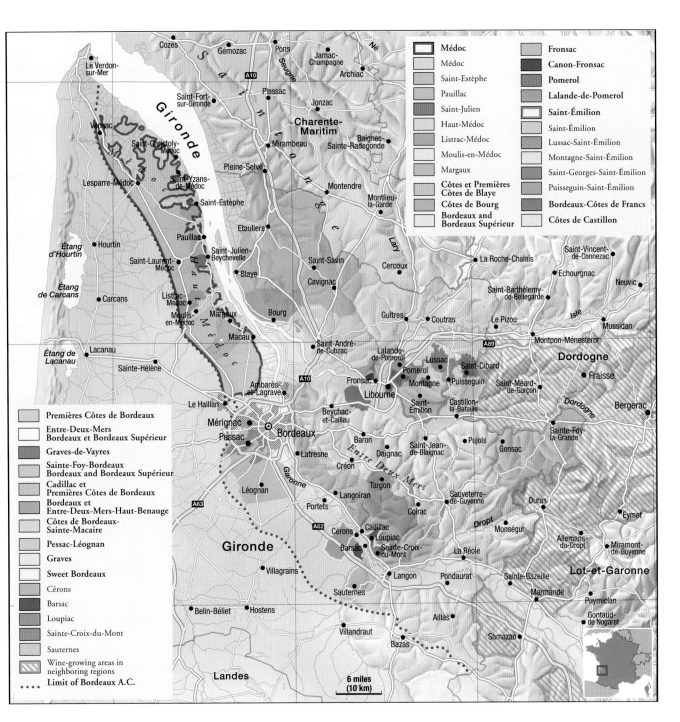

Médoc
- Médoc
- Saint-Estèphe
- Pauillac
- Saint-Julien
- Haut-Médoc
- Listrac-Médoc
- Moulis-en-Médoc
- Margaux
- **Côtes et Premières Côtes de Blaye**
- **Côtes de Bourg**
- **Bordeaux and Bordeaux Supérieur**

- Fronsac
- **Canon-Fronsac**
- **Pomerol**
- **Lalande-de-Pomerol**
- **Saint-Émilion**
- Saint-Émilion
- Lussac-Saint-Émilion
- Montagne-Saint-Émilion
- Saint-Georges-Saint-Émilion
- Puisseguin-Saint-Émilion
- **Bordeaux-Côtes de Francs**
- Côtes de Castillon

- Premières Côtes de Bordeaux
- Entre-Deux-Mers / Bordeaux et Bordeaux Supérieur
- Graves-de-Vayres
- Sainte-Foy-Bordeaux / Bordeaux and Bordeaux Supérieur
- Cadillac et Premières Côtes de Bordeaux
- Bordeaux et Entre-Deux-Mers-Haut-Benauge
- Côtes de Bordeaux-Sainte-Macaire
- Pessac-Léognan
- Graves
- Sweet Bordeaux
- Cérons
- Barsac
- Loupiac
- Sainte-Croix-du-Mont
- Sauternes
- Wine-growing areas in neighboring regions
- ···· Limit of Bordeaux A.C.

6 miles (10 km)

hierarchical arrangement. Instead, a higher—quality *appellation* of Pessac-Léognan has been created for the northern end—as an equivalent of the communal A.C.s of the Médoc—and the Sauternes label at the southern end.

The structure is similar in Entre-Deux-Mers. The *rive droite*, or right bank, of the Dordogne is more complicated. It comprises a row of individual *appellations* that do not constitute part of any official hierarchical arrangement with each other, even though their prestige varies widely. In the northwest are the vineyards of Bourg and Blaye, in the southeast Fronsac with Canon-Fronsac and the Libournais, which is subdivided into Pomerol and Saint-Émilion and a series of satellites—the areas are so labeled

that the name of the more prestigious A.C. forms part of their own *appellation*, like Lalande-de-Pomerol or Puisseguin-Saint-Émilion. The final label in the east is the Côtes-de-Castillon.

HIERARCHICAL RELATIONSHIPS

One of the milestones in the success story of Bordeaux wines was the classification of the various *crus*, first officially undertaken in 1855. Thomas Jefferson had made a previous attempt with the Médocs *crus* during his visit in 1787, with the names of Latour, Lafite, Margaux, and Haut-Brion—still dominant today—top of the list. However, another half-century was to pass before the world exposition of 1855 in Paris provided the occasion to designate the best châteaux officially as such. The Bordeaux chamber of commerce—the Libournais did not belong to it and therefore did not participate in the classification exercise—was asked to draw up lists. This was done with the help of *courtiers* from the Bordeaux exchange, who had long operated on the basis of such classifications for their own purposes. In contrast to Burgundy, where the monasteries especially had been practicing the art of classifying individual vineyards for centuries, the *courtiers* allowed not only for the factor of the *terroir* but also for the human achievement involved—more precisely, the reputation of the châteaux and the average prices that their wines had commanded in the markets over a long period. Their scheme distinguished five classes, ranging from the *premier* to the *cinquième grand cru classé*, the first to the fifth growth. However difficult as such an exercise appears, the *courtiers* carried out their work in such model fashion that their assessments have remained in forced virtually

The barrels of the Château Lafite-Rothschild are stored in the cellars under the vineyard.

Every year since 1945, a different well-known artist has been commissioned to design the label for the Premier Grand Cru Classé Château Mouton-Rothschild.

unchanged—only Château Mouton-Rothschild was added in 1973 as a fifth member to the illustrious family of *premiers crus* first nominated by Jefferson. Overall, 87 châteaux are included in this classification.

Château Haut-Brion is the only representative of Graves in the *premier cru*. Sixty Médoc *domaines* are ranked (including four *premiers*, 14 *deuxièmes*, 14 *troisièmes*, 10 *quatrièmes*, and 18 *cinquièmes*) and 26 châteaux of Sauternes and Barsac, with only the Sauternes Château Yquem given the top title of Premier Cru Supérieur. Below these *crus classés*, the Crus Bourgeois, a further classification of 444 wines in the Médoc, was worked out in the 1930s. Updated and officially sanctioned in 1972, 322 châteaux belong to this group today, still representing almost 50 percent of the total Médoc output.

SETTING AN EXAMPLE

Of course, the success of Médoc, the classification of which had been one of the triggers of a huge commercial success, attracted jealousy. However, it would take until 1936—and the crises that the French wine industry had undergone in the previous 150 years were certainly in part to blame—before a similar venture was undertaken in Saint-Émilion on the right bank of the Dordogne. It became reality only after the Second World War, in 1954–55. The classification was much simpler here than in the Médoc. In the first place, a distinction was made between the *appellations* Saint-Émilion and Saint-Émilion Grand Cru, with only the latter having the right to further subclassification. Overall, 75 châteaux in this group are labeled once again as *grands crus classés*, and 11 of them are graded one rank higher, as *premiers grands crus classés*.

The real top rank of the *appellation* is occupied by only two estates, Château Cheval Blanc and Château Ausone, which form an A group within the *premiers grands crus*, while the other nine have to make do with B-group membership. Apart from being somewhat simpler, the Saint-Émilion system has a further substantial advantage. Whereas the Médoc classification does not in principle allow for modification—this being one reason why Mouton took decades to be acknowledged as *premier cru classé* despite the obvious quality of its wines—

The permitted yields per hectare* of individual *appellations*

One of the vital features of each classification in France is, beside the *terroir* designation, the limit of the maximum permitted yield per hectare for each *appellation*. Depending on the prestige of the given *appellation*, these permitted maximum yields are specified more or less liberally.

For the regional *appellation* Bordeaux it is 55 or 65 hl/ha, for Bordeaux Supérieur 50 hl/ha. For years, however, the possibility has existed of moving this limit upwards, as a result of which it can reach 68 or 78 hl/ha for Bordeaux Rouge and Blanc and 66 for Bordeaux Supérieur.

The base and highest values for the most important *appellations* are set as follows: Médoc 50/66, Haut-Médoc 48/66, communal *appellations* (Pauillac etc.) 47/66, Graves 50, Pessac-Léognan 45 (red) and 48 (white) / 66, Sauternes, Barsac 25/28, Entre-deux-Mers 60/75, Premières Côtes de Bordeaux 50/66 (red) and 50/55 (white), Pomerol 42/60, Fronsac 47/65, Côtes de Bourg 50/60 (red) and 60/75 (white).

*1 ha = 2.47 acres; 1 hl = 26.42 U.S. gallons

such revision is prescribed in Saint-Émilion every ten years. This periodic check offers a real incentive to growers to keep the quality of their work and their products at a level that matches their grading. Such motivation is alas lacking in the Médoc, if we judge only by the downright lamentable image that some classified *crus* present time and again.

producers more freedom of movement here, in 1989 an additional category of *cru artisan* was introduced. This offers connoisseurs the opportunity to buy really top wines at very favorable prices, which is hardly possible any more within the classified growths.

Crus Artisans: Tips for Connoisseurs

Particularly in the Médoc, it often happens that wines only labeled as *cru bourgeois*, if we just follow the hierarchical system, are markedly better presented than many a fifth or even fourth growth, and occasionally better even than châteaux ranked still higher. To allow

The dry wines of the Médoc and Graves

MÉDOC
37 million bottles, 127 crus bourgeois, 113 crus artisans, 5 caves coopératives
A broad range of red wines, many of which are lighter and therefore more accessible in character, while others are rounder and take more time in the bottle; often Merlot provides a certain softness and harmony.

SAINT-ESTÈPHE
8.3 million bottles, 5 crus classés, 43 crus bourgeois, 25 crus artisans and others, 1 cave coopérative
They are known for marked and spirited tannins which, mingling with the often present acidity of the wines, guarantee long aging. They then manifest characterful, often earthy tones.

PAUILLAC
8.1 million bottles, 18 crus classés, 16 crus bourgeois, 7 crus artisans and others, 1 cave coopérative
Wines with body and structure which contain powerful tannins and age magnificently to reveal their second character trait—elegance and finesse.

SAINT-JULIEN
6 million bottles, 11 crus classés, 8 crus bourgeois, 11 crus artisans and others
Much harmony and finesse, both in the bouquet and on the palate, but with firm

tannins and a good structure that often confer great potential.

LISTRAC-MÉDOC
4.8 million bottles, 29 crus bourgeois, 12 crus artisans and others, 1 cave coopérative
Often very inaccessible when young, these wines are solid and rich in tannins, but their usually relatively high Merlot content gives them a full, velvety character when mature.

MOULIS-EN-MÉDOC
4 million bottles, 31 crus bourgeois, 13 crus artisans and others
The wines of Moulis are as varied as the soils, with a broad range from soft to full and more tannin-rich growths that reach their peak after about a decade.

MARGAUX
9 million bottles, 21 crus classés, 25 crus bourgeois, 38 crus artisans and others
Elegance is the key concept of Margaux, combined with delicious fruit when young. The subtle tannins hold firm during long aging, leading, in the case of the greatest wines, to fantastic refinement.

HAUT-MÉDOC
30 million bottles, 5 crus classés, 140 crus bourgeois, 116 crus artisans and other crus, 5 caves coopératives

Comprises the famous crus, and its wines often show strength and solidity with strongly marked Cabernet Sauvignon, usually intense aromas and after some years of aging a complex bouquet and balance.

PESSAC-LÉOGNAN
9 million bottles, 15 crus classés: 6 for red and white wines, 7 only for red, 2 only for white wine; another 41 châteaux
Four-fifths red wines with elegant character, intense, sometimes floral aromas and an occasional special smoky overtone, fleshy, well-structured and with great aging ability. A fifth is dry, very aromatic white wines with astonishing durability and a remarkable roundness and finish.

GRAVES
About 24 million bottles, 400 producers
The red wines have pleasant aromas of ripe red berries, a good fullness and juiciness, and with aging, finesse and harmony. About an eighth of the production constitutes intensely perfumed white wines. They are characterized by good *nervosité* and at the same time typical roundness, which improves with aging in the bottle.

MÉDOC: A SEA OF VINES IN TWO PARTS

The Médoc, a coastal strip no more than 6 miles (10 km) wide on the left bank of the Gironde, that stretches almost 50 miles (80 km) from Bordeaux almost to the Atlantic, is far better known than its neighbors and rivals, and its classified *crus* account for a large part of the prestige of the region. About 37,100 acres (15,000 ha) planted to vines produce on average 18,500,000 gallons (700,000 hl) of wine per annum.

Prior to the 17th century, the region was so marshy that large parts of it could only be reached by boat. With the arrival of the Dutch—experts in drainage—the nobility of the Bordelais region began to use the overwhelmingly flat landscape with its gravel soils for wine. The division into a northern part, the Médoc *appellation* proper, and the southern half or Haut-Médoc, established itself quickly and is still valid. The Haut-Médoc in particular, where numerous châteaux and mansions have documented the wealth of their owners since the 18th century, has proved an outstanding area to produce top wines.

Only about a third of the total Médoc production comes from the northern part. The vineyard holdings here are divided among over 650 owners, of whom almost a third market their own wines. There are no *crus classés* here, but about 130 châteaux, who account for more than half of the production, belong to the group of *crus bourgeois*. For all the variety of the *terroirs*, Médoc wines are not so firmly structured nor so complex and ageable as those of the Haut Médoc, but they often display great charm and are drinkable young.

The situation is quite different further upriver in Haut-Médoc, home of the most famous *crus classés* and the prestigious communal *appellations* Saint-Estèphe, Pauillac, Saint-Julien, Listrac, Moulis, and Margaux. Though this part of the overall region includes two-thirds of the cultivated area, because of the special situation of the localities mentioned, only something over 9,880 acres (4,000 ha) are classed as Haut-Médoc proper, which produce on average 5,020,000 gallons (190,000 hl) of wine. The Haut-Médoc *appellation* also possesses only a small number of classified estates, which account for a mere 8 percent of the total production, whereas the 140 *crus bourgeois* make up 70 percent.

THE REALM OF CABERNET

Médoc, Haut-Médoc, and the communal *appellations* are the real home of the most famous red wine grape of Bordeaux, the Cabernet Sauvignon. A late-ripening variety that easily

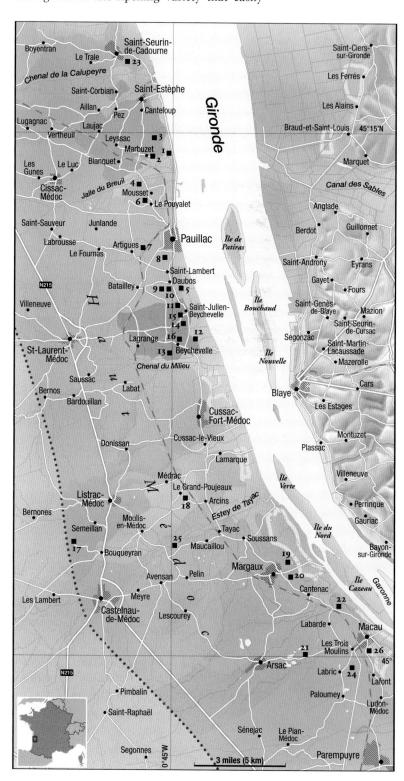

Château Comtesse de
Lalande in Pauillac.

Médoc

Saint-Estèphe
■ 1 Cos d'Estournel
■ 2 Haut-Marbuzet
■ 3 Montrose

Pauillac
■ 4 Lafite-Rothschild
■ 5 Latour
■ 6 Mouton-Rothschild
■ 7 Grand-Puy-Lacoste
■ 8 Lynch Bages
■ 9 Pichon
    Longueville-Baron
■ 10 Pichon Longueville
     Comtesse de Lalande

Saint-Julien
■ 11 Léoville-Las-Cases
■ 12 Ducru-Beaucaillon
■ 13 Gruaud-Larose
■ 14 Léoville Barton
■ 15 Léoville Poyferré
■ 16 Beycheville

Listrac-Médoc
■ 17 Mayne Lalande

Moulis-en-Médoc
■ 18 Poujeaux

Margaux
■ 19 Margaux
■ 20 Palmer
■ 21 Monbrison
■ 22 Siran

Haut-Médoc
■ 23 Sociando-Mallet
■ 24 Cantemerle
■ 25 Citran
■ 26 Maucamps

Côtes and Premières
Côtes de Blaye

Côtes de Bourg

Bordeaux and
Bordeaux Supérieur

•••• Limit of
    Bordeaux A.C.s

adapts to the most wide-ranging climatic and geological conditions, it makes wines of unequaled greatness and complexity on the gravel soils of the Gironde, which allow its roots to explore to great depths.

Of course, the otherwise really quite hardy Cabernet needs a lot of sun, or its wines manifest the grassy, unpleasant flavor of green paprika pods and hard, bitter tannins that do not become more harmonious during aging. The enormous concentration of tannin in the wine derives from the small berries with their thick skins, which requires much skill from the vintner in balancing the *cuvées*. For this, the growers and winemakers of the Médoc have four other varieties of grape available: Merlot, Cabernet Franc, Malbec, and Petit Verdot. They are used in a wide range of quantities and ratios, though the lively but (from a grower's point of view) rather troublesome Petit Verdot, is cultivated less and less. Of course,

wines with a high Cabernet Sauvignon content need long maturing to establish a balance and allow the bouquet to unfold. Changing consumer patterns and the trend to quicker, early-maturing wines has also changed the structure of Médoc wines to some extent. This has meant a higher proportion of Merlot, especially in *appellations* with lighter, simpler wines.

In the best-known châteaux of the Médoc, Cabernet Sauvignon continues to reign supreme, and is allowed to unfurl its great glories. There was such a run on the great names of Médoc viticulture, particularly during the 1990s, that prices reached astronomical levels once again. It is a situation not without risk for the châteaux, especially if the trade profits more than they do.

Bourgeois, artisans, and paysans

Although everyone seems to talk only about the *crus classés*, the real development of recent decades has been in the *crus bourgeois*, and to a lesser extent in the *crus artisans* and *paysans* as well. While the *crus classés* represent only 23 percent of total production, the *bourgeois* make almost 50 percent, the *artisans* and *paysans* about 11 percent. The remaining production is processed by the cooperatives.

Although the term *cru bourgeois* is probably much older, it was first used commercially in the Bordeaux region in the 19th century. The same *courtiers* who had drawn up the 1855 classification also classified all the wines in the area into various types: *paysans*, *artisans*, *artisans supérieurs*, *premiers artisans*, *bourgeois*, *premiers bourgeois*, and *bourgeois supérieurs*, with the famous *crus classés* really being just the top end of the *bourgeois*, or *crus bourgeois classés*, to be precise.

That social classifications were used to describe a wine hierarchy has historic reasons. An observer had already noted in the 18th century that given two plots of land, one belonging to a leading personality, the other to a peasant, the wines of the former always obtained better prices.

The economic crises of the 1920s and 1930s and a series of bad harvests prompted the gradation of 444 (now 322) châteaux as *crus bourgeois*, of which 99 were classed as *supérieurs* and 6 as *supérieurs exceptionnels*. The labeling within the category was modified again in 1962. The *supérieurs* became *grand crus bourgeois* and the *exceptionnels* turned into *crus grands bourgeois exceptionnels*, but like the distinction of the 1930s this was not backed by legal recognition. Only in recent years has the community of the *crus bourgeois* come to an understanding about working out a formal hierarchical classification of member châteaux and getting it officially recognized.

A Class of its Own

Château Pichon Longueville-Baron and its avantgarde winery.

One of the continuing strengths of the Bordeaux region lies in the classification of its vineyards and its wines that the growers and the trade carried out themselves. In contrast to many other areas, where jealousy and misconstrued egalitarianism do not permit such hierarchical gradations, here they dared to assess which wines were the best, and also used this as a prime marketing instrument for the whole region. Ultimately, Bordeaux became the most famous wine-growing district in the world because of the enormous prestige of the *crus classés*, and the whole industry, whether classified or not, benefited from it.

On the occasion of the 1855 exposition in Paris, Napoleon III asked the Bordeaux region chamber of commerce to undertake a selection of the best wine-growing estates to represent the region in Paris. The job was passed to the syndicate of wine-brokers (*courtiers*), who had long worked with such classifications, albeit unofficially. The basis of their system was the prices that could be achieved by the various growths. With the exception of the Château Haut-Brion from Graves, the system applied only to the Médoc and the sweet wines of Sauternes and Barsac. The wines of the right bank of the Dordogne were not included because their areas of cultivation came under the auspices of the Libourne Chamber of Commerce, whose reputation would develop only later anyway.

Attempts at classification had begun much earlier. Even in 1730 brokers on the Quai des Chartrons in Bordeaux, where the best-known shippers had their offices, were already working with lists of this sort. Of course, at this date the lists had little relevance for the consumer as the wines were exported in barrels, blended in London and reached the end consumer as anonymous products. Somewhat earlier, at the end of the 17th century, Arnaud de Pontac, owner of the Château Haut-Brion, had gone directly to the English market, dissatisfied with the prices he was getting from the system, and had begun to sell the wines under the name of the *domaine*. Haut-Brion soon became the most sought-after and expensive wine of its day.

Spurred on by this success, the interest of the Bordelais families was now directed at sites whose wines displayed similar potential that could be turned into hard cash. Their eye fell on the flat hilltops of the Médoc, where the Margaux, Lafite, and Latour estates looked particularly promising. Margaux belonged to the Lestonnac family, who had allied themselves at the time with the Pontacs by intermarriage, and in the early 18th century Margaux became the second Bordeaux estate to cause a stir in London. Only a few years later, Lafite and Latour followed suit. Thus today's ruling elite of the Bordeaux wine industry were firmly established three hundred years ago.

A Solid System to Stand the Test of Time

During the 18th century, the other Médoc *domaines* developed that were classified later. The first more or less reliable ratings began to circulate, including that by Thomas Jefferson, who had unerringly picked out the above four châteaux as the absolute top *crus*. The ratings only became obligatory, however, with the official classification of 1855, which was backed by statute. The amazing thing about it is that it has remained virtually unchanged to this day. Although time and again various *domaines* were merged or others were split up, although the owners and the winemakers changed and some names disappeared altogether, the 1855 list is still valid today.

Countless attempts have been made to amend, abolish, or replace the original classifications with alternative ratings, but in vain. This is not to overlook the disadvantages that the Bordeaux classification system had (and still has), even if you ignore the confusion sown in the consumer's mind by the co-existence of such widely differing schemes in the Médoc, Saint-Émilion, and Graves. However, the greatest handicap of the Médoc list lies rather in the very result that its enormous success first made possible—its permanence and stability. It took decades of lobbying for a top château like Mouton to be admitted to the illustrious elite of the *premiers crus classés*. On the other hand, even the prolonged crisis at many Margaux *domaines* in the 1970s did not pose a threat to their membership for a single moment. Regular revision of the ratings, say many critics of the Médoc system, would not only give consumers better quality and more up-to-date information, but also motivate the estates not to rest on their laurels. They would have to keep their quality standards up.

Great wines deserve great respect even in packing.

The châteaux keep bottles from every vintage as a reference.

Even a standardization of the various classification systems, and their extension to as yet unclassified *appellations* such as Pomerol, would certainly be considered progress by many consumers. This would make the *premiers crus* of individual areas comparable with each other—an idea that the Bordelais folk fear like the Devil fears holy water. Their argument is that wines of different *appellations* cannot be assessed in confrontation: they are not better or worse, just different. It is a fig leaf whose logic makes an absurdity of the whole classification to which the Bordelais have become so attached. After all, it was they who with their system of hierarchically graded *appellations*—Pauillac ranks higher than Haut-Médoc, which ranks higher than Bordeaux, even if the wines all come from one and the same parish—that made such comparisons the basis of their wine legislation in the first place.

CONCENTRATED STRENGTH IN A TRIO

In contrast to the southern part of the Médoc, where lavishly constructed châteaux and wine-growing estates were created in the 18th and 19th centuries, the northern half of the Haut-Médoc cannot offer massive splendor. Instead, this area shines with a unique concentration of great wines—34 of the 60 classified growths of the Médoc: 18 in the Pauillac area alone, 11 in Saint-Julien, and five in Saint-Estèphe.

In the days when large parts of the marshy Médoc were inaccessible by land, the harbors of Saint-Estèphe—the Port de la Chapelle—and Pauillac played a key role as the only points of access. Particularly in times of crisis, Pauillac offered a good alternative facility in maritime trade for ships that could not berth in Bordeaux.

Saint-Estèphe—which was called Saint-Estèphe de Calon until the 18th century, *calon* meaning "wood," and occurring also in the name of the famous Calon-Ségur estate, for example—is the most northerly of the trio. Wine was produced here even in Roman days, and the industry developed enormously in the 13th century. Prestigious *premiers crus classés* are, however, not to be found. All the *crus classés* together account for only about 20 percent of the output by volume, which is the lowest proportion for all communal *appellations* of the Médoc. This compares with 54 percent for the *crus bourgeois*, including some outstanding names such

Château Ducru-Beaucailloux, a *deuxième grand cru classé* in Saint-Julien, stands on a gently rounded hill rising directly from the bank of the Gironde.

The large bottles of the best *grands crus* of the Médoc, which come on to the market in very limited numbers, are coveted collectors' items.

as Phélan-Ségur, Ormes des Pez, Lilian Ladouys, Tour de Pez, or even Pez.

CHARACTER NEEDS AGE

In comparison with its more southerly neighbors, Saint-Estèphe suffers from spread: the best localities of the over 3,060 acres (1,240 ha) under vine are distributed over three rather widely separated areas: the Cos d'Estournel area in the south, the area around Montrose in the east and the sites around Château Calon-Ségur in the north. The soils consist primarily of gravel and sand with silicate elements, though the ferrous or chalky substrata are responsible for the differing characters of the wines.

The intense color of the Saint-Estèphe wines is considered a strong *terroir* feature. The wines often seem somewhat heavier than those of Pauillac or Saint-Julien, their strong tannins being very challenging, and when young they can seem very austere, to which their marked acidity contributes. This is offset by a higher proportion of Merlot compared with Pauillac or Saint-Julien.

Although the area under vine in Pauillac, the southern neighbor of Saint-Estèphe, is somewhat smaller with 2,970 acres (1,200 ha), the *appellation* has incomparably greater prestige, above all because its wines exude pure *noblesse*. The only village in the region with a promenade along the Gironde embankment has been systematically involved in viticulture only since Louis XV's day, but even so is home to three of the five *premiers crus classés* (the classic Lafite and Latour plus the "newcomer" Mouton) and 15 other classified *crus*. In its total number of *crus* it is surpassed only by Margaux.

BLACKCURRANT, MINT, AND CEDARWOOD

A good 84 percent of Pauillac's annual output comes from the famous châteaux—only in Saint-Julien is the proportion still higher. The rest is divided among 16 *crus bourgeois* and seven *artisans*. Like Saint-Estèphe, Pauillac also has varying soil formations, which can, for example, lead to wines from Château Lafite revealing a finesse untypical of Pauillac and being compared more often with Margaux *crus*. Certainly this is one of the limitations of the *appellation* system, which is ultimately directed at administrative parish boundaries that do not always reflect real *terroir* borders. It is one reason why Château Lafite has special permission to run vineyards in the neighboring Saint-Estèphe area.

Overall the soils of Pauillac are very barren but deep, and consist of predominantly iron-bearing gravels. The best growths are on two flat hilltops called *plateaux*, with Latour and the two Pichon-Lalandes in the Saint-Lambert part that once belonged to Saint-Julien, and Mouton and Lafite on Le Pouyalet in the north. In the distribution of grape varieties, Pauillac has the highest Cabernet Sauvignon proportion of any Bordeaux wine. It is normally between 60 and 80 percent, and only falls below 50 percent in a few cases, such as Pichon Comtesse.

Cabernet Franc and Merlot share a rather meager proportion of the area under vine, while Petit Verdot is unusually strongly represented and sometimes can make 10 percent of the blend. The special combination of varieties is what ensures the specially firm, well-structured, and powerful wines of Pauillac, whose rich bouquet manifests the typical Cabernet aromas of blackcurrant, mint, and cedarwood, and which possess great aging ability.

Not so forceful, but possessing unsurpassed harmony and balance, are the wines of Pauillac's southern neighbor Saint-Julien, which with only 2,220 acres (900 ha) is the smallest of the three northern *appellations*. Fruit and juice on the one hand, and structure and tannins on the other, make up perhaps the most modern wines of the Médoc.

BALANCED IN EVERY RESPECT

Although the village of Saint-Julien-Beychevelle can offer no *premier cru*, it does have five seconds, two thirds and four fourth growths. These 11 produce a noteworthy 85 percent of total production, which is a record for the region. As the other châteaux grow virtually only good *bourgeois* and *artisans*, you can buy wines from Saint-Julien really almost blindly.

Like in Pauillac, the best vineyard localities are on two hilltops, with that of the village itself including the three Léovilles *appellations* and Talbot, while the other, called Beychevelle, including Ducru-Beaucaillou, Gruaud-Larose, and Beychevelle itself. These hilltops are separated from each other by small water courses and drainage ditches. As everywhere in the Médoc, the best wines are in the direct vicinity of these ditches and channels.

On the large estates of Saint-Julien the Cabernet Sauvignon proportion is between 65 percent and 70 percent, 25 to 30 percent is Merlot, leaving only a small proportion of Cabernet Franc.

In the damp cellars of Bordeaux, wines often keep for decades.

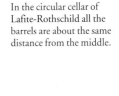

In the circular cellar of Lafite-Rothschild all the barrels are about the same distance from the middle.

Médoc

Château Potensac****
Ordonnac

131 acres (53 ha); 300,000 bottles • Wine: Médoc
Potensac has been in the hands of the Delon family
for 250 years and over the last twenty years it has
established itself as the most reliable Médoc—always
very dark, rounded, finely spiced with a typical cedar
note and with potential.

Château Rollan de By****
Begadan

*98.8 acres (40 ha); 220,000 bottles • Wines: Médoc,
→Haut-Condissas*
Starting with an initial plot acquired in 1989, Jean
Guyon has created not only a sizable estate, but also a
wine which due to its quality, fruit and concentration
has achieved international recognition today. The Cuvée
Haut-Condissas has just that little bit extra.

Haut-Médoc

Château Sénéjac
Le Pian-Médoc

*81.5 acres (33 ha); 120,000 bottles • Wines: Haut-
Médoc, Karolus*
In only a short time, Thierry Rustman from Talbot
has helped this fine estate to produce worthy wines.

Château Sociando-Mallet****–*****
Cadourne

*143 acres (58 ha); 400,000 bottles • Wines: →Haut-
Médoc Cru Bourgeois, Demoiselle*
The superstar of the *crus bourgeois* captivates with
good consistency, the wines with their depth of fruit
and extract sweetness. Has long deserved the status
of a classified growth.

Pauillac

Château Clerc Milon***–****
Pauillac

*74 acres (30 ha); 185,000 bottles • Wines: Pauillac
Cinquième Cru Classé*
The château in the Mouton empire works with the
unusually high Merlot proportion of the well-known
Pauillac estates. Nevertheless, the wines display the
typical firm structure of the good growths of the
appellation.

Château Coufran***–****
Pauillac

*188 acres (76 ha); 600,000 bottles • Wines: Pauillac
Cru Bourgeois*
The château is close to the banks of the Gironde,
and has a fine barrel cellar in which a remarkably
consistent quality of wine has been stored over the
years. Even the trace of vegetal overtones (paprika pods)
in some vintages works well, integrated into the overall
bouquet.

Château Duhart-Milon-Rothschild***–****
Pauillac

*185 acres (75 ha); 220,000 bottles • Wines: Pauillac
Quatrième Cru Classé*
As the vineyards of Duhart had to be replanted in the
1970s, it has taken a long time to realize the potential.
The first vintages are a little Pinot-like and too thin, but
more recent vintages have produced wines with good
concentration.

Château Grand-Puy-Lacoste****
Pauillac

*124 acres (50 ha); 180,000 bottles • Wines: Pauillac
Cinquième Cru Classé*
Characterized by its 70 percent Sauvignon content, this
cru is a classic Pauillac, with a firm structure and great
potential. In recent years its has been gaining in
roundedness and texture.

Château Lafite-Rothschild*****
Pauillac

*222 acres (90 ha); 250,000 bottles • Wines: Pauillac
Premier Cru Classé, Moulin des Carruades*
The Margaux among the Pauillacs is how Latour is
frequently called. Finesse controls the strength, even
though the grape combination (70 percent Cabernet
Sauvignon) is wholly typical for the *appellation*. The
best Lafite years do not always coincide with those of
Bordeaux generally.

Château Latour*****
Pauillac

*161 acres (65 ha); 400,000 bottles • Wines: Pauillac
Premier Cru Classé, Les Forts de Latour*
75 percent Cabernet Sauvignon make Latour a Pauillac
par excellence—firm, big, ageable—that is considered
the most consistent of the *premiers crus*. The reason: the
vineyards lie close to the water surface of the Gironde.
At the end of the 18th century, Thomas Jefferson
described this wine as one of the best of Bordeaux. The
second wine, Les Forts de Latour, is qualitatively not far
behind the Grand Vin.

Château Lynch-Bages****–*****
Pauillac

*235 acres (95 ha); 420,000 bottles • Wines: Pauillac
Cinquième Cru Classé*
Founded in the 17th century by Irish immigrants,
Lynch's vineyards are widely scattered in the south of
Pauillac. A high proportion of the vines are very old—
The foundation of the unusually full-bodied, velvety,
spicy style of this top vineyard.

Château Mouton-Rothschild*****
Pauillac

*203 acres (82 ha); 300,000 bottles • Wines: Pauillac
Premier Cru Classé, Pauillac Le Petit Mouton de
Mouton-Rothschild, Bordeaux Blanc Aile d'Argent*
Mouton was not admitted to the illustrious circle of
the *premiers crus* until 1973. It owes its character to
the special nature of the barren gravel layers that run
several yards deep and contain a lot of iron and silicate.
The Cabernet (Sauvignon and Franc) proportion is
unusually high at 90 percent, which also makes it
more dependent on climatic fluctuations between
the vintages.

Château Pichon-Longueville****–*****
Pauillac

*180 acres (73 ha); 420,000 bottles • Wines: Pauillac
Deuxième Cru Classé*
The better known of the two Pichons, called Pichon
Baron for short, lies on the border with Saint-Julien in
the south of the *appellation*. Year after year, the two
Pichons compete to surpass each other, with varying
outcomes. However, with 65 percent Cabernet
Sauvignon-in the 1980s it was still 75 percent—the
Pichon Baron usually produces the firmer, more
structured wines.

Château Pichon-Longueville Comtesse de Lalande****–*****
Pauillac

185 acres (75 ha); 400,000 bottles • Wines: Pauillac Deuxième Cru Classé, La Réserve de la Comtesse

The wines of Pichon Comtesse have an unusually high Merlot content for Pauillac (35 percent, compared with only 45 percent for Cabernet Sauvignon, with this ratio remaining unchanged in recent decades), and it is therefore softer and more harmonious than is usual in the *appellation*, although highly complex.

Château Pontet-Canet****
Pauillac

195 acres (79 ha); 480,000 bottles • Wines: Pauillac Cinquième Cru Classé, Pauillac Château Les Hauts de Pontet

The estate is adjacent to Mouton in the south, and has developed astonishingly since the 1980s. With their tobacco bouquet, the wines are considered a classic expression of Pauillac, and in good years can vie with the better-known *crus*.

Saint-Estèphe
Château Calon-Ségur***–****
Saint-Estèphe

232 acres (94 ha); 400,000 bottles • Wines: →Saint-Estèphe Troisième Cru Classé

Calon-Ségur has a high *terroir* potential which has fortunately become noticeable again in recent years.

Château Cos d'Estournel*****
Saint-Estèphe

161 acres (65 ha); 200,000 bottles • Wines: →Saint-Estèphe Deuxième Cru Classé, Les Pagodes de Cos

Now managed by Jean-Guillaime Prats, this estate is the undisputed star of Saint-Estèphe and some critics esteem it more highly than many *premiers crus*. 60 percent Cabernet Sauvignon and 40 percent Merlot make a powerful but always round, harmonious ensemble.

Château Haut-Marbuzet****
Saint-Estèphe

143 acres (58 ha); 300,000 bottles • Wines: Saint-Estèphe

Cabernet and Merlot virtually in a 1:1 ratio tends to be rare in Pauillac. The quality of Haut-Marbuzet is therefore all the more astonishing, and is achieved year after year.

Château Montrose****–*****
Saint-Estèphe

168 acres (68 ha); 330,000 bottles • Wines: Saint-Estèphe →Deuxième Cru Classé, La Dame de Montrose

The Cabernet Sauvignon proportion for Montrose is very high for the *appellation* at 65 percent, which makes the wines still firmer and capable of greater aging. In good years, when the grapes ripen completely, Jean-Louis Charmolüe achieves absolute top quality.

Château Ormes de Pez****
Saint-Estèphe

81.5 acres (33 ha); 200,000 bottles • Wines: Saint-Estèphe Cru Bourgeois

The estate belongs to the portfolio of Jean-Michel Cazes (Lynch-Bages, Cantenac-Brown). Despite a high Cabernet ratio, the wines often seem very soft and show their flavors more in the nose than on the palate.

Château Phélan Ségur***–****
Saint-Estèphe

158 acres (64 ha); 340,000 bottles • Wines: Saint-Estèphe Cru Bourgeois, Frank Phélan

Thanks to efforts of the Gardinier family, Phélan-Ségur has been completely renovated in recent years, and the

wines have reached a superb standard. Around 60 percent Cabernet Sauvignon, which gives them their stimulating, spicy, animal aromas in good vintages.

Saint-Julien
Château Beychevelle***–*****
Saint-Julien

225 acres (91 ha); 460,000 bottles • Wines: Saint-Julien Quatrième Cru Classé, Amiral de Beychevelle

One of the most spectacular châteaux, built in the mid-18th century. If other wines have become steadily softer and round in recent decades, Beychevelle has gained in structure—and quality.

Château Ducru-Beaucaillou***–*****
Saint-Julien

124 acres (50 ha); 210,000 bottles • Wines: Saint-Julien Deuxième Cru Classé

The vineyards of Ducru are scattered all over the parish, with the largest plot squeezed between two Beychevelle sites. The wines are elegant, and always manifest a clear tannin structure. In lesser years some of the glow and extract sweetness may occasionally be absent.

Château Gruaud-Larose****–*****
Saint-Julien

203 acres (82 ha); 450,000 bottles • Wines: Saint-Julien Deuxième Cru Classé, Saint-Julien Sarget de Gruaud-Larose

In the 1980s, the quality of the wines of Gruaud-Larose was legendary, and wheeled into the 1990s at a very high standard. The huge vineyard, almost a single site, is among the most impressive in the Médoc.

Château Léoville Barton*****
Saint-Julien

124 acres (50 ha); 230,000 bottles • Wines: Saint-Julien Deuxième Cru Classé, La Réserve de Léoville Barton

In recent years Anthony Barton has brought his *cru* to the highest level. When young, it is unusually dense and attractive, and it matures to an incomparable harmony and balance.

Château Léoville Las Cases*****
Saint-Julien

240 acres (97 ha) • Wines: Saint-Julien Deuxième Cru Classé

Léoville Las Cases really should have been included in the ranks of the *premiers crus*. It is no accident that the wine is considered the Latour of Léoville, because the vineyards of Léoville abut those of the *premiers crus* in the north. The legendary vintages such as 1982 or 1985—and those of the second half of the 1990s—take decades to unfold their full splendors.

Château Léoville-Poyferré****–*****
Saint-Julien

198 acres (80 ha); 450,000 bottles • Wines: Saint-Julien Deuxième Cru Classé, Château Moulin Riche

In good years, the wines are on a par with Las Cases, but they develop more quickly. The winery is considered the model of technical perfection, and is supervised by the well-known enologist Michel Rolland.

Château Talbot***–****
Saint-Julien

252 acres (102 ha); 600,000 bottles • Wines: Saint-Julien Quatrième Cru Classé

Over 247 acres (100 ha) in one site—only 15 percent planted to Merlot—west of Saint-Julien is a vineyard holding such as few can boast of. Many consider Talbot far better than its rating would suggest.

Pure Finesse

In contrast to Graves, where the vineyards still extend almost into the center of Bordeaux, there is in the north a relatively broad strip between the city and the Margaux district and its neighboring parishes.

Margaux, Listrac, and Moulis are the three communal *appellations* of this southernmost part of Haut-Médoc. The natural conditions are not markedly different from those of Pauillac, Saint-Julien, or Saint-Estèphe. The typical sandy, pebbly Graves gravels with limestone subsoils are the characteristic soil structure, and in terms of climate the proximity to the Gironde plays the same stabilizing role as in the more northerly districts. Here, too, small rounded hillocks, called *croupes* or *plateaux*, on which the soils are well drained and the gravel layers particularly deep, offer the best conditions for the vines.

On the western edge of this half of the Haut-Médoc are the two territories of Moulis-en-Médoc and Listrac-Médoc. Neither has a *cru classé*, but they do have a large number of good to very good *bourgeois*. In Listrac, the more northerly of the two areas with about 1,730 acres (700 ha) of vineyards, three zones are particularly suited to viticulture—Fonréaud in the south and Fourcas in the north of the commune, and finally Listrac itself—and at up to 400 feet (122 m) high are some of the highest sites in the whole of the Médoc.

A Lot of Merlot in Médoc

The soils of these areas, despite the common features, are very different in detail. Fourcas, whose *crus* are the best of the *appellation*, has silicate-rich sandy soils on which Cabernet

Château Palmer has equipped itself with thoroughly modern winery technology.

Left
Château Lascombes in Margaux is an architectural gem but in wine terms it is still searching for an individual style.

Right
Under young Claire Villars, Château Chasse-Spleen is making a name as one of the best Moulis.

ripens well and gives the wine strength, whereas Merlot turns out better on the limestone formations in the other areas. Generally, Cabernet and Merlot are planted in a ratio of 2:1 or 1:1, with a slightly rising trend in the Merlot, which yields soft, fruity wines.

Still smaller than Listrac is Moulis, adjoining in the southeast, where there is a similar spectrum of grape varieties: Cabernet ranges from 50–70 percent, Merlot from 20–50 percent. The vineyards are split up and scattered all over the parish territory, though some of the dominant *crus bourgeois* here—especially Poujeaux and Chasse-Spleen—display a level of quality that can bear comparison with that of many *crus classés* of neighboring parishes.

Vines that grow on sandier soils tend to resemble those of Margaux, those on limestone soils Pauillac. Undoubtedly the greatest prestige name of the southern Haut-Médoc is the Margaux *appellation*, which includes the villages of Arsac, Labarde, Cantenac, Issan, and Soussans. With 3,210 acres (1,300 ha) planted to vine, this is the largest of the Médoc individual areas, and also includes the most *crus classés*. The wines of Margaux may be 60–75 percent Cabernet Sauvignon, but they are considered to have more finesse and a stronger bouquet than the other *appellations*, and to be unsurpassed in elegance, almost like burgundies

from Bordeaux, as they are often apostrophized. This particular quality resides in a combination of the particularly sheltered climate of the zone and the extremely barren gravel soils on top of limestone or marls. The characteristic climate is brought about by the long islands in the Gironde opposite the district, which keep off the cold north winds that occasionally blow up from the estuary.

Even the incomparable prestige of the *appellation* could not save it from a profound crisis that struck in the 1970s. The general tendency in the European wine industry to go for quantity instead of quality, in combination with the great scandal of the adulterated Médoc wines and the preceding overheating of market prices, led to a collapse in the market. After some very modest vintages, the wines of the area have now regained their position.

SELECT PRODUCERS IN LISTRAC, MOULIS, AND MARGAUX

LISTRAC

CHÂTEAU CLARKE***–****
LISTRAC-MÉDOC
173 acres (70 ha); 350,000 bottles • Wines: Listrac Cru Bougeois, Le Merle Blanc
Baron Edmond de Rothschild has built up this estate from scratch since 1973. Wine was first produced in the newly constructed cellar in 1978. Today the vines have reached an age that ensures better quality, and Clarke has risen to become one of the best Listrac producers.

CHÂTEAU FOURCAS-HOSTEN***–****
LISTRAC
116 acres (47 ha); 320,000 bottles • Wines: Listrac Cru Bourgeois, Les Cèdres d'Hosten
The best of the four Fourcas châteaux, belonging to Peter Sichel, Bertrand de Rivoyre and Patrice Pagès. In good years, the wine carries clear aromas of berries and vanilla, but can also turn out very cedary and rather austere.

CHÂTEAU MAYNE LALANDE***–****
LISTRAC
49.5 acres (20 ha); 100,000 bottles • Wines: Listrac Cru Bourgeois, Château Malbec Lartigue, Château Myon de l'Enclos, La Grande Réserve du Château Mayne Lalande
Bernard Lartigue has built up this *domaine* from scratch since 1991. In the marvelous modern *barrique-chai* fine cedary wines are produced with a lot of fruit.

MARGAUX

CHÂTEAU BRANE-CANTENAC****
MARGAUX
210 acres (85 ha); 140,000 bottles • Wines: Margaux Deuxième Cru Classé
Rising to ever higher standards since 1996.

CHÂTEAU DAUZAC***–****
MARGAUX
111 acres (45 ha); 280,000 bottles • Wines: Margaux Cinquième Cru Classé, La Bastide Dauzac, Haut-Médoc Château Labarde
Another remolded Margaux given luster and harmony by its high Merlot content. Dauzac belongs to the M.A.I.F. insurance group, but is run by the Lurton family from Entre-deux-Mers.

CHÂTEAU KIRWAN****
MARGAUX
86.5 acres (35 ha); 170,000 bottles • Wines: Margaux Troisième Cru Classé, Les Charmes de Kirwan
Under the guidance of enologist Michel Rolland, this Margaux *cru* has undergone a renaissance.

CHÂTEAU MARGAUX*****
MARGAUX
245 acres (99 ha); 390,000 bottles • Wines: Margaux Premier Cru Classé, Margaux Pavillon Rouge, Pavillon Blanc
The only *premier cru* of the *appellation*. Since the 1980s, the fate of the house has been in the hands of Paul Pontallier, one of the best enologists in France. The wines have since re-discovered their unique elegance and character.

CHÂTEAU PALMER****–*****
MARGAUX
126 acres (51 ha); 240,000 bottles • Wines: Margaux Troisième Cru Classé, Alter Ego
Palmer has been esteemed for decades because of its consistent quality and velvetiness. Since 1998 it has offered serious competition to the *premier cru* on its northern borders.

CHÂTEAU RAUZAN-SÉGLA****
MARGAUX
124 acres (50 ha); 200,000 bottles • Wines: Margaux Deuxième Cru Classé, Ségla
The Rauzan estate, well-known since the 17th century, is now in the hands of the Wertheimer family, who own Chanel. It displays its highly elegant style in a masterly fashion.

CHÂTEAU SIRAN***–****
MARGAUX
99 acres (40 ha); 160,000 bottles • Wines: Margaux Cru Bourgeois
A bourgeois that can hold its own among so many *crus classés* of its *appellation*. Siran is unusually firmly structured for Margaux, which is due both to the relatively high Petit Verdot content and the *terroir*.

MOULIS

CHÂTEAU CHASSE-SPLEEN****
MOULIS-EN-MÉDOC
210 acres (85 ha); 600,000 bottles • Wines: Moulis Cru Bourgeois, Haut-Médoc L'Ermitage de Chasse-Spleen, Bordeaux Blanc
The better known of the two top Moulis *crus* is 75 percent Cabernet Sauvignon, and in good years manifests an extract density without equal in the *appellation*.

CHÂTEAU POUJEAUX***–****
MOULIS-EN-MÉDOC
124 acres (50 ha); 240,000 bottles • Wines: Moulis Cru Bourgeois, Château La Salle de Poujeaux
The *grand vin* of Poujeaux consists only half of Cabernet. The wine is harmonious and more accessible, but no longer has the density and depth of earlier years.

GRAVELLY GRAVES

The oldest vineyards of the Bordeaux area were planted in the direct vicinity of the trading center of Burdigala—the region that now belongs viticulturally to the Graves region. Geographically the famous alluvial gravels of the left banks of the Garonne and Gironde are also Graves (gravels), but for wine purposes only the vineyards adjacent to the city and up the Garonne carry the name as a designation of origin. The Graves district, which stretches for about 30 miles (50 km) from Bordeaux in a southerly direction, is planted to vines over about 12,400 acres (5,000 ha), and is therefore one of the smaller zones of the Bordelais area, which overall covers a good 247,000 acres (100,000 ha). Two thirds of the Graves area is planted to red varieties, one third to white, and the region is the only one which can boast of outstanding reds and superb whites as well as overwhelming sweet wines. Geographically, the district is divided up much more simply than Médoc, north of the city. Here there is only one large *appellation* of Graves (around 7,410 acres/3,000 ha), which incorporates the small *appellation* Cérons and—in the extreme north—the still very young district of Pessac-Léognan. In the south, Graves encompasses the sweet wine districts of Sauternes and Barsac (4,940 acres/2,000 ha).

Whereas the Graves *appellation* is now reserved for dry whites, the Graves Supérieur label is for dessert wines that do not come from the Sauternes-Barsac or Cérons *appellations*, while Pessac-Léognan provides excellent whites and reds alike. The reason for this is not so much the pebbly, gravelly soils, which are comparable to those of the Médoc, but the more prominent landscape relief compared with its northern neighbor, which is responsible for a series of differing microclimates. The best vineyards in the region are scattered in the higher wooded areas as small or even extensive clearings, or surrounded by the relentlessly expanding sprawl of Bordeaux. At the end of the 19th century, Graves still covered about 247,000 acres (100,000 ha), but urbanization has reduced this to little more than 12,400 (5,000 ha). The red wines are made from the Cabernet Sauvignon, Cabernet Franc and Merlot grape varieties that predominate in the Médoc as well, and bear a strong resemblance to Médoc wines. But the real stars of this part of the Bordelais region are Sémillon and Sauvignon Blanc, which make the dry whites, the dessert wines of Cérons and the sumptuous sweet Sauternes and Barsacs. A strong

Pessac-Léognan
■ 1 Haut-Brion
■ 2 La Mission Haut-Brion
■ 3 Laville Haut-Brion
■ 4 Pape Clément
■ 5 Domaine de Chevalier
■ 6 Haut-Bailly
■ 7 Carbonnieux
■ 8 Fieuzal
■ 9 Smith Haut-Lafitte

Graves

Cérons

Barsac
■ 10 Coutet
■ 11 Crus Barréjats
■ 12 Climens
■ 13 Doisy Daëne

Sauternes
■ 14 Gilette
■ 15 De Malle
■ 16 Suduiraut
■ 17 Sigalas Rabaud
■ 18 Lafaurie-Peyraguey
■ 19 Clos Haut-Peyraguey
■ 20 D'Yquem
■ 21 La Tour Blanche
■ 22 Rieussec
■ 23 Guiraud
■ 24 De Fargues

Bordeaux and Bordeaux Supérieur

Premières Côtes de Bordeaux

Entre-Deux-Mers Bordeaux and Bordeaux Supérieur

Saint-Émilion

Côtes de Castillon

Cadillac and Premières Côtes de Bordeaux

Bordeaux and Entre-Deux-Mers-Haut-Benauge

Côtes de Bordeaux-Sainte-Macaire

Loupiac

Sainte-Croix-du-Mont

• • • • Limit of Bordeaux A.C.s

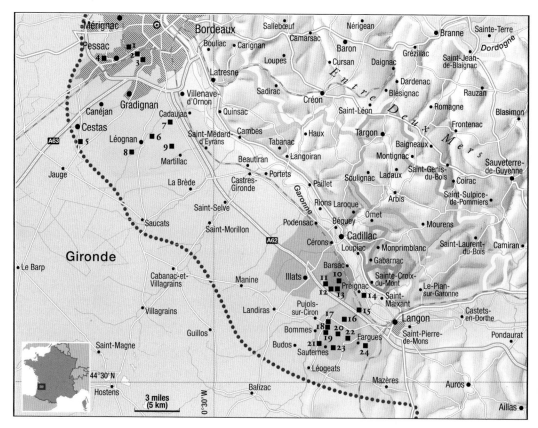

SELECT PRODUCERS IN THE GRAVES REGION

CHÂTEAU D'ARDENNES***–****
ILLATS
153 acres (62 ha); 350,000 bottles • Wines: Graves Blanc, Graves Rouge
François Dubrey produces white and red Graves that are among the most elegant in the region and are also excellent value for money.

CHÂTEAU DE CHANTEGRIVE**–****
PODENSAC
217 acres (88 ha); 560,000 bottles • Wines: Graves Blanc, Graves Rouge, Graves Blanc Caroline, Cérons
Famous for many years for its white wines, and in particular for its Cuvée Caroline, fermented in the barrel, this estate's reds have now made considerable progress and display good concentration and ripe fruit.

CHÂTEAU RESPIDE MÉDEVILLE***–****
TOULENNE
30 acres (12 ha); 70,000 bottles • Wines: Graves Blanc, Graves Rouge
The region around Langon is better known for its Sauternes, but Respide Médeville proves that good reds can be grown here too. Cabernet Sauvignon and Merlot are used in a 60:40 ratio. In the estate's whites, a relatively high proportion of Muscadelle is introduced.

CLOS FLORIDÈNE****
PUJOL-SUR-CIRON
47 acres (19 ha); 100,000 bottles • Wines: Graves
Denis Dubourdieu is professor of enology at the University of Bordeaux and runs not only the Château Reynon in the Premières Côtes but also this Graves estate, whose modern whites and reds with their consistent quality are on a par with many a Pessac-Léognan.

VIEUX CHÂTEAU GAUBERT***
PORTETS
34.5 acres (14 ha); 120,000 bottles • Wines: Graves Blanc, Graves Rouge
Good whites, mainly made of Sémillon and fermented in the barrel, are the ace products of the Haverlan family's estate.

VILLA BEL AIR***
SAINT-MORILLON
114 acres (46 ha); 280,000 bottles • Wines: Graves Blanc, Graves Rouge
Jean-Michel Cazes of Château Lynch-Bages founded the estate in 1990, and has since then convinced with his round, fruity reds, which consist about half and half of Cabernet and Merlot.

---

proportion of Sauvignon Blanc is often found in the more emphatically fruity whites. When young or picked early, the variety shows its customary grassy, vegetal aromas, and only acquires its more complex, riper fruity overtones when fully ripe or over-ripe.

Some of the classified growths contain up to 50 percent Sémillon. This is considered one of the world's great grape varieties not only because of its tendency to botrytization (which makes it pre-eminent for producing the great sweet wines of the Sauternes area), but also because of its legendary aging ability. The wine styles of the individual white wine *appellations* and the châteaux themselves are distinct not only in the way they combine the varieties, but also in the use of different aging techniques. The use of new barrels is not unchallenged because individual

Left
Classiness is in the detail—spittoon at Château La-Mission Haut-Brion.

Right
Château Haut-Brion is the oldest wine estate of Bordeaux to have made an individual name for itself.

growths can become coarse, thereby losing their finesse. On the other hand, the better *barrique* whites are certainly of higher quality than the superficial fruity representatives of the variety from steel tanks, whose youthful charm is often quickly dissipated.

Going from Bordeaux in a southerly direction, the proportion of Sémillon in the vineyards increases, as does the residue sugar content of the white wines. Far removed from the sweet power packs of Sauternes but still clearly mellow or even sweet are the wines of Cérons, a small *appellation* in the south of the Grave region. Though red wines are indeed also produced in the villages of Podensac, Illats, and Cérons, the whites are more important, the medium-dry output being bottled as Bordeaux Supérieur, the sweet wines as Cérons.

A Rising Star: Pessac-Léognan

A cathedral of wine—the winery of the Domaine de Chevalier.

this legendary birthplace of wine in the Bordelais region. The numerical decline was of course more than offset by the qualitative improvement in the *appellation*, which has two Bordelais standard bearers in Haut-Brion and Pape Clément and whose other *crus*, classified in 1959, are of rare consistency and high quality.

Red-White Alliance

Pessac-Léognan is also the only top wine-growing area in the Bordeaux that produces outstanding whites as well as reds. The quickly established prestige and consequent rising revenues have ensured that the retreat of the planted area has been stopped and in individual cases even reversed. The fast-improving image results from the inclusion of all wines in the new A.C. that were first ennobled as Graves Crus Classés only in 1959. This is incidentally also why the classified growths of Pessac-Léognan continue to be labeled as *crus* of Graves, i.e. they now effectively carry a double A.C.

The classification of the area applies of course equally to red and white wines. The châteaux that dance at both weddings include Bouscaut, Carbonnieux, Domaine de Chevalier, Malartic-Lagravière, Olivier, and La Tour Martillac. For Couhins, Couhins-Lurton, and Laville Haut-Brion only the whites, for Fieuzal, Haut-Bailly, Haut-Brion, La Mission Haut-Brion, Pape

Only in 1987 did Pessac-Léognan become the most important *appellation* of the Graves region, occupying the northern third of it closest to the city of Bordeaux. Basically, this independence was established much too late. The number of wine-growing estates, particularly in the areas closest to the city, has fallen drastically since the mid-19th century. In Mérignac, the number dropped from 22 to only one, in Pessac from 12 to four, in Talence from 19 to three, and viticulture threatened to vanish altogether from

The oldest châteaux in the Bordelais region

When Bertrand de Goth, youngest son of a rich noble family, was appointed Archbishop of Bordeaux in 1299, his elder brother presented him with a wine estate in Pessac, now within the city borders. Only six years later he was elected Pope, upon which he named the estate Pape Clément, thus establishing the name of the oldest extant wine estate in the region. Although its existence was threatened more than once in the course of its history (notably by the French Revolution and 20th-century urbanization), wine has been produced uninterruptedly at Pape Clément ever since. With less than 74 acres (30 ha) planted to vines, 90 percent of them red varieties—60 percent Cabernet Sauvignon, 40 percent Merlot—Pape Clément is certainly no giant, and until recently certain other *crus* had a better reputation for quality. Nonetheless, in recent years the quality has stabilized and in the 1990s reached a level that is surpassed by few Graves reds.

The wines of the second historic estate, Château Haut-Brion, a few miles closer to the city, have always been at this level. Since its early days in the 17th century, Haut-Brion has been among the small group of elite Bordelais *crus*, and has never disappointed. It was the only Graves *premier cru classé* château in the Médoc classification in the 1855 listing and again in the 1973 revision. The peculiar situation of the vineyards, surrounded by outlying districts of the city of Bordeaux, has a positive effect climatically. In order to be able to maintain constant top quality, in recent years the winery of the estate has been updated with the very latest technology.

Haut-Brion's neighbor La Mission Haut-Brion also benefits from the special climatic situation and soils of Haut-Brion, where a second wine (La Tour Haut-Brion) and a white wine (Laville Haut-Brion) are also made. As the estate has belonged to the

Château La Mission Haut Brion in Pessac-Léognan is the sister of Haut Brion opposite it.

owners of Haut-Brion for nearly 20 years, the wines are now produced by the same team with the same perfection.

Clément, Smith-Haut Lafite, and La Tour Haut-Brion only the reds were classified, while the non-classified wines of these châteaux are labeled Graves sec. About 3,210 acres (1,300 ha) of the communities of Cadaujac, Canéjan, Gradignan, Léognan, Martillac, Mérignac, Pessac, Saint-Médard-d'Eyrans, Talence, and Villeneuve-D'Ornon are planted three-quarters to red and only a quarter to white varieties of grape, though Cabernet Sauvignon scarcely exceeds 60 percent among the reds. In some cases, it is only marginally present in the make-up of the wines. With Les Carmes de Haut-Brion for example, it only accounts for 10 percent of the mix, with Cabernet Franc making 40 percent and Merlot up to half the grape total.

SELECT PRODUCERS IN PESSAC-LÉOGNAN

CHÂTEAU CARBONNIEUX***–****
LÉOGNAN
222 acres (90 ha); 540,000 bottles • Wines: Pessac-Léognan Cru Classé Blanc, Le Sartre Rouge; La Tour Léognan
In terms of area, one of the largest estates in Graves, with both its reds and whites classified. Although the whites with their strong Sauvignon content must be considered the better-known Carbonnieux wines, the reds also attain the same standard.

CHÂTEAU DE FRANCE***–****
LÉOGNAN
84 acres (34 ha); 190,000 bottles • Wines: Pessac-Léognan Blanc, Rouge
Château de France is a splendidly situated *domaine*, whose commercial buildings reflect a piece of Bordeaux history. Under the young Arnaud Thomassin, white and red wines have gained in clarity and character.

CHÂTEAU HAUT-BAILLY****
LÉOGNAN
69 acres (28 ha); 120,000 bottles • Wines: Pessac-Léognan Cru Classé
Consistent qualities at a very high level are the trademark of Haut-Bailly, whose exclusive red traditionally belongs among the best Léognans and is 65 percent Cabernet Sauvignon.

CHÂTEAU HAUT-BRION*****
PESSAC
114 acres (46 ha); 270,000 bottles • Wines: Pessac-Léognan Rouge Premier Cru Classé, Pessac-Léognan Blanc, Bahans Haut-Brion, Les Plantiers du Haut-Brion
One of the best wine-growing estates of the whole Bordeaux region, whose whites and reds are equally convincing (*see page 252*).

CHÂTEAU LA LOUVIÈRE***–****
LÉOGNAN
119 acres (48 ha); 250,000 bottles • Wines: Pessac-Léognan Blanc, Rouge, Pessac-Léognan L de Louvière Blanc, Rouge, Bordeaux Rosé L de Louvière, Pessac-Léognan Le Louvetier Blanc, Rouge
This holding, part of André Lurton's empire, produces equally good whites and reds that are excellent value for money.

CHÂTEAU MALARTIC-LAGRAVIÈRE****
LÉOGNAN
104 acres (42 ha); 150,000 bottles • Wines: Pessac-Léognan Cru Classé
Pierre de Malartic bought the estate known as Lagravière in 1803. Since the 1998 change of

ownership, this estate has woken up out of its long sleep and its wines, both white and red, display a notable finesse and polish.

CHÂTEAU LA MISSION HAUT-BRION***–*****
PESSAC
52 acres (21 ha); 100,000 bottles • Wines: Pessac-Léognan Cru Classé, La Chapelle de la Mission
An eternal rival of Haut-Brion, La Mission—separated from its more famous neighbor only by a road—is now under the same ownership and has achieved almost the same quality.

CHÂTEAU OLIVIER***
LÉOGNAN
111 acres (45 ha); 230,000 bottles • Wines: Pessac-Léognan Cru Classé Blanc, Rouge
A most fascinating castle and house set in a lovely park. The Olivier wines—both white and red are classified—are less rounded and have less depth than the other *crus classés*, but age well and develop in harmonious fashion.

CHÂTEAU PAPE CLÉMENT****–*****
PESSAC
80 acres (32.5 ha); 160,000 bottles • Wines: Pessac-Léognan Cru Classé
The oldest wine-growing estate of Bordeaux brought forth a very convincing series of red wines in the second half of the 1990s. The whites, in which Sémillon and Sauvignon are about equal, also reach very high levels.

CHÂTEAU SMITH HAUT-LAFITTE****
LA BRÈDE
136 acres (55 ha); 200,000 bottles • Wines: Pessac-Léognan Cru Classé
Château Smith Haut-Lafite is no longer satisfied just with turning out excellent whites and reds. In recent times, a luxury hotel complex has grown up alongside the architecturally notable château, where treatments based on wine and grape products are offered.

DOMAINE DE CHEVALIER****
LÉOGNAN
84 acres (34 ha); 140,000 bottles • Wines: Pessac-Léognan Cru Classé Blanc, Rouge; L'Esprit de Chevalier Blanc, Rouge
The former Chibaley was already an established leading light in Léognan in the 18th century. Under Olivier Bernard, not only the famous whites, but now also the red wines are once again among the best in this *appellation*.

The Sweet Desserts of Château d'Yquem and its Neighbors

Probably like no other wine-growing area in the world—an exception in the last two decades is the Seewinkel in Austria's Burgenland—the hilly landscape north of the small town of Langon on the Garonne has concentrated on producing sweet white wines. Unlike, for example, the Rhein and Moselle, these are not marginal quantities that put a dot on the "i" of production but are the main and often the only product the châteaux in the region have to offer.

In the 18th and 19th centuries, the sweet wines were the real stars of the Bordeaux region, and this was probably why, unlike all the other *appellations*, they were classified at the same time as the Médoc *crus*. Top of the list is a *premier cru supérieur*, Château d'Yquem, which thus occupies a unique position compared with all other *premiers crus*. Behind it, nine other Sauternes were selected for the *premiers crus* grading and seven *deuxièmes crus*. In addition, neighboring Barsac registered two *premiers* and seven *deuxièmes crus*.

The basis for the rare specialization of the area is the interplay of early morning mists and warm afternoon sunshine, which at the confluence of the cold Cirons with the warmer Garonne, offers ideal climatic conditions for the development of *Botrytis cinerea*, a sporal fungus. This pierces the skin of the berries, which leads to the water evaporating and consequently to enormous concentrations of sugar, acids and extracts. A situation to be feared in the case of red grapes—the fungus destroys the

The vineyards of Sauternes are close to the villages of Barsac and Sauternes.

Opposite
A Sauternes grower who sticks to tradition.

Without the early morning mist there would be no noble rot wines at the Château d'Yquem.

pigments in the skin—can in the case of whites produce golden, honeyed wines that have almost unlimited aging ability and seem made for eternity. The Sémillon grape in particular finds the pebbly soil with a clayey, chalky subsoil the ideal *terroir* to attain the necessary over-ripeness without which the botrytis fungus cannot develop.

The first lovers of the Sauternes area crus were the Dutch shippers on the Quai des Chartrons in Bordeaux, who launched these wines on an unparalleled career. The crises of the late 19th and first half of the 20th centuries brought a decline of the sweet *crus*, of course, which was stopped only by the growth of a new generation of wine-lovers, combined with a series of great vintages in the 1980s.

Incomparable Effort

Even with the best climatic conditions, the producers of great sweet wines must work in the vineyards with a rigor unnecessary for any other kind of wine. The major requirement is a strict limitation of yields—at best, only one or two glasses of wine can be pressed from each vine—to provide the necessary ripeness and concentration. The weather in the harvesting period must also help, otherwise all the effort would be wasted. At Château d'Yquem, 280 feet (86 m) above sea level and the highest part of the *appellation*, Comte Alexandre de Lur Saluces has presided since 1968, showing how legendary qualities are to be attained. The château employs

put overnight in refrigerated chambers, where they freeze depending on their sugar concentration. When pressed, only the juice of the ripe unfrozen berries is released—a tiny quantity of thick, uncommonly extract-rich must. Of course, wines of this sort are not really of the same sweet quality as the real thing. They resemble more closely the EISWEIN product of Canada or California. What they chiefly lack are all the typical taste-forming trace elements that only botrytization can give—for example the exotic aroma overtones or extreme glycerine content—which surface fully only after long aging. Such wines using the most modern technology can be very pleasant to drink when young, with their strong emphasis on fruit, but they virtually never attain the greatness of mature, naturally produced *crus*.

50 people all year in the 250 or so acres (100 ha) of vineyard, for a yield of less than 20 gallons per acre. No pesticides are used here, and manuring is done at most every three or four years with horse manure. Instead, plowing is carried out, the plants are hugely cut back in winter, and in summer the leaves are removed from around the grapes, to permit maximum sunlight to reach the grapes. At harvesting, up to 120 seasonal workers are employed, who over three or more weeks effect up to ten or eleven gleanings—in years when botrytization develops quickly and evenly it can be fewer—to pick only botrytized berries. The must is pressed in three stages, fermented in new oak barrels and left to age in them for up to three years, with racking and transferring to another barrel every three months. In bad years there is no Yquem, as last happened in 1992. In good years, the nectar produced is incredibly intense, with a bouquet of honey, nuts, sultanas, apricots, and candied oranges, together with enormous strength, fullness, sweetness, and spice on the palate.

Not all wine estates in Sauternes—and still fewer in the other sweet wine *appellations*—can afford or want to incur such expense, or risk not producing any wine at all. For this reason, many businesses have been content in botrytis-less years to harvest over-ripe but non-botrytized grapes. The wines from them—although established at the same high price levels as the botrytized *crus*—achieved a quality that sometimes rated no higher than high-grade *sélections* and at an international level scarcely reached the standard of German or Austrian Auslese wines. For this reason, in the last decade the technique of CRYOEXTRACTION has been increasingly used, borrowed from the New World. The grapes are

These wooden blocks are used to close the barrels.

Opposite, above
Botrytized grapes for Sauternes.

The grapes are picked in several stages, with only the botrytized grapes being selected. The rest are given further time to become over-ripe.

Select Producers in Sauternes

Château Clos Haut-Peyraguey**
BOMMES
42 acres (17 ha); 37,000 bottles • Wines: Sauternes Premier Cru Classé, Sauternes Château Haut-Bommes
The vines of Jacques Pauly grow in the immediate vicinity of Yquem. His wines of the 1990s display remarkable concentration, but take a long time to unfold their charms.

Château De Fargues**–*****
FARGUES-DE-LANGON
37 acres (15 ha); 12,000 bottles • Wines: Sauternes
The wines that Alexandre de Lur-Saluces produces on his small private estate are scarcely below those of Yquem in quality, and the yields are hardly any higher.

Château Gilette**–*****
PREIGNAC
11 acres (4.5 ha); 7,000 bottles • Wines: Sauternes
This small estate produces sumptuous wines with marked, fruity and exotic bouquets that are of consistent quality year after year.

Château Guiraud*–****
SAUTERNES
247 acres (100 ha); 100,000 bottles • Wines: Sauternes Premier Cru Classé, Bordeaux Blanc Sec
With approximately 270 acres (100 ha), Guiraud is one of the very large estates of the Sauternes region. Despite excellent growth in good years, the quality of the wine is subject to a degree of fluctuation.

Château Lafaurie-Peyraguey*–*****
BOMMES
99 acres (40 ha); 75,000 bottles • Wines: Sauternes Premier Cru Classé
The château below Yquem dates to the 17th century. Virtually all the somewhat scattered vineyard areas are planted to Sémillon.

Château Raymond-Lafon**–*****
SAUTERNES
44.5 acres (18 ha); 20,000 bottles • Wine: Sauternes
This unclassified estate in the Yquem neighborhood was taken over by Pierre and Francine Meslier in 1972. Since then, it has gained a place alongside the *crus classés* purely through the outstanding quality of its wines. Today, it is managed by the next generation but in the same spirit.

Château Rieussec**–*****
FARGUES-DE-LANGON
185 acres (75 ha); 90,000 bottles • Wines: Sauternes Premier Cru Classé, Sauternes Clos Labère, Bordeaux Blanc R. de Rieussec
Rieussec is one of the best-known names of Sauternes, which is undoubtedly due to the successful marketing of the dry R. de Rieussec whites. The estate belongs to the empire of the Baron de Rothschild (Lafite) *domaines*.

Château Sigalas Rabaud**–*****
BOMMES
34.5 acres (14 ha); 30,000 bottles • Wines: Sauternes Premier Cru Classé
Conditions at the highly-esteemed Sigalas Rabaud are virtually as ideal for the development of botrytis as in Yquem. The 17th-century estate now belongs to the Cordier wine firm and is considered one of the best in the area.

Château Suduiraut**
PREIGNAC
217 acres (88 ha); 130,000 bottles • Wines: Sauternes Premier Cru Classé
The wines of Suduiraut stand out more for finesse than for body and strength, which is in part due to the subtle touch of acidity. The bouquet often displays overtones of exotic fruits and figs.

Château La Tour Blanche**
BOMMES
104 acres (42 ha); 60,000 bottles • Wines: Sauternes Premier Grand Cru Classé, Sauternes Les Charmilles de Tour Blanche, Bordeaux Blanc Sec Isis, Bordeaux Blanc Osiris, Bordeaux Rouge Cru du Cinquet
The wines of La Tour Blanche have joined the top ranks of the region only since the end of the 1980s.

Château d'Yquem***
YQUEM
255 acres (103 ha); 95,000 bottles • Wines: Sauternes Premier Cru Supérieur Classé, Ygrec
Château Yquem belonged to the Lur-Saluces family from 1785, but the family is now only a minority shareholder. However, Comte Alexandre continues to guarantee the legendary quality of the wines by his personal management.

Sweet, Sweeter ...

Although Sauternes is a symbol for the prestige of all the sweet wines of the Bordelais region in general and of Graves in particular, it is not the only *appellation* under which semi-sweet or sweet wines are produced. Barsac, for example, is a region adjacent to Sauternes in the north, whose yields can be bottled under its own A.C. or that of its better known neighbor. Château Coutet is one example of such a wine. This rule only applies in one direction, and it probably wouldn't make much sense the other way around. Additional areas that generate sweet wines include Cérons on the left bank of the Garonne, and Loupiac, Cadillac and Sainte-Croix-du-Monde on the right.

Barsac, which under English rule had been the leading village in the area and was its principal port (Sauternes was also shipped from here) produced the best-known wines of the southern Graves district at the time. Nowadays its name is overshadowed by that of its neighbor, even though the A.C. specifications are virtually identical and ten Barsac châteaux were included in the 1855 classification of Sauternes, including the Climens and Coutet *premiers crus*. The *crus classés* today still account for 30 percent of production by volume, and Barsac's wines are considered by many observers just as good, even if they are occasionally somewhat lighter than the best Sauternes.

North of Barsac is the district of Cérons, where two different sweet wine types are made:

Château d'Yquem has occupied a special position for over 150 years because of the quality of its wine.

on the one hand a kind of medium sweet *sélections*, which are mostly marketed as Graves Supérieurs by the trade; on the other sweet and dessert wines marketed as Cérons. The latter *appellation* is scarcely known even to avowed wine specialists, so it is not surprising that only 20 percent of the wines of the area carry the label, and Cérons as a sweet-wine *appellation* is becoming increasingly sidelined by Sauternes and Barsac. Dry whites and red wines are also grown here and labeled Graves, while the small quantities of dry whites from Sauternes and Barsac are sold under these labels themselves.

Right of the Garonne

A series of villages along the right bank of the Garonne at the same height as Sauternes and Barsac have also specialized in sweet wines. To some extent, they benefit from similar climatic conditions as those on the opposite bank, but the landscape is quite distinct from that in Sauternes and surroundings. The relief is livelier, and more recent alluvial soils alternate with limestone plateaus of maritime origin, on whose slopes the vineyards can be pitched very steeply. The best-known of the *appellations* here is probably Loupiac, on whose 988 acres (400 ha) the vines are planted mainly on south-facing sites with good conditions for over-ripeness and botrytization. The high Sémillon content in the vineyards, which can reach 70–80 percent, would seem natural terrain for good sweet wines, yet the style of the wine tends to resemble fruity *sélections*, and is quite distinct in concentration and structure from Barsac or Sauternes. Cadillac, an *appellation* of a series of villages around the town of that name (founded by the

If the sun smiles on the grapes in late autumn, a great vintage is imminent.

English in the 13th century) produces mostly light, at best aromatic and decidedly fruity wines, though they are rarely really expressive. As part of the Premières Côtes de Bordeaux—a designation of origin that is only used for dry *crus*, the name Cadillac being reserved exceptionally for the sweet wines—the area would basically not have merited any *appellation* at all, but in 1973 the legislation was of a different view. In terms of potential, the best sweet wines of the right bank of the Garonne comes from the 1,480-acre (600-ha) *appellation* of Sainte-Croix-du-Mont, which lies directly opposite Sauternes and Barsac and the Cirons tributary.

Though the sometimes very steep slopes of the vineyards are clearly geographically different from those in Sauternes, the wines reflect a markedly higher incidence of botrytization than is the case in Loupiac or Cadillac. In alcohol content and sweetness, they are on a par with their famous counterparts, even if they are relatively deficient in structure and aging ability. Here too, dry whites and reds of the district are generally bottled as Bordeaux or Bordeaux Supérieur.

SELECT PRODUCERS IN BARSAC, LOUPIAC, AND SAINT-CROIX-DU-MONT

CHÂTEAU CAILLOU***—****
BARSAC
44.5 acres (18 ha); 30,000 bottles • Wines: Barsac Cru Classé
Though a neighbor of the great Climens, Caillou used to be different in the style of its wines, which were much less sumptuous; they are now much more concentrated.

CHÂTEAU CLIMENS*****
BARSAC
71 acres (29 ha); 40,000 bottles • Wines: Barsac Premier Cru Classé, Cyprès de Climens
Climens is the Yquem of Barsac. Sometimes the *premier cru* of less famous *appellation* is ranked higher than that of the illustrious Sauternes château. The wines from the higher sites develop an uncommonly rich exotic and fruity bouquet as they age.

CHÂTEAU CLOSIOT**—****
BARSAC
19.8 acres (8 ha); 18,000 bottles • Wines: Barsac: Château Closiot, Passion de Closiot, Château Camperos
Françoise Sirot and her husband Bernard, a popular Belgian wine journalist, offer a finely graded range of sweet wines, from the rich and refined to the fruity and delicate. They belong to the circle of new Sauternes producers who dare to experiment with different balance of wine.

CHÂTEAU COUTET****—*****
BARSAC
95 acres (38.5 ha); 60,000 bottles. Wine: Barsac Premier Cru Classé
One of the Barsac estates which markets its wines under the more prestigious neighboring *appellation*. Despite fairly high yields compared to the most famous names in the regions, the wines nonetheless have great aromatic finesse and are long-lasting.

CHÂTEAU DOISY DAËNE***—****
BARSAC
37 acres (15 ha); 40,000 bottles • Wines: Sauternes Cru Classé
The wines of this estate were once made entirely from Sémillon, but today 20 percent Sauvignon Blanc is part of

the *cuvée*. They are vinified by Denis Dubourdieu, son of the owner, who prefers a very aromatic style.

CHÂTEAU LOUBENS***—****
SAINTE-CROIX-DU-MONT
57 acres (23 ha); 80,000 bottles • Wines: Sainte-Croix-du-Mont
In good years, the sweet wines of Loubens can easily outdo many a Barsac or even a Sauternes in quality.

CHÂTEAU DE MYRAT***—****
BARSAC
54.5 acres (22 ha); 40,000 bottles • Wines: Barsac Cru Classé
Following a period of difficulty, Myrat was able to recover its previous high quality only in the second half of the 1990s.

CHÂTEAU LA RAME***—****
SAINTE-CROIX DU-MONDE
49.4 acres (20 ha); 100,000 bottles • Wine Sainte-Croix-du-Mont
Yves Armand knows how to give his Réserve du Château sweet wines a sweetness and complexity in good years that can stand any comparison. In lighter years, the Cuvée Tradition enchants wine drinkers with its clear aromatics and balance.

CRU BARREJATS****
PUJOLS-SUR-CIRON
12.3 acres (5 ha); 6,000 bottles • Wine: Sauternes
In ten years, Mireille Daret and Philippe Anurand have shown what can be achieved with passion and skilled work. Their wines are full of refinement and brilliant character. They belong to the number of young wine-makers who are breaking new ground for Sauternes and Barsac.

DOMAINE DU NOBLE****
LOUPIAC
37 acres (15 ha); 55,000 bottles • Wines: Loupiac
Pleasing fruit aromas and great aromatic elegance are the well-known and esteemed trademarks of Loupiac wines, even though they are lacking the sumptuousness and full sweetness of the great Sauternes. In their style, the wines of the Domaine du Noble attain a standard of excellence, and must be considered a bargain at their price.

RIVE DROITE

In the Bordelais region, the *rive droite* (right bank) is the whole area north of the Dordogne, one of the two great rivers that run together as the Gironde not far downriver of Bordeaux.

Just as the Graves district on the left bank of the Garonne is divided into the zones of the Médoc and the Graves proper, so the right bank is also divided into two zones with distinctive characters. One is the Libournais with the Fronsadais on the Garonne in the southeast, the other the area of Bourg and Blaye in the northwest, which lies partly on the Gironde, directly opposite Margaux. Altogether, about a quarter of the total area planted to vine of the whole wine-growing region belongs to this part of the Bordelais area, with the Libournais 32,100 acres (13,000 hectares) getting the lion's share.

Viticulture was certainly carried on here in Roman times. In the 4th century, the poet Ausonius, for whom one of the most famous châteaux in France is named, boasted that his wine was drunk even in the Eternal City. Some centuries later Charlemagne stayed in Fronsac, and in the Middle Ages Pomerol and Saint-Émilion were celebrated stopping places on the pilgrim route to Santiago de Compostela. After the Hundred Years' War between England and France the wine trade developed on this side of the Gironde as well, and the Dordogne served

The vineyards of the Côte de Bourg lie on the right bank of the Gironde.

as a transport route along which the red wines of Bergerac could be carried to England.

The rise of the wine industry in the 17th and 18th centuries was nevertheless much less pronounced than in the Médoc. The classification of 1855 also passed the Libournais by, and it took till the middle of the 20th century for Saint-Émilion to get a classification of its own, while Pomerol, the second famous *appellation* of the region, still has none.

An unequal couple—Merlot and Cabernet Franc

The diversity of the wines of Saint-Émilion and Pomerol and those of the individual châteaux within the two *appellations* is primarily attributable to differences in the *terroirs*—Pétrus for example has very chalky soils—and microclimatic zones. Further variety, however, comes from the different mix of grape varieties—in contrast to the Médoc-Cabernet Sauvignon, which requires the warmest of sites to be able to ripen fully, is only a very small component in the blends.

The difference in the ripening patterns of the varieties means that in the Saint-Émilion district Merlot constitutes 50–70 percent (and in exceptional cases such as at Château Troplong Mondot even 80 percent) of the content, with Cabernet Franc making the other 20–50 percent, whereas in the best Pomerol *crus* the Merlot proportion tends to be even higher. The art of *assemblage*, or blending, begins therefore not in the winery or *cuvier* but in the vineyard, where the grower has to plant the most suitable varieties of vine. While

Old Merlot vine stock.

Cabernet Franc achieves remarkable results on pebbly or sandy soils, Merlot benefits more from loamier soils.

The differing responses to the given *terroir* explains at least in part the considerable differences in the ratios of grape varieties within individual *appellations*. In Saint-Émilion, for example, there are châteaux such

as Ausone and Canon La Gaffellière that grow half and half Cabernet Franc and Merlot, whereas at others (e.g. Cheval Blanc) Cabernet Franc predominates, with up to 60 percent. In the Pomerol area, the Merlot proportion can vary from over 90 percent, such as at Trotanoy and Pétrus, for example (observers even believe that in recent years the latter has consisted entirely of Merlot), to just 65–70 percent, only marginally above Saint-Émilion, as at La Conseillante, L'Evangile, or Nenin.

In order to find the perfect ratio of the two varieties for the given vintage, the grapes from the individual parcels of land are initially vinified and aged separately in the cellar. This allows the vintner the opportunity to react to the moods of nature. Independently of conditions in the vineyard, he can increase the proportion of early ripening Merlot in the finished wine in bad years, or after very hot autumn days step up the proportion of later ripening Cabernet.

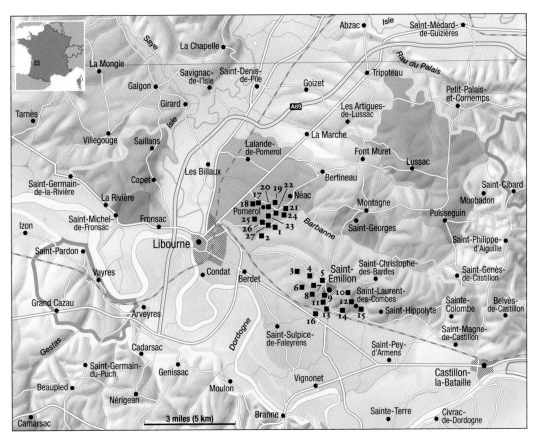

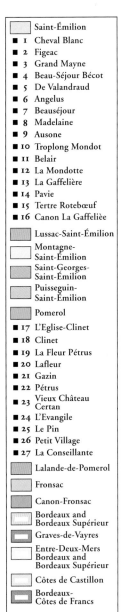

Saint-Émilion

- ■ 1 Cheval Blanc
- ■ 2 Figeac
- ■ 3 Grand Mayne
- ■ 4 Beau-Séjour Bécot
- ■ 5 De Valandraud
- ■ 6 Angelus
- ■ 7 Beauséjour
- ■ 8 Madelaine
- ■ 9 Ausone
- ■ 10 Troplong Mondot
- ■ 11 Belair
- ■ 12 La Mondotte
- ■ 13 La Gaffelière
- ■ 14 Pavie
- ■ 15 Tertre Rotebœuf
- ■ 16 Canon La Gaffelièe

Lussac-Saint-Émilion
Montagne-Saint-Émilion
Saint-Georges-Saint-Émilion
Puisseguin-Saint-Émilion
Pomerol

- ■ 17 L'Eglise-Clinet
- ■ 18 Clinet
- ■ 19 La Fleur Pétrus
- ■ 20 Lafleur
- ■ 21 Gazin
- ■ 22 Pétrus
- ■ 23 Vieux Château Certan
- ■ 24 L'Evangile
- ■ 25 Le Pin
- ■ 26 Petit Village
- ■ 27 La Conseillante

Lalande-de-Pomerol
Fronsac
Canon-Fronsac
Bordeaux and Bordeaux Supérieur
Graves-de-Vayres
Entre-Deux-Mers Bordeaux and Bordeaux Supérieur
Côtes de Castillon
Bordeaux-Côtes de Francs

THE RED WINE COUNTRY OF LIBOURNE

Whereas both red and white wines are grown in the more northerly Bourgais, the Libournais is almost exclusively red-wine country. In contrast to Médoc and Graves, where Cabernet Sauvignon rules supreme, here it is Cabernet Franc (alias Bouchet) and Merlot that dominate. The way they are put together during blending—along with the influences of differing *terroirs*—distinguishes the individual *appellations*, which are grouped in a semi-circle around Libourne. In the immediate vicinity of the town itself, in its northeastern suburbs, are the vineyards of Pomerol, which cover a total area of under 1,980 acres (800 ha) divided among 180 or so châteaux.

In the southeast of Libourne, but already a certain distance away from the town center, is Saint-Émilion, where wine was grown even in Roman times. With almost 13,600 acres (5,500 ha) between them, the two *appellations*, Saint-Émilion and Saint-Émilion Grand Cru, cover the greatest area and, because of their classification system, are the best known. The next circle of viticulture, often only a few paces from this center of prestige, is constituted by the "satellites" of these *appellations*, Lalande-de-Pomerol (Pomerol) and Montagne, Lussac, Saint-Georges, and Puisseguin (Saint-Émilion), whose *appellations* include the cognomen Saint-

Émilion as well. The eastern and southeastern end of the Libournais is formed by two relatively unknown cultivation districts, Côtes de Castillon and Côtes de Francs. They form the border of the Gironde department toward the Dordogne and comprise a total of somewhat over 7,410 acres (3,000 ha) of vineyards.

Castillon-La-Bataille, the main commune in Côtes de Castillon, has important historical associations for the Bordelais region, if not for the whole of France. At the confluence of the Lidoire and Dordogne, the decisive battle that ended the Hundred Years' War in the French king's favor took place, bringing to an end the English domination of Gascony.

Both *appellations* are the most recent in Bordeaux: Francs was made a separate A.C. in 1967, Castillon only in 1989. Côtes de Francs also produces a small quantity (less than 1 percent of the total production) of white or sweet wines from the usual varieties of Bordeaux, the only area anywhere in the Libournais area to do so.

The real strength of the two areas is of course in their reds, which turn out much more complex and structured than the products sold under the regional Bordeaux label, but at the same time are much better value for money than the other much better-known communes of the Libournais district.

THE CAPITAL OF MERLOT: SAINT-ÉMILION

Saint-Émilion with its stately old houses has been designated a cultural monument. It stands on a limestone hill whose cellar galleries are as legendary as the wines that are aged in them.

developed by erosion from the first area, and differ less in their composition than in the angle and direction of the slope. The third major zone is defined as the Graves (pebbly and gravelly soils) in the northwest, on the border with Pomerol, while the fourth is the Sables, the sandy plateaus west and east of the town. The last area is that of the alluvial gravels of the Dordogne plain directly below the town.

HISTORIC LOCALITIES WITH RECENT PRESTIGE

Wine has been produced in this part of the Bordelais since the 3rd century, and thus has perhaps the most longstanding tradition in the whole wine-growing area. A start was made by Roman legionaries, who cleared the Saint-Émilion plateau and neighboring Pomerol. Not far from the present town the poet Ausonius cultivated his own grapes and made the first documented record of viticulture in the area.

In the 8th century, a Breton hermit called Emilion settled in a cave near the old villa, and the town took its name from him. His spiritual aura attracted numerous believers, who in the centuries that followed extended the grotto into a monolithic rock church, which is impressive even today for its dimensions and atmosphere. The limestone from the countless caves that arose at that time and served as wine cellars with their ideal climate were used by the residents of the village to build their houses, whose pale yellowy white tones lend the place a great deal of its fascination today.

At the end of the 12th century, King John of England, son of Henry II and brother of Richard the Lionheart, gave the town a charter, which meant it could elect its own council, the *jurade*, which still exists. Even though this no longer functions as a town council but more as a kind of wine fraternity, it is more than just another piece of folklore. It acted and still acts as an important supervisory body for the wine industry in Saint-Émilion, and in earlier days branded barrels that in its judgment contained high-quality wine with a *marque du vinetier*. Wines that did not carry this seal of quality had to be destroyed.

The later history of the town was notable more for its wars than its wines. During the Hundred Years' War and the French Revolution it was repeatedly the object of military conflict,

Every wine pilgrimage in the Bordelais region has one not-to-be-missed destination—the lovely little town of Saint-Émilion, which clings to the slopes of the Dordogne Valley less than 25 miles (40 km) east of Bordeaux. Narrow alleys wind between old stone houses up to the plateau where the imposing parish church towers over all the surrounding vineyards. Although elsewhere the name Saint-Émilion is synonymous with the white Ugni Blanc grape variety, the town on the Dordogne is—like almost all the Libournais—a purely red wine district, and moreover one of the best in the region.

Though the circumference of the area is scarcely 30 miles, virtually the entire 13,600-acre (5,500 ha) wine-growing area is completely covered with rows of vines, making this one of the most intensive monocultures of the entire Bordelais region. There are around 1,000 wine-making businesses making a living from it, of which over 400 are only mini-estates just growing grapes. Four or five sub-areas are usually distinguished, though some experts identify up to 17 *terroirs*, each of which has its own soil formation and individual wine types. The most important *terroir* of the *appellation* is certainly the "plateau" with its limestone formations, on top of which are flatter layers of argillocalcite or sandy clay. The second area is the *Côtes*, the slopes off this plateau. Their soils perhaps one reason why Saint-Émilion took a long time to catch up with the prestige of the Médoc and Graves.

COMPLEX CLASSIFICATION

Although a wine syndicate was established back in 1884 and the district was declared an *appellation d'origine* in 1936, it took until the 1950s before the best *crus* were classified here. In 1951, the *jurade* introduced a new quality control of wines which in 1954—almost 100 years later than in the Médoc—led to a separate rating system. Its classification would be revised every ten years, unlike in its long-established neighbor. The new system provided for five grades overall, for which two separate *appellations* were set up: Saint-Émilion and Saint-Émilion Grand Cru. Astonishingly, the latter more prestigious label produces somewhat over 3 million gallons (130,000 hl), i.e. a good third more wine than the basic *appellation*. The *grands crus* themselves were subdivided into four classes: plain *grand crus*, *grands crus classés* and finally the small group of *premiers grands crus classés*, which in turn were subdivided into A and B. Whereas only two châteaux were admitted to this top A group

of *premiers grands crus* (Ausone and Cheval-Blanc), the B group includes 11 names: L'Angélus, Beau-Séjour-Bécot, Beauséjour, Belair, Canon, Figeac, Clos Fourtet, La Gaffelière, Magdelaine, Pavie, and Trottevieille.

Their wines are distinctive not only because of the differing soils on which the vines grow but also because of the greatly differing proportions of the three main grape varieties used in the blending, though the precise ratios are not always explicable directly in terms of geographical situation. Thus the top estates both on the plateau and on the Côtes have examples of balanced Merlot-Cabernet proportions, and also of wines where the Merlot is clearly more prominent. On the boundary with Pomerol, where the Merlot content is in general much higher than in Saint-Émilion, paradoxically the Cabernet proportion rises, such as Cheval-Blanc, for example, where Cabernet Franc makes 60 percent. In turn, Cabernet Sauvignon is unusually high both on the *côte* near Pavie and on the Pomerol boundary at Figeac.

Château Canon La Gaffelière, an estate of almost 50 acres (20 ha) at the foot of Saint-Émilion, has come along amazingly under Stephan von Neipperg, and now produces one of the best wines of the famous *appellation* year after year.

SATELLITES IN ORBIT

Although the character of the individual *crus* of Saint-Émilion differ from each other, they do share some features compared with the wines of their satellites: they have more structure, more character, greater density, and greater aging ability.

The satellites of Saint-Émilion include four *appellations* that enclose the district to the north and northeast: Montagne, Saint-Georges, Lussac, and Puisseguin. These are allowed to use "Saint-Émilion" as a cognomen to their own names.

In landscape terms, all four districts resemble Saint-Émilion, but in respect of the *terroir*—the soils are to some extent cooler and wetter, and as the distance from the Dordogne grows, so the moderating temperature influence wanes—and the grape varieties used, there are clear differences.

Not infrequently Merlot rules the roost almost alone, reaching a proportion of 90 percent in the grape mix. Even though the wines of these *appellations* cannot rival those of their famous neighbors, they are excellent value for money, more than just possible alternatives compared with the often over-priced *grands crus* of Saint-Émilion. In addition, part of the output is not even sold under the satellite *appellation* but as Bordeaux or Bordeaux Supérieur, and thus falls into an even more reasonable price bracket.

SELECT PRODUCERS IN SAINT-ÉMILION

CHÂTEAU L'ANGÉLUS*****
SAINT-ÉMILION
59 acres (24 ha); 70,000 bottles • Wines: Saint-Émilion Premier Grand Cru Classé B, Saint-Émilion Carillon de l'Angélus
Although Hubert de Boüard's estate caught up with the *premiers grands crus* only at the last revision, in terms of the consistent quality of its wines it could almost demand an A rating. Its ideal situation on the edge of the plateau, the balanced blending of Cabernet and Merlot, and the vinification make this one of the most modern great Bordeaux reds.

CHÂTEAU AUSONE*****
SAINT-ÉMILION
17 acres (7 ha); 22,000 bottles • Wines: Saint-Émilion Premier Grand Cru Classé A
The vine stocks of Ausone, the modern estate on the site where the Roman poet Ausonius had his villa, are on average 50 years old. Alain Vauthier, with his philosophy linked to nature and the cosmos, has in recent years succeeded in bringing Ausone to what is probably the highest level in its history.

CHÂTEAU BEAU-SÉJOUR-BÉCOT****
SAINT-ÉMILION
40.5 acres (16.5 ha); 90,000 bottles • Wines: Saint-Émilion Premier Grand Cru Classé B
That adjacent *domaines* should have the same or a similar name is not uncommon in the Bordelais region. In such cases the owner then adds his own name. The Bécot family produces a wine strongly dominated by Merlot, which becomes uncommonly subtle and complex as it ages.

CHÂTEAU BEAUSÉJOUR****
SAINT-ÉMILION
17 acres (7 ha); 35,000 bottles • Wines: Saint-Émilion Premier Grand Cru Classé B
Like its namesake and neighbor, Beauséjour is a blend with a Merlot predominance. The vintages of the late 1980s were among the best of the *appellation*.

CHÂTEAU BELAIR****
SAINT-ÉMILION
31 acres (12.5 ha); 60,000 bottles • Wines: Saint-Émilion Premier Grand Cru Classé
Since the beginning of the 1990s, Belair has exploited the potential of the site to the full. The wines are complex, full, rich, and have unique finesse.

CHÂTEAU CANON*****
SAINT-ÉMILION
44.5 acres (18 ha); 80,000 bottles • Wines: Saint-Émilion Premier Grand Cru Classé B
At the end of the 1980s, Canon produced a series of splendid, complex wines. The 1990s, on the other hand, were notable for the problems in the winery. After the complete rebuild of the *chai*, we may expect the high quality of former years again.

CHÂTEAU CANON LA GAFFELIÈRE****–*****
SAINT-ÉMILION
48.5 acres (19.5 ha); 65,000 bottles • Wines: Saint-Émilion Grand Cru Classé, Saint-Émilion Grand Cru La Mondotte
Stephan von Neipperg, who runs a whole series of wine estates on the *rive droite*, is the scion of old Württemberg nobility. His brother manages the estate attached to the family castle at Schwaigern in Germany. For years, Canon La Gaffelière has been of the highest quality and has moved up into the elite of the *grands crus*. A 10-acre (4-ha) plot planted 100 percent with Merlot provides the mini-quantities needed for the excellent Mondotte, which now fetches prices at the level of Cheval-Blanc.

CHÂTEAU CAP DE MOURLIN***–****
SAINT-ÉMILION
34.5 acres (14 ha); 72,000 bottles • Wines: St.-Émilion Grand Cru Classé
Jacques Capdemoulin produces a classic wine that is noticeable for a more pronounced tannin overtone than is usual in Saint-Émilion.

Château Cheval-Blanc*****
Saint-Émilion
91.5 acres (37 ha); 150,000 bottles • Wines: Saint-Émilion Premier Grand Cru Classé A
Almost with one foot in Pomerol terrain and not far from Château Pétrus, Cheval-Blanc—astonishingly—grows not preponderantly Merlot but almost 60 percent Cabernet Franc. The wines are among the legends of the Bordelais region, and stand out for the incredible consistency of their quality even in lesser years.

Château Dassault****
Saint-Émilion
59 acres (24 ha); 80,000 bottles • Wines: Saint-Émilion Grand Cru Classé, Saint-Émilion D de Dassault
Originally founded as Château Couperie, in 1955 the estate passed into the hands of the industrialist Marcel Dassault, who renamed it. The wines now have a good but fine structure, and maturing in the barrel has been mastered.

Château Faugères****
Saint-Émilion
74 acres (30 ha); 250,000 bottles • Wines: Saint-Émilion Grand Cru, Côtes de Castillon Cap de Faugères
Much has been invested in modernization at Faugères since the end of the 1980s. The quality of the wines has settled to a consistent high standard.

Château Figeac****–*****
Saint-Émilion
99 acres (40 ha); 150,000 bottles • Wines: Saint-Émilion Premier Grand Cru Classé
Figeac is unique among the great châteaux of Saint-Émilion in devoting a third of its vineyards to Cabernet Sauvignon. The reason for this is the particular character of the soils in the region of Cheval-Blanc, which resemble those of the *rive gauche*. Figeac, thanks to careful work in the vineyard, is now back among the top estates.

Château La Gaffelière***–****
Saint-Émilion
54.5 acres (22 ha); 110,000 bottles • Wines: Saint-Émilion Premier Grand Cru Classé B, Clos La Gaffelière
Grapes have been grown at the foot of the *côte* since Roman times. The superb situation below Saint-Émilion has been fully exploited once again since the mid-1990s and produces wines with rich aromas of fruit and fresh woods and mature, harmonious tannins.

Château Pavie****–*****
Saint-Émilion
91.5 acres (37 ha); 95,000 bottles • Wines: Saint-Émilion Premier Grand Cru Classé B
Pavie, like Château Monbousquet, is undergoing a sensational renaissance. Its owner, Gérard Perse, obviously has the will and the means to follow the most rigorous principles of quality laid down by the star enologist Michel Rolland.

Château Pavie-Macquin****
Saint-Émilion
37 acres (15 ha); 60,000 bottles • Wines: Saint-Émilion Grand Cru Classé
Although only rated as a *grand cru*, in the 1990s Pavie-Macquin often overtook its more famous namesake in terms of quality, as it cares for its vineyards in a most comprehensive and natural-based manner. The mark of the wines is full, firm tannins that promise a good aging ability.

Château Soutard***–****
Saint-Émilion
54.5 acres (22 ha); 120,000 bottles • Wines: Saint-Émilion Grand Cru Classé
The imposing château is one of the oldest in the locality. Despite the splendid unified vineyard, the grapes are vinified separately per plot, so that variations in grape and ripeness can be taken into account. Soutard is one of the classics of Saint-Émilion.

Château le Tertre Rotebœuf****–*****
Saint-Émilion
15 acres (6 ha); 26,000 bottles • Wines: Saint-Émilion Grand Cru
The wines of François Mitjavile have been among the densest, most sumptuous, and most eloquent of the *appellation* for more than a decade, and in the next revision of the classification would merit ranking with the *premiers crus*.

Château la Tour Figeac****
Saint-Émilion
35.8 acres (14.5 ha); 48,000 bottles • Wine: Saint-Émilion Grand Cru
Using biodynamic cultivation, Otto Rettenmaier has succeeded in clearly expressing his *terroir* in his wines, and increasing the quality of the wines to the point where they are approaching that of their famous neighbor.

Château Troplong Mondot****–*****
Saint-Émilion
74 acres (30 ha); 100,000 bottles • Wines: Saint-Émilion Grand Cru Classé
Troplong Mondot is placed at the highest point of Saint-Émilion. The wines show much spice, licorice and fruit, good tannins on the palate, and a firm structure, but also need a lot of time to unfold completely.

Château Valandraud****–*****
Saint-Émilion
19.5 acres (8 ha); 12,000 bottles • Wines: Saint-Émilion Grand Cru
In the space of a few years, Jean-Luc Thunevin has managed to turn his wine into one of the most sought-after and expensive of the *appellation*. The very first *vin de garage* has now been extended and has indisputably gained in complexity.

Clos Fourtet****
Saint-Émilion
49.5 acres (20 ha); 80,000 bottles • Wines: Saint-Émilion Premier Cru Classé, Domaine des Martialis
Directly outside the walls of Saint-Émilion, the *clos* is now producing wines with high concentration but fine tannins and outstanding length.

Clos de l'Oratoire****
Saint-Émilion
24.5 acres (10 ha); 50,000 bottles • Wines: Saint-Émilion Grand Cru Classé
Another estate run by Stephan von Neipperg. In many years, the wines turn out even better than those of Canon La Gaffalière. They display fine fruit aromas with overtones of cedarwood, and when young stand out on the palate for their classic, firm tannin structure.

Pomerol: Favored by Pétrus

Pomerol is downright flat. Where other wine-growing areas boast of their landscape charms, the 1,980 acres (800 ha) of Pomerol stretch north of the old port of Libourne, flat as far as the eye can see. The only eye-catcher in the district is the tall, much photographed church tower. There is no real village, at best smallish hamlets and any number of scattered wine-growing estates, over 150 in all, of which some of the best-known have under 24.5 acres (10 ha) to manage.

1,980 acres (800 ha) of vine stocks is not much, particularly as the wine yields are the lowest of all Bordeaux reds. But what a list of names: Pétrus, Trotanoy, Clinet, Gazin, La Conseillante, …! Very few wine regions of the world can boast prestige of that sort. Yet during all the centuries when Médoc and Graves or even neighboring Saint-Émilion were busily building their reputations, Pomerol always remained to one side. Although wine growing goes back a long way, there was no historical continuity to it. It was only at the beginning of the 20th century that the Belgians and Dutch began to take an interest in the wines from the front gardens of Libourne, and it took until the 1950s for Pétrus and its neighbors to become anything approaching celebrities—and that for a *cru* that is now frequently called the most expensive single wine in the world! Its late discovery also accounts for the fact that all attempts at classification have passed it by without a trace. More than such attempts at classification,

The Vieux Château Certan supplies outstanding Pomerol.

Château Pétrus is the home of one of the most sought-after red wines in the world.

it is outstanding personalities that brought Pomerol prestige.

Undoubtedly Jean-Pierre Moueix is among these. Not only has he made a series of châteaux in the Bordelais area famous, he has also successfully steered the Dominus project in California to prestige. Also a great influence in the development of the wine industry, not only in Pomerol but in Bordeaux generally and in the Midi and distant Spain, is the enologist Michel Rolland of Pomerol-Château Le Bon Pasteur.

The Mark of the Terroir

Though Merlot is important in Saint-Émilion, it features still more prominently in Pomerol. Château Pétrus, for example, the icon of Pomerol, cultivates Cabernet Franc on one of its 28 acres, but this virtually never ends up in the final *cuvée*. For some decades, the rest has been planted entirely with Merlot stocks. Even in the early 1950s, Cabernet Franc still constituted 30 percent. The vineyards of Pétrus lie in the north-eastern part of the *appellation* on its highest elevation. The specialty of Pétrus is its *terroir*: the soils of the plateau consist predominantly of loam with ferrous layers in the subsoil. The loam give the wines their sumptuous, round fullness, which always prevails over the noticeable tannins, while the iron is purportedly responsible for the truffle aromas that develop as the wine ages. Top Pomerols are highly modern red wines. Responsive even when young, they are at

least as capable of aging as good Médocs. The best are dark, velvety, voluminous, and meaty. When young, they display black berry fruits and spiciness, whereas as they age delightful truffle aromas develop.

The Heath Behind Pomerol

Other major or minor celebrity châteaux are grouped round the hillock of Pétrus, their soils containing not only loam but also a lot of sand and gravel. It is not the structure their wines lack so much as the sumptuous fullness that make Pétrus and its immediate neighbors so unusual. This phenomenon is even more noticeable in the wines of Pomerol's northern neighbor, the Lalande-de-Pomerol district. Although the mix of grape varieties is comparable with Pomerol here, and although the permitted maximum yields are the same, like the satellites of Saint-Émilion the wines manifest less density and eloquence than their better-known cousins. There are of course exceptions even here, with outstanding wineries whose wines in good years easily bear comparison with Pomerol and are excellent value for money.

Select Producers in Pomerol

Château Clinet****
Libourne-Pomerol
22 acres (9 ha); 45,000 bottles • Wines: Pomerol
Clinet is situated not far from Château Pétrus in the best part of Pomerol. With their rather higher Cabernet-Sauvignon ratio, the wines are inaccessible longer but also have greater aging ability than many of their neighbors.

Château La Conseillante****–*****
Libourne-Pomerol
30 acres (12 ha); 55,000 bottles • Wines: Pomerol
Although La Conseillante is directly beside the Saint-Émilion star Cheval-Blanc, its wines are clearly distinct for their higher Merlot content. Dense color, fruit in the nose and on the palate, dense extracts but also remarkable finesse are the characteristics of its quality.

Château La Croix de Gay***–****
Libourne-Pomerol
30 acres (12 ha); 72,000 bottles • Wines: Pomerol
An almost direct neighbor of Pétrus, but much quicker in the development of the wines. Lesser vintages generally turn out very well here.

Château l'Église-Clinet****–*****
Libourne-Pomerol
15 acres (6 ha); 12,000 bottles • Wines: Pomerol, La Petite Église
A small production at top prices but also with top qualities: its fullness and complexity are already evident when very young.

Château l'Évangile****–*****
Libourne-Pomerol
34.5 acres (14 ha); 60,000 bottles • Wines: Pomerol
The scent of violets and great structure distinguish the wines of this château, a neighbor of Conseillante and lying exactly between Pétrus and Cheval-Blanc. The 1990s wines were an excellent series.

Château Lafleur*****
Mouillac
11.1 acres (4.5 ha); 20,000 bottles • Wine: Pomerol
This small estate has, since 1998, risen to the top of the *appellation*. This is due to the particular *terroir*, which is ideally suited to the distribution of the grape varieties—half each of Merlot and Cabernet Sauvignon—and the most painstakingly delicate vinification.

Château La Fleur Pétrus***–****
Libourne-Pomerol
26 acres (10.5 ha); 42,000 bottles • Wines: Pomerol
The name betrays the location of the château in the Jean-Pierre Moueix empire. The wines are finer but also clearly less structured than those of its two neighbors.

Château Latour à Pomerol***–****
Libourne-Pomerol
20 acres (8 ha); 46,000 bottles • Wines: Pomerol
Another château of Jean-Pierre Moueix. The wines with their high Merlot content usually turn out very dense and powerful.

Château Pétrus****–*****
Libourne-Pomerol
28 acres (11.4 ha); 30,000 bottles • Wines: Pomerol
The apotheosis of Pomerol and Jean-Pierre Moueix's empire. Made almost exclusively from Merlot, Pétrus was long considered the most expensive single wine in the world. Despite the high Merlot proportion, the wines manifest enormous structure and aging potential.

Château Le Pin***–****
Libourne-Pomerol
5 acres (2 ha); 8,000 bottles • Wines: Pomerol
Le Pin was long considered an absolute insider tip and cult wine. Great volume, delightful charm and rarity were responsible for prices rising to astronomical heights, but quality is lagging behind.

Château Trotanoy****–*****
Libourne-Pomerol
18 acres (7.2 ha); 26,000 bottles • Wines: Pomerol
The second great name from the portfolio of the Moueix dynasty displays a lot of fruit and structure. Since 1997 Trotanoy has clearly been gaining in density and character and is now scarcely below the standard of Pétrus.

Vieux Château Certan****–*****
Libourne-Pomerol
33.5 acres (13.5 ha); 55,000 bottles • Wines: Pomerol
The wines of this neighbor of Pétrus are powerful and firm and display spicy aromas and finesse. The increased share of Cabernet gives it great potential for aging and its own personality.

TIPS FROM THE RIGHT BANK

Apart from Saint-Émilion and Pomerol, there are a number of other *appellations* along the right bank of the Dordogne and Gironde. Here too, just as in the two world-famous *appellations*, Merlot dominates in the blending of red wines, apart from a few rare exceptions. The wines owe their special charm, their delightful fruit, and their attractive roundedness—not to mention their commercial success—to Merlot.

In the Côtes de Castillon and Côtes de France, to the east of Saint-Émilion, wine-makers had already decided in the 1980s to apply stricter quality measures such as increased planting density of at least 5,000 vines per hectare and reduced yield. They soon succeeded in producing the first wines with markedly increased concentration and denser fruit. A new generation has now established itself , which has learned how to improve on their efforts, and is creating fascinatingly full-bodied and complex wines. The same also applies to the other "small" *appellations* on the right bank.

Fronsac and Canon-Fronsac were in high esteem in the 17th century, in the time of the Duc de Richelieu, when they were served at court in Versailles. In the picturesque area to the north-west of Libourne they are now building on their former fame. The two *appellations* together cover 2,790 acres (1,130 hectares) and consist of several ranges of hills with valleys, peaks and some direct slopes. *Terroirs* and soil vary corre-spondingly. Canon-Fronsac covers locations with a shell limestone base. However, the wines are linked by a common character, comprising both body and strength and also intensive berry aromas and truffle and spice notes.

Since Roman times—the Romans planted the first vines on the nearby slopes—Bourg-sur-Gironde has been an important port. When Aquitaine was under English rule, a lot of wine was shipped from this port. In this "little Switzerland on the Gironde," villages, farms and châteaux are mostly enthroned on hilltops, often giving a view of the ever-brown Gironde. In the 15 wine-growing communities, with just under 9,700 acres (3,900 hectares) of vines, the soils are mostly argillaceous limestone or clay sand and gravel. The underlying rock is hard limestone, which used to be quarried. In creating the *assemblages*, winemakers often fall back on Malbec, which gives the wine liquorice notes.

Wine-growing in the Blayais underwent a major boom in the 17th century, when simple whites were produced for Cognac. Left over from those times is a certain preference for whites (495 acres/200 hectares), often consisting solely of Sauvignon or blended with Sémillon. Red varieties are cultivated on 1,309 acres (5,300 hectares) and, due to the usually high proportion of Merlot, produce wines with plenty of charm and a particularly good price-to-performance ratio.

The best vineyards of Fronsac and Canon-Fronsac, where local conditions are ideal in the favorable, very mild local micro-climate, provide a magnificent view of the Dordogne.

SELECT PRODUCERS: CÔTES DE BOURG, CÔTES DE CASTILLON, CÔTES DE FRANCS, FRONSAC/CANON-FRONSAC, AND PREMIÈRES CÔTES DE BLAYE

CÔTES DE BOURG

CHÂTEAU BRÛLESECAILLE***
TAURIAC
69.2 acres (28 ha); 170,000 bottles • Wine: Côtes de Bourg
Very balanced red wines with well judged barrel maturation, ripe fruit, discreet spice and pleasantly full body.

CHÂTEAU FALFAS***–****
BAYON
54.4 acres (22 ha); 120,000 bottles • Wines: Côtes de Bourg, Tradition, → Le Chevalier de Falfas
This beautiful château dating from the 16th century has a biodynamically cultivated slope facing the Gironde. The top wine, Le Chevalier de Falfas, has a typical liquorice note, high concentration and firm tannins, and ages outstandingly.

CHÂTEAU ROC DE CAMBES****–*****
BOURG-SUR-GIRONDE
24.7 acres (10 ha); 45,000 bottles • Wine: Côtes de Bourg
On the first and most famous range of hills, right by the river, these over 30 year old vines provide grapes of enchanting fruit and concentration. François Mitjavile uses them to create sensational, full-bodied, deeply aromatic wines.

CHÂTEAU TAYAC***
BOURG-SUR-GIRONDE
74.1 acres (30 ha); 200,000 bottles • Wines: Côtes de Bourg: Tradition, → Cuvée Réserve, Prestige
For many years, this château with the most beautiful location in the *appellation* has been creating typical wines with good structure. After a few years of maturing in the bottle, they achieve a complex bouquet and convincing harmony on the palate.

CÔTES DE CASTILLON

CHÂTEAU D'AIGUILHE****
SAINT-PHILLIPPE D'AIGUILHE
103.8 acres (42 ha); 110,000 bottles • Wine: Côtes de Castillon
Since Stephan von Neipperg took charge of this estate, the wines have reached an unprecedented level of structure and body.

DOMAINE DE L'A****
SAINTE-COLOMBE
9.9 acres (4 ha); bottles not recorded • Wine: Côtes de Castillon
Stéphane de Derencourt advises estates such as Pavie-Macquin and others on biodynamic cultivation. He himself produces a deliciously fruity wine with a velvet texture and excellent profile.

CÔTES DE FRANCS

CHÂTEAU PUYGUERAUD****
SAINT-CIBARD
74.1 acres (30 ha); 200,000 bottles • Wine: Bordeaux Côtes de France
The Thienponts have been running this estate since 1938 and both it and they have been instrumental in making the *appellation* famous. The quality is excellent and reliable even in lesser vintages.

FRONSAC/CANON-FRONSAC

CHÂTEAU CASSAGEN HAUT-CANON**–***
SAINT-MICHEL-DE-FRONSAC
32.1 acres (13 ha); 70,000 bottles • Wines: Canon-Fronsac: Fronsac, Cuvée La Truffière

In the neighborhood of his truffle oaks, Jean-Jacques Dubois produces an impressive, truffely wine.

CHÂTEAU DALEM***–****
SAILLANS
37.1 acres (15 ha); 80,000 bottles • Wine: Fronsac
Known for the complexity and unusual spiciness of the mature wines, Dalem always displays a solid tannin structure. A good nine-tenths of the wine consists of Merlot.

CHÂTEAU MOULIN HAUT-LAROQUE****
SAILLANS
37.1 acres (15 ha); 60,000 bottles • Wine: Fronsac
Year after year, Jean-Noël Hervé demonstrates the standard that Fronsac wines can achieve. Thanks to optimum grape ripeness and masterly extraction, the wines develop impressive texture and the finest tannins.

CHÂTEAU DE LA RIVIÈRE***–****
LA RIVIÈRE
145.7 acres (59 ha); 300,000 bottles • Wines: Fronsac, Aria
In this impressive château with spectacular rock cellars and vineyards facing the Gironde, Xavier Péneau produces exceedingly aromatic wines with ripe tannins. Aria is his dense top *cru*.

CHÂTEAU VILLARS***–****
SAILLANS
74.1 acres (30 ha); 200,000 bottles • Wine: Fronsac
Thierry Gaudrie, a tireless ambassador for Fronsac and Canon-Fronsac, provides his wines with intensive fruit, fine spiciness, ripe tannins and a pleasant roundedness.

PREMIÈRES CÔTES DE BLAYE

CHÂTEAU CHARRON**–***
BERSON
61.8 acres (25 ha); 180,000 bottles • Wine: Premières Côtes de Blaye
Bernard Germain's wine empire originated here. Peyredoulle and Lacaussade-Saint-Martin are part of the same group in the *appellation*. The quality is always reliable and the Acacia is always one of the best whites on the right bank.

CHÂTEAU HAUT-BERTINERIE***–****
CUBNEZAIS
150.7 acres (61 ha); 400,000 bottles • Wine: Premières Côtes de Blaye
Vines trained in a lyre shape, which give improved grape ripeness, and maturing in new barrels form the foundation of the Bantegnies family's excellent white and red wines.

CHÂTEAU LES-JONQUEYRES****
SAINT-PAUL
37.1 acres (15 ha); 55,000 bottles • Wine: Premières Côtes de Blaye
Pascal and Isabelle Montaut were among the first to show how full of character the wines around Blaye could be. Dense and complex red wines.

CHÂTEAU PEYBONHOMME-LES-TOURS**–***
CARS
158.2 acres (64 ha); 420,000 bottles • Wine: Premières Côtes de Blaye
Jean-Luc Hubert has converted the estate to organic cultivation. He offers red wines which are always balanced and of solid quality. At Château de Grolet, in the Côtes de Bourg, he is working on ever more concentrated wines.

ENTRE-DEUX-MERS

Right of the Dordogne and left of the Garonne is the concentrated prestige of the Bordelais area. This is where the *grands crus* are grown, where you find the most famous château wines in the world. That does not mean that no wine is made between the two rivers. Quite the contrary. Called Entre-Deux-Mers (Between Two Seas), as the Garonne and Dordogne are circumscribed, it is a very productive wine landscape. Its intensively cultivated vineyards are punctuated by picturesque villages, superb châteaux and buildings of great historic importance. The region is hardly well known, however. At best, the French themselves appreciate Entre-Deux-Mers as a hearty, fresh white wine that goes well with seafood of all kinds. The reason for this is that most of the production of this wedge-shaped territory, that steadily widens as it gets further from Bordeaux, is not marketed under one of its own *appellations* but under the anonymous *appellations* Bordeaux or Bordeaux Supérieur. Around 40 percent of all Bordelais reds and as much as 70 percent of all Bordelais whites are bottled under these two labels. Many of these wines are processed not by the growers themselves but by cooperatives, and reach the market by the million under the labels of the great shippers. The lack of prestige of the actual cultivation areas of Entre-Deux-Mers—there are six of them in all, ranging from less than 247 acres (100 ha) under vines to over 6,180 acres (2,500 ha)—also suffer from the fact that qualitatively the greater part of their wines hardly stand out from the generic white and red Bordeaux, and many of the popular brand wines seem to be technically better made and cleaner.

SIX APPELLATIONS IN SEARCH OF AN IDENTITY

The largest of these areas is the *appellation* of the whole region, Entre-Deux-Mers. Although Merlot and both the Cabernets are cultivated in the area that occupies the larger part of the land between the rivers, the *appellation* applies only to whites made predominantly of Sémillon, Sauvignon Blanc, and Muscadelle, though the rare Merlot Blanc, Colombard, Mauzac, and Ugni Blanc are also used. Despite the not overhigh standard that predominates here, it is quite astonishing what some of the estates from Grézillac, Sadirac, Moulon or Créon can turn out in red and white qualities, particularly if you

In the 19th century, the vineyards of Fronsac east of the town of Libourne produced wines that rated more highly than those of Pomerol.

bear the prices of their wines in mind, which can be half or a third those of the better-known *appellations* of the Médoc and Libournais.

The second largest A.C. district in the area is called Premières Côtes de Bordeaux. It is over 37 miles (60 km) long, no more than 3 miles (5 km) wide and stretches like a frontier wall of Entre-Deux-Mers from the confluence of the Garonne with the Dordogne in a southeasterly direction.

In the Middle Ages, this was one of the best-known winemaking areas of the Bordelais region overall, and the wines had almost as good a reputation as Graves on the opposite bank of the Garonne. Embedded in the Premières Côtes, in the northern part of which mainly reds and in the south sugar-residue whites are produced, are the three sweet-wine districts of Loupiac, Cadillac, and Sainte-Croix.

On the southeastern edge of Premières Côtes are two smaller *appellations* called Côtes de Bordeaux Saint-Macaire—lying directly beside the Garonne—and Premières Côtes Haut-Benauge. Saint-Macaire is an *appellation* without any market significance whatsoever, which can only be used for sweet whites and which, apart from its sugar residues, scarcely manifests any organoleptic features. The greatest part of the production of this area is therefore sold as

Bordeaux or Bordeaux Supérieur, in order to have any chance at all of selling.

The same applies to Haut-Benauge, and the question naturally arises why the legislators provided two separate designations. If the whites of the district were sold as Entre-Deux-Mers and the reds as Premières Côtes de Bordeaux, this would be of more use to both producers and consumers.

The two smaller *appellations* at each end of Entre-Deux-Mers would similarly win no prizes in the familiarity stakes. One is Graves de Vayre in the extreme northwest, directly opposite Libourne, whose 1,240 acres (500 ha) of sandy and gravelly soils produce light reds predominantly from Merlot. Although these *appella-tions* are expressly for red wines, the greater part of the wine is sold as Bordeaux A.C. Somewhat more self-assured is Sainte-Foy-Bordeaux in the extreme east of the Bordelais region, on the border of the Lot-et-Garonne department and only 12 miles (20 km) from Bergerac, where red wines and sweet whites are bottled under the town's own *appellation*. In sum, it must be said that these small districts scarcely justify their labels.

Select Producers in Entre-Deux-Mers & other Bordeaux Appellations

Château Bonnet**‒****
Branne-Grézillac
667 acres (270 ha); 1,500,000 bottles • Wines: Bordeaux: include Réserve, rosé; Entre-Deux-Mers: Château Guibon Blanc, Rouge, Château Grossombre Rosé, Rouge
The Lurton family owns *crus* all over the Bordelais area with a total production of 4.5 million bottles. The heart of the empire in Entre-deux-Mers is not only a tourist sight of significance for the history of wine but produces a Réserve in barrels that has often beaten better-known *appellations* in blind tastings and is unsurpassed as value for money. The Lurtons also own Couhins-Lurton and Cruzeau in Pessac-Léognan.

Château de Chelivette***‒****
Sainte-Eulalie
24.5 acres (10 ha); 16,000 bottles • Wines: Premières Côtes de Bordeaux, Cuvée Elisabeth, Bordeaux Supérieur, Cru de Manoir
Juicy wines with clear signs of aging in the barrel. Chelivette has stepped up the quality in recent years and has modernized his winemaking.

Château Mongiron**‒****
Nérigean
12.3 acres (5 ha); 36,000 bottles • Wines: Bordeaux and Bordeaux Supérieure
The young Jean-Michel Quéron offers three clearly differentiated *cuvées*. The prize example is the outstandingly good La Fleur Mongiron.

Château De Reignac***
Saint-Loubès
190 acres (77 ha); 400,000 bottles • Wines: Bordeaux: Supérieur, Prestige
The château illustrates the fact that with adequate ambition very convincing red wines can be created even in sites with lesser reputations.

Château Reynon***‒****
Beguey
71 acres (29 ha); 300,000 bottles • Wines: Cadillac, Premières Côtes de Bordeaux, Bordeaux Sec Vieilles Vignes
Reynon is the best estate owned by professor of enology Denis Dubourdieu, and is where he makes white

Bordeaux, red Premières Côtes and one of the rare, interesting Cadillacs. He also owns Clos Floridène and Château Cantegril on the opposite bank of the Garonne.

Château Thieuley**‒****
Créon
198 acres (80 ha); 700,000 bottles • Wines: Bordeaux, Premières Côtes de Bordeaux, Cadillac Liquoreux, →Bordeaux Supérieur Francis Courselle
Such a range of products is rare in the Bordelais area. The top product is the Bordeaux Supérieur Cuvée Francis Courselle, which is a successful synthesis of fruit and the use of wood.

Château Tour de Mirambeau**‒****
Naujan-et-Postiac
222.4 acres (90 ha); 650,000 bottles • Wines: Bordeaux, Bordeaux Supérieure, Entre-Deux-Mers
Jean-Louis Despagne, now actively supported by his son Thibault, shows how you can produce modern and excellent whites and reds in the Entre-Deux-Mers region if you make use of your perfectionist tendencies in the vineyards and winery. At present he is experimenting with 10,000 vines per hectare in order to achieve the very best quality. Rauzan Despagne and Bel Air Perpoucher, another 222 acres (90 hectares), also belong to the same family.

Château Trocard**‒***
Les-Artigues-de-Lussac
222 acres (90 ha); 650,000 bottles • Wines: Bordeaux Supérieur Monrepos, Bordeaux Rosé
Good Merlot wines that are sold at astonishingly low prices under the Bordeaux Supérieur label. Jean-Louis Trocard owns a whole series of other estates in the Libournais, of which Saint-Émilion Grand Cru Château Franc La Rose and Pomerol Clos de la Vieille Église have the best reputation.

Domaine de Courteillac***
Ruch
42 acres (27 ha); 150,000 bottles • Wines: Bordeaux, Bordeaux Supérieur, Antholien
Interesting whites and reds are the products of this estate, which has proved to be very reliable.

THE SOUTHWEST: IN THE SHADOW OF MIGHTY BORDEAUX

To define southwest France precisely in wine-growing terms is a matter that requires instinctive feeling. Geographically, after all, Bordeaux also belongs to the Southwest, but there they do not want to be too closely associated with the "poor neighbor," and insist on their status as an independent wine region. The winegrowers of Bergerac or Cahors do just the same, being unwilling to have their *appellations* identified with the Southwest. But such local sensibilities can be overlooked, because geography provides a ready orientation.

HISTORIC TRADING CENTER

In viticultural terms, the *Sud-Ouest* is a wine region like Loire, Bordeaux, or Rhone. Historically there is much more to it: it comprises the whole territory upriver from Bordeaux to the edge of the Pyrenees and the distant Massif Central. Earlier, the whole region whose wines had to be transported on the Garonne or Dordogne to the sea, to be shipped to ports in England or Holland, was known as the *Haut-Pays*, an expression that now refers only to the northern hinterland of Agen and Toulouse around Gaillac and Cahors.

Winemaking started much earlier in the Haut-Pays than along the Gironde, but suffered terrible setbacks, first when the port of La Rochelle was closed to ships from northern

Opposite
The Dordogne region with its rivers, villages, and vineyards is one of the most romantic landscapes of France.

Below
Bergerac could never hold its own against Bordeaux as a trading center, but its wine association, based in the historic town center, is providing fresh impulses.

Europe, and subsequently as the Bordelais region began to develop its own wines, boosted by numerous tax and excise privileges from the English crown.

Bordeaux had functioned as the main trading center for the wines of the region ever since Roman times. Unfortunately, in the course of time the harbor proved to be more of an obstacle for the hinterland than a gateway to the world. Time and again the burghers of the city managed to ship their own wines in their entirety before the other regions had a look in. By the time its turn finally arrived in the spring, many an Haut-Pays wine had already turned to vinegar.

UP AND DOWN IN HISTORY

Nonetheless, the winegrowers of Bergerac or Cahors, Gascony, and Gaillac managed again and again to find a market for their products. In the Middle Ages, the monasteries had done much to promote wine growing in the area. In the 17th century, the Dutch began to take an interest in the *crus*. What they chiefly wanted was thin brandywines or intense sweet wines. Bergerac decided to go for it, thus creating the basis for Monbazillac, which developed a great reputation in the 18th century.

Though the trade restrictions that Bordeaux set up like a fortified wall around itself have long gone, the region around the Gironde established such supremacy in the markets of the world that all other wine-growing areas of the hinterland were bound to get a raw deal. In the 1940s, a handful of pioneers sought to plant out new areas and construct a modest image, such as for example the Vignerons de Buzet. But only in the last decade or two has the region—especially individual growers in the areas nearer Bordeaux—begun not just to catch up but also to produce some outstanding *crus* that have caught the attention of wine lovers everywhere. For the latter, the southwest of France has, meantime, become a treasure trove of good-quality wines of high standard.

ONE BECOMES FIVE

The climate and grape varieties in the Southwest have features in common with the Bordelais region. As in Gironde, an Atlantic climate prevails over a large part of the Haut-Pays, which is subjugated only by continental influences in the Massif Central. As in the Bordelais region, the range of grape varieties is dominated by the Cabernets, Merlot, Sémillon, and Sauvignon Blanc, though in many areas interesting native varieties developed only in recent times must be added to these.

In general, five sub-regions are distinguished in the Southwest, which in turn comprise a series of areas of cultivation and *appellations*. Closest to Bordeaux is the Bordure Aquitaine or fringe region of Aquitaine, which covers the north and south banks of the Garonne from just behind Langon up to Agen. Marmande is the center of a region directly adjacent to Graves and the beef-producing region Bazadais. Here mainly fruity whites and full-bodied reds are produced. North of that are the Côtes du Duras, which border Entre-deux-Mers in the west and once specialized in mellow white wines. These days, the output is overwhelmingly of dry Sauvignon Blanc and red wine from Bordeaux varieties. Finally there is Buzet, occupying the left bank of the Garonne between Agen and

Marmande, producing principally powerful red wines from Cabernet and Merlot.

Only a few miles further from Bordeaux and contiguous with the Bordure Aquitaine in the north is the Bergeracois, which includes *appellations* such as Monbazillac and Pécharmant. The Bergerac *appellation* proper, growing white wines very similar to Bordeaux and beginning directly beyond the easternmost cultivation area of the Gironde, Sainte-Foy, has a counterpart called Côtes-de-Bergerac, which produces sweet whites as well. A further seven districts are included in this part of the Southwest: Pécharmant with outstanding reds, Montravel (also approved as a red wine since the 2001 vintage) and Haut-Montravel with their aromatic whites, and the sweet white specialists of Monbazillac, Rosette, Saussignac, and Côtes de Montravel.

FROM GASCONY TO THE MASSIF CENTRAL

The southern part of the region between the Landes and Gascony is dominated by the wines of the Pyrenees. Among these are Madiran, which has risen to become a new star in the French wine firmament, and which owes its

Bergerac
Côtes de Montravel
Haut-Montravel
Montravel
Rosette
Pécharmant
Saussignac
Monbazillac
Côtes de Duras
Côtes du Marmandais
Cahors
Entraygues and du Fel wines
Estaing wines
Marcillac
Côtes de Millau
Buzet
Côtes du Brulhois
Lavilledieu wines
Côtes du Frontonnais
Gaillac
Tursan
Côtes de Saint-Mont
Madiran, Pacherenc du Vic-Bilh
Béarn
Jurançon
Irouléguy
Wine-growing areas in neighboring regions

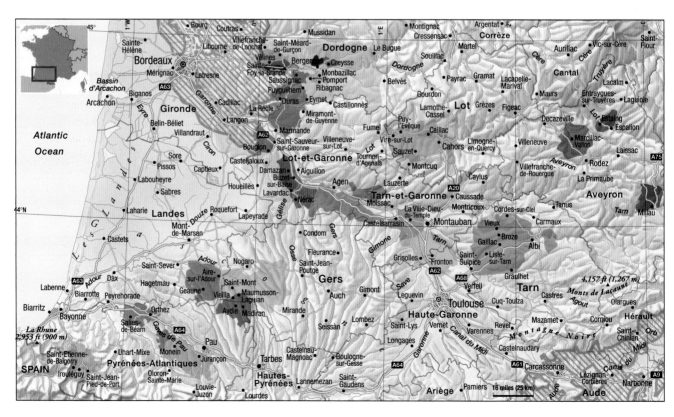

character to the Tannat variety. Jurançon, which flourishes southwest of Pau, is considered the best quality wine of the Southwest, both sweet and dry. Irouléguy, in the Basque country, provides wines of attractive quality, while the small Béarn region is still searching for its identity.

Further to the north and east lie the districts of Madiran and Côtes-de-Saint-Mont, in which strong reds are produced from the native Tannat grape. Finally, Tursan and Pacherenc du Vic-Bilh are dedicated to wines from white grapes, with the latter district being better known for sweet versions.

North and northwest of the industrial and university city of Toulouse is the Haut-Pays proper—the region of Cahors, Gaillac and neighboring *appellations*. Cahors specializes mainly in red wines made from Malbec, whereas Gaillac, on the boundary between Atlantic and Mediterranean-influenced viticulture, offers a broad range of different types of wine.

A small group of V.D.Q.S. cultivation areas are to be found even in the distant Massif Central. They constitute an eastern boundary of the Southwest toward Languedoc and the Rhône Valley. The best-known wine of the Aveyron, first made in the 10th century by monks from the famous abbey of Conques north of Rodez, is Marcillac, an *appellation* first established in 1990. A good 334 acres (135 ha) in a climatically sheltered valley is turned over to the earthy Fer Servadou, here called Mansoi, which furnishes a unique red wine scented with aromas of raspberries and other fruits that is usually drunk very young.

The valley of the Lot north of here is home to the *appellations* Entraygues and Le Fel, with the vines crowded into narrow terraces of around 49.5 acres (20 ha) each. White Entraygues is made from Chenin Blanc grown on loamy silica and granite, while red Le Fel comes from Fer Servadou and the Cabernets grown on schist.

A little further up the Lot Valley is the tiny V.D.Q.S. label of Estaing, established in 1965 with a mere 37 acres (15 ha) of vineyard on schist and argillaceous limestone soils. Chenin and a little Mauzac go into the white wine, while Gamay, Fer, and the Cabernets into the fruity rosés and reds.

Somewhat further east, around the town of Millau, about 136 acres (55 ha) of the Côtes de Millau *appellation* are scattered along the Tarn. Here too Chenin and Mauzac turn out fresh, simple white wines, while the rosés and reds, both for young drinking, are made of Gamay, Syrah, and Cabernet Sauvignon.

Petit and Gros Manseng are the two grape varieties that go into Jurançon south of Pau. The vine stocks are grown to a height of over six feet (2 m), and propped up very accurately by the growers.

Jurançon is a balanced sweet wine with a delicate acidity. The lips of the newly born infant who became King Henry IV were symbolically wetted with it. A delightful dry version also exists.

HISTORIC WINES AND CHANGING TIMES

With over 32,100 acres (13,000 ha) planted to vines in a total of 93 parishes around the town of Bergerac, the Bergerac *appellation* is the largest and possibly the best-known *appellation* in the direct vicinity of the Bordelais region. Although whites, reds, and sweet wines are produced, the name is often associated just with red wines—a real paradox, bearing in mind that the town itself is ringed by a series of markedly sweet-wine *appellations*.

Vines have been grown here since Roman times, and in the Middle Ages this was one of the monasteries' chief fields of activity. With their rich color and high alcohol content, the wines long served to improve clarets from Bordeaux. However, when the Dutch supplanted the English as traders in this region, they began to shift development more toward sweet wines, for which there was strong demand in their homeland. The reds, which are now bottled as Bergerac A.C., are so similar to generic Bordeaux A.C. they can easily be confused. However, under the Côtes de Bergerac label stronger wines are turned out with more tannin emphasis, also some mellow (*moelleux*) white wines.

The best reds come from the Pécharmant *appellation* in the northeastern corner of the Bergerac area. The *grand cru* of the Dordogne wines covers about 741 acres (300 ha) of sloping south-facing sites, whose gravel, clay, and limestone soils are rich in iron, which gives the wines their firm structure. The top wines of this area,

like the best Côtes de Bergerac, are aged in the barrel and require a degree of maturing in the bottle before their pronounced tannins become soft and the bouquet becomes complex and elegant.

Sweet Wines with Fruit and Elegance

Unlike the eastern part of the Bergeracois, where red wines dominate the scene, the three *appellations* of Montravel apply only to wines from white grapes. Under the plain Montravel designation, which covers the southern half of this district, fruity, fresh wines are made principally from Sauvignon grapes. On the other hand, Côtes de Montravel, the northern half, produces mellow wines in which Sémillon plays an important part. Haut-Montravel, the smallest and most easterly of Montravel's subdivisions—where the chalky soil helps the Sémillon to higher concentrations, but the wines always appear remarkably balanced because of the ever present acidity—gets the third independent *appellation*.

The sweet wines, which were already famous in the heyday of the Dutch, deserve mention as a specialty of the region. While the small Rosette district to the northwest of the town of Bergerac is almost totally forgotten, Monbazillac and Saussignac enjoy a certain celebrity. After a long crisis, Monbazillac has for some time been at pains to re-establish its former renown. Sémillon is the lead grape in this, and the vineyards profit from the special climatic conditions at the confluence of two rivers, the Gardonette and the Dordogne. However, botrytization is less common here than in the Sauternes district, and the wines are consequently somewhat lighter but perhaps more elegant.

Left
The regular topping up of the barrel—*ouillage* in French—stops the wines oxidizing.

Right
Only conscientious care of vines wards off diseases.

Opposite
The Ramonteu family offers a tasting of its excellent Jurançon at the Domaine Cauhape.

The Bordure Aquitaine

The western parts of the Bordure Aquitaine are even closer to the Bordelais region than are the Bergeracois. To be more precise, the Côtes du Marmande are simply a continuation of Graves in the south and Entre-deux-Mers in the north. Its 4,450 or so acres (1,800 ha) are given over to producing full-bodied, balanced red wines and rosés, with the palette of grape varieties including not only the usual Bordeaux crop but also Fer, Gamay, Syrah, Malbec, and the native Abouriou. Only a small area is planted to white-wine varieties corresponding to those of Graves.

However, Buzet, an *appellation* established in 1973, lies somewhat further up the left bank of the Garonne, and in the south spills over into the production area of Armagnac brandy. Its loamy, partly gravelly soils produce mostly red wines. These are made mainly from the Bordelais varieties, with Merlot playing a predominant role. Great efforts have been made in recent years by the Vignerons du Buzet cooperative, which vinifies a wide range of different *cuvées* and ages them in barrels.

The last zone of cultivation in this area is squeezed between the Côtes du Marmandais in the south and Bergerac in the north. Like the Marmandais, it borders the Gironde in the west, and here too Bordelais varieties are grown. In the past, Sémillon used to dominate, from which mainly mellow wines were made. Nowadays production has largely gone over to producing white wines from the more aromatic Sauvignon. The red wines from the two Cabernets, Merlot and some Malbec—here called Cot—are often aged separately per variety, and they range from the light, uncomplicated bistro wines to the stronger, tannin-rich crus aged in the barrel.

In the Shadow of the Pyrenees

acreage had shrunk to 124 (50 ha), even though Madiran had been recognized as an *appellation* only two years previously. However, the low point prompted rethinking. New *domaines* were established, whose wines revealed good qualities. Even so, Madiran was on the verge of losing its soul. The state viticultural office I.N.A.O. set a limit of only 40–60 percent on the prescribed proportion of the native, tannin-rich Tannat grape variety and recommended the addition of the more popular Cabernets or Fer Servadou to the wines.

This was the last straw for the winegrowers. Young Alain Brumont, a grower's son who had taken over the rundown Château Montus, spearheaded the revolution, stocking the excellent gravelly soils of the estate with the now unfavored Tannat. Adopting greatly limited yields, three weeks of mash fermentation, long aging in new barrels and frequent racking of the wines in the cellar, he succeeded in taming the Tannat. When he first aged the varieties separately in 1985, a new star appeared in the wine firmament. The *prestige-cuvée* at Montus beat even the best-known Bordeaux in blind tastings, and opened the market to Madiran wines.

The countryside between the Garonne and the Pyrenees is probably better known for Armagnac, or for its culinary specialties than for its wines, but the latter do have something to offer. A range of *appellations* stretch from Agen in the northeast to Pau in the southwest that are among the best in the Southwest.

The first among equals is the Madiran cultivation area. Vines here date back to Roman times. From the 12th century, when Gascony belonged to the English crown, it quickly prospered, and the wines were shipped via the Adour and Bayonne to northern Europe.

In the 19th century, the area was still planted to vines on 3,460 acres (1,400 ha). By 1950, the

The vineyards of the Domaine Brana near Saint-Jean-Pied-de-Ports—one of the most spectacular sites in the Irouléguy *appellation*.

Charles Hours at Clos Uroulat, and Henri Ramonteu—two musketeers of Jurançon.

New Methods for Aging

Since then, numerous growers have followed his example. However, not everyone was satisfied with the traditional methods of aging difficult varieties. Among those seeking a new approach was Patrick Ducourneau, inventor of MICRO-OXYGENATION. In this, the wines are given a carefully judged dose of oxygen even before malolactic acid conversion, using a

ceramic probe in the tank. This rounds off the tannins more quickly and makes the wine drinkable at an earlier stage. Critics see it as a manipulation of the wine that diminishes its aging potential. However, this has had no effect on the success of the method, which is used today in thousands of wineries in countries all over the world.

The dynamism that had seized the Madiran area was bound to awaken the sleeping beauty of the area—the Pacherenc du Vic-Bilh. This is made from a range of grape varieties that include Manseng, Courbu, Sauvignon, and Sémillon as well as the native Arrufiac. The dry whites are unusually aromatic, but the grapes for the best products—golden yellow, dense sweet whites which need not stand in awe even of Jurançons and Sauternes—are harvested between October and the New Year.

A neighbor of Madiran is the red or white Côtes de Saint-Mont, made of regional varieties of grape. It is not only the spicy, often more lightly structured reds, but above all the highly aromatic whites that display interesting qualities. Almost the entire output is marketed by a single high-quality cooperative. Much less well known is a wine that grows not far from here, the Tursan, which also exists in white and red versions.

In the hilly region south of Mont-de-Marsan, the hardy Baroque variety has been cultivated ever since the phylloxera disaster, a white-wine variety that produces rustic, dry, strongly alcoholic wines. With Manseng and Sauvignon, these are acquiring much more freshness and complexity than before, and enjoy even greater popularity.

BÉARNAIS: NOT JUST A SAUCE

Apart from the world-famous *béarnaise* sauce, the hills between Gascony and the Pyrenean massif also have excellent wines to offer. Béarn itself has lent its name to an *appellation* on whose 395 acres (160 ha) of vines—90 percent of them lie on the secluded slopes of Bellocq parish—both strong rosés and red wines are made from Tannat and marketed under the Béarn label, like the lighter Cabernet Franc, which is bottled under the double label of Béarn-Bellocq. However, the only really important wine in Béarn is, of course, Jurançon.

In the undulating hills of the Béarnais area, vines are planted at heights of up to 1,000–1,300 feet (300–400 m) exclusively on south-facing slopes. Even though it can be cold and rainy here in spring, the area enjoys long, sunny autumns. This is when a warmer

southerly wind blows over the Pyrenees, which allows growers to wait to the end of November, sometimes even into December, before harvesting. Only at this point does the showy Petit Manseng variety display its true grandeur. The small, airily dangling grapes get darker, their skins begin to wrinkle and the berries dry out. Under the influence of hot days and cool night, the next stage is the *passerillage*, a kind of exaggerated over-ripeness.

The must of these grapes makes great sweet wines, which have precisely the right amount of fine, fresh acidity to give them spirit and balance. Of course, this quality is obtained only at the price of very low yields—yields that in bad times would not give growers a living. For this reason, they prefer to plant the plumper sibling of the Manseng, the Gros Manseng, and to a lesser extent Courbu as well. However, since neither of these reaches full maturity in lesser years, the idea arose of also making a dry Jurançon, which in 1975 was allowed a separate *appellation*, Jurançon *sec*.

The last French wine-growing area in the direction of the mountains and Spain is the other side of Pau, close to the peaks of the Basque country. This is the home of Irouléguy, planted to vines on a little over 494 acres (200 ha) on the slopes of the Tize and Arradoy valleys, where elegant reds, scented rosés, and very interesting whites are made.

Alain Brumont's massive new tower house at Château Bouscassé has become a symbol for the new Madiran. Thanks to a group of committed growers and winemakers, this tannin-rich red wine once again enjoys a high reputation.

Select Producers in the Southwest

Bergerac

Château Bélingard**–****
Sigoulès

217 acres (88 ha); 500,000 bottles • Wines: Bergerac Sec, Bergerac Rouge, Côtes de Bergerac, → Côtes de Bergerac Prestige Sélection parcellaire, → Monbazillac; Cuvée Blanche de Bosredon

Laurent de Bosredon has made his name with Monbazillac Blanche de Bosredon. The estate's other premium wines also bear his grandmother's name. The dry whites and the red wines have now gained in concentration and profile.

Château Laulerie***–****
Domaine de Gouyat
Saint-Méard-de-Gurçon

103.8 acres (42 ha); 350,000 bottles • Wines include: Bergerac Sec, → Montravel, Bergerac Rouge, → La Cuvée, Côtes de Bergerac

Each half stocked with either red or white varieties, Serge Dubard's double estate provides excellent quality in both types. The red La Cuvée, offered only after six years of maturing, is excellent and individual.

Château Panisseau**–****
Thénac

173 acres (70 ha); 300,000 bottles • Wines include: Bergerac Sec, Tradition, Nymphéa, → Divin; Bergerac rouge; Côtes de Bergerac: Tradition, → Baccarat, Moelleux

Since Daniel and Bernadette Evrad took over this historic estate with its handsome residential 12th-century castle in 1999, Panisseau has been undergoing a renaissance. The Belgian couple have drastically reduced the yields and are employing the best in wine-making technology.

Château Tirecul la Gravière****–*****
Monbazillac

22.7 acres (9.2 ha); 17,000 bottles • Wines: Monbazillac and → Cuvée Madame, → Vin de Pays de Périgord Blanc Sec

Here on the famous Côte Nord of Monbazillac, Bruno Bilanchini selects the grapes for his famous sweet wines in several sessions. His traditional blend—50% Muscadelle, 45% Sémillion and 5% Sauvignon—adds to the wines' depth and typical character. The Cuvée Madame can hold its own among the world's greatest *liquoreux*.

Château Tour des Gendres****–*****
Ribagnac

106 acres (43 ha); 280,000 bottles • Wines include: Bergerac Sec: → Moulin des Dames, → Anthologia, Cuvée des Conti; Bergerac Rouge: Classique, Moulin des Dames, → Anthologia; → Côtes de Bergerac La Gloire de mon Père

Luc de Conti has shown the wine world that Bergerac has great *terroirs* which give the wines extra ordinary qualities. This is based on conscientious, nature-based work in the vineyard and a great winemaking talent.

Vignobles des Verdots**–****
Conne de Labarde

81.5 acres (33 ha); 170,000 bottles • Wines: Bergerac Sec: Clos de Verdots, → Les Tours de Verdots, → Le Vin; Côtes de Bergerac: Clos de Verdots, Les Tours de Verdots, → Les Verdots selon David Fourtout, Monbazillac

A fourth-generation wine-maker, David Fourtout has caught the bug for making great wines. All his wines are excellent, but Les Verdots and the white Le Vin are absolute top quality.

Buzet

Les Vignerons du Buzet**–***
Buzet-sur-Baïse

4,917.4 acres (1,990 ha); 13,000,000 bottles • Wines include: Buzet Blanc, Rosé, Rouge; Baron d'Ardeuil, → Grand Réserve, Cuvée Jean-Marie Hébrard, Château de Gueyze

Decades ago, this cooperative was already among the pioneers in this region. Even today, its wines have no true rivals.

Côtes du Marmandais

Cave Cocumont**–***
Cocumont

2,720 acres (1,100 ha); 1,000,000 bottles • Wines: Côtes du Marmandais Blanc, Rosé, Rouge; Tradition, → Prioret, Grains de Bonheur, → Dignité Prieur, La Bastide

The cooperative stands out for its red wines, with the top *cuvées* being clearly aged in the wood. In recent years, the quality of the various wines has stabilized at a high level.

Domaine Elian da Ros****
Cocumont

39.5 acres (16 ha); 45,000 bottles • Wines include: Côtes du Marmandais: → Chante Coucou, → Clos Bacqueys, → Vignoble d'Elian

After years working for Zind-Humbrecht in Alsace, Elian da Ros took over the family estate and immediately began to demonstrate what impressive wines the Marmandais can offer if vineyard and winery are tended with passion and knowledge. Unusually full, fruity reds with splendid tannins, dense texture and great length.

Côtes de Saint-Mont

Plaimont**–****
Saint-Mont

6,180 acres (2,500 ha); 25,000,000 bottles • Wines: Côtes de Saint-Mont Blanc, Rouge: Château de Sabazan, → Château Saint-Gô, → Le Faite; Madiran: → Château Viella Village, Arte Benedicte, Plénitude; Pacherenc du Vic-Bilh: Collection, → de la Saint-Sylvestre; Vins de Pays des Côtes de Gascogne: Colombelle, Prestige de Gascogne

André Dubosc, the head of Producteurs Plaimont, created the Côtes de Saint-Mont *appellation* from nothing in the 1970s. The quality of his wines, for which he prefers to use native varieties, has reached a high standard and has gained international success together with the aromatic fresh whites from Colombard and other varieties.

Irouléguy

Domaine Brana***–****
Saint-Jean-Pied-de-Port

96 acres (39 ha); 150,000 bottles • Wines: Irouléguy Blanc, Rose, Harri Gorri → rouge; Cuvée

Jean Brana uses biodynamic cultivation on the spectacular hill terraces created by his father Étienne, the great pioneer of this *appellation*. His wines are astonishingly well-balanced. His sister Martine distills one of the best *eau de vie de Poire Williams*.

Domaine Etxegaraya***–****
Saint-Étienne-de-Bagorry

18.5 acres (7.5 ha); 35,000 bottles • Wines: Irouléguy Rosé, Rouge, → Cuvée Lehengoa

Joseph and Marianne Hillau stock half their vineyards with Tannat and the rest supplies two varieties of Cabernet. Their top *cuvée*, from hundred-year-old vines, displays an excellent harmony between fruit, tannin and velvety texture.

Les Vignernons du Pays de Basque***–****
Saint-Étienne-de-Bagorry
321.2 acres (130 ha); 700,000 bottles • Wines include: Irouléguy Blanc; Xuri d'Ansa; → Andarena, → Mendia; Irouléguy Rosé: → Elorri; Irouléguy rouge: Les Terrasses de l'Arradoy, → Domaine de Mignaberry, → Gorri d'Ansa
Michel Bergouignan has made this small cooperative one of the most dynamic in the Southwest. Using the most modern winemaking technology, the quality achieved is even better than before.

Jurançon
Clos Lapeyre****
La Chappelle de Rousse
19.8 acres (8 ha); 55,000 bottles • Wines: Jurançon Sec, Jurançon and → Sélection, → Vent Balaguer
Bernard Larrieu cultivates what is probably the most beautiful vineyard in Jurançon; a magical amphitheater of vine terraces. It provides him with unusually aromatic wines, which he is able to give additional variety and finesse by the carefully judged use of *barriques*.

Clos Uroulat****
Monein
18.5 acres (7.5 ha); 35,000 • Wines: Jurançon Sec Cuvée Marie, → Jurançon
Charles Hours is the soul of Jurançon. Now assisted by his daughter Marie, he produces only two wines, one dry and one sweet. Year after year, both are among the best and most balanced in the *appellation*.

Domaine Bru-Baché***–****
Monein
19.5 acres (8 ha); 40,000 bottles • Wines: Jurançon Sec, Casterrasses, → L'Éminence, Quintessence
Claude Loustalot has now stepped completely into the shoes of his legendary uncle Georges Bru-Baché, and the sweet wines, mainly produced from Petit Masteng, are once again of a high standard.

Domaine Cauhapé****–*****
Monein
99 acres (40 ha); 200,000 bottles • Wines include: Jurançon Sec: Sève d'Automne, → Noblesse du Petit Manseng; Jurançon: Symphonie de Novembre, Noblesse du Temps, Quintessence du Petit Manseng, Folie du Janvier
Henri Ramonteu was the first in the Southwest to go only as far as Nature allows. His sweet Jurançons are masterpieces of variety and an ever-changing interplay of texture, residual sugar and the classiest acidity. The dry whites are extremely aromatic and refined.

Madiran
Alain Brumont***–*****
Maumusson-Laguian
450 acres (182 ha); 2,000,000 bottles • Wines: Madiran: Meinjarre, Torus, Château Montus, → Château Montus Prestige, Château Bouscassé, → Château Bouscassée Vieilles Vignes, → La Pacherenc du Vic-Bilh Sec Tyre; and Doux: → Vendemiaire, Brumaire, Frimaire
The founder of modern Madiran has constructed a gem of a winery and cellar at Montus, where everything is done by the very latest methods. Brumont administers his wine-growing empire from Bouscassé. As far as the quality of the wines—which age exceedingly well—is concerned, Montus and Bouscassé balance each other.

Chapelle Lenclos***
Maumusson-Laguian
44.5 acres (18 ha); 130,000 bottles • Wines: Madiran: Domaine Mouréou, → Chapelle Lenclos; Pacherenc du Vic-Bilh

Patrick Ducourneau is the inventor of micro-oxygenation, which he first used on his own two red wines. The spread of his method, which has gained world-wide recognition, unfortunately means that he has not been able to devote as much attention to his vineyards. The more recent vintages therefore fall short of the magnificent heights of those of 1989 and 1990.

Château d'Aydie****
Aydie
136 acres (55 ha); some bought-in grapes; 600,000 bottles • Wines include: Madiran: → Château d'Aydie, Odé d'Aydie; Pacherenc du Vic-Bilh: → Château d'Aydie, sec Cuvée Frédéric Laplace; → Vin de Liqueur Maydie Tannat Vintage
For years the Laplace family has contributed to the fame of Madiran. Their reds contain a high proportion of Tannat: 95% for the Château, which has a little Cabernet Sauvignon added. In recent years the wines have acquired a denser texture and ripe tannins. Micro-oxygenation is also used here. Maydie is the original delicious treat which shows the ripe fruit of Tannat to advantage.

Château Laffitte-Teston***–****
Maumusson-Laguian
101 acres (41 ha); 180,000 bottles • Wines: Madiran: Joris Laffitte, Tradition, → Vieilles Vignes; Pacherenc du Vic-Bilh Doux Rêve d'Automne sowie sec, → Cuvée Ericka
Jean-Marc Laffitte is one of the most talented growers of Madiran. In his modern, beautifully designed cellar he produces an excellent *sélection* from old vines such as a dry Pacherenc called Ericka with a lot of body, lemony aromas and a fine acidity.

Château de Viella***–****
Viella
57 acres (23 ha); 150,000 bottles • Wines: Madiran: Tradition, → Prestige; → Pacherenc du Vic-Bilh
Alain Bortulucci, a wine-maker with ancestors from Friuli, knows how to exploit the outstanding *terroir* of his hillside locations to best advantage. His reds are ranked among the best in the *appellation*, and his Moelluex is equal to them in all respects.

Domaine Berthoumieu***–****
Viella
64 acres (26 ha); 160,000 bottles • Wines: Madiran: Tradition, → Charles de Batz; Pacherenc du Vic-Bilh Sec and Doux
Didier Barré is the sixth generation to run this family estate. Besides the good classic Madiran with a somewhat higher than usual share of Cabernet, he produces an excellent Cuvée Charles de Batz from his oldest Tannat vines.

Domaine Labranche-Laffont***–****
Maumusson
47 acres (19 ha); 120,000 bottles • Wines: Madiran: Tradition, 'Vieilles Vignes; 'Pacherenc du Vic-Bilh Sec and Doux
Christine Dupuy keeps her winery as personal as her living room. Her wines also have their own individual signature, which favors fruit, juice and harmony.

Domaine Laffont****–*****
Maumusson
9.4 (3.8 ha); bottles not recorded • Wines: Madiran: Tradition, → Erigone, Hecate; → Pacherenc du Vic-Bilh
Madiran was love at first sight—and taste—for the Belgian wine enthusiast Pierre Speyer. His passion now manifests itself in magnificent reds with scents of chocolate, berry and blackcurrant leaves, which offer dense, sweet extracts and fine *barrique* notes, and are among the best wines in the Southwest.

Haut-Pays: Between the Atlantic and the Mediterranean

The Haut-Pays today, much reduced compared with earlier times, consists of a total of five designations of origin lying east of Agen and north and northeast of Toulouse between the Garonne, Tarn, and Massif Central. Probably the oldest, largest, and at the same time easternmost of these areas is Gaillac, which extends to the walls of mighty Albi. It is assumed that Gaillac was one of the first wine-growing centers in Gaul. Later the wines were carried down the Tarn and Garonne to the Atlantic, from where they were shipped to England throughout the Middle Ages. Until the early 19th century, the practice persisted of blending lighter-colored clarets from Bordeaux with the more intensely colored reds from Gaillac.

Not much is left of the old glory. Though the *appellation's* 3,950 or so acres (1,600 ha) planted to vines provide ideal conditions for the numerous grape varieties cultivated here, in recent decades really convincing products have been turned out by only a few individual growers. Most of them offer a wide range of wines, with single-variety wines being quite common even where production regulations for the *appellation* require blending. In white wines, the stars of the Bordelais region are grown along with the native Mauzac, Ondenc, and Len de l'El. In red wines, the Cabernets and Merlot are

Above
Cartier chief Alain Dominique Perrin produces wine at Château Lagrezette near Cahors.

Opposite
Robert Plageoles' unconventional Gaillac wines are very successful.

just tolerated at best, Fer (here called Braucol) being much preferred, but Gamay and Syrah are increasingly finding support.

At the confluence of the Tarn with the Garonne, a V.D.Q.S. area called Lavilledieu was established in 1947, with a good 346 acres (140 ha) planted to vines on barren, gravelly alluvial soils. Cabernet Franc, Gamay, and Syrah cover a quarter of the area, and are supplemented by Negrette and Tannat. Lavilledieu wines are strongly fruity and best drunk chilled.

A few dozen miles down the Garonne are the Côtes du Frontonnais, which still covers 4,940 acres (2,000 ha) planted to the red varieties of the Bordelais and the native Negrette, whose delicate, aromatic rosés and reds are quite fascinating in their overtones of violets, licorice, and blackcurrants. A small number of growers produce increasingly complex, full-bodied *cuvées* that keep well.

A similar situation prevails in the Côtes du Brulhois, a small region west of Agen that sank into a kind of coma in the 1930s and was only reawakened by a cooperative in 1965. Nowadays 494 acres (200 ha) are stocked with Tannat, Cabernet, Merlot, Cot, and Fer Servadou.

The Black Wine of Cahors

The northern end of the Haut-Pays, and the most interesting *appellation* is found in the Lot Valley. In earlier centuries the dark red wine from the Cahors area was among the most famous and most sought-after *crus* in France. Here too wine production received an enormous boost when Gascony came under the English crown. The barrels could be transported down the Lot, which runs into the Garonne near Aiguillon, to Bordeaux, from where they could be shipped to England. Despite endless machinations by the growers of Bordeaux, the success of the "black wine" could not be prevented. Cahors's golden age was around 1720, when the area planted to vines swelled to an impressive 98,800 acres (40,000 ha). As in all other wine-growing regions of France, phylloxera wiped out all the vineyards. Even more their undoing, however, was the subsequent mistake in the matter of resistant graft stocks. Those they selected proved too productive and too early for Cot, alias Malbec or Auxerrois, which ripens late and has a strong tendency to seep.

In the era of mass wine, which reached a peak after the First World War, growers survived only by planting out high-yield hybrid varieties. During this time, the great black wine of Cahors passed almost into oblivion. It was only after 1947 that some growers evinced a desire to replant the characterful Cot. The renaissance of Cahors started ten years later. It's available once again—the black wine with its intensive aromas of berries, licorice, and herbs, its strong structure and noble tannins, which are the armory for long aging.

Select Producers of the Haut-Pays

Cahors

Château du Cèdre****
Vire-sur-Lot
62 acres (25 ha); 120,000 bottles • Wines: Cahors: →Le Cèdre, →Le Prestige, GL
The reds of the Château du Cèdre are very dark and densely structured on the palate. On 5 acres (2 ha), Viognier is one of the varieties grown.

Château Lagrezette***–****
Caillac
158 acres (64 ha); 360,000 bottles • Wines: Cahors: Dame d'Honneur, Moulin Lagrezette, →Le Pigeonnier
Cartier chief Perrin was one of the first Parisian V.I.P.s to try his hand at winemaking. He has for some years been advised by the famous Bordelais enologist Michel Rolland. The quality of the wines has risen rapidly.

Château Lamartine**–****
Saturac
69 acres (28 ha); 150,000 bottles • Wines: Cahors: Tradition, Expressions, →Cuvée Particulière
Alain Gayraud's wines are perfect in their soft, fruity and tannin-rich style as well as excellent value for money.

Clos de Gamot**–***
Prayssac
30 acres (12 ha); 50,000 bottles • Wines: Cahors: Tradition, Vignes Centenaires
This is the bastion of tradition. The wines are never very attractive when young, but the older vintages from the time of Jean Jouffreau (deceased) are legendary.

Clos Triguedina***–****
Puy-l'Évêque
146 acres (59 ha); 340,000 bottles • Wines: Cahors: Tradition, →Prince Probus, New Black Wine
One of the best-known names of Cahors, the Probus *cuvée* achieves a level of quality in good years scarcely matched by any other wine in the *appellation*.

Primo Palatum****
Morizes
45,000 bottles • Wines include: →Cahors, Madiran, Graves, Bordeaux, Côtes du Roussillon, Minervois; →Jurançon Sec, Sauternes, Limoux, Vin de Pays d'Oc.

The enologist Xavier Copel has set new standards with his small company based in the Bordelais region. He purchases wine from the best *terroirs* belonging to the best winegrowers between the Atlantic and the Mediterranean, and matures it with the greatest skill. The Mythologia series is particularly concentrated and has great volume.

Côtes du Frontonnais

Château Bellevue La Forêt***
Fronton
277 acres (112 ha); 800,000 bottles • Wines include: Côtes du Frontonnais: →Ce Vin, Prestige, Allégresse, Cuvée d'Or, →Optimum
Soft, straight wines with harmonious fruit are the strengths of this large *domaine* from Fronton.

Domaine Le Roc***–****
Fronton
62 acres (25 ha); 100,000 bottles • Wines: Côtes du Frontonnais: Classique Réserve, →Don Quichotte, →La Soignée
The Ribes brothers use the Negrette and Cabernet varieties to blend wonderfully fruity and rounded wines. Particularly excellent is the Cuvée Don Quichotte.

Gaillac

Domaine Casses Marines***–****
Vieux
33.6 acres (13.6 ha); 70,000 bottles • Wines include: Les Greilles, Peyrouzelles, →Rasdu, Grain de Folie Doucé, Mysterre, Préambule; →Délire d'Automne, Graal; →Vin de Table Zacmu
Patrice Lescarret uses organic methods to entice deliciously sweet nectar from his vineyard plots on the limestone plateau. His dry whites and reds are also excellent, with clean fruit.

Domaine Robert Plageoles***–****
Cahuzac-sur-Vère
44.5 acres (18 ha); 72,000 bottles • Wines: Gaillac: →Ondenc, Muscadelle, →Vin d'Autan, Mauzac Vert, Mauzac Roux, Mauzac Nature
Robert Plageoles has created highly original wines from the traditional varieties of Gaillac.

The Rhône Valley and the Savoie

Wine of Two Worlds

Few regions of France can boast of a wine-growing tradition as ancient as that of the Rhône Valley. The Phocaeans, Greek settlers from the city of Phocaea in Asia Minor who founded Marseille in 600 BC, already knew that the region was particularly suitable for viticulture, and they planted vines. Under the rule of the Romans, who are supposed to have learned the art of improvement from the Gauls, viticulture then spread to the central and northern part of the valley, where Gaulish tribes were certainly cultivating vines by 71 AD in the Côtes Rôtie and Hermitage areas.

However, the career of Côte du Rhône wines was checked by the powerful Duchy of Burgundy, which wanted to supply its own wines to the most important markets of London and Paris. They therefore imposed high transit duties on Rhône growths or banned their transport down the only route available at the time, the Saône, as was the position from the 14th to the 16th centuries. Only in the 17th century, when conditions for overland transport improved, and still more in the 19th century when the first railways were built, did Rhône wines become popular in Paris.

Rasteau is known not only for its full reds but also its fortified *vin doux naturel*.

The period after the Second World War brought a dramatic loss of image. The cheap sources of wines in the former French colonies of North Africa, used as blending wines to provide color and alcoholic strength, dried up, prompting many a Bordeaux château—quite illegally, of course—to try Rhône wines instead. Slack sales in the barreled wine market did not exactly motivate growers in the Valley to develop their own qualities. What reached consumers under the Côtes du Rhône label were at best simple but palatable reds in the lowest price brackets. It was only in the 1980s that growers of the region realized the size of the potential available to them thanks to their unique *terroir* and still better grape varieties.

Northern and Southern Climate

Along with the Rhine, Danube, Loire, Douro, Garonne, and Moselle, the Rhône is one of the most important wine rivers in the world. Even in its uppermost reaches in Valais, in Switzerland, there is an extensive wine industry with splendid products. In the main part of the French section, from Lyons, the broad river valley runs almost dead straight southwards for almost 125 miles (200 km), with the foothills of the Alps on one side and the Massif Central on the other side. For almost the entire stretch, the valley is covered with steep vineyards and large fields of vines, which between Vienne in the north and Avignon in the south constitutes one of the most varied vine-growing regions in the country. Around 124,000 acres (50,000 ha) are planted with vines in six departments and 163 localities; the region also boasts the most-produced red-wine *appellation* (Côtes du Rhône rouge) in France. The Rhône in a wider sense also includes a series of fringe areas such as Diois, Côtes du Ventoux, Coteaux du Tricastin, Costières du Gard, and the Muscat de Lunel region, with the two last-named constituting a transition to Languedoc-Roussillon.

The diversity of the wines is due principally to a special geographical constellation. In the northern part of the Rhône Valley, where vines are planted mainly on the terraces of steep granite slopes, a markedly cooler continental climate prevails than in the southern part with its broad alluvial and sandy plains, where it can be very hot in the summer and remains pleasantly mild in winter. These climatic differences are also the reason the northern sites produce single-variety wines, as is the case in most northern wine-growing regions of Europe, while in the south *cuvées* predominate.

The greatest resource of the region is its white and red grape varieties which—although largely ignored, especially in France itself—are among the best in the world and have long produced splendid wines outside their region of origin. The

Syrah (left) is the star variety of Rhône red wines, while Marsanne, Rousanne, and Viognier (right) go into the white specialties.

pride and joy is the blue Syrah, which in recent years has developed into a sort of designer grape. As far back as the Romans, the dark grapes with their small berries were known to have a special quality. In the best conditions for ripening, the dark and at the same time fruity, tannin-rich wines can prove very complex and extremely ageable, and they accord with the image of firm and yet harmonious wines such as are popular with modern consumers. Pure Syrah wines are produced under the Côte Rôtie, Hermitage, Saint-Joseph, or Crozes-Hermitage *appellations* of the northern Rhône, but they are being planted more and more often in the vineyards of the south as well.

Séguret, one of the loveliest villages of France and home of one of the best Rhône red wines.

Rhône Varieties in the New World

Even before the French became aware of the real qualities of the variety, the Australians made it their showpiece variety under the name Shiraz, gaining their greatest and most important successes with it in international markets in the 1970s and 1980s. The top Australian cult wine of all, Penfolds' Grange, was once made solely from Syrah, and even today contains only small quantities of Cabernet Sauvignon. How conscious the Australians were of the origin of their favorite is evident from the fact that the strong reds made from the Rhône grape were long sold as Hermitage. The success of the Australians inspired not only the Rhône growers. In the last two decades, numerous vineyards in California and South Africa have also been planted with Syrah, while in France itself the grape has conquered many vineyards in the Languedoc.

The second important red-wine variety, the high-yield Grenache, also had to adopt an Australian-Californian accent. Unlike Syrah, this came not from the Rhône itself but from Aragón, spreading along the Mediterranean coast and into the southern reaches of the Rhône. Anyone who hastily dismisses it as a characterless mass-market variety forgets that some of the finest reds from Châteauneuf-du-Pape and the Villages *appellations* are made from Grenache vines where the yield is kept low. How full, dense, and full-bodied these wines can be has recently been demonstrated by the Spanish Priorat area.

Mourvèdre too, a late-ripening variety that needs a lot of warmth, whereupon it produces wines with a lot of tannin, has become more and more popular in the southern Rhône as well as in the hotter areas of the New World.

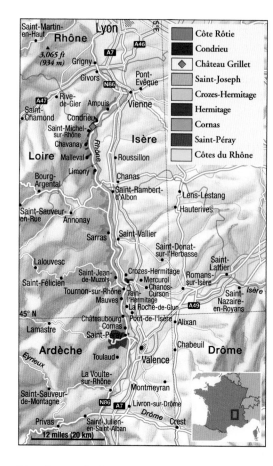

Left
Syrah is allowed to attain its most profound eloquence in the vineyards of the Hermitage.

Right
At Chapoutier in Tain-l'Hermitage, the *pigeage* is carried out in the traditional way.

Together with the above varieties and the soft, fruity Cinsault or the deep red, strongly alcoholic Carignan, it forms the basis of practically all the red wines of the southern Rhône. In the white wines, on the other hand, the most interesting varieties come undoubtedly from the north. Wines sold under the Condrieu A.C. made from 100 percent Viognier grapes stand out particularly, with their dense, intense aromas of honey, apricots, and peaches.

In recent years, the white Marsanne and Roussanne varieties have become popular in the New World and won a real fan club among growers and winemakers, whose members like to call themselves Rhône Rangers. On the

Rhône itself, these two varieties are responsible for the great wines of the Hermitage, but together with Clairette, Grenache Blanc, Counoise, Bourboulenc, and others also form the basis for the white Villages wines and crus on the southern reaches of the river.

VILLAGES, CRUS, AND RÉGIONAUX

One of the strengths of the Rhône wine industry is at the same time one of its weaknesses, namely the ingenious *appellation* system. At the base of this quality pyramid you find the mainly red wines of the regional Côtes du Rhône *appellation*, which is produced principally in the lower reaches of the river. A step above this are wines labeled Côtes du Rhône Villages. Products of a total of 95 communes in the departments of Drôme, Gard, and Vaucluse belong to this group, with 16 communes of the A.C. designation being able to add their own village names to this. At the top are the *crus*, geographically demarcated *appellations* such as Gigondas or Côte Rôtie, whose labels no longer bear any reference to their belonging to the Rhône family.

IN THE REALM OF SYRAH AND VIOGNIER

Founded as a Roman garrison town in 121, and with a now picturesquely ruined Roman amphitheater that still offers views over the Rhône Valley, Vienne is the northernmost point of the Côtes du Rhône *appellation*. In the mostly rather narrow valley, the vines clamber up steep granite slopes. This is an area with a largely continental climate and warm summers, in which the sunlight is exploited to the full by terraced vineyards but the heat is tempered by a permanent wind. Winters are unusually cold for the latitude. The northern part of the Rhône, in which mainly single-variety wines are grown, constitutes the southern boundary of the viticultural regions of France where chaptalization is carried out. Heat and coolness together give the wines their rich aromatic character and elegant structure.

The production of this part of the overall *appellation* is bottled almost exclusively under the name of the local *appellations* of the more prestigious *crus*, of which the area has eight. (The south has only five.) Labels of the Côtes-du Rhône regional *appellation* are practically non-existent here. The best-known *crus* also include the most northerly quality wines of the Rhône, apart from a small table-wine output in the direct vicinity of the town of Vienne. This is the Côte Rôtie, home of wonderful Syrah

Marcel Guigal can well smile—his cellar in Ampuis is full of liquid treasure.

wines, in which up to 20 percent of the white Viognier is officially permitted but rarely effected by growers.

Although wine growing here dates back to Roman times and perhaps even a few centuries earlier, the name of the *appellation*, which means "scorched slope," only goes back to the 19th century. Until the 1950s the wine had virtually no reputation, and the area planted out even in past centuries rarely exceeded the current 494 acres (200 ha). A specialty of the growing area is cultivation on pyramidal stilts, which appears to be the only sensible arrangement on the narrow terraces.

THE CRUS OF THE NORTH

Directly south of the Côte Rôtie is the small white wine district of Condrieu, in which Viognier is the star. The name of the administrative and commercial town with its distinctive Rhône bridge means *coin du rieux*, or "stream place." Chalky soils on rock, with schist and mica in the upper strata provide a basis for subtle, multi-layered Viognier wines. The constant ventilation of the steep slopes is of great benefit, because the variety is prone to rot. Although some Condrieu wines from good vintages are wholly suited to aging, it is best to drink them young, when aroma and fruit in the nose are still accompanied by sumptuous juiciness on the palate. The largest *appellation* in the north territorially is Saint-Joseph, with almost 2,220 acres (900 ha) planted to vines, scattered over a riverine strip almost 30 miles (50 km) long. It is also the first in which both reds and whites are made, with Marsanne and Roussanne taking the place of Viognier. Dense, fruity red wines—the whites are less interesting—are found more and more often, and at very reasonable prices. In the area around the town of Tain l'Hermitage the vineyards move to the left bank. This is where the 331 acres (134 ha) of the Hermitage hills are, the famous *appellation* which has lent its name to many an overseas Syrah wine, and the less famous Crozes-Hermitage, with more than 2,970 acres (1,200 ha) planted to vines producing both 100 percent Syrah reds and white wines blended from Marsanne and Rousanne. While the granite-based, south-facing slopes of the Hermitage generate firm, dense, and ageable growths, the Crozes wines grown on flatter gravels or loess sites are much lighter.

The last of the northern Rhône districts are the Cornas and Saint-Péray *appellations*, both directly opposite Valence on the right bank of

In his own steep vineyards at Les Ruchets, enologist Jean-Luc Colombo has created a paradigm of a modern northern Rhône wine, which is particularly convincing even in lesser years.

the Rhône. Saint-Péray used to be known exclusively for simple sparkling wines, but in recent years has forged a reputation for good still whites, although the total acreage is only a little over 148 (60 ha), hardly enough to establish a real market presence.

Cornas is not much larger. It also used to produce whites, but now makes only reds from Syrah. The wines are somewhat lighter than the Côte Rôtie, but can have a lot of character.

Select Producers from the Northern Rhône

Thierry Allemand**
Cornas
9 acres (3.5 ha); 12,000 bottles • Wine: Cornas: → Chaillot
Allemand's Cornas wines have strong character, excellent structure and firm tannins. Only after a few years' maturing in the bottle do they display their aromatic variety.

Bernard Burgaud**
Ampuis
10 acres (4 ha); 15,000 bottles • Wine: Côte Rôtie
A deep color and concentrated, clear Syrah fruit notes are the trademark of Bernard Burgaud's wines.

M. Chapoutier*−*****
Tain L'Hermitage
395 acres (160 ha); 3,000,000 bottles • Wines include: Condrieu, → Hermitage Blanc De Lorée, Côte Rôtie de la Mordorée, Hermitage: Le Pavillon, → Monier de la Sizeranne, Crozes-Hermitage, Châteauneuf-du-Pape La Bernardine
Ever-busy Michel Chapoutier makes some of the best Hermitage and Côte Rôtie wines. He also produces wines from the southern Rhône *appellations* and even Australia.

Jean-Louis Chave*−****
Mauves
37 acres (15 ha); 48,000 bottles • Wines: Hermitage → Blanc, Rouge; E. Catelain, → Vin de Paille
This old master of Hermitage is one of the largest vineyard owners of this prestigious *cru*. The white Hermitage combines an elegant honey, vanilla and flower bouquet with a rich, fresh structure in the mouth, and the red is in no way inferior.

Yann Chave*−****
Mercurol
41 acres (16.5 ha); 80,000 bottles • Wines: Crozes-Hermitage Blanc: Cuvée, → Le Rouvre; Rouge: Tradition, → Tête de Cuvée, Hermitage

In 2001, Yann Chave took over the estate which his parents Bernard and Nicole had founded in 1970. The main wine produced is the red Crozes, and the Tête de Cuvée is excellent. The quality of the wines has been rising recently. A new cellar was ready for use in 2003.

Louis Chèze*−****
Limony
49 acres (20 ha); 80,000 bottles • Wines include: → Condrieu; Saint-Joseph: Blanc, Rouge, → Cuvée des Anges
The reserved Louis Chèze produces delightful Condrieus and better and better Saint-Josephs.

A. Clape**
Cornas
15 acres (6 ha); 25,000 bottles • Wines: → Cornas, Saint-Péray, Côtes du Rhône
Auguste Clape runs his 15-acre (6-ha) estate in Cornas, with the help of his son Pierre Marie. Some of his wine stocks are well over 60 years old.

Jean-Luc Colombo**−*****
Cornas
Acres: not recorded; 300,000 bottles • Wines include: Cornas: Les Ruchets, Saint-Péray, Côtes du Rhône; Hermitage, Saint-Joseph; → Coteaux d'Aix-en-Provence Domaine de la Côte Bleue, Coteaux du Languedoc Domaine de la Salente, → Côtes du Roussillon Domaine Saint-Luc
Colombo is to the Rhône what Rolland is for Bordeaux: the most inspiring of wine experts. At the same time, he is an excellent winemaker based in Cornas and now also in the Gulf of Marseille. His company offers carefully selected *appellations*.

Laurent & Dominique Courbis*−****
Châteaubourg
64 acres (26 ha); 120,000 bottles • Wines include: Cornas: Eygats, → La Sabarotte, → Champelrose, Saint-Joseph

Laurent Courbis is considered the best wine-maker in the community. His Cornas Cuvées display a dense color, a many-layered bouquet and plenty of body and fine tannins.

YVES CUILLERON***–*****
CHAVANAY
76.5 acres (31 ha); 150,000 bottles • Wines include: Condrieu: →Chaillets, Vertige, Ayguets; Saint-Joseph Blanc: Lyceras, Saint-Pierre; rouge: L'Amarybelle, →Les Sérines; Côte Rôtie: Bassenon, →Terres sombres
You may become enthusiastic about the very ripe Viogniers, but the red Saint-Josephs show increasing potential, as do the first-class Côtes Rôties.

DELAS***–*****
SAINT-JEAN DE MUZOLS
30 acres (12 ha); 1,500,000 bottles • Wines include: Condrieu: →Clos Bucher, →Vin de Pays Viognier; Côte Rôtie: →Seigneur de Maugiron; Hermitage: →Marquise de la Tourette; Crozes-Hermitage: →Tour d'Albon; Saint-Joseph
Founded in 1835, Delas rather missed the boat in the 1980s, when it was owned by Champagne Deutz. Since 1993 it has belonged to Roederer, and the general manager Fabrice Rosset has made considerable investments. In Jacques Grange, a former Colombo employee, he has gained an outstanding winery manager. Since 1999, Delas has once again assumed its rightful place alongside Chapoutier and Jaboulet with excellent red wines.

DOMAINE COMBIER***–****
PONT DE L'ISÈRE
34.5 acres (14 ha); 50,000 bottles • Wines: Crozes-Hermitage: Blanc, Rouge, →Clos de Grives
The Clos is a masterpiece of density and harmony, not least because of many years of organic cultivation.

DOMAINE ALAIN GRAILLOT****
PONT DE L'ISÈRE
49 acres (20 ha); 100,000 bottles • Wines: Crozes-Hermitage: Blanc, Rouge, La Guirade
A master of Syrah, which has a unique clear fruit at Graillot.

DOMAINE ROCHEPERTUIS—JEAN LIONNET***
CORNAS
37 acres (15 ha); 35,000 bottles • Wines: St. Péray, Cornas
Lionnet produces superb Cornas—the top selection is Rochepertuis—and a white wine with 50% new wood fermentation.

PIERRE GAILLARD***–****
MALLEVAL
39.5 acres (16 ha); 100,000 bottles • Wines include: Jean Elise, Condrieu: →Côte Rôtie; Rose Pourpre, →Côte Brune et Blonde, Saint-Joseph; Les Pierres, Clos de Cuminaille
For many years, Pierre Gaillard was *chef de culture* in the vineyards of Guigal, and he thoroughly mastered his trade there. He uses cold maceration before fermentation, subsequently fermenting at 90°F (32°C) with frequent punchdown. His rich, sweet Condrieu Jeanne Elise reaches the highest level.

YVES GANGLOFF****
CONDRIEU
7.5 acres (3 ha); 15,000 bottles • Wines: →Côte Rôtie La Barbarine, Condrieu
Yves Gangloff has 5 acres (2 ha) for Côte Rôtie and 2.5 acres (1 ha) for Condrieu—and a rare obsession with quality.

JEAN-MICHEL GÉRIN***–*****
AMPUIS
12 acres (5 ha); 40,000 bottles • Wines include: Condrieu, →Côte Rôtie: Les Grandes Places, →Champin Le Seigneur, Ladone

Grandes Places is the gem of the Gérin family, who have been producing wine in Ampuis for five generations. With La Landone, they have now added another splendid example.

E. GUIGAL***–*****
AMPUIS
160.5 acres (65 ha); 5,500,000 bottles • Wines include: Condrieu, Hermitage: Blanc, Rouge, Côte Rôtie: Château d'Ampuis, →La Landonne, Côte Brune La Turque, →Côte Blonde La Mouline, →Saint-Joseph Vignes de l'Hospice, Côtes du Rhône, →Gigondas, Tavel, Châteauneuf-du-Pape
The great magician, undisputed best vinifier and *négociant* of the northern Rhône, has recently fitted out his business as one of the most modern in France. In 2001, Guigal took over two other estates with an excellent reputation: that of Jean-Louis Grippat and the Domaine de Vallouit.

PAUL JABOULET AÎNÉ***–*****
TAIN DE L'HERMITAGE
247 acres (100 ha); 200,000 bottles • Wines include: Hermitage: →Blanc Chevalier de Sterimberg, La Chapelle, Crozes-Hermitage, Côtes Rôtie Les Jumelles, Cornas, Saint-Joseph, Châteauneuf-du-Pape, Gigondas, Vacqueyras, Côtes du Rhône, Tavel
The Hermitage La Chapelle of this venerable winery is still one of the greatest and most consistent elite wines of France. In 2001, the winery opened a spectacular cellar for aging in a quarry dating back to Roman times.

JEAN-PAUL & JEAN-LUC JAMET***–****
AMPUIS
17 acres (7 ha); 20,000 bottles • Wine: Côte Rôtie, Côte Rôtie Côte Brune
Jean-Paul and Jean-Luc Jamet cultivate only Syrah on the edge of the high plateau behind Ampuis and make excellent Côte Rôtie from it. The wines are aged for 20 months in small oak barrels.

ANDRÉ PERRET***–****
CHAVANNAY
27 acres (11 ha); 50,000 bottles • Wines: Condrieu, →Clos Chanson Coteau Chéry, Saint-Joseph: Les Grisières
Although the Condrieu is considered Perret's showpiece wine, the Saint-Joseph has remarkable fruit and structure.

GEORGES VERNAY****
CONDRIEU
39 acres (16 ha); 100,000 bottles • Wines include: →Condrieu: Coteau de Vernon, Les Chaillés d'Enfer; Côte Rôtie
One of the Condrieu classics with various *cuvées* of very consistent quality.

FRANÇOIS VILLARD****–*****
SAINT-MICHEL-SUR-RHÔNE
25 acres (10 ha); 45,000 bottles • Wines: →Condrieu: →Grand Vallou, →Deponcius; Côte Rôtie, →Saint-Joseph Le Reflet
In only a few years, this young ex-chef has turned out to be a driving force on the northern Rhône. White and red wines of the highest standard.

LES VINS DE VIENNE****
SEYSSUEL
25 acres (10 ha); 200,000 bottles • Wines include: →Vin de Pays des Collines Rhodanéenes: Sotanum, →Taburnum; Côtes du Rhône and Villages, Condrieu, Côte Rôtie, Hermitage, Cornas, Vacqueyras, Gigondas
The three friends Yves Cuilleron, Pierre Gaillard and François Villard have helped the historic location of Seyssuel near Vienne to achieve a comeback. They have also created a small trading company and, with an unmistakable trained nose, have been maturing and bottling small quantities of excellent wines.

Gateway to the South

As you travel southward, it becomes markedly hotter between Valence and Montélimar and the landscape and towns take on a more Mediterranean appearance. The Tricastin area, the gateway to Provence, is firmly in the truffle, fruit, and lavender-growing businesses, and instead of the steep terraces of the north, the grapes are cultivated here in great fields on a landscape that is slightly undulating at most. The larger part of the planted area of this southern half of the Rhône Valley, which accounts for at least 95 percent of the total production, is marketable only under the regional *appellation* Côtes du Rhône. Despite the generally hot, dry climate with optimum ripening conditions for the grapes, the weather also has its latent risks—for example in the

If the Brunel ancestors knew what class their Château La Gardine had attained today…!

form of the often unpredictable, and even violent Mistral wind.

Traditionally 13 different red and white varieties of grape are grown that go into the wines in greater or lesser ratios, with white wine grapes occasionally finding use in red wines. The area is of course mainly planted to red varieties, with Grenache, Mourvèdre, and Syrah making at least 70 percent of the total. The whites must be made at least 80 percent from Grenache Blanc, Clairette, Marsanne, Roussanne, Bourboulenc, and Viognier. Unlike in the Bordeaux area, where blending of different grape varieties takes place only after the completion of fermentation, wines here in the southern Rhône Valley are fermented together whenever the *vendange* (harvest) permits. In the reds of the regional *appellation*, carbonic maceration has been increasingly used in recent years. One of the characteristics of the district is the key position of the viticultural cooperatives, apart from that in the prestige *appellations* such as Châteauneuf-du-Pape, while a *négoce* of the reputation of the great houses in the northern Rhône could not develop here.

The Complete Hierarchy

Besides the huge regional *appellation*, the south also has five *crus*, plus more than 14,800 acres (6,000 ha) classified as Côtes du Rhône Villages. Unlike in the north, there are no exclusively white *crus*—only Châteauneuf-du-Pape, Lirac, and Vacqueyras have a smallish white wine production. More significant is the position of the rosés, which are bottled under the designations Gigondas, Lirac, Vacqueyras, and Tavel (the latter exclusively for rosés). Gigondas, at the foot of the climbers' paradise of the Dentelles du Montmirail, is, after Châteauneuf-du-Pape, the best known of the southern *appellations*. Because of the differences in the *terroirs* within the 2,970 acres (1,200 ha) of the parish—the higher, warmer sites are chalky and sandy, the lower ones are loamy and pebbly—the wines turn out very differently. The best growths are deep in color, emphatically fruity, strongly alcoholic, and powerful, without being overfull of tannins.

A similar division occurs in neighboring Vacqueyras, which is almost the same size, where the soils contain both loam and chalk and pebbly gravel. The wines here are somewhat less massive, show more finesse than

---

Sweet wines from the Rhône

A specialty and rarity of the southern Rhône are the two fortified *vins doux naturels* (V.D.N.s) Muscat Beaumes-de-Venise and Rasteau, which are produced only here and in Languedoc-Roussillon. The name (natural sweet wines) is misleading, as the residual sweetness arises not from a natural end of fermentation but as a result of the conversion of sugar into alcohol being artificially terminated. If the two sweet wines of the famous *villages* parishes of Beaumes-de-Venise and Rasteau share a sweet taste and winery technique, however, they are distinct in one key point: the Muscat de Beaumes-de-Venise is produced from Muscat Blanc à Petits Grains, a variety of grape introduced to southern France by the popes in the 14th century that displays typical Muscat aromas. The Rasteau on the other hand is mainly the product of the classic red wine varieties of the *appellation*, and is more like a very thick red or brown port.

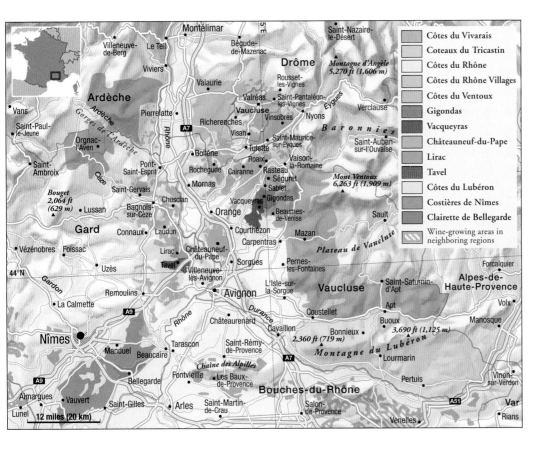

strength and are thus as clearly distinct from the growths of Gigondas as those of nearby Châteauneuf-du-Pape.

The two remaining *crus* lie on the right bank of the Rhône. Here, the hilly limestone formations come much closer to the river, offering the grapes optimum conditions with their good drainage. The historical roots of viticulture here go back at least as far as they do on the eastern bank of the Rhône, but Lirac and Tavel first enjoyed a cautious upturn only after the Second World War. Lirac was one of the first districts of France infected by phylloxera (in 1863), as a château owner had imported seedlings from America and with them the destructive pest. Although under wine legislation they do not belong to the Rhône *appellations* proper, there are a series of peripheral cultivation areas attached to the region. The most northerly of these is Diois, where the Crémant de Die is found—once called Clairette de Die and produced from the Clairette grape—and a sparkling wine produced from Muscat with a single fermentation, an approach described as *méthode ancestrale*. Not far from this are the Coteaux du Tricastin, where the wine industry has developed at breakneck speed in recent years. Here mainly red wines from the usual southern Rhône varieties are grown that are pleasantly fruity and seem soft enough, but rarely show much character. On the southern flank of Mont Ventoux is the cultivation area called Côtes du Ventoux, which has had a separate *appellation* since 1973 and with a total of 51 communes in all is one of the most extensive in the Rhône. The area produces white wines, rosés, and reds, with the ratios of varieties in the blending slightly differing from the neighboring villages on the west flank of Ventoux.

The hierarchy of *appellations* in the Rhône Valley

r = red wine, rs = rosé, w = white wine

A—Côtes du Rhône (r, rs, w)

B—Côtes du Rhône Villages (r, rs, w) without mention of the commune (wines from a total of 95 communes in the departments of Drôme, Gard, and Vaucluse)

C—Côtes du Rhône Villages with the name of the commune added (16 communes in the departments of Drôme, Gard, and Vaucluse. They are: Cusclan (r, rs), Laudun (r, rs, w), and St.-Gervais (r, rs, w), in Gard, Rochegude (r, rs, w), St.-Maurice (r, rs, w), St.-Pantaléon-les-Vignes (r, rs, w), Roussets-les-Vignes (r, rs, w) and Vinsobres (r, rs, w) in Drôme, Beaumes-de-Venise (r, rs, w), Cairanne (r, rs, w), Rasteau (r, rs, w), Roaix (r, rs, w), Sablet (r, rs, w), Séguret (r, rs, w), Valréas (r, rs, w) and Visan (r, rs, w) in Vaucluse.)

D—13 *crus* (geographically localized *appellations*) of the northern and southern Rhône that no longer contain any reference to Côtes du Rhône in the name. They are the Côte Rôtie (r), Condrieu (w), Château Grillet (w), Saint-Joseph (r, w), Crozes Hermitage (r, w), Hermitage (r, w), Cornas (r) and St-Péray (w, sparkling wine) in the north, Châteauneuf-du-Pape (r, w), Gigondas (r, rs), Vacqueyras (r, rs, w), Lirac (r, rs, w), Tavel (rs) in the south.

Villages with Character

The greatest development in the Rhône wine industry has been the progress in the *villages appellations* in the southern part of the region, with around 15,300 acres (6,200 ha) planted to vines. Amazing quality was produced mainly in the parishes that were granted the right to use their own names on the label together with the *appellation*, which applies to 16 out of the 95, though they in fact have more than half the total acreage.

Even more than in the case of the *crus*, the *villages* parishes are largely on the left bank of the Rhône, where the hills are quite gentle and rise toward the Alps quite slowly, and a total of 13 of the small cultivation areas are situated. The remaining three *villages appellations* are in the hills and on the high plateau on the right bank of the Rhône.

Whereas the permitted yield is 548 gallons per acre (52 hl/ha) for the regional *appellation* and 476 gallons per acre (45 hl/ha) for the simple *villages* labels, for the *villages* labels with the parish name as well the limit is only 440 gallons (42 hl/ha). The grape variety ratios in the reds

Cairanne is among the Rhône villages that has established a position at the top of the *appellation* thanks to the qualities of its *terroir* and skills of its growers.

must contain at least 50 percent Grenache and at least 20 percent Syrah or Mourvèdre, while with whites a minimum proportion of 80 percent of the principal varieties such as Clairette, Viognier, Bourboulenc, Marsanne, Roussanne, and Grenache Blanc is specified. Unlike in many wine-producing areas in the rest of Europe, the rosés can include up to 20 percent of white grape varieties, and with the exception of Chusclan, white, red and rosé wines can all carry the *villages appellations* in all the *villages* parishes.

The least-known *villages* lie on the right bank of the Rhône in the area of Bagnols-sur-Cèze. They are Laudun, Chusclan, and Saint-Gervais, with Laudun alone comprising almost two-thirds of the 1,560 acres (630 ha) under cultivation. The preponderantly dry, sandy and gravelly soil—only in Saint-Gervais do you find limestone with layers of loess and clay—produce fine, elegant wines that are largely made and sold by cooperatives.

There are, of course, also a number of splendidly functioning estates in the districts selling their own wines, but they often sell their products under the simple *villages appellation* or even the regional Côtes du Rhône label.

The Left Bank

The concentration of the prestige *villages* labels bearing parish name is on the left bank, and the parishes lie in the departments of Drôme and Vaucluse. The most northerly group, which includes Rousset-les-Vignes, Saint-Pantaléon-les-Vignes, Valréas, Vinsobres, Visan, and Saint-Maurice, lies well within the foothills of the Alps and here the landscape provides the best scenery in the whole region.

For their part, the best wines undoubtedly come from Vinsobres, a small parish on the edge of the former papal enclave around Valréas—and also the largest *villages* parish, where notably very fruity reds with low tannin content are made. Its hilly vineyards on clay and limestone-bearing soils turn out dense wines with a fine balance between fruit and tannins. The "three Vs"—Valréas, Vinsobres, and neighboring Visan—are also the best-known *appellations* of the zone, while Saint-Pantaléon and Rousset have a rather low profile. In the central area of the region are the four parishes of Cairanne, Roaix, Rasteau, and Rochegude.

Cairanne and Rochegude have come up with some very good wines in recent years, and have produced perhaps the most consistent *villages* products anywhere. Both are located on the last undulations of the Alpine foothills towards the Rhône Valley before the backdrop of the Dentelles du Montmirail and Mont Ventoux. The best reds are made just along the boundary between the two parishes, whose loamy soils are excellently suited to the production of dense, tannin-rich reds that need not fear competition from much more prestigious *crus* in the area.

In the immediate vicinity of this *cru*, right on the slopes of the Dentelles du Montmirail, are the last three *villages* parishes: Séguret, Sablet, north of Gigondas, and Beaumes-de-Venise, south of Vacqueyras. The hill of Sablet is a particularly remarkable phenomenon, with entirely sandy soils in part. Some of the vineyards look as if the vines had been planted on the beach, and the hill itself is riddled with grottoes buried beneath the compacted masses of sand. The wines here turn out much softer and finer, which the growers to some extent offset by increasing the proportion of Mourvèdre.

Séguret too, the old romantic neighboring village built into the slope and protected as a conservation area, produces very soft wines, though they do not always have the expressiveness and character of the wines of Sablet. The absolute star of the *villages appellations* is Beaumes-de-Venise, though it is better known

Sablet [*sable* = sand] did not acquire its name by accident, because both the hill and the vineyard soils are made of sand.

for its Muscat than the splendid red wines produced here.

In good years, the local cooperative, which is considered the best of the *villages* cooperatives, produces *cuvées* and prestige bottlings of a standard well up to that of the best wines of the neighboring *crus* of Vacqueyras, and they can vie even with good Gigondas.

In Gigondas, the growers are proud of the sturdy character of their *grand cru*.

Select Producers in the Southern Rhône

CAVE COOPÉRATIVE CAIRANNE**–****
CAIRANNE
2,964 acres (1,200 ha); 3,700,000 bottles • Wines include: Côtes du Rhône: Les Grandes Vignes; Côtes du Rhône Villages Cairanne: →Cuvée Antique, Cuvée des Voconnes, →Temptation; Cairanne Blanc: →Grande Réserve, →Cuvée Passion; Vin de Pays de la Principauté d'Orange
The top *cuvée* of this cooperative is the Antique, and a very high quality wine it is. Alongside this, the firm sells a wide range of good to very good wines.

CHÂTEAU D'AQUÉRIA***–****
TAVEL
161 acres (65 ha); 400,000 bottles • Wines: Lirac Blanc, Rosé, Rouge; l'Héritage, Tavel
Known as the best producer of the strongest Rhône rosé, the estate also endeavors to shine with its reds. The Cuvée l'Héritage is excellent.

CHÂTEAU DE LA CANORGUE***
BONNIEUX
74 acres (30 ha); 100,000 bottles • Wines: Côtes du Lubéron →Blanc, Rosé, →Rouge and Cuvée Vendange de Nathalie
Jean-Pierre Margan is one of the pioneers of organic wine growing in the South. His wines are unusually consistent in quality. The reds age superbly.

CHÂTEAU SIGNAC***–****
BAGNOLS-SUR-CÈZE
94 acres (38 ha); 200,000 bottles • Wines include: Côtes Rhône Villages: →Come d'Enfer, →Terra Amata
Alain Dugas, owner of La Nerthe in Châteauneuf, bought the rather rundown estate some years ago and has rebuilt its reputation. Already the wines are of the high quality associated with La Nerthe.

CHÂTEAU DU TRIGNON***–****
GIGONDAS
161 acres (65 ha); 250,000 bottles • Wines include: Côtes du Rhône, →Cuvée Bois des Dames, →Gigondas, →Sablet, →Rasteau
Few other growers in the area can boast of Gigondas, Sablet and Rasteau of such consistent quality, and the Côtes du Rhône Cuvée Bois des Dames is also excellent.

CLOS DU JONCUAS—F. CHASTAN***–****
GIGONDAS
71 acres (29 ha); 125,000 bottles • Wines include: Gigondas: rosé, →Clos Joncuas, →Vacqueyras La Font de Papier, →Séguret Domaine de la Garancière
Dany Chastan, who runs this organically cultivated estate together with her father Fernand, proves with her wines—regularly among the best of the three *appellations*—that organic estates can turn out excellent products and that she is among the best winemakers of the Côtes du Rhône.

DOMAINE BRUSSET****
CAIRANNE
215 acres (87 ha); 400,000 bottles • Wines include: Côtes du Rhône Villages Cairanne: Coteaux des Travers, →Vendange Chabrille, →Cuvée Hommage; Gigondas: Le Grand and →Le Hauts de Montmirail; Côtes du Ventoux
The wines of this important estate, especially the Gigondas, have reached a very high standard.

DOMAINE DE CABASSE***–****
SÉGURET
49.5 acres (20 ha); 80,000 bottles • Wines include: Sablet Les Deux Anges, Séguret Rosé, Séguret Rouge, Cuvée Garnacho, Cuvée de la Casa Bassa, Les Deux, Gigondas

Swiss grower Alfred Haeni bought the estate and soon made it one of the best in the *appellation*. He grafted Syrah on Cinsault rootstocks by the row, and is still experimenting both in the vineyard and the winery.

DOMAINE DIDIER CHARAVIN**–****
RASTEAU
133 acres (54 ha); 80,000 bottles • Wines include: Côtes du Rhône Blanc, Rosé, Rouge; Côtes du Rhône Villages Rasteau: Cuvée Prestige, →Cuvée de Parpaioune, Rasteux Vin Doux Naturel: Doré, Rouge
Originally founded as the Domaine Papillon, the firm shines today with its dense, firm Rasteau reds, whose star number is the Cuvée de Parpaioune.

DOMAINE LES GOUBERT**–****
GIGONDAS
57 acres (23 ha); 90,000 bottles • Wines include: Gigondas: Cuvée Florence, Sablet, Beaumes-de-Venise, Séguret
Jean-Pierre Cartier manages 40 different plots in Gigondas, Séguret, Beaumes and Sablet. His best wine, the Cuvée Florence, is made from Grenache and Syrah vines. Half of this wine is aged for a year in new wood and blended before bottling with the other half from the tanks.

DOMAINE GOURT DE MAUTENS****–*****
RASTEAU
35 acres (14 ha); 30,000 bottles • Wines: Côtes du Rhône Villages Blanc, Rouge
In only a few years Jérôme Bressy has joined the elite of the Rhône valley. His secret is passion, unremitting discipline and a great talent.

DOMAINE DE L'ORATOIRE SAINT MARTIN****
CAIRANNE
57 acres (23 ha); 120,000 bottles • Wines include: Côtes du Rhône Blanc, Rosé, Rouge, Côtes du Rhône Villages Cairanne Haut-Coustias, →Cairanne: Réserve des Seigneurs, →Cuvée Prestige, Haut-Coustias
The Alary family has been growing wine in Cairanne for 300 years. Frédéric and Françoise Alary offer quality products of very consistent standards, particularly in the red *cuvées*.

DOMAINE DE PIAUGIER***–****
SABLET
64 acres (26 ha); 110,000 bottles • Wines include: Côtes du Rhône Villages Blanc, Rouge, Sablet Montmartel
Solid, vigorously structured wines that need a few years to age in the bottle.

DOMAINE DE LA RÉMÉJEAN***–*****
SABRAN
86.5 acres (35 ha); 150,000 bottles • Wines: Côtes du Rhône: Arbousiers, Chèvrefeuilles; Côtes du Rhône Villages: Églantiers, Genévriers
Set apart from the well-known *appellations*, Ouahi and Rémy Klein—he is from Alsace, she is from Morocco—make outstanding *cuvées* under the regional and generic *villages appellation*. The Églantiers is on a par with the best representatives of the prestigious *crus*.

DOMAINE MARCEL RICHAUD****
CAIRANNE
99 acres (40 ha); 120,000 bottles • Wines include: Côtes du Rhône Villages Cairanne: Blanc, Rouge, →L'Esbrescade
Marcel Richaud sets the example for optimum ripeness and thus produces wines of great roundness and finesse.

DOMAINE DOMINIQUE ROCHER***–****
CAIRANNE
37 acres (15 ha); 75,000 bottles • Wines include: Côtes du Rhône Villages, Cairanne, Monsieur Paul
This still very young estate produces most modern wines of the *appellation*. The Cuvée Monsieur Paul is superb.

DOMAINE SAINTE-ANNE***–****
SAINT-GERVAIS
76.5 acres (31 ha); 125,000 bottles • Wines include: Côtes du Rhône, Côtes du Rhône Villages and Saint-Gervais
This estate was the first to show the heights that Côtes du Rhône Villages from the right bank can reach.

DOMAINE DE LA SOUMADE***–*****
RASTEAU
66.5 acres (27 ha); 170,000 bottles • Wines: Côtes du Rhône Villages Rasteau: Cuvée Confiance, Prestige, →Rasteau Vin Doux Naturel: Rouge, Doré
The Roméros' two top red *cuvées* and the red Vin Doux have long been among the best of the southern Rhône area. The Cuvée Confiance especially is in no way second to the *crus* of the north in terms of elegance.

DOMAINE VIRET***–*****
SAINT-MAURICE-SUR-EYGES
74 acres (30 ha); 110,000 bottles • Wines include: Côtes du Rhône Villages Saint-Maurice: →Maréotis, Colonnades, →Emergence, →La TriLoGie
Philippe Viret and his father André have created a spectacular *domaine* in only a short time. They use biodynamic methods.

MAS DE LIBIAN**–****
SAINT-MARCEL-D'ARDÈCHE
42 acres (17 ha); bottles not recorded • Wines include: Côtes du Rhône Blanc, Rouge; Côtes du Rhône Villages Rouge, →La Calade

On this charming estate on the right bank of the Rhône, the young winemaking couple Hélène Thibon and Alain Macagno produce high quality wines with their own distinctive style.

MONTIRUS**–****
SARRIANS
133 acres (54 ha); 220,000 bottles • Wines include: Vacqueyras Blanc, Rosé, Rouge; Montirius; Clos Montirius; Gigondas
Christine and Eric Saurel have converted the old family estate to biodynamic cultivation and now produce finely fruity, balanced wines of great depth in their own winery.

TARDIEU-LAURENT****–******
LOURMARIN
90,000 bottles • Wines include: Côtes du Rhône, Côtes du Lubéron, Côtes du Rhône Villages Rasteau, Gigondas, Châteauneuf-du-Pape, Condrieu, Hermitage, Côte Rôtie
As wine dealers, Michel Tardieu and Dominique Laurent set the standard. Their selection from the Rhône valley is of the very highest quality.

LES VIGNERONS BEAUMES-DE-VENISE*–****
BEAUMES-DE-VENISE
2,970 acres (1,200 ha); 6,000,000 bottles • Wines include: Muscat de Beaumes-de-Venise: Carte Or, Bois Doré; Vacqueyras, Côtes du Rhône Villages; Beaumes-de-Venise: Terroir du Trias, →Carte Noire; Notre Dame d'Aubune Blanc, Rosé, Rouge; Côtes du Rhône: Cuvée des Tocques; Côtes du Ventoux: Cuvée Spéciale, Cuvée des Tocques
The most celebrated cooperative of the southernmost Rhône stands out particularly for its red Beaumes-de-Venise *cuvées* and of course for its Muscat.

Papal Wines: Châteauneuf-du-Pape

By far the best-known, largest, and highly regarded single *appellation* in the Rhône Valley is Châteauneuf-du-Pape, which has over 7,410 acres (3,000 ha) planted to vines in only five localities (Châteauneuf, Courthézon, Bédarrides, Orange, and Sorgues), where predominantly red wine varieties are grown. In 1157, the Templars settled on the site of the ancient decisive battle (in 121 BC) between the Romans, led by Quintus Fabius Maximus, and the Gaulish tribe of the Allobroges. They named the place Castrum Novum. Pope John XXII, who is believed to have encouraged viticulture, had a castle built on the Templars' former property in 1323. The castle was used mainly as a papal summer residence. The present name is 19th-century. Despite the long history, the reputation of the *appellation* is of recent date, because up to the Second World War the wines were mostly sold in Burgundy.

Châteauneuf is an exception in every respect. Lying on a rocky hill visible from a great distance, the town clings picturesquely to its sandy clay slopes surrounded by a plain densely overlaid with a deposit of reddish pebbles, a relic of the Rhône glacier. There are also sandy and loamy soils, and the fragmentation of vineyard ownership in most *domaines* means that the majority of *cuvées* are blends of wines from

Despite the stream of visitors to the former summer residence of the popes, Châteauneuf-du-Pape has retained an air of quiet and tranquillity. Its wine has recently re-established its former reputation.

a great variety of *terroirs*, which engenders balance and at the same time helps to minimize the risks associated with ripening.

Overall, 13 varieties of grape are permitted in the *appellation*, of which Grenache, Cinsault, Mourvèdre, Syrah, Muscardin, Counoise, Clairette, and Bourboulenc are those mainly used. Many of the top growers consider Grenache as the most complex variety, while Mourvèdre, which is hard when young and inclined to reduction, gives the wines aging ability. In recent years, more Syrah has been planted, but in the hot southerly climate it does not display much of the subtlety and complexity it reveals in the northern Rhône. Much has also changed in recent decades during the winemaking. Whereas the reds used to be left on the mash for two or three months and then aged for five to ten years in the barrel, the equivalent periods now are two weeks and two years respectively. Experiments were also made with carbonic maceration, but this does not make much sense with a wine whose typical features are great strength and density.

Unusual Reds

The most unconventional way of making red wine is probably that found at the famous Domaine Beaucastel, located on a site dominated by giant red pebbles. On the Perrin brothers' estate they follow an old family recipe in which the mash is heated to 176°F (80°C) immediately after leaving the wine press, in order to improve the extraction of tannins. In good vintages, these wines are among the most characterful in the *appellation*, but in lesser years they can seem over-extracted and over-structured. The changing style of Beaucastel wines, however, suggests that the mash is not being heated with quite the same rigor as before. In many firms in Châteauneuf, very traditional methods are still used despite much shorter times together with the mash. Large wooden barrels or even old concrete tanks for fermentation are, with the exception of estates such as Mont Redon, encountered far less often than barrels, except with whites, whose best representatives are fermented in small oak barrels.

Select Producers of Châteauneuf-Du-Pape

Château de Beaucastel★★★★–★★★★★
Courthézon
247 acres (100 ha); 330,000 bottles • Wines:
→ *Châteauneuf-du-Pape Blanc, Rouge; Roussane Vieilles Vignes, Côtes du Rhône Coudoulet de Beaucastel, La Vieille Ferme*
However unusual the vinification of the red Châteauneuf-du-Pape by forced heating of the mash may seem, the quality in good years is incontestable. However, the estate's top wine is the white Châteauneuf. The estate also sells good generic Côtes du Rhône and wines under the Perrin & Fils brand.

Château la Gardine★★★–★★★★
Châteauneuf-du-Pape
124 acres (50 ha); 220,000 bottles • Wines include: Châteauneuf-du-Pape Blanc, Rouge: Tradition, → *Cuvée Les Générations*
The Brunel family has turned La Gardine into one of the best examples of the modern, balanced Châteauneuf style with excellent barrel maturing.

Château Mont Redon★★★–★★★★
Châteauneuf-du-Pape
358 acres (145 ha); 640,000 bottles • Wines:
→ *Châteauneuf-du-Pape Blanc, Rouge; Côtes du Rhône: Blanc, Rosé, Rouge, Lirac*
Mont Redon is one of the largest and most consistent wine-growing estates of the *appellation*. The Abeille and Fabre families have in recent years replaced the old concrete tank and wooden barrels of the winery with a modern stainless steel system. The Lirac Château Cantegril has also belonged to the estate for some time.

Château la Nerthe★★★★–★★★★★
Châteauneuf-du-Pape
222 acres (90 ha); 175,000 bottles • Wines: Châteauneuf-du-Pape: Cuvée des Cadettes, → *Blanc Clos de Beauvenir*
La Nerthe was the place where the 13 grape varieties that became the foundation of Châteauneuf-du-Pape were first planted after the phylloxera disaster. The former Parisian tax consultant Alain Dugas took over the state in 1990, brought it right up to date technically, and systematically reduced the Grenache constituent of the vineyard in favor of Syrah and Mourvèdre.

Château Rayas★★★★
Châteauneuf-du-Pape
63 acres (25.5 ha); bottles not recorded • Wines: Châteauneuf-du-Pape Blanc, Rouge, Cuvée Pignan
One of the most fashionable wines of the *appellation* comes from Rayas, whose owner also runs the Château des Tours and Château de Fonsalette in the Villages. Rayas is a high class, finely structured wine that ages superbly.

Clos du Mont-Olivet★★★–★★★★
Châteauneuf-du-Pape
99 acres (40 ha); 200,000 bottles • Wines include: Châteauneuf-du-Pape: Blanc, Rouge, → *Cuvée du Papet; Côtes du Rhône*
As traditional as this estate are its wines, in which tertiary aromas of brushwood, fungus and leather can quickly be detected. The top wine is Cuvée du Papet.

Domaine de la Janasse★★★★–★★★★★
Courthézon
124 acres (50 ha); 150,000 bottles • Wines: Châteauneuf-du-Pape Blanc, Rouge, Tradition, → *Chaupin,* → *Vieilles Vignes, Côtes du Rhône:* → *Le Chastelet, Les Garrigues*
Since young Christophe Sabon took over the winery side of the estate, the quality of the wine has stabilized at a

spectacularly high level, both for the three Châteauneuf *cuvées* and for the selection of Côtes du Rhône. The white wines are also of the same high standard.

Domaine de Marcoux★★★★
Orange
47 acres (19 ha); 40,000 bottles • Wines: Châteauneuf-du-Pape Blanc, → *Rouge; Côtes du Rhône*
Catherine and Sophie Armenier, two sisters, use biodynamic cultivation in their vineyards and harvest very elegant, deep reds with fine tannins.

Domaine de la Mordorée★★★–★★★★
Lirac
136 acres (55 ha); 280,000 bottles • Wines include: Châteauneuf-du-Pape, → *Lirac Cuvée de la Reine des Bois, Lirac Blanc, Tavel, Côtes du Rhône Blanc, Rosé, Rouge*
Although the estate is outside the *appellation*, it has been among the best producers of Châteauneuf for some time. In terms of quality, however, the red Lirac *cuvée* is on the same level.

Domaine du Pegaü★★★–★★★★★
Châteauneuf-du-Pape
52 acres (21 ha); 90,000 bottles • Wines: Châteauneuf-du-Pape: Cuvée Laurence, Da Capo, Cuvée Réservée
Father Paul and daughter Laurence jointly run the estate, which has been marketing its own wine only since 1989. The whites are fermented after a short time in used barrels, the reds in concrete. No clarification or filtration is undertaken. The style is classic, powerful and full of volume.

Domaine Pierre Usseglio★★★★
Châteauneuf-du-Pape
52 acres (21 ha); 60,000 bottles • Wines: Châteauneuf-du-Pape: Blanc, → *Rouge,* → *Cuvée de Mon Aïeul*
In recent years, Jean-Pierre and Thierry Usseglio have given their wines more body, but also more polish. Outstanding quality.

Domaine Vieux Télégraphe★★★★
Bédarrides
173 acres (70 ha); 220,000 bottles • Wines: Châteauneuf-du-Pape Blanc, Rouge; Vieux Mas des Papes
The Brunier bothers' estate stands somewhat apart from Châteauneuf—they also own the Domaine de la Roquette directly in the heart of the locality. The quality of their wines is founded on the top location at La Crau, one of the highest points in the locality. Wine-making is traditional and yields are low.

Domaine de Villeneuve★★★★
Orange
20.7 acres (8.4 ha); 29,000 bottles • Wine: Châteauneuf-du-Pape
Philippe and Marie-Christine du Roy de Blicquey have been running the state since 1993, using biodynamic methods. With admirable reliability, they produce a single wine full of finesse and complexity.

Vielle Julienne★★★–★★★★★
Orange
76.5 acres (31 ha); bottles not recorded • Wines: Châteauneuf-du-Pape: → *Vieilles Vignes, Blanc, Côtes du Rhône Villages Vieilles Vignes*
That the normal version and the Special Cuvée of the Châteauneuf are of virtually the same high standard and in any case far above most rivals is a rare phenomenon. This estate is hidden behind the façade of a small farmhouse and produces absolutely top class wines without exaggerated attention to technology.

THE WINES OF THE SAVOIE

The Alpine Region of eastern France, which consists of the departments of Savoie and Haut-Savoie, used to be an independent kingdom that stretched a long way into modern Italy. The bilingualism of the neighboring Aosta Vallay goes back to this time. The individuality and seclusion of the area have meant that its wines are only rarely seen outside regional borders. Vines are grown on about 3,950 acres (1,600 ha), two thirds with white varieties and mainly in the Rhône Valley between Lake Geneva and the Lac du Bourget and south thereof as far as Chambéry and the Isère Valley, supplemented by smaller enclaves in the north and northeast. Unlike most French areas of cultivation, which are laid out compactly over large areas, the vineyards of the narrow valleys make a patchwork quilt. Despite this, there is only one larger *appellation*, Vin de Savoie, which covers a whole series of grape-variety wines, and besides this a number of mini-districts such as Crépy or Seyssel, plus a special *appellation* for the Roussette grape and Prickler Mousseux and Pétillant de Savoie.

The most notable feature of the wines is the range of native grape varieties, which probably owe their existence to the special political position of the former kingdom. Apart from the white Jacquère grape, which alone covers 2,470 of the 3,950 acres (1,000 of the 1,600 ha), and is notable mainly for its high yield and neutral character, it is the red Mondeuse and white Roussette that carry the banner for quality, alongside which even the increasingly cultivated Gamay or Chardonnay have a hard time.

NATIVE VARIETIES WITH FLAIR

In particular, the wines from the Mondeuse grapes—dark, juicy, and with a light peppery overtone—come up with astonishing quality. The variety is possibly related or even identical to the Refosco grape of North Italy. Nowadays it is unfortunately only cultivated on about 494 acres (200 ha), Gamay (which is easier to grow) having replaced it in many vineyards. Its white equivalent is Roussette, also called Altesse, a late-ripening variety that is possibly related or identical to the Hungarian Furmint grape. Roussette wines with their pronounced acidity and high aging ability can be among the best white wines of France, and this special position is recognized by the legislation with a separate

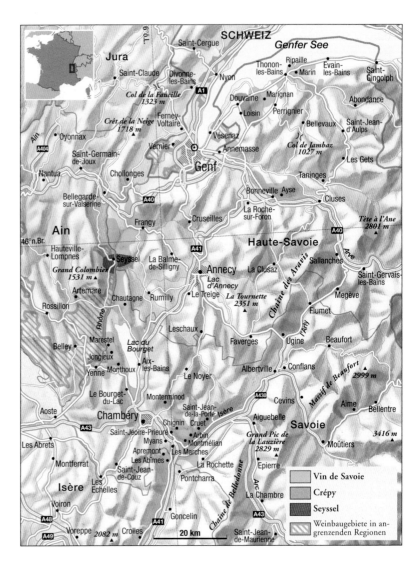

Opposite
Unusual grape varieties flourish in the alpine landscape that give Vin de Savoie quite a distinctive character.

appellation within the overall Vin de Savoie designation. Single-variety Roussette wines from low yields can also be marketed under the village name. If the latter is absent, the wines are made with up to 50 percent Chardonnay.

Chasselas, otherwise more popular in Switzerland and Alemannic areas, dominates not only the vineyards nearest Lake Geneva-where it has its own *appellation* in the Crépy mini-district, but is also the predominant variety in the Seyssel cultivation area north of the Lac du Bourget. In both areas, light, fruity, and sometimes fizzy wines are produced, though the fizzy and sparkling wines are generally sold as Mousseux and Pétillant de Savoie.

The larger part of the regional production reaches the market as Vin de Savoie, with the label also carrying the name of the commune in a number of cases. The red varieties allowed under this *appellation*, which are often single-variety, are Gamay, Mondeuse, Pinot Noir, Cabernet Franc, Cabernet Sauvignon and others, with a proportion of white grapes also being acceptable. Among the permitted white varieties are Aligoté, Roussette, the mass grape Jacquère, Chardonnay, and Mondeuse Blanche.

A similar range of varieties is found in Bugey, adjacent to western Savoie, even though it belongs neither administratively nor geographically to the departments of the former kingdom. The wines likewise show great affinities, apart from the absence of Chasselas. Here Montagnieu, Manicle, Machuraz, Virieu-le-Grand, and Cerdon have *villages* rights, and Cerdon even has a separate *appellation* for Mousseux and Pétillant.

Select Producers

Patrick Charlin***–****
Groslée
12 acres (5 ha); 40,000 bottles. Wines: Bugey: Montagnieu: → Brut and → Altesse, Pinot Noir, Pressurage de Novembre
Patrick Charlin has had great success with his sparkling wine and the Altesse from the vineyards on the slopes of Montagnieu. The Pinot is more unreliable, depending on location.

Château de la Violette**–***
Les Marches
20 acres (8 ha); 80,000 bottles • Wines: Abymes, Apremont, Roussette de Savoie, Vin de Savoie Rouge
The fact that the vineyards of Daniel Fustinoni contain two-thirds Jacquère does not necessarily make his drive for quality any easier. Nonetheless, he keeps coming up with good white wines of various *villages*.

Domaine de Manicle & Virieu**–***
Murs
25 acres (10 ha); 65,000 bottles • Wines: Roussette Virieu, Manicle Blanc, → Manicle Rouge, Mondeuse
Christian and Christiane Beaulieu are among the few winemakers of Bugey whose wines can hold their own in a national context. Their red Manicle in particular is worth noting.

Domaine du Prieuré Saint-Christophe***
Fréterive
16 acres (6.5 ha); Wines: Mondeuse Cuvée Prestige, Roussette de Savoie
As one of the pioneers of the Savoie *appellation*, Michel Grisard has specialized in the two native varieties, the red Mondeuse and white Roussette. His Roussette shows that the variety can stand aging in the barrel. The Mondeuse is not only of unusual density and intensity but also ageable.

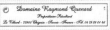

Louis Magnin***–****
Arbin
15 acres (6 ha); 35,000 bottles • Wines: Roussette de Savoie, → Arbin Mondeuse Vieilles Vignes, → Chignin-Bergeron
Béatrice and Louis Magnin have marketed their own wines since 1978. Their white Chignon-Bergeron from Roussette grapes and the red Arbin from old stocks are both convincing.

André & Michel Quénard***–****
Chignin
54 acres (22 ha); 150,000 bottles • Wines: Abymes, Chignin, → Chignin-Bergeron, Chignin-Gamay, → Chignin-Mondeuse
The strength of the Quénards father and son lies in their reds made from Gamay and Mondeuse, but the whites, especially the Chignin-Bergeron Les Terrasses, show consistently good quality.

Raymond Quénard***
Chignin
15 acres (6 ha); 50,000 bottles • Wines: Chignin Blanc, Chignin-Bergeron, Chignin Rouge, Chignon Gamay, Chignin Mondeuse
The ace up the sleeve of Raymond Quénard is the almost century-old stocks of his vineyards. Apart from Mondeuse, he has specialized mainly in white wines, which he develops into particularly soft and round wines by systematically converting the acidity.

Charles Trosset***
Arbin
8.5 acres (3.5 ha); 25,000 bottles • Wines: Arbin Mondeuse
Charles Trosset produces one of the strongest and most expressive Mondeuses of the Vin de Savoie *appellation*.

PROVENCE: THE SEA, THE SUN, AND MORE

Provence has a magic power of attraction. The name alone evokes a yearning for sunshine, azure blue skies, and rocky bays with clear blue water, umbrella pines and the intense scent of wild herbs such as thyme and lavender, leisure and carefree enjoyment. But only connoisseurs will appreciate that Provence is also an El Dorado for wine.

The first vine stocks were brought here in the 6th century BC by Phoenicians from the coast of the Levant and Phocaean Greeks from Asia Minor. After the Romans established their Provincia Romana in 154 BC, meritorious Roman veteran soldiers would be given, by way of a pension, a small estate here that they could develop to grow vines and other produce. In Fréjus, the launching point for Roman colonization, and Marseille, major potteries were established where amphorae were made to ship Provençal wine to the most distant imperial legionaries. In the Middle Ages, it was—like everywhere else—the monasteries that carried on the cultivation.

The first holiday guests—aristocrats from northern Europe—arrived in the 18th century. In the 19th century, the Côte d'Azur was defi-

Provence is one of the lushest fruit- and vegetable-growing areas of France, but also produces top wines.

Opposite
The intense aromas of herbs, flowers, and fruit are often found in the bouquet of the wines.

nitely a fashionable destination in winter for the rich and powerful. The year-round stream of tourists, which had a major effect on Provence in general and its wine industry in particular, began in 1936, when the Front Populaire government introduced paid holidays for everyone. After the Second World War, summer tourism exploded, plastering the whole coast with accommodation buildings of all kinds in order to absorb the hundreds of thousands of sun-seeking visitors. Holiday eating habits also assumed Provençal guise, consisting of *mesclun* (mixed green salad), tomatoes, ratatouille, grilled fish, lamb cutlets, and *aïoli* (garlic mayonnaise). Provence sold its most suitable accompaniment—ice-cooled rosé.

Following the succession of disasters (phylloxera, wars, and economic crises), and like most of their colleagues elsewhere, Provençal growers went over to mass production, and planted mainly Carignan, Cinsault, and Grenache vines for the *gros rouge*. The scratchy red was better suited to the world of the industrial cities of the north than to the summery Mediterranean atmosphere. But, pressed quickly or racked after only a short period on the mash, the lighter,

making red wines of much higher quality. White wines are made only in small quantities and are often of only average quality. The region has four small areas of cultivation that have long been famous and in the top rank: Bandol, Cassis, Bellet, and Palette. Their *terroirs* consistently produce convincing and fascinating wines of great expressiveness and quality.

Newcomers Then and Now

Two factors have exerted influence on the Provençal wine industry. The first was a stream of *pieds noirs*, Algerian French who left Algeria after 1962 and settled in Provence and the Midi mainly for climatic reasons. They put enormous effort into rebuilding their lives, not infrequently in the wine business. They often already had practical experience of growing wine in the dry heat of Algeria, and were therefore open to major innovations in matters such as temperature controls.

From around 1980, the wine estates also awoke the interest of other newcomers. Apart from the fascination of the landscape itself, it was the love of wine that they had in common, which had previously manifested itself generally in an enthusiasm for the great Bordeaux and Burgundies. On the basis of their expertise and often with the introduction of great financial resources, numerous *domaines* were completely renovated and restructured, laying the basis for the current explosion in quality. The newcomers hailed not just from other parts of France but also from other countries such as Germany, England, Scotland, Holland, Sweden, Denmark, Switzerland, and the U.S.A., often bringing with them great attention and devotion to natural winemaking that has shown up in the quality and expressiveness of the wines.

tannin-deficient rosés could be pressed from the same grapes and tossed down the throat—well chilled, of course.

Nothing has changed in this even today. Up to four-fifths of the total wine production of Provence is turned into rosé. What better outcome could there be for a grower than to have his product sold off a bare half year after the harvest and drunk before the following harvest? The cash till is quickly replenished, and work in the winery is gratifyingly minimal. Most estates and cooperatives are not reluctant to exploit the opportunity.

Quality, of course, often falls by the wayside in the process. It is no wonder, therefore, that rosé's image is that of a minor wine that need not be taken seriously. However, increasingly numerous excellent rosés are being produced, whether immediately pressed to make elegant pale wines or made by the alternative method into somewhat stronger raspberry-colored wines.

Moreover, along with the seasonal rosé there is another less obvious trend. Provence is developing no less rapidly than the other regions of southern France. More and more estates are

Raimond de Villeneuve has restored the Château de Roquefort estate with great zeal.

Tireless champions of Bandol—Comte Henri de Saint-Victor and his son Eric.

The extraordinarily broad range of grape varieties in Provence came in very handy for this upturn. Apart from the three varieties mentioned above there are Syrah, Mourvèdre, Cabernet plus Vermentino, Sémillon, Sauvignon, and Marsanne. Most businesses operate on a two-quality basis: simple, cleanly vinified, and cheap wines for everyday use and the general public, who often drive over from Marseille, Aix-en-Provence, and Nice to buy direct; and more ambitious and more expensive *cuvées* for connoisseurs and the many restaurants of the Côte d'Azur, that are only too happy to promote and give precedence to local growers. After

The quality of the wines of Château Simone is a match for the splendid appearance of the estate.

Provençal *restanques*—flat terraces shored up by stones.

locals, restaurants, and tourists have stocked up at cooperatives and estates, not much is left of the best wines of Provence and Corsica for export. If you want to get an impression of the best wines you are more or less obliged to visit them at home. The same is true in Corsica (see page 314), where the wines show an enchanting character of their own.

Coteaux d'Aix and Les Baux de Provence

On the chalk cliffs above the Étang de Berre are the ruins of one of the oldest settlements in Provence.

Coteaux d'Aix: A Mini-region with a Microclimate

Aix itself is not a wine-producing city, apart from the tiny Palette *appellation*, whose north-facing slopes overlook part of it. Things were different in the 18th century: the total area planted to vines covered 56,800 acres (23,000 ha), reaching right up to the city. Only 8,150 acres (3,300 ha) of this remain, keeping the city at a respectful distance and lying mainly southwest, west and north of it. In the east, the Montagne Sainte-Victoire marks the beginning of the Côtes de Provence region.

In the north, the Durance constitutes the boundary, establishing its course between the Montagne du Lubéron and the Chaîne de Trévarasse. The loamy, sandy soils of the valley here are covered with extensive vineyards. Eastward, there is an exceptional area between Jouques and Rians, which belongs to the Var department, as does the neighboring Artigues, while the other 47 localities of the *appellation* belong to Bouches-du-Rhône. At a height of over 1,000 feet (300 m), it has a special microclimate that is much cooler than one would expect in Provence. This delays the ripening of the grapes, involving greater risks for the grower, but does wonders for the structure and aroma of the wines. The first grower to show what could be done was Georges Brunet, former owner of

Aix-en-Provence has been able to buff up its reputation as a city of arts and literature only in recent decades. In the 15th century, it was a stronghold of the arts under René the Good, Count of Provence and "Last of the Troubadors," who granted the city privileges and popularized its wines. The French Revolution, 300 years later, brought hard times. Marseille ousted Aix, and the latter struggled to establish an identity. Today the university city shines once again, not least because of its famous festival, for which a special *cuvée* is bottled.

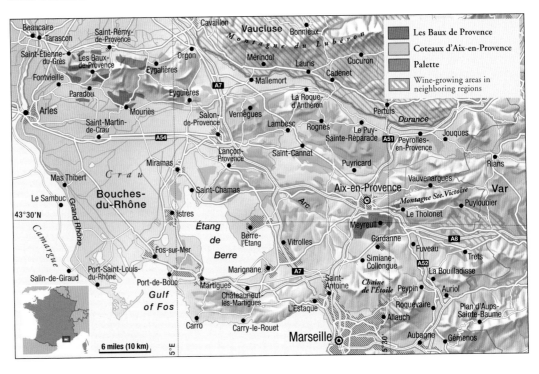

the 3ème Cru Classé La Lagune at Vignelaure. From the 1989 vintage, Californian-trained German grower Peter Fischer at Château Revelette spearheaded development in the mini-region with his Grand Vin assembled from Syrah and Cabernet, which has a good ten-year aging potential. The other reds in the region are generally allowed a life of three to five years.

A New Generation of Red Wines

Syrah and Cabernet Sauvignon have become the basis of the red wines that are to be taken seriously in the Coteaux d'Aix. Bordeaux's superstar grape has a distinctly non-Atlantic character of its own in Provence, whether in the Coteaux d'Aix or the Côtes de Provence. Mostly the weather is just right for the late-ripening Cabernet, so that the green vegetal aromas and tannins are replaced by full-bodied blackberry fruit tones. When combined with Syrah, the aromas and fruit take on a distinctly southern quality, though in the Coteaux d'Aix they do not seem awkward or heavy.

Other zones in the *appellation*, such as the areas around Saint-Cannat and Lambesc, lie between 650 and 1,000 feet (200 and 300 m) above sea-level and thus retain a moderate Mediterranean climate with a later ripening date. The wines mostly manifest slight increased acidity, giving balance and freshness to the rosés, which even here make up over half the production and are often more than 50 percent Grenache Noir. The occasional whites, for which growers have a choice of Clairette, Ugni Blanc,

Peacocks are the mascots of Château Revelette.

The wines of Mas de la Dame are best sampled in the courtyard of the farmhouse.

Rolle, Sémillon, or Grenache Blanc, have a pleasant freshness that is generally lacking in hotter localities. However, all estates offer all three types, often with a choice of two levels of quality.

The areas planted to vine around the Étang de Berre enjoy a particularly mild climate with higher humidity, producing grapes that ripen early and yield round, harmonious wines. On the limestone cliffs near Lançon, which belong to the 2,470-acre (1,000-ha) estate of Château Calissane, the ruins of a fortified village can be discerned, built by the Ligurian Celts in the 4th century BC before the Romans conquered the area. Grapes grow here alongside olive trees and almonds, and depending on the yield, selection, and vinification, produce wines with fruity, aromatic charm or—most notably after aging in the bottle for four or five years—that emphasize the dense, complex expressiveness of the *terroir*.

Les Baux de Provence

The Alpilles are undoubtedly one of the most captivating landscapes in Provence. The fissured chalk cliffs contrast with the azure blue of the sky. Pines and wild herbs dominate the flora and vine stocks. In the small district comprising only six villages south of Avignon and northeast of the Camargue, the climate is hotter and more humid than in the Coteaux d'Aix and thus earlier-ripening than in the Coteaux d'Aix, to which it used to belong. The number of sunshine hours per annum varies between 2,700 and 2,900, enough to guarantee best ripening. In

The Cabernet dispute

The potential of the Les Baux district for wine is evident from the story of a newcomer to the area, architect Eloi Durrbach. In 1974, he took over his grandmother's summer residence on the northern side of the Alpilles and developed it into the wine-growing estate of Domaine de Trévallon, which he planted with his favorite varieties Cabernet and Syrah in equal proportions. Using natural methods and a dramatic reduction of yields, he made a red wine from young vines that caused a sensation internationally, and triggered off fierce controversy in Les Baux as to what percentage of Cabernet would compromise the typical character of the district. Despite Trévallon with its handmade, uncompromising wines having done more for the reputation of Les Baux than all the others put together, a majority of the

growers' association voted to link the *appellation* they were seeking with a condition limiting the proportion of Cabernet in the *assemblage* to 15 percent. Therefore, when Les Baux became an independent A.C., the 1995 Domaine de Trévallon was downgraded on the label to a Vin de Pays de Bouches-du-Rhône, even though the vintages since then have been still better, bearing incomparable witness to an outstanding *terroir*. The delightful and rare white wine is based on Marsanne and Rousanne fermented in the bottle, and far outstrips the other whites of Les Baux, which follow the specifications of the Coteaux d'Aix.

Just as his father carved sculptures, so too Eloi Durrbach has created works of art from the stony soil of the Alpilles.

addition, the Mistral with its violent gusts helps to keep vine diseases in check. The first to exploit the natural conditions of this exceptional region was Noël Michelin, a scion of the famous tire family, with his great experience plantations and of the world. From 1968, he structured his Domaine des Terres Blanches on sound ecological principles, making it one of the first bio-estates in France. His example set a trend. There are only 14 estates that make up the 741-acre (300-ha) *appellation*, but a majority of them use mostly natural methods on the predominantly very stony, argillocalcitic soil. Two estates follow biodynamic principles, and four others are biologically recognized.

No less important is the self-discipline that the *domaines* had to accept when they achieved their own *appellation* in 1995. With a higher

density of plants, stricter cutting back, lower yields, and a minimum aging in the winery of 12 months for red wines, they were nailing their colors to the mast. The rosé is limited to about one fifth of the harvest instead of the four fifths of Côtes de Provence.

In reds, a range of varieties was deliberately opted for in which Grenache and Syrah predominate, with Mourvèdre and Cabernet in the supporting role, in order to obtain a distinct Provençal character. Thanks to the high quality of the wines, the tourist appeal of the spectacular village of Les Baux and the Alpilles, together with the luxury restaurants, the fame of and demand for the Les Baux de Provence A.C. is guaranteed.

An exceptional Palette

Managed by the Rougier family since 1850, Château Simone enjoys unchallenged special status, not just in Provence but in France. Its 42 acres (17 ha) account for four fifths of the Palette *appellation*, and because of its fame was declared an A.C. back in 1948. The north-facing slopes of Montaiguer on the southeastern boundaries of Aix provide a cool *terroir* in an otherwise hot environment. In the 16th century, monks of the Grands Carmes d'Aix laid out plots to vines and dug a vaulted cellar into the hillside. They also built the core of the château, to which later owners added the arrowhead turrets and lateral wings. Under the Rougiers, all that was kept in excellent condition along with the dozen 'olde-worlde' varieties that populate the vineyards along with Grenache, Mourvèdre, and Cinsault, plus Clairette, Ugni, and Grenache Blanc. Many vine stocks are 50 or more years

old, and, being on north-facing slopes, ripen slowly and continuously. The main consideration here is to preserve and continue tradition with care and prudence. The most unusual wine is the white, which is fermented in the barrel, aged in wood until the end of the second year after the harvest and can mature for decades, when it manifests itself as a highly elegant wine with toasty, nutty overtones. The tannin-rich reds have no less class. Both are wines beyond any fashion. They are testimony to a wine culture that goes back centuries and these days is rarely found so unadulterated. Let us hope that Château Simone will continue to remain true to its principles.

No other Crus de Provence age so excellently as the white and red Palettes from Château Simone. After 40 years in the cellar, the white wine is a subtle joy.

Select Producers in Coteaux d'Aix and Les Baux de Provence

Château Bas**—***
Vernègues

173 acres (70 ha); 450,000 bottles • Wines: Coteaux d'Aix: Alvernègues, Pierre du Sud, Cuvée du Temple: Blanc, → Rosé, → Rouge
Built right beside a Roman temple, the château is undergoing a renaissance thank to former Gaggenau chef George von Blanquet. Since 1995, the Cuvées du Temple in particular have gone from strength to strength.

Château de Beaupré***
Saint-Cannat

99 acres (40 ha); 200,000 bottles • Wines: Coteau d'Aix including Château de Beaupré Blanc, Rosé, Rouge; Collection du Château Blanc, → Rouge
Baron Émile Double laid out the first vineyards and cellerage beside the neat château in 1980. Today his direct descendants are still running the estate. The Collection features wines with good aging ability matured in the barrel.

Château Calissane**—****
Lançon-Provence

247 acres (100 ha); 600,000 bottles • Wines: Coteau d'Aix: Cuvée du Château, Cuvée Prestige, Clos Victoire: Blanc, Rosé, Rouge
Director Jean Bonnet has turned the historic 2,470 acre (1,000 ha) estate beside the Étang de Berre into a topflight operation. Convincing quality is produced on three clearly distinct levels, the top being Clos Victoire Rouge, one of the best reds in Provence.

Château Revelette***—****
Jouques

63 acres (25 ha); 120,000 bottles • Wines: Coteau d'Aix: Blanc, Rosé, Rouge; Grand Vin: → Blanc, Rosé, → Rouge
Peter Fischer has achieved very aromatic, fine-fruited Peacock wines—the living symbol of the estate—and challenging, ambitious and (especially with the red) long-aging first-rate wines using organic cultivation and Californian expertise.

Château Romanin**—****
Saint-Rémy-de-Provence

141 acres (57 ha); 180,000 bottles • Wines: Les Baux de Provence: Château Romanin: Blanc, Rosé, → Rouge; La Chapelle de Romanin, Cuvée Le Coeur
With biodynamic techniques and tiny yields, the eminently ageable wines produced by Jean-André Charial (*patron* of the celebrated nearby restaurant L'Oustau de Baumanière) and Jean-Pierre Reyraud get better and better.

Château du Seuil***
Puyricard

128 acres (52 ha); 250,000 bottles • Wines: Coteau d'Aix Blanc; Le Grand Seuil: Rosé, Rouge; → Le Grand Seuil Prestige
This stately estate north of Aix-en-Provence first established a reputation with its aromatic whites, but the red wines are also convincing.

Château Simone****—*****
Meyreuil

42 acres (17 ha); 80,000 bottles • Wines: Palette: → Blanc, Rosé, → Rouge
Château Simone (see lower panel on previous page) is a living vinological monument. Its white wines in particular are legendary and age for 30 years or more.

Domaine des Béates**—****
Lambesc

57 acres (23 ha); 100,000 bottles • Wines: Coteau d'Aix: Les Mantines: Blanc, Rosé, Rouge; Béates: Rosé, → Rouge; → Terra d'Or
The house of Chapoutier was responsible for the changeover of the estate to biodynamic cultivation in 1996. Top of the range is the highly concentrated Terra d'Or, matured in new barrels. The different *domaines* now each follow their own way.

Domaine d'Eole***—****
Eygalières

57 acres (23 ha); 100,000 bottles • Wines: Coteau d'Aix including Tradition Rosé, Cuvée Caprice Rosé; Tradition Rouge, → Cuvée Léa
Christian Raimont has used organic methods in his vineyards since the estate was founded in 1993. The lively, elegant Cuvée Léa, based on Grenache and Syrah, is among the most interesting wines of the *appellation*, as is the Cuvée Caprice rosé.

Domaine Hauvette***—****
Saint-Rémy-de-Provence

30 acres (12 ha); 40,000 bottles • Wines include: → Coteau d'Aix Blanc; Les Baux de Provence: Rosé, → Rouge
Horse-lover Dominique Hauvette runs her small estate using organic methods, doing the work herself from the vineyard to the bottling. Very concentrated and complex reds.

Domaine Terres Blanches***—****
Saint-Rémy-de-Provence

86.5 acres (35 ha); 140,000 bottles • Wines: Coteau d'Aix Blanc; Les Baux de Provence: Rosé, → Rouge; → Cuvée Aurélia
Noël Michelin, scion of the tire family, created the first French organic wine-growing estate here in 1968. The outstanding Cuvée Aurélia, a blend of Syrah, Grenache and Cabernet, is made only in the best years.

Domaine de Trévallon****—*****
Saint-Étienne-du-Grès

49.5 acres (20 ha); 65,000 bottles • Wines: Vin de Pays des Bouches-du-Rhône: → Blanc, → Rouge
On one of the best *terroirs* of Les Baux, Eloi Durrbach produces its greatest wines—but outside the A.C. (see upper panel on previous page). The white wine consist of only 3,500 bottles.

Mas de la Dame***—****
Les Baux de Provence

143 acres (58 ha); 240,000 bottles • Wines include: Les Baux de Provence: Rosé du Mas; Cuvée de la Stéle, → Coin Caché
Two female growers are successfully developing the idyllic estate using organic methods to make it one of the best . The white wine is also a success.

Mas Sainte-Berthe**—***
Les Baux de Provence

94 acres (38 ha); 150,000 bottles • Wines: Coteaux d'Aix Blanc; Les Baux de Provence: Passe Rosé; Tradition, → Cuvée Louis David
The vineyards of this much visited estate lie at the foot of the castle of Le Baux. The estate is steadily enhancing the quality of its wines (especially the reds), undistracted by the stream of tourists.

CÔTES DE PROVENCE AND COTEAUX VAROIS

Aix, Toulon, and Fréjus are the three points that roughly mark out the main cultivation area of Provençal wines. It is an enormous triangle in which over 51,900 acres (21,000 ha) are classed as A.C., not to mention the additional areas under vine that furnish various *vins de pays*. The ancient Provincia Romana offers excellent conditions for viticulture, which has been carried out here on a large scale since antiquity. In summer, the temperature can rise far above 86°F (30°C), especially in the interior, but the Mistral often provides a touch of freshness and keeps the vine stocks healthy, because fungal and other diseases can scarcely tolerate its dry draft. Precipitation is low, and most common in spring and autumn. Growers have mostly storms and hail to fear, which can destroy their work and the harvest in minutes. Climatic conditions are modified by the great diversity of the sites and their alignment, because several chains of hills give the landscape a variegated aspect.

Geologically speaking, two elements dominate: a crystalline rock base dating back to the Paleozoic and later chalk formations. When the Alps folded upward, the limestone was thrust westward, while the rock base was folded upward in the east, and still shows visible influences of volcanic activity. There it constitutes the major massifs of the Maures, Esterel, and Tanneron. In the west, limestone sediments characterize the Bandol and Cassis areas and also the Montagne Sainte-Victoire near Aix.

On the Domaine Richeaume at the foot of the Montagne Sainte-Victoire an integrated concept was put into practice.

Parade in pastel tones: tank test at the Domaine Sant-André, near La-Londe-des-Maures.

The Côtes de Provence A.C. has been an umbrella designation for the cultivated areas of the Var department since 1977, from which only the cooperative growers around Brignoles gained nothing at the time. Their *appellation* Coteaux Varois was obtained only in 1993. It includes 28 parishes with 4,450 acres (1,800 ha) under vine overall, with a good two thirds of the production being sold as rosé, a quarter as red and the rest as white wine. In the meantime, there are an increasing number of independent estates with a concern for quality.

In the sister *appellation* there has been much renewed discussion about sites, with a view to subdividing the almost 47,000 acres (19,000 ha) under vine into *terroirs*. A provisional classification exists that follows geography and is based on five zones.

• La Bordure Maritime: the coastal strip between Saint-Raphael and Hyères;
• Les Collines du Haut-Pays: the hilly region around Lorgues and Draguignan, rising towards the north;
• La Vallée Intérieure: the valley stretching from Vidauban to Toulon behind the Massif des Maures;
• Le Bassin du Beausset: the Beausset basin adjacent to the *appellations* of Cassis and Bandol;
• La Sainte-Victoire: the vineyards at the foot of the Montagne Sainte-Victoire in the north and the Monts Auréliens in the south. La Sainte-Victoire was the first of these areas to obtain an official recognition.

The name of the mountain which Paul Cézanne painted again and again, almost obsessively, is now synonymous with the most highly

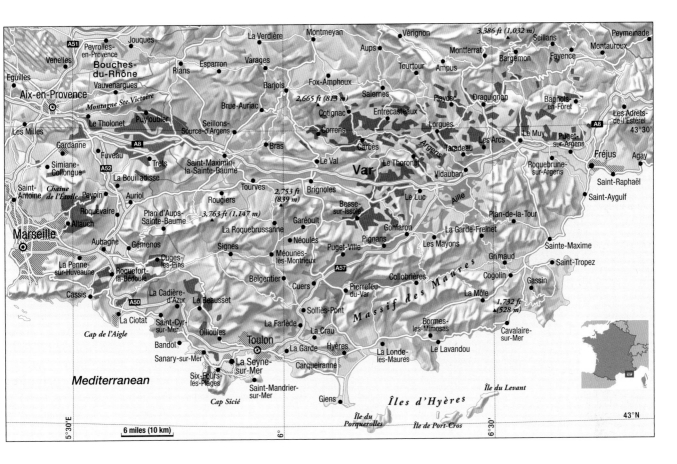

developed Côtes de Provence area—in terms of cohesion, image, and the quality of the wines produced.

WINE STYLES AND GRAPE VARIETIES

Rosé is an important economic factor for Provençal growers. The chief varieties used are Grenache Noir and Cinsault, the former making the fruitier style, the latter the floral, fuller-bodied style. If the rosé is vinified like a white wine by immediate pressing, the color turns out very pale and the aromas are discreet but elegant. With the rosé derived by the *saignée* process, the must remains on the skins until it reaches the color tone the vintner requires, after which it is bottled without pressing. In this case, it often displays a slight violet shimmer and gives off aromas of small red fruits. A specialty is the Tibouren variety, which produces inherently little color but has a lot of body and liveliness.

The Roman past and the proximity of Italy are also evident in the range of grape varieties. The Trebbiano, here called Ugni Blanc, is particularly common in Provence and is really not serviceable for more than pleasant whites or to add a touch of acidity to the traditional, slightly oxidizing Clairette. However, the Ligurian Vermentino or Rolle is attracting renewed interest on the basis of its fresh aromas and lively structure. Sémillon has long been

Côtes de Provence

- La Sainte-Victoire
- Le Bassin du Beausset
- Les Collines du Haut Pays
- La Vallée Intérieure
- La Bordure Maritime
- **Coteaux Varois**
- **Bandol**
- **Cassis**
- Wine-growing areas in neighboring regions

common, and can produce very elegant wines, especially if fermented in the barrel. Recently some growers have been trying the Sauvignon and Marsanne varieties.

The more interesting wines of Provence are the reds. They have a wide range of varieties to draw on, with Syrah and Mourvèdre setting the pace today, but also quite a lot of Cabernet Sauvignon, domesticated for over a century. Enrichment comes from Grenache Noir and occasionally old Carignan. Although modern expertise is applied, the predominant character of the red wines is linked with tradition in the best sense, and unfurls a many-layered bouquet only after some years. They keep on the whole for about five years, but the aging potential of the concentrated top *cuvées* is often twice as long.

Coteaux de Pierrevert

In the very north of Provence, the district around the towns of Manosque, Forcalquier, and Peyrus succeeded in gaining A.C. status for a cultivated area of 642 acres (260 ha) in 1999. At the foot of the Provençal Alps cooler climatic conditions prevail that are reflected in the freshness of the wines. Rosé is made, of course, plus some white wine, but here too the best wines are the reds, particularly when they contain a healthy dose of Syrah.

Bandol

but very fine tannins derived from the chalk-rich slopes. This gives the wines an aging potential that is extraordinary for the south. Because of this, it became one of the most in-demand export wines in the 18th century, and over 1.5 million gallons (60,000 hl) of wine—more than is produced today—was shipped abroad every year from Bandol in barrels marked with a large B.

Right from the start Bandol was lucky to have devoted growers who believed in their wines and their estates. No *grand cru* comes about anywhere without people of this kind. Starting over after the phylloxera catastrophe was slow and difficult, but the growers worked at it and got their *appellation* in 1941. They themselves set up a strict discipline, namely a minimum 50 percent of the difficult Mourvèdre and a maximum yield of 428 gallons per acre (40 hl per ha). In addition, grapes for red wine could come from young stocks only from the eighth harvest or later. As far as aging was concerned, 18 months in the barrel was prescribed. With these criteria, which are far more rigorous than all *appellations* granted later, they consciously established the basis for the future of red Bandol.

In order to ripen best on Bandol's *terroir*, Mourvèdre requires special treatment. It must be thinned out. Long before growers in other regions realized that this is a means to master the yields and improve quality, the practice was quite the usual thing in the wine-growing

Bandol is among the rare spots in the world where all conditions coincide to make a completely original wine. Its slopes face the sea and are protected from cold north winds, making it ideal for viticulture. This awoke the interest of the Phocaeans almost immediately after they had established a base in what is now Marseille. Bandol is among the very first areas on the European side of the Mediterranean where vines were planted from the 6th century BC However, what predestined the small area for viticulture so early on was the natural harbor at Bandol, which lent the wine in the interior its name.

The fame of Bandol depends on a single grape variety, the Mourvèdre. It comes from Catalonia, where there are towns called Murviedro near Valencia and Mataró near Barcelona, as the extremely late-ripening variety is often called internationally. It is widely distributed in southern Spain, without, however, having brought forth any really remarkable wines so far. Things are different in the south of France. Mourvèdre is here a component of Châteauneuf-du-Pape, where it is documented as long ago as the 17th century and from where it is thought to have spread through Provence. Before phylloxera destroyed the vineyards, it had become one of the leading varieties there, and had established a solid position especially in Bandol along with Grenache and Cinsault.

One quality of Mourvèdre in particular contributed to the rise of Bandol, namely its marked

Clos Sainte-Magdeleine, a dream of an estate at the foot of Cap Canaille, France's tallest cliff, produces one of the best-known Cassis.

A vineyard stands on this promontory extending into the Mediterranean. Small wonder that its Cassis should give off a delicate aroma of iodine from time to time.

communities of Saint-Cyr-sur-Mer, La Cadière d'Azur, Le Castellet, Le Beausset, and their immediate neighbors. Despite almost record levels of sunshine (3,000 hours a year) and the sheltered sites, Mourvèdre would otherwise not ripen and reach a potential alcohol content of 12.5 abv, without which it possesses no quality.

Bandol has not escaped the rosé problem. A substantial proportion of the grapes from the 3,210-acre (1,300-ha) *appellation* is turned into rosé. But however much this product displays a style of its own and shows more strength and finish on the palate than some other rosés, it is still only a small lad compared with a mature red.

In the south of France, Mourvèdre is valued for its intense fruit, often reminiscent of blackberries. But these primary aromas, which in Bandol are often accompanied by overtones of pepper, spices and even meaty tones, give but a slight intimation of the actual character of the wine, which becomes evident generally only eight years after the harvest. Leather and underwood then become the keynotes, accompanied by complex overtones of ripe and cooked berries, licorice, herbs, and spices, though the wines continue to manifest an amazing elegance and harmony.

Thanks to self-discipline and commitment, the *appellation* shows an astonishingly high

Left
Jean-Pierre Gaussen and his family swear by Mourvèdre.

Right
Nature and animal lover Laurent Bunan samples the aromas of a Bandol.

Cassis is one of the rarest white wines of Provence, and goes excellently with Mediterranean fish dishes.

overall level across its 50 estates and five *caves coopératives*, with a whole series of wineries standing out. That you can find still more convincing wines in Bandol has—as elsewhere—to do with hard work in the vineyard and winery and the associated investment. Part of this is a rigorous selection of grapes from special sites and from particularly old vine stocks. Since the end of the 1980s, more and more winemakers have gone over either to greatly increasing the proportion of Mourvèdre in their red *cuvées* or producing a second *cuvée* (almost) solely from Mourvèdre using the best selected grapes. The resulting wines include some of supreme quality. The growers of Bandol have also shown much sensitivity in the use of aging in wood. Most still work with large old tuns, to avoid masking the lively natural tannins of their wines. As far as vintages are concerned, Bandol is a total exception. Though difficult weather conditions may prevail everywhere else, when the Mourvèdre is ripening here in October, the sun is mostly doing its work properly. In contrast, the very rare white wines remain a Mediterranean curiosity, with growers going wherever the mood takes them.

Cassis and Bellet

The small port and neat coastal town of Cap Canaille, in the shadow of the highest cliff in France, offers growers no less favorable conditions for viticulture on their 420 acres (170 ha) planted to vine than Bandol. However, in contrast to the latter, its growers have oriented themselves more to white wines, which now constitute three quarters of total output. They are based on Ugni Blanc, Clairette, Sémillon, and Marsanne. Bulky, characterful and dry, the wines often smell of

almonds, white flowers, peaches, apricots, or even exotic fruits such as lychees or mangoes, and occasionally toss in an overtone of iodine.

The vines thrive on terraces facing the sea. Intent focus on quality reaped the first A.C. for the growers in Provence back in 1936. The remaining quarter of the output is made up of very light (i.e. mostly directly pressed) rosés of Grenache, Cinsault, and Carignan, while reds are a rarity.

Bellet, Nice's own *cru*, is cultivated in the heights above the city and produces barely 100,000 bottles a year. However, the area now exceeds 99 acres (40 ha). The 11 independent estates and single cooperative make very aromatic whites from Rolle, small additions of other southern varieties and some Chardonnay. Thanks to Braquet and Fuella (or Folle Noire), two local varieties, assembled with Grenache and Cinsault, the reds acquire charm and finesse. The rosés are agreeable and lively.

Select Producers of Bandol, Cassis, and Côtes de Provence

Château de Bellet***—****
Nice
25 acres (10 ha); 30,000 bottles • Wines: Bellet: Blanc, Rosé, Rouge; → Rouge Baron 'G'
The château, run by Ghislaine de Charnacé, has for years been the leading estate of the Bellet mini-*appellation* just above Nice. Wines of very individual character.

Château de Fontcreuse***
Cassis
57 acres (23 ha); 110,000 bottles • Wines: Cassis: Blanc, Rosé
Vines have been grown on this site since ancient times. The very aromatic white is based on Ugni, Clairette and Marsanne, the rosé mainly on Grenache.

Château Jean-Pierre Gaussen***—****
La Cadière-d'Azur
30 acres (12 ha); 100,000 bottles • Wines: Bandol: Blanc, Rosé, Rouge; Longue Garde
Jean-Pierre Gaussen, whose wines were previously marketed as Domaine de la Noblesse, goes for strong character in his wines. They are among the most impressive in Bandol, especially the Longue Garde.

Château des Launes***
La Garde Freinet
37 acres (15 ha); 52,000 bottles • Wines: Côtes de Provence: → Blanc, Rosé, Rouge, → Grand Réserve, → Cuvée Prestige
Installed at the foot of the Maures massif since 1981, the Handtmanns from Germany have steadily improved the quality of their wines using natural methods. The fruity white is based on Rolle, the very harmonious reds on Grenache, Syrah, and Cabernet.

Château de Pibarnon****—*****
La Cadière-d'Azur
119 acres (48 ha); 220,000 bottles • Wines: Bandol: Blanc, Rosé, Rouge
Since Comte Henri de Saint-Victor discovered and bought the estate in 1977, Pibarnon has become a model of modern Bandol, not least thanks to the commitment of his son Eric. The terraces face the sea, their blue limestone marls resembling those of Yquem. They produce almost 100% Mourvèdre wines of elegance, complexity, depth, and excellent aging potential.

Château Pradeux****
Saint-Cyr-sur-Mer
52 acres (21 ha); 60,000 bottles • Wines: Bandol: Rosé, → Rouge
Pradeux is the bastion of traditional Bandol with a high aging potential, which Cyril Portalis champions and produces with unwavering commitment.

Château de Roquefort****
Roquefort-la-Bédoule
57 acres (23 ha); 130,000 bottles • Wines include: Côtes de Provence: Blanc, Rosé; Rouge Les Mures, → Rubrum Obscurum
Since 1995, when Raimond de Villeneuve took over the family estate, this has become one of the most interesting *domaines* in Provence. Especially good are the reds and the characterful Rosé Sémiramis.

Château Sainte-Anne**—****
Sainte-Anne-d'Evenos
62 acres (25 ha); 75,000 bottles • Wines: Côtes de Provence and Bandol: Blanc, Rosé, Rouge, → Cuvée Mourvèdre

Françoise Dutheil de la Rochère produces convincing wines using organic methods. The flagship is the 100% Mourvèdre *cuvée*.

Château Sainte-Marguerite***
La Londe-des-Maures
64 acres (26 ha); 120,000 bottles • Wines: Côtes de Provence: L'Esprit and Cuvée Prestige: Blanc, Rosé, Rouge; Cuvée Symphonie: Blanc, Rouge
This *cru classé* gained its elegant, fruit style from Jean-Pierre Fayard. Particularly successful is the Rosé Saint-Pons, produced from very old vines.

Château de Selle***—****
Taradeau
142 acres (58 ha); 150,000 bottles • Wines: Côtes de Provence: Blanc, → Rosé, Rouge, → Longue Garde
This core of the Ott *domaine* supplies the famous barrel-matured Rosé Cœur de Grain and a strong red wine. Also remarkable are the white wines from the Clos de Mireille estate in La Londe-des-Maures.

Château Vannières****
La Cadière-d'Azur
79 acres (32 ha); 160,000 bottles • Wines: Côtes de Provence: Rosé, → Rouge; Bandol: Rosé, Rouge
On his estate in the Le Beausset basin, Burgundy-born Eric Boisseaux cultivates an individual, softer and more elegant style of Bandol, yet the wines still have good aging potential and do not lose any of their typical character. Consistent high quality.

Clos Sainte-Magdeleine***—****
Cassis
30 acres (12 ha); 60,000 bottles • Wines: Cassis: → Blanc, Rosé
This idyllic estate on the bay of Cassis, with vine terraces under Cap Canaille, has belonged to the Zafiropulo family since 1920. The fruity white consists of Marsanne, Clairette, Ugni Blanc and a touch of Sauvignon; the rosé is pressed directly.

Domaine Bunan**—****
La Cadière-d'Azur
158 acres (64 ha); 340,000 bottles • Wines include; Bandol: Blanc, Rosé, Rouge; Moulin des Costes, Château La Rouvière, Mas de la Rouvière, Domaine de Bélouvé; Côtes de Provence
The Bunan family is one of the pioneers of Bandol, where since 1961 they have been restructuring and expanding their various estates. The red Bandols in particular are of very high quality and age superbly.

Domaine de la Courtade***—****
Île de Porquerolles
74 acres (30 ha); 130,000 bottles • Wines: Côtes de Provence: Alycastre and La Courtade: Blanc, Rosé, Rouge
The Alsatian Richard Auther grows complex wines on this idyllic island off Hyères, among them a striking red based on Mourvèdre.

Domaine du Deffends***
Saint-Maximin
34.5 acres (14 ha); 70,000 bottles • Wines: Coteaux Varois including: → Le Champ du Sesterce Blanc, Rosé, Rouge, → Le Clos de la Truffière
Since the 1970s Jacques and Suzel Lanverson have grown mainly red wines on their hard chalky soils using Cabernet and Syrah with added *pigeage* to produce dense but nonetheless elegant wines.

Domaine la Ferme blanche***
Cassis

74 acres (30 ha); 140,000 bottles • Wines: Cassis Blanc, Rosé, Rouge

Although a quarter of this very old estate is planted with red varieties, white wine is of course in the foreground, given a slightly exotic overtone by a touch of Sauvignon.

Domaine Gavoty***–****
Cabasse

62 acres (25 ha); 170,000 bottles • Wines include: Côtes de Provence: →Tradition; Cuvée Clarendon: →Blanc, →Rosé, →Rouge

This estate, run by Pierre Gavoty and his daughter, has acquired a solid reputation over the years, thanks mainly to its white wine, which ages well and has plenty of finesse, and its excellent rosé.

Domaine Lafran-Veyrolles***–****
La Cadière-d'Azur

247 acres (10 ha); 35,000 • Wines: Bandol: Blanc, Rosé; Rouge Classique, →Longue Garde

Ever since the creation of their top, entirely Mourvèdre-based cuvée of 1993, which is only partially separated from the stalks, Madame Claude Jouve-Férec and her vintner Jean-Marie Castell have produced extraordinary improvements at this very tradition-conscious estate.

Domaine des Planes***
Roquebrune-sur-Agens

66.5 acres (27 ha); 110,000 bottles • Wines include: Côtes de Provence: Blanc, Elegance; Rosé Cuvée Tibouren, →Rouge Cuvée Réservée

Ilse and Christophe Rieder use natural methods to produce a whole range of delightful, often single-variety wines on their estate above Saint-Raffaels. The Sémillon, Tibouren, and Mourvèdre stand out particularly.

Domaine Richeaume****
Puyloubier

54 acres (22 ha); 80,000 bottles • Wines include: Côtes de Provence: Blanc, Rosé, Rouge; Tradition, →Columelle, →Syrah

Hennig Hoesch, from the Dueren industrial dynasty, runs this idyllic estate at the foot of the Montagne Sainte-Victoire on ecological and holistic lines. He is now energetically assisted by his son Sylvain, and the red wines of the domaine are among the best in the region.

Domaine de Rimauresque***–****
Pignans

86.5 acres (35 ha); 200,000 bottles • Wines: Côtes de Provence: Blanc, Rosé, Rouge

Under the guidance of the Wemys industrial family from Scotland, this cru classé has steadily piles on the quality since 1988, with the reds now catching up on and even exceeding the high quality of the whites and rosés.

Domaine Saint-André de Figuière***–****
La Londe-des-Maures

42 acres (17 ha); 110,000 bottles • Wines: Côtes de Provence including Blanc, Rosé, Rouge; Grand Cuvée, →Réserve

Alain Combard first gained experience in Chablis before he moved to Maures and became an organic winegrower. Not only his elegant white wine but also the rosé and red display a finesse reminiscent of Burgundy. The Réserve wines are of the best quality.

Domaine Sorin***–****
Saint-Cyr-sur-Mer

30 acres (12 ha) • Wines: Bandol: Rosé, →Rouge; Côtes de Provence: Blanc, Rosé, Rouge

Luc Sorin learned the wine business in Burgundy, and now displays his skills with bravura in Provence. His strength is full red wines loaded with fruit and fine tannins.

Domaine Tempier****
Le Castellet

74 acres (30 ha); 100,000 bottles • Wines: Bandol Rouge: Cuvée Spéciale, La Migona, La Tourtine, Cabassaou

In this core business of the Bandol appellation the sons of Lucien Peyraud pursue an unwavering course. With natural cultivation, a high proportion of Mourvèdre and selection according to terroir, they produce high quality classics.

Domaine de la Tour de Bon***–****
Le Beausset

30 acres (12 ha); 40,000 bottles • Wines: Bandol: →Blanc, Rosé, Rouge, →Saint-Ferréol

Since Agnes Henry-Hocquard turned her back on Paris and took over the estate bought by her father in the 1970s, the wines have become still more aromatic, concentrated, and stylish.

Domaine de Triennes**–****
Nans-les-Pins

102.5 acres (41.5 ha); 260,000 bottles • Wines: Vins de Pays du Var including Chardonnay, →Viognier Sainte-Fleur, →Les Auréliens, Merlot, Syrah, Cabernet Sauvignon, Sainte-Auguste

In 1990, Aubert de Villaine for the Domaine de la Romanée-Conti and Jacques Seysses from the Domaine Dujac joined forces to produce wine together in Provence. Their greatest successes so far have been their Viognier and the Cuvée Saint-Auguste.

Les Maîtres Vignerons de Saint-Tropez**–***
Gassin

1,610 acres (650 ha); 2,700,000 bottles • Wines include: Côtes de Provence: Carte Noire, Château de Pampelonne, Domaine Pouverel, Château Farambert: Blanc, Rosé, Rouge

In 1964, eight estate owners joined forces to bottle and sell their wines together. However, the wines are vinified on the estates. Under their director Robert Zimmer, the master vintners have become a highly successful institution with very reliable wines. Their top cru is the red Château Pampelonne.

Françoise Dutheil de la Rochère uses a sensitive nose to track the development of the new red Château Saint-Anne.

Corsica

Corsica is one of the oldest wine regions in the world. Wild grapes were growing on the Île de Beauté 6,000 years ago. The Phocaeans founded a settlement on the east coast in 565 BC and began growing wine. The island came under Roman rule in 238 BC.

The collapse of the Roman Empire led to unsettled times in Corsica and its attractive coasts, and the vineyards fell into disuse. Only when Pisa gained supremacy in 1020 did viticulture return. At the end of the 13th century, Pisa lost out to Genoa, which remained in control for 450 years. The commercially-minded Genoans secured a monopoly on Corsican wine, which became the most important industry on the island, and introduced a legislative framework for it in the 16th century. Corsicans rose repeatedly in revolt against the occupation, inducing the city state to sell the island to France in 1768.

This did not change anything in the wine trade. On the contrary. Ajaccio-born Napoleon Bonaparte granted the islanders the right to sell their wine free of excise. Around 1850, Corsica had 49,400 acres (20,000 ha) planted to vine, and three-quarters of its population lived from wine-growing. Less than 50 years later, phylloxera ravaged the vineyards. A second blow came in the First World War, when a large part of the male population was killed. The final blow to viticulture was the flight from the land.

New life was brought in the 1960s by Algerian Frenchmen. They extended the culti-

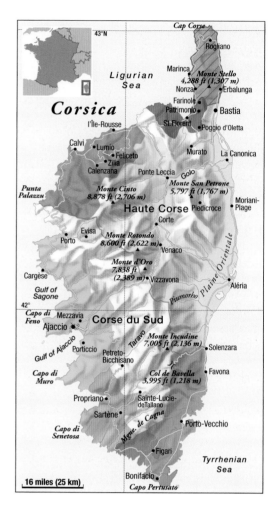

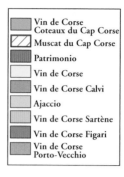

| | Vin de Corse Coteaux du Cap Corse |
| Muscat du Cap Corse |
| Patrimonio |
| Vin de Corse |
| Vin de Corse Calvi |
| Ajaccio |
| Vin de Corse Sartène |
| Vin de Corse Figari |
| Vin de Corse Porto-Vecchio |

vated area, so that by 1976 over 66,700 acres (27,000 ha) were turning out 50 million gallons (1.9m hl) of wine. This was followed by another drastic change, as a new generation of winegrowers headed for quality and traditional grape varieties. At the same time, the E.U. launched a program of vine clearance. The

---

The nine wine regions

Patrimonio
The oldest *appellation*, awarded in 1968, with rare argillocitic soils. Its small estates produce individual wines, with the reds being based on Nielluccio, the whites on Vermentino, the latter having great fruit and finish.

Ajaccio
The second *cru* after Patrimonio was awarded its *appellation* in 1984. It does justice to the local Sciacarello variety, which thrives on granite soils. From 2000, vines must be at least 60 percent of this variety. In the rosé, a lot of white Vermentino is often included, which gives it body.

Vin de Corse
The global *appellation* applies to all classified sites on the island, but the accessible, easy-drinking wines that carry it grow mostly on

the eastern plain. Reds and rosés are often based on Nielluccio and Sciacarello, while whites must have at least 75 percent Vermentino.

Vin de Corse Calvi
Seneca praised these wines. These days, they are no longer found near the town of Calvi but are at home in the northwestern region of Balagne, the Tuscany of Corsica.

Vin de Corse Coteaux du Cap Corse
A substantial wine-growing region in the 19th century with 5,680 acres (2,300 ha) under vine, it now has only 74 acres (30 ha), where good, round Vermentinos are grown.

Vin de Corse Figari
At the southern tip, one of the oldest regions of cultivation, grapes thrive on granite-based soils to produce strong, rustic wines.

Vin de Corse Porto Vecchio
Founded in 383 BC, the mountainous hinterland of the former Portus Syracusanus supplies reds to be laid down, robust whites, and agreeable rosés.

Vin de Corse Sartène
In the cultivated areas around the capital of the south, the reds often have aromas of red berries and a robust structure, while the white wines are fine and aromatic.

Muscat du Cap Corse
Though it was already famous in the 16th century, the *Vin Doux Naturel* based on Muscat Blanc à Petits Grains was awarded the *appellation* only in 1993. The wines often manifest lemony aromas, and are drunk cold as an aperitif or dessert.

area planted to vines in Corsica shrank dramatically. Between 1978 and 1998 the total output fell by 80 percent from 50 million gallons to 10 million gallons (1,897,500 hl to 384,000 hl) Over the same period, the volume of A.C. wines rose from 1.7 million gallons to 2.4 million gallons (67,000 to 91,000 hl). In the meantime, the A.C. area approaches 6,180 acres out of 15,800 acres (2,500 out of 6,400 ha). Irrigation of the vineyards and chaptalization are banned with these wines. Red wines make 50 percent, whites 10 percent, and rosés 40 percent.

Apart from the Côte Orientale, where over 13,100 acres (5,300 ha) of the total planted area are concentrated, the other cultivation areas are small, and each has its distinctive features. Geologically the island is a mosaic of schist, gneiss, sandy marls, clay, chalk, and granite. The surrounding Mediterranean absorbs the heat of the sun during the day and radiates it back at nights. But the Sirocco, which blows throughout the year, especially in the Patrimonio area, tempers the summer heat.

Some twenty grape varieties are planted out on the island, including Cinsault, Ugni Blanc, Syrah, Carignan, Grenache, Merlot, and Alicante. However, the interest of A.C. growers and wine-lovers alike focuses on three varieties:
• the white Vermentino, which in Corsica is also called Malvoisie and is known in Provence

One of the best Patrimonios grows on the Domaine Leccia, not far from Bastia.

as Rolle. Often strongly alcoholic, the wines have a floral bouquet and aromatic fullness;
• the red Nielluccio, identical with Sangiovese, yields deep-colored wines with a lot of body;
• the red Sciacarello is the main indigenous variety of Ajaccio, where it produces light red wines that exude the scent of wild herbs of the *maquis* and taste slightly peppery. It is usually assembled with other varieties, so that it becomes rounder.

SELECT PRODUCERS OF CORSICA

DOMAINE ANTOINE ARENA****
PATRIMONIO
27 acres (11 ha); 40,000 bottles • *Wines include:*
Patrimonio: Blanc, Vieilles Vignes, Carco; Vendange Tardive: Rosé, Rouge; Vieilles Vignes: →*Muscat de Cap Corse; Grotte di Sole: Blanc, Rouge, Muscat*
Antoine Arena is a specialist in white grapes, whether developed as dry, sweet or *vin doux naturel*. His top range is convincing in all its variations.

DOMAINE COMTE PERALDI***–****
MEZZAVIA
124 acres (50 ha); 190,000 bottles • *Wines: Ajaccio: Blanc, Rosé, Rouge;* →*Clos du Cardinal*
Well-made wines from one of the largest and most reputable estates. The Clos, made solely from Sciacarello and matured in the barrel, is outstanding.

DOMAINE LECCIA****
POGGIO-D'OLETA
54 acres (22 ha); 90,000 bottles • *Wines: Patrimonio: Blanc, E Croce: Rosé, Rouge,* →*Petra Bianca; Muscat de Cap Corse*
All Yves Leccia's wines are of high quality, but his red Nielluccio Petra Bianca combines body, roundness and finish in exemplary fashion.

DOMAINE MAESTRACCI***
MURO
67 acres (27 ha); 120,000 bottles • *Vin de Corse Calvi: Clos Reginu and E Prove: Blanc, Rosé, Rouge*
Maestracci makes two series of wines in differing styles, with E Prove being the more engaging, especially the red wines.

DOMAINE ORENGA DE GAFFORY**–***
PATRIMONIO
183 acres (74 ha); 290,000 bottles • *Wines include: Patrimonio: Blanc, Rosé, Rouge; Muscat du Cap Corse*
The family on the domaine Orenga de Gaffory and at San Quilio produce a wide spectrum of wines of different quality. Those matured in the barrel are designated 'Cuvée des Gouverneurs'.

DOMAINE DE TORRACCIA***
PORTO VECCHIO
104 acres (42 ha); 210,000 bottles • *Wines: Vin de Corse Porto-Vecchio: Blanc, Rosé, Rouge,* →*Oriu*
Christian Imbert began to build up his estate in the south of the island in 1964, and his Oriu—made four fifths of Nielluccio and one fifth of Sciacarello—has long asserted its position among the best Corsican reds.

Languedoc and Roussillon

Revolution in the Midi

A wind of change has been blowing through the earthy vine-growing villages between the Rhône and the Spanish border. Instead of automatically tugging the forelock to the famous growths of Bordeaux and Burgundy, the growers of the Midi have rolled up their sleeves and got down to making their own superwines. These days, wine buffs around the world scramble to obtain the wines of the star growers of Languedoc and Roussillon. This did not happen by chance.

Ultimately it was no historical accident that France's viticulture outside Provence started 2,000 years ago at the gates of Narbonne. Barren slopes, a dry climate, and record annual hours of sunshine offer extraordinarily good natural conditions for healthy, aromatic, and concentrated wines.

Viticulture in the southernmost tip of France reached its first heyday under the Romans, when amphorae full of wine from Gallia Narbonensis enjoyed a good reputation even in Rome, and were exported as far as Germania.

Behind the bathing resort of Banyuls rise the steep foothills of the Pyrenees, where growers have worked for centuries to establish a unique vineyard architecture.

With the fall of the Roman Empire, viticulture lost its supra-regional importance. Though wine was grown by the numerous monasteries that sprang up from the 9th century, in the Middle Ages it was all drunk within the region. Only when the infrastructure was substantially improved at the end of the 17th century by the construction of a harbor at Sète, the Canal du Midi, and various cross-country roads was there an upturn in the wine industry. At that time there was great demand for eau-de-vie-brandy to fortify wine and conserve it. The result was that a major part of the local output was distilled. On the plains, this meant planting robust, high-yield varieties such as Aramon or Carignan. Growers in higher-placed villages went more for quality on their stony slopes and planted Grenache or Mourvèdre. The reputation of individual communities and vineyards dates from this period.

Rapid industrialization of the cities of northern France in the 19th century brought a decisive change in the market. A new class of consumer developed for whom wine had a firm place in providing nourishment and pleasure in an otherwise miserable working-class environment. Railways furnished the transport. The business was so lucrative that vines ousted all other crops from the Midi. With 1,140,000 acres (460,000 ha) planted to vines, Languedoc became the greatest wine-growing area in the world. This put paid to the better growths. Instead of being kept apart, their stronger, darker qualities only served to make thinner brews more tolerable. Through phylloxera, economic collapses, two World Wars, the growers of Languedoc persisted with mass production. Only the dramatic consequences of over-production brought a belated change of heart.

From 1970 on, the wine-growing region began to take on a new, very differentiated structure. On the plains, where irrigation was possible, more lucrative fruit and vegetable crops drove the vines out of the fields. However, wherever a long history of wine production had mastered sites that were good for particular quality and individual character, growers were rewarded with an A.C., the highest grade in the French vineyard classification system. To gain this accolade, however, the growers had to plant better varieties of vine and show that they took quality seriously. Thus, many aromatic varieties such as red Syrah, Mourvèdre, and Grenache Noir became domesticated on the schist, granite, or argillocitic soils; in the case of the whites, the main varieties were Roussanne,

Marsanne, Rolle, and Viognier. In deference to tradition, they are assembled with each other and with ancestral, less expressive varieties to produce complex, balanced wines.

VIN DE PAYS WITH CHARACTER

When another crisis hit the wine industry in the mid-1980s, a number of pioneers took the lead in establishing a growers' association (1987). They created a Vin de Pays d'Oc designation, with regional character and a guarantee of quality. They backed chiefly the internationally popular grape varieties and the more fertile vineyards classified as *vin de pays* on which higher but nonetheless restricted yields are permitted. Using modern winery techniques, especially temperature controls, they began to produce single-variety wines that matched market and consumer demand—and match it now even more. Initially the syndicate was launched with 200 members producing 5.2 million gallons (200,000 hl) of *vin de pays*. By the end of the millennium, it comprised over 1,000 firms who between them turned out over 68.7 million gallons (2.6 million hl), of which 80 percent is exported. And the trend is still upward. From a viticultural perspective, Languedoc-Roussillon has become one of the most attractive areas of cultivation worldwide, drawing investors from France and abroad to the Mediterranean coastal areas.

Apart from forests and wild herbs, only vines grow on the hot schist soils of Faugères—but what a wine they produce!

Though the present *appellations* gradually developed in Roussillon and Languedoc, in the early 1980s there were very few estates producing convincing wines. Top-ranking wines were not even a prospect. The region's main handicap was in the minds of its growers. The long history of mass production had left a deep sense of inferiority, and robbed the Midi of a proper wine culture. There was scarcely a grower who was familiar with the great Bordeaux and Burgundies, let alone the concept of what a great Midi wine might be like.

Red wine is unquestionably an essential feature of Mediterranean life. The *gobelet* (or goblet) profile of the vine stocks goes back to Roman times.

THE EMERGENCE OF GREAT WINES

Then the incomprehensible happened. At the beginning of the 1980s, a wine from Languedoc, called Mas de Daumas Gassac, pushed various Médoc *crus classés* off the rostrum. It was moreover just a *vin de pays* that had first come on the market in 1978. Aimé Guibert, a former leather manufacturer from Millau, was the very first to show the incredible potential of the region. Admittedly, he relied predominantly on the Bordelais Cabernet Sauvignon grape.

A more potent symbol of the revolution in attitudes and quality quickly followed—a whirlwind called Olivier Jullien, who hit the Midi in 1985. He might have seemed an unlikely candi-

In fact, a storm of inspiration suddenly blew out of nowhere that has not abated one jot since. On the contrary—initially only a few, but every year more and more growers have come to realize the opportunity offered them by the vineyards and their *terroirs*. They have caught on to how to make great wines, i.e. with the precisely the same great rigor that *grands crus* and *crus classés* require. At the same time they are lowering the yields, increasing the density of stocks on new plantations, and selecting the best plots. The first pioneers are going over to bottling their wines separately as well.

Since then, Languedoc and Roussillon have come up with outstanding wines of quite unique (i.e. Mediterranean) character. Even so, you have to know what you are looking for when you opt for wines from Languedoc or Roussillon. As a general rule, growers operate to different quality levels according to the age of the stocks, the grandeur of the *terroir*, and the varying levels of expense during vinification and aging. Just as car buyers accept that a car manufacturer can produce small, medium-sized family cars, and luxury vehicles, wine lovers have to get used to the idea that top growers here, whose super *cuvées* are the source of international wonder, also produce everyday tipple at reasonable prices. And that has its good side too.

Roses serve as warning indicators. Like vines, they are affected by mildew, but more quickly than the vines, giving the grower time to undertake preventive spraying in the vineyard.

date to show the world that Languedoc was in a position and mind to produce great wine. At the age of 20, when he was a first-year student of enology at Montpellier, the opportunity to lease vineyards came up. He acted quickly, and immediately set about building his winery himself. Olivier and the other pioneers of the first days had two things in common: enormous idealism and empty pockets. With healthy respect for the barren land and old vine stocks, the young grower of Mas Jullien produced *cuvées* of unheard-of density, spirit, and expressiveness. Others such as Michel Louison at the Château des Estanilles plumbed the potential especially of Syrah on very barren soils, with minimal yields, and using barrels for the aging.

Coteaux du Languedoc

The success of the single-variety Syrah wines (they are often wholly Syrah, though this is not officially recognized) extends even to the *vin de pays*. At the same time, there has also been a growing regard for Grenache and Mourvèdre among the best producers. The latter is tricky to cultivate, and produces satisfactory results only in suitable localities that have still to be identified. Grenache Noir, notorious for its tendency to seepage and oxidation, has given growers something to ponder, chiefly because it has demonstrated its potential in Châteauneuf-du-Pape and Catalonia's Priorat.

Two attempts have been made to provide a suitable hierarchical classification for the geological and geographical diversity of the Coteaux du Languedoc. The older one (see map on opposite page) defines 12 *terroirs* that, regardless of size, manifest an identity of their own on the basis of their natural characteristics and earlier reputations. Eight of these *terroirs* lie mainly or predominantly on the terrain of a single commune. Among these, Picpoul-de-Pinet is the outsider, a white wine made from the Picpoul variety, which grows near the Bassin de Thau. Saint-Georges d'Orques, outside the gates of Montpellier and once a famous *cru*, is again attracting attention with concentrated, elegant red wines. Pic-Saint-Loup has leapt to the head of the *terroirs* thanks to its quality consciousness and solidarity of its growers; the smaller Montpeyroux is hot on its trail. La Clape, too, has produced convincing products of more reliable and sometimes even remarkable nature. The delightful ex-island near Narbonne was, like Pic and Pinet, classified with the *zones climatiques* encompassing larger territories, in order to allow more producers to look forward to possible upgrading to the benefits of an *appellation*.

Whether this system will match the reality in the glass, only the future can prove. The other zones are called Terre de Sommières, Terrasses du Larzac, Grès de Montpellier, and Terrasses de Béziers.

Clairette du Languedoc

Awarded in 1948, this A.C. acknowledged the grape variety of the same name, which has been cultivated for centuries in 11 villages between Pézénas and Clermont-l'Hérault, initially to produce a sherry-like Madeirized wine and subsequently the raw material for the vermouth

The islands of quality that its *appellations* represent still lie in an ocean of vines in the Languedoc, with around 741,000 acres (300,000 ha) under vine. The largest is the Coteaux du Languedoc, 20,800 acres (8,400 ha) in an area that begins south of Nîmes and ends in Narbonne. It stretches almost 80 miles (130 km) along the Mediterranean and extends 30 miles (50 km) into the interior, comprising 168 communes and a wide range of localities. Apart from history and political structure, sun, wind, and relative dryness, their common denominator is the red grape varieties. Hard action has been taken against Carignan. Though still the most widespread variety, its proportion in Coteaux du Languedoc has been restricted to 40 percent, while Pic Saint-Loup allows 10 percent, a qualitative maximum for the region. Among the three main varieties of Grenache, Mourvèdre, and Syrah, the latter has come to the fore. As an early ripening, high-colour, and aromatically complex variety, the grape acquires a fuller, warmer character on the barren upland sites, and to some extent even an extraordinarily dense structure with pronounced aromas of the *garrigue*, the Mediterranean moor.

Château Moulin de Ciffre is undergoing a renaissance under the management of Bordelais grower Jacques Lésinau.

industry. Only in recent years has modern winery technology brought out a wholly different aspect of the variety, which is cultivated on only 173 acres (70 ha), i.e. a fresh, fruity character with aromas of dried fruits, aniseed, and almonds.

FAUGÈRES

Faugères is a wild, thinly populated and thickly forested area that begins 10 miles (15 km) north of Béziers. Of the 12,400 acres (5,000 ha) that were included in the *appellation* in 1982, only 4,450 acres (1,800 ha) have been planted. Faugères is the only A.C. of Languedoc with homogeneous soils based on schist that are suited to high-quality red wines. Following the pioneering example of the Château des Estanilles, more estates have gone over to *cuvées* with high Syrah proportions aged in barrels, wines that are in demand for their complexity, concentration, and elegance. The fine fruit and often floral aromas of the rosés make them a popular choice for many restaurants.

SAINT-CHINIAN

Saint-Chinian lies between Minervois and Faugères, obtaining its A.C. status in the same year as the latter (1982). Center of the 7,410-acre (3,000-ha) *appellation* is the town of this name, which lies on a notable geological boundary. The area of cultivation is divided in two.

The southern zone possesses limey clay soils on which reds with body and much tannin prosper. The north stretches over the foothills of the Monts de l'Espinouse, and is made of schist. After a series of estates and the cooperatives of Berloup and Roquebrun had produced wines of reliable quality in the 1980s, from the mid-1990s a group of younger firms began to cause a stir with intensive, complex, and concentrated red wines. Some of the older estates have caught their enthusiasm. As in Faugères, only the rosé is also classified, whites being covered by the Coteaux du Languedoc *appellation*.

With his Château des Estanilles Michel Louson was the first to show the dimensions that Syrah can take on in Languedoc.

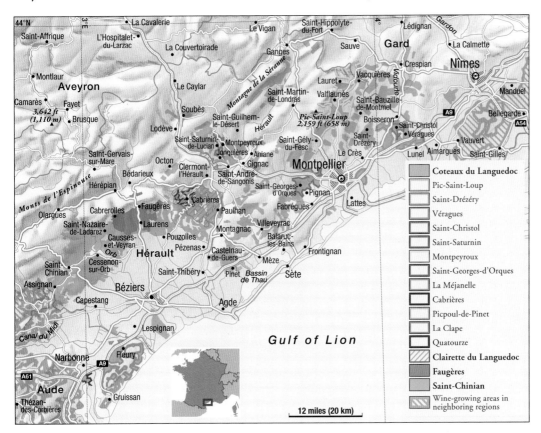

Coteaux du Languedoc
Pic-Saint-Loup
Saint-Drézéry
Véragues
Saint-Christol
Saint-Saturnin
Montpeyroux
Saint-Georges-d'Orques
La Méjanelle
Cabrières
Picpoul-de-Pinet
La Clape
Quatourze
Clairette du Languedoc
Faugères
Saint-Chinian
Wine-growing areas in neighboring regions

12 miles (20 km)

MINERVOIS

Minervois runs from the outcrops of the Montagne Noire to the Canal du Midi and from there down to the River Aude. In the south, the boundary runs between Narbonne and Carcassonne. Four rivers have created extensive, not very fertile terraces where mainly chalk, but also gravel, sand, and some slate form the soils. The area of cultivation, in which 11,100 acres (4,500 ha) furnish A.C. wines, is distributed among 45 communes of the Aude department and 16 of Hérault.

The center includes the stony terraces of the Argent Double, the Balcons de l'Aude with their brown marl, the great wine-growing community of Laure, and the hilly Petite Causse region with the famous wine locality of La Livinière. The latter was the first officially recognized *cru* of Minervois along with five neighboring parishes including Siran, in 1998. The barren *terroir* of the high plain gives the red wines a special full-bodied character. Toward the charming villages of Caunes schist and the famous pink marble are the determinative soil components. Here the climate manifests clear Atlantic influences and the wines display greater freshness. Around Minerve, the historic capital of the region, lie the Montagnes du Causse. Here the climate is dry but often cold, the soils are chalky, and the wines very individual.

To the east, where the vineyards stretch for 20 miles (35 km) toward Béziers, Mediterranean influences are most prominent. Often, an occasionally violent wind from the sea reaches right up to the Serres, Mourels, and the Terrasses de la Cesse, the hottest and driest area, where the wines turn out bulky and strong.

In 1990, the growers launched a quality initiative, which lowered yields to 481 gallons per acre (45 hl/ha) and limited the proportion of Carignan to 40 percent at most. Grenache Noir and Syrah dominate the *assemblage*. The traditional Cinsault also retains its place, giving the reds and rosés finesse. The Cinsault wines made from old vinestocks and vinified with *pigeage* are filigree from the soft *attaque* right up to the taste, but also have surprising finish.

Though some rosés and whites are vinified, including a number of delightful wines now made mainly with Marsanne and Roussanne, the forte of the district is its reds. More and more cooperatives and growers are coming up with well-structured growths that are matured in the barrel, often very spicy wines with fine ripe fruit and convincing body, that develop very advantageously.

LIMOUX

In the upper reaches of the Aude—16 miles (25 km) south of Carcassonne—sparkling wine was available as far back as 1544. The Benedictines of the abbey of Saint-Hilaire, who discovered

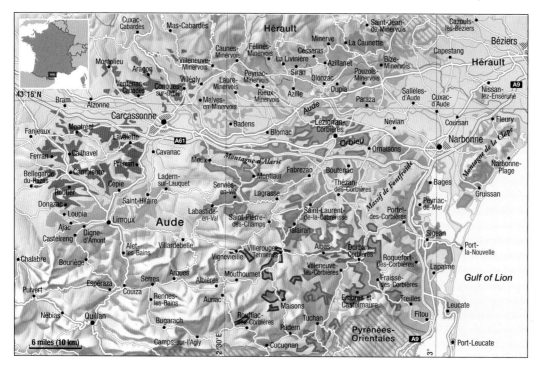

	Minervois
	Minervois-La Livinière
	Muscat de Saint-Jean-de-Minervois
	Corbières
	Montagne d'Alaric
	Lézignan
	Serviès
	Lagrasse
	Boutenac
	Fontfroide
	Saint-Victor
	Termenès
	Quéribus
	Durban
	Sigean
	Fitou
	Cabardès
	Côtes de la Malepère
	Limoux
	Wine-growing areas in neighboring regions

the *prise de mousse* in 1531, were 150 years ahead of Champagne. The native grape variety Blanquette, elsewhere called Mauzac, is what made it possible. It tends not to ferment the sugar completely. If the wine is drawn off into barrels or bottles, the yeast begins to revive in spring and convert the sugar residue into alcohol, producing carbonic acid. The *méthode ancestrale* following this process is still used, but since the end of the 19th century, Limoux has gone over to the *méthode champenoise* for sparkling wines.

Though Limoux gained its *appellation* for the sparkling wine back in 1938, its growers failed to gain the reputation it deserved. Since then, one or two things have happened, particularly to the grape varieties, where Chenin and Chardonnay have replaced the unsuitable Clairette. Since 1991 there has been a Crémant de Limoux, where the Chardonnay stands out. Several excellent wines exist under this *appellation* at a comparatively low price.

Meanwhile, Limoux means much more than this. With over 34,600 acres (14,000 ha) of vineyard, other products had to be made besides Blanquette, so bearing in mind the Atlantic aspects of their climate, the growers took to planting Bordelais varieties such as Sauvignon and others for the *vin de pays*. However, it is Chardonnay that has brought the

Midday meal at Clos Centeilles, where former bookseller Daniel Domergues (left) and his wife Patricia Boyer show what finesse Cinsault is capable of.

greatest success. The large cooperative, Les Caves du Sieur d'Arques, carried out an expensive *sélection* of the vineyard sites which culminated in the definition of four *terroirs* that reflect mainly different climatic conditions: Autan, Méditerranéen, Océanique, and Haute Vallée, with the latter featuring as *grand cru* and aging very well. The decidedly high quality of their wines gained the growers the *appellation* Limoux, reserved for dry white wines, for which Mauzac, Chenin, and Chardonnay are vinified and aged in the barrel.

Cabardès

Northwest of Carcassonne and adjacent to Minervois and therefore strongly exposed to Atlantic weather, the growers of this small region have the opportunity to combine Mediterranean and Bordelais grape varieties for their reds and rosés. Most prominent on the 988 or so acres (400 ha) planted to vines are Grenache and Syrah, Cabernet Sauvignon, and Merlot. Besides pleasing, fruity, substantial reds, the best *cuvées* show greater strength, structure, and interesting tannins. A tenth of the output is rosé.

Malepère

Situated on the hills southwest of Carcassonne and alongside the Limoux region, the 1,980-acre (800-ha) vineyards of Malepère are climatically exposed to the same wetter and cooler Atlantic climate, despite the southern position. Here, too, Mediterranean and Bordelais varieties thrive side by side, with Cabernet Franc being added to Cabernet Sauvignon and Merlot, plus Syrah, Grenache, and Cinsault. Its special strength lies in its fruity, aromatic, agreeable, and elegant reds and rosé wines.

CORBIÈRES AND FITOU

Corbières forms an enormous rectangle covering 1,150 square miles (3,000 km²) south of a line from Narbonne to Carcassonne in the department of Aude. To the west, the hills rise to a height where it is too cold for vines. In the east, they thrust toward the lagoons of Leucate and Bages and the Mediterranean. In the south their realm ends in the rocky cliffs crowned by the Cathar castles of Quéribus and Peyrepertuse. The large area of cultivation—the A.C. covers 37,100 acres (15,000 ha)—is distinguished by a wealth of different soils and climates. Vine stocks grow on schist from the Primary, chalk and sandstone from the Secondary, layers of marls from the Tertiary and gravelly alluvium brought down in the Quaternary.

The proximity of the Mediterranean determines the climate, of course, but Atlantic influences are also perceptible depending on height and the degree of westerliness. In 1990, work was begun on a scheme to define 11 major areas that took account of these differing characteristics. They are the *terroirs* shown on the map (p. 155): Sigean, Durban, Quéribus, Termenès, Saint-Victor, Fontfroide, Lagrasse, Serviès, Montagne d'Alaric, Lézignan, and Boutenac.

The growers of Corbières have also replanted thousands of their acres with Grenache, Syrah, Mourvèdre and—to a much lesser extent—white varieties such as Grenache Blanc, Rolle, Marsanne, and Roussanne. But, above all, they have succeeded in mastering Carignan, much

A typical vineyard hut in Corbières, which provides shelter from weather.

Near Limoux, irises grow wild on the edge of many vineyards.

abused as a mass-wine grape. They kept vineyards with stocks where old Carignan furnished low yields but optimum quality, and developed a vinification method that suited it. From the mid-1960s, the general practice in Languedoc-Roussillon was to go over to vinifying Carignan by carbonic maceration.

In this, hand-selected grapes are put whole into a tank saturated in carbon dioxide, so that every berry is forced to ferment within its skin. The alcohol thus produced extracts the maximum possible content from the skins. If this fermentation is interrupted early by pressing after six to eight days, the wine has acquired color and aroma but loses structure and tannin. Carignan becomes more pleasant, i.e. commercial, but receives a typical, slightly animal overtone.

However, in Corbières many growers are able to extend the maceration period and achieve additional EXTRACTION in a grand finale, which gives the wine great strength and fine tannins. The Carignan thus becomes eminently keepable, acquires a spicy bouquet often reminiscent of wild herbs, and overtones of game and underwood which increase with age.

A preponderance of Carignan assembled with Grenache and Syrah, or more rarely Mourvèdre, produces a style of wine that gives Corbières a common denominator. By the end of the 1980s, Corbières growers were surpassing other Midi *appellations* with good, comparatively homogeneous quality. The feeling seemed to spread that they had cracked it. However, at the same time energy was expended in internecine strife within the association. And suddenly Corbières had been left behind. Inspired red wines with a hitherto unsuspected profile of fruit and zing sprang up in all corners of Languedoc—except here. This has changed in recent times, with *cuvées* that open up new, unsuspected dimensions.

The proportions of rosés and whites are 4 percent and 2 percent respectively. Cinsault is an important factor in the rosés, giving many wines their pale tones and rather floral nose. The dry white wines deserve notice. The Corbières growers were the first in Languedoc-Roussillon to take due note of interesting aspects of the Grenache Blanc, especially its Mediterranean character. Instead of vainly trying to imitate the acidity of northern wines, they went for equal amounts of taste and finish.

FITOU

Fitou has a story of its own, although all Fitous can be bottled as Corbières. In 1948, just by way of a hint to the winegrowers of Languedoc and Roussillon, the national wine institute I.N.A.O. awarded it an *appellation*, the first to a dry red wine of the region. The message was: "top honors await you beyond mass wines and sweet wines—but with low yields." However, such a red wine hardly existed in those days, because all the producers turned out Rivesaltes, the decidedly more lucrative sweet wine. When a crisis struck this at the beginning of the 1980s, Fitou pulled its finger out. Today, a mere 6,420 acres (2,600 ha) provide a good 13 million bottles of wine.

As an *appellation*, Fitou is nonetheless an oddball. It consists of two enclaves only six miles (10 km) apart within Corbières, under whose A.C. its growers bottle rosés and whites, and sometimes even reds. Fitou *maritime* stretches as far as the eastern foothills of the Corbières, on argillocitic, often stony and barren soils, and borders the Mediterranean. Moisture from the latter provides good ripening, and offers ideal conditions for the tricky but high-quality Mourvèdre. The A.C. belongs to the villages of Fitou, Caves, Treilles, La Palme, and Leucate. The other zone is called Fitou de Hautes-Corbières, as it lies right in the heart of Corbières. The classified vineyards of the villages of Cascatel, Villeneuve-les-Corbières, Tuchan, and Durban are the only cultivated spots in the wild, fissured, hilly landscape, where a diversity of Mediterranean herbs, bushes, and orchids prosper. The predominantly schist soils provide excellent conditions for Syrah vines. In the two zones, which together add up to 6,180 acres (2,500 ha) of vines, the summers are hot and rain is very rare. Though producers nowadays—who include seven wine-growing cooperatives and about 35 estates—are very keen on the newly introduced varieties, Fitou owes its character to old Carignan stocks and Grenache Noir.

The strong, rustic reds, which are aged for at least nine months but often much longer in large tuns, were popular in Britain, Belgium, and Denmark before 1982, in a period when Languedoc and Roussillon otherwise had little quality to offer. Since then, Fitou has undergone a cautious change. Carignan has been made more accessible by means of carbonic maceration, while the Syrah or Mourvèdre in the *assemblage* furnish finer tannins and spicier aromas. New small barrels give overtones of body and elegance. Meanwhile, competition to Fitou has grown up in all regions of the Midi, and the former huge commercial advantage has melted away.

The oldest sparkling wine in the world flows in long streams during the carnival of Limoux.

Unloved Carignan has found a refuge in the wild, dry landscape of Corbières, generating dense reds with good aging ability.

ABBAYE SYLVA PLANA**–***
ALAIGNAN DU VENT
77 acres (31 ha); 130,000 bottles • Wines: Faugères: La Closerie, → Le Songe de l'Abbé.
Henri Ferdinand and Nicholas Bouchard, owners of the respected Domaine Deshenrys in the Côtes de Thongue, have taken over this former monastery estate near Laurens and, with the cooperation of Cédric Guy, are producing full-bodied, spicy reds.

ABBAYE DE VALMAGNE**–***
VILLVEYRAC
161 acres (65 ha); 200,000 bottles • Wines: Vins de Pays d'Oc; Coteaux du Languedoc: Blanc, Rosé, Rouge
The imposing abbey has offered reliable wines for many years. It is now run using natural methods, and the Cuvée Turenne in particular has gained in concentration and depth.

BORIE DE LA VITARÈLE***–****
CAUSSES ET VEYRAN
32 acres (13 ha); 37,000 bottles • Wines include: Coteaux du Languedoc Les Terres Blanches; Saint-Chinian: Les Schistes, → Les Crés; → Vin de Pays La Combe; Lou Festéjaïre
Cathy Planès and Jean-François Izard have come a long way since founding their *domaine* in 1990. Their powerful reds are now differentiated according to *terroir* and have well-defined character.

CHÂTEAU CAZAL VIEL**–****
CESSENON-SUR-ORB
205 acres (83 ha); 600,000 bottles • Wines include: Saint-Chinian: L'Antenne, → Cuvée des Fées, Larmes des Fées
The young, dynamic Laurent Miquel is currently giving this established estate a new impulse of quality. He also advises other wine-makers and offers an interesting collection of wines under his name.

CHÂTEAU DES ESTANILLES****
LENTHÉRIC
84 acres (34 ha); 200,000 bottles • Wines: → Coteaux du Languedoc Blanc; Faugères Rosé; Rouge: Tradition, Prestige, Château
Michel Louison is an example to today's young guard, he was the first to demonstrate what grandeur Syrah could achieve in the Midi. His white wine is also excellent.

CHÂTEAU GRÈS SAINT-PAUL**–***
LUNEL
59 acres (24 ha); 130,000 bottles • Wines include: Muscat de Lunel; → Bohémienne; Coteau du Languedoc: Romanis, → Antonin, → Syrhus, Vins de Pays d'Oc
The old family estate near Lunel produces attractive dry and sweet Muscat wines and balanced, rounded reds with ripe tannins.

CHÂTEAU DE LASCAUX***
VACQUIÈRES
86.5 acres (35 ha); 150,000 bottles • Wines: Coteaux du Languedoc: Blanc, Rosé, Rouge; → Pic Saint-Loup
Syrah and Grenache dominate the vineyards of Jean-Benoît Cavalier, who has run the estate since 1984, and produces one of the most interesting whites in Languedoc from Viognier, Marsanne, Roussanne, and Rolle.

CHÂTEAU MANSENOBLE***–****
49.5 acres (20 ha); 110,000 bottles • Wines include: Vins de Pays, Corbières Rouge, → Réserve, → Cuvée Marie-Annick
The Flemish wine enthusiast Guido Janseger has shown in only a few years how to apply skill, nose, and enthusiasm to producing excellent red Corbières.

CHÂTEAU MOULIN DE CIFFRE**–***
AUTIGNAC
74 acres (30 ha); 90,000 bottles • Wines: Coteau du Languedoc, Saint-Chinian, Faugères, Vin de Pays Val Tarou
Jacques and Bernadette Lésineau, growers in Pessac-Léognan, are bringing about a stylish renaissance with the three A.O.C.s at their outstandingly well restored estate. The Cuvée Eole shows first-class Bordelais barrel aging.

CHÂTEAU SAINT-AURIOL***
LAGRASSE
124 acres (50 ha); 300,000 bottles • Wines: Corbières: Blanc, Rosé, Rouge
Claude Vialade and Jean-Paul Salvagnac are among the pioneers of quality in Corbières. Their whites and reds vinified and aged in the barrel offer consistently good quality.

CHÂTEAU SAINT-MARTIN DE LA GARRIGUE***–****
MONTAGNAC
148 acres (60 ha); 300,000 bottles • Wines include: Vins de Pays, Picpoul-de-Pinet, Coteaux du Languedoc, → Bronzinelle, Cuvée Réservée, → Saint-Martin
In the space of only a few years Umberto and Gregory Guida have made a byword of the imposing château and its large estate, both for their fresh and aromatic whites and the characterful reds with good aging ability.

CHÂTEAU LA VOULTE-GASPARETS***–****
BOUTENAC
136 acres (55 ha); 230,000 bottles • Wines: Corbières: Cuvée Réservée, → Cuvée Romain Pauc
For many years the estate has been producing one of the most typical and best Corbières from its excellent *terroir*.

LES CHEMINS DE BASSAC***–****
PUIMISSON
35 acres (14 ha); 50,000 bottles • Wines: Vins de Pays des Côtes de Thongue: Blanc, Rosé, Rouge; Pierre Elie, → Cap de l'Homme, Camille Léonie
The Ducelliers and their friend Regis Abbal very aromatic, elegant, expressive wines with the best of vineyard techniques and controlled low yields.

CLOS BAGATELLE**–****
SAINT-CHINIAN
136 acres (55 ha); 250,000 bottles • Wines include Vins de Pays; Saint-Chinain: Rosé, Rouge; Mathieu, → La Gloire de Mon Père,; → Muscat de Saint Jean de Minervois
The Simon family has lived on the estate since 1623. In the last 40 years, its wines have always been among the most solid in the region, but the younger generation is now giving them fruit and structure.

CLOS CENTEILLES****
SIRAN
35 acres (14 ha); 50,000 bottles • Wines include: Minervois Rouge: Capitelle, Campagne, Clos de Centeilles, Vin de Pays
No one understands how to give wines such subtlety and individual character—thanks to old stocks and a barren *terroir*—as well as Daniel and Patricia Boyer-Domergue.

JEAN-LOUIS DENOIS***–****
ROQUETAILLADE
17 acres (7 ha); 36,000 bottles • Wines include: Vin de Pays d'Oc: → Sainte-Marie, La Rivière, → Chloé; → Tradition Brut

Jean-Louis Denois from Champagne caused a stir in Limoux for his experiments with Riesling. He has now sold part of his Domaine de l'Aigle to Antonin Rodet and is making a convincing new start with new wines from old vines.

DOMAINE DES AIRES HAUTES**—****
SIRAN
59 acres (24 ha); 90,000 bottles • Wines include: Vins de Pays; → Minervois La Livinière, Minervois Domaine des Aires Hautes: Blanc, Rosé, Rouge
Gilles Chabbert offers consistent, velvety Minervois wines from the Domaine des Aires Hautes, but his Clos de l'Escandil in La Livinière always beats them in terms of body, structure, spice and finish.

DOMAINE JEAN-MICHEL ALQUIER****
FAUGÈRES
31 acres (12.5 ha); 40,000 bottles • Wines include: Faugères: Générique, Réserve: La Maison Jaune, → Les Bastides
Jean-Michel Alquier has produced excellent reds with *assemblages* of Grenache, Syrah and Mourvèdre and much more sensitive barrel aging. His white *vin de pays* made from Marsanne and Roussane is simply exquisite.

DOMAINE BAILLAT***—****
MONTLAUR
34.5 acres (14 ha); 50,000 bottles • Wines: Corbières: Rosé, Rouge; Domaine: → Clos de la Miro, → Cuvée Emilien Baillat
Both Austrian and Occitan wine-producing blood runs in Christian Baillat's veins. Steadfast in the search for perfection, he has graded his wines into three categories, with the top one being close to heaven. All the wines have a surprisingly enlivening character.

DOMAINE LEON BARRAL***—****
CABREROLLES
57 acres (23 ha); 95,000 bottles • Wines: Coteaux du Languedoc Blanc; Faugères
With conscientious work in the vineyard and winery, Didier Barral has taken the family estate into the select top ranks of Faugères. Outstanding white wine vinified in the barrel.

DOMAINE BORIE DE MAUREL***
FÉLINES MINERVOIS
66.5 acres (27 ha); 150,000 bottles • Wines include: Minervois Blanc, Rosé, Rouge; Belle de Nuits, Maxime, La Livinière, Sylla
An interesting range of red wines based on grape varieties of various degrees of dominance and always showing willingness to experiment. The best is Sylla, made wholly from Syrah.

DOMAINE CANET-VALETTE***—****
CESSENON-SUR-ORB
44.5 acres (18 ha); 80,000 bottles • Wines: Saint-Chinian Rouge: Domaine, → Le Vin Maghani
Marc Valette is one of the leading figures of the new guard in Saint-Chinian and produces concentrated reds full of spice, fruit, finish, and potential.

DOMAINE DE L'HORTUS***—****
VALFLAUNES
136 acres (55 ha); 310,000 bottles • Wines: Coteaux de Languedoc: Bergerie: Blanc, Rosé, Rouge; Domaine: Blanc, → Rouge, Grande Cuvée, Clos Prieur
Jean Orliac discovered his estate in 1980 while climbing Pic-Saint-Loup; he has since developed it through his own unique combination of natural methods and modern technology, making it one of the best of the Pic.

DOMAINE RAMBERT***—****
BERLOU
49 acres (20 ha); 90,000 bottles • Wines: Saint-Chinian: Le Travers de Marceau, → Mas au Schiste; Coteaux du Languedoc Blanc, Vin de Table: → Le Chant de Marjolaine, → Carignator 1er
Jean-Marie Rimbert founded his estate on the schist slopes of Berlou in 1996. Here he produces highly individual, extremely juicy, full-bodied, fruity wines, with two made only from Carignan.

DOMAINE JEAN-BAPTISTE SENAT**—****
TRAUSSE-MINERVOIS
39.5 acres (16 ha); 50,000 bottles • Wines: Minervois: La Line, Enclos de l'Ane, → Le Bois de Merveilles
Jean-Baptiste and Charlotte Senat abandoned the student life in Paris in 1996 and took over the family estate in the Minervois. With old vines, many of them Grenache, plenty of hard work and their own philosophy, they are on their way to working miracles.

MAS CHAMPART***
BRAMEFAN
39.5 acres (16 ha); 40,000 bottles • Wines include: Saint-Chinian: → Côte d'Arbo, → Causse du Bousquet; Coteaux du Languedoc
From 1976 onwards, Isabelle and Matthieu de Champart have been putting their estate together piece by piece. Replanting has been done, with mass removal of unsatisfactory vines. Their wines show plenty of fruit and harmony.

MAS DE DAUMAS-GASSAC****—*****
ANIANE
124 acres (50 ha); 200,000 bottles • Wines: Vin de Pays: Blanc, Rouge
Aimé Guibert was the first to demonstrate the unexploited potential of Languedoc with his 1978 vintage red wine. Since then his red has become ever finer, more polished, and profound, while the highly aromatic white wine is superb. Both wines age extremely well.

MAS JULLIEN****—*****
JONQUIÈRES
42 acres (17 ha); 60,000 bottles • Wines include: Les Etats d'âmes; Coteaux du Languedoc: Blanc, Rosé, Rouge
Olivier Jullien is a mild revolutionary and member of the awkward squad, who has probably done more than anybody to inspire his wine-growing colleagues—and continues to do so. His wines are classics of the new and up-and-coming Languedoc and beyond all fashion.

PRIEURÉ DE SAINT-JEAN DE BÉBIAN****
PÉZENAS
74 acres (30 ha); 88,000 bottles • Wines: Coteaux du Languedoc: Blanc, Rouge, Chapelle, Prieuré
Since 1994, this already legendary estate, which was producing superb, very Mediterranean red wines at the same time as Daumas-Gassac, has belonged to Chantal Lecouty and Jean-Claude Le Brun, who used to run the *Revue du Vin du France*. With great commitment, they have restored the vineyards and winery and deliberately modernized the general style of the wine. White and red wines reach high standards.

SOCIÉTE COOPÉRATIVE VINICOLE DE CASTELMAURE*—****
EMBRES-ET-CASTELMAURE
741 acres (300 ha); bottles not recorded • Wines include: Corbières: Blanc, Rosé, Rouge, → Envie de Raisin, → Cuvée Pompadour, → Grande Cuvée, → No. 3, Vin de Pays
In 20 years, president Patrick de Marien and director Bernard Pueyo have turned this small, remote cooperative into a flourishing, ground-breaking new company. The quality has been rising spectacularly for some years.

Côtes du Roussillon and Villages

Few regions of Europe present such a fascinating variety of landscapes and such contrasts as Roussillon. It is just 30 miles (50 km) from the sandy beaches of the bathing resorts to the 9,133-foot (2,784-m) peak of Canigou. The upward folding of the Pyrenees in the Tertiary provided the variegated potpourri of schist, granite, gneiss, clay, chalk, gravel, and shingle. Only Alsace offers a comparable wealth of such diverse geological structures. Created at the same time was the impressive panorama from the slopes facing the Mediterranean. The vine stocks reach a height of 2,000 feet (600 m), but only where there is an unambiguously Mediterranean climate. The sun shines here more intensely, the average annual temperature is 59°F (15°C) and the northwest wind blows through the foliage of the vines on average every third day, doing wonders for their health.

Red varieties thrive best in these circumstances. Even in the 1960s, when Carignan reigned almost supreme, there was a far-sighted initiative to plant "improving" varieties such as the fruity, round Grenache Noir, the dark, complex Syrah, which is gaining ground enormously, and the ticklish but subtle Mourvèdre.

The winegrowers' commitment was acknowledged in 1977 by the award of the A.C., long before Corbières, Minervois, or Coteaux du Languedoc, which followed only in 1985. The Côtes du Roussillon A.C. comprises overall about 16,100 acres (6,500 ha) planted to vines, scattered over 125 parishes in the departments of the Pyrénées Orientales. In the particularly hilly north of the cultivation area, where schist, granite, and chalk predominate, the red wine was given a higher rating as Côtes du Roussillon Villages. The villages of Caramany and Latour-de-France and very recently Lesquerde and finally Tautavel were singled out as individual communal *appellations*. Since the mid-1990s, only Tautavel, which includes the neighboring

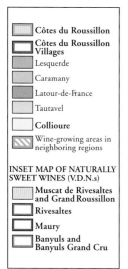

Côtes du Roussillon
Côtes du Roussillon Villages
Lesquerde
Caramany
Latour-de-France
Tautavel
Collioure
Wine-growing areas in neighboring regions

INSET MAP OF NATURALLY SWEET WINES (V.D.N.s)

Muscat de Rivesaltes and Grand Roussillon
Rivesaltes
Maury
Banyuls and Banyuls Grand Cru

parish of Vingrau, has produced wines that really prove how excellent their *terroir* is. In the other three communal *appellations* cooperatives run things, and only a fraction of their output meets the quality one could expect from the given specifications. The white and rosé wines are labeled Côtes du Roussillon even in the Villages.

In the more southerly part of Roussillon there are no common denominators in the soil conditions, and the vineyards are often flatter and more extensive. An interesting feature is the natural terraces of the Aspres consisting of large alluvial or worn slate pebbles. Devoted growers produce convincing wines even here, but it does not always work, and requires stricter selection of plots and grapes. The normal reds, still strongly Carignan in make-up, display rough tannins that take several years to acquire polish.

Red wine occupies the foreground in Roussillon, but rosé has also experienced an upturn in recent times. In the last two decades the wineries were brought in line with modern enological requirements, and temperature control in particular—a vital feature especially in the hot south—has become the norm.

As generally in the Midi—except in the few areas that specialize in it—white wine plays a subordinate role, and accounts for only 5 percent of the volume. While most of it is at best easy-drinking tipple lacking acidity, there are some delightful exceptions with very individual profiles. Instead of imitating northern freshness that they can never attain, they are based on concentrated grapes picked when ripe and fermented in the barrel. The result is wines of extraordinary strength and finish, which go extremely well with strongly seasoned Mediterranean or exotic cuisine.

Their secret—like that of all great wines—lies not least in selecting the right plots, i.e. identifying the *terroir*. This work is still at an early

Collioure and its light inspired Henri Matisse and the Fauvist painters. Nowadays its red wines excite the countless tourists.

stage in Roussillon, as in Languedoc. Although the first purely schist wine was bottled in 1984 and many estates and cooperatives have gone over to consciously planting particular sites with particular grape varieties, it is a lengthy enterprise, and only in recent times have individual growers had the courage to bottle and sell wines from specified *terroirs* separately.

Collioure

Collioure is the jewel among the coastal resorts of Roussillon. The medieval castle and picturesque fortified church have been immortalized countless times since Matisse and the Fauvistes first discovered and enthused about the legendary light of the former fishing township and port from 1905 onwards. Here at the French end of the Costa Brava, the slate core of the Pyrenees dips steeply into the Mediterranean. The Greeks were the first to hack out the slopes into terraces and cultivate vines. The *appellation* now covers 815 acres (330 ha) planted to vines.

Grenache ripens completely in this area and became famous as naturally sweet wine under the name of neighboring Banyuls (see following two pages). The traditional dry, strong red gained its *appellation* only 32 years later, in 1971.

Made from vines growing on barren soil, smiled on by the sun and with a degree of moisture arising from the sea, the wines acquire particular fullness and structure on a maximum yield of 429 gallons per acres (40 hl/ha).

Though Collioure often used to be just a country tipple stored in great tuns, it has now developed into one of the most delightful *crus* of the Midi region. The most exciting Collioures still come from the vintages that favor Grenache Noir, but thanks to Syrah and/or Mourvèdre, which have been permitted since 1982, there are deep red, spicy, polished, and yet clearly southern red wines that are nowadays often aged in the barrel. In addition, the three cooperatives and 20 or so estates produce a strong raspberry-colored rosé, which goes excellently with grilled fish.

The best white wines of the coast are made of immediately pressed Grenache Gris and Grenache Blanc and are (still) bottled as Vin de Pays de la Côte Vermeille.

Naturally Sweet Wines:
Banyuls, Maury, and Rivesaltes

The majestic peak of Canigou and its iron ore attracted Ligurians, Iberians, Greeks, and Romans even in antiquity. The Greeks, who reached the coast of Roussillon around 600 BC, introduced vine growing here. The schist terraces of the Côte Vermeille, the French end of the Costa Brava, were excellently suited to it, and produced strong, sugar-rich wines. The Romans were likewise very partial to them. In the 1st century AD Pliny enthused about the fiery tipple of Roussillon.

Wine production flourished again under the kingdom of Mallorca that Jaime the Conqueror had forged in 1276 out of the Balearics, Roussillon, and Montpellier for his youngest son, a man whose inclinations tended toward peace, the arts and crafts. Nine years later, the doctor and celebrated scholar Arnaldus of Villanova succeeded in distilling alcohol from wine at the estate of the Templars south of Perpignan, using an Arab recipe. Called *eau-de-vie* because of its exciting effects, he used this spirits of wine to carry out experiments. Thus he discovered that adding spirits of wine stopped fermentation, preserved part of the natural sugar in the wine and prevented it turning to vinegar. This was the birth of *vin doux naturel* (V.D.N.), naturally sweet wine. The method, called *mutage* or muting, ensured these durable wines a considerable success throughout the Middle Ages.

After he had finally gobbled up Roussillon in 1659, the French king Louis XIV introduced

Unusual wine specialties have been produced along the rocky coast between delightful Collioure and the Spanish Costa Brava since the Middle Ages.

Unusual wine specialties have been produced along the rocky coast between delightful Collioure and the Spanish Costa Brava since the Middle Ages.

the wines to his court in Versailles, and Voltaire became a great fan of Muscat de Rivesaltes.

Its long and fascinating history was turned to good advantage by Roussillon-born astronomer and politician François Aragon to get the special characteristics of *vin doux naturel* legally recognized in 1872. An *appellation* followed in 1936, when areas of cultivation, grape varieties, degrees of ripeness, yields, vinification, and minimum aging were specified. The driest and hottest slopes and terraces of Roussillon are reserved for V.D.N.s. The grapes must have developed a minimum 9 ounces (252 g) of sugar per quart (liter), corresponding to a potential alcohol content of 14.4 percent. Such a high degree of ripeness was attained not just by the sun, but also by limited yields of 321 gallons per acre (30 hl/ha) or less. After fermentation set in, the grower or vintner monitored conversion of sugar into alcohol. He chose the moment to add the pure and tasteless spirits of wine to the fermenting must, thus determining the character of the finished wine. The earlier he interrupted the fermentation, the higher the residual sugar content. The longer he waited, the drier the wine. The specifications say that the sugar residue value must be between 1.5 ounces and 4.5 ounces (50 g and 125 g) and the finished wine should have a total rating—alcohol + sugar residue—of 21.5 percent. The spirits of wine added thus varies between 5 percent and 10 percent by volume, the alcoholic strength between 16 percent and 18.5 percent. Roussillon produces 90 percent of French *vin doux naturels*.

Of the four varieties mainly permitted for them (Muscat, Macabeo, Malvoisie, and

Grenache), the last-named, or to be more precise, Grenache Noir and not the likewise cultivated variants Grenache Blanc and Gris, has special status in that it gives the highest-quality Banyuls, Maury, and Rivesaltes their character. Whereas with simpler qualities, the spirits of wine is added to the must, with the best wines it is poured over the macerated grapes—which is called *mutage sur grains*—and macerated with them for several days, or often up to two to four weeks. During this period, the increased alcohol content releases pigments, aromatic substances, and tannins from the skins before pressing is carried out and part of the alcohol is thereby lost.

Traditional Banyuls, Maury, and Rivesaltes are aged in great tuns, in which they are intentionally exposed to oxidation.

To speed up the development of aromas, the wines are in part exposed to the high temperature contrasts between day and night, summer and winter by being placed outside in the open air in *demi-muids* (tuns holding 159 gallons (600 liters)) or even in demijohns, as at Mas Amiel. The bouquet and flavor of traditional V.D.N.s in the first phase of aging are reminiscent of stewed fruits, fresh figs, peaches, and candied cherries. There follows a phase in which dried fruits such as prunes, raisins, figs, and apricots dominate. Further aging—from around the seventh year—brings out roasting aromas such as rusks, roast nuts, and caramel. Then come cocoa, coffee, and later tobacco until finally, after 15 to 20 years, RANCIO tones, the same as one finds in very old cognacs, old dry sherries and *vins jaunes* from the Jura, reminiscent of the aroma of green walnut husks.

Since 1975 an additional type of sweet wine has been added to the range—Vintage, which is often called *Rimage* in Banyuls. These are usually dark red wines bottled early, and are highly juicy and thick. Their intense smell is principally that of fresh ripe cherries with overtones of berries, and the sweetness of the grape sugar hides the mostly very marked tannins. They age like great red wines, as the sweetness becomes steadily more discreet.

V.D.N.s are also made from white varieties (or a combination of them with Grenache Noir) that age beautifully. After ten or more years they often develop aromas of dried apricots, orange peel and—with some Muscat—a touch of pine resin. In their young days, Macabeo and Grenache Blanc remain rather reserved as sweet wines. In popularity and quality they are far outstripped by Muscat de Rivesaltes. This is based on Muscat of Alexandria with its large berries and Muscat Blanc à Petits Grains, which

Traditionally, Banyuls wines are aged in 159-gallon (600-liter) tuns in the open air. The radically forced oxidation thereby attained helps their complex aromas to unfurl.

has very small ripe golden berries. Vinified as a white wine at lower temperatures, in Roussillon it possesses very intensive fresh aromas of lemons or peaches, and occasional overtones of broom, fennel, and aniseed. A young Muscat should always have a very pale tone. In Languedoc, Muscat wines are also produced in St-Jean-de-Minervois, Frontignan, Lunel and Mireval, and at Beaumes-de-Venise in the Rhône area. The only dark V.D.N. outside Roussillon comes from Rasteau.

Chilled to 53–59°F (12–15°C), Banyuls, Maury, and Rivesaltes are pleasant aperitifs, and despite their intense aromas do not impair following wines. They are excellent with *foie gras* and duck dishes prepared with fruit, and go well with goat's cheeses and blue cheeses. As a dessert, they are served with cakes, and their association with chocolate desserts is legendary, the only wines that can easily cope with them, especially the young vintages or dry Banyuls. Once they develop ripe aromas, the connoisseur drinks them as a digestive and enjoys their stunning complexity.

SELECTED PRODUCERS IN ROUSSILLON

CAVE COOPÉRATIVE DE MAURY*–****
MAURY

3,705 acres (1,500 ha); 550,000 bottles • Wines include: Côtes de Rousillon and Villages; Maury: 6 ans d'age, → Vieille Réserve, Recolte Millésimé; Chabert de Barbaira

The Maury wine cooperative has been fighting for decades to get its *vin doux naturel* wines, which grow on schist soils, officially recognized. Besides those aged traditionally, the wines of the annual vintage are steadily improving.

CELLIERS DE TEMPLIERS**–*****
BANYULS-SUR-MER

2,420 acres (980 ha); 1,100,000 bottles • Wines include: Collioure: Blanc, Rosé, Rouge; Banyuls: Rimage, Viviane Le Roy, → Amiral Vilarem, → Président Henri Vidal

The sign of G.I.C.B, a merger of five cooperatives, produces some of the best Banyuls year after year. Their subsidiary La Cave de l'Abbé Rous offers wines under the Mas Cornet label, including a fruity Collioure and a complex Banyuls Mise Tardive.

CHÂTEAU DE CALADROY*–***
BÉLESTA-DE-LA-FRONTIÈRE

321 acres (130 ha); 450,000 bottles • Wines include: Côtes du Roussillon: Rosé, Rouge; → Cuvée La Juliane, → Cuvée La Tour Carrée, Cuvée Saint-Michel, Rivesaltes, Vin de Pays

Along with the new owners, a new quality-conscious spirit has moved in on this grand estate with first class schist locations. This is bearing its first fruits.

CLOS DES FÉES****
VINGRAU

27 acres (11 ha); 35,000 bottles • Wines: Côtes du Roussillon Villages: Les Sorcières, → Tradition, Vieilles Vignes, → Le Clos des Fées, La Petit Sibérie

Ex-wine waiter, publisher, and TV wine journalist Hervé Bizeul has changed sides and become a grower. He has a nose for the right sites and has built up his estate from them. Since his début in 1998 he has been producing wines of great density and powerful structure.

CLOT DE L'OUM****
BÉLESTA-DE-LA-FRONTIÈRE

44.5 (18 ha); 35,000 bottles • Wines: Côtes du Roussillon Villages: La Campagnie des Papillons, Saint Bart, Numéro Uno

Éric and Lèia Monnè have taken a step sideways to a new career, and have shot to success. For years they have been acquiring small plots of old vines on gneiss, granite and schist, at heights of 1,150–1,640 feet (350 to 500 m). At their first attempt, in 2001, they succeeded in producing three wines of incredible sophistication and complexity.

COUME DEL MAS**–****
BANYULS-SUR-MER

25 acres (10 ha); 20,000 bottles • Wines: Collioure: → Blanc, Rosé, Rouge, → Quadratur; Banyuls: Blanc Les Amandiers, Tradition, → Quintessence

Fascinated by the spectacular Banyuls *terroir*, the agrarian and enologist Philippe Gard has dared the impossible. He has created a new *domaine* out of nothing. With extremely hard work, considerable expertise and plenty of passion he immediately produced three outstanding wines.

DOMAINE CAZES FRÈRES**–*****
RIVESALTES

395 acres (160 ha); 800,000 bottles • Wines include: Vin de Pays: Canon de Maréchal, → Credo; Côtes du

Roussillon: → Blanc, Rosé, Rouge; Côtes du Roussillon Villages: → Alter Ego, → Trilogy; Rivesaltes: Vintage, Ambré, Tuilé, → Aimé Cazes; Muscat de Rivesaltes

Brothes André and Bernard Cazes have been the driving force of Roussillon since the early 1980s. Their own estate has grown, but convinces at every level. Today, working together with their children, they work on biodynamic lines. Top of the range are the *vins doux naturels*.

DOMAINE DES CHÊNES***–****
TAUTAVEL

98 acres (36 ha); 90,000 bottles • Wines include: → Côtes du Roussillon Blanc Les Magdaléniens; Côtes du Roussillon Villages: → La Carissa, Tautavel; → Muscat de Rivesaltes, → Rivesaltes Tuilé

Alain Razungles, an enthusiastic enologist at the university in Montpellier, and his father Gilbert are masters of the techniques of producing seductively fruity and solid barrel wines, as well as excellent *vins doux*.

DOMAINE FONTANEL**–****
TAUTAVEL

86.5 acres (35 ha); 175,000 bottles • Wines include: Côtes du Roussillon: Blanc, Rosé; Côtes du Roussillon Villages: Tradition, → Prieuré; Rivesaltes: → Ambré, Rouge, Muscat

Pierre Fontanel and his wife Marie-Claude are an unassuming and untiring wine-growing couple. Their red wine *cuvées* are well differentiated and the Cuvée Prieuré in particular is convincingly well-structured and spicy.

DOMAINE DE FORÇA RÉAL***–****
MILLAS

99 acres (40 ha); 150,000 bottles • Wines include: → Côtes du Roussillon Blanc; Côtes du Roussillon Villages: → Les Haut de Força Réal; Rivesaltes: → Hors d'Age, Muscat

Wine dealer Jean-Paul Henriques has turned into a wine producer on the excellent schist-based sites of a hermitage-topped hill, on which he produces high quality wines.

DOMAINE GARDIÈS****
VINGRAU

111 acres (45 ha); 130,000 bottles • Wines include Vin de Pays Blanc; Côtes du Roussillon Villages: Les Millères, → La Torre, Les Falaises; Rivesaltes, Muscat de Rivesaltes

Since he took over the family estate, which is half in Vingrau, half in Espira d'Algy, in 1990, Jean Gardiès has wrought real miracles. His red wines, conceived as *assemblages* and aged in the barrel, are among the best in the region.

DOMAINE GAUBY*****
CALCE

86.5 acres (35 ha); 80,000 bottles • Wines include: Vin de Pays Blanc: → Vieilles Vignes, L'Oum, → La Roque; Côtes du Roussillon: Les Calcinaires; Côtes du Roussillon Villages: → Vieilles Vignes; → Muntada

Ghislaine and Gérard Gauby have set new standards with their continual search for perfection. They select their plots, give the vines the best possible care, use only sorted grapes and have mastered perfectly judged barrel aging. Reds and whites have now become much more mineral and complex and display outstanding freshness. Must be decanted a few hours before drinking.

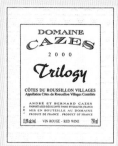

DOMAINE DE LA CASENOVE**–****
TROUILLAS

124 acres (50 ha); 120,000 bottles • Wines include:
Côtes du Roussillon: La Garrigue, → Torrespeyre,
→ Amiral François Jaubert, Vin de Pays: → Macabeu-
Tourbat, → Dominis 'M'; Rivesaltes: Domaine de Saint
Luc: Pla del Rei
The wine-growing estate has been in the family for over
400 years. It has long been the custom for the eldest
Montés son to take over the former Templar estate only
after another professional career. Once an excellent
photo-journalist, Étienne is now just as outstanding a
grower. His wines have full character.

DOMAINE MARCEVOL**–***
ARBOUSSOLS

25 acres (10 ha); 27,000 bottles • Wines: Vin de Pays
Blanc, Côtes du Roussillon: Tradition, → Prestige
Guy Predal, from northern Catalonia, has joined forces
with Pascal Verhaeghe from Cahors. With lots of hard
work in the vineyard and plenty of commitment, they
have succeeded in producing juicy wines with clean
fruit and spice.

DOMAINE DU MAS CRÉMAT***–****
ESPIRA D'AGLY

74 acres (30 ha); 90,000 bottles • Wines include: Vin de
Pays, Muscat Sec, → Grenache Blanc Vieilles Vignes; Côtes
du Roussillon and Fût de Chêne; Muscat de Rivesaltes
Using his Burgundian origin and experience, top grower
Jean-Marc Jeannin created a wine style all his own in
Roussillon that links strength and finesse in an unusual
way. Since his premature death, his wife Cathérine
Mongeard from Vosne-Romanée has run the estate
with admirable courage.

DOMAINE PIQUEMAL***–****
ESPIRA D'AGLY

143 acres (58 ha); 285,000 bottles • Wines include:
Côtes du Roussillon: → Blanc, Les Terres Grillées,
Rouge, Fûts de Chêne, Les Terres Grillées; → Muscat de
Rivesaltes Coup de Foudre; Vins de Pays
By dint of much effort, knowledge, and vision, plus the
help of their son Franck, the Picquemals have created
an interesting and homogeneous range of wines. The
Muscat from the barrel is delightful.

DOMAINE OLIVIER PITHON***–****
CALCE

33 acres (13.5 ha); 23,500 bottles • Wines: Côtes du
Roussillon Blanc: → Cuvée Laïs, 'La D 18'; Côtes du
Roussillon Villages: La Coulée, Saturne
Olivier Pithon gained his first experiences of vineyard
and winery working with his brother Jo in Anjou. Now
he is applying these in Roussillon and conjuring up
wines of astonishing freshness and fruit.

DOMAINE DE LA RECTORIE****
BANYULS-SUR-MER

57 acres (23 ha); 110,000 bottles • Wines include:
Collioure: Blanc L'Argile, Rosé, Rouge Le Seris,
→ Coume Pascole; Banyuls: Vintage, Elisabeth,
→ Léon Parcé; → Vin de Pierre, → L'Oriental
Since their first Banyuls vintage in 1984, Marc and
Thierry Parcé have come up with stunning wine
creations again and again. They have now joined forces
with three winegrowers from Maury to found the
Perceptorie de Centernach and have extended their
range to include Côtes du Roussillon and Maury.

DOMAINE SARDA MALET****
PERPIGNAN

119 acres (48 ha); 200,000 bottles • Wines include: Côtes
du Roussillon: → Blanc, Rosé, Rouge; → Réserve, →
Terroir de Mailloles; Rivesaltes, Muscat, → La Carbasse

Thanks to reliable quality at a high level, Suzy Malet has
made an international name for her estate. However, since
son Jérôme started to use his nose for wine-making, they
have gained in concentration and precision and have risen
to become some of the best in the region.

DOMAINE DES SCHISTES***–****
ESTAGEL

124 acres (50 ha); 125,000 bottles • Wines: Vin de Pays:
Merlot, → Cabernet; Côtes du Roussillon: → Tradition,
Les Terrasses; Rivesaltes: → Maury Vintage
Jacques and Nadine Sire run their estate at the foot of
the south wall of the Corbières, turning out quality
wines which get better from year to year. Since 1999
they have also offered an excellent young Maury.

DOMAINE DE LA TOUR VIEILLE***–****
COLLIOURE

32 acres (13 ha); 52,000 bottles • Wines include:
Collioure: → Blanc Les Canadells, Rosé des Roches,
Rouge La Pinède, → Puig Oriol; Banyuls: → Vendanges,
Millésimé; → Mémoire d'automne
The wines that Christine Campadieu and Vincent
Cantié produce from their traditionally maintained
vineyards in Collioure and Banyuls give a varied and
authentic impression of their Catalan *terroir*.

DOMAINE VIAL MAGNÈRES****
BANYULS-SUR-MER

32 acres (13 ha); 30,000 bottles • Wines include:
Collioure: → Blanc Armenn, Rouge Les Espérades;
Banyuls: Blanc Rivage, → Gaby Vial 1993, → Al Tragou;
→ Ranfio Seco
Bernard Saperas maintains the old schist terraces above
the sea with passion. His range of Banyuls is notably
well differentiated. He was a pioneer of the white wine
styles of the Côte Vermeille, re-introducing the Ranfio
Seco, a *fino*. The old Rancio is legendary.

L'ÉTOILE**–*****
BANYULS-SUR-MER

348 acres (141 ha); 182,000 bottles • Wines include:
Collioure: Rosé, Rouge; Banyuls: → Blanc Doux Paillé;
Rouge: Rimage, → Macéré Tuilé, Grande Réserve,
→ Extra Vieux, → Select Vieux
The oldest grower cooperative of the Côte Vermeille is
at the same time a bastion of traditional Banyuls aged
oxidatively, where it offers a real miracle. Fluctuating
quality with dry wines.

MAS AMIEL***–*****
MAURY

395 acres (160 ha); 300,000 bottles • Wines include: Côtes
du Roussillon: Hautes Terres; Côtes du Roussillon Villages
Carrerades; Maury: 10 ans d'age, 15 ans d'age, → 1980;
Maury Vintage: → Privilège, Réserve, Charles Dupuy
Olivier Decelle has brought the famous Mas into a new
epoch. The new range offers not only convincing dry
wines—the *vins doux* have also gained in style and
quality.

VIGNOBLES JEAN ET BERNARD DAURÉ**–****
CASES-DE-PINE

331 acres (134 ha)+222 acres (90 ha) + 15 acres (6 ha);
750,000 + 220,000 + 20,000 bottles • Wines include:
Côtes du Roussillon Villages: Blanc, Rouge, → Talon
Rouge, Muscat de Rivesaltes; Vin de Pays Jaja de Jau;
Collioure: Rosé, Rouge; Banyuls: Rimage, Cap Béar;
Rivesaltes
Estelle Dauré now runs the family estates of Château de
Jau, Les Clos de Paulilles and Mas Christine, together
with Viña del Nuevo Mondo in Chile, with a great
deal of verve and feminine intuition. She produces
top quality in her Collioures and the intensive,
complex Banyuls.

ECKHARD SUPP, DUNJA ULBRICHT, STEFFEN MAUS

ITALY

The History of Italian Wine

Not only is Italy one of the most important wine-producing countries in Europe today, it is also one of the continent's oldest producers. Recent archeological finds have shown that the vine was first systematically cultivated in Italy by the Etruscans in the 8th century BC although viticulture did not arrive in France until the 6th century BC when the Greeks introduced it from their colony Massalia (Marseille). We can assume that efforts were made to cultivate the vine even earlier though clear proof of this has not yet been established. With the advent of the Roman Empire advanced skills and expertise in viticulture and winemaking spread throughout Western and Central Europe. The Romans were also responsible for the development of the wine trade into a very profitable economic activity. Pompeii, the port at the foot of Mount Vesuvius, evolved into the most important wine-trading city in the ancient world, and its destruction as a result of the volcanic eruption of AD 79 paved the way for the establishment of regional wine centers throughout the Roman Empire. The resulting rise of wine may have contributed to the fact that the total ban on the drunken revelry of the Bacchanalia (the Roman variant of the Greek cult of Dionysus), which was pronounced as early as 186 BC, was more honored in the breach than in the observance. With the rise of Christianity and up to its recognition as a state religion in the 4th century, the consumption of wine in the context of cult activities became more moderate.

No other Italian wine matures for so long and with such *grandezza* as Barolo, the great wine of Piedmont.

The city of Florence—renowned not only for culture and art but also for the wines of Tuscany, grown and produced on its doorstep.

Regional wine production figures		*Source: Ismea, Istat 2003*
Region	Vineyards in acres (ha) (2000)	Production in 1,000 gal (1,000 hl) (1997–2001)
Abruzzi	82,780 (33,500)	104,185 (3,959)
Apulia	210,030 (85,000)	202,235 (7,685)
Basilicata	19,025 (7,700)	13,158 (500)
Calabria	148,010 (59,900)	170,525 (6,480)
Campania	43,985 (17,800)	29,790 (1,132)
Emilia Romagna	33,360 (13,500)	21,050 (800)
Friuli-Venezia Giulia	71,900 (29,100)	53,235 (2,023)
Lazio	71,410 (28,900)	87,765 (3,335)
Liguria	7,410 (3,000)	3,945 (150)
Lombardy	54,360 (22,000)	38,155 (1,450)
Marches	48,925 (19,800)	45,235 (1,719)
Molise	14,580 (5,900)	9,210 (350)
Piedmont	129,970 (52,600)	84,765 (3,221)
Sardinia	63,255 (25,600)	24,370 (926)
Sicily	275,760 (111,600)	208,895 (7,938)
Trentino-Alto Adige	144,055 (58,300)	63,870 (2,427)
Tuscany	34,100 (13,800)	30,735 (1,168)
Umbria	35,090 (14,200)	23,685 (900)
Valle d'Aosta	1,235 (500)	790 (30)
Veneto	181,865 (73,600)	220,105 (8,364)
Total	1,671,114 (676,300)	1,282,703 (54,557)

The fall of the Western Roman Empire in AD 476 heralded a period of fundamental change in Italy, and the unrest arising from the migration of the peoples had a detrimental effect on all activities which require generations of peace and tranquillity. Wine growing and production, and particularly the creation of fine wines, declined. When a market for wine re-emerged with the rise of the trade centers of Genoa, Florence, and Venice, and the growth in the affluence enjoyed by their inhabitants, trade in wines from Bordeaux, Burgundy, the Rhine, and the Danube developed into a profitable business. Some of the names which are still well known in the world of wine today were established as early as the 13th and 14th centuries. These include the Antinoris, whose wealth was initially based on the silk trade, and the Frescobaldis, who financed the brisk trade in goods between Bordeaux and the English crown, and collected taxes in London on behalf of the popes.

While Italian bankers and traders made good profits from wine imports, vine cultivation in Italy itself survived only in the form of a subsistence activity among the—mainly extremely poor—rural population. In some regions of Italy, the wine-growing tradition only survived due to the work of the monasteries. This decline lasted into

the 19th century when signs of a new beginning finally emerged in Piedmont and Tuscany. Vine varieties such as Barolo, Brunello, and Chianti were developed on the basis of the French models with the active involvement of French enologists. Within 150 years these wines were among the most popular and best in the world. The Italian schools of ENOLOGY, and wineries such as Gancia, Cinzano, and Bolla, which remain famous to the present day, were founded at this time.

In Italy, the ravages of PHYLLOXERA almost succeeded in bringing the aspiring wine culture to a standstill and the two world wars of the 20th century also played their part in blocking its development. During the difficult years in the aftermath of the Second World War, an approach which favored the planting of highly productive vineyards and the selection of high-yielding rather than qualitatively superior vine varieties became established. This trend was also supported by the French wine industry which provided a growing market for Italian "plonk" to mix with its own table wines, following the decline in supplies from its former colony Algeria.

Upturn and Obstacles

This trend toward increasingly high yields in Italy reflected the fact that during the food shortages of the post-war years, wine was not a luxury but considered to be an important source of calories. Consumer behavior did not begin to change in this regard until the 1960s when the annual per capita consumption of wine by the Italians initially decreased from 30 to 16 gallons (110 to 60 l).

At the same time, there was a radical shift in viticulture to an emphasis on quality, despite the scandal which shocked the entire country in the mid-1980s when it emerged that a group of irresponsible producers had sought to "improve" cheap wine through the addition of methanol.

Within a few weeks over 20 people died after drinking the contaminated wine.

The upturn in the fortunes of winemaking started in Tuscany where a completely new category of wines emerged: the Supertuscan table wines, which were made with the hitherto uncommon French vine varieties Cabernet Sauvignon, Merlot, Chardonnay, and Syrah and generally matured in small *barriques* made of new oak wood. Throughout the 1970s and 1980s, the new generations of winegrowers and producers looked to France and the New World for inspiration and tried to implement the new insights they gained there at home in Italy.

It was shortly after this that the equally radical process of the modernization of Barolo and Barbera started in Piedmont, with the aim

of producing more intensely-colored, fruitier wines to satisfy the sophisticated tastes of the international market. While this development initially only affected winery practices, in the 1990s the focus shifted to the vineyards. Old and obsolete vineyards were cleared and replaced with modern more quality-oriented cultivation systems.

At the same time, Italian wine legislation was at least partly adapted to the new realities and requirements of the international markets. A new category of wine was created, that of the table wine with denomination of origin (*Indicazione Geografica Tipica*, I.G.T.), and thanks to changes in production regulations, a series of former table wines could be marketed as quality wines with denominated (and guar-

anteed) origin (*Denominazione di Origine Controllata/ e Garantita*, D.O.C./D.O.C.G.).

Finally, Italian wine producers began to appreciate and exploit the country's vast but largely unused stock of indigenous vine varieties and took the first steps toward improving the stocks. This is where the most important challenge and opportunity for the future of winemaking in Italy lies, as the fashion for "international" grape varieties may well die and consumers will once again favor the specialties and unique characteristics of wines from individual countries.

The Nebbiolo grape matures to unique perfection on the slopes surrounding Barolo, the Piedmontese village which gave its name to Italy's most famous red wine.

HIERARCHY, ITALIAN STYLE

Although Cosimo III de'Medici first defined the Chianti area in 1716, and awarded the world's first binding *appellation* to Carmignano red wine, the legislation defining categories of wine and geographical provenance in Italy did not come into force until 1963. The principles of this law, which give legal protection to controlled production zones and wines, are still in place today. The law divided wine production into two classes in accordance with the European standard: table wines (*vini da tavola*) and quality or D.O.C. wines (DENOMINAZIONE DI ORIGINE CONTROLLATA) which were henceforth subject to precise regulations with respect to the vine varieties used in their production, the geographical provenance of the grapes, and vine cultivation and winery practices. The production statute for the first D.O.C. zone was developed for the Tuscan white wine Vernaccia di San Gimignano, three years after the passing of the new legislation. In subsequent years, over 300 of these D.O.C. denominations were established.

A MISSED OPPORTUNITY

The increase in the number of D.O.C. zones was accompanied by a growing criticism of the inadequacy of the options available to differentiate between the quality of individual *appellations*. While the market had long since created clear price-based distinctions, high-quality wines were otherwise deemed the equals of their basic mass-produced counterparts. Thus an additional classification was created at the top of the quality pyramid to designate wines whose quality was both controlled and guaranteed (DENOMINAZIONE DI ORIGINE CONTROLLATA E GARANTITA,

Morning mists in Carmignano, west of Florence.

D.O.C.G.). These wines were subject to more stringent production regulations, lower maximum yields, and longer aging. This mark of distinction was conferred on some of Italy's most prestigious wines, such as Barolo, Barbaresco, Brunello, Chianti, and Vino Nobile di Montalcino. However, when it was awarded to wines of less distinguished provenance, such as Albana di Romagna, Asti Spumante, and Vernaccia di San Gimignano, an important opportunity to establish a real quality hierarchy was missed.

Moreover, with their combination of bureaucratic detail and *laissez-faire* implementation, the production regulations were soon perceived by many top producers as a hindrance. Innovative growers realized that their efforts to improve their wines, for example through the introduction of changes in the composition of blends, were irreconcilable with the excessively precise regulations prescribed by the law. A winemaker who wanted to produce a Chianti Classico from 100 percent Sangiovese grapes, instead of the mandatory blend of red and white grapes, was just as far outside the legal framework as one who wanted to mature Barolo or Brunello in smaller new wooden barrels, or one wishing to process some of the indigenous Friulian vine varieties.

The most important Italian D.O.C.G. wines		
D.O.C.G. designation	Region	Main vine variety
Asti	Piedmont	Moscato
Barbaresco	Piedmont	Nebbiolo (single-varietal)
Barolo	Piedmont	Nebbiolo (single-varietal)
Brunello di Montalcino	Tuscany	Sangiovese (single-varietal)
Carmignano	Tuscany	Sangiovese, Cabernet
Chianti	Tuscany	Sangiovese
Chianti Classico	Tuscany	Sangiovese
Franciacorta	Lombardy	Chardonnay, Pinot Noir
Sagrantino di Montefalco	Umbria	Sagrantino
Taurasi	Campania	Aglianico (single-varietal)
Torgiano Rosso Riserva	Umbria	Sangiovese
Valtellina Superiore	Valtellina	Nebbiolo
Vernaccia di San Gimignano	Tuscany	Vernaccia
Vino Nobile di Montepulciano	Tuscany	Sangiovese

However, the Italian winegrowers were very resourceful. They simply defined their new wines as table wines, ignoring the fact that, for example, it was not possible to specify the year on the label. Thanks to their outstanding quality and some clever marketing, they quickly achieved prices which made most quality wines with protected *appellations* look like cheap mass-produced goods. Legislators were not pleased by the undermining of the quality hierarchy, and responded by revising the law in the 1990s. Under the new regulations, there is greater flexibility in the definition of the D.O.C.s and D.O.C.G.s and the ridiculously long cask-aging periods were reduced. Many of the super table wines were then marketed with an official denomination of origin and year, under the name *vini da tavola con indicazione geografica* or *Indicazione Geografica Tipica* (I.G.T.), while others were reclassified as D.O.C.s. Under the new hierarchy there are four categories:

• Table wines (*vini da tavola*) whose labels do not include information about the wine's geographical origin and year.
• I.G.T. wines whose labels include information about the geographical provenance, vine variety, specific vineyard, and year.
• D.O.C. wines (*Denominazione di Origine Controllata*).

Production volumes and regions of the main D.O.C. and D.O.C.G. wines		Source: Federdoc 2001
Designation of origin	Region	Volume 1,000 gal (1,000 hl)
Asti Spumante or Moscato d'Asti D.O.C.G.	Piedmont	20,000 (760)
Barbera d'Asti D.O.C.	Piemont	7,895 (300)
Oltrepò pavese D.O.C.	Lombardy	21,580 (820)
Bardolino D.O.C.	Veneto	7,630 (290)
Prosecco D.O.C.	Veneto	11,050 (420)
Soave D.O.C.	Veneto	18,420 (700)
Valpolicella D.O.C.	Veneto	13,945 (530)
Trentino D.O.C.	Trentino	12,105 (460)
Südtirol D.O.C.	Alto-Adige	9,210 (350)
Friaul Grave D.O.C.	Friuli	15,265 (580)
Colli Piacentini D.O.C.	Emilia Romagna	8,945 (340)
Lambrusco D.O.C.	Emilia Romagna	14,210 (540)
Sangiovese di Romagna D.O.C.	Emilia Romagna	7,370 (280)
Chianti Classico D.O.C.G.	Tuscany	8,685 (330)
Chianti D.O.C.G.	Tuscany	26,315 (1,000)
Verdicchio D.O.C.	Marche	7,630 (290)
Frascati D.O.C.	Lazio	6,840 (260)
Montepulciano d'Abruzzo D.O.C.	Abruzzi	21,840 (830)
Salice Salentino D.O.C.	Apulia	8,160 (310)

• D.O.C.G. quality wines (*Denominazione di Origine Controllata e Garantita*), with various additional labels, including RISERVA (longer cask aging); *superiore* (relating to alcohol content or maximum yield); *classico* (wine originating from the historical center of the cultivation area); and *vigna/vigneto* (single-vineyard bottling).

The towers of San Gimignano—symbols of the quest for power in medieval Italy.

VARIETIES FOR THE FUTURE

Italy's vineyards offer what is probably the largest resource of different types of the species *Vitis vinifera*. While the 12 most common varieties (see table on page 343) account for what is grown in more than half of the country's vineyards, dozens of other economically relevant varieties exist, in addition to probably hundreds of subspecies which survive hidden on a few acres of vineyard waiting to be rediscovered and transformed into quality wines.

Although the white varieties can easily compete with red in terms of quantity, Italy's truly great wines, with a few exceptions, are red. The prestige of all Italian viticulture rests on two grape varieties: Sangiovese and Nebbiolo (which is cultivated in less than one percent of Italian vineyards and is only really successful in a few locations).

NEBBIOLO

Barolo and Barbaresco, Piedmont's top-quality wines, are pressed from Nebbiolo grapes. Nebbiolo is also the basis of other single-varietal and blended D.O.C. and D.O.C.G. wines, such as Gattinara, Ghemme, Roero, and the Lombardy *appellation*, Valtellina. This vine, which is also known as Spanna, Picutener, and Chiavennasca, is grown in cooler areas and is far less suited to excessive yields than other varieties. Its small fruit give a dark tannic wine. The distinctive features of the great Nebbiolo wines include

their dense, ruby-red, shimmering color and their aroma of tea leaves, spices, roses, and sometimes even a hint of tar. Extremely harsh and tannic when young, they age into outstanding, soft, alluring, and gratifying wines.

SANGIOVESE AND ITS FRENCH PARTNERS

Sangiovese, Italy's second top red variety, provides the basis for very famous wines, such as Brunello, Chianti, and Vino Nobile which are all produced in Tuscany. Torgiano and Montefalco, two other major representatives of the variety, are produced in Umbria. Romagna also has extensive tracts of Sangiovese. Here, however, in contrast to the fine, complex wines of Tuscany, it mainly yields rather light and sweet everyday wines, except for those produced from grapes harvested on the higher slopes.

The variety probably originated in Tuscany and is believed to have been known to the Etruscans. Its wines are characterized by a lively acidity and complex TANNIN structure which is why they lack the powerful and compact effect of Cabernet, for example. To compensate for this late-ripening variety's vulnerability in cooler weather conditions—causing high acidity and forcing the tannins to remain green and raw—it has generally been blended with other varieties to provide color, fruit, sweetness, and mildness. The traditional recipe for Chianti Classico, which actually used white grapes, is rarely used now, and single-varietal Sangiovese or blends with French varieties are more common—smooth and fruity Merlot has become a particular favorite in recent years.

As well as their use for blending with Sangiovese, the French Cabernet Sauvignon and Merlot varieties are well established in Italy in their own right. Introduced in the late 19th century, particularly in the north in response to the phylloxera disaster, up to the post-war years, Merlot was, in fact, Italy's most common variety. The advent of the Tuscan wine revolution brought these vines into focus once again. Sassicaia, the country's first major Cabernet Sauvignon wine, proved that this variety was suited to conditions in Italy. The Supertuscan table wines, which earned an international reputation for quality Italian winemaking, were based on this model. The fact that their Cabernet was almost impossible to distinguish

Hitherto, modern wine production tended to concentrate on only a dozen varieties. However, Italy's vineyards are host to a wealth of old, indigenous, and often unresearched varieties which are now attracting increasing interest among enologists and producers.

from French and Californian ones did not occur to critical Italian winemakers and producers until a very late stage.

In contrast, for many decades Merlot was merely used in the production of thin, acidic, mass-produced wines. It was not until the late 1980s and early 1990s that Tuscan and then Friulian Merlots came onto the market. These wines finally exploited the potential of this excellent variety to create intensely-colored, soft, full-bodied wines with a firm tannin structure and lovely fruit AROMAS. The fact that the two joint-venture companies in Tuscany, founded by the Californian Mondavi producers, have taken to blending Merlot with Sangiovese, is an indication of the potential of this early-maturing variety which, with its fruity wines, is perhaps more suitable than the originally favored Cabernet Sauvignon.

BARBERA AND UNDISCOVERED TREASURES

Since the 1980s, Italian producers have worked more intensively with other native varieties. The Piedmontese wine Barbera has enjoyed one of the most astonishing careers in European wine-making. Originally an acidic outsider, it developed to earn a reputation as a dense, spicy, modern, top-quality red. The major southern varieties, Aglianico, Negroamaro, Primitivo, Nero d'Avola, and Uva di Troia have also finally been enjoying a little of the attention they richly deserve. Northern Friuli is something of an exception. Here, the three outstanding red varieties, Refosco, Pignolo, and Schioppettino, survived and have been used to produce high-quality wines in recent decades. Finally, when Corvina—the basis for the great Amarone wine of the Veneto—is added to the list, Italy indeed emerges as a rich treasure-house which will continue to inspire great creativity in future decades.

WHITE VARIETIES

The story of the Italian white grape varieties couldn't be more different. Few areas in Italy are really suited to the production of great white wines. And while, for red wines, high-quality Sangiovese also leads the field in terms of quantity, the quantity league for whites is mainly led by grape varieties whose good wines are the exception rather than the rule. For example, Moscato Bianco—used in the production of the single-varietal Moscato d'Asti as well as the wonderful dessert wines of the island of Pantelleria—and Malvasia can give very interesting wines, but they are mostly used in mass

There can be no doubt the future lies with unique varieties like Sangiovese as opposed to the virtually ubiquitous international varieties. Sangiovese is the key to the outstanding character of the great Tuscan reds but it has yet to yield convincing results in other areas.

production where excessive yields are incompatible with high-quality production. Of the Trebbiano wines, none stands out in terms of complexity of taste; in France this variety is justifiably used in brandy distillation under the name "Ugni Blanc." The same applies to the Venetian Garganega variety, although it occasionally produces delightful sweet wines of the *appellation* Recioto di Soave. Along with the Tuscan white Vernaccia, the Piedmontese Arneis and Cortese, and Verdicchio from the Marches, it has failed to turn Italy into a country of white wines. Producers finally latched onto the French varieties Chardonnay and Sauvignon Blanc as part of the Italian wine revolution, but they have quickly discovered that these varieties are only really suited for cultivation in a few areas, such as Alto Adige (Southern Tyrol), eastern Friuli and a few upland areas in central and southern Italy. In addition, the enthusiasm of the international markets for these varieties, which are cultivated in vast quantities throughout the world, is threatening to wane in the not-too-distant future.

Varieties and their area of cultivation in 1,000s of acres (hectares)			*Source: Ismea, Istat 2003*
Rebsorte	1990	2000	Change
Sangiovese	213 (86.2)	172.2 (69.7)	–19%
Catarrato Bianco	160.6 (65)	106.7 (43.2)	–33%
Trebbiano Toscano	144.6 (58.5)	105 (42.5)	–27%
Montepulciano	76.6 (31)	73.6 (29.8)	–4%
Barbera	116.4 (47.1)	69.9 (28.3)	–40%
Merlot	78.8 (31.9)	63.2 (25.6)	–20%
Trebbiano Romagnolo	52.6 (21.3)	49.4 (20)	–6%
Negroamaro	77.6 (31.4)	41.5 (16.8)	–47%
Moscato Bianco	33.3 (13.5)	32.9 (13.3)	–2%
Chardonnay	15.3 (6.2)	29.1 (11.8)	+90%
Garganega	32.1 (13)	28.6 (11.6)	–11%
Nero d'Avola	35 (14.2)	28.1 (11.4)	–20%

THE NORTHWEST: THE ALPS, THE APENNINES, AND THE PO

A view of Alberetto della Torre in Piedmont against the snow-capped Alps.

Northwest Italy consists of four regions whose landscapes and climate vary considerably: Valle d'Aosta, Piedmont, Liguria, and Lombardy.

Piedmont lies sheltered by the western flank of the Alps which runs almost seamlessly into the Ligurian Apennines in the west and opens out onto the plain of the river Po. Its varied hilly landscape and soils are eminently suited to viticulture—the lime-rich marl of the Langhe hills in particular providing optimum conditions for top-quality wines. The region is the home of one of the world's best red varieties, Nebbiolo, and one of today's most popular sparkling wines, Asti or Asti Spumante.

A CONTINENTAL CLIMATE

Although Alba, Piedmont's most famous wine-producing area, is on the same latitude as Bordeaux, the two regions enjoy completely different climatic conditions. Unlike the Bordelais region, where the extremely mild sea climate is particularly suitable for vine cultivation, the seasons in Piedmont are dominated by a rather continental climate. With its short, dry summers, long and often foggy autumns, and very cold winters, the region does not conform to the stereotype of the Italian climate.

Viticulture is therefore only found in areas which are exposed to the alleviating influence of river valleys or on protected south-facing slopes where the heat of the sun can be exploited to the full. The Valle d'Aosta, for example, enjoys this combination of features, and sophis-ticated red varieties positively thrive in its Alpine setting. It is surprisingly warm and dry here during the mid-year period, and the steep wine terraces benefit from every ray of sunlight. Similar conditions can be found in the Valtellina and Veltlin, on the Swiss border of Lombardy, where some of the most interesting results are obtained from Nebbiolo vines.

THE RIVIERA AND THE ADRIATIC COASTS

The situation in the rest of Lombardy, which opens out to the wide, misty plain of the Po toward the Adriatic Sea and is subject to its climatic influence, couldn't be more different. Even northern Italy can offer Mediterranean conditions in places where large expanses of water contribute to the regulation of the temperature, for example Lakes Iseo and Garda with their mineral-rich, gravelly, moraine soils. However, most Lombardian wines originate from the climatically less fortunate areas of Oltrepò Pavese on the northern foothills of the Ligurian Apennines, facing the Lombardy plain.

The vines that grow in elongated Liguria, the southernmost of the northwestern regions which extends along the southern edge of the Apennines, enjoy excesses of heat and sun. The sea-facing vineyards enjoy optimum conditions for quality production but, given the extremely difficult working conditions, they are rarely exploited to the full.

YOUNG GROWERS, NEW WINES

A fresh wind is blowing throughout the Northwest. The developments that have taken place over the past two decades, particularly in the Barolo area, can be described without hesitation as a revolution in winemaking. It all started with work on the vineyards. Inspired by experience gained in visits to France during the 1970s and 1980s, many young growers decided to reduce yields, mainly by means of radical crop-thinning in summer, to enable them to harvest fully ripe and extremely concentrated grapes in autumn.

The changes in winery practices were even more radical. Many producers replaced their stock of wooden casks—in which the Barolo was often stored, to its detriment, for excessive periods—with temperature-controlled stainless steel FERMENTATION tanks, and *barriques* for

aging. While traditionalists were originally critical of the extremely brief fermentation and MACERATION periods, and the practice of aging the wines in new *barriques*, most were eventually spurred on to introduce one or more carefully considered innovations and often produced amazingly good wines in the 1980s and 1990s.

NEW METHODS, ALL VARIETIES

The producers in Barbaresco and areas around Langhe, Roero, and Monferrato tentatively followed the example of the *Barolisti*. The results of the Barolo experiments also helped to improve the results obtained from other grape varieties: Barbera, which attained the status of a top international wine thanks of barrel-aging; Dolcetto, whose more clearly-defined fruit was greeted with enthusiasm; and, finally, Grignolino, Freisa, and the imported French varieties.

Even the white wines started to make progress but they failed to mirror the successes of the reds. Gavi and Arneis, from Roero, initially seemed to be capable of developing into fashionable wines, but their taste profile remained too neutral to withstand the competition from

Modern wine production in *barriques* and stainless steel tanks at Rocche de Manzoni.

Brachetto is a rare Piedmontese variety used to produce very unusual light red sparkling wines with an intense raspberry aroma.

French, German, and overseas whites. Asti only succeeded in meeting the increasing requirements of the international markets with its light, fruity variety, Moscato d'Asti, and, despite its elevation to D.O.C.G. status, still lost ground.

PROGRESS IN LOMBARDY

While the response to the new quality philosophy was tentative in Valle d'Aosta and Liguria, which mainly produce for the domestic market, the successes achieved in parts of Lombardy were almost as impressive as those of Piedmont. The Franciacorta area, in particular, distinguished itself. The producers from Lake Iseo achieved major successes in the quality of both bottle-fermented sparkling wines and still wines, which are usually based on blends of indigenous and international grape varieties.

Northwest Italy is, therefore, well armed for the future. The excessive price trends in the case of certain *appellations* is, however, casting a shadow. This is less true of the producers of the really top-quality wines than of those lower down the scale who sometimes demand top prices for wines which could not be described as top-quality.

Regional grape varieties in the Northwest

The Northwest is home to a wide variety of enological treasures in the form of indigenous vine varieties which have only been introduced to a wider audience in recent decades, particularly Dolcetto, which is popular in Piedmont and Liguria. This early-ripening, unproblematic variety yields fruity red wines which are low in acidity and have a characteristic cherry and pepper aroma. They should be drunk in their first two or three years.

The other Piedmontese red VARIETALS, such as Freisa which is often available in fizzy or semi-sparkling form, the light and intensely aromatic Grignolino, Pelaverga, Ruchè (Rouchet), Croatina, Bonarda, Vespolina, and the Muscat-like Brachetto, have hitherto been undervalued, even at regional level.

With its Petite Arvine, Premetta, and Petit Rouge, the Valle d'Aosta also has its indigenous red varieties whose sometimes very interesting wines receive no international attention. The same applies to Lombardy where, in addition to the native Groppello, varieties from the neighboring regions of Trentino, Veneto, and Emilia Romagna are also vinified: Schiava, Marzemino, Corvina, and Lambrusco.

Two exceptional regional white varieties can be found in Liguria: Vermentino, which is

also cultivated in Sardinia, Tuscany, and France, and the indigenous Pigato, which yields pleasant fruity wines. The other whites tend to be more neutral in character and this is particularly true of the Piedmontese varieties Cortese (which is the base wine for Gavi), Arneis, and Favorita. The acidic Erbaluce is only suitable for the production of sparkling wine and sugary sweet wines. The Valle d'Aosta can add a Pinot Gris—known here as Malvasia—to the list, and the indigenous specialty of Blanc de Morgex. In Lombardy, Garganega, a variety from the neighboring region of the Veneto, deservedly attracts some attention.

VALLE D'AOSTA:
SPECIALTIES FROM THE FOOT OF THE ALPS

Wine production reached this strategically important valley at the latest with the Roman legionaries. From their fortress of Augusta Praetoria, today known as Aosta, the Romans controlled the Alpine passes via the Great and Little St. Bernhard and also started to cultivate the land. The Aosta valley, which was a constant object of tension between France, Italy, and Switzerland right into modern times, is a unique viticultural world. The spectacular narrow vine terraces on the steep cliff walls are the highest in Europe and climb to heights of up to 4,265 feet (1,300 m). They lend the numerous indigenous vine varieties their distinctive character and the valley's most individual wines originate here.

The producers have benefited since time immemorial from the special climatic conditions along the Dora Baltea river. This horseshoe-shaped valley, framed by the Valais and French Alps, which are 13,120 feet (4,000 m) high, is one of Europe's most protected and driest areas. The climate is characterized by extreme winters and hot summers. Day and night temperatures differ significantly, which ensures ideal conditions for the formation of strong, fruity aromas during the growing season. While many of the high regions are suitable for growing white wine varieties with a good acidic balance, the south-facing terraces of the central valley—the best locations of all—are also suitable for the production of full-bodied reds.

After Roman times, wine production in this area was continued by Italian monks. The valley has the clergy to thank not only for planting the

Amphitheater of vines near Donnas (in the lower Valle d'Aosta).

terrace vineyards but also for their contribution to the preservation of this labor-intensive mountain viticulture right into the 20th century. Some of the monks made a name for themselves and their wines which spread beyond the region's borders, for example Don Augusto Pramontton, who produced a legendary Malvoisie de Nus from raisined Pinot Gris grapes. Although the area under cultivation continuously decreased in size over the 20th century, from around 7,410 to 1,235 acres (3,000 to 500 ha), it is now believed that a turning point has been reached in the valley. With financial aid from the state, the region's 2,400—mostly part-time—wine producers have rekindled their interest and ambitions for the business.

VARIETIES AND SPECIALTIES

Around three quarters of the regional wineries have now regained D.O.C. status and are marketed under the D.O.C. *appellation* "Valle d'Aosta/Vallée d'Aoste" (the bilingualism is a legacy from the 9th century, when the Aosta valley belonged to the French kingdom of Savoie), with 27 types of wine and 22 authorized grape varieties defined in the regulations. Of these, the specialties produced from the indigenous vine varieties are particularly interesting.

Of the whites, the Petite Arvine—which is also cultivated in Valais in neighboring Switzerland—and the Blanc de Valdigne yield the most distinctive wines. The latter is used in the production of the well-known Blanc de Morgex et La Salle from the upper end of the valley. Its origin in Europe's highest mountain vineyards has earned it the nickname *Bianco dei ghiacciai*, "wine of the glaciers." Its producers, most of whom are members of the local cooperative, only work

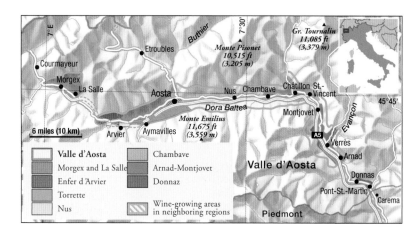

around 37 acres (15 ha) of vineyards and the vines are mainly cultivated on low pergolas. The Blanc de Valdigne, which is highly resistant to phylloxera, is one of the few European varieties which are not grafted onto American rootstocks but planted with its original roots. The climatic conditions of the steep terraces produce grapes which yield light-colored, spirited and often slightly fizzy wines with a citrus-like freshness and the aroma of mountain herbs.

Of the remaining white varieties, Moscato di Chambave stands out. This wine is produced in both a dry version and from raisined fruit for dessert wine (called PASSITO or Flétry in one of the local dialects). White wines are also produced from Müller-Thurgau, Pinot Blanc, Pinot Gris, Pinot Noir, and Chardonnay.

PETIT ROUGE—"THE LITTLE RED"

The indigenous Petit Rouge is used in the production of single-varietal and blended red wines which offer a unique embodiment of the raw, earthy character of the landscape. In Enfer d'Arvier, with its clear berry aroma, underlined with pepper and spice notes, it represents 85 percent of the total volume and is complemented by the native varieties Vien de Nus, Neyret, Gamay, and Pinot Noir. Torette, which originates from the Nus area and is cask-aged for six to eight months, consists of 70 percent Petit Rouge to which Fumin, Neyret, and Vien de Nus as well as Dolcetto, Gamay, and Pinot Noir are added.

The sensitive Nebbiolo matures on the central and lower reaches of the Dora Baltea valley. In high areas of up to 1,970 feet (600 m), above Pont-St-Martin, it is blended with small volumes

The Valle d'Aosta is enclosed by the Valais Alps, Mont Blanc, and the Graian Alps. One of the main trading routes near the region's most important vineyards was guarded from Fénis castle.

Grollo dell'amicizia — the wooden friendship drinking-vessel with six lips from Valle d'Aosta.

of Freisa, Neyret, or Vien de Nus to produce Donnas or Donnaz, a fruity and acidic, slightly rustic wine which is aged in wood for two years. Although it is lighter in structure than the famous Nebbiolo wines of Piedmont, after three to five years of bottle aging, Donnas can be an elegant and classy wine.

Needless to say, the advance of the international varieties did not halt at the high mountain backdrop of the Valle d'Aosta. Chardonnay, Cabernet, Merlot, and even Syrah can be found on numerous terraces. In some cases they yield interesting wines but in most, rather pedestrian products. Anyone wishing to become aquainted with the rare specialties of the Valle d'Aosta will find many treasures awaiting in the region's wineries and restaurants.

SELECT PRODUCERS OF THE VALLE D'AOSTA

COSTANTINO CHARRÈRE**–****
AYMAVILLES
27 acres (11 ha); bought-in grapes; 500,000 bottles
• *Wines include: Premetta, Vin de La Sabla, Les Fourches,*
→*Le Crête di Costantino Charrère, Chardonnay Cuvée La Frissonière les Crêtes, Petite Arvine Champorette, Torrette Les Toules, La Tour: Fumin, Pinot Noir, Syrah*
In addition to the family estate which was established in 1955, Charrère also runs the Les Crêtes winery which is fitted out with the very latest equipment. With its almost full spectrum of Aosta D.O.C. varieties, this is one of the valley's few truly important producers.

COOPERATIVA CROTTA DI VEGNERON**
CHAMBAVE
74 acres (30 ha); 200,000 bottles • *Wines include: Chambave Moscato, Nus Malvoisie Passito, Nus Rosso, Müller-Thurgau, Pinot Noir, Gamay, Fumin*
The wines produced by this cooperative include some of the interesting types from the Valle d'Aosta. Its

Chambave Moscato and Müller-Thurgau are particularly consistent in terms of quality.

FONDAZIONE INSTITUT AGRICOLE RÉGIONAL***
AOSTA
17 acres (7 ha); 50,000 bottles • *Wines: Gamay, Pinot Noir, Petit Rouge, Müller-Thurgau, Pinot Gris, Trésor du Caveau, Sang des Salasses*
The red and white wines produced from the grapes grown in the institute's own vineyards are among the best of the Valle d'Aosta.

EZIO VOYAT**
CHAMBAVE
5 acres (2 ha); 15,000 bottles • *Wines: Rosso le Muraglie, Passito Le Muraglie, La Gazella*
Specialty: Moscato, Moscato Passito. The fourth generation of the Voyats appears to have missed the opportunity to become part of the new wave of quality Aosta wines.

PIEDMONT

Great past, great future—
top estate Elio Altare
(in La Morra).

Piedmont is mainly known as the home of two outstanding red wines: Barolo and Barbaresco. The former is often eulogized as the "wine of kings and king of wines," which suggests that it has enjoyed many centuries of tradition. However, neither of these cult wines was created until the second half of the 19th century, and the form in which they are known today did not emerge until the late 1970s. Nonetheless, Piedmont is a region with a long history of wine-making. The northwestern flank of the Alps, along with the Apennine mountain range, dictate climatic conditions which favor wine growing almost throughout the region, but above all in the provinces of Cuneo, Asti and Alessandria, Langhe, and Monferrato.

GREEKS OR ETRUSCANS?

It is not known whether the Greeks or Etruscans were responsible for introducing viticulture to this region. However, the long-established tradition of allowing the vines to be grown up trees or tall posts—*etrusco*—is at least a clue. The Romans did not value the wines of Piedmont very highly; Pliny the Elder does not include them in his list of the best Italian wines (although he mentions in his natural history an *"uvea spinea … quae sola alitur nebulis"* [a climbing vine … that is the only one which can withstand fog] which may refer to today's Nebbiolo). Following the fall of the Roman Empire, Piedmont became a passage area at the mercy of rival powers. During this period of economic insecurity, it was mainly the monks who engaged in wine production; it was not until the 13th century that Piedmont wine-making experienced a new lease of life. A reference to "Nibiol" appears in a document of 1268, from which it can be concluded that Nebbiolo is indeed an indigenous variety which

Grinzane Cavour—the birthplace of dry Nebbiolo.

is particularly well suited to the region's climate. A chronicle of the community of La Morra, on the northern periphery of today's Barolo area, contains a document dated 1512 which contains a reference to a "Nebiolum." In 1758 the town of Alba passed a decree prohibiting the import and use of wines from other wine-growing areas for blending, and specified a date for the start of harvesting. In addition to Nebbiolo, described at the time as being sweet and slightly fizzy, the main varieties cultivated in the area were Malvasia and Moscato.

The first dry Nebbiolo was created in the 19th century on the initiative of Camillo Cavour, the statesman who is renowned as the father of Italian unification. Around 1850 he employed the French enologist Louis Oudart to develop a dry red wine with good keeping properties, based on the Bordeaux model, for his own winery in Grinzane near Alba and for that of Marquise Giuletta Faletti von Barolo, a French-woman by birth. The result of Oudart's endeavors, a dry, full-bodied red wine which was given the name Barolo, enjoyed a privileged position from the beginning of its career. A successful politician with contacts in the royal house of Savoy and the aristocracy in the royal court in Turin, Cavour was well placed to launch his new wine. By 1896 it was one of Italy's best wines. Shortly before this, Domizio Cavazza had also succeeded in producing a dry Nebbiolo wine by fermenting all of the sugars. As the independent *appellation* Barbaresco, the latter at times enjoyed even greater appreciation than the more famous Barolo. Even phylloxera appears to have been impressed by this prestige, as Nebbiolo was spared when most of Piedmont's vines succumbed to its ravages in the late 19th century.

SMALL PRODUCERS VERSUS LARGE DOMAINS

Despite its prestige, the variety remained insignificant in terms of the quantity produced. Today barely three percent of Piedmontese wines are produced from this variety, a fact which is explained not least by its difficult requirements with respect to soil and climate. Instead, producers tended to favor the indigenous early-ripening Dolcetto and high-yielding Barbera, a choice largely dictated by economic factors.

In contrast to Tuscany, for example, ownership of the vineyards in Piedmont is extremely

fragmented; for a long time many producers did not have sufficient capital to allow them to adopt a sophisticated quality-based approach. Unlike the rest of Italy, farmers here obtained relative freedom from the nobility at an early stage, but this brought no guarantees of economic independence as they still remained locked into a lease system. They were able to farm their smallholdings largely at their own discretion but the high taxes they were forced to pay ensured that they remained poor. Therefore, although viticulture had been part of the mixed-farming system since time immemorial, hardly any farmers had sufficient resources or enough land to sustain viable individual wine production. Even today, the region's largest estate, the Dogliani brothers' Batasiolo, has a mere 277 acres (112 ha) of vineyards. Consequently, the growers were forced to sell their products to a few wineries which, up to the 1980s, continued to exploit their position to obtain grapes, MUST, and even young wine at low prices.

The developments of recent decades, with quality wines yielding far better profits, has shifted the balance in favor of the individual producers. Whereas in the 19th century, only a few large landowners and affluent bourgeoisie established their own domains—including

Fog is a common phenomenon in the Langhe hills where some of the most popular wine regions are located, particularly near the river Tanaro which flows through the town of Alba.

Barale in Barolo (1870) and Pio Cesare in Alba (1881)—the upturn in recent decades afforded many others an opportunity to consolidate their holdings.

BAROLO LEADS THE WAY

Piedmont's success as a wine-producing region rests on Barolo. At one time known only to a select group of loyal followers, its more modern and accessible version, along with the Super-tuscans, has become a symbol for the quality renaissance in Italian winemaking. Other wines also assumed a new revitalized allure in its wake: first the Barberas, whose vines occupy about half of the region's vineyard area, but also Dolcetto, Nebbiolo d'Alba, and Roero. Even the once famous, but subsequently almost forgotten, northern Piedmontese Gattinara and Ghemme attained new levels of quality and access to new markets.

With the exception of individual products from a handful of talented producers, the region's white wines fail to keep pace with the progress of the reds. This is true of the high-volume sparkling wine Asti as well as Gavi and Arneis, the blighted fashion wines whose celebrated career was limited to a single, fairly short and lukewarm season.

Northern Piedmont: Carema and Gattinara

The Nebbiolo vineyards of northern Piedmont are strung out like pearls on a necklace, along the Sesia river valley. Boca and Bramaterra are the northernmost D.O.C. zones situated on the foothills of the Monte Rosa massif. Bramaterra, Gattinara, Coste della Sesia, Lessona, Ghemme, Sizzano, Fara, and Colline Novaresi line the left and right banks of the Sesia downriver. The small vineyards in the narrow, mainly morainic hills, which roll gently down to the Lombardy plain in one direction and climb steeply to the protective main Alpine ridge in the other, are located at a height of between 660 and 980 feet (200 and 300 m). The orientation, height, and microclimatic conditions often vary significantly from one vineyard to the next, with damp and mist causing major problems in some areas. The soil composition also varies considerably and ranges from fine limestone gravel to volcanic porphyry.

Most of the northern Piedmontese D.O.C.s are concentrated around the fertile valley of the river Sesia, northwest of Novara, where vineyards, fields, and meadows alternate and vines are grown only in the most suitable sites.

Gattinara and Ghemme

Gattinara, the most famous wine-growing area in the foothills of the Piedmontese Alps, is the region's largest and it is mainly stocked with Spanna (Nebbiolo) vines. The widespread, fine, gravelly, volcanic soil yields well-structured wine with floral and fruit notes which is a serious rival to Barolo and can have similar aging qualities. The more interesting Gattinara wines are generally made from unblended Nebbiolo grapes, even if the D.O.C.G. regulations, which were defined in 1991, authorize the addition of ten percent Vespolina and Bonarda to soften the wine a little. In line with

the general trend for shorter aging periods, Gattinara need only age in wooden casks for one year, or two years for reserve quality.

Ghemme lies just a short distance away on the eastern side of the Sesia valley and belongs to the province of Novara. Its approximately 210 acres (85 ha) of vineyard slopes were awarded D.O.C.G. status in 1997. Up to 25 percent Vespolina and Uva Rara (the local variety of Bonarda) may be blended with the Nebbiolo. Good Ghemme is characterized by a silky bitter-sweet taste.

Varied Wines from Spanna Grapes

Four other D.O.C. zones with Spanna wines can be found not far from Gattinara, on the mountain range west of the Sesia and north of the town of Cossato. Bramaterra, which thrives on approximately 74 acres (30 ha) of volcanic soil, yields wines which are generally less full-bodied but develop an elegant aroma of violets and roses. The mandatory addition of 30 percent or more of Cratina, Bonarda, or Vespolina injects a fruity acidic character.

In the village of Lessona, with its mere 20 acres (8 ha) of vineyard, Spanna, which thrives on the very gravelly, lime-poor soils, can be produced as a single-varietal but it is generally blended with Vespolina and Bonarda to give robust, full-bodied, sometimes almost salty

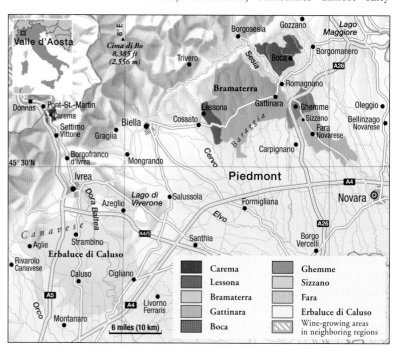

Select Producers in Northern Piedmont

Antoniolo***–****
Gattinara
49 acres (20 ha); 60,000 bottles • Wines include: Gattinara → Vigneto Osso San Grato, → Vigneto Castelle, → San Francesco; Coste della Sesia: Nebbiolo Juvenia, Bricco Lorella
Founded in 1949. The single-vineyard Gattinara Osso San Grato is one of the region's finest wines.

Cieck***
Aglié–San Grato
11 acres (4.5 ha); 25,000 bottles • Wines include: → Erbaluce di Caluso, Spumante, Caluso Passito Alladium Vigneto Runc, Canavese Rosso Neretto di San Giorgio
Lodovico Bardesono and Remo Falconieri's estate is one of the few reputable Caluso wineries. The Spumante is particularly good.

Luigi Ferrando & Figlio***–****
Ivrea
11 acres (4.5 ha); 30,000 bottles • Wines include: Erbaluce di Caluso, Cariola, Caluso Passito, → Carema Etichetta Nera, Canavese Rosso Montodo, → Cariola Brut
Rich complex Nebbiolo and Erbaluce wines.

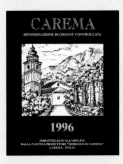

Nervi***
Gattinara
74 acres (30 ha); 80,000 bottles • Wines include: → Gattinara Vigneto Mosino, Coste della Sesia Spanna, Amore
The Bocciolone family manages one of Gattinara's biggest wine estates. In addition to the outstanding single-vineyard Gattinara, they also produce a good Nebbiolo, Cabernet, and Merlot blend known as Amore.

Produttori Nebbiolo di Carema***–****
Carema
49 acres (20 ha); 70,000 bottles • Wines include: Carema, → Carema Carema
This cooperative was founded in 1959 and is financed using the members' own capital. Production is concentrated on two versions of red Carema.

Travaglini****
Gattinara
74 acres (30 ha); 180,000 bottles • Wines include: Gattinara, Gattinara Riserva Numerata
Following the closure of the Le Colline estate, Travaglini assumed the top position for this *appellation*.

---

wines. Wines with a vigorous tannin structure and a bouquet which starts with violets and wild berries and is followed by notes of tea, spices, and rust thrive in the 37 acres (15 ha) of the Boca zone. The recently-created D.O.C., Coste della Sesia, allows the producers in these zones to make wines which lie outside previous D.O.C. boundaries and are dominated by Bonarda, Vespolina, and Croatina grapes.

In the neighboring province of Novara, this cross-boundary role is fulfilled by the D.O.C. *appellation* Connine Novaresi. In the D.O.C. zones of Sizzano (99 acres/40 ha) and Fara (54 acres/22 ha) which are located here, Nebbiolo represents merely 30 to 60 percent of the volumes harvested. This accounts for the less overtly tannic character of the wines produced here, which also develop more quickly.

The Erbaluce di Caluso zone is close to the Valle d'Aosta and the Alps. Snow is a common feature of winters here.

The Veteran of Monte Rosa

Nebbiolo changes its name once again at the entrance to the Aosta valley where it is known as Picutener. The steep terraces of moraine gravel soil, which climb to a height of up to 2,300 feet (700 m), go back to Roman times. Even then the yields were low; no other result is possible with such barren, stony soils and raw climate. The 99-acre (40-ha) D.O.C. region named after the mountain village of Carema produces original wines, whose aroma of wilting roses and tar, and hesitantly-unfolding flavor, are an impressive reflection of their unique *terroir*. This acidic wine needs at least five years' aging.

Sweet Gold

Erbaluce, a light, acidic grape which only fully ripens in extremely sunny positions, can be found in the morainic lands of Canavese and the environs of the industrial town of Ivrea. Fully ripened, it makes wines with a straw-yellow color, an aroma of yeast, bread, and hay, and a spicy finish. The natural acidity makes Erbaluce an ideal base wine for sparkling wine although its real strength lies in the dessert versions, Passito. The grapes for this wine must originate from the best locations and are not harvested until they are extremely ripe. Before pressing, they are dried for months in well-aired rooms and the wines are aged for years in small wooden casks. Then the refined sweet Erbaluce will finally develop its rich aroma of dried fruit, orange peel, and hazelnuts.

Asti and Monferrato

Monferrato and the more famous Langhe were once groups of islands in the Adriatic Sea which, in prehistoric times, covered the plain of the river Po. Both regions have the same geological formation, though their sediments differ in one respect which is important for wine growing: whereas the soils south of Alba are mainly lime and marl, the soils on the hills around the towns of Asti, Alessandria, and Acqui are more sandy.

A Modern Mass-produced Wine

Alto Monferrato, the area including the southern part of the hill group and the town of Canelli, is synonymous with Asti Spumante. With an annual production level which is approaching 18,480,000 gallons (700,000 hl), it is the second most extensively produced Italian quality wine.

Moscato d'Asti—this has been a Muscat Mecca for five hundred years.

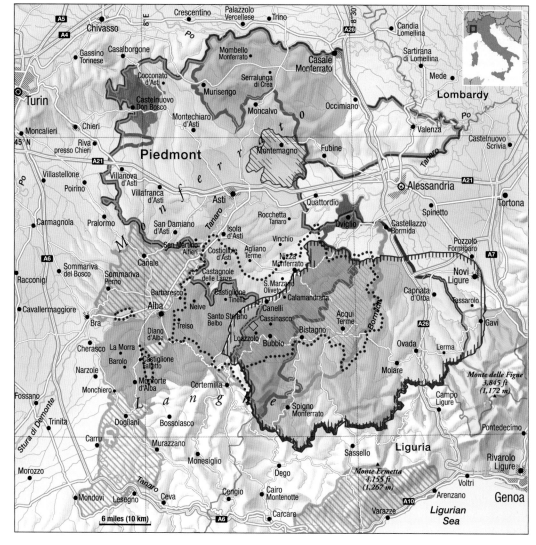

Legend:
- Barbera del Monferrato
- Barbera d'Asti
- Freisa d'Asti
- Malvasia di Castelnuovo Don Bosco
- Grignolino del Monferrato Casalese
- Grignolino d'Asti
- Ruchè di Castagnole Monferrato
- Piedmont
- Cortese dell'Alto Monferrato
- Brachetto d'Acqui
- Loazzolo
- Asti
- Dolcetto d'Alba
- Dolcetto d'Asti
- Dolcetto d'Acqui
- Dolcetto d'Ovada
- Gavi
- Wine-growing areas in neighboring regions

SELECT PRODUCERS OF ASTI AND MONFERRATO

CAUDRINA**
CASTIGLIONE TINELLA
62 acres (25 ha); 150,000 bottles • Wines: Asti La Selvatica, Moscato d'Asti La Caudrina, La Galeisa, →Barbera d'Asti La Solista, Montevenere, Piemonte Chardonnay Mej
Romano Dogliotti and his consultant Guilano Noè produce convincing Moscato and Barbera wines, which are among the best in Piedmont.

GUISEPPE CONTRATTO*−****
CANELLI
• Wines: Barolo Cerequio Tenuta Secolo, →Asti De Miranda, →Barbera d'Asti, Solus Ad, →Spumante Brut Riserva Guiseppe Contratto, Piemonte Chardonnay La Sabauda
This traditional winery was acquired by the Bocchino Grappa dynasty in 1994. The quality of the wines stabilized under the new owners; Contratto is once again one of the best names in Canelli.

FRATELLI GANCIA & C.−***
CANELLI
6 acres (2.5 ha); some bought-in grapes; 23,000,000 bottles • Wines include: Barolo Mirafiore, →Asti, →Pinot di Pinot, Gancia dei Ganci Riserva Brut, Vermouth, Americano
Carlo Gancia founded his company in 1850 on completion of an apprenticeship in Champagne. Gancia is one of the leading Asti producers. Most famous wine: Pinot di Pinot.

PIERO GATTI*−****
SANTO STEFANO BELBO
18.5 acres (7.5 ha); 35,000 bottles • Wines: Piemonte Moscato, Moscato d'Asti, Langhe Freisa La Violetta

Pietro Gatti, one of the longest established Asti producers, is famous for his Moscato d'Asti. If it makes sense to bring harvesting forward, he simply labels the wine as Piemonte Moscato.

ELIO PERRONE*−****
CASTIGLIONE TINELLA
22 acres (9 ha); 60,000 bottles • Wines: Moscato d'Asti Clartè, Sourgal, Barbera d'Asti Grivò, Dolcetto d'Alba Guilin
For years, Stefano Perrone in Castiglione Tinella has been producing sparkling aromatic Moscato d'Asti wine.

PAOLO SARACCO**−*****
CASTIGLIONE TINELLA
33 acres (13.5 ha); 110,000 bottles • Wines include: Moscato d'Asti, Moscato d'Autunno, Langhe: Bianco Graffagno, Chardonnay Bianch del Luv and Prasuë
One of the best names for Moscato d'Asti, but the various Chardonnays have also long been among the most interesting of their kind in Piedmont.

LA SPINETTA-RIVETTI***
CASTAGNOLE LANZE
79 acres (32 ha); 210,000 bottles • Wines include: Moscato d'Asti: Bricco Quaglia, Biancospina; Barbera d'Alba: Ca' di Pian, Vigneto Gallina; Monferrato Rosso Pin, Barbaresco Vursu Vigneto: Gallina, Starderi, Valeirano; Piemonte Chardonnay Lidia
The family attracted some attention in the mid-1980s with their single-vineyard Moscato, and—in red wines—with the Nebbiolo-Barbera-Cabernet blend Pin; in recent years also with their three outstanding single-vineyard Barbarescos and a Barolo.

This sparkling wine, which was surprisingly awarded D.O.C.G. status in 1994, is a single variety wine produced from Moscato Bianco, a descendant of the Muscat family. The D.O.C.G. regulations allow a maximum yield of 800 gallons per acre (75 hl/ha). To ensure survival against international competition, quantity is the sole priority.

When Spumante production was introduced in Piedmont in the mid-19th century, BOTTLE-FERMENTATION or the MÉTHODE CHAMPENOISE was used. Nowadays, the approximately 80 million bottles which flood the market annually are produced using the Charmat method whereby fermentation takes place in pressurized tanks. This eliminates the need to RIDDLE the bottles and makes it possible to prevent fermentation of almost one third of the grape sugar, ensuring that the wine remains sweet.

THE SCENT OF MUSCAT

Moscato d'Asti offers a newly fashionable alternative to Asti Spumante. It, too comes from Moscato Bianco and is fermented in pressurized tanks, but it differs from Asti Spumante in that it has more RESIDUAL SUGAR and is less alcoholic and fizzy. About two million bottles of Moscato d'Asti are produced each year. Compared with Asti Spumante, the wine generally exudes a more aromatic complex bouquet, with notes of orange, elderberry, and pear, mainly due to the origin and quality of the grapes. Unlike the industrial producers, the wineries which have specialized in Moscato d'Asti can mostly work with their own grapes from good locations. Muscat was cultivated as early as 500 years ago around Santo Stefano Belbo, Castiglione Tinella, and between Canelli and Alba where the microclimate ensures a distinctive bouquet.

The Mecca of Muscat wines can be found in the Loazzolo D.O.C. zone. Here a few producers have concentrated on a Passito from late-harvested, partly dried grapes. Their dessert wine, with its complex aromas of roses, violets, melon, and mint, is as rare as it is expensive. Another still sweet wine from Moscato Bianco is produced in the Strevi area of the province of Alessandria. This is a rather light dessert wine which has a fine, appealing aroma, although it has not yet been awarded D.O.C. status. Brachetto, on the other hand, has had D.O.C.G. status since 1996 and is enjoying increasing popularity. The light red grape is currently grown on 148 acres (60 ha) of vineyard which produce approximately one million bottles per year.

ALBA AND ASTI:
THE RISE OF BARBERA AND ITS PEERS

Nebbiolo may be the driving force behind Piedmont's prestige as a wine-producing region but the locals have always drunk Barbera wines. Almost half of the vineyards in the region are stocked with this variety. For decades, it produced the highest yields and by far the worst wines. Barbera has probably been known in Monferrato since the 13th century, but its victorious march through the vineyards of Piedmont did not take place until after the phylloxera disaster, when it proved to be particularly adept at producing high yields on American rootstocks. It gave abundant harvests on almost all soil types at a time when quality was of necessity neglected by the crisis-shaken producers.

In the mid-1980s, Barbera found itself at the center of what became known as the methanol scandal. Criminal producers had "refined" the cheapest Barbera wines with methanol, killing over 20 people. At a time when the reputation of the grape could hardly sink any lower, a group of innovative and quality-oriented producers, notably Giacomo Bologna, had already started to work on this unjustly maligned variety. ACID adjustment and barrel aging were the magic formulae used to transform the robust acidic grapes into spicy, complex and longer-lived wines. Bologna's elegant Bricco dell'Uccellone was the first of the new Barberas produced in this way.

Concentrated elegance: Giacomo Bologna was the first to reveal the great qualities of Barbera with his Bricco dell'Uccellone.

Numerous small family wineries where the land and vineyards are farmed with basic implements can be found in the area surrounding the two rival towns. Many of them sell their grapes or wine to large producers or traditional *négociant* houses.

ANOTHER NEBBIOLO TRIUMPH

In the area around Alba, where producers were in the process of modernizing Barolo, they also started to experiment with the Barbera grapes which had been stocked in most of that area's vineyards for generations. The action of the *terroir*, combined with the experience gained in winery techniques by the *Barolisti*, could only have a positive outcome, and Barbera d'Alba became the prime D.O.C. of the new full-bodied, international-style reds. The Asti producers later made equally successful inroads with the new approach. Since the early 1990s, magnificent fruity and tannic wines, the best of which have sufficient structure to age for years, have been mainly produced from very old Barbera vines bearing concentrated grapes.

FREISA, GRIGNOLINO, AND RUCHÈ

The two indigenous grape varieties, Freisa and Grignolino, survived phylloxera in the provinces of Asti and Monferrato. However, due to their sensitivity and low yields, they were not very popular with producers.

Light-colored, with a fresh and light taste, Grignolino wines once offered a welcome change to the heavy red wines of Langhe and were even popular at the royal court of Savoie. The best representatives of this variety, with their typical scent of roses, nuts, and white pepper and which, despite their lightness, are surprisingly tannic and full-bodied, thrive on the dry, loose soils of northern Monferrato.

In contrast, Freisa was never a very important variety. Although its presence in Piedmont can be traced back to 1799, the slightly fizzy, short-lived wines it produces have never enjoyed much popularity. The best of the remaining 4,920-acre (2,000-ha) Freisa sites can be found in the Asti region. Here, and in a small area east of Turin (D.O.C. Freisa di Chieri), particularly concentrated barrel-aged wines are now being produced from Freisa Piccola.

With their 247 acres (100 ha) of Ruchè or Rouchet, the producers in the area of Castagnole Monferrato have saved a red grape variety of unknown origin from decline and extinction. Ruchè wines have a balsamic aroma of roses and red fruit, a silky taste with good tannin structure, and hence the capacity to age for some years.

Select Producers of Barbera

Marchesi Alfieri****−*****
San Martino Alfieri
37 acres (15 ha); 60,000 bottles • Wines include:
Barbera d'Asti: La Tota, →Alfiera; Monteferrato: Il
Bianco dei Marchesi, Il Rosso dei Marchesi, Piemonte
Grignolino Sansoero
Machesi Alfiera produce wonderful densely fruity
Barberas.

Bava***−****
Cocconato
49 acres (20 ha); some bought-in grapes; 600,000 bottles
• Wines include: Barbera d'Asti Stradivario, , Arbest and
Piano Alto; Monferrato Bianco Alteserre, Giulio Cocchi
Spumate Brut, Gavi Cor de Chasse, Malvasia di
Castelnuovo Don Bosco, Moscato d'Asti Bass Tuba
The best wines produced by this well-known estate
are the Barbera Stradivario and Piano Alto.

Bertelli****
Costogliole d'Asti
15 acres (6 ha); 25,000 bottles • Wines include: Barbera
d'Asti: Montetusa, San Antonio, Cabernet 1 Fossareti
All the wines produced here are matured in barriques;
the various Barberas are impressive.

Alfiero Boffa, Vigne Uniche****
San Marzano Oliveto
37 acres (15 ha); some bought-in grapes; 200,000
bottles • Wines include: Barbera d'Asti: →Collina della
Vedova; Moscato d'Asti, Dolcetto, Spumante
Five single-vineyard Barberas prove that there are some
remarkable terroirs between Nizza Monferrato and
Costigliole d'Asti.

Braida di Giacomo Bologna***−*****
Rocchetta Tanaro
43 acres (17 ha); 200,000 bottles • Wines include:
Barbera d'Asti: Bricco dell'Uccellone, →Ai Suma,
→Bricco della Bigotta; Langhe Bianco Il Fiore di Serra
dei Fiori, Pinot Nero del Monferrato Il Bacialé, Barbera
La Monella, Moscato d'Asti Vigna Senza Nome
The single-vineyard Barberas are still top of the league
in the Astigiano. An exemplary operation.

Cascina la Barbatella****
Nizza Monferrato
10 acres (4 ha); 15,000 bottles • Wines: Barbera d'Asti
La Vigna dell'Angelo, Monferrato Bianco Noë, La
Vigna di Sonvico
Low yields, careful treatment of the grapes and modern
vinification ensure top wines such as Vigna di Sonvico
(made from Cabernet and Barbera) are produced.

Cascina Castlet***
Costiglione d'Asti
25 acres (10 ha); 65,000 bottles • Wines include: Barbera
d'Asti: →Passum and Policalpo; Moscato Passito Avié
A dry Barbera called Passum, matured as a dry, is
produced here from partly dried grapes.

Andrea Oberto***−****
La Morra
20 acres (8 ha); 50,000 bottles • Wines include: Barolo:
→Vigneto Rocche; Barbera d'Alba: Vigneto Boiolo,
→Giada,; Dolcetto d'Alba: Vantrino Albarella, San
Francesco, Langhe Rosso Fabio
The estate is actually in the Barolo area but its best
wine is a Barbera d'Alba called Giada, followed by
the Rocche vineyard Barolo Langhe Fabio and
three Dolcetto versions.

Visitors to the Braida di
Giacomo Bologna winery are
greeted by a stylish interior
with a view of the brand
new barriques.

La Tenaglia**−****
Serralunga di Crea
32.5 acres (13 ha); 55,000 bottles • Wines: Chardonnay,
Oltre, Grignolino del Monferrato, Barbera del
Monferrato, Chiaro di Crea, Barbera d'Asti: Bricco
Crea, Emozione, Giorgio Tenaglia
In Serralunga di Crea, somewhat removed from the
center of Barbera production, La Tenaglia produces
notable Barbera d'Asti selections and Chardonnay
Oltre in good years.

Tenuta Garetto***−****
Agliano Terme
30 acres (12 ha); 70,000 bottles • Wines: Barbera d'Asti
Superiore Favà, In Pectore, →Tra Neuit e Dì, Piemonte
Chardonnay Diversamente
Allessandro Garetto took over the family business as a
very young man, and has followed an unwavering and
single-minded course to join the circle of the best
Barbera d'Asti producers.

Villa Terlina*****
Agliano d'Asti
15 acres (6 ha); 25,000 bottles • Wines: Barbera d'Asti
Gradale, →Barbera d'Asti Monsciuro
Paolo Alliata and Bettina Eickelberg produce wonderful
dense and expressive wines from old vines on their
unproductive soils.

Vinchia e Vaglio Serra**−****
Vinchio
320 ha; 150,000 bottles • Wines include: Barbera
d'Asti: →Vigne Vecchie, →V.V. Bricco Laudana; Barbera
del Monferrato Vivace, Cortese del Monferrato Dorato,
Grignolino d'Asti, Chardonnay d'Asti
For a long time, the members of the Vinchio cooperative
supplied the most famous wineries in the area with the
raw materials for their top wines. However, since they
began bottling and also marketing the Barbera d'Asti
Vigne Vecchie, this has indisputably become one of the
best wines of the region.

Alba, Langhe, and Roero

The hill landscape of Langhe covers an area of approximately 772 square miles (2,000 sq. km) enclosed by the plains of Turin and Cuneo, Monferrato and the Ligurian Maritime Alps. The unique geological formation of these hills emerged together with those of Monferrato and Roero during the tertiary period when the area now known as the Po plain was still flooded by the Adriatic Sea. The gray-white, limy, marl soils formed from the maritime deposits are rich in minerals and trace elements: iron, potassium, phosphorus, copper, manganese, and magnesium in varying volumes dictate the special character (*terroir*) of the vineyards here. Thanks to the exceptional potential of the Langhe soils, in 1881 King Umberto I founded an agricultural college in Alba, which was specially devoted to wine production.

On the Left Bank of the Tanaro

Roero, the continuation of the Langhe hills on the west bank of the Tanaro northwest of Alba, may have been formed at the same time as the last wave of the Alpine massif. However, unlike the Langhe hills, its ranges run almost parallel to each other. Lime marl is rare here; the soils are based on Ice Age deposits which formed the deep valleys and steep slopes. Piedmont's most famous grape is indigenous here and the wine is marketed under the D.O.C. Nebbiolo d'Alba. Its cultivation area extends to the other side of the Tanaro. For almost too long, the local producers used the Nebbiolo grape to produce a sweet wine suitable only for drinking while young.

Finally, however, the modern age arrived with the introduction of restrictions on volume, controlled fermentation and barrel-aging. Wines from the better wineries now offer a serious alternative to Barolo, not quite as complex and long-lived as their model, but at least affordable.

In general, the wines from this *appellation* become lighter and less complex with the shift from south to north. The very sandy soils of the northern part of the zone yield very finely-structured wines which were popular in aristocratic circles in Turin as early as the 16th and 17th centuries. In 1985 a separate D.O.C. zone was created for Nebbiolo and Arneis in recognition of the individuality of the Roero wines.

Modest Dolcetto

To make use of the less blessed wine-growing sites, the Piedmontese producers have always

One of life's small pleasures —a wine bar in Roero.

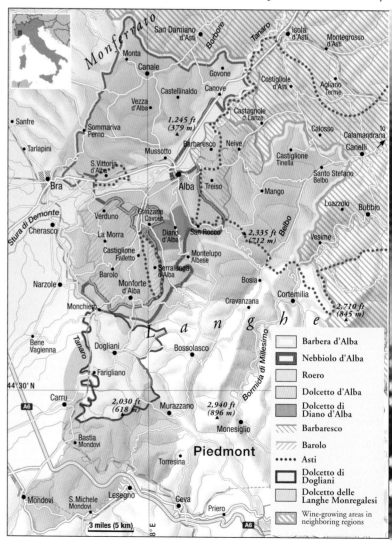

Legend:
- Barbera d'Alba
- Nebbiolo d'Alba
- Roero
- Dolcetto d'Alba
- Dolcetto di Diano d'Alba
- Barbaresco
- Barolo
- Asti
- Dolcetto di Dogliani
- Dolcetto delle Langhe Monregalesi
- Wine-growing areas in neighboring regions

planted Dolcetto on the cooler slopes. This low-acid variety ripens around four weeks before the sensitive Nebbiolo, which not only reduces the risk that it will be spoilt by fall rains but also has organizational advantages when it comes to harvesting. Having been ignored for many years, these mild, fruity, relatively light, everyday wines designed to be drunk when young, now enjoy seven individual D.O.C.s with more than half of production dedicated to Dolcetto d'Alba.

One of the most interesting Dolcetto wines is bottled by the producers in the area around Diano d'Alba. Here, the variety is not planted on the less favorable sites but instead is cultivated on the best south-facing slopes. This, combined with stringent production regulations—a maximum yield of 600 gallons per acre (56 hl/ha) and 12 percent minimum alcohol strength—brought the Diano producers the first official recognition of individual vineyard sites (*sori*) in Italy.

One of the most charming of red wines, Dolcetto can be drunk when young and has intense fruit aromas. The best Dolcettos, however, have considerable depth.

Another D.O.C. designation exists in Dogliani, which is probably the true home of Dolcetto. After above-average increases in quality, Dolcetto di Dogliani has developed into a relatively firm complex wine with fine fruit and lasting taste.

FRAGRANT RARITIES

The much respected Barbera is also cultivated in Roero and Langhe, and other regional specialties await discovery here, such as Pelaverga, an absolute rarity, which grows in the D.O.C. zones of Verduno and Colline Saluzzesi. It was one of the most popular varieties in the province of Cuneo between the 13th and 16th centuries. Its bright red wines with a color reminiscent of onion skins and the aroma of white pepper, are sometimes blended with Nebbiolo and Barbera. This undoubtedly does little to hamper their supposed aphrodisiac effects.

SELECT PRODUCERS IN AND AROUND ALBA

CLAUDIO ALARIO***–****
DIANO D'ALBA
15 acres (6 ha); 30,000 bottles • Wines: →Dolcetto di Diano d'Alba, →Barbera d'Alba Valletta, Nebbiolo d'Alba, Langhe
The best Diano Dolcettos as well as an excellent single-vineyard Barbera are produced here today.

CERETTO***–****
ALBA
247 acres (100 ha); 700,000 bottles • Wines include: Barbaresco Bricco Asili. Barolo Bricco Roche, Monsordo Langhe: Chardonnay, Cabernet, Pinot, Dolcetto d'Alba Rossana
The Cerettos manage three wineries from La Bernadina. Two produce single-vineyard Barolos and Barbarescos.

PIO CESARE***–*****
ALBA
74 acres (30 ha); some bought-in grapes; 320,000 bottles • Wines include: Barolo, →Barolo Ornato, →Barbaresco Il Bricco, Nebbiolo d'Alba, Dolcetto d'Alba, →Barbera d'Alba Fides, Moscato d'Asti, Il Nebbio, Gavi, Langhe Chardonnay Piodilei
A traditional winery in the center of Alba, its Barolo and Barbaresco are dense, modern, single-vineyard wines.

MATTEO CORREGIA****–*****
CANALE
45.5 acres (17 ha); 70,000 bottles • Wines include: →Barbera d'Alba Bricco Marun, →Nebbiolo d'Alba La Val del Preti, Roero, Roero Arneis
The Barberas are sensational, as is a Nebbiolo.

CARLO DELTETTO**–****
CANALE
25 acres (10 ha); 80,000 bottles • Wines include: Barbera d'Alba, Dolcetto d'Alba, Gavi, →Roero Madonna dei Boschi, →Roero Arneis San Michele
The Deltetto winery produces a top Arneis and has a good reputation for its Roero and Barbera d'Alba.

MALVIRÀ-FRATELLI DAMONTE***–****
CANALE
89 acres (36 ha); 70,000 bottles • Wines include Roero, →Roero Arneis Trinità, Langhe San Gugliemo Bianco and Rosso
This winery specializes in Arneis wine. Three of the five types of wine are fermented or matured in barrels.

PELISSERO****
TREISO
49 acres (20 ha); 90,000 bottles • Wines: Barbaresco, Barbaresco Vanotu, Barbera d'Alba Piani, Dolcetto d'Alba Augenta and Munfrina, Langhe Nebbiolo, →Langhe Long Now
Using Dolcetto and Barbera, Giorgio Pelissero produces modern wines characterized by barrel fermentation.

ALFREDO PRONUTTO***–****
ALBA
175 acres (70 ha); some bought-in grapes; 700,000 bottles • Wines include: Barolo: Bussia, Cannubi; Barbaresco: Montestefano, Rabajà; Barbera Pian Romualdo, Nebbiolo Occhetti
Barolo Bussia and Barbaresco Montestefano are the great wines of this winery, now part of the Florence-based Antinori empire.

PUNSET***–****
NEIVE
47 acres (30 ha); 50,000 bottles • Wines: Barbaresco, →Barbaresco Campo Quadro, Barbera d'Alba Superiore Vigneto Zocco, →Dolcetto d'Alba Campo Re, Langhe Rosso Dualis
On this organically managed estate run by Marina Marcarino, the selected harvests Campo Quadro and Campo Re are now among the top wines in Piedmont.

TENIMENTI DI BAROLO E FONTANAFREDDA*–****
SERRALUNGA D'ALBA
173 acres (70 ha); some bought-in grapes; 6,000,000 bottles • Wines include: →Barolo La Delizia, →Lazzarito, Barbaresco, Dolcetto d'Alba, Pinot Nero, Roero, Roero Arneis, Gavi, Spumante Brut Gattinera, Asti
This winery, owned by a Sienese bank, produces very good single-vineyard Barolos, matured by enologist Danilo Drocco.

BAROLO:
A UNIQUE COMBINATION

The special qualities of the variety, and the vineyards which enabled it to unfold to its maximum potential, have together created what is now acknowledged as one of Italy's greatest red wines.

FEW TERROIRS ARE CHOSEN

Nebbiolo vines mostly mature to their maximum potential on the calcareous marl soils of the Tortonian epoch. These top-quality sites are distributed among the south and southwest slopes of three high ridges which rise from Alba in a southerly direction. There are 11 townships in the Barolo area and together they have a mere 3,200 acres (1,300 ha) of vineyards—Bordeaux, by comparison, covers 250,000 acres (100,000 ha). However, the truly outstanding sites are concentrated around five core townships. The entire prestige of the *appellation* is concentrated in Barolo itself, La Morra, Castiglione Falletto, Serralunga d'Alba, and Monteforte d'Alba, while Verduno, Grinzane Cavour, Diano d'Alba, Cherasco, Novello, and Roddi have only small Barolo areas.

THE TORTONIAN AND HELVETIAN EPOCHS

Despite the shared history of their formation, the soils within the Barolo area vary significantly in type. To the west, at the level of La Morra, Barolo, and Novello, the calcareous marl is more compact, fresher, and more fertile than in the rest of the area and produces softer, fruitier, rounder wines. Geologists have defined this zone as Tortonian. In contrast, the eastern range of hills of Castiglione, Serralunga, and Monforte has been identified as originating in the Helvetian epoch and has a higher proportion of reddish weathered sandstone or contains quartziferous sand. These soils are, in general, less fertile and yield more intense, structured, tannic wines that mature more slowly.

Nebbiolo reacts very sensitively to all the soil variations and to the varying climatic conditions found in the different sites. There is a good reason why, even in the most prestigious Barolo vineyards, you are more likely to find Dolcetto vines than Nebbiolo on the lower slopes, as the latter simply would not ripen there. The varying chemical composition of the soils also influences the character of the wines. For example, the high manganese and magnesium content of the

Probably the most reputable, if not the most popular, fine Italian wine, Barolo takes its name from a small town which lies around 9 miles (15 km) south of Alba in the Langhe hills. Even in this landscape which is dotted with numerous castles, the town's imposing *castello* and fortifications tower impressively over surrounding rooftops. On clear days, the sky-scraping Alpine peaks can be seen in the distance from the castle. In autumn, however, the fog, after which the region's best-known vine variety is named (*nebbia* means fog), rises from the Tanaro valley which separates the Langhe hills from Roero.

Barolo has Marquise Giulietta Faletti and her enologist Louis Oudart to thank for its prestige. They were the first to allow the must from the Nebbiolo grapes to ferment systematically and, with the resulting very powerful, dry but elegant wine, revealed the potential for quality concealed on the slopes and peaks around Alba. A difficult and demanding variety, which needs extremely high doses of summer sun, even in previous centuries Nebbiolo had conquered the best south-facing sites in the Barolo, Castiglione, Falleto, Serralunga, and Monteforte d'Alba areas which were generally accepted as its ideal *terroir*.

Nebbiolo is grown only in the southern zones of the Barolo township where it matures best. The calcareous marl ensures round and silky wines.

producing areas. In the past, this repeatedly facilitated the misuse of the names of famous sites. On the other hand, in the case of Barolo, the highly varied character of the wines from the different sites prompted the development of the perfect Barolo, blended from grapes of different origins, taking their positive and negative characteristics into account. This was made easier by the fact that the area's vineyards are extremely fragmented in terms of ownership, and no individual producer would have been able to harvest sufficient volumes from a single site to produce estate or single-vineyard bottlings.

Furthermore, this situation very much suited the zone's major NÉGOCIANT houses which, in the past, processed most of the grapes and marketed the wine. The best known of these, companies like Prunotto and Bruno Giacosa, acquired such a detailed and intimate knowledge of the characteristics of the individual sites over time, and established such a solid base of suppliers of good grapes that, even today, their wines remain virtually untouchable in terms of high quality.

soils in La Morra lies behind the expressive bouquet and clear liquorice notes of the wines produced there. On the opposite hill chain, the higher levels of iron in the topsoil clearly intensify the youthful harshness of the wines produced in this area. While the wines from Serralunga and Monforte are among the area's top representatives in good warm years, under less advantageous conditions, the acidity combined with the tannins can yield bitter and unsatisfactory wines.

In addition to Barolo, the Langhe hills near Alba are home to the famous white truffle. In autumn, many winegrowers can be seen scouring the hills with their dogs in the hope of making a valuable find.

A gourmet's paradise— Barolo and truffles.

BLENDS AND ESTATE/ SINGLE-VINEYARD BOTTLINGS

Although it was always known that the quality of the Nebbiolo depended on conditions in the vineyard, it took almost a century to come to the conclusion that the wines from these estates and vineyards should be bottled separately. There were several reasons for this. First, unlike France and Germany, Italy never had an estate or vineyard definition policy. To the present day, there is no comprehensive register of vineyards with a precise and unambiguous definition of the best sites, even in the most reputable wine-

Barolo: Past and Present

Classical Barolo is usually blended from a selection of musts produced in the area. In the 1960s, in an effort to achieve a more rounded and, if possible, reproducible taste, there was a move toward estate or single-vineyard bottling. Given that the quality of the grapes differs significantly in the different holdings in the Barolo and Barbaresco areas, the idea was that the best sources should be identified and receive the recognition they deserved. This development was pioneered by Alfredo Prunotto and his enologists, Beppe Colla and Renato Ratti, as well as the wine critic, Luigi Veronelli, a supporter of the French system of domain classification. Veronelli had in fact tried to persuade Prunotto and Colla to produce their wines as single-vineyard bottlings as early as the 1950s. The outstanding vintage of 1961 marked the birth of the estate/single-vineyard bottlings in Langhe. Renato Ratti, who had set up his winery in the former monastery, Abbazia dell'Annunziata near La Morra, soon followed suit and undertook extensive studies to identify the most suitable vineyard plots in the area. Ratti's research resulted in a map which is still the most comprehensive record available of the Barolo estates and their quality potential.

Mixing or Separating

Other wine producers and merchants such as Bruno Giacosa, the Ceretto brothers, Angelo Gaja, the Fontanafredda winery, and the

Wintry vineyards in Barolo where estate and single-vineyard bottlings are now the norm. Top producers try to reduce yields and achieve higher grape concentration through vigorous winter pruning.

Produttori di Barbaresco cooperative adopted this idea in the 1960s and over the following decades almost all the producers tried to win greater prestige and higher prices for their traditional wines. When the wave of estate bottlings spread to other Italian regions, such as Tuscany, the zone name was included as an official element of distinction in the D.O.C.G. legislation, and the option of higher-quality possibilities for individual estates was also created.

Today, some excellent Barolo is still blended using grapes from different zones in the area, but the best individual products are mostly bottled separately, while the rest are marketed with the generic D.O.C. label. It is admissable to drop the estate *appellation* for smaller vintages and this further increases the prestige of the estate and single-vineyard bottlings.

Downside

This development led to serious inflation in the price of estate and single-vineyard bottlings in the 1990s. The enormous commercial success prompted many producers to vinify the grapes separately, even if they had little potential to yield higher-quality wines. While most producers and consumers were still concentrating on the vineyard—known locally as *vigna* or *cru*—the innovative houses had already set to work on a new quality dimension. Strict limitations in yield were achieved through heavy winter pruning and radical summer thinning until the harvested yields matched those of the top French *crus* and lay well below the mandatory volumes prescribed in the legislation.

Revolution in the Wineries

The new viticultural practices were matched by changes in winery techniques. As was the practice almost everywhere in Piedmont, producers in the Barolo area traditionally allowed the must to stay in contact with the LEES for three, four, or more weeks to give the Nebbiolo sufficient structure, body, and, in particular, good aging capacity. Once racked, the wine was then left to the forces of nature and, when fully fermented, stored for years in large wooden barrels. Nebbiolo could only withstand this process in better years when its grapes were full, almost over-ripe, and correspondingly high in alcohol content.

In weaker years, generous tannins were released from the grape skins, pips, and stems, but the wines lacked the fruit to balance their harshness. By the time the tannins matured during the over-long cask-aging, the fruit had long faded and the presence of maturation acids rendered the wines bitter and aggressive.

WHAT HAPPENS IF THE TANNINS ARE HEATED?

A young generation of producers, led by Elio Altare from La Morra, followed the example of their colleagues in Bordeaux and Burgundy and radically reduced the fermentation period to between 48 and 72 hours, or at most eight to ten days. They learned that, if the fermenting mass is carefully heated, both the color achieved and tannin extracted during the first hours are completely adequate. The tannins extracted at the beginning of the fermentation process also have the major advantage of being sweet and round as opposed to bitter and harsh. The wines started in this revolutionary new way were then aged in *barriques* which in turn added pleasant tannins, spicy tastes, and aromas. It is occasionally rumored that the complex taste of modernist wines may also originate from varieties not defined in the D.O.C.G. rules, but this remains as yet unproven.

Elio Altare from La Morra is one of the most fervent and convincing of modernists: his Vigna Aborina has become legendary.

Bruno Giacosa is a traditionalist who as both a producer and *négociant* believes in long fermentation and maceration periods and has no interest in *barriques*.

Elio Altare is cautious with new wood and has not completely turned his back on the traditional, tried and trusted tuns.

THE LAW AND SUCCESS

The legal regulations governing the production of Barolo and Barbaresco have been updated in the meantime. The wines must still consist of 100 percent Nebbiolo—even the traditional addition of Barbera is no longer allowed—and yield is now restricted to $3^1/_2$ tons of grapes per acre (8 tonnes/ha). Quality-conscious producers still feel this is too much. The regulations prescribe two years of cask-aging for Barolo and one for Barbaresco, then both wines must mature in the bottle for one year before being put on the market. The traditionalists doubted the aging capacity of the modern wines, but now, 15 years on, the first vintages have proved that the new types of Barolo and Barbaresco have developed well and acquired more refined tastes with time.

The war over production techniques has petered out with no clear victor. Many excellent traditional wines can now stand alongside the "modern," top-quality products, as the traditionalists have also been making greater efforts with respect to quality. International success has vindicated all Barolo producers, traditionalists and modernists alike. In 1967 only 1,593 acres (645 ha) in the area were stocked with Nebbiolo vines, but by 1990 this had more than doubled to 3,228 acres (1,307 ha). Barolo and, to a lesser extent, Barbaresco, are now among Europe's most expensive wines, although the extension of the cultivation areas has also had a negative impact on quality. The threat of an unequal price-performance ratio, which has already resulted in economic turmoil in northern Piedmont in the recent past, should not be underestimated as a possible future scenario in the Northwest.

BARBARESCO

If Barbaresco was left in the shadow of Barolo up to the 1960s, this was a reflection not of its quality but of the class of its consumers: Barolo was to some extent produced for aristocratic and upper-class circles. The Barbaresco area, which stretches beyond the village of the same name and along neighboring townships of Treiso, Neive, and San Rocco Seno d'Elvio, had a major disadvantage to overcome: its producers included neither kings, aristocrats, nor government members who could give the wine the attention and inspiration it needed.

AN INDEPENDENT AREA

Castello di Neive, the castle in the village center, is an exception. Its owners commissioned Louis Oudart, the enologist responsible for the creation of dry Barolo, to work in its winery. In 1862 the Castello wines convinced a panel of experts in London, although at the time Neive did not belong to the Barbaresco area. Its sites were not in fact linked with those of the famous neighboring township until 1933.

The link with the development of Barolo was forged in the last decade of the 19th century by the enologist Domizio Cavazza, director of the Enological School of Alba, when he also produced dry red wines from the Nebbiolo grapes from Barbaresco. Cavazza carried out exemplary work in his role as director of the wine producers' cooperative founded in 1894, and his Produttori del Barbaresco are among the *appellation's* best producers to the present day.

The current boundaries of the area, which includes 1,250 acres (500 ha) of vineyards producing around three million bottles per year, were drawn in 1966. The fact that the new *appellation* was given the name Barbaresco is due mainly to the quality of the grapes in the best zones, such as Asili and Rabajà. At the same time, the wine began gradually to regain popularity, largely thanks to the efforts of Giovanni Gaja and the wine trader Bruno Giacosa. Almost two decades later, Giovanni's son, Angelo Gaja succeeded in bringing Barbaresco to the point of its international breakthrough.

In today's D.O.C.G. area, the best vineyards are located at a height of between 590 and 1,050 feet (180 and 320 m). This comparatively low altitude is the factor behind some of the differences between Barbaresco wines and Barolo. The warmer microclimate allows the grapes to ripen more quickly, which means that they ripen with lower levels of sugar than the Barolo. This is reflected in the legislation by a minimum alcoholic strength of 12.5 percent which is half a percent lower than Barolo. On the other hand, in difficult years the producers can often fully or at least partly harvest the grapes before the weather changes and thus avoid major differences between VINTAGES, which is a factor with Barolo. The homogenous calcareous marl soils of the Barbaresco area are similar to the Tortonian soils of the La Morra and Barolo townships. There are differences, however, in the mineral composition. Here, instead of manganese we find copper and zinc, which give rise to a different range of aromas in the wine.

In the 1960s, the Barbaresco producers also experimented with single-vineyard bottling and the debate between modernism and traditionalism also took place here, although it was less controversial than the Barolo version. The D.O.C. regulations were subsequently modified here, too, and the prescribed cask-aging period reduced by one year.

A wine-producing area with a bright future— Barbaresco.

Elegance versus Strength

Barbaresco is well able to compensate for what it sometimes seems to lack in structure and power with the balance of its alcoholic strength, tannins, and acidity as well as its intense aromatic qualities which initially evoke violets and fresh berries. At its best between ten and fifteen years old, it ages significantly less well than Barolo, and can reach optimum maturity at between five and ten years.

The wines from zones with above-average temperatures and a damp microclimate are particularly aromatic and elegant. They are mostly very small plots which open onto the river Tanaro, for example the Asili and Rabajà zones in the Barbaresco township, which manage to produce complex wines with fine fruit even in mediocre years. In contrast, the wines produced from the best vines in Neive have an excellent reputation for their outstanding power and structure. Their youthful rawness is often

Left
Angelo Gaja's old cellar full of wood casks.

Right
Wine shops like this one in Neive, one of the centers in the Barbaresco zone, offer great shopping opportunities for the region's numerous visitors as they mainly offer locally produced and traded wines. They often keep vintages which have long been sold out at the wineries themselves.

Angelo Nazionale, Italy's most unusual producer.

even reminiscent of Barolo, which is why their producers often describe themselves as *baroleggianti*. They need longer cask- and bottle-aging to achieve their full potential. Gallina has the reputation of being the best site in Neive but other neighboring sites also now enjoy considerable prestige. Further south, in Treiso, where the soils are heavier and the wines more tannic, from among the small estates usually owned by individuals, only Pajorè has emerged as distinctive.

During Barolo's victory march, critics often accused the producers of Barbaresco of lacking concentration and paying insufficient attention to quality. However, in recent years, the situation has improved immensely. A small group of producers has emerged, making wines which have no problem measuring up to some Barolos. The future has just begun for Barbaresco.

Angelo Gaja, Barbaresco

"Angelo Nazionale," as people like to call him, is the master of winemaking in Piedmont, if not in all of Italy. His single-vineyard bottlings, Sorì San Lorenzo, Sorì Tildin, and Costa Russi, which are among the country's most expensive wines, have enabled Barbaresco to shine impressively. Since the 1996 vintage, they have, however, been produced under the Langhe D.O.C. *appellation* and as a registered trademark. Since then, Gaja has been fighting the multitude of increasingly futile single-vineyard bottlings and campaigning for the strengths of a general Barbaresco.

As a son of one of the region's first wine-producing families—his father Giovanni had acquired the zone's largest wine-growing estate as early as the 1950s and 1960s and converted it from mixed to monoculture—Angelo was predestined for his role as the leading figure in the world of winemaking in his home town of Barbaresco. With his unerring instinct for innovations and unique marketing talents, he has established an outstanding international reputation in a very short time. He brought back new ideas from France: the quality-enhancing strategies of controlled fermentation temperatures, early biological acid conversion, and new *barriques* were among them, as well as rigorous yield restrictions; and the planting of Cabernet and Chardonnay vines in good Barbaresco vineyards, which led to considerable disputes with his father. However, success has vindicated him with the building of his wine-importing company, his acquisition of the Barbaresco Castello and the best Barbaresco vineyards, and his involvement in the vineyards of Chiesa di Santa Restituta in Montalcino and the Cá Marcanda estate in Maremma in Tuscany. Gaja's glory has faded somewhat with the international success of a whole raft of Piedmont producers in the 1990s.

SELECT PRODUCERS OF BAROLO AND BARBARESCO

ELIO ALTARE*****
LA MORRA
20 acres (8 ha); 50,000 bottles • Wines include: Barolo: Vigneto Arborina; Barbera d'Alba, Dolcetto d'Alba, Langhe: →Vigna Larigi, →Vigna Arborina; →Langhe La Villa
Altare's Aborina proves that even less prestigious vineyards can produce top quality wines. The mash is left to stand for the shortest possible time and barrel maturing is as long as possible, resulting in plenty of fruit and perfectly ripe tannins.

AZELIA—LUIGI SCAVINO***−*****
CASTIGLIONE FALLETTO
20 acres (8 ha); 50,000 bottles • Wines: Barolo, →Barolo Bricco Fiasco, →Barbera d'Alba Bricco Punta, Dolcetto d'Alba Bricco Oriolo
Thanks to grape selection and barrel aging, the Dolcetto vineyard in Montelupo Albese and the Barolo sites in Fiasco provide the top quality Azelia wines.

MICHELE CHIARLO**−****
CALAMANDRANA
250 acres (104 ha); some bought-in grapes; 1,100,000 bottles • Wines include: Barbaresco Rabajà, Barolo: →Cannubi, →Cerequio, →Rocche di Castiglione; Barbera d'Asti Valle del Sole, Dolcetto d'Alba, Gavi Fornaci di Tassarolo, Gavi di Gavi Rovereto, Barilot, Countacc
Recently this producer has been concentrating on fine Barolo, Barbaresco and Barbera wines.

DOMENICO CLERICO*****
MONFORTE D'ALBA
37 acres (15 ha); 65,000 bottles • Wines: Barbera d'Alba, Barolo: →Ciabot Menti Ginestra, Per Cristina, →Pajana, Briccotto Bussia; Langhe Arte Langhe Freisa La Ginestrina
This estate produces two of the best single-vineyard Barolos in the area and, with Arte, one of the most fascinating Nebbiolo and Barbera blends.

ALDO CONTERNO****−*****
MONFORTE D'ALBA
59 acres (24 ha); 160,000 bottles • Wines include: Barolo: 'Vigna Colonello, Vigna Cicala, →Granbussia, →Bussia, Soprana, Romirasco; Barbera Conca Tre Pile, Langhe: Favot, Bianco Printanié, Chardonnay
Conterno combines the best of traditional and modern, and his single-vineyard Barolos are legendary.

GIACOMO CONTERNO***−****
MONFORTE D'ALBA
37 acres (15 ha); 65,000 bottles • Wines include: Barolo; →Cascina Francia, →Monfortino; Barbera d'Alba, Dolcetto d'Alba, Langhe Freisa
Giovanni Conterno is best known as the region's defender of tradition and Monfortino is his showpiece.

PAOLO CONTERNO***−****
MONFORTE D'ALBA
17 acres (7 ha); 40,000 bottles • Wines: Barolo Ginestra, Dolcetto d'Alba Ginestra, Barbera d'Alba Ginestra
With their balance of fruit and flavor, these wines are always among the most notable in the region.

CONTERNO-FANTINO***−*****
MONFORTE D'ALBA
32 acres (13 ha); 90,000 bottles • Wines: Barolo: Vigna del Gris, →Sori Ginestra; Barbera d'Albi Vignota, →Langhe Rosso Monprà, Langhe Chardonnay Bastia
Recommended: the Ginestra single-vineyard Barolo and the half-and-half Nebbiolo Barbera blend Monprà.

Barolo is famous for its longevity.

GIOVANNI CORRINO****
LA MORRA
25 acres (10 ha); 20,000 bottles • Wines: Barolo: →Vigneto Rocche, →Vigna Giachini; Barbera d'Alba Vigna Pozzo, →Barbera d'Alba, Dolcetto d'Alba
Renato and Giuliano have attracted attention with their single-vineyard Barolos and excellent Barbera Pozzo.

ERBALUNA—S. & A. OBERTO**−***
LA MORRA
18.5 acres (7.5 ha); 40,000 bottles • Wines: Barbera d'Alba, Dolcetto d'Alba, Nebbiolo Langhe, Grignolino Langhe, Barolo Vigna Rocche
With its Rocche dell'Annunziata, Piedmont's best-known organic estate has one of the finest vineyards, and also produces a high quality Barolo.

GAJA*****
BARBARESCO
238 acres (96 ha); 350,000 bottles • Wines include: Barbaresco: →Costa Russi, →Sorì San Lorenzo, Sorì Tildin; Barolo Sperss, →Langhe Darmagi, Barbera Sitorey, Dolcetto Langhe Cremes, Sito Moresco, →Langhe Chardonnay: Gaja & Rey and Rossj-Bass
The leading light of Italian wine production (see panel on preceding page).

BRUNO GIACOSA****−*****
NEIVE
37 acres (15 ha); some bought-in grapes; 550,000 bottles • Wines include: Barbaresco: →Santo Stefano, Gallina, Basarin; Barolo: →Falletto, Villero, →Collina Rionda, →Rocche di Castiglione Falletto; Nebbiolo d'Alba Valmaggiore, Roero Arneis, Spumante Giacosa
Every year, Giacosa sources the best grapes for his Barbaresco Santo Stefano and the traditional single-vineyard Barolos. The Spumante is one of the best in Italy.

FRATELLI GIACOSA***−****
NEIVE
49 acres (20 ha); some bought-in grapes; 500,000 bottles • Wines include: Barolo: Bussia, La Mandorla,; Barbaresco: →Rio Sordo, Roccalini; Barbera d'Alba: Bussia, Maria Gioana; Dolcetto San Rocco, Chardonnay, Roero Arneis
This négociant house moved out of the shadow of its famous namesake in the early 1990s, primarily because of its Barbaresco Rio Sordo and Barolo Bussia.

ELIO GRASSO****−*****
MONFORTE D'ALBA
33 acres (13.4 ha); 50,000 bottles • Wines include: Barbera Langhe Vigna Martina, Barolo: →Ginestra Casa Matè, →Barolo Gavarini Vigna Chiniera, Dolcetto d'Alba Gavarini Vigna dei Grassi, Langhe Chardonnay
Grasso made the leap into the Piedmontese elite with his outstanding vintages of the late 1980s.

SILVIO GRASSO***−****
LA MORRA
17 acres (7 ha); 40,000 bottles • Wines: Barolo: →Bricco Luciani, →Ciabòt Manzoni, Langhe Nebbiolo, Barbera d'Alba Fontanile
This house has made tentative steps toward modernization.

BARTOLO MASCARELLO***−****
BAROLO
12 acres (5 ha); 35,000 bottles • Wines: Barolo, Dolcetto d'Alba, Barbera d'Alba Vigna San Lorenzo
Excellent traditional wines up till the 1980s, after which there was something of a decline. There are no single-vineyard wines.

GIUSEPPE MASCARELLO & FIGLIO**−****
MONCHIERO

124 acres (50 ha); 50,000 bottles • Wines include: Barolo: →Monprivato, Bricco, →Villero, Codana; Barbaresco Macarini, Barbera d'Alba, Dolcetto d'Alba: Bricco, Pian Romualdo; Nebbiolo d'Alba San Rocco
In good years, Monprivato is among the top group of traditionalist wines. The estate vineyards vary in quality.

VIGNA RIONDA—G. MASSOLINO & FIGLI***−****
SERRALUNGA D'ALBA

40 acres (16 ha); 90,000 bottles • Wines include: Barolo: Vigna Rionda, Parafada, Margheria; Barbera d'Alba, Dolcetto d'Alba Barilot, Piria, Moscato d'Asti, Chardonnay Langhe
Vigna Rionda is one of the best Barolo vineyards and its grapes yield the Massolinos' best wine.

MOCCAGATTA**−*****
BARBARESCO

27 acres (11 ha); 50,000 bottles • Wines include: Barbaresco: →Bric Balin,→Cole; Barbera d'Alba Vigneto Basarin' Dolcetto d'Alba Vigna Buschet, →Langhe Chardonnay Bric Buschet
This modern operation—the third generation of Minutos—has made a very good name for itself with single-vineyard Barbarescos and Chardonnay.

MONFALLETTO-CORDERO DI MONTEZEMOLO**−****
LA MORRA

67 acres (27 ha); 120,000 bottles • Wines: Barolo: →Monfalletto, →Enrico VI, Chardonnay Langhe Elioro, Barbera d'Alba, Dolcetto d'Alba, Pinot Nero
This traditional estate became famous for its Barolo Enrico VI. The current owners have also given the wine a more modern touch.

NADA***−****
TREISO

16 acres (6.5 ha); 20,000 bottles • Wines: Barbaresco, Dolcetto d'Alba, Langhe Rosso Seifile
With its Barbaresco and Nebbiolo blend, in good years, Nada is among the area's best, although it has no top quality Nebbiolo sites in Treiso.

FRATELLI ODDERO**−*****
LA MORRA

131 acres (53 ha); 250,000 bottles • Wines include: Barbaresco, Barolo: →Mondoca di Bussia, →Rocche di Castiglione, →Vigna Rionda; Langhe: Furesté, Chardonnay; Collaretto, Barbera d'Alba, Dolcetto d'Alba
The single-vineyard Barolos, particularly the Rionda, embody a good compromise between traditional and more modern styles.

ARMANDO PARUSSO***−*****
MONFORTE D'ALBA

20 acres (8 ha); 50,000 bottles • Wines include: Barolo: →Bussia Vigna Munie, →Bussia Vigna Rocche; Dolcetto d'Alba, Barbera d'Alba Ornati, Langhe Bricco Rovella Bianco, →Rosso
Marco and Tiziana Parusso are among the top group of modernists in the Langhe region. Of their wines, Barolo Bussia Rocche and the red Bricco Rovella are of particular high quality.

E. PIRA & FIGLI****−*****
BAROLO

9 acres (3.5 ha); 15,000 bottles • Wines: Barolo, →Barolo Cannubi
This estate is run by Chiara Boschis and is part of the Borgogno négociant company in Barolo. It has attracted attention with its very good single-vineyard Barolo Cannubi.

PODERI ROCCHE DEI MANZONI***−****
MONFORTE D'ALBA

148 acres (60 ha); 180,000 bottles • Wines include: Barolo: →Vigna d'la Roul, →Vigna Big; Bricco dei Manzoni
A convinced modernist, Valentino Migniori shines with his elegant single-vineyard Barolo, but also produces excellent sparkling wine fermented in the bottle.

PRINCIPIANO FERDINANDO***−****
MONFORTE D'ALBA

22 acres (9 ha); 25,000 bottles • Wines include: Barolo Boscareto, Barbera d'Alba Pian Romualdo, Dolcetto d'Alba
The abundantly fruity aroma and taste of the barrel-fermented, single-vineyard Barolo Boscareto is popular.

ALBINO ROCCA****−*****
BARBARESCO

22 acres (9 ha); 65,000 bottles • Wines: →Dolcetto d'Alba Vignalunga, Barbera d'Alba Gepin, Barbaresco: →Vigneto Loreto and Brich Ronchi; Langhe Bianco La Rocca
Angelo Rocca emerged from his cousin Bruno's shadow in the 1990s. The Loreto vineyard yields top class Barbaresco.

BRUNO ROCCA—RABAJ***−****
BARBARESCO

15 acres (6 ha); 30,000 bottles • Wines: Barbaresco: →Rabajà, Coparossa; Barbera d'Alba, Langhe Chardonnay Cadet, Dolcetto d'Alba Trifolé
One of Barbaresco's top estates of the 1980s, now a little tired, but still producing some very good wines.

LUCIANO SANDRONE****−*****
BAROLO

27 acres (11 ha); 40,000 bottles • Wines: →Barolo Cannubi Boschis, Barolo, Dolcetto d'Alba, →Barbera d'Alba, →Nebbiolo d'Alba Valmaggiore
Sandrone achieved world fame with his Cannubi Boschi single-vineyard Barolo and blotted out the memory of the difficult years in the early 1990s with his Barolo and Nebbiolo of 1995.

PAOLO SCAVINO*****
CASTIGLIONE FALLETTO

30 acres (12 ha); 65,000 bottles • Wines: Barolo: →Bric del Fiasc, →Cannubi, →Rocche dell'Annunzata; Barbera Carati
Enrico Scavoni's Barolo del Fiasco is legendary and he also sets standards with his barrel-aged Barbera.

SETIMO AURELIO***
LA MORRA

17 acres (7 ha); 40,000 bottles • Wines: Barolo, Barolo Vigneti Rocche, Dolcetto d'Alba, Langhe Nebbiolo
Tiziana Settimo is a woman who maintains the traditional style of Barolo. The single-vineyard Barolo Rocche is powerful and long-lasting.

MARO VEGLIO***−****
LA MORRA

25 acres (10 ha); 30,000 bottles • Wines: →Barolo Castelletto, Barolo Vigneto Arborina, Gattera, Rocche, →Barbera d'Alba Cascina Nuova, L'Insieme
Young Mauro and his wife Daniela have learned a lot from their neighbor Elio Altare, as is shown by the reliable quality of their barrel-aged wines.

ROBERTO VOERZIO*****
LA MORRA

25 acres (10 ha); 45,000 bottles • Wines: Barolo: La Serra, Cerequio, Brunate; Barbera d'Alba Vignasse, Vignaserra, Dolcetto d'Alba Priavino, Langhe Chardonnay Fossati e Roscaleto
Voerzio's best wines are Barolo La Serra and Cerequio, the Vignaserra and the Barbera Vignasse.

Piedmontese White Wines

Apart from Moscato, which is mainly made into sparkling wine, Cortese is the only vine variety from which large quantities of white wine are produced in Piedmont. It grows in the Monferrato hills, north and south of Alessandria, and in the mountains around Gavi, where it provides the basis for one of Italy's favorite white wines, Gavi or Cortesi di Gavi.

Cortese di Gavi

Vittorio Soldati, an ambitious amateur producer, was the first to demonstrate successfully, in the 1950s, that Gavi could be more than a very basic *trattoria* wine. He quickly recognized the relationship between the restriction of yields and the quality of the wine produced. After initial, very promising successes on the La Scolca estate, Soldati invested in a minimum of technology. In the winery, he concentrated on slow, controlled-temperature fermentation and reductive aging. In acknowledgment of the value of his wine, he called it Gavi di Gavi. International recognition was not long coming, and in 1998 the quality was legally prescribed and Cortese di Gavi, as it is now called, was awarded D.O.C.G. status.

A Little More, Perhaps?

The authorized yield is surprisingly generous: a maximum yield of 4.2 tons per acre (9.5 tonnes/ha) which corresponds to a must volume of almost 1,850 gallons (70 hl). If the 20 percent excess permitted in Italy, which winemakers almost always take advantage of, is added, this gives more than 850 gallons per acre (80 hl/ha). The 10.5 percent minimum alcohol content is probably an acknowledgment of the climatic conditions—because it is relatively cool in the vineyards, the must weight usually remains lower —and it is also an acknowledgment of the high vineyard yields, which at a minimum stock density of 1,340 vines per acre (3,300 vines/ha) translate into a yield of approximately seven pounds (3 kg) of grapes per vine or more. Top varieties generally yield less than two pounds (1 kg).

Quality-conscious producers try to compensate for the short growth period with vineyard work—denser planting, leaf work during the summer, and, above all, thinning the grapes to reduce the yield per vine, which brings the risk of a very late harvest. When its potential is

Arneis was groomed to become the white counterpart of the region's great reds. Despite its pleasant aromatic qualities, however, it lacks the pedigree and potential to become a truly great wine.

exploited to the full, Gavi is between straw yellow and golden yellow in color, its scent is based on exotic fruit notes as well as apricots and apple, and the taste is generally accompanied by a soft almond tone.

Some producers process their best grapes separately on a single-vineyard basis and age the wine partly in *barriques*. Wood-aging lends a fine, light, sweetish note to both the aroma and taste which balances the rather acidic Gavi well. However, most of what is produced from Cortese, under the original *appellation* Gavi, and in the D.O.C. areas Colli Tortonesi, Monferrato, and in the Piedmont area in general, remains little more than a light, fresh, pedestrian wine.

Arneis in Roero and Langhe

In the hills north of the Tanaro, the two regional white wine varieties, Arneis and Favorita, are arousing interest. For a long time they were used only for blending in red wines or as table grapes, and were threatened with complete neglect and extinction, until some innovative producers took up their cause. Today Arneis grows once again on around 1,235 acres (500 ha) of vineyard, a fact which is mainly due to the efforts of the Bruno Giacosa and Ceretto *négociant* houses. On the conical mountains of Roero, and in Langhe, the variety was even awarded D.O.C. status in 1989, but it yields very varied wines. Two types of Arneis wines have emerged, based on the production techniques used: the first displays a very one-dimensional fruit with a light almond taste and mild acid; the second is more complex, with an abundant aroma of blossoms, apples, peaches, or nuts.

Quality starts in the vineyard.

Favorita and Chardonnay

The Favorita—another variety that is indigenous to Roero and Langhe—also seemed to have been completely forgotten and was almost forced to make way for Chardonnay. In all of Piedmont only 370 acres (150 ha) are planted with the variety. It is closely related (or even identical) to Ligurian Vermentino, whose taste characteristics it shares. Thirteen producers cultivate this variety and bottle fresh, fruity wines with a consistently good acid structure. When fermented in *barriques* they tend to have a sweeter bouquet and full, spicy taste.

Consumer popularity explains the unparalleled rise of Chardonnay. This popular grape was mainly grown in vineyards which had grown Dolcetto or indigenous white varieties.

Chardonnay is now usually part of the standard repertoire of the larger Piedmontese estates. Its wines enjoy D.O.C. status with the general *appellations* of Piedmont and Langhe. A prestigious wine, it is generally fermented and aged in small oak barrels, following the French and Californian models.

Finally, the dry, often bottle-fermented white sparkling wines deserve a mention. They do not have D.O.C. status in Piedmont and their existence depends entirely on the efforts of individual producers and wineries, but they often attain impressive levels of quality. The grapes are often purchased from neighboring Lombardy, vinification and bottle fermentation, however, are only carried out in Piedmontese wineries.

Pergola cultivation—as seen here in Carema—has only survived in areas close to the mountains where vines are threatened by frost.

SELECT PRODUCERS OF GAVI

Castellari Bergaglio***—****
Gavi
25 acres (10 ha); 70,000 bottles • Wines: Gavi di Gavi Fornaci Rollona, →Gavi di Gavi Roverto Vigna Vecchia, Pilin
For years Marco Bergaglio has been committed to Gavi of outstanding quality, making him an exemplary winemaker. Bergaglio has broken ground in Gavi with his barrel-aged whites.

La Scolca***
Gavi
111 acres (45 ha); 350,000 bottles • Wines include: Gavi Villa Scolca, Gavi di Gavi, Soldati La Scolca Spumante Brut

Vittorio Soldati started bottling Gavi as early as the 1950s, and with his Etichetta Nera in 1966 he created a model which had a stimulating effect on the entire region. He also produces notable sparkling wines.

Tenuta san Pietro***
Tassarolo
37 acres (15 ha); 100,000 bottles • Wines: Gavi: →San Pietro, Bricco del Mandorlo, Vigneto La Gorrina
Maria Rosa Gazzinga's estate in Tassarolo, only a few miles north of Gavi, is one of the historic founding estates in the Gavi region. The wines are light and harmonious but generally rather neutral in character.

LIGURIA

As well as Dolcetto, which is known as Ormeasco here, the varieties Vermentino, Pigato, and Rossese are cultivated near towns such as Triora in the mountainous hinterland of the western Riviera.

The orange and lemon blossoms are a real give-away: the climate in Liguria bears no resemblance to that of its neighboring regions. Its location on the Gulf of Genoa, nestled into the southern slopes of the western Maritime Alps, makes this half-moon stretch of coastline an almost tropical enclave in the predominantly cool regions of northern Italy. The Ligurian Alps, which climb to heights of over 8,120 feet (2,500 m), and the Ligurian Apennines, provide effective shelter from cold winds. The sea also stores and slowly releases the sun's heat so annual mean temperatures here are even higher than in Tuscany.

However, the topography of the region places significant obstacles in the way of agriculture. For even the most basic farming purposes, the Mediterranean *maquis* had to be cut back and terraces had to be dug into the steep slopes and

secured. As a result, a unique cultivated landscape has developed in Liguria over the centuries and has survived to the present day.

TRADITIONAL VITICULTURE

However, the survival of this landscape comes at a cost. Villages stand empty and terraces have fallen into decay. Wine production here has adhered to its traditions, or, to be more precise, winemaking is too unimportant in Liguria for anyone to have bothered to change it. Neither the quantitative euphoria of the 1960s nor the technological evangelism of the 1970s and 1980s made any impression here. However, with current yields at around 375 gallons per acre (35 hl/ha), it would appear that some quality-oriented producers are returning to Ligurian standards. Nowhere else in Italy have so many indigenous vine varieties managed to survive. At the last count, there were over 100, some merely covering a few acres. However, each abandoned vineyard means the potential loss of valuable varieties.

CINQUETERRE

The name of the steep coastal cliff on the Riviera del Levante, north of the town of La Spezia, is associated with a white wine produced from the local varieties of Bosco, Albarola, and Vermentino. When good, its slightly salty taste makes it an excellent accompaniment to the fish dishes which are a mainstay of the local cuisine.

Sciacchetrà, the dessert wine version produced from the same blend of grapes, was once well

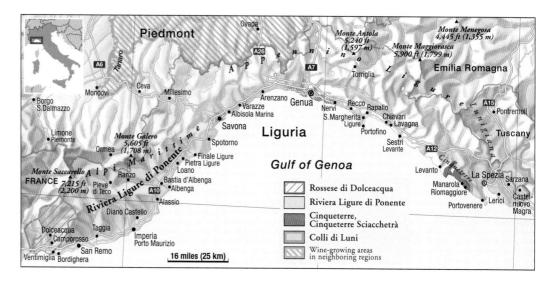

Select Producers in Liguria

Maria Donata Bianchi***–****
Diano Castello
6 acres (2.5 ha); 20,000 bottles • Wines: Riviera Ligure di Ponente: Vermentino, Pigato; →Eretico: Vermetino, Pigato
Emanuele Trevia, a pioneer of modern winery techniques in Liguria, produces powerful, structured whites.

Bruna***
Ranzo
13.6 acres (5.5 ha); 37,000 bottles • Wines: Riviera Ligure di Ponente: Pigato Le Russeghine, Pigato Villa Torrachetta, Rossese Le Russeghine, →Pigato U Baccan
Francesca Bruna's specialty is the Pigato grape and the very individual U Baccan from over-ripe selected grapes.

Cascina Feipu dei Massaretti***
Bastia d'Albenga
11 acres (4.5 ha); 45,000 bottles • Wines: Riviera di Ponente: Pigato, Rossese; Russu du Feipu, Due Anelli

The diligence of Agostino 'Pippo' Parodi turns the sensitive Pigato grape into high quality wines.

Tommaso e Angelo Lupi***–****
Pieve di Teco
34.5 acres (14 ha); 150,000 bottles • Wines: Riviera Ligure di Ponente: Pigato, Vermentino, Ormeasco; Vignamare
The very clean, pure wines are vinified in collaboration with Donato Lanati, considered the best enologist in Piedmont, who learned his skills from the Tuscan Giacomo Tachis.

Terre Rosse***
Finale Ligure
11 acres (4.5 ha); 25,000 bottles • Wines: Vermentino, Pigato, →L'Acerbina, Le Banche, →Solitario, Passito Terre Rosse
The minerals which give the vineyards soils their red color (terre rosse) are also found in the wines; there are vine varieties such as Lumassina, now considered extinct.

known far beyond the borders of Liguria but is now only produced in small quantities.

A Mediterranean Herb Garden

The few quality-oriented producers in Liguria have hitherto devoted all of their innovative energies to the white varieties of Vermentino and Pigato, the latter being one of the varieties exclusive to Liguria which was probably established here by the Ancient Greeks. This variety is mainly cultivated on around 490 acres (200 ha) in the Val d'Arroscia valley near Ranzo, and in the Albenga enclave.

As charming as towns like Triora look with their nooks and crannies, conditions for wine growing are difficult here and few producers succeed in providing more than simple table wines.

Pigato acquires its typical bouquet, with notes of wild herbs and wild flowers, on the sun-drenched terraces. The low yields and favorable climatic conditions ensure that even average years give structured wines with a high alcohol content. As a sweet dried-grape Passito—a kind of "straw wine" (VIN DE PAILLE)—this variety exudes rich honey and apricot aromas.

Vermentino, Liguria's best-known white variety, has D.O.C. status in the Riviera Ligure di Ponente zone, between Genoa and the French border, and in Colli di Luni between La Spezia and Tuscany. Although less sophisticated than Pigato, this variety also has aromas of Mediterranean herbs and its soft taste has subtle lemon notes and pleasant spicy undertones.

Ligurian Red Wines

Rossese di Dolceaqua, from the mountains behind Ventimiglia, Bordighera, and San Remo, is a ruby-red wine of rustic simplicity. Just a few producers succeed in creating wines from Rossese grapes, which combine an aroma of dried roses and fruits of the forest with a subtle note of almonds. In the Albenga zone of the Savona province, where Rossese is bottled under the Riviera Ligure di Ponente D.O.C., it generally yields paler-colored and light-tasting everyday wine which is similar to the dry rosé from the indigenous Barbarossa grape.

Ormeasco is the name given here to the Piedmontese variety Dolcetto. When aged in wood, it can produce good, competitive wines. Finally, the best-known Tuscan variety, Sangiovese, also deserves a mention as it is occasionally found in the eastern part of Liguria under the Colli di Luni D.O.C.

LOMBARDY

With its metropolis, Milan, Lombardy is the industrial heart of Italy and its most densely populated region. Its image as an agricultural region is dominated by the widespread cultivation of rice, maize, wheat, and vines. Vines can be seen growing everywhere in the region, from Veltlin in the narrow Alpine valley of the Adda, the west bank of Lake Garda, the plain of the river Po near Mantua, the hills to the south of Pavia and, finally, to the slopes near Bergamo and Brescia. A lot of wine is produced here but not much is of high quality. The enormous market for everyday and bulk wines in metropolitan Milan has hindered the development of a leading regional wine or even a uniform style of production. Local wines are in demand as a basis for sparkling wine production in other regions, and it is only in recent decades that smaller areas like Franciacorta have succeeded in establishing an independent image.

The climate is subject to continental Alpine and Mediterranean influences. With its hot summers and often very cold winters, high humidity levels, and fresh fertile soils, only a few parts of the Po plain are suitable for viticulture. However, the hill and mountain landscapes provide better locations for growing vines, thanks to their almost Mediterranean climate and the shelter of the Alps.

Left
Bottles are stored neck-down and shaken daily to move the yeast deposits to the neck of the bottle. This is done by hand at the Lorenzo Faccoli winery.

Right
Franciacorta is produced using the bottle-fermentation method. The Spumante is left lying on the lees for years. At the end of the storage period, the yeast deposit is removed by disgorgement.

A MODERN SPARKLING WINE

Today, Lombardy's most reputable individual zone is without doubt Franciacorta, where Italy's best dry sparkling wines have been produced for some years now, some of which enjoy D.O.C.G. status. In recent decades, a veritable Spumante industry, consisting of 80 wineries using the Champagne method, has established itself on the slopes around Lake Iseo. Since the changes in legislation, the area's still wines, some of which are truly excellent, also have their own D.O.C. designation, Terre di Franciacorta. At four million bottles, the total volume produced in the area is, however, too low to make an impact on the international market: by comparison, 270 million bottles are produced in Champagne each year.

Cellatico, a light red wine, is produced north of Brescia and is a blend of Schiava, Barbera, Marzemino, and Incrocio Terzi No. I, a hybrid of Cabernet Franc and Barbera, only cultivated in Italy. Cellatico, and the *appellations* Capriano del Colle and Botticino, are unknown outside the locality and the same applies for the D.O.C. wines of the Riviera del Garda Brescino, where Groppello is the main variety cultivated. The rather neutral white wine, Lugana, produced from Trebbiano grapes on the south bank of Lake Garda, is slightly better known.

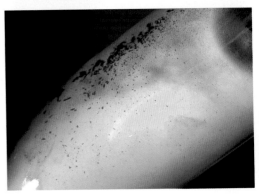

Farmsteads nestled into the vineyard slopes in Valtellina.

■	Valtellina
▨	Valcalepio
▢	Franciacorta, Terre di Franciacorta
▨	Cellatica
▨	Capriano del Colle
◇	Botticino
▢	Riviera del Garda Bresciano
▢	Tocai di San Martino della Battaglia
◆	Lugana
▨	Colli Morenici Mantovani del Garda
▨	Lambrusco Mantovano
▨	Oltrepò Pavese
▨	Wine-growing areas in neighboring regions

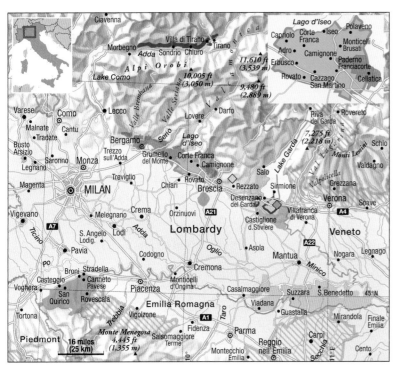

MOUNTAIN NEBBIOLO

Previously, the Veltlin (known as Valtellina in Italian) region was mainly a supplier of bulk wine to the neighboring Swiss canton of Grisons. The main grape variety grown in Veltlin is Piedmontese Nebbiolo, known here as Chiavennasca; however, it does not always reach full maturity on the slopes of the narrow, steep Adda valley. Although the Rhaetian and Lepontine Alps deflect a lot of the rain and cold north winds, only the terraces on the southern slopes provide conditions that are adequate for vine cultivation.

Vines from these southern terraces, which develop a minimum alcohol content of 12 percent, have enjoyed D.O.C.G. status since 1998, and can bear the vineyard designations of Sassella, Grumello, Inferno, and Valgella, as can the D.O.C. Valtellina Superiore. As the Veltlin Nebbiolo generally produces rather bitter and acidic wines, the valley's producers

Franciacorta—the champagne of Italy

The name of the moraine landscape on the southern periphery of Lake Iseo between Bergamo and Brescia is probably derived from the *"francae curtes,"* the tax exemption granted to the Benedictine Order in the area during the Middle Ages. Up to the mid-20th century, the area produced little more than ordinary wine for local consumption.

Franciacorta's rise to become the "Champagne of Italy" started in 1961 when Guido Berlucchi's enologist persuaded him to produce a sparkling wine. The success of the venture was so conclusive that in the 1970s Milanese industrialists started to invest in the area's growing Spumante industry. Following

Berlucchi's example—his winery produces over four million bottles annually from wines originating from Oltrepò and Trentino—local producers began to specialize in bottle-fermented sparkling wines produced using the Champagne method and based on Pinot and Chardonnay.

In 1995, Franciacorta was honored as Italy's first and (still) only bottle-fermented D.O.C.G. sparkling wine, and, unlike the other inglorious D.O.C.G. white wines, Albana di Romagna, Asti, and Vernaccia di San Gimignano, it actually deserved it.

The Franciacorta label may only be sported by wines produced from Chardonnay, Pinot Blanc, Pinot Noir, and a maximum of 15 percent of Pinot Gris, which mature on the

lees for at least 18 months, or 30 months in the case of vintage production.

The best Franciacorta Spumantes are BRUT. A sweetening dosage is not really necessary, as the temperatures enjoyed in the area are significantly higher than in the Champagne region of France. Body and aromatic richness, as well as additional subtleties of flavor, are provided by the storage of the basic wine in *barriques*. In addition to standard white sparkling wines, the area also produces rosé sparkling wines and the Franciacorta specialty, Satèn, which is aged for longer than normal sparkling wine and based on grapes originating from vineyards whose maximum official yield is around 20 percent lower than that allowed for the standard wines.

Beyond the Po

With its 42,000 acres (17,000 ha) of vines, Oltrepò Pavese, a hilly landscape to the south of Pavia, is Lombardy's most important viticultural area, both in terms of its size and the volumes produced there. However, half of its produce is still dispatched to neighboring Piedmont as a basic wine for Spumante production. This commercial relationship has encouraged the emphasis on exclusively quantity-oriented wine production from an early stage. The wide range of varieties cultivated here, from Chardonnay, Sauvignon, Pinot Gris, Riesling Italico, and Riesling Renano to Pinot Noir, Cabernet Sauvignon, Barbera, Bonarda, and regional vines, has done little to promote the production of high-quality local wines. Noteworthy initiatives in recent decades, however, have focused not only on local sparkling-wine production but also on indigenous red wines. Promising experiments with high-quality Pinot Noir clones have yielded interesting barrel-aged wines.

The few local Lombardian specialties include Buttafuoco, a sometimes light fizzy red wine produced from a mix of Croatina, Barbera, and Uva Rara; these varieties are also used in the production of Sangue di Giuda (Judas's blood), a red sparkling wine with a very fruity flavor.

have developed a kind of dried grape wine or *vin de paille* based on the Amarone model. The wine is called Sfursat or Sforzato (i.e. forced or strained) because, in order to concentrate their sugar content, the grapes are dried for a short period before PRESSING and fermentation. The few truly excellent wines marketed under this name are very luxurious, with a high alcohol content and rich spicy aromas.

Oltrepò Pavese—vineyards as far as the eye can see whose produce mainly provides base wines for the sparkling wine industry. However, the better wineries are also successfully experimenting with a wider range of varieties.

Select Producers in Lombardy

BARBACARLO***
BRONI
40 acres (16 ha); 25,000 bottles • Wines: Oltrepò Pavese: Barbacarlo, Montegbuono, Ronchetto
Lino Maga has completely dedicated his efforts to the care and maintenance of the Barbacarlo vineyard, one of the first in Oltrepò whose wines established a reputation outside of Lombardy.

BELLAVISTA****
ERBUSCO
290 acres (117 ha); 600,000 bottles • Wines include: Franciacorta Gran Cuvée: Rosé, Brut, →Pas Opérée, →Satèn, →Riserva Vittorio Moretti, Terre di Franciacorta Bianco: →Ucellanda, →Convento dell'Annunciata, Rosso; Casotte, →Solesine
Vittorio Moretti has developed one of the best wineries in the Franciacorta area, where his family has lived for centuries. Thirty percent of the base wines ferment in *barriques* and the estate is known for its famous Spumante bottlings and its excellent still white wines.

GUIDO BERLUCCHI**
CORTEFRANCA
173 acres (70 ha); bought-in grapes; 4,500,000 bottles • Wines: Spumante Cuvée Impériale: Brut, →Max Rosé, Millésimato, Franciacorta Antica Cantina Fratta Millesimato
This winery generally obtains its grapes and base wines from Oltrepò and Trentino. The Cuvée Imperiale is Italy's best-known quality sparkling wine.

CA' DEI FRATI***–****
SIRMIONE
55.5 acres (22.5 ha); 160,000 bottles • Wines: Lugana Vigna I Frati, →Lugana Brolettino, Riviera del Garda Bresciano Chiaretto, Tre Filer, →Vigna Pratto
Piero Dal Cero's estate made a name for itself with its barrel-aged Lugana Brolettino. Today, the red Pratto is also one of Lombardy's finest wines.

CA' DEL BOSCO*****
ERBUSCO
237 acres (96 ha); 450,000 bottles • Wines: Franciacorta: Brut, Millesimato, →Dosage Zero, →Cuvée Anna Maria Clementi; →Terre di Franciacorta Chardonnay, →I.G.T. Sebino Maurizio Zanella, Pinero, Elfo
Along with Angelo Gaja and Giacomo Bologna, Maurizio Zanella was one of Italy's main innovators in winemaking during the 1980s. Today, along with his sparkling wines, his still reds and whites are among the best in the country, for example the Chardonnay, the red Sebino which bears the name of its producer, and the new Elfo. Outstanding Pinot Pinero.

CASTELLO DI LUZZANO—M. & G. FUGAZZA***
ROVESCALA
173 acres (70 ha) • Wines: Oltrepò Pavese: Pinot Nero, Barbera, Rosso 270, Bonarda; Gutturnio Colli Piacentini Romeo
The efforts made to improve the quality of the wines produced on this estate on the Piedmont border are already showing good results.

Gian Paolo e Giovanni Cavalleri**−****
Erbusco
69 acres (28 ha); 175,000 bottles • Wines: Franciacorta: Brut, →Collezione Brut, Crémant, Pas dosé, Rosé, Rosé Collezione, Rosso Vigna Tarjadino; Terre di Franciacorta: Rampaneto, Seradina →I.G.T. Merlot del Sebino Corniole
The five sparkling wines have no problem standing up to the French competition; perfect sparkle, a fine, slightly yeasty bouquet, and a creamy taste.

Gualberto Ricci Curbastro & Figli**−****
Capriolo
37 acres (15 ha); 80,000 bottles • Wines include: Franciacorta: →Extra Brut, Satèn; Terre di Franciacorta: Bianco, Chardonnay, Rosso, →Vigna Bosco Alto, Vigna Santella del Grom; Pinot Nero Sebino, Brolo del Passoni Chardonnay Passito Sebino, Grappa
Riccardo Ricci Curbastro has established the family estate as one of the top wineries in the Franciacorta area in recent years. Both the sparkling wines and the still white Bosco Alto have considerable stature.

Contadi Gastaldi***−****
Adro
• Wines: Franciacorta: Satèn, Pinodisé, Rosé, Brut, Pas Dosé; Terre di Franciacorta Bianco
Within a few years of its establishment, Vittorio Moretti's second operation (see Bellavista) has built a solid reputation for good sparkling wines.

Enrico Gatti***−****
Erbusco
22 acres (9 ha); 60,000 bottles • Wines: Franciacorta Brut, Terre di Franciacorta: Bianco, Rosso; →Gatti Rosso, →Gatti Bianco
In the early 1970s, estate agent Gatti acquired the land in Erbusco and planted vines. His son-in-law Enzo Balzarini then developed the business into one of the best-known in the Franciacorta region. Its reputation does not, however, rest on sparkling wine but on its Cabernet Gatti Rosso.

Monte Rossa****
Cazzago San Martino
96 acres (39 ha); 200,000 bottles • Wines include: Franciacorta: →Brut Cabochon, Extra Brut Millesimato, →Brut Satèn, Brut Rosé; Terre di Franciacorta Ravellino
One of the area's traditional houses, this winery has regularly improved the quality of its wines in recent years and is now one of the elite in the Franciacorta area.

Nino Negri**−***
Chiuro
94 acres (38 ha); some bought-in grapes; 1,200,000 bottles • Wines include: Valtellina: Superiore, Inferno, Sassella Le Botti d'oro, →Sfursat 5 Stelle; Chiavennasca, Vergiano, Vigneto Ca'Brione, Vigneto I Grigioni
The best-known Veltlin winery belongs to the Italiano Vino group. Its "Five-Star-Sfursat" has great density and depth in good years.

Provenza**−***
Dezenzano del Garda
74 acres (30 ha); 400,000 bottles • Wines: Lugana: Brut Charmat Sebastian, →Brut Metodo Classico Ca'Maiol, Fabio Contato Riserva, Garda Classico: Chiaretto, Tenuta Maiolo, VdT Sol Dorè
In Provenza, the Contato family has united four historic wine estates in one. Although this has created the largest operation in the *appellation*, the wines here are not the mass-produced ones typical of the region. The sparkling

wines—Ca'Maiol remains on the yeast for 36 months— are distinguished by their freshness and finesse.

Conti Sertoli Salis-Salis 1637***
Tirano
18.5 acres (7.5 ha); some bought-in grapes; 125,000 bottles • Wines include: Valtellina: Superiore Sassella, Inferno, Grumello, →Sforzato Canua, →Superiore Conte della Meridiana
This traditional house has been producing Valtellina's most modern and elegant wines since the early 1990s. The Saloncello and the Torre della Sirena table wines are remarkable.

Stefano Spezia***
Mariana Mantovana (Mantua)
5 acres (2 ha); 30,000 bottles • Wines: →Lambrusco Etichetta Rossa, →Ancellotta Barrique, Ancellotta Frizzante, Rosso Spezia Merlot
In Lombardy, Spezia proves that Lambrusco can be an interesting product. Specialties include a bottle fermented red sparkling wine as well as a barrel-aged Ancellotta, a dark, rich, spicy and complex wine.

Tenuta Mazzolino**−****
Corvino San Quirico
42 acres (17 ha); 65,000 bottles • Wines: →Noir, Corvino, Oltrepò Pavese; Barbera, Bonarda, Riesling italico Guarnazzola, Pinot Camarà
The Tenuta is located on the slopes of the Oltrepò facing the plain of the Po. With the help of Piedmontese enologist Giancarlo Scaglione, it succeeded in producing one of the region's best wines from Pinot Noir.

G. & G.A. Uberti***−****
Erbusco
35 acres (14 ha); 90,000 bottles • Wines include: Franciacorta: Brut Francesco I, →Extra Brut Comari del Salemi, →Magnificentia; →Terre di Franciacorta: Bianco dei Frati Priori and Maria Medici, Rosso dei Frati Priori
Unpretentious wines with a total emphasis on quality. The best products are the still white Bianco dei Frati Priori and the Franciacorta Extra Brut Comari del Salemi.

Bruno Verdi**−****
Canneto Pavese
• Wines include: →Barnera Campo del Marrone, Bonarda Possessione di Vergomberra, Buttafuoco, Sangue di Giuda, Pinot Nero, Moscato Volpara, Vergomberra Brut
This estate, run by the seventh generation of the Verdi family, produces surprisingly high quality reds. Apart from the single vineyard Barbera, the Bonarda and the Pinot Noir, all the red wines are *cuvées* based on the Croatina grape variety, which is considered a mass production grape, but here produces wines full of fruit and aroma.

The Northeast: Between the Habsburg Empire and Venice

The landscapes in this large region comprising Trentino, Alto Adige (Southern Tyrol), Friuli-Venezia Giulia, Veneto, and Emilia Romagna are formed by the Alps in the north, the Apennines in the south, the Po plain in the middle and the Adriatic coastal lands in the east. The soils available for viticulture vary as widely as these geological formations: the barren and highly porous soils of the deep Alpine valleys are composed of gravel and morainic scree with a high proportion of limestone; the soils found in floodplains of the Adige river valley are highly fertile; the barren dry soils of the morainic hills on the southern edge of the Alpine foothills are interspersed with glacial gravel; and the marine deposits of the coastal strips and the plain of the river Po, which was once almost completely flooded by the Adriatic Sea, are dominated by calcareous marl with sandstone inclusions. The foothills of the Apennines are less subject to erosion than those of the Alps, and their soils are dominated by lime gravel, sandstone, marl, and clay. The numerous rivers with their deposits create fertile soils in the valleys.

The climate in northeastern Italy varies as widely as its landscapes and soils. Although Trentino-Alto Adige enjoys a cool, Alpine-continental climate, the terraces of the Adige valley and its tributaries are blessed with around 2,000 hours of sun annually and an average temperature of 63°F (17°C), and are hence highly suited to viticulture. In contrast, the climate of the Po

With its Vinitaly trade fair, Verona becomes Italy's wine capital every April. However, there are many other wine-related events throughout the year and particularly in the Bottega del Vino, the city's best-known wine bar.

Silvio Jermann flouts Friulian tradition by creating his wines from blends of different varieties. He bottles them as table wines, gives them striking names, and lets their quality speak for itself.

plain is characterized by Mediterranean influences. This balancing effect on temperatures extends right up to the west of the region—the shores of Lake Garda boast typical southern vegetation with cypress and palm trees. The higher locations on the edge of the Dolomites and the Alps experience a typical mountain climate, with significant differences between day and night temperatures. However, the peaks of up to 9,750 feet (3,000 m) provide shelter from the northern frosts and this significantly extends the growing season, particularly in spring. Thus, vine varieties which require relatively long growth and ripening periods can be cultivated in the higher locations in Friuli which are unlikely to be reached by the sea's temperate influence. Heavy storms, often with hail, which are capable of destroying entire harvests, are the main climatic problem on the southern edge of the Alps.

Variety in the Vineyards

The diversity of the region's soil and climate poses a real challenge to the range of indigenous and imported vine varieties cultivated there, and to the types of wine produced from them. International Merlot grows alongside local specialties such as Marzemino or Pignolo, and the weighty Amarone with its high alcohol content is produced along with fresh, light whites and delicate dessert wines. However, this diversity cannot be explained by the natural conditions alone. Just like the Tyroleans, Habsburgs, Venetians, and French of more recent periods, the Etruscans, Romans, Carelians, and Illyrians left their mark on this landscape. They all influenced viticulture, which to the present day remains partly based on old political boundaries or on wine growing in neighboring countries.

In the recent past also, developments in wine production in the various zones have followed anything but a simultaneous course. While in Alto Adige the emphasis on quality production started at a very early stage, thanks mainly to the efforts of the cooperatives and large wineries, in the neighboring province of Trentino, where wine growing was still largely in the hands of smaller operations, the quality movement did not really take hold until ten years later—one of the consequences of the area's traditional role as a supplier of base wine for the local and

international sparkling wine industry. In the 1980s, the producers in Friuli concentrated their energies on the production of fruity, light, modern white wines which were aimed at the gap in the Italian market which previously was only served successfully by Alto Adige. The developments of recent years indicate, however, that the main opportunities in the future could lie with the red or strongly structured white wines.

QUALITY OR QUANTITY?

Veneto, which is one of Italy's most prolific wine-producing regions and a traditional center of international wine trade with northern Europe, paints a contradictory picture. Winemaking in the areas around the city of Verona, for example Valpolicella, Soave, and Bardolino, yields both outstanding quality and anonymous mass-produced wines, as the vines here are cultivated not only on the slopes, which are best for quality, but also in the fertile flood plain of the river

Adige. The west of the region has established a good reputation in the past two decades, with products such as the heavy red wine Amarone and individual dessert wines.

In the east of Veneto, apart from the successful efforts of a minority of producers, a mass-production ideology still reigns. Prosecco —which can vary significantly in quality—is the only well-known wine produced here. As long as the region can find a secure market for its cheaper products, there will be little incentive to exploit the ideal conditions it enjoys for quality production. A change of heart with respect to quality can only be expected if the competition from other European or overseas countries becomes more acute.

This is even more true of Emilia Romagna, whose development has been blocked for decades by the huge volumes of basic Lambrusco produced there. The efforts of individual producers to improve quality are even more rare here, and all the more valuable.

Contrasting wine-growing landscapes in northern Italy: from Mezzolombardo, Trentino to Laimburg, Alto Adige.

Regional vine varieties

The international vine varieties have established a firmer foothold in the northeast than in any other part of Italy. Merlot (Friuli), Cabernet Sauvignon, Cabernet Franc, and Pinot Noir (Alto Adige) have been cultivated here since the phylloxera catastrophe of the late 19th century, and in some cases with very good results. Pinot Gris, or Pinot Grigio as it is known here, has become Italy's most popular wine. It is found together with Chardonnay in most of the region's newly established vineyards, while the only common Italian varieties are Sangiovese, Barbera, and Trebbiano (mainly in Emilia Romagna).

All of the other vines cultivated in the Northeast are regional varieties. The most popular is the Schiava or Vernatsch (called Trollinger in

Germany) in Trentino-Alto Adige which is mainly used in the production of the Lago di Caldaro (Kalterer See) D.O.C. Lagrein, Teroldego, and Marzemino are not very strongly represented in terms of volume, but there is currently a revived interest in their red wines.

Corvina, the main variety used in the production of Valpolicella, Bardolino, and Amarone, is widely planted in Veneto. The Po plain is stocked with sub-varieties of the Lambrusco family (Grasparossa, Marani, Maestri, Salamino, Monterico, di Sorbara). Other red varieties worthy of mention in this context include: Raboso (Veneto), Refosco Dal Peduncolo Rosso (Friuli), Pignolo (Friuli), Schioppettino (Friuli), and Tazzelenghe (Friuli).

With 32,000 acres (13,000 ha), the most widely-planted white variety in Veneto is Garganega, which is the main constituent of

Soave. White varieties from German-speaking areas, such as Riesling, Müller-Thurgau, Veltliner, Kerner, Silvaner, and Gewürztraminer, are common in Alto Adige, Trentino, and Friuli. In Trentino they are complemented by the indigenous Nosiola and Moscato Giallo/Rosa varieties. The indigenous variety Malvasia di Candia thrives in Emilia Romagna as does Albana, the first white wine variety to be awarded D.O.C.G. status. Albana can also be found in Friuli along with the other white varieties Tocai Friulano/Italico, Verduzzo, Ribolla Gialla, Picolit, and Vitovska.

In Italy, the Northeast is the region with the most interesting potential in terms of varieties. Their systematic improvement and use could inject badly-needed inspiration into a global market dominated by increasingly homogeneous wines.

Trentino

Trentino has the Etruscans, rather than the Romans, to thank for establishing viticulture in the region. It is even said that the Romans, who did much to spread wine growing within and outside of Italy, learned some of their vineyard and winery techniques, including the use of wooden casks as fermentation and storage containers, from the Etruscan cultures of northern Italy. As in the neighboring province of Alto Adige, wine production is mainly concentrated in and around the valley of the Adige river and its tributaries. Vines are cultivated on around 22,240 acres (9,000 ha)—partly in the fertile flood plain, and partly on the barren slopes whose soils mainly consist of moraine gravel. Seventy percent of the vines are distributed among five D.O.C. areas and four I.G.T. designations are available for the rest.

Artistically stacked bottles of Trento, a Spumante produced from Chardonnay and the Pinot varieties. This wine matures on the racks.

Marzemino and Teroldego

The wines of this province were first exposed to a wider public during the Counter-Reformation Council of Trent, the third session of which opened in Trent in 1545 and was completed, after repeated interruptions, in 1563. The participants may have focused their attention on the more delightful aspects of the sacrament of the mass after the actual council sessions, as some of the vine varieties used to produce the region's wines today were available at the time, for example Marzemino and Teroldego. Marzemino is one of the less well-known indigenous vine varieties of northern Italy. This late-ripening, resistant variety can produce full-bodied aromatic wines but it is often used as a high-volume base for lightly sparkling wines. Its

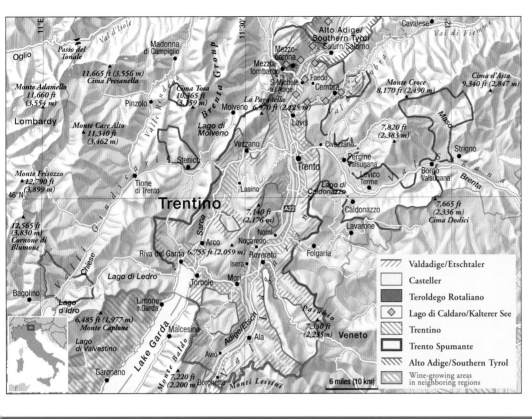

Trentino is a fascinating wine landscape located for the most part in the valley of the river Adige and framed by high mountains which protect it from inclement weather.

valley of lakes to the north of Riva del Garda—the range of vines cultivated here is dominated by international varieties. Chardonnay and Pinot Gris have had a major impact on the white wines, while interesting reds are being produced using Cabernet and Merlot.

MODERN WHITE AND RED WINES

The miles of wine-growing areas lining both sides of the Brenner expressway are dominated by high pergolas (a form of overhead vine training) which protect the grapes from excessive heat, decay, and disease. The disadvantage of this form of protection lies in the fact that it promotes excessive yields. This is reflected in the D.O.C. regulations, with their over-generous upper limits of up to 7 tons per acre (15 tonnes/ha) and the clear emphasis on quantity in Trentino viticulture. Individual producers have, meanwhile, proved that fresh, aromatic white wines can be yielded on the mountain slopes, despite their barren soils and significant variations between day and night temperatures. Most of the production, particularly from the major D.O.C. zone of Valdadige, can at best be described as "clean but inconsequential."

In addition to white varieties, large quantities of red grapes are also cultivated in this province.

potential can only fully unfold on suitable soils, for example the black basalt of the villages of Isera and Nomi in the Trentino D.O.C. zone. Isera Marzemino, an elegant wine with a subtle almond aroma, which was immortalized by Mozart in his opera *Don Giovanni*, can include the domain name in its designation.

Teroldego, the only Italian variety which thrives on flat ground as opposed to slopes, has even greater potential if cultivated in soils that are not too fertile. This vine variety, which is grown almost exclusively on the very gravelly flood plain of the Campo Rotaliano near Mezzocorona and Mezzolombardo in Trentino, yields deep-colored red wines with complex aromas. Its outstanding character won it the award of its own D.O.C., Teroldego Rotaliano. However, the D.O.C. regulations authorize yields of up to 1,335 gallons per acre (125 hl/ha) which is difficult to reconcile with modern quality standards. The best Teroldego producers in Campo Rotaliano limit themselves to yields of no more than 425–535 gallons per acre (40–50 hl/ha). The barrel-aged vintages, in particular, can display a depth and complexity of taste which is rarely found in the province. These wines have aromas of liquorice, plums, cherries, and violets, plenty of power and even some aging capacity.

In addition to the indigenous varieties, which also include red Schiava (called Vernatsch or Trollinger in Alto Adige) in its various variants, and white Nosiola—from which an interesting VIN SANTO is produced in Valle dei Laghi, the

Mezzolombardo against a mountain backdrop.

From *négociant* house to quality wine estate— Endrizzi in San Michele.

The top varieties include Merlot and Cabernet Franc, and to a lesser extent Cabernet Sauvignon, which are often bottled as single varietals. Some producers are experimenting with a Bordeaux blend which can yield successful, and powerful, wines. As with the whites, most of the Trentino reds bear the D.O.C. designation Trentino or Valdadige, of which the latter was mainly established for light, simple types of wine. The grassy notes often found in the Cabernet and Merlot wines and their blends can be explained by both the high yields and the restriction of ripening opportunities for the grapes growing under the shadows of the pergolas, which are not very suitable for use with these varieties.

SPARKLING AND FRUITY

The School of Enology of San Michele all'Adige on the border of Alto Adige which, along with the Geisenheim School of Enology in Rheingau, Germany, and Davis University in Sacramento, California, is one of the best research institutes in the wine world, works in and for Trentino. The insights gained by the institute's scientists are often put directly into practice by the producers of the Adige valley in their vineyards and wineries.

A real quality movement did not emerge, however, until the 1990s, when the large cooperatives recognized the importance of high-quality premium wines, and some of the wineries, which had previously concentrated on the production of bulk wine for export, implemented successful measures to improve the quality of their products.

In economic terms, the sparkling wine industry is the most important sector of the Trentino wine industry. It produces five million bottles of sparkling wine each year, some of which is very high in quality. Most of it is produced using tank fermentation, known in Italy as the CHARMAT METHOD. However, some wineries produce sparkling wines using bottle-fermentation, a method introduced from Champagne in the early 20th century by the Ferrari winery. Some of these sparkling wines, which bear the Trento D.O.C. designation, are among Italy's best and are marketed internationally. A separate *appellation* also exists for bottle-fermented Trentino sparkling wines. However, unlike Franciacorta, they do not have D.O.C.G. status. Their name, "Trento D.O.C.," is easily confused with the still wine *appellation* "Trentino D.O.C." and, when combined with the brand name of the most important private alliance of sparkling wine producers, gives the rather unwieldy name of Trento Talento.

The old billboard in the Ferrari winery in Trento shows the different stages in the production of Spumante, from the vineyard, casks, and bottle fermentation to disgorgement and dosage, which in essence remain unchanged to the present day.

Alto Adige

The Alto Adige (Southern Tyrol), a region which enjoys close historical and cultural links with the Austrian region of Northern Tyrol, has been part of Italy since the First World War and, together with Trentino, forms an autonomous region. Most of the vineyards in this most northerly province of Italy are located in the valley of the Adige (Etsch) river and its tributaries, in particular the Isarco (Eisach) which flows from Bolzano (Bozen) in the north.

The quality center in Alto Adige is located in the Überretsch area, a mountain terrace which lies above the Adige valley between Bolzano in the north and Ora (Auer) in the south. This is the most attractive section of the Alto Adige wine route. Smaller centers of quality can also be found in the area around Terlano (Terlan), Merano (Meran), and Santa Maddalena (Sankt Magdalen) as well as Mazzon and the left bank of the Adige.

The close links with German and Austrian models of viticulture, as well as its bilingualism,

An invitation to dine with Alto Adige red wine.

reflect the region's long association with Tyrol, and the German-speaking world. This starts with some of the 18 vine varieties cultivated here, which include typical German varieties, such as Riesling, Sylvaner, Müller-Thurgau, Gewürztraminer, Kerner, and Trollinger (also known as Schiava or Vernatsch), continues with the way in which zones are named, and extends to harvesting practices such as AUSLESE (selected harvest), which have been included in the D.O.C. regulations. Although 90 percent of wines produced in Alto Adige are legally defined as quality wines, this means as little here as it does in Germany. And yet, Alto Adige has emerged as one of Italy's most quality-conscious regions.

WINERIES AND COOPERATIVES

Unlike other regions, for example Piedmont, the quality initiative did not originate with the individual estates and small wineries but with the larger commercial wineries and cooperatives. Lageder and Hofstätter, and later also Niedermayer and a few others on the one hand, and Girlan, Schreckbichl, Terlan, and Cortaccia (Kurtatsch) on the other were the protagonists of the quality contest which radically changed vinification practices in Alto Adige from the mid-1980s. The cooperatives, which processed two thirds of the region's total grape harvest, assumed a central role in this process, as they were responsible for spreading the movement. Their payment of their member producers on a quality, as opposed to quantity, basis, their policy of separate vinification of wines from particularly suitable areas, in which yields were drastically reduced, and, not least, their delight in experimenting in the winery with steel tanks and *barriques*, became a model for producers throughout the province and beyond.

The withdrawal from the marketing of excessive volumes of cheap and simple Schiava (Vernatsch) wines (mainly sold as Lago di Caldero/Kalterer See, Colli di Bolzano/Bozner Leiten and Santa Maddalena/Sankt Magdalener) proved to be the making of the region. Taste was traditionally sacrificed for high volumes in the cultivation of the Schiava variety. However, its more careful treatment in recent decades allowed the astonishing qualities of the variety to come to the fore. Now it is often sold not as Lago di Caldero/Kalterer See, but under the variety *appellation*. Wines based on this variety are bright red in color, with an aroma of violets.

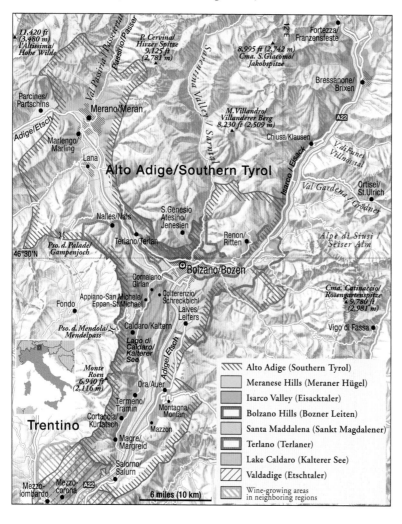

Alto Adige (Southern Tyrol)
Meranese Hills (Meraner Hügel)
Isarco Valley (Eisacktaler)
Bolzano Hills (Bozner Leiten)
Santa Maddalena (Sankt Magdalener)
Terlano (Terlaner)
Lake Caldaro (Kalterer See)
Valdadige (Etschtaler)
Wine-growing areas in neighboring regions

Varieties on the Move

The excessive planting of Schiava, in increasingly large and productive vineyards, resulted in the almost complete elimination of Gewürztraminer, which is one of the oldest known varieties in Italy. This grape, with its rich aroma, was present in the area now known as Alto Adige as early as the end of the first millennium. Like other varieties of German-Austrian origin, it managed to survive to the present day but now faces enormous competition. For, despite the fact that the varieties from German-speaking areas are still the most common in Alto Adige, the province's undisputed best wines are made from imported varieties such as Chardonnay, Sauvignon Blanc, Cabernet Sauvignon, and Pinot Noir.

The area's producers now enjoy a good international reputation, particularly for their clean, fresh, white wines. The trend toward firm-structured, dense white wines also prompted many wineries here to experiment with barrel-aging, although large wooden casks are also coming back into fashion when it comes to giving the wines maximum complexity while retaining their fruit.

In contrast, the red wines are more adversely affected by the consequences of the nonsensical policy of mass-production. In particular, the region's characteristic use of pergolas, and pruning for maximum yield, give rise to wines with strong herbaceous notes and high levels of acidity. However, in the best zones, and in those in which yields have been reduced, in good years Cabernet Sauvignon and Pinot Noir give results which undoubtedly stand comparison with the best wines in Italy—and perhaps even with those in France.

The province's most interesting red variety is the native Lagrein which has been experiencing something of a renaissance in recent years.

Behind the idyllic exterior of the Georg Baron Widmann estate in Cortaccia/Kurtatsch, a virtual revolution has been taking place in the vineyards and cellar. The estate now markets its own top-quality products.

An astonishing paradox: the ice which protects the vines from frost is produced by sprinkling.

Formerly used mainly in the production of an unprepossessing rosé known as Kretzer, over a very short period its wines have blossomed into powerful spicy wines that are valued for their color, tannins, and aging capacity. They now enjoy increasing popularity among wine connoisseurs. Of course, once again, strict limitation of volume is the key to quality. For a long time, it was believed that only the sandy, gravelly soils of Gris, a district of Bolzano where the best Lagrein vines thrive, could produce good wines. In the meantime, however, more and more producers in other locations have discovered that this belief is ill-founded and proved that it is possible to yield excellent Lagrein Scuro (Lagrein Dunkel) in other areas of Alto Adige.

Two Innovators on the Wine Lake

Just a few years ago, it was likely that someone talking about the Alto Adige wine lake was not referring to Lake Caldaro (Kalterer See) but rather to the enormous volume of the wine—of the same name and very questionable quality—which flooded the markets in countries bordering Alto Adige for decades. The fact that this is no longer the case is mainly thanks to the services of two winemaking protagonists in the Überretsch area, Alois Lageder, a winery owner, and Luis Raifer, the head of the Colterenzio/Schreckbichl cooperative winery.

The restored castle of Löwengang in Magré (Magreid) is the operative center of the Lageder winery, which was founded in 1855 and located, until a few years ago, on the outskirts of Bolzano. After four generations of exclusively buying in and vinifying grapes, the current owner of the company, Alois Lageder, did a radical turnabout and dedicated his efforts to acquiring the best wine-growing sites and traditional wineries. With Römigberg on Lake Caldaro and the Löwengang and Hirschprunn sites in Magré, Lageder is now the owner of the best domains in Alto Adige. Moreover, in addition to introducing modern, natural viticulture practices in his own vineyards, he also inspired his suppliers—most of his grape supplies are still bought in—to concentrate on maximum quality, rather than on quantity.

While his ancestors were mainly interested in the wine trade, Alois Lageder targeted his efforts on the expansion of his vineyards. Natural cultivation practices ensure that Löwengang is now one of the region's top vineyards.

wooden casks to enhance their complexity and structure is also standard practice at Lageder. Their Löwengang Chardonnay was one of the first in Alto Adige to be fermented in *barriques*.

This dynamic company's best asset remains, however, the many vineyards whose grapes Lageder transforms into a wide range of distinctive estate bottlings. Haberlehof, Tannhammerhof, Benefizium Porer, Lindenburg, and Oberingramhof were recently joined by the unequaled top-quality plot at Römigberg, where one of Italy's best Cabernet Sauvignons is grown.

The company's latest gem is the newly acquired wine estate of Hirschprunn, which was formerly used to house refugees fleeing Mussolini's fascist regime and then stood empty for many years. Its grapes are still processed at Löwengang with all of the other Lageder products, but it is planned to develop the estate into a separate domain with a "château character."

Stylishly renovated historic environment for the wines of the future.

Traditional Methods and Modern Techniques

After the upgrading of the old winery in the 1970s and 1980s, the construction of a new winery behind the Löwengang estate triggered another significant shift toward modernization. With a capacity in excess of 790,000 gallons (30,000 hl) and production stages distributed on four levels, at a total height of 49 feet (15 m), so that the grapes and musts are transported almost exclusively by gravity and without pumps, the new winery is one of the most modern to be found in Alto Adige today. For example, the fermenting tanks are arranged in a circle so that all of the musts and wines cover the same path to reach the casks.

Of course, at Lageder many red wines are no longer pumped over, but, as in ancient times, the cap (i.e. layer of grape solids) is pressed down into the must automatically. The aging of better quality reds and whites in small or large

THE COOPERATIVES HOLD THEIR OWN

The Colterenzio/Schreckbichl cooperative in Girlano (Girlan), the Cornelianum of Roman times, proved that the cooperatives were in a position to emulate the quality efforts of private producers and wineries, or even provide a model for them, during the very decade in which Lageder developed his new exemplary winery. Founded in 1960 by only 28 producers, within a few decades it became one of the leading forces in wine production in northern Italy. Today, its 350 members farm over 980 acres (400 ha) of vines in Girlano, Appiano (Eppan), and Salorno (Salurn).

Under the directorship of Luis Raifer, the winery is successfully run in accordance with the very latest principles. Above all, attention has been paid to work in the vineyards, something which is far from automatic in Italy's cooperatives. The almost complete elimination of chemical products, whose previously unrestricted use was replaced by a policy of maintaining beneficial insects, is as much a part of the Colterenzio/Schreckbichl philosophy today as the separate vinification and bottling of wines from the best locations.

Thanks to these new efforts in the area of quality, the Cornell series of wines—above all the red Cornelius, a blend of Cabernet Sauvignon and Merlot, and the barrel-fermented Chardonnay—and the excellent Praedium varietals from the Coreth, Puiten,

Lake Caldaro (Kalterer See) and its vineyards.

Left
Luis Raifer—visionary director of the region's foremost cooperative.

Right
Alois Lageder—a producer with foresight.

Prail, Siebeneich, Weißhaus, and Mantsch vineyards were created as early as the 1980s.

Equal virtuosity was shown with fruity wines reductively aged in steel tanks and with barrel-aged wines. Thanks to the rigid yield restrictions, which Raifer succeeded in motivating his producers to observe, the reds, in particular, show unusual density and complexity for wines from a northern climate zone.

Raifer has proved that his expertise in winery practices also extends to marketing in his own estate of Lafòa, whose Cabernet Sauvignon and Sauvignon Blanc grapes are now being separately bottled. Both products are among the Alto Adige wines which have successfully attained international standards and can even stand their ground in the face of heavy French competition.

The altitudes of the vineyards of Cortaccia/Kurtatsch in Alto Adige/Southern Tyrol vary between 800 and 1,600 feet (250 and 500 m) above sea level.

SELECT PRODUCERS IN TRENTINO AND ALTO ADIGE

TRENTINO

ENDRIZZI**–****
SAN MICHELE ALL'ADIGE
41 acres (16.5 ha); some bought-in grapes; 200,000 bottles • Wines include: Trento Masetto Brut; Trentino; Traminer Aromatico, Müller-Thurgau, →Chardonnay and →Cabernet Collezione, Pinot Grigio, →Teroldego Rotaliano, Dulcis in Fundo
This former *négociant* winery has been transformed into a quality-oriented estate under the management of Paolo and Christine Endrici. The best wines are marketed with artists' labels.

FERRARI—FRATELLI LUNELLI****
TRENTO
153 acres (62 ha); some bought-in grapes; 3,000,000 bottles • Wines include: Trento: Maximum Brut , Rosé, →Riserva del Fondatore
This sparkling wine house is not only the region's biggest, it also produces some of the best bottle-fermented products. In the last decade a mineral water label has also been acquired.

FORADORI****–*****
MEZZOLOMBARDO
37 acres (15 ha); 100,000 bottles • Wines include: →Granato, →Karanar, →Teroldego Rotaliano Vigneto Morei; Trentino: Pinot Bianco, Chardonnay, Myrto
Elisabetta Foradori has not only transformed the old family estate into Trentino's top winery, she has also begun to develop the potential of Sicilian winemaking through a joint venture. Her three Teroldego wines, particularly the Granato, are top class.

LA VIS***–****
LAVIS
1,976 acres (800 ha); 1,700,000 bottles • Wines include: Trentino Ritratti: Chardonnay, Cabernet Sauvignon, Pinot Nero, →Rosso Vigneti delle Dolomiti, Trentino Traminer Aromatico Maso Tratta, Mandolaia Vendemia Tardiva
Initially, this cooperative supplied the basic materials for some well-known Trentino wines, and today it very successfully bottles its own. Some of the wines, matured according to the individual vineyards, are among the best in the region.

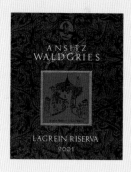

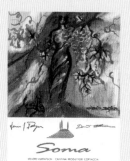

POJER & SANDRI***–****
FAEDO
44.5 acres (18 ha); 200,000 bottles • Wines: Trentino: Müller-Thurgau, Nosiola, Sauvignon, →Rosso and Bianco Fayé, →Essenzia Vendemmia Tardiva, Spumante Cuvée Brut
The go-getting producers, Mario Pojer and Fiorentino Sandri, are known for their white and red wines, and also for their outstanding pomace brandies (*grappa*). Their Rosso Fayè is one of Trentino's best reds.

SAN LEONARDO***
BORGHETTO
40 acres (16 ha); 80,000 bottles • Wines: Trentino: Merlot, Cabernet, San Leonardo, Villa Gresti
The wines of the Bordelais region influence Carlo Guerrieri Gonzaga's San Leonardo, produced from Cabernet Sauvignon, Cabernet Franc and Merlot. It is a source of contention: some celebrate it as Trentino's greatest red, others consider it a soulless and lackluster drink.

ALTO ADIGE

ANSITZ ALTGRIES***
BOLZANO
12 acres (5 ha); 60,000 bottles • Wines include: Alto Adige: Cabernet Sauvignon, →Lagrein Dunkel Riserva, →Rosenmuskateller Passito, St. Magdalener Classico
A traditional estate, with origins in the 12th century, which also has a museum. In the old cellars there are now also *barriques* for Cabernet Sauvignon and Lagrein. The grapes for the luscious aromatic Rosenmuskateller are dried till February.

J. HOFSTÄTTER****
TRAMIN
111 acres (45 ha); some bought-in grapes • Wines include: Alto Adige: →Blauburgunder Barthenau, Lagrein Steinraffler, →Cabernet Sauvignon Yngram, Gewürztraminer Kolbenhof
In quality and quantity, this tradition-conscious winery is Alois Lageder's main rival. The grapes for the top wines of the Foradori family estate come from five different sites to the right and left of the Adige, growing at height of up to 2,000 feet (600 m). The Blauburgunder Barthenau Vigna S. Urbano sets standards.

KELLEREIGENOSSENSCHAFT BOZEN**−****
BOLZANO
*741 acres (300 ha); 1,500,000 bottles • Wines include:
Alto Adige: St. Magdalener Huck am Bach, →Lagrein
Collection Baron Eyrl, Lagrein Perl, →Lagrein Taber,
Blauburgunder Greel, Blauburgunder Sandlahner,
Riesling Leitach, Gewürztraminer Kleinstein*
The Kellerei Bozen was created in 2001, merging the
Gries and St. Magdalena wineries. The average level of
the three dozen different wines is remarkably high. The
good reputation of the winery is primarily based on the
Lagrein wines.

KELLEREIGENOSSENSCHAFT GIRLAN**−****
GIRLANO
*667 acres (270 ha); 650,000 bottles • Wines: Südtiroler
including Blauburgunder Trattmannhof, Vernatsch Fass
Nr. 9, Weissburgunder Plattenriegl*
Girlano's second cooperative demonstrated years ago
that Schiava is not only suitable for the production of
thin Lago di Caldaro (Kalterer See), but can also yield
complex red wines suitable for aging. On the initiative of
Hartmuth Spitaler, manager of the cooperative for many
years, artists' labels were introduced at a very early stage.

KELLEREIGENOSSENSCHAFT KURTATSCH***−****
CORTACCIO
*544 acres (221 ha); 2,500,000 bottles • Wines include:
Alto Adige: Cabernet Freienfeld, Merlot Brenntal,
Cabernet/Merlot Soma, Blauburgunder Frotzenhof,
Gewürztraminer Brenntal, →Chardonnay Eberlehof,
Lagrein Fohrhof, Grauvenatsch Sonntaler*
The 250 members of this winery own some of the best
sites surrounding the historic wine-growing village of
Cortaccio (Kurtatsch). The Soma is a *cuvée* produced
on Bordelais lines.

ALOIS LAGEDER/ANSITZ HIRSCHPRUNN**−*****
MAGRÉ
*119 acres (49 ha); some bought-in grapes; 950,000
bottles • Wines include: Südtiroler →Chardonnay and
Cabernet Löwengang, →Cabernet C.O.R. Römigberg,
Pinot Grigio Benefizium Porer, Pinot Bianco Haberlehof,
Sauvignon Lehenhof, →Hirschprunn I.G.T. Mitterberg
Bianco Contest, Etelle and Dronach, →Rosso Corolle*
Alois Lageder is one of the main players in Alto Adige
wine production, a role which he reinforced by
acquiring the Hirschprunn estate and building the
modern new winery in Magré.

2001
MANDOLAIA
VENDEMMIA TARDIVA

LA VIS

BARTHENAU
VIGNA S. URBANO
2000
J. Hofstätter

Lafòa
CABERNET SAUVIGNON

TIEFENBRUNNER
Feldmarschall
von Fenner zu Fennberg

MANINCOR***−*****
CALDARO
*87 acres (35 ha); 100,000 bottles • Wines: Alto Adige:
Terlaner Classico, Kalterer See Auslese, Moscato Giallo,
Cuvée Sophie, Lieben Aich, Pinot Noir Mason di
Mason, Merlot/Cabernet Sauvignon Cassiano*
Michael Graf Enzenberg's spectacular new winery building
generally produces decided individual wines, spontaneously
fermented and matured for a long time on fine yeasts.

JOSEF NIEDERMAYR**−*****
GIRLANO
*37 acres (15 ha); some bought-in grapes; 860,000
bottles • Wines: Südtiroler: →Sauvignon Naun
Barrique, →Lagrein from Gries Blacedelle and Riserva,
Gewürztraminer Doss; Kalterer See Auslese Ascherhof,
Terlaner Hof zu Pramol, →Aureus, →Euforius*
For a long time, Josef Niedermayr's winery stood in the
shadow of its more famous counterparts, but thanks to
the work of master winemaker Lorenz Martin, it has
recently begun to shine with its Lagrein, Pinot Noir and
Cabernet Sauvignon.

SCHRECKBICHL/COLTERNZIO****−*****
GIRLANO
*790 acres (320 ha); 1,200,000 bottles • Wines: Alto
Adige including Cabernet Sauvignon Lafòa, →Lagrein
Cornell, →Cabernet/Merlot Cornelius, Pinot Nero
Cornell Schwarzhaus Riserva, Gerwürztraminer
Cornell, Sauvignon Praedium Prail, Chardonnay
Praedium Pinay, →Pinot Nero Praedium St. Daniel*
With strict control of grape quality of the cooperative,
which numbers 310 members, Luis Raifer has made it
into one of the leading wineries in Alto Adige. The wine
comes in three quality levels, with the best wine being
marketed under the brand of Cornell.

TIEFENBRUNNER CASTELL TURMHOF***−****
CORTACCIO
*54 acres (22 ha); some bought-in grapes; 500,000
bottles • Wines include: →Müller-Thurgau
Feldmarschal von Fenner, Alto Adige: Gewürztraminer,
Lagrein, →Chardonnay Castel Turmhof,
→Rosenmuskateller Linticlarus*
Seldom has a Müller-Thurgau established such an
international reputation as has Feldmarschall von Fenner.
It grows at over 3,000 feet (1,000 m) on the Fennberg and
produces a sophisticated wine reminiscent of Sauvignon.
The best wines of the estate are sold under the brand name
Linticlarus.

Careful handling of the grapes.

Down the slope, step by step.

Wine harvesting as in olden times.

Friuli-Venezia Giulia

Friuli-Venezia Giulia, known as Friuli for short, reflects more than most other regions of Italy the myriad contrasts and different ethnic, cultural, and political influences of the country's past. This strip of land was inhabited as early as the Stone Age, over 40,000 years ago, and, like Veneto, the Karst plateau, or Carso as it is known locally, was populated by highly-developed Bronze Age cultures. The area has long been a transitory region for different ethnic groups, some of which engaged in viticulture at least 3,000 years ago.

One particular political development in the 15th century was to have a significant effect on culture and viticulture in Friuli. In 1420, Venice conquered the western part of the region, with Udine as its center, while the Habsburg empire gained control of the eastern part around Gorizia. The border along the river Judrio today still separates the best cultivation areas of Friuli, Colli Orientali, and Collio. The division of the western zone into one with more red varieties and the eastern zone into one with a preponderance of white varieties, reflects the wine preferences of the two former powers. While the red varieties benefit from the many hours of sunshine and an annual mean temperature of 50°F (15°C), the constant movement of air between the Alps and the sea, which gives rise to significant variations between the day and night temperatures, is ideal for the white varieties and enhances their aromas.

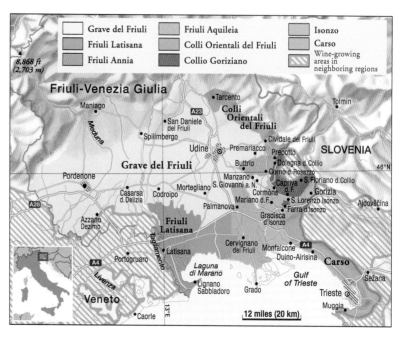

The Marco Felluga family successfully combines a medieval legacy with modern winery practices on its prestigious Russiz Superior estate where the winery is in a tunnel built into the slope.

In geological terms, Friuli is divided into two almost equally sized areas, the northernmost of which—the Alps and Alpine foothills—is unsuitable for vine cultivation. In contrast, the plains and hills of the southern area are dominated by soils which offer good conditions for viticulture: the morainic hills have dry, mineral-poor soils; the soils of the volcanic deposits are rich in minerals and trace elements; the alluvial plain has dry pebbly soil; and the soil in the coastal strip has sand, peat, and a high lime content. On the hills in the central area, the Cormòns *flysch*, a mix of marl and sandstone layers from the Eocene epoch, yields very lively complex wines.

Friuli's viticulture has a clearly identifiable structure. The region's eight viticulture zones line up, one next to the other, inside the protective arc of the Alps, and a specific range of vine varieties is authorized under each D.O.C. designation. The largest area is Grave del Friuli, which is located on the alluvial plain of the Tagliamento river. The coastal zones—Friuli Latisana, the newly-established Friuli Annia, and Friuli Aquileia—lie south of Grave del Friuli. With their excellent soils and ideal climate conditions, the hillside zones of Colli Orientali del Friuli and Collio (Collio Goriziano) yield wines which are the main source of the considerable prestige which the region has earned over the past two decades. Collio is bordered to the south by the Isonzo area, whose southeastern flank in turn borders the Carso, the Karst plateau which extends across the Slovenian border.

From Red to White to Red

Although Friuli is now best known as a white wine region, up to a few decades ago the region's winemaking was dominated by red varieties. In 1965, 80 percent of wines were based on dark grapes, mainly Merlot, the variety of preference following the ravages of phylloxera. It was only with the rise in consumer demand for clean white wines in the 1970s and 1980s that Friulian producers began to concentrate on Chardonnay, Pinot Gris, Sauvignon, and the indigenous variety Tocai Friulano. With the help of European Union subsidies, around 5,000 acres (2,000 ha) of mixed cultivation was transformed into specialized vineyards and many indigenous varieties eliminated in favor of popular international vines. Meanwhile, steel tanks and cooling machines for temperature-controlled reductive fermentation also arrived in the wineries, heralding a radical departure from the traditional style of production which tended to promote OXIDATION. The resulting success on national and international markets was impressive. The powerful aromatic white wines reflected contemporary tastes and quickly began to achieve astronomical prices.

In the 1990s, it was the turn of the red wines of Friuli to regain their prestige: initially Bordeaux blends, later single-varietal Merlot wines (whose name is all they have in common with the acidic sweet versions of the post-war period), and finally outstanding wines from indigenous varieties which had almost been allowed to die out.

If they can be used to produce expressive, individual wines which will stand out from the uniform products of other countries, these indigenous varieties represent the main opportunity available for future winemaking in Friuli. Great things are expected of the reds Refosco dal Peduncolo Rosso, Scioppettino, Pignolo, and Tazzelenghe, and the whites Tocai Friulano, Ribolla Gialla, Verduzzo, and Picolit.

Between Udine and Gorizia

The Colli Orientali hills, with their *flysch* soils, form a half-moon around the region's capital Udine and constitute the northwestern flank of the massif which includes Collio. They have great potential for red wines. High-quality Merlot, Cabernet, Schioppettino, Refosco, and Pignolo grapes thrive here, in particular on the southern slopes facing the Adriatic Sea. The single varietals and blends (often barrel-aged) produced from these grapes are powerful but elegant, combining a robust tannin structure with abundant fruit. In good years, they are among the best red wines produced in Italy.

The climate on the northern slopes of these hills is significantly cooler, making them eminently suited to the production of particularly powerful, interesting white wines which have a good alcohol content and benefit from barrel-aging. The sweet white wine Picolit is a regional specialty which, in terms of quality, is often exceeded by the similarly indigenous but not always sweet Verduzzo. This is particularly true of the Verduzzo wines originating from the separate D.O.C. zone Ramandolo, on the northwest flank of the Colli Orientali.

The great individual reds and the best Friulian whites come from Collio. Many Collio producers have vineyards on Slovenian soil and, thanks to a special E.U. regulation, are allowed to market them with Collio labels. The specialties from Collio include Sauvignon Blanc and Chardonnay, complemented by the indigenous Ribolla Gialla. Thanks to their good acid content, the wines from this area—which represent 85 percent of the region's production—retain their freshness when aged in *barriques* and are among the few white wines Italy has to offer that can truly compete at international level.

The carefully cultivated vineyards in Capriva del Friuli near Gorizia bear witness to the ambition of the region's producers who cultivate impressive red varieties on the southern slopes and very pure white Collio on northern slopes.

THE FRIULIAN PLAINS AND THE CARSO

While Collio and Colli Orientali enhanced the reputation of Friulian wine production, developments in the region's other zones followed quite a different course. Grave, Aquileia, Latisana, and Annia offer little more than well-made, pleasant, everyday reds. Some expressive varieties are grown in the Carso (Karst) area, but their wines are rather unusual for international tastes. Around a dozen of the Isonzo producers have succeeded in making the transition to the regional and, in some cases, national elite.

With more than 15,000 acres (6,000 ha) of vineyard, the Grave del Friuli zone represents only about one third of the total Friulian area, though it produces two thirds of the region's volume. The area starts in the west at the Livenza plain, and continues along the Tagliamento and Judrio rivers which form the border with Veneto, and across to the hills of Collio and Colli Orientali. The zone's name, Grave, is derived from the gravelly soils of the alluvial plain. While the fertile limy soils of the zone's south and western areas are only suited to industrial viniculture and the production of basic wines, the barren stony soils of the moraine landscape in the Tagliamento valley and the alluvial deposits produce rather appealing wines.

The Grave del Friuli whites of distinctive freshness and character are produced from the vines grown near the mountains on soils composed of glacier deposits.

ALONG THE COAST

The D.O.C. zones of Aquileia, Annia, and Latisana are located along the coast between the town of Grado and the Veneto border. The deep fertile soils of Aquileia, which lies furthest east and is named after the Roman garrison whose ruins can be visited there, yield light wines which must be drunk when young. There is little to report about Friuli Annia, the youngest D.O.C. area, as its establishment was the outcome of the granting of a political favor to one of Italy's largest private wineries. In the Latisana area, enormous volumes of grapes are ripened in vast vineyards for the production of uninteresting wines. The areas where the deep loamy soils are richer in minerals sometimes yield pleasant, light, everyday wines.

The situation in Isonzo, which lies south of Collio in the region of the same name, is somewhat better. This predominantly flat area, whose soils are heavy and calcareous, particularly in the south, was underestimated for a long time. The producers in northern Isonzo have meanwhile proved that the white and red wines they produced on sandy and gravelly soils could earn a place at the top of the Friulian league.

The Carso zone is located on a barren, elevated plateau with calcareous soil, an unusual site whose Bora vines are generally unprotected from the cold east winds. Despite the raw climate, wine has been produced here for centuries, with varieties such as Malvasia and Terrano—a Refosco variant—dominating. Terrano, with its hard tannins, is undrinkable when young and can only be appreciated by experienced palates. Few producers succeed in creating a pleasant wine with this variety. Finally, one last Carso rarity deserves a mention: white Vitovska, whose stringent aroma is unlikely to find appreciation outside of the region.

Picolit and Verduzzo

Friuli provides one of the best-known sweet wines of northern Italy, based on and named after the indigenous variety of Picolit. For a long time, Picolit was one of the most famous wines of the land; it was cultivated extensively in the late 18th century, and from the mid-19th century it was consumed in the royal courts of Austria, France, England, Russia, and Tuscany. However, the legendary reputation of this sweet wine, which was often compared with Château d'Yquem, failed to last in the 20th century. The vine now survives on barely 500 acres (200 ha) and only around 100,000 bottles are produced each year. Picolit can develop a rich aroma of flowers, honey, and figs with notes of ripe apple and pears. Although the wines are much sought-after and expensive, their quality is, for the most part, questionable.

Verduzzo, the second of Friuli's sweet varieties, yields delightful and dense dessert wines, particularly in Ramandolo. The vineyards climb to heights of 1,200 feet (370 m) along the ridges of Monte Bernadia where intensive daytime sun and a drastic reduction in temperatures at night ensure the development of its clear aromas. The yields are low and, following the drying of the grapes, the volumes seldom exceed 320 gallons per acre (30 hl/ha). Verduzzo does not enjoy the same prestige and reputation as Picolit and is hence less expensive.

Select Producers in Friuli-Venezia Giulia

Borc Dodòn****–*****
Villa Vicentina Udine
21 acres (8.5 ha); 8,500 bottles • Wines: →Cabernet Franc/Cabernet Sauvignon Uìs Neris, Tocai/Sauvignon/Verduzzo Uìs Blàncis, →Refosco dal Pedunculo Rosso
Denis Montanar has been using biodynamic methods for years. The reds are among the finest in Friuli.

Dorigo****–*****
Buttrio
79 acres (32 ha); 180,000 bottles • Wines include C.O.F. Ronc di Jury: →Chardonnay, Sauvignon, Pinot Nero, →Pignolo; Picolit Vigneto Montsclapade; Refosco; Spumante Pinot Nero Pas Dosé
Modern vineyard practices with high stock density and low-growing vines were introduced in the 1980s.

Il Carpino****
Oslavia
37 acres (15 ha); 60,000 bottles • Wines: Il Carpino Collio: Ribolla Gialla, →Sauvignon, Malvasia, Chardonnay, Cabernet Sauvignon-Merlot Rosso Carpino, Vigna Runc: Pinot Grigio, Chardonnay, Sauvignon
Half of the permitted maximum yields, thorough grape selection, and fermenting in wooden barrels give the Il Carpino white wines character and volume. Vigna Runc is produced by the estate's younger vines and is matured in steel tanks.

Livio Felluga***–****
Cormòns
334 acres (135 ha); 650,000 Bottles • Wines: C.O.F.: Tocai Friulano, Pinot Grigio, Sauvignon, Refosco, Picolit; →Merlot Riserva Rosazzo Sossò, →Terre Alte
Merlot Sossò is one of Friuli's most lively whites.

Marco Felluga/Russiz Superiore***–****
Gradisca/Capriva
479 acres (194 ha); 850,000 bottles • Wines include: Collio: Chardonnay, Tocai Friulano, Pinot Bianco, Pinot Grigio, Sauvignon; →Molamatta, →Carantan; Russiz Superiore Collio: Pinot Bianco, →Rosso degli Orzoni
Apart from the winery in Gradisca, this house also owns estates in Capriva (Russiz Superiore), Buttrio and in the Chianti Classico region.

Ronco del Gnemiz****–*****
San Giovanni al Natisone
26 acres (10.5 ha); 65,000 bottles • Wines include: C.O.F.: Ribolla Gialla, Sauvignon, Müller-Thurgau, Pinot Grigio, Tocai Friulano, →Chardonnay, Picolit, Verduzzo, →Rosso del Gnemiz, Schiopettino
Recommended: Chardonnay, Rosso del Gnemiz, Sauvignon, Pinot Grigio, Müller-Thurgau.

Josko Gravner***–*****
Gorizia
43 acres (17.5 ha); 40,000 bottles • Wines: Ribolla Collio, →Breg, Rosso Gravner, →Ruino
Instead of *barriques*, this house now uses gigantic earthenware amphorae in its winery. The oxidized and concentrated wines do not really fit into the Friuli range of tastes, but are nonetheless among the greatest wines of Italy.

Vinnaioli Jermann***–****
Farra d'Isonzo
106 acres (43 ha); 28,000 bottles • Wines: Vinnae, →Vintage Tunina, →Where the Dreams have no End..., Sogno Terra Promessa..., Capo Martino, Chardonnay, Riesling Renano, Pinot Bianco, Moscato Rosa Vigna Bellina, Engelwhite, Cabernet, Traminer Aromatico, Pinot Grigio, Sauvignon, Tocai Italico
The wines from this house enjoy cult status.

Livon***–****
San Giovanni al Natisone
272 acres (110 ha); 450,000 bottles • Wines include: C.O.F. Pinot Grigio, Braide Grande, Refosco Riûl; Collio: Chardonnay Tre Clâs, Masarotte, Tocai Fruilano Ronc di Zorz, Sauvignon Gravalunga, Pinot Bianco Cavezzo, Plazate, →Tiareblù, Schioppettino Picotis, →Picolit Cumins, Moscato Giallo Planeces, Verduzzo Casali Godia
This estate has vineyards in the region's best locations.

Miani–Enzo Pontoni*****
Buttrio
28.5 acres (11.5 ha); 12,000 bottles • Wines: C.O.F.: Tocai Friulano, →Ribolla Gialla, Sauvignon, Merlot; →Miani Rosso, Miani Bianco
The old Merlot, Tocai and Refosco vines yield some of Friuli's best wines.

Mario Schipetto***–****
Capriva
74 acres (30 ha); 200,000 bottles • Wines: Collio: Tocai Friulano, Pinot Bianco, Pinot Grigio, Sauvignon, Malvasia Istriana; Merlot, Cabernet Franc; Rivarossa, Blanc des Rosis, Müller-Thurgau, Riesling Renano, Ribolla Gialla
Mario Schipetto has made sound investments in a modern winery and new vineyards in Collio and Colli Orientali.

Borgo del Tiglio/Nicola Maerrari****–*****
Cormons
20 acres (8 ha); 40,000 bottles • Wines: Collio including Tocai Friulano Ronco della Chiesa, Sauvignon, Chardonnay; Collio Bianco, Collio Rosso, →Rosso della Centa, →Studio
Recommended: Merlot Rosso della Centa. The quality of the white wines improved even more in the 1990s.

Vie de Romans—S. Gallio****
Mariano del Friuli
40 acres (16 ha); 100,000 bottles • Wines include: Isonzo: →Chardonnay Ciampagnis Vieris and Vie di Romans, Pinot Grigio Dessimis, Tocai Friulano, →Sauvignon Piere and Vieris, →Flors de Uis, Voos dai Ciamps
Sauvignon Vieris is one of the first Friulian quality wines to be produced from this variety.

Le Vigne di Zamò***–*****
Manzano
111 acres (45 ha); 250,000 bottles • Wines include: Series →Abazzia di Rosazzo, →Vigne dal Leon and Villa Belvedere
Estate bottled by three estates in Colli Orientali. The white Ronco delle Acacie, Cabernet Sauvignon, Pignolo and Refosco, plus the red Ronco dei Roseti blend, are among the best in Friuli.

Villa Russiz****
Capriva
74 acres (30 ha); 130,000 bottles • Wines: Collio: Malvasia Istriana, Pinot Bianco, Pinot Grigio, Tocai Friulano, Sauvignon; →Sauvignon de la Tour, Merlot Collio, →Gräfin de la Tour, →Graf de la Tour
Top wines for a good cause: Villa Russiz also boasts a foundation for orphans.

Zidarich***–****
Duino-Aurisina
15 acres (6 ha); 13,000 bottles • Wines: Carso: Vitovska, →Malvasia, Terrano, Prulke
Benjamin Zidarich will have no truck with fashionable vines. In the vineyards which he took over from his father, he grows Terrano, Vitovska and Malvasia. In the winery, too, all up-to-date equipment is lacking, but instead there are large wooden barrels which are used for the fermentation and solid aging of the wines.

VENETO: THE WEST

Along with Sicily and Apulia, Veneto is one of Italy's most prolific winemaking regions. Around 211 million gallons (8 million hl) are produced from its approximately 40 cultivated vine varieties, a quarter of which enjoy D.O.C. status. This means that the region produces almost one fifth of Italian quality wines. However, a sharp west-east divide exists in terms of the reputation and quality of its wines. While the province of Verona in the west, with its Soave, Valpolicella, and Bardolino, produces some of the most popular Italian wines—and, with Amarone, one of the country's great reds—the wines of the Breganze, Colli Berici, and Colli Euganei, Pave, and Lison-Pramaggiore zones are virtually anonymous. Prosecco is the only wine produced in the east which has succeeded in establishing a strong D.O.C. designation and its quality varies considerably.

The region's wine-growing areas extend from Lake Garda along the Alpine foothills to the Adriatic lagoon at Venice and the borders of Friuli. The vineyards on the slopes are south-facing and are effectively sheltered from the cold north winds by the Alps. Soil types include morainic gravel at Lake Garda, mainly Dolomite residual gravel as well as fertile fields and alluvial deposits in the plains.

The predominant white vine variety cultivated in Veneto is the high-yielding Garganega which is the main constituent of Soave and Gambellara wines. Its aromatic potential can only fully unfold on particularly thin soils where it can yield fragrant white wines with fine lemon and almond aromas. The red varieties cultivated in the region include Corvina Veronese, Corvinone, Rondinella, and Molinara. Corvina is also the base wine for Recioto, the sweet variant of Valpolicella. The ubiquitous international varieties Chardonnay, Cabernet, and Merlot are also cultivated in the vineyards of Veneto.

Soave is undoubtedly Veneto's best-known wine and its most important in terms of quantity. It is produced from Garganega supplemented with Chardonnay, Pinot Blanc, or Trebbiano and cultivated on around 16,000 acres (6,500 ha) of vineyard, most of which lie within the alluvial plain of the river Adige, whose fertile soils make it difficult to control the yields. The fresh, delicate wines, with fine, almond notes which lie behind Soave's widespread success only thrive on the volcanic soils of the Classico zone around Soave and Monteforte d'Alpone.

Valpolicella, the red counterpart of Soave, originates from the valleys to the north of Verona. As in the case of Soave, the Valpolicella zone is divided into two parts. The Classico zone around San Pietro in Cariano, Fumane, and Negrar produces very interesting, intense wines from grapes which ripen at heights between 490 and 1,500 feet (150 and 450 m). Meanwhile, the mass-consumption wines that line supermarket shelves throughout Europe are produced in the areas in the Adige valley, which were added to the zone in 1968.

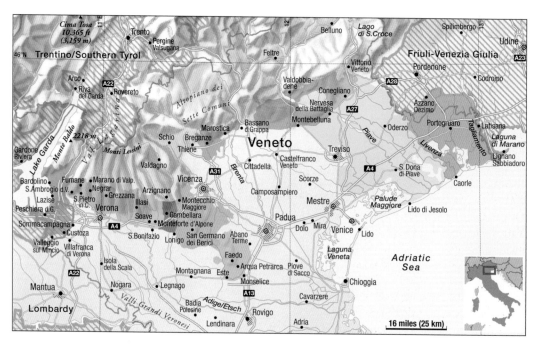

Quintarelli

The estate on the hills above Negrar has almost 30 acres (12 ha) of vineyards, most of which belong to the Classico zone of Valpolicella. The barren soils consist of volcanic basalt. Good ventilation of the rows of vines prevents rotting and other diseases, largely avoiding the need for spraying.

Quintarelli started testing new varieties as early as the 1980s when Cabernet Franc and Sauvignon, Sangiovese, Nebbiolo, Croatina, Garganega, Saorin, and Trebbiano Toscano joined the traditional Valpolicella varieties Corvina, Rondinella, and Molinara. Some of them were used in the production of Valpolicella and a Cabernet table wine called Alzero was created, produced in a similar way to Amarone.

Perfect raisining, i.e. drying, is the key to Quintarelli winemaking. Unripe or rotting grapes are eliminated during harvesting which is carried out by hand. Following a second check, the grapes are spread out in flat slatted boxes. During the slow drying process, depending on the ventilation, humidity, and

Negrar, a wine-producing village in the Valpolicella zone.

temperature, BOTRYTIS CINEREA develops and Quintarelli has worked out exactly how to control the NOBLE ROT to prevent premature oxidation and ensure that the wines are perfectly matured.

In early February, when three quarters of the water has evaporated from the grapes, they are pressed and macerated. After around 20 days, alcoholic fermentation with the natural yeasts

begins. This takes 45 to 50 days. Recioto and Amarone age for seven years in Slovenian oak casks. Alzero spends 30 months in French *barriques* and the same period again in large Slovenian oak containers. The residual sugar results in further fermentation during cask maturation, which gives the wines their high alcohol content of 14 to 15 percent and particularly luxurious aromas. While Amarone and Alzero are mostly dry when bottled, only Recioto from the best years still has a high level of residual sugar. Amarone Riserva and Recioto Riserva are rare highlights: the best casks in the best years yield little more than 2,500 bottles of each.

At Quintarelli, normal Valpolicella also enjoys careful handling. Macerated, fermented on the skins for seven days and filled in tanks, it is then left waiting until April when the Amarone is racked off and it is then pumped onto the Amarone skins. The residual sugar triggers the second fermentation of the Valpolicella which gives it the strength it needs to ferment for six years in Slovenian oak casks without wasting away.

A proportion of the Valpolicella grapes—above all Corvina, Rondinella, and Molinara—has always been dried on timber racks after harvesting. The grapes were then pressed in December or January and their high sugar concentration prevented the musts from fermenting fully. The sweet wine yielded by this process was Recioto della Valpolicella. However, some of the zone's natural yeasts are capable of converting the high sugar content of raisined grapes into alcohol. Amarone, an opulent powerful red wine with a high alcohol content, was born when this phenomenon was systematically exploited for the first time in the 1950s. Its production has been perfected in the interim: the wines are now produced in accordance with modern enological methods and sometimes also aged in *barriques*, an innovation which has served them well. In the second half of the 1990s production of Amarone wines was more than doubled in response to growing demand, and prices rose as well. Many wine lovers now regard Amarone as one of the top Italian wines, comparable with Barolo and Brunello di Montalcino.

A third Valpolicella variant was created in the 1970s and 1980s when the producers reflected on the Ripasso technique and added fermented Valpolicella to the pressed skins of the fermented Recioto or Amarone to re-ferment it with the residual sugars and yeasts. These wines are often bottled under the D.O.C. designation Superiore or as table wines.

Bianco di Custoza dominates the large group of neutral white wines produced in Veneto. Its zone extends from the southwest of Verona to Lake Garda. Its taste is characterized by the Soave grape Garganega as well as the "grape-of-all-trades," Trebbiano Toscano.

Custoza's next-door neighbor is red Bardolino. Although this is produced from the same grapes as Valpolicella, it is a lighter-tasting wine. The rosé version, Bardolino Chiaretto, is often more interesting than actual Bardolino.

Recioto and Amarone of astounding quality are bottled in the village of Garganago near Sant' Ambrogio di Valpolicella.

VENETO: THE EAST

In Veneto, few quality wines are found outside of the province of Verona. Despite the fact that the eastern part of the region has extensive vineyards, high-quality production is a rarity. The few examples of quality production in the east are down to the efforts of individual maverick producers rather than the established characteristics of the region as a whole. The eastern zones start in the Gambarella area, the counterpart of Soave in the province of Vicenza—where, apart from a well-known large winery which has holdings and production centers in all of the important regions, only one single small producer occasionally attracts attention—and extend along two strips to the east, the first in a more southerly direction via Colli Berici and Colli Euganei toward the Po delta,

Does such a ripe firm Trebbiano grape justify the pride of the Soave producer?

and the second from Breganze along the edge of the Alps up to Conegliano and further east to the border of Friuli. It is difficult to understand why Colli Berici and Colli Euganei remain unknown to a wider public, as the morainic and volcanic soils of these hills, between the Alpine foothills and the Adriatic Sea, offer ideal conditions for the production of high-quality wines. This is borne out by a small group of producers who have been producing lively whites and dense reds for years. The international varieties Chardonnay, Pinot Blanc, Sauvignon, and Tocai are as common there as the red varieties Cabernet and Merlot. The Moscato wine, Fior d'Arancio, is a particular specialty of Colli Euganei. In its best guise as a Passito, it has a dense golden-yellow color and

Prosecco

The origin of the Prosecco grape, which yields a fresh neutral white wine suitable for sparkling production, is disputed. Some say it comes from the village of the same name near Udine and is similar to the indigenous Friulian variety Grela, others say it originates from Dalmatia.

The sparkling version of this wine can probably be explained by a quirk of nature. The fermentation of the late-ripening Prosecco grapes was sometimes interrupted by frost in the winter months so that the wine still has some carbon dioxide and residual sugar in spring. The history of the success of this wine started in the 19th century when Antonio Carpené and three partners founded a company with the intention of producing champagne. However, they did not produce champagne and instead, Prosecco di Conegliano-Valdobbiadene became a very popular and fashionable tipple. Nowadays, around 20 million bottles of Spumante are produced annually by means of secondary fermentation in pressurized tanks. If the product of this tank fermentation process is bottled after one month of storage with a bottle pressure of at least three atmospheres, it may legally be labeled *Spumante*, i.e. sparkling wine. If it does not reach this pressure, it must be labeled *Frizzante*, i.e. fizzy or semi-sparkling wine. Prosecco Spumante clearly yields higher prices than Frizzante; however, in qualitative terms the difference between the two is not always detectable. The Prosecco wines from the Cartizze zone, which generally have more residual sugar, are controversial. They are often more expensive but seldom better than Prosecco originating from the zone of the same name.

Prosecco needs a protective wire cap to prevent it from popping open.

Good Prosecco is also bottled in the Cartizze hills.

Prosecco develops its delicate bubbles in pressurized stainless steel tanks.

Select Producers in Veneto

Allegrini***−*****
Fumane
104 acres (42 ha); 370,000 bottles • Wines include: Valpolicella Classico: →Superiore La Grola, →Palazzo della Torre; →Amarone, Amarone Fieramonte, →Recioto Giovanni Allegrini, →La Poja
This house was behind the innovation in Valpolicella and produces noteworthy wines from the grapes of the La Grola vineyard in Sant'Ambrosio and from the highest plot, La Poja. These wines are among the most lively in the region.

Roberto Anselmi***−*****
Monteforte d'Alpone
111 acres (45 ha); 350,000 bottles • Wines include: Capitel Croce, Soave Classico Capitel Foscarino, Recioto I Capitelli, Cabernet Realda
With barrel aging, single-vineyard bottlings and an outstanding dessert wine, Ansemi in the 1980s served as an inspiration to the region's producers in more than one respect.

Ca'La Bionda***−*****
Marano dal Valpolicella
49 acres (20 ha); 110,000 bottles • Wines: Amarone della Valpolicella Vigneti di Ravazol, Recioto, →Valpolicella Classico Superiore
The Castellanis have been cultivating their hillside locations in the heart of Valpolicella for four generations. Since Allessandro took over running the winery, the estate has gone up in quality; the wines are amazingly mineral and cool.

Ca'Lustra***−****
Faedo di Cinto Euganio
52 acres (21 ha); 150,000 bottles • Wines: Cabernet Vigna Girapoggio, Chardonnay Vigna Marco, Sauvignon del Veneto, Spumante Fior d'Arancio
The single vineyard wines come from the best granite soils and provide a high degree of smooth, rounded drinking pleasure.

Romano dal Forno****−*****
Cellore d'Illasi
62 acres (25 ha); 26,000 bottles • Wines: Valpolicella superiore, →Amarone, Recioto
Extremely concentrated, dense, dark-colored wines. Despite long aging in new *barriques*, the wood does not dominate. The Amarone is of cult status and is usually sold out in advance.

Roccolo Grassi**−****
Mezzane di Sotto
30 acres (12 ha); 23,000 bottles • Wines: Soave Superiore La Broia, Valpolicella Superiore Roccolo Grassi, Amarone Roccolo Grassi, →Recioto Valpolicella, Recioto Soave
A young, modern operation with polished, elegant wines with a *barrique* note: the Roccolo Grassi vineyard is impressive, in particular the Recioto Valpolicella.

Maculan***−*****
Breganze
87 acres (35 ha); some bought-in grapes; 600,000 bottles • Wines include: Prato di Canzio; Breganze: di Breganze, Rosso Brentino and Marchesante, Cabernet, Cabernet Palazotto, →Cabernet Fratta and Ferrara, →Chardonnay Ferrata, Sauvignon Ferrata, Torcolato, Acini Nobili
Part vineyard with revolutionary dense planting of vines, based on the French model, and part winery, Macula produces extraordinary wines. The specialty is the sweet Acini Nobili, which however does develop its noble rot in a climate-controlled room.

Masi/Boscaini**−****
Sant'Ambrogio
395 acres (160 ha); some bought-in grapes; 9,000,000 bottles • Wines include: Masi: Amarone: →Mazzano, →Campolongo di Torbe, →Vajo Amaron Serego Alighieri; Recioto Classico: Mezzanella, Casal dei Ronchi Serego Alighieri; Valpolicella Classico, Soave Classico, Bardolino Classico, I.G.T. Veronese: Brolo di Campofiorin, Rosso Osar, →Toar
In addtion to simple consumer wines, this house can offer all the region's top products, including the Ripasso wine Brolo di Campofiorin and Toar, which is mainly produced from almost extinct grape varieties.

Leonildo Pieropan****
Soave
79 acres (32 ha); 300,000 bottles • Wines: Soave Classico: Vigneto Calvarino and →Vigneto La Rocca, Recioto di Soave Le Colombare
The single-vineyard La Rocca (100% Garganega) and Calvarino (70% Garganega, 30% Trebbiano di Soave) wines are convincing due to their concentration, lush fruit and freshness. Good aging potential.

Giuseppe Quintarelli****
Negrar
38 acres (15.5 ha); 60,000 bottles • Wines: Amarone, Recioto Classico, Valpolicella Classico Superiore Monte Paletta (Rosso Ca' del Merlo), Alzero Cabernet Franc
The legend of the Valpolicella zone (see panel on preceding double page).

Serafini & Vidotto***−****
Nervesa della Battaglia
31 acres (12.5 ha); 65,000 bottles • Wines: Montello e Colli Asolani: Prosecco, Chardonnay, Cabernet, Merlot; Rosso dell' Abbazia, Pinot Nero
The Rosso d'Abbazia, a classic Bordeaux blend, is evidence that distinctive wines can also be produced in the eastern Veneto.

Fratelli Speri***−****
San Pietro in Cariano
148 acres (60 ha); 500,000 bottles • Wines: →Valpolicella Classico, →Amarone, Recioto
A large part of the harvest is sold to wine houses in the neighborhood, where they are used in the most famous *cuvées* of the Valpolicella region. But the product with the Speri label also belong to the elite.

Fratelli Tedeschi***−****
San Pietro in Cariano
52 acres (21 ha); some bought-in grapes; 400,000 bottles • Wines: Valpolicella Classico Superiore Capitel delle Lucchine, Amarone del la Fabriseria, →Capitel Monte Olmi, Recioto Classico Monte Fontana, →Vin de la Fabriseria San Rocco, Capitel San Rocco delle Lucchine, →Soave Classico Monte Tenda, Capitel San Rocco Bianco
The Amarone selections, Recioto, and the Ripasso wine Capitel Monte Olmi are among the best Valpolicella has to offer.

Villa dal Ferra***
San Germano dei Berici
15 acres (6.25 ha); 60,000 bottles • Wines: Colli Berici: Cabernet Le Rive Rosse, Merlot Campo del Lago, Pinot Bianco Bianco del Rocolo, Sauvignon Monte Cavallo, Tocai Costiera Granda; Pinot Nero Rosso del Rocolo, Riesling del Veneto Busa Calcara
The only Colli Berici house which produces distinctive quality wines. Donato Lanati, one of Italy's best enologists, is employed there. Radical new vineyard plantings ensure a good foundation for the future.

Not only indigenous varieties, such as Vespaiolo or Gropello, grow on the flat hills and gravelly soils near Breganze, but, thanks to the warm microclimate, Cabernet Sauvignon also matures well.

an aroma of honey and exotic fruit combined with a clear but successfully integrated sweetness. It is one of Veneto's most impressive dessert wines.

REVOLUTIONARY VINEYARDS

Breganze, the wine-growing area around the small town on the edge of the Alps, has the Maculan winery to thank for the prestige it now enjoys. In the late 1980s, Maculan initiated a modest revolution in its vineyards when it replaced its traditional, very high-yielding, tall cultivation systems with new vines planted in

the best French manner at a density of up to 4,000 vines per acre (10,000 vines/ha). The vines were pruned to unusually low heights in accordance with the Guyot system of cane pruning, which is named after the French scientist who was responsible for its promulgation in the 19th century. Unusual things also started to happen in the Maculan winery. After harvesting, the grapes were stored in a specially constructed, extremely humid, climate chamber until they developed the botrytis rot which they did not form naturally in the vineyard.

In the Montello e Colli Asolani zone, Serafini and Vitotto were responsible for the introduction

of similarly revolutionary modern winemaking techniques and achieved results which left the Venegazzù estate of Conte Gasparini, who was the area's most prestigious producer in the 1970s, far behind.

The Prosecco zone starts on the far side of the Colli Asolani. Under the regulations defined for the D.O.C. Prosecco di Conegliano-Valdobbiadene, irrespective of where the grapes were actually grown, the wine may bear the name of either of the two townships as its designation of origin. This is intended to guarantee a certain level of quality, while offering the producers a degree of flexibility.

The wide Piave plain and the area bordering Friuli north of the Venetian lagoon complete the account of winemaking in this region. The extensive vineyards yield simple, mass-consumption wines which have no distinctive characteristics. Here, Ornella Molon, Conte Collalto, Rechsteiner, and some other producers have shown that with rigorous yield control and careful vinification it is possible to produce decent wines even on the fertile soils of Piave. Their Cabernet-Merlot blends were impressive but the influence of the wines made from the extremely acidic native Raboso variety has failed to penetrate beyond the immediate locality.

EMILIA ROMAGNA

Cozy wine bars are part of the national culture.

which are flushed out by the numerous rivers winding their way to the Adriatic Sea. As is the case all over the Po plain, the climate is very damp and precipitation often takes the form of dense fog. The summers are hot and humid while the winters are rainy and cold. The mountains and hills include the northern end of the Tuscan-Emilian Apennines. The soils here are more barren—depending on the zone, they consist of residual pebbles and red loam—and, thanks to the good air circulation, the climate is also less humid.

With an annual production volume in excess of 158 million gallons (six million hl), Emilia Romagna is Italy's fourth biggest wine producer after Sicily, Apulia, and Veneto. Most of the vines grow in heavy fertile soils on flat ground and, like the adjacent wheat and sugar beet crops, give particularly high yields. Depending on the year, only 12 to 15 percent of the total production is accounted for by quality wines.

If Lombardy and Milan are identified as Italy's head, Emilia Romagna can confidently be described as its stomach. This region, which ranges from the northern slopes of the Apennines to the southeast of the Po plain, mainly cultivates wheat and sugar beet on its 150,000 farms. Reflecting the advanced mechanization of agricultural processes and optimum use of agrichemicals, more crops are produced here per acre of agricultural land than in any other region in Italy.

In topographical terms, the region is divided into an extensive plain and the Apennine mountains. The lowlands consist of alluvial soils

IT DOESN'T ALWAYS HAVE TO BUBBLE

The belief that only fizzy semi-sparkling wines go well with the heavy local cuisine, with its fatty pork specialties, appears to be widely held in Parma, Modena, Reggio, and surroundings. Not only is Lambrusco bottled with varying degrees of fizz, but Barbera and other varieties also sparkle. Dry still wines are more a specialty of Romagna, the eastern part of the region which nestles into the Adriatic and borders the

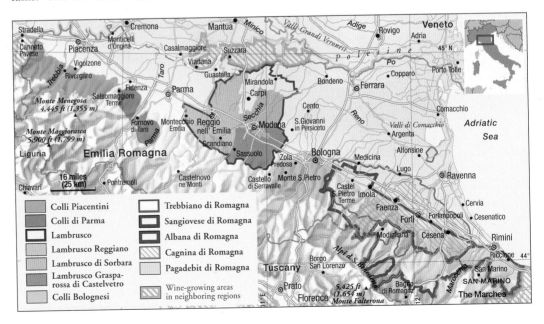

Colli Piacentini
Colli di Parma
Lambrusco
Lambrusco Reggiano
Lambrusco di Sorbara
Lambrusco Graspa-rossa di Castelvetro
Colli Bolognesi

Trebbiano di Romagna
Sangiovese di Romagna
Albana di Romagna
Cagnina di Romagna
Pagadebit di Romagna

Wine-growing areas in neighboring regions

Select Producers in Emilia Romagna

Castelluccio**
Modigliana
47 acres (19 ha); 40,000 bottles • Wines: Ronco della Simia, →Ronco delle Ginestre, →Ronco dei Ciliegi, Le More, Lunaria
Standards are being maintained even in the wake of the departure of Gian Matteo Baldi, who was responsible for the development of the Sangiovese variants and blends.

Umberto Cesari−****
Castel San Pietro Terme
222 acres (90 ha); bought-in grapes; 1,400,000 bottles • Wines include: →Sangiovese Riserva, Liano, Albana Passita, Colle del Re, Trebbiano, Vigneto del Parolino
Recommended: Cabernet/Sangiovese Liano.

Fattoria Zerbina – Germiniani*−****
Faenza
74 acres (30 ha); 190,000 bottles • Wines: Sangiovese di Romagna: Ceregio, Pietramora, Torre di Ceparano; →Albana di Romagna Scacco Matto, →Marzeno di Marzeno

This producer's top wine, the Albana Passito Scacco Matto, has attained D.O.C.G. status.

La Stoppa**
Rivergaro
59 acres (24 ha); 220,000 bottles • Wines: Bianco Ancarano, Sauvignon Colli Piacentini, Chardonnay Spumante Brut, Rosso Ancarano Frizzante; Colli Piacentini: Malvasia, Gutturnio, Barbera; →Macchiona, →Alfeo, →Stoppa, Buca delle Canne
Elena Pantaleone offers quality that is a rarity in this region, while maintaining regional flair.

La Tosa – Pizzamiglio*−****
Vigolzone
25 acres (10 ha); 60,000 bottles • Wines: Colli Piacentini: including Valnure, Sauvignon, Malvasia Sorriso di Cielo, Gutturnio Vignamorello, Cabernet; Luna Selvatica
This winery produces some of the best Emilian wines from the classical varieties of the Nure valley.

Marches. Albana di Romagna, the first Italian white wine to be awarded D.O.C.G. status, is produced here. This thriving variety, which needs abundant humidity, is extremely high-yielding as is reflected in the D.O.C.G. regulations which authorize a yield of 1,070 gallons per acre (100 hl/ha). Its sweet Passito version is, however, more interesting.

The other white varieties found in Romagna, Pagadebit and Trebbiano di Romagna, are

Legendary balsamic vinegar

Aceto Balsamico Tradizionale di Modena (traditional balsamic vinegar of Modena) and Aceto Balsamico Tradizionale di Reggio Emilia (traditional balsamic vinegar of Emilia Romagna) are the finest thing that can be made from Trebbiano grapes. The mean annual volumes produced do not exceed 795 gallons (3,000 l). Balsamic vinegar is made from concentrated Trebbiano must and aged for at least 12 years in a series of barrels that are usually made from a variety of woods. It is sold in bottles containing around 3 fluid ounces (100 ml) and, used sparingly by the drop, adds an exquisite taste to refined dishes.

equally prone to excessive yields. The situation with respect to the red variety Sangiovese di Romagna is somewhat better, at least in parts of the region, although it does not achieve anything like the results yielded by its Tuscan cousin. The most that can be expected from this *appellation* is clean, drinkable wines. The wines from the other Emilia Romagna D.O.C. zones—Colli Bolognesi, Colli di Parma, and Colli Piacentini—are mostly light, semi-sparkling, and more or less sweet, and seldom display any interesting qualities.

The almost hopeless situation in winemaking in this region is down to the dominant position of the cooperatives. Almost all of the producers are cooperative members and the largest of these processes grapes from 67,000 acres (27,000 ha) of vineyards, which is more than one quarter of the area covered by Germany's vineyards. The cooperatives pursue a volume-oriented market policy and wield significant influence.

Lambrusco

Like Prosecco, Lambrusco is first a grape variety, or more specifically a whole group of more than 40 different varieties. Traditional Lambrusco can be a wine of excellent quality which bears very little or no resemblance to the inferior product which has flooded the pizzerias of the world in recent decades. Unfortunately, the cooperatives have allowed this artisan wine to decline into a sticky sweet oddity and have even packaged their product in aluminum cans in order to create better marketing opportunities.

The qualities of traditional Lambrusco are, however, being rediscovered. Smaller producers are now offering wines under the Lambrusco di Sorbara, Lambrusco di Castelvetro, and Lambrusco di Salamino di Santa Croce *appellations* which are relatively dry with a bitter-fruity taste and which, in this—and only this!—guise, are truly a suitable accompaniment to the region's robust cuisine.

The Marches

The Marches alternates between worlds, both geographically and in its wines. At its northern end, it is an extension of Romagna with its popular beaches, at its southern, the wilder landscape of Abruzzi. The Marches shares varieties, soils, and climate with almost all of the neighboring regions—and hence also its wine types—which is one of the reasons why, in the past, its reputation as a winemaking region was underdeveloped. Although its proximity to the popular resorts of Rimini and Riccione traditionally provided a captive market for its products, this factor also stifled efforts to establish quality winemaking. Why invest all that effort and money when it wasn't really necessary? For decades, white Verdicchio wine was the only product which succeeded in establishing a reputation beyond the region's borders, and the wine's amphora-shaped bottle—a stroke of genius of the Milanese marketing specialists—probably had more to do with its fame than the quality of the content.

And yet traditionally in the Marches, better quality-quantity balance was struck between white and red wines than in Umbria, where Orvieto prevails, or in the Sangiovese stronghold of Tuscany. In recent decades, the region's quality spectrum shifted from white to red wines based on the Montepulciano and Sangiovese varieties. Viticulture in the Marches covers large expanses of the hills in the hinterland of the

Adriatic beaches and occasionally even extends right down to the coast, for example the cliff massifs south of the regional capital Ancona. The temperate influence of the sea, which reaches inland as far as the first hill ranges, contrasts with the climate of the Apennine and Abruzzian valleys which are buried deep in the region's interior. The cooler harsher climate here brings its own characteristics to the fore and appears to have a particularly good influence on the white wines, which are fresher and more lively than those produced from coastal vines.

Red Wine with a Sea View

The Marches' best-known and best-quality red wine, Rosso Conero, grows almost directly by the sea in the coastal area around Ancona. Often a single variety made from Montepulciano grapes, the finesse of some of its representatives would suggest the occasional addition of small volumes of Sangiovese. A small group of Conero producers have been demonstrating the area's potential for some years now. Some of their barrel-aged wines can fully withstand comparison with top Tuscan wines. They have sought advice from Tuscany's most famous enologists, including the former chief Antinori enologist, Giacomo Tachis.

In the 1990s, Rosso Conero developed into a very interesting product which also represents

For a long time, quality was not a top priority in the Adriatic hinterland, which is also a fruit-growing area. However, this is gradually changing, and the Castelli di Jesi Verdicchio is a good example of the new trends.

Select Producers in the Marches

Fazi Battaglia***
Castelplanio
865 acres (350 ha); 3,000,000 bottles • Wines include:
Verdicchio dei Castelli di Jesi: Le Moie, San Sisto
This winery in Castelplanio is owned by
pharmaceuticals magnate Angelini (as are the Tuscan
estates Val di Suga, San Leonino, and Trerose). Today
the estate is once again one of the most consistent
producers in the region.

Le Caniette****
Ripatransone
32 acres (13 ha); 50,000 bottles • Wines: Falerio Lucrezia,
Veronica, →Rosso Piceno Morellone, Rosso Bello, →Rosso
Piceno Riserva Nero di Vite, Sibilla Passerina
Raffaele Vagnoni is identified with the red wines Nero
di Vite and Morellone, which are considered among the
top Sangiovese-Montepulciano wines, not only in the
Marches but throughout the whole of Italy.

Gioacchino garofoli**−****
Loreto
62 acres (25 ha); some bought-in grapes; 1,300,000
bottles • Wines include: Verdicchio Castelli di Jesi: Serra
del Conte, Macrina, →Serra Fiorese, →Podium; Rosso
Conero: Piancarda, →Agontano; Kòmaros, Grillo,
Guelfo Verde, Spumante
Both the Rosso Conero and the Verdicchio bottlings are
impressive.

Cocci Grifoni***
Ripatransone
111 acres (45 ha); 130,000 bottles • Wines: Falerio Colli
Asoclani San Basso, Rosso Piceno Superiore Le Torri,
Vina Messieri, →Il Grifone, Poder Colle Vecchio
Marche Bianco, Passerina Spumante Brut
The Cocci Grifoni family produces as range of good
wines from native grape varieties. Il Grifone is the top
red wine of the collection.

Lanari****
Varano
32 acres (13 ha); 40,000 bottles • Wines: Rosso Conero,
→Rosso Conero Fibbio
Owner Luca Lanari and winemaker Giancarlo Soverchia
make a good team, as is impressively demonstrated by the
Fibbio, a red made from Montepulciano grapes.

Umani Ronchi***−*****
Osimo
360 acres (146 ha); some bought-in grapes; 4,500,000
bottles • Wines include: Verdicchio Castelli di Jesi:
→Casal di Serra, Viall Bianchi; →Le Busche; Rosso
Conero: Cùmaro, →San Lorenzo; Bianchello del
Metauro, Rosso Piceno, Montepulciano d'Abruzzo,
Maximo, Pelago, Tajano
Indisputably number one, thanks to Giacomo Tachis. This
house also produces the top reds Cùmaro and San Lorenza,
excellent Verdicchios, and a lovely, refined sweet wine.

good value for money. Rosso Piceno, its
counterpart produced in the south of the region,
is officially a Sangiovese-Montepulciano blend
but fails to achieve the same power and complexity.

The New Face of Verdicchio

The white wines are dominated by Verdicchio
from the two D.O.C. zones, Castelli di Jesi
and Matelica, which together supply almost
80 percent of the total volume. This powerful rustic white often used to lack elegance,
fruit, and freshness. Since the producers of the
Marches stopped fermenting it on its skins and
abandoned the *governo* technique—whereby
dried grapes are added to the fermented wine to
restart the fermentation—Verdicchio has evolved
into a pleasantly fruity, light-to-medium-strength
white wine. More powerful barrel-fermented
wines have recently joined the fresh, light, original version.

The Bianchello del Metauro, Colli Maceratesi,
Falerio dei Colli Scolani, Lacrima di Morro
d'Alba, and Vernaccia di Serrapetrono *appella-*
tions are not even familiar in Italy and are unlikely to attract attention beyond their localities
in the future. Thus, the fate of winemaking in
the Marches is in the hands of the producers of a
small number of *appellations*. The fact that the
region's most famous producers turned their
backs on their native region decades ago may go

some way to explaining the current situation:
the Mondavi family, which emigrated in the
1920s and has been making wine in the Napa
Valley in California since the 1960s, is now one
of the world's best-known producers.

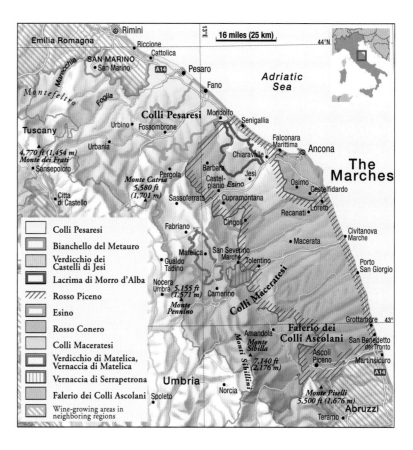

CENTRAL ITALY: THE REGION OF TUSCANY

Central Italy cannot be defined in terms of its geography alone. Whether the prosperous city of Bologna is still considered the north and Abruzzi the south, or whether they are both in the center of the country, is more a political, and most certainly a social, matter. Italy's poor south is everything that the rich north abhors—despite the fact that in the past the north not infrequently profited from the south and was even partly responsible for its poverty. The regions of the Marches, Tuscany, and Umbria are indisputably central Italian. The case of Lazio is less clear-cut; although its wines do exhibit strongly meridional traits, its classification in the center of the country can be justified by pointing to the example of Umbria, whose most important wine-growing region encroaches on the area around Rome. Abruzzi on the other hand is thought of as southern for historical and social reasons, although its topography, climate, and wines are not dissimilar to those of the Marches.

IDEAL GROWING CONDITIONS

The natural conditions for growing top wines are ideal virtually throughout central Italy. Whether it is the eastern Adriatic foothills of the Apennines or their western slopes, or the mountainous volcanic landscapes of the Tyrrhenian coast from Siena southwards, the region's soils and climate favor powerful aromatic wines. The climate of the various growing regions is determined more by altitude than latitude: in the higher regions,

The vineyards of Nippozano are part of the Rufina area, which produces a wine which was long valued as a robust red before it was declared a Chianti.

such as Pomino between Florence and Arezzo, conditions are much cooler than in the more northern, populated area of the Po valley. The general tendency to grow grapes and olives on the slopes while cultivating grain and fruit on the plains is altogether beneficial for wine growing because it means the vineyards are situated on chalky, volcanic soils—conditions which are regarded as ideal for wine in Italy.

GRAPE VARIETIES AND TYPES OF WINE

Top-quality wines are more likely to be produced if the correct grape varieties are grown on these soils. The star among the local red varieties is the Sangiovese, a grape which forms the basis of Chianti Classico, Brunello di Montalcino, and Nobile di Montepulciano. Of the imported varieties Cabernet Sauvignon, Merlot, and, perhaps, Syrah do best. Together with other varieties such as Ciliegiolo or Montepulciano, the region has an enormous potential for red wines.

The range of white varieties still leaves something to be desired. Apart from some interesting grapes like Verdicchio or Vernaccia, along with the various successful applications of Chardonnay or Sauvignon, the spectrum is much too strongly dominated by the rather bland Trebbiano Toscano. There are even a number of critics who maintain that central Italy is simply not suited to growing high-quality white wines.

A WHITE PAST

While the wines of Tuscany have caused a sensation in the last two decades, the other central Italian regions have not been able to emerge from their neighbor's shadow despite ideal growing conditions and some excellent vines. Traditionally, Lazio, the Marches, and Umbria were—and still are—specialists in the production of precisely that type of white wine which finds no resonance on the international market. There are the beginnings of a new approach, however, and these have given cause for hope. In the Marches, the Rosso Conero has been especially impressive, while in Umbria, Torgiano and the heavy Sagrantino di Montefalco have provided a fresh stimulus to producers. In addition, the Antinori estate of Castello della Sala has inspired Orvieto producers to make good-quality whites.

The great success of Tuscan wines is largely due to an influx of enthusiastic amateurs and specialists who came from northern Italy and from abroad to seek a new start in Tuscany. Because they lacked experience themselves, they hired professional enologists to bring about a modernization of both vineyard practices and winery techniques.

THE TURN OF THE SOUTH

Together with the great wine merchants of Florence, who positioned themselves at the head of the movement for change, the newcomers revolutionized the region's most outstanding wine, Chianti. With their Supertuscans or *vini da tavola eccellenti* they created a new wine category which became a model for the entire country. These moves were sparked by general dissatisfaction with the rigid D.O.C.

Left
The real Tuscany—the estate of Vignamaggio in Greve.

Right
Traditional but always trendy—Cantinetta Antinori in Florence.

The ubiquitous Trebbiano.

definitions, which hindered quality work and stifled any attempts at experimentation with grape varieties and aging methods. Eventually the authorities accepted a *fait accompli* and retrospectively legalized Chianti Classico which has no white wine content. They also removed restrictions which compelled overly long cellaring periods, and permitted aging in small *barriques* as well as the addition of international grape varieties. At the same time, the list of D.O.C. and D.O.C.G. names of origin was extended, and I.G.T. definitions were introduced under which the super table wines of approved origin could also be marketed—as had long been common practice in France, Spain, and Germany. In the past few years central Italian wine has increasingly turned to largely untapped but high-quality growing regions such as the Maremma and Morellino areas, as well as others in the Marches and Umbria.

Regional varieties

Central Italy has comparatively few grape varieties, but with the Sangiovese it can lay claim to one of the finest red varieties in the world. Known as Sangiovese in the Romagna and Chianti regions, the same grape is called Brunello in Montalcino, and Prugnolo Gentile in the growing areas of the Vino Nobile di Montepulciano—although it is still a matter of debate whether these types really do constitute independent clones or subspecies as has long been maintained.

In terms of quality and quantity, the Montepulciano of the Marches and Abruzzi takes second place among the red varieties; the round, soft, full wines may be pleasing and attractive but they never achieve the complexity and range of a really great Sangiovese. In the Chianti region, Canaiolo

Nero, Malvasia Nera, and Colorino are represented in smaller quantities. Previously they were used to enrich the color, aroma or taste of Sangiovese, but have clearly forfeited this role with the rise of Cabernet Sauvignon and Merlot. The latter varieties—either on their own or as blends—have enhanced the spectrum of Tuscan wines: Cabernet Sauvignon, especially in the shape of the cult wine Sassicaia, has even chalked up a number of triumphs in international competitions.

Trebbiano Toscano, the dominant white variety, is primarily used for distilling spirits in France (where it goes under the name Ugni Blanc)—a fact which can hardly be considered a mark of quality. Light, neutral wines are the best one can hope to achieve with this variety. It was formerly used as a blend in Chianti to reduce the astringency and youthful aggression of the Sangiovese grape.

Since Trebbiano lost its main *raison d'être*, the Galestro wine made from it has probably been the most intelligent, if short-term, attempt to use the enormous quantities of wine available. At the end of the 1980s and start of the 1990s Galestro even stood on the threshold of becoming a fashionable wine. The Verdicchio of the the Marches region is rarely able to exceed the quality of Trebbiano; and the growers of Vernaccia—the first Italian wine in San Gimignano to achieve D.O.C. honors and the first Italian white to gain D.O.C.G. status—have yet to outline a convincing concept for producing quality. Respectable white wines are occasionally made from Greco, Grechetto, Vermentino, and the various Malvasia varieties (Malvasia di Candia, Malvasia del Lazio, Malvasia del Chianti), but even in their growing regions in Umbria and Lazio it is quantity rather than quality that is emphasized.

TUSCANY AND ITS WINES

Tuscany is home to the most common Italian quality wine: Chianti. But Tuscany has more to offer than this popular red wine which is grown in the hills between Florence and Siena, Arezzo and Pisa. Around half of the harvest from Tuscany's 148,260 acres (60,000 ha) of vineyards is marketed as quality wine. In addition to Chianti, wines such as Brunello di Montalcino, Vino Nobile di Montepulciano, and Vernaccio di San Gimignano, along with other individual wines and brands, such as Tignanello or the famous Sassicaia, have made Tuscan wines renowned throughout the world.

Imitators have always been a problem: some of the Tuscan growing regions were so popular that their names had to be protected from forgers and those seeking to capitalize on their reputation. Designations of origin such as Carmignano, which was granted in 1716, are some of the oldest protected *appellations* in the world.

The variety of wines in the region is reflected in the variety of *terroirs*. The spectrum ranges from the great curve of the Apennines in the north and east to the hills of central Tuscany, and from the volcanic formations of the south to the coastal landscape of Livorno and Grosseto provinces. Hills and mountains cover more than two thirds of Tuscany, natural features which have provided ideal growing conditions for wine for thousands of years.

Roman art treasures still provide evidence of Florence's ancient glories. Wines from the surrounding hills include the reds Carmignano and Pomino.

Siena is the real capital of Tuscan wine. Vino Nobile, Brunello, and the majority of Chianti Classico wines are grown in the surrounding province.

The Etruscans brought viticulture and a wine industry to perfection, and their achievements established the model for Roman wine growing. In the Middle Ages it was mainly the Florentine nobility that was associated with wine, if more as merchants than growers. Names famous today, such as Antinori and Frescobaldi, have been linked to Tuscan wines since the 13th and 14th centuries.

THE BEGINNINGS OF WINE TOURISM

As the once powerful and wealthy patrons of Leonardo, Michelangelo, and other artists, the great Tuscan noble families are not only associated with wine but also with the region's art history. This artistic legacy, preserved in the historical cities studding one of Italy's most attractive landscapes, turned Tuscany into a popular tourist destination at an early stage. When wine tourism became fashionable in Tuscany, it was able to profit from a highly developed tourist infrastructure long before the advantages of the idea were recognized in the other wine-growing regions of Italy.

In spite of—or perhaps because of—its rich viticultural heritage, Tuscany, and indeed the whole of Italy, came close to completely losing contact with developments in other countries after the Second World War due to the disastrous effects on the wine industry of rural migration. Not until the 1970s did the great wine houses of Florence hesitantly begin to look for a new approach.

RIPE FOR THE VINEYARD

It was mainly wealthy city dwellers from the Italian north or abroad who were responsible for the turnaround; after settling in Tuscany to realize their long-cherished dreams of a quiet country life, they turned to wine growing either out of passion or as a means of realizing a return on their large investments. Most of them had absolutely no experience and so had to take advantage of the specialist skills of professional enologists. Quality was their mantra and they introduced essential elements from the vine-growing and wine-making practices of other countries to Tuscany, such as the use of French grape varieties, temperature-controlled fermentation and the technique of aging wines in

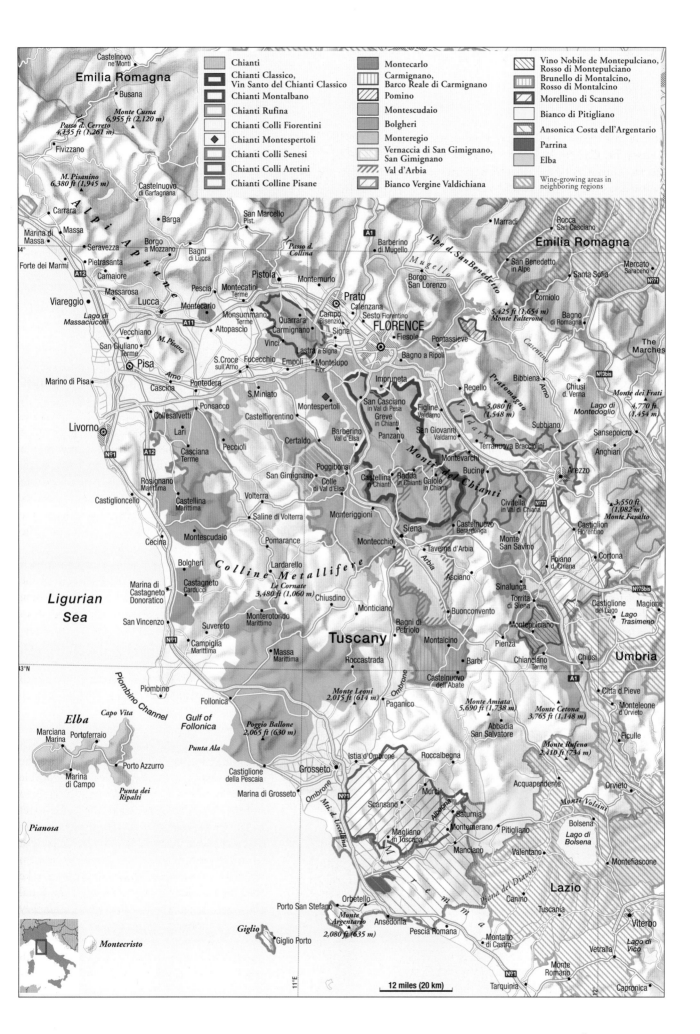

barriques. Uninhibited by history or tradition, they began to create a whole new generation of top class wines.

It was therefore unavoidable that these new wines, which were conceived according to international criteria, came into conflict with bureaucratic D.O.C. rules. Over the years these had fixed regulations for all sorts of irrelevant details: the recipes for blending varieties in a given wine were hopelessly out-of-date; barrel-aging often took several years; and the maximum yields allowed were wildly excessive. The "revolution" swept all the wine-growing areas of the region, beginning in the heart of the Chianti district, before spreading to the coastal vineyards near Bogheri and the Rufina hills at the foot of the Apennines and on up to Montalcino and Montepulciano, where two of the most famous regional red varieties—Brunello and Vino Nobile—grew in abundance. Not only did these new wines signal that a fresh wind was blowing through traditional designations of origin; the sense of change they inspired brought about entirely new designations. Many of the best products which had previously had to trade as table wines, because they contained Cabernet Sauvignon or because they had not undergone the requisite aging process, have now been legitimized through the allocation of new D.O.C. or I.G.T. names. Even the production restrictions on Chianti Classico were adjusted— varietals as well as wines with added Cabernet and Merlot have since been permitted—and Classico was granted a D.O.C.G. status separate from the other Chianti *appellations*.

But the Tuscan wine industry still has a major task ahead of it, namely the comprehensive over-

Cypress trees—the green symbol of Tuscany.

Opposite
Above vineyards at the Fattoria di Felsina estate in Castelnuovo Berardenga.

Arezzo—a Mecca for fans of antiques and bric-a-brac.

haul of most vineyards. The proportion of white varieties for which there is no longer any place in the modernized D.O.C. statutes is still too high, and there are still too many old and inferior vines even in the renowned vineyards. Many of the vineyards are so exhausted or riddled with viruses that one wonders how the growers are able to exploit their depleted stock to reach the maximum yield restrictions. The suspicion that some wines are purchased secretly from outside the region is today considered to be (more or less) an established fact.

In many areas, however, efforts have been undertaken to renovate vineyards and their vines. In the Chianti Classico area, for example, a far-reaching research program was initiated in the 1980s which is now beginning to bear the first fruits. In the past few years, the main centers of activity have shifted to the coast and southern Tuscany. Areas like Bolgheri, Montescudaio, or the region of Morellino di Scansano on the edge of the Maremma plain have, for some time now, been the targets of massive investment and new plantings by the greatest and most important houses of Tuscany.

Super Tuscans

Italian wine laws are like no others in Europe. Legislation has been devoted to the regulation of even the most trivial details, hindering the early efforts toward achieving quality in Tuscany and, later, in Piedmont.

Outdated prescriptions of the varieties allowed to make up a given wine or antiquated methods for pressing and aging did not, in the opinion of experts, allow for the development of the best quality. Winegrowers and producers preferred to experiment with French varieties such as Cabernet, Chardonnay, Syrah, and Merlot, as these types seemed to hold out the promise of greater success than that gained by the arduous, time-consuming propagation of superior Sangiovese or Trebbiano vines. Growers chose to expose their wines to the piquant effects of new wood, instead of allowing them to molder away for years in enormous, old wooden barrels. Ideas and processes developed in France and California seemed to make it a quicker and less complicated matter to endow wines with more body and concentration, greater elegance, a more pronounced longevity, and aromatic complexity.

Innovative growers in Italy who wanted to proceed in this direction were forced to downgrade the classification of their high-value wines and market them as simple table wines. The first examples of this new style came on the market at the start of the 1970s: these were Incisa's Sassicaia and Antinori's Tignanello. It was the Tignanello especially—a blend of Sangiovese and Cabernet in a ratio of 80:20— that paved the way for famous names such as Camartina, Vigorello, Grifi, I Sodi di San Nicolò, Siepi, Balifico, Cabero Il Borgo, Monte Vertine, and Convivio.

Gianni Nunziante, the owner of Vignamaggio in Greve.

Other wines were Sangiovese varietals such as San Martino, Solatio Basilica, Cappanelle, Cetinaia, Le Pergole Torte, Cepparello, Percarlo, and Flaccianello della Pieve; or they consisted mainly—if not entirely—of Cabernet Sauvignon, such as Campora, Solaia, Sammarco, Cortaccio, Nemo, Saffredi, Guado al Tasso, Maestro Raro, Il Pareto, Ornellaia, and Tassinaia. What the Italian authorities rejected with short shrift was speedily and enthusiastically embraced by the market. Within a short period of time supposedly simple wines began to win prizes and this caused a number of quality wine producers to begin reflecting on their own practices. In the mid-1980s the lessons learned had spread far beyond Tuscany and there was scarcely an estate without at least one of the new top-notch table wines, which American critics enthusiastically celebrated as Supertuscans.

A mere ten years later the controversy was no more: the authorities had established new D.O.C. areas in many of the regions, adjusted production regulations in line with existing practices, and assented to the category of *indicazione geografica*—the table wine with a geographical designation of origin. Many of the table wines that were previously considered so exceptional are today to be found under D.O.C. or I.G.T. names.

The Reinvention of Chianti

In the 1970s and '80s the new ambitious estate owners in Tuscany had but one goal: to produce great, complex red wines which would improve on aging. Some of them pinned their hopes on French varieties and a broad range of wines while others perfected the native Sangiovese grape to produce a top-quality varietal. Two companies whose histories, strategies and quality are representative of the group are Castello di Ama, located several kilometers south of Gaiole in Chianti, and Fattoria di Felsina, situated in Castelnuovo Berardenga on the outermost edge of the Chianti Classico region.

The Adventure of Chianti Classico

In 1977 a group of Roman families decided to purchase a neglected estate above the hamlet of Monti, just south of Gaiole, in one of the best areas in the Chianti Classico region in order to pursue quality viticulture at the highest level. They had money but little in the way of wine-making skills to invest and so they hired, as their enologist, Marco Pallanti, a man who was to prove one of the most talented Italians in his field. Head of the operation was Silvano Formigli, an individual with a clear strategic concept as well as excellent contacts in the trade press.

Castello di Ama began by developing a series of single-vineyard variations on Chianti Classico which were later produced in three—then four—versions, each with its own blend and characteristics. Most made use of traditional Tuscan grape varieties—San Lorenzo with its mixture of Sangiovese and Canaiolo; Bellavista, which complemented these two

Left
Some of the oldest and most famous estates such as Badia a Coltibuono and Castello di Brolio are situated in Gaiolo, in the southwest of the Chianti Classico region.

Right
In spite of a rich wine-growing tradition, the Fattoria di Felsina in Castelnuovo Berardenga did not break into the elite group of Chianti Classicos until the end of the 1990s.

varieties with a dash of Malvasia; and the classic Chianti blend of Bertinga. Vigneto La Casuccia, however, was an innovative blend of Sangiovese with Canaiolo and the French grape, Merlot.

Merlot Makes a Career for Itself

It became clear that Merlot had fallen onto fertile soil here: 1985 saw the first vintage of a Merlot varietal, a table wine, from Vigna l'Apparita. Together with the 1987 vintage, it rose to become one of the very best Tuscan reds. In numerous tastings it outclassed all the most renowned Merlot wines from countries around the world including Petrus, Le Pin, and the Californian wines.

In France, Merlot—with few exceptions—is the variety responsible for the softer, fruitier components of the great Bordeaux wines. In Ama and on the other Tuscan estates which experimented with the variety, it was unusually high in tannins, exhibiting a complex, diverse nose and palate; Merlot was even able to absorb effortlessly the enormous boost in aroma and taste from the wooden casks used in the aging process.

Along with his top wines, Marco Pallanti presents an impressive range of good to very good wines to an astonished public every year. Whether it be Pinot Grigio from Vigna Bellaria, his two Chardonnays, the Pinot Nero Vigna Il Chiuso, the Sauvignon or the simple Colline di Ama from the classical white Chianti varieties—Pallanti's wines are almost always among the best in the region.

New Techniques

Pallanti caused a new sensation in the catastrophic year of 1992. At a time when the renowned firm of Antinori was unable to bottle a single one of its top wines and was only able to bring the high-volume Santa Cristina onto the market, Pallanti triumphed with another top vintage of Merlot l'Apparita, which bore comparisons with its legendary predecessor from 1988.

Rigorous selection and propagation in the vineyard, a meticulously supervised vinification process and the controlled, balanced aging of the wine had worked real wonders. These improvements were supported by the most modern cellaring technology, which included the somewhat controversial use of concentration equipment.

The Character of the Terroir

The wines of Fattoria di Felsina in Castelnuovo Berardenga, on the southern edge of the *appellation*, are more closely tied to the peculiarities of the *terroir* than at Ama, where the variety of vineyards has again been reduced. Felsina was purchased in 1966 by businessman Domenico Poggiali and systematically built up by his son-in-law, Giuseppe Mazzocolin, together with his friend, Franco Bernabei, a well-known enologist and also one of the most famous winemakers in Italy.

The vineyard is situated on the final gentle foothills of the Monti del Chianti as it runs down into the Ombrone Valley, and covers about 865 acres (350 ha) of land, of which only a seventh is given over to wine growing. The geological composition of the vineyards reflects this border location: there are blue-gray marlaceous soils—or *galestro*—rocky *albarese*, loamy and alluvial soils as well as marine sediments, and it is to this diversity that the wines of Felsina owe their extraordinary complexity and range.

Felsina is especially renowned for its Chianti Classico and even the normal version, supported by a clever mix of small and medium barrels in the aging process, makes an uncommonly rich and complex impression. The *riserva* is in fact a single vineyard wine from Rancia, Mazzocolin's favorite vineyard. The most mature vines on this quartzy, marlaceous soil with its strips of sand and loam are 35 years old. The stock has been carefully renewed and seedlings from the best vines have been propped up on existing plants in order to achieve a uniform improvement in the quality.

The cellar at Castello di Ama.

Sangiovese with Cabernet

In good years, the Vigneto Rancia is one the best wines in the entire growing region, but the real stars of Fattoria are two varietal table wines: Fontalloro from Sangiovese and Maestro Raro from Cabernet Sauvignon. They are aged in *barriques* and both perfectly harmonize structure and elegance, as well as fruity density and the ability to improve with age.

Mazzocolin and Bernabei have not ignored their white wines either. The barrel-fermented Chardonnay, I Sistri, initially suffered from a lack of structure and definition but by the 1991 vintage it had developed into one of the finest of its kind in Tuscany. When there is so much quality to be had, the cost-benefit relationship is particularly favorable for the more basic products.

Since the start of the 1990s, Mazzocolin has owned Castello di Farnetella in Sinalunga, outside the Chianti Classico area and close to the growing region of Nobile di Montepulciano. At the beginning of the 1980s the concentration of Sangiovese vines had been increased here and the vineyards cultivated according to modern methods. In addition, young Pinot Noir and Cabernet Sauvignon plants were propped up on older vines, and the wines improved with micro-vinification techniques to the point where, today, they are able to compete with produce from neighboring D.O.C.G. regions. The most interesting wines from the higher altitude vineyards are a Chianti Colli Senesi, in which a Merlot component reinforces the structure and fruit, and a very aromatic Sauvignon Blanc.

Italy's Most Popular Wines: The Chianti Family

The name "Chianti" has been in common usage since the 13th century when it was associated with the hills around Radda, Gaiole, and Castellina, and referred to as a white wine. It is only since the 1930s that the Chianti growing region has undergone continuous expansion, and it now covers a large part of Tuscany. Even the characteristic mixture of varieties that make up Chianti is comparatively recent. Before the 19th century Chianti—the name by then had come to mean a red wine—was made mainly from Canaiolo grapes, to which a Sangiovese or Malvasia component was added.

The Recipe

Bettino Ricasoli, Prime Minister of a newly united Italy from 1861, was the scion of an old Tuscan noble family and owner of the Ricasoli firm of wine merchants. He is also renowned for having developed the traditional Chianti recipe of 70 percent Sangiovese, 15 percent Canaiolo Nero, 10 percent white varieties—such as Trebbiano Toscano and Malvasia del Chianti—and five percent from other varieties. The addition of white wine was intended to take the edge off the harshness of the young, inaccessible Sangiovese and enable it to be consumed at an earlier date—a characteristic which was encouraged by the so-called *governo* process. This

The *gallo nero*, or black rooster, is the symbol of Chianti Classico. Its growing region was defined for the first time by Grand Duke Cosimo III de Medici in 1716.

Rufina is today the smallest of the seven Chianti zones. The region has enormous potential which is far from being fully exploited.

consisted of setting part of the grape harvest aside and drying it before adding it to the wine after fermentation had finished. Fermentation would then begin again, giving the wine not only a higher alcohol content, making it fuller and rounder, but also ensuring that the carbon dioxide remained in solution thus making it seem fresher and lighter. This type of blend, however, did not endow the wine with genuine quality.

The Growing Region

With production of around 26½ million gallons (one million hl) a year, Chianti has the largest volume of the officially recognized quality wines in Italy today. Behind the famous name, however, there lurks a contradictory reality. All wines with the name "Chianti" share a common basis in the robust Sangiovese variety. But because the extensive growing region provides such a variety of different *terroirs* and climatic conditions, the consumer is faced with a puzzling array of wines. For this reason eight different subregions have been instituted and these are stated on the label (although the designation "Chianti" without a geographical suffix is also permitted). The most important of these is the Classico region which has had its own D.O.C.G. statute since the mid-1980s and which is treated separately here. Around the central Classico area are distributed the growing regions of Chianti Rufina, Chianti Colli Fiorentini, Chianti Colli Aretini, Chianti Colli Senesi, Chianti Colline Pisane, Chianti Montalbano, and the most recent, Chianti Montespertoli.

Relatives both Rich and Poor

The most interesting wines, with the longest tradition of quality, are from the Chianti Rufina area. In some cases they have even surpassed many of the Classico wines. The growing region stretches across the slopes above the town of Pontassieve in the Arno valley and is part of the former Pomino region—a name which is also a designation of origin today, being reserved for the highest sites up to 2,950 feet (900 m). Most of the vineyards belong to the Frescobaldi and Giuntini Antinori families who also produce the best wines. The cool climate of the higher sites, together with their superb chalky, marl soils, provide the conditions for elegant, multifaceted wines.

Chianti and Chianti Classico both enjoy D.O.C.G. status but since the end of the 1990s they have had separate designations of origin. Chianti Classico, with an annual production volume of more than six million gallons (230,000 hl), is one of Italy's biggest quality wines. It must have at least 12 percent alcohol by volume and its maximum yield is limited to 3 tons per acre (7.5 tonnes/ha) while a simple Chianti needs only 11.5 percent alcohol and can produce 4 tons per acre (9 tonnes/ha). The maximum yield of the other Chianti varieties is set at $3^1/_4$ tons per acre (8.5 tonnes/ha), and they are allowed a minimum alcohol content of 11.5–12 percent by volume.

The varieties permitted for all types of Chianti are Sangiovese, Canaiolo Nero, Trebbiano Toscano, Malvasia Nera, as well as a few others. The proportion of white wine in Chianti was significantly reduced in 1984, and since 1995 Chiantis which are Sangiovese varietals have been permitted. These days Merlot and Cabernet Sauvignon are allowed to constitute 15–20 percent of the blend, and aging in *barriques* has largely replaced the unnecessarily long aging process of former times, in which the large barrels were often inadequately maintained.

For Chiantis without any additional designation—the *putto*—there is a *superiore* version which is regulated by requiring a smaller harvest than for the *riserva*; the period it must age in the barrel is not prescribed.

Much simpler in structure and aromatic expression are the wines of the Colli Fiorentini, which come from the hills between the Arno valley and the Chianti Classico area. While it is undoubtedly true that this damp, cool growing region is less suited to producing high-grade wines, the continuing urban sprawl from Florence is also harming the area's grape crops.

The same can be said of the Chianti zones of Colli Aretini in the area around the city of Arezzo, as well as Colli Senesi, whose growing regions cover the eastern and central southern parts of Tuscany below Siena. The Colli Senesi also have to share their growing region with more famous wines like Brunello di Montalcino and Nobile di Montepulciano, which claim the best fruit from the top sites, leaving hardly anything for their poorer cousins.

Montalbano includes the small Carmignano region and is therefore fated to stand in the shadow of a superior wine—a position which it has to endure often enough as Carmignano's secondary wine in any case. The creation of Barco Reale has actually exacerbated the situation, as Carmignano itself—in spite of being awarded D.O.C.G.—has now been forced to contend with image problems.

Although its growing region undoubtedly has more potential, the Chianti Colline Pisane is the lightest member of the Chianti family.

Chianti history in the Frescobaldis' cellar.

In Chianti, wine and woods are neighbors.

With the exceptions of Classico—whose prestige and qualities seem to have consolidated—and the independent Chianti Rufina, the region offers little to impress the consumer. Growers on the edge of the area have sought to emphasize their connection with Classico in their use of the Chianti name, and Classico growers in turn demanded their own D.O.C.G. status at the end of the 1980s in order to distinguish themselves more clearly from these other regions. It is, in fact, high time that the definition of the Chianti family was given a thorough overhaul.

Carmignano is grown on the northern slopes of Monte Albano, a small ridge of mountains on the northern banks of the river Arno, west of Florence. This wine's designation of origin was protected under threat of legal sanction in the first-ever document to define a Chianti area, signed by Cosimo III de' Medici in 1716. Carmignano was therefore the first wine in Italy to be given a legal designation of origin and is perhaps the first *appellation* in the world to have enjoyed legal protection.

Centuries later, Carmignano was the first Tuscan wine to be officially blended with the French variety of Cabernet Sauvignon, long before growers elsewhere conducted similar experiments.

Carmignano has had D.O.C.G. status for a number of years; it must contain at least 12.5 percent alcohol by volume and must age for at least 21 months in the barrel; *riserva* wines require at least two years.

When made by top growers Carmignano is an intensely colored, complex wine which is powerful in good years and ages satisfactorily. All other versions—such as the Rosato and the various Vin Santo types which can be dry, sweet, white or light red—are only classified at the D.O.C. level, though some of the Vin Santos must be aged for four years.

Apart from the Chianti Montalbano, which is made as a secondary wine by some growers in the same area, the region now has another quality wine with D.O.C. status—the Barco Reale di Carmignano. It is predominantly blended from Sangiovese and Canaiolo grapes, requires a minimum alcohol content of only 11 percent, and has no obligatory aging period before it may be bottled.

Classical Chianti at the Peak

During the Middle Ages and shortly after, "Chianti" meant the communes of Radda, Gaiole, and Castellina, which formed a political and military whole in the *Lega del Chianti*. Grand Duke Cosimo III de' Medici (1670–1723) extended the area in his edict of 1716 to include the commune of Greve. After 1932 other areas were also added: parts of San Casciano Val di Pesa and Barberino Val d'Elsa—a group of villages close to Florence—as well as Castelnuovo Berardenga in the south. Even after the concept of "Chianti" was widened to include peripheral growing regions, the definition of its heartland remained unchanged. The countryside in Chianti is some of the most beautiful in Tuscany and it enjoys an excellent reputation not only through its wines—around a tenth of the total area is covered in vineyards—but also through its proximity to centers of art in Florence and Siena.

Vineyards in Transition

In the 1960s and 1970s many of the vineyards were restocked, although in the course of this work less attention was paid to quality than to maximizing yields and rationalizing working methods. As it turned out, this approach was to demand a high price: samples taken from older Chianti vintages today clearly prove that wines from this era are less expressive than the Chiantis of earlier decades, or even those from more recent years, all of which have aged extremely well.

The silhouette of Greve, one of the oldest growing centers in the very heart of the Chianti Classico region.

These were painful lessons. At the end of the 1970s the Chianti Classico region—one of the first regions in Italy to do so—began to take a more innovative tack. New, international grape varieties, more sophisticated aging techniques and modern marketing methods were already in full swing here when other regions were still intent on producing surpluses. These efforts at first bore fruit only in the table wines. At the time, Italy's rigid production regulations were intent on protecting quality wines, many of which had ceased to be as good as their reputations. The result was that some table wines were better than those which carried the region's prestigious designation of origin. Several years went by before it was ultimately decided to redefine the production regulations for Chianti Classico according to the quality criteria of the table wines. Furthermore, growers began to renew their interest in the local Sangiovese variety.

The Best Terroir

Sangiovese is one of those varieties which needs a great deal of warmth and dry conditions in order to ripen, and the Chianti Classico area is exceptionally suited to these growing conditions. The large number of hillside vineyards allows an optimal orientation of the vines at an ideal height of between 820 and 1,640 feet (250 and 500 m) above sea level. The good drainage provided by the loose, blue-gray, chalky, marlaceous soils (*galestro*) or weathered sandstone (*albarese*) means that the vineyards rarely

Chianti Classico
San Casciano in Val di Pesa
Greve in Chianti
Tavarnelle Val di Pesa
Barberino Val d'Elsa
Poggibonsi
Castellina in Chianti
Radda in Chianti
Gaiole in Chianti
Castelnuovo Berardenga
Chianti
Chianti Colli Fiorentini
Chianti Colli Senesi
Chianti Colli Aretini

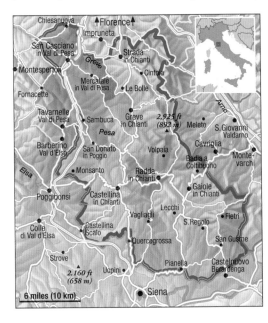

Nobility with red wine in its veins

In 1180 Ugo and Antinoro di Rinuccino were officially named owners of the Castello di Combiate. One hundred years later the family, which had in the meantime moved to Florence, was entered in the register of the silk trade corporation. In 1385 a certain Giovanni di Piero, son of a subsidiary line of the family, was apprenticed to the winemakers' guild. Since that date the wine-growing tradition of the Antinoris has proceeded without interruption, reaching a temporary peak in 1895 with the founding of the trading house of Marchesi Antinori. In 1898 the cellars in San Casciano Val di Pesa were built and today these function as the center of a diverse concern, with interests in all the important growing regions of Tuscany, Umbria, Piedmont, Apulia, and even California. This traditional firm owes much of its prestige to its former head enologist, Giacomo Tachis, who was responsible for such extraordinary wines as Sassicaia, Tignanello (largely made from Sangiovese), Solaia (mainly Cabernet), and many others. In addition, the enologist Renzo Cotarella created one of Italy's best Chardonnays on the Umbrian estate of Castello della Sala.

Piero Antinori, director of his family's estate, with more than 600 years of tradition.

The aristocratic banking family of Frescobaldi has been active in growing and trading wine since the 14th century. With estates in both the Classico and Rufina regions, a virtual monopoly in Pomino, large interests in Montalcino, and new vineyards in the Maremma region, the Frescobaldis are today one of the biggest and best producers in Italy. Their best-known products are their Chianti Rufina wines, Pomino variants and the Luce della Vita. This latter wine is the result of a joint venture with the Californian firm of Mondavi.

Wine was thought to be an occupation suited to the upper classes, and other noble families also pursued the trade for this reason. Giuntini Antinori, distant relations of Marchesi Antinori, owned the Rufina estate of Selvapiana. In the 19th century they also owned the abbey of Badia a Coltibuono, which today belongs to another branch of their descendants, the banking family of Stucchi Prinetti. The Prinettis had formed an alliance with one of the most powerful Tuscan dynasties—the Medici—through the marriage of Piero Stucchi Prinetti to Lorenza de' Medici.

After a less than successful intermezzo in Australia, descendants of Baron Ricasoli, who developed the Chianti blend, are once again proud owners of the Castello di Brolio, which they manage together with another family with a long-standing tradition, the Mazzei from Castello di Fonterutoli. The Ricasoli name also resonates in the name of the proprietors of the Castello di Cacchiano, the Ricasoli Firidolfi family.

become too wet, even when there is heavy rainfall. Even the Bordeaux varieties of Cabernet Sauvignon and Merlot achieve good results on this *terroir*.

While in the past the acidity of Sangiovese often gave a sharp and immature impression—white grapes were added during fermentation to soften the tannins—modern Chianti Classico with a predominant or even exclusive Sangiovese component, forms a single, harmonious unit. As a young wine, its bouquet is floral and slightly spicy, taking on leather and tobacco notes as it ages; its tannins are elegantly structured and redolent of cinnamon, with a sophistication well supported by a slightly acidic tone. It is well-suited to most Tuscan dishes such as pasta, wild game, lamb, and beef.

The best wines of the Chianti Classico region come from medium altitude sites south of Greve and north of Radda and Castellina, as well as from the slopes stretching from Gaiole in the south into Castelnuovo, toward the Arbia valley. One of the very best *terroirs* is the Conco d'Oro at Panzano, part of the Greve commune.

GALLO NERO

Chianti, along with other Tuscan wines, was given a fresh lease of life by the traditional wine houses and the "newcomers" from the north and abroad, but developments in the last couple of decades have been dominated by the

The Castello di Brolio—long in the hands of the Ricasoli family—is thought to be the oldest vineyard in the world. It was here that Baron Bettino Ricasoli developed the recipe for Chianti in the 19th century.

sign of the black rooster, or *gallo nero* in Italian. This is the world-famous symbol of the Consorzio Chianti Classico, the region's federation of winegrowers, an organization to whom Chianti Classico owes its D.O.C.G. status. The federation also undertook the renovation of vineyards in the heart of Tuscany. Under the title "Chianti 2000," a long-term research project was instituted at the end of the 1980s to carry out research into the best varieties, clones, and systems of cultivation. Although many Chianti vineyards are still in need of an overhaul at the start of the new millennium, the knowledge gained from the project has already led to a series of new facilities being established.

Select Producers in Northern Tuscany

Agricola san Felice**–****
Castelnuovo Berardenga
494 acres (200 ha); 1,200,000 bottles • Wines include: Chianti Classico: Riserva Il Grigio, Poggio Rosso, →I.G.T. Toscana Vigorello, Brunello di Montalcino Campogiovanni
This large estate in the southern Chianti Classico region belongs to the German Allianz group. The wines' quality is good to very good; the single-vineyard Chianti Poggio Rosso is ranked among the best in the region.

Badia a Coltibuono**–****
Gaiole
143 acres (58 ha); 330,000 bottles • Wines: Chianti Classico, Chianti Classico Riserva, →I.G.T. Toscana Sangioveto, Chianti Cetamura, Trapploine Bianco, Sella del Boscone, Chardonnay, Vin Santo del Chianti Classico
The Stucchi Prinettis' Sangioveto and Chianti Classico are among Tuscany's prize wines.

Capannelle**–****
Gaiole
15 acres (6 ha); 25,000 bottles • Wines: Capanelle: Riserva, →Barrique, Chardonnay, →50:50
Rosetti is considered a Sangiovese specialist. He set the standard with his 50:50, a Sangiovese-Merlot blend (the latter comes from Avignonesi vineyards in Montepulciano) and a red made from Syrah. Since 1997, the estate has been owned by J. Sherwood.

Castello di Ama***–****
Gaiole
222 acres (90 ha); 300,000 bottles • Wines include: Chianti Classico: →Vigneto San Lorenzo, →Vigneto La Casuccia; I.G.T. Toscana: →Merlot, Chardonnay, Pinot Grigio, Pinot Nero, Vin Santo
This premium estate in the southern Chianti Classico region suffered severe competition in the 1980s.

Castello di Fonterutoli***–*****
Castellina
171 acres (69 ha); 450,000 bottles • Wines: Chianti Classico Castello di Fonterutoli, , I.G.T. Toscana: →Siepi, →Poggio alla Badiola; Morellino di Scansano Belguardo
For years the Mazzeis' Sangiovese-Cabernet blend Concerto was one of the best of the Supertuscans, but production was terminated in favor of a Riserva Chianti. The new premier wine is the Merlot-Sangiovese blend Siepi. Castello di Fonterutoli also handles the wines of the neighboring estate of La Brancaia; until recently these underwent vinification in the Fonterutoli cellars.

Castello di Monsanto***–*****
Barberino Val d'Elsa
124 acres (50 ha); 270,000 bottles • Wines: Chianti Classico Riserva Il Poggio, →I.G.T. Toscana: Nemo, →Tinscvil, Chardonnay, Sangiovese, Vin Santo
Fabrizio Bianchi's Poggio was the first single-vineyard Chianti, and his Tincsvil the first really good successor to Tiganello. Nemo is a successful Cabernet.

Chianti Ruffino and Tenuta Nozzole**–****
Pontassieve
1,483 acres (600 ha); some bought-in grapes; 16,000,000 bottles • Wines include: Brunello Riserva Greppone Mazzi, Chianti Classico: →Riserva Ducale Oro, →La Forra; Nero del Tondo, Nobile di Montepulciano, →Il Pareto, Le Bruniche
In the 1950s Ruffino was know for its bottles of Chianti in raffia baskets, but its Riserva Ducale was also a top quality wine. The best estate is Tenuta Nozzole in Greve, which produces outstanding Chianti and the great Cabernet Pareto.

Le Cinciole****
Greve/Panzano
27 acres (11 ha); 40,000 bottles • Wines: Chianti Classico, →Chinati Classico Riserva Il Petresco
Luca Orsini and Valeria Vigano rely on their splendid unadorned Sangiovese from the hills south of Florence.

Collelungo****
Castellina
27 acres (11 ha); 30,000 bottles • Wines: Chianti Classico, →Chianti Classico Riserva, Campocerchio
All of the wines display the special quality of the soil and location in the vineyard near Castellina. Winemaker Alberto Antonini manages to transfer the quality of the grapes to the bottle in a convincing manner.

Corzano & Paterno****
San Casciano Val di Pesa
27 acres (11 ha); 50,000 bottles • Wines: Chianti Terre di Corzano, Chianti Riserva Tre Borri, Il Corzano, Aglaia Chardonnay, Passito di Corzano
Under Alyosha Goldschmidt's management, the estate produces characterful wines typical of the region. The Passito di Corzano, made in Vin Santo fashion, is also impressive.

Fattoria di Felsina***–*****
Castelnuovo Berardenga
128 acres (52 ha); 250,000 bottles • Wines: →Chinati Classico Vigneto Rancia; I.G.T. Toscana: →Fontalloro,→Maestro Raro, →I Sistri; Vin Santo
Fattoria's superb Chiantis, Chardonnays and Cabernets are made at the edge of the Chianti Classico region under the direction of Giuseppe Mazzocolin.

Fattoria la Massa****–*****
Greve
67 acres (27 ha); 90,000 bottles • Wines: Chianti Classico, Chianti Classico Giorgio Primo
Motta's' Chianti Classico variants, particularly the Giorgio Primo, have been among the greatest of Italian wines since the mid-1990s, with their fruity and cedary nose and wealth of essences on the palate.

Fattoria San Giusto a Rentennano***–*****
Gaiole
82 acres (33 ha); 60,000 bottles • Wines: Chianti Classico, I.G.T. Toscana: Percarlo, La Ricolma, Vin Santo del Chianti Classico
The fattoria run by Luca, Francesco and Elisabetta Martin di Cigala has for years been one of the best estates in the Chianti Classico region. The vintage Chianti has a very good price-to-performance ratio. Percarlo is a single-variety Sangiovese in a class of its own.

Fattoria Selvapiana***–****
Pontassieve
101 acres (41 ha); 100,000 bottles • Wines: Chianti Rufina: Riserva, →Vigneto Bucerchiale; Borro Lastricato, Vin Santo
Francesco Giuntini-Antinori owns some of the best vineyards in the region as well as a cellar whose bottles, some of them decades old, prove just how well a good Chianti Rufina ages.

Fontodi***–****
Greve
116 acres (47 ha); 16,000 bottles • Wines: Chianti Classico, →Chianti Classico Vigna del Sorbo, →I.G.T. Toscana Flaccianello della Pieve, Pinot Bianco Meriggio, →Pinot Nero Casa Via, Syrah Casa Via, Vin Santo, Solstizio

In the 1980's Manetti's Flaccianello della Pieve, a single-variety Sangiovese, enjoyed great success, and in the 1990s experiments were undertaken with Syrah and Pinot Nero. Fontodi has almost completely restocked its vineyards.

ISOLE E OLENA***–*****
BARBERINO VAL D'ELSA
101 acres (41 ha); 200,000 bottles • Wines: Chianti Classico, →I.G.T. Toscana Ceparello, Collezione De Marchi: →Cabernet, →Syrah, Vin Santo
Paolo De Marchi was one of the first to modernize his vineyards systematically. The results of his efforts are internationally famous Sangiovese, Cabernet and even Syrah wines. The Vin Santo is impressive.

LIVERNANO****–*****
RADDA IN CHIANTI
30 acres (12 ha); 30,000 bottles • Wines: Anima Toscana Bianco, Livernano Rosso Toscana, Puro Sange Rosso Toscana
Marco Montanari bought the estate in 1990 and has replanted the vineyards. Today he produces three wines, two reds and a white, which are all excellent in quality.

MARCHESI ANTINORI***–****
FLORENCE
2,964 acres (1,200 ha); some bought-in grapes; 15,000,000 bottles • Wines include: Orvieto Classico Campogrande, Santa Cristina, Chianti Classico: Pèppoli, Badia a Passignana Riserva, →Tenute del Marchese; Vino Nobile di Montepulciano La Braccesca, Brunello di Montalcino Pian delle Vigne, →I.G.T. Toscana Tignanello and →Solaia, Bolgheri Guado al Tasso, Spumante
For decades this firm has been among the very best in the region.

MARCHESI FRESCOBALDI***–****
FLORENCE
2,125 acres (860 ha); some bought-in grapes; 8,000,000 bottles • Wines include: Chianti Rufina: →Castello di Nipozzano Riserva, →Montesodi; →I.G.T. Toscana Mormoreto and →Lamaione, Chianti Rémole, Ablaze, →Brunello di Montalcino Riserva Castelgiocondo, →Pomino Bianco Il Benefizio, Pomino Rosso, →Luce della Vita, Lucente, Dazante
The Frescobaldi produce one of the broadest ranges of wines in Tuscany, but no Chianti Classico.

MONTE VERTINE***–****
RADDA IN CHIANTI
22 acres (9 ha); 50,000 bottles • Wines: →Le Pergole Torte, →Montevertine, Il Sodaccio, M, Bianco di Montevertine, Pian del Ciampolo, Thea di Maggio
Sergio Mannetti, whose products rose to become cult wines in the 1980s, remained loyal to Sangiovese, complementing it only with the other local varieties Caniolo and Colorino.

PODERE IL PALAZZINO***–****
GAIOLE
30 acres (12 ha); 40,000 bottles • Wines: Chianti Classico, Chianti Classico Grosso Sanese, Rosso del Palazzino
The Sderci brought Rosso Sanese onto the market in the early 1980s, and it is still the firm's premier wine.

POGGERINO***–****
RADDA IN CHIANTI
17 acres (7 ha); 30,000 bottles • Wines: Chianti Classico, →Chianti Classico Riserva Bugialla, I.G.T. Toscana Primamateria, I.G.T. Rosato di Toscana Aurora

The Folonari family who took over the Chianti house of Ruffino in 1913 invested heavily in their own domains such as Santedame, Nozzole, Zano and Marzi (see below). They are among the best and most renowned producers of Chianti.

With the assistance of the enologist Nicolò d'Afflitto, the Lanzas developed their Chianti Riserva Bugialla into one of the region's most elegant wines.

RIECINE**–****
GAIOLE
10 acres (4 ha); 18,000 bottles • Wines: Chianti Classico Riserva, →I.G.T. Toscana La Gioia, Bianco di Riecine
La Gioia, a great Sangiovese wine, was created here with the help of enologist Sean O'Callaghan.

SAN VINCENTI****
GAIOLE
20 acres (8 ha); 30,000 bottles • Wines: Chianti Classico, Chianti Classico Riserva, →Stignano
Roberto Puccis owns unique, stony vineyard sites. Here, winegrower Carlo Ferrini produces mineral wines of outstanding quality.

TENUTA CAPEZZANA***–****
CARMIGNANO
235 acres (95 ha); 460,000 bottles • Wines: Carmignano: Villa di Capezzana, →Riserva; →Ghiaie della Furba, Barco Reale, Chianti Montalbano, Trebbiano di Toscana, Chardonnay, Tremisse, Vin Santo Riserva, Vin Ruspo
Apart from their two Carmignano versions, the top wine of the Contini Bonacossi is the Cabernet Merlot bled, Ghiaie della Furba.

VECCHIE TERRE DI MONTEFILI***–*****
GREVE
23 acres (9.5 ha); 45,000 bottles • Wines: Chianti Classico, Anfiteatro, Bruno di Rocca, Vigna Regis
Roccaldo Acuti and his enologist, Vittorio Fiore, produce premium quality wines, Including a Chianti Classico, the Sangiovese wine Anfiteatro, and the Cabernet-Sangiovese blend, Bruno di Rocca.

A Not So Holy Dessert Wine

Grapes hanging up to dry near Selvapiana in Rufina.

the additional suffix of *occhio di pernice* (partridge eye). Vin Santo is processed in a similar manner to a "straw wine" (*vin de paille*), although today the fruit is no longer laid out to dry on straw matting but is instead hung up in well-ventilated rooms or placed on wooden grates. Not until the fruit has almost reached the raisin stage can it be pressed; the must which is produced is then so concentrated and sugary that the fermented wine achieves levels of 15 and 16 percent alcohol by volume while still containing residues of unfermented sugar.

A Second Fermentation in the Attic

After fermentation, barrels are half-filled with the young wine and then sealed. In the past these barrels were generally constructed from Italian chestnut but, since the 1980s, French oak, as elsewhere, has come into increasing use. The barrels are stored in the *Vinsantaia* which is normally the attic of the estate's buildings. Over a period of years the residual sugar undergoes fermentation again in the summer heat, due to the influence of yeast, and in time this seals up the staves of the barrel. The swings in temperature between the warmth of summer and the cold of winter give rise to the rich aromas of nuts, apricots, honey, spices, and flowers which are the mark of a good Vin Santo. The aging process is complete after between two and six years, the different periods of time producing different types of wine, all of which are defined by D.O.C. regulations. The range encompasses dry wines similar to a Fino sherry, as well as medium and sweet varieties.

Vin Santo, holy wine, is the name given to Italy's famous sweet or sherry-like dessert wine. Its natural home is Tuscany but it is widely produced throughout central Italy and even in the northern region of Trentino. Normally Vin Santo is made from white grapes, especially Trebbiano Toscano and Malvasia which several decades ago were still cultivated in vast quantities in the Chianti region. Today, Sangiovese or other red varieties are only occasionally used, and in such cases the wine is often given

Vernaccia di San Gimignano

Tuscany produces a small number of remarkable white wines including some interesting Chardonnays, and several good Montecarlo Biancos, as well as some Vermentino wines from the coast. The only really well-known white wine, however, comes from a small city to the northeast of Siena whose characteristic towers have made it one of the most popular tourist destinations in the region: San Gimignano. Vernaccia vines, particularly a white variant, have been grown here since the 13th century. The term "Vernaccia" refers to a large group of varieties—both white and red—which are not related to each other. These grapes can be found in a swathe stretching from the island of Sardinia and the far south to

the far north and Alto Adige. Despite its name, it is thought that San Gimignano's Vernaccia is not related to any of the other varieties within the group, but is instead native to its region and a genuine local specialty.

In 1966 Vernaccia di San Gimignano was the first Italian quality wine to be given D.O.C. status—a measure which probably saved this rather unpopular variety from being permanently displaced by Trebbiano and Malvasia. The fortuitousness of its elevation to a D.O.C. wine was borne out by subsequent events when it became apparent that the wines of San Gimignano had far more interesting aroma and flavor traits than standard Tuscan blends of white wine. In spite of its undeniably unique character however, the wines were never really successful: national and

international tastes increasingly turned to the red wines of Tuscany. Fermented in steel tanks, and often quite simply structured, these whites were only slowly accepted by the market. Even the awarding of D.O.C.G. status in the 1990s was unable to bring about a fundamental change.

The local designation of origin of San Gimignano, awarded simultaneously for rosés, red wines and Vin Santo, will have a more clearly defined impact on the local industry. It appears that the reds trading under this name—many of the Sangiovese varietals are similar to a moderately powerful Chianti—are achieving more interesting qualities with some growers than the more famous Vernaccia.

San Gimignano, the home of Vernaccia, and a popular tourist destination.

EACH TO HIS OWN

Almost every D.O.C. region in Tuscany that takes itself seriously has its own definition for the local Vin Santo. Sometimes they are Canaiolo Bianco varietals (Bianco della Valdinievole), while in other places they are blends of Sangiovese and Malvasia Nera (Bianco dell'Empolese, Binaco Pisano di San Torpé, Bolgheri). Candia di Colli Apuani, Carmignano, Colli dell' Etruria Centrale have both white and red Vin Santo; Colline Lucchesi limits itself to red only; Elba, Montecarlo, and Monteregio have white and red varieties; Montescudaio is red; while Pomino, San Gimignano, and Val d'Arbia are white. Three of Tuscany's famous growing regions have created their own independent designation of origin for Vin Santo. These are Chianti, Chianti Classico, and Montepulciano where three, four or even more kinds are produced: *secco*, *amabile*, *occhio di pernice*, and *riserva*. Most of Tuscany's Vin Santo, however, is sold without a D.O.C. designation.

As with the wines, so it is with their quality—i.e. there is considerable variation. Almost every grower in Tuscany produces this traditional wine himself—irrespective of his grapes, *terroir*, or skill. Because the wines are aged for years in barrels of dubious quality and the proscription against moving the wine encourages the formation of short-lived acids, molds, and undesirable aromas, the production of Vin Santo is a demanding process and only a few are ever able to master it. Good Vin Santo, of the type made by around two dozen growers, stands comparison with any sweet or fortified wine from another country. For the most part, however, the Tuscan habit of dunking hard almond cookies into a glass of Vin Santo after a meal appears to be its only proper use.

Moscadello Montalcino

The Muscatel family has really only made a home for itself in the extreme north and south of Italy. The many variations on this grape variety—one of the most ancient in the world—produce both Asti and the sweet wines of Pantelleria. In Trentino (Alto Adige) they are noted for their delicate aromas, while in Loazzolo they excel in exotic fullness. It is only in the small commune of Montalcino, home of the Sangiovese classic Brunello, and Rosso di Montalcino, that Muscatel has been able to find a niche in central Italy, in the form of Moscadello. For years it was largely ignored until, at the end of the 1980s, several large and renowned Brunello producers took an interest in the grape, the result being a rather light, sweet wine.

The enormous commercial success of this wine contrasts with a small production volume of 39,600 gallons (1,500 hl) which is, in turn, shared among various different types of wine: there is a semi-sweet still Moscadello; a light, sweet, bubbly wine and a dense, sweet, alcoholic variety called Vendemmia Tardiva whose fruit is harvested late, and which is modeled closely on Vin Santo or the sweet wines of cooler wine-growing countries.

Vin Santo, the traditional Tuscan welcoming drink, is available in a wide range of styles, from those resembling liqueurs through to dry varieties. The best are aged for up to ten years before bottling and are fascinatingly complex.

THE OTHER SANGIOVESE

If Chianti is one of the most popular designations of origin in Italy today, then Brunello is without doubt one of the most prestigious. Its growing region is, for the most part, identical with the commune of Montalcino, a small town perched atop the northernmost salient of the 1,970-feet (600-m) high range running between the Ombrone and Arbia valleys, about 25 miles (40 km) south of Siena. With its steep, winding streets snaking between narrow medieval buildings, Montalcino has remained one of the best-preserved towns in Tuscany. However, in the last few years it has increasingly been opened up to tourism.

Like most red wines in Tuscany, Brunello di Montalcino is made with Sangiovese grapes, though in contrast to Chianti or Vino Nobile it is unblended. A good Brunello is an unmistakable wine. Remarkably robust throughout, the young wine is characterized by solid, though sometimes rough tannins. After aging for an appropriate period in a wooden barrel as well as in the bottle it develops a wonderful bouquet reminiscent of spices, game, and sweet tobacco.

Montalcino, south of Siena, did not become famous for its great Brunello until the 1960s; since then, the area devoted to wine growing has increased several times over.

MULTIFACETED TERROIRS

The climate in Montalcino is dry and moderately Mediterranean. The massif of the 5,700-feet (1,738-m) high Monte Amiata in the south, which towers over the hilly countryside, shields the region from storms, while the high altitude means there is a clear contrast between daytime and night temperatures which encourages the development of a sophisticated bouquet. The higher vineyards in particular are characterized most years by the excellent quality of their fruit from which elegant wines with an overwhelming fullness of aroma are made. In difficult years, however, the thin-skinned Sangiovese has problems ripening and suffers from attacks of mold. In the southwest of Montalcino, on the other hand, and in Castelnuovo dell'Abate, it is somewhat warmer than in the northeast in the middle of the year and this explains why denser, more mineral wines are made here.

The soils, too, vary greatly and this influences the character of the wines. At the foot of the mountain of Montalcino clayey limestone alternates with stony, loamy soils, while the higher reaches are much sandier. As one approaches Monte Amiata deposits of volcanic tuff become more evident.

The sheer variety of natural conditions means that, in the past, wine was blended from fruit from several *terroirs*; by combining the grapes it was hoped that the advantages from some would compensate for the disadvantages of others. It was not until recently that the leading estates decided to attempt single-vineyard wines, though only the most exceptional of these have come to anything.

BRUNELLO THEN AND NOW

Wine growing can be traced back to the Romans and Etruscans here. The designation Brunello appeared for the first time at the end of the 14th century in documents from Montalcino but it is unclear what type of wine was meant. There is no evidence for a red wine based on Sangiovese—which was then still called Vermiglio—having been made before the 18th century, and Brunello in its present form only dates from the end of the 19th century. Brunello owes its existence to the work of Ferruccio Biondi-Santi (see page 417). Even after the war the name "Brunello" was only used by

the Biondi-Santi family for the wines made on their Il Greppo estate.

Although a cooperative was formed in the 1930s, the name of the wine so familiar today did not catch on until the end of the 1950s and beginning of the 1960s. Even in 1970 Montalcino only had 161 acres (65 ha) of specialized vines; at that time Brunello's prestige was based on the fact that it was so rare. In 1980 Brunello was awarded the highest stamp of approval—the D.O.C.G.—from the Italian wine authorities. The legal provisions relating to its production, however, also proved too inflexible for Brunello. Winegrowers were compelled to age their Brunello for at least four years in wooden barrels—a year longer for the *riserva* wines—and were not allowed to sell it before January 1 in the fifth year. The more concentrated wines of previous years had easily coped with conditions which now proved disastrous for the much greater yields of destalked grapes, which were harvested earlier and left to stand as must for shorter periods. The result was thin wine which was only lent a certain

Left
Olives, the second crop for many producers in Tuscany.

Right
Castello Banfi—a wine empire in Montalcino.

freshness and fruitiness by the addition of younger wines. From the mid 1990s, therefore, regulations were modified. The total period of cellaring is now only two years; aging in *barriques* is permitted, and the wines may be sold at an earlier date.

In addition the simpler, second-class D.O.C. wine of Rosso di Montalcino was allowed to be made from Brunello grapes, using fruit taken from younger vines, cooler locations or suboptimal vintages. In the last few years, interest in this wine has grown much faster than in the more expensive Brunello. On average, around half the total production is bottled under the name Rosso and sold at an earlier date.

Worldwide demand has led to a great expansion in Brunello production. In the space of 30 years the area devoted to this variety grew from 247 to 3,706 acres (100 to 1,500 ha). At the same time the DOC Sant Antimo within the Montalcino district, which is still relatively young, is becoming increasingly popular for wines based on Cabernet-Sauvignon and Merlot.

A family and its wine

The history of Brunello is closely tied to that of the Biondi-Santi family. Some 150 years ago, Clemente Santi noticed that some of his vines grew more compact grapes, and he undertook the first experiments in the vineyards of his Il Greppo estate to isolate and propagate suitable Sangiovese rootstock. The berries from these vines were especially thick-skinned, and the resulting wine was more expressive than the rest of the estate's Sangiovese. In the following decades he perfected his propagation technique. His grandson, Ferruccio, was finally able to stock most of the vineyard with these selected vines and in 1888 the first wine to be called "Brunello" was bottled.

In those days Brunello was only bottled in exceptionally good years: the must was left to stand for a long period with its skins and stalks, making an acidic, tannic wine. There was a lower yield from these new vines, which made it more concentrated than today's equivalent. In order to make it more accessible and give it greater balance, Biondi-Santi left the wine to mature for several years in large barrels of Slovenian oak. The resulting wine aged well; it had the fine, ethereal scent of dried roses and a velvety but lively palate.

The estate's cellars still house rare bottles of the 1888 and 1891 vintages as well as bottles from the best years of the 20th century. These

rarities are regularly tested and recorked—a service provided for passionate Brunello collectors around the world.

Unfortunately the fame of Il Greppo has faded considerably in the last few years. The restocking of the vineyards, long an urgent necessity, has been put off, and the barrels used in the cellars are now simply too old. The concentration achieved by the older vintages has not been attained for some time. Nevertheless the reputation of Biondi-Santi Brunello continues to be high. For those consumers conscious of quality, however, Il Greppo wines cannot compete with today's top products from Montalcino.

A Noble Wine
from Montepulciano

From afar, this medieval town looks like something from a picture book: its historic buildings are in superb condition and many of them conceal a wealth of artistic treasures. It is no wonder, then, that Montepulciano is one of the most popular tourist destinations in southern Tuscany. The town is perched atop the extinct volcano of Monte Poliziano, from which it gets its name, and looks down over Lake Trasimeno and the Chiana valley, famed for its white cattle. In the Montepulciano region, Sangiovese is known as Prugnolo Gentile, and the local wine made from a blend similar to that of Chianti is called Vino Nobile di Montepulciano, or Nobile for short.

A D.O.C.G. wine since 1980, the growing area for Nobile is small. A mere 2,965 acres (1,200 ha), mostly in eastern and southeastern locations, are licensed for the production of Nobile. The soils here consist for the most part of yellow sand and clayey sandstone, while limestone formations, which produce the best wines in the Chianti Classico region, are completely absent because of the volcanic nature of the soil. As with Montalcino, the climate here is considerably warmer than in central Tuscany and the summers can occasionally be too hot. In dry years, therefore, it is mainly those vineyards facing Lake Trasimeno that provide the best results; in these locations, even a modicum of moisture is useful for promoting the growth and maturity of the grapes.

The hillside town of Montepulciano is famed for its stunning beauty and rich cultural history; it also has a long tradition of wine growing.

Vino Nobile, a wine based on the Sangiovese grape, began to be recognized for its quality in the 18th century long before its neighbor, Brunello. The newcomer, however, has since come to overshadow the reputation of Nobile.

Backing a Winner

The history of wine growing in Montepulciano dates back to the Middle Ages and is closely tied to the changing political and military fortunes of the commune. In the wars between Siena and Florence, Montepulciano—despite its geographical proximity to Siena—allied itself with the Medicis in Florence and it was they who, out of gratitude, later transformed the isolated hilltown into a center for the arts. Wine growing was a flourishing industry at that time and one from which the wealthy and noble families of the city profited. In the 16th century Popes Paul III and Sixtus V praised Nobile as Italy's "most perfect wine."

Whether the designation "Vino Nobile" derives from the involvement of the elite merchant class in the wine trade or from the harvest of the best fruit is unclear. In the 17th century the Nobile was still honored as the "King of Wines" but its reputation then began to diminish steadily.

It was not until the 20th century that it underwent a certain renaissance when Adamo Fanetti, the owner of an estate in Montepulciano, set out to make a high-quality wine on the model of Brunello, which he dubbed "Vino Nobile." Tancredi Biondi-Santi, one of the guardians of Brunello, assisted him with technical advice and provided ideas on how to market the new product.

Fanetti took the assortment of varieties which Ricasoli had established for Chianti Classico as the model for his new wine. Sangiovese provides the base, to which may be added 20 percent Canaiolo Nero, 20 percent from other red varieties, and 10 percent white wine. In spite of this, comparison between the two D.O.C.G. wines is not straightforward. As a rule, Vino Nobile has more body and a higher alcohol content than Chianti, which can largely be attributed to the more favorable climate of Montepulciano.

In spite of its strength, the Nobile consistently makes a relatively fruity impression and occasionally exhibits distinct floral aromas—connoisseurs speak of the scent of violets—and it has an unmistakable aftertaste somewhere between that of Chianti and Brunello. It is, of course, best suited to drinking as a hearty accompaniment to a juicy Chiana steak.

Resting on its Laurels

Since 1989 Vino Nobile may be produced without the addition of white grapes, and this has had a beneficial effect on its quality. Today *riserva* wines are occasionally Sangiovese varietals, or a small amount of Cabernet Sauvignon may be added to lend the wine greater density and aromatic complexity. After obvious advances in recent decades, Nobile has been able to match the quality of the new styles of Chianti and Brunello. The maximum yield is restricted to 1,500 gallons (56 hl), as for Brunello, but the wines generated by a small group of top producers is now providing impressive proof that this limit is set at too generous a level to achieve quality.

For many years a second, pressing problem concerned the region's ancient wineries whose standards of hygiene often left much to be desired—though this is something that has recently begun to improve. D.O.C. guidelines had also laid down cellaring times which were simply too long: at least two years for Nobile and three years for *riserva* wines. Following the example of Brunello, however, this obligatory aging period was reduced by half. Including the prescribed final cellaring period in bottles, a Nobile today may be sold two years—the *riserva* three years—after the New Year following the harvest.

An increase in the minimum content of dried EXTRACTIONS, together with a lowering in the acid content of the wines, has done much to improve the average quality. Since the end of the 1980s a series of winegrowers has enthusiastically pursued new types of quality wines. It is hoped that careful selection of vines and a denser planting in the vineyards will lead to better fruit, while in the wineries there has been an emphasis on gentler pressing and pumping techniques, as well as on meticulous hygiene in the fermenting vats and wooden barrels.

A certain internationalization in the taste of the wine has also become apparent; this, it was supposed, would make it easier to sell wines at higher prices. Furthermore, the use of *barriques* and the internationally familiar varieties of Cabernet Sauvignon, Merlot, and Syrah would help many firms achieve greater success with their Nobile. The regional character of the wines and the specific qualities of the individual varieties, however, do not always appear to have been preserved in the process.

As with the system of secondary wines in Montalcino, simpler wines in Montepulciano may be declared Rosso di Montepulciano. This is a lighter, fresher wine, made primarily with the fruit of younger vineyards, which may be drunk earlier. The taste of Rosso can vary widely however. There are, for instance, Rosso di Montepulciano wines on the market which are the equal of Vino Nobile in their density and power, though they make a fresher and more vivacious impression because of their shorter aging period. Sometimes the Rosso even brings out the typical aroma and taste of Sangiovese better than some of the considerably more expensive Nobile brands. Nevertheless, the demand is almost entirely for Nobile wines, and an increasing number of vineyards are now producing a wine under their own label in addition to their Riserva wines.

Impressive Renaissance palaces frame the Piazza Grande in Montepulciano, which is the birthplace of the poet and humanist Poliziano. (His real name was Agnolo Ambrogini, but he adopted the old name of his native town, Politianus.) He was Chancellor under Lorenzo de' Medici.

WINE GROWING ON THE COAST

For years the Tuscan coast between Livorno and Grosseto was considered a no man's land in terms of wine growing. There were only a few growers cultivating vines in the region and the wine they produced paled beside the reputation of the D.O.C. wines of central Tuscany. The area's climatic conditions are, in fact, extremely well-suited to growing good red wines. Apart from on the smaller islands, however, there was no wine-growing tradition to build on. The arable areas of the Arno delta and the coastal plain were already taken up with other types of agriculture, and the mountainsides were covered by forests and *maquis*, dense scrub vegetation common to the coasts of the Mediterranean.

THE GRAVEL OF BOLGHERI

This area of Tuscany is dominated by sandy, loamy soils similar to the Colline Pisane area and the mountains of Montescudaio, so that grapes grown here produce both light, fruity wines and great reds which age well. In the region of Bolgheri, a small city in Livorno province, there are gravelly, chalky formations, known as Sassicaia, which provide conditions

Piermario Meletti Cavallari created the cult wine Grattamacco from Cabernet and Sangiovese. He has now stocked a new vineyard with Merlot.

ideally conducive to wine production. It is no coincidence, then, that the most famous wine in Italy today, the marchese Incisa della Roccheta's Sassicaia, was developed here after the Second World War. Made from Cabernet Sauvignon and a small amount of Cabernet Franc, and aged in French *barriques*, it became a model for Italian quality wine production in the 1980s.

MERLOT AND SANGIOVESE

Up to this time, the region had only produced the rather weak D.O.C. wine Rosé of Bolgheri, but word of its real potential quickly spread. The producers of the cult wine Sassicaia—the marchese Mario Incisa della Rocchetta, together with his cellarmaster Giacomo Tachis—quickly found that they had numerous imitators. Among them was one of the Antinori brothers, Lodovico, who, together with André Tchelistcheff, the famous enologist from Napa, developed a Californian-style estate close to San Guido. His Ornellaia and Masseto wines, which are based on Cabernet and Merlot, quickly won over an enthusiastic international audience.

Meanwhile in the small medieval town of Castagneto Carducci, near Bolgheri, Piermario Meletti Cavallari went about things rather more quietly. Cavallari, an urban refugee from Brescia, focused on Sangiovese; his red Grattamacco contains only a small portion of Cabernet Sauvignon to round off the aroma and taste. And the house of the Marchesi Antinori—which had neglected the region somewhat since their collaboration with Incisa—finally joined the ranks of the producers of excellent Tuscan coastal wines with a Cabernet called Guardo al Tasso.

In the 1990s this activity spread to the gentle slopes behind the coastal town of Cecina under whose red, compact, sandy soil there lay a stratum of gravel similar to that at Sassicaia. The region of Montescudaio in Cecina's hinterland is not as blessed by nature but is nevertheless capable of producing respectable, full-bodied red wines. Sea breezes here mean that the climate—as with all areas of the Tuscan coast—is mild and the differences between the seasons are far less marked than they are in many other regions, for example in Chianti Classico inland.

ON THE FRINGES

Sea breezes also regulate the climate on the island of Elba and in dry years they can even damage the grape harvest. As with the Tuscan mainland, wine has been grown here since the days of the Etruscans, although today only a few producers make good wines such as the sweet, red Aleatico which is the real specialty of the island.

In the northern part of the Tuscan coast, at the foot of the Alpi Apuane, as the Apennines are somewhat confusingly referred to here, lie the Colli di Luni, a continuation of a Ligurian range. This area's white Vermentino can be very fruity and well-balanced. The white Candia dei Colli Apuani, on the other hand, is almost unknown

Left
Ornellaia brought Californian concepts to Bolgheri and first caused a stir toward the end of the 1980s with its Merlot wine, Masseto.

Right
The horses of Sassicaia— winners on the racetracks of the world.

outside the region. The same applies to Colline Lucchesi, from the hills around the city of Lucca, where both white and red versions are made.

Probably the best and—at least among connoisseurs—best-known white wines in the region come from Montecarlo (not to be confused with the capital of Monaco), though they are native to a more inland area. Here, the neutral Trebbiano grape is enhanced by the addition of other interesting varieties which lend the wines a certain *terroir* character—a compliment that one is not able to pay to Bianco Pisano di San Torpé, whose only claim to fame seems to be that it was being made as long ago as the time of the Roman Empire.

Thoroughbred horses, thoroughbred wines

Sassicaia initiated the wave of Tuscan "super table wines." The process of aging the wine in *barriques*, and frequent addition of French varieties, enabled it to achieve a level of quality previously thought unattainable in the region. Although its name is closely tied to more recent developments in Italian wine growing, the origins of this red wine from Bolgheri reach further back than some of the most prestigious Italian D.O.C. wines.

The history of Sassicaia began after the Second World War when the marchese Mario Incisa della Rocchetta moved from Rome to his country estate of San Guido, in Bolgheri. He loved all things French, and, as the breeder of internationally successful racehorses, he was friendly with the Rothschilds, owners of some of the finest châteaux in the Bordeaux region. Francophilia and friendship therefore helped to transport Cabernet seedlings from the Gironde to Bolgheri.

During the 1960s, Incisa's nephew, Piero Antinori, his chief winemaker Giacomo Tachis, and the French enologist Emile Peynaud expressed an interest in this experiment. At

Marchese Incisa della Rocchetta, creator of Sassicaia.

their suggestion, a second vineyard was established; the first products to reach the market were 3,000 bottles from the 1968 vintage.

Around 1970—at about the same time as Antinori's Sangiovese table wine, Tignanello, was making waves—Sassicaia began to take off. Much of the wine's success was due to Giacomo Tachis, who had managed to perfect Sassicaia's

vinification and aging process to the point where it was able to compete with the most reputable of its Californian and French peers.

Production expanded under the direction of Mario's son, Nicolò. The original vineyard area of 4 acres (1.6 ha) was extended to around 74 acres (30 ha) and the annual yield increased to almost 200,000 bottles, making Sassicaia one of the highest volume, top-quality wines in Italy. The vineyards of Tenuta San Guido are today divided into four parcels: Sassicaia, Castiglioncello, Aia Nuova, and Quercione. Apart from the 1,150-feet (350-m) high Castiglioncello—a site which would be eminently suited to its own *cru*—none of the vineyards is higher than 320 feet (100 m) above sea level.

Since the 1980s Grattamacco, Ornellaia, Guado al Tasso and Tenuta Terriccio have also given proof of the potential for wine production offered by the Tuscan coast. And in the 2000 vintage the vineyard at last brought out a second wine. This wine is named Guido Alberto.

Tuscany's New El Dorado

One of the most interesting areas under development in Tuscany—and perhaps in all Italy—is on the southern stretch of coast and its hinterland, which extends as far as the foothills of Monte Amiata and the Brunello area. This is the Maremma area, a landscape which has traditionally been more famous for its nature parks and cattle breeding than for its wines. Today its name has come to refer to all the wine-growing areas of southwest Tuscany.

In Maremma the red Sangiovese grape is dominant, and forms the basis of that most important *appellation*, the Morellino di Scansano, which is grown on the border between the coastal plain of Grosseto and the volcanic hills. Although little known to a wider public, this designation of origin has an undeniable potential, particularly when the vineyards are clayey and slaty soils stocked with mature Sangiovese vines.

Maremma stretches from the coast into the hinterland in the most southerly tip of Tuscany. It has considerable quality potential and has already attracted many investors.

An Attractive Combination of Varieties

The expressive character of Morellino wines is due both to the *terroir* and the unique composition of varieties to be found in many of the older vineyards. Apart from the dominant Sangiovese grape there are also Grenache—called Alicante here, a name which betrays its Spanish origins—Ciliegolo, Canaiolo, and Malvasia Nera, which provide aromatic complexity and a soft, full, fruity taste in some of the most interesting wines of the region. In addition, some of the estates have planted Cabernet Sauvignon, Merlot, or Chardonnay, though these are largely used for the high-quality table wines, the Supertuscans.

The unrealized potential of Maremma, especially the Morellino area, has been discovered by the more established estates and producers from northern Tuscany and the Chianti region. They have invested in new vineyards which have been organized according to the latest

The future of the Maremma region

The growing region of Morellino di Scansano, at the edge of Maremma, has become a magnet for investors in the past few years. The list of those who have either purchased new land for planting vines, or bought existing vineyards and established businesses, is quite extensive and encompasses a number of famous names from the Tuscan wine industry. They include large producers like Luigi Cecchi in Castellina and the Mazzei family, who own the famous Castello di Fonterutoli; Federico Carletti, the owner of the Poliziano estate in Montepulciano; and the Widmers, a Swiss couple whose Brancaia estate collaborates closely with Fonterutoli.

Even the Marchesi Frescobaldi have bought into the Maremma area. Their most recent company, Luce della Vita—a joint venture between the Tuscans and the Californian house of Robert Mondavi—includes new

Winegrowers were never interested before in the Morellino di Scansano region southeast of Grosseto, but today investors throng here.

vineyards, which the Frescobaldis had long had an eye on, inland from the Tuscan coast. Their 290 acres (120 ha) in the D.O.C. area

of Morellino complement the 1,800 acres (740 ha) of vineyards the family already owns in central Tuscany and in the Brunello region; they are to be stocked with Sangiovese and Merlot at a density of 2,225 vines per acre (5,500 vines/ha).

Estates like those of Erik Banti, Le Pupille, or Moris Farms, which in the last few decades have produced good wines more or less anonymously, have undoubtedly played their part in this unusually hectic activity. Another motive for the decision to invest in Maremma was probably the sheer availability of cheap land suitable for viniculture that was not being fully exploited.

The tranquility and isolation of the region may soon be over forever: established producers in Chianti Classics and Montalcino have invested heavily in Maremma.

techniques and with an eye to the mistakes made by previous generations.

The reason for these investments is not hard to find. The success of Tuscan wine in the last 20 years has meant that the restricted area under cultivation has not been able to meet the demand for Chianti, Brunello, etc., especially as the vines themselves were older and yielded only limited harvests. The southern Tuscan areas offered a welcome opportunity for producing new wines with a Tuscan designation of origin—especially I.G.T. Toscana—without having to resort to less reputable Apulian or Sicilian *appellations*.

But even here the risks are not inconsiderable. Large areas have had to be freshly stocked and, on past experience, this means that top-quality wines cannot usually be expected for several years. On the other hand, only in exceptional cases do the sites of Maremma have a potential for quality which would put them on a level with central Tuscany: most of the vineyards are clearly inferior.

This problem of patchy vineyard quality is one that the growers of other designations of origin in southern Tuscany are having to come to terms with. As with southern Italy, it is often the case here that the list of wine types allowed by law is inversely proportional to the quality and reputation of the individual wines. On the slopes of the Massa Marittima, where the D.O.C. region of Monteregio has been established, there are at least still good Sangiovese, Cabernet, and Ciliegiolo wines. The same cannot be said of Parrina, whose whites, reds, and rosés from the Grosseto plain are virtually unknown, and the

Tradition and technology go hand in hand: on some estates the grapes are still brought in using baskets, and the wine is bottled in demijohns. In the surrounding area, however, there are also vast winemaking firms growing fashionable varieties and building hi-tech cellars.

Ansonica Costa dell'Argentario region is one of the new, highly productive regions which it might have been better not to have established in the first place.

The only white wine from southern Tuscany to enjoy a degree of popularity at the regional level is Bianco di Pitigliano, a Trebbiano blend with Greco and Malvasia, which finds a market in Rome. To claim that there is more than a mere handful of companies producing proper wines, however, would be an exaggeration—despite the fact that southern Tuscany has in recent years become the plaything of the large Chianti estates as well as other investors. If growers' achievements up until now are critically examined, one is forced to ask whether the optimism connected with all this hectic business activity has in fact been justified.

Select Producers in Southern Tuscany

Avignonesi***−****
MONTEPULCIANO

208 acres (84 ha); 500,000 bottles • Wines: →Nobile di Montepulciano, Rosso di Montepulciano, Vignola, Marzocco, Pinot Nero, →Merlot, →Grifi, →50:50, Aleatico, Vin Santo, →Vin Santo Occhio di Pernice
The Falvo brothers created new trends for the region with their wines such as Grifi, a Sangiovese-Cabernet blend, the single-variety Merlot Desiderio, the internationally competitive sweet wine Vin Santo Occhio di Pernice, and the Chardonnay Marzocco.

Castello Banfi**−****
MONTALCINO

1,730 acres (700 ha); some bought-in grapes; 5,000,000 bottles • Wines include: →Brunello di Montalcino Poggio all'Oro, Rosso di Montalcine Centine, →Summus Castello Banfi, Col di Sasso, Collalto, Pinot Nero Belnero, Merlot Mandrielle, Tavernelle, Chardonnay Fontanelle
The *castello* Poggio alla Mura, which belongs to Banfi, is well worth seeing. The range of wines from this American-owned winery has remained consistently high in quality for many years.

Ciacci Piccolomini d'Aragona***−****
MONTALCINO

86 acres (35 ha); 90,000 bottles • Wines: →Brunello di Montalcino Vigna Pianrosso, Rosso di Montalcino Vigna della Fonte, →I.G.T. Toscana Ateo, →I.G.T. Sant'Animo Rosso Fabius
In recent years the estate has experienced an upturn in quality. The best vintages are bottled as single-vineyard wines. The Brunello and the table wine Ateo (which has 15% Cabernet Sauvignon) are around the same level of quality.

Andrea Costanti****−*****
MONTALCINO

25 acres (10 ha); 40,000 bottles • Wines: →Brunello di Montalcino, Rosso di Montalcino, Vermiglio
Constanti's estate is one of the historical giants of Montalcino. The south-southwest orientation of the vineyards and the *galestro* soils of Eocene origin offer ideal conditions for Sangiovese. Constanti's wines are generally very elegant and fruity. The house olive oil is also outstanding.

Croce di Mezzo***−***
MONTALCINO

9 acres (3.5 ha); 15,000 bottles • Wines: Brunello di Montalcino, Rosso di Montalcino, Rosso della Croce
Paolo Nanetti and Fiorella Vannoni's estate has only recently begun producing above average quality wines.

Fattoria dei Barbi e del Casato**−****
DONATELLA

133 acres (53 ha); 350,000 bottles • Wines: →Brunello di Montalcino Vigna del Fiore, Rosso di Montalcino, Vin Santo, →Bruscone dei Barbi, Brusco dei Barbi
Francesca Colombini-Cinelli's estate is a true farm, which raises sheep and pigs as well as producing wines. You can find its produce on the menu in the restaurant. The *fattoria* was one of the first to take up Biondi-Santi's idea of calling the local wine Brunello.

Eredi Fuligni****−*****
MONTALCINO

20 acres (8 ha); 50,000 bottles • Wines: →Brunello di Montalcino Riserva Vigneti dei Cottimelli, Brunello di Montalcino, Rosso di Montalcino Ginestreto, Fuligni San Jacopo

The Fuligni family rely on maturing in big wooden barrels, and every year they produce one of the best wines within the Brunello di Montalcino boundaries.

Grattamacco***−****
CASTAGNETO CARDUCCI

19 acres (7.5 ha); 50,000 bottles • Wines: Grattamacco Rosso, Grattamacco Bianco
The family of Paola and Piermario Meletti Cavallari has, since 2002, leased the estate for twelve years to Claudio Tipa.

Gualdo del Re****−*****
SUVERETO

35 acres (14 ha); 60,000 bottles • Wines: Val de Cornia Rosso Gualdo del Re, Val di Cornia Rossa and Bianco Esordio, →Federico Primo, →Rennero, Strale Pinot Bianco, Vermentino Valentina
The owners, Nico Rossi and Maria Teresa Cabella, produce outstanding wines, with the aid of the wine-maker Barbara Tamburini. The single-variety Cabernet Sauvignon Federico Primo and the Merlot Rennero are among the top wines in Italy.

Lisini***−****
MONTALCINO

25 acres (10 ha); 50,000 bottles • Wines: →Brunello di Montalcino Ugolaia, Rosso di Montalcino
Wines have long been produced here under the guidance of the famous oenologist Franco Bernabei; they are characterized by elegance and a fruity, floral bouquet.

Montepeloso*****
SUVERETO

15 acres (6 ha); 20,000 bottles • Wines: Val di Cornia Rosso, →Gabbro, →Nardo
Facio Chiarelotto is uncompromising in his pursuit of quality. The red Gabbro and Nardo wines, made from Sangiovese and Cabernet Sauvignon, are among the most concentrated wines in Italy.

Casanova di Neri***−****
MONTALCINO

37 acres (15 ha); 70,000 bottles • Wines: →Brunello di Montalcino Cerretalto, →Tenuta Nuova, Rosso di Montalcino
Giacomo Neri's firm in Montalcino specializes in wines from selected vineyard sites. Neri is experimenting with aging in various kinds of wood and swears by the new *barriques*, which lend his complex, fruity wines a slight vanilla note, soft tannins and—most importantly—a long, powerful finish.

Poderi Boscarelli***−*****
MONTEPULCIANO

32 acres (13 ha); 60,000 bottles • Wines: Vino Nobile di Montepulciano, Rosso di Montepulciano
The Riserva del Nocio produced by Paolo di Ferrari Corradi and Sons is unanimously considered one of the best Nobiles. Also of consistent high quality are the Nobile and the Boscarelli I.G.T.

Poggio Antico**−****
MONTALCINO

49 acres (20 ha); 60,000 bottles • Wines: Brunello di Montalcino, Rosso di Montalcino, →Altero
This estate has superbly situated vineyards whose enormous potential has begun to be better exploited over the last few years. One of the very best Tuscan restaurants is also situated here.

POLIZIANO****–*****
MONTALCINO

297 acres (120 ha); 500,000 bottles • Wines: Nobile di Montepulciano: →Vigna Asinone and Caggiole; Rosso di Montepulciano, Chianti Colli Senesi, Bianco Valdichiana, →Elegia, Ambra, →Le Stanze, Vin Santo

With his Cabernet Le Stanze and Riserva Nobile Asinone, Federico Carletti is one of the very best wine producers in the Montepulciano region. Recently, a very good Morellino from the Lhosa estate has been added to the range. The wines are modern, but not too woody, and even the simpler quality wines attain a very high standard.

SALICUTTI****–*****
MONTALCINO

• Wines: →Brunello di Montalcino, Rosso di Montalcino

The organic grower Francesco Leanza surpassed all the elite wines in the region with his outstandingly excellent 1995 Brunello.

SAN GUIDO—INCISA DELLA ROCCHETTA****–*****
CASTAGNETO CARDUCCI—BOLGHERI

74 acres (30 ha); 200,000 bottles • Wines: →Sassicaia, →Guido Alberto

This estate is home to the cult wine Sassicaia.

SANTA RESTITUTA****–*****
MONTALCINO

37 acres (15 ha); 45,000 bottles • Wines: →Brunello di Montalcino Sugarile, Rosso di Montalcino, →Chiesa di Santa Restituta, Vin Santo

This famous Brunello estate was acquired some years ago by Angelo Gaia. The top Sangiovese, Chiesa di Santa Restituta, and the single-vineyard Brunello Sugarile are among the best wines in southern Tuscany.

VASCO SASSETTI***–****
CASTELNUOVO DELL'ABATE

• Wines: →Brunello di Montalcino, Rosso di Montalcino

Sassetti runs one of the up and coming estates in the region, along with a butcher's shop and the popular *trattoria-osteria* Bassomondo.

SASSOTONDO****–*****
SOVANA

27 acres (11 ha); 20,000 bottles • Wines: Franze Rosso Toscana, Sassotondo Rosso, San Lorenzo Rosso

Here in the most southerly corner of Tuscany, Carla Benigni Ventimiglia and her winemaker, Attilio Pagli, produce outstanding wines from the promising Ciliegiolo variety, as well as from Alicante and Sangiovese.

MICHELE SATTA****
CASTAGNETO CARDUCCI

74 acres (30 ha); 160,000 bottles • Wines: Bolgheri Bianco, Rosso Diambra, →Bolgherei Rosso Piastraia, I.G.T. Toscana Cavaliere Sangiovese, Costa di Giulia Bianco, Il Giovane Re Viognier

In the vineyard, Michele Satta relies on the natural balance of the vines. His wines express this close to nature philosophy.

TENUTA CAPARZO**–****
MONTALCINO

215 acres (87 ha); 420,000 bottles • Wines: Brunello di Montalcino, →Brunello di Montalcino La Casa, Rosso di Montalcino La Caduta, Chianti Classico, →I.G.T. Toscana Ca' del Pazzo, I.G.T. Sant'Animo Le Grance

Good vintages of the barrel-aged single-vineyard Brunello La Casa from Sante Turnone are considered among the best in the region. There is also a premium quality Cabernet-Sangiovese blend, Ca' del Pazzo.

Biondi Santi, originator of Brunelli, with his oldest wine.

TENUTA GHIZZANO***–****
PECCIOLI

40 acres (16 ha); 70,000 bottles • Wines: Chianti Colline Pisane, →Veneroso, →Nambrot, Vin Santo San Germano

The *tenuta* has been owned by the Venerosi Pasciolini family since the 14th century. The first Veneroso vintage garnered the highest praise. A high quality Merlot single variety, Nambrot, is produced.

TENUTA DELL'ORNELLAIA***–*****
CASTAGNETO CARDUCCI—BOLGHERI

148 acres (60 ha); 200,000 bottles • Wines: →Ornellaia, →Masseto, Poggio alle Gazze, Le Volte, Serre Nuove

Established by Ludovico Antinori with the assistance of the veteran Californian master, André Tchelistcheff. Largely focused on Merlot, the estate made a name for itself with a blend, Ornellaia, and a single variety Merlot called Masseto. It has since been bought by the Californian firm of Mondavi. Since 1997, the range has been extended by an interesting secondary wine, Serre Nuove, and the basic wine Le Volte.

TENUTA DI TERRICCIO***–****
CASTELLINA MARITTIMA

62 acres (25 ha); 50,000 bottles • Wines: Rondinaia, →Lupicaia, →Tassinaia, →Saluccio, Con Vento

The Luicaia, Tassinaia, Rondinaia, and Saluccio wines of the former showjumper Gain Annibale Rossi have fulfilled all expectations fueled by the ideal growing conditions of this estate.

VAL DI SUGA***–****
MONTALCINO

91 acres (37 ha); 180,000 bottles • Wines: →Brunello di Montalcino Vigna del Lago and →Spuntali, Rosso di Montalcino

Val di Suga, one of the best Brunello estates, was bought in the mid-1980s by the Angelini group, together with Tenuta Trerose in Montepulciano and San Leonino in the Chianti Classico region. The quality of all the wines has remained at the high level achieved.

UMBRIA

Despite its wine-growing potential, Umbria—like other central Italian regions—is overshadowed by its neighbor, Tuscany. In the green heart of Italy (as the tourist brochures call this part of the country), only Orvieto is familiar to a wider audience. Of the four and three quarter million gallons (180,000 hl) of quality wine produced in the region—a fifth of total Umbrian production—Orvieto accounts for two thirds.

Orvieto and Orvieto Classico are made from neutral local varieties such as Trebbiano

Sangiovese has a great future.

Toscano, Verdello, Grechetto, and Canaiolo Bianco, and are seldom more than merely drinkable, pleasant wines for everyday occasions. Previously the region preferred its wines sweet or medium-dry but today there are more intense tasting products—occasionally even barrel-fermented ones—which can provide a good accompaniment to strong-tasting dishes.

Although Orvieto production is largely in the hands of three cooperatives, a few small to medium-sized businesses have emerged since the 1980s with new ideas and remarkably good wines. One of these is the Chardonnay Cervaro from Antinori's Castello della Sala, an exceptional table wine which brilliantly exploits all the potential of modern Italian viticulture.

If Antinori's Umbrian wines at first profited from their association with this reputable Tuscan firm, they soon earned the industry's respect and established their own, independent image. This process was hastened along by a series of other companies in the Orvieto region who made similar efforts—including the largest cooperative in the area which produced some above-average, quality wines.

RED BEATS WHITE: TORGIANO

Although the dominance of Orvieto means that Umbria is mainly a white wine region, international acclaim was first achieved by a red wine. Torgiano, a wine with a Sangiovese base, was created virtually single-handed by Giorgio Lungarotti, and later awarded D.O.C. honors. In the 1970s Lungarotti ensured that the fame of this small commune *appellation*, close to the regional capital of Perugia, spread beyond Italy, and the Rubesco—especially the Riserva Monticchio—became a cult wine on the international wine scene.

The success of Torgiano was short-lived, however, in spite of the elevation of *riserva* wines to D.O.C.G. status in 1992. Lungarotti was practically the only producer of this designation of origin but he undermined the entire *appellation* by allowing the wines made by his company to stagnate in the 1990s. Nevertheless, Lungarotti's considerable achievements—he was also the initiator of the annual *Banco d'Assaggio dei Vini d'Italia*, one of the country's most important wine competitions, and the driving force behind a wine museum in Torgiano—provided an important stimulus to the Umbrian wine industry.

Map

The Marches

4,460 ft (1,414 m) Monte il Castello
Sansepolcro
Anghiari
43°30'
Arezzo
3,195 ft (974 m)
Citta di Castello
3,550 ft (1,082 m) Monte Favalto
Castiglion Fiorentino
Tuscany
Colli Altotiberini
Cortona
Umbertide
Umbria
Gualdo Tadino
Lago Trasimeno
Magione
Castiglione del Lago
Chiascio
Nocera Umbra
Lago di Chiusi
Perugia
Assisi
Colli del Trasimeno
Chiusi
Monte Subasio 4,235 ft (1,290 m) Spello
Torgiano
43°
Colli Perugini
Bettona
Deruta
Citta di Pieve
Tiber
Foligno
Bevagna
Marsciano
Montefalco
Trevi
Montefalco
Ficulle
Colli Martani
3,590 ft (1,094 m)
Monte Rufino 2,410 ft (734 m) Paglia
Todi
Orvieto
Spoleto
Castel Giorgio
Orvieto
Lago di Corbara
Acquasparta
Monte Fionci 4,385 ft (1,337 m)
Monti Volsini
Baschi
San Gemini
3,675 ft (1,121 m)
Ferentillo
Bolsena
Bagnoregio
Lago di Alviano
Amelia
Terni
Piediluco
Lago di Bolsena
Montefiascone
Colli Amerini
Narni
Lago di Piediluco
42°30'N
Lazio
Orte
Tuscania
Viterbo
Soriano nel Cimino
3,455 ft (1,053 m)

Legend:
Colli Altotiberini
Colli del Trasimeno
Colli Perugini
Torgiano / Torgiano Rosso Riserva
Colli Martani
Montefalco / Montefalco Sagrantino
Orvieto
Orvieto Classico
Colli Amerini
Wine-growing areas in neighboring regions

6 miles (10 km)

Umbria's North Gets Going

New designations of origin were created throughout the region, especially in the north at the upper reaches of the river Tiber and around Perugia. The commune of Montefalco, with its dry or sweet red wines from native Sagrantino and Sangiovese varieties, has been particularly impressive. The Sagrantino di Montefalco varietal, which has been promoted to a D.O.C.G. wine, shows a great deal of power and fullness accompanied by rich, spicy aromas. The sweet version, the Sagrantino di Montefalco Passito, is a specialty only found in this region. Good red and white wines from Sangiovese, Merlot, Cabernet Sauvignon, Trebbiano, Grechetto, and Chardonnay can be found here as Colli del Trasimeno and Colli Perugini. Even the more recent Umbrian designations of origin like Colli Martani and Colli Amerini—areas in the center and extreme south of the region which were defined in 1989 and 1990 respectively—have impressed in the wines made by several of the region's more interesting producers.

With the revived Orvieto (Classico), a powerful Montefalco, and a workhorse like Torgiano —providing the qualities of the latter stabilize— Umbria's future seems secure.

Left
In Orvieto more engaging white wines from traditional varieties are now being made, including a *barrique*-aged Classico from Tenuta Vellette.

Right
Visitors to Umbria and its wine-growing regions should include Assisi on their itinerary, a town famous for both its art and its religious history.

Select Producers in Umbria

Castello della Sala—Antinori**–****
Ficule
346 acres (140 ha); 300,000 bottles • Wines: Orvieto Classico, →Cervaro della Sala, →Muffato della Sala, →Pinot Nero Vigneto Consola
The Florentine house of Antinori was one of the first to invest outside its home region. Here, it produces one of the best Chardonnays in central Italy.

Giorgio Lungarotti***
Torgiano
692 acres (280 ha); 2,800,000 bottles • Wines include: San Giorgio, Torgiano: Torre di Giano Riserva Il Pino, Rubesco Riserva Vigna Monticchio; Chardonnay: Vigna I Palazzi, di Miralduolo; Caernet, Pinot Grigio, Buffaloro, Castel Grifone, Solleone, Metodo Classico Brut, Falò, Brezza, Pergoleto, Rondò, Vin Santo
In spite of a few new and sometimes insignificant wines, the backbone of this former leading vineyard is formed the red classics Rubesco Riserva Monticchio, which is only bottled in exceptional years, and San Giorgio, a 50:50 blend of Cabernet and the Tuscan varieties Sangiovese and Canaiolo.

Il Palazzone****
Orvieto
57 acres (23 ha); 45,000 bottles • Wines: I.G.T. Umbria Grechetto L'Ultima Speranza, Orvieto Classico: Terre Vineate, →Campo del Guardiano; →I.G.T. Umbria Rubbio

Giovanni Dubini has built up one of the few outstanding houses in the region. Strengths are the Orvieto variants and the Rubbio.

Tenuta Vellette***
Orvieto
247 acres (100 ha); 350,000 bottles • Wines include: Orvieto Classico: Velico, Amabile; Calanco, Rosso di Spicca, Monaldesco
The classic Orvieto of the Bottais is marked by density and expressive power. Since 1989, the estate has also added a barrel-fermented Orvieto Classico, Velico and the Sangiovese-Cabernet blend Calanco to its repertoire.

Val di Maggio—A. Caprai****–*****
Montefalco
116 acres (47 ha); 500,000 bottles • Wines include: →Sagrantino di Montefalco, Rosso di Montefalco
Marco Caprai has invested a great deal, and his wines are impressive, even in an international context. The top wine, Sagrantino "25 anni" is one of the great wines of Italy.

Vallesanta—L. A. Barberani***
Baschi
99 acres (40 ha); 300,000 bottles • Wines: Orvieto Classico: Secco Castagnolo, Amabile Pulicchio, Muffa Nobile; Calcaia, Pomaio, Foresco, Polvento, Grechetto, Pinot
Barberani and enologist Maurizio Castelli create an impressive palette of products. Painstaking work in the vineyard and winery yields cleaned-toned, good quality wines (with typical grape variety characteristics).

Lazio

Few people know that a large area of the Eternal City is given over to vineyards. The names Frascati and Colli Albani are familiar, but they are not necessarily connected with Rome. However, with 74,130 acres (30,000 ha) under production the region is by no means insignificant. Lazio does not grow outstanding D.O.C.s to compare with other regions, and the few good Frascati wines (the biggest D.O.C. in Lazio) are outnumbered by the many mass products. But the region does have a growing number of quality-oriented producers who are offering reds that can certainly compete well.

In antiquity the farms surrounding the city served as both bread baskets and wine cellars to the state. The house wine of the Romans— Falernian, usually a red—was made from the native Aminea variety, though this is now probably extinct. The Roman writers Horace, Virgil, Martial, and Pliny the Elder recorded its popularity and variety. White Falernian was also made, and this family of wines could be anything from light to heavy, and from sweet to dry.

White Wines Predominate

More than 85 percent of Lazio wines are white, mainly blended from Trebbiano Toscano and Malvasia. Vineyards in the south of Rome, which penetrate into the city itself, produce Frascati, one of Italy's best-loved quality wines. For a long time the producers of this generally sweet white wine trusted blindly in tradition and the loyalty of the consumer so that the shelves of European supermarkets became choked with Frascati, and its reputation degenerated into that of a cheap wine.

Another popular white wine in the region is Est! Est!! Est!!! di Montefiascone which is produced from Trebbiano and Malvasia grapes in Viterbo province, close to the Orvieto area. Its strange name is popularly explained by an anecdote which recounts how, whilst making a journey to Rome, a German bishop sent his priest ahead to find appropriate accommodation and seek out the best wines which were to be clearly marked with the word "Est!." The priest is said to have been so enthused by the white wines of Montefiascone that he wrote the expression three times—Est! Est!! Est!!! This wine was formerly highly thought of but it, too, has now found its way onto the supermarket shelves.

From around the end of the 1980s it was apparent that efforts were under way—especially on the Falesco estate—to produce real quality wines in the region again. The vineyards which face the banks of Lake Bolsena enjoy a mild climate which, together with the volcanic soil, provides excellent growing conditions for producing outstanding white wines.

Of the remaining areas in Lazio suited to quality vintages, the D.O.C. wines of Colli Albani, Colli Lanuvini, Marino, and Zagarolo, as well as the white variants from the regions of Castelli Romani, Cori, Velletri, and Cerveteri, all have similar characteristics to Frascati. Some growers are experimenting with imported vines such as Chardonnay or Sauvignon Blanc, but few have so far succeeded in producing wines capable of competing on the international or even national markets.

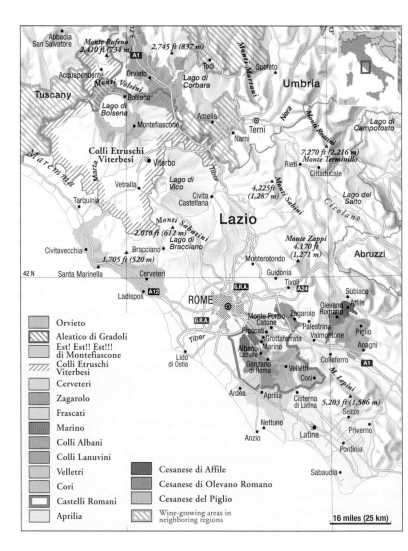

Select Producers of Lazio

Colacicchi***–****
Anagni
12 acres (5 ha); 18,000 bottles • Wines: →Torre Ercolana, Romagnano Bianco, Romagnano Rosso
The family of wine merchant Trimani from Rome purchased this old estate in the 1980s and made great efforts to revive its potential. Under the direction of Giacomo Tachis and Attilio Scienza they produced one of Lazio's best red wines in the Ercolano, a Cabernet-Merlot blend with a small Cesanese component.

Castel De Paolis—A. Croce***–****
Grottaferrata
25 acres (10 ha); 55,000 bottles • Wines: →Frascati: Vigna Adriana, →Selve Vecchio; Muffa Nobile, Moscato Rosa Rosathea, →I Quattro Mori
From the beginning of the 1990s Giulio Santarelli has been proving just how good a Frascati can be. His single vineyard Frascati, Vigna Ariana, is magnificent. Even more remarkable are the wines from his newly organized vineyards which grow Merlot, Cabernet, Syrah, Sauvignon, and Viognier grapes.

Colle Picchioni – P. Di Mauro***–****
Marino
23 acres (9.5 ha); bought-in grapes; 110,000 bottles • Wines: Marino Colle Picchioni Oro, →Colle Picchioni Rosso Vigna del Vassallo, Vignole
Paola di Mauro was one of the first to pursue quality wine growing in Lazio. The basis of her best red wines, such as the excellent Vigna del Vassallo, are French vines up to 60 years of age (which she discovered quite by chance on a newly purchased property). In good years the Colle Picchioni Oro is considered one of the best white wines in the entire region.

Falesco****
Montefiascone
22 acres (9 ha); bought-in grapes; 220,000 bottles • Wines: →Est! Est!! Est!!! di Montefiascone, Poggio dei Gelsi, also Vendemmia Tardiva, →Montiano
Riccardo Cotarella (his brother is head enologist with the Marchesi Antinori) is not only one of the few producers of really good Est! Est!! Est!!!, but he also acts as a consultant to numerous Italian estates, and this work has provided him with many occasions on which to prove his talent. The estate's top wine is the red Montiano.

A Glimmer of Hope for Reds

It is not by concentrating on long-established white wines that the region's future is likely to flourish, however; instead, in recent years, it has been the attempts made with imported red varieties such as Cabernet and Merlot which have produced impressive results. A few of these French varieties had already reached the region at the beginning of the 20th century; some vineyards in the Colli Romani have vines up to 70 years old which are the source of small quantities of exceptional wines. Merlot, Cabernet, and recently even Syrah have provided complex wines, capable of aging, which reveal the potential of the region for good red wines, in stark contrast to the traditional dominance of white wines.

Cesanese, the local standard red variety, seldom amounts to much, however. At their best, Cesanese wines are simple, harmless, fruity, and drinkable affairs for the everyday table. Even today, most growers are reducing the Cesanese proportion in their wines where this is allowed in the statutes of the various *appellations*. Instead, they are planting Sangiovese vines in order to profit from the great reputation of this premium Tuscan variety.

In contrast to neighboring Umbria, Lazio has not been able to stir itself into launching a really serious quality offensive at the turn of the millennium. While it is true that some of the large producers are bringing respectable products onto the market, and that there is even a small group of ambitious estates, the region's many cooperatives, who still control the wine-growing business according to their own whims, have yet to come up with a single competitive wine. Without real entrepreneurial initiative, the region's potential will remain unrealized in the future.

This grand gateway into a vineyard recalls the fame once possessed by wines grown to the south and east of Rome. Today, Lazio is known only for its mass-produced wines.

SOUTHERN ITALY AND THE ISLANDS: A REAWAKENING

According to one's perspective, southern Italy begins either in Rome or in Naples. From the point of view of wine growing, however, the border is marked by Abruzzi on the Adriatic, and Campania on the Tyrhennian coast of the Italian peninsula. The south then encompasses Molise, Apulia, Basilicata, and Calabria, as well as the large islands of Sicily and Sardinia.

A succession of cultures and dynasties have left their mark on southern Italy in the past: Greeks, Albanians, Arabs, Spaniards, Etruscans, and Romans, as well as the Vatican, and the great houses of the Hohenstaufens and Bourbons. In antiquity, wine growing owed much to the great contribution made by the Greeks. Later, the slopes of both Vesuvius and Etna, and the hills of Apulia and Campania, became the greatest suppliers of wine to Republican and Imperial Rome.

The southern latitudes of Italy are inevitably associated with heat and aridity, but it is surprising just how often the region is subject to very cold weather. Climatic conditions in this part of the country are marked by extremes, as are the soil types. From the fertile coastal strips of Apulia, with their maritime climate, to the bleak, rocky countryside of Basilicata and the Sicilian mountains, there is a diverse range of *terroirs* which provide the conditions for a wide spectrum of grape types, most of them local varieties. Several of these, for example the reds Aglianico, Nero d'Avola, and Montepulciano, are so promising that growers from the New World are starting to show an interest in them.

RICH AND POOR REGIONS

Although there are hardly any of these varieties to be encountered in Abruzzi—Montepulciano and Trebbiano almost completely dominate the field—this northernmost region of the south has been able to build up a lucrative wine industry. Its good-value, easily drinkable wines are very much in demand, both at home and abroad.

The range on offer is sparser in Basilicata, where a single, superb variety—Aglianico—overshadows all others, though this has not helped the industry achieve even moderate prosperity. Calabria—the poorhouse of Italy—has few varieties with which it might cause a stir on the international scene, and its industry is the most archaic in the country.

In Calabria time seems to have stood still.

A magnificent view of Etna can be had from Taormina. At the foot of the volcano is a large wine-growing region which, despite its promising soils, has yet to produce anything of significant quality.

Such is not the case in Apulia, whose broad plains produce wine in industrial quantities, most of it being shipped abroad in tankers, or blended with inferior northern Italian wines; up until the 1970s the region's production ended up almost entirely as vermouth. In spite of this, efforts have been undertaken to match northern Italian standards for quality—standards which Calabria or Molise seem destined never to equal.

Enormous strides have been made toward producing quality wines on Sicily recently. For years the island produced nothing except sickly Marsalas, but since the start of the 1990s superb wines—barrel-aged Chardonnays, good local reds, opulent and exotic sweet wines from Pantelleria and the Eolian Islands—demonstrate that, in Sicily, too, a new age has dawned. In Apulia it was small and medium-sized wine companies that showed the courage to strive for quality, but in Sicily the avant-garde included large companies like the high-volume wine producer Corvo, which quickly recognized the possibility and even necessity of establishing a solid reputation with quality wines.

SIGNS OF CHANGE

The vinicultural methods and winery techniques of northern Italy may have established themselves in most regions of southern Italy, but the south has been slow to respond to the popular international varieties—mainly Cabernet and Chardonnay—which are so much in demand elsewhere. Only some of the top Sicilian wines are made from these grapes; most are still produced from local varieties.

This is especially the case in Campania and Sardinia, which have had no difficulty in finding a market, thanks to their healthy tourist industries. But on Sardinia, and in Basilicata and

Most of the vineyards in Abruzzi lie, like the countryside near Alba Adriatica, in the hilly hinterlands of the Adriatic where the climate is decidedly mild.

Calabria, time seems to have stood still in the last few years and there have been no enological advances. In Sicily the long-established ranks of the elite have at least been swelled by additional names.

The most positive picture is offered by the wine industry in Apulia where hitherto unknown firms have emerged with some astonishing wines. Apulia, Sicily, and perhaps also Campania and Abruzzi show that the conditions for achieving success on the national and international wine markets do exist, but growers must seize the initiative themselves. When this does finally happen, the prestige regions of northern and southern Italy will sit up and take notice.

Regional grape varieties

The great wealth of the vineyards of Apulia, Campania, and Sicily lies in largely undiscovered or untested grape varieties. Just how much might be slumbering away in these regions becomes clear when one realizes that a variety called Primitivo was leading a marginal existence in Apulia but became a superstar in California under the name of Zinfandel.

Even in southern Italy international varieties such as Chardonnay, Cabernet, and Merlot have taken root more or less successfully, as have national greats such as Barbera, Sangiovese, and Trebbiano. Of the red varieties, Montepulciano, Aglianico, Negroamaro, and Nero d'Avola dominate the quality wine scene. They share a vivid color, a relatively high alcohol content, and a neutral, aromatic base which makes them suitable for use in blending. What they might develop in terms of tannin structure and elegance, given the opportunity to grow in really good locations, has still not been sufficiently investigated.

Typical Trulli near Locorotondo in Apulia.

The red varieties also include Primitivo, Uva di Troia, and Piedirosso in Apulia, Gaglioppo in Calabria, and Nerello Mascalese and others in Sicily.

White varieties are no less interesting. Along with the international varieties already mentioned, Moscato and Malvasia also produce some interesting and complex sweet wines.

Probably the best white variety in the south is Fiano which is, unfortunately, cultivated on far too few vineyards in Campania. The more widespread Greco—not to be confused with the Umbrian Grechetto—is grown in only marginal quantities in Calabria, where it is used to make sweet wines.

The fruity, light wines which are made from Falanghina and Biancolella—two other white varieties from Campania—are familiar to whole armies of tourists. Less well known—but no less capable of producing quality wines—are the Sicilian varieties, Inzolia and Grecanico Dorato, and Sardinia's Vermentino.

The other indigenous white wine varieties in the south—such as Bombino, Forastera, Asprinio, Coda di Volpe, Monica, Cataratto, and Grillo—are generally processed into simple, rustic wines. Enormous efforts will still be required in both the vineyard and the cellar to reveal their true potential for the future.

Abruzzi and Molise

Trebbiano and Montepulciano

The spectrum of varieties grown here is one of the least diverse in Italy: for many years there was only one white variety, Trebbiano, and one red, Montepulciano. It is only in recent decades that varieties such as Ciliegiolo, Passerina, Merlot, Cabernet, and even Riesling have gained a tentative foothold here. White wines are dominated by Trebbiano d'Abruzzo, a variant of a widespread varietal group; wines of the same name with a D.O.C. designation are rarely suited for anything more than the daily table.

There are still a few growers who make expressive vintages from old vines, but their yields are now greatly reduced, and the distinctive aromas of the wines they produce are not to everyone's taste. The widespread cultivation of red Montepulciano d'Abruzzo grapes—not to be confused with the Sangiovese wine, Nobile di Montepulciano—which can produce wines with low acid and pleasant tannins, is more in line with international trends.

It is considered unlikely that Montepulciano is related to the Sangiovese of Tuscany, as its wines are markedly different from those of the great Tuscan red. Although they often share the same density, Montepulciano rarely attains the same elegance and longevity of its compatriot.

Abruzzi is one of the less well-known wine-growing regions in Italy, although it is home to the popular red wine, Montepulciano d'Abruzzo. One of the most productive regions in the country, it is bounded by Lazio to the west, Umbria and the Marches to the north and the small province of Molise to the south. Abruzzi also has the highest mountains in the Apennines, the Gran Sasso group, with peaks reaching 9,500 feet (2,912 m).

From a geographic and viticultural perspective Abruzzi is closely related to the neighboring, northern, province of the Marches which not only has a similar landscape and comparable climate but whose vineyards are also partly stocked with the red Montepulciano variety from Abruzzi.

Politically and socially, however, the region must be considered as belonging to the chronically underdeveloped south—which is why, in the past, wine growing had, and indeed still has, few chances of competing with northern and central Italian regions. At the foot of the mighty Apennine massif facing the Adriatic, slopes up to a height of 1,900 feet (600 m) are covered in vines. These hill sites, like the vineyards on the Adriatic, profit from an equable, almost mild climate despite their southern situation. This balance between sunshine and a cooler climate results in rich but not overly heavy wines.

Like a toy village: a huddle of houses in Scanno.

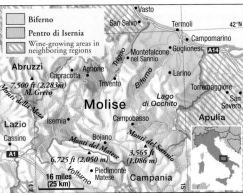

A good Montepulciano d'Abruzzo can, however, surprise with its unusual aromas and tannin structure, making it the ideal accompaniment to game dishes.

Alternative Types of Wine

Cerasuolo, the rosé variant of Montepulciano, is characterized by a pleasant fruitiness. Its often rather dark wines frequently have a high alcohol content, making them less suitable as light summer rosés.

The monotonous panorama of Abruzzi wine has recently been enriched. In the far north of the region, around the town of Controguerra on the borders with the Marches, a new D.O.C. region was established. Later, the hills to the south received the status of a sub-zone of D.O.C. Montepulciano d'Abruzzo as D.O.C. Colline Terre. As was the case in Tuscany and elsewhere in Italy, attempts were initially made to stem the tide of prestige table wines which were achieving better prices than D.O.C. vintages from the same areas. This was an especially risky strategy in Abruzzi; Montepulciano was able to build up a good position in that sector of the market which

Vineyards on the slopes produce the round, often tannic, Montepulciano d'Abruzzo, while flatter sites near the coast produce high yields and simpler wines.

Molise

Italy's second smallest region produces vast quantities of grapes but hardly any of these go into producing quality wines. Biferno and Pentro di Isernia, which were awarded D.O.C. designation in the 1980s, and the new I.G.T. names have achieved at best only a national reputation. This is not to say, however, that the region has no potential for top-ranking wines.

The climate in the hills, where wine is grown at up to 1,900 feet (600 m), is almost continental, and it is only on the slopes facing the coast that Mediterranean conditions prevail. The assortment of grape varieties is modeled on that of Abruzzi and there is an increasing experimentation with varieties from Campania such as Greco, Fiano, and Aglianico. Most wine is still made for domestic consumption and commercial wines are marketed almost exclusively by the cooperatives. Private estates have, to date, been very rare.

accounts for simple, well-balanced wines of origin because of its excellent value for money. In spite of all the efforts of individual growers, though, it has still not been possible to establish a prestigious reputation which would allow it to command a higher price. Thanks to new outside investment, a further upturn is to be expected.

Select Producers of Abruzzi

Barone Cornacchia***
Torano Nuovo
82 acres (33 ha); 450,000 bottles • Wines: Controguerra Cabernet Villa Torri, Montepulciano d'Abruzzo Poggio Varano and Vigna La Costa, Trebbiano d'Abruzzo
For years the Cornacchia family have been among the top producers in the Abruzzi, where they produce wines very typical of the area.

Gianni Masciarelli****–*****
San Martino sulla Marrucina (Abruzzi)
• Wines: Montepulciano d'Abruzzo Villa Gemma, Chardonnay Marina Cvetic, Trebbiano d'Abruzzo Marina Cvetic, Villa Gemma Bianco
Produces some of the best wines for miles around, such as the single-vineyard Montepulciano and the barrel-fermented Chardonnay. The newly laid out vineyards, with up to 3,200 vines per acre (8,000 per hectare) are an intriguing development.

Tenuta Cataldi Madonna***
Ofena (Abruzzi)
47 acres (19 ha); 90,000 bottles • Wines: Montepulciano d'Abruzzo and →Cerasuolo Pié delle Vigne, Trebbiano d'Abruzzo, Malandrino, Pecorino, Vigna Cona Rosso
The estate's vineyards, which lie at about 1,400 feet (450 m) above sea level, produce especially fruity wines. The specialty is the rosé version of Montepulciano. The white wines have a simple but refreshing character.

La Valentina***
Spoltore
74 acres (30 ha); 210,000 bottles • Wines: Montepulciano d'Abruzzo, →Montepulciano d'Abruzzo Spelt, Trebbiano d'Abruzzo
Sabatino di Properzio has invested heavily in the estate, and the results can be seen in the very good quality of the wines.

APULIA

Apulia is often referred to as the wine cellar of Italy. Its 210,000 acres (85,000 hectares) do indeed account for almost an eighth of the total grape-growing area in Italy, and with its 185 to 210 million gallons (7 to 8 million hl) it is, along with Sicily, the country's most productive region. Upon closer examination, however, Apulia's wine industry resembles a gigantic wine factory instead of a well-kept wine cellar. Yields are higher here than anywhere else in Italy. There are many vineyards which harvest up to 16 tons of grapes per acre (40 tons/ha)—four times the upper limit if wines are to be of moderate quality and retain the characteristics typical of their variety. It is not surprising therefore that only two percent of Apulian wines have D.O.C. status and that most of the production from the region is either distilled into industrial alcohol, converted to grape must concentrate, or sold in barrels to large northern Italian or French wine producers.

The small number of D.O.C. wines from the region are spread over 25 designations of origin, none of which commands a significant share of the market. In the case of most of these *appellations*, the quantities bottled and sold outside Apulia are negligible. Funds allocated by the European Union for clearing vineyards have only exacerbated the situation; instead of converting their large-scale industrial vineyards to other uses, Apulia's growers have abandoned their old, high-quality vines which were planted

on awkward sites in the hills. And although more than 50,000 growers gave up their profession in the 1980s, Apulia's wine lake still refused to dry up. Conditions for quality wine growing in this region are almost ideal, in terms of both the climate and the intriguing local grape varieties. Even in Roman times the area was praised for its excellent wines and other agricultural products. In Rome's early days, the civilizing influence of Greek culture was particularly apparent here, and there are still traces of the Greek language in the region's dialect today.

In contrast to neighboring regions, which are dominated by the Apennines and characterized by desolate, stony soils, Apulia boasts broad, fertile, coastal plains with gentler hills in its interior. The fecundity of most its soil types, together with its relatively flat countryside, is a virtual utopia for highly productive industrial vineyards.

NATIVE TO APULIA?

As elsewhere in Italy, in Apulia the better wines are grown in bleaker locations with well-drained soils, such as the karst plateau of Le Murge, home to Castel del Monte. The region's indigenous varieties produce only a few great wines. The most widespread variety is Negro-amaro, which goes into making the D.O.C. wines Alezio, Brindisi, Leverano, and Salice Salentino. Wines of this variety are generally very dark and high in tannins—*negro amaro* means "bitter black"—and exhibit a powerful, occasionally rough, primitive taste.

Primitivo vines, a variety which produces a full-bodied red wine but seldom attains its best form in Apulia, cover a huge area. Primitivo is more renowned and of better quality in California, where it is known as Zinfandel; in the U.S. it produces a wine full of fruit which occasionally achieves great elegance and a capacity to age. It was previously—incorrectly—believed that Zinfandel was descended from Primitivo, but it has since been proved that the variety first appeared in Italy after it had already become firmly established in the northeast of the U.S. and later in California. In all probability, the vine originated in one of the Balkan lands and was taken to America before being reimported to the Old World.

Uva di Troia is Apulia's third premium grape variety. The name indicates the legacy left by

Aleatico di Puglia	
San Severo	
Cacc'e Mmitte di Lucera	
Rosso Barletta	
Moscato di Trani	
Rosso Canosa	
Castel del Monte	
Gioia del Colle	
Martina Franca	
Locorotondo	
Ostuni	
Brindisi	
Primitivo di Manduria	
Lizzano	
Salice Salentino	
Squinzano	
Copertino	
Leverano	
Alezio	
Wine-growing areas in neighboring regions	

The ancient city of Ostuni with its almost African ambience gave its name to a wine-growing region northwest of Brindisi in which southern grape varieties produce unusually dry, rather light wines.

Greek culture in the region. This grape makes the majority of red wines from Castel del Monte, a region in northern Apulia named after an octagonal castle built by the Hohenstaufen monarch, Frederick II, in the 13th century. The elite, D.O.C.-named wines of Castel del Monte include more than just this powerful red which ages well, however; they also embrace varieties such as Aglianico, Spätburgunder, Chardonnay, Pinot Blanc, and Sauvignon.

The wines with the best prospects for the future come from the far south and were previously bottled under one of the mini-D.O.C. desig-nations. Many of these *appellations*—such as Copertino, Brindisi, Salice Salentino, San Severo, and Alezio—are used for red as well as white wines. Occasionally, the *appellations* encompass a diverse array of other wine types—which, in the past, has been confusing for both growers and consumers.

Some of the best-known names in Italian wine—including the Marchesi Antinori from Florence and the Pasqua brothers in Verona—have recently begun to invest in Apulia, and this fact must surely confirm the region's potential for quality.

Select Producers in Apulia

AGRICOLE VALLONE**—****
LECCE
336 acres (136 ha); 200,000 bottles • Wines: →Brindisi: Rosso Vigna Flaminio, Rosato Vigna Flaminio; →Graticciaia Rosso, Salice Salentino: Vereto, Rosso
The specialty is the Graticciaia, produced on the model of the Patriglione.

FRANCESCO CANDIDO***
SANDONACI BEI GUAGNANO
339 acres (137 ha); 900,000 bottles • Wines: Duca d'Aragona, →Cappello di Prete, Salice Salentino: Bianco Vigna Vinera, Rosso, Rosato Le Pozzelle; I.G.T. Salente Chardonnay Casina Cucci
The best products are generally made from Negroamaro; its aromas of tea and fruit and its full body, demonstrating the high potential of this Apulian variety.

CONTI LEONE DE CASTRIS**—****
SALICE SALENTINO
988 acres (400 ha); 4,000,000 bottles • Wines include: →Five Roses, Salice Salentino: →Rosso Donna Lisa, Bianco, Rosato and Rosso Maiana, Sauvignon Vigna Case Alte Bianco, Messapia Bianco, Aleatico Negrini
As well as its rosé, this estate is known for its excellent reds and good white wines.

FELLINE****
MANDURIA
• Wines: →Primitivo di Manduria, Salento Rosso Alberello, →Vigna del Feudo

The Perrucci make impressive red wines, including a very good Primitivo (known in California as Zinfandel).

ROSA DI GOLFO—D. CALÒ***
ALEZIO
99 acres (40 ha); 180,000 bottles • Wines: I.G.T. Salento: →Rosa del Golfo, Quarantale, →Portulano, Bianco Bolina
Known initially for remarkable rosés, but now has a good selection of whites and reds.

MASSERIA MONACI**—***
COPERTINO
40 acres (16 ha); 650,000 bottles • Wines: Copertino Rosso Eloquenzia, I Censi Salento Rosso, Sant Brigida Salento Bianco, Simposia Salento Rosso
Severino Garofano has brought to the family estate all the experience gained over decades as Apulia's most important wine consultant.

CONTI ZECCA****—*****
LEVERANO
791 acres (320 ha); 1,500,000 bottles • Wines: Leverano: →Malvasia Vigna del Saraceno, Rosato Vigna del Saraceno; Salice Salentino: Rosso Cantalupi, Rosato, Bianco; Cantalupi, I.G.T. Salento Donna Marzia Bianco / Rosato / Rosso
Three lines of wines—one from Leverano, one from Salice Salentino, and one sold under I.G.T. Salento, have for years been noted for their quality.

CAMPANIA

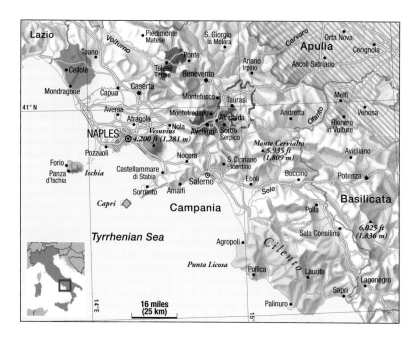

Campania stretches along the Tyrrhenian coast in the southwest of Italy. Its broad coastal plains are repeatedly broken by hills of sedimentary or volcanic origin, the most famous of these being Vesuvius, southeast of Naples. With around 74,000 acres (30,000 ha) of vines, Campania lies in ninth position nationally, just behind Sardinia. Of the approximately 53 million gallons (2 million hl) of wine produced here every year, less than six percent have D.O.C. status.

It was in the present-day province of Campania, however, that the Italian wine industry was born around 3,000 years ago. Greek settlers established their OINOTRIA ("Wineland") here. The later Latin expression *Enotria* came to be used as a synonym for all of Italy's wine-growing areas. The Greeks passed on much of their winemaking expertise to the native Etruscan inhabitants. The Romans later developed the region into the center of their wine trade. The eruption of Mount Vesuvius in AD 79, however, brought profound changes; the volcano's destruction of Pompeii meant that the Empire's greatest commercial harbor for wine was eliminated in a single blow, and Rome was compelled to develop the wine industry systematically in other parts of the Empire.

CHARACTER WINES

Campania's Mediterranean climate, in which the nearby sea and mountains prevent temperatures from becoming too hot, provides ideal conditions

	Falerno del Massico
	Solopaca
	Sant' Agata de' Goti
	Aglianico del Taburno
	Greco di Tufo
	Taurasi
	Fiano di Avellino
	Vesuvio
	Cilento
	Ischia
	Capri
	Wine-growing areas in neighboring regions

for a series of local white and red varieties, especially in the provinces of Avellino and Benevento. The most respected of these is Taurasi, whose *riserva* version has been awarded D.O.C.G. status. The best representatives of this powerful red, blended from Aglianico grapes and a small percentage of other varieties, age well and can easily stand comparison with the great red wines of northern and central Italy. The best known of the wines in Campania, Greco di Tufo and Fiano di Avellino, are also worthy of interest; the grape varieties which form their base were probably brought to Italy by the Greeks. They achieve their best form in the regions which bear their name: the Greco, with its scent of citrus fruit and almonds, from the village of Tufo (where it is generally blended with Falanghina and Biancolella), and Fiano from the region of Avellino.

FRUITY SUMMER WINES

In the area around Avellino a good Fiano, which the Romans praised as *vitis apianae*, has the potential to combine freshness and power with the scent of peaches and nuts. It therefore displays a greater complexity than the neutral whites of central and northern Italy, or the fruity but one-dimensional Biancolella and Falanghina summer wines made on the coast and the islands of Ischia and Capri.

Attempts to revive the once-famous wines of the region, such as Falerno, Lettere, Asprinio, and Lacryma Christi, should be seen as more archeo-

Aglianico—southern Italy's top variety

Aglianico produces full-bodied, intensely colored and aromatic wines, especially when grown on volcanic soils; a brilliant ruby red when young, it transforms on ageing into a mahogany hue. Good wines have a bouquet of maraschino cherry and violet notes, later becoming delicately spicy. The best-known wine made from Aglianico is Taurasi, from the mountains north of the town of Avellino in Campania. The *riserva* wines have even been awarded D.O.C.G. status. Aglianico del Vulture, from the slopes of the extinct volcano of the same name in the neighboring region of Basilicata, is almost as good. Recently, the region of Taburno has proved that it is also capable of growing superb wines. When used for blending, Aglianico enhances the final product—a role it performs in Falerno del Massico, Biferno, Castel del Monte, Cilento, Solopaca, Vesuvio, and Sant'Agata de'Goti.

Naples is the beating heart of an ancient land in which present-day winemakers are finding it difficult to achieve the fame of their antique forebears. Lacryma Christi, a wine once much in demand but now almost forgotten, is still made on the slopes of Vesuvius. This can be red, rosé or white, fortified or sparkling, but only occasionally is it anything other than mediocre.

logical than enological in nature. In spite of modern efforts, these varieties probably have little in common with their antique forebears.

The same is true for the red wines from the region of Lacryma Christi, which are sold as Vesuvio. The more interesting wines in recent years have come from one of the most beautiful coastlines in Europe, the Costa Amalfitana, where the vineyards have to be carved out of steep slopes, or in the Sant'Agata de'Goti and Solopaca *appellations*, between Caserta and Avellino in the north of the region.

Wine growing in Campania, as in other southern Italian regions, suffers from the general social and economic deprivation of the area, and an unnecessarily complex patchwork of *appellations*. As in Apulia, however, several producers have increased their efforts in the last few years and have been rewarded with some measure of success. By and large, the wine industry in Campania has not been active enough and the large investments that have had such a beneficial effect on Sicily and in Apulia tend to be rare in this region.

SELECT PRODUCERS OF CAMPANIA

CASA D'AMBRA VINI D'ISCHIA***–****
FORIO
17 acres (7 ha); some bought-in grapes; 320,000 bottles.
• *Wines include:* →*Biancolella Tenuta Frassitelli and Vigna di Piellero, I.G.T. Ischia: Per'e Palummo Tenuta Montecorvo, Forastera:* →*Cimentorosso Forastera, Arime*
Has earned an excellent reputation mainly for its fruity, fresh white wines made from Biancolella and Forastera. Also has a remarkable barrel-fermented white wine, Arime, made from local varieties.

FEUDI DI SAN GREGORIO***–*****
SORBO SERPICO
173 acres (70 ha); 2,500,000 bottles • *Wines:*
→*Campanaro,* →*Taurasi,* →*Fiano di Avellino Pietracalda, Falanghina, Greco di Tufo Cutizzi, Serpico*
Probably Campania's best producer, this estate is still in the developing stage, but already has a series of excellent red and white wines.

MONTEVETRANO****
SAN CIPRIANO PICENTINO
10 acres (4 ha); 20,000 bottles • *Wines:* →*Montebetrano*
Silvia Imparato is the owner and Riccardo Cotarello makes the single wine.

OCONE—AGRICOLA DEL MONTE**–***
PONTE
114 acres (46 ha); 120,000 bottles • *Wines: Aglianico Del Taburno: Vigna Pezza la Corte and Diomede, Fanaghina del Taburno Vigna del Monaco; Calidonio*
Good to very good wines, of which the various Aglianico versions are the most impressive.

TERRADORA DI PAOLO***
MONTEFUSCO
371 acres (150 ha); 600,000 bottles • *Wines: Fiano di Avellino Terra di Dora, Campo Re, Greco di Tufo Loggioa della Serra, Terre degli Angheli,* →*Aglianico Irpinia, Falanghina Irpinia, Taurasi Fatica Contadina*
Paolo, Lucio, Walter and Daniela Mastroberardino have left the parent company. They are concentrating particularly on local grape varieties.

VILLA MATILDE**
CELLOLE
153 acres (62 ha); 200,000 bottles • *Wines include: Falerno del Massico: Bianco Vigna Caracci,* →*Rosso,* →*Vigna Camarato, Cecubo, Terre Cerase, Falanghina, Piedirosso*
Not only the red Falerno, but also the self-contained nature of the whole range of wines is impressive.

Calabria and Basilicata

The Aglianico del Vulture is only rarely aged in the grottoes of Barile, in the heart of its growing region; this greatest of the southern red wines is also slowly being modernized.

Together with the neighboring region of Basilicata, Calabria is structurally one of the weaker regions of Italy. It was the worst affected by the exodus of labor in the 1960s and 70s, and it was hardly able to develop a single sector of the economy with which to secure some measure of prosperity.

The wine industry shows little economic potential either, although with 32,120 acres (13,000 ha) Calabria has a considerable area given over to viticulture. Much of the fault for this must lie with the region's topography; its largely inaccessible mountains make it difficult to achieve any degree of agricultural efficiency. Nevertheless, the fundamental conditions for growing quality wines—as elsewhere in southern Italy—are more than favorable. In antiquity

Calabria's wines enjoyed the best of reputations, and it was no coincidence that the area belonged to *Oinotria*, the "Wineland" of the Greek settlers. In many parts of Calabria the heat of the southern climate is compensated for by the altitude of the vineyards, and the native varieties of grape also show great promise. Calabria is above all the home of Gaglioppo, also known as Montonico Nero, whose wines with their conspicuous tannins form the basis for most regional D.O.C. reds. The best known of these D.O.C. wines is Cirò, from the slopes of the Sila massif, which is said to have its origins in the wines of Kremissa—or Cremissa—fabled in antiquity for being presented to victors in the games at Olympia. A few producers have the skill necessary to make a well-balanced wine from this initially rather prickly, acidic product. Occasionally, it is matured in a *barrique* and exhibits a rich red color, a spicy palate, and even, given certain conditions, an ability to age well.

Origins Unknown

On the southern slopes of the Pollino mountains an eponymous D.O.C. wine is made from Gaglioppo and is marketed exclusively by the local cooperative. Savuto, from the other side of the Sila massif to Cirò, has a still greater potential. Here Gaglioppo is partly blended with Sangiovese which, given the altitude of the vineyards, leads to fine, expressive wines. The really interesting products in this area are sold by just a small group of growers. The other D.O.C. regions in Calabria like Lamezia, Sant'Anna di Isola Capo Rizzuto, and Melissa, on the other hand, have yet to come up with either appealing quality wines or regionally renowned products; they are among the numerous regions of origin in Italy which were set up simply to satisfy the ambitions of a political clientele.

Even Calabria's best dessert wine, the Greco di Bianco, makes virtually no impression on the market. It comes from Bianco, on the toe of the Italian "boot," where it is made from partially dried grapes. Under this name, dense, amber-colored wines with fine, fruity aromas and a marked spiciness are made by a small group of growers. The example of Greco di Bianco proves what can be achieved in Calabria—and makes one regret all the more the region's lack of real quality wines.

Pollino	
Cirò	
Melissa	
Sant'Anna di Isola Capo Rizzuto	
Donnici	
Savuto	
Lamezia	
Greco di Bianco	
Wine-growing areas in neighboring regions	

The fruit-bearing shoots must be correctly tied in winter to allow the grapes to develop.

Young, flexible willow stems are used as ties, though these have largely been replaced by modern binding materials.

To avoid wind damage, the branches are tied to wire frames stretched between the vines.

Instead of the skillfully tied knots of former years, today's growers generally use mechanical binding.

At the end of April the young shoots appear from the buds of the year-old wood.

Pruning in winter is crucial for the healthy growth of the shoots.

Basilicata—volcanic wines

Basilicata's 19,765 acres (8,000 ha) of vineyards makes its wine-growing region twice as large as that of Trentino/Alto Adige, though only around 10 percent of this area produces quality wines. The almost completely landlocked and mountainous terrain of Basilicata, which only becomes flatter in the southeast on the coast, has a single designation of origin—the red Aglianico del Vulture. Most of the region's wine production is shipped in tankers to the north of the country and abroad. Unique to Italy are the region's underground cellars. In the area around Barile, the main town of the *appellation*, they can reach depths of more than 39 feet (12 m) in the loess soils of this rugged landscape. In the past they were used by growers for pressing grapes and storing their wines. Just as unique is the traditional method of training the vines on posts, which requires the plants to be bound together to form pyramids. According to experts, this method allows high-quality fruit to mature better than on modern, efficient wire frames.

Grown on the slopes of Monte Vulture, an extinct volcano in the north of the region, Aglianico is becoming one of the most popular southern Italian wines. Its dark color, strong aroma, and powerful, tannic accents make a good Aglianico del Vulture one of the best wines in Italy.

SELECT PRODUCERS IN CALABRIA AND BASILICATA

D'ANGELO**−***
RIONERO IN VULTURE (BASILICATA)
49 acres (20 ha); some bought-in grapes; 300,000 bottles • Wines include: Aglianico del Vulture: →Riserva Vigna Caselle; I.G.T. Basilicata: →Rosso Canneto, Bianco Vigna dei Pini
Canneto is harvested late and matured for 15 months in small oak barrels. With various Aglianico wines, Vigna dei Pini is an interesting Chardonnay-Pinot Bianco blend.

FATTORIA SAN FRANCESCO**−***
CIRÒ (CALABRIA)
173 acres (70 ha;) 120,000 bottles • Wines: Cirò Rosso Classico: →Ronco dei Quattor Venti, Superiore Donna Madda, Superiore; Cirò Bianco
The premium wine Quattro Venti was one of the earliest *barrique* versions of Cirò.

LIBRANDI***−****
CIRÒ MARINA (CALABRIA)
408 acres (165 ha); some bought-in grapes; 2,000,000 bottles • Wines: →Gravello, Cirò Rosso Duca San Felice, Critone, Le Passule

Top wines: Gravello, a Gaglioppo and Cabernet blend; Magno Megonio, made from Magliocco, and the white wine Mantonico.

ODOARDI**−***
COSENZA (CALABRIA)
124 acres (50 ha) • Wines: →Savuto Superiore: Vigna Mortilla, →Vigna Vecchia; →Scavigna: Vigna Garrone, Pian del Corte; →Valeo
The D.O.C. wines Savuto and Scavigna are still the only really excellent representatives of their respective designations of origin.

PATERNOSTER**−***
BARILE (BASILICATA)
16 acres (6.5 ha); some bought-in grapes; 130,000 bottles • Wines include: Aglianico del Vulture: Don Anselmo Riserva del Fondatore; Barigliott, Clivus, L'Antico, Il Moscato
A slightly bubbly wine called Barigliott is made from Aglianico, and there is even a red sparkling wines, L'Antico. Notable for its consistently high quality.

SARDINIA

Cannonau di
Sardegna,
Malvasia di Cagliari,
Monica di Cagliari,
Moscato di Cagliari,
Vermentino di
Gallura
Moscato di
Sorso-Sennori
Alghero
Nuragus di Cagliari
Giro di Cagliari
Vernaccia di Oristano
Mandrolisai
Carignano del Sulcis

Sardinia has preserved one of the most archaic wine cultures in Italy but also one of the richest, in terms of the spectrum of its grape varieties and the diversity of wine styles. Around 21¼ million gallons (800,000 hl) of wine is produced annually on more than 61,775 acres (25,000 ha)—the area has been greatly reduced in recent years. However, only a few designations of origin, such as Alghero or Vermentino di

Gallura, are able to achieve significant production volumes. A series of D.O.C. wines do not achieve more than 2,600 or, at best, 5,000 gallons (100 to 200 hl) per year.

Over the centuries the island has been subject to a wide range of cultural influences: Byzantines, Arabs, and Catalans settled here, and the Spanish influence on Sardinian wine growing is unmistakable even today. This legacy manifests itself, above all, in the island's most important red wine varieties—in Cannonau, which is nothing less than that most Spanish of wines, Garnacha; in Carignano, also known as Cariñena, or Carignan; and in Vermentino.

CANNONAU: A BACKGROUND WINE

It is Cannonau, in particular, that has a potential for quality which, until now, has not received sufficient attention by international experts. Only in the south of France and in the New World has Cannonau been properly cultivated. Insiders have been murmuring for some time that some of the renowned Supertuscans may have been drawing their particular strengths from a relatively high proportion of Cannonau (which, in a further indication of its Spanish origins, is called Alicante on the Tuscan coast).

Cannonau produces full-bodied wines, high in alcohol but not unduly overshadowed by their tannins. They not only age well and exhibit complex aromas, these wines are also superbly suited for use as a blend—for example, with Cabernet Sauvignon. In Spain and southern France, Carignano is wrongly considered to be a simple, characterless wine, suitable for mass production or blending. On Sardinia, though, it is capable of producing interesting wines with a sustained aroma and a round full taste. The best of these wines is marketed under the D.O.C. designation of Carignano del Sulcis.

From the province of Gallura, on the northern tip of this sun-drenched island, comes Vermentino, a pleasantly fruity, fresh white wine with occasional exotic, aromatic nuances which harmonize perfectly with the region's fish dishes. This variety, which is cultivated in Liguria as well as in southern France—where it is known as Rolle—can produce outstanding results, provided growers keep to strict limits on the yields from their vineyards: only in this way can the grape harvest produce more intense-tasting wines.

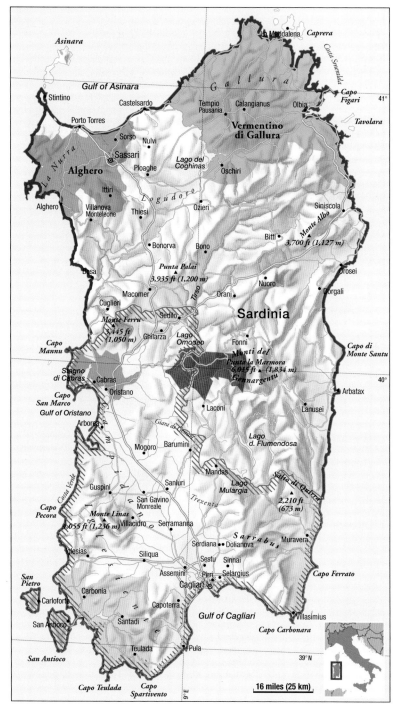

Sweet Wines
from the Sunny Isle

Apart from the internationally familiar grape varieties introduced from the European mainland, Sardinia has a number of indigenous varieties—though a recitation of their names (Caricagiola, Pascale, Gregu Nieddu, Caddiu, Carenisca, Retagliadu, Nieddu Mannu, etc.) would probably not ring any bells with non-specialists on the island. Less well known is a scent-laden red wine, Monica. This is bottled under the D.O.C. names of Monica di Cagliari and Monica di Sardegna. Malvasia, which is mainly made into Liquoroso—a fortified dessert wine—is sold under a regional name of origin, and is familiar to consumers on the mainland. Powerful, dry white wines as well as sherry-like Liquoroso products are made under the name Vernaccia di Oristano. The name Vernaccia does not imply a relationship with the Tuscan Vernaccia di San Gimignano nor with Vernatsch from Alto Adige: the word is used in Italy for a wide variety of white and red wines.

Good whites, reds, and rosés are being made in increasing quantities in the D.O.C. region of Alghero, the largest and most productive on the island, whose wines are generally blended from a number of native varieties.

If Sardinia's wines are still unable to establish a significant position on international markets, in spite of a fascinating, high-quality selection of both grapes and wines, then blame should be leveled at the structure of the island's wine industry which is still mainly dominated by the large cooperatives. Only two or three big producers and a handful of growers have been able to lay claim to a national, let alone an international, reputation. Most of the region's production is still consumed on the island itself or ends up in tankers to be shipped to the European mainland for use as a blend with more renowned wines.

A Vernaccia from the Contini estate.

Traditional dress is still held in great esteem.

Select Producers in Sardinia

Antonio Argiolas**−*****
Serdiana
494 acres (200 ha); 600,000 bottles • Wines include: →*Turriga,* →*Angialis, Nuragus di Cagliari Sèlegas, Vermentino di Sardegna Costamolino, Monica di Sardegna Perdera, Cannonau di Sardegna Costera, Serralori, Alasi*
The potential of Grenache—alias Cannonau—is proved by Turriga, a wine with Carignano and Malvasia Rossa components, which is aged for 18 months in French oak. The dessert wine, Angialis, is also excellent.

Attilio Contini**−****
Cabras
Bought-in grapes • Wines include: →*Vernaccia di Oristano Riserva,* →*Nieddera Rosso, Pontis, Cannonau di Sardegna, Antico Gregori, Elibaria, Karmis, Vermentino di Sardegna*
The firm buys in all of its grapes and it led the movement for quality on the island in the 1980s. Its range encompasses most of Sicily's important designations of origin.

Cantina Sociale Santadi**−****
Santadi
700,000 bottles • Wines include: Terre Brune, Latinia, Villa di Chiesa, Carignano del Sulcis Riserva Rocca

Rubia, Cala Silente, Vermentino di Sardegna Villa Solais, Monica di Sardegna Antigua, Nuragus di Cagliari Pedraia, Carignano del Sulcis Tre Torri
This cooperative has for years been making some of the best wines on the island, especially the red Terre Brune. Much of the thanks for this must go to the dedicated enologist, Giacomo Tachis.

Tenuta Sella & Mosca**
Alghero
1,236 acres (500 ha); bought-in grapes; 4,500,000 bottles • Wines include: →*Alghero Marchese di Villamarina, Vermentino di Sardegna la Cala,* →*Alghero Le Arenarie,* →*Anghelu Ruju, Cannonau di Sardegna Riserva,* →*Alghero, Torbato Terre Bianche, Monteluce, Rubicante, Tanca Farrà, Aliante, Spumante Brut di Torbato, Oleandro, Vermentino di Gallura Monteoro*
This 100-year-old producer in Alghero is one of the most dynamic on the island and its range includes the top wines in a broad range of designations of origin. The red Alghero Villamarina has repeatedly won the highest honors from leaders in the Italian industry. A good blend of Carignano, Cabernet, and Merlot has now also been added.

SICILY

This, too, is Sicily: in the autumn when the new Cabernet Sauvignon vineyards are displaying their first beautiful shades of red, the mountains of Madonie are already capped with snow.

Sicily is an island of contradictions. With Apulia it shares top place in Italy for the yield of its grape harvest and the amount of land dedicated to viticulture. On average, 211 million gallons (eight million hl) of wine are produced from 271,800 acres (110,000 ha) of vineyards. But more than any other region in southern Italy, Sicily has discovered its potential for creating really top-quality wines. The natural conditions for wine growing could not be better: long hours of sunshine, a warm climate and low rainfall provide optimal conditions for bringing the grapes to maturity. The island's barren soils result in expressive wines, while vineyards on highland slopes at up to 2,900 feet (900 m) produce particularly elegant, aromatic vintages.

Sicily was famed for its wines and agricultural produce even among the Greek settlers of antiquity. Vines were brought to the island by the Phoenicians, but the Greeks introduced new techniques and varieties such as Grecanico from their homeland—along with their native gods and mythology. The poetess, Sappho, who had been banished from her island home of Lesbos, is said to have cultivated wine here, and the Romans later thought Sicilian wine a welcome change from the famous Falernian.

Centuries later, under Arab rule, the island's viticulture did not suffer any real setbacks. The new rulers not only tolerated wine growing—despite the ban on alcohol in the Koran—they even introduced the technique of distillation. Throughout the entire Middle Ages it was mainly monks who distilled these mysterious "waters of life" with which they increased the wealth of their large estates. Sicily was therefore one of the few parts of Italy in which the traditions of wine growing were kept alive over centuries of social and political decline.

	Marsala
	Alcamo
	Contessa Entellina
	Menfi
	Etna
	Cerasuolo di Vittoria
	Moscato di Noto
	Malvasia delle Lipari
	Moscato di Pantelleria, Moscato Passito di Pantelleria

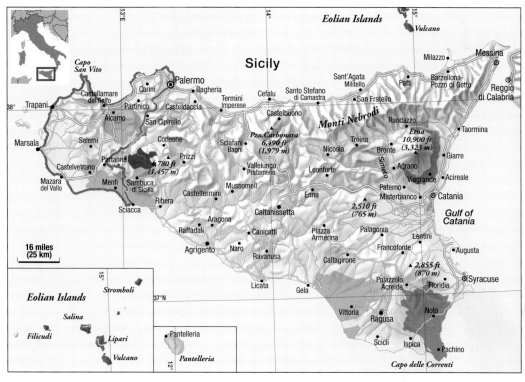

A Crisis—In Spite of Marsala

It was only when Spanish viceroys ruled the island that Sicily's viticultural star began to wane. Under the Spaniards, grain was grown in preference to wine, and it was not until the end of the 18th century that an Englishman, John Woodhouse, began to revive Sicily's wine industry when he discovered Marsala, an alternative to the expensive commodity of sherry. Unfortunately, despite its isolated location, the island was not immune to the effects of phylloxera, and even the fame of Marsala began to fade. Today it is Trapani, in the west of the island, that is the largest wine-growing province on the island, with an annual production of 119 million gallons (4.5 million hl); this area is also home to the D.O.C. region of Marsala which is still the best known of the designations of origin. There is also a large continuous area of viticulture on both the southern and northern coasts, while in the east—with the exception of the area around Etna—mainly table grapes are grown.

Some of the most interesting Sicilian products are not grown on the main island but on the tiny Eolian islands to the northeast—including the volcanic island of Stromboli—and on Pantelleria, halfway between Sicily and Tunisia. A variety of dessert wines is made here, from Malvasia (on Lipari) and Zibibbo (on Pantelleria), also known as Muscat of Alexandria. All of these enjoy enormous popularity with Italian wine connoisseurs and they are even beginning to celebrate their first foreign successes.

The initial spark for this revival of older traditions was provided by Carlo Hauner, who had already caused a sensation in the 1980s with his Malvasia delle Lipari, and it was mainly the indigenous Malvasia and Corinto Nero varieties that were used. Hauner's example was not taken up by other producers, though this probably had more to do with the rather marginal nature of vineyards on Salina and its neighboring islands than with a lack of will on the part of the region's few growers.

Moscato di Pantelleria has since become more consistent and of better quality across a broad geographical area; several producers in the region around Marsala have now begun to invest in the wine. The sweet Passito and fortified Liquoroso versions are now numbered among the best sweet wines in the country.

Investing in Whites and Reds

The real revolution in the 1990s took place among the white and red wines. Apart from a

The Tasca d'Almerita bought the imposing estate of Regealeali in 1834. Today, it is one of the greatest and best-managed private domains in Italy.

Marsala—a sweet wine with a checkered history.

few successful attempts with Cabernet and Chardonnay wines, the protagonists of this new trend took advantage of the wide range of local varieties, some of which, in the course of time, proved they had greater potential than their previous incarnations as cheap, anonymous, mass-produced wines. Of the white wines, this role was played by Inzolia, alias Ansonica, the Cataratto grape, and possibly Grecanico Dorato. Grillo, on the other hand, is with few exceptions really only suited to producing Marsala.

Alcamo, a white wine from the largest D.O.C. region on the island (more than 49,000 acres/ 20,000 ha), demonstrates, however, that a limited harvest and careful cultivation of this traditionally high-volume variety can produce pleasant, full, dry whites.

Among red wines, the Nero d'Avola, alias Calabrese, has shown good potential, and the intensely colored, dense wines which it has produced since the mid-1980s exhibit at least the same levels of quality as those derived from Aglianico on the mainland. In the last few years some good wines made from Frappato and Nerello Mascalese grapes have come on the market: Frappato, in particular, which forms the basis for Cerasuolo di Vittoria on Sicily's southeastern corner, corresponds to the image of fruity and sunblessed red wine with its cherry-like, fruity aromas.

In contrast to Apulia or Campania, the drive to achieve quality did not occur through the initiative of the smaller producer (bearing in mind that, of the more than 100,000 producers in the region, only around 180 bottle and sell their own wines). Instead, the impetus came from large companies, including Settesoli, the biggest cooperative in Menfi on the south coast. This tendency has been reinforced by the recent investments by large Italian wine-producers such as Zonin or GIV in vineyards and production facilities, a development which expresses the confidence that Italy's wine industry has placed in what was once its sickest patient.

Sicilian Marsala

Sicily owes its greatest success in wine growing to Marsala, a fortified wine which was discovered almost by chance by a young Englishman. In 1770 John Woodhouse, a merchant's son from Liverpool, found himself in the harbor at Marshallà (present-day Marsala) where he was served a local wine which he thought equal to the Spanish sherries and Portuguese Madeiras so popular in Britain at the time. After long preparations and a three-year experimental phase, Woodhouse made his first shipment to England.

The real breakthrough came in 1800, when Admiral Nelson ordered a yearly delivery of 500 barrels to his fleet. Although grapes were, at first, in plentiful supply and cheaply priced, the wine's sudden success created problems in meeting the demand. Woodhouse therefore lent growers the necessary capital for new vineyards, receiving in return long-term price guarantees for both grapes and the base wines.

Woodhouse's example was, of course, not without its imitators. In 1812 Benjamin Ingham opened a new, larger, and technically superior operation close to Woodhouse in Marsala, and in 1833 businessman Vincenzo Florio became the first Sicilian to involve himself in this profitable trade. He purchased land between Woodhouse's and Ingham's cellars through a third party, establishing his own production site for a wine which the company's constitution described as "Madeira style."

For a century Sicily's wine industry basked in Marsala's success, but then came an inexorable, if slow, decline in the 20th century. The phylloxera disaster, new competition in the form of

Nets protect the slow-ripening Marsala grapes around Palermo against birds.

The Planeta estate in Sambuca is now ranked among Sicily's top producers, largely due to its French varietals.

Conte Tasca d'Almerita—specialist in Sicilian varieties.

mainly Australian wines (large areas of the hot, dry Australian interior had been given over to the production of fortified wines), and the usual spiral of overproduction and falling prices led to a deterioration in the quality of Marsala. Soon only the artificially scented versions of this once noble drink were available on the European market—including Marsala all'uovo which was mixed with an egg yolk—and customers simply lost interest.

It was not until the 1980s that there were again laborious and careful attempts by a few growers—such as Marco di Bartoli's Vecchio Samperi—to reconstruct the prestige of the old-style Marsala. Di Bartoli was unable to attract more than half a dozen followers, however, particularly as the interest of the wine world had shifted in the direction of the island's dry whites and reds. Today, high-quality Marsala is produced by a handful of companies in a variety of styles, and a cloud of forgetfulness has descended on the mistakes of the past. The most interesting products bear the designations *Fine*, *Superiore*, *Vergine*, and *Vergine Stravecchio*. These are wines with an alcohol level of 18 percent by volume, which are aged from four to ten years in a barrel before becoming available on the market. Good Marsala has an amber-yellow or brown color and generally develops rich honey aromas or the typical RANCIO of sherry. They are excellent as aperitifs or as an accompaniment to dessert. The very best exhibit an astonishing variety of aromas which makes Marsala's negative reputation seem all the more incomprehensible.

Select Producers of Sicily

ABBAZIA SANT'ANASTASIA****
CASTELBUONO
• *Wines: Santa Anastasia Rosso, Passomaggio, Baccante, Zurrica, →Litra*
This company, in Palermo province, produces impressive wines from local as well as French variants.

MARCO DE BARTOLI—VECCHIO SAMPERI***−****
MARSALA
62 acres (25 ha); 60,000 bottles • Wines: Vecchio Samperi Riserva 20 Anni Solera, Moscato Passito di Pantelleria Bukkuram, Marsala Superiore: Oro Vigna La Miccia, Riserva 20 Anni Solera; Josephine Doré, Zibibbo, Vigna Verde, Grappoli del Grillo, Rosso di Marco
The Riserva Marsala Vecchio Samperi is exemplary: a non-fortified wine, its levels of alcohol and density are derived from over mature-grapes and a high degree of concentration, as well as up to 30 years of aging in the barrel.

CALATRASI—TERRE DI GINESTRA*−***
SAN CIPIRELLO
618 acres (250 ha); some bought-in grapes; 7,000,000 bottles • Wines: Terre di Ginestra: Bianco, Rosso; Calatrasi Terrale: Bianco, Rosso; Tenuta Calalbaio Olmobianco, Tenuta Calalbaio Rubilio, Pelavet di Ginestra, D'Istinto: Syrah, Cataratto / Chardonnay, Sangiovese /Merlot, Sangiovese
Maurizio Miccichè runs the successful winery. The Terre di Ginestra, Accademia del Sole 2001, and Distinto series offer a lot of wine for not much money. Miccichè also produces wine in Apulia and Tunisia.

CASA VINICOLA DUCA DI GINESTRA**−***
CASTELDACCIA
Some bought-in grapes; 9,500,000 bottles • Wines: Corvo: Bianco, Rosso, Glicine, Novello, Spumante Brut; Terre d'Agala, →Colomba Platino, Bianca di Valguarnera, →Duca Enrico, Portale d'Aspra
The red Duca Enrico was the first wine on the island to receive the highest praise. The winery has now returned to its old strengths.

COS***
VITTORIA
35 acres (15 ha); 25,000 bottles • Wines: Cerasuolo di Vittoria, Frappato di Vittoria, Vignalunga, Ramingallo, Le Vigne di C.O.S.: Rosso, Bianco; Aestas Siciliae
The focus here is on the red wines from the Cerasuolo di Vittoria *appellation*: good Chardonnay and Cabernet.

CUSUMANO***−****
PARTINICO
124 acres (50 ha); 400,000 bottles • Wines: Alcamo Bianco Nandaria, Benuara Sicilia Rosso, Nadaria Inzolia Sicilia Bianco, →Nadaria Nero d'Avola, Nadaria Syrah, Noa Silicia Rosso, Sagana Rosso
The Cusumano brothers are young, ambitious producers, and they and their estate have rapidly risen to become one of the top operations in Sicily, thanks to very good wine quality and professional marketing.

PLANETA****
SAMBUCA DI SICILIA
• *Wines: La Segreta: Bianco, Rosso; Alastro, Chardonnay, Santa Cecilia, Merlot, Cabernet*
Single-variety wines made from French grape varieties, including one of the best Chardonnays in Sicily, and also balanced blends of local and French varieties.

SETTESOLI*−***
MENFI
18,530 acres (7,500 ha); 13,000,000 bottles • Wines: Settesoli: Bianco, Rosato, Rosso, Feudo del Fiori,

Bonera, Soltero Rosso, Chardonnay Sicilia, Nero d'Avola / Cabernet, Nero d'Avola / Merlot, Porto Palo Bianco
The largest cooperative and biggest bottler on the island makes plain, crisp products for everyday purposes as well as high quality varietals and blends.

SPADAFORA***−****
PALERMO
222 acres (90 ha); 200,000 bottles • Wines: I.G.T. Sicilia: DiVino Bianco, Don Pietro Rosso, →Schietto Rosso, →Incanto, Vigna Virzi: Rosso, Bianco: Bianco d'Alcamo
An exemplary estate with consistent high quality; produces an outstanding red Schietto as well as Incanto, a sweet wine.

CONTE TASCA D'ALMERITA—REGALEALI***
SCIAFANI BAGNI
988 acres (400 ha); 2,300,000 bottles • Wines: Cabernet, Chardonnay, Regaleali: Bainco, Rosso, Rosato, →Rosso del Conte, Nozze d'Oro, Villa Tasca, Conti d'Almerita Crèmant, Almerita Brut
The standard for native Sicilian varieties. Rosse del Conte, made from Nero d'Avola grapes, is a classic, as is the white Nozze d'Oro: both age exceptionally well. There is also excellent Cabernet and Chardonnay, both from recently established vineyards.

TENUTA DI DONNAFUGATA**−****
MARSALA
420 acres (170 ha); 1,500,000 bottles • Wines: Contessa Entellina, I.G.T. Sicilia, Donnafugata: Bianco, Rosso, Rosato; Vigna di Gabri, →Chiarandà del Merlo, Tancredi, Damaskino, Moscato di Pantelleria, Lighea, Passito di Pantelleria Ben Ryé, Opera Unica, Milleunanotte
Mainly dry wines, with the focus on white varieties. The firm's best wine is the barrel-aged Chardonnay Chiarandà del Merlo.

VINICOLA ITALIANA FLORIO***
MARSALA
Bought-in grapes; 3,000,000 bottles • Wines: Marsala Superiore: Secco Ambra, Riserva Targa 1840, Baglio Florio, Vergine Terre Arse; Morsi di Luce
The traditional house of Marsala, owned by the Cinzano empire, is again producing clean, complex Marsala versions. The oenoligist is Marco Rabino.

One of the best addresses for Marsala: Florio.

ECKHARD SUPP

GERMANY

WINEMAKING IN GERMANY

The Romans were the first to succeed in the systematic cultivation of vines along the rivers Mosel and Rhine. Diocletian had initially intended Trier to be a transit camp for the trade in Roman wines to the British provinces, but it soon became clear that production locally was more profitable. Probus, a successor of Diocletian, introduced the cultivation of grapes to the Mosel. Soon the slopes of the Rhine and Mosel, the hills of the Pfalz, the Bergstraße, and even Franconia and Württemberg were covered with vines. Around the year 800 Charlemagne began to encourage the selection of grape varieties of good quality, ensuring that the best sites for vineyards were identified, and passing laws to protect winemakers and wine traders.

The treasury of the monastery of Eberbach in the Rheingau.

Legend:
- Ahr
- Mittelrhein
- Mosel · Saar · Ruwer
- Rheingau
- Nahe
- Rheinhessen
- Hessische Bergstraße
- Pfalz
- Baden
- Württemberg
- Franconia
- Saale · Unstrut
- Saxony
- Wine-growing areas in neighboring countries

At the turn of the millennium, monasteries were the leading producers of wine. Cistercians from the Burgundian parent house of Cîteaux founded the monastery of Eberbach in the Rheingau in the 12th century, and it became Europe's largest and best known winemaking center. German wines were soon in demand all over Europe. In the 16th century, records show that vines were grown on an area of 740,000 acres (300,000 ha)—three times as large as the vine-growing area of Germany today—and that wine consumption per head was 32 gallons (120 liters) a year, almost five times the present quantity.

These record figures were followed by a crisis. Drastic deterioration in the climate of Central Europe, together with the wars that shook the continent, also destroyed the foundations of viticulture. It was not until toward the end of the 17th century that the economy began to revive.

While the Burgundian monks had at first grown the French Pinot Noir grape, here known as Spätburgunder, in German vineyards, a different, white grape variety soon conquered the banks of the Mosel and the Rhine-Riesling. With careful selection, it became the area's leading variety.

German winemaking suffered a severe setback in the second half of the 19th century when it was affected by the PHYLLOXERA louse from France. The devastating effects of phylloxera reduced the vine-growing area to a third of what it had once been. Two world wars and the economic crisis of the inter-war years prevented any real resurgence until the 1950s.

Mass Production Versus Quality

In the 1960s, winemaking in the Federal Republic of the time saw perhaps its greatest period of expansion. By the beginning of the 1990s vines grew on over 245,000 acres (100,000 ha). Yields rose in the same period from 534 to over 1,070 gallons per acre (50 to 100 hl/ha): wine production had more than doubled in barely three decades.

This was the result of improved methods of vineyard cultivation, mechanization, and systematic pest control, and of the breeding of more resistant and higher-yielding grape varieties. The winemaking economy concentrated chiefly on its export trade, relying heavily on mass production: sweet or medium-sweet Liebfraumilch became synonymous with German wine in general in the British and American markets.

The German Wine Law, dating from 1971 but revised in the 1990s, did little to enhance the

Burg Rheinstein stands proudly above the vineyards opposite Assmannshausen. It was built around the year 900 for customs and excise purposes.

Bacchante on an ornamental panel from the Mosel.

reputation of German wines. Its refusal to adopt an estate classification system, and the legally equal standing of small top vineyards and *Großlagen* ("large sites," or groups of vineyards) without the potential to produce wines of high quality, denied consumers the opportunity to distinguish between the huge range of wines on offer. Leading viticulturists have called for the introduction of estate classification on the French model. However, the proposal is criticized by those winemakers who through their individual efforts make wines that are among the very best in their respective districts but who may not own vineyards in locations which would usually be considered worthy of classification.

The rise in quality during the 1990s was also the result of individual effort. Winemakers set about producing wines which took account of the public's higher expectations. Modern methods of vinification and concentration on the best grape varieties raised the international reputation of German white wines, both dry and sweet. The latest trend—toward the growing of black grapes, and the making of a number of intensely colored, complex, and powerful red wines—is also promising.

Vine-growing areas and quantities produced in winemaking regions 2001 figures, source: DWI and Enzyklopädie des deutschen Weins (Eno-Verlag)				
Cultural region	Vine-growing area in acres (ha)		Average annual production for the 1990s in millions of gallons (hl)	
Ahr	1,282	(519)	1.15	(43,690)
Baden	39,204	(15,866)	31.6	(1,195,330)
Franconia	14,924	(6,040)	13.3	(503,420)
Hessische Bergstraße	1,126	(456)	.9	(37,660)
Mittelrhein	1,388	(562)	1.9	(72,830)
Mosel-Saar-Ruwer	25,678	(10,392)	40.0	(1,520,520)
Nahe	10,840	(4,387)	9.5	(362,520)
Pfalz	57,875	(23,422)	63.9	(2,420,710)
Rheingau	7,919	(3,205)	6.5	(246,130)
Rheinhessen	65,068	(26,333)	67.4	(2,552,790)
Saale-Unstrut	1,608	(651)	.4	(17,920)
Saxony	1,102	(446)	.3	(13,430)
Württemberg	28,010	(11,336)	29.4	(1,114,050)
Total	256,029	(103,615)	267.0	(10,101,000)

THE WINE LAW AND STYLES OF WINES

Classic and Selection

In the late 1990s two categories were added to the German legislation on wine, *Classic* and *Selection*. As additions to the existing quality range they were intended to make orientation and the choice of a wine easier for the consumer by providing a more precise definition of taste. *Classic* wines are defined as full-bodied (*gehaltvoll*) and dry, and they must be from varieties of grape that are typical of their area. Yields may not exceed 60 hl/ha. Between one and eight varieties whose wines may bear the new designation were established for each area of cultivation. The residual sugar content may not exceed 15 g/l or twice the acid content, and the alcohol content must be one volume percentage higher than required for the corresponding quality classification in that area. For *Selection* wines the range is narrower; the residual sugar content may not exceed 9 g/l or twice the acid content, with a limit of 12 g/l or one and a half times the acid content for Riesling.

German wines are divided by the Wine Law into four categories: *Tafelwein* (table wine), *Landwein* (country wine), QUALITÄTSWEIN *Bestimmer Anbaugebeite* (quality wine from defined regions), abbreviated to Q.b.A., and *Qualitätswein mit Prädikat* or *Prädikatswein* (wine with a distinction), Q.m.P. The majority of wines produced fall into the two last-named categories. Unlike the French wine law, its German equivalent does not classify wines on a geographical basis, but distinguishes between Q.b.A. only on the basis of the sugar content of the grape MUST. The "distinctions" are: KABINETT (cabinet), SPÄTLESE (late harvest), AUSLESE (select harvest), BEERENAUSLESE (select berry harvest), and TROCKENBEERENAUSLESE (T.B.A.) (select dried berry harvest), as well as the special case of EISWEIN (ice wine).

By German law, only *Tafelwein*, *Landwein*, and Q.b.A. wines can have extra sugar added. The minimum must weights for each grade of

Vinothèque wines from the Ratzenberger vineyard estate in the Mittelrhein. Old vintages were kept as a kind of reference library or archive.

The hydrometer or areometer used in determining the weight of the must measures its specific weight and thus its sugar content.

quality vary slightly, depending on where the vines are grown, and are expressed in degrees OECHSLE. As well as stating the minimum weight of the must, a finished wine must also have a minimum alcohol content. *Tafelwein* and *Landwein*, however, must not exceed a total alcohol content of 15 percent vol.

One of the prerequisites for describing the distinctions between categories of German wine was created by the Pforzheim physicist Ferdinand Oechsle (1774–1852) when he invented the hydrometer, also known as the areometer. This hollow glass instrument weighted with mercury (or lead) is marked with a scale and resembles a thermometer. If the hydrometer is placed in water (SPECIFIC GRAVITY 1) the weight of the amount displaced will be equal to the weight of the immersed instrument. If the density of the fluid is altered by the substances dissolved in the fluid of the must, the hydrometer will not sink so far in. It thus shows how many grams heavier a liter of

Lage, Großlage, Bereich

According to the definitions of the German Wine Law, the term *Lage* (site) or *Einzellage* (literally, single site) usually means a vineyard of at least 19 acres (8 ha) with a distinct name and a defined geographical extent and boundaries. The Wine Law states that the grapes from such a vineyard must produce wines of consistent flavor if it is to be granted the status of *Einzellage*.

Old rural place names were given to vineyards from the middle of the 19th century onward, although at first only the top wines bottled on the great estates—particularly *Spätlese* and *Auslese* wines—were identified in this way. After the passing of the 1971 Wine Law such vineyard descriptions became the general rule, since the Law drastically reduced the number of legally recognized names, and made it compulsory to state the geographical origin of a *Qualitätswein* on the label.

The Wine Law also defines the *Großlage* (literally "large site," a group made up of several *Einzellagen*) and the *Bereich* ("district," consisting of several *Großlagen*). But as these larger units cannot be distinguished from *Einzellagen* simply by the names on the label, the consumer cannot tell what kind of description of origin is conveyed. For a long time there has been criticism of the failure of the German Wine Law to classify geographical areas in terms of their potential for quality, as in France.

must is than a liter of water, and the difference in the sugar content can be calculated. Must with a specific weight of 1.050 is 50 degrees Oechsle (°Oe), corresponding to about 6 percent vol potential alcohol (1 oz = 28 g; 1 quart = 1 l).

In the 1970s German winegrowers and consumers alike favored *Spätlese* wines, and the market was positively flooded with cheap, so-called *Prädikat* wines, which could often be made drinkable only by the addition of "sweet reserve," unfermented grape juice.

Such wines were not to be confused with the great *edelsüß* (nobly sweet) wines made from over-ripe grapes affected by the BOTRYTIS CINEREA fungus. These fine wines have been made since the 18th century, and it is on them that the reputation of German wine, particularly the highly esteemed Rieslings from the Rheingau and Mosel, was at least partly founded until well into the first half of the 20th century. In contrast, the fashionably sweet wines of the 1960s and 1970s were to some extent the result of viticultural mass production, and the results, in the cool German climate, were bound to be thin and sour without an added dose of sugar.

SWEETNESS: LESS IS MORE

In the middle of the 1970s wines with a dry finish—first and foremost Edelzwicker wines from Alsace—became increasingly popular with wine lovers around the world, and German winemakers intent on quality began making their own wines dry and sometimes even "bone-dry": such wines could contain practically no residual sugar, and were no longer "improved" with sweet reserve, which did not always suit the acidic wines of the Mosel, Nahe, and Rheingau. Dry wines from more southerly vineyards were naturally better balanced and easier to drink than these German products.

It was not long before winemakers remembered the real criteria for wine of good quality: a full flavor and the right balance. A slight amount of RESIDUAL SUGAR is now tolerated, and the popularity of *edelsüß* wines is growing. Attempts were made to produce wines of a more "international" style. Burgundy vine varieties were more often grown, and even Chardonnay made its way into German vineyards. Experiments have also been made with *barrique* maturation and acidity conversion.

As a result of this development, the styles of wines made by leading German winemakers cover a broad range, with the makers' individual style now often determining the character of the wine more strongly than the idiosyncrasies of particular vineyards or regions. At the same time,

	1. Logo and name of vineyard
	2. Year
	3. Grape variety
	4. Nature of distinction in Q.m.P.
	5. Indication of flavor
	6. Designation of origin (*Bereich, Großlage, Einzellage, Gemeinde* (parish, community)
	7. Identification as Q.m.P. (or Q.b.A., *Tafelwein*, or *Landwein*)
	8. Region of cultivation of *Qualitätswein, Tafelwein,* or *Landwein*
	9. Official inspection number for *Qualitätswein*
	10. Name of firm bottling the wine (if estate-bottled, the winemaker's name and address)
	11. Number of ecological inspection office
	12. Volume contained in bottle
	13. Alcohol percentage by volume (rounded to the nearest 0.5 percent)
	14. Logo of winemaker(s)

the increasingly technological aspect of winemaking has ensured that the simpler wines in particular have become more uniform.

The range of German wines, then, has become wider, and can hold its own on the international market. Strong, dry, but well-balanced white wines, and expressive, rich, rounded red wines now stand side by side with the classic fruity Rieslings of the northern wine-growing regions, and their top quality *edelsüß* products.

THE LABEL

The labels of German wines have to provide certain facts, to which further information may be voluntarily added. It is compulsory to state the category of the wine (*Tafelwein, Landwein,* Q.b.A., or Q.m.P.), and also the region of cultivation or origin of a *Tafelwein*. In addition, the names of the winemaker and the place where the wine was bottled must be given, as well as the volume in the bottle and the alcohol content. *Qualitätsweine* also have an official inspection number and a "lot number," allowing precise identification of the details of its bottling. In a *Prädikatswein* the "*Prädikat*" must be defined.

Optional information includes precise identification of the area of origin, the names of up to two grape varieties, the year the wine was made, an indication of whether the wine was bottled by the maker, the name of the vineyard, and a description of the flavor (dry, medium-dry, sweet, etc.).

Bottles with designer labels, perhaps mentioning only the name of the wine, the vineyard, and the year it was made, must carry an additional label, as specified by the Wine Law, giving the compulsory information.

Just as wine is the winemaker's creation, the design of the labels is often entrusted to experienced artists.

The Main Vine Varieties

Germany is first and foremost the land of the Riesling grape, but it is also a country of vine breeders. A great number of grape varieties developed here, for instance Müller-Thurgau and Scheurebe, spread to other countries during the 20th century. At the same time, such a wide range of varieties was introduced that today only Riesling and Müller-Thurgau can be said to occupy really large vineyard areas. Three other grape varieties have more than five percent of the share, while many of the rest are cultivated on less than one percent of the entire area on which vines are grown in Germany.

Riesling and Riesling Crosses

Riesling is probably descended from the wild vine *Vitis vinifera silvestris* growing in the forests on the Upper Rhine. There are records of grapes being grown here in the 11th century, but viticulture did not become really widespread until the 17th and 18th centuries. The best results with the Riesling grape are achieved when it is grown in temperate to cool climatic zones, providing conditions for as strong as possible a development of the AROMAS, and for a good balance of sugar and acidity. Together with Chardonnay, Riesling is regarded as having the most distinctive character of all white grape varieties. As a late-ripening grape, it produces wines suitable for drinking young and fresh, as well as growths capable of long maturing, and complex, concentrated dessert wines. Its ability to retain acidity as the grapes continue ripening makes it the ideal variety for *Spätlese* and *Auslese* wines.

More than almost any other variety, Riesling takes on the characteristics of the locality where it is grown, and brings them out in its wines. Riesling wines from the schist formations of the Mosel, the clay and loessial slopes of the Rheingau, the lower red sandstone strata of Rheinhessen, from Baden, Alsace, or the primary rocks of the Wachau district of Austria, can all be clearly distinguished from each other. Styles extend from wine with a mineral or fruity character, to a note of honey in a *Prädikat* wine. The wines are pale yellow with greenish reflections, or yellow to golden-yellow among the finest of the *Prädikat* wines. They have a fine fruitiness to the nose, with an aroma of apples, peaches, grapefruit, and other citrus fruits, or in the top quality *Prädikat* wines of honey and

The 12 most widely grown grape varieties (2001)		
Variety	Area of stocks in acres (ha)	% of grape-growing area
Riesling	53,160 (21,514)	20.8%
Müller-Thurgau	45,982 (18,609)	18.4%
Spätburgunder	23,736 (9,606)	9.5%
Silvaner	15,868 (6,422)	6.2%
Kerner	14,959 (6,054)	5.8%
Portugieser	13,664 (5,530)	5.3%
Bacchus	12,451 (5,039)	4.9%
Scheurebe	7,331 (2,967)	2.9%
Dornfelder	7,178 (2,905)	2.8%
Grauburgunder	6,654 (2,693)	2.6%
Trollinger	6,461 (2,615)	2.5%
Schwarzriesling	6,130 (2,481)	2.4%

exotic fruits. On the palate, fine Rieslings have a lively acidity and good body—a high concentration of EXTRACTIONS compensates for their sometimes low alcohol content—and their flavor is almost always intense.

In the last few decades there has been increasing cultivation of Riesling in the New World. California, Australia, New Zealand, and other countries have tried to imitate the winegrowers of the Rhine, the Mosel, and the Danube. The second largest Riesling-growing area in the world lies in the countries of the former Soviet Union, but although little is known of the vines grown there, the end products, with a few exceptions, are rather disappointing. The climate is too mild in general for the grapes to reach their potential: outside Central Europe wines made from the Riesling variety tend to be neutral and uninteresting in flavor. Quite often so-called Riesling wines are made without any Riesling grapes at all, for instance in Australia, where the well-known Hunter Riesling was previously made from Semillon grapes.

There is also some confusion in Europe, and not only because of the diversity of names given to "genuine," white Riesling, also called Rheinriesling in Austria. This confusion is caused by the so-called Welschriesling ("foreign" Riesling), known in Italy as Riesling Italico, which is in fact a completely independent grape variety and has nothing in common with the great Riesling grape.

At least as popular in Germany as Riesling is the Müller-Thurgau variety, a cross between Riesling and Gutedel, raised in 1882 by Hermann Müller of Thurgau in Geisenheim. This early-ripening variety needs fertile soil and produces a very high yield, and for that very reason its yield must be considerably restricted if it is to give good results. Usually wines made from Müller-Thurgau, with its mild acidity, are soft and rounded. The wines from grapes not yet fully ripe have a slightly aromatic, muscat note, which they lose as they mature further, often after two or three years.

The Kerner variety is the result of a cross between Trollinger and Riesling vines in 1969. This variety is regarded as robust, guaranteeing a good yield, and is therefore to be found in all German wine-growing areas today. Its wines resemble Rieslings, but cannot achieve the same high quality.

In terms of quantity, Silvaner was the major German grape variety grown in the 1950s, not least because it was the first to promise a really guaranteed yield. In time it was ousted in many regions by Riesling, Kerner, and Müller-Thurgau, but at present interest in Silvaner wines is increasing again. Their BOUQUET is rather restrained, they have moderate acidity, and are strong on the palate.

In 1916 Georg Scheu crossed Silvaner with Riesling to raise the Scheurebe variety (also known in Austria as Sämling 88). In the lower quality categories the wines made from this strong, lime-tolerant variety are often neutral, but it can produce fine, sweet *Auslese* wines.

The Bacchus grape was bred by crossing Silvaner, Riesling, and Müller-Thurgau. This variety has a high yield with good must weight, and its wines often have a slight muscat flavor, sometimes also showing a similarity to Riesling.

Particularly striking white wines—at their best they are rich in extracts, dense, and spicy— are made from Pinot Gris, known in Germany as Grauburgunder ("gray Burgundy") or Ruländer, and in Italy as Pinot Grigio. The grapes have skins of a grayish red color, and the variety is a direct descendant of Pinot Noir.

RED WINES IN SECOND PLACE

The most popular red wine variety grown in Germany is Spätburgunder (late Burgundy), known in Austria as Blauburgunder (blue Burgundy). In its native France, as Pinot Noir, it has one of the finest reputations of any red wine variety. The best wines made from Spätburgunder in Germany are those from grapes grown on the Ahr, in Baden, and in the Pfalz and Rheingau regions.

The Portugieser or Blaue Portugieser (blue Portuguese) variety came to Germany from Austria. Simple, straightforward wines are often made from this early-ripening variety, which has a reliable yield, but it can also produce dense,

powerful, fruity wines. The Portugieser variety is often used for Weißherbst wines (a kind of rosé).

Dornfelder is a cross between the Helfensteiner and Heroldrebe varieties, making wines notable for strong acidity and a spicy fruitiness. Originally it was bred to improve other varieties by intensifying their color. However, it has become established as a variety in itself and is now actually very fashionable. The grapes are also used to make Sekt, the German sparkling wine.

Trollinger, known as Schiava in Italy, and as Vernatsch in the South Tyrol, is the favorite variety of growers in Württemberg. The wines are light red and fruity, and are notable for their striking acidity. In other parts of Germany, Trollinger is not very often grown, because it ripens extremely late in the season.

Schwarzriesling (black Riesling) is not related to Riesling at all, but is one of the Burgundy varieties, and is known in France as Pinot Meunier. Despite its more intense color and stronger character it slightly resembles Spätburgunder, the Pinot Noir variety.

Grapes from old Riesling vines make concentrated wines expressing the character of their *terroir*, particularly when they are grown by biological methods.

MAKING WHITE WINES

This medieval print shows the three most important stages of winemaking: first harvesting the grapes, then treading with the feet and finally pressing in a table press.

It used to be so easy: the grapes were crushed in a vat at the vineyard itself, the must was put through a basket press in the PRESSING room, so that the YEASTS could then begin to work on it in the large and often ancient FERMENTATION tub, known as a *Fuder* on the Mosel. If the grapes were healthy, they produced a clear, clean must and a wonderful wine typical of its variety and locality. Unfortunately everything did not always go well, and countless ruses were devised to help the fermentation along quickly. Many of these techniques came from overseas, where research had long since revolutionized vineyard and winery work. These early successes led in time to an unlimited belief in the value of high-tech methods. Pumps and tubes, steel tanks for temperature-controlled fermentation, centrifuges, cross-flow filters, cultured yeasts, bacteria, enzymes, and finally concentrators working by evaporation or osmosis took over the wineries, while improved machines for pruning the vines, thinning the leaves, and finally for harvesting itself were introduced into the vineyards.

THE BLESSINGS OF TECHNOLOGY

The grape juice has to go through a lengthy process, particularly in large wineries. It is filtered in the separator, and may be pasteurized to ensure that no remains of wild or "ambient" yeast survive. Then it is fermented with exotic aromatic yeasts from Australia or America to emphasize the primary note of the fruit. Starter cultures of appropriate bacteria or enzymes set the conversion of acidity going, and the wine passes through a microfilter again before it is bottled under sterile conditions.

Such wines cannot really be faulted, but they have less and less individuality. Clean wines of neutral aroma and flavor are the inevitable outcome of wine made in this way.

RESPECTING THE GRAPES

In the early 1990s, when mechanization and the use of chemical aids, enzymes, and aromatic yeasts were being heavily promoted for purposes of mass production, leading winemakers put their minds to the real qualities of their wines. The guiding principle today is to treat the grapes

Battery of silvery stainless steel tanks, Brackenheim vineyard estate, Württemberg.

View of the winery of the Haarti vineyards in Piesport on the Mosel.

Barriques and fermentation casks at the Koehler-Ruprecht vineyard estate in the Pfalz.

SOUR GRAPES

Germany's viticultural areas are among the most northerly in the world. The average annual temperature is lower here than in Italy, Spain, or large parts of France, and there is less sunshine. While in the south musts and wines low in acidity usually have to be additionally acidified, German winemakers are more likely to have to counter excess acidity.

Modern winery technique follows two main methods of dealing with acidity in the must or the wine: de-acidification by the addition of calcium carbonate, and the biological conversion of acidity, a process in which the more aggressive malic acid, which with tartaric acid makes up most of the total acidic content, is split by enzymes and bacteria into lactic and carbon dioxide, a process known as MALO-LACTIC FERMENTATION.

A certain lively play of acidity is in fact one of the best qualities of German white wines: the correct amount and kinds of acids give it freshness and contribute to its ability to mature. The advantage of the biological conversion of ACID over chemical de-acidification is that only the malic acid is affected. Furthermore, any unwanted milky or buttery notes produced by the process, once a potential drawback to the biological conversion of acid, can now be avoided by the use of special enzymes.

But while large wineries use malolactic fermentation to give wines a more rounded or "international" character, leading German winemakers now abstain from either method. Since acid content is high as a result of early harvesting, in their view there is only one recipe for rich, rounded, wines: to leave the grapes on the vine until they have ripened fully.

as gently as possible, using only as much technology as necessary; an example is the practice of pressing the whole grapes without previously removing the skins or crushing the berries. Even letting the must stand for a time to give the wines more structure and ability to mature is "permitted" again these days, and is no longer the sign of a hopelessly conservative attitude.

When wines are made with sweet reserve, the fermentation is interrupted (by pressure, or chilling and FILTRATION) so that the aromas typical of the variety are preserved. The major new development, however, is experimentation with *barrique* maturation for white as well as red wines—particularly those made from the Burgundy grape varieties. At the time of writing, German winemakers are in a forward-looking mood for which they deserve credit. The standard model of white winemaking in Germany is now definitely a thing of the past.

Picking grapes in steep hillside vineyards—as shown here in the Piesport on the Mosel—will still have to be done by hand in the future.

Mechanical concentrators

Attempts have always been made to concentrate the must, in particular its sugar content, which produces alcohol during fermentation. French winemakers have practiced *saignée* (bleeding), in which a little juice is drained from the crushed grapes for red wine in order to give a more intense color and richness to the rest of the must, which will then ferment on the grape skins.

In Austria and the Mediterranean countries wine is concentrated by leaving the grapes to dry for a certain time after harvesting—a procedure banned in Germany by the German Wine Law. The *vins de paille* (straw wines) thus produced are often very sweet, or like Italian Amarone, may be strongly alcoholic.

For more than ten years there have been experiments, particularly in France, with mechanical concentrators. Essentially, two procedures are involved: water is removed from the must in a vacuum evaporator at 77–86°F (25–30°C), or in a process known as REVERSE OSMOSIS the must is forced at high pressure against a membrane which holds back certain molecules, depending on the size of the pores. In this way fluid molecules as well as unwanted by-products of fermentation, such as volatile acids, are filtered out of the wine.

The advantage of this method is obvious. If, for instance, the year's weather was satisfactory until extensive rainfalls just before harvest, excess water can be removed from the must in this way. If the wine seems to be threatened by bacterial action, the damage can be rectified later. But there is no denying the disadvantages: first, the must or finished wine is subjected to violent treatment in clear contradiction to the gentler winemaking procedures which leading winemakers value so highly; and second, concentration of the must levels out differences between years and local origins. The wines become more and more uniform over time, and those from different vineyards or regions are more and more like each other.

Such procedures could seriously undermine the German Wine Law, which defines qualitative categories in terms of degrees Oechsle in the must. Instead of waiting for the grapes to reach the requisite ripeness on the vine, the winemaker can simply manufacture *Auslese* and *Beerenauslese* qualities in the winery.

Mosel—Saar—Ruwer

The Mosel

The valley of the Mosel is one of the most impressive viticultural landscapes in the world. The river runs northwest toward the Rhine between the Hunsrück mountain range and the Eifel region, and almost everywhere the steep slopes on its banks are thickly planted with vines. The Mosel produces perhaps the most characteristic wines of Germany, and its finely fruity, dry, or sweet Rieslings are unsurpassed.

The reason is an extreme geographical situation with the ideal microclimate of the steep hillsides, where the sun can reach every grape. Its warmth is also stored in the argillaceous slate soil, based on Devonian rock, along the central and lower course of the river, while shelly limestone formations predominate on the Upper Mosel. The surface of the water has a moderating effect on the temperature, and as a result the climate has the right amount of warmth to ripen the grapes, but is mild enough to develop the aromatic characteristics of Riesling fully.

Work in these sloping vineyards, some of them extremely steep, is very arduous. The vines are often grown on narrow, almost inaccessible terraces which foil any attempt to mechanize vineyard work. Small single-track railroads have been built on the Lower Mosel in the last few years to transport vineyard workers up to even the highest plots of land, but that makes little difference to the intensity of labor involved. In such vineyards it is still five or even ten times as great as the labor invested in growing vines on more level sites. Nonetheless, and leaving aside certain top wines, Mosel wines are on average the least expensive in the whole of the Federal German Republic, and yields are the highest here, at up to 1,315 gallons per acres (123 hl/ha).

After the dissolution of the great ecclesiastical estates at the time of secularization, the most powerful wine trade in Germany established itself here. Today, the valley of the Mosel is the home of half a dozen of the country's largest wineries, bottling not only the wines of the Mosel itself but almost everything that can be made from grapes in and beyond Europe.

Riesling and Elbling

Those who think of nothing but Riesling in connection with the Mosel forget that only every second vine grown here is in fact of the Riesling variety. Müller-Thurgau represents almost 20 percent of the grapes grown, and the old indigenous Elbling variety, once particularly popular as the basis for sparkling wine and re-evaluated in recent years, still accounts for almost ten percent.

The Elbling variety, perhaps originally Roman, has asserted itself against the omnipresent Riesling on the Upper Mosel in particular, between Trier and the border with Luxembourg, although it cannot seriously compete. Today the variety produces fresh, straightforward, and usually dry Q.b.A. wines which, with their more neutral fruit aromas, have become a specialty of the area.

Trier is the center of viticulture on the Upper Mosel. The old winemaking traditions of the episcopal wine-growing estates, of the Stiftung Staatliches Friedrich Wilhelm Gymnasium, and of the Vereinigte Hospitien are a refreshing contrast to the huge modern Sekt factories.

Selected single vineyards
1 Nies'chen
2 Braune Kupp
3 Kupp
4 Bockstein
5 Rausch
6 Würtzberg

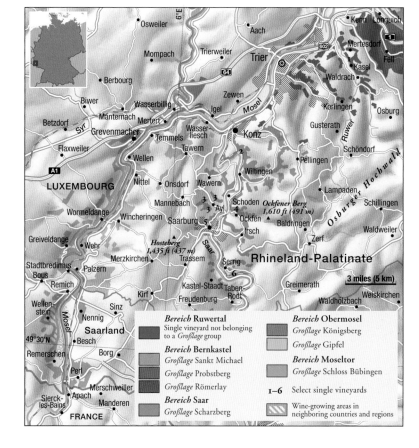

THE SAAR

The upper reaches of the Saar are the natural setting of the most southerly part of the Mosel-Saar-Ruwer region, which is almost level with the southern Rheinhessen or northern Pfalz, but is nonetheless regarded very much as a northerly winemaking area. Wines from the Saar often have strong acidity, but in good years they can be among the most elegant produced in this region of cultivation. The reason for the lively character of Saar Rieslings lies in the structure of the vineyards, which have much gentler slopes than the hillsides of the central Mosel further north, and seldom face south, so that they receive far less warmth and sunlight.

Unlike the great valley of the Mosel, the vineyards here are much more sparsely situated. The wines of the Wiltinger Scharzhofberg are famous, and should not be confused with those of the Großlage Scharzberg, terminology with which the German Wine Law seeks to confuse consumers. The uniform southern aspect of the Wiltinger vineyard and the residual schist Devonian soil, with extreme oscillations of temperature and ancient vine stocks, ensure the production of wines which are unsurpassed for their fullness of bouquet and complexity, particularly the finer *Auslese* wines.

The Saarburger Rausch, where red clay mingles with the schist, also produces grapes with delicately fruity notes which more than compensate even for very high concentrations of sugar. The Serriger Würtzberg, Ockfener Bockstein, and Wiltinger Braune Kupp vineyards, as well as the Ayler Kupp, all have very high potential for quality, although it has sometimes—as in the case of the Ayler Kupp vineyard—been eroded by the excessive importance given to the *Einzellage* or single vineyard by the 1971 Wine Law, and even today is fully exploited only by a few winemakers.

THE RUWER

The upper course of the Ruwer lies only about a mile from that of the Saar, but the wines of the two areas are clearly distinct. This part of the Mosel-Saar-Ruwer region, the smallest, grows grapes which can be extremely sour in cool years and sometimes put a severe strain on the wine lover's palate, particularly in the years when great efforts were being made to produce dry wines. At the same time, however, in both good and bad years they always have a markedly fruity character, which comes out fully in fine *Prädikat* wines. The best wines come from the Grünhäuser Abtsberg, Karthäuserhofberg, Lorenzhofer Felslay, and Kaseler Nis'chen vineyards, and grow on gray and red schist soils. A few of the estates in the Ruwer which produce top-quality wines are world-famous, and include the vineyards of Maximin Grünhaus, the Karthäuserhof, and Karlsmühle.

Left
In Ockfen on the Saar near Saaburg, the argillaceous residual schist soils are suitable for growing grapes to make well-concentrated, elegantly fruity wines.

Right
This vineyard hut on the Saar recalls the days when winegrowers could reach their vineyards only on foot, and had to have some means of shelter overnight or in bad weather.

A winemaking estate with a fine tradition—Maximin Grünhaus on the Ruwer.

Sweet Wines

Germany's sweet wines, in particular its legendary *Eiswein*, are specialties in great demand worldwide. Germany's sweet *Auslese*, *Beerenauslese*, and *Trockenbeerenauslese* wines can hold their own with those made anywhere else in the world, such as the Sauternes and Tokajis.

Because of rapid alternation between damp, cool weather and sunny warmth in the autumn, the Mosel and the vineyards on the banks of the rivers Rhine and Main are particularly suitable for producing *Beerenauslese* and *Trockenbeerenauslese* wines, whereas the grapes for *Eiswein* can be picked in most low-lying and therefore colder vineyards.

A prerequisite for the making of *Prädikat* wines of high quality is that the grapes should remain on the vine until so much sugar has accumulated in them that it cannot be entirely converted into alcohol during fermentation. While *Beerenauslese* and *Trockenbeerenauslese* wines are the result of the action of *Botrytis cinerea*, the fungus which affects the grapes with NOBLE ROT, *Eiswein* is the child of night and cold.

The destructive force of botrytis can turn into its opposite under the right climatic conditions. Its spores perforate the grape-skins of affected berries, which become thinner as they go on ripening, and thus causes evaporation of the water in the flesh of the fruit. The result is an even higher concentration of sugar and acidity, and of aromatic and flavoring substances, in grapes which in any case are already rich in extracts.

Winegrowers working carefully to pick grapes at the "noble rot" stage, or even when they are dried like raisins—there will often be only a few suitable grapes in a bunch—pass through the vineyard several times in the autumn. At that season in Germany the weather seldom allows viticulturists to pick the dried berries in up to eight harvesting procedures, as with the famous Sauternes of Château d'Yquem, but it is perfectly possible to pick in two, three, or four stages.

Eiswein: A Nocturnal Adventure

Of course wines cannot be made from over-ripe grapes or those affected by noble rot every year, although in principle modern technology and its mechanical concentrators have superseded these old winemaking rules. However, differences between the years of production of the other kind of sweet wine, *Eiswein*, are even more important. The grapes need not have been affected by botrytis to make *Eiswein*; they must be frozen when they are picked and pressed. Only then will

Grapes for *Eiswein* are picked by night.

Frosty morning at 3°F (–16 °C).

Grapes coated with ice.

Plastic protects the grapes on the vine.

The grapes reach the winery still frozen.

Selecting the grapes by hand before pressing.

Most of the winemakers of the Mosel have great difficulty in getting anything like a good price for their wines, and therefore resort to mass production—but Egon Müller of the Wiltinger Scharzhof vineyard on the Saar auctions his fine wines for one to two thousand euros (about US $1,215–2,430) a half bottle.

Müller Junior, who has been running the estate for some time, is unmoved by the fact that one of the best-known German wine writers once described his dry range as "a disaster." In fact, he is no longer making any dry wines, but he produces some astonishing sweet wines, bottles which are regarded as great treasures, in particular the *Beerenauslese* and *Trockenbeerenauslese* wines with their gold caps, and a rare *Eiswein* which can hardly be matched anywhere.

Only five percent of the total production of this estate at the foot of the Scharzhofberg—one of the finest Riesling vineyards in the world—is offered at the annual auctions of the Großer Ring of winemakers in Trier. But at prices from 230 euros (US $280) for the humblest *Kabinett* wine, and 2,400 euros (US $2,920) for a *Trockenbeerenauslese*, these few bottles easily account for a large part of the Scharzhof vineyard's sales. Those figures are a world record for young wines; with his old wines, Müller recently achieved a price of 6,650 euros (US $8,090) for a 1959 *Trockenbeerenauslese*.

The prices paid at auction for his wines, and their quality, have made the name of Müller internationally famous. And of course Müller himself knows that such prices are a fashionable market phenomenon dependent on many factors, with little the winemaker can do to influence them, and cannot be fully explained by the fame of the vineyard and the high quality of its wines.

---

the liquid from the fruit retain the form of ice crystals as the grapes are being pressed, while the concentrated juice runs off in drops.

The temperature should be seven, eight, or even better ten or twelve degrees below freezing (32°F/0°C) for the grapes to be thoroughly frozen. The winemaker who leaves some bunches of grapes on the vine, hoping for an *Eiswein* harvest, is constantly on the alert as winter sets in. As soon as the night temperature falls below that magic mark, he summons his picking team, who must bring in the grape harvest by lamplight before dawn.

Unlike grapes affected by noble rot, in which the acid content has decreased as the fruit ripens further, grapes for *Eiswein*, if they are sound, have very high acidity, and like the sugar and the aromatic and flavoring substances, this acidity is concentrated by the crystallization of the liquid. Particularly in more northerly areas, on the Mosel, the Saar, and the central Rhine, an *Eiswein* therefore often has a noticeably fruity acidity, while rather fuller, rounder wines are pressed in most other areas. High amounts of extracts, high acidity, and even higher sweetness, as well as aromas of honey, roses, quinces, and exotic fruits are the characteristics of really good examples of *Eiswein*, in addition to the notes typical of the grape variety used.

NOTHING VENTURED, NOTHING GAINED

A considerable number of grape varieties is suitable for the production of *edelsüß* wine or *Eiswein*, including varieties such as the Scheurebe or Rieslaner which are scarcely worth mentioning in connection with simple, dry *Qualitätsweine*, but develop unsuspected qualities of flavor in the higher reaches of *Prädikat* wines. But the grape variety *par excellence* for making sweet wines is the Riesling,

The Eiswein made in the C. von Schubert Schlosskellerei, in Mertesdorf on the Ruwer, from grapes grown in the Maximum Grünhäuser Abtsberg vineyard, is one of the best known of sweet German wines.

one of the few which, as it ripens, retains a good part of its acidity to give bite and structure to the finished wine.

However, considerable risks are involved—starlings love sweet grapes, heavy rain can make short work of a plot set aside for *Eiswein*—and the extremely labor-intensive work necessary in the winery to produce very small quantities raises the cost of making this kind of wine a great deal. It is not surprising, then, that *Beerenauslese* and *Trockenbeerenauslese* wines, like *Eiswein*, are among the most expensive to be found. Lovers of these most noble of wines are happy to pay large sums for half a bottle, and enjoy the wine drop by drop after long years of maturing.

The Großer Ring and the Bernkasteler Ring

The Großer Ring (Great Ring) of winemakers offering *Prädikat* grades of Mosel, Saar, and Ruwer wines at auction was founded in the early 20th century by the mayor of the city of Trier, where the annual auctions are still held. The Großer Ring comprises only those firms which are members of the regional Mosel-Saar-Ruwer association and of the association of German *Prädikat* wine estates (the V.D.P.). A number of top firms in the Mosel region which do not belong to the V.D.P. have formed a similar group called the Bernkasteler Ring. The highest prices by far, however, are still reached at the annual auctions of the Großer Ring.

THE CENTRAL MOSEL
AND THE TERRACED MOSEL

THE CENTRAL MOSEL

The Central Mosel, which in the latest changes to the definition of districts was classed with the Trier vineyards, is the best-known part of the Mosel region, and also the most popular with tourists. There are good reasons for this, since the narrow valley of the meandering river, bending sharply at Trittenheim, Piesport, Zeltingen, and Traben-Trarbach, offers increasingly impressive panoramas with miles of enclosed vineyard slopes, and these views have established the image of the Mosel worldwide.

The soils of gray and red schist here, together with the ideal south or southwest aspect of the slopes, give the Rieslings made in the Central Mosel an unusual amount of fullness and balance. The wines are more substantial than those of the Upper Mosel, and can sometimes be quite powerful. However, there are clear differences in the character of the wines made by the top vineyards of the Central Mosel. The Rieslings of the Trittenheimer Apotheke are both substantial and elegant. Even more powerful are those of the Piesporter Goldtröpfchen vineyard, although

it must be remembered that this vineyard wa over-promoted by the Wine Law, and has been enlarged by the addition of less valuable plots o land. The Brauneberger Juffer-Sonnenuhr, one o the most famous of the vineyards, produces excel lent wines from its predominantly very dry so even in damp, cool years.

Almost as good as the wines of the Juffer-Sonnenuhr are those of the Kestene Paulinshofberger, although the potential of this vineyard has not really been fully exploited by winemakers. The most expensive vineyard in Germany—and surely one of the most expensive in the world—is the Bernkasteler Doctor, which makes wines of great elegance. The *Gemeinden* (communities) of Wehlen and Zeltingen divide the famous Sonnenuhr vineyard between them, with Wehlen clearly having the better part of the deal. It is no coincidence that an unusually large number of top winemakers have settled here. Different again are the wines from the vineyards of the Ürziger Würzgarten, with its red sandstone soil, and the Erdener Prälaten. Both vineyards make wines which unite strength and spiciness with the elegance of the Riesling grape.

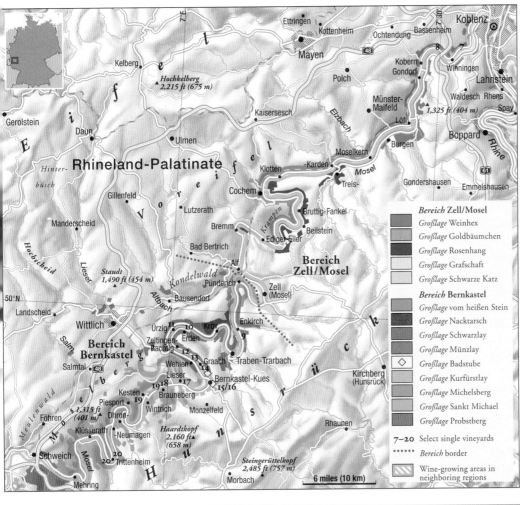

Select single vineyards

7 Im Röttgen
8 Uhlen
9 Batterieberg
10 Treppchen
11 Würzgarten
12 Sonnenuhr
13 Sonnenuhr
14 Dompropst
15 Graben
16 Doctor
17 Niederberg-Helden
18 Juffer-Sonnenuhr
19 Paulinshofberger
20 Apotheke

Even a glance at the steep vineyard slopes at Kröv shows their remarkable potential, although that has been somewhat impaired by the institution of the Kröver Nacktarsch Großlage.

Bereich Zell/Mosel
Großlage Weinhex
Großlage Goldbäumchen
Großlage Rosenhang
Großlage Grafschaft
Großlage Schwarze Katz

Bereich Bernkastel
Großlage vom heißen Stein
Großlage Nacktarsch
Großlage Schwarzlay
Großlage Münzlay
⬦ Großlage Badstube
Großlage Kurfürstlay
Großlage Michelsberg
Großlage Sankt Michael
Großlage Probstberg

7–20 Select single vineyards
••••• Bereich border
Wine-growing areas in neighboring regions

6 miles (10 km)

This final section of the course of the river owes its name of the Terraced Mosel to the grayish brown, narrow stone terraces, which in winter can look very forbidding, and which seem to cover the landscape from this point on. Countless such terraces are crammed into a very narrow space, utilizing every patch of ground and leaving hardly any room for the vines themselves, so that the work of the winegrower is considerably more difficult.

Although more northerly than the vineyards of Brauneberg, Kasel, Trier, and Saarburg, the Terraced Mosel produces rounded wines with fewer acid notes. They are achieved not only by the perfect south-facing aspect of the terraces and the moderating influence of the river Mosel, a very broad expanse of water at this point, but also by the stony, poor soils, which demand all that the vines can give.

In order to keep up with the well-known and popular wine-producing areas of the Middle and Upper Mosel, the best winemakers and gastronomic experts of the area have joined together to form the "Terrassenmosel" association, which attracts tourists to the region in summer with culinary and cultural events.

A Return to High Quality

The Lower or Terraced Mosel with its steep vineyards—the steepest anywhere on the river—is the crown and conclusion of this unusual viticultural area. Despite its outstanding potential, in the 1970s the Mosel region stood for simple and usually sugary wines, which were especially popular in northern Germany and the English-speaking countries. Its image is still determined by the sweet wines it produces, yet 50 percent of the wines from the Mosel now on the market are dry, and another 30 percent medium-dry.

In addition, over the last ten years leading winemakers between Saarburg and Winningen have won over lovers of high-quality Rieslings. They began by making wines in the best vineyards of Wiltingen, Piesport, Bernkastel, and Ürzig, wines which were once again worthy of the fine Riesling grape variety and the region. The secret was in concentrating on winemaking methods producing only 430 or 530 gallons per acre (40 or 50 hl/ha), from vineyards which contain vines growing on their own roots and up to 100 years old, instead of the usual 1,068 or even 1,388 gallons (100/130 hl). This movement, promoted by growers on the Central Mosel in particular, is now being emulated everywhere in the region.

The Terraced Mosel

Before the Mosel turns to meet the Rhine it becomes truly spectacular once again. While the river here describes more of a straight line than on its course between Cochem, Zell, Bernkastel, and Piesport, the slopes on its banks become steeper, more rugged, and inaccessible, increasing the picturesque charm of its banks. The Bremmer Calmont in the border area between the Lower and Central Mosel is the steepest vineyard in Germany, although Kobern, and Uhlen and Röttgen in Winningen, do not lag far behind in this respect.

The leading Winninger Uhlen vineyard grows grapes which make several of the liveliest Rieslings along the Mosel, with a distinct mineral note.

Opposite
In vineyards on a steep gradient such as the Ürziger Würzgarten viticulturalists install tackle blocks to bring equipment up and take the grape harvest down.

Select Producers in the Mosel-Saar-Ruwer Area

Maximin Grünhaus★★★★
Mertesdorf

4 acres (34 ha); 220,000 bottles • Wines: Riesling from the Bruderberg, →Abstberg, and →Herrenberg vineyards

The three top vineyards of the Maximin Grünhaus winery were named in the past after the ecclesiastical hierarchy—Abtsberg, Herrenberg, and Bruderberg in descending order, and C.F. von Schubert has shown today that this was an accurate assessment. The wines are predominantly dry, but the firm also makes high-quality *edelsüß* wines and *Eiswein*.

Fritz Haag★★★★–★★★★★
Brauneberg

19 acres (7.8 ha); 70,000 bottles • Wines: Riesling Brauneberger Juffer, →Brauneberger Juffer-Sonnenuhr

Wilhelm Haag has risen to international fame with his Rieslings from the Brauneberger Juffer and its heart, the Juffer-Sonnenuhr vineyard. Elegance is lent to Haag's wines by traces of peaches, roses, and sometimes blackcurrant in the aromas, and by an almost always perfect balance between acidity and residual sugar.

Reinhold Haart★★★★–★★★★★
Piesport

15 acres (6 ha); 50,000 bottles • Wines: Riesling, Weißburgunder from the Piesporter Kreuzwingert, Domherr and →Goldtröpfen vineyards, also from the Wintrich Ohlingsbert vineyard

Gentle handling of the best grapes with the use of modern technology is Theo Haart's recipe for success. His dry wines are dominated in general by a striking acidity when young, while the *edelsüß* wines are notable for a luxuriant, fruity sweetness.

Heymann-Löwenstein★★★★
Winningen

32 acres (13 ha); 80,000 bottles • Wines: Riesling, Müller-Thurgau, Weißburgunder from the Winninger vineyards →Röttgen and →Uhlen

Reinhard Löwenstein, the scion of an old winemaking family, has been running his vineyard since 1992. Using grapes from the steep schist terraces of Uhlen and Röttgen, he makes mainly dry wines which, with their strength and spiciness, are in marked contrast to the idea of Mosel Riesling as delicately fruity in character.

Carl A. Immich★★★★
Batterieberg, Enkirch

18 acres (7.5 ha); 25,000 bottles • Wines: Riesling from Enkircher Steffensberg and →Batterieberg vineyards

Gert Basten still cultivates ten acres (4 ha) of what used to be Germany's third largest private winemaking estate around the monopoly vineyard of Batterieberg. Clean, fruity Rieslings are made in the oldest wine cellars still intact in the country, dating from the year 1200.

Karlsmühle★★★–★★★★
Mertesdorf

33 acres (13.5 ha); 65,000 bottles • Wines: Riesling and Weißburgunder from the Lorenzhöfer →Felslay and →Mäuerchen vineyards, also from the Kasler →Nies'chen and Felsnagel vineyards

Peter Geiben is regarded as one of the rising stars of the 1990s. His wines from the monopoly vineyards of Felslay and Mäuerchen have subtlety and a strong play of acidity.

Karthäuserhof★★★★
Trier-Eitelsbach

47 acres (19 ha); 100,000 bottles • Wines: Riesling and Weißburgunder from Eitelsbacher →Karthäuserhofberg

A Mosel estate particularly rich in tradition is run today by Christoph Tyrell. Tyrell's Ruwer wines are distinguished for their great density and power, and have above-average ability to mature.

R. & B. Knebel★★★★–★★★★★
Winningen

13 acres (5.5 ha); 30,000 bottles • Wines: Riesling, Weißburgunder, Kerner from Winningen vineyards, →Hamm, →Röttgen, →Uhlen

Reinhard and Beate Knebel have devoted themselves to the making of dry Mosel Riesling, and have achieved a rare perfection. Their wines from Hamm and Röttgen are both delicate and distinctive, and have an expressive bouquet, qualities which they retain in the highest ranges of *Prädikat* wines.

Dr. Loosen★★★★–★★★★★
Bernkastel

27 acres (11 ha); 70,000 bottles • Wines: Riesling, Müller-Thurgau from vineyards in Erden, Ürzig, Graach, Wehlen and Bernkastel: →Treppchen, →Prälat, →Sonnenuhr, →Himmelreich

The bouquet, density, extract content, and very high alcohol content of Loosen's wines distinguish them from the usual fruity Mosel style. The stocks of vines from which the grapes for these wines are harvested are up to 100 years old, and most of them grow on their own roots. The best are from the vineyards of Prälat in Erden and Sonnenuhr in Wehlen, although unlike many of his colleagues Loosen has made a name not just for his *edelsüß* wines but for dry wines too.

Egon Müller★★★★★
Scharzhof und Le Gallais, Wiltingen

31 acres (12.5 ha); 100,000 bottles • Wines: Riesling from Scharzhofberg, including edelsüß wines, and from →Wiltinger Braune Kupp (monopoly, Le Gallais)

Egon Müller's *edelsüß* products are sold for record prices at almost every wine auction. The grapes of the famous Scharzhofberg are used almost exclusively to make high-quality *Prädikat* wines. They also concentrate on *edelsüß* wines at Le Gallais, again cultivated by Müller, a vineyard which makes its wines at the Scharzhof.

Dr. Pauly-Bergweiler★★★–★★★★
Bernkastel

37 acres (15 ha); 125,000 bottles • Wines: Riesling, Spätburgunder, Müller-Thurgau from many top vineyards in Bernkastel, Ürzig, Brauneberg, Graach, Erden, and Zeltingen

Peter Pauly has the best vineyards in the Bernkastel district in the Alte Badstube on the Doctorberg, and has had to fight for decades for their recognition. The wines are made in an ultra-modern winery, fermented in stainless steel tanks, and only some of them are aged in wooden casks.

Joh. Jos. Prüm★★★–★★★★
Wehlen

36 acres (14.5 ha); 120,000 bottles • Wines: Riesling from Wehlen and Zeltingen →Sonnenuhr vineyards, Graacher Himmelreich, Bernkasteler Badstube

Manfred Prüm is one of the best-known and most controversial winemakers in the Mosel region. Critics find fault with the frequent off notes in his young wines, but lovers of Rieslings praise their extremely good capacity to mature.

S. A. PRÜM****
WEHLEN
41 acres (16.5 ha); 100,000 bottles • Wines: Riesling from vineyards in Bernkastel, Wehlen (→Sonnenuhr), and Graach
Since the mid-1990s, and after years of economic problems, Raimund Prüm, with the help of investors, has once again been able to feature as a producer of the best Rieslings. They come from the Sonnenuhr vineyard in Wehlen, and are in the medium-dry to sweet category of *Spätlese* and *Auslese* wines.

WILLI SCHAEFER*****
GRAACH
8 acres (3.2 ha); 30,000 bottles • Wines: Riesling from the Graach Himmelreich and →Dompropst vineyards, and Wehlen →Sonnenuhr vineyards
In most years Schäfer's Rieslings from the Graacher Dompropst in particular—from dry Spätlese to exotic *Beerenauslese* wines—are among the best growths of the region: they have a nose of apricots, fine citrus fruits, and sometimes of smoke, and they are always full of fruity acidity and dense extracts on the palate.

SCHLOSS LIESER****
LIESER
18 acres (7.5 ha); 50,000 bottles • Wines: Riesling from Lieser Niederberg-Helden
Since taking over the running of Schloss Lieser, Thomas Haag has shown that the long-neglected Niederberg-Helden vineyard is among the best in the Central Mosel. A pronounced citrus character is a feature of these elegantly fruity wines.

SELBACH-OSTER***−****
ZELTINGEN
35 acres (14 ha); 100,000 bottles • Wines: Riesling from vineyards in Zeltingen (→Sonnenuhr, →Schlossberg), Graach (→Dompropst), Wehlen (→Sonnenuhr), and Bernkastel
Besides running their well-known export business, the Selbachs manage their own wine-producing estate with a series of top vineyards between Bernkastel and Zeltingen. Gentle treatment of the grapes, and careful concentration on only the most essential procedures in the winery, produce wines which in many cases are the perfect expression of their *terroir*.

WITWE DR. H. THANISCH— ERBEN THANISCH****−*****
BERNKASTEL-KUES
16 acres (6.5 ha); 60,000 bottles • Wines: Riesling from the Bernkastel (→Doctor), Graach (→Dompropst), and Brauneberg (→Juffer-Sonnenuhr) vineyards
In the middle of the 1980s the inheritance left by Dr. Thanisch was the basis of, among other things, the winemaking estate of Sofia Spier, which since then has made its mark with top-quality growths from famous vineyards such as Doctorberg or Juffer-Sonnenuhr. They do not think much of dry Mosel Rieslings here, preferring the fruity, lively style with light or even more emphatic residual sweetness, which gives a good balance to the fruit acid of the wines.

WITWE DR. H. THANISCH— ERBEN MÜLLER-BURGGRAEF***−****
BERNKASTEL-KUES
34.5 acres (14 ha); 90,000 bottles • Wines: Riesling from many vineyards in Bernkastel (→Doctor),

Brauneberg (→Juffer-Sonnenuhr), Graach, Lieser (→Niederberg-Helden), and Wehlen (→Sonnenuhr)
The second half of the Thanisch inheritance belongs to the Müller-Burggraef family, but is not so much in the public eye as the Spier estate. Here too, however, the quality of the wines from the most famous vineyards of the Central Mosel is considerable.

GEHEIMRAT J. WEGELER ERBEN****−*****
BERNKASTEL-KUES
37 acres (15 ha); 250,000 bottles • Wines: Riesling and Müller-Thurgau from the Bernkastel (→Doctor), Kasel (→Nies'chen), and Wehlen (→Sonnenuhr) vineyards, and estate wines
The stainless steel tanks of the great vaulted cellars in Kues produce clean Rieslings; even the simple estate-made Riesling is impressive in its fruity and well-balanced style. The *Spätlese* and *Auslese* wines made by the firm from the grapes of the famous Bernkastel and Wehlen vineyards, and above all those of the Kasel Nies'chen vineyard, are of top quality.

DR. F. WEINS-PRÜM****−*****
WEHLEN
10 acres (4 ha); 40,000 bottles • Wines: Riesling from the Wehlen →Sonnenuhr, Graach Himmelreich, Dompropst and Erden →Prälaat vineyards
Hubert Selbach, a banker before he took over the family estate, has managed his share in the property of the Prüm dynasty of Wehlen very unobtrusively and has taken it to the top. He works in a very traditional way, and concentrates on ensuring that his wines display the aromatic density and fullness of flavor which the grapes from the firm's excellent vineyards can give them.

FORSTMEISTER GELTZ—ZILLIKEN****−*****
SAARBURG
25 acres (10 ha); 60,000 bottles • Wines: Riesling from the Saarburger Antoniusbrunnen,→Rausch, Bergschlösschen and Ockfener→Bockstein vineyards
The cellars of Hans-Joachim Zilliken contain one of the most spectacular settings for winemaking in the Mosel region. Waterbearing veins in the surrounding rock make the cellars extremely humid and guarantee perfect conditions for the wines to mature. Zilliken's wines are models of elegance and lightness, even in the higher *Auslese* qualities.

Famous and controversial: the J.J. Prüm estate in Wehlen on the Mosel.

THE AHR

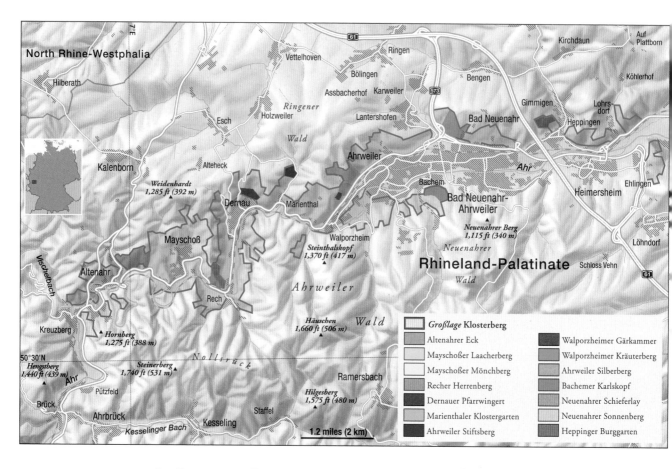

AN ISLAND OF RED WINE

An island of red wine in northern Germany—such is the description aptly given to the valley of the Ahr, a river which makes its way between Koblenz and Bonn on the left of the Rhine, passing through the volcanic landscape of the Eifel area. Wooded hillsides, pretty villages, and little towns like historic Ahrweiler and romantic Mayschoß, are the setting for one of Germany's smallest wine-growing regions: it is only around 18 miles (30 km) long, and less than 1,200 acres (500 ha) in total are devoted to the growing of vines.

Vines were being grown on the schist and basalt soils in the center of the Ahr valley and the gravel soil of the Lower Ahr as early as the 8th century. French monks planted the black grapes of their native country here, just as they did on the Rhine, and in contrast to almost all other German viticultural regions Pinot Noir, otherwise Spätburgunder, managed to hold its own against the Riesling grape on the Ahr.

Even today, by far the larger part of the area is stocked with black grapes, and Spätburgunder alone accounts for the vines in over half the

vineyards between Sinzig and Altenahr. The overall picture of the black grape monopoly of the Ahr valley is completed by the Portugieser variety, although it produces amounts barely worth mentioning here, and Frühburgunder, which has become increasingly prominent in recent years, while Riesling has to be content with less than ten percent of the entire vineyard area, and the heavy bearers of other viticultural areas, such as Müller-Thurgau, are merely tolerated here.

THE MOST NORTHERLY RED WINES IN THE WORLD

Because of its northerly situation, the Ahr is among the most demanding and climatically difficult vine-growing areas in the world. Why, then, do black grapes in particular do so well here, hungry for the sun as they are? The answer lies in the ideal situation of the steep slopes with their schist soils. The southern aspect of the vineyards catches all the sun available, and the schist stores its warmth to pamper the sensitive vines. At the same time, the narrow valley and wooded hilltops ensure that warmth is built up over the

The sensitive Spätburgunder variety growing in an ideal situation at Ahrweiler.

vineyards, greatly to their benefit, and they also give effective protection from cold winds.

Different as the Ahr is from the other German vine-growing landscapes, there is one point in which, until very recently, it fitted into the general philosophy of viticulture in Germany. Here too, only thin and pale wines were made over several decades, often either sweetly insipid or massively acid. Record yields were achieved, sometimes of over 1,068 gallons per acre (100 hl/ha) of vineyard area, but the quality of the wines was better left unmentioned.

Yet the region undoubtedly has great potential for producing wonderful wines. They may not be as rounded or as high in alcohol as those from more southerly vineyards, but their richness of aroma and fruity character will satisfy high requirements. This is particularly true of those velvety Spätburgunder wines matured to dryness, which can sometimes even benefit by a time spent aging in the *barrique*, a demanding method.

The prerequisite for making such wines is of course a carefully chosen situation (sites in the central valley of the Ahr between Bad Neuenahr and Altenahr are the best), a favorable climate and a good season, careful work in the vineyard

and winery, and rigorous limitation of yields, although it is still very difficult to convince most winemakers of this. A small group of producers willing to experiment, however, has shown more than once over the last decade how good the red burgundies of the Ahr can be. It is a pity, but understandable, that year after year the wines made by these producers sell out within a very short time.

STRIVING FOR QUALITY

Werner Näkel was one of the first to realize that an improvement in quality was essential. Even in the early 1980s Näkel, a native of Dernau, was dissatisfied with the thin, sweet, undistinguished wines which most of his local colleagues were content to make from the Portugieser or Spätburgunder varieties. He had learned his trade on the red wines of the 1970s, which all struck him as being made too simply and with too much technology, matured too fast, and with poor keeping qualities, let alone having any ability to age well. Above all, he did not like their flavor.

Yet there were countless examples of the way a good red wine ought to look and taste—after

all, the Germans were already importing large quantities of fine foreign wines at this time. However, the search for the right path to take was not an easy one. As early as 1983 Näkel was experimenting with the *barrique* maturation of wine, but his inexperience and the paucity of literature on the subject led to a series of setbacks, since the wines still had nothing like the requisite structure to overcome the influence on their flavor of the new wood of the casks.

Fortunately Näkel was not alone in his endeavors. A few of his colleagues began following his example in the mid-1980s, and at the beginning of the 1990s efforts to achieve quality were being made by a good dozen winemakers in the Ahr valley.

The first revolution was in the vineyard: planting out many clones of different kinds, adapting the cultivation of the vines to new requirements, clearing the area around them to get healthy grapes and consequently a deeper

The spa of Bad Neuenahr-Ahrweiler is also the center of the best-known German red wine growing district.

color and cleaner-tasting wines, thinning out to at most ten or twelve bunches of grapes a vine, restricting yield to 530 or often even to only 430 or 320 gallons per acre (50, 40, or 30 hl/ha), and rigorous selection of the best grapes in up to three or four picking processes in the autumn—all these were soon part of the repertory of all really serious producers.

However, Näkel does not care for terms like "natural" and "biological," although to a great extent he works on the same principles as ecologically orientated winemakers. He is concerned primarily to cultivate the vineyard in such a way as to produce the best possible grapes with the minimum strain on the environment.

Methods of working have undergone radical alteration in the winery too. Instead of following the old practice of making what were really just red white wines, fermentation now takes place on the must (sometimes even on the whole grapes), the wines mature in new or used wooden casks, and as a general principle there is rather less use of modern winery techniques. "A coarse filter is enough to keep any particles from floating in red wine," today's innovators say, to explain their abstention from many of the new high-tech devices which are now part of the basic equipment elsewhere.

These tireless workers first showed that their new approach really could be successful with the vintages of 1988 and 1990, when the season's weather played a part. By now the new style has been largely accepted. Beside the Meyer-Näkel estate, Deutzerhof, Kreuzberg, Adeneuer, Nelles, Stodden, Sonnenberg, and several other vineyards have made themselves a solid reputation. Genuine red wine is being made again in the north of Germany.

Wine-tasting at the Meyer-Näkel winery in Dernau.

Werner Näkel of the Meyer-Näkel estate.

Wolfgang Hehle of Deutzerhof in Mayschoß.

Always good for a superior rating: the Deutzerhof estate in Mayschoß

SELECT PRODUCERS ON THE AHR

J. J. ADENEUER***
BAD NEUENAHR-AHRWEILER

22 acres (9 ha); 80,000 bottles • Wines: Spätburgunder and Frühburgunder, Portugieser, Dornfelder, from the Walporzheim →Gärkammer (a monopoly) and other vineyards

Since 1714 the miniature Gärkammer vineyard has been in the possession of the Adeneuer family estate, which has held a leading position in the region's winemaking trade since 1984. Thanks to reduced yields in its integrated viticulture the growths of this estate, which produces only red wine, have good concentration and a fine bouquet.

DEUTZERHOF—COSSMANN-HEHLE****−*****
MAYSCHOSS

17 acres (7 ha); 50,000 bottles • Wines: Spätburgunder and Frühburgunder, Dornfelder, Portugieser, Riesling and Chardonnay from vineyards in Altenahr and Heimersheim, →Caspar C, →Grand Duc Select, Catharina C

After marrying into the Cossmann family estate Wolfgang Hehle, a former tax adviser, devoted himself entirely to its wines, introducing new momentum and innovative ideas. His Spätburgunder *barrique*-matured wines are now consistently among the best in the Ahr region. The *Trockenbeerenauslesen* and *Eiswein* made from the Riesling grape are also of top quality.

H. J. KREUZBERG***−****
DERNAU

20 acres (8 ha); 45,000 bottles • Wines: →Spätburgunder and Frühburgunder, Portugieser, Dornfelder, Riesling from Dernau (→Pfarrwingert) and Bad Neuenahr (→Schieferlay, →Sonnenberg), →Spätburgunder Devon

The Kreuzberg brothers have made their estate one of the most famous in the Ahr region by virtue of skillful division of labor and a willingness to experiment in the winery. All their red wines are aged in wooden casks, and the best of them in the smaller *barrique*.

MEYER-NÄKEL****−*****
DERNAU

32 acres (13 ha); 100,000 bottles • Wines: Spätburgunder and Frühburgunder, Dornfelder, Riesling from Dernau and Bad Neuenahr, →"S," →"G," Blauschiefer, →Illusion

A wide range of really top-quality wines, the best of them *barrique*-matured over a long period. Werner Näkel's methods include a natural approach to cultivation and strict selection in the vineyard. In the winery, Näkel is concerned to transfer the quality achieved in the vineyard to the bottle in as unadulterated a form as possible.

NELLES****
HEIMERSHEIM

12 acres (5 ha); 50,000 bottles • Wines: Spätburgunder and Frühburgunder, Portugieser, Domina, Riesling, Grauburgunder from vineyards in Heimersheim and Bad Neuenahr, the Triumvirat line: →Albus, →Clarus, →Ruber, →B, →Futura

The labels of this estate give prominence to the year of its first mention in the records, 1479, a date which illustrates the length of the family tradition. The estate's best wines today are matured in *barriques*, and both vineyard and winery work to avoid drastic methods. The top wines made by Nelles go under the overall name of Triumvirat.

SONNENBERG—GÖRRES & LINDEN***
BAD NEUENAHR-AHRWEILER

12 acres (5 ha); 50,000 bottles • Wines: Spätburgunder and Frühburgunder, Portugieser, Domina, Dornfelder, Riesling, Kerner from vineyards in Bad Neuenahr, →Schieferlay, →Sonnenberg and Ahrweiler, Tradition, Selection F.H.

Norbert Görres and Manfred Linden turned to viticulture only in 1980, but they soon acquired a high reputation beyond the Ahr region itself. Their wines are light and easy to drink, and they do not use *barriques* even to mature red wines.

THE MITTELRHEIN

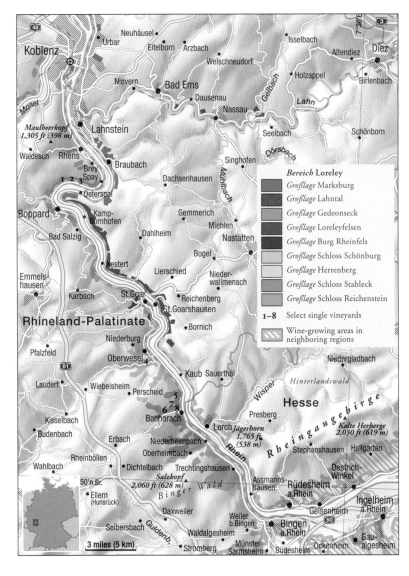

It was the Romans again who were responsible for planting the first vineyards at the foot of the Siebengebirge range. Much later the Franks extended these plantations. Many of the towns they founded have been connected with wine-making ever since, for instance Königswingert, now Königswinter, where grapes still grow near the ruins of Drachenfels, a popular tourist attraction. The vineyards of Oberdollendorf and Niederdollendorf were once cultivated by the Cistercians of the monastery of Heisterbach, now a ruin. The wines made here come from over 50 acres (24 ha) of land which have been reorganized and are part of the Petersberg Großlage group. Over a length of 30 miles (50 km) up the Rhine toward Koblenz, vine growing is successful only on the southern slopes of the right bank of the river. The best known winemaking villages here are Hammerstein and Leutesdorf. Vines are also grown at Ehrenbreitstein opposite the Deutsches Eck, and on the lower course of the Lahn, particularly in Weinähr and Oberndorf.

South of Koblenz and Lahnstein, not only does the Rhine display its full romantic beauty but the hillside vineyards here, some of them extremely steep, produce wines of better quality than those from further north. However, many of the old terraces cut into the slate slopes are very difficult to reach, and cultivating them is so cost-intensive that they have now been abandoned.

The largest vineyard of the Mittelrhein region is the Bopparder Hamm, running for four miles (6 km) down the left bank of the river, and with a full southern aspect. From the bend in the Rhine to St. Goarshausen there are steep vine-

Select single vineyards
1 Mandelstein
2 Feuerley
3 Ohlenberg
4 Bernstein
5 Hahn
6 St. Jost
7 Wolfshöhle
8 Posten

yards on the right bank which offer more favorable conditions for the Riesling grape to ripen, while the best vineyards on the other bank lie opposite Kestert and at Burg Rheinfels. Only here does the left bank of the Rhine, with the valleys running off it, offer well-protected and sunny situations. The narrow, densely wooded valley of the Rhine and the broad surface of the river create the climatic prerequisites for vine growing in the Mittelrhein, but really outstanding wines can be produced only in the extreme south of the region.

The vineyards of the Mittelrhein and the Rheingau meet further along the right bank of the Rhine with its romantic castles, to the southeast; the first Rheingau vines grow at Lorchhausen, in sight of Bacharach, a place probably more visited by tourists than anywhere else in the Mittelrhein viticultural region, which on the left bank of the river extends to Bingerbrück.

The Other Side of the Coin

Tourists visiting the border region between the Mittelrhein and Thurgau wine-growing areas are usually less interested in vineyards than in the fortresses, castles, romantic little towns, and the mysterious Lorelei, all of which have made this landscape a world-class tourist destination. Tourism may have brought benefits to the wine producers of the Mittelrhein (providing them with a guaranteed market for very little effort), but the other side of the coin is that the wine itself suffered: why go to the trouble of trying to make wines of high quality when tourists would drink anything on offer? But all that is in the past: today the producers of Sekt can buy their basic wines more cheaply in Italy and Spain, and consumers will no longer be fobbed off with poor wines of the kind made in the 1970s and 1980s.

About a dozen winemakers have seen the signs of the times. These viticulturalists have planted their vines with care on steep, south-facing vineyards in the bends of the Rhine and its lateral valleys, at Boppard, Oberwesel, Bacharach, and Steeg, and in the Kaub area on the right bank of the Rhine, and they make robust wines from the Riesling which covers three-quarters of the vineyard area.

Although the Mittelrhein used to be a much more important wine-growing region in past centuries—around 1900 there were still 4,940 acres (2000 ha) of vines under cultivation here, while today only 1,482 acres (600 ha) are cultivated—its wines are well on the way to making a fine name for themselves.

Rheinfels Castle high above St. Goar sponsored the organization of the *Großlage* vineyards on the left bank of the Rhine.

Opposite
Plowing steep vineyards like this one above Bacharach calls for skill and strength.

Select Producers of the Mittelrhein

Fritz Bastian****
Bacharach
23.5 acres (9.5 ha); 30,000 bottles • Wines: Riesling, Spätburgunder, Portugieser, Scheurebe from Bacharach vineyards (→Heyles'en Werth [a monopoly]), →Posten
The Bastians run the inn "Zum grünen Baum" (The Green Tree), and they also own the only island vineyard in Germany, the Heyles'en Werth. Their best wines are from the Posten vineyard.

Toni Jost, Hahnenhof***–****
Bacharach
30 acres (12 ha); 90,000 bottles • Wines: Riesling, Spätburgunder from Bacharach (→Hahn) and the Rheingau →(Wallufer Walkenberg)
Peter Jost also manages vineyards in the Rheingau producing grapes which are vinified in Bacharach. His wines in the *Spätlese* and *Auslese* ranges are full and strong, and the *edelsüß* variants are also excellent.

Martina & Dr. Randolf Kauer***–****
Bacharach
7 acres (3 ha); 20,000 bottles • Wines: Riesling from Bacharach (→Kloster Fürstental, Wolfshöhle) and Urbar (→Beulsberg)
Dry/medium-dry Rieslings made by biological methods.

Heinrich Müller***–****
Spay
15 acres (6 ha); 55,000 bottles • Wines: Riesling, Grauburgunder, Kerner, Spätburgunder from Boppard (Hamm, →Feuerlay, →Mandelstein)
One of the oldest wine-growing firms in Boppard.

August Perll***–****
Bacharach
17 acres (7 ha); 90,000 bottles • Wines: Riesling, Spätburgunder from Boppard vineyards (→Feuerlay, →Mandelstein, Fässerlay, Ohlenberg)
The best Rieslings from Bopparder Hamm come from Lakes Mandelstein and Feuerlay.

Walter Perll***–****
Bacharach
15 acres (6 ha); 55,000 bottles • Wines: Riesling, Müller-Thurgau, Spätburgunder from the Bopparder Hamm (Mandelstein, →Fässerlay, Feuerlay, →Ohlenberg)
The best wines come from Fässerlay, where it is sometimes even possible to make *Beerenauslese* wines from Spätburgunder, and from Ohlenberg.

Ratzenberger****
Steeg
20 acres (8 ha); 55,000 bottles • Wines: Riesling, Spätburgunder, Müller-Thurgau from Bacharach (Wolfshöhle, Kloster Fürstental) and Steeg (→St. Jost)
Pressing the whole grapes, fermentation at a very cool temperature, and maturing in large wooden casks are processes producing clean, rich Rieslings.

Florian Weingart***–****
Spay
15 acres (6 ha); 85,000 bottles • Wines: Riesling, Müller-Thurgau, Grauburgunder from vineyards in Spay and Boppard (→Feuerlay, Ohlenberg, Engelstein)
One of the last three full-time viticulturalist families of Spay harvests some of the grapes for its Rieslings, which are clear as glass.

The Rheingau

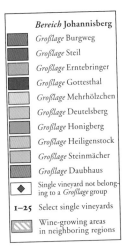

The Rheingau holds the record for Riesling production.

Müller-Thurgau grapes. At present, the average yield per acre is less than 965 gallons (90 hl/ha) in the Rheingau, in marked contrast to yields of 1,068–1,388 gallons per acre (100–130 hl/ha) in other German winemaking regions.

The situation of the vineyards on the right bank of the Rhine, an area which between Wiesbaden and Rüdesheim constitutes the only part of the river running east to west for any length between Basel and the North Sea, offers ideal ripening conditions for the sensitive Riesling grape. The rows of vines face south, and are protected from cold north winds by the first of the Taunus heights on one side, while on the other they benefit from the broad surface of the river, which is over half-a-mile wide at this point.

A Unique Character: the Erste Lagen

Study of the local soils shows that the Rheingau is clearly distinct from the other great Riesling-growing region of Germany, the Mosel with its variety of schist and shelly limestone formations. Here on the Rhine, the soils are predominantly deep and often calcareous, consisting of sand, loess, gravel, and occasionally sandstone, while the steep Rüdesheim vineyards stand out clearly from the flatter central part of the area between Eltville and Johannisberg, which in turn is distinct from the slopes running gently down to the Main at Hochheim and Wicker.

It is hardly necessary to mention that the soils also influence the character of the wines, which do not have the light-hearted fruitiness of the Mosel Rieslings, but often show more breeding and character, without resembling the even more powerful Rieslings of Alsace and Austria. For some years, since the fashion for

Together with the Mosel, the Rheingau is the best known of the German wine-growing regions both at home and abroad. The Romans laid out their vineyards here on the Rhine at an early date, and Charlemagne is said to have recognized the suitability of the steep Rüdesheim slopes for growing vines when he observed that the snow always melted from them very quickly every year.

At just 18 miles (30 km) in length, and with a vine-growing area of 7,904 acres (3,200 ha), the Rheingau is one of the smaller German winemaking regions (although not so much so, perhaps, with respect to its extent, for the last vineyard which is officially part of the region is the Lohrberg near Frankfurt). Much the greater part of the vineyard area is stocked with Riesling vines—80 percent, and here the Rheingau holds the record—while the rest is planted mainly with Spätburgunder and

Legend

Bereich **Johannisberg**

- *Großlage* Burgweg
- *Großlage* Steil
- *Großlage* Erntebringer
- *Großlage* Gottesthal
- *Großlage* Mehrhölzchen
- *Großlage* Deutelsberg
- *Großlage* Honigberg
- *Großlage* Heiligenstock
- *Großlage* Steinmächer
- *Großlage* Daubhaus
- ◆ Single vineyard not belonging to a *Großlage* group
- **1–25** Select single vineyards
- Wine-growing areas in neighboring regions

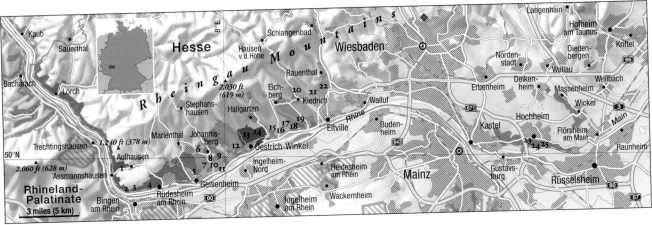

What is the V.D.P.?

The Verband Deutscher Prädikats- und Qualitätsweingüter (Association of German Prädikat and Qualität Winemaking Estates), which has its headquarters at Bad Kreuznach on the Nahe, goes back to the beginning of the 20th century. Originally founded as the Verband Deutscher Naturweinsteiger (Association of German Auctioneers of Natural Wine), the association had to change its name after the enactment of the Wine Law of 1971, since mention of such terms as "natural" was no longer allowed in the marketing of wine. Members of the association originally had to be vine-growing estates which regularly auctioned their products, but this aspect has become of subsidiary importance with the passing of time. Today, other aims are more prominent: the V.D.P. implements the quality requirements laid down in its statutes by means of regular tastings and inspections, the members market their products jointly, and they introduce the work of the association to the outside world.

Today the V.D.P. has 197 members cultivating 9,365 acres (3,790 ha) in all, 3.5 percent of the total German vine-growing area. Small and medium estates predominate, and only twelve firms own or manage areas of over 123 acres (50 ha). The members pledge themselves not to claim membership of any *Großlage* group, to sell wines of the higher qualities only after they have matured for several months, and to pick all grapes from *Auslese* quality upward by hand. In addition, the V.D.P. has concentrated on cultivation of the steep vineyards which produce fine wines, and it works together with the Naturland-Verband.

The V.D.P. Classification

The most important V.D.P. project in recent years was to establish the category *Erstes Gewächs* or *Grosses Gewächs* in Germany, analogous to *premier crus* and *grand crus* in France. In 2002 a statute was passed restricting the designation *Erstes* or *Grosses Gewächs* to top quality dry wines from the best slopes, which were to be sold under special labels. The relatively liberal assignment of the classification to a large number of vineyards aroused criticism and the policy actually caused one of the initiators to leave the V.D.P.

The restriction to dry wines was treated with particular reserve on the Mosel, which is famous for its top quality sweet wines. Now that sweet wines may also be classified as *Erstes Gewächs* the Mosel V.D.P. has accepted the new statutes.

The walled vineyards of the monastery of Eberbach in the Rheingau bear the stamp of the Burgundian monks who laid them out.

Select single vineyards
1 Höllenberg
2 Berg Schlossberg
3 Berg Roseneck
4 Berg Rottland
5 Rothenberg
6 Hölle
7 Kläuserweg
8 Schloss Johannisberg
9 Hasensprung
10 Klaus
11 Jesuitengarten
12 St. Nikolaus
13 Lenchen
14 Doosberg
15 Engelmannsberg
16 Nussbrunnen
17 Wisselbrunnen
18 Marcobrunn
19 Hohenrain
20 Gräfenberg
21 Baiken
22 Rothenberg
23 Domdechaney
24 Kirchenstück
25 Hölle

the sweet, thin wines of the 1960s and 1970s passed, leading winemakers, organized into the Vereinigung der Charta-Winzer, "Association of Charta Winemakers," have been encouraging this individuality in the character of their wines. In the mid-1990s the Charta Association merged with the Rheingau V.D.P., believing it would be able to realise its objectives better within that prestigious organization.

EBERBACH MONASTERY

The Rheingau has a long tradition of quality, and a high reputation. As early as the 12th century Cistercians from Burgundy founded what is still the most famous monastery in the area, Eberbach. It was mainly thanks to them that viticulture in the Rheingau took off to such a remarkable extent in following centuries. Eberbach became the most important wine-making estate and center of the wine trade in the whole of Europe. The famous treasury of the monastery, the old presses, and the lay brothers' dormitory, now used for tastings and wine

auctions which are great occasions, became the focal point of winemaking in the Rheingau.

At its very heart, and symbolic of the achievements of monastic wine growing, was a vineyard which is marked off from the surrounding vineyards by a wall, on the model of the French *clos*. It is known as the Steinberg. The vines were planted here as early as 1232, but the surrounding wall was not completed until 1766. Today the Steinberg, with the slopes of Schloss Johannisberg, is an area granted special status by the Wine Law. Officially it is defined as part of a locality, but can also be mentioned on labels without the usually obligatory addition of the parish or community name.

The Steinberg, which is a rather cool vineyard, produces wines which are definitely not very opulent, and in poor years can even suffer from a harsh, green acidity. In great years, however, particularly when it is possible to gather grapes for high-quality *Auslese* wines or even *Eiswein*, the wines of the Steinberg display all their expressive power, their full aromatic potential, and a rich spiciness.

The Hotel Krone in picturesque Assmannshausen, where the Rheingau begins and where its best red wines are made.

Left
In the autumn of 1775 the grapes were harvested late at Schloss Johannisberg by mistake. According to the legend, this was the origin of Spätlese wines.

Right
The residential tower of Schloss Vollrads in Oestrich-Winkel. The estate, now under new management, is once again producing top-quality Rheingau wines.

Eberbach monastery, secularized in the Napoleonic period, is now part of the Hesse state vineyards managed from nearby Eltville, where the wines are also made. In addition, the red wine estate of Assmannshausen, where by common consent the best Spätburgunder grapes of the Rheingau are now pressed, the estate of Bensheim on the Bergstraße, and a winemaking business in Hochheim on the Main, are part of this small but nevertheless distinguished German wine empire.

JOHANNISBERG AND OTHER WINEMAKING CASTLES

It is to the Benedictines that Schloss Johannisberg, the other famous name of the Rheingau, owes its existence. The original monastery building, a foundation of the beginning of the 12th century, had only a moderate length of life. By 1716 it was in a state of dilapidation and was bought by the princely abbey of Fulda, which demolished it and then replaced it with the present castle, visible from afar above the rows of vines in the single vineyard of the same name, both a landmark and the best-known architectural monument in the Rheingau.

Schloss Johannisberg was not only one of the first winemaking estates in the region, it was also here that the first pure-variety Riesling vineyard was planted in the early 18th century, amidst what had previously been the "red" or at least a predominantly mixed panorama of Rhenish vine growing. A century later, the estate's possessions were secularized under Napoleonic rule, and after the Vienna Congress of 1815 they passed into the hands of the Metternich family, whose descendants still live here. The landed property which used to belong to the castle is now owned by the firm of Oetker.

Together with the professional viticultural competence of the monks, the private interests of the old noble families formed the real backbone of the historical winemaking of the Rheingau. The lords of Schönborn, Vollrads, and Knyphausen, the princes of Hesse, and the princes of Prussia at Schloss Reinhartshausen worked at least as energetically as the monks to establish its reputation as a viticultural region.

Over a long period, the outstanding position of the Rheingau in German viticulture was also reflected in the progressive development of vineyard and winery technologies. The first wine filters were used here, it was here that *Spätlese* wines were "invented" and the selection of grapes with noble rot perfected, and one of the most famous schools of viticulture in the world—the Geisenheim research institute—indeed still is situated in the region.

Despite the famous past and the international renown of the wines of the Rheingau, which at the beginning of the 20th century were among the most expensive in Europe—even more expensive

State-owned vineyard estates

All the states of the Federal Republic of Germany where wine is made have state-run vineyards or trial vineyards. The state-owned vineyards of Hesse in the Rheingau and on the Bergstraße are probably the best known to the general public.

With the historic monastery of Eberbach, the wineries in nearby Eltville, and the distributors in Assmanshausen and Bensheim, the state-run wine businesses of Hesse have good potential for making and marketing wine, and own some excellent vineyards, for instance the historic Steinberg, one of the oldest vineyards of the Rheingau to be mentioned in documentary records. The crucial improvement in the development of quality in state vineyards came with the change from a camaralistic approach to one following the principles of managerial economics.

As was the case in Hesse, the quality of wines made by the Staatlicher Hofkeller in Würzburg, which is the property of the Free State of Bavaria, left much to be desired, but here too great progress has been made since about the 1980s. The Saxon estate of Schloss Wackerbarth, which failed as a result of economic difficulties, was less lucky. Once highly regarded, little of its former reputation adheres to the now state-owned viticultural estates of the Rheinland-Pfalz, of Oppenheim in Rheinhessen, Niederhausen in the Nahe region, Mariental in the Ahr region, and Trier in the Mosel.

Baden-Württemberg, on the other hand, has a number of state-owned viticultural estates, some of which are able to offer products of outstanding quality. Weinsberg in particular (an estate associated with the teaching and experimental institute there) and Freiburg (with the Blankenhornsberg estate) have an excellent reputation, while at present Karlsruhe and Meersburg are on the whole known only to insiders.

than claret, champagne, and burgundy—the decades after the Second World War saw this region of Germany, like others, suffering a deep identity crisis which affected the quality of its products. Even the famous monastic wine estates and those of the castles found it difficult to keep up with the rise in quality evident in other viticultural regions: the flagship of the Rheingau was close to foundering.

In recent years the situation has improved considerably, and Reinhartshausen, Vollrads, Schönborn, and Knyphausen may be well on the way to taking their place among the elite of the region again, and perhaps even among the top winemakers of Germany.

WINEGROWERS OF THE NOBILITY AND THE BOURGEOISIE

While in the 1920s the wines of the Rheingau could still fetch prices on the international market which made even the winemakers of Bordeaux and the great champagne houses green with envy, today that state of affairs is only a wistful memory. In the second half of the 20th century the history of the Rheingau, like that of almost all German wine-producing regions, was determined more by a policy of rationally managed mass production than by any concern for quality.

There has now been a return to something more like the higher standards of the past, at least in the making of *Qualität* wines, although that fact is not yet generally acknowledged. Obviously, expectations are particularly high in a viticultural region with such historic associations. Some uncertainty about the typical style of Rheingau Riesling still exists. First a flood of exaggeratedly dry wines with acid notes came on the market in reaction to the years of sweet wines, but at present stronger medium-dry wines are being made. This may be a logical development, but if residual sugar is to act as a substitute for fullness and density it is as difficult as it ever was to judge the right balance. Winemakers almost find it easier to satisfy the rising demand for *edelsüß* growths with fine *Beerenauslese* and *Trockenbeerenauslese* wines, or even *Eiswein*.

Progress in the region today, however, is being made not so much by the old-established noble estates as by family-owned vineyards. Names like those of Gunter Künstler, Bernhard Breuer, Robert Weil, Diefenhardt, Querbach, Eser, Johannishof, Lang, and Ress have long denoted quality and have produced fine growths, something which can be said only with reservations of the Johannisberg, Knyphausen, Oetinger, Schönborn, Langwerth, and Löwenstein estates. It was also the bourgeoisie who strongly promoted discussion of the vineyard classification system, although the wines they have introduced as their "First Growths" in recent years have tended to prove quite disappointing in one way or another.

MON DIEU
WENN ICH DOCH SO VIEL GLAUBEN IN MIR HÄTTE
DAß ICH BERGE VERSETZEN KÖNNTE, DER
JOHANNISBERG
WÄRE JUST DERJENIGE BERG
DEN ICH MIR ÜBERALL NACHKOMMEN LIEßE

H. HEINE 1797 – 1856

Heinrich Heine's pious wish was not a modest one, for in his time Schloss Johannisberg was at the height of its fame.

Select Producers in Rheingau

Georg Breuer*—*****
Rüdesheim
64 acres (26 ha); 140,000 bottles • Wines: Riesling, Grauburgunder, Spätburgunder from Rüdesheim (→Schlossberg, →Rottland, Roseneck, Bischofsberg) and Rauenthal →Nonnenberg), Montosa, → Winzersekt
Bernhard Breuer has not only been a prominent figure in the regional V.D.P. and the Charta association, he was also one of the first to commission designer labels, and to experiment with aging Spätburgunder wines in *barriques*. He is always impressive in the consistent quality of his best Rieslings, which are grown in the most famous vineyards of Rüdesheim.

Diefenhardt*—*****
Marienthal
40 acres (16 ha); 100,000 bottles • Wines: Riesling
Uncomplicated, modern winemaking is the rule here, and the wines are equally straightforward and uncomplicated. They are particularly good tasted in the *vinothèque* or at the inn on the estate itself.

August Eser*—*****
Oestrich-Winkel
25 acres (10 ha); 100,000 bottles • Wines: Riesling, Spätburgunder from a large number of very good vineyards in Oestrich, Rauenthal, Erbach, Hattenheim, Hallgarten, Winkel, and Rüdesheim
Although this estate has been much divided into different plots, and there is a correspondingly wide variety of labels, Joachim Eser succeeds in achieving very high quality in all the wines he makes. The best are the Rieslings from the Hattenheim and Oestrich vineyards.

Prinz von Hessen*—*****
Geisenheim
118.5 acres (48 ha); 350,000 bottles • Wines: Riesling, Spätburgunder in Johannisberg (→Klaus), Winkel and Kiedrich, estate wines
The estate of the Landgrave of Hesse is one of the largest in the Rheingau, and in recent years has attracted attention through great improvements in the quality of its wines. The Johannisberger Hölle and Klaus vineyards provide grapes for the best of the Rieslings made here.

Hupfeld*—*****
Königin Victoriaberg und Oestrich-Winkel
28.5 acres (11.5 ha); 70,000 bottles • Wines: Riesling, Spätburgunder from vineyards in Hochheim (→Victoriaberg), Winkel, Oestrich, and Johannisberg
As the name indicates, the Hupfeld vineyard estate is in two parts: one has its center in Oestrich, the other, including the famous Victoriaberg, is in Hochheim am Main. Here Queen Victoria is said to have been delighted by the wine of Hochheim on a picnic in 1845. The Hochheim Rieslings are the best products of the house today.

Weinbau-Domäne Schloss Johannisberg*—*****
Geisenheim
86.5 acres (35 ha); 260,000 bottles • Wines: →Riesling Schloss Johannisberg (a monopoly)
Schloss Johannisberg is the winemaking establishment of the Rheingau *par excellence*. Benedictine monks helped to found the viticulture of the Rheingau here in the 12th century, in answer to the work of the Cistercian monastery of Eberbach. By way of Napoleon and Prince Metternich, the castle finally passed into the possession of the Oetker group, which in recent years has been making various efforts to restore the slightly tarnished reputation of the estate's wines to its old glory.

Johannishof*—*****
Geisenheim
49.5 acres (20 ha); 130,000 bottles • Wines: Riesling from many vineyards in Johannisberg, Winkel, Geisenheim, and Rüdesheim
Johannes Eser has been responsible for work in the winery on his father's estate since 1985. He makes fruity, fresh wines to a consistently high standard from grapes supplied by many vineyards. Eser's simple estate Riesling is of outstanding quality.

Baron zu Knyphausen*—*****
Erbach
54 acres (22 ha); 100,000 bottles • Wines: Riesling, Spätburgunder from vineyards in Erbach (→Marcobrunn) and Hattenheim (→Wisselbrunnen)
The Knyphausen family own plots in the top-ranking Marcobrunn and Wisselbrunn vineyards, and make their wines with particular care. The estate wines consistently have a powerful acidity, and are usually matured for longer than rival products before going on the market.

Franz Künstler**—*****
Hochheim
59 acres (24 ha); 240,000 bottles • Wines: Riesling, Spätburgunder from vineyards in Hochheim (→Hölle, →Domdechaney, Kirchenstück, Reichestal, Stielweg, Herrnberg)
Gunter Künstler is considered one of the best of all German winemakers. His Rieslings from Hölle, Domdechaney, and Reichestal—whether *Spätlese, Auslese*, or *edelsüß*—are among the finest in Germany. However, the Spätburgunder wines are also very fine in good years. Künstler also manages the Hochheim vineyard of Geheimrat Aschrott'sche Erben.

Hans Lang*—*****
Hattenheim
44 acres (18 ha); 120,000 bottles • Wines: Riesling, Silvaner, Weißburgunder, Spätburgunder from vineyards in Hattenheim (→Wisselbrunnen, Schönhell), Hallgarten (→Jungfer), Erbach (→Marcobrunn), and Kiedrich, Riesling & Spätburgunder Johann Maximilian
Johannes Lang has systematically built up a range of wines of high quality, and in recent years has also had some success in experimenting with the maturing of red wines in *barriques*.

Freiherrlich Langwerth von Simmern'sches Rentamt*—*****
Eltville
81.5 acres (33 ha); 180,000 bottles • Wines: Riesling, Chardonnay, Weißburgunder, Spätburgunder from vineyards in Rauenthal, Erbach, Hattenheim, Eltville, and Kiedrich
This historic estate has been managed for some years by Baron Georg Reinhard. All the wines of the estate are fermented and matured in old, used wooden casks. The latest efforts made to improve the range have obviously suited the wines.

Dr. Heinrich Nägler*—*****
Rüdesheim
21 acres (8.5 ha); 20,000 bottles • Wines: Riesling, Spätburgunder, Ehrenfelser from vineyards in Rüdesheim (→Schlossberg, →Rottland, Rosenberg, Bischofsberg, Drachenstein)

Heinrich Nägler, a self-taught winemaker, still works largely by traditional methods, an approach that could change with the entry of his son Tilbert into the firm.

WILFRIED QUERBACH***−****
OESTRICH-WINKEL

23.5 acres (9.5 ha); 70,000 bottles • Wines: Riesling, Spätburgunder from Oestrich (Lenchen, →Doosberg, Klosterberg), Hallgarten →Schönhell), Mittelheim (Edelmann) and Winkel (Hasensprung, Dachsberg)
Typical of the Querbach estate is a strong awareness of tradition. Nonetheless, the most modern methods are employed in both vineyard and winery, including mechanical harvesting, and have been very successful, as the clean, straightforward, and expressive Rieslings prove. The best of them come from the Doosberg vineyard in Oestrich.

BALTHASAR RESS**−****
HATTENHEIM

89 acres (36 ha); 250,000 bottles • Wines: Riesling, Spätburgunder and other varieties from Hattenheim (Nussbrunnen, Engelmannsberg), Rüdesheim (Schlossberg, Rottland) and Schloss Reichhartshausen, Ress-Wein, Gutsriesling Von Unserem
Stefan Ress has made his name as both a viticulturalist and an organizer of many cultural events. The former wine-dealing business has become a top winemaking estate—the line marketed by the winery itself is only a small part of its activities. For some years the wines have no longer been made at the historic manor house, but in the buildings of the former viticultural cooperative of Hattenheim.

SCHLOSS REINHARTSHAUSEN***−*****
ERBACH

215 acres (87 ha); 550,000 bottles • Wines: Riesling, Weißburgunder, Chardonnay, Spätburgunder from Erbach (→Marcobrunn, Schlossberg, Siegelsberg), Hattenheim (Wisselbrunnen, Nussbrunnen), and Erbach (→Rheinhell)
The estate of the Leibbrand family has had to be sold along with the hotel which was part of it, and its future does not yet seem fully secure. Over the last two decades, the rise of the estate to the very top group of winemaking firms in the Rheingau had been constant. Systematic experiments with Chardonnay and with *barrique* maturing were made here earlier than in other German viticultural areas. In the last few years the firm's blend of Weißburgunder and Chardonnay has made a wine of genuinely high quality, and the *Auslese* wines made with Riesling from Schlossberg and Siegelsberg need fear no competition.

SCHLOSS SCHÖNBORN**−****
HATTENHEIM

113.5 acres (46 ha); 300,000 bottles • Wines: Riesling, Spätburgunder, Weißburgunder from Hattenheim, Erbach (→Marcobrunn), Hochheim (→Domdechaney), and Rüdesheim (→Schlossberg)
The estate of the counts of Schönborn has maintained its high reputation through all the vicissitudes of recent decades. Now, under the management of Günter Thies, there has been a further upward trend for some years, particularly evident in the wines from the famous Marcobrunn vineyard in Erbach.

SCHLOSS VOLLRADS***−****
OESTRICH-WINKEL

118.5 acres (48 ha); 500,000 bottles • Wines: Riesling from the single vineyard of Schloss Vollrads and from vineyards in Hattenheim
After the suicide of Erwein Count Matuschka von Greiffenclau, owner of Schloss Vollrads, who was heavily in debt, this famous estate spent some time

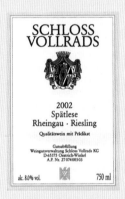

in uncertain waters, but was soon able to regain its former stature under the management of Rowald Hepp. Although it was the subject of sharp criticism for a long period, the quality of the wines from Vollrads had in fact already risen to its old high standards in the second half of the 1990s.

STAATSWEINGÜTER KLOSTER EBERBACH**−****
ELTVILLE UND ASSMANNSHAUSEN

375.5 acres (152 ha); 1,000,000 bottles • Wines: Riesling, Weißburgunder, Spätburgunder and Frühburgunder from Assmannshausen (→Höllenberg), Hattenheim (Engelmannsberg), Erbach (→Marcobrunn, Sigelsberg), Rauenthal (→Baiken), Rüdesheim (→Baiken), Hochheim (→Hölle, Kirchenstück, Domdechaney), and from the monopoly vineyard of the Steinberg, →Champion-Wein
The Rheingau estates owned by the *Land* of Hesse are among the most famous of German state-owned vineyards. In Assmannshausen, they have specialized very successfully in the traditional aging of red wines, while Rieslings are vinified in the great winery at Eltville. In Kloster Eberbach and the historic *clos* of Steinberg, the state-owned vineyard possesses two jewels in the crown of the history of viticulture in the Rheingau region. Under the management of Rowald Hepp, there was increased emphasis on quality in Eltville at the end of the 1980s, a line which is being futher pursued by current director Dieter Greiner.

GEHEIMRAT J. WEGELER ERBEN****−*****
OESTRICH-WINKEL

119 acres (48 ha); 450,000 bottles • Wines: Riesling, Müller-Thurgau, Gewürztraminer, Grauburgunder from vineyards in Oestrich (→Lenchen), Winkel (→Jesuitengarten), Rüdesheim (→Rottland, →Schlossberg), and Geisenheim (→Rothenberg), Geheimrat J
This Oestrich firm is not only the control center of the three Wegeler estates in the Rheingau, Pfalz, and Mosel, but also the home of the famous brand name of Geheimrat J, made as both a Riesling and a Sekt. Under the management of Norbert Holderieth, the Rheingau estate in particular has become a model winemaking business over the last few years. The Rieslings from the Geisenheimer Rothenberg and Rüdesheimer Berg Schlossberg vineyards in particular, and the *edelsüß* wines from the Lenchen vineyard in Oestrich, are often unsurpassed.

ROBERT WEIL***−*****
KIEDRICH

161 acres (65 ha); 350,000 bottles • Wines: Riesling from Kiedrich →Gräfenberg, estate wines
It is true that Wilhelm Weil has not, like Egon Müller in the Saar region, specialized entirely in sweet wines, but it is here that the estate's strength lies. Not for nothing do the wines auctioned by this firm, which has belonged for some time to the Japan-based multinational Suntory company, regularly compete for the highest prices with those of the Scharzhofberg. By means of careful work in the vineyards—very ripe grapes, for instance, are covered with plastic over a large area—Weil has managed to harvest grapes for *Trockenbeerenauslese* wines and even *Eiswein* year after year, achieving spectacular must weights and extract values. Rather more powerful in style than the delicate wines of the Mosel, Weil's *Prädikat* wines are at least as long-lived and complex in aroma and flavor.

THE NAHE

The Nahe winemaking region appears at first glance to have more contradictions in it than the Mosel. At the beginning of the 20th century the wines from Bad Kreuznach, Schlossböckelheim, Niederhausen, and Dorsheim—for the viticultural region of the Nahe as it exists today was created only by the 1971 Wine Law—were at least as famous and sought after as those of the neighboring Rheingau. After the Second World War this region too concentrated almost entirely on mass production, doubled the area under cultivation by planting vines even in valleys and on level land which was not particularly suitable for them, and sought its salvation in the production of wines for blending to make the famous—or infamous—Liebfraumilch, and other popular and often even more dubious exports of German post-war viticulture.

As in the neighboring Rheinhessen area, a kind of mass hysteria quickly came to dominate the entire viticultural panorama of the region. It is no coincidence that its southern border merges so seamlessly with the vineyards of the Rheinhessen hinterland that the frontier is barely visible to the impartial eye. The result of this development is the fact, almost unique in Germany, that while individual estates on the Nahe may have a high

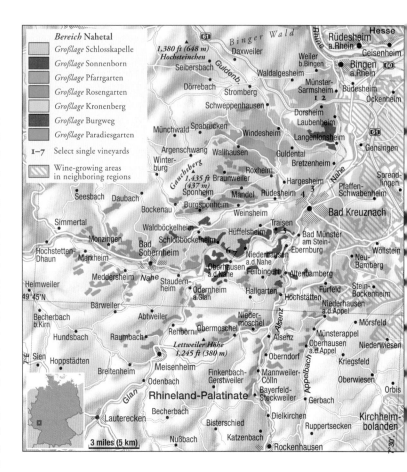

Traisen, southwest of Bad Kreuznach, little more than 74 acres (30 ha), is regarded as one of the best wine-making communities on the Nahe.

reputation, and some are even among the best in the country, the Nahe as an entire region, unlike the Mosel, Pfalz, Rheingau, or Franconia, is almost unknown to the general public, or at least seems to have little character.

EXPORT WINES IN CRISIS

To meet consumer demand, over a long period only small quantities of dry or medium-dry wines were made here, although it is in that area that one of the strengths of the region could lie. The mild climate and the many different soil formations are ideal for growing and developing Reisling in particular—and Riesling accounts for over a quarter of the vineyard area, which amounts to a good 11,115 acres (4,500 ha). However, other varieties, for instance Müller-Thurgau, which covers only a

slightly smaller area than Riesling, Silvaner, Kerner, Scheurebe, and Grauburgunder, have not yet been able to establish their own image, and are usually submerged in the anonymity of mass-market brand names.

As long as the tankers of Liebfraumilch and other popular "delicacies" were still driving all over the world at regular intervals, this lack of image and individuality could not do the viticulture of the region much harm. Or such at least was the idea at the time, but the easy profits from the success of sweet wines did not pay off in the end. As other wine-producing

Select single vineyards
1 Pittermännchen
2 Goldloch
3 Brückes
4 Krötenpfuhl
5 Bastei
6 Hermannsberg
7 Hermannshöhle

SELECT PRODUCERS IN THE NAHE

CRUSIUS***–****
TRAISEN
31 acres (12.5 ha); 90,000 bottles • Wines: Riesling, Weißburgunder, Müller-Thurgau, Spätburgunder from vineyards in locations including Taisen, Schlossböckelheim, Niederhausen, Norheim
Although Peter Crusius largely converted his vinification procedures to the use of stainless steel tanks in the 1990s, the better Riesling qualities are still matured in wooden casks. His *edelsüß* qualities in particular are among the top wines of the Nahe.

HERMANN DÖNNHOFF****–*****
OBERHAUSEN
37 acres (15 ha); 100,000 bottles • Wines: Riesling, Grauburgunder and Weißburgunder from Oberhausen (→Brücke, Felsenberg, Leistenberg), Niederhausen (Hermannshöhle), Schlossböckelheim (Felsenberg), and Norheim, estate Riesling
Helmut Dönnhoff shows remarkable skill in bringing out the characteristics of the various *terroirs*—the family has owned plots in the best vineyards for generations. Dönnhoff restricts winery work to the minimum, treating the wines as gently as possible. They are matured in oak casks, without fining agents, and sweet reserve is used only for the simplest qualities. Only the *edelsüß* wines, in which Dönnhoff is regarded as a leading specialist, are fermented in small stainless steel vessels.

EMRICH-SCHÖNLEBER****
MONZINGEN
36 acres (14.5 ha); 110,000 bottles • Wines: Riesling, Grauburgunder and Weißburgunder, Kerner, Rivaner from estates in Monzingen
Because of its sheltered position, Monzingen has the benefit of a milder, drier climate than the rest of the Nahe, and Werner Schönleber exploits these natural conditions to make top-quality Rieslings.

HAHNMÜHLE***–****
MANNWEILER-CÖLLN
23 acres (9.5 ha); 60,000 bottles • Wines: Riesling, Traminer, Silvaner, Weißburgunder, Spätburgunder from vineyards in Oberndorf, Alsenz, Cölln, estate wines, →Silvaner Secco
Riesling and Traminer are probably the most unusual combination of vines grown on Martina and Peter Linxweiler's estate, particularly when they are planted together and ecologically cultivated and picked. Acidity in the wines made from them is generally very marked.

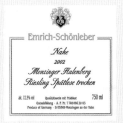

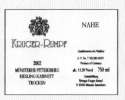

KRUGER-RUMPFF***–****
MÜNSTER-SARMSHEIM
49 acres (20 ha); 150,000 bottles • Wines include: Riesling, Silvaner, burgundy varieties from vineyards in Münster-Sarmsheim (→Dautenpflänzer, Pittersberg, Rheinberg, Kapellenberg)
Stefan and Cornelia Rumpf manage not only one of the best wine-growing estates in the Nahe region, but also a famous inn. The Rumpfs' wines, always straightforward, are particularly good in the higher *Prädikat* grades, where the typical rather rustic acidity is tempered by alcohol, sweet reserve, or extracts.

PRINZ ZU SALM-DALBERG***
WALLHAUSEN
28.5 acres (11.5 ha); 70,000 bottles • Wines include: Riesling, Grauburgunder, Spätburgunder from vineyards in Wallhausen and Roxheim, estate Riesling, Prinz Salm Qualitätsweine
Michael Prince of Salm-Salm is not only one of the famous winemakers of the Nahe, but also Federal German chairman of the V.D.P. and a politician. The range of wines produced at Schloss Wallhausen, where biological cultivation is practised, is of good quality and easy to survey. Vineyard details are given only on the labels of the best wines made by the firm.

SCHLOSSGUT DIEL***–*****
BURG LAYEN
42 acres (17 ha); 120,000 bottles • Wines: Riesling, Grauburgunder, Weißburgunder, Spätburgunder from vineyards in Dorsheim (Goldloch, →Pittermännchen, Burgberg), estate wine Diel de Diel, →Victor
The Rieslings made by the controversial winemaker and wine writer Armin Diel, particularly those from the Pittermännchen vineyard with its slaty soil, are model examples of wines from the Nahe.

BÜRGERMEISTER WILLI SCHWEINHARDT
NACHFAHREN**–****
LANGENLONSHEIM
80 acres (32.5 ha); 180,000 bottles • Wines include: Riesling, Weißburgunder, Grauburgunder, Chardonnay, Spätburgunder, Portugieser from vineyards in Langenlonsheim, →Scala
One of the largest and at the same time best firms in the region (an unusual combination). As well as making white wines fermented in steel or plastic tanks, Schweinhardt is one of the few German producers to be experimenting with Cabernet Sauvignon.

Gutenberg on the Gräfenbach, with other viticultural villages, lies in a lateral valley of the Nahe running northwest.

The Bastei lies at the foot of the Roter Fels, a massive porphyry cliff near Traisen. It is the best vineyard in the community, and its grapes make remarkably complex Rieslings with a mineral note.

countries responded to the change in consumer taste, as well as competing in price with their now more popular product, these brands found that they were experiencing setbacks on the international markets. As a result, the Nahe seems to have suffered even more economic problems than other regions. Quite recently the largest winemakers' cooperative of the area was forced to give up its independence as it was subsumed under the roof of the Mosel cooperative, nor did the state viticultural estates in Niederhausen-Schlossböckelheim survive the crisis.

SOME OUTSTANDING WINES

The efforts and courage of a small group of leading winemakers within the regional V.D.P. association is all the more admirable. Once again they seek top quality in the wines they now produce, and they lead the way in the discussion of vineyard classification. Because for a long time the Wine Law did not allow them to put descriptions such as *erster Lage* or *grand cru* on their labels, they introduced through voluntary agreement among their members the principle that only well-established vineyard names classified within the area may appear on labels, while all other products must be marketed as simple estate wines. They dispense entirely with any mention of *Großlage* names for their wines, and indeed the practice of naming a *Großlage* has recently come under criticism.

The Nahe does have potential for the production of top quality wines, particularly because the wine styles of the three most important subdivisions of the region, the Upper Nahe, the area around Bad Kreuznach, and finally the Lower Nahe are clearly distinct from each other.

Steep, rocky hillsides leaving little space for vines are typical of the landscape along the course of the Nahe above Bad Kreuznach. The porphyry formations and the river are valuable here for the storage of warmth, and ensure the necessary conditions in which the grapes can

ripen and give the wines their characteristically delicate fruity character. Viticultural centers acknowledged to have the best vineyards are Schlossböckelheim, Niederhausen, and Traisen, and the names of vineyards such as the Traisener Bastei, Niederhausener Herrmannshöhle and Hermannsberg, Oberhäuser Brücke, and Schlossböckelheimer Felsenberg are good references in themselves.

The natural conditions in and around Bad Kreuznach are very different. Here deep, heavy soil predominates, and the wines are denser and more powerful in style, making what is clearly a more southern general impression. The best vineyards are the Kreuznacher Brückes, Krötenpfuhl, and Kahlenberg, but unfortunately most of the once famous winemaking estates owned by the town of Kreuznach seem to have allowed the qualititative improvements of the region in recent years pass them by.

Viticulture does not become interesting again until we reach the Lower Nahe and its side valleys. The river, here flowing north and straight toward the Rhine, is accompanied on its eastern bank by the extensive vineyards of Rheinhessen, while the hillside vineyards of the Nahe region on the western bank are to some extent hidden behind hills, villages, and church towers.

The side valleys of the Nahe in particular, with their sunny south aspects, offer the Riesling grape optimum conditions, as the Dorsheim vineyards of Pittermännchen and Goldloch, and the Münster vineyards of Pittersberg and Dautenpflänzer brilliantly show. Once again, however, there is an enormous range of diversity in the styles of wines made from vineyard to vineyard, and even from one winemaker to another, with Riesling sometimes tending toward the Mosel style, sometimes toward the neighboring Mittelrhein. The question of whether the wines of the Lower Nahe find their ideal expression in the dry, the medium-dry, or the very sweet range is much discussed by the leading winemakers of the region.

The fermentation tanks in the castle estate of Diehl in Burg Layen are artistically embellished. The estate's Auslese wines, made from Riesling grapes from the Dorsheimer Goldloch vineyard, are among the best on the Nahe.

Michael Prince of Salm-Salm, president of the V.D.P.

Helmut Dönnhoff, a leading viticulturist in Oberhausen on the Nahe.

RHEINHESSEN

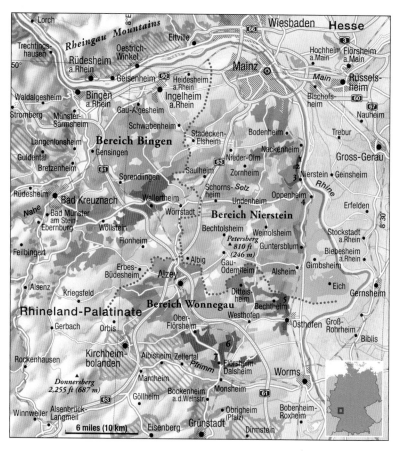

Rheinhessen has a total vineyard area of over 64,000 acres (26,000 ha), divided into 24 Großlagen and an impressive 432 Einzellagen, and with yields per acre of only a little more than 1,068 gallons (100 hl/ha) (quite modest by comparison with the Mosel, Württemberg, and the Pfalz), it is indisputably the largest wine-producing region of Germany. Grapes and wine seem to be present everywhere, and there are only three communities in the entire region which do not have their own vineyards.

Rheinhessen is more firmly connected with Liebfraumilch than any other viticultural region, and indeed the vineyard which gives that famous mass-produced brand its name is on its territory: the Liebfrauenstift-Kirchenstück in Worms, a genuine clos within the walls of the collegiate church of the Virgin Mary. Large quantities of this blend of varieties and wines from different districts have continued to be produced in Rheinhessen in recent decades. It is the only such blend allowed by the German Wine Law to describe itself as a Qualitätswein.

Internationally, Liebfraumilch has become synonymous with German wine in general, and has undoubtedly contributed to the decline in its reputation. That being so, it was almost a symbol of a radical new start in German viticulture when the vineyard, which had fallen into neglect, was put back into good order a few years ago by the energetic efforts of a famous Nierstein winemaking estate.

It was also in Rheinhessen that the unfortunate philosophy of the German Wine Law in grouping vineyards into Großlagen found its most notorious expression: the Großlagen of Oppenheimer Krötenbrunnen and the neighboring Niersteiner Gutes Domtal may stand today as perfect examples of a wrong-headed policy, which ultimately achieved nothing but to destroy any justification for the wines of these Großlagen to stake a claim to quality for almost two decades.

BEYOND LIEBFRAUMILCH

Fortunately Rheinhessen has much more to offer than Liebfraumilch, Krötenbrunnen, and Gutes Domtal. Today, outstanding wines are being made again, in particular on what is known as the Rhine Front, where the Rheinhessen plateau falls steeply to the left bank of the river between Nackenheim in the north and Alsheim in the south. Rieslings which can easily hold their own with the best products of the Rheingau, the Mosel, and the Pfalz grow on the red sandstone of Nierstein, a schist formation resulting from a geological rift which runs right through the Rhine valley. They combine the elegance of wines from the north with the power and spiciness of southern wines.

As a result the best vineyards of the region, such as the Rothenberg in Nackenheim, Pettenthal, Brudersberg, Hipping, Ölberg, and Orbel in Nierstein, have re-established themselves on a firm foundation in recent years. Oppenheim, too, has a consistently top-quality vineyard in the Sackträger, where the soils are no longer red sandstone schist formations, but consist of loess and calcareous marl.

Few people know what a wide spectrum of vines Rheinhessen grows. Most of the postwar crosses were raised at the Alzeyer vine-breeding institute, and varieties such as Scheurebe and Dornfelder, which attracted attention during the recent move toward making red wines, come from its trial grounds. Because of this extensive range of classic grape varieties and various crosses, no one variety can be said to dominate the viticulture of Rheinhessen. Müller-Thurgau grows on about 20 percent of the vineyard area, Silvaner occupies some 15 percent, but all the other varieties—Riesling, Kerner, Scheurebe, Bacchus, Portugieser, Faberrebe, Morio-Muskat, Spätburgunder, Huxelrebe, Ortega, and Siegerreber—occupy positions somewhere below the 10 percent mark.

Finally, it should not be forgotten that environmentally friendly and ecological viticulture was first introduced on German soil in Rheinhessen in the 1970s, and such methods have found many followers in the region since.

Select single vineyards
(see map opposite)

1 Pettenthal
2 Hipping
3 Ölberg
4 Sackträger
5 Geyersberg
6 Hubacker
7 Bürgel

Nierstein has some excellent sites on the Rhine, including the Brudersberg, Hipping, Pettenthal, and Ölberg vineyards, and a few leading winemakers are active there as well.

The Hessische Bergstraße (Hessian Mountain Road)

As a wine-growing area, the Bergstraße comprises the vineyard slopes on the borders of the Odenwald, between Darmstadt in the north and Weinheim in the south, where the soils and the climate are very suitable for viticulture.

The rugged terrain makes the steep vineyards difficult and cost-intensive to work, and there are many economic problems in cultivating them. Consequently almost 90 percent of winegrowers supply the largest of the regional cooperatives, in Heppenheim. If we remember also that the Bensheim estate alone cultivates around ten percent of the entire vineyard area, and that most of the wine produced stays in southern Hesse, it is obvious why wines made on the Bergstraße are almost unknown outside the region.

The strength of the Bergstraße lies in its Rieslings, which approach the quality of Rheingau Rieslings, and in its burgundy varieties. Although production here is restricted to two groups of varieties and kinds of wines, the great diversity of the local vineyards and soils is expressed in many different nuances. The Bergstraße Rieslings, most of which grow in the higher vineyards, have less acidity than in more northerly regions and generally have a more mineral character, which in turn varies between the granite and sandstone soils on which the vines grow. Burgundy varieties ripen on lower-lying plots, some with very deep loessial soils, and differ from their cousins made in Baden chiefly in their lower alcohol content.

The fact that almost no winegrowers on the Bergstraße market their own products, and cooperatives dominate the scene, has done little to encourage the development of quality wines in the area. Over the years, only the state-run vineyards and one or two private winemakers have succeeded in producing wines which can claim to be of high quality.

STAATSWEINGUT BERGSTRASSE*—**** BENSHEIM**
94 acres (38 ha); 250,000 bottles
• *Wines: Riesling, Grauburgunder, Weißburgunder, Spätburgunder, Gewürztraminer from vineyards in Heppenheim (→Centgericht, Steinkopf), Schönberg, Bensheim (Kalkgasse, Streichling)*

SIMON-BÜRKLE*** **ZWINGENBERG**
40 acres (16 ha); 80,000 bottles
• *Wines: Riesling, Weißburgunder, Grauburgunder, Silvaner, Spätburgunder, Lemberger, and Cabernet Sauvignon from the northern Bergstraße*

Map legend

HESSISCHE BERGSTRASSE
Bereich Starkenburg
Großlage Rott
Großlage Wolfsmagen
Großlage Schlossberg
Single vineyard not part of a *Großlage* group
BADISCHE BERGSTRASSE
1–2 Select single vineyards

Select single vineyards

1 Centgericht
2 Steinkopf

The Heart of the Area: Nackenheim to Dienheim

No other viticultural region of Germany contains such great contrasts and differences of quality between its various districts as Rheinhessen. In the past it was notable almost exclusively for the mass production of wine and certain new strains of grapes, some of them of dubious quality and apparently bred with a view not so much to the quality of the wine as to at a kind of clinically clean production on an industrial scale. There are good reasons why the unspeakable Liebfraumilch is so firmly linked to the name of the region.

Nonetheless, a number of top winemakers producing wines of high quality have attracted attention in Rheinhessen in recent years. This trend begins on the excellent argillaceous slate soils of the Rhine Front, where some of the best vineyards in the region are found. On the steep slopes of the Rhine rift between Nackenheim and Dienheim such estates as Gunderloch, Heyl zu Herrnsheim, and Sankt Antony have shown for years that they are among the absolute elite of German viticulture, and houses like Schneider,

Seebrich, and Kühling-Gillot consistently produce wines of high quality. Unfortunately, the poor image of Rheinhessen wines in general has so far made it difficult for the producers to market these products adequately, or to get suitable prices for them.

There are other remarkably good vineyards, for instance in the area between Bechtheim, Westhofen (particularly the Aulerde vineyard), and Flörsheim-Dalheim on the border with the Pfalz, where another group of leading wine producers has established itself, with names including Keller, Groebe, Schales, and Wittmann. It is true that in the hinterland of Rheinhessen top-quality wines are few and far between, but with a certain amount of effort good to very good wines can be made here, as they also can in the north, in the once-famous vineyards of Bingen and Ingelheim. Here, however, the policy of earning money quickly and easily from the tanker wine trade still predominates. It is an attitude which may also endanger future efforts to improve the image of Rheinhessen.

Select Producers in Rheinhessen

Brüder Dr. Becker*−****
Ludwigshöhe
28 acres (11.5 ha); 80,000 bottles • Wines include: Riesling, Silvaner, Scheurebe, burgundy varieties from vineyards in Dienheim and Ludwigshöhe
In the 1970s Helmut Pfeffer was one of the first Germany viticulturalists to practice biological winemaking, at the same time proving that such methods did not necessarily mean a lower quality of wine. His daughter Lotte is continuing his work with the same energy. Recently the estate has tended to return to making medium-dry wines.

K. F. Groebe*
Biebesheim
17 acres (7 ha); 50,000 bottles • Wines include: Riesling, Silvaner, Grauburgunder, Spätburgunder from vineyards in Westhofen (→Aulerde)
Although the Aulerde vineyard in Westhofen is not on the famous Rhine Front, its calcareous soil makes it an excellent site. Friedrich Groebe presses his best wines from its grapes. Grauburgunder and Spätburgunder wines of reliable good quality are marketed as *Tafelwein*.

Gunderloch**
Nackenheim
31 acres (12.5 ha); 70,000 bottles • Wines include: Riesling, Silvaner from the →Nackenheimer Rothenberg vineyard, also from →Pettenthal and →Hipping in Nierstein, →Jean Baptiste
Since the middle of the 1980s Agnes and Fritz Hasselbach have brought their estate gradually into the top rank of

wine producers in Rheinhessen. Their success was founded on the possession of large areas in the leading vineyards of Rothenberg, Pettenthal, and Hipping. The Rothenberg site in particular, with its argillaceous slate soil, regularly produces excellent Rieslings with plenty of fruit, bouquet, and a firm, well-structured body. Their travels in other winemaking countries persuaded the Hasselbachs to modernize their vineyard work and winery techniques. One of their wines is called Jean Baptiste, in reference to Zuckmayer's play *Der fröhliche Weinberg* (The Merry Vineyard), which is a tribute to Carl Gunderloch, founder of the estate.

Louis Guntrum*
Nierstein
49 acres (20 ha); 200,000 bottles • Wines include: Riesling, Müller-Thurgau, Silvaner, Scheurebe from many vineyards in Nierstein and Oppenheim, Guntrum Classic, Villa Guntrum, Louis Philipp
As a large-scale winery this old-established Nierstein firm did not enjoy a particularly good reputation for the quality of its wines. However, there has been a change since the estate began concentrating on the growths from its own vineyards—it is sole owner of a number of them. The Oppenheim wines in particular, including some made from Gewürztraminer and Silvaner, are of a good to very good standard.

Freiherr Heyl zu Herrnsheim*−****
Nierstein
46 acres (18.5 ha); 180,000 bottles • Wines: Riesling, Silvaner, Müller-Thurgau, burgundy varieties from

vineyards in Nierstein (→Brudersberg, →Pettenthal, →Ölberg, Hipping, Orbel), →Liebfrauenstift Kirchenstück, →Arcadia

Peter von Weymarn made the Heyl estate not only one of the top winemaking estates in Rheinhessen, but one of the leading firms working with ecological methods in the whole of Germany. The best wines, which bear their vineyard names, are entirely fermented and matured in large wooden casks. Since the sale of the estate to the Ahr family, Markus Ahr and the estate manager Michael Burgdorf have continued to run the business in Weymarn's spirit.

KELLER****
FLÖRSHEIM-DALSHEIM

32 acres (13 ha); 120,000 bottles • Wines: Riesling, burgundy varieties, Huxelrebe from vineyards in Dalsheim (→Hubacker), Niederflörsheim, and Monsheim

The fact that the estate of Klaus and Hedwig Keller is among those to have won most awards in Germany might appear something of a paradox from the point of view of any classification of vineyards—which only goes to prove that the winemaker's feeling for quality counts for a great deal in viticulture. The Hubacker Rieslings are among the best of the estate's wines. The burgundy varieties are also remarkable.

KRUG'SCHER HOF***
GAU-ODERNHEIM

136 acres (55 ha); 250,000 bottles • Wines: Chardonnay, Weißburgunder, Spätburgunder, Riesling, Menger-Krug Sekt

The real center of the Menger-Krug business is the estate of Motzenbäcker at Deidenheim in the Pfalz, but the majority of its vineyards lie here in Rheinhessen, where most of the family's famous Sekts are also made. Since the middle of the 1980s Chardonnay has been grown for use in making Sekt and as a single-variety still wine—and the occasional *edelsüß* specimens are also remarkable.

KÜHLING-GILLOT****
BODENHEIM

22 acres (9 ha); 70,000 bottles • Wines: Riesling, Grauburgunder, Scheurebe, Portugieser, Spätburgunder and others, from vineyards in Oppenheim and Bodenheim, Sekt

The estate of Gabi and Roland Gillot dates from the 18th century. The Gillots' wines, particularly the *edelsüß* growths and the *barrique*-matured burgundies, are among the best in Rheinhessen, and the inn managed by Gabi Gillot makes its guests very comfortable.

MICHEL-PFANNEBECKER***
FLOMBORN

29 acres (11.8 ha); 70,000 bottles • Wines: Silvaner, Riesling, burgundy varieties, Müller-Thurgau from vineyards in Westhofen and Flomborn

This estate in Flomborn, where excellent Rieslings are made from the grapes of the Westhofener Steingrube, shows that the vineyards of Westhofen can make outstanding wines. The white burgundy varieties and the Chardonnay are also above average.

RAPPENHOF—DR. MUTH**–***
ALSHEIM

128.5 acres (52 ha); 300,000 bottles • Wines include: Riesling, burgundy varieties, Chardonnay, Kerner from vineyards in Alsheim, Diensheim, Guntersblum, Oppenheim and Nierstein

The estate of Reinhard Muth, formerly chairman of the German Winegrowers' Association, passed into the hands of his son Klaus some years ago. Muth was one of the pioneers of Chardonnay in Germany, using *barriques* for fermentation.

SANKT ANTONY***–*****
NIERSTEIN

54 acres (22 ha); 160,000 bottles • Wines: Riesling, Silvaner, etc., from vineyards in Nierstein (→Ölberg, →Hipping, →Pettental, →Orbel, Rosenberg, Heiligenbaum, Paterberg), Vom Rotliegenden

Alexander Michalsky makes delicately elegant wines with concentrated extracts on the estate originally founded by the Gutehoffnung works and now part of the M.A.N. company. With a wide range of Rieslings from the vineyards of the "Rotliegend" area, as it is called, Michalsky's business is one of the three best in Rheinhessen, and is among the elite viticultural estates of the whole of Germany.

SCHALES****
FLÖRSHEIM-DALHEIM

99 acres (40 ha); 400,000 bottles • Wines include: Riesling, Müller-Thurgau, Weißburgunder, Spätburgunder from vineyards in Dalsheim, →Trullo, Schales Selection

The Schales brothers are among the best winemakers in Rheinhessen. Their Trullo is a blend of Weißburgunder, Kerner, and Riesling grapes. Their *edelsüß* and *Eiswein* products are also good.

GEORG ALBRECHT SCHNEIDER***–****
NIERSTEIN

43 acres (17.5 ha); 90,000 bottles • Wines include: Riesling, Müller-Thurgau, Kerner, Silvaner from vineyards in Nierstein (→Orbel, →Hipping, →Ölberg, →Pettenthal and others)

When this traditional Nierstein estate moved to larger premises and changed its winery methods to fermentation in stainless steel tanks, its wines improved noticeably. Georg Schneider's Rieslings from the best vineyards of Nierstein, and his Grauburgunder from the Paterberg, are well above average in quality.

HEINRICH SEEBRICH***
NIERSTEIN

25 acres (10 ha); 80,000 bottles • Wines include: Riesling, Müller-Thurgau, Kerner, Silvaner, Dornfelder, Spätburgunder from vineyards in Nierstein (→Ölberg, →Hipping)

Heinrich Seebrich works with the same gentle methods in both vineyard and winery, and sets much store by the early bottling of his *Prädikat* wines, which will then mature in bottle before they are put on the market.

VILLA SACHSEN***
BINGEN

41 acres (16.5 ha); 130,000 bottles • Wines include: Riesling, Müller-Thurgau, Kerner, Silvaner from vineyards in Bingen (→Scharlachberg)

The Villa Sachsen estate was in deep trouble before Prince Salm, master of Schloss Wallhausen in the Nahe region, and his team took over its management and became co-owners. Today the firm is again doing well with its Rieslings from the once-famous vineyard of Scharlachberg in Bingen.

WITTMANN****
WESTHOFEN

62 acres (25 ha); 130,000 bottles • Wines include: Riesling, Müller-Thurgau, Silvaner, Huxelrebe, Spätburgunder from vineyards in Bechtheim and Westhofen (→Aulerde)

Although the estate has for some time been among the leading group of wine makers in Rheinhessen—and those using ecological methods—it was only recently accepted into the V.D.P. Its wines, particularly the Rieslings from vineyards in Westhofen, show that even beyond the Rhine Front the region has great potential for quality.

The Biological Heyl zu Herrnsheim Estate

The mediocre standards of winemaking in Rheinhessen during the 1970s may help to account for the fact that the movement toward ecological viticulture in Germany first developed in that area. Any producers who hoped to rise above the crowd making standard Liebfraumilch were obliged to draw attention to themselves, if only by adding new descriptions to the label. Another cause of this trend may have been that winemaking in Rheinhessen had gone too far in the use of technology and chemicals, and younger viticulturalists—inspired by the revolutionary ideas of environmentalists in the Rhine-Main area in general—thought they should make wines differently in response to the products of conventional vineyard and winery work. However that may be, the early stages of the ecological winemaking movement were motivated not so much by concern for the quality of the product as by general political and ideological concepts.

Nonetheless, the estate of Freiherr Heyl zu Herrnsheim in Nierstein has provided proof over many years that there are also other and far more personal reasons for turning to natural winemaking, reasons which can be reconciled with the idea of qualitatively excellent production. The motivation of Peter von Weymarn, who was then running the estate, was of a very personal nature. As a scientist, he had begun thinking about his own diet and making radical changes in it, and ultimately he could hardly avoid applying his own health-conscious attitude to the products and operating methods of his firm.

However, there are also other reasons why Heyl is an ecological vineyard of a kind not typical of German conditions, with its relatively large size and its established place among the best winemaking firms in Germany. From the first, the idea of quality played a dominant part. The wine was to be produced with ecological factors in mind to make it even better: it was to be a genuinely top-quality product.

Markus Ahr, the present head of the firm of Heyl, has a philosophy of quality which continues from Weymarn's ideas. It is a long way from the dogmatism of purely ecological doctrine. His version of natural viticulture rests mainly on three principles. He does not use synthetic fertilizers, only compost and green manure. As a substitute for herbicides, the soil is mechanically worked. His third principle is to refrain from using pesticides and fungicides—only Bordeaux mixture, a solution of copper sulfate, is permissible under the strict regulations of the European Union.

The young vineyard owner is of course also aware of the drawbacks of ecological viticulture, and in many respects has to agree with its critics. Growing vines by biological methods means driving machinery around the vineyards too often, and the tractors compact the ground. In addition, copper accumulates in the soil as time goes on, and—so the critics say—there is therefore still no sound ecological balance, particularly as frequent driving through the vineyards involves environmental pollution.

To Ahr, the biological arguments of recent years have been something of a distraction from truly relevant enological problems, allowing a series of dubious practices and such technological devices as concentrators, or the addition of enzymes and aromatic substances, to creep into the world of wine through the back door unnoticed. Nonetheless, he plans to continue with

Left
The interior of the estate, which dates back to the 16th century.

Right
The green manure, now often sown between the rows in certain regions by growers who prefer biological methods of viticulture, is cut with this mowing machine.

environmentally conscious methods at Heyl zu Herrnsheim. "Our estate has such a good name for the quality of its wines that on purely economic grounds I could have allowed myself to stop working with biological viticulture. But then I would probably have had to wave goodbye to some of my claims to quality as well!"

The Ahr family has now taken over the famous estate in Rheinhessen, but Markus Winfried Ahr and the estate manager Michael Burgdorf continue to practice methods of biological viticulture, and pursue a policy aiming for quality.

Ecological viticulture

Ecological viticulture, like biological agriculture in general, refrains from using chemical synthetic fertilizers, weedkillers, insecticides, fungicides, and acaricides. Instead it prefers a holistic approach involving the maintenance of soils and pure groundwater, the protection of species and the landscape, and ecological cultivation and waste disposal. The soil in the vineyard is at the root of everything. Ecological viticulturalists use organic materials to activate, encourage, and feed it. The principal role is played by compost, made from grapeskins (MARC), stable manure, chaff, straw, and vegetable matter. Often the vineyards have to bring in raw materials from outside, since only a very few concerns can build up a self-contained agricultural cycle of their own. However, some vineyards do keep pure-bred livestock so as to have valuable manure available.

In ecological viticulture sowing green plants among the vines is particularly important, and is the counterpart of the rotation of crops in biological agriculture. The dense root systems running through the soil have a positive long-term effect on the wealth of micro-organisms present. The various mixtures sown—leguminous plants, clovers, grain, grasses, and herbs, mown and used as mulch two or three times a year—serve as excellent green manure and help the formation of humus. The flowers bring insects back to the vineyards, and beneficial insects keep down the populations of red spider and vine moth. Green plants prevent erosion of the vineyards, and are a factor in maintaining the water balance. The practice must, however, be precisely adjusted to the conditions of the particular situation, and long-term green planting is not suitable everywhere.

In general the difference from conventional viticulture consists of a fundamental approach, not just to the cultivation of the soil but also to tending the vines and protecting them from disease. European viticulture has to face the constant threat of powdery mildew (*Oidium*) and downy mildew (*Plasmopara*). While winegrowers using traditional methods rely from the first on chemical substances, ecological winegrowers aim to reduce the risks of infection. To achieve this objective they begin with the selection:

- of suitable locations
- of the right variety of grapes
- of the correct distance between lines and rows, and
- of the best way of growing vines and continue by:
- reducing the number of shoots left during winter pruning
- breaking off shoots in spring to reduce the number of shoots per vine to the optimum
- carefully trimming the foliage to ensure good ventilation during the growing season
- thinning the bunches of grapes as needed.

These measures are not usually employed in conventional viticulture, the only exceptions usually being those estates which aim chiefly for top quality and are already to some extent adopting an ecological approach. The ecological viticulturalist finds it essential to avoid difficult sites and particularly vulnerable grape varieties. Liquid plant manure, plant preparations, ground minerals and so on can be used to strengthen the vines effectively.

The biological viticulturalist must also work considerably more carefully and thoughtfully than his conventional colleague. The result is that ecological vineyards, naturally enough, have lower yields than those of conventional concerns aiming for high quality. But successful ecological viticulture is reflected in fewer variations in yield and quality, and often in high must weights even in bad years.

As for the quality of the wine itself, viticulturalists are agreed that it is decided in the vineyard, so it is possible that ecological viticulture may point the way to the future.

A. Dominé

SEKT

Although the most famous of all sparkling wines comes from Champagne in France, and in recent years Italy has been very successful with its Prosecco and Spain with its Cava, the Germans have no equals in the production—and consumption—of their own sparkling wine, SEKT. While their average annual wine consumption per person, just over 5 gallons (20 liters), is not outstanding, when it comes to sparkling wine the Germans easily lead the field with almost 1.3 gallons (5 liters) per person.

This liking for sparkling wine pre-dates the Sekt industry of Germany itself. Several enterprising young Germans were attracted to the idea of making champagne in the early 19th century: Krug, Bollinger, Geldermann, Mumm, and Deutz went abroad to found the champagne-making firms whose products are still among the best and best known of brands.

The word Sekt was still unusual at this time, and is first recorded in Berlin around 1825. Its invention is usually ascribed to the actor Ludwig Devrient, and it is said to derive from either French *sec* (dry), or from "sack," in allusion to a kind of sherry popular in England.

The major German Sekt-making wineries, situated with only a few exceptions on the Rhine and Mosel, were founded in the second half of the 19th century, and the houses dating from that time—Kessler, Henkell, Söhnlein, Deinhard, Kupferberg, Kloss & Foerster, Schloss Vaux, and Faber—still have the largest turnover today, selling 30, 40, or 100 million or more bottles a year (by way of comparison, the annual production of French champagne is some 250–300 million bottles).

Such quantities cannot be made by the classic bottle fermentation process, and therefore German Sekt is usually made by tank or Charmat fermentation, with the second fermentation introduced in large pressurized containers from which the finished wine is filtered, still under pressure, and then bottled.

Many enologists prefer tank to bottle fermentation, since it has the advantage of maintaining

Amounts of sugar contained in different forms of Sekt	
naturherb, brut nature	under 3 g per liter
extra herb, extra brut	up to 6 g per liter
herb, brut	up to 15 g per liter
extra dry, *extra trocken*	12 to 20 g per liter
dry, *trocken, sec*	17 to 35 g per liter
medium dry, *halbtrocken, demi-sec*	33 to 50 g per liter
sweet, *mild, süß, doux*	over 50 g per liter

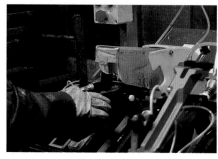
Various base wines are used to full the *cuvée*, and sugar and yeast are added.

For bottle fermentation, the bottle is closed with a crown cork and stored on slats.

In viticultural firms and small Sekt-making houses, *remuage* is still done by hand in the traditional way.

Remuage leaves the yeast sediment deposited in the neck of the bottle, and it must then be disgorged.

The bottle is topped up with the correct amount of wine, and is then finally corked.

The last step is to add the decorative bucket-shaped capsule typical of most Sekt bottles.

a standard quality in every bottle. However, the yeast makes more contact with the wine in the smaller volume of a bottle than in a tank, where it sinks to the bottom. In addition, second fermentation in the bottle takes longer than the Wine Law will allow for the same process in a tank, and lengthy yeast contact is a crucial factor in the quality of the finished sparkling wine.

Sekt made by the time-consuming traditional method of bottle fermentation is a complex sparkling wine with small bubbles and a delicate, attractive mousse.

BOTTLE FERMENTATION AND WINZERSEKT

It is not surprising, then, that the great Sekt wineries use the more elaborate bottle fermentation process with its long maturing period for their top products, which are made either from Riesling or from the classic Burgundy grape varieties. Obviously this sector of the market will not produce quantities running into six-figure numbers, but the leading *cuvées* of the German Sekt wineries can compete with central Champagne itself in quality, quantity, and price.

While certain brands in this premium area are made entirely from German wines, the same, obviously, cannot be said for the great mass of German Sekt. If the huge quantities sold were to be made entirely from grapes grown in the country, not only would the final product be

considerably more expensive, but German vineyards would very soon have reached the limits of their capacity. As a result, 90 percent of the base wines in the huge tanks of the Rhine and Mosel Sekt wineries come from Italy, Spain, or other parts of the European Union.

Together with the classic Sekt brands, a very interesting new category of product has made its mark in the last decade: Winzersekt, or winegrower's Sekt. It differs from the traditional branded products in that it may properly be regarded as an estate-bottled wine, although the actual second fermentation, with the *remuage* and *dégorgement* processes, is contracted out to other establishments, the best known of them being situated in the Sprendlingen area of Rheinhessen.

More and more viticulturalists have now begun fermenting their own wines to make Sekt, so that they can be sure of the quality of the finished wine. Only the finest grape varieties are used for the base wine: in the north the characteristic fruity Riesling of the area, in the south the burgundy varieties, which once they have undergone secondary fermentation are almost reminiscent of champagne with their winey, yeasty character.

While the Sekt market in general seems to have been stagnating for some time, Winzersekt is becoming increasingly popular: first with the viticulturalists themselves, since it offers the welcome opportunity of an interesting and profitable sideline, and second with consumers, who find them a change from the familiar Sekt brands and a pleasing alternative.

HENKELL, SÖHNLEIN, DEINHARD

The firm of Henkell did not intend to specialize in sparkling wine. When Adam Henkell founded his wine business in Mainz in 1832, he was thinking primarily of the export trade, in which good money could still be made at the time. The firm did not begin making Sekt until some 25 years later, still working from Mainz, where the family had set up a "champagne factory"—at this time there were no legal rulings prohibiting the use of the name.

Two generations after it was founded, the business had become a Sekt winery, production was moved to Henkellsfeld near Biebrich, and in 1898 the name Henkell Trocken was registered and patented as a trade mark. Today, a Sekt empire is run from the present suburb of Wiesbaden, and in many sectors of the field it has become the market leader. The original sternly neo-classical building of the time, its style softened by decorative elements of a more

Select German Producers of Sekt

Geldermann***–****
Breisach

2,900,000 bottles • Wines: Geldermann, Odeon, Cuvée Privée, Carte Blanche, Carte Rouge, Carte Noire
After leaving the champagne house of Deutz, René Lallier made his Sekt winery one of the most quality-conscious in Germany. However, a drastic fall in sales in 2003 led to a takeover by the Rotkäppchen-Mumm Sekt companies.

Godefroy H. von Mumm**–***
Hochheim

• Wines: Mumm, Jules Mumm
This Sekt winery in Hochheim, which once formed part of the Seagram empire, was bought in 2002 by the Rotkäppchen company. The popular brand, MM, has been world-famous since 1850 and is protected by patents.

Günter Reh*–**
Trier

200,000,000 bottles • Wines: Schloss Wachenheim, Faber, Feist, Schloss Böchingen, Rondel
The company of Reh is one of the largest winery groups in Europe. Originally best known for its Faber Sekt, the group has also expanded into the higher grades of Sekt and wines in the last decade, particularly with Schloss Wachenheim and the wine-growing estate of Reichsgraf von Kesselstatt.

Rotkäppchen-Sektkellerei**–***
Freyburg

92,000,000 bottles • Wines: Rotkäppchen Sekt, Riesling, Weißburgunder fom Saale-Unstrut
The Rotkäppchen winery is one of the large former East German businesses to have profited from reunification. Founded at the end of the 19th century, the firm was taken over by the state under the D.D.R. regime. Besides classic Sekts it makes still wines and aromatic, sweet sparkling wines.

Rüdesheimer Sektkellereien Kloss & Foerster und Ohlig & Co.**–***
Rüdesheim

2,400,000 bottles • Wines: Riesling Sekts, E.G.-Cuvée, red and rosé Sekt
After the expropriation of the Rotkäppchen winery in Freyburg, its founding families made their new home in Rüdesheim and found a suitable partner in the Ohlig winery. Although the two brands retain their independence, their products are identical.

Sektkellereien Henkell & Söhnlein***–****
Wiesbaden

234,000,000 bottles • Wines: Henkell Trocken, Fürst von Metternich, Adam Henkell, Söhnlein Rheingold, Söhnlein Brillant, Carstens S.C., Rüttgers Club, Deinhard, Lutter & Wegner
Some years ago what is easily the best known German Sekt winery took over the famous Sekt-making firm of Deinhard of Koblenz, and since then has been the market leader in every respect. The range includes such premium products as Adam Henkell and the Riesling Sekt Fürst von Metternich.

Sektkellerei C. A. Kupferberg & Cie**–***
Mainz

16,000,000 bottles • Wines: Kupferberg Gold
This Sekt winery in Mainz, rich in tradition and with old cellars well worth a visit, now belongs to the Racke G.m.b.H. empire.

Sektkellerei Schloss Vaux***
Trier

5 acres (2 ha); 250,000 bottles • Wines: Riesling Sekts from leading Rheingau vineyards
This firm, originally founded in Berlin, has specialized in the production of Rheingau Riesling Sekts. It uses only *Qualitätswein* to make Sekt, and sometimes bottles the base wine as a still wine.

Baroque nature, contrasts with the down-to-earth working atmosphere of the four cubic, green winemaking halls adjoining the main building at the back, where almost two thirds of the wine and Sekt made by the present company of Henkell & Söhnlein are produced.

The success of Henkell, and later of Söhnlein too, was founded on a willingness to make large quantities of a branded product and market it with a great deal of publicity. To this day, over five percent of the firm's turnover is set aside for marketing purposes. Not for nothing is Henkell Trocken still the best known brand of Sekt in Germany.

The Henkell family itself retired from the actual running of the winery some time ago. In parallel to the career of the Henkells, Johann Jacob Söhnlein had founded a "Rheingau Sparkling Wine Factory" in nearby Schierstein. Contact with the Metternich family, which then owned Schloss Johannisberg, ensured a supply of the best base wines in Germany, and a right to use

Opposite
Kupferberg was founded in 1850 by Christian Adalbert Kupferberg, who created what is still the leading brand of Kupferberg Gold. The reception hall of the original building in Mainz was extended during the Jugendstil period.

one of the best-known trade names in the sector. Söhnlein was bought up by the industrialist Oetker family in 1958, and in 1987 they merged with Henkell, their keenest competitors in the field of branded Sekts. Investments in Hungary and Poland followed, and a decade after the merger another large company, Deinhard of Koblenz, was added to what is now the leading German Sekt empire. Today it produces over 100 million bottles of Sekt, and with its production of spirits, wines, and other drinks, output amounts to almost 240 million bottles a year.

The leader among the many brands made by the firm is Söhnlein Brillant, with a good 36 million bottles, followed by Henkell Trocken and Rüttgers Club. In addition, prestigious *cuvées* are made, for instance the single-variety Chardonnay Sekt Adam Henkell, a wine that can hold its own even on the international stage, or the Fürst Metternich Riesling Sekt, also a single-variety product, with all the base wine coming from the Rheingau.

The Pfalz

The Pfalz (Palatinate), an area around 50 miles (80 km) in length, is the second largest wine-growing region in Germany, with around 57,820 acres (23,400 ha) under vines, and the beauty of its landscape makes it a popular tourist attraction. The region is also interesting in connection with the history of wine, for many winemaking cellars which lay buried beneath vineyards for centuries, and have only recently been discovered and restored, show that grapes were being grown on the slopes of the Palatine Forest as early as the Roman period.

The southern part of the region is the sunniest and warmest of German viticultural regions after Baden. In situations entirely sheltered from cold winds, for instance the low-lying valley of Birkweiler near Landau, the vegetation sometimes assumes an almost Mediterranean aspect. And the diversity of soil formations suits the expressive power of the wines. Sandstone, clay, marl, red marl, shelly limestone, porphyry, granite, and schist—practically every kind of soil on which vines will grow well is here in the Pfalz.

In accordance with the Wine Law, the Pfalz is divided into two regions, but we should really distinguish between three: the northern third, the Deutsche Weinstraße (German Wine Road), extends from the border with Rheinhessen

The Mittelhaardt area extends north and south of Bad Dürkheim. Almond trees thrive here, evidence of the mild climate which also grows an excellent fine and fruity Riesling.

at Worms to Grünstadt; the second, the Mittelhaardt area, runs to south of Neustadt; and finally the third, the Südliche Weinstraße (Southern Wine Road), extends to the Alsatian border at Wissembourg.

The Best Vineyards in the Mittelhaardt Area

The wine-growing district with the highest claims to quality, and with the greatest reputation as a tourist attraction, is the area between Herxheim and Neustadt known as the Mittelhaardt. Its aspects and its weathered sandstone soil are recognized as the best in the Pfalz. Vineyard names such as Ungeheuer and Reiterpfad are internationally famous, representating the high prestige of the wines of the Pfalz, especially its Rieslings.

Although the Pfalz, unlike the more northerly wine-growing regions, is not regarded as purely Riesling country, Riesling is still the variety most strongly represented here, accounting for rather more than one-fifth of the total vineyard area. Müller-Thurgau comes only a little way behind, while Kerner, Portugieser, Silvaner, and Scheurebe are of less importance.

The top vineyards of the Mittelhaardt would probably fall into the top group in any classification of German vineyards, along with those of the Mosel and the Rheingau. The estate registers of the 19th century, evaluating individual vineyards in accordance with their potential, show that such was already the case then. Rieslings from these leading vineyards are usually firmer in structure than their northern counterparts, with a higher alcohol content, and are matured to a drier finish.

The Rise of the Southern Pfalz

The third part of the Pfalz, the Südliche Weinstraße, is unforunately still dominated by a kind of viticulture which seems to aim above all for production of the maximum amount of grapes to fill the large tank installations of the winemakers' cooperatives. The mania for quantity which infected many winemakers more than three decades ago led to the restocking of about 2,500 acres (1,000 ha) of vineyards between 1979 and 1982 alone—and they were of course planted with high-yielding varieties on level ground, where viticultural quality

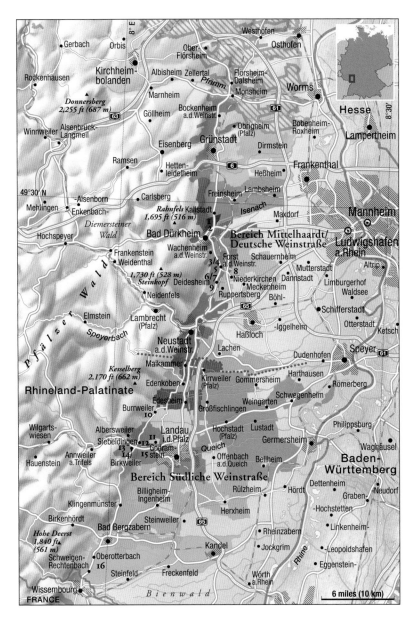

8° E

Westhofen
Gerbach · Orbis
Ober-Flörsheim
Osthofen
Rockenhausen
Kirchheim-bolanden
Albisheim · Zellertal
Flörsheim-Dalsheim
Monsheim
Worms
Donnersberg 2,255 ft (687 m)
Marnheim
Bockenheim a.d.Weinstr.
Bobenheim-Roxheim
Hesse
Winnweiler · Alsenbrück-Langmeil
Göllheim
Obrigheim (Pfalz)
Lampertheim
Eisenberg
Grünstadt
Dirmstein
Frankenthal
Ramsen
Hetten-leidesheim
Heßheim
Lambsheim
49°30′ N
Alsenborn
Carlsberg
Freinsheim
Isenach
Maxdorf
Mannheim
Mehlingen · Enkenbach-
Diemersteiner Wald
Rahnfels Kallstadt 1,695 ft (516 m)
Ludwigshafen a.Rhein
Hochspeyer
Bad Dürkheim
Bereich Mittelhaardt/ Deutsche Weinstraße
Frankenstein Wachenheim a.d.Weinstr.
Weidenthal
Forst a.d.Weinstr. Schauernheim
1,730 ft (528 m) *Steinkopf* Deidesheim
Niederkirchen Dannstadt
Mutterstadt
Meckenheim
Limburgerhof
Altrip
Neidenfels
Ruppertsberg
Böhl-
Waldsee
Elmstein
Lambrecht (Pfalz)
Speyerbach
Haßloch
Iggelheim
Schifferstadt
Otterstadt
Ketsch
Neustadt a.d.Weinstr.
Lachen
Dudenhofen
Speyer
Kesselberg 2,170 ft (662 m)
Maikammer
Harthausen
Rhineland-Palatinate
Edenkoben
Kirrweiler (Pfalz) Gommersheim
Römerberg
Burrweiler
Schwegenheim
Wilgarts-wiesen
Albersweiler
Großfischlingen
Weingarten
Philippsburg
Siebeldingen
Landau i.d.Pfalz
Hochstadt (Pfalz)
Lustadt
Germersheim
Waghäusel
Annweiler a.Trifels
Godram-stein
Queich
Offenbach a.d.Queich
Bellheim
Baden-Württemberg
Hauenstein
Birkweiler
Bereich Südliche Weinstraße
Billigheim-Ingenheim
Rülzheim
Hördt
Dettenheim
Neudorf
Klingenmünster
Herxheim
Graben-Hochstetten
Birkenhördt
Steinweiler
Rheinzabern
Linkenheim-
Hohe Deerst 1,840 ft (561 m)
Bad Bergzabern
Kandel
Jockgrim
Leopoldshafen
Schweigen-Rechtenbach
Oberotterbach
Steinfeld
Freckenfeld
Wörth a.Rhein
Eggenstein-
Wissembourg
FRANCE
Bienwald
Rhine
6 miles (10 km)

Pfälzer Wald

Legend:

Bereich Mittelhaardt/ Deutsche Weinstraße

- *Großlage* Schnepfenflug vom Zellertal
- *Großlage* Grafenstück
- *Großlage* Höllenpfad
- *Großlage* Schwarzerde
- *Großlage* Feuerberg
- *Großlage* Kobnert
- *Großlage* Rosenbühl
- *Großlage* Hochmess
- *Großlage* Honigsäckel
- *Großlage* Schenkenböhl
- *Großlage* Schnepfenflug an der Weinstraße
- *Großlage* Hofstück
- *Großlage* Mariengarten
- *Großlage* Meerspinne
- *Großlage* Rebstöckel
- *Großlage* Pfaffengrund

Bereich Südliche Weinstraße

- *Großlage* Mandelhöhe
- *Großlage* Schloss Ludwigshöhe
- *Großlage* Trappenberg
- *Großlage* Ordensgut
- *Großlage* Bischofskreuz
- *Großlage* Königsgärten
- *Großlage* Herrlich
- *Großlage* Kloster Liebfrauenberg
- *Großlage* Guttenberg

1–16   Select single vineyards
•••••   *Bereich* border
▨▨▨   Wine-growing areas in neighboring regions

Selected single vineyards

1 Spielberg
2 Michelsberg
3 Jesuitengarten
4 Kirchenstück
5 Ungeheuer
6 Kalkofen
7 Grainhübel
8 Klostergarten
9 Reiterpfad
10 Schäwer
11 Münzberg
12 Im Sonnenschein
13 Kastanienbusch
14 Mandelberg
15 Rosenberg
16 Sonnenberg

could hardly be achieved. Until recently, therefore, the southern Pfalz was active mainly in the sale of wine in casks. In 1971, when it was still permissible to blend wines of different areas, the sourest products of the Mosel were made drinkable by the addition of Pfalz wines, and later large quantities made their way into the wine trade as Liebfraumilch. To this day, about half the wines of the Pfalz are bottled outside the region.

Even in the southern Pfalz, however, there are some outstanding vineyards, for instance the Godramsteiner Münzberg, the Siebeldinger Im Sonnenschein, and the Kastanienbusch and Mandelberg vineyards in Birkweiler. The rather rich, deep soils, with their high lime content, are particularly suitable for the burgundy varieties. With the growing popularity of these burgundies, and their suitability as the ideal accompaniment to food—in contrast to Riesling, which today is often bottled and drunk much too early

to be much good for that—the southern Pfalz is to the forefront of present fashion.

While the famous large estates of the Mittelhaardt were still seeking some way out of the quality crisis they themselves had created, some dynamic young winegrowers emerged in the late 1980s in the southern Pfalz in particular, and were soon regarded as among the most innovative in the whole of Germany. With colleagues from other parts of the region, they modernized work in the winery, introducing steel tanks and wooden casks for the fermentation and VINIFICATION of their wines, making great efforts to limit yields, and even trying to make internationally acceptable red wines. Above all, they showed how the enormous potential for quality of the Pfalz vineyards could be fully exploited, following the tradition of the great estates of the Mittelhaardt which had been created as the result of secularization under Napoleon.

This attractive wayside shrine is the emblem of the Kirchenstück in Forst, one of the best Riesling vineyards in the Pfalz, situated in the Mittelhaardt not far from Deidesheim.

RED WINE IN THE LAND OF RIESLING

The Müller-Catoir vineyard in Haardt, near Neustadt, has been in existence for over 250 years, and is famous for its outstanding white wines. Its Spätburgunder wines are made with equal care.

The Pfalz is one of the most attractive wine-growing regions of Germany, and is notable for its hospitality. Burg Battenberg, southwest of Grünstadt, is surrounded by vines. Here visitors can enjoy a drink in a pleasant garden in good weather.

Two or three centuries ago, the majority of vineyards in Germany were still stocked with black grape varieties—something that may seem impossible today in the land of Riesling, Silvaner, and Müller-Thurgau. Yet it is a fact that even on the Mosel and in the Rheingau, Riesling did not embark on its triumphal progress until modern times. Before that, and perhaps owing to the influence over several centuries of Burgundian monks such as the Cistercians, black burgundy grape varieties had dominated the range of vines grown.

From the 1970s onward, consumption of white wines in German households steadily fell, and in the last decade of the 20th century red wines were in such demand that German supply could not keep pace with it. The classic red wine regions such as Württemberg and the Ahr, not to mention the few vineyards stocked with black grape varieties in the west of the Rheingau, were severely overstretched; the people of Württemberg still drink almost all the red wine produced there themselves—even if they did not, the red wines of the region do not on the whole satisfy the new taste for red wine which has been formed by powerful wines from southern countries—and the area of vineyards in the Ahr and Rheingau growing black grape varieties is simply too small to meet demand.

Fortunately other regions were in a position to help. They included Franconia: while previously its merits had clearly lain in the area of dry white wines, it now filled this gap in the market with red burgundies from the vineyards of Burgstädt, and with the new Domina grape variety, a cross of Portugieser and Spätburgunder,

distinguished for its intensity of color and powerful fruit acidity.

It was an obvious move for southern Baden to be taken over by the making of red wines, if only because of its climate—amounts of sunlight and warmth reach top levels here—and in fact for the last few years several of the best *barrique*-matured Spätburgunder wines in Germany have been made here. Winegrowers such as Fritz Keller, Karl-Heinz Johner, Joachim Heger, and the Bercher brothers, as well as the cooperatives of Wasenweiler and Königschaffhausen, have now even seen their wines succeed outside the country.

THE DORNFELDER GRAPE

However, the Pfalz has a part of its own to play on the German red wine scene. The region has almost as good a climate as neighboring Baden, and consequently over the last few years many viticulturalists have enlarged the areas given over to varieties for making red wines. They not only plant the classic Spätburgunder grape, but are ready to risk experimenting with a whole range of varieties.

The best results have been achieved by the Sankt Laurent grape, possibly a descendant of Spätburgunder which originated in France in the and arrived in Austria by way of Germany, then to return to Germany from Austria again. If the good results achieved by Knipser and Messmer are emulated, then yet more may be expected of this variety in the country. The same may be said of the Dornfelder grape, a cross between Helfensteiner and Heroldrebe bred at the Weinsberg viticultural school, and already one of the three most widespread red wine varieties in Germany.

From the same breeding program come the new crosses based on Cabernet and only recently introduced to the public. They bear exotic names such as Cabernet Cubin and Cabernet Mitos, both of them crosses with Lemburger, and Cabernet Dorio and Cabernet Dorsa, where the Dornfelder variety was also involved in the breeding. In view of the poor results as yet achieved by German crosses in terms of quality, however, one may wonder whether the reliable old Cabernet Sauvignon very successfully grown by such viticulturalists as Knipser and Philippi in the Pfalz, and Männler and Keller in Baden, might not have served the purpose better.

Five Friends

All used to be straightforward in the world of the Pfalz. A handful of vineyards with names well known to wine lovers existed in the Mittelhaardt area, and the wine-growing estates were dominated by the three Bs: Bassermann-Jordan, Reichsrat von Buhl, and Bürklin-Wolf, the first two located in Deidesheim and the last in Wachenheim. Almost no one else could compete with these distinguished names.

The three estates had been the outcome of secularization in the Napoleonic period. At the beginning of the 19th century, Andreas Jordan began to extend his parents' estate in Deidesheim and systematically enlarge the former ecclesiastical property. He planted Riesling and, unusually for the time, made single-variety wines from it. After Jordan's death the business was divided between his three children, laying the foundations of what were to become the estates of Reichsrat von Buhl and Dr. Deinhard. In neighboring Wachenheim the Bürkling-Wolf estate began to attract attention with its wines, and these two villages had a monopoly of quality that was soon known well beyond the region.

The crisis in the viticulture of the Pfalz did not leave the "three Bs" unaffected, for they had been unable to keep up their standards. In the mid-1980s, a group of younger and then little-known viticulturalists tried to turn the tide, and decided to coordinate their efforts. They soon found the formula that was to make them famous, and called themselves the Five Friends (though they were originally only four). Their names were Becker, Kessler, Rebholz, Siegrist, and Wehrheim. They all operated on the principle of team work, sharing their experience, and offering frank criticism within the group.

At first the Five merely held wine tastings together, but in 1991, they devised their first joint brochure and announced their first presentation of the year's wines. It was quickly evident that as a group they could attract greater public attention, and joint marketing activities had far more advantages than disadvantages, since they were not competing with each other on the market. They all sold mainly straight from the vineyard to private customers, supplying only small quantities to restaurants or the professional wine trade.

Most profitable of all, however, were their discussions among themselves. In order to increase their own expertise, the five organized visits together to Burgundy, Tuscany, Ribera del

The "Five Friends" wine-growing association was founded in 1991.

2002er Deidesheimer Kieselberg Riesling Kabinett trocken

Burg Ortenberg stands proudly above its Schlossberg vineyard, one of the most outstanding sites in Baden, which makes excellent Traminer and Riesling wines.

Duero, and Bordeaux, where they profited as viticulturalists and winemakers from their hosts' open-minded attitude.

To further the learning process, they organized a professional symposium in conjunction with the annual presentation of their wines. Subjects of discussion included the aging of red and white wines in *barriques*, analysis of the influence of vineyard situations, and the importance of soil and climate.

For all their common interests, the Five do not try to bind themselves too closely together; theirs is a flexible cooperation. They deliberately encourage the individuality of their own styles of winemaking and the independent marketing of their products.

In many ways the tale of the Five Friends from the southern Pfalz symbolizes the modern viticulture of the region. It symbolizes the new atmosphere that has entered the business with the younger generation of winegrowers. The desire to achieve quality now infects even the former suppliers of cheap wines in casks, and there is greater self-confidence among winegrowers on the Südliche Weinstraße, who not so long ago were regarded as the outsiders of the Pfalz.

Nor will progress stop here, and the best evidence of that is the sudden changes in the estates of the "three Bs" over the last few years. It was as if they and other estates in the Mittelhaardt and Deutsche Weinstraße areas had woken from a long sleep; their wines suddenly regained their former quality. The future of the Pfalz looks bright.

SELECT PRODUCERS IN THE PFALZ

DR. VON BASSERMANN-JORDAN****
DEIDESHEIM
104 acres (42 ha); 350,000 bottles • Wines: Riesling from vineyards in Forst (→Kirchenstück, Jesuitengarten), Ruppertsberg (→Reiterpfad, Nussbien), and Deidesheim (Hohenmorgen, →Kalkofen)
After Ulrich Mell joined this estate as cellarmaster, its wines rapidly improved. The potential of the estate's vineyards is one of the highest in the Pfalz.

FRIEDRICH BECKER***–****
SCHWEIGEN
35 acres (14 ha); 100,000 bottles • Wines include: Spätburgunder, Riesling, Chardonnay, Weißburgunder, Grauburgunder from the →Sonnenberg vineyard in Schweigen
Like the other members of the Five Friends, Friedrich Becker and his cellarmaster Stefan Dorst are among the innovative producers of the southern Pfalz. Their preference is for Pinot varieties, and French Burgundy is the example they emulate. Their program includes careful work in cultivating the vineyards by natural methods.

BERGDOLT–ST. LAMPRECHT***–*****
DUTTWEILER
45.5 acres (18.5 ha); 140,000 bottles • Wines include: Riesling, Weißburgunder, Spätburgunder, Dornfelder from vineyards in Kirweil (Mandelberg) and Duttweil (Mandelberg, Kalkberg, Kreuzberg)
The vineyards of thus monastic estate produce top-quality wines year after year. These wines—particularly those made from the Weißburgunder and Chardonnay grapes—are powerful, with good keeping quality.

JOSEF BIFFAR****
DEIDESHEIM
32 acres (13 ha); 80,000 bottles • Wines include: Riesling, Weißburgunder, Dornfelder from vineyards in Ruppertsberg (→Reiterpfad, Nussbien), Deidesheim (→Grainhubel, →Kalkofen, Kieselberg), and Wachenheim (Gerümpel, Goldbächel)
Under the management of Ulrich Mell, the Biffar estate was one of the most successful of the 1980s and 1990s, making a particular impression with its fresh, fragrant Rieslings. Time will show whether the new cellarmaster, Dirk Roth, can match his predecessor's achievements.

REICHSRAT VON BUHL****
DEIDESHEIM
124 acres (50 ha); 400,000 bottles • Wines: Riesling, Weißburgunder, Spätburgunder from vineyards in Forst (→Jesuitengarten, →Kirchenstück), Deidesheim (Leinhöhle, Kieselberg) and Ruppertsberg (Reiterpfad), →Buhl Classic, Riesling Sekt
Recently, and after a period of crisis lasting some time, the quality of the wines produced by the second largest of the "three Bs" of the Pfalz has again become evident, particularly in the *Auslese* and *edelsüß* area. The *Beerenauslese* wines from the Jesuitengarten are among the best in the region.

DR. BÜRKLIN-WOLF***–*****
WACHENHEIM
296 acres (120 ha); 670,000 bottles • Wines: Riesling, Weißburgunder and others from vineyards in Forst (→Kirchenstück, →Jesuitengarten, Pechstein, →Ungeheuer), Deidesheim (Hohenmorgen, Langenmorgen, →Kalkofen), Ruppertsberg (→Geisboehl), and Wachenheim (Gerümpel, Rechbächel, Goldbächel), Villa Eckel

Bettina Bürklin-Guradze and her husband Christian von Guradze have reduced their range of varieties to the essentials. Since the middle of the 1990s their wines have once again been among the best of the region, and 1996 was an outstanding vintage. Rieslings from the Forster Kirchenstück and Ruppertsberger Geisboehl vineyards are classified within the region as First Growths. The latter in particular are worthy of that status.

A. CHRISTMANN***–*****
GIMMELDINGEN
35 acres (14 ha); 100,000 bottles • Wines include: Riesling, Grauburgunder, Weißburgunder, Spätburgunder, Portugieser, St. Laurent from vineyards in Gimmeldingen (Meerspinne, →Mandelgarten), Königsbach (→Idig, Ölberg), Deidesheim (Hohenmorgen), and Ruppertsberg (→Reiterpfad, Linsenbusch, Nussbien), →Selektion "S."
The growths here are elegant, with fruity notes; Steffen Christmann does not make broad, heavy wines. Although the firm produces large quantities of red wines from the burgundy varieties, its leading products are still Rieslings from the Idig, Hohenmorgen, Mandelgarten, and Reiterpfad vineyards.

EYMANN***
GÖNNHEIM
42 acres (17 ha); 150,000 bottles • Wines: Riesling, Silvaner, Weißburgunder, Grauburgunder, Spätburgunder, Chardonnay, Gewürztraminer, Muskateller, Müller-Thurgau; St. Laurent, Portugieser, Dornfelder, Regent, Sekt from vineyards in Gönnheim
Rainer Eymann has been managing the family estate since 1983 by ecological methods, sowing green plants among the vines, using natural fertilizers and natural means of combating pests and disease, and reducing yields in order to increase the quality of the grapes. The estate now offers some very good wines, particularly in the Toreye-Selektion range, as well as *Auslese* wines made from Riesling, Muskateller wines, and Spätburgunder vinified as a white wine.

FITZ-RITTER****
BAD DÜRKHEIM
52 acres (21 ha); 160,000 bottles • Wines include: Riesling, Grauburgunder, Weißburgunder, Chardonnay, Gewürztraminer, Spätburgunder, Dornfelder from vineyards in Dürkheim and Ungstein, barrique wines, Ritterhof Sekts
The half-timbered house with its fine grounds belongs to one of the most beautiful wine-growing estates in Germany. Konrad Fitz and his cellarmaster Rolf Hanewald make Rieslings with a clean note, very good in the *edelsüß* area in particular, and also a delicate Gewürztraminer. The red wines of the estate are matured in *barriques*. The Sekt winery of Ritterhof, founded in 1837, is also part of the estate.

WINFRIED FREY U. SÖHNE***–****
ESSINGEN
25 acres (10 ha); 60,000 bottles • Wines: Riesling, burgundy varieties, Dornfelder, Portugieser, St. Laurent, from vineyards in Essingen
Winfried Frey and his sons use biological methods to cultivate vineyards in Essingen, aiming chiefly to produce *edelsüß* qualities. The broad spectrum of *edelsüß* wines and *Eiswein*, and the diversity of grape varieties grown, are evidence of the satisfaction the winemaker feels in being able to offer small quantities of as many products as possible.

KNIPSER***–*****
LAUMERSHEIM

62 acres (25 ha); 200,000 bottles • Wines include:
Riesling from vineyards in Dirmstein, Großkarlbach,
and Laumersheim

The Knipser brothers produce some remarkable wines:
dense St. Laurents and Dornfelders with good maturing
qualities, Cabernet Sauvignons which are unusually
mature and strong for Germany, top-quality *edelsüß*
wines made from the Scheurebe grape, and most of all
dense, intensely flavored Chardonnays, Weißburgunder
and Grauburgunder wines.

KOEHLER-RUPRECHT****–*****
KALLSTADT

35 acres (14 ha); 80,000 bottles • Wines include:
Riesling, Weißburgunder, Grauburgunder, Chardonnay,
Spätburgunder from vineyards in Kallstadt
(→Saumagen, Steinacker, Kronenberg), →Philippi,
Riesling "R.," Pinot Noir "R.R.," barrique-matured
wines, Cuvée Elysium

Bernd Philippi is regarded as one of the best
viticulturalists and winemakers in Germany. He
shows as much virtuosity in making Rieslings (the
best are from the Kallstadter Saumagen vineyard) as
he does with wines from the Burgundy varieties. The
best of his wines bear the selection mark "R." on the
label, and an *edelsüß* cuvée is marketed under the
evocative name Elysium. Philippi's methods are
traditional—selective picking by hand, fermentation
using natural yeasts—but the wines are unmistakably
modern in character.

HERBERT MESSMER***–****
BURRWEILER

49.5 acres (20 ha); 190,000 bottles • Wines include:
Riesling, Weißburgunder, Grauburgunder, Chardonnay,
St. Laurent, Spätburgunder from vineyards in
Burrweiler (→Schäwer) and Gleisweiler

Wines of excellent quality, not just in the special
selection lines marketed but in the standard range too,
are the trademarks of this estate. The *edelsüß* wines are
top-quality products, and the estate's white wines are
unusually fruity and delicate.

GEORG MOSBACHER****
FORST

35 acres (14 ha); 110,000 bottles • Wines include:
Riesling from vineyards in Forst (Ungeheuer,
Pechstein, Freundstück, Stift) and Deidesheim
(Herrgottsacker)

The large amount of Rieslings is noticeable among the
wines made by this estate, and they are surpassed only
by a few leading winemaking firms. In the 1990s the
Forst vineyard of Ungeheuer almost always produced
some of the best wines in the area.

MÜLLER-CATOIR****
NEUSTADT-HAARDT

49.5 acres (20 ha); 140,000 bottles • Wines:
Riesling, Rieslander, Weißburgunder, Grauburgunder,
Scheurebe, Muskateller, Spätburgunder from Haardt
(→Bürgergarten and Mandelring) and the →Mußbacher
Eselshaut and →Gimmeldinger Schlössel vineyards
(Trockenbeerenauslese)

Over the last 250 years, the firm has established a
reputation as one of the best wine-growing estates in
Germany. For 25 years, Jakob Heinrich Catoir and his
excellent cellarmaster Hans-Günther Schwarz, now
retired, have carried this banner. His successor, Martin
Franzen, has continued the house tradition of refined
style since 2002. As he continues to accumulate
experience, he should continue to produce top quality
edelsüß Rieslaners and spirited Rieslings.

MÜNZBERG – LOTHAR KESSLER & SÖHNE****
GODRAMSTEIN

27 acres (11 ha); 90,000 bottles • Wines include:
Weißburgunder, Riesling, Spätburgunder, Dornfelder
from the Münzberg vineyard in Godramstein

The dry *Spätlese* and *Auslese* wines made by the Kessler
family from Weißburgunder are proof that this variety
can sometimes be more interesting than the omnipresent
Chardonnay. The close attention paid to *barrique* aging
of the burgundy varieties is the great strength of the
estate, which is a member of the Five Friends Society.

ÖKONOMIERAT REBHOLZ****
SIEBELDINGEN

32 acres (13 ha); 90,000 bottles • Wines include:
Riesling, Weißburgunder, Grauburgunder, Chardonnay,
Spätburgunder from Siebeldingen (→Im Sonnenschein,
Rosenberg), Birkweiler (Kastanienberg), and
Godramstein (→Münzburg), Hansjörg Rebholz "R."

Rebholz makes wines of unusual density and
complexity for this region, particularly in the special
selection lines. The motto of the house is the name
of one of its *Trockenbeerenauslese* wines: *Zeit und
Geduld* (Time and Patience).

THOMAS SIEGRIST***–****
LEINSWEILER

31 acres (12.5 ha); 80,000 bottles • Wines include:
Riesling, Müller-Thurgau, Weissburgunder,
Grauburgunder, Chardonnay, Silvaner, Spätburgunder,
Dornfelder from vineyards in Leinswiler, Ilbesheim, and
Wollmersheim, barrique-aged wines, Cuvée Johann
Adam Hauck

Thomas Siegrist has made a name as one of the best
producers of red wines in the southern Pfalz. Maturing in
barriques has also become one of his specialties; the wood
notes, which were very noticeable at first, have now been
moderated, making way for a delicate fruitiness.

STIFTSWEINGUT FRANK MEYER**–***
KLINGENMÜNSTER

20 acres (8 ha); 70,000 bottles • Wines: Silvaner,
Riesling, Weißburgunder, Grauburgunder and other
white varieties, Sekt, Portugieser, Spätburgunder,
new red crosses such as Cabernet Cubin

Meyer uses natural methods in cultivating vineyards
with soils ranging from sandy gravel to calcareous
clay, and picks by hand. His two dozen wines are
dominated by dry *Spätlesen* made from Riesling and
burgundy varieties, and his *barrique*-matured red
wines made from Portugieser (!) and Spätburgunder
are worth noting.

DR. WEHRHEIM***–****
BIRKWEILER

25 acres (10 ha); 80,000 bottles • Wines include:
Riesling, Weißburgunder, Chardonnay, Spätburgunder
from vineyards in Birkweiler (Kastanienbusch,
Mandelberg, Rosenberg)

Wehrheim is almost unsurpassed in the Pfalz for
Burgundy varieties and Chardonnay. The reason lies
not only in the good vineyards, with soils of weathered
sandstone or calcareous clay, but also in the
professionalism shown in both vineyard and winery:
sensible restriction of the yield is followed by gentle
methods of cultivation and minimum filtration.

Baden

With its 39,040 acres (15,800 ha) of vineyards, Baden is only the third largest viticultural area of Germany, but it is by far the most extensive. The region runs for nearly 300 miles (500 km) in an almost perfect north–south direction along the Upper Rhine, from the Rhine-Neckar area around Mannheim and Heidelberg to Basel. The larger part of the Baden viticultural region lies in the rift valley of the Rhine and the river's side valleys, with the exception of some small "islands" of vineyards on Lake Constance and the valley of the Tauber in Franconia.

The European wine-growing laws, which divide all vineyard districts on the Continent into various categories, place Baden in Zone B. This is not an arbitrary decision, since the upper valley of the Rhine is generally considered the warmest part of the whole Federal German Republic. While there can be considerable climatic differences in the various parts of Baden, the valley of the Rhine as a whole enjoys the protection of the Black Forest massif against rough east winds, while on the French side of the Rhine the Vosges Mountains successfully ward off rain. The Breisgau area near Freiburg can boast more hours of sunlight and thus higher average temperatures than any other German wine-growing district, and the Ihringer Winklerberg in the Kaiserstuhl area is considered to be the most reliably warm vineyard between the Lower Rhine and Lake Constance, and between Trier and Dresden.

A romantic vineyard castle, Ortenburg.

There are considerable differences between the constitution of the soil in the various vine-growing areas. Limestone, clay, and marl soils alternate, loess and volcanic rock predominate in the Kaiserstuhl, there is shelly limestone and red marl in the northeast, and the hills of Lake Constance consist of coarse moraine gravel.

Success with Burgundy Varieties

With all these climatic and geological differences, the various styles of wines made in the different parts of Baden sometimes display clearly marked individual characteristics.

White burgundy grape varieties do best along the Badische Bergstraße and in the Kraichgau, since they get sufficient sun there, while the climate provides the necessary fruit and elegance. In spite of high potential for quality and the efforts of individual viticulturalists, these areas have not yet managed to make a really distinctive name for themselves, which may be due partly to prejudices and ingrained ideas on the part of wine writers and consumers. In the

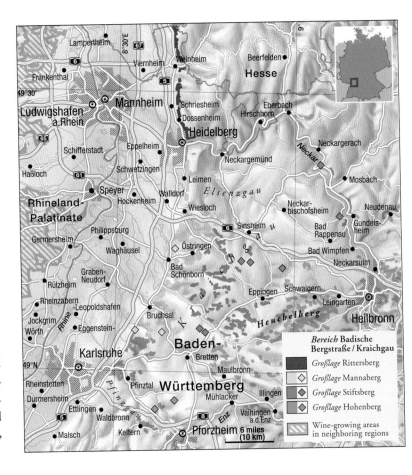

Bereich Tauberfranken, where the winegrowers have to expect frost and as a result vines are planted only on hillsides, the wines resemble those of neighboring Franconia. The favorite grape variety here is Müller-Thurgau, which covers two thirds of the area under vines.

Very different is the Ortenau, where vineyards thread their way through the Black Forest in the beautiful landscape of the valleys running off to the side of the Rhine. Riesling predominates here, and is also known in the area as Klingelberger, after the first vineyard in the Ortenau at Durbach, where it was originally planted as a single variety at the end of the 18th century. However, the little wine-growing village of Durbach shows that the Ortenau vineyards can be just as suitable for red wines made from the Spätburgunder grape.

The Spätburgunder is also the best and now the most widely grown variety in the warm, sunny Breisgau, with its calcareous soils. In the nearby Kaiserstuhl area and on the Tuniberg the range of varieties becomes more extensive again. Grauburgunder is used to make a dry wine fermented in wooden casks, invented here after the sweet, thick wines known by the variety's alternative name Ruländer fell out of fashion, and it does so well in this region that it can hold its own even with French growths. The same can be said of Spätburgunder and Müller-Thurgau; the latter is often labeled as Rivaner, and reaches a degree of ripeness which can give even this high-yielding grape an interesting structure or flavor.

Less impressive is the situation in the Markgräflerland, where viticulturalists have predominantly planted the Gutedel vine. This rather neutral grape variety has its charms, and can even achieve interesting quality, for instance in Switzerland and neighboring Alsace, where Gutedel is known as Chasselas. However, most of the Markgräfler viticulturalists seem to find realizing this potential in the bottle as hard as squaring the circle. The tourist attractions of the area, and consequently the absence of any problem in the marketing of wines, have probably tended to block motivation for making wines of really top quality.

AWARENESS OF QUALITY

The yields at harvest in particular, now almost a third less than the yields of the 1980s, show that some growers in Baden have taken the effort to achieve quality really seriously. At that earlier time Baden, like the other wine-growing regions of Germany, had its eye on the ideal of rationalized viticulture covering a large area,

Durbach is the unofficial capital of the Ortenau area. It has well-protected vineyards with favorable aspects, for instance the Schlossberg, Schloss Staufenberg, and Steinberg vineyards, and in good years the Rieslings grown there make wines of unique fullness.

Wine from Lake Constance

The vineyards around Lake Constance lie in two German states and three viticultural areas: Bavaria, Württemberg, and Baden. Baden, with around 988 acres (400 ha), is much the largest of the three.

The southern aspect here and the wide surface of the lake, which acts like a gigantic mirror and reflects back sunlight, are a guarantee of particularly mild climatic conditions, but as the vineyards are at a comparatively high altitude—up to 1,650 feet (500 m)—the wines made here are fruity in character as a rule, but not so concentrated and powerful as those of the Upper Rhine. High amounts of rainfall and rising mists are complicating factors.

Most of the wine from the Spätburgunder grape, which has been cultivated for over 200 years on the northern banks of the lake, is used to make Weißherbst wines. This pale rosé wine is the main product of the highly regarded state wine-growing estate of Meersburg, which with 148 acres (60 ha) is the largest estate on Lake Constance and grows Spätburgunder in half of its vineyards. Its Weißherbst is considered one of the best in Germany. With Spätburgunder, the main variety grown here is Müller-Thurgau. Vineyards on the Hohentwieler Olgaberg near Singen, the highest vineyard of Germany, at 1,840 feet (560 m), also belong to the state.

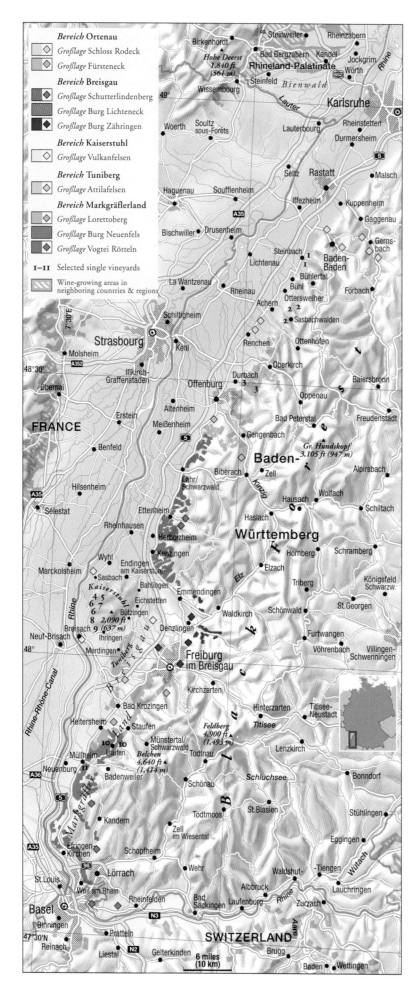

Bereich Ortenau
◇ *Großlage* Schloss Rodeck
▢ *Großlage* Fürsteneck

Bereich Breisgau
◈ *Großlage* Schutterlindenberg
◈ *Großlage* Burg Lichteneck
◆ *Großlage* Burg Zähringen

Bereich Kaiserstuhl
◇ *Großlage* Vulkanfelsen

Bereich Tuniberg
◇ *Großlage* Attilafelsen

Bereich Markgräflerland
◇ *Großlage* Lorettoberg
◈ *Großlage* Burg Neuenfels
◆ *Großlage* Vogtei Rötteln

I–II Selected single vineyards

Wine-growing areas in neighboring countries & regions

6 miles
(10 km)

with the production of expressive wines of high quality taking only second place. The most notable example of this policy was the gigantic operation involved in the restructuring of land in the Kaiserstuhl area.

Baden is in fact organized by the Wine Law into very large wine-growing units: this extensive region is subdivided into no more than nine *Bereiche*, with only 16 *Großlagen* and 314 *Einzellagen*—obviously a more functional structure than prevails, for instance, in the comparatively small Mosel region with its 19 *Großlagen* and 500 *Einzellagen*. In addition, 85 percent of the vine-growing area is run by

Weißherbst wine made from Spätburgunder

Weißherbst is a term introduced to describe German and Swiss rosé wines. Such wines are based on a single grape variety, which must be identified on the label. The variety most commonly used is Spätburgunder, vinified as white wine: that is to say, the grapes are pressed immediately they are delivered to the winery, so that the must can absorb only a few coloring substances from the skins, and this process gives Weißherbst its typical pale pink hue. Its charm resides in the freshness of its fruity and floral aromas, and it should therefore always be drunk young and chilled. The Weißherbst wines of the Kaiserstuhl and Lake Constance are famous. Badisch-Rotgold, known as a "Rotling" and made of white or red grapes pressed together, is usually of lower quality. This rosé, which comes into the *Qualitätswein* category, is often made of mixed Ruländer (otherwise Grauburgunder) and Spätburgunder grapes. Rotling from Württemberg can be labelled as a "Schilcher" wine, a term also denoting that it is made from white and black grapes that have been mixed.

members of cooperatives, a ratio greater than any in Germany except for the small Hessische Bergstraße area and Franconia.

This has not prevented the growers of Baden from uniting their forces to promote quality in their products. Leading Baden wine-growing estates have combined not so much *with* one another—for the gulf between those who market their own products and the cooperatives is as great here as anywhere—but side by side with each other, in a minor viticultural revolution which has made a considerable difference to the styles and quality of the wines they produce.

Today, over half the wines of Baden are made dry, and another third are medium-dry. It is most obvious in the wine made from the Grauburgunder variety, alias Ruländer; with modern fermentation, and sometimes matured in *barriques*, it is no longer highly colored and sweet, and has become a modern, fruity wine. Unlike the wine made from its Italian counterpart Pinot Grigio, it is full-bodied. Spätburgunder and Weißburgunder wines also profit from concentration on the essentials, and even from *barrique*-maturing. This product of the burgundy varieties is certainly the most interesting wine that Baden has to offer.

The Restructuring of Vineyards

Since the 1950s, systematic efforts have been made in German viticulture to restructure the land under vines. These efforts began with the realization that the splintering of vineyards into small plots in many areas called for an econom-

Select single vineyards
(see map opposite)
1 Stich den Buben
2 Alde Gott
3 Plauelrain
4 Steinbuck
5 Enselberg
6 Henkenberg
7 Eichberg
8 Schlossberg
9 Winklerberg
10 Altenberg
11 Reggenhag

The Kaiserstuhl is an example of misconceived land restructuring; the vineyards here were artificially remodeled for purely economic reasons, and no account was taken of their original and natural qualities.

ically unjustifiable expenditure of labor, and was increasingly becoming an obstacle to any kind of rational viticulture. The reorganization of landed property not only created larger areas which were easier to cultivate, but also meant that drainage systems could be installed and suitable paths laid out to take machinery. The aim was to restock vineyards with higher-yielding cloned varieties—and all these measures were clearly likely to raise production.

Apart from the fact that such measures seldom increased quality, there were some undesirable side effects. On the Kaiserstuhl, for instance, the whole landscape of the loessial terraces of the volcanic hills was comprehensively remodeled, so that today, seen from the valley, it looks like a collection of huge slag heaps in an opencast mining landscape covered with the green of the vines. As a prime concern was to lay out the large terraces so that they would be suitable for machinery, there was a tendency to plant some of the vineyards inclining toward the slopes—with the unfortunate result that cold air cannot flow off but actually builds up in these vineyard valleys created by human hand, so that frost damage can now occur in regions once famous for their mild climate.

The restructuring of land was not wholly bad, and there are more successful examples in the Mosel and on the Rhine Front in Rheinhessen, where the appearance of the landscape was preserved and deteriorations in quality were on the whole kept within bounds.

Select Producers in Baden

Abril***–****
Bischoffingen

16 acres (6.5 ha); 40,000 bottles • Wines include: Grauburgunder, Weißburgunder, Müller-Thurgau, Silvaner, Riesling, Spätburgunder from vineyards in Bischoffingen and Schelingen, Weisse Linie, barrique-matured wines

The Bischoffingen vineyards seem particularly suitable for growing both red and white burgundy varieties. At least, it is from these grapes that Hans-Friedrich Abril makes the wines on which the good reputation of his little estate is founded. The *barrique*-matured whites are intense in color, and derive their aroma and flavor from the fact that the grapes are picked very ripe.

Affentaler W.G.**–***
Bühl-Eisental

612.5 acres (248 ha); 3,500,000 bottles • Wines include: Riesling, Spätburgunder, Müller-Thurgau from many vineyards around Bühl, Huber Althof, Orblie Secco

The Affental cooperative is one of the many such cooperatives in Baden working with a view to quality. In the past, nuns grew vines in what was then called Avetal, mainly to make wine for church use. Today the Affental cooperative has many outlets for its wines, including the top echelons of the restaurant trade.

Bercher***–*****
Burkheim

59 acres (24 ha); 170,000 bottles • Wines include: Riesling, Weißburgunder, Grauburgunder, Müller-Thurgau, Spätburgunder from Burkheim (→Feuerburg) and Sasbach

In the last decade Rainer and Eckhardt Bercher have made their estate one of the market leaders in Baden. The emphasis of their work is on the burgundy varieties, which do particularly well on the weathered volcanic soil of the Feuerberg, as their *barrique*-matured special selection wines and their dry Spätburgunder *Auslese* wines in particular show.

Duijn****
Bühl

20 acres (8 ha); 25,000 bottles • Wines: Spätburgunder from Bühlertal Engelsfelsen, Sterneberg, Laufen

Jakob Duijn is Baden's vertical take-off in Spätburgunder. Within a few years the Dutchman has established his reds among Baden's top quality wines.

Freiherr von Gleichenstein***–****
Oberrotweil

59 acres (24 ha); 150,000 bottles • Wines include: Spätburgunder, Weißburgunder, Grauburgunder, Müller-Thurgau from Oberrotweil (→Henkenberg), Amolten, and Achkarren (→Schlossberg)

Unlike many of his colleagues, Hans-Joachim von Gleichenstein, an opponent of *barrique*-maturing, seldom attracts much public attention. However, he quietly makes excellent Grauburgunder wines from the Henkenberg vineyard in Oberrotweil, and the time they spend maturing in new wooden casks does not detract in the least from their quality.

Dr. Heger***–*****
Ihringen

40 acres (16 ha); 120,000 bottles • Wines include: Riesling, Grauburgunder, Weißburgunder, Silvaner, Chardonnay, Spätburgunder from Ihringen (→Winklerberg), Achkarren (→Schlossberg), Merdingen (Bühl), and Freiburg (Schlossberg), →Spätburgunder Mimus

On entering the family firm, Joachim Heger found himself in possession of some very good vineyards. The Winklerberg of Ihringen in particular, Germany's warmest vineyard, regularly produces outstanding grapes. Riesling, Silvaner, Muskateller, and the burgundy varieties all thrive here in harmony together. The Grauburgunder and Weißburgunder wines have much power, as well as attractive fruit.

Albert Heitlinger***–*****
Östringen-Tiefenbach

86 acres (35 ha); 210,000 bottles • Wines include: Riesling, Grauburgunder, Weißburgunder, Müller-Thurgau, Spätburgunder barrique-matured wines, Dialog, Grand Étage

Although it took Erhard Heitlinger a little longer than some other winegrowers to present his wines in the right light to appeal to a critical public, the reason lay less in their quality than in the position of his estate, which lies in a part of Baden not generally thought capable of anything but simple wines. Today, however, this energetic viticulturalist has made it abundantly clear that his is one of the elite estates of Baden, particularly with his Grauburgunders and other *barrique*-matured wines.

Reichsgraf und Marquis zu Hoensbroech****
Angelbachtal-Michelfeld

54 acres (22 ha); 120,000 bottles • Wines include: Weißburgunder, Grauburgunder, Riesling, Silvaner, Spätburgunder from vineyards in Michelfeld and Eichelberg

Rüdiger zu Hoensbroech founded his firm in 1968, and his wines soon attracted attention in following decades. He was one of the founding members of the V.D.P. in Baden. His Chardonnay and Weißburgunder from the Himmelberg vineyard in Michelfeld represent the best quality in his range.

Bernhard Huber***–****
Malterdingen

32 acres (13 ha); 80,000 bottles • Wines: Spätburgunder, Chardonnay, Weißburgunder, Grauburgunder, Müller-Thurgau, Riesling, from vineyards in Malterdingen and Hecklingen

Bernhard Huber was one of the first German viticulturalists to make an international impression with *barrique*-fermented Chardonnays. He is also regarded as a Spätburgunder specialist. His Weißburgunder and Grauburgunder wines from Malterdingen vineyards are above average too.

Karl H. Johner****–*****
Bischoffingen

33 acres (13.5 ha); 85,000 bottles • Wines: Spätburgunder, Grauburgunder, Weißburgunder, Chardonnay, Müller-Thurgau, "S.J."

After having spent years helping to develop English wines, Johner began building up his own estate in his native Kaiserstuhl at the end of the 1980s. In less than five years, the new winegrower had already become something of a superstar in German viticulture. He does not take much notice of the absurdities of the German Wine Law and the discussion of vineyard classifications—he simply bottles his products as *Tafelwein*, and they still fetch top prices. His Spätburgunder, Chardonnay, and Grauburgunder wines, and even the rather plain Müller-Thurgau which Johner sells as Rivaner, have a fullness of flavor which raises them well above the average.

Franz Keller—Schwarzer Adler****–*****
Oberbergen

*81.5 acres (33 ha); 200,000 bottles • Wines:
Grauburgunder, Weißburgunder, Müller-Thurgau,
Spätburgunder, from vineyards in Oberrotweil
(Kirchberg, Eichberg) and Oberbergen (Bassgeige,
Pulverbuck), Kellers Keller, barrique-matured wines,
Classik, special selection lines "A." and "S."*

The Schwarze Adler in Oberbergen is much better
known as a top restaurant than for the wine-growing
estate which is part of the property. However, the
wines bottled under the management of Fritz Keller
are more than adequate to match the restaurant's
culinary achievements. This is true not only of classic
wines from the vineyards of Bassgeige and Pulverbuck,
but even more so of the *barrique*-matured special
selections which go under the unpretentious names
of "A." and "S." Wines made from Weißburgunder,
Grauburgunder, Spätburgunder, and Chardonnay
have reached a standard that can stand up to foreign
competition.

Andreas Laible****
Durbach

*10 acres (4 ha); 35,000 bottles • Wines include:
Riesling, Traminer, Scheurebe, Spätburgunder
from the →Durbacher Plauelrein vineyard*

The talented and ambitious Andreas Laible runs his
small estate on the outskirts of Durbach with exemplary
commitment. The secret of his dense, fruity, and spicy
Riesling, Scheurebe, and Weißburgunder wines lies in
choosing the best vineyard plots and aiming for
moderate yields.

Lämmlin-Schindler***
Schliengen-Mauchen

*47 acres (19 ha); 170,000 bottles • Wines include:
Spätburgunder, Weißburgunder, Grauburgunder,
Gutedel, Chardonnay from vineyards in Mauchen*

Some wine lovers may be surprised to find that a
viticulturalist using biological methods, and with
vineyards in a remote Black Forest valley of the
Markgräflerland at that, can produce top quality wines,
but Gerhard Schindler really does make outstanding
white and red wines from the burgundy varieties and
Chardonnay.

Heinrich Männle****
Durbach

*13.5 acres (5.5 ha); 40,000 bottles • Wines include:
Spätburgunder, Weißburgunder, Grauburgunder,
Scheurebe, Riesling, Traminer from the Kochberg
vineyard in Durbach*

Unusually for Durbach, Heinrich Männle's vineyards
are mainly stocked with black grape varieties. Even
more unusual is the quality of the red wines he makes,
some of them matured in *barriques*. Recently Männle
has also been experimenting with Cabernet Sauvignon,
and has shown that this variety can produce good
results in Germany.

Salwey***–****
Oberrotweil

*49.5 acres (20 ha); 150,000 bottles • Wines include:
Spätburgunder, Grauburgunder, Weißburgunder,
Riesling, Silvaner from vineyards in Oberrotweil
and Glottertal (Eichberg)*

Wolf-Dieter Salwey took over his parents' business
in 1964, and through the years has confirmed his
reputation as a fine viticulturalist and winemaker.
His Grauburgunder wines are among the very best
in Baden.

Seeger****
Leimen

*20 acres (8 ha); 40,000 bottles • Wines include:
Riesling, Weißburgunder, Grauburgunder,
Spätburgunder from the Heidelberger and Leimener
Herrenberg, barrique-matured wines*

Thomas Seeger began maturing his red and white
burgundy varieties in the middle of the 1980s. He has
been one of the most unconventional viticulturalists
in Baden, but is also recognized as one of the best.
As well as his single variety growths, he shines with
an unusual Cuvée Anna, made from Spätburgunder,
Schwarzriesling, Lemberger, and Portugieser grapes.

Max Markgraf von Baden
Schloss Staufenberg**–****
Durbach

*66.5 acres (27 ha); 100,000 bottles • Wines include:
Riesling, Müller-Thurgau, Spätburgunder from
vineyards in Durbach (→Klingelberg)*

Of the Margrave's two estates, Staufenberg and Salem,
this is easily the better, although the wines themselves
are vinified at Salem. The Riesling made here takes its
name, specifying its Ortenau origin, from the estate's
top vineyard, the Klingelberg. The Chardonnay and
Gewürztraminer wines are of top quality.

W.G. Ehrenstetten***
Ehrenstetten

*350 acres (140 ha); 1,500,000 bottles • Wines include:
Gutedel, Müller-Thurgau, burgundy varieties from
vineyards in Ehrenstetten, Chasslie*

This viticulturalists' cooperative in the Markgräfler
area, managed by Franz Herbster and his cellarmaster
Norbert Faller, has attracted attention in recent years
not only with its Chasslie, a Gutedel wine bottled *sur lie*,
but also with good Spätburgunder wines from the
Ölberg, marketed in modern designer bottles.

W.G. Königschaffhausen***–****
Königschaffhausen

*889 acres (360 ha); 1,300,000 bottles • Wines include:
Spätburgunder, Müller-Thurgau, Weißburgunder,
Grauburgunder from vineyards in Königschaffhausen,
Regnum, "S.L."*

The Königschaffhausen cooperative was one of the first in
Baden to aim its production deliberately at the market for
wines of top quality, and from the first it was also one of
the most successful. In particular, the *barrique*-matured
Spätburgunder wines from the Steingrüble—named
Regnum or "S.L."—have been widely appreciated.

W.G. Oberbergen**–***
Oberbergen

*691 acres (280 ha); 2,800,000 bottles • Wines include:
Müller-Thurgau, Spätburgunder, Grauburgunder,
Silvaner from vineyards in Oberbergen (Baßgeige,
Pulverbuck), Frühlingsbote, Konrad*

The majority of the wines are from the large single
vineyard of the Baßgeige in Oberbergen, and the
Grauburgunder and Spätburgunder wines are even
a little better than the rest of the excellent range.

W.G. Wasenweiler am Kaiserstuhl**–****
Wasenweiler

*222 acres (90 ha); 650,000 bottles • Wines include:
Spätburgunder, Müller-Thurgau, Silvaner, Weißburgunder,
Grauburgunder from vineyards in Wasenweiler, Die Neun*

A German cooperative which succeeds in attracting
attention with its red wines in Italy is something out
of the ordinary. Johann Haberl, who manages the
cooperative in Wasenweiler, did just that, and brilliantly,
with his 1990 vintage. The best wines are from the
Kreuzhalde vineyard. Biologically made wines are
marketed under the name of "Die Neun."

WÜRTTEMBERG

As others see them, and indeed as they see themselves, the people of Württemberg are almost exclusively drinkers of red wine, most of it made from the black Trollinger grape. However, that idea is only partly accurate. It is true that the viticultural area of Württemberg—at about 27,920 acres (11,300 ha), this state is the fifth largest wine-growing region in Germany—is predominantly stocked with black grapes, but of the individual varieties Riesling in fact holds first place. Its lead over Trollinger is narrow but undeniable, however little this may suit the self-image of the Württembergers. As for the rest, the amount of black grape varieties planted does not necessarily mean that the red wines made

from them are actually drunk in Württemberg. On the whole the wines made from Trollinger, Lemberger, and Schwarzriesling grapes are still rather thin and colorless, and in the past they rightly attracted little critical attention outside the region.

Vines in Württemberg grow mainly in the valley of the Neckar and on the hills around it, but the outskirts of the region officially extend to the valley of the Tauber in the northeast and as far as Tübingen and Reutlingen in the south, with a small self-contained area of vineyards by Lake Constance, between Friedrichshafen and Lindau. The cool, continental climate, with only the surface of the river Neckar exerting

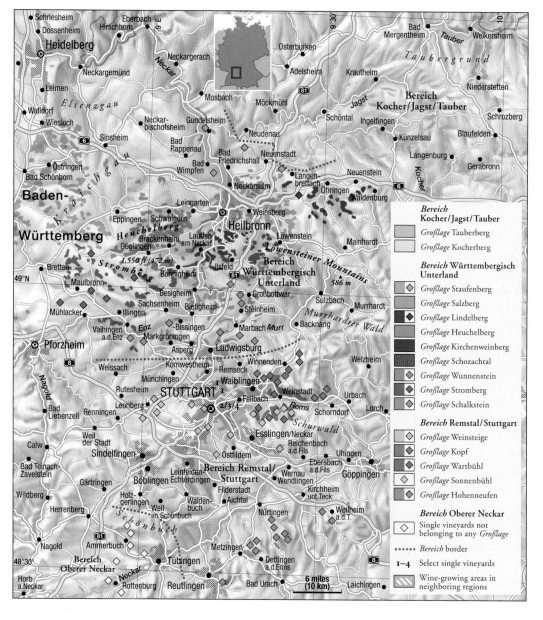

Select single vineyards
1 Zuckerle
2 Herzogenberg
3 Gips
4 Mönchberg

Opposite
If it weren't for the Neckar, pictured here at Mundelheim, and its influence on the temperature, the grapes would find it difficult to ripen in cool Württemberg.

a moderating influence, can make viticulture a very arduous task, although it is perhaps less difficult to grow Riesling, which is the dominant variety in the south of the area around Stuttgart in particular, since such conditions suit the grape well. In more northerly vineyards the predominant variety is Lemberger, known in Austria as Blaufränkish. Similarly, the Trollinger grape is known as Vernatsch in its native South Tyrol.

FROM MERELY DRINKABLE TO BIG RED WINES

It seemed for a long time that the fate of Württemberg was to make red wines which were pleasing and drinkable, but seldom really interesting. The situation was not improved by the cooperatives' winery techniques, involving methods of what was almost the mass production of simple wines: ready to drink young, but without expressiveness or elegance. A favorite method was to heat the must briefly to a temperature of 185°F (85°C) to hasten color extraction, instead of achieving it by the classic process of must fermentation. As a result most of the so-called red wines supplied by these wineries were sadly lacking in both structure and character. Only around ten years ago did some of the Württemberg estates again start to make

These viticulturalists and cellarmasters are the outstanding proponents of *barrique* maturation in Württemberg: the initial letters of their names form the word HADES, the title of their association. They worked together to optimize methods of maturing in small oak casks, and have made an international reputation for themselves.

powerful, genuinely red wines with an intense flavor again, wines to which the increasingly popular practice of *barrique* maturation even lent a certain international character.

Some of the leading viticulturalists of Württemberg joined together in an association known as "Hades" in order to pool their experience of *barrique*-maturation. The name consists of the initial letters of the five member estates: Hohenlohe-Öhringen, Adelmann, Drautz-Able, Ellwanger, and the state-owned Weinsberg estate. The Hades group has succeeded in persuading even the most critical among wine writers of the potential of their vineyards.

In the future, much may be expected of Württemberg. A potential reservoir of quality, as yet unexploited but very promising, exists in the region's Riesling and also in its Lemberger, which is successful in Austria under the name of Blaufränkisch, and in Württemberg is also suitable for blending with other varieties. The first results are already making their mark, but longer and more intensive efforts will probably be needed before the merely drinkable wines of Württemberg become genuine, fully developed products of European stature.

Select Producers in Württemberg

Graf Adelmann* – ****
Kleinbottwar**

49 acres (20 ha); 120,000 bottles • Wines include: Riesling, Trollinger, Lemberger, Samtrot, Frühburgunder, Spätburgunder from solely owned vineyards in Kleinbottwar, Die Mauern von Schaubeck, Cuvée Vignette I, Brüssele'r Spitze

It seems natural to look in the field of red wine for the best wines made by one of the pioneers of the *barrique* maturation of red wines in Germany; they are marketed under the name of Brüssele'r Spitze. However, the estate's top Rieslings are also very good, and so is the red Cuvée Vignette I, made from Lemberger, Samtrot, and Spätburgunder grapes.

Gerhard Aldinger* – ****
Fellbach**

79 acres (32 ha); 160,000 bottles • Wines include: Trollinger, Spätburgunder, Riesling from the →Untertürkheimer Gips (a solely owned vineyard), and vineyards in Fellbach, Hanweiler, Uhlbach, and Rotenberg, Cuvée C., G.A. Weisswein, G.A. Rotwein

Gert Aldinger is the 15th generation of his family to run this estate. Its most valuable item of capital lies in its sole ownership of the Untertürkheimer Gips, an excellent vineyard for growing Riesling and Spätburgunder. Aldinger uses mainly traditional methods in the winery, but presents his wines in a very up-to-date style, in conical bottles with designer labels.

Ernst Dautel**
Bönnigheim**

26 acres (10.5 ha); 80,000 bottles • Wines include: Riesling, Chardonnay, Trollinger, Lemberger, Schwarzriesling from vineyards in Bönnigheim, Besigheim, and Meimsheim, Kreation (white and red), Selektion "S.," Essenz

As a member of the German Barrique Forum, Ernst Dautel naturally pays special attention to his red and white wines matured in wooden casks, including those made not only from his experimental plantings of Cabernet Sauvignon and Merlot vines, but also from the Trollinger and Lemberger varieties traditionally grown in Württemberg. By sensibly restricting yields, he succeeds in making wines of great density and structure.

Drautz-Able – ****
Heilbronn**

36 acres (14.5 ha); 150,000 bottles • Wines: many varieties from Leben in Neckarsulm, Heilbronn, Lauffen, and Erlenbach, →Jodokus, barrique-aged wines, Composition L., Häusles-Wein

Richard Drautz represents the letter D in the name of the Hades association which has attracted attention with its experiments in *barrique* maturing. The name of Jodokus given to his best red wines (made from the Dornfelder and Lemberger varieties) is that of an ancestor of the Drautz family.

Karl Haidle**
Kernen-Stetten**

42 acres (17 ha) 150,000 bottles • Wines include: Riesling, Kerner, Trollinger, Spätburgunder from vineyards in Stetten and Schnait, Selektion "S."

Karl Haidle's estate was thoroughly modernized in 1992, and since then this viticulturalist has been among the best in the whole area around Stuttgart. He still likes to ferment his wines in wooden casks, and also works with *barriques*. His best *Einzellage* wines are his Riesling Pulvermächer and the Spätburgunder wines from the Burghalde. Some of his top wines are bottled without

any mention of the vineyard on the label, including Dornfelder, Lemberger, the Dornfelder-Lemberger "S.," and his Weißburgunder "S."

Graf von Neipperg – ****
Schwaigern**

78 acres (31.5 ha); 240,000 bottles • Wines include: Riesling, Lemberger, Schwarzriesling, Spätburgunder, Samtrot, Trollinger from vineyards in Neipperg (Schlossberg), Schwaigen (Ruthe), and Klingenburg (Schlossberg)

Besides its main seat in Neipperg, the family owns a series of famous wine-growing estates in Bordeaux. The castle accommodates the fermentation plant and storage cellars. The estate's Lembergers and Rieslings are in the top category of Württemberg wines.

Schlossgut Hohenbeilstein**
Beilstein**

33 acres (13.5 ha); 100,000 bottles • Wines include: Riesling, Trollinger, Samtrot, Lemberger, Spätburgunder from the Beilsteiner Schlosswingert vineyard

Schloss Hohenbeilstein is only 100 years old, and has a modern wine-growing estate behind its handsome façade. The vineyards are cultivated by biological methods, and only the Spätburgunder wines may carry the vineyard name of Schlosswingert. The wines themselves are of consistently good to very good quality.

Staatsweingut Weinsberg* – ****
Weinsberg**

99 acres (40 ha); 250,000 bottles • Wines include: Riesling, Lemberger, Trollinger, Spätburgunder, Samtrot from vineyards in Gundelsheim, Abstatt, and Weinsberg, "G.V."

The Weinsberg state-owned estate has long had a good reputation in the world of wine, and not just since its recent introduction of a number of new Cabernet crosses. It has been practicing biological methods of winemaking at Burg Wildeck for some time. An interesting wine is its blend of Kerner, Silvaner, and Burgundy varieties sold under the name of "G.V."

W.G. Grantschen – ***
Grantschen**

346 acres (140 ha); 1,600,000 bottles • Wines include: Riesling, Trollinger, Lemberger, Schwarzriesling from vineyards in Grantschen, "S.M.," Grandor, Schwarze Serie

In contrast to Baden, where a whole series of cooperatives makes outstanding wines, the Grantschen cooperative is alone in Württemberg in producing wines of really top quality. Its Auslese made from Lemberger and called Grandor, and "S.M.," a blend of Dornfelder and Lemberger, reach a very high standard in good years.

Albert Wöhrwag* – ****
Stuttgart-Untertürkheim**

45.5 acres (18.5 ha); 160,000 bottles • Wines: Riesling, Trollinger, Lemberger, Spätburgunder, etc., from the Untertürkheimer Herzogenberg vineyard, →Phillip

Hans-Peter Wöhrwag's estate has been known to lovers of wine for some time, and not just since the introduction of his magnificent Riesling *Eiswein* of 1994. He regularly makes outstanding wines from Riesling, Trollinger, and Spätburgunder grapes on his premises. The blend of Lemberger, Spätburgunder, and Dornfelder marketed under the name of Phillip is also very good.

FRANCONIA

Franconia is one of the most soundly established and popular viticultural regions of Germany. The vineyard slopes on the river Main and in the Steigerwald, their furthest outposts running to the Rhine-Main area in the west and the diocese of Bamberg in the east, have long attracted wine lovers from far and wide who appreciate the clear, straightforward style of the indigenous Franconian wines.

The focal point of the area is the old episcopal city of Würzburg, with its fortress of the Marienberg and the Renaissance and Rococo buildings in the city center: architectural jewels which were destroyed in the war but have been restored with loving care and admirable attention to detail. The city is dominated by the famous vineyard Am Stein, which seen from a distance appears to tower above the rooftops like a wall. A good mile long, and with a surface area of 227 acres (92 ha), it is the largest of all self-contained German hillside vineyards, and the best part of it, known as the Stein/Harfe vineyard, is in the sole ownership of the Bürgerspital.

For the rest, Franconia is dominated by a continental climate, with cold winters scarcely tempered by the river Main and its smaller tributaries, and warm, very dry summers, providing the grapes with optimum conditions in which to ripen. Franconia has few soil formations by comparison with the geological diversity of the Pfalz or Baden. The soils of the Mainviereck (the "square" of the Main), the eastern part of the region, are mainly of residual primary rock and red sandstone, and further to the east the

soils are clay, loess, and shelly limestone. Red marl dominates the Steigerwald area.

BACK TO THE ORIGINAL FRANCONIAN WINES

Monks began growing vines in Franconia as early as the 8th century, and in the Middle Ages the vineyard area of the region was enlarged to almost 247,000 acres (100,000 ha), as large as the entire area down to vines in Germany today. At the time Franconia was the largest viticultural area of the German Empire, with a vineyard area far exceeding that of the Mosel or the banks of the Rhine.

Today the situation has clearly changed: with little more than 14,800 acres (6,000 ha) under vines, Franconian viticulture comes only sixth among the German wine-growing regions. Less than ten percent of the viticulturalists active in this region (over 7,000 of them) market their own wines. The overwhelming majority deliver their grape harvest to the various cooperatives, which then supply must or wines for bottling and marketing, most of these supplies going to the large local winemakers' cooperative in Kitzingen.

In the past Franconia was known principally as the land of the Silvaner grape. This variety, low in acidity and of rather subdued character, did very well on the shelly limestone soil of the Maindreieck (the "triangle" of the Main), where it developed a strong style with a slightly earthy touch. Today, however, the picture is

Select single vineyards
1 Stein
2 Stein/Harfe
3 Innere Leiste
4 Teufelskeller
5 Pfülben
6 Sonnenstuhl
7 Ratsherr
8 Lump
9 Schwanleite
10 Küchenmeister
11 Julius-Echter-Berg
12 Kalb

FRANCONIA
Bereich Mainviereck
Großlage Reuschberg
Großlage Heiligenthal

Bereich Maindreieck
Großlage Burg
Großlage Rosstal
Großlage Ravensburg
Großlage Kirchberg
Großlage Engelsberg
Großlage Marienberg
Großlage Honigberg
Großlage Ewig Leben
Großlage Hofrat
Großlage Teufelstor
Großlage Ölspiel
Großlage Markgraf Babenberg

Bereich Steigerwald
Großlage Kapellenberg
Großlage Zabelstein
Großlage Steige
Großlage Schild
Großlage Schlossberg
Großlage Herrenberg
Großlage Burgweg
Großlage Frankenberger Schlossstück
Großlage Ipsheimer Burgberg

Single vineyards not belonging to any *Großlage*

BADEN
Bereich Tauberfranken

Bereich border

1–12 Select single vineyards

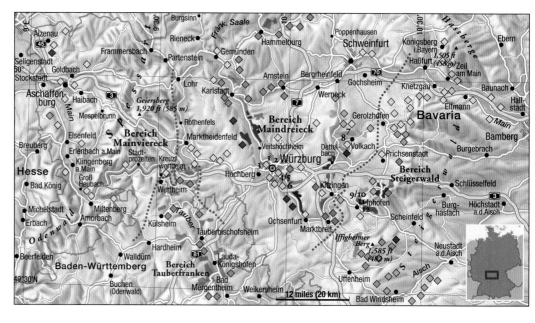

recent years a small group of winemakers has shown that the region also has good potential for red wines. The Frühburgunder and Spätburgunder wines from Bürgstadt were known in the past for their good qualities, and for some time now good quality red wines have also been made from the Domina and Schwarzriesling varieties in the Randersacker and Nordheim area.

TEUFELSKELLER AND KÜCHENMEISTER

Although the region is divided into only three *Bereiche* (if we leave aside the Bavarian part of Lake Constance, which is of only minor viticultural importance), several centers of winemaking can be easily distinguished, each having its own independent wine typology. And one of the undisputed centers of Franconian winemaking lies at the geographical heart of the region, from Würzburg to Sommerhausen by way of Randersacker.

This area contains a large number of the really famous vineyards of Franconia, including the Würzburg Stein, Innere Leiste, and Abtsleite, and the vineyards of Pfülben, Teufelskeller (Devil's Cellar), and Sonnenstuhl around Randersack. Expressive Rieslings and spicy Silvaners are the local specialties, but even Müller-Thurgau can sometimes produce impressive *Spätlese* wines, and as mentioned above, experiments with red wines have been made near Randersack and the results promise well for the future.

Going upstream along the river and past the knee-shaped bend of the Main triangle, one comes to Sulzfeld and Kitzingen, where the region's large winemaking cooperative is located,

very different. Many viticulturalists decided that the variety was too difficult to grow, and consumers, out of ignorance, believed them. Today the old-established Silvaner grape has to be content with one-fifth of its original area, ceding the rest to Müller-Thurgau, which in some places even approaches the 50 percent mark. Luckily recent years have seen a reversal of the trend, and more and more consumers are re-discovering the superiority of the native and old-established Silvaner vine to the heavy-yielding Müller-Thurgau grape.

The region grows few other varieties. Only the white, densely-berried Bacchus variety with its faint muscat note occupies any amount of the entire vineyard area worth mentioning— about one-tenth—although Riesling and Rieslaner can produce excellent results, especially in the field of *edelsüß* wines. However, in contrast to almost all other winemaking areas of Germany, Franconia make no wines with any residual sugar worth mentioning. The majority of its products are dry, and the Franconians even use a special term to describe the flavor of their wines: if they have less than four grams of residual sugar they are called *Fränkisch trocken* (Franconian dry).

A good 95 percent of the vineyards of Franconia are planted with white grapes, but in

Escherndorf is a charming wine-growing village in an attractive area of country where the river Main describes a curve. It is well known for the Lump, its best vineyard.

The historic cellar with its barrels in the Bürgerspital in Würzburg.

and where, apart from a few undaunted viticulturalists, few people hope to make quality products. The situation is much more hopeful a few miles to the east, where a completely different viticultural landscape begins in the Steigerwald at Iphofen. Here the river no longer exerts any perceptible moderating influence, and but for the protection of the mountains to the east and north there could be little question of growing vines in this fundamentally bleak climate.

However, the major wine-growing areas of the Steigerwald at Iphofen include the world-famous Julius-Echter-Berg and Kalb vineyards, the nearby Rödelsee with the Küchenmeister

Left
Franconian wine with fish—a harmonious partnership of flavors.

Right
The cellarmasters still wear their traditional leather aprons for wine-tastings in the Hofkeller of Würzburg.

Drinking wine in comfort in the Juliusspital, Würzburg.

vineyard—the name means literally "kitchen-master," and one can only speculate on what it originally implied about the quality of its wines—the Schwanleite vineyard, and finally Castell, further to the northeast, with the Schlossberg. The vineyards at high altitude here produce excellent Riesling and Silvaner. The Franconian-bred Rieslaner and Kerner, Scheurebe, and burgundy varieties also do very well, sometimes producing outstanding *Beerenauslese* and *Trockenauslese* wines, as does the rare Huxelrebe grape.

The Heart of Red Wine

As the river Main continues its course northward from Kitzingen, it describes three huge loops; some of the most popular vineyards in Franconia stand on their banks. The leading vineyards of this *terroir* are the Escherndorfer Lump and Volkacher Ratsherr, to which the names of the Nordheimer Vögelein and the Dettelbacher Berg Rondell should perhaps be joined. Unfortunately, it must be said that the fame of the vineyards and the attractions of the picturesque towns and villages of the area are not always calculated to promote the quality of the wine. As elsewhere, meticulous care in vineyard and winery does not seem worth so much trouble when it is too easy to sell the wines which are the end product.

The last large viticultural center of the region is situated on the southern flank of the "square of the Main," between Bürgstadt in the west and Kreuzwertheim and Marktheidenfeld in the east, and some of the estates here also own vineyards in the neighboring Bavarian Tauber valley. This is the center of Franconian red winemaking. Bürgstadt, with its Centgrafenberg vineyard and its red sandstone soil, has always been known for this specialty, but the red burgundies produced in Erlenbach near Marktheidenfeld are also good, while classic Riesling and Silvaner varieties predominate again in the neighboring Homburger Kallmuth vineyard. This is one of the most remarkable hillside vineyards on shelly limestone soil in Franconia, and is even under a preservation order.

Silvaner and Domina Grapes

Hardly any other viticultural area of Germany grows as many different vine varieties as Franconia, and nowhere else is the policy of choosing which varieties to grow so strongly marked by tradition and progress alike. Today it seems scarcely credible that the vineyards of Franconia were once dominated by Silvaner, which until just three decades ago was grown even more widely than Riesling, not only here but in all the German wine-growing regions. At the time Franconia and Silvaner were synonymous with the indigenous spicy, full-bodied wines made between Würzburg and Iphofen, Volkach and Wertheim.

However, with the spread of such new crosses as Müller-Thurgau, Scheurebe, and Rieslaner, which guaranteed the winemaker musts with more weight, or greater ease of picking, or both, the Silvaner grape increasingly fell out of favor: it is not entirely straightforward to grow and does not produce above average yields. Now grown in just under one-fifth of the entire viticultural area of Franconia, it occupies only about half the space given over to Müller-Thurgau.

Nonetheless, the genuine white wines of Franconia can still be found. The best grapes for them grow on the Escherndorfer Lump, the Randersackerer Pfülben, the Iphofener Julius-Echter-Berg, the Homberger Kallmuth, and the Würzburger Stein, and have survived all the modernization of vineyard and winery work, still tasting as good as they did years ago: spicy, nutty, earthy, and smoky, powerful on the palate, and even with a faint suggestion of honey when the grapes are fully ripe.

Not so with Domina, the fashionable variety among the new crosses. When the local viticulturalists of Kitzingen took the name of the variety too literally and put the picture of a genuine dominatrix on their labels—along with her accessories and attributes—there was great indignation among puritans in the wine world. In fact the wines made from Domina deserve more respect, for this variety has given evidence of Franconia's potential to produce red wines even more convincing than Spätburgunder.

The powerful and intensely colored Domina, a Portugieser–Spätburgunder cross, has aromas of jam and berries, is very suitable for *barrique* aging, and with its astringent, rustic tannins benefits by being left to mature for some time. It is even possible to make *Beerenauslese* and *Trockenbeerenauslese* wines from Domina.

Going up the Main from Würzburg, the principal estates of this wine-growing district own large plots of land in the best of the Randersacker vineyards, for instance the Pfülben, Teufelskeller, Marsberg, and Sonnenstuhl.

The Bocksbeutel

In the 18th century there was concern among German viticulturalists over the increasing number of fakes then beginning to undermine the wine trade on an extensive scale. The famous Würzburger Stein in particular attracted the attention of the makers of adulterated wines, and at the time there was no wine law to ban imitations. To the Würzburgers of the time, the only proven method of giving some protection to the genuine Stein wines was a special bottle, sending the consumer an unmistakable signal that he had the genuine article before him and had not purchased a forgery. In 1718 the shape of bottle

known as the BOCKSBEUTEL was developed at the Bürgerspital in Würzburg, then the largest vineyard estate of the region. It is a squat flask, convex in front but flat when seen from the side, and it has become been the emblem of Franconian wine in general. Today the shape is protected by law, and elsewhere in Germany it can be used only for wines from the Ortenau area in Baden. Products from other countries can be marketed in bottles resembling the Bocksbeutel only when there is a proven tradition of that shape in their areas of origin, for instance in parts of Portugal.

Select Producers in Franconia

Waldemar Braun*—*****
Nordheim
15 acres (6 ha); 55,000 bottles • Wines include: Müller-Thurgau, Silvaner, Bacchus, Riesling, Chardonnay from vineyards in Nordheim (Vögelein, Kreuzberg) and Sommerach (Katzenkopf), barrique-matured wines
Braun ferments and matures his wines exclusively in steel tanks and new *barriques*. His reds are among the best in Franconia. Braun also sometimes produces such exotic wines as his Weißherbst *Beerenauslese* of 1994, made from Domina grapes.

Bürgerspital zum Heiligen Geist**—****
Würzburg
297 acres (120 ha); 900,000 bottles • Wines include: Riesling, Silvaner, Weißburgunder, Grauburgunder from vineyards in Würzburg (→Stein, →Stein/Harfe, Abtsleite, Pfaffenberg) Randersacker (→Teufelskeller, →Pfülben, Marsberg), Michelau, and Gössenheim
The smallest of the famous "Three Hospitals" owns not only the largest plot in the famous Stein vineyard of Würzburg, but also the heart of that vineyard, known as the Stein/Harfe. The range of varieties embraces the entire spectrum of Franconian wine growing, although with a rather disproportionate amount of white varieties.

Fürstlich Castell'sches Domänenamt***
Castell
161 acres (65 ha); 400,000 bottles • Wines include: Silvaner, Müller-Thurgau, Rieslander, Riesling from vineyards in Castell (→Schlossberg, etc.), Sommer-Linie
This traditional estate on the slopes of the Steigerwald works its vineyards according to the guidelines of the Naturland association. Its Riesling and Rieslaner wines, its red wine *cuvée*, and its *edelsüß* wines are good to very good, although occasionally it does not seem to exploit its potential to the full.

Rudolf Fürst****
Bürgstadt
30 acres (12 ha); 100,000 bottles • Wines include: Spätburgunder, Frühburgunder, Riesling, Weißburgunder from the Bürgstadter →Centgrafenberg and Großheubacher Bischofsberg vineyards, →Parzival
Paul Fürst is the only winegrower of any great reputation in Bürgstadt, and has long been regarded

as one of the few German red wine specialists; his red wines grown on the weathered red sandstone soil of the Centgrafenberg are of top quality. His Frühburgunder wine is his great pride, but his Rieslings and occasional *edelsüß* wines are also outstanding.

Glaser—Himmelstoss***
Nordheim
25 acres (10 ha); 100,000 bottles • Wines include: Müller-Thurgau, Silvaner, Bacchus, Kerner, Scheurebe, Spätburgunder from vineyards in Nordheim, Sommerach, Obervolkach, Dettelbach, and Neusses
The estate is in two parts, and the wines are made in the Nordheim buildings constructed in 1979. Modern winery techniques—the estate management, formerly opposed to *barrique*-maturing, has recently adopted the practice of aging the wines in small wooden casks—and moderate yields give straightforward, clean whites, and excellent sweet wines.

Martin Göbel***
Randersacker
15 acres (6 ha); 55,000 bottles • Wines include: Silvaner, Müller-Thurgau, Riesling, Domina, Spätburgunder from vineyards in Randersacker (→Teufelskeller, →Pfülben, Sonnenstuhl, Marsberg, Lämmerberg)
Hubert Göbel cultivates 14 different grape varieties on his 15 acres (6 ha) of vineyards. This committed winemaker turns them into wines which are notable even in Randersacker, a place which is spoilt for choice. Especially good are his Rieslaner, Silvaner, and Domina wines, and his *edelsüß* growths.

Juliusspital***—****
Würzburg
402 acres (163 ha); 1,000,000 bottles • Wines include: Silvaner, Müller-Thurgau, Riesling from many of the best vineyards in Franconia (→Würzburger Stein, Iphöfen Julius-Echter-Berg, Randersackerer Pfülben, Escherndorfer Lump, Rödelseer Küchenmeister)
The largest of the "Three Hospitals" of Würzburg is accommodated in the historic buildings of the Juliusspital, which can boast a spectacular cellar 273 yards (250 m) long containing wooden casks, as well as the oldest pharmacy still operating in Germany. Its wines have long placed it among the leading viticultural groups of Franconia.

FÜRST LÖWENSTEIN***–****
KREUZWERTHEIM

74 acres (30 ha); 150,000 bottles • Wines include:
Silvaner, Müller-Thurgau, Riesling, Spätburgunder
from vineyards in Franconia (→Homburger Kallmuth,
→ Richolzheimer Satzenberg) and Baden (in the Tauber
valley), Fürst von Löwenstein in Hallgarten/Rheingau
This family estate owns the Homburger Kallmuth, one
of the best vineyards on shelly limestone soil in
Franconia. Recently the estate has also resumed
operating its Rheingau vineyards.

JOHANN RUCK****–*****
IPHOFEN

27 acres (11 ha); 120,000 bottles • Wines include:
Silvaner, Müller-Thurgau, Riesling, from vineyards
in Iphöfen (→Julius-Echter-Berg, Kalb, Kronsberg,
Burgweg) and Rödelsee →Schwanleite,
(Küchenmeister), →Dolce Vita, Johann Rosé
Ruck has built a modern winemaking and storage
plant behind the firm's traditional façade on the historic
market place of Iphofen. The wines are among the best
made in Franconia, with unusual size and elegance in
the *Auslese* wines made from Huxelrebe and Rivaner
in particular. Also to be recommended are wines made
from the Kerner, Silvaner, Riesling, and Grauburgunder
varieties.

EGON SCHÄFFER****
ESCHERNDORF

17 acres (7 ha); 30,000 bottles • Wines include:
Silvaner, Müller-Thurgau, Riesling from vineyards in
Escherndorf (Fürstenberg, Lump) and Untereisenheim
(Sonnenberg)
Almost all of Egon Schäffer's few wines are sold to
private customers—apart from certain quantities
exported to Japan. The Silvaners in particular are
well above average in quality.

RICHARD SCHMITT***–****
RANDERSACKER

27 acres (11 ha); 90,000 bottles • Wines include: Müller-
Thurgau, Silvaner, Kerner, Riesling from vineyards in
Randersacker (→Pfülben, →Teufelskeller, Sonnenstuhl)
Using gentle methods, Bernhard Schmitt gets the very
best out of the grapes in his top vineyards. His method
of working produces excellent results in his Riesling,
Silvaner, and Rieslaner wines, as well as those made
from the less usual Traminer.

TROCKENE SCHMITTS**–****
RANDERSACKER

31 acres (12.5 ha); 110,000 bottles • Wines include:
Müller-Thurgau, Silvaner, Kerner, Riesling from
vineyards in Randersacker (→Pfülben, Sonnenstuhl)
and Würzburg (Abtsleite), table wines
Bruno Schmitt is the successor to his legendary uncle
Robert, and makes mainly dry wines very much in the
spirit of the founder of the business. His dry *Spätlese*
and *Auslese* wines made from Riesling and Silvaner in
particular are among the best in the region.

SCHMITT'S KINDER****
RANDERSACKER

32 acres (13 ha); 100,000 bottles • Wines: Silvaner,
Müller-Thurgau, Bacchus, Riesling, etc., from vineyards
in Randersacker (→Pfülben, Sonnenstuhl, Marsberg)
Since 1984 Karl Martin Schmitt has been working on
old agricultural land outside the gates of Randersacker.
Only the force of gravity will take the grapes here from
one stage of vinification to the next, and it obviously
does the wines good. Schmitt even succeeds in making
excellent wines from the Müller-Thurgau variety,
otherwise known as Rivaner, and in good years his
Dominas are among the best red wines of the region.

SCHLOSS SOMMERHAUSEN***
SOMMERHAUSEN

49.5 acres (20 ha); 200,000 bottles • Wines: a full range
of varieties from vineyards in Iphofen, Radnersacker,
Eibelstadt, and Sommerhausen
The Steinmann family was better known in the past for
its viticultural college than for the estate belonging to it.
Today, the firm makes wine from an impressive number
of different varieties, some as exotic as Blaue Silvaner,
and bottles fine sweet wines made from the Scheurebe
variety.

ZUR SCHWANE—JOSEF PFAFF****
VOLKACH

44 acres (18 ha); 150,000 bottles • Wines include:
Silvaner, Riesling, Müller-Thurgau from vineyards in
Volkach (→Ratsherr), Obereisenheim, Escherndorf
(→Lump), Iphofen, and Wipfeld, →Schwanen
Modern vinification and modern marketing are very
much part of the operation here, despite the wealth of
tradition in the background. The firm's strength lies in
soft Silvaners, delicate Rieslings, and rounded, well-
balanced wines made from Spätburgunder grapes.

STAATLICHER HOFKELLER***–****
WÜRZBURG

297 acres (120 ha); 1,000,000 bottles • Wines include:
Riesling, Silvaner, Müller-Thurgau, Rieslaner,
Spätburgunder from many leading Franconian
vineyards (the Würzburger Stein, Randersackerer
Pfülben, Hörsteiner Abtsberg), →Tiepolo
Although the Residence Palace in Würzburg was
never devoted to the care of the sick, the Staatlicher
Hofkeller here is counted as one of the "Three
Hospitals." The estate saw its fortunes revive rapidly
in the 1990s under the management of Rowald
Hepp, who brought it back into the top group
of Franconian winegrowers. The best results are
obtained from the Würzburg and Randersacker
vineyards. Hepp had made some truly spectacular
wines here before moving on to the Rheingau estate
of Schloss Vollrads in 1999.

JOSEF STÖRRLEIN***–****
RANDERSACKER

18.5 acres (7.5 ha); 75,000 bottles • Wines: Müller-
Thurgau, Silvaner, Riesling, and red varieties from
vineyards in Randersacker (Sonnenstuhl, Marsberg)
Armin Störrlein makes 80 percent of his wines dry, and
does not make *edelsüß Auslese* wines, so that the very
best grapes of his grapes can go into the basic range.
Even better than his good Rieslings are the red wines
he makes from Domina and the usually disregarded
Schwarzriesling.

HANS WIRSCHING***–****
IPHOFEN

155 acres (63 ha); 500,000 bottles • Wines include:
Silvaner, Riesling, Müller-Thurgau, Scheurebe from
vineyards in Iphofen (→Julius-Echter-Berg, Kronsberg,
Kalb) and Rödelsee (→Küchenmeister), Sommerweine,
barrique-matured wines
This estate is one of the biggest and best in Germany,
and produces mainly Franconian dry wines, which are
carefully matured, keep their freshness for a long time,
and are capable of aging well.

ZEHNTHOF—THEO LUCKERT***–****
SULZFELD

30 acres (12 ha); 70,000 bottles • Wines include:
Silvaner, Müller-Thurgau, Weißburgunder, Riesling
from vineyards in Sulzfeld, barrique-matured wines
The only estate in Sulzfeld which can claim to be really
well known. Luckert's wines are dense on the palate,
with a clean tone.

The Three Hospitals

There are really only two "hospitals," the Juliusspital and the Bürgerspital, but traditionally the number three has a good ring to it, and the Staatlicher Hofkeller belonging to the Residential Palace in Würzburg was associated with the two real hospitals, so that it is now customary to speak of the "Three Hospitals."

The Bürgerspital is the oldest of these three institutions, which have connections with other aspects of the daily life of Würzburg besides winemaking, although their vineyards are indisputably their most famous property. Founded in 1319 as a civic institution for the care of the aged, it acquired its first vineyards a few years later, and today has been growing wine for almost 700 years. The secular counterpart to the episcopal Juliusspital, which still fulfils its original medical purpose, it works some 415 acres (168 ha) of vineyards, and is thus the fourth largest winemaking estate in Germany. Its famous cellar containing old wooden casks is also the largest of its kind that remains fully functional.

The reputation of the Bürgerspital is founded chiefly on the Würzburger Stein/Harfe, a *clos* in the center of the famous Stein vineyard itself, solely owned by the foundation and recognized as one of the best vineyards in Franconia. The Rieslings from the other parts of the Bürgerspital's plots in the Stein and its Randersacker vineyards are also of outstanding quality, and remarkable white wines are even made from the burgundy varieties from the Würzburger Pfaffenberg, which cannot really be considered one of the very top vineyards of the region.

Tastings in the Department of Anatomy

While the strength of the Bürgerspital tends to lie in its sweet *Auslese* wines, it is with the dry or medium-dry *Qualität* and *Kabinett* wines that the neighboring Juliusspital excels. Fully integrated into the medical hospital which gives the institution its name, and which was completed in 1576 under Julius Echter of Mespelbrunn, after whom the famous Iphofen vineyard is named, the estate also enjoys the luxury of its historic setting, a jewel among the architectural monuments of Würzburg. The princely building itself—with its 820-foot (250-m) cellar containing wooden barrels, the beautiful Rococo pharmacy (the oldest still in use in Germany), and the old Department of Anatomy, a hall now used for wine tastings and other events—make a visit to it an unforgettable experience.

With its top vineyards in the Stein, Pfülben, Julius-Echter-Berg, Küchenmeister, and Lump, the Juliusspital can boast the most consistent production of high-quality wines of all three hospitals in recent decades. One might be tempted to regard the estate as a pure Silvaner specialist, but that would not do justice to its outstanding Rieslings, and even Müller-Thurgau and the rarely grown Traminer can sometimes be matured into very fine wines here.

The two hospital vineyard estates are complemented by the Staatlicher Hofkeller, located in the Würzburg Residence Palace. We need hardly say that all the plots owned by this institution

 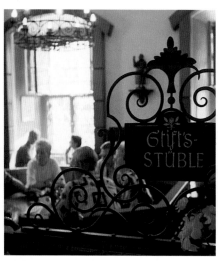 

The three great Würzburg winemaking institutions: the oldest is the Bürgerspital, founded in 1319.

The Juliusspital was founded in 1576 and established itself as the second largest wine-growing estate in Germany.

The Staatlicher Hofkeller, part of the residence palace of Würzburg, can hold its own with the other two in the extent of the area its owns and the quality of the wines produced.

too, the largest wine-growing estate in Franconia with its 370 acre (150 ha) of vineyards, are in the best situations of the region, and that it is not unusual for grapes to be brought here after picking from 60 miles (100 km) away, to be vinified and matured in the great building in the city center of Würzburg.

Although the wines of the Hofkeller were neglected too long, that situation was to change fundamentally in the middle of the 1990s. Rowald Hepp, who had previously been managing the state-owned vineyards in the Rheingau, helped the estate to make a new start, and the results showed within a very short time. Modernized fermentation procedures and a new stock of barrels created the right conditions for vinifying the grapes from the estate's top vineyards to bring out their potential for quality effectively.

Würzburg, a winemaking metropolis combining a taste for good living with remarkable cultural achievements. The inner city is bounded to the north by the famous Stein vineyard.

The largest German vineyards and wineries

The largest businesses in the German wine economy are found not among the wine-growing estate owners, but in the big wineries and the cooperatives. However, it is difficult to find reliable statistics on the amounts produced. Among the cooperatives the leaders in the field are the Badischer Winzerkeller in Breisach (ca. 30 million bottles) and the Weingärtner-Zentralgenossenschaft of Möglingen in Württemberg (ca. 27 million bottles), closely followed by the Moselland-Kellerei in the Mosel region and the Franconian Gebietswinzergenossenschaft.

However, by comparison with the amounts produced in the large privately-owned wineries, these are very modest figures. The output of the Reh-Gruppe alone is estimated at 200 to 300 million bottles. The volume produced by the Sekt winery of Henkell-Söhnlein in Wiesbaden is similar (including Deinhard Sekts and products other than wines, the firm produces 234 million bottles a year). The winery of Peter Mertes in Bernkastel-Kues is usually estimated to produce 100 to 200 million bottles, Peter Herres in Trier markets about 70 million, and a group of other firms (Zimmermann-Graeff, Langguth Erben, Pieroth, Rheinberg-Edeka, Kupferberg-Racke, A. Oster, and Rotkäppchen) produce somewhere between 40 and 60 million bottles a year.

Assessment of wine-growing estates must take into account the total area under vines and the quantities of wines bottled. The list is headed by the state-owned estates of Hesse,

An enormous and impressive cellar for storing casks lies below the historic princely building of the Juliusspital.

cultivating just under 470 acres (190 ha) of vineyards and producing 1,250,000 bottles a year. Next come Franconian firms: the Juliusspital (415 acres/168 ha; 1,000,000 bottles), the Staatlicher Hofkeller (297 acres/120 ha; 1,000,000 bottles), and finally the Bürgerspital (297 acres/120 ha; 900,000 bottles).

The largest family estates are in the Pfalz: Heinrich Vollmer in Ellerstadt (311 acres/126 ha; 1,500,000 bottles), and Dr. Bürklin-Wolf in Wachenheim (297 acres/120 ha; 670,000 bottles). Only two other estates in Germany (if we leave aside the very heterogeneous property of the state of Baden-Württemberg) have more than 247 acres (100 ha) of vines under cultiva-

tion (for the fate of Schloss Wackerbarth in Saxony, with its 300 acres/121 ha of vineyards, seems to be sealed). They are the Margrave of Baden's estates of Salem and Schloss Staufenberg (279 acres/113 ha; 900,000 bottles), and the episcopal estates in Trier (254 acres/103 ha; 850,000 bottles).

In all 14 major vineyard estates cultivate between 125 and 247 acres (50 and 100 ha): Schloss Reinhartshausen (Rheingau; 214 acres/87 ha; 550,000 bottles), the three Wegeler estates (Rheingau/Mosel/Pfalz; 175 acres/71 ha; 750,000 bottles), the two properties of the Menger-Krug family (Pfalz/Rheinhessen; 185 acres/75 ha; 500,000 bottles), the Fürstlich Castell'sche Domänenamt (Franconia; 173 acres/70 ha; 600,000 bottles), Paul Anheuser (Nahe; 160 acres/65 ha; 500,000 bottles), Hans Wirsching (Franconia; 170 acres/69 ha; 500,000 bottles), the state-owned Meersburg estate (Baden; 153 acres/62 ha; 450,000 bottles; however, the state-owned vineyards in Baden-Württemberg in all cultivate over 247 acres/100 ha), Reichsgraf von Kesselstatt (Mosel; 150 acres/61 ha; 400,000 bottles), the state-owned Kloster Pforta estate (Saale·Unstrut; 148 acres/60 ha; 300,000 bottles), Fritz Allendorf (Rheingau; 131 acres/53 ha; 700,000 bottles), the Rappenhof-Muth estate (Rheinhessen; 128 acres/52 ha; 300,000 bottles) and the Reichsrat von Buhl estate in Deidesheim (Pfalz; 124 acres/50 ha; 400,000 bottles).

SAALE-UNSTRUT AND SAXONY

Vines were already being grown in the Middle Ages in almost the whole of what are now the eastern states of the Federal Republic of Germany. At that time the vineyards extended to the Baltic coast, covering an area many times greater than they do today. The inexorable decline began during the Thirty Years' War, to which countless vineyards fell victim, and those spared by the mercenaries fell victim to phylloxera at the end of the 19th century. Viticulture in the east of the country today, therefore, is confined to small parcels of land in the states of Saxony and Saxony-Anhalt, more precisely in the valleys of the rivers Elbe, Saale, and Unstrut. Naturally, vines continued to be grown here during the years of the German Democratic Republic, but even more than in the west growers concentrated almost exclusively on the amounts that could be harvested, and the quality of the products took second place in the planned economy.

Although the move toward quality began in the west in the 1980s and 1990s, the comparable process in the east set in only very hesitantly after the reunification of the country. The economic difficulties facing most firms in former East Germany, and the absence of any structure of small and medium-sized wine-growing businesses, made the production of top quality wines almost impossible. In addition, viticulture in the

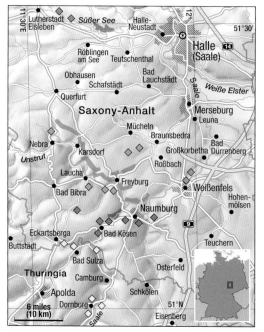

new wine-growing regions of Saale-Unstrut and Saxony had to be organized in difficult climatic conditions. These are the two most northerly wine-growing areas in Germany, and come up against the viticultural limit beyond which grapes cannot be expected to ripen regularly. As in Franconia and Württemberg, the climate is continental in nature, but here the mild summers are counteracted by even colder winters.

Freyburg on the Unstrut is the center of viticulture in the Saale-Unstrut region: there is little rain, the sun ripens the grapes well, and yields are naturally low.

Saale-Unstrut

In the Saale and Unstrut region, vines have been cultivated for a thousand years. There are documentary records as early as 1066 showing that grapes were grown by the Cistercian monks of Kloster Pforta, today a state-owned vineyard. The grapes which ripen on the slopes rising above the banks of the rivers Saale, Unstrut, and Ilm and the lake called the Süßer See are mainly white. The most important factor in the favorable climate here is the slight amount of rainfall, only 19.5 inches (50 cm) a year.

The principal grape grown in the 20 single vineyards of the area is a rather insipid Müller-Thurgau, which accounts for a quarter of the bottles of wine here, although its stocks have been considerably reduced since 1991. Silvaner and Weißburgunder each occupy one-tenth of the cultivated vineyards, followed by Kerner, Riesling, and Traminer. Of the 235 acres (95 ha) stocked with black grape varieties, Portugieser is grown on 99 acres (40 ha). At the time of writing experiments are in progress with Zweigelt, Lemberger, and the cross known as Regent. The entire cultivated vineyard area is 1,284 acres (520 ha), of which 864 acres (350 ha) are part of the viticulturalists' association of Freyburg, comprising some 500 part-time winegrowers and six agrarian cooperatives. Of the 18 vineyard estates, ten are run by full-time viticulturalists.

Uwe Lützkendorf and his father Udo make wines which give evidence of the potential of former East German wine-growing areas, particularly in wines from the Pfortenser Köppelberg, a vineyard laid out by the monks of the monastery of Pforta as early as 1154.

Saxony

The smallest wine-growing area of Germany, in the valley of the Elbe between Dresden and Meissen is also dominated by Müller-Thurgau. However, through the extension of the cultivated vineyard area from about 495 acres (200 ha) in the days of the D.D.R. to over 865 acres (350 ha) at present, with the support of a reunification bonus from the European Union,

The Rotkäppchen Fairy Tale

Children are not aware of this, but their parents have suspected it for a long time and several tests have revealed that generations of parents, grandparents, brothers, and sisters have unwittingly spread a false fact. What the innocent granddaughter was given to take to her sick grandmother in the woods by her mother, was not any old wine, it was Sekt! And the name of a Sekt brand has become so linked to the fairytale character, that experts still believe the sparkling wine was named after this girl.

That may be a fairytale in itself, but what is true is the one success of the former East Germany's winemaking industry: the story of Rotkäppchen (Little Red Riding Hood) Sekt. The winery in Freyburg on the Unstrut, founded in 1856 by the families of Kloss and Foerster, had sold the brand name which they had used since 1894 (and which originally referred to the red foil caps on the bottles), to a Rüdesheim winery making Sekt founded in

The Rotkäppchenhaus—the scene of Sekt production.

1919. After reunification the name was sold back to Freyburg, and this incident marked the start of an astonishing rise in the firm's fortunes.

Although the Sekt market was in crisis, the winery, which had scarcely managed to sell 15 million bottles before reunification, was very soon marketing 25 million, then after the purchase of Mumm 92 million bottles a year, and Rotkäppchen became one of the most widely drunk German sparkling wines. Of course the base wines to make such quantities do not now come from East German vineyards, but are bought in from various European countries, as is the case with almost all German Sekt wineries. This success has been made possible by modern winemaking technology and exemplary management, and Rotkäppchen could perhaps motivate other viticulturalists and cellarmasters on the Elbe, Saale, and Unstrut to provide wine growing in the east with a future.

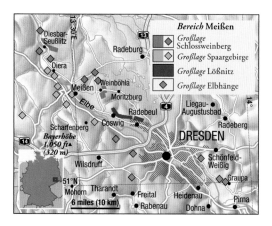

Riesling and above all Weißburgunder have increased in importance.

Viticulture can look back over a long history on the Elbe as well, as a document of 1161 shows. The vineyards of Pillnitz and Wachwitz where the kings of Saxony grew their own wine are famous. The vines here were planted on particularly steep slopes so that they would be less exposed to the frequent spring frosts. In many years, however, extremely low temperatures reduce yields considerably. But the small amount of rainfall, on average amounting to no more than 19.5 inches (50 cm) a year, also restricts the yield. Where harvests yield no more than 320 to 530 gallons per acre (30 to 50 hl/ha) the environmental conditions in themselves will ensure that the best wines have

This winemaker's sign in Roßbach near Naumburg illustrates the pride in viticulture felt in the East.

Opposite
One of the finest opera houses in the world—the Dresden Opera House, built by Gottfried Semper.

a good concentration, despite their northern origins.

By far the largest number of vineyards, most of them only a few acres in extent, are cultivated today by part-time winegrowers who have organized themselves into the Meissen viticultural cooperative. The grapes picked in about half the vineyard area of the state as a whole are processed by this cooperative.

The state of Saxony originally ran the estate of Schloss Wackerbarth near Radebeul, which once comprised 299 acres (121 ha), with considerable success, and its Sekt was famous. However, as most of the vineyards were only leased, and many of them have now had to be returned to their owners, the future of this estate is uncertain, since its economic infrastructure has been withdrawn. On the other hand, Schloss Proschwitz, under Georg Prinz zur Lippe, is seeing a period of revival, and viticulturalists such as Vincenz Richter, Walter Schuh, and Klaus Zimmerling, who cultivates his vines by biological methods, are already offering wines of good quality.

The wine-growing area of Saxony, like the Saale-Unstrut area, is a favorite tourist attraction. Neither region has any problem in disposing of its wines at the moment, and both sell most of their products at high prices to day trippers. The rest strike a regional note on the wine lists of East German hotels and restaurants.

SELECT PRODUCERS IN SAALE-UNSTRUT AND SAXONY

GÜNTER BORN***
HÖHNSTEDT
21 acres (8.5 ha); 30,000 bottles • Wines include Müller-Thurgau, Weißburgunder, Silvaner, Riesling from vineyards in Höhnstedt
The Born family have built up a good reputation for the dry, straightforward white wines made on their estate, one of the first new estates founded in former East Germany after reunification.

LANDESWEINGUT KLOSTER PFORTA***
BAD KÖSEN
148 acres (60 ha); 300,000 bottles • Wines include: Müller-Thurgau, Weißburgunder, Silvaner, Riesling from vineyards in Bad Kösen, Schulpforte and Goseck
Originally founded by the Prussian state, Kloster Pforta passed into the hands of the state of Saxe-Anhalt after reunification. Today it makes mainly dry, light wines, although most of them are matured only in stainless steel tanks.

LEHMANN***
SEUSSLITZ
5 acres (2 ha); 20,000 bottles • Wines include: Müller-Thurgau, Riesling, Weißburgunder, Traminer, Spätburgunder from the Heinrichsberg vineyard in Seusslitz
Joachim Lehmann was endeavoring to produce grapes of high quality even in the days of the D.D.R. His wines,

which he has made and marketed himself since reunification, are fresh, with a clean note. Most of his output is sold through the estate wine shop and the inn also attached to the winery.

LÜTZKENDORF***
BAD KÖSEN
27 acres (11 ha); 55,000 bottles • Wines include: Silvaner, Riesling, Weißburgunder, Portugieser, Spätburgunder from vineyards in Karsdorf and Freyburg
Uwe Lützkendorf is now one of the best (and best-known) winegrowers in the east German viticultural regions. With his father Udo, formerly the cellarmaster of a state-owned winery, he has made the estate one of the most important in the Saale-Unstrut region.

SCHLOSS PROSCHWITZ—PRINZ ZUR LIPPE***
MEISSEN
78 acres (31.5 ha); 95,000 bottles • Wines include: Müller-Thurgau, Grauburgunder, Riesling, Scheurebe, Spätburgunder
As the first V.D.P. member from former East Germany, the castle estate of Georg Prinz zur Lippe deservedly enjoys a high reputation. The Prince courageously built it up after being one of the first to have his former family property restored. His wines have a clean note, with a good bouquet, and are almost all dry.

ULRICH SAUTTER, ECKHARD SUPP, PATRICK FIÉVEZ, ANTHONY ROSE

WESTERN EUROPE

Switzerland

Switzerland is world-famous for banks, watches, and cheese, but beyond its borders you rarely hear about Swiss wines. You might just be offered a few rather mediocre examples in the course of some quaint promotional event where fondue, cowbells, and alpenhorns will probably be featured as the essence of Swiss lifestyle.

And yet there are grapes aplenty thriving on the 37,000 acres (15,000 ha) of Swiss vineyards, and the wines produced from them speak for themselves. Not a few achieve international standards of quality these days, and yet they hardly receive the recognition they deserve. Even in areas close to the Swiss border the people are more likely to have tried New Zealand or Chilean wine than to know anything about the products of one of the oldest wine-growing regions in the heart of Europe.

A Complex History

Switzerland is a federated state which unites people and regions of varying different cultural backgrounds. There are four official languages:

This vineyard with its vineyard hut in Beringen, not far from Rheinfelden in the northwestern corner of Switzerland, belongs to the widely scattered region of eastern Switzerland, stretching from Basel to Liechtenstein.

German, French, Italian, and Rhaeto-Romanic. The history of wine growing in Switzerland reflects this diversity of cultural influences and historical developments. There are probably several ways by which wine cultivation reached the lands of present-day Switzerland:

• From Massilia (Marseille), the ancient Greek entryway for central European wine growing,

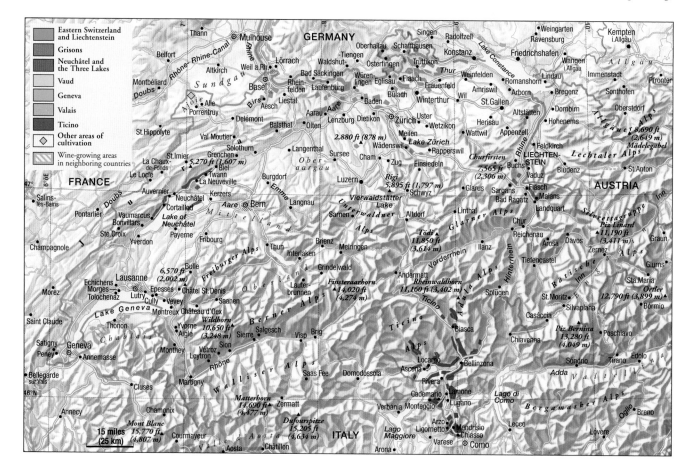

up the Rhône valley to Lac Léman (Lake Geneva) and into the lower Valais;

• From the Rhône through the Doubs valley to the Burgundian Gate and from there by one route to the Swiss side of the Jura mountains, by another to the upper Rhine and Lake Constance;

• From Lombardy to Ticino and from there via the San Bernadino pass to the Rhine valley in Grisons;

• From the Aosta valley via the Great Saint Bernard pass to Valais.

The history of Swiss wine growing is generally traced back to the Roman era, although their records of viticulture are poor. In the 6th century, more numerous traces were left by the Burgundian monks. They not only founded the monastery of St. Maurice (near Aigle), but also brought to Lake Geneva the first rudimentary wine legislation. In the following years, viticulture grew along with the monasteries. There is evidence of wine growing at Mont Vully in the early 7th century. In the mid-8th century there is proof of vineyards in the Rhine valley in Chur and along Lake Constance. Finally, by the high Middle Ages, no part of the country was without vines. They even grew in the Bernese Oberland. However, despite the quantities produced, the domestic consumption of wine could only be satisfied, right up until the 16th century, by additional imports from Alsace and the southern Baden region.

The 19th century brought about events that were to develop into a crisis by the early 20th. When the states of Baden, Württemberg, and Bavaria joined the German Customs Union in 1835, the eastern Swiss border cantons lost a market which had been significant. Things were made worse by the opening of the Gotthard tunnel in 1882, which allowed for cheap imports from Italy. Between 1874 and 1907, the vine parasite PHYLLOXERA devastated all the major Swiss wine growing areas. The situation was further complicated by creeping outbreaks of mildew. The vast extent of cultivated vines, some 84,920 acres (34,380 ha) in 1884, had fallen to almost a third, 30,769 acres (12,457 ha), by 1932. Not until the 1970s did increasing internal demand boost the wine-growing economy once more. At present, Switzerland's 13 gallons (49 l) per person demonstrates a fairly high annual wine consumption. The wine-growing area today amounts to almost 37,000 acres (15,000 ha), with a relatively stable trend.

GEOLOGY, TOPOGRAPHY, AND CLIMATE

Almost everywhere in Switzerland, the Alps and their foothills set the conditions for wine growing. Close to the Alps there are TERROIRS which were created as the mountains pushed upwards. In the Pre-Alpine valleys and along the lakes, most vines grow on glacial moraines. The climate conditions also depend on the direct proximity of the mountains. The Alpine foothills vary the height and steepness of the vineyards, the mountain ranges themselves

Swiss wine economy in figures				
Areas of cultivation (in 2002)				
Eastern Switzerland	6,397 acres	(2,590 ha)	72% red	28% white
Ticino and Misox	2,548 acres	(1,031 ha)	94% red	6% white
Romandie	28,144 acres	(11,390 ha)	46% red	54% white
Total area	37,089 acres	(15,011 ha)	53% red	47% white

The most important wine cantons Areas of cultivation in acres (ha)		The most important varieties Areas of cultivation in acres (ha)		
			1998	2001
Valais	12,911 (5,225)	Chasselas	13,336 (5,399)	12,970 (5,249)
Vaud	9,577 (3,876)	Pinot Noir	11,320 (4,583)	11,389 (4,609)
Geneva	3,294 (1,333)	Gamay	4,925 (1,994)	4,687 (1,897)
Ticino	2,471 (1,000)	Merlot	2,038 (825)	2,165 (876)
Zürich	1,542 (624)	Müller-Thurgau	1,712 (693)	1,611 (652)
Neuchâtel	1,497 (606)	Chardonnay	541 (219)	625 (253)
Schaffhausen	1,189 (481)	Sylvaner	516 (209)	516 (209)
Grisons	1,021 (413)	Pinot Gris	358 (145)	410 (166)
Aargau	981 (397)	Gamaret	121 (49)	272 (110)
Thurgau	657 (266)	Red Hybrids	111 (45)	250 (101)

View over Epesses on Lake Geneva with its impressive vineyards.

The Maison Carré in Auvernier, by Lake of Neuchâtel, has some old tools and equipment as well as some equally traditional wines.

constantly provide rain shadow and often serve as wind tunnels.

The unique topographical and climatic qualities of the different regions of the country each have their own very special strengths. On the southern side of the Alps, the sun shines at an annual average of well over 2,000 hours. However, excellent red wines can be found both in dry Valais, with 16 inches (41 cm) of rain a year, and in Ticino, which, with its 71 inches (180 cm), is definitely heavy on precipitation. On the northern side of the Alps, Grisons, with its 1,700 hours of sunshine, brings a comparable expressiveness to a glassful. Here, the southern föhn wind, so picturesquely known as the "grape boiler," blows along the Rhine valley. Other areas, such as Neuchâtel at the foot of the Jura, profit from the marked differences in temperature between day and night. Steep slopes in the vicinity of water are also considered indicators of quality in Swiss viticulture.

QUESTIONABLE CLASSIFICATION

Switzerland has no national wine legislation. The Foodstuffs Act of 1909 regulates the basics as regards the protection of consumer health. Wine-growing policy is mainly a matter for the 26 cantons. The Federal Resolution on Viticulture passed in 1992 is an attempt to define a set of uniform conditions. However, the situation has not fundamentally changed. On the one hand, the generously set upper yield limits (for instance, 25 gallons per 120 square yards (96 l/100 sq. m) for top-quality red wine), formulated in this paper, make the avowed declaration to promote quality wines appear questionable. On the other hand, the definitions of the *appellations contrôlées* sketched out in the above-mentioned resolution are, in the end, still going to be a matter for the cantons. In the 1990s, several cantons did decide on A.O.C. statutes. However, the intended reliability of quality often suffered from political concessions, so much so that in the late 1990s some winegrowers of high standing in cantons with an A.O.C. statute preferred to label their wines as *vin de table* in protest.

Due to the unalterable topographical conditions and climatic risks, Swiss wine growing has to live with high operating costs, which means that the country's wines are only represented internation-

ally in the top price groups. Switzerland as a wine country therefore faces the task of justifying the fact that most of its large vineyards are stocked with Chasselas—a grape that is seen in other countries as being more of a dessert fruit. Such justification would be made easier with a less half-hearted official quality policy. Indeed, in the best situations in the Romandie, the Chasselas grape achieves a high degree of expressive power, depending on the *terroir*. In addition, Switzerland also

produces remarkable red wines. The Merlot of Ticino has already developed into a variety of international caliber.

But Switzerland is also, not least, a treasure house of Pinot Noir. Almost unnoticed by the international wine markets, there are Pinot Noir wines ripening in some regions of Switzerland which seem to approach considerably closer than many others in the world to the Burgundian ideal.

The Château d'Aigle in the midst of the vineyards of the Chablais by Lake Geneva, where the Chasselas grape rules. Pinot Noir, in particular, also gets interesting results here.

Eastern Switzerland

Eastern Switzerland, with 6,175 acres (2,500 ha), is a small and scattered wine-growing region. The largest single area is the Hallauer Berg in the canton of Schaffhausen, covering about 370 acres (150 ha). The geographical term "eastern Switzerland" is used simply to separate it from French-speaking "western Switzerland." The vineyards of central and northwestern Switzerland are thus also counted as part of the "east." A unifying factor for the eastern Swiss regions is the predominance of two varieties of grape. The dominant red wines are almost exclusively prepared from Pinot Noir. For the whites, the leading grape is Müller-Thurgau. More sophisticated white wines are, however, produced from Pinot Blanc and Pinot Gris, while the best vineyards also use Chardonnay and Sauvignon Blanc. There are, in addition, two interesting native white varieties: in Grisons, the oily and at the same time robust Completer, and the fine, delicate Räuschling along Lake Zürich.

Small-scale vineyards in this area tend to encourage the opinion that its wines are provincial. In the 1970s, some producers further fostered this assumption with bland *vins de pays*. Nowadays, however, many family concerns cultivate a great variety of local and regional varieties of wine to a high standard. The present active generation of growers and producers is highly qualified, has a broad viticultural horizon, and can avail itself, even in smaller companies, of high quality (and expensive) winery techniques. It is the Pinot Noir wines, from grapes of strongly limited yields, must-fermented and aged in wooden casks, which are raising the reputation here.

In the föhn wind tunnel of the Grisons Rhine valley, the Pinot Noir is heavy and well structured. These wines, because of their expressive power, are made as if for oak-cask aging. The southern autumn wind also favors the remaining vineyards along the Walensee and in the inner Swiss cantons. In both Appenzell half-cantons, vines grow up to an altitude of 2,130 feet (650 m). The northern Rhine valley in Sankt Gallen forms a stylistic and climatic bridge to the viticulture of Lake Constance.

As the Swiss shore of Lake Constance faces north, the best wines here are grown on moraine hills behind the lake, along the Thur and Seebach valleys, and at Stein am Rhein, where the Rhine leaves the lake. The local Pinots possess a fruity, robust quality. The Pinots Noirs from the low rainfall Klettgau region are as a rule softer and fleshier. This also applies to the area known as the "Zürich Wine Country" (Zürcher Weinland) which lies between Schaffhausen and Winterthur. Its lush Pinots Noirs are drunk, almost without exception, in the capital. Along the upper Rhine and its tributaries are the lowest lying wine-growing areas of Switzerland: 1,165 feet (355 m) above sea level at Eglisau, 1,116 feet (340 m) at Döttingen in Aargau, 1,024 feet (312 m) at Aesch in the Birs valley in the Basel-Land canton.

In the canton of Aargau, the regional style of the Pinot is decided mainly by winery techniques. The almost universally practiced blending of fermented MUST and warmed must parts allows for balanced, accessible wines. In the Limmat valley and along Lake Zürich you can find robust, firmly structured Pinots Noirs. It is from this area, from the village of Stäfa, that one of the Pinot Noir clones originates. The Mariafeld clone is widely distributed throughout eastern Switzerland and southern Germany.

Since 1998 Schaffhausen, Aargau, and Zurich have passed A.O.C. statutes. However, it is not yet apparent that this has had more than a symbolic significance. In addition, just as in Germany, the quality labels *Spätlese* and *Auslese* have always been used. However, in contrast to their use in that country, their use here is down solely to the judgment of the producer.

This picture is deceptive. The old traditions are today being kept up by the younger, excellently trained generation of winemakers.

Bad Osterfingen****
Osterfingen (Schaffhausen)

acres (2 ha); bought-in grapes; 20,000 bottles • Wines: Pinot Blanc; Pinot, → Pinot Badreben (Barrique)

From their gravelly, poor soil the Meyer family produce very stylish gastronomic wines. The vineyard also has a restaurant.

Georg Fromm****
Malans (Graubünden)

10 acres (4 ha); 35,000 bottles • Wines: Riesling x Sylvaner, → Pinot Gris; → Pinot Noir Barrique, Merlot

Georg Fromm produces delicate but highly flavored wines. He has another vineyard in Blenheim, New Zealand, which has an international reputation.

Martha and Daniel Gantenbein****
Fläsch (Graubünden)

12.4 acres (5 ha); 25,000 bottles • Wines: Chardonnay, Riesling, Pinot Blanc, → sweet wines; Pinot

The Gantenbeins have great versatility. Their Chardonnay has long been the peak of excellence in Switzerland, and the Pinot, aged in oak casks, is an independent interpretation of this variety, repeatedly discussed by wine critics. With the help of the föhn, here known as the "grape boiler," they have had repeated success in producing excellent sweet wines.

Hofkellerei des Fürsten von Liechtenstein**—***
Vaduz

5 acres (2 ha); 10,000 bottles • Wines: Chardonnay; Pinot

Recommended rarities from the enclosed vineyard of the Prince of Liechtenstein in the historic royal residence city of Vaduz. The princely house also owns vineyards in the Weinviertel area of Lower Austria, and it is from here that interesting tasting trips to the former Liechtenstein-owned estates in the Czech Republic are organized. The wines from the Austrian estates—the Merlot especially worthy of mention—are in part marketed via Vaduz.

Toni Kilchsperger***
Flaach (Zürich)

9.4 acres (3.8 ha); 30,000 bottles • Wines: Riesling x Sylvaner, Räuschling, Chardonnay, Gewürztraminer, → Worrenberger Räuschling; Pinot

Very good white wines, clear as a bell. The complexity of the fruit is quite consciously placed in the foreground. A finely adjusted oak cask note in the Worrenberger Chardonnay.

Urs Pircher****
Eglisau (Zürich)

13 acres (5.3 ha); 25,000 bottles • Wines include Riesling x Sylvaner, Pinot Gris, → Räuschling, Gewürztraminer; Pinot, Eglisauer Stadtberg Blauburgunder Barrique

Spectacularly situated vineyards along the upper Rhine, and wines that are just as exceptional: delicacy and body in great harmony.

Rebgut Bächi***
Truttikon (Zürich)

17.3 acres (7 ha); 50,000 bottles • Wines include: Riesling x Sylvaner, Pinot Blanc, Gewürztraminer; Pinot vineyard wines, Truttiker Pinot Spätlese Barrique

The Zahner family's Pinot Noir wines are immensely loaded with tannin and strongly woody—and they ripen to a warmth of Burgundy quality.

Schlossgut Bachtobel****
Weinfelden (Thurgau)

13.6 acres (5.5 ha); 30,000 bottles • Wines: Riesling x Sylvaner, Pinot Gris, Weißriesling, Sauvignon Blanc; Pinot, Claret, → Blauburgunder Auslese No. 2

A perfectionist pace-setting concern with three different stylish varieties of Pinot Noir. Hans Ulrich Kesselring now also produces white specialties and the Bordeaux Cuvée Claret.

Hermann Schwarzenbach***
Meilen (Zürich)

16 acres (6.5 ha); 40,000 bottles • Wines include: Sauvignon, Chardonnay, Sémillon, Pinot Gris, Completer, Freisamer, → Meilener Riesling x Sylvaner Spätlese, Meilener Seehalden Räuschling; Pinot, Lemberger

If a vintner exists who can convince you that Müller-Thurgau is a high-quality grape, Hermann Schwarzenbach would be the man. The many different trial varieties are worthy of recognition.

Gian Battista von Tscharner***—****
Reichenau (Graubünden)

15 acres (6 ha); 30,000 bottles • Wines include: Pinot Gris, Maienfelder Brisig, Sauvignon, → Jeninser Completer, Gewürztraminer, Traminer; Pinot, Z'blau Wunder us Jenins, Jeninser Blauburgunder Mariafeld, Churer Blauburgunder Barrique, Cuvée Anna

Gian Battista von Tscharner grows Blauburgunder grapes, from which he produces strong tannin reds which require aging; he also produces high profiled white wines.

Weinbau Scadena****
Malans (Graubünden)

11 acres (4.5 ha); 20,000 bottles • Wines: Kerner, Completer, Aligoté; Pinot, → Blauburgunder Spätlese Barrique

Peter Wegelin's Pinots, aged in oak casks, have a fullness and intensity that make them stand out even among the best wines of Grisons.

Weingut Baumann***—****
Oberhallau (Schaffhausen)

18 acres (7.3 ha); 50,000 bottles • Wines: Müller-Thurgau, Chardonnay; Pinot, 'Blauburgunder Trockenbeere

This family concern ages typical—in the best sense of the word—Klettgau wines. There is also a high-quality range of oak-aged wines.

Zum Ochsen***—****
Malans (Graubünden)

12 acres (4.7 ha); bought-in grapes; 50,000 bottles • Wines include: → Chardonnay Malanser Selvenen, Pinot Gris and Blanc, Sauvignon, Completer; Cabernet, Pinot Malanser Spiger, Pi-Ca-Do

After a long period of training in the Domaine de la Romanée-Conti, Thomas Donatsch began aging wines in oak in 1974. Today he is an almost unrivaled expert in this method.

Zum Sternen***
Würenlingen (Aargau)

17.3 acres (7 ha); 60,000 bottles • Wines include: Pinot Gris, Sauvignon, Gewürztraminer; Pinot, Malbec, Garanoir, Regent, → Blauburgunder Barrique

The Meier family is famous for their impressively finely structured Blauburgunder, and for fat, Australian-style Sauvignon.

THE THREE LAKES

The Lake of Neuchâtel, the Lake of Biel and the Lake of Morat make a picturesque scene, forming a bridge between Alemannic influences and the lifestyle of the Romandie—and this also applies to wine growing. Pinot Noir and Chasselas, representatives of the eastern and western Swiss wine-growing areas, each have about a half share of the area devoted to vines. The wines here have an excellent reputation among initiates.

NEUCHÂTEL

The main wine-growing area, some 1,500 acres (606 ha), is on the Neuchâtel side of the Three Lakes area. It begins at the canton border near Vaumarcus, continuing above the northwestern shore, through the Béroche region toward Bevaix, Cortaillod, and Auvernier. Neuchâtel and its outlying areas also have magnificent vineyards, and wine growing continues through Cressier, through the region famous as Entre-deux-Lacs, to Le Landeron, on the Lake of Biel. White wine production is dominated by Chasselas, and the Neuchâtel Blanc is a light wine, extremely refreshing due to the residual carbon dioxide from fermentation. Pinot Noir is the only variety of red wine in the canton. Even the clones, with their reduced yield, are prescribed—Pinot Noir de Cortaillod supplies a delicate and yet well-structured Burgundy, and is given character by the climate and limy soil at the foot of the Jura. The Pinots aged in oak are particularly reminiscent of the Côtes de Nuits wines. Another specialty is the salmon-pink Œil de Perdrix—a fruity elegant rosé produced

Auvernier is one of the most important wine-growing communities by the Lake of Neuchâtel. Here, a number of mainly smaller estates mostly produce the slightly sparkling Neuchâtel Blanc.

Above the wine village of Auvernier, the vineyards spread up the slopes and offer a far-reaching view over Lake Neuchâtel.

without botrytis. Perdrix Blanche is a Pinot Noir vinified as a white. Chardonnay and Pinot Gris are also grown in small quantities.

Neuchâtel's discipline in matters of yield is proverbial in Switzerland. On an average taken over many years, the Pinot Noir produces just over 13 gallons per 120 square yards (just under 50 l/100 sq. m). For Chasselas, an upper limit of 2.2 pounds per 1.2 square yards (1 kg/sq. m) was set as early as 1990. An A.O.C. regulation finally came into existence in Neuchâtel in 1993.

LAKE OF BIEL/BERN

The wine-growing villages of the Bern region along the Lake of Biel lie tightly and idyllically enclosed by their vineyards. Chasselas wines here are less tangy and somewhat fuller. The Pinot Noir is brighter and lighter, but some of the Bern producers clearly demonstrate its potential with their more extract-rich wines. La Neuveville, Twann, Schernelz, Schafis, and Ligerz are the most important wine-growing communities. Erlach, on the southwest shore of the Lake of Biel, at the foot of the Jolimont mountain, also grows vines. The entire wine-growing area along the Lake of Biel covers 603 acres (244 ha). There has been an A.O.C. statute since 1996. The Bern canton also has about 35 acres (14 ha) of vines growing near Spiez and Oberhofen along the Lake of Thun.

LAKE OF MORAT/FRIBOURG

Mont Vully is a moraine hill with a slope falling steeply down toward the Lake of Morat. The microclimate on the terraces running across the slope above the villages of Môtier, Praz, and Sugiez is exceptionally favorable and produces some spectacular wines. The Chasselas is mostly soft and smooth, but the Pinot Noir, in contrast, is robust and dense. Specialties such as Traminer, Pinot Gris, and the Freisamer—cultivated here as Freiburger (Sylvaner x Ruländer)—are as a rule substantial and aromatic. As the entire CRU, including the part in Vaud, covers a mere 296 acres (120 ha), it has remained a connoisseur's secret.

In the Broye area on the southern shore of the Lake of Neuchâtel, just under 30 acres (12 ha) of vines grow and Fribourg canton has had an A.O.C. system since 1997.

Select Producers of the Three Lakes Region

Neuchâtel

Cave du Prieuré**–***
Cormondrèche
111 acres (45 ha); 400,000 bottles • Wines: Chasselas: Perdrix Blanche; Œil de Perdrix; Pinot; →Domaine de Chambleau
Reliable cooperative with vineyards in Auvernier, Colombier and Cormondrèche.

Cave de la Ville de Neuchâtel***
Neuchâtel
30 acres (12 ha); 100,000 bottles • Wines: Chasselas (Neuchâtel Blanc, →Cru de Champrevèyres), Pinot Gris, Chardonnay; Perdrix Blanche, Œil de Perdrix; Pinot
Very reliable production; the fruity, rounded Pinot Noir wines are very good.

Château d'Auvernier***–****
Auvernier
86.5 acres (35 ha); some bought-in grapes; 400,000 bottles • Wines: Chasselas (Neuchâtel Blanc, also Non Filtré) Pinot Gris, Chardonnay; Œil de Perdrix; Pinot Noir
A historic estate with wines to match; recommended standard quality →Château d'Auvernier Blanc, exemplary →Œil de Perdrix.

Encavage de la Maison Carré***
Auvernier
24 acres (9.5 ha); 50,000 bottles • Wines: Chasselas (Auvernier), Pinot Gris, Chardonnay; Perdrix Blanche, Œil de Perdrix; Pinot (Auvernier)
Wines produced with traditional equipment, sometimes rough, sometimes inspired; the →Pinot Noir is packed with body and oaky flavor.

Alain Gerber***–****
Hauterive
17 acres (7 ha); 50,000 bottles • Wines: Chasselas (Neuchâtel Blanc, also Non Filtré), Pinot Gris, Chardonnay; Perdrix Blanche, Œil de Perdrix; Pinot
Particularly good are the extract-rich Pinot →Cru de Hauterive and the delicate, intense →Chardonnay made from old vines.

Grillette—Domaine de Cressier****
Boudry
49 acres (20 ha); 160,000 bottles • Wines: Chasselas, →Chardonnay "Premier," →Sauvignon Blanc "Premier," Viognier, →Pinot Noir "Graf Zeppelin"
Impressive, dynamic developments in quality in recent years: the wines have strength and elegance. Despite their international style, they don't deny their Neuchâtel origins.

Olivier Lavanchy***
Neuchâtel-la-Courdre
17 acres (7 ha); 50,000 bottles • Wines: Chasselas (Neuchâtel Blanc, Cru de Champrevèyres), Pinot Gris, Chardonnay; Perdrix Blanche, Œil de Perdrix; Pinot
Very clean, elegant wines and stylishly barrel-aged →Pinot.

A. Porret & Fils***–****
Cortaillod
17 acres (7 ha); 60,000 bottles • Wines: Chasselas (Cortaillod, also Non Filtré) Pinot Gris, Chardonnay; Œil de Perdrix; Pinot
A concern with traditions, its own Pinot clone and a well-maturing prestige product, →Pinot Noir Cortaillod; in good years, there is a *non égrappé* version which is pressed.

Vins Keller**–***
Vaumarcus
32 acres (13 ha); some bought-in grapes; 100,000 bottles • Wines include: Chasselas "Cru des Terrasses" (Neuchâtel Blanc), Pinot Noir, Œil de Perdrix, Perdrix Blanche, Pinot Gris, Riesling x Sylvaner, Chardonnay, Garanoir, Gamaret
A well introduced traditional range and innovative wines, for instance the sweet →Lune de Mielle (Pinot Gris) and →Claire de Lune (Riesling x Sylvaner).

Bern

Erich Andrey***
Ligerz
27 acres (11 ha); 70,000 bottles • Wines include: Chasselas, Sylvaner, Pinot Gris, Chardonnay; Œil de Perdrix, Pinot
Smooth, popular vineyard Chasselas, occasionally rounded off by a remnant of sugar; Schafiser, →Les Planches and →Marnin display mineral notes.

Johanniterkeller Martin Hubacher***
Twann
12 acres (5 ha); 60,000 bottles • Wines include: Chasselas, Pinot Gris, Chardonnay, Sauvignon; Gamaret, Sankt Laurent, Pinot
Modern wines; clean, Twann Chasselas, typical, lightly wood-influenced →Chardonnay.

Rebgut der Stadt Bern**–***
La Neuveville
52 acres (21 ha); 180,000 bottles • Wines: Chasselas, Pinot Gris, Pinot
Traditional, rarely exceptional but always reliable.

Heinz Teutsch****
Schafis
7.5 acres (3 ha); bought-in grapes; 70,000 bottles • Wines: Chasselas, Pinot Gris, Chardonnay, Blanc de Noirs; Œil de Perdrix; Pinot
A very reliable operation; even standard product →Gutedel Schlössliwy is of extraordinary stature.

Fribourg

Château de Praz***
Praz
30 acres (12 ha); 75,000 bottles • Wines: Chasselas, →Pinot Gris, Pinot Blanc, Freiburger, →Traminer, Riesling x Sylvaner, Œil de Perdrix, Pinot
Powerful, mineral wines, which can be laid down.

Albert Derron***
Môtier
12 acres (5 ha); bought-in grapes; 100,000 bottles • Wines include: Chasselas (Vully Bataille de Morat), Freiburger, Pinot Gris; Œil de Perdrix; Gamay, Pinot (Vully)
The Freiburger (new variety of Freisamer), a Sylvaner and Ruländer cross, is outstanding.

Jura

Centre Ajoie***
Alle
12 acres (5 ha); 25,000 bottles • Wines: Riesling x Sylvaner, Pinot Gris; Garanoir, Pinot
In 1986 and 1992 a cooperative planted two areas of vineyards. This rare wine is seen in Switzerland as a symbol of a democratic federalism, and as such is held in high honor.

The Cantons of Vaud and Geneva

Vaud

Some of the finest wine-growing areas are by Lake Geneva, in the Vaud canton. These vineyards cover a total area of 9,577 acres (3,876 ha), and are divided into the three areas of La Côte, Lavaux, and Chablais. Chasselas is the dominant vine. Red wines comprise only a fifth of the total, and of these the typical Vaud red wine of the A.O.C. Salvagnin is a blend of Gamay and Pinot Noir. An A.O.C. system has defined terms for regions and communities since 1995, though it seems dubious to allow not only the two historic crus of the Lavaux area, Dézaley and Calamin, to call themselves GRAND CRU, but all wines bear the description "*Château*," "*Clos*," *Abbaye*," or "*Domaine*."

On the moraine soil of La Côte, producers prepared to take a risk have raised the reputation of the previously average wines.

The steep vine-growing slopes of the Lavaux, especially the great vineyards of Dézaley and Calamin above Lake Geneva, are spectacular. Dézaley, inherited from Cistercian monks, produces fat, full-bodied Chasselas wines from granite soil. Its only problem is that its smoothness can overpower due to a lack of acidity. The particularly exquisite wine of the neighboring *cru* of Calamin is usually more classical. Wines of the surrounding communities also stand comparison. When the Alps arose, the tectonic displacement in the Lavaux region, exposed a great variety of geological strata. The diversity of the *terroirs* created is fascinating. Full, fruity red wines are also produced in the Lavaux in tiny quantities, usually *cuvées*, mostly from Pinot Noir. In Cully, there is also an interesting native red variety, Plant Robez.

The name Chablais is not a sad attempt at plagiarism; it derives from *caput laci*, head of the lake. The center of this region, known for Chasselas wines of great refinement, is Aigle, with its castle and museum of viticulture. Here, at the entrance to the Rhône valley, the northern föhn of Valais can already be felt. Typical for the region are shingly alluvial land and vineyards on landslip rubble. The soils also contain plenty of lime (Yvorne), magnesium (Aigle) or gypsum (Ollon and Bex). As far as body is concerned, the wines of Chablais lie between those of La Côte and Lavaux. Apart from Chasselas, Chablais also produces small quantities of red wine and some Pinot Gris.

The winemaker Dubois from Cully has plenty of reason to feel happy: around Lake Geneva, there are very interesting *terroirs* for vines, and there's no need to worry about demand.

The medieval castle of Vufflens le Château, to the west of Lausanne, lies in the midst of the best vineyard sites. From the tower, you can see Lake Geneva.

Geneva

At 3,347 acres (1,355 ha), the Geneva canton is the third largest wine-growing canton. Only a small part of this area lies by the lake. The majority of production is in the Mandement, between the bank of the Rhône and the Swiss border. Here lies Satigny, at 1,205 acres (488 ha), the largest wine-growing community. The soils are rich in lime, clay and gravel.

Wine growing in the Geneva canton is highly mechanized, even using pick-up loader harvesting. The lower level of climate risk also sets wine growing in Geneva apart from that in other regions. The range of varieties is still dominated by Chasselas, and nearly a third of the area is given over to Gamay. Until the early 1980s, mainly plain wines sold by the liter were produced from both. The cooperative "Vin Union," which produced four-fifths of the wines in Geneva, failed to take advantage of new developments, and its operations were bought up in 1999 by the ecological vintner Jean-Daniel Schlaepfer, to shut them down for good. Today there are innovative vintners who sell their own products, creating interesting wines. However, the A.O.C. laws passed in 1988, which allow exaggerated upper yield limits and the adding of sugar at up to 9 pounds per 26 gallons (4 kg/hl), do still damage the area's reputation.

Select Producers of the Vaud and Geneva Cantons

Chablais

Henri Badoux**
Aigle

124 acres (50 ha); some bought-in grapes; 750,000 bottles • Wines include: Petit Vignoble Yvorne, →Aigle Les Murailles, Ollon Domaine Grange Volet, St. Saphorin, Pinot, Gamay
The company is famous mainly for its "lizard wine." High yields and an unclear branding policy have damage the reliability of the quality in recent years. These recent weaknesses have given rise to speculation as to whether all the grapes for the Aigle Les Murailles do in fact come from steep slope sites.

Cave de la Commune de Yvorne****
Yvorne

15 acres (6 ha); 45,000 bottles • Wines: Chasselas, Pinot
Wines which combine strength and refinement; the Chasselas →Trechene, which comes from a single, very low yield vineyard covering just under two and a half acres, is outstanding, as is the fruity Clos de l'Abbayé.

Domaine de la Pierre Latine***
Yvorne

22 acres (9 ha); 65,000 bottles • Wines: Chasselas, Pinot Gris, Gamay, →Pinot, Merlot, Gamaret, Garanoir, Diolnoir
The mayor of Yvorne is also a successful winegrower, producing harmonious and aromatic wines.

La Côte

Henri Cruchon****
Echichens

25 acres (10 ha); some bought-in grapes, 250,000 bottles. • Wines include: Chasselas, Pinot Blanc, Altesse, Viognier, Roquentin, →Sauvignon Barrique, Gamay, Pinot, Cabernet, Cabernet Franc, Merlot, Gamaret, Garanoir, Syrah
Because of his high quality and innovative experiments with different varieties, Henri Cruchon has become a pioneering figure in La Côte.

Domaine la Colombe***
Féchy

25 acres (10 ha); 75,000 bottles • Wines: →Chasselas, Chardonnay, Pinot Noir, Gamaret, Garanoir
Raymond Paccot is attempting, with great success, to rehabilitate the typical Chasselas places of origin of Féchy and Mont-sur-Rolle. Biodynamic cultivation and extract-rich, aromatic, clear wines.

Domaine Rolaz-Hammel**−***
Rolle

114 acres (46 ha); 300,000 bottles • Wines: Chasselas, Chardonnay, Viognier, Merlot, Syrah, Cabernet Sauvignon, Cabernet Franc, Pinot Noir, Gamay
A subsidiary of the mass producers Hammel, the company is experimenting with mainly international varieties. Of most interest are the *cuvées* of the →Domaine de Crochet.

Uvavins**−****
Tolochenaz

1,112 acres (450 ha); 2,000,000 bottles • Wines: a diverse range of product lines; varieties include Chasselas, Charmont, Aligoté, Sauvignon, Pinot Gris, Doral, Kerner, Pinot, Diolnoir, Gamaret, Garanoir, Cabernet, Merlot

A very good cooperative, which is working together with a renowned chef (of the same name) to produce the outstanding →Collection "Le vin vivant" de Bernard Ravet.

Geneva

Domaine des Balisiers***
Peney

62 acres (25 ha); 160,000 bottles • Wines include: Chardonnay, Sauvignon, Pinot Blanc and Gris, Chasselas, Aligoté, Cabernet Comte de Peney, Gamay Dame Noir, Gamaret
Jean Daniel Schlaepfer and his companion Gérard Pillon are important forces in the Geneva wine industry. Their vines are cultivated using the lyre system; the local hero Chasselas is being pushed ever further into the background in favor of more noble varieties. Red wine is prepared with a long standing time for the mash and partial barrel aging. Organic vines have been cultivated since 1980, and 66 percent of production today is red.

Domaine le Grand Clos****
Satigny

17 acres (7 ha); 35,000 bottles • Wines include: Chasselas, Chardonnay, Pinot Blanc and Gris, Sauvignon, Petite Arvine, Muscat, Gewürztraminer, Viognier, Petit Manseng, Pinot, Gamay, Syrah, Cabernet, Cabernet Franc, Merlot
The unconventional Jean Michel Novelle is Geneva's star winegrower and attracts attention every year with spectacular different *cuvées*.

Lavaux

Louis Bovard**−****
Cully

42 acres (17 ha); some bought-in grapes; 250,000 bottles • Wines include: Dézaley La Medinette, Epesses Terre à Boire, →Calamin Cuvée Speciale Collection Louis-Philippe Bovard, St. Saphorin, Sauvignon, →Dézaley Rouge, St. Saphiron Rouge Cuvée Louis
This house, rich in traditions, also values innovations such as the recent remarkable →Chasselas-Chenin *assemblage* from St. Saphorin.

Jean-François Chevalley***−****
Treytorrens

13.6 acres (5.5 ha); 30,000 bottles • Wine: Chasselas
A traditional family operation which manages to make the mineral qualities of Chasselas stand out. Particularly recommended are the two *grands crus* Dézaley "Es Embleyres" and →Calamin "Réserve du Margis."

Vincent & Blaise Duboux****
Epesses

6.2 acres (2.5 ha); 15,000 bottles • Wines: Chasselas: →Calamin Cuvée du Père Vincent, →Dézaley Haut de Pierre, Marsanne, Chardonnay, Pinot, Cabernet Franc, Syrah, Merlot
Duboux is one of the most distinguished family concerns in Lavaux, with small-scale but perfectionist production. The *grand cru* location brings a complex aroma profile previously considered almost impossible and a great elegance to the Dézaley Marsanne and Chardonnay.

Luc Massy***
Epesses

25 acres (10 ha); some bought-in grapes; 150,000 bottles • Wines include: Epesses Clos du Box, Dézaley Chemin de Fer, Dézaley Marsens, St. Saphorin Sous les Roces, Sauvignon Blanc de Epesses
Modern, very clean and smooth wines from the vineyards at the heart of the Lavaux region.

Valais

With 12,911 acres (5,225 ha) of vines Valais is the largest of the Swiss wine-growing cantons. The valley rises from 1,509 feet (460 m) to 1,556 feet (630 m) over a distance of 31 miles (50 km). Some of the vineyards are even higher. There are gentle slopes where the vines spread out into the distance, and there are, as at Lake Geneva, spectacular terraces with vineyard walls many feet high. Despite the high altitude, the intense sunlight and the effects of the föhn create unique ripening conditions. As Valais is a very dry region, the winegrowers have to irrigate their vines in many places.

The region divides into three geographical zones. There is a small area in Lower Valais between Lake Geneva and the bend in the Rhône at Martigny. The heartland of Valais wine growing is spread out along the south-facing right-hand bank of the Rhône from Martigny to Leuk. This almost-enclosed wine-growing area has many different types of soil. In Fully and Martigny, the ground is poor in lime. In Leytron and Chamoson, the vines are grown on cones of volcanic debris. There are slate-based vineyards in the Sion area. As far as Salgesch and Leuk, the soils are poor in clay and rich in lime. Upper Valais is famous for the Visperterminen vineyard, which rises to a height of 3,609 feet (1,100 m). The oxidative "Glacier Wine," aged in the SOLERA manner (as with FINO sherry), is not from this area but from Val d'Anniviers near Sierre.

Visperterminen, in the Upper Valais, holds the altitude record for wine growing on the continent of Europe. The wine terraces rise to 3,610 feet (1,100 m), but the south-facing aspect and the warm föhn winds provide enough ripeness.

Vineyards in Sion— extremely steep and stony.

For many centuries wine growing in Valais satisfied only the canton's own requirements. Not until after the Second World War did commercialization produce yields that enabled wines to pass beyond the region's borders. The boom led to ill-advised speculation and excessive yields. Many vines were planted on the "wrong" bank of the Rhône, where there are no south-facing slopes for the vineyards. In the 1970s and 1980s, the Valais wine industry was in danger of losing its way in mass production.

Today, 50 different varieties of wine are cultivated in Valais. Some 22,000 owners share the wine-growing areas. However, over the past ten years Valais has succeeded in fixing and further refining its identity. The A.O.C. regulation of 1993, while establishing a few grand crus, has helped to achieve this. But even more important were the efforts of small- and medium-scale winegrowers, which have in turn influenced the cooperatives and wholesalers.

In the case of Fendant, the traditionally rather broad white Chasselas wine of Valais, biological ACID conversion (see page 125) is now no longer an irrefutable dogma. More and more, Fendant is bringing honor to its name by displaying the firm consistency of the flesh of the Chasselas clone in question, an indication of depth of AROMA and structure. The standard red wine, Dôle, produced from Pinot Noir and Gamay, and recently also from up to 20 percent of other varieties, was once a feeble imitation of the Bourgogne Passe-Tout-Grains. It has remained a juicy, easy-going wine, even though it could have gained in refinement—and has made room for alternative reds alongside it, such as the single-variety aged Pinot Noir. One specialty is the baroque Johannisberg, here a Sylvaner rather than a Riesling. The Malvoisie (Pinot Gris) is available in medium dry to sweet and fruity (mi-flétri or flétri) versions. Furthermore, highly successful wines are being created along the line of the Rhône, because varieties such as Marsanne (Ermitage) and Syrah thrive even on the banks of the northernmost section of the river.

In recent years the Valais winegrowers have rediscovered their great historic wealth of different native varieties. Humagne Rouge and Cornalin are striking, many-faceted red wine grapes, while Petite Arvine and Amigne are very, aromatic and also unusually independent white wine varieties.

Select Producers in Valais

Gérald Besse****
Martigny-Combes
36 acres (14.5 ha); 100,000 bottles • Wines include: Fendant, Malvoisie Flétri, Petite Arvine, Ermitage, Johannisberg, Pinot Noir, → Gamay, Dôle, Syrah
A leading producer of the new, elegant Fendant. The Gamay (three different pressings from three communities) and Syrah are also remarkable.

Charles Bonvin***
Sion
74 acres (30 ha); some bought-in grapes; 500,000 bottles • Wines include: Fendant, Petite Arvine, Amigne, Muscat, Ermitage, Pinot Blanc, → Dôle, Syrah Domaine Blûlefer, Humagne Rouge
Well-mannered, characteristic, accessible wines such as the very typical Dôle Clos du Château.

Oskar Chanton***
Visp
22 acres (9 ha); 60,000 bottles • Wines include: Gwäss, Lafnetscha, Himbertscha, Réze, Heida, Petite Arvine, Amigne, Humagne Blanche, Malvoisie, Hibou-Eyholzer Roter, Humagne Rouge, Cornalin
This pioneer of native varieties ages nearly 20 different single-variety wines.

Marie-Thérèse Chappaz****
Fully
17 acres (7 ha); 40,000 bottles • Wines include: Chasselas, Hermitage, Petite Arvine, Malvoisie, Rosé, Gamay, Dôle, Pinot, Cabernet, Cabernet Franc, Humagne Rouge
She is a specialist in sweet delicacies, but her other wines also display style and quality.

Domaine du Mont d'Or***
Pont-de-la-Morge
49 acres (20 ha); 200,000 bottles • Wines include: Riesling, Johannisberg, Fendant, → Petite Arvine "Sous l'Escalier," Malvoisie, Ermitage, Dôle, Syrah, Cornalin
This winery produces independent Rieslings, which sometimes take a little getting used to, from clayey calcareous schist soils; the acidity is low due to malolactic acid conversion.

Benoît Dorsaz***−****
Fully
12 acres (5 ha); 30,000 bottles • Wines include: Chasselas, Petite Arvine, Pinot, Humagne Rouge, Cornalin
Benoît Dorsaz is one of the younger producers who concentrate mainly on the local varieties of Valais, and use modern winemaking methods and stylish barrel maturing to give them polish.

Bon Père Germanier***−****
Vétroz
27 acres (11 ha); 300,000 bottles • Wines include: Fendant Les Terrasses, → Amigne, → Mitis, Petite Arvine, Syrah, → Grand Cru Balavaud: Pinot and Dôle
Reliable medium-sized operation. The wines from the *grand cru* sites are to be recommended, as are the exemplary sweet Amigne Mitis and the exquisite oak-aged Syrah Cayas.

Robert Gilliard S.A.**
Sion
99 acres (40 ha); some bought-in grapes; 1,000,000 bottles • Wines include: Fendant Les Murettes, Ermitage, Amigne, Muscat, Humagne Rouge, Syrah, Cornalin, Diolnoir, Dôle, Antares
Fendant "Les Murettes" is the best known Fendant outside Switzerland. Robert Gilliard produces very good quality wines.

Imesch Vins**−***
Sierre
30 acres (12 ha); some bought-in grapes; 360,000 bottles • Wines include: Soleil de Sierre: Fendant, Johannisberg, Œil de Perdix, Dôle, Pinot; Nobles Cépages: Chardonnay, Marsanne, → Petite Arvine, Marsanne, Pinot, Humagne Rouge, → Cornalin, Syrah
This *négociant* company is over 100 years old and is now managed with great commitment by Yvon Roduit. From 120 contracted winegrowers, it only orders grapes cultivated according to principles of integrated viticulture.

Didier Jorbis****−*****
Chamoson
6.2 acres (2.5 ha); 10,000 bottles • Wines: Chardonnay, Savagnin, Pinot, Cabernet Sauvignon, Cabernet Franc, → Syrah
Didier Joris carries out his small-scale production using the techniques of his craft, aims for appropriate oxidizing in aging, and produces concentrated, stylish, top quality wines such as the deep, intense Syrah "Près de Pierre," which need fear no international comparison.

Simon Maye et Fils***−****
St. Pierre-de-Clages
27 acres (11 ha); 75,000 bottles • Wines include: Fendant Trémazières, Chasselas Cuvée Fauconnier, Petite Arvine, Pinot, → Syrah, → Humagne Rouge, → Païen
Simon Maye is on the small side as a producer, but always has very high-quality wines with a high proportion of specialties such as Syrah de Chamoson Vieilles Vignes, Humagne Rouge or the barrel-fermented Païen, rounded with residual sweetness.

Denis Mercier****−*****
Sierre
14 acres (5.5 ha); 35,000 bottles • Wines: Fendant de Pradec, Johannisberg de Sierre, Pinot Blanc de Gouning, Petite Arvine de Pradec, Ermitage de Pradec, Dôle Blanche de Sierre, Pinot de Sierre, → Cornalin de Sierre, → Syrah de Pradec
Mercier is one of the most consistent, exceptionally perfectionist concerns in the region. The Syrah has cult status; the Cornalin's density and fineness are exemplary.

Provins Valais**−****
Sion
3,112 acres (1,260 ha); 11,000,000 bottles • Wines include: Capsule Dorée series; Specialités series; → Sélection du Grand Métral series: Petite Ariven, Amigne, Marsanne, Pinot Blanc; Syrah, Païen; → Cuvée du Maître de Chais series: Fendant St.-Léonard, Johannisberg Chamoson, Sauvignon, Humagne Blanche, Petite Arvine Fully, Grains de Malice; Pinot Ardon. Cabernet, Syrah, Cornalin, Humagne Rouge
The cooperative, with its 5,250 members, processes a quarter of all the Valais wine harvest, and two thirds of this—mostly of good quality—is bottled by the cooperative itself. The premium ranges Sélection du Grand Métral and Cuvée du Maître de Chais (barrel-aged wines) are even among the top quality products in the region.

Rouvinez Vins***−****
Sierre
109 acres (44 ha); some bought-in grapes; 1,200,000 bottles. Wines include: Fendant de Sierre, Dôle de Sierre, Muscat, Johannisberg, Ermitage, Malvoisie, Noble Contrée, Les Grains Nobles, → La Trémaille, Château Lichten Blanc and Rouge, Gamay, Pinot, → Le Tourmentin
This concern has taken on a leading role with ground-breaking *cuvée* wines. In the late 1990s the family took over the important dealer Cave Ostat.

TICINO

Ticino canton is considered the sun-terrace of Switzerland—and especially of its German-speaking regions. This opinion mixes truth and tourist legends into a long-lived clichée. Nowadays, Ticino is indeed one of the most interesting wine-growing regions in Switzerland. In the Merlot of Ticino, Switzerland has a wine which is a trend-setter even on an international scale.

In the mid-19th century, when mildew had destroyed the previously customary mixture of red European grapes such as Freisa and Barbera, the people of Ticino substituted more resistant American varieties. The wines from the hybrids may have been noticeably less tasty, but at least they ensured economic survival. The various trials with different varieties, carried out after 1900 by the canton's research station, must also be viewed with this aim in mind. The cultivation of Merlot has been encouraged since 1907. By the end of the Second World War, Merlot had made itself at home, although for a long time it was only used for unsophisticated, light-colored table wines. Hesitant attempts by larger wine dealers to expand their ranges with prestige wines largely met with no response. Only when a group of immigrants to Ticino from eastern Switzerland started to subscribe to the Bordeaux model in every detail did a movement toward improved quality begin, which has continued to the present day.

Geographically, Ticino is divided into the areas north and south of Monte Ceneri. In the Sopraceneri, on sandy alluvial soils in the Magadin plain and around Lake Locarno, light, fruity wines dominate. In the side valleys and

The vines grow on steep slopes high above Lake Lugano. Here, the preference is for planting Merlot of Ticino, which has acquired a good reputation thanks to a series of excellent winemakers.

The grapes cultivated all around the picturesque little town of Riva San Vitale are almost exclusively red varieties, as is the case everywhere in Ticino. In the Italian part of Switzerland, white wine is the outsider; white varieties cover barely a sixteenth of the area under vine.

along the Ticino river the soils are richer in granite and poorer in humus, and the local Merlot is correspondingly firmer and more substantial. The Misox—a mountain valley near Bellinzona, which politically speaking is part of Grisons—is also counted as part of the Sopraceneri. In the Sottoceneri, the rugged Malcantone produces robust, maturable wines, while the Mendrisiotto, with its moraine soils of lime and clay, is associated with particularly full-bodied, fiery wines. In the Lugano area, we find berry-rich, soft Merlots. Apart from Merlot, small quantities of Nostrani—rustic red wines made from a blend of mainly Piedmontese varieties—are produced all over Ticino. The Uva Americana, still cultivated here and there on trellises, is mainly used to make an aromatic grappa. The proportion of the total vine area of 2,471 acres (1,000 ha) given over to white varieties is at present a mere six percent.

A D.O.C. system has operated in Ticino since 1997. The upper yield limits of 2.2 pounds of grapes per 1.2 square yards (1 kg/sq. m), giving around 20 gallons per 120 square yards (75 l/100 sq. m) are so generously set that you can even find Merlots sold by the liter with D.O.C. On top of this, up to 10 percent of other wines (including foreign imports) may be blended with a D.O.C. wine. This regulation will, in 2005, come under pressure to be adjusted to the E.U. wine legislation. However, the Ticino D.O.C. statute has already resulted in a considerable loss of trust. Some growers (Kaufmann, Klausener, Stucki, Zündel) therefore prefer to market their wines as *vino da tavola della svizzera italiana*.

Select Producers in Ticino

Agriloro S.A.**−****
Arzo (Mendrisiotto)
18.5 acres (7.5 ha); 40,000 bottles • Wines:
Chardonnay, Pinot Gris, Pinot Blanc; Sottibosco,
→ Merlot Riserva
The domaine white wines are overloaded with wood
notes, but the velvety reds are impressive.

Cantina Kopp von der Crone***
Castel San Pietro
15 acres (6 ha); 19,000 bottles • Wines: Merlot
"Gorla," → Merlot "Balino"
Anna Barbara von der Crone, like many of her
colleagues, avoids the A.O.C., disputed because of their
lax regulations, and markets her intensive Merlot as
Vino di Tavola.

Chiodi S.A.***
Ascona (Locarnese)
7.4 acres (3 ha); some bought-in grapes; 20,000 bottles.
• Wines: Merlot: Preludio (Bianco); Ria (Rosato), Tre
Terre, → Rompidée
Rompidée, with its strong oak-aged character, has
acquired a good reputation in recent years.

Gialdi S.A.***
Mendrisio (Mendrisiotto)
Bought-in grapes from 148 acres (60 ha); 400,000
bottles • Wines: Riserva Gionico, Sassi Grossi
A new dealership with great ambitions. The excellently
structured barrel-aged Merlot → Sassi Grossi, partly
produced from air-dried grapes, lives up to them.

Daniel Huber****
Monteggio (Malcantone)
16.8 acres (6.8 ha); 25,000 bottles • Wines:
→ Montagna Magica Ronco di Persico, Fusto 4
Pioneering family concern, very consistent in quality.
The 1985 Ronco di Perrico gave the company the
breakthrough into the top echelons of Swiss wine
producers. Since then, wines have steadily been refined
in quality. The Montagna Magica, produced from five
varieties, can reliably be counted among the most
delicate, most complex and most dense of Ticino wines.

Adriano Kaufmann***−****
Beride (Malcantone)
9.4 acres (3.8 ha); 18,000 bottles • Wines: Sauvignon,
Vino de la Meditazione Sémillon; Pio della Rocca, Pio
del Sabato, Rubino
Adriano Kaufmann produces powerful red wines
based on Merlot and/or Cabernet. He also specializes
in high quality white wine production, in part using
cryoextraction (concentration by freezing) to
emphasize the fruit.

Erick Klausener****
Purasca (Malcantone)
7.4 acres (3 ha); 15,000 bottles • Wines: Merlot:
Trevano, → Gran Riserva di Trevano, Château de la
Musique, → Rosso di Sera VdT
Extreme must fermentation here probably produces the
most extract-rich Merlots in Ticino. It will be a long
time before any final judgment can be made on some
Gran Riserva di Trevano vintages.

Sergio Monti****
Cademario (Malcantone)
8.6 acres (3.5 ha); bought-in grapes from 2.5 acres
(1 ha); 20,000 bottles • Wines: Bianco; Rovere,
→ Malcantone Rosso dei Ronchi

Sergio Monte runs an exceedingly experimental estate
above Lake Lugano, and he makes extraordinarily
velvety, deeply fruit barrel-aged wines.

Mauro Ortelli***−****
Corteglia (Mendrisiotto)
8.6 acres (3.5 ha); 20,000 bottles • Wines: Bianco:
Corteglia, Novi dal Drunpa, I Trii Pin, Novi dal
Drunpa
Ortelli's high-quality wines go their very own Ticino
way. His extract-rich I Trii Pin, matured in steel tanks,
skillfully questions the often rather uncritical use of
barriques.

Werner Stucki****
Rivera (Monte Ceneri)
8.6 acres (3.5 ha); 15,000 bottles • Wines: Bianco:
Temenos, Conte di Luna, → Tracce di Sassi
Werner Stucki is devoted to small, hand-finished
production. His outstanding red wines—especially from
the Merlot variety—are distinguished by tannins that
gather softness and structure together, and at the same
time the perfect proportions of fruit and wood are
impressive. This innovative winegrower demonstrated
his international commitment with the reorganization
of La Brancaia in the Chianti Classico region.

Tamborini**−***
Lamone (Luganese)
124 acres (50 ha); 350,000 bottles • Wines: Merlot:
Collivo Rosso, Collivo Riserva, Riserva San Zeno,
Vegneto Comano, → Castello di Morcote
Old established dealers near Lugano. Over the last few
years quality has been somewhat variable. Many of the
red wines appear thin and over-extracted.

Tenuta Bally****
Breganzona (Luganese)
17 acres (7 ha); 35,000 bottles • Wines: Bianco,
Cresperino, Riserva Crespera, Topazio
Most interesting here are the robust red wine *cuvées*; the
premium ranges, matured in the barrel, have become
better and better in recent years.

Valsangiacomo**
Chiasso (Mendrisiotto)
62 acres (25 ha); some bought-in grapes; 500,000
bottles • Wines include: Bianco: Il Mattirolo, Il
Symposion, Ronco Grande; Il Forno di Pedrinate,
Merlot: L'Ariete, Piccolo, Riserva di Bacco, Cuvée
Speciale, Roncobello di Morbio Inferiore, Don
Giovanni, Rubro, Dioniso
Valsangiacomo's by now admittedly somewhat dusty
range of wines is due to be restructured.

Vinattiere***−****
Ligornetto (Mendrisiotto)
128 acres (52 ha); 200,000 bottles • Wines: Merlot:
Castello Luigi, Vinatierri, Ligornetto
Luigi Zanini produces modern, accessible Merlots with
body and strength. You could fairly easily mistake them
for wines from Chile or California.

Christian Zündel****
Beride (Malcantone)
10 acres (4 ha); 15,000 bottles • Wines: Bianco:
Velabona; Orizzonte, Terraferma
As well as his white Velabona, Christian Zündel from
Beride produces wood-flavored, firmly structured and
very elegant red wines, which are now among the most
sought-after in Switzerland.

AUSTRIA

In some respects Austria is a newcomer to top-quality European wine growing, although it is one of the oldest wine-drinking cultures in central Europe. The Celts may or may not have grown vines along the banks of the Danube, but they were certainly familiar with the value of grapes. Systematic viticulture, however, was introduced by Romans to the Pannonia Superior province.

Austrian wine legislation is similar in many ways to the German and, as in Germany, in AD 280 Roman emperor Probus authorized the garrisons of the imperial provinces to cultivate wines to provide their legions with the desired mood enhancer. A few centuries later, Charlemagne allowed for further development with his selection of the best vines—which he called "Frankish," differentiating them from the "Hunnish." He also saw to it that wine growing received a secure economic basis by granting the right of vintners to serve their own product.

The first written evidence of wine growing in Austria comes from Mautern in the Wachau. Here St. Severin carried out his charitable works in the 5th century. Krems, the famous viticultural town, is first mentioned in 995, and in the 11th, 12th and 13th centuries nearly all the major monasteries of the Austrian and Bavarian Pre-Alpine region had agricultural estates here, leading to the first blossoming of Austrian viticulture.

It was to be the late 18th century, however, before any more significant developments occurred. Emperor Joseph II, in 1784 confirmed the right of HEURIGER inns to serve wine, and brought new energy to the wine business. The

tradition endures and even today, in Vienna, vintners can sell their wines direct from the vat in their own inns (see page 546). Emperor Joseph invested great efforts in the quest for growing quality wine that could be taken seriously. These efforts culminated, in the mid-19th century, in the foundation of the viticultural college of Klosterneuburg—one of the first such institutions in the world.

Not even the vine parasite, phylloxera, could slow down this progress, which early in the 20th century led to the cultivation of several different varieties such as Zweigelt, Blauburger, Goldburger, or Jubiläumsrebe, and, in the 1930s, to the development of high trellis growing by Professor Lenz Moser. In this method of cultivation, the vine stem is forced to grow very tall, and with an equally tall wall of foliage it allows more efficient working in the vineyard and guarantees a high number of healthy grapes.

Rapid expansion of the wine-growing area followed after the Second World War, as did the

Kapfenstein is in the southeast of Styria, near the Slovenian and Hungarian borders.

division of the country into particular areas. This steady growth continued until 1985. However, as in other European wine-growing nations, Austria was then ruled by the ill-fated idea of untrammeled mass production. The deep crisis into which a small group of adulterators threw the Austrian wine industry in 1985 when they brought *Spätlese* wines with added glycol onto the market was a nasty shock. The Austrian wine industry reacted quickly and forcefully, implementing a new wine law, the strictest in the world of European wine. With firm determination, the best winegrowers in the Wachau, Burgenland, and Styria began producing wines that were soon to draw attention to themselves for wholly positive reasons.

Since that time, at least, Austrian wines have counted among the very top quality products in dry white wines and sweet wines. And since then, Austrian winegrowers have been and still are inundated with national and international awards for their Rieslings, Veltliner, *Beerenauslese* or Ausbrüche. The focus on these varieties is due to the climate conditions in this Alpine republic, which favor the noble white wines, as these owe their delicacy but also their capacity for aging to such conditions. It is well known that Riesling produces wines of the very top quality in the Wachau region, but even Grüner Veltliner, often underestimated as a mass yield vine, can rise above itself in good vineyards with controlled yield. However, the real surprises are the wines produced in Burgenland or Styria from varieties such as Bouvier, Muscatel, or Welschriesling, conjuring up lush exotic character or the most delicate fruit according to VINTAGE and vineyard.

Through careful work in the vineyards, the introduction of oak casks in cellaring, and rigid control of yield, the winegrowers of the Burgenland in particular have succeeded in recent years in producing red wines of an almost Mediterranean quality. The fruit and the elegance of the wines, together with perfect VINIFICATION, have aroused a good deal of interest, even internationally. Austrian viticulture has, so to speak, three red aces up its sleeve: the native Blaufränkisch and the St. Laurent, introduced from France via Germany, from which the third ace, Zweigelt, was cultivated in the 1920s and 1930s. Individually or blended, these varieties have such potential that neither Cabernet Sauvignon nor Spätburgunder—despite their suitability for some of the warmer vineyard sites in the country—have really had a chance to develop. These aces could become trump cards, given that world wine production looks set to become more and more uniform in future.

The Wine Regions of Austria

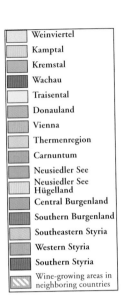

	Weinviertel
	Kamptal
	Kremstal
	Wachau
	Traisental
	Donauland
	Vienna
	Thermenregion
	Carnuntum
	Neusiedler See
	Neusiedler See Hügelland
	Central Burgenland
	Southern Burgenland
	Southeastern Styria
	Western Styria
	Southern Styria
	Wine-growing areas in neighboring countries

Austria's wine growing areas are, with the exception of a few acres of vines in the Vorarlberg, shaped like a crescent around the eastern half of the country and the capital Vienna, and they form a bridge from the cooler northern to the southern, warmer climate zones of Europe. Warmer climatic features are evident in the two main growing areas of Lower Austria and Burgenland, particularly in the meeting of the continental Waldviertel and the hot, Pannonian (southeast European) climate. The large areas of water provided by the Danube and the Neusiedler See also function as a buffer between extremes of climate. In cool weather, they provide reserves of warmth, but in the summer heat they lower the temperature. Under these conditions, the varieties that thrive are primarily those that are given body by the heat but which can obtain the necessary potential for aroma from the cool nights of late summer and autumn.

The coolest wine-growing areas of the country are those which are the furthest from the great Pannonian region and the Hungarian plain. This applies particularly to the Wachau, Kremstal and Kamptal, and to the northwestern Weinviertel in Lower Austria and the southern and western parts of Styria. It is no accident that the finest and fruitiest white wines are produced here; Grüner Veltliner dominates above all in Lower Austria, and Riesling—although cultivated only on an insignificant percentage of the wine-growing area—here achieves some of its best wines in the world. In Styria, the white whites can be even more delicate, but sometimes a little thinner, and here, alongside the international varieties of Chardonnay and Sauvignon Blanc, the often somewhat pale and neutral-seeming Welschriesling produces surprisingly fine, fruity wines of good character.

A Bridge between North and South

The situation is different in eastern parts of Lower Austria and in the Burgenland, especially around the Neusiedler See. Among the white varieties here the dominant ones are those which can stand a lot of warmth and which are suitable for producing rich, often sweet white wines. The red wine varieties, too, such as Blaufränkisch, Zweigelt, St. Laurent, Pinot Noir, even Cabernet Sauvignon, which all need more warmth and sun to ripen, have found their ideal TERROIR here. With the possible exception of Blaufränkisch, it is mainly blends of two or three of these varieties which have made news in recent years.

A healthy mixture of the two cooler areas and the hot, southeast European region is found in Vienna and the Thermenregion which adjoins it to the south. The white varieties may traditionally be the main grapes cultivated in Vienna, but some of the younger wine producers have, in the last few years, changed the wine world's mind with splendid red wines. In the Thermenregion, the division of red and white wines can even be set out geographically, with a line drawn between the slopes of the Vienna Woods and the lowlands toward the Neusiedler See, where conditions are already very similar to those in the easternmost areas of vine cultivation. Finally, mention should be made of Vorarlberg, the most westerly federal state in Austria, where small quantities of fine white wines are produced, which have, however, not been able to achieve any real commercial importance.

Left
The most beautiful part of the Wachau: Dürnstein in the Danube valley.

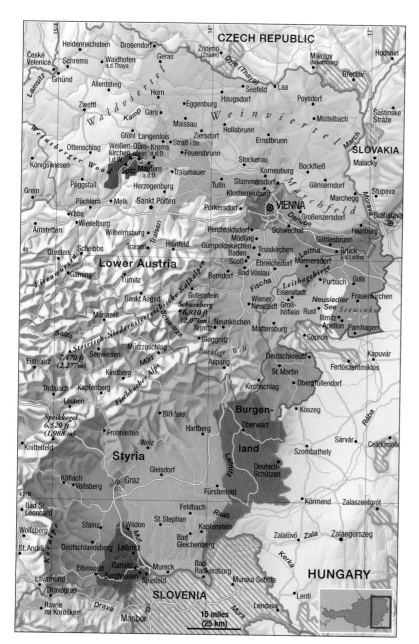

Areas of cultivation and production quantities

Federal state area of cultivation	Vine-growing area in acres (hectares) in 1999		Ave. annual prod. in the 1990s in 1,000s gallons (hectoliters)	
Lower Austria	74,067	(29,975)	38,280	(1,450,000)
Wachau	3,435	(1,390)		
Kremstal	5,364	(2,171)		
Kamptal	9,555	(3,867)		
Danubelands	6,748	(2,731)		
Traisental	1,685	(682)		
Carnuntum	2,204	(892)		
Weinviertel	39,234	(15,878)		
Thermenregion	5,747	(2,326)		
Without wine-growing area	94	(38)		
Burgenland	35,925	(14,539)	20,460	(775,000)
Neusiedler See	20,521	(8,305)		
Neusiedlersee-Hügelland	9,664	(3,911)		
Central Burgenland	4,633	(1,875)		
Southern Burgenland	1,107	(448)		
Styria	8,112	(3,283)	3,828	(145,000)
Southern Styria	4,297	(1,739)		
Western Styria	1,067	(432)		
Southeastern Styria	2,743	(1,110)		
Without wine-growing area	5	(2)		
Vienna	1,675	(678)	581	(22,000)
Outside the areas under cultivation	52	(21)		n n
Total	119,832	(48,496)	63,360	(2,392,000)

Figures from 2002/1999. Source: Ö.W.M.

The weather in the famous wine village of Spielfeld in southern Styria is like the Mediterranean in summer, but snowy in winter.

New Wine Law

The Austrians are currently working on a new wine law. This is within the framework of the European Community, where the aim is to achieve uniform community wine regulations in every member state in the longer term. Following the controls on designation of the place of origin in France, Italy and Spain, Austria has also started to introduce the D.A.C. labelling for quality wines that are typical of their area. The classification *Districtus Austriae Controllatus* is being introduced on the basis of the present 16 wine-growing districts and their quality requirements. The growers will be able to decide themselves whether to adopt the marking, which will be applied through inter-professional committees. D.A.C. will replace the older commercial classifications *Qualitätswein* or *Prädikatswein* and the individual quality classes. The Weinviertel district has pioneered the application of D.A.C.

THE DANUBE LANDS

The best-known wine lands of Austria lie along the banks of the Danube, only about 60 miles (100 km) upriver from the capital of Vienna. Krems, the old wine city, is the center of a collection of wine-growing areas whose present shape has been determined only over the past two decades. The most famous of these areas, without a doubt, is the Wachau. Vines were grown here as early as the middle of the first millennium AD. The gently winding Danube valley between Melk and Mautern, with terraced vineyards growing on the slopes of the northern bank, rivals the most beautiful wine landscapes of Europe, and not least for that reason attracts and enchants hundreds of thousands of visitors every year.

The special climate conditions of the Danube valley arise from its particular position at the point where the southeast European climate region meets that of the Waldviertel, which is still Atlantic in type. Here there is a continuous exchange of warm and cold masses of air, which provides the grapes with the warmth to ripen and the nighttime coolness to develop their aroma.

As far as the ground is concerned, the vineyard hills of the Wachau—the Loibenberg,

In Austria, organic farming has become more widespread than in any other country. A "green" vineyard such as this one in the Wachau is no longer an unusual sight.

Dürnsteiner Kellerberg, Achleiten, Klaus, and the Spitzer Singerriedel are famous—are characterized by ancient rock formations of iron-rich gneiss, granite or slate, though in the lower-lying regions loess, sand, and alluvial gravel may predominate.

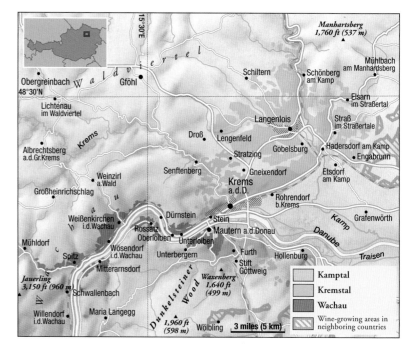

The Wachau: quality and individuality

From both an Austrian and a European point of view, the Wachau is a unique case among wine growing regions. Not only because its vineyards almost exclusively produce Rieslings and Grüner Veltliner, but also because in the 1980s the region's producers organized themselves into a powerful association, the "Vinea Wachau Nobilis Districtus."

With great political skill, this organization pushed through a regulation creating new wine terms, unique to the Wachau. Accepted even by the strict state wine legislation, which usually tended rather toward uniformity, these new regulations left existing wine quality labels well behind them in terms of naming and conditions of production. The *Qualitätsweine* of Wachau are not divided into the levels KABINETT, SPÄT-

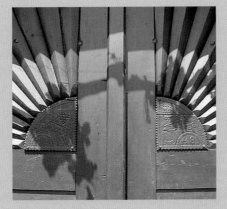

The vineyard gates in the Wachau are unusual—as are the region's wine laws.

LESE, and AUSLESE, but are labeled STEINFEDER, FEDERSPIEL, and SMARAGD.

• *Steinfeder* wines are the lightest within this classification. They have a must weight of 15 to 17 K.M.W. (Klosterneuburger Mostwaage, Klosterneuburg must gauge: corresponding to just under 82 OECHSLE) and an alcohol content of 10.8 percent alcohol by volume.

• *Federspiel* is equivalent to a level between *Kabinett* and *Spätlese*. The wines need a must weight of at least 17 K.M.W. and an alcohol content of no more than 11.9 percent by volume, with a maximum of 0.14 ounces of RESIDUAL SUGAR per 34 fluid ounces (4 g per liter).

• *Smaragd*, the highest level, comes between *Spätlese* and *Auslese* and needs a must weight of at least 18.2 K.M.W., but is permitted a maximum of only 0.28 ounces of residual sugar per 34 fluid ounces (8 g/l) of wine.

THE WACHAU

In the Wachau, Riesling reigns supreme. Indeed, many Austrians like to believe the grape originated here. However, because of the different types of soil, there is a wide range of vines grown here, each of which can find its own best environment. Apart from Riesling, Grüner Veltliner is the best known variety, which rarely develops a similar degree of aroma and flavor anywhere else. But even Sauvignon Blanc or Chardonnay (which the inhabitants of the Wachau, set on their claim to uniqueness, have tried to rename "Feinburgunder") may find their optimum *terroir* here, where they can develop all their delicacy.

Epitomizing the individuality, much prized by the people of the Wachau, is the "Vinea Wachau Nobilis Districtus" association, formed in the

On the road to the vineyard: everyday life in Loiben.

1980s and now highly respected. The association defined and named its own levels of quality and successfully fought for the right to use them officially as wine names. You will seek in vain for *Kabinett*, *Spätlese* or *Auslese* wines in the Wachau. Here they drink *Steinfeder*, *Federspiel*, or *Smaragd* instead.

KREMSTAL AND KAMPTAL

Much less well known than the Wachau, but with no less potential for quality, the two other wine-growing regions in the environs of the city of Krems are Kremstal and Kamptal. This is not surprising since the western vineyards of the Kremstal, on the Pfaffenberg and the Steinerne Hund, are geologically and climatically speaking still part of the Wachau, from which they were removed for purely political reasons.

Only a few hundred yards further on, where the Danube leaves the narrow valley of the Wachau and flows into the broad plain, there are noticeably stronger eastern European climate conditions, and the difference from the Wachau is also undeniable when it comes to soils. Mighty terraces of loess stretch out from the city to the northeast and form an outstanding *terroir* for Grüner Veltliner, which here sometimes produces wine more dense, but rarely more fine than in the Wachau. On the clay and conglomerate soils of the other parts of Kremstal and Kamptal, too, excellent Grüner Veltliner, Chardonnay, and even red varieties grow.

One of the few ancient rock formations of the Kamptal is the Heiligenstein, a monolithic crag towering above the villages of Zöbing and Langenlois. Its Rieslings are the absolute equals of any produced by the top Wachau vineyards, especially if they are pressed from grapes of old vines.

Select Producers in Wachau, Kremstal, and Kamptal

Leo Alzinger***–****
Dürnstein-Unterloiben

11 acres (4.5 ha); 36,000 bottles • Wines: Grüner Veltliner, Riesling, Chardonnay from Frauenweingarten, Mühlpoint, →Loibenberg, →Steinertal, Hollerin, Höhereck

Leo Alzinger's golden rule is to treat the grapes and the musts very carefully. The grapes are removed from the stalks, moved on without the use of pumps, fermented with their own yeasts and then matured in wooden casks or steel tanks. The resulting wines are always honest and complex, and of a convincing quality.

Wilhelm. Bründlmayer/
Schloss Gobelsburg***–*****
Langenlois/Gobelsburg

203 acres (82 ha); 79 acres (32 ha); 350,000 bottles/ 350,000 bottles • Wines: Grüner Veltliner, →Riesling, →Chardonnay, Zweigelt, Blauer Burgunder, St. Laurent, Merlot and others from →Heiligenstein, →Spiegel, Loiserberg, →Berg Vogelsang, Dechant, Gaisberg, Hussen, →Lamm

In the late 1980s, Willi Bründelmayer was one of the first producers whose wines were successful abroad. His Chardonnay, in particular, attracted attention and often emerged favorably from comparisons with more famous vines. However, it is the Rieslings from Heiligenstein which are his best wines. Since 1996, Bründelmayer has also been managing the estate at Schloss Gobelsburg and has once more made its wines into what they should be, given the potential of their vineyard sites: top of the Kamptal range.

Peter Dolle**–****
Strass

74 acres (30 ha); 200,000 bottles • Wines: Grüner Veltliner, Riesling, Weißburgunder, St. Laurent and others from →Gaisberg, Brunngasse, Hasel, Sandgrube

While other wine producers in Lower Austria tried their hand at Chardonnay, Peter Dolle put his trust primarily in Weißburgunder. However, the highest position in current production is held by his Veltliner and Riesling.

Ludwig Ehn***–****
Langenlois

35 acres (14 ha); 70,000 bottles • Wines: Grüner Veltliner, Riesling, Chardonnay, Sauvignon, Blauer Burgunder and others from →Seeberg, →Panzaun, →Heiligenstein, →Titan

Modern, fruity, rounded wines, where the sometimes clearly noticeable residual sweetness has a harmonious effect—these are the characteristic wines from Ludwig and Michael Ehn's estate in the center of Langenlois. The top wine is a Grüner Veltliner, aged in oak, called Titan.

Freie Weingärtner Wachau**–****
Dürnstein

1,610 acres (650 ha); 3,200,000 bottles • Wines: Grüner Veltliner, Riesling, Neuburger, Müller-Thurgau, Weißburgunder from Loibenberg, →Kellerberg, →Achleiten, Vorderseiber, →Singerriedel, Tausendeimerberg

The good value offered by this cooperative is astonishing. It can compete with the best wine producers in the Wachau as regards quality, but its pricing is not at all ambitious. Pressing is done in five houses, and the center of the operation is in Dürnstein, near the impressive little Baroque palace of the vintners, whose trump card, apart from a very high quality management team, is the large share they own of the top vineyard sites at Kellerberg.

Geyerhof, Familie Maier**–****
Furth/Gottweig

41 acres (16.5 ha); 55,000 bottles • Wines: Grüner Veltliner, Weißburgunder, Riesling, Zweigelt and others from Richtern, Hoher Rain, Gaisberg, Rosensteig, →Sprintzenberg, 'Steinleithn

Outstanding red wines. However, the company's strengths lie in the Veltliner from the various different vineyards. Since the early 1990s, the company has been run on organic lines.

Ludwig Hiedler***–****
Langenlois

57 acres (23 ha); 150,000 bottles • Wines: Grüner Veltliner, Weißburgunder, Riesling, Chardonnay and others from →Thal, 'Speigel, →Heiligenstein, Loiserberg, Kittmannsberg, →Liubisa

Hiedler has rigorously converted his winery to the most modern technology and methods. Liubisa, one of his best, is blended from Spätburgunder and Sangiovese and is one of Austria's most extravagant *cuvées*.

Franz Hirtzberger***–*****
Spitz

27 acres (11 ha); 120,000 bottles • Wines: Grüner Veltliner, Riesling, Weißburgunder, Chardonnay and others from →Singerriedel, Hochrain, Rotes Tor, Steinporz, Donaugarten, →Grüner Veltliner Honivogl

The leader of the "Vinea Wachau" association not only owns large chunks of the absolute top quality vineyard site in the Wachau—the Singerriedel in Spitz—but is also an absolute perfectionist in the winery. His Rieslings are characterized by strength, elegance and structure, but the Honivogl and the Chardonnay are not far behind in quality.

Josef Högl***–*****
Spitz

15 acres (6 ha); 35,000 bottles • Wines: Riesling, Grüner Veltliner, Sauvignon and others from →Bruck, →Schön, Birn, Riesling Terassengärten, Grüner Veltliner Gärten Loiben

Before taking over his father's business, Högl worked for several years with Franz Xaver Pichler and Franz Prager. His wines, especially the Veltliner from Schön and Riesling from Bruck, have been among the very top wines produced in the Wachau since the early 1990s, and in density and complexity, rival those of his teachers.

Jamek*–****
Weissenkirchen

98 acres (25 ha); 195,000 bottles • Wines: Riesling, Grüner Veltliner, Chardonnay, Spätburgunder and others from →Klaus, →Achleiten, Zweikreuzgarten, Pichl, Stein am Rain, Marienfeld

In the 1990s, Jamek missed out somewhat on new developments, and his wines appeared tired and old-fashioned. His successor gives cause for hope.

Emmerich Knoll***–*****
Dürnstein-Unterloiben

23.5 acres (9.5 ha); 65,000 bottles • Wines: Grüner Veltliner, Riesling, Chardonnay and others from Loibenberg, Kreutles, →Schütt, Kellerberg, Pfaffenberg

Good vineyard sites such as Schütt, Kellerberg and Pfaffenberg form the foundation for Emmerich Knoll's excellent range of wines. In the vineyard, he works with the most natural methods possible; in the winery, he prefers using natural grape yeasts to pure yeast cultures, and his wines must be stored for six to nine months before they come onto the market.

KARL LAGLER**–****
SPITZ
20 acres (8 ha); 60,000 bottles • Wines, Grüner Veltliner, → Riesling and others from → Steinborz, Hartberg, Burgberg, Donaugarten, → Tausendeimerberg, Vorderseiber
Karl Lagler is one of the most famous winemakers in Spitz. His Rieslings from Steinborz and Tausendeimerberg are firm and spicy, at times really lush. From his winery, recently rebuilt in the midst of his vineyards, the family runs a comfortable hotel.

FRED LOIMER***–****
LANGENLOIS
39.5 acres (16 ha); 60,000 bottles • Wines: Grüner Veltliner, Chardonnay, Weißburgunder, Grauburgunder, Riesling and others from → Spiegel, Käferberg, Seeberg, Steinmassel, Ladner, Sachsenberg
Loimer's Grüner Veltliner from Spiegel, made from old vines, is consistently one of the best wines of this variety in the whole of Austria with an impressive dense fruit, complex bouquet, body, strength, and, occasionally, also harmoniously integrated residual sweetness.

GERALD MALAT***–****
FURTH/GÖTTWEIG
89 acres (36 ha); 200,000 bottles • Wines: Grüner Veltliner, Chardonnay, Riesling; Blauer Burgunder, Cabernet and others from Höhlgraben, Steinbühel, Hochrain, Pinot Blanc Sur Lie, → Das Beste vom Veltliner, → Das Beste vom Riesling.
Unlike many colleagues, Malat relies less on the selection of the vineyard than on *cuvées* for his top quality wines, with the label "*Das Beste von...*" (The Best of...). In his modern well-equipped winery, he also produces a convincingly good Chardonnay. Malat was one of the first to plant Cabernet Sauvignon.

MANTLERHOF***–****
BRUNN IM FELDE
39.5 acres (16 ha); 70,000 bottles • Wines: Grüner Veltliner, → Roter Veltliner, Riesling, Chardonnay and others from Weitgasse, → Spiegel, Tiefenthal, Wieland, → Reisenthal
Sepp Mantler is known as a specialist in a rare vine variety, the Roter Veltliner, from which, in good years, he produces intensive, substantial wines, often with residual sweetness. His Rieslings and Veltliner have also gained in expression and balance over recent years.

SEPP MOSER***–****
ROHRENDORF
128 acres (52 ha); 300,000 bottles • Wines: Grüner Veltliner, Chardonnay, Riesling, Zweigelt, Cabernet and others from → Gebling, Wolfsgraben, → Schnabel, Hedwigshof, Siebenhand, Hollabern, → Sauvignon Blanc Atriumweingärten
Moser, a member of the famous Rohrendorf wine dynasty, founded his wine-growing business at a late stage, but soon established himself as a top producer. He not only bottles outstanding Kremstal wines, but also owns excellent red wine vineyards.

NIKOLAIHOF, FAMILIE SAAHS***–*****
MAUTERN
39.5 acres (16 ha); 140,000 bottles • Wines: in Krems-Stein: Riesling, Grüner Veltliner, Weißburgunder, Neuburger and others from → Steiner Hund, → Im Weingebirge, → Vom Stein, Baumgarten, Burggarten, Süßenberg
Vines have been cultivated on the former estate of the archdiocese of Passau since 985. Klaus and Christine Saahs, the present owners, turned to organic wine growing early on and over the years they have demonstrated that top quality and organic methods of

cultivation and production certainly can go together. Their Rieslings and Veltliner from the Kremstal and Wachau vineyards have great capacity for aging.

FRANZ XAVER PICHLER****–*****
DÜRNSTEIN-OBERLOIBEN
18.5 acres (7.5 ha); 80,000 bottles • Wines: Grüner Veltliner, Riesling, Sauvignon and others from Loibenberg, Steinertal, → Kellerberg, → M.
The widely famed star of Wachau wine production almost places more trust in Veltliner than in Riesling. Franz Xaver Pichler produces monumental wines: dense, spicy, full of body (rather too much for some critics). The secret of his vines lies in the excellent vineyard plots, in the traditional methods of wine preparation—here, wine is still fermented with natural grape yeasts in wooden casks—and in rigid selection and limitation of yield. In good years the best casks are filled and designated "M.," no matter whether with Riesling or Veltliner.

RUDI PICHLER***–****
WEISSENKIRCHEN
22 acres (9 ha); 30,000 bottles • Wines: Grüner Veltliner, Riesling, Weißburgunder and others from → Achleiten, Kollmütz, → Hochrain, Hall, Kirchweg
Rudi Pichler has established himself over the last few years among the top echelons of the Wachau wine producers. His modern, extract-rich wines are fermented in steel tanks and then aged in wooden casks.

PRAGER**–****
WEISSENKIRCHEN
32 acres (13 ha); 85,000 bottles • Wines: Riesling, Grüner Veltliner, Chardonnay and others from → Achleiten, → Steinriegel, → Klaus, Hinter der Burg, Hollerin, Kaiserberg, Kollmitzberg
The company has been managed for over ten years by Prager's son-in-law Toni Bodenstein. A supporter of vineyard classification and author of a map of Wachau vineyards, he produces top quality wines in good years, but the levels of quality sometimes seem a little disjointed.

SCHLOSS GOBELSBURG****
LANGENLOIS
111 acres (45 ha); 180,000 bottles. • Wines: Riesling and Grüner Veltliner von Heiligenstein, Gaisberg, Grub, Renner, Lamm, Steinsetz, Spiegel and Alte Haide.
The old monastery vineyard of Schloss Gobelsberg transformed itself a few years ago. Under the direction of Michael Mossbrugger and with Willi Bründlmayer as adviser it has now secured itself a place among the top quality producers in Kamptal, chiefly with its outstanding Grüner Veltliner.

SONNHOF, FAMILIE JURTSCHITSCH**–****
LANGENLOIS
148 acres (60 ha); 360,000 bottles • Wines: Grüner Veltliner, Riesling, Chardonnay and others from → Loiserberg, → Steinhaus, Fahnberg, Spiegel, Ladner, Heiligenstein
Three brothers share the work on this exemplary Langenlois estate, which has made an outstanding name for itself, above all with its Grüner Veltliner wines.

UNDHOF, ERICH SALOMON**–****
KREMS-STEIN
49 acres (20 ha); 100,000 bottles • Wines: Grüner Veltliner, Riesling and others from Undhof-Wieden, Kögl, Wachtberg, Pfaffenberg, Hund
This traditional wine-growing estate in a monastery went through a crisis in the late 1980s, but after an all-round renewal of its stock of casks and modernization of wine production, it is once again among the elite of Kremstal. In Kögl and Pfaffenberg, it owns two of the best Riesling vineyards, while very good Veltliner grows directly behind the monastery.

THE WEINVIERTEL

The Weinviertel, or "wine quarter", is the largest and most productive wine-growing area in the country, and covers the whole northeastern part of Lower Austria. Here, around one-third of the total area of vines in Austria is cultivated, and individual wine-growing communities alone, such as Retz, can achieve similar quantities of production to the whole of the Wachau. However, for many years the reputation of this region's wines, with regard to quality, was questionable. This is by no means due to a lack of potential, but to the fact that here—perhaps thanks to the region's position at the edge of the former Iron Curtain—growers for too long limited themselves to supplying only basic wines.

The Weinviertel also lies on the border area of the Pannonian southeast European climate zone and therefore enjoys some of the best conditions for viticulture. Here thick layers of loess are to be found, suitable for Grüner Veltliner, but soil maps also register lime and silicate soils, clay,

The inner court of the Pfaffl vineyard in Stetten, only a short distance northeast of Vienna. The producers in this quiet retreat specialize in Grüner Veltliner and red wines.

sand, and even ancient rock formations such as are found in the Wachau, with the result that Pinot varieties, Traminer and even Riesling are at home here in certain vineyards.

The two wine-growing centers of this region are Retz in the west and Falkenstein in the northeast, both of which were independent regions in years gone by. Even if white wine dominates the Weinviertel, there are one or two definite "red wine islands" in the north along the border with the Czech Republic. In recent years these have shown interesting qualities which have attracted attention.

Along its southern edge, the western Weinviertel borders the Danube lands (Donauland). One of the youngest wine-growing regions of Austria, its present extent is made up of Carnuntum in the east, and the rather insignificant Traisental to the southwest. It stretches from the loess terraces of Kamptal to the foothills of the Vienna Woods at the gates of the capital. Most of its vineyards lie to the left of the Danube on the slopes of the Wagram; on the other side of the Danube, there are vines only at Klosterneuburg and on the northern slopes of the Kahlenberg.

Simple, fruity, full-bodied wines are produced here, from Grüner Veltliner and Müller-Thurgau; there is also a little Riesling, Roter and Frühroter Veltliner, Portugieser and Zweigelt.

Until around ten years ago, Carnuntum was part of the Danube lands. In the area of this old Roman garrison—which long before Vienna became the political and cultural center of Austria or rather of the then Roman province of Pannonia Superior—there are only around 2,470 acres (1,000 ha) stocked with vines. The vineyards on the foothills of the Thermenberge are particularly suited to the production of full-bodied white and red wines.

The mixture of thick strata of loess, gravel deposits from the Danube and occasional outcrops of loam provide an ideal *terroir*, above all for red wines. The young winegrowers and producers of Carnuntum have recognized this fact, and over the last few years they have caused quite a stir with their excellent products. The brand association "Rubin Carnuntum" has created publicity for them, and a few years ago they even successfully launched a white *primeur* wine called Primus Carnuntum.

SELECT PRODUCERS IN THE WEINVIERTEL

WALTER GLATZER * – ******
GÖTTLESBRUNN
22 acres (9 ha); 80,000 bottles • Wines: Grüner Veltliner, Welschriesling, Zweigelt, Blaufränkisch and others from Kräften, Heideacker, Schüttenberg, Aubühel, Zwiering
In recent years this company has switched to various red varieties. The Blaufränkisch, Zweigelt Dornenvogel and Cuvée Gotinsprun are excellent.

SCHLOSS WEINGUT GRAF HARDEGG ** – ****
SEEFELD-KADOLZ
102 acres (43 ha); 200,000 bottles • Wines: Grüner Veltliner, Riesling, Weißburgunder, Merlot, Zweigelt and others from Dreikreuzer, Lange Riede, Neuriß, Steinbügel, Sonnbergen, Zeiselberg, → Maximilian, → Merlot/Cabernet Max
Peter Veyder-Malberg is responsible for boost in quality, and for recent trials, including Rhône variety Viognier.

GERHARD MARKOWITSCH * – ******
GÖTTLESBRUNN
30 acres (10.5 ha); 70,000 bottles • Wines: Grüner Veltliner, Chardonnay, Riesling, Zweigelt, Blaufränkisch, Cabernet from → Rosenberg, Rubin Carnuntum, Redmont
Markowitsch is setting new standards for the region.

ROLAND MINKOWITSCH * – ******
MANNERSDORF
18.5 acres (7.5 ha); 30,000 bottles • Wines: Riesling, Welschriesling, Grüner Veltliner, Gewürztraminer and others from Zweifelhab, Kapellenfeld, Jäbelissen, Kohler
Traditional production in wooden casks and even an old log press. Wines are clear toned, at the same time complex.

BERNHARD OTT ** – ****
FEUERSBRUNN
25 acres (10 ha); 60,000 bottles • Wines: Grüner Veltliner, Riesling and others from → Rosenberg, Stiegl, Storz, → Brenner
Very good Veltliner, Sauvignon Blanc and even Riesling.

R. & A. PFAFFL * – ******
STETTEN/SCHLOSSGUT BOCKFLIESS
47 acres (19 ha); 150,000 bottles • Wines: Grüner Veltliner, Riesling, Weißburgunder, Chardonnay, St. Laurent, Zweigelt and others from Seiser am Eck, Sandlern, Zeiseneck, → Hundsleiten, Rossern, Haidviertel, Sandtal, Neuberg, Hochfeld, → Cabernet Excellent, Chardonnay Exclusive
The Grüner Veltliner wines are particularly successful.

FAMILIE PITNAUER * – ******
GÖTTLESBRUNN
23.5 acres (9.5 ha); 50,000 bottles • Wines: Grüner Veltliner, St. Laurent, Zweigelt, Cabernet and others from Kräften, Bärenreiser, Hagelsberg, Schüttenberg, Franz Josef, → Pegasos, Bienenfresser
Their latest creation, the 80 percent Syrah Pegasos, is most unusual in Austria.

ANTON WÖBER * – ******
ZIERSDORF
22 acres (9 ha); 40,000 bottles • Wines: Grüner Veltliner, → Roter Veltliner, Riesling and others from Katzensprung, → End des Berges, In der Schablau, Hirtenthal, Matinée
Wöber only took over the estate in 1993, but has acquired a solid reputation with very good Rieslings, Welschrieslings, Roter Veltliner and Grüner Veltliner.

THE HEURIGER

The bush is displayed on the Wieninger estate.

If you visit Vienna, you won't be able to avoid them. The *Heuriger* pubs are among the most popular tourist attractions in the Austrian capital. Every evening, dozens of tourist buses take crowds of visitors from all over the world to Grinzing, so that they can sit there by candlelight and enjoy the friendly, easy-going atmosphere. To be precise, the Viennese *Heuriger* should be called a *Buschenschank* (Bush Inn). The actual *Heuriger* is the young wine of the current year, which may be served in the *Buschenschänke* from St. Martin's Day, November 11, to the end of the year.

Exactly what *Buschenschänke* are and what they can do was laid down in the dim and distant past in 795 in Charlemagne's edict *Capitulare de villis*, and then revived by the Emperor Joseph II in his famous circular of 1784. A true *Heuriger* may sell only wines of its own production, i.e. from the grapes of its own vineyards. It may only do this on 300 days of the year, and only in the wine-growing suburbs of the city, definitely not in the city center. The signal for the "season" is given by green bushes which are displayed in front of the pub. In addition to their own wines, which must come from vineyards no more than six miles (10 km) outside the city, only juices, water and a single soft drink may be sold, but certainly never coffee or beer.

Even the menu of a genuine *Buschenschank* is regulated by law: sausages, cheese, ham, smoked meats or bacon, bread, vegetables, and fruit are allowed. However, with the menus, as with the wines, things are becoming less rigid. Most of the pubs in Vienna's surrounding belt of vineyards offer their tourist visitors complete menus, on which, alongside many and varied hot dishes, even bottled wines from other producers may occasionally be found.

In spite of these changes, the true *Heurige* do still exist, though you may have to search a little off the beaten track, in towns like Nußdorf or Heiligenstadt, for example. Even better, you could go to the other side of the Danube, to Stammersdorf, Jedlersdorf, or Strebersdorf. Here you will find not only a truly Viennese sociable atmosphere, but you will also be served really good wine.

COFFEE CITY

In the center of Vienna, however, the coffee-house is the life and soul of the city. In contrast to the Parisian café, where the atmosphere is always a little worldly and sophisticated, or the Italian bar, where espresso is tipped down in a few seconds, the Viennese coffee house has its own particular rhythm. It is the most accurate mirror of the city and its inhabitants, being both a place of rest and a place to meet up with people.

The study of Viennese coffee varieties is something of an arcane science, and only the true connoisseur will ever be able to distinguish *kleine Schwarze*, *große Braune*, *Melange*, *Einspänner*, *Fiaker*, *Mokka g'spritzt*, or *Türkische*. A proper coffee should of course be accompanied by a tempting *Mehlspeise*—cake or gâteau—but quite a few coffeehouses serve hot meals as well. Most of the coffeehouses in the city share an ambiance which combines plush comfort and vibrant city life, and which often does not wind down until the early hours of the morning.

The *Heurige* present quite a different prospect. Most of them do not open until the afternoon, and then the wooden tables are firmly occupied by gentlemen of the older generation. But the longer the evening goes on, the more mixed the company gets, until finally, at closing time, young and old are not infrequently united in cheerful if somewhat tipsy company. You could almost believe that wine really did have rejuvenating qualities.

Select Heuriger Pubs

Note: as *Heuriger* pubs are only open at certain times which differ from year to year, it is advisable to make a prior reservation.

Leopold Breyer
Amtsstrasse 15, Vienna-Jedlersdorf
Tel.: +43–1–2924148
At first sight, this is one of the typical *Buschenschänke* for tourists, but the Viennese themselves come to Breyer's. The wines are of above-average quality, and Breyer is recognized as being one of the best vintners in the city.

Franz Christ
Amtsstrasse 12–14, Vienna-Jedlersdorf
Tel.: +43–1–2955152
Traditional pub with well cared for, simple furnishings and excellent wines, which are aged in steel tanks, small oak casks or large wooden casks. Weißburgunder and Chardonnay are usually very successful.

Hans Peter Göbel
Hagenbrunner Strasse 151
Vienna-Stammersdorf
Tel.: +43–1–2948420
This rising young vintner with his modern designer Heurige right next to the vineyards specializes in red wines and even manages a good Cabernet Sauvignon—highly unusual in Vienna.

Hengl-Haselbrunner
Iglaseegasse 10, Vienna-Grinzing
Tel.: +43–1–3203330
Away from the tourist stretch in the center of Grinzing, the Hengl family runs one of the few *Heuriger* pubs on the right bank of the Danube, mainly patronized by Viennese, among them many local celebrities. The wine and the food are excellent.

Am Reisenberg
Oberer Reisenbergweg 15, Vienna-Grinzing
Tel.: +43–1–3209393
A secret among initiates—to get there, you have to climb the last 550 yards (500 m) up a steep hill on foot. The splendid view, the cozy atmosphere and good wines are ample compensation for your trouble.

Sankt Peter
Rupertusplatz 5, Vienna-Dornbach
Tel.: +43–1–4864675
The wines are no longer produced in the monastery itself, but in a contract winery. However, the atmosphere in the Dornbacher Pfarrer (Dornbach Vicarage), as the *Heuriger* is popularly known, is straight out of the good old days: rustic, with local clientele and clean, full-bodied wines.

Schilling
Langenzersdorfer Strasse 52 / 54
Vienna-Strebersdorf
Tel.: +43–1–2924189
"Wiener Augustin" is Herbert Schilling's own brand. His estate is one of the most respected in the city. His red Cuvée Camilla displays a fine bouquet and plenty of fruit. Food and service in the pub are of the same standard as the wines.

Wieninger
Stammersdorfer Strasse 78
Vienna-Stammersdorf
Tel.: +43–1– 292 41 06
The best wines and outstanding food are characteristic of this *Heuriger*, whose youthful manager, Fritz Wieninger, is seen as the absolute star of Viennese wine making. The food alone is worth the trip to Stammersdorf.

From top to bottom:
Impressions of *Heuriger* pubs.

Treat yourself to a Chardonnay or Blauburgunder with the excellent cuisine at Wieninger's in Stammersdorf, the top Viennese wine producer.

Peter Bernreiter in the Amtsstrasse is considered an expert on Burgunder grapes. His excellent Grauburgunder, especially, has become a legend in Vienna.

Vienna and the Thermenregion

There are vines growing even in the neighborhood of the Schönbrunn palace, although most of the 1,730 acres (700 ha) of vines cultivated in the city area are in the north of Vienna.

It is possible that as early as pre-Roman times the Celts were growing vines on the slopes of the Vienna Woods, although systematic viticulture did not arrive until the legions of the Roman Empire introduced it. Even the famous Stephansdom (St. Stephen's Cathedral), the symbol of Vienna, to some extent owes its existence to wine—the Babenberg dynasty could not begin building the church until, in the 12th century, they had exchanged some of their vineyards in the Wachau for parish rights in Vienna.

Wine growing in Vienna is divided into two areas of approximately equal importance: the slopes of the Kahlenberg, with its shell limestone soils, in the northwest, and the Bisamberg, with its gravely loess and loam, in the northeast. The two areas also have considerable differences in climate, although the whole of Vienna is on the border of the half-oceanic climate of western Europe and the Pannonian climate of the southeast. While lighter, fruitier wines are produced on the cooler Kahlenberg, the grapes of the Bisamberg display a good deal more structure and complexity.

In earlier times, wine was grown even in the center of Vienna itself, and as late as 1547 there were vines quite close to the Hofburg. By the 1950s, wine growing in the city was markedly decreasing and only received a new boost in the second half of the 20th century. Today there are some 1,730 productive acres (700 ha) in the Vienna wine-growing region, worked by 400 winegrowers.

Although the *Gemischte Satz* (mixed blend), which formed the traditional *Heuriger* wine, is now only to be found on some 15 percent of the wine-growing areas, 85 percent of the wines are still produced from white varieties. In this region, too, pure varieties of Veltliner, Weißburgunder, Riesling, or Chardonnay have established themselves. The majority, even today, are served directly in the *Heuriger* pubs of the city, for production does not even cover the city's own needs.

The different companies often display great differences in quality. Where the customers are more or less uncritical, either because they are wedded to tradition or simply too comfortable, the vintner is also under no particular pressure, which is clearly to be seen in the wines served. On the other hand, there are an increasing number of wineries which over the last 15 years have made quite considerable efforts to establish their position among the elite of Austrian wine production.

THERMENREGION

In the past, the most famous wines from the area around Vienna have come from the southern continuation of the slopes of the Kahlenberg. Under the name "Gumpoldskirchen"—in those days, you could still call wine-growing regions

---

SELECT PRODUCERS IN VIENNA

KARL ALPHART ***−*****
TRAISKIRCHEN
35 acres (14 ha); 45,000 bottles • Wines: Riesling, Rotgipfler, Neuburger, Chardonnay, Zweigelt, Spätburgunder from Zistl, Rodauner, Hausberg, Mandl-Höh
Sparse, dry vineyards on the slopes of the Vienna Woods and rigid limitation of yield to a company average of no more than 11 gallons per 2.5 acres (40 hl per ha) are the secret behind the quality of the Alphart wines. The excellent Rotgipfler *Trockenbeerenauslese* wines are particularly remarkable. But the dry and medium-dry Zierfandler-Rotgipfler, Rieslings, and Chardonnays are also above average for this area.

MANFRED BIEGLER ***−****
GUMPOLDSKIRCHEN
20 acres (8 ha); 40,000 bottles • Wines: in Gumpoldskirchen: Riesling, Zierfandler, Rotgipfler and others—no vineyard origins
Manfred Biegler's company has long been among the best in the Thermenregion, but ever since his son Othmar started work in the winery, the level of wine quality has gone up still further. Rotgipfler wines, oak-aged or unoaked, are the specialty of the two Bieglers, who also produce successful Chardonnays and Rieslings. Their wines combine modern lushness with classical structure.

E. & C. FISCHER **−****
SOOSS
44 acres (18 ha); 80,000 bottles • Wines: Grüner Veltliner; Zweigelt, Portugieser, Cabernet, Spätburgunder and others from Paitzbreite, In den Robbingen, →Fasangarten, →Gradenthal, Aderhags, Steinhäufel, →Pinot Noir Barrique, Cabernet Barrique
Engelbert and Christian Fischer run a winery in one of the so-called *Urhäuser* (original houses) in Sooss. Modern, cool fermented wines are produced here, but the best products are made from Zweigelt, Pinot Noir and Portugieser and aged in oak casks, with the vineyards of Fasangarten and Gradenthal offering the greatest potential.

JOHANNESHOF, J. & V. REINISCH **−****
TATTENDORF
99 acres (40 ha); 120,000 bottles • Wines: Chardonnay; →Cabernet, →Blauburgunder, St. Laurent and others from Dornfeld, Mitterfeld, Holzspur
Just outside the gates of Tattendorf, the Reinisch family has set up an almost Californian-style estate. Here, they produce excellent Cabernet Sauvignon, St. Laurent, Chardonnay and Pinot Noir. This modern winery not only has an inviting sales room, but it also accommodates a very commendable *Heuriger*, built over an ecological pond and now popular with the locals for excursions.

FAMILIE SCHWERTFÜHRER **−*****
70,000 bottles • Wines: Chardonnay; Zweigelt, Pinot, Cabernet, Portugieser and others, →Spada
The Schwertführers call their best wines, made from Zweigelt, Pinot Noir, St. Laurent and Cabernet Sauvignon, *Spada* or "sword." Although Chardonnay and Weißburgunder are good, the red varieties dominate in quality as in quantity: their harmonious unity makes them unparalleled over a wide area.

FRITZ WIENINGER ***−*****
VIENNA-STAMMERSDORF
32 acres (13 ha); 120,000 bottles • Wines: Grüner Veltliner, →Chardonnay, Riesling, →Blauer Burgunder and others from Jungenberg, Rothen, Gabrissen, Herrenholz, Wiethalen, Breiten, Wiener Trilogie, Select, →Grand Select
Wieninger is not only the star among Viennese wine producers, he is also one of the top winemakers in Austria. In his Chardonnay and Spätburgunder he has created two ranges of products which are unequaled far and wide, especially as far as the oak-aged wines Select and Grand Select are concerned. But Grüner Veltliner and Riesling, too, make lush and fruity wines here in most years. The Danubis blend and the Wiener Trilogie made from Zweigelt, Blauburgunder, Cabernet, and Merlot complete the outstanding range.

Opposite
Every member of the family is needed at grape harvest time.

Below
The Viennese love to go south out of the city, in order to eat well and drink good wine in the villages of the Thermenregion, of which the best known is Gumpoldskirchen, and to walk in the vineyards.

by place names, as was also the case with Rust and Retz—wines were produced which were famous and popular throughout Austria. The success of the region is mainly derived from its reputation as a much-visited excursion and vacation center for the Viennese. In the distant past, the Romans appreciated the spas between the present-day towns of Mödling and Bad Voslau, and, more recently, even Beethoven preferred to compose in Gumpoldskirchen. After 1985 however, the newly renamed region disappeared into anonymity for quite a considerable time.

This explains why today, many of the top wine producers of the region are better known than the Thermenregion, which, with over 5,683 acres (2,300 ha) of vines is by no means one of the smallest in the country. Around 60 percent of the vineyards are stocked with white varieties, among which are two unique specialties of the Thermenregion: Zierfandler and Rotgipfel. Both may be bottled together as a *cuvée* and are then put on the market under the name of Spätrot-Rotgipfler.

As far as climate is concerned, the Thermenregion belongs to the Pannonian region. With

egard to soils, it is divided into two. In the
orthwest heavy clay and lime soils predomi-
ate, while the south, the plain of the Steinfeld,
s characterized by alluvial gravel. Of course
hese different soils each bear different varieties:
nainly white along the slopes of the Vienna
Voods, red in the Steinfeld. The best wines of
he Thermenregion are full-bodied, expressive,
nd even reasonably long-lived, which applies
o both white and red wines. Here, too, many
vine producers over the last few years have
nade strenuous efforts to make their wines
ationally and internationally competitive.

Glass Making

The History of the Wine Glass

The search for a specialized glass perfectly suited to the properties of wine is relatively recent. The great masters of early glass production were the 13th-century Venetians, who, through fear of catastrophic fires, exiled their glassblowers to the nearby island of Murano. Over the centuries, the costly works of the glassblower's art, sold primarily to royal courts throughout Europe and the Middle East by Venetian merchants, were considered the ultimate in drinking vessels. As artistic as they were, these are unsuited to enjoying wine, and apart from the thinness of the glass, they have few advantages over the plain beaker-like glasses used to serve wine in all Mediterranean countries in home and simple restaurants. The main defect of these glasses is that they widen as they reach the top and so instead of concentrating the BOUQUET they allow it to disperse rapidly.

The Bohemian glassblowers showed rather more feeling for the actual purpose of the wine glass, although they succumbed to a tendency for excessive decoration. This was expressed in cut glass, which is as artistically skilled as it is irritating.

In general, early glass shapes are exceedingly generous in the opening, but usually very sparing in the body. The most absurd example is the bowl-shaped champagne glass, a miniature

The Riedel family glassworks in Kufstein in Tyrol.

The composition of glass has not changed for 4,000 years.

The natural basic materials—quartz, lime and alkali—are melted at 2,120°F (1,000°C).

In this famous glass factory, the glassmakers still use traditional methods today.

bathtub on a stem, shaped so that if you want to balance your glass, you are obliged to hold the body, which quickly warms up cool sparkling wines.

Two classic forms have remained popular today, the balloon glass and the tulip. The simple French balloon glass, which you can buy in French supermarkets, often for very little more than decorated paper cups, does its job reasonably well as long as it is not filled too full. A variation of this basic form has been used in different countries and wine regions. In Alsace, the addition of a tall green stem and foot became the customary glass for white wine; on the Rhine, it had a thick, fluted green glass foot, and was called the *Römer*, to name only two of

the most common examples. Apart from being too wide at the top, and lacking a chimney for the full appreciation of the aroma, their major disadvantage is in their everyday use—they have become more of a unit of wine than a glass for enjoying your wine. The tulip glass, with its tall chimney, is generally more suitable, especially for white wines, but it has too little surface area to permit the best possible development of aroma.

Among the traditional glasses, the Andalusian and Manzanilla sherry drinkers deserve praise, for their COPITA is the original type of tasting glass, with a comparatively tall chimney that centers the aroma and guarantees full enjoyment.

The glassblower begins work on a still unformed lump, the "gob."

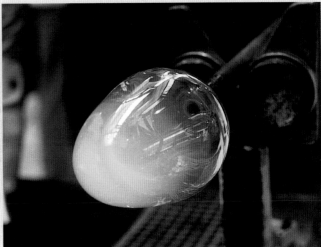

The glassmaker's pipe was used in a similar form 2,000 years ago in Rome.

The glass "gob" has little in common with the finished wine glass.

The work of art takes shape—in special molds for each type of glass.

BURGENLAND

With just under 35,829 acres (14,500 ha) devoted to vines and an annual production of 20,475,561 gallons (775,000 hl) the Burgenland is Austria's second largest wine growing area after Lower Austria. On the edge of the Hungarian plain, it profits from the hot Pannonian climate and is therefore better suited than any other region of the country to producing white wines from fully or over-ripe grapes, as well as for dense wines with the emphasis on fruit and tannin.

The major part of the vineyards lies close to or not very far away from the Neusiedler See, a body of water which has a decisive influence on the climate conditions of the region. While the land to the northeast is largely flat, on the western shore of the lake there are gentle rolling hills and steep slopes along the Leitha range. And, just as in the Bordeaux region, even slightly rising slopes may be of importance for the quality of the wine. In central and south Burgenland, on the other hand, the slopes are for the most part shallower. As far as viticulture

Reliable guests, the storks come back year after year to their nests on the rooftops of Rust.

The "Türkenturm" (Turk Tower) of Breitenbrunn can be seen from a great distance.

is concerned, the region is divided into four unequal areas, which for one thing have been rather unfortunately chosen, and to add to that they have been given unclear definitions, such as the awkward double-barreled name "Neusiedlersee-Hügelland" (Neusiedler Lake Hill Country). Many wine producers would therefore be grateful to see the whole of the Burgenland declared as a single wine region.

To the northeast lies the Neusiedlersee region, which is mainly known for its sweet wines. Full-bodied white wines are also made here, and among these are some of the best Chardonnays produced in the country. The red wines here are usually most successful as blends, either of various native varieties or native and international varieties. Particularly worthy of note are the wines from the "Pannobile" marketing cooperative, a small group of top producers who all age their wines in oak.

Along the northwest and west shores of the lake lies the region of Neusiedlersee-Hügelland. Here the variety of vineyard sites is much greater, as the lakeshore differs greatly from the neighboring hills on the one hand and slopes of the Leitha range on the other, not only in climate conditions but also in the composition of the soil. Apart from excellent Blaufränkisch and Zweigelt, outstanding white wines also thrive here, with not only Chardonnay, but even Sauvignon Blanc producing very good results. Even if the center of the area, the lakeside town of Rust, is mainly famous for its Ausbruch dessert wine, the actual strengths of the Neusiedler-Hügelland undoubtedly lie in

the dry matured white and red wines, which have plenty of body and refinement.

To the south, the countryside becomes increasingly more hilly, but the range of varieties decreases. Especially in the central Burgenland, which borders the southern shore of the lake, the Blaufränkisch grape almost has a monopoly in the vineyards. Aged in a classic wooden cask, or in a BARRIQUE, it can produce magnificent results. The same variety is slightly less dominant, but nonetheless responsible for the best wines in the south Burgenland close to the borders of Styria. In what is perhaps the best-kept secret of the wine-growing areas of Europe, this is made into wonderfully fruity, spicy red wines, whose only real defect is the small quantities which arrive on the market.

STUDENTS OF WINE, HUNGRY FOR KNOWLEDGE

In the wine town of Rust—which is also worth seeing because of its protected historic old town—the Weinakademie Österreich (Austrian Wine Academy) represents a special center of wine knowledge. From introductory courses on the experience of wine and culinary weekends, as well as preparation for the much sought after title "Master of Wine," the institute offers a broad range of courses for development at many different levels.

Above
As in this vineyard on the Neusiedler See the growers in Burgenland often sow rape to loosen the soil and provide natural nutrients.

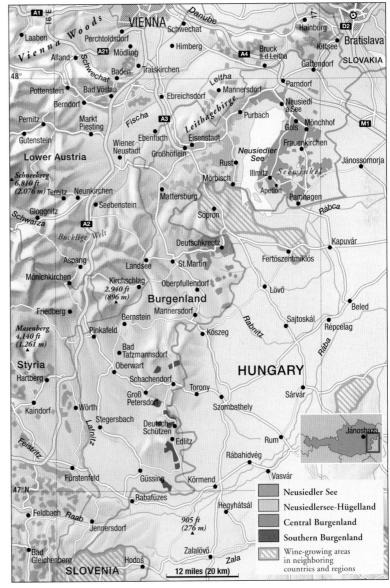

Sweet Wines from Seewinkel and Ausbruch from Rust

Anyone who has ever traveled in the Seewinkel area, Austria's last piece of wine-growing land on the far side of the Neusiedler See just before the Hungarian border, will probably have smiled at house inscriptions along the lines of "Here we serve the wine of world masters." However, it cannot be denied that the vineyards of the northern Burgenland are most excellently suited to the production of sweet wines and that some of the local wine producers have in recent years been overwhelmed with international awards.

The production of these sweet wines, marked by the NOBLE ROT of the BOTRYTIS CINEREA fungus, requires an interplay of sufficient warmth and humidity. There is, of course, an abundance of warmth in the Pannonian climate zone, almost an over-abundance in summer. Larger-scale rainfall may be lacking, but the huge water surface of the Neusiedler See, from which the mists rise in autumn, supplies the required humidity.

Given these ideal conditions, the people of Seewinkel succeed every year in producing wines which, in other centers of sweet wine production, such as Germany or the Sauternes region, are only possible now and again or by employing masses of technology. They make their *Beerenauslese* and *Trockenbeerenauslese* wines from well-known varieties or from even less well-known grapes such as the Welschriesling, Bouvier, Neuburger, Scheurebe, Weißburgunder, or Muscatel-Ottonel. The result is the harmo-

The Kellergassen with their wine cellars are a popular destination for cyclists.

Even if the vines in Weiden am See are planted in long lines, this does not affect the quality of the Seewinkel wines.

nious combination of a high degree of sweetness with a rich fruit and extract content and a refreshing acidity.

In recent years two special styles of wine have developed here, with vinification processes that are in part very different from one another. The one emphasizes the refinement and fruit of its wines, and the other uses a high alcohol content and a great deal of aging in new wood to produce body, density, and a rather more international structure. Both have found devotees and success outside the borders of Austria, so the Seewinkel will probably be the object of plenty of attention in the future.

However, the most severe competition for the people of Illmitz and Apetlon and their neighbors does not come from abroad, but from nearby. The old and honored community of Rust is less than four miles (6 km) away, on the west shore of the Neusiedler, and in recent years it too has attracted attention for its spectacular sweet wines. In the past, the term of origin "Rust" was applied to all wines with residual sweetness from eastern Austria, but this bad habit, which encouraged forgery and adulteration, was ended for good by the wine law of 1985.

However, right up to the present day, the name of the town has been closely linked with a special kind of wine production, the AUSBRUCH, a type of winemaking that originally came from Hungary, where it was used in the production of Tokaji. It consists of combining carefully

selected noble rot grapes with MUST of *Spätlese* or *Auslese* quality and letting them ferment. From the fruit of the must and noble rot character of the grapes onto which it is poured, an extraordinary sweet wine is produced, which according to Austrian law has to have a must weight that lies between that of *Beerenauslese* and *Trockenbeerenauslese*.

Over the last few years, Ausbruch has undergone an unexpected renaissance. A group of winemakers who joined together to form the "Cercle Ruster Ausbruch" has done much to revive the old wine name. However, the production of the wine has in part been rather drastically modernized. In many places today the grapes no longer have must poured over them, but noble rot grapes of *Beerenauslese* quality are simply left to ferment, not infrequently in an oak cask. Lovers of the genuine Ausbruch of Rust feel torn in two: they cannot but respect the outstanding quality of the wines, but at the same time they mourn the distortion of the true idea of Ausbruch.

RED WINE IN THE BURGENLAND

While Austria was recovering in the second half of the 1980s from the shock of the glycol scandal, the first signs of a new beginning came from the Burgenland, of all places, where adulteration had led to the greatest loss of prestige. However, it was not white or sweet wines which now stepped into the limelight, but red wines, and one of the most respected journals of the wine industry even donated a special red wine prize to encourage the few wine producers who, at that time, had recognized its potential.

The centers of attention were mainly wines made from the Blaufränkisch grape that came from the western and southern shores of the Neusiedler. Strict selection of grapes, rigorous limitation of yield and the experimental aging of the wines in oak casks led some winemakers to succeed in turning this variety, once greeted with condescending amusement, into truly interesting wines which soon found recognition among consumers.

Newly introduced international varieties such as Cabernet Sauvignon or even Pinot Noir were the first to attract attention abroad. When, a few years later, the vintners were able markedly to improve the Zweigelt and the St. Laurent by giving them color, bouquet, structure, and the capacity for aging, the breakthrough had been made.

After a learning process that has lasted a decade, Austria's red wine producers have today achieved a respectable reputation. Their

In the Seewinkel and in Rust the botrytis fungus, which dehydrates the grapes, provides good concentration and sweetness and is responsible for what are probably the most splendid sweet wines in Austria.

Rust, the old Free City on Neusiedler See, has a great number of wineries and inns within its walls, and you can try the famous Ausbruch wine in all of them.

strengths mainly lie in the fact that they have gone back to authentic native vines, such as the very traditional Austrian Blaufränkisch or the Klosterneuburg cultivation, the Zweigelt, not forgetting the St. Laurent, which also appears in other parts of central Europe but is not of any great importance there.

Efforts were originally concentrated on the Blaufränkisch. This late ripening variety with its intensely colored wines and typical deeply fruity AROMA had the advantage of, in some areas such as the central Burgenland, dominating the vineyards. Anyone who wanted to produce red wine simply could not ignore this grape. The case of the Zweigelt, the cross of St. Laurent and Blaufränkisch, which had been planted since the 1930s because of its undemanding nature, and which today even outranks Blaufränkisch in terms of area covered, is different. Only gradually did the winemakers of the Burgenland come to work out the character and the hidden qualities of these densely fruity wines and, above all, to make use of their perfect suitability for blending.

As pure varieties, but to a far greater extent as blends—occasionally with Pinot or Cabernet—these grapes also demonstrate a great capacity for aging. The first red wines have in the meantime reached a maturity where this claim can comfortably be made, and as far as the products of the 1990s are concerned, experience has shown that they are even better.

In terms of quantity, the Burgenland will never be able to compete with the great wine regions of Europe. However, in quality, the fruity Austrian red wines, structured by elegant TANNINS, have gained their place as a high-quality niche product.

STYRIA

Only around five percent of the Austrian wine-growing area is in Styria, in the south of the country. Of the 86,450 acres (35,000 ha) under vines here in the 16th century, scarcely a tenth remains. However, the wines of the "Tuscany of Austria," as the south of Styria in particular is often known, have been among the most popular in the country since at least the mid-1980s. On the one hand, this is because Styrian wine makers were hardly involved at all in the glycol scandal, and on the other, because they developed early a sense of what customers wanted. Their wines are dry, as a rule, light and fruity, and therefore more adapted to the changes in taste of the 1990s.

As far as climate is concerned, Styria is influenced by Mediterranean conditions, but the altitude of the vineyards—on the southern slopes of the Alps—ensures mild temperatures. It is no accident that a quarter of the wine-growing area is covered with Welschriesling, a sixth with Weißburgunder and Chardonnay, and a further fifth with other members of the white range such as Müller-Thurgau, Sauvignon Blanc, Traminer, Muscat, or Grauburgunder. Of the reds, only Zweigelt and Blauer Wildbacher have been able to establish themselves over about a quarter of the wine-growing area. The latter however is hardly ever made into red wine, but almost exclusively into Schilcher, the characteristic Styrian rosé.

The most famous Styrian region, and as far as area is concerned the largest, is southern

Styria (Südsteiermark) on the borders of Slovenia, where in the Maribor area the cultivation of vines has continued almost seamlessly from imperial times. A good proportion of the wine has the right to bear the Austrian title *Bergwein*, as it comes from vineyards with a slope of more than 26 percent.

It is almost exclusively white wines that are produced, and the Welschriesling, seen in other regions merely as a base for mass-produced wine, here develops into a multifaceted, fruity

In the autumn mist fills the valleys of southern Styria. On the high slopes where *Bergwein* is picked the skies are clear. The altitude means that production is almost exclusively limited to white wines and the rosé Schilcher.

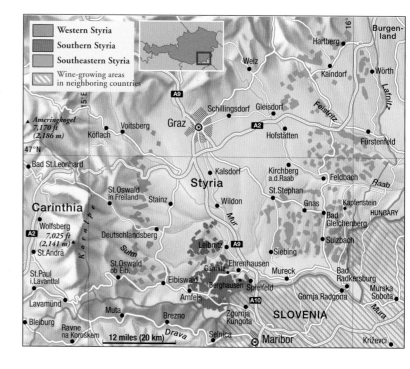

Welcome to Schilcher-Land

While the vineyards of southern and south-eastern Styria are mainly stocked with white varieties, a red grape, the Blauer Wildbacher, rules in western Styria. Its origins probably go back to the 4th century, but it never spread much outside the southeastern part of the Austro-Hungarian Empire. In Styria, the Wildbacher is mainly used to produce the rosé wine Schilcher. It is a genuine regional specialty, but often displays such a high degree of crisp acidity that the wine seems almost undrinkable to unaccustomed palates. Although the major part of this rosé is consumed within the region itself and therefore there are no problems with sales, a number of wine producers have been attempting to give the Schilcher a more pleasing, rounded aspect over the last few years. Occasionally, longer must standing times are used to mature the Blauer Wildbacher as an actual red wine, fruity and to be drunk young.

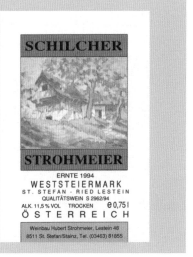

and classy wine. In addition, particularly over the last 20 years, Sauvignon Blanc has made a name for itself. Aged in steel tanks or in barrels, Styrian Sauvignons are today considered the fiercest rivals to the wines from the New World, which often cannot show nearly as much fruitiness and structure.

Apart from Sauvignon, the wine producers here cultivate another international variety, but one which has been at home in this region for so long that it almost counts as a Styrian specialty. Chardonnay has been cultivated in Styria for more than a hundred years under the name of *Morillon*, and here it shows its fruitiest, most exciting aspect, the complete opposite of those solid, broad, often buttery-seeming Chardonnays which today are mostly imported from overseas.

Around 2,718 acres (1,100 ha) of vineyards belong to the second wine-growing area in Styria, southeastern Styria (Südoststeiermark), which stretches from east of the Mur to the border of the Burgenland. Here, white varieties dominate, even more so than in southern Styria, covering a good 90 percent of the area. Welschriesling joins Traminer, Sauvignon Blanc, Weißburgunder, and Müller-Thurgau in a whole range of light and fruit-accented varieties. The Traminer is considered the specialty of the area, and in the past many wine producers have repeatedly attempted to make it known in the international arena, but the competition from Alsace, Germany, and southern Tyrol is probably too overwhelming, and the quantities harvested in Styria are too small, for this really to be successful.

Although southeastern Styria has no less than four designated wine routes in its tiny territory, it is still possible to count true quality wineries on your fingers. While southern Styria increased its presence in international markets in the 1990s, and was able to claim a respectable position with its wines, its winemaking colleagues from the east have not been able to follow this development as yet.

Finally, western Styria (Weststeiermark), smallest part of Styria, with its mere 988 acres (400 ha) of vines, is much more open to developments. At least as pretty in terms of landscape as the southern Styrian wine route, this area is in an almost unique position. In contrast to the rest of the region, it is a red variety that dominates here, the Blauer Wildbacher, which covers around 70 percent of the wine-growing area. Worries about sales are almost unknown in western Styria, because the great majority of the small amounts of wine produced from the steep slopes around Deutschlandsberg, Stainz, or St. Stefan is consumed by weekend vacationers in the *Heuriger* pubs of the estates themselves.

In Styria, wine-growing families often cultivate small vineyards and harvest by hand. Among the grapes harvested is a very finely structured Chardonnay, which has been grown here for a hundred years or more.

SELECT PRODUCERS IN BURGENLAND AND STYRIA

BIRGIT BRAUNSTEIN****
PURBACH
49 acres (20 ha); 70,000 bottles • Wines: in Purbach: Welschriesling, Weißburgunder, Blaufränkisch, Zweigelt 15 and others from → Burgstall, Rosenberg, Eisner, Heide, Glabarinza, Kirchtal, → Oxhoft Weiß, → Oxhoft Rot
Paul and Birgit Braunstein, father and daughter, are at present the most successful team in Purbach. Their estate has excelled itself with its lovely clean wines. Specially recommended is the red Oxhoft made from Cabernet and Blaufränkisch, with lots of elegance and complexity. The family also runs a notably good inn.

FAMILIE FAULHAMMER, SCHÜTZENHOF****—****
DEUTSCH-SCHÜTZEN
54 acres (22 ha) • Wines: in Deutsch-Schützen: Welschriesling, Blaufränkisch, Zweigelt, among others, from Ratschen, Weinberg, Katzenjäger, Szápari, Paigl, Bergwiesen, → Senior, → Kastellan, Allegria
At 30 percent, the Körper-Faulhammer family estate's share of Blaufränkisch is comparatively low for South Burgenland, but the wines produced from it, such as the single variety Senior and Castellan, are very good. The estate's white wines are also of respectable quality, and when circumstances allow, they bottle an interesting *Schilfwein*, the Burgenland equivalent of *Strohwein* or *vin de paille*.

FEILER-ARTINGER****—*****
RUST
77 acres (31 ha); 130,000 bottles • Wines: Welschriesling, Weißburgunder, → Pinot Cuvée; Blaufränkisch, Zweigelt, Cabernet and others from Greiner, Vogelsang, Mitterkräften, Gemärk, Umriss, → Ausbruch, → Solitaire
In Rust, on the other side of the famous Seewinkel, Hans Feiler has created a whole range of monumentally outstanding sweet wines. His Pinot Cuvée, mainly fermented and aged in the traditional wooden barrels, has hardly any serious rivals within the country. The estate, in which his son Kurt is taking on more and more responsibility, also produces an interesting selection of single variety Ausbruch alternatives. The red Solitaire, made from Blaufränkisch, Zweigelt, and Cabernet Sauvignon, can also be highly recommended.

JOSEF GAGER****—*****
DEUTSCHKREUTZ
49 acres (20 ha); 100,000 bottles • Wines: Zweigelt, Blaufränkisch, Cabernet, Merlot, from Mitterberg, Kart, Fabian, → Cuvée Quattro, → Cablot
Gager's Cablot, a blend of Cabernet and Merlot, and his Quattro, blended from the four varieties Cabernet, Zweigelt, Blaufränkisch, and St. Laurent, are truly interesting exceptions to the Blaufränkisch-dominated central Burgenland.

FAMILIE GESELLMANN****—****
DEUTSCHKREUTZ
94 acres (38 ha); 150,000 bottles • Wines include: Chardonnay, Blaufränkisch, Cabernet, from among other vineyards Steinriegel, Hochacker, Mitterberg, Siglos, Fabian, Creitzer, → Opus Eximium, → Bela Rex
The whole range of red and white wines possible in the Burgenland is produced by Engelbert Gesselmann and his son Albert, who provides the top wines such as Blaufränkisch Creitzer and the *cuvées* Bela Rex and Opus Eximium with noticeably more fruit and harmony.

PINOT BLANC

WEINHOF PAUL & MARIA BRAUNSTEIN 7083 PURBACH/SEE
HAUPTGASSE 18 TEL. 0 26 83/55 130 o. 59 13 BURGENLAND
ÖSTERREICH

FEILER-ARTINGER

2000
RUSTER AUSBRUCH
ESSENZ
WELSCHRIESLING

BURGENLAND

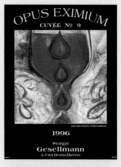

Gabarinza
2000

BURGENLAND

GERNOT & HEIKE HEINRICH***—*****
GOLS
74 acres (30 ha); 350,000 bottles • Wines: Pannobile Weiß, Muskateller, Chardonnay; → Gabarinza, Pannobile Rot, → Zweigelt
Gernot Heinrich is one of the most successful young wine makers of the last ten years. His Gabarinza red blend, made from Zweigelt, Blaufränkisch, and St. Laurent, thanks to sensibly reduced yields and careful aging, is a model of what a high-quality red wine produced from native grapes should be. The company's second top wine is, surprisingly, the dry white Pannobile.

HANS IGLER***—*****
DEUTSCHKREUTZ
25 acres (10 ha); 75,000 bottles • Wines: → Blaufränkisch, Cabernet and others from Hochberg, Kart, Goldberg, → Vulcano
Even before the death of her father, Waltraud Reisner-Igler was famed as one of the pioneers of red wine cultivation in Austria. In the late 1990s, she brought a new level of perfection to her wines. Inside the bottles lies density and complexity: on the outside, decorative artist-designed labels.

FAMILIE KOLLWENTZ, RÖMERHOF***—*****
GROSSHÖFLEIN
49 acres (20 ha); 85,000 bottles • Wines: Welschriesling, Chardonnay, Sauvignon, Blaufränkisch, Cabernet, Zweigelt, among others, from Tatschler, Haussatz, Point, Steinmühle, → Cuvée Eichkopf, → Steinzeiler, → Trockenbeerenauslese
Anton Kollwentz, supported for some years now by his son Andi, is one of the pioneers of Burgenland red wine, but has also excelled with his white wines. The superb single variety Blaufränkisch and the top quality *cuvée* Steinzeiler have been joined from the 1997 vintage onwards by an outstanding *cuvée* of Blaufränkisch and Zweigelt.

ALOIS KRACHER****—*****
ILLMITZ
18.5 acres (7.5 ha); 50,000 bottles • Wines: Welschriesling, Chardonnay and others, → Nouvelle Vague, → Zwischen den Seen, Beerenauslese, Trockenbeerenauslese
The Austrian winemaker who probably currently has the best international reputation comes from the Seewinkel. His sweet wines are among the most sought-after delicacies throughout Europe. He has chosen a full-bodied, lush, often oak-aged style for his wines, which comes through most noticeably in his Nouvelle Vague wines. Recently Kracher has demonstrated with two *cuvées* that he understands the production not just of white, but also of red wines of quality.

KRUTZLER***—*****
DEUTSCH-SCHÜTZEN
15 acres (6 ha); 50,000 bottles • Wines: Blaufränkisch, Zweigelt, Cabernet Sauvignon and others from Ratschen, Bründlgfangen, Weinberg, → Perwolff, → Alter Weingarten
In their almost unknown winery, the Krutzers created two top red wines based on Blaufränkisch which always find a place among the top 20 wines of the country. Their trump cards are the old Blaufränkisch vine stocks in excellent vineyard sites and the absolute will to create the topmost quality.

ACKNER-TINNACHER***–****
GAMLITZ
..o acres (16 ha); 95,000 bottles • Wines:
..elschriesling, Weißburgunder, Grauburgunder,
..hardonnay, Sauvignon and others from →Steinbach,
..ckberg
..ine fruity wines of character are the specialty of Wilma
..nd Fritz Tinnacher, such as their Sauvignon Blanc, the
..hite Burgundy varieties and the Gelber Muskateller.
..he Welschriesling also often comes out surprisingly
..romatic and many-layered.

HELMUT LANG***–*****
LLMITZ
..9 acres (12 ha); 40,000 bottles • Wines: Chardonnay,
..elschriesling, Weißburgunder, Sämling 88, Sauvignon;
..weigelt, Blaufränkisch, Blauer Burgunder, from
..ömerstein, Sandriegel,→ Ausbruch, → Beerenauslese,
..→Trockenbeerenauslese
..n the Neusiedler See area, known more for its lush
..xotic wines, this combination of fruit and delicate
..legance gives a quite unique dimension, in particular
..o Helmut Lang's sweet single variety wines.

JOSEF LEBERL***–*****
GROSSHÖFLEIN
..5 acres (14 ha); 70,000 bottles • Wines: Sauvignon,
..laufränkisch, Cabernet, from among other vineyards
..atschler, Reisbühel, Haussatz, Folligberg, →Peccatum
..uvée
..f Joseph Leberl wasn't so reserved and didn't have his
..eet so firmly on the ground, he would undoubtedly be
..ne of the superstars of Burgenland. His excellent
..ines, above all the Cabernet, Zweigelt, and Cuvée
..eccatum, combine a fine fruity character with a
..uccessfully maturing blend, both in large wooden
..arrels and in *barriques*.

HANS AND ANITA NITTNAUS***–****
GOLS
..2 acres (13 ha); 70,000 bottles • Wines:
..elschriesling; Cabernet, Blaufränkisch, St. Laurent,
..mong others, from →Altenberg, Ungerberg, Spiegel,
..delgrund, Hochlust, Pannobile Weiß, →Pannobile
..ot, →Comondor, Ausbruch
..ohn Nittnaus is one of the pioneers of the Pannobile
..ssociation and also one of the most experimentally
..minded of the group. In the early 1990s his wines often
..uffered from an excess of hard tannins from the grape
..nd the wooden barrel, but since the mid-1990s fruit
..as regained its rightful place in his wines.

ERICH AND WALTER POLZ /
REBENHOF AUBELL***–****
SPIELFELD/OTTENBERG
..136 acres (55 ha); 500,000 bottles • Wines:
..elschriesling, Chardonnay, Sauvignon,
..eißburgunder among others from
..→Hochgraßnitzberg, →Obegg, Nussberg, Herrenberg.
..The Polzes run their wine estate, right on the borders of
..lovenia, with the combined energy of an extended
..amily. They had made a good name for themselves as
..arly as the late 1980s with Chardonnay and Sauvignon
..and in the mid-1990s they leased the vineyards of the
..Dr. Aubell estate to add to their own.

FAMILIE SATTLER, SATTLERHOF**–****
GAMLITZ
..30 acres (12 ha); 80,000 bottles • Wines: Sauvignon,
..Chardonnay, Weißburgunder, Welschriesling, among
..others, from Sernauberg, →Pfarrweingarten,
..Kranachberg, Steirische Klassik
..One of the best wines of Styria and in addition one of
..the best restaurants in the area, both in the hands of the
..same family—surely a rare stroke of luck. As head of the

VIGOR RUBEUS

BURGENLAND

»ZIEREGG«
SAUVIGNON
BLANC

TEMENT
BERGHAUSEN

ERNST
TRIEBAUMER
RUST
BLAUFRÄNKISCH
RIED MARIENTAL

Steirische Klassik association, Wilhelm Sattler is in
charge of the fruity, honest range which is the subject of
this brand.

E. & M. TEMENT****
BERGHAUSEN
136 acres (55 ha); 300,000 bottles • Wines:
Welschriesling, Morillon, Sauvignon, Weißburgunder,
among others, from → Zieregg, → Graßnitzberg,
Wielitsch, Steirische Klassik
Manfred Tement is a perfectionist and also a man
who likes fiddling about with things, so it is no
wonder that his cellar, only a stone's throw away
from the Slovenian border, is one of the best
equipped over a wide area. He made a name for
himself early on with his wines, especially the
oak-aged ones from the Zieregg vineyards, and for
ten years he has been among the top producers in
Styria. He also, along with Franz Xaver Pichler from
the Wachau and Tibor Szémes from Burgenland,
produces a very impressive red wine.

TRIEBAUMER***–*****
RUST
52 acres (21 ha); 92,000 bottles • Wines: in Rust:
Chardonnay, Weißburgunder, Blaufränkisch, Cabernet,
Merlot, among others, from Satz, Vogelsang, Greiner,
Pandkräften, Mitterkräften, → Oberer Wald, Gmärk,
→Mariental, Hartmisch,→Ausbruch
Ernst Triebaumer's Blaufränkisch wines from Corallian
limestone and marl soils of the Mariental were already a
red wine legend in the late 1980s. They were among the
first to undergo the radical aging in new oak wood,
and since then they have increased in complexity and
balance. As for the Rust specialty, Ausbruch,
Triebaumer is also one of the best and regularly has
fruity, multi-layered white wines.

VELICH***–*****
APETLON
7.5 acres (3 ha); 30,000 bottles • Wines: Welschriesling,
Chardonnay, Neuburger, among others, from Rohrung,
Hedwigshof, →Tiglat, Darscho, → Vitezfeld,
→Beerenauslese, Trockenbeerenauslese
In the mid-1990s, Heinz and Roland Velich progressed
very rapidly to make their breakthrough into the elite
group of Austrian winemakers. First of all, the pair
convinced their amazed public with their bright and
clean *Beerenauslesen* and *Trockenbeerenauslesen* from
Seewinkel. However, their undisputed masterpieces
were their barrel-fermented Chardonnay and Pinot Gris
wines. Their Tiglat, without a doubt, is one of the really
great European Chardonnays and perfectly unites the
mineral character of Burgundy with the lush fruit of
good New World Chardonnay.

WINKLER-HERMADEN**–****
KAPFENSTEIN
36 acres (14.5 ha); 80,000 bottles • Wines:
Welschriesling, Weißburgunder, Chardonnay,
Sauvignon; Zweigelt, among others, from Kirchleiten,
Winzenkogel, An der Kapelle, Schlosskogel,
Rosenleiten, Steirische Klassik, → Olivin, Caphenstein
As one of the few wine producers of Southeast
Styria, Georg Winkler-Hermaden, in his castle of
Burg Kapfenstein, has attracted attention from
outside the region. His Burgundies are particularly
strong and expressive and his Traminer—a specialty
of the company—and a *barrique*-aged Zweigelt by
the name of Olivin, leave no room for doubt that
this region can produce interesting red wines in
good years.

LUXEMBOURG

Wine has been grown on the left bank of the Mosel since the time of the Romans. Wormeldange is one of the most important wine-growing communities of the Duchy.

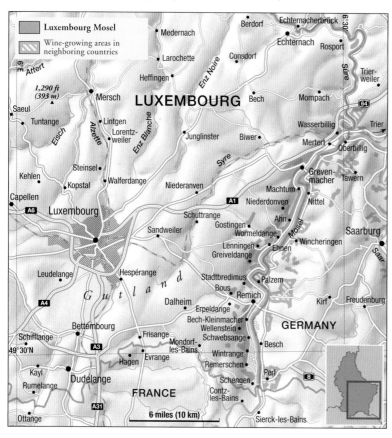

From Wasserbillig in the north to Schengen in the south, the wine-growing lands of Luxembourg follow the Mosel, covering 3,316 acres (1,342 ha). Ten years ago there were 3,469 acres (1,404 ha). The decline is mainly due to growers leaving the business. This tiny wine-growing district produces almost exclusively dry aromatic white wines, but although the area under cultivation is small, Luxembourg can look back on a long history of viticulture. Excavations on the banks of the Mosel have unearthed burial artefacts from the 5th century BC decorated with depictions of grapes and wine leaves.

The Mosel in Luxembourg consists mainly of slopes, some of them steep and in a few cases even spectacular, most of which face southeast or southward. A boat trip along the river shows the steep slopes at their most impressive, and you get an idea of the effort required of the winegrowers to work their plots of land. For some years now, restructuring has been accompanied by a notable improvement in the working conditions in the vineyards, thanks to the effects of numerous mergers. In only ten years the number of individual estates was reduced by 637. The already difficult growing conditions are exacerbated in this northern

Wine hierarchy in Luxembourg

The Weinbauinstitut (Institute of Viticulture) in Remich was founded in 1925 and represents the will of the Luxembourg government to have a wine industry strongly oriented toward quality. In 1935 the Institute created the *Marque Nationale du Vin Luxembourgeois* with the declared aim of guaranteeing the origin and a regulated standard of quality for the consumer.

A further step in the direction of a more clearly quality-oriented viticulture was taken by the government in 1959 when it introduced several additional categories with the terms *Vin Classé*, *Premier Cru*, and *Grand Premier Cru*. In 1971 the *Marque Nationale* was adjusted to match European legislation,

and since 1980 the *Marque Nationale-Appellation Contrôlée* has been issued as a guarantee of quality. This and additional signs of recognition of higher quality are awarded after tasting the wine, which is evaluated by experts according to the 20 points system:

less than 12	*Vin de Table*
12–13.9	*Vin de Qualité (V.d.Q.)*
14–15.9	*V.d.Q. – Vin Classé*
16–17.9	*V.d.Q. – Premier Cru*
18–20	*V.d.Q. – Grand Premier Cru*

All wines that bear the *Vin de Qualité* label must be bottled in Luxembourg and have to carry a prescribed sticker or label on the back

with the guarantee term and a control number.

It should be pointed out that the wines are classified strictly according to criteria of quality, so that their origin has no part in their evaluation.

The "hit list" of Luxembourg varieties:

Rivaner	32.6%	decreasing
Auxerrois	13.2%	increasing
Pinot Gris	13.0%	strongly increasing
Riesling	12.8%	level
Elbling	11.0%	strongly decreasing
Pinot Blanc	10.0%	increasing
Pinot Noir	6.2%	strongly increasing
Gewürztraminer	1.0%	level

climate by frequent rainfall. The annual average rainfall is 28 inches (72.5 cm). In this rather modest-sized wine-growing area, which is 26 miles (42 km) long and some 357–433 yards (330–400 m) wide, it makes little sense to emphasize local features. However, there is a clear difference in the soil between the canton of Grevenmacher in the north and that of Remich in the south. In the north, the soil is formed by shell limestone, and the valley is narrower. The wines there are more polished and after a few years of MATURING they gain in class. In the more southern area, from the community of Stadtbredimus on, the soils mainly consist of red and clay marl, and the valley here is wider, producing fuller, more harmonious wines which, however, sometimes may be lacking in character.

The Rivaner grape rules in Luxembourg, a crossing of Riesling and Gutedel developed toward the end of the 19th century and better known as Müller-Thurgau. In the early 1980s it still dominated almost half of all the vineyards, but since then its share has fallen to some 32.6 percent. The Rivaner, a grape with a decidedly high yield, gives lightly fruity and pleasant but rather plain wines. The Elbling, too, which has been cultivated here since Roman times, has come under pressure in some years due to its extraordinarily high acidity. Even when climate conditions are good, it produces only a light, effervescent wine. It is an ideal thirst quencher, but otherwise ends up being used in sparkling wine production.

With increasing decisiveness, Luxembourg winemakers are turning to varieties which are of higher quality and better able to express their particular *terroir*. Riesling, which ripens particularly late on the Mosel slopes and is fermented to make dry, light wines, here also represents elegance and a mineral quality and develops an

attractive, intensive bouquet. It is among the best varieties, but Pinot Gris and Auxerrois have surpassed it in the meantime. The success of the Auxerrois may be surprising as it does not have the best of reputations. It finds its own character along the Luxembourg Mosel; well-rounded, well-structured, and with aromas often determined by citrus, it can undoubtedly be seen as a specialty. Auxerrois plainly outdoes Pinot Blanc in the wine producers' favor—the latter mostly produces somewhat more sinewy, but rather less fruity wines.

Apart from Riesling, the most notable success in the Grand Duchy has been with Pinot Gris. Its advantage lies in its low acidity, intensive aromas and generosity, which in sunny years gives it a certain opulence. Auxerrois, Pinot Blanc and Pinot Gris cultivation has doubled within the last thirty years. Pinot Noir has also become immensely popular, its area increasing tenfold in ten years. Gewürztraminer and Chardonnay are rare exceptions in Luxembourg wine growing.

Just beyond the pretty wine villages of Luxembourg, which lie in the valley, the vineyards begin, often rising very steeply.

Cooperatives and Individual Winemakers

In Ahn the winegrowers have made use of the more level south and southeast facing slopes and divided these into broad terraces.

Opposite
In the northern part of the region shell limestone determines the soils and the wines. The latter are pleasingly slender-bodied and have a lot of class.

As happened to so many other wine regions, the Moselle Luxembourgeoise experienced a serious crisis in the early 20th century, which led to the formation of wine producers' cooperatives in the years after the First World War. In the wineries built at the time, in Grevenmacher, Wormeldange, Greiveldange, Stadtbredimus, Wellenstein, and Remerschen, it was possible to get a better grip on the problems of viticulture, wine production and sales. A further step was taken in 1966, when all the cooperatives joined together to form "Les Domaines de Vinsmoselles." Its approximately 800 members own two thirds of Luxembourg's wine-growing land, with the majority of the wine producers only working their vineyard plots part-time, as most of them own less than two and a half acres

(1 ha) of vineyard. Today 62 percent of total production comes from the Vinsmoselle wineries. Over the last ten years, however, their area of land has decreased, because the independent sale of grapes has proved more lucrative for the winegrowers.

There are now 53 independent wine estates which largely vinify the grapes from their own vineyards themselves, and these are increasing in importance. All of them mainly produce dry, completely fermented wines, but often also crémant. In recent years there have been more and more examples of *barrique* aging, introduced in 1982 by the Domaine Aly Duhr, and even of EISWEIN. To date, there have been practically no *Spätlese* or *Beerenlese* wines produced.

The third important power in the alliance of Luxembourg wine production is the wine trade. Its 35 companies bottle 17 percent of the total production of around 4,277,200 gallons (160,000 hl). The wine trade is responsible for introducing crémant, production of which began in the 1920s. The wine trading companies are mainly supplied with grapes by estates and contracted winegrowers.

Crémant de Luxembourg

The production of sparkling wines has a certain tradition in Luxembourg. Just as in neighboring Germany, in Luxembourg, too, grapes are imported from abroad, among other places from northern Italy. Alongside these branded sparkling wines, which are produced by the Charmat method, though some are also bottle fermented, the true Crémant de Luxembourg has asserted itself. Since 1991, this has been the only *appellation* recognized outside France. Vinsmoselle lead

Yields and chaptalization

The maximum yield has been reduced in Luxembourg since 1993. For Rivaner and Elbling, only 3,700 gallons per 2.5 acres (140 hl per ha) are permissible; for other, better quality grapes, it can be only 3,170 (120 hl). Many wine producers in the Grand Duchy today regret following the German model and setting quantity above quality. Today, a more French philosophy of cultivation generally prevails, as expressed in the *Appellation d'Origine Contrôlée* system, which is seen as the proper example to follow on this bank of the Mosel.

The E.U. limited the amount of CHAPTALIZATION, or adding grape juice to increase the sugar levels, in Luxembourg to 3.5 degrees and thereby set the maximum value. However, a new directive has lowered this level for wines of at least 9.5% alcohol per volume to 2.5 degrees and prohibited producers from exceeding 12.5 percent alcohol. The aim is to encourage wine producers to improve the quality of their grapes in order to create wines with a higher alcohol content. In the Grand Duchy, it is recognized that wines with a relatively low alcohol content cannot be objectively compared with foreign products, which for the same variety of grape will often show a higher alcohol content.

Select Producers in Luxembourg

Mathias Bastian**
REMICH
29 acres (11.7 ha); 85,000 bottles • Wines include: →Riesling, Pinot Gris, →Auxerrois, Gewürztraminer, Chardonnay; Pinot
The family estate has well-placed vineyard sites on the slopes of Remich and Wellenstein. Grapes are picked by hand in several repeated harvests and the wines aged in stainless steel, but oak casks are used for Chardonnay and Pinot.

Domaine Clos des Rochers**
GREVENMACHER
23.5 acres (9.5 ha); 50,000 bottles • Wines: →Pinot Gris, Riesling, Auxerrois, Pinot Blanc
The Clasen family, who also own the well-known sparkling wine house Bernard-Massard, have created this estate. It was one of the first to introduce low yields, grape selection during harvesting, and modern winery techniques.

Domaine Mme Aly Duhr**
AHN
22 acres (9 ha); 70,000 bottles • Wines: →Riesling, Pinot Gris, Pinot Blanc, Auxerrois, Gewürztraminer; Pinot Noir; Crémant
For over 300 years the Duhrs have been producing wine along the Mosel and they cultivate steep slopes in the Ahn area. One of the best estates of Luxembourg, working with a very high planting density of 7,500 vines, strict pruning and selection of grapes harvested.

Domaine Mathes**
WORMELDANGE
22 acres (9 ha) • Wines: →Riesling, Auxerrois, Pinot Blanc, Pinot Gris, →Crémant
The Mathes family has planted 60 percent of their vineyards with Riesling. Thanks to low yields, they

have won numerous awards for the Crémant and for their *grand premier cru* wines.

Domaine Sunnen-Hoffmann**
REMERSCHEN
12 acres (5 ha); 40,000 bottles • Wines: →Riesling, Auxerrois, Pinot Blanc, Pinot Gris, Gewürztraminer; Pinot Noir
This domaine, founded in 1872, has vineyard plots on the best sites of Remerschen, Schengen and Wormeldange. After pneumatic pressing, vinification is carried out in stainless steel, and some wines are aged in old tuns of 265 gallons (1,000 l).

Domaine Thill Frères*–****
SCHENGEN
30 acres (12 ha); 70,000 bottles • Wines: →Château de Schengen Pinot Gris, →Pinot Blanc, Auxerrois, →Riesling, Gewürztraminer
The house of Bernard-Masset has, since 1986, also been responsible for the management of one of the largest wine companies of the country. Rich soils combined with strict quality criteria in the vineyard and during harvesting result in full, maturable wines.

Les Domaines de Vinsmoselle*–**
STADTBREDIMUS
2,124 acres (860 ha) • Wines: all grape varieties, Art et Vin, →Schengen Markusberg Pinot Blanc, →Wormeldange Koeppchen Riesling, →Crémant Poll-Fabaire
This association, formed in 1966 from six wine producers' cooperatives, has around 800 members and produces some 2,642,000 gallons (100,000 hl) per year, which makes it the most important producer of still and sparkling wines in the Grand Duchy by a considerable margin. From simple Rivaner and Elbling to classy *grand premier cru* wines, Vinsmoselle offers an astonishing range of differing varieties.

---

in this branch of the industry, too, with three quarters of crémant production. The conditions of production set down that the wine has to consist exclusively of the grapes from its own wine region, and it is mostly Elbling, Pinot Blanc, Auxerrois, Riesling, Pinot Noir and in increasing quantities Chardonnay that are used. In addition, the wine must spend nine months on the yeasts before DÉGORGEMENT.

Whether the wines are crémant or still, the people of Luxembourg are their own best customers. They are the world's leading wine consumers, with an annual consumption of 15 gallons (55 litres) per person. Although they very much enjoy a cultivated cuisine and test which wine to drink with what dish, people enjoy a glass of wine at any time of the day. In cafés, wine is usually served in a glass with a green foot, similar to those in Alsace or along the Rhine. It is usually drunk very cold. Just as in Alsace, no meal is complete without wine, as people along this part of the Mosel prefer a French lifestyle.

ENGLAND AND WALES

Despite being home to many of the great consumers and connoisseurs of the world's wines, England is only a minor player on the wine production stage. This apparent paradox is explicable: it is precisely because England is not a major wine producing nation that it has come to appreciate as a consumer wines from the four quarters of the globe. And, because the English are so fond of their wines, despite high latitudes and the depredations of an inhospitable climate for quality *Vitis vinifera* grapes, they have applied a typically stiff upper lip to the production of grapes and have done the best that they can in trying circumstances. If the English wine industry had a motto, it might adopt the words of William Edward Hickson: "If at first you don't succeed, try, try again."

Based on the discovery of the pollen of *vinifera* vines in Essex and Suffolk, it is believed that the vine was introduced to Britain long before Julius Caesar came, saw, and conquered. From findings of amphorae on the sites of Roman towns, it appears that wine consumption increased considerably after the Roman invasion of Britain. It is not clear whether the vine was widely cultivated in Britain during the Roman Empire but, from the discovery in 1995 of a 20-acre (8 ha) Roman vineyard in Northamptonshire, it seems clear that a certain amount of wine at least was made. In 731, Bede

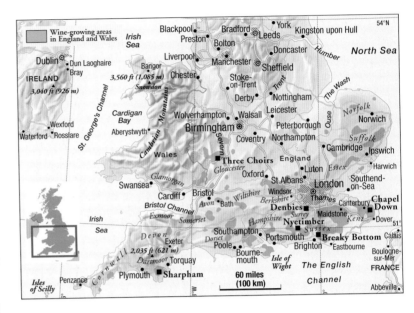

records in his *Ecclesiastical History* that "wines are cultivated in several localities," and by the 9th century, vineyards made an appearance in the law code of Alfred the Great.

By the time of the Domesday Book, there is a record of 38 vineyards, only 12 of which were monastic. Vineyards steadily grew in size and number, so much so that the number rose to 300. Two factors intervened to check this progress, however. First, Henry II's marriage to Eleanor of Aquitaine in 1152 saw a huge increase in trade in wine with France. Secondly, the Black Death stopped England's nascent wine industry in its tracks. By the time of the dissolution of the monasteries in 1536, English vineyards had become virtually extinct.

English viticulture did not cease entirely after the Middle Ages, however. Domestic wine growing continued, albeit on a very minor scale, more as the hobby of a handful of well-to-do landowners. The seeds of the modern industry were sown in 1946 by a research chemist, Ray Barrington Brock, in his four-acre garden in Oxted in Surrey. The first commercial vineyard of the modern era was established by Sir Guy Salisbury-Jones at Hambledon in Hampshire in 1951. The pioneering Major-General was followed by a handful of other enthusiasts, none however with much experience either of viticulture or winemaking. Most of the styles of this early era were based on Germanic crossings and hybrids planted to ripen in England's cool, maritime climate, and the early style of English wine was, consequently, Germanic.

St. George's Winery has well cared for, closely planted vineyards in East Sussex and is well known for its fresh and fruity Müller-Thurgau.

A boom of sorts occurred in the early 1970s and by 1985 the area under vine was 1,060 acres (430 ha). On 10 June 1992, as evidence that English wine had come of age, the Queen served the 1988 Chiddingstone Pinot to President Mitterand at a state banquet. By the turn of the century, England had almost 2,470 acres (1,000 ha) under vine, producing an average of over two million bottles a year. Gradually styles have evolved from the Germanic toward drier unoaked and oaked styles for whites along with botrytized sweet whites, and toward champagne-method sparkling wines and a smattering of oak-aged reds. While most vineyards in England and Wales are of modest size and rely on tourists and cellar-door sales, there are a number of growers who sell direct to wineries, as well as a handful of commercial vineyards, notably Denbies at Dorking in Surrey with some 250 acres (101 ha) under vine, Chapel Down at Tenterden in Kent, and Three Choirs in Newent, Gloucestershire.

The 400-odd vineyards of England and Wales are concentrated in the relatively mild, southern regions of the country, in particular in the Home Counties of East and West Sussex and Kent, with the most northerly planted in Durham close to the 55th latitude. Although with fewer than 1,000 sunshine hours England is too cool for winemaking according to the WINKLER SCALE (see page 812), the harshness of the northerly climate is mitigated by the warming influence of the Gulf Stream. Given England's geographical location, selecting early-ripening, disease-resistant grapes for south-facing sites is important, along with protection from spring and late frosts and wind, relatively low rainfall, and altitudes of not much more than 325 feet (100 m) above sea level. As it is, the English harvest does not normally take place until late October or early November.

It is probably too early to say that English wine has specific regional characteristics; nonetheless,

Wine harvest on the Hambledon estate in Hampshire.

the United Kingdom Vineyard Association recognizes six specific wine regions. Weald and Downland covers the vineyards of East and West Sussex and Kent and is relatively mild with clay and chalk soils. Wessex covers the more temperate climate counties on the south coast, of Dorset, Hampshire, Wiltshire, and the Isle of Wight. South West and Wales, which comprises the western tip of the British Isles, tends to be dominated by westerly winds blowing in off the Atlantic and with them, wet weather. Thames and Chiltern covers the Home Counties of Berkshire, Buckinghamshire, London West, and Oxfordshire and is the warmest of the regions. East Anglia comprises the flat, windy counties on the east coast, and, finally, Mercia, covers the Midlands and the North.

Not to be confused with British wine, which is made from imported grape concentrate, English wine is made from fresh grapes grown in England. Most of England's grape varieties are early ripeners, the most widely planted of which is Müller-Thurgau, which produces a fragrant floral, off-dry or medium dry. Müller-Thurgau is followed by Reichensteiner and then the hybrid Seyval Blanc, which suits the English climate and can be made in both unoaked and oaked

Denbies, the largest wine estate in England, in Surrey, southwest of London. Technically, it is state of the art. Harvesting here is done by machine.

The Hidden Spring Winery is not far from Hastings and the south coast. Apart from the fashionable red, their Seyval Blanc is of interest.

styles to produce, respectively, a Sauvignon-like or Burgundian-style dry white. It is controversial, however, in the sense that it has made it difficult for the English wine industry to gain recognition from the European Union whose Quality Wine Scheme excludes hybrid varieties. Aromatic whites are made from Huxelrebe, Schönburger, and Bacchus, while Madeleine Angevine is also a relatively popular white variety which can, on occasions, be characterful.

There are as many as 44 grape varieties grown to make wine in England and Wales, most of them hybrids or crossings of Germanic origin, although there are some premium varieties in the form of Chardonnay, Pinot Noir and even Cabernet Sauvignon. The Chardonnay and Pinot Noir is for the most part used to make sparkling wine with at least two estates, Nyetimber and Ridgeview, set up to make sparkling wine exclusively. Indeed there are those who believe that England's future, if it has one as a wine producer, lies in sparkling wines. Cabernet Sauvignon is grown with Merlot in polytunnels at Sharpham in Devon, where it is blended and aged in French oak to produce a light, cool-climate red table wine in the Loire Valley or New Zealand style.

Bill Darey from Denbies is happy with the ripeness of his Pinot grapes.

SELECT PRODUCERS IN ENGLAND

BREAKY BOTTOM***
RODMELL, EAST SUSSEX
5.5 acres (2.5 ha) • Wines: Müller-Thurgau, →Seyval Blanc, Cuvée Rémy Alexandre
Thanks to the dedication of its owner Peter Hall, this tiny vineyard in its lovely, isolated hollow of the southern Downs has become one of England's most sought-after addresses. Hall is celebrated because of the quality of his wines, which are based on low yields of the unfashionable hybrid Seyval Blanc. Some plots are having their stocks renewed with Chardonnay, Pinot Noir, and Pinot Meunier for sparkling wine.

CHAPEL DOWN**
TENTERDEN, KENT
27 acres (11 ha); some bought-in grapes • Wines include: Pinot Blanc, Bacchus, Schönburger, Reichensteiner, Pinot Noir
Britain's largest commercial winery produces a range of very interesting and also prize-winning wines, among them the Chapel Down sparkling wine, some remarkable reds, and aromatic dry whites under the Curious Grape label. The wines are made by Owen Elias, U.K. Winemaker of the Year in 2001 and 2002. Visitors' centers in the Tenterden and Lamberhurst vineyards are open daily.

DENBIES**
DORKING, SURREY
250 acres (101 ha) • Wines: 20 different grape varieties including Dornfelder and Pinot Noir; Brands: →Surrey Gold, →Special Late Harvest
With over 250 acres (100 ha) of wines, this company with its visitors' center and Napa-style winery in the hills near Dorking is England's biggest wine estate. It produces a variety of different styles of wine, including white and red table wines and sparkling wine. Surrey Gold was chosen for the House of Commons wine list.

NYETIMBER***
WEST CHILTINGTON, WEST SUSSEX
37 acres (15 ha) • Wines: Chardonnay, Pinot Meunier, Pinot Noir, Première Cuvée, Blanc de Blanc Brut, Classic Cuvée
This medieval estate, renovated by Stuart and Sandy Moss from Chicago, now belongs to the songwriter Andy Hill. Set in rolling downland near the south coast, it was the first estate in England to be planned and

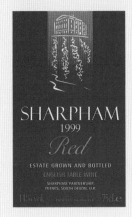

planted so as to meet the exact requirements of the champagne method. The estate has gained recognition because of the excellent quality of its sparkling wine aged on the yeasts, and the most recently released vintages have won gold medals at the *Vinalies* in Paris and top awards in Britain.

RIDGE VIEW WINE ESTATE****
SUSSEX
16 acres (6.5 ha); some bought-in grapes; 30,000 bottles • Wines include: Blanc de Blancs, Blanc de Noirs
Mike Roberts has equipped his prize-winning estate to produce the best quality sparkling wines from classic champagne varieties. He uses traditional methods to create a series of five different wines. For the *assemblages*, he and his son, together with the assistant winemaker Simon, use a number of different grafts and clones.

SHARPHAM**
DART VALLEY, DEVON
10 acres (4 ha) • Wines include: Madeleine Angevine, Dart Valley Reserve, Sharpham Red, Beenleigh Red
Planted mainly to Madeleine Angevine, the estate produces, alongside cold-fermented, dry white wines, a barrel-fermented white. Pinot Noir, Cabernet, and Merlot are grown at nearby Beenleigh Manor. Sharpham's founder, the philanthropist Maurice Ash, died in 2003, but the partnership is continuing to develop estate activities such as wine growing, cheese-making, and organic milk production.

THREE CHOIRS**
NEWENT, GLOUCESTERSHIRE
74 acres (30 ha) • Wines include: Phoenix, Premium Selection; Classic Cuvée
Britain's second largest producer, which has invested a million pounds in a new winery, produces a series of commercial wines made from, among other varieties, Seyval Blanc, Schönburger, Bacchus, Huxelrebe, and Phoenix. It also makes a red and a white which are both barrel aged, a nouveau and a sparkling wine. The estate also operates an award-winning restaurant and hotel, and in 2003 it opened a small brewery.

David Schwarzwälder

SPAIN

Spain as a Wine-producing Country

Spanish wine production can be followed right back to the second millennium BC. The Phoenicians gained a foothold in Spain around 1900 BC and subsequently left the first traces. The first references to systematic cultivation of extensive vineyards date back to the Greek colonization of Spain from 700 BC. Near the Bay of Roses in the modern day province of Girona, the Greeks founded the city of Empúries. Today, the quality wine-producing area of Empordà-Costa Brava is regarded as the true starting point for the spread of *Vitis vinifera* in Spain.

The remains of significant wine-pressing equipment can be found in Catalonia and also in Navarra, La Rioja, and Valdepeñas. The mash was fermented in tanks hewn out of the rock and then flowed through channels, also cut into the rock, and collected in earthenware containers. This method is still used today, particularly in La Rioja, where the peasant winegrowers ferment their COSECHERO wine in the traditional way in open tanks made of brick or hewn from the rock.

A few centuries later, the Romans managed to industrialize wine production, distributing the wines pressed in the various provinces throughout the Mediterranean region. After the fall of the Roman Empire and the rule of the Visigoths, the Arab conquerors tolerated wine growing in their Christian territories, although they did not promote it. The Arabs distilled wine spirit for medicinal purposes, and careful study of the literature on the Court of Córdoba reveals repeated references to the cheering effect of wine, which leads to the conclusion that the

The Finca San Cristóbal estate near Jerez de la Frontera.

Islamic rule of abstinence was not taken too literally during Arab rule.

In the period of armed conflict that existed between the Christians and Arabs until the Moors were finally defeated in 1492 and the Christian *Reconquista* of the Iberian Peninsula, wine growing was often the only method of cultivation to survive the ravages and pillaging reasonably intact. The rootstocks proved extremely difficult to remove since they had spread out over a wide area due to the dry climate.

The Beginnings in Jerez

As the first wine-growing regions of any significance, Jerez and Málaga developed an important market in the 16th century, extending beyond Spain. Lured by the tax privileges, the first foreign merchants settled in today's capital of Manzanilla, Sanlúcar de Barrameda. The *sack* or *saca* that denotes Spanish exports was the favorite drink of the English court at that

The New Spanish Wine Law

The new Spanish wine law, *La Nueva Ley de la Viña y el Vino*, will bring far-reaching changes, and discussion is still going on over the new legislation, which was passed on June 28, 2003. The biggest problem is that the various wine-producing regions of Spain are implementing the law in different ways. The future quality classifications are a key point. Until now the only classes have been table wines, country wines, and D.O. and D.O.Ca wines. The new list contains two further classes, table wines of designated geographical origin (*Vinos de Mesa con Indicación Geográfica*) and the highly controversial class of estate wines (*Vinos de Pago*), which represents the new peak of Spanish quality wines. Some are accusing the new list of being too vague. Others fear it will cause confusion among buyers. The discussion over the definition of estate wines is particularly keen. Theoretically, the term *Vino de Pago* means estate wines from the table, country, D.O. and D.O.Ca. growers. An estate wine from a normal D.O. area (V.C.P.R.D.) could initially be thought to be the same as one from a table wine district, although for years the quality control for a D.O. has been much more stringent in every respect than that for the *Vinos de Mesa*, which are subject to only minimal control. To give one example, the La Mancha district in Castile anticipated the new legislation last year and introduced its own interpretation of estate wines, simply assigning their own D.O. to the recognized *Pagos*, of which there are only two so far, Dominio de Valdepusa (Marqués de Grinon) and Finca Elez (Manuel Manzaneque), both of which used to be recognized as simple country wines. It is an open question whether a wine produced in La Mancha in the past within a D.O. can be recognized as an estate wine. We are also still waiting for an exact definition by the central government of, for example, the maximum size a *Pago* (estate) may have, how far away its cellars may be, and what methods of control the wines will be subject to. These open questions must be settled by June 2004. Another important point is the regulation of the names of the wines. Under the new regulation a company could market wines from different appellations under one and the same brand name.

time. At the end of the 18th century, it saw a return to favor. It was during this period that such famous companies as Osborne and Garvey came into being.

BODEGAS AND COOPERATIVES

In Castile, meanwhile, wine-growing regions such as that around the Medina del Campo had reached the peak of their fame. For a while, the town had almost 500 *bodegas*, or wineries. In the mid-19th century, people began to lay the foundations of modern Spanish viticulture in La Rioja, and in 1850, Luciano de Murrieta produced the first "modern Rioja" using vat-fermenting methods, thereby establishing the basis for an impressive success story. In 1872 Josep Raventós founded the Codorníu sparkling winery. After 1930, the first *Denominación de Origen* (D.O.) regions came into being: Jerez in 1935, Málaga in 1937, and Montilla-Moriles in 1945. As early as the 1920s, La Rioja was given an initial, provisional regulatory mechanism, but did not become a D.O. in its present sense until 1947, and then only in conjunction with the region of Tarragona.

The consequences of the Civil War, which ended in 1939 with victory for Franco's army, crippled the Spanish wine-growing industry. People tried to bring this decline under control by re-establishing cooperatives and by processing the huge quantities of grapes in a more efficient and economical way. This led to the creation not only of the upper-middle-class *bodegas* but also of the second of the two types of winery that still dominate most of the Spanish wine market today.

To understand the Spanish wine situation, it is essential to know that even now, among the winegrowers, there is only a small middle stratum that markets its own products. Famous regions such as the D.O.Ca. Rioja or Jerez are dominated by large wineries, the traditional *bodegas*, which have only a small wine-growing area of their own and procure grapes or even young wine under contract from winegrowers within the region. Traditionally, in addition to VINIFICATION, the *bodegas* believed their work lay in vat fermenting and in bottle-aging wines. In this way, they met the wishes of Spanish wine drinkers, who appreciated mature wines of consistent quality each year.

The number of wooden vats offered large *bodegas* many opportunities to blend wines. This enabled cellarmen to guarantee that quality remained as consistent as possible each year. They also took care to add a limited amount of older wine. In many northern Spanish wine shops,

The old Contino estate with its impressive cellar stands on a bend in the river Ebro, not far from Logroño. It produces an excellent estate-bottled Rioja.

people attached greater importance to maturity than to the VINTAGE, and as a result a label would describe a wine as being "in its fifth year," displaying the actual vintage only on the back label. The cooperatives, on the other hand, aged only a very small quantity of their wine in the barrel, and concentrated on supplying branded producers and selling simple young wines.

Nowadays, the distinctions that were once so strict are becoming blurred. Nearly all *bodegas* have become modern wineries that are now working very hard toward attaining vintage character. The only feature that remains is their dependence on other people's wine harvest; the same is true of the cooperatives. Many now age an excellent drop of wine in the barrel. There has also been a palpable change in those growers who bottle their own wine. In the past few years, many have broken free of the large concerns and taken a step toward autonomy. They are responsible for a major part of the revolution in the quality of Spanish wines over the last 10 years, creating several top-quality wine specialties that point the way for the entire Spanish wine-producing industry, especially the large traditional wineries.

The château concept, or *concepto de château* as the Spanish call it, is another new development. In line with the French model, a considerable number of producers have become established within a relatively short period of time, adhering more or less strictly to the claim of making wines using only their own grapes. It has to be said that soil and position have not been typical considerations when looking at the history of Spanish wine. But this is exactly where the future lies, because hardly any other country in mainland Europe has so many good situations and soils for wine growing as Spain.

Colossus under Control

When speaking of Spain as a wine-producing country, two salient points spring to mind. First, it has the largest wine-growing area in the world, with 2.89 million acres (1.17 million ha); 15 years ago, it was even greater at 3.75 million acres (1.5 million ha). Second, it is the most mountainous important wine-producing country. Within Europe, only Switzerland and Austria have more mountain ranges running through them and naturally this has an effect on growing conditions. It goes some way toward explaining why Spain is not one of the mass producers of wine, but has an annual output of around 925 million gallons (35 million hl), with one acre of land producing, on average, considerably less wine than in the other western European wine-producing countries.

Contrary to the obvious assumption that nothing could be simpler than producing wine in the Spanish sunshine, the opposite has often proved to be the case. For one thing, the arid conditions in some areas makes intensive planting impossible, while in many upland parts of the country, and thus throughout central Spain, the sprouting vines are at risk from spring frost. Spanish vines are just as susceptible to cold and drought as any other vines. It therefore comes as no surprise that in a country covering such a large area, the yield is comparatively low.

The maxim "a vine that has to fight produces good quality wine" is still applicable in wine growing today. And so it was only a matter of

Vines pruned in the traditional goblet shape are often low growing. This protects them from the wind, but means harvesting is a backbreaking job.

Freixenet in Sant Sadurní d'Anoia in the Penedès region has become one of the world's major sparkling wine producers.

time before Spanish winegrowers began to exploit the opportunities and turn toward quality production. During the 1980s and 1990s, Spanish viticulture experienced a period of modernization and reorganization. Special attention was paid to raising the quality throughout the wine-producing region and to promoting many small wine regions, which were encouraged to produce quality wines that complied with the strict regulations of the *Denominaciónes de Origen* (D.O.). Between 1987 and 1997, more than 20 new D.O. regions were created in this way. Many long-forgotten traditional grape varieties were prevented from disappearing completely, and new cellar technology helped create wines of hitherto undreamed-of qualities. Spain's wine range has changed considerably, and today a thoroughly impressive variety of the most diverse wines is pressed in more than 62 D.O. regions.

Not just Mediterranean

The division of Spain into D.O. regions is as simple as it is incomplete, because high-quality table wines gradually appear at the edge of these *appellations*. To get a general idea, it might be helpful to have a brief look at the various climatic zones that define the country. The variety and diversity of Spanish wines is the result of the interactions of the three main zones: the Atlantic climate, the continental climate, and the influences of the Mediterranean. There are

also many areas of overlap, and mini-climates caused by the extremely variable orography of the Iberian Peninsula.

The Cantabrian mountains in the north form a natural barrier that protects inland Spain from the moist Atlantic air currents. Similarly, the Sierra Morena mountain range to a great extent protects the broad plain of La Mancha, south of the capital, Madrid, from the Mediterranean influences that dominate Andalusia. La Mancha accounts for roughly half of total Spanish production. Between these two mountainous areas, mainly in Castile–La Mancha, Castile–León, and Aragón, the harsh continental climate prevails. West of Gibraltar, on the other hand, Atlantic influences once again predominate, transforming the region around Jerez into an in-between zone, creating the unique conditions for making sherry and Manzanilla.

In the east, the climatic zone influenced by the Mediterranean is very narrow, since the mountain ranges extend practically to the coast here. There are, however, gaps in this barrier, such as the Ebro valley, which conducts warm air currents inland. This gives rise to the special climatic situation of the La Rioja region, where Atlantic, Mediterranean, and to a lesser extent continental influences overlap. Navarra also exhibits a similarly complex situation. There are always little pockets of isolated climatic zones, such as Toro in Castile–León, for example, which experiences extremely low rainfall. As a result of this complex climatic situation, no clear distinctions can be made in terms of wine style. The wines are greatly influenced by the variety of grape. For this reason, typical wines can be attributed to climatic zones only to a limited extent.

The region of La Rioja, with its Atlantic climate, produces fine wines that bear little resemblance to the commonly held idea of fiery, glowing red wines. In good years, they have the potential to keep exceptionally well. The same is true of Navarra and Somontano. In the northwest of the country, and the transitional area of El Bierzo in northwestern Castile–León, there are exceptionally fruity red wines. On the plateau north of Madrid grow quality grapes of a totally different type. They are distinctive for being full-bodied, often with a slightly higher alcohol content. There is also no doubt that the wines of the Duero valley are excellent. Catalonia is famous for cava, but also for soft, Mediterranean red wines, ripe Chardonnays, and opulent Priorats, which are some of the most sought-after wines in the country.

Galicia
Castile–León
Basque Country
La Rioja
Navarra
Aragón
Catalonia
Extremadura
Madrid
Castile–La Mancha
Valencia
Murcia
Andalusia
Balearic Islands
Canary Islands
La Palma
El Hierro
Tacoronte-Acentejo
Valle de Güímar
Valle de Orotava
Ycoden-Daute-Isora
Abona
Lanzarote
Wine-growing areas in neighboring countries

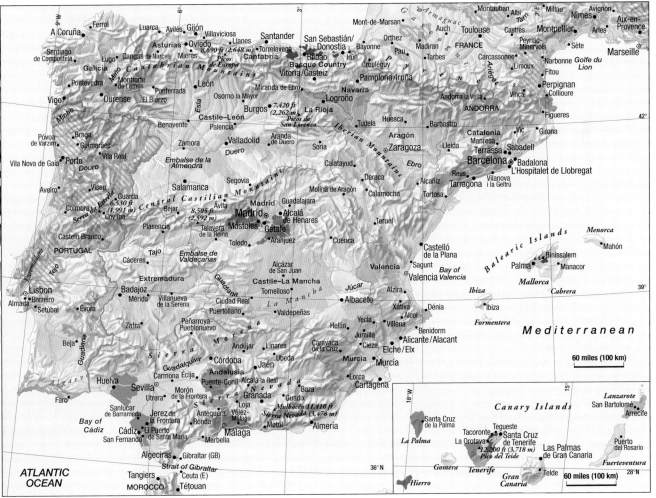

Further to the southeast, you can take a walk through the history of Spanish wine. There are all sorts of sweet wines to taste, made from Muscatel, Monastrell (or Mourvèdre), and Malvasía grapes. Some of these wines are still produced in the same way that they were 300 years ago, when they were drunk in all the royal houses of Europe, together with the equivalent wines from Andalusia. The highlands of Valencia and Murcia produce a large quantity of red wine, which is traditionally sold for blending or in barrels as top-up wine. The large stocks of old vines have in the last few years prepared the soil for red wines of increasingly high quality. Jumilla has played a pioneering part in this development.

The region of La Mancha extends south of the mountain range that dissects Castile, and is famous for its good champagne base wines, which are mainly exported; light, clean white wines and sometimes earthy, soft, easy-drinking *tintos*. White grapes still clearly predominate, easily accounting for 70 percent of all grapes grown. The D.O. Valdepeñas lies like an enclave in the southern part of the D.O. La Mancha. It produces full-bodied and soft red wines that are sold fully aged in wooden casks in true Spanish style.

Andalusia has its own unique range of wines. The distinctive Finos, Manzanillas, and Olorosos, which occur here solely due to a vagary of nature, are indigenous to the province of Cádiz. Sea air, FLOR YEAST, the addition of wine spirits, and MATURING by a method of decanting vertically from one row of casks into another

produces wines worthy of a much more exalted status than mere aperitifs. Nor should we forget the respectable dessert wines from Málaga, which do not deserve the stigma of being cheap and mass-produced. Here, too, renewed efforts are being made to raise quality.

Extremadura in the Southwest is in a state of flux between modern and rustic wines. With only a few exceptions, the wines produced here are simple but smooth and rich, as you would expect Spanish wines to be. The range of grape varieties grown is as wide as the various soil conditions. Extremadura is both the underdog and the future of Spanish wine growing. This situation can also be applied to the islands in the Atlantic Ocean and Mediterranean Sea. The Balearic Islands, in particular Mallorca, offer the right climate and soil to produce original wines, but the range of varieties is an unknown quantity for many wine producers. The vintners there are beginning to exploit this potential. The classical Tintos, which now seem obsolete, are being replaced by modern qualities with greatly improved character. Some of the dessert wines produced on the Canary Islands are of excellent quality. Overall, the situation can be viewed in a positive light: the wines need to have a more consistent finish, and further research needs to be carried out into varieties. BARRIQUE wines are rare; young wines that can be quickly consumed are the order of the day. However, the potential is excellent.

Cádiz—the capital of the region of Andalusia, and the traditional home of sherry—still feels the effects of the raid led by Francis Drake. In 1587, he purloined 2,900 barrels of sack, as the sherry intended for export was known, from the harbor, loaded them onto ships he had seized, and dispatched them to England, where they received a very enthusiastic welcome.

SPANISH GRAPE VARIETIES

There is such a wide range of Spanish grape varieties that even experts find it bewildering. The picture becomes clearer only if you concentrate on the most important ones. Of the practically indeterminable number of grape varieties that grow in Spain—there are reputed to be approximately 600 varieties—about 15 principal varieties can be described as truly Spanish. These account for about 75 percent of the total wine-growing area. It is not only the names of some of these grapes that vary from region to region. The wines they produce also vary greatly due to the wide variations in climate and soil conditions.

At the top of the list are two black grapes that are Spanish grapes *par excellence*: the Tempranillo (called *Tinta del País* in Ribera del Duero, *Cencibel* in La Mancha and Valdepeñas, and *Ull de Llebre* in Catalonia) and the Garnacha.

To a great extent, Spanish winegrowers owe their top-quality wines to the blue-black-red Tempranillo, which develops magnificent fruit notes of cherry, raspberry, and blackberry and, because of its well-balanced tannin structure, ages excellently in oak. This most noble Spanish variety is the main black grape variety in the wine-growing regions of La Rioja, Ribera del Duera, Valdepeñas, and Penedès, and plays a prominent role in some smaller D.O.s.

The Garnacha Tinta is the black variety most commonly grown in Spain. It is found practically everywhere. However, it plays a very important part in La Rioja, Navarra, Campo de Borja, Cariñena, Calatayud (Aragón), Madrid, and in the D.O.s of the province of Tarragona in Catalonia. Until recently, experts were rather dismissive of this grape because of its tendency to oxidize. It had a sound reputation only as a grape for producing *rosado*. Since the splendid wines of the D.O. Priorat brought it to fame overnight, it has aroused great interest. The Garnacha Tinta combines wonderful strawberry and raspberry fruit notes with strong spicy tones, giving it a very distinctive character. Some French wine enthusiasts know this grape, which originated in Spain, as Grenache, which produces spectacular results in Châteauneuf-du-Pape, for example.

Other important indigenous black varieties are Cariñena, Graciano, Tinta de Toro, Mencía, Monastrell, and Bobal. There is no doubt that the last three produce good wines, but like the Garnacha they tend to oxidize rapidly and so do not age well in oak casks. Wine producers counter this shortcoming by adding more stable varieties. The potential of these varieties has barely been explored, and undoubtedly in future it will be possible to produce wines that can be aged from them.

Spain has several hundred grape varieties.

There are already examples of good Monastrell wines aged in oak. These require old vines that produce small quantities of grapes with a strong TANNIN structure, and Spain still has enough of these. Cabernet Sauvignon, Merlot, and Syrah, the three most important French red wine grapes, have acclimatized very successfully in many areas and have for many years now produced presentable results both as single-VARIETAL and blended wines. In Spain, the Cabernet matures to produce a soft wine. In the Mediterranean regions, this variety, with its marginally increased complexity due to its pronounced tannins, nearly always matures fully, but in the case of high yields it develops a roundness that lacks character. In areas where Cabernet is not grown in large quantities, it can produce excellent results. The best Spanish Cabernets are juicy, full-bodied, and extremely heavy.

The Syrah is worth a special look. It took Spanish wine producers a long time to recognize that this variety from the Middle East produces fantastic results in some areas, such as the Priorat region, the upland areas of Penedès, the highlands of the Levant (Jumilla), and Castile–La Mancha. At present, Syrah is grown in only very small areas, but it should have an important part to play among Spain's red wines in the future.

RARE AND MASS-PRODUCED WHITE WINES

The white varieties are led by two grapes, the Albariño from Galicia and the Verdejo from Rueda in Castile, both of which have only recently won the fame they deserve. They may not be widespread, but their potential and distinctive character place them at the top of the list of Spanish white wines. Verdejo produces expressive wines with good acidity, high glycerin content, and delicate citrus AROMAS. The strength of these wines does not lie in their fruitiness but in their mineral notes, coupled with slight hints of aniseed and a very typical, delicately spicy bitterness in the finish. This very unusual composition of BOUQUET and flavor gives Verdejo a character of its own among the white grapes of Europe. It is the main variety in the Castilian D.O. Rueda.

The Albariño, on the other hand, thrives on its impressive apricot, kiwi, and passionfruit notes. At home in the far northwest of the peninsula, it is the principle variety in the D.O. Rías Baixas of Galicia.

The most common white grape varieties are the Airén—indigenous to the largest consolidated wine-growing region in the world, La

Tempranillo or *Tinta del País* is the top-quality Spanish grape variety and is a defining feature of the best Rioja and Ribera del Duero wines.

The Albariño grape is Galicia's top variety and is responsible for making the Rías Baixas into a cult wine, blending freshness and strength to perfection.

Uva Palomino is really a very ordinary variety that does not reveal its true quality until the sherry *flor* yeast sets to work, when it develops its distinctive character.

Mancha, and the most frequently grown white wine grape in the world—and the Viura, also called Macabeo. It is no secret that the quality of the Airén bears no relation to its distribution. But with the help of modern technology, it can be used to make perfectly respectable, clean, if rather bland young wines.

The Viura, on the other hand, is a much classier grape altogether. It forms the basis for cavas and attractive white wines and is just as at home in La Rioja as it is in Navarra, the new D.O. Ribera del Guadiana in the southwest of the country, or in Costers del Segre in Lleida. In terms of distribution, it can be regarded as the counterpart of Garnacha Tinta. The wines it produces are accessible and have a floral, fresh fruit character with a pleasing acidity.

SWEET AND SPICY SPECIALTIES

The grape varieties used to produce wines from Jerez, Córdoba, Málaga, and Huelva merit special mention. Palomina is the grape that grows on the white *albariza* soils around Jerez de la Frontera in the province of Cádiz. Wines from the Montilla-Moriles region are produced mainly from the famous Pedro Ximénez grape, while the D.O. Málaga makes its astonishing wines partly by using sun-dried Moscatel grapes. Two varieties of Moscatel are at home in Spain. In the case of the large-berried Muscatel, which produces the famous sweet wines of the Levant area and Málaga, it is the popular Muscat of Alexandria grape, found throughout the world. Thanks to plenty of sun, its wines are extremely full-bodied and aromatic. The small-berried Muscatel, found in Navarra, is much more delicate and displays greater acidity, as can be seen from the fine, elegant Moscatel wines from this region.

This list of Spanish varieties is by no means exhaustive. Less common specialties can be found on the islands, but also in damp Galicia or in the hot Levant. They are nearly always used in *cuvée* wines or for blending, but definitely make their mark on the wines. These and other varieties will be discussed later, together with the more famous grape varieties.

PIONEERING CATALONIA

Several times in the eventful history of Spanish wine Catalonia has been the starting point for fundamental developments. Archeological finds suggest that the Greeks produced Spain's first wine in modern-day D.O. Empordà–Costa Brava. The Roman emperors were already drinking wines from today's D.O. Alella, and made it famous within their empire. Over 100 years ago, modern viticulture was started in Spain in the Penedès region with the introduction of the bottle-fermenting process for making cava, adopted from Champagne in France. Finally, in the 1970s, the Catalan wine pioneers laid the foundations for scientific and contemporary wine production and set a technical standard that is acknowledged everywhere. It is therefore all the more remarkable that after such a technical fresh start it took Catalonia such a long time to leap to the top of the quality league. A large number of producers worked solidly, but outstanding wines were still rare until relatively recently. Now Catalonia produces some very attractive wines.

At the foot of the Montserrat mountain, home to Catalonia's most important shrine, stretch the vineyards of the Penedès area, famous not only for its extremely successful sparkling wine, cava, but also for producing top quality dry wines.

Although the various regions of Catalonia have much in common, the new D.O.s developed differently. Catalonia's range of wines reflects that of the rest of the country, and wine specialists all over the world use it as a barometer for all of Spain. This is mainly because Catalonia is one of the most dynamic wine-producing regions in the world. One of the most recent signs of this dynamism was the introduction of an umbrella *appellation*—the dream of many wine regions, even outside Spain—which involved grouping the nine individual D.O. wine-growing regions together to form the V.C.P.R.D. (*Vinos de Calidad Producidos en Regiones Determinados*) Cataluña. This umbrella *appellation* guarantees quality wine from a clearly defined growing region. Although it serves the interests of the major producers, who operate at an international level, committed winegrowers such as those in Priorat are campaigning for their vineyards to be recognized and protected.

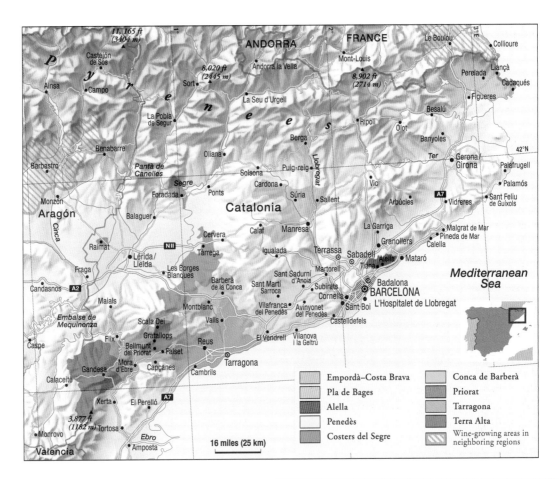

Empordà–Costa Brava		Conca de Barberà	
Pla de Bages		Priorat	
Alella		Tarragona	
Penedès		Terra Alta	
Costers del Segre		Wine-growing areas in neighboring regions	

16 miles (25 km)

The quality *barrique* cellar of the Bodegas Mont Marsal illustrates the fact that dry red and white wines are also a good bet in the Penedès region.

An Adventurous Choice of Varieties

Catalonia's wine regions offer an astounding range of varieties. In addition to the indigenous varieties, in particular some other native varieties that are needed to produce cava (see pages 584–5) and the Tempranillo, known here as Ull de Llebre, the Catalans were very forward-looking and quickly accepted high quality French grapes. Catalonia was the first place in Spain to produce the single-varietal Cabernet and the first successful vintages from indigenous and Bordelais grapes. The first such vineyards are now at least 20 years old and are able to produce deep and well-structured wines.

The cava *bodegas* now reserve the traditional, hand-operated vibrating racks solely for their prestige wines.

The cellarmen of Catalonia have been very resourceful. On the one hand, they have managed to keep up with fashion trends and produce some excellent barreled Chardonnay wines, for example, by being quick to make use of varieties that have now become international. On the other hand, they are aware of the astonishing wealth of native varieties that enables them to create wines with very individual styles. There is still great potential in this area, which enological grand masters such as Miguel Torres, José Luis Pérez (Mas Martinet), or the Albet y Noya brothers are only now beginning to exploit. Over 30 grape varieties that were under threat of extinction are now being grown again in trial plots belonging to major Catalan wineries and perfected by means of clone selection. A large part of the proceeds from wine production is invested in research in the field of enology, which is developing apace in this region.

Ecological Trends

In the last few years, the development of organically produced wines has caused a stir in Catalonia. With almost 50 recognized organic winegrowers, the region has more organic winegrowers than any other country. As a result of the ideal conditions for environmentally friendly cultivation (the dry and warm climate and the poor soils make it easy to do without chemical plant and grape treatments), winegrowers in Catalonia comply strictly with legislation, which pleases clients who are still mostly outside Spain.

Most of the estates are in the Penedès region, but there are also some in Tarragona. Top wine producers such as the Albet y Noya brothers or Antoni Capel (Masia Freixe), whose wines are mentioned in the same breath as the very best Catalonian vintages, insist that the wines produced by these organic winegrowers must be taken seriously. Low yields from the most carefully tended vineyards are another factor in attaining success.

Undiscovered Tradition

As in most regions that have gradually made a name for themselves with modern wines, the old styles of wine have by no means died out. In the small D.O.s, wines known as *vinos rancios* have a certain part to play in Spain's wine-growing history. These are dry wines made from Garnacha Blanca or Tinta, which are picked when very ripe and stored for many years in large tuns without the addition of any wine spirit. They are often stored in the open air, and occasionally glass containers are also used. The sweet *vino generoso* is another variety that a few producers continue to make. In its preparation, once FERMENTATION has begun, wine spirit is added to stop it, thereby retaining a considerable amount of RESIDUAL SUGAR. Unlike the southern Levant, Garnacha is the main predomi-nant grape used to make the MUST, with Moscatel being used more rarely. Sweet Mistela grapes are also an old winegrowers' tradition. These are used to make unfermented sweet must, which is prevented from fermenting by adding wine spirit. Tasting these archaic wines is just like going back in time, but after a good meal, the dessert wines still prove that they have an important place.

Apart from the Penedès region and the Costers del Segre, the Garnacha and Tinta grape varieties account for a significant proportion of the vineyards in the Catalan *appellations*, a fact that is bemoaned by forward-thinking winegrowers. After the dramatic turn-around in the fortunes of wine in Priorat, whose new wines rely at least in part on musts from old Garnacha vines, people have come to recognize that the black Garnacha, if harvested in small quantities, can produce full-fruit and exceptionally rich wines. The problem facing the small D.O.s is how to break up the rigid, old structures, and to encourage winegrowers to allow new techniques to influence their wine-making methods. Priorat is not the same thing as Catalonia, but even the less well-known wine-growing areas of the region are still full of possibilities.

With its numerous restaurants, Barcelona is one of the most important buyers of its provincial wines, whether white, rosé, or red. But nothing tickles the Catalans' taste buds more than cava.

Harmonious Sparkling Wine: Cava

Along with Antoni Gili, who bottled the first Catalan sparkling wine as early as 1862, Josep Raventós has a very important place in the history of CAVA. Raventós studied the classic production process in Champagne itself. He put his experience into practice on the 100-year-old Can Codorníu estate in Sant Sadurní d'Anoia, 30 miles (50 km) west of Barcelona, using indigenous grape varieties. When, in 1872, he officially presented his first sparkling wine in Barcelona, it was the start of a new era for the Penedès region and the enological modern age for Catalonia.

Ever since the first bottles were produced, the Penedès cava has been pressed from the same grape varieties the Catalan varietal triumvirate of Xarel·lo, Macabeo, and Parellada. Paralleda can spoil easily, thereby reducing the quality of the wine, unlike the increasingly widespread Chardonnay, which improves the quality considerably if grown in the right sites.

Like many cava buildings, the reception hall at Rondel was built by architects of the *Modernisme* movement, the Catalan equivalent of Art Nouveau.

Torreblanca is one of the smallest and best cava wineries.

Traditional Method

For a wine to bear the cava quality mark it must be made using the traditional method of BOTTLE FERMENTATION, which is basically the French MÉTHODE CHAMPENOISE. Thus, the differences between cava and champagne lie in the choice of grape, the soil, and the climatic conditions.

After harvest, the grapes are de-stemmed and carefully pressed. The must is usually filtered straightaway and individual varieties ferment separately. After careful tasting, the cellar masters decide the blending of the various CUVÉES for the final wines. Before bottling selected yeast and sugar, or must-concentrate, are added to produce the second fermentation in the bottle. The quality of the yeast is critical to the final taste. Good yeast can make average base wines into good cava, but not the other way round.

After fermenting in the bottle and storing on the yeast for at least nine months, the now dead yeast is shaken down into the neck of the bottle. This is usually done using a *girasol* or gyropallet. The neck and yeast are frozen, the bottle is opened, and the frozen yeast plug is removed. The bottle is then topped up with the producer's own secret mixture, usually older wine and sugar. This DOSAGE decides the type and the sugar content of the cava and its appropriate description.

A spicy and aromatic dosage is important for small artisan wine producers, as it gives each cava its individuality. Once topped up, the bottle is sealed with a cork with a star on its base to show quality and authenticity.

In the case of better-quality wines, the *cavistas* go well beyond the minimum nine months, because until the cava reaches a certain age, and depending on the quality of the yeast, its complexity of flavor increases considerably during this aging period. The title of *gran reserva* refers to this aging period and can be used only for cavas that have been aged on the yeast for at least 30 months. The term *reserva*, on the other hand, is purely a marketing ploy. The *cavistas* wish to emphasize a product that is merely special in their opinion.

A good cava should be soft, fresh, have a slightly fruity-yeasty flavor, and no excess acidity. Unlike champagne, there is an extremely important rule for cava: once on sale, even if it is a vintage cava of the very best quality, it should be drunk as soon as possible, because a cava leaves the cellar when the producer considers it to be ready for drinking.

SELECT CAVA PRODUCERS

ALSINA & SARDÀ***–****
VILAFRANCA DEL PENEDÈS
131 acres (53 ha); 50,000 bottles • Wines: Alsina & Sardà Extra Brut, Alsina & Sardà Brut Reserva
The concern is situated right in the heart of the Penedès. The family's specialties are soft, harmonious cavas with a consistent mild yeasty flavor. The top-of-the-range cava, Brut Nature Sello, which is aged for up to three years, is supple and full-bodied.

CAVAS DEL CASTILLO DE PERELADA
PERELADA
247 acres (100 ha); bought-in grapes; 1,250,000 bottles • Wines: Castillo Perelada Brut Nature, Castillo Perelada Rosado Brut, →Castillo Perelada Gran Claustro Extra Brut, Rosado Dalí
The prestige brand name of Gran Claustro (60,000 bottles are sold every year) is still made in the company's original premises in Girona. A wonderful example of a classic soft cava with a light *fines-herbes* finish.

CAVAS FERRET***–****
GUARDIOLA DE FONT-RUBÍ
25 acres (10 ha); bought-in grapes; 280,000 bottles • Wines: Ferret Novíssim Brut, Ferret Brut Reserva, Ferret Rosado Extra Brut, Ezequiel Ferret Extra Brut
Ferret is one of the Penedès region's small but distinguished firms. The cavas contain a high proportion of the Parellada grape, which is harvested in the upper Penedès area near the *bodega*. The highly aromatic Rosado cava deserves special mention as it is one of the stars of its class.

CAVAS LLOPART***–****
SANT SADURNÍ D'ANOIA
148 acres (60 ha); 220,000 bottles • Wines: Llopart Reserva Brut Natural, Integral Brut, →Leopardi Brut
This family concern, founded 1887, ensures that its cavas are left to mature on the yeast for a long time. The wines are complex and full-bodied. The estate's vineyards, on slopes with a high calcium content, are among the best in Penedès and are worked organically.

CAVAS MONT FERRANT***–****
BLANES
Bought-in grapes; 300,000 bottles • Wines: Blanes Nature Extra Brut, Mont Ferrant Brut, Mont Ferrant Gran Reserva Brut
One of the few important wineries not in Penedès. The grapes, however, are bought from top vineyards in upper and central Penedès. The wines are always wonderfully fruity. The top-quality →Reserva Brut vintage is full-bodied, with a good structure and texture.

CAVAS NAVERÁN***
SANT MARTÍN SADEVESA
247 acres (100 ha); 350,000 bottles • Wines: Naverán Extra Brut, Naverán Brut, →Naverán Chardonnay
A traditional winery. Although famous for its cava, it produces more non-sparkling wine. Cavas are full-bodied rather than elegant, but are described as typical because of aromas. The single-varietal Chardonnay cava →Dama de Naverán is worth noting, as it displays a masterful combination of yeast and fruit aromas.

CODORNÍU***–*****
SANT SADURNÍ D'ANOIA
6,672 acres (2,700 ha) • Wines: 1551 Extra Brut, Mediterrania Extra Brut, Gran Codorníu Brut, Non Plus Ultra Extra Brut, →Ana de Codorníu Brut, →Cuvée Raventós Brut

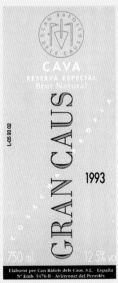

The Penedès classic and the pioneer of cava production using the traditional champagne method. During the last 100 years the company has invested more than almost any other in technical research into wine production. It has introduced Chardonnay, and is experimenting with Pinot Noir. This group includes Raimat, which also produces high-quality cavas, Masia Bach, Rondel, and Bodegas Bilbainas in La Rioja. Codorníu is the market leader in Spain and even its basic products are more than all right. Its top-of-the-range cavas are among the best in the country. →Cuvée Raventós with a high Chardonnay content, the *fines-herbes* →Ana de Codorníu, and →Jaume de Codorníu.

FREIXENET**–****
SANT SADURNÍ D'ANOIA
1,038 acres (420 ha); bought-in grapes • Wines: Carta Nevada, Cordon Negro Brut, Freixenet Brut Extra, Freixenet Reserva Real Brut, →Freixenet Vintage Brut Natural, Brut Barroco
Freixenet has long been the name for the best cava throughout the world. The group also owns the wineries of René Barbier, Castellblanch, and Segura Viudas, which, with its →Reserva Heredad, was one of the first producers to make champagne-quality wines, and also the Champagne firm Henri Abelé. The largest sparkling wine producer in the world also produces wines under its own name, which was coined in 1915 from the La Freixeneda estate. Such wines are of remarkable quality and include the rich, rather conservative Brut Barroco. The →Reserva Real with its fresh, pleasantly yeasty character, and the smooth Freixenet Vintage are highly recommended. From a technical point, the cellar is the most modern *Denominación Cava* producer at present.

GRAMONA****–*****
SANT SADURNÍ D'ANOIA
72 acres (29 ha); 160,000 bottles • Wines: Tres Lustros Brut Natural, Gramona Tira Extra Brut, →Celler Batlle Brut, Gramona Imperial Brut
This famous company still uses very artisan production methods, but is known for its balanced *cuvées*. The young Jaume Gramona, professor of enology at the University of Tarragona, is an expert in maturing cava. His →Tres Lustros and the legendary →Celler Batlle (fermented *sur lie* for seven years!) are particularly good examples of complexity and delicacy.

ROVELLATS***–****
SANT MARTÍ SARROCA
519 acres (210 ha); 350,000 bottles • Wines: Rovellats Brut Nature, Rovellats Brute Nature Chardonnay, Rovellats Grand Cru Masia S. XV Extra Brut, →Rovellats Brut Imperial
Not just famous for its star-shaped cellar tunnel, this dream estate produces smooth, lively, and elegant cavas that never disappoint with their clear character and clean taste. The →Brut Nature is a very lively yet complex cava made by the company. Rovellats is a Chardonnay veteran in the Penedès region.

AGUSTÍ TORELLÓ****
SANT SADURNÍ D'ANOIA
63 acres (25 ha); bought-in grapes; 180,000 bottles • Wines: Agustí Torelló Mata, Brut Natural, →Kripta, Quercus
Traditional company producing smooth, very fruity cavas. Quercus came to fame with its top-quality →Kripta wine, which was guaranteed to cause a stir simply because of its amphora-shaped bottle. It is a very mature cava with a floral aroma and strong notes of freshly baked bread and dried fruits.

Catalan Wine Regions I

Empordà–Costa Brava

Ampurdán, or Empordà in Catalan, where 6,178 acres (2,500 ha) of vineyards are now cultivated, was once the cradle of Spanish viticulture. From the medieval period onward, people here, as in neighboring French Banyuls, produced naturally sweet wines from Garnatxa, the Garnacha grape, or characterful *rancios* with their high alcohol content. More recently, they failed to catch on to modern trends and consoled themselves with producing rosé wines, which met with the approval of tourists. Only in the last few years have black French varieties been planted, vinified using modern methods, and sometimes blended with the indigenous Garnacha and Cariñena grapes to create well-rounded, harmonious red wines. The Castillo Perelada gives an indication of their great potential.

Parellada—a traditional cava grape.

Pla de Bages

The few winegrowers and cellarmen of the 1,236-acre (500-ha) region around Manresa, northwest of Barcelona, made a conscious effort to gain independence, which they achieved in 1995 by becoming a D.O. Prior to that, their grapes had gone to the cava industry. Since then, large areas have been replanted, particularly with the Cabernet, Merlot, and Tempranillo grapes, which enrich the traditional Garnacha and Sumoll grapes. The vineyards in the central mountains influenced by the Mediterranean are particularly suitable for well-balanced red wines.

Alella

Pressure from the expansion of nearby Barcelona threatened to engulf the vineyards of Alella, which became a D.O. as long ago as 1956. Luckily, in 1989, the D.O. situated next to the Costa Brava was extended into the hinterland on four plateaus known as the Vallès, which reach altitudes of up to 813 feet (250 m), so that there are now 1,297 acres (525 ha) of vineyards. At the same time, the region's few producers revolutionized their style and took to producing light and fresh white wines using modern vinification methods and the traditional Pansà Blanca grape (as the Xarel·lo is called here), and the newly planted Chardonnay. The pleasant red wines, usually made from Tempranillo, Cabernet, and Merlot, are in the minority. The region's best-known label is Marqués de Alella from Parxet.

Penedès

Penedès is considered to be the cradle of modern Spanish wine growing. After the PHYLLOXERA outbreak, the region went over to supplying mass-produced wine to meet the rising demand from abroad for cheap vatted wine. Although famed for centuries for robust red wines, the dominance of white grapes came about with the rapid development of the cava industry. Nowadays, two-thirds of the 66,717 acres (27,000 ha) of the region's vineyards are planted with white grapes, most of which are used to produce cava. Whereas in the past they produced champagne base wines for markets throughout Europe, the thriving cava industry now uses almost all the region's grapes.

The Mediterranean climate usually enables the grapes to reach an enviable degree of ripeness, making the *tintos* soft and juicy, and the white wines aromatic. A total of 15 varieties can be used. Alongside the traditional cava grapes of Xarel·lo, Parellada, and Macabeo, and indigenous black varieties such as Ull de Llebre (Tempranillo), Garnacha, Monastrell, Cariñena, and Samsó, Bordeaux varieties are also grown, together with Pinot Noir,

Most winegrowers in and around Sant Sadurní d'Anoia harvest their grapes themselves and sell them to one of the major cava wineries.

Sauvignon Blanc, and even Riesling. Penedès offers suitable conditions for practically every variety of grape, because the vineyards extend from the Mediterranean Sea up to a height of 2,600 feet (800 m).

The D.O. is divided, unofficially yet logically, into three sub-zones according to topography: lower Penedès, which stretches along the coast from Sitges to El Vendrell; central Penedès, protected from the sea by a coastal mountain range; and upper Penedès, which is bordered to the east by the Serra Litoral mountain range.

The breakthrough for still wines did not come until the 1960s and 1970s. A few enterprising wine producers, led by Miguel A. Torres, had started to plant foreign varieties alongside Spanish quality grapes such as Tempranillo (Ull de Llebre). Modern cellars with stainless steel tanks and new barrels sprang up in just a few years. Temperature-regulated fermentation had become the norm in cava production, and still wines benefited from this experience. The fact that for years all the wines that left the *bodegas* were merely average occurred to only a very few enologists. People were interested only in technology, and forgot about the soul and regional character of the wine in their quest for perfection. But wine-growers failed to reduce the yield and concentrate on specific *pagos* (sites). As a result, the wines, although they were still rich and round, threatened to become too smooth and bland, as can be seen in the case of many Cabernets, the most frequently grown foreign black grape variety. An increasing number of smaller producers are now giving Penedès a fresh treatment. They recognize that quantity is not the same as quality and that it is the *pagos* which gives the wines their identity.

Miguel A. Torres is one of Spain's most respected wine producers. This old barrel cellar is at his head office in Vilafranca del Penedès.

Whereas new plantings in the Penedès region and elsewhere in Spain now use state-of-the-art viticultural methods, in all older vineyards the vines are kept in the traditional goblet shape.

COSTERS DEL SEGRE

The only *appellation* of the province of Lleida takes its name from the river Segre. The four sub-zones of the D.O. Costers del Segre, ratified in 1988, have three things in common: extreme fluctuations in temperature; high sunshine levels; low rainfall. With barely 9,884 acres (4,000 ha) of vineyards this D.O. came into being at the initiative of the Codorníu Cava group, which built one of Europe's most impressive wineries here, named the Raimat estate. When the project began in 1914, most wine experts shook their heads at the idea of building a winery in this location. The soil around the estate had a very high salt content and was almost desert-like. Healthy soil had to be spread over hundreds of acres, and it was possible to cultivate grapes only thanks to an irrigation system that was extremely modern for its time, using the river Ebro.

Most of the vineyards are in the eastern area of the D.O., in the Vall del Riu Corb and Les Garrigues. Nearly all the new concerns, for instance Car Vinícolas Reunidas, or Celler de Cantonella, started up here and so followed the top producer, Castell del Remei. The red wines pressed from Garnacha, Ull de Llebre, Cabernet, Monastrell, Trepat, Samsó, Pinot Noir, or even Syrah grapes, usually have a wealth of character because of the harsh climatic conditions. The top-quality wines are also very good for laying down. On the southeastern border, there are old vineyards stocked with Garnacha Tinta. The chalky soils there also offer ideal conditions for top varieties such as Tempranillo. As far as white grapes are concerned, the cava varieties dominate, together with Chardonnay and Sauvignon Blanc, because even here Catalan sparkling wine can be produced.

CONCA DE BARBERÀ

Cava wine producers are also very interested in this 9,883-acre (4,000-ha) wine-growing area that lies between the Penedès region and Costers del Segre, especially as at 1,625 feet (500 m), and on predominantly chalky soil, it produces extremely fresh and fruity wines. The dominant grape varieties of Macabeo and Parellada are mostly used for producing cava wine. The area, which did not become a D.O. until 1989, has many new plantings, including a large amount of Chardonnay, but Cabernet, Merlot, and Pinot Noir also find favorable conditions here. Only a few of the wines are bottled under the D.O., which is renowned for its fresh, young white wines.

Catalan Wine Regions II

Priorat

In the last few years, Priorat's economy has experienced a dramatic upturn, and its red wines are now some of the most expensive and sought-after in Spain. The rediscovery of this region, which had more inhabitants in Roman times than it does today and which was one of the most famous agricultural regions in medieval times, has sparked interest in Spain in forgotten wine-growing areas.

René Barbier, whose predecessors created the cava of the same name, was the instigator. He got to know and love the Priorat region at the end of the 1970s, and in 1979 began to redevelop an old vineyard there, Clos Mogador, which opened like a Roman amphitheater on to the Siurana river valley. Friends and acquaintances followed his example, namely Carlos Pastrana (Clos de L'Obac) and José Luis Pérez (Clos Martinet).

The unique feature of the Priorat area lies in its situation. It is a geologically isolated wine-growing region, surrounded by a ring of precipitous mountains that only descend slightly in the southeast to the sea. Within these natural barriers, the fascinating landscape of narrow valleys and hills rises to between 800 and almost 2,000 feet (250–600 m) above sea level. The vineyards are laid out in steep rows and terraces which can usually only be cultivated by hand. The soils are characterized by slate remains, called *licorella*, which produce only

small yields, because the vine has to penetrate to great depths to find water. For a long time, Garnacha grapes were grown, then Cariñena after the phylloxera outbreak. Yields rarely exceed 1,800 lb per acre (2,000 kg per ha), which is why the musts are so rich in EXTRACTS and produce wines of great depth and intensity, with warm, luscious fruit, typically mineral notes, and an alcohol content that, although 14 to 15 percent, is never obtrusive. Garnacha is undisputedly the star grape of the Priorat region, even if Cabernet and Syrah (which is predicted to have a bright future here) also exhibit great character on this unique soil.

René Barbier and his friends, who include Álvaro Palacios (L'Ermita, Finca Dofí) and Daphne Glorian (Clos Erasmus), recognized star quality. The immigrants, as the newcomers were called, first set up a small, primitive cooperative and put their first wine (of 1989) on the market in 1991. This wine was a joint vintage which each of them bottled under their own label and which was sold outside the Spanish aging system. It quickly caused a stir, and only two years later four of the five immigrants had wineries of their own.

These wineries owe their breakthrough into the top-price bracket for Spanish wines to Álvaro Palacios. This young man from La Rioja had managed to take on a magnificent vineyard, topped with a hermitage, which was planted with Garnacha vines in 1940. When he

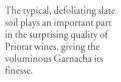

The typical, defoliating slate soil plays an important part in the surprising quality of Priorat wines, giving the voluminous Garnacha its finesse.

bottled his L'Ermita in 1993, he thought it was better than the only really expensive Spanish red wine, Vega Sicilia. Bravely and confidently he put L'Ermita on the market at an even higher price—and met with success.

José Luis Pérez was no less revolutionary when, together with the Catalan singer Lluís Llach, and on condition that they cooperate, he urged the winegrowers of the village of Porrera to demand six times the usual price for grapes at that time. He realized that this was the only way to maintain the old wine terraces that now provide excellent Cims de Porrera. Today, the wines produced by these five pioneers are among the most sought after in Spain. In 2000 the district was designated Spain's second D.O.Ca., and it now has nearly 40 producers bottling under their own labels. With the rise into the top league the *appellation* now includes nearly all the 1,600 hectares of vineyards. However, the labor-intensive work, together with a labor shortage, place restrictions on such expansion. The top wines to date require so much work that the venture deters industrial wine producers. At present, production runs at only 450,000 gallons (17,000 hectoliters) per year. Grapes are rare in Priorat and thereby expensive, so flight from the land has been stopped, with local people even beginning to return. The only new-generation wine produced in any quantity, Les Terrasses from Álvaro Palacios, came about only by virtue of an agreement with the Bellmunt cooperative.

Tarragona

Long before most of the red wine regions we know today in Spain had begun, the red wines from Tarragona were regarded as soft, robust, and fiery. But in the 1960s they gained a reputation for being coarse and too alcoholic. Committed wine producers are now showing renewed interest in this *appellation*, which is so rich in tradition.

Falset split off as a sub-zone in autumn 2000, and it is now the autonomous D.O. of Montsant. Formerly best known for full-bodied red wines, the D.O. Tarragona still has 18,038 acres (7,300 ha) registered, most of which are now growing white grapes. The main varieties are Macabeo and Parellada, with the reds Ull de Llebre, Carinena, and Garnacha Tinta. Most of the 22 registered bottlers are cooperatives producing modern and generally simple wines. The very aromatic, sweet liqueur wines should not be forgotten—they are made from white and red Garnacha grapes.

With his L'Ermita, the young, La Rioja-born Álvaro Palacios was the first to catapult a Priorat wine to the top of the Spanish wine hierarchy.

Montsant

The former sub-zone of Tarragona, which directly borders Priorat, produces very good red wines of strong color and commendable body. The soil conditions are only slightly similar to those of its famous neighbor, consisting mainly of chalk and clay. The vintners grow chiefly red grapes, Garnacha, Cariñena, and Ull de Llebre, on 4,448 acres (1,800 ha).

Terra Alta

On the 20,622-acre (8,200-ha) large, relatively unknown D.O. Terra Alta region, southwest of Tarragona, the main grapes are Macabeo, Garnacha Blanca, Garnacha Tinta, and Cariñena. The differences in altitude in this mostly mountainous region are considerable, and the great fluctuations in temperature are reminiscent of an almost continental climate. The River Ebro exerts a balancing influence, especially on cold nights. Originally, the red wines here were considered to be just as rough as the climate. Thanks to modern technology and increased planting of Tempranillo and Syrah grapes, these wines have now become softer and more complex. Soil and climate seem to be designed to produce the highly structured, well-rounded red wines that are in such demand throughout the world at present. Since top producers such as Bàrbara Forés-Ferrer have shown that full-bodied red wines and smooth, extract-rich white wines can be made from old vineyards, Spain's top enologists consider Terra Alta to be one of the greatest hopes.

Select Producers in Catalonia

Albet y Noya*–******
Subirats (D.O. Penedès)
*109 acres (44 ha); some bought-in grapes; 800,000
bottles • Wines include: Albet y Noya Macabeo
Col.lecció, Tinto Tempranillo D'Anyada, Nuria,
→Reserva Martí Syrah Col.lecció, Dolç Adria*
The brothers Albet y Noya are the Spanish pioneers of
organic wine growing. Their top wines are the single
varietal Col.lecció wines and →Reserva Martí, their
only reserva wine. Good cavas, remarkable young wines
bearing the Anyada title, and convincing Priorato under
the brand name of Mas Igneus.

Alvaro Palacios**–*******
Gratallops (D.O.Ca. Priorato)
*62 acres (25 ha); some bought-in grapes; 150,000
bottles • Wines: Les Terrasses, →Finca Dofí, L'Eremitá*
Alvaro Palacios became world-famous with his quality
red wine →L'Eremitá from the eponymous vineyard. The
second wine, Finca Dofí, which also comes from a single
vineyard, exhibits extra class and great refinement. This
winemaker is regarded as one of the best cask specialists
in the country, especially as he earned the starting capital
for his winery by trading in barrels.

Can Ráfols dels Caus*–******
Avinyonet del Penedès (D.O. Penedès)
*109 acres (44 ha); 375,000 bottles • Wines: Petit Caus
Blanco, Gran Caus Rosado, →Gran Caus Tinto
Reserva, →Caus Lubis*
On this dream estate, Carles Esteve produces his famous
Gran Caus wines as well as an excellent Caus Lubis, The
vineyards, which are planted with 18 different varieties
of vine, are exposed in steep areas to a variety of microclimates, on the basis of which he makes the selections
for his top wines. Even his second wine, Petit Caus, is of
pretty good quality.

Castell del Remei*–******
Castell del Remei (D.O. Costers del Segre)
*198 acres (80 ha); 700,000 bottles • Wines: Castell del
Remei Blanco Chardonnay, Tinto Crianza Merlot, Tinto
Reserva Cabernet Sauvingon, →Tinto 1780 Añada, Oda*
The winery is a figurehead for fruity, modern wines in
the D.O. The Merlot and Gotim Bru are always sure to
provide a consistent quality. The Coupage 1780 stands
out, with good density and potential. The small,
exquisite sister estate, at 124 acres (50 ha), produces
one of the top wines of Catalonia, the Cervelo Seleció.

Cavas del Castillo de Perelada*
Perelada (D.O. Empordá-Costa Brava)
*297 acres (120 ha); some bought-in grapes; 7,000,000
bottles • Wines: Castillo Perelada Chardonnay, Castillo
Perelada Reserva, →Castillo Perelada Gran Claustro,
XX1, Malaveina*
Although it used to be known for simple wines and
good cavas, the winery is now increasingly producing
more and more quality still wines. The →Gran Claustro,
made from five different varieties of grape, comes highly
recommended, as does the simpler Reserva Perelada.
Fortified estate buildings, converted to form a state-of-
the-art winery, supply the outstanding single-vineyard
wine Malaveina. XX 1 has now been introduced as the
first of a series of limited edition wines.

Celler Alcover Jofre*–******
La Vilella Alta (D.O.Ca. Priorato)
*6.2 acres (2.5 ha); some bought-in grapes; 7,000 bottles
• Wine: Fra Fulco*
After a difficult new start, Toni Alcover is once again
one of the top producers in Priorat. He selects the grapes

for his juicy and very ripe Fra Fulco from the oldest
vineyards in the village.

Celler Bárbara Forés-Ferrer Escoda*
Gandesa (D.O. Terra Alta)
*42 acres (17 ha); 50,000 bottles • Wine: →Coma d'en
Pou Tinto*
A small estate with a great future and the juiciest
Crianza in the region. The estate, founded in 1989, has
old Garnacha vines and the advisor is the Priorato
pioneer José Luis Pérez.

Celler de Capçanes*–******
Capçanes (D.O. Tarragona)
*568 acres (250 ha); 750,000 bottles • Wines: Mas Donis
Tinto, Lasendal Tinto Crianza, Vall del Calas Tinto
Crianza, Costers del Gravet Tinto Crianza, →Cabrida
Tinto Crianza, →Flor de Primavera Kosher*
The cooperative was one of the first to effect a profound
quality revolution in Tarragona. It now bottles the
majority of its collection itself and, in Flor de
Primavera, produces one of the world's best kosher
wines. The wines consistently have personality and
display a charming, warm character. The top wine,
→Cabrida from an old Garnacha vineyard, joins the
ranks of Catalonia's best wines.

Clos Erasmus**
Gratallops (D.O.Ca. Priorato)
25 acres (10 ha); 6,000 bottles • Wine: Clos Erasmus
Having vinified and aged her superb reds in René
Barbier's cellar for the first years, the young Swiss-
American Daphne Glorian has now taken over Alvaro
Palacio's old cellar.

Clos Mogador***
Gratallops
*49 acres (20 ha); 25,000 bottles • Wines: Clos Mogador
Tinto Reserva*
With his Clos Mogador, René Barbier has created one of
Spain's really great wines. He presses the grapes using a
former olive oil press, so that only half the potential juice is
extracted from the grape. The wine is beefy with a lot of
ripe tannins, but is very distinguished. The blend, especially
the addition of Syrah, is adapted for each year's vintage.

Finca Son Bordils*
Inca (Mallorca, Baleares)
*84 acres (34 ha); 200,000 bottles • Wines: Son Bordils
Muscat, Son Bordils Negre, Son Bordils Cabernet
Sauvignon, Son Bordils Syrah*
In the center of Mallorca, outside the two D.O. regions,
the brothers Pedro and Ramón Coll have been producing
fruity, modern wines since 1998. Apart from the Muscat,
typical of its grape variety, the simple but juicy and firm
Negre and the extraordinary Syrah deserve attention.
Despite the youth of the vines, this wine is loaded with
energy and displays structure and elegance.

Jean Léon*–******
Torrelavid (D.O. Penedès)
*131 acres (53 ha); 270,000 bottles • Wines: Jean Léon
Petit Chardonnay, Jean Léon Chardonnay Fermentado
en Barrica, →Jean Léon Cabernet Sauvignon Reserva*
This traditional firm has the best vineyards growing
traditional grapes in the region, and is renowned for its
extremely ripe Cabernet Sauvignon *reservas*. The
Chardonnays are also in a class of their own. They
generally need three years, however, to display their full
aroma. Since the death of its founder, Jean Léon, the
firm has belonged to the Torres group.

The Balearic Islands

The long-faded fame of Mallorcan wines dates back to a sweet Malvasía aged for a long time in a barrel, which in the 19th century was just as sought after as the wines from Madeira. After the phylloxera outbreak, rough table wines dominated production on the Balearic main island until, in the 1960s, people once again became more aware of quality. Of the 4,900 acres (2,000 ha) of vines on the islands, the D.O. Binissalem and the recently appointed *appellation* of Pla i Llevant hold 1,600 acres (650 ha) between them. The main black grape variety is the indigenous Manto Negro, grown in the area around Binissalem on the high plateau in the center of the islands. Unlike most other black grape varieties, this large-berried fruit produces astonishingly stable wines that age well in the barrel. For this reason, Manto Negro must account for at least half of the grapes that are pressed to make red wines, in the hope that they will be awarded the D.O. *appellation*. Unfortunately, the main area of production is

still the traditional, rather bland *tintos*, which hardly do justice to the potential of this variety, particularly its elegance. However, there are signs that a more contemporary style, based more on concentration, is in the offing. Blends

with Cabernet Sauvignon, Tempranillo, and Callet point the way forward. White wine production, which accounts for less than a fifth, is based on the Moll grape variety, as well as the Macabeo, Parellada, and a little Chardonnay. They are pleasantly spicy and fresh when drunk young. Pla i Llevant in the east may have a much broader range of varieties, but the real difference lies in the large proportion of Callet plantings. The wines produced from the red Callet grape are different from the others because of their typical earthy aroma mixed with ripe fruits. There is no doubt that Callet has a distinctive character. It is important for the quality of this wine, however, that the yield from this leading variety remains low. Since the end of the 1990s, the island's wine scene as undergone an amazing renaissance. *Bodega* wine producers such as Miquel and Toni Gelabert or Anima Negra now vinify *tintos* of the highest quality. By comparison, the vines on the neighboring islands are hardly worth mentioning.

JOSEP ANGUERA BEYME***
DARMÓS (D.O. MONTSANT)
74 acres (30 ha); 75,000 bottles • Wines: Joan D' Angeura Tinto, Joan D' Angeura Vi Dolç, Joan D' Angeura Finca L'Argata
Old family wine estate that successful converted to bottled wines in the mid-1980s. The young red wine is of an exceptionally firm structure with a lot of soft fruit. The single vineyard wine →Finca L'Argata is playful, with an attractive finish, due to the skilled blending of four red varieties.

MAS MARTINET VITICULTORS****
FALSET (D.O. PRIORATO)
25 acres (10 ha); some bought-in grapes; 70,000 bottles • Wines: Martinet Bru, →Mas Martinet
The spiritual father of the new Priorat winegrowers, José Luis Pérez, produces well-balanced, mature, deep and fruity Prioratos that can be drunk very young. Now his daughter Sarah controls the style of the wines. Together with the songwriter Luis Lach, Don José has created an independent *bodega* project and founded the magnificent Cims de Porrera.

MAS ESTELA**-****
SELVA DE MAR (D.O. EMPORDÁ-COSTA BRAVA)
20 acres (8 ha); 42,000 bottles • Wines: Vinya Selva de Mar Tinto: Crianza, Reserva, Garnatxa, Moscatel
Didier Soto and Nuria Dalmau cultivated their small estate on the Costa Brava using organic methods. The reds are well-structured, but have woody notes. The real specialties and stars are still the natural sweet Garnatxa and Moscatel with their huge intensity and highly individual character.

MIGUEL TORRES**-*****
VILAFRANCA DEL PENEDÈS (D.O. PENEDÈS)
3,200 acres (1,300 ha); some bought-in grapes; 25,000,000 bottles • Wines include: Viña Sol, De Casta, Sangre de Toro, Gran Coronas Reserva, →Milmanda, Fransola Etiqueta Verde, Gran Coronas Mas la Plana, Grans Muralles, →Reserva Real
The standard of wine in Catalonia (and Chile) would not be what it is today without Miguel Torres. Without exception, the company's range of wines is compelling.

Outstanding single-varietal wines such as →Chardonnay Milmanda, →Fránsola Etiqueta Verde and →Gran Coronas Mas La Plana. The new red →Grans Muralles, made from grape varieties that had almost disappeared, is very interesting.

PARXET***
TIANA (D.O. ALELLA)
148 acres (60 ha); some bought-in grapes; 1,000,000 bottles • Wines: Marqués de Alella, Chardonnay, Marqués de Alella Classico, Parxet Cava Brut, →Marqués de Alella Fermentado in Barrica
The still wines and cavas made by this firm on the outskirts of Barcelona have style and class. The various white wines sold under the Marqués de Alella label, according to type, display fine fruit and acidity (Chardonnay) or are very harmonious with residual sugar (Classico).

RAIMAT**-****
RAIMAT (D.O. COSTERS DEL SEGRE)
4,200 acres (1,700 ha); 7,000,000 bottles • Wines: Raimat Chardonnay, Raimat Cava Gran Brut, Raimat Abadia, Raimat El Molí, →Raimat Mas Castell, Raimat Vallcorba
The estate was acquired by Cordorníu in 1914 and transformed, with great effort, into one of the most impressive wine estates in Spain. The research work that the cava producer had to conduct there led to a vital step forward in wine growing throughout the country. The spicy Reserva Abadía and the standard Cabernet offer consistent good quality, and there are the excellent Cabernet special *cuvées* →El Molí, →Vallcorba and →Mas Castell.

VITICULTORS MAS D'EN GIL***-****
BELLMUNT DEL PRIORAT (D.O. PRIORATO)
86.5 acres (35 ha); 70,000 bottles • Wines: Coma Blanca, Coma Vella, →Clos Fontá, Gran Buig
The Rovira wine family took over the former Mas Barril, with 309 acres (125 ha) of land, in the lower Priorat region. They restored it and introduced state-of-the-art technology. The top wine Clos Fontá is a serious Priorat with full fruit and fine spices, and the substantial white Coma Blanca is also compelling. In special years, the powerful top *cru* Gran Buig is produced.

THE HISTORY OF LA RIOJA

The numerous Roman wine-fermenting vessels found cut into the rock in the region of La Rioja, and which can still be seen there, bear witness to the fact that the area was a wine-growing center way back in classical times. Later, it was the monasteries that encouraged wine growing and also supervised quality. A deed of donation, in which the king of Navarra transferred land and vineyards to the monastery of San Millán de la Cogolla, provides evidence that vines were also grown in the early medieval period. The pilgrims who went in their hundreds of thousands to Santiago de Compostela in distant Galicia to see the grave of James the Apostle were served the alcoholic grape juice in pilgrims' hostelries run by the monasteries. They spread the word about La Rioja wine far and wide.

Wine has always been very important for the region, and in 1560 the winegrowers formed an association and agreed on a standard brand mark for their barrels to guarantee the wine's origin. Even at that time, the wine from La Rioja enjoyed a certain reputation and its name was often wrongly applied, even though the region did not have any good transport routes to the distant coasts and large cities until the 19th century. The first wine companies—as we know them today with their huge cellars filled with thousands of BARRIQUES, or barrel, casks—did not come into being until the second half of the 20th century.

THE RISE OF BARRIQUE CASKS

The wine region took off only after the introduction of barrel production, which meant that the wine could be kept. Wines finished in small oak casks were unknown in La Rioja until 1862,

In the Middle Ages, when hundreds of thousands of St. James' pilgrims passed through La Rioja on their way to Santiago de Compostela, the region's towns and viticulture experienced the first major upturn in their economic fortunes. Many of their buildings date back to this period, including those located in Calahorra in the La Rioja Baja.

although as early as 1786 Manuel Esteban Quintano had experimented to some extent with oak casks after visiting the Bordeaux region. His wines passed the acid test of an ocean-crossing to the Latin-American colonies with flying colors, but he could not cash in on this new type of wine by charging a higher price, and Señor Quintano's pioneering enological experiment drifted back into oblivion. During his exile in London, Colonel Luciano de Murrieta acquired a taste for Bordeaux wines. Before returning to Spain to take over a *bodega* in La Rioja, he went to Bordeaux to study the wine preparation methods there. He had barrels brought from Bilbao, which he filled for the first time in 1850. Then he dispatched some of the 19-gallon (72-liter) barrels to Cuba, where he sold them for a good price. Encouraged by this success, he continued with barrel production. Around 1850, Camilo Hurtado de Amézaga, the Marqués de Riscal, also began to speculate on the future of La Rioja as a wine-growing region. He too had spent many years of his exile in Bordeaux, where he became a devotee of the wines of the Médoc. In

1860, he had a *bodega*, based on the Bordeaux model, built at Elciego. In that same year, the Marqués had vines from Bordeaux planted on a quarter of his 494-acre (200-ha) estate.

When Bordeaux lost much of its harvest to a serious mildew epidemic and the phylloxera disaster, the region even took in wines from La Rioja. However, the traditional Rioja wines were often of poor quality and did not travel well, so on the advice of the Marqués the administration of the province of Álava decided to engage the services of a French expert by the name of Jean Pineau. He taught a select group of estate owners to appreciate the French method of mashing in large wooden barrels and then finishing the wines in small oak casks. This he did with no little success, for Monsieur Pineau was soon able to report to his patrons, *"que el año próximo casi todos los propietarios hagan el vino al estilo de Burdeos"* (that in the next year nearly all the proprietors should produce Bordeaux-style wines).

Despite the initial good results, however, most winegrowers fought shy, because finishing the wines in small oak casks seemed to them to be a nuisance and too costly. Pineau then entered the services of Riscal, and this *bodega* began to mature red Rioja wines in barrel casks in their cellar tunnels. Convincing other winemakers was a gradual process, and it was some time before some *bodegueros* adopted these techniques once more, impressed by the success of the wines at international wine exhibitions. Subsequently, many wine estates based on the French model grew up within a very short space of time. Many French people settled in La Rioja, and so began the history of a wine that now enjoys a widespread international reputation.

A century of viticultural history in the traditional winemaking firm of Tondonia in Haro.

THE WINE-GROWING REGION OF LA RIOJA

La Rioja is Spain's best-known wine region. High quality wines have been produced here since the second half of the 19th century. With the exception of only a few individual *bodegas* in other wine-growing areas, La Rioja supplied all of Spain's notable wines right up to the 1980s. It was not until the 1990s that La Rioja had to begin to take seriously the increasing competition from other regions. This, however, actually had a positive effect, since it made the old-established *bodegas* make more effort, which in turn led to the creation of a new generation of wines that could hold their own with the competitors from Ribera del Duero, Priorat, or anywhere else. It was no accident that, in 1991, in view of its long history as a distinct wine-growing region, La Rioja was awarded the *Denominación de Origen Calificada*, Spain's highest *appellation*.

The wine-growing area of the upper Ebro has various natural conditions that make it perfect for producing outstanding wines. The fact that it lies so close to the Bay of Biscay means that its climate is governed primarily by Atlantic influences, but also by Mediterranean air currents coming in from the east. This delicate meteorological balance of moderate temperatures, sufficient rainfall, and sometimes hard frost creates the preconditions for producing wines of an elegant character. Climatic conditions, which are not always favorable, mean that the quality of Rioja wines depends very much on the wine year.

The wine-growing area of the D.O.Ca. Rioja is not restricted to the political boundaries of the

The river Ebro is the backbone of La Rioja and confirms once again that major wine-growing regions definitely need major rivers.

These old citizens of San Sebastián are courageously tending a small vineyard, where their sparkling Txakolí thrives looking out over the Bay of Biscay.

autonomous region and can be divided into three sub-zones, each producing distinctive types of wine. La Rioja Alta in the west is famous for fine, elegant wines with only a moderate alcohol content. The Basque sector, La Rioja Alavesa, is known for its exceptionally fruity wines. In La Rioja Baja, which stretches eastward from Logroño as far as Navarra, the extremely dark grapes that have the potential to produce a higher alcohol content are grown on the alluvial soils of the Ebro river.

There is no clear classification according to location in the region of La Rioja, but the best quality wines come from La Rioja Alta and La Rioja Alavesa. Here, the system of small winegrowers has for the most part been retained: around 2,500 families cultivate almost half of the 32,123 acres (13,000 ha) north of the Ebro. La Rioja Alavesa also has the highest proportion of Tempranillo grapes (94 percent) among the red varieties planted there. The carefully cultivated, for the most part relatively small parcels of land are reputed to produce the best grape harvest. Here the vineyards on the steep slopes of the Cantabrian mountains are nearly all south facing, and the chalky deposits of the mountains provide ideal soil conditions. Vineyards that are half way between the low-lying, fog- and frost-prone river banks and the mountains are regarded as especially valuable, because in such areas the wind dries the grapes when it rains and cools them in the heat of the summer.

La Rioja Alta on the other side of the Ebro is the region of the big, old *bodegas*. The chalk

content of the soil is lower, the parcels of land more generous. The legendary vineyards that have been producing top-quality wines for many centuries are to be found in the rolling hills of this area. With more than 64,245 acres (26,000 ha), also planted mainly with Tempranillo, La Rioja Alta supplies most of La Rioja.

La Rioja Baja extends south of Logroño over a considerably larger area to Alfaro in the east, but as far as the wine-growing area is concerned, at around 54,360 acres (22,000 ha) it can only attain second place. Eight districts in Navarra are also classified. The high temperatures produce an early harvest and make it essential to have a high proportion of Garnacha grapes, since they are the best at withstanding the heat. The cooperatives play an important role here.

Many classic *bodegas* in La Rioja have no vineyards, or very few, of their own. They buy the harvest from all three sub-zones and adapt their *cuvées* to the conditions of the respective wine years. Any climatic shortcomings—such as frost or hail—in one area can be compensated for by undamaged grapes from other zones. These classic *bodegas*, which produce fine wines, glowing ruby-red in color and aged for long periods in barrel casks, now have to face up to the new generation château wine estates. They press their wines from a single harvest, leave the red musts in contact with the skins for longer to attain a deeper color and higher extraction, and age them for a shorter period in wood, but use new *barrique* casks. This trend toward fruitier and more easy-drinking wines seems to be catching on more and more in La Rioja.

La Rioja does not only produce wines that are aged in wood. There is a tradition of using

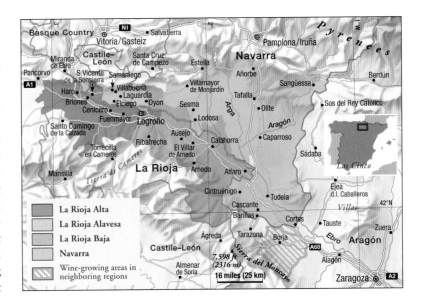

the carbonic MACERATION method typical of the Beaujolais region to make red wines, known as *cosechero*, and almost every winery produces white wines as well as *rosados*.

Without a doubt, La Rioja's most important grape is the Tempranillo, which has fine tannins and the potential to age for an incredibly long time. It is regarded as Spain's top-quality variety. It is supplemented by the Garnacha, which provides color and body, and the highly individual, acidic Graciano, together with the coarser Mazuelo (with its more intense color and tannin structure), called Cariñena in other parts of Spain. White grapes account for only an eleventh of the wine-growing area of around 123,600 acres (50,000 ha), with the Viura grape being the most important. Malvasía and Garnacha Blanca are used only in small quantities for blending. Although it has a few interesting white wines, La Rioja is and will always be a red wine area.

Txakolí

Chacolí, or Txakolí in Basque, is an acquired taste, according to the Basques. This is particularly true of the coarse, acidic wines that are still served to visitors in some *caseríos* or Basque farms. The name may actually be derived from the Arab *chacalet*, meaning "thin" or "light." In the past, this grape used to cover a considerably larger area than it does now, and in 1801 Wilhelm von Humboldt described the wines, then called *chacolín*, as being a blend of champagne and Mosel wines. Even today the wines fermented from the indigenous varieties of Hondarribi Zuri (white) and Hondarribi Beltza (red), and sometimes the full-bodied Folle Blanche, are bottled with their natural carbon dioxide, giving them a distinctive sparkling character and making them an ideal accompaniment to local seafood.

The traditional way to pour Txakolí.

Since 1990, 210 acres (85 ha) of Txakolí vines west of San Sebastián, around the village of Guetaria, have been protected by a mark of origin. The D.O. Chacolí de Vizcaya followed, and by 2003 the D.O. Txakolí de Álava had finally gained protected status. Today, both D.O.s produce some notable wines, although at 11.5 percent vol, they are usually slightly stronger than the traditional ones. They are no longer vinified in the traditional fermenting vats, but in small stainless steel tanks. Txakolí should be slightly yeasty, because it is left on the yeast lees after fermenting. It should also taste of blossom, peach, and citrus, and have a lively acidity. There are barely 70 producers, mostly with modest production. Two excellent wineries are Txomín Etxániz in Guetaria and Itsasmendi in Muskitz.

How Wine is Made in La Rioja

In the old town of Logroño, the capital of La Rioja, there is one wine store after another. Each specializes in different *tapas*, and each is especially proud of its wine, usually a *vino joven*, served in large beakers. These young wines, a deep glowing purple in color, decidedly fruity, usually with cherry aromas and flavors, are a traditional specialty of the region and are rated particularly highly by the Basques. Even until just a few years ago, *vino joven* accounted for more than 50 percent of La Rioja's wine. The more costly wines that could be sold at a higher price

In La Rioja, good wines are finished in barrels. *Bodegas* have thousands of *barricas*, which have to be cleaned thoroughly after each wine.

Left and center
Opening old bottles using a pair of glowing-red tongs.

Right
The cellar man at Marqués de Riscal appreciates the excellent 1936 vintage.

after a longer aging period did not come into fashion until the price of grapes was pushed up considerably by the wine boom that came at the end of the 1990s.

These easy-to-drink young wines represent the region's original style of wine, produced by the winegrowers themselves, known as *cosecheros*. They use simple, open basins dug into the soil, known as *lagar*, which hold around 5,283 gallons (20,000 liters), or nowadays, fermenting tanks. The grapes—almost exclusively Tempranillo—are poured in unpressed. The initial fermentation releases carbon dioxide gas, which saturates the atmosphere in the *lagar*, so that all the grapes ferment without coming into contact with the air. In large *bodegas*, this carbonic maceration method is applied by adding carbon dioxide to a sealed, stainless steel tank. This produces red wines with plenty of fresh fruit, slightly peppery notes, and soft tannins, very closely related to the Beaujolais Primeur, and intended to be enjoyed young. Recently, blending processes have come into fashion, whereby the winemakers start a carbonic maceration process, but squeeze out the wine earlier, leaving it to complete its fermentation in the usual way, before giving it a short aging period in small oak casks.

La Rioja's reputation is based, however, on more expensive wines aged in wood. For these wines, the stems are removed from the red grapes, which are then pressed before being pumped into the MASH tank. During fermentation, care is taken to ensure that the mash solids

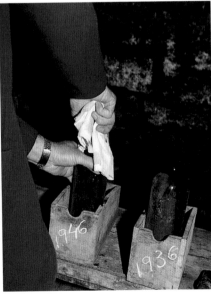

Spain's classification system

The classifications within the *Denominación de Origen Calificada* (D.O.Ca.) Rioja relate to the length of time the wines are aged either in the cask or in the bottle. Information on the quality grade of a wine is given on the label on the back of the wine bottle. The D.O.Ca. Rioja awards the following classifications:

• *Vino joven*, the young Rioja, bears only the classification *garantía de origen*. This wine, whether white, rosé, or red comes onto the market only a few months after the grape harvest. Even so, it can still have been aged in wood for a short period.

• *Crianza* wines must mature in the *bodega* for at least two years, one of them in the barrel, six months being sufficient for white and *rosado* wines.

• *Reserva* wines are not allowed to leave the *bodegas* for three years, one of which must be spent in the barrel. White *reservas* require six months in the barrel and six in the bottle. *rosado reservas* are hardly ever sold now.

• *Gran reserva* wines age for at least 24 months in oak barrels and for a further 36 months in the bottle. Some traditional *bodegas* still produce white *gran reservas*, which are some of the best white wines in the world. They have to spend at least six months in oak and 42 months in the bottle.

These classifications represent only the legally stipulated minimum aging period. A large number of traditional concerns in La Rioja extend the aging period far beyond the stipulated guidelines, producing a highly individual range of great wines in the region.

This aging and classification system for table wines, which offers the consumer ready-to-drink wines, has spread out from La Rioja to the whole country. However, the same aging periods do not apply everywhere. It is striking that areas with cooler climates, such as La Rioja, Navarra, and Ribera del Duero, have to prove 12 months' aging in the barrel if the red wine is to be of *crianza* quality, whereas in warmer areas six months is sufficient.

Red wines with great aging potential, and which the consumer himself must leave to mature, are a new development in Spain.

floating on the top do not become dry, because it is the skins and fruit flesh that give the must its tannins, color, and fruit. The must is therefore regularly sucked down into the tank and pumped up to the top to cover and thus moisten the mash or MARC. It is up to the cellarmen how long the must ferments on the mash. It used to be the case that even for the best quality wines, the maximum period the wine could be left on the mash was 15 days, but in extreme cases this period can now be doubled. The wine is then drawn off, the mash pressed once, and the wines transferred either to stainless steel tanks or large wooden barrels for MACOLACTIC FERMENTATION to convert the aggressive malic acid into milder lactic acid.

La Rioja is now also starting to apply quality control even in the vineyard, so that early selections can also be made. After several RACKINGS, the wine is poured into barrel casks and then stored in a large barrel cellar either above or below ground.

The young wines are transferred after a few months, when the cloudiness that is still present starts to clear. This liquid SEDIMENT, which accounts for three percent of the contents of the barrel during the first transfers, is subsequently filtered and in many cases given to employees. Afterwards, the wine is generally transferred only every six months. In some *bodegas* this is still done by hand, a process that, depending on the number of barrels, occupies several teams the whole year through, because it is not that unusual for large *bodegas* to have tens of thousands of barrels.

The red wines spend a specific period in oak, depending on the quality. Such periods often exceed the aging periods stipulated by the *Consejo Regulador*. Wood aging stabilizes the wines and gives them extra aging potential as an added bonus. To complete the aging process, all qualities of wine spend a certain amount of

time after FILTRATION and bottling in the bottle cellar to harmonize them before they are sold.

Classic Riojas are basically fine wines, a clear, ruby-red in color through being aged in wood, and are not renowned for being particularly full-bodied. The new-generation Riojas are something else altogether. The wines spend longer on the mash, giving them more color and tannins. The wine is aged in wood for only the legal minimum period, and the barrels are new, giving a greater woody or toasty flavor to the wine. In the last few years, a series of "super *reservas*" has come onto the market, which are made in the following way. The musts for these top quality wines are always based on a strict selection of grapes, which not only produces robust and concentrated wines but also places great emphasis on the fruit. These Riojas are usually very deep in color and robust, clearly much more in keeping with contemporary international tastes than the delicate classic Riojas with their fine acidity and long aging in barrels.

The fruity *vino joven* still tastes good even when drunk from an ordinary glass.

Select Producers in La Rioja

Bodegas Bilbainas*
Haro

642 acres (260 ha); some bought-in grapes; 1,800,000 bottles • Wines: Viña Paceta, Viña Pomal Reserva, Viña Zaco Reserva, →Viña Pomal Gran Reserva, La Vicalanda Reserva

A classic produced along modern lines by one of Spain's most renowned enologists, José Hidalgo. One result of this new direction is the top quality La Vicalanda wine, made from 100% Tempranillo. The Viña Pomal wines have also gained in intensity. The *bodega* has also been awarded the right to produce sparkling wines under the *Denominación Cava*.

Bodegas Bretón*****
Logroño

262 acres (106 ha); some bought-in grapes; 1,100,000 bottles • Wines: Loriñon Blanco Fermetado en Barrica, Loriñon Crianza, Loriñon Reserva, Loriñon Gran Reserva, →Dominio de Conte Reserva, Alba de Bretón

Founded in 1983 and regarded as being neo-classical, this firm ages traditional blends in American oak. The wines however have more density and fresher fruit than traditional Riojas.

Bodegas Faustino*
Oyón

1,285 acres (520 ha); some bought-in grapes; 7,000,000 bottles • Wines: Faustino V Rosada, Faustino V Reserva, →Faustino I Gran Reserva

Faustino is an exception among the large bodegas of La Rioja in that most of its wines are made from grapes from the producer's own vineyards. This must be one reason why the Faustino I Gran Reserva consistently offers exceptional quality from one year to the next. The family firm still owns Bodegas Campillo, a so-called "château" estate, which presses top quality Tempranillo wines only from its own grapes.

Bodegas Marqués de Murrieta******
Logroño

556 acres (225 ha); 1,500,000 bottles • Wines include: Marqués de Murrieta, Dalmau Reserva, Castillo Ygay Reserva Especial

A house with traditions, which began to make some concessions to modernity in the mid-1990s with its concentrated, fruity Dalmau. The Castillo Ygays are legendary—two of these wines are always offered in parallel, one "early bottling" and one "historic vintage," which has as a rule been aged in the barrel for decades and is hardly to be surpassed in its refinement.

Bodegas Muga*****
Haro

173 acres (70 ha); some bought-in grapes; 1,250,000 bottles • Wines: Muga Blanco, Muga Crianza, Muga Reserva, Muga Gran Reserva, →Torre Muga Reserva

One of the few traditional firms to have managed a smooth transition from old to modern ways, while still retaining the distinctive character of its wines. The firm uses only wooden barrels, producing fine wines with a distinctive woody character and elegant acidity, suitable for laying down.

Bodegas Fernández Remírez de Ganuza*****
Samaniego

148 acres (60 ha); 80,000 bottles • Wines: Remírez de Ganuza Reserva, Gran Reserva

Remírez de Ganuza is regarded as the most quality-obsessed wine producer in La Rioja. Almost no one else selects grapes with such strict criteria as this former

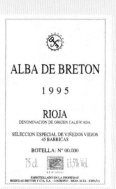

vineyard speculator. He even cuts the grape clusters in half horizontally, using the lower half to produce young wines and the upper half, known as the shoulders, to produce *reserva* wines. His wines were among the most exciting new discoveries of the 1990s.

Bodegas Riojanas****—****
Cenicero

494 acres (200 ha); some bought-in grapes; 2,500,000 bottles • Wines: Monte Real Blanco Crianza; Monte Real Reserva, Viña Albina Reserva, →Monte Real Gran Reserva, Viña Albina Gran Reserva

Call in at this family-run concern if you want to sample perfect, traditional Riojas. Viña Albina and Monte Real have fine fruit and a ruby-red color. All wines are based on classic blends, with Tempranillo accounting for 80%.

Bodegas Roda*****
Haro

124 acres (50 ha); some bought-in grapes; 140,000 bottles • Wines: Roda II Reserva, →Roda I Reserva, Cirsion

This *bodega* was founded in 1989 and produces a premier (Roda I) and a secondary wine (Roda II). For these *reservas*, the grapes must come from vines that are at least 30 years old. In 2000, the special selection Cirsion was introduced, which comes from ancient vineyards.

Bodegas y Viñedos del Marqués de Vargas*****
Logroño

148 acres (60 ha); 220,000 bottles • Wines: Marqués de Vargas: Reserva, →Reserva Privada

Wine was not produced on the estate until 1989. Using the most modern technology, fine, concentrated Rioja *reservas* with a firm woody structure are made here. The top wine, Reserva Privada, has some Cabernet in the blend. The estate is one of the few producers that sometimes work with Russian oak.

Cosecheros Alaveses****—*****
Laguardia

173 acres (70 ha); some bought-in grapes; 800,000 bottles • Wines: Viñas de Gain Crianza, Viña El Pisón Reserva, →Pagos Viejos Reserva, Grandes Añadas Reserva

The winery produces excellent Crianzas, Reservas, single-vineyard wines, and the exceptional Grandes Añadas range. The wines are beguiling, with full body, plenty of fruit and great intensity. Juan Carlos de Lacalle is extremely creative and has played a major role in the revival of Rioja wines.

Finca Allende*****
Briones

54 acres (22 ha); some bought-in grapes; 180,000 bottles • Wine: Finca Allende Crianza, →Aurus, →Calvario

The renowned winemaker Miguel Angel de Gregorio set up his own business with this project in 1995 and, with his elegant and balanced single-vineyard wine Calvario, he produces one of the most remarkable wines of the "new guard" in La Rioja.

Finaca Valpiedra*****
Fuenmayor

198 acres (80 ha); 125,000 bottles • Wines: Finca Valpiedra Reserva

This jewel of the Martínez-Bujanda group lies directly above a loop of the river Ebro and is surrounded by first-class terraced vineyards. To date only one wine, Finca Valpiedra Reserva, has been produced each year. The wine always exhibits perfect maturity, is impressively differentiated and displays a gentle elegance.

Granja Nuestra Señora de Remelluri****
Labastida
222 acres (90 ha); 500,000 bottles • Wines: Remelluri Blanco; Reserva
Jaime Rodriguez acquired this old monastery estate at the foot of the Sierra Cantabria in 1968 and turned it into one of the premier châteaux estates in La Rioja. His son Telmo is now in charge and has recently given the wines a previously unachieved sophistication and depth.

Marqués de Cacéres***–****
Union Viti-Vinicola, Cenicero
Bought-in grapes; 8,400,000 bottles • Wines include: Blanco Seco, Antea, Satinela; Rosado; Crianza, →Reserva, →Gran Reserva, →Gaudium
After reviving the Médoc châteaux estates of Camensac and Larose-Trintaudon during his French exile, Enrique Forner returned to Spain at the end of the 1960s. Since 1970, initially working with the enologist Emile Peynaud and today with Michel Rolland as consultant, he has created a modern yet classic Rioja type which has become a standard throughout the world. This is due not least to the commitment of his daughter Christine.

La Rioja Alta****
Haro
741 acres (300 ha); some bought-in grapes; 2,000,000 bottles • Wines: Viña Alberdi Crianza, Viña Ardanza Crianza, →Gran Reserva 904, Gran Reserva 890
A timeless Rioja style, 51,000 *barrique* casks and two *gran reserva* brands, 904 and 809, appreciated by Rioja connoisseurs the world over. The wines from this *bodega*, which was founded in 1890, are fine and complex. The *gran reservas* have smoky aromas and finish. The wines are aged for an extremely long time in American oak, leaving them wholesome and perfectly clean.

Señorio de San Vicente***–****
San Vicente de la Sonsierra
45 acres (18 ha); 70,000 bottles • Wines: Reserva
The pride of the Eguren brothers, who have already proved with the Bodegas Sierra Cantabria that they can

In Spain the donkey is still an essential means of transport.

produce quality wine. The single-vineyard wine is not so full-bodied, but is still wonderfully fruity, juicy, and very harmonious, with a personality of its own.

Viña Tondonia, R. López de Heredia**–****
Haro
420 acres (170 ha); some bought-in grapes; 1,200,000 bottles • Wines: →Viña Tondonia Blanco Reserva; Viña Cubillo Crianza, Viña Bosconia Crianza, Viña Tondonia Gran Reserva
A monument to the old Rioja traditions: large wooden tuns, long cellar tunnels, old *barrique* casks. This is the place for you if you like light but firm classic Riojas. The white wines are unique and their aromas of wood barrel, fruit, honey, and flowers combine to create an unmistakable complexity, making them some of the best old white wines in the world.

Viñedas del Contino**–****
Laserna
153 acres (62 ha), but is being extended; 350,000 bottles • Wines: Contino Tinto Crianza, Reserva, Gran Reserva, Graciano, Reserva del Olino
This winery, launched by the owners of the famous C.U.N.E. *bodega*, lies in a loop of the Ebro river, and the excellent quality of the wine gives it convincing credibility.

Viños de los Herederos del Marqués de Riscal****–*****
Elciego
519 acres (210 ha); some bought-in grapes; 4,000,000 bottles • Wines: Marqués de Riscal Reserva, Marqués de Riscal Gran Reserva, →Barón de Chirel Reserva
This *bodega* produces only *reserva* and *gran reserva* wines. Even the ordinary *reserva* made by the firm has in recent years been one of the best Riojas. The super-*reserva* Barón de Chirel, with its high proportion of Cabernet (the sole producer, Riscal has always been able to use this French variety with official approval) has set the quality standards in Spain.

Navarra

The vineyards of Navarra extend between the river Ebro and the Pyrenees over gently rolling hills. Initially, it was the fruity rosé wines that attracted attention, but Navarra has long proved to be one of the most promising Spanish red wine regions.

The cellars that have been excavated near the small village of Funes give an indication of just how important wine must have been to the Romans in Navarra. The capacity of the site is estimated at around 20,000 gallons (75,000 liters). In the early medieval period, wine production centered on the monasteries that gradually sprang up along the pilgrim route to Santiago de Compostela. Wine and bread were also given to the hungry and sick pilgrims in the hospitals. The economic significance of this agricultural sector peaked when the king of Navarra's territory stretched from Bordeaux right into La Rioja, enclosing three important wine centers. It was then that French grape varieties first entered the region.

Until the 1980s, Navarra was known mainly for its *rosados*, which represented the wine-growing of this region more than any other wine, for reasons both good and bad.

Rosé was pressed here as far back as the 17th century, but the real *rosado* came into being much later. The reason for the dominance of the *rosados* can be found in the huge Garnacha plantings that took place after the phylloxera disaster in the first quarter of the 20th century. Moreover, the best *bodegas* produced wines in

the classic Rioja style—for part of Navarra i classified as D.O.Ca. Rioja.

To get away from the image of the pleasan but simple and reasonably cheap rosé wines, th autonomous government of La Rioja allowed it quality wine region to implement one of th most liberal D.O. regulatory systems in Spain This permitted a huge range of varieties an allowed wine growing practically everywher where it was climatically possible.

Convinced that they too could produce majo red and white wines, a few pioneers, such a Juan Magaña and the Guelbenzu family begar to cultivate French and Spanish quality grape varieties. Only a few *bodegas*, such as th Navarran Chivite wine dynasty, whose younges offspring, Fernando Chivite, is one of the vision aries among Spanish enologists, and the win research institute E.V.E.N.A., under the direc torship of the enologist Javier Ochoa, had don the necessary spade work. This led to the crea tion over the last 20 years of a range of wines o unparalleled individuality.

The diversity of the wines from the quality wine region of Navarra is in part due to th varied climatic conditions of the five sub-zones In four of the five sub-regions, winegrowers roduce white wines, *rosados*, young and cask-ged red wines, both single-varietal and lended. Usually, all they have in common is a igh quality standard and a highly individual oncept of winemaking. Baja Montaña, which as long been better than any other bottled vine producer worth mentioning, is the excep-ion. It supplies many Garnacha grapes or nusts to top producers in other zones.

The trend is clearly toward concentrated and ruity red wines. Many of the *cuvées* from ndigenous and French varieties have been very uccessful, as have single-varietal Tempranillos, Cabernet Sauvignons, or Merlots, the most ignificant variety, which is vinified to a high tandard. Most red Navarra wines tend to be ncreasingly full-bodied and have left the rather ine style based on classic Riojas almost totally behind. Some of the new *bodegas* have devel-oped red wines with strong tannins.

Tierra Estella is the northwestern agricultural area of Navarra. The climatic conditions in the far north of this area are very difficult for wine growing. As a result of Atlantic meteorological influences, it produces wines that are almost central European in character, including excel-lent Chardonnays. Valdizarbe in the central northern area of the region has similar condi-tions and produces wines with delicate fruit.

Baja Montaña is the eastern sub-zone account-ing for about 15 percent of the wine-growing area. It produces mainly *rosados*. Ribera Alta represents the center of the wine-growing region of Navarra, producing juicy, extract-rich wines that are reminiscent of the Mediterranean cli-mate. Ribera Baja is the southernmost sub-zone and has 30 percent of the wine-growing area. Robust, expressive wines with intensive color are produced from extremely arid, sandy chalk soils. In this region especially, winegrowers have redis-covered the possibilities presented by the old Garnacha vineyards, and now single-varietal Garnacha red wines are beginning to appear in the range of wines sold from the *bodegas*. The *crianzas* made from this most Spanish of grape varieties are particularly worth watching.

Select Producers in Navarra

Bodegas Julián Chivite***–*****
Cintruénigo (D.O. Navarra)
890 acres (360 ha); bought-in grapes; 3,000,000 bottles
• *Wines include: Chivite Colección 125 Blanco Dulce,*
→*Chivite 125 Colección Chardonnay Fermentado en Barrica; Gran Feudo Reserva, Gran Feuda Viñas Viejas, Chivite Colección 125 Tinto Reserva, Chivite 125 Colección Gran Reserva*
In addition to reliable *rosados* and classic *tintos*, the family also produces a range of top-quality wines on its Arínzano estate at Estella. They are sold under the Chivite Colección 125 label and combine northern elegance with southern maturity. The Chardonnay, regarded in a good year as the best in the country, and the red Reserva, are as delicate as they are intense.

Bodegas Guelbenzu**–****
Cascante (Navarra)
104 acres (42 ha); 230,000 bottles • *Wines include: Guelbenzu Tinto, Guelbenzu Evo,* →*Lautus*
Ricardo Guelbenzu and his enologist Joseba Altuna produce balanced *tintos* blended to produce an international flavor, but which are Spanish through and through. The cask-aging is kept short, and large wooden tuns are used during the winemaking process.

Bodegas Magaña***–****
Barrillas (D.O. Navarra)
309 acres (125 ha); 325,000 bottles • *Wines: Viña Magaña Reserva, Dignus Crianza,* →*Barón de Magaña, Viña Magaña Merlot Reserva*
The star wine has to be the renowned Merlot. In the last few years, however, the reasonably priced Dignus, a blend of four varieties, has shown true class. Juan Magaña, one of the pioneers of French varieties in Spain, makes a modern *tinto*, Barón de Magaña, which is sold after aging in the barrel without being bottle-stored.

Bodegas Nekeas***–****
Añorbe (D.O. Navarra)
556 acres (225 ha); bought-in grapes; 1,200,000 bottles
• *Wines include:* →*Nekeas Chardonnay Fermentado en Barrica; Nekeas Merlot, El Chaparral, Nekeas Reserva,* →*Izar de Nekeas*
This *bodega* was founded in 1993 as an ultramodern cooperative. The cool north of Navarra produces wonderfully fruity Chardonnays and concentrated red wines. The enologist Concha Vecino equips her *tintos* for a long life and provides them with a robust tannin structure.

Bodegas Ochoa***–****
Olite (D.O. Navarra)
358 acres (145 ha); 800,000 bottles • *Wines include: Ochoa Moscatel;* →*Ochoa Vendimia Seleccionada, Ochoa Tempranillo Crianza,* →*Ochoa Reserva, Ochoa Gran Reserva*
Together with Chivite, Javier Ochoa produced the region's first *reservas* and *gran reservas* keeping wines. These top-quality wines are firm with powerful tannin structures that need time. His single-varietal *tintos* are juicy and easy-drinking, and display only discreet woody flavors.

Castillo de Monjardín***–****
Villamayor de Monjardín (D.O. Navarra)
395 acres (160 ha); 450,000 bottles • *Wines include: Castillo de Monjardín:* →*Chardonnay, Reserva Chardonnay; Crianza, Reserva*
Victor del Villar owns several of Navarra's highest vineyards. He is regarded as a Chardonnay-lover and makes three different wines from this grape, including Navarra's only *reserva*. As an experiment, he has ventured to produce a sweet wine made from grapes that have been exposed to frost. The red wines are meaty with lots of fresh fruit.

The Wine-growing Regions of Aragón

Campo de Borja

South of Navarra, on the opposite side of the Ebro river, lies Campo de Borja, awarded D.O. status in 1980. For over 600 years, the monks of the Monasterio de Veruela west of Borja saw to wine growing, and the wine festival is still held in the restored monastery to this day. The vineyards are in the hilly countryside between the Sierra del Moncayo, which is over 6,500 feet (2,000 m) high, and the banks of the Ebro at 1,150–2,300 feet (350–700 m) above sea level. The climate, with its cold winters and short, hot summers, is very continental, and practically every year the harvest is reduced due to frost damage. This D.O. of 15,570 acres (6,300 ha) usually produces a harvest of only about 22,050 short tons (20 million kg) of grapes. The plus side is that the raw climate has its advantages in that the vines have to fight to survive in the most intriguing sites in the foothills of the mountain, thus promising concentrated, well-structured wines. The authorized grape varieties are the red Garnacha, Tempranillo, Mazuela, and Cabernet Sauvignon, and the white Viura (Macabeo) and Moscatel, although white wine accounts for barely 11 percent of total production. The Garnacha grape accounts for more than 74 percent. Old plantings of Garnacha combined with other varieties produce expansive yet robust wines.

Aragón's poor soils provide favorable conditions for wine growing.

Modern cellar technology and finishing in new *barriques* have long been applied even in less well-known wine regions.

Calatayud

Good *rosados* and honest *tintos* are the trademark of the D.O. Calatayud. The name of this still relatively unknown wine-growing region, which gained D.O. status in 1990, is derived from the Arabic and means "fortress (*kalat*) of the Ayud," which can still be visited today in the town of the same name. Here, the red grape varieties of Garnacha, Tempranillo, Mazuela, and Monastrell grow on the steep, semi-arid soil. With the exception of Viura, the white varieties are insignificant here. The D.O. produces 18,500–21,000 short tons (17–19 million kg) of grapes. The soils are rocky and friable, and the yield from the D.O.'s 18,040 acres (7,300 ha) very low indeed. The climate is cooler and rainfall is somewhat higher than in neighboring regions, and this produces slightly lighter and more acidic wines. In addition to very fresh *rosados*, the region produces mainly young red wines based on the Garnacha grape, and also *crianzas*.

Cariñena

The very alcoholic wines of earlier times have almost disappeared from Aragón's oldest D.O., which, with its 49,420 acres (20,000 ha), is also the largest. The majority of the vines grow on

Select Producers in Aragón

Bodegas Borsao***
Borja (D.O. Campo de Borja)
3,583 acres (1,450 ha); 1,600,000 bottles
• Wines include: Borsao Tinto, Borsao Crianza,
Gran Campellas, Señor de Atares, Tres Picos
With its Borsao Joven and Crianza this big winery has
created pleasing *tintos* based on Tempranillo and
Garnacha grapes; the spectacular full-bodied Garnacha
Tres Picos has now been added to the range.

Bodegas Val de Pablo**–***
Terrer (D.O. Calatayud)
Bought-in grapes; 450,000 bottles • Wines include: Señorío
de San Vicén: Rosado, Tempranillo, Don Diago Tinto
The concern was not included in the D.O. until 1999.
The quality of the *tintos* is convincing, because the
winemaker procures good-quality Tempranillo grapes
from the cooperatives. The coming *crianza* differs very
pleasingly from the region's typical Garnacha wines.

Grandes Vinos y Viñedos***
Cariñena (D.O. Cariñena)
12,360 acres (5,000 ha); 9,000,000 bottles • Wines:
Valdemadera Tinto, Monasterio de las Viñas Tinto,
Corona de Aragón: →Crianza, Reserva
Despite its size, this winery has produced some fine and
juicy red wines. Founded in 1997, it is already one of
the most interesting producers in Cariñena.

Viñas del Vero***–****
Barbastro (D.O. Somontano)
1,433 acres (580 ha); 6,000,000 bottles • Wines: Viñas
del Vero: Clarión, Tempranillo, Val de Vos Crianza,
Merlot, →Gran Vos
The range of single-varietal wines with their extremely
clear fruit and good structure has enjoyed great success.
The business has acquired a quality wine vineyard in its
immediate neighborhood. It has produced one of the
two best *tintos* of the district, marketed under the name
of Blecua.

Viñedos y Crianzas del Alto Aragón***–****
Salas Bajas (D.O. Somontano)
593 acres (240 ha); bought-in grapes; 2,200,000 bottles
• Wines include: Enate: Chardonnay 234, Macabeo-
Chardonnay; Tempranillo-Cabernet Sauvignon
Crianza, →Tinto Reserva Especial
The wines produced by this winery are exceptionally
clear yet slightly international in style. The wines are
precise, always manifesting the distinct flavor of the
grape varieties from which they have been made, and
the red wines at least are now very full-bodied. With its
Enate Reserva Especial, the *bodega* has created one of
Spain's best *tintos*.

---

an undulating, rocky plateau surrounded by a
range of hills that shelter it from the cold winds
of the Pyrenees. The climate is therefore dry
with hot summers, giving the grapes the potential to develop a high alcohol content, as well as
robust yet sweet tannins. The name of the
region may lead people to believe that the red
Cariñena grape, known as the Mazuelo in other
regions, is the main variety. Although it is represented, Garnacha and Tempranillo are the
preferred varieties. Cariñena offers a host of
crianza and *reserva* wines that are practically
unbeatable in terms of price and quality, being
exceptionally soft and mature. Many producers
have gradually started to plant Cabernet
Sauvignon, which develops a greater maturity
here than in the other wine-growing regions of
northern Spain. The white Macabeo grape
continues to play a major role, covering almost
a fifth of the total surface area. It is usually sold
in the barrel, because within the D.O. region
there is a famous cava manufacturer.

Somontano

The small, top-quality region of Somontano has
something exotic about it. The wines of this
D.O. have very little in common with the wines
of Aragón's other quality wine-producing areas.
This is partly due to the climate. Strangely,
despite its proximity to the mountains,

Somontano is a fast-rising
star of Spanish wine-
growing regions, with
single-varietal wines taking
center stage. The Moristel
produced by the Bodega
Pirineos in Barbastro is
very convincing.

Somontano, which is situated in the north of the
province of Huesca, is the most balanced D.O.
in the autonomous region in terms of climate.
The quality of its vineyards and commitment of
its producers also play a critical role.

In the flat-bottomed valleys around Barbasto,
the region's capital, the soils are interspersed
with minerals from long-extinct volcanoes,
which provide excellent conditions for wine
growing. Planted with the usual varieties until
the beginning of the 1980s, the Sobrarbe cooperative (now Bodegas Pirineos) gradually began
to restock the vineyards with high-quality
Spanish and foreign grape varieties with the
benefit of the latest viticultural knowledge. The
range of authorized grape varieties grown in this
D.O., founded in 1985, now comprises 12 varieties, with red grapes accounting for 75 percent.
There are only ten concerns that bottle wines,
with 93 percent of the bottling being carried out
by the big three: Enate, Viñas del Vero, and
Bodegas Pirineos, the heart and soul of the turn-
around in the fortunes of wine in Somontano.

The results of this plan—consistent selection
in the vineyard, separate-site production, and
investment in cutting-edge technology—have
caused a furore, especially abroad. The wines,
which come from the 5,189 acres (2,100 ha)
registered to the estate, are elegant, very delicate, with vibrant fruit, repeatedly described as
the New-World wines of southern Europe.

CASTILE–LEÓN

With its nine provinces, Castile–León is the largest regional entity in the European Union to have its own parliament. It is primarily agricultural, but with only 173,000 acres (70,000 ha) of vines, the area devoted to wine growing is relatively small in Spanish terms. So far, less than half of this area has D.O. status. There are currently five *Denominaciones de Origen*, but the district of Ribera de Arlanza in the province of Burgos will shortly be designated the sixth D.O.

In Castile, there is a long tradition of wine growing, which blossomed for the first time in the 16th and 17th centuries. The court in Madrid was the driving force, and the huge demand from the rapidly expanding new capital just had to be met. There was also great demand from abroad, which led to the wine-growing area spreading throughout the country. It is hard to calculate the precise extent of the total area in Castile–León at the end of the 19th century before the outbreak of the phylloxera disaster, but the small region of Rueda provides a starting point. It used to cover 222,400 acres (90,000 ha), but has now shrunk to less than a

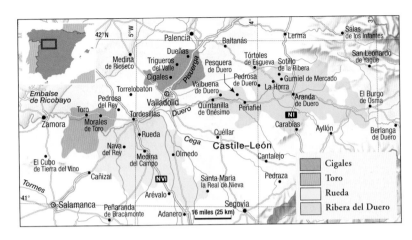

tenth of that figure. Despite massive replanting after the damage caused by the phylloxera outbreak, the wine-growing area has never regained its 19th-century proportions. Furthermore, in the 1950s when the national plan of the Franco regime turned large tracts of Castile over to cornfields, many vines had to give way to grain.

Castile has an excellent reputation among connoisseurs of Spanish wine, and this is not restricted to the Ribera del Duero. The wines are generally regarded as being full-bodied with character and intense fruit. There is no doubt that the soil and climatic conditions are responsible for much of the wines' profile. Castile–León has poor soils, extremes of hot and cold, and to a lesser extent, repeated periods of drought. El Bierzo in León provides an example of the low yield produced from the vines. This low yield is often further decimated by the inclement weather.

Barren plateaus and a wide temperature range are features of the wine-growing regions in Castile-León. They ensure that the wines are balanced and expressive. Some of the region's best-known wines come from Pesquera del Duero in the Ribera del Duero area.

FIVE QUALITY WINE AREAS

Even as recently as the 1960s, the wine region of Castile was regarded as being antiquated. La Rioja was at its height of popularity. Today, however, many of the major Spanish wines are concentrated in this autonomous region. In addition to the Ribera del Duero, four more zones are classified as quality wine regions. El Bierzo, in the northwestern tip, produces the lightest wines, and Cigales, not far from Valladolid, supplies red- and rosé-lovers with robust wines. Together with the Catalan Priorats, Toro offers the most full-bodied wines of all Spain, which is not surprising, since Zamora has the third lowest rainfall of the country's provinces. Rueda deserves special

quality that they have tempted famous wine-makers from La Rioja and Galicia, who believe they have found a distinctive new style of red wine here. The red wines from Valdevimbre-Los Oteros between Benavente and León are some of Spain's classic table wines.

Production of top-quality table wines has generally increased around the Duero basin. *Bodegas* such as Abadía Retuerta, Mauro, and Alta Pavina have basically reversed the sad reputation of table wines. Most of the country's famous table-wine producers are now concentrated in Castile.

To complete the picture, reference should be made to the wines right on the Portuguese border. The loops of the river Duero, where Castile's largest river becomes the border, are shared by the provinces of Salamanca and Zamora. *Rosados* and medium-bodied red wines are produced here, and after Ribera de Arlanza could possibly be regulated by a seventh D.O. in the region going by the name of Los Arribes.

In terms of winemaking technology, the region of Castile is definitely at the forefront. Yet the trend is leaning toward a controlled naturalness. The wine is not filtered so thoroughly, and the chemical treatment of vineyards is kept to a bare minimum. This is not particularly difficult in a region that is so bleak that its climate manages to make life miserable and difficult even for pests.

mention, because the change from oxidation-finished white wines to the fruity, delicate wines of today has been dramatic. Rueda could soon be giving Spain its first smooth white wines suitable for laying down, for the possibilities of the Verdejo grape variety have in no way been fully exploited.

However, the quality wine regions of Castile–León are not the only places to produce attractive wines. Cebreros in the province of Ávila produces robust and soft red wines of such

The rustic surroundings of the Bodega Monjardín in Navarra.

Toro, Spain's new viticultural heaven

When the wine-growing region around the small town of Toro, where monks grew wine as early as the 13th century, was finally recognized as a D.O., its wines immediately began to attract attention. But no one anticipated that only 11 years later some of Spain's most renowned enologists would rush to set up wineries in the D.O. Toro. The original area under cultivation has now been doubled to 14,826 acres (6,000 ha) and is still growing. Tinta de Toro is only native to this area; it is simply a clone of Tempranillo, created through the special climate conditions in Toro, and it provides 90 percent of the total harvest. Garnacha Tinta and the white

Malvasía and Verdejo grapes also play some part. The Tinta de Toro produces very dark red wines with high extract and tannin levels and is responsible for the fact that, alongside the Ribera del Duero and the Priorat, Toro is considered to be a new wine miracle. The young wines mostly contain a high proportion of Garnacha grapes, whereas the Tinta de Toro predominates in the barrel-aged quality wines. Most of the 30 winegrowers registered so far— the number of winegrowers selling their own wine should double shortly—produce the main variety as a single-varietal wine. The *appellation* regulations stipulate that a *crianza* wine should be aged in oak for at least six months. The white Malvasía provides soft wines that should be drunk when they are young.

Of the region's D.O.s, this area is the warmest and the driest. With 3,000 hours of sunshine each year, the grapes attain an enviable degree of ripeness. To avoid the development of an excessive alcohol content, the grapes are harvested here as early as the beginning of September. The Tinta de Toro with its 13.5 percent vol develops the best spicy-fruity character. Top wineries such as Vega Sicilia, Mauro, and Pesquera like the Tinta de Toro for its opulent fruit and soft tannins, which make this red wine smooth, yet profound, and give it considerable keeping potential. In the opinion of experienced winemakers, the Tinta de Toro is the only real alternative to Tempranillo. It is therefore assured a place in the Spanish wine Olympics.

Ribera del Duero

This wine-growing area extends for more than 68 miles (109 km) along both sides of the river Duero through parts of four provinces. Around 85 percent of the whole region lies within the province of Burgos, even though many of the *bodegas* are in the province of Valladolid. When, in 1982, the *Denominación de Origen* was first established, only a few wine producers existed alongside cooperatives. Today there are well over 150 *bodegas*, with more springing up. Scarcely any region growing quality wines has made such rapid progress as the Ribera del Duero, which has become a byword for excellence throughout the world.

The secret of this success lies in the region's red wines, which are exceptionally dark, superbly fruity, richly robust and remarkably well able to age. Apart from the main variety, Tinta del País, the following reds: Garnacha, Cabernet Sauvignon, Merlot, and Malbec, and the white, Albillo, are licensed.

The D.O. Ribera del Duero is best known for high-quality red wines aged in wood, which must contain at least three-quarters Tinta del País, as Tempranillo is called hereabouts. However, many top companies produce pure varietals from the best Castilian grapes. The continuing vast variation in styles and qualities is due largely to preparation methods and very variable harvests. The best vineyards are in the province of Burgos near the villages of Roa, La Horra, Gumiel, and Sotilla—these are also called the heartland of the

La Horra is one of the most famous wine areas in the Ribera del Duero.

Ribera. Nevertheless, we must avoid geographical classification, since the harvest from any area may circulate throughout the D.O. region. Styles are also determined by different oakwood, not only classic American oak but also French barrels are used.

The region has a greater variety of *terroirs* than is usual in Castile, and these mainly influence the personalities of small growers' wines. Thus, Ribera is not simply confined to Ribera. The 37,064 acres (15,000 ha) of vineyards, 80 percent stocked with the red main varietal, are sited not only on the Duero's banks, but also on surrounding hills. Most top-quality growing areas lie on south-facing, highly chalky slopes, which descend to the river from high ground. At several points the region reaches deep inland, up to nearly 22 miles (35 km). The extreme highland climate—many vineyards lie over 2,624 feet (800 m) up—often brings late frosts. These radically reduce harvests in a number of years, which explains the scarcity and consequent popularity of reds.

Cigales

Cigales, the smallest of the four D.O. regions in central Castile, lies on a tributary of the Duero, the Río Pisuerga. It is nearly 30 miles (48 km) long and 9 miles (15 km) wide. Currently the vineyards cover over 6,792 acres (2,750 ha), almost all sited in the north of Valladolid province. Only one district in the neighboring province, Palencia, is a D.O. area. Climatically, Cigales is somewhere between the warmish Toro region and the cooler Ribera del Duero, whose western edge lies only 15 miles (24 km) away. The landscape is generally flat, broken up by occasional table-mountains. Historically, the village after which the D.O. is named is a legendary center of Spanish winemaking.

From early mediaeval times the Claretes of Cigales, very full-bodied *rosados* (pinks), were considered the best in Spain. Juicy *rosados* are still trodden here, although recently sturdy but

In the twilight of an autumn day, the rich green vineyards stand out sharply against the burnt landscape of Castile–León.

palatable Tintos have found more favor. The permitted varieties are the whites Albillo, Verdejo and Viura, but they account for less than 10 percent of the total area under cultivation. The main varieties are Tinta del Pais and Garnacha. Ten years ago the red wines still

only accounted for just under 10 percent of the total wine output of this region; now their share has risen to 45 percent. Particularly the super-modern and largely unknown wine producers who have entered the market in recent years—the area now has around 20 bottling plants—are increasingly concentrating on pure Tinta del Pais wines, which age excellently in the small oak vats. The potential for high-quality Tintos is certainly there, but so far the Cigales Tintos have only in exceptional cases reached the heights of their neighbor's top quality products.

The expressive *rosados*, described on their back-label as "Cigales Nuevo," still account for most D.O. production. These wines are trodden from at least 60 percent Tinta del País, and released by the D.O. regulators as early as November. They have a fine freshness and an opulent bouquet.

Many wine drinkers will wonder how Riberas differ from Riojas, if the Tinta del País and Tempranillo are identical. In the Ribera region only a few wines are aged as long as traditional Riojas. Instead, they are often marketed soon after fermentation in small oak barrels. Thus, Ribera wines often have a relatively deeper color, sweeter tannins, and a darker fruitiness tending toward plum, while Riojas frequently exude stronger aromas of red berries. Recently, many new-generation Riojas, along with several Riberas, have acquired distinct vanilla and cinnamon aromas after fermenting in new wood.

RUEDA

The establishment of the first D.O. dedicated—at first—solely to white wine, Rueda, inaugurated the triumphal progress of a grape practically unknown before. The Verdejo grape is indigenous to this region, stocked with some 16,800 acres (6,800 ha) of vines, extending north of the Duero into Valladolid province and is also present in small areas of Ávila and Segovia. It constitutes nearly half the total vineyards. Alongside this main variety, Viura, Sauvignon Blanc, and Palomina are also licensed, though the latter must not be newly planted. The D.O. named after the small village of Rueda has one of the country's best wine cellar infrastructures and all of the 30 bottling plants have hyper-modern cellar facilities. The making of white wine, with temperature-controlled fermentation, is now standard practice, and cooling the harvested grapes before PRESSING, selection-tables, and cold maceration are no longer exceptional. Many old cave-cellars, with kilometer-long tunnels, have been redesigned into real showcases. Some store the sparkling wine: Rueda Espumoso, whose yeast needs at least nine months to mature, must contain up to 75 percent Verdejo. However, the region's stars are Rueda Verdejo, also with at least 75 percent Verdejo, and the intensely pure varietals of Sauvigon Blanc wines, which have developed a unique, robust structure on the bare high plains.

The strong point of Verdejo wine is its floral rather than distinctly fruity bouquet, underscored with a delicate bitterness and a strongly herbal taste. One of this varietal's outstanding features is its high extract-value, which can be seen from the substantial streaks in the glass. But this should cause no anxiety—far from indicating too much alcohol, it promises denseness and quality. The third variety is a straightforward Rueda, made with 50 percent Verdejo. Since 2000 the red varieties grown here, chief of which is Tinta del Pais, have

also had D.O. protection. The red Ruedas are not as complex as the Riberas, but this could change in a few years.

EL BIERZO

Bordering on Galicia, El Bierzo D.O. definitely has the best balanced climate of any D.O. region in Castile–León. Atlantic rain and Castilian sun make El Bierzo's valleys one of the most productive of Spain's landscapes. Most vineyards lie on flat slopes in the valleys, scarcely over 1,641 feet (500 m) high. Sheltering mountain ranges ensure that late frosts rarely strike.

Main varieties are the whites Doña Blanca and Godello and the principal wine, the indigenous red, Mencía. All red wines must contain at least 75 percent of this grape. It has a delicate, red fruit aroma and produces fruity, subtle red wines with sturdy acidity and a characteristic mineral quality. If grown on old vines, blackberry notes predominate. Mencía wines are normally offered as *vino joven*, but the best producers prove that aging in barrels can add concentration and complexity.

The Prada a Tope vineyards with a taproom in Cacabelos independently produce red and white wines of the D.O. El Bierzo.

VEGA SICILIA, PESQUERA, AND PINGUS

The following three great vineyards have established, confirmed and constantly renewed the reputation of the Ribera region. Vega Sicilia, Bodega Alejandro Fernández-Tinto Pesquera, and Dominio de Pingus are not only some of Spain's best wines but also rank with the world's top labels.

VEGA SICILIA

Back in 1864, the first vines were planted in the western section of the present D.O. Ribera del Duero. However, only from 1915–17, under the Herrero family who gave the estate its current name, was a quality red wine produced that could be considered a forerunner of present-day varieties. Alongside viticulture, the house of Vega Sicilia has devoted most of its energy to a highly elaborate, sophisticated process of maturing wines—the key to the uniquely Baroque style of the Único, the estate's main *cuvée*. In good vintages the Único proves itself one of the world's most versatile reds, whilst its inimitably deep aromas evoke a unique character of fruit dried under southern sun. It also smells of dry fruit such as figs and plums, of forest berries, tobacco, coffee, and spices. In the mouth a very special velvety fullness develops, underscored by melting tannins.

The 445 acres (180 ha) of the estate's vineyards are dominated by the Tinta del País, which, in some of the oldest plots, is mixed with Cabernet Sauvignon vines. The hand-picked grapes are first taken in small crates to the cellar, where they are completely hulled and moved by conveyor-belt to the fermenting tanks. The best plots' harvest has already been pre-selected for the Único, and is fermented in wooden vats. The second-ranking wine, Valbuena, is stored in stainless steel tanks. After malolactic fermentation, which also takes place in large wooden tanks, the Único is first left to settle for six months in old barrels. Then all the wines are tasted and tested and their future decided. The second-rank wine, Valbuena, which is marketed after five years' fermentation, is now poured into pre-used barrels of French oak for 11 to 14 months. Then it is matured in bottles for at least 18 months more. What will become Único now proceeds on its complex way, by carefully selected steps, to ultimate perfection. Initially, the wine ferments for up to two years in new

Vega Sicilia, with its stately chapel and buildings around a courtyard, can be seen as the original core of the Ribera region that is so much in demand today.

French barrels, before maturing for five years or more in ever-older barrels, mainly American oak, until the day of bottling finally arrives.

The usual blending of the Único reflects the distribution of different wine varieties in the estate's vineyards. Tinta del País represents at least four-fifths, followed by Cabernet Sauvignon, Malbec, Merlot, and a drop of Albillo, the crowning glory. The Unico goes unfiltered into bottles, where it must mature for at least three years. The owner family, Álvarez, would leave an interval of at least 11 years before releasing it into the world of paying wine collectors and gourmets. In outstanding vintages like 1970 and 1981, the Tinto Fino often constitutes only two thirds of the *cuvée*, while the Cabernet Sauvignon rises to a fifth, reinforced by Merlot and Malbec. Then the Único will be commercially sold as a *reserva especial* only after several more years' aging.

The Vega Sicilia vine strips in the Duero valley extend between the river's left bank and the adjoining chain of hills in the western corner of the Ribera region.

Long before the Ribera del Duero had earned a reputation as a wine-growing region, Vega Sicilia was already legendary. It is reassuring for the wine world to know that this estate and its unique wines with their long tradition are still cared for so lovingly. This is at least partly due to the sensitivity with which innovations have been introduced. Yet Alión, the second estate which the Álvarez family stocked in 1992 only a few kilometers nearer Peñafiel, shows how carefully this legacy has been fostered. Here, on 124 acres (50 ha), only Tinta del País grapes were planted. When ripe, the grapes are selected with utmost care. They are generally macerated for three weeks at most, before the wine is matured in new French barrels for a maximum of 16 months. The result is a supremely smooth, fruity and spicy wine, which can stand comparison with any other modern Spanish red wine.

Pesquera

If Vega Sicilia is the Ribera region's grandfather, Alejandro Fernández is its father. He not only created the modern Ribera style, but also inaugurated a new kind of Spanish wine, combining the maturity of grapes grown under southern sun with full-bodied fruitiness and great finesse. Today this formula inspires great wines not only in the Ribera del Duero but all over Spain, especially in the region of La Rioja.

When he was young, Alejandro Fernández earned his living repairing and constructing agricultural machines of all kinds. Simultaneously, however, he managed several vine-

Left
The old wine cellars in Pesquera perforate the village hill. Only the acorn-like airshafts betray the fact that outstanding reds are slumbering here.

Right
Only when the vintage is exceptional will Alejandro Fernández bottle his Janus, which he produces by consciously conservative methods.

Tinto Pesquera consists exclusively of Tinta del País, as Tempranillo is called hereabouts.

yards in his home locality, Pesquera del Duero, which were left to him by his father. At that time grapes or young wines were still sold to those areas whose wines suffered from lack of color or body—for example, La Mancha. The more color a wine had, the more it cost. In 1972, angered by the contempt in which cooperatives held his excellent wines, Don Alejandro established his *bodega*. Without hulling his grapes, he fermented his harvest and pressed them in the old winepress that still stands near the estate. Initially, he kept his reds in champagne bottles with spring fasteners, and began marketing them throughout the region. Gradually, news of the quality of his wine

spread throughout Castile. An American importer helped him achieve his breakthrough. "Wine Pope" Robert Parker received a sample of Pesquera 1992 from Don Alejandro, and he christened this "the Petrus of Spain." World renown for Pesqueras and Alejandro Fernández were assured.

Pesquera wines always use pure-varietal Tinta del País grapes, which are harvested in deliberately limited quantities. After alcoholic fermentation, up to a fortnight of maceration generally follows. To mature the wines, and for the malolactic fermentation, barrels of American oak are selected—a technique that consciously upholds the region's tradition. The wines never become woody, yet age superbly. Different Pesquera qualities are manifested according to the age of the vines, the choice of grape, the age of the barrels used, and the duration of the aging in wood. Only the Janus Special Reserve, prepared in the most successful years, follows traditional methods of preparation, whereby the stems are also macerated with the juice, as if to remind people of the wines that have made Pesquera famous.

PINGUS

Pingus, at present Spain's most popular and dearest red wine, has given the Ribera region immediate renown. Since 1990 the young Dane, Peter Sisseck, has managed the estate, the Hacienda el Monasterio. He learned the craft of winemaking in Bordeaux and was inspired by Valandraud in Saint-Émilion. In the locality of la Horra he has also planted four plots of land with over nine acres (3.8 ha) of old Tinta del País—land which he used to rent in 1995 but has since purchased. With utmost care and following ecological principles, he still tends his vineyards, which lie in probably the best *terroirs* of the Ribera region, restricting his yields drastically. Then he waits patiently for the grapes' optimum ripeness, before they are hand-picked and taken 25 miles (40 km) in small crates by refrigerated truck to his wine cellar in distant Quintanilla de Onésimo. Here, ten women de-stalk the grapes by hand, before lightly crushing them underfoot in small stainless steel fermenting containers. By this time it is already early October and the nights are cool. The grapes lie in their own must for ten days before fermentation sets in; and this usually lasts another eight days. Generally, Peter Sissek lets the wine macerate for only a few days before he takes off the stems and pours the juice into new French barrels. In these, in the warmer spring weather, malolactic

fermentation follows automatically. Then every single barrel is tasted and every wine, whose exceptionally strong nose suggests intense concentration, is further aged in another barrel—a process called "maturing in 200 percent new oak."

After nearly two years in a barrel, the Pingus is bottled. Since Robert Parker awarded the first vintage 98 out of 100 points in 1995, precipitating it into the small circle of the world's top wines, wine lovers all over the globe have been battling for one of the 7,000 bottles produced annually. This truly hand-made wine bewitches the nose with an intense aroma of fig, smoke, and tar, and the palate with its enormous body; here it develops similar aromas, and also dark chocolate, spices, and a prodigious length. It is altogether a dramatic wine with a thoroughbred backbone. Recently, Peter Sisseck has taken over other vineyards, which produce the more wood-oriented, less complex second-rank wine, Flor de Pingus.

By means of well-established vines and very sophisticated cellar work, the young Dane Peter Sisseck, called Pingus by friends and relatives, created the most expensive cult-wine in Spain—the Pingus.

Select Wine Producers in Castile–Léon

Bodegas Alejandro Fernández****
Pesquera de Duero (D.O. Ribera del Duero)
543 acres (220 ha); 850,000 bottles • Wines: Tinto Pesquera: Crianza, Reserva, Gran Reserva, Janus Reserva and Gran Reserva
Ribera owes its current prominence to Alejandro Fernández and his Pesquera wines. He also manages the excellent Condado de Haza estate near Roa de Duero.

Bodegas Arzuaga Navarra***–****
Quintanilla de Onésimo (D.O. Ribera del Duero)
346 acres (140 ha); some bought-in grapes: 450,000 bottles • Wines: Tinto Arzuaga Crianza, Tinto Arguaza Reserva, →Tinto Arzuaga Gran Reserva
The *bodega* belongs to the younger generation on the Duero. The vines are striking for their elegance and harmony. The better the quality (Reserva and Gran Reserva), the higher the proportion of Cabernet and French oak.

Bodegas de Crainza Castilla la Vieja***–****
Rueda (D.O. Rueda)
247 acres (100 ha); some bought-in grapes; 2,000,000 bottles • Wines: Palacio de Bornos: Rueda Superior, Fermentado en Barrica, →Sauvignon Blanc
Antonio Sanz and his son Ricardo are among Castile's most respected winegrowers. Alongside their very fruity Sauvignon and the crystal-clear Rueda Superior, the estate is experimenting with wood-aged Ruedas and white wines with residual sugar. The reds have no D.O.

Bodegas Emilio Moro**–*****
Pesquera de Duero (D.O. Ribera del Duero)
148 acres (60 ha); some bought-in grapes; 425,000 bottles • Wines: Finca Resalso, Emilio Moro, Malleolus, Malleolus de Valdemiro
The Moro family has gained in standing since 1991, when their first wine was bottled. Their selections from old vines, Malleolus and Malleolus de Valdemiro, have set the standards in the western Ribera region. Their style is lush and beefy with definite mineral notes.

Bodegas Hermanos Sastre***–****
La Horra (D.O. Ribera del Duero)
99 acres (40 ha); 140,000 bottles • Wines include: Via Sastre Crianza, Pago de Santa Cruz, Regina Vides, Pesus
Sastre is one of the top wine estates in Ribera del Duero. Production is small, and expensive specialties such as the single vineyard wine Pago de Santa Cruz or the wonderfully harmonious Regina Vides have character and great depth. The Merlot-dominated Pesus is one of the most exclusive wines in Spain.

Bodegas Hermanos del Villar***–****
Rueda (D.O. Rueda)
222 acres (90 ha); 300,000 bottles • Wines: Oro de Castila: Sauvignon Blanc, Fermentada en Barrica, →Rueda Superior
A serious *bodega* established in 1994. The estate, however, has old tunnel cellars. The wines are exceptionally fruity and soft, which gives them great charm. Pablo del Villar is one of the region's great hopes for the future.

Bodegas Ismael Arroyo****–*****
Sotillo de la Ribera (D.O. Ribera del Duero)
30 acres (12 ha); 360,000 bottles • Wines: Valsotillo: Crianza, Reserva, →Gran Reserva
The traditional yet fruity and deep-colored style of the Arroyo brothers lifted the *bodega* to the peak of Spanish

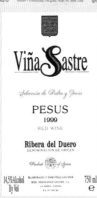

winemaking. The single-variety wines are matured only in American oak and show great aging potential.

Bodegas Lezcano***
Trigueros del Valle (D.O. Cigales)
35 acres (14 ha); 120,000 bottles • Wines: Docetañidos, Lezcano Crianza, Lezcano Reserva
Young Félix Lezcano did not found his small wine estate until 1991. However, his still immature wines are in an excellent location. Alongside a fine *rosado*, he produces complex if slightly woody *tintos*, which are getting finer every year.

Bodegas Mauro****
Tudela de Duero (no D.O.)
Pedrosa del Rey (D.O. Toro)
136 acres (55 ha); 225,000 bottles • Wines: Mauro, Terreus, →Vendima Seleccionada
This *bodega* was among the first in Castile to produce an outstanding, non-D.O. red wine. Since 1997 there has been an additional red wine from Toro, of which some 40,000 bottles are produced under the brand name Viña San Román. All the brands, from Terreus through to Mauro and San Román, reveal a brilliant and noble structure.

Bodegas Peñalba López***–****
Aranda de Duero (D.O. Ribera del Duero)
500 acres (200 ha); 800,000 bottles • Wines: Torremilanos: Crianza, Reserva; Torre Albéniz Reserva
In recent years the *bodega* owned by Pablo Peñalba and Pilar Albéniz has risen to join the best companies in the D.O. The Torremilanos wines are single variety, prepared from Tempranillo; the Reserva Torre Albéniz contains a little Cabernet. The vines produce wine that is full-bodied and with finish, and has great aging potential. The *bodega's* own cask maker has switched all the barrels to French wood.

Bodega Pérez Pascuas****
Pedrosa de Duero (D.O. Ribera del Duero)
210 acres (85 ha); 350,000 bottles • Wines include: Viña Pedrosa: Reserva, Gran Reserva, Pérez Pascuas Gran Selección
The very complex, fine and acidic *tintos* of the Viña Pedros brand are intended to age, but can seem rather inaccessible in youth. The *bodega* has very old vineyards 2,625 feet (800 m) up. The Selección Pérez Pascuas is one of the D.O.'s supreme wines.

Bodegas Rodera***–****
Pedrosa de Duero (D.O. Ribera del Duero)
161 acres (65 ha); 200,000 bottles • Wines: Carmelo Rodero: Crianza, Reserva, →Gran Reserva
For years Camelo Rodero sent his grapes to Vega Sicilia; then he made himself self-sufficient. His *tintos* always have a robust consistency, underscored with plump tannins. He owns one of the best Cabernet vineyards in the Ribera region, a small percentage of whose grapes go into the *reservas* and *gran reservas*.

Bodegas Vega Sauco***
Morales de Toro (D.O. Toro)
30 acres (12 ha); 190,000 bottles • Wines: Vega Sauco Tinto, Vega Sauco Crianza, Vega Sauco Reserva, →Adoremus
The strength of Wenceslao Gil's wines lies in their exceptional color and intense taste. Although the enologist has prescribed long aging in American oak, the wood is not dominant, thanks to the concentration of Vega Saucos.

Bodegas y Viñedos Vega Sicilia✶✶✶✶✶
Valbuena de Duero (D.O. Ribera del Duero)
445 acres (180 ha); 220,000 bottles • Wines: Unico
Tinto: Gran Reserva, Reserva Especial, Valbuena Tinta
Reserva
Since 1982, this has been owned by the Alvarez family,
who keep this historic estate and its wines in top
condition. They also own the nearby *bodega* Alíon,
where an impressive modern Ribera is produced from
124 acres (50 ha) of Tempranillo.

Dominio de Pingus✶✶✶✶–✶✶✶✶✶
Quintanilla de Onésimo (Ribera del Duero)
12 acres (5 ha); 25 acres (10 ha) leased; 37,000 bottles
• Wines: Pingus, Flor de Pingus
The Dane Peter Sissek succeeded in creating the Ribera's
most sought-after cult wine. He cleverly exploited the
success of his wine to give his estate a more extensive
future base.

Dominio de Tares✶✶✶
San Román de Bembibre (D.O. Bierzo)
Bought-in grapes, 220,000 bottles • Wines: Domenico
de Tares, Godello Fermentado en Barrica, Tinto Roble,
Cepas Viejas
From the very beginning, this young company relied on
grape varieties native to the region and uses the most
modern technology in the production of both red and
white wines. Even the grapes for the standard Roble
come from old vineyards. Cepas Viejas comes from
schist slope vineyards which are more than 60 years old.

Dos Victorias✶✶✶–✶✶✶✶
San Román de Hornija (D.O. Toro)
Nava del Rey (D.O. Rueda)
20 acres (8 ha); some bought-in grapes; 25,000 bottles
• Wines: Jose Pariente Rueda Superior, →Gran Elías Mora
In 1999 the two Victorias, both qualified enologists,
followed two vintages of their white Rueda José
Pariente with the first red table wine from the Toro
region, where the two Castilian women are building a
bodega. The 2000 vintage of their red wine, Elías
Moroa, was the first to bear the Toro *appellation*. Both
wines come from old vineyards and are outstandingly
fruity and well-structured.

Explotaciones Valduero✶✶✶–✶✶✶✶
Gumiel del Mercado (D.O. Ribera del Duero)
494 acres (200 ha); 1,200,000 bottles • Wines:
Valduero Crianza, Reserva, →Gran Reserva, Reserva
Primium
This family business stands by long aging in wood, and
always markets very mature wines, which seem well
balanced, subtle, yet also dense. The reds are generally
trodden as pure varietals from Tempranillo, and are
among the most reliable and reasonably priced wines on
the Duero.

Hacienda Monasterio✶✶✶✶
Pesquera de Duero (D.O. Ribera del Duero)
173 acres (70 ha); 320,000 bottles • Wines: Hacienda
Monasterio: Crianza, Reserva
A juicy Ribera type with an international profile,
intensely fruity, with soft tannins. The hyper-modern
estate and all its vines, working almost exclusively with
French oak, was conceived by the Dane Peter Sisseck.
Special emphasis is given to grape-selection and careful
wine preparation. Nothing is filtered.

Pago de Carraovejas✶✶✶✶
Peñafiel (D.O. Ribera del Duero)
148 acres (60 ha); 320,000 bottles • Wines: Pago de
Carraovejas: Crianza, Reserva
Highly aromatic wines of a very dark color are the
bodega's specialty. The first vines were planted in the

late 1980s by chief enologist, Tomás Postigo—including
a perfectly balanced Cabernet vine. All the *bodega's*
wines contain 25 percent of the French grape.

Vinos Blancos de Castilla✶✶✶–✶✶✶✶
Rueda (D.O. Rueda)
371 acres (150 ha); bought-in grapes; 1,500,800 bottles
• Wines: Marqués de Riscal: Reserva Limousin,
Sauvignon, →Rueda Superior
The undisputed pioneer of modern white wine
preparation in Rueda uses the very latest techniques to
tread his classic Marqués de Riscal Rueda Superior,
made from Verdejo and a dash of Viura. The wine also
exudes clean aromas of fruit and blossoms, and is a
perfect balance between body and stylishness. The same
applies to the Sauvignon Blanc.

Vinos Sanz✶✶✶
Rueda (D.O. Rueda)
247 acres (100 ha); 350,000 bottles • Wines: Sanz
Rueda Superior, Sanz Sauvignon, →Finca La Colina
The estate has the largest and oldest Sauvignon Blanc
vineyard in the D.O. Rueda. So it is no surprise that the
enologist Juan Carlos Ayala regularly treads one of the
country's best Sauvignon Blancs.

Teófilo Reyes's extensive knowledge of the Ribera expresses itself in his wines' complex style.

GALICIA

Galicia, a region where nature is wild and rampant, lies in the northwest of the Iberian Peninsula. Celtic traces remain not only in the language, Gallego, which is related to Portuguese, but also in a certain tendency toward mysticism. Pre-Christian and Christian elements mingle as in virtually no other area of Spain. Perhaps this also explains a recurring sense of reserve. That said, the switch from an almost medieval agrarian structure to avant-garde techniques in the modern cellars of Rías Baixas, home of the Albariño, has been so swift that it can hardly be said to be a transition.

Galicia produces roughly 26.5 million gallons (1 million hectoliters) of wine each year, and not so long ago there was the problem that no one knew where to put it all. Most of the wine-growing estates in Galicia are highly productive; the frequent rain and the temperate climate in the river valleys where most vines grow, do their work. On the one hand, the region of Galicia is plagued by excessive quantity and mediocrity, while on the other it can produce wines of such originality and quality that any enterprising wine lover will constantly find new surprises.

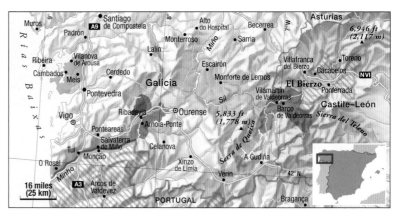

▨	Rías Baixas
▨	Ribeiro
▨	Ribeira Sacra
▨	Valdeorras
▨	Monterrei
▨	Wine-growing areas in neighboring regions

Opposite
Small land holdings, on which, in addition, livestock are kept and vegetables grown, share those areas of the Ribeira Sacra suitable for wine growing.

Even in the hinterland Galicia remains green and moist. In Ribeira Sacra many farmers cultivate only small terraces, which extend along south-facing slopes.

RIBEIRA SACRA

From an enological viewpoint, the Ribeira Sacra is certainly one of the most fascinating D.O. wines of recent years. Not least because in Galicia of northwestern Spain, a bastion of white wine production, it is the only region where reds exceed 75 percent of total winemaking. The quality varietal indigenous to this area is Mencía, and is probably derived from Cabernet Franc. The grape is only partially suitable for aging in wood and so it is marketed as a young wine. As a result, the region produces no *crianza*-quality wines.

The exquisite charm of these wines lies in their slender style and delicate fruitiness, which, according to vintage, can taste of licorice, plum, blackberry, or added fruit so that all Mencía wines from the Ribeira Sacra have undeniable

Valdeorras is another wine-growing region where time seems to have stood still in many villages and hamlets.

body. Climatic conditions are ideal: the combination of moderate rainfall with quasi-Mediterranean sunshine means that in the average temperature of 56.3°F (13.5°C) the grapes always mature fully. In Spain this varietal soon aroused attention, as its profile differs strikingly from the rounded, fully ripe red wine personalities which the country produces otherwise, and the prices for a red aged in the tank are almost disgracefully high. There are several reasons for this. First, 90 percent of the 2,965 acres (1,200 ha) of vineyards in the Ribeira Sacra (meaning "the holy bank" and referring to the numerous monasteries founded here in the 12th and 13th centuries) are on steep or very steep slopes. Over the millennia, viticulturalists have laboriously wrested an almost surreal-looking network of tiny terraces from these extremely unresponsive surfaces, on which any mechanical work is impossible. Prior to this, harvesters with full baskets were lowered on ropes to the river, where boats were waiting to take the grape harvest away. The slopes are so steep that it was often impossible to climb them with a full load of grapes.

New Pathways Along the Holy Bank

The soil consists of residual shale and granite, which give the wines a very individual mineral note. As the gorge-like geography of the river valleys of the Sil and Miños and their tributaries offer no opportunity for extending the vineyards, other paths have to be trodden here. For the younger generation of winegrowers their only chance is to manage their companies in a competitive way, by eliminating inferior varieties and replacing them with quality grapes. At present, the top-quality varietal, Mencía, accounts for only 49 percent of the vineyards. Another 30 percent is occupied by weaker varieties such as Garnacha Tintoreta and others. At the moment astronomical sums are paid for 2.2 lb (1 kg) of Mencía grapes, because according to the 2004 Consejo Regulador's scheme for quality control in the D.O., at least 85 percent of this grape must grow in the Ribeira Sacra. By this date the vineyards' total transformation must be complete.

Even the whites that have been settled here are not exempt. The two white grapes planted here, Godello and Albariño produce excellent results on the slate soil. Their percentage share is due to increase from an unlikely 6 percent to at least 15 percent.

Monterrei

In the neighboring province, Ourense, is the small D.O. Monterrei, whose vines offer a mirror image. Here, white wines predominate, with the varieties Doña Blanca, Godello, and Treixadura, ahead of the reds Mencía and Bastardo. Yet here, too, the regulatory authorities must suffer grapes, including the white sherry grape Palomino Fino or the Garnacha Tintorera, which do not produce optimum results in a northern climate. Another drawback is that for the only varietal really characteristic of the region—the Blanca de Monterrei or even Monstruosa—only 99 acres (40 ha) remain free. Recently, however, vines have again become available, and reconstruction of the vineyards has begun, principally to increase the proportion of straw-colored Godello, with its stylish apple and lime aromas.

The whites produced by the ten registered *bodegas* include some good quality wines. Of the 7,410 acres (3,000 ha) of vineyard available in the Támega valley area only the best 650 are allocated to quality wine making. Here, whites with a high proportion of Godello and Treixadura predominate, as they display fruitiness, body, and superb acidity. Sampling the available D.O. wines, however, quickly shows that despite a clean, harmonious taste, many wines demand clear definition, which will undoubtedly come in time. The bottling plants have good technical standards, because sufficient investment has been made recently. Training new vines on wires, which allows better sanitary care for the fruit, will swiftly raise the white Monterrei wines' overall quality. Whether the reds will achieve importance outside the region in future is less certain.

The soil, which is very rich compared to the Ribeira Sacra, together with the temperate climate, is not ideal for robust reds. Only extreme revenue-limitation, to maximize the Mencía's advantages, could help here.

Valdeorras

Also in Ourense, with some 3,705 acres (1,500 ha), is the D.O. Valdeorras. This regularly hits the headlines in the Spanish trade press, being the home of the recently re-discovered white Godello grape. Certainly, this cannot be compared with the aromatic opulence of a good Albariño, but produces middle-strength whites rich in extract and exuding fresh lemon, almonds, and very special earthy herbal aromas. Thanks to their distinctive personality the Godellos are slowly becoming a sought-after specialty. They are the pride of the D.O. and a bridge to the past, which threatened to disappear in the rather backward, rural Galician environment. Earlier, this role was taken by the main variety of white wine near the Sil. Looking at current varietals, it seems that the Garnacha, which normally needs limitless sun, is important. Nevertheless, most of the young wines are absorbed anonymously into table wine. Instead, *bodegas* in Valdeorras can turn to red Mencía, which has already been mentioned. This now forms the basis of some serious production of highly delicious, juicy red, but no longer very cheap young wines, which thanks to modern stainless steel techniques are trodden in many of the region's small cellars. The very limited quantities produced obviate distribution difficulties, especially as these wines are mostly consumed in Galicia itself.

Left
In Valdeorras one can often speak of vines that are literally trained by hand.

Right
The Río Sil region enjoys an especially temperate climate—ideal for wine—so that every well-situated terrace is used for wine growing. Recently more extensive vineyards, which are easier to cultivate, have been added.

RÍAS BAIXAS

Winemaking and fishing are the economic cornerstones of the Rías Baixas.

Only 20 years ago white wines from the D.O. Rías Baixas were completely unknown, and the vineyards covered less than a third of the present area of some 6,175 acres (2,500 ha). What is now celebrated as a Spanish white wine miracle then comprised a group of totally outmoded cooperative cellar owners. These accepted the harvest of thousands of part-purchase winegrowers and trod ungainly white wines, most of which soon became grassy and oxidated, ending up as barrel-fillers in large urban bottling plants. The farmers stored the only halfway pure vintage Albariño for themselves, and from April even this was hardly drinkable. Once the Franco era had ended, there were a few enterprising individuals who invested in wine production, and proved that the despised Albariño grape could result in white wines that equaled any northern quality variety. Initially, winemakers wanted to create an exclusively Albariño *denominación*. However, since in the southwestern corner of Pontevedra province vines were traditional to certain areas, it was decided to uphold at least this tradition and include all long-established varietals in the arrangements. The provisional description, Albariño, was changed to Rías Baixas, which in Galician means the lower (southern) estuaries.

The D.O. divides into five sub-zones with different soil and climate conditions. As in other regions, producers can purchase harvests throughout the whole D.O. As a result, only a few ADEGAS—Galician for *bodegas*—can reckon on area-specific vines. The recent plethora of small vineyards will undoubtedly make *terroir* occupation more significant in future. Pure vintage Albariños are customary throughout the region. The center for this vine is the sub-zone El Salnés, with the appealing small town, Cambados, which has an annual festival celebrating this grape.

The Albariño is a very aromatic varietal, which has stylish fruit, an excellent extract, and subtle acidity. To be called Rías Baixas, a wine must contain at least 70 percent Albariño, and, depending on the region, the varieties Caiño, Loureira, Torrontés, or Treixadura. The production of red wines in this region is of little significance.

Ribeiro

The D.O. Ribeiro is the only region in Galicia to have always had a certain degree of renown. The reason is the myriad Galician taverns, which in all the largish towns serve this wine as a cheap tipple to wash down their particular specialties. Considering the cloudy, sour little wine that was produced in the past, wine drinkers must consider themselves very grateful to the winegrowers, cooperatives, and appropriate regulators for having improved Ribeiro wines beyond all recognition in recent years. The present-day quality rests mainly on the potential of the traditional white varieties, such as Treixadura, Loureira, and Torrontés, which are grown separately on raised posts. These have proved themselves against negligible mass-market products such as Palomino. This particular grape was a typical relic of the post-phylloxera phase—planted for financial reasons, to recoup losses quickly. The old varietal whites prove fruity, light and pleasantly sparkly. The Ribeiros still stand for youth and freshness. Aging the wines in barrels is not usual. The wines have a substantial yet aggressive acidity. In their nose, dominant aromas are fruit and vegetable notes such as freshly mown grass and herbs. This region also produces reds—primarily from Caiño Tinto and Brancellano—that are simpler in character. The specialty

Vilariño: This picturesque village nestles among the Ribeiro vineyards.

of this region by the Río Miño is still young white wine.

Albariño and Seafood

In the north, near Santiago, lies the small sub-region of Val de Ulloa. Near the provincial capital of Pontevedra some 400 winegrowers in and around Soutomaior cultivate vineyards planted almost exclusively to Albariño. Further south, directly on the Portuguese frontier, the partial regions of O Rosal and Condado are sited. The Condado area has a most inclement climate, with late frosts. Otherwise the climate is very mild, with rainfall figures more reminiscent of northern Europe than the Iberian Peninsula.

Galicia is a land of Cockaigne for gourmets, and the Gallegos are famous in Spain for their tendency to eat a large amount of good food, especially seafood, which is uniquely plentiful in their estuaries. Rías-Baixas wines accompany this to perfection. Their superlative fruit, which often assumes exotic notes, and the slender but robust body, make these wines ideal accompaniments to meals. Almost all companies mature their wines in modern steel tanks. Some wines are marketed before Christmas, and these sparkle with fresh fruit. A good Rías Baixas is always highly aromatic. In recent years, however, the best wines have been left in the tank for longer—generally eight months—to achieve more complex fruit aromas and extra harmony. Nevertheless, all Galician white wines should be drunk, at the latest, two years after being harvested.

Select Wine Producers in Galicia

Adegas Galegas*–****
Salvaterra do Miño (D.O. Rías Baixas)
99 acres (40 ha); some bought-in grapes; 500,000 bottles • Wines include: Don Pedro de Soutomaior, Don Pedro de Soutomaior Neve, Tempo, Veigadares
With Don Pedro de Soutomaior, wine producer José Rodriguez succeeds year after year in creating a fine, clear, fruity but hard Albariño. Veigadares, due to the sensitive use of wood, holds a special place among the cask-fermented wines in the region.

Adegas Moure*
Escairón (D.O. Ribeira Scara)
17 acres (7 ha); some bought-in grapes; 150,000 bottles.
• Wines: Abadía da Cova, Albariño, Mencía
The two winemakers and owners of the small adega have taken enormous trouble to restore the old terraces on the steeps slopes of the Miño ravine. One famous wine is their extremely fruity young red from Mencía, and another is a crianza which is surprisingly fresh and delicate. In good years the Albariño, which is not actually typical of the region, displays a noticeably mineral, individual terroir character.

Bodegas del Palacio de Fefiñanes**
Cambados (D.O. Rías Baixas)
Bought-in grapes; 50,000 bottles • Wines: Albariño de Fefiñanes, 1583 Albariño de Fefiñanes
In recent years this winery, housed in a medieval castle, has greatly improved its quality. The 1583, barrel-aged, powerful and with good finish, is a success, but it still takes second place to the brilliant, intense and complex wines not aged in wood.

Bodegas Terras Gauda*–****
As Eiras-O Rosal (D.O. Rías Baixas)
173 acres (70 ha); 750,000 bottles • Wines: Abadía San Campio, Terras Gauda Etiqueta Negra, →Terras Gauda
In terms of size, the Terras Gauda is the most important bodega foundation in the recent history of the D.O. Rías Baixas. In an area which is noticeable for very small estates, the investors cleared an area of 148 acres (60 ha) of hill country to plant vines, thereby creating the largest connected vineyard in the D.O. In many years, Terras Gauda is one of Spain's five most aromatic dry white wines.

Martín Códax*–****
Vilariño-Cambados (D.O. Rías Baixas)
371 acres (150 ha); some bought-in grapes: 1,250,000 bottles • Wines: Martín Códax, Burgáns, Gallaeca, Organistrum
Galicia's most popular Albariño is a byword for quality. This wine company started as a cooperative and has first-rate vineyards. Alongside Martín Códax, a juicy young wine, there is Gallaeca, a late harvest, plus Organistrum, a barrel fermented Albariño, and a wine with residual sweetness.

Godeval*
Barco de Valdeorras (D.O. Valdeorras)
42 acres (17 ha); some bought-in grapes; 200,000 bottles • Wines: Viña Godeval, Viña Godeval Fermentado en Barrica
Horacio Fernández is one of the fathers of the revival program that saved the Valdeorrs' white wine grape, Godello. The vineyards of the estate, some on barely accessible slopes, are cultivated with technical perfection, and produce a very flowery, clear Godello.

Granja Fillaboa**
Salvaterra do Miño (D.O. Rías Baixas)
371 acres (25 ha); 180,000 bottles • Wines: Fillaboa Fermentado en Barrica, →Fillaboa
This estate produces two wines: the young Fillaboa, which is striking for its fresh, stylish quality, and an exemplary cask-aged Albariño, which is produced only in small quantities.

Pazo de Señorans**–*****
Meis (D.O. Rías Baixas)
25 acres (10 ha); some bought-in grapes; 180,000 bottles • Wines: Pazo de Señorans, Pazo de Señorans Selección de Añada
On this estate, owned by María Soleda Bueno, working together with the enologist Ana Quintela, harvesting is by vineyard, and some of the D.O.'s best structured Albariño is fermented separately in tanks. In outstanding years, a selection from the best vineyards is matured for eighteen months in steel tanks.

Emilio Rojo*
Arnoia-Ponte (D.O. Ribeiro)
7 acres (3 ha); 11,000 bottles • Wines: Emilio Rojo
Emilio Rojo helped Lado make a comeback. His only wine, white Emilio Rojo, has power and fine flower notes.

CASTILE–LA MANCHA

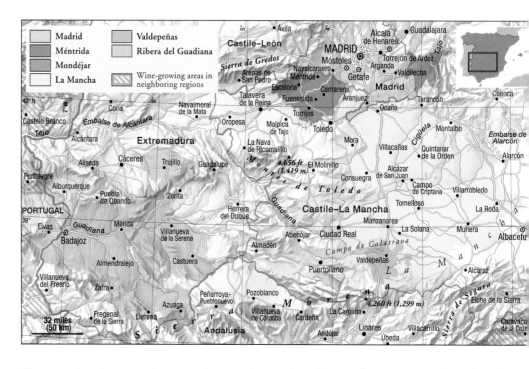

The central region, as wine connoisseurs also call Castile–La Mancha (or New Castile), is the world's largest connected wine-growing region. It was a major talking point for the European Commissioners when, in 1986, Spain joined what was then the European Community. It was finally agreed that part of the vineyards would, for a compensation premium, be laid fallow. After almost a third of the vines have been removed, the region still has six D.O. areas: Méntrida, Mondéjar, La Mancha, Ribera del Júcar, Valdepeñas, and Almansa (east of Albacete, off the map). With these, and its impressive table wine area, the region still gathers half of Spain's annual wine harvest, which totals between 30 and 45 million gallons (15–20 million hectoliters) according to year.

La Mancha, as the whole region is laconically known, is not to be confused with the D.O. area of the same name, which only covers part of it. The region's problem is the predominance of one grape, the white Airén, the world's most frequently planted vine variety. Because of its resistance to climatic extremes, it was planted profusely as a rescue measure after the phylloxera devastation, though it produces only average-quality wine. Many conscientious winemakers marketed part of their produce as the basis of sparkling wines. Nevertheless, in La Mancha's D.O. regions and also in Valdepeñas and some other *appellations*, there are many

Left
To some extent in La Mancha wine is still fermented in these amphorae—called *tinajas*—which are as tall as a man.

Right
La Mancha, the largest wine region in Spain, extends across the broad, dry highlands of the Meseta.

good, even excellent producers. A few ambitious winemakers have accepted the challenge of creating first-rate wines of character outside the areas designated as quality-wine regions, partly by means of indigenous wines, partly by French varieties.

Discounting a few exceptions, the region's most remarkable wines are not whites, but made from red grapes, which cover only a quarter of over 1,235,500 acres (500,000 ha) of vineyards. In the D.O. La Mancha, the heart of New Castile, foremost among the reds are Cencibel or Tempranillo. The red *barrique* wines are generally soft, proverbially "spoilt" by the sun, fragrant, and often have a slightly earthy note. Modern, very fruity wines with a

Windmills are the landmarks of La Mancha. In Consuegra they stand beside the ruined fortress, towering above the endless fields and vineyards.

robust note of wood are also fermented and often blended with Cabernet Sauvignon. In Mondéjar and Méntrida good reds are still planted very thinly. The brand new, pure red D.O. Ribera del Júcar in the east of the region produces harmonious Tintos, mainly from Cencibel grown on stony ground 2,460 feet (750 m) above sea level. But Cabernet, Merlot, Syrah and the Bobal variety from the Levant are also permitted. Almansa primarily produces table wines from a grape of the Garnacha family, called Garnacha Tintorera, one of the world's very few grapes to have red fruit flesh. Mondéjar is also famous for deep-colored red wines. However, most of the 9,880 acres (4,000 ha) of vines are devoted to the white variety, Malvar.

D.O. Ribera del Guadiana

More for administrative reasons than because of shared characteristics, from 1997 this macro-D.O., consisting of some 17,290 acres (7,000 ha), brought together a small portion of the Extremadura vineyards in the southwest of the country. The wines vary enormously, for they originate from six different sub-regions, and are prepared on the basis of over 20 varieties, some of Portuguese origin. Definitive reds can be found in the sub-region of Tierra de Barros, around the city of Almendralejo. Here you also find some of the oldest wine cellars. The styles of the often very robust reds are scarcely comparable. Very

rustic and rounded wines rub shoulders with immaculately fruity, soft ones. The best reds are usually produced from Tempranillo blended with Garnacha, or even Cabernet. In good *bodegas*, aging in barrels is standard practice. In the other sub-zones there are also some very pleasant wines pressed. Up in the north, in the Sierra de Gata, in the Cañamero Mountains, near the monastery of Guadalupe, and in the far southwest on the Portuguese border, some wine producers have achieved success with clean, fruitily juicy reds that are nothing like the traditional, broad reds often encountered in more southerly parts.

Enormous *barrique* cellar with fine red wines in Almendralejo.

Bodegas Ayuso**–***
Villarrobledo (D.O. La Mancha)
Bought-in grapes; 5,500,000 bottles
• Wines include: Armiño Viña Q. Estola Reserva
Despite its large size, this is a totally reliable wine cellar, owned by the same family for over 50 years. Its best known wine is the velvety, appealing red, Estola. The pioneer of barrel-aging in La Mancha now has a *barrique* park of over 12,000 barrels.

Bodegas Centro Españolas***
Tomelloso (D.O. La Mancha)
543 acres (220 ha); bought-in grapes; 2,000,000 bottles
• Wines include: Verdial; Allozo Crianza, Allozo Reserva
One of the most spectacular *bodegas* of the last generation in La Mancha. Over three-quarters of the production comprises reds, for which almost all the vines had to be planted. With Allozo line reds, fruit and structural harmony are always more evident than oakiness. The young wines generally come out very aromatic and limpid.

Bodegas Alejandro Fernández***–****
Campo de Criptana, (D.O. La Mancha)
Bought-in grapes; 200,000 bottles • Wine: El Vinculo
In the late 1990s Alejandro Fernández, father of the famous Tinto Pesquera, bought an old *bodega* in the little windmill town of Campo de Criptana. Through contacts in La Mancha from the early Pesquera days, he was able to acquire excellent grapes and thus produce a wood-aged Cencibel and a Tempranillo. The wine is extremely concentrated, rich in tannins and powerful.

Bodegas Mariscal**
Mondéjar (D.O. Mondéjar)
247 acres (100 ha) • Wines: Vega Tajuna, Blanco, Rosado: Tinto; Señorío de Mariscal Crianza
Mariscal was the first wine cellar in Modéjar to age wines in oak, as it still does with the convincing Crianza. Nevertheless, its strength lies in the clean, fruity young wines. The Tinto is macerated carbonically.

Bodegas Piqueras**–****
Almansa (D.O. Almansa)
Bought-in grapes; 600,000 bottles • Wines include: Marius, Crianza, Reserva; Castillo de Almansa; Blanco; Rosado; Crianza, Reserva, Gran Reserva
This family firm, founded in 1915, has for years been the region's only plausible producer north of Yecla. The best reds often contain about three-quarters Cencibel and one quarter Monastrell. They are persuasively fruity and well balanced.

Bodegas Torres Filoso**–***
Villarrobledo (D.O. La Mancha)
99 acres (40 ha); 100,000 bottles • Wines: Arboles de Castillejo, Torres Filoso, →Juan José
Within a few years this hitherto large-scale producer has reduced his production of a million bottles by a tenth. His wines have great personality and—unusually for Mancha Tintos—need a lot of time. This is because they reveal a strong barrel oakiness, with an underlying subtle acidity; in time, they taste subtle, last well, and have limpid fruit.

Dehesa del Cabrizal****
Retuerta del Bullaque (Viña de Terra de Castillo)
37 acres (15 ha); 130,000 bottles • Wine: Dehesa del Carrizal
After an apprenticeship with Carlos Falcó, Ignacio de Miguel decided to create an equally sophisticated table

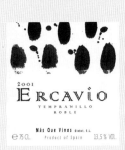

Left
The wine of La Mancha has history on its side. It thrives in the shadow of ancient castles such as this one in Almansa.

wine in the neighboring province of Ciudad Real, in the heart of La Mancha. The resulting cask-aged Cabernet is wonderfully mature, yet fresh and marvelously well balanced.

Manuel Manzaneque***–****
El Bonillo (D.O. Finca Elez)
91 acres (37 ha); 300,000 bottles • Wines: Manuel Manzaneque: Chardonnay, Crianza, Reserva, →Syrah; Finca Elez Crianza
In the bleak mountainous landscape of Albacete province, theater producer Manuel Manzaneque has created a small wine paradise. At a height of 3,280 feet (1,000 m) his French winemaker produces very fruity yet well-structured and full-bodied wines—quite different from the norm in La Mancha. The *bodega* emphasizes strict selection of grapes in the vineyard and works only with French oak.

Marqués de Griñon****
Malpica de Tajo (D.O. Dominio de Valdepusa)
104 acres (42 ha); 330,000 bottles • Wines: Marqués de Griñon: Cabernet Sauvignon, Eméritus, →Petit Verdot, Syrah
The wines of the Marqués de Griñon, also known as Carlos Falcó, are a must among Spanish wines. In 1970 he risked planting French grapes at his family estate in the hot, dry climate of Toledo, using the most up-to-date viticultural methods. His single variety wines are elegant, fine and very complex. His top red *cuvée*, Eméritus, shows a great deal of volume and depth.

Mas Que Viños**–****
Dos Barrios (no D.O.)
25 acres (10 ha); some bought-in grapes; 125,000 grapes • Wines: Ercavio: Joven, Roble, Reserva; La Plazuela
The three enologists, Madrigal, Rodríguez and Schmedes, have been working since 1999 on a dense and fruity La Mancha type wine with soft, ripe tannins. The vines are in Toledo province, and the winery is being built. In 2003, they introduced the opulent and juicy elite Cencibel La Plazuela.

Viñedos y Bodegas El Barro***
Camarena (D.O. Méntrida)
247 acres (100 ha); 60,000 bottles • Wines: Grand Vulture
One of the few interesting producers in the D.O. Méntrida, south of the city of Toledo, which is dominated by wines aged in wood. The brand Grand Vulture sets a standard other *bodegas* will follow. The wine is soft, and the mature, sweet tannins give it class. Including this, El Barro shares some of the best vines in the D.O.

Vinícola de Tomelloso***
Tomelloso (D.O. La Mancha)
4,446 acres (1,800 ha); 1,000,000 bottles • Wines: Añil, Torre de Gazate, Rosado, Crianza, →Reserva
Everything that this company makes has quality—from white as a basis for sparkling wine to bottled wines. The *tintos*, especially the *reservas* of the brand Torre de Gazate, which are sometimes made from pure Cabernet varietal, sometimes blended with Cencibel, reveal respectable structure and depth. This is due to the strict selection of the harvest.

VALDEPEÑAS

The region of Valdepeñas, with its *Denominación de Origen*, covers 188 sq. miles (487 sq. km), and fits like an enclave into the southern section of the D.O. La Mancha. The city that has given the region its name lies in the center of a broad, very flat valley. On both sides rise small chains of hills, which bring some variation to the landscape and announce the first foothills of the Sierra Morena. *Val de peñas* is Castilian for "valley of rocks."

The glory days of the city and its wines go back to the mid-19th century. In those days the Madrid wine market had become so important that both cities were connected by rail. Every day the so-called "wine train" transported 2,500 skins of wine to the capital. Export trade also developed from Valencia's harbor. At this time a light red wine was produced, blended with 20 percent white. This fresh, light red—also

In summer it grows exceedingly hot in Valdepeñas. Only darkening the windows in good time offers any prospect of slight cooling.

called Clarete—achieved worldwide renown and was as sought-after in South America as in the Philippines. It still exists, though today white and red musts are blended, rather than finished wines. Although phylloxera attacked Valdepeñas 30 years late (La Mancha's extreme climate had delayed its incidence) the effects on the vineyards were just as devastating as in the rest of Europe. However, the city had such massive reserves in its cellars that trade in wine could continue.

Typical vessels for wine preparation and storage were *tinajas*, clay jugs, which from time immemorial had been covered with straw mats or wooden lids. Although *tinajas* are still in use in most *bodegas*, now they are mainly used for storage, rather than wine preparation. The colossal *tinajas* of the last generation are no longer made of clay, but cement, and fulfil the tasks of normal concrete tanks as found throughout Europe. In the age of modern fermentation tanks, only a few small-scale wine producers still ferment wine in classic *tinajas*. These small wine producers also press the earlier oxidating, but sometimes very expressive, Valdepeñas variety of wine. Nowadays, these wines are increasingly rare. The region's major *bodegas* started a full 20 years ago to make their wine production as modern as possible.

In the mid-1970s foundations were laid for the production of quality bottle wines. Modern cellar facilities, with stainless steel fermenting tanks that can be cooled down, stabilization casks, modern filters, and other equipment are now standard issue. Recently, almost all wine bottlers have started to use considerable quantities of

---

Madrid

Geographically, the small D.O. Madrid should be included in La Mancha. It sweeps round in a semicircle to the south of the capital, then extends into the wide plain of the central region. In earlier times, vineyards extended deep into the city. Madrid's main street, the Paseo de la Castellana, even had vines growing along it. The sub-region around Arganda comprises half of the 29,157 acres (11,800 ha) of vineyards. It produces mild, slightly nutty white wines from the Malvar grape, and by far the largest part of the *appellation's* Tinto-Fino (Tempranillo) reds. These represent the region's true potential, for the best Tinto Finos have a dark color, plenty of fruit, and robust

tannins. So far, unfortunately, there are only a few examples of this variety of red wine. Other sub-zones, around Navalcarnero and San Martín de Valdeiglesias, make up another 13,585 acres (5,500 ha). Neutral white cask-wines—as well as *rosados* and *tintos* from Garnacha—are produced here. An exception is wine from the white Albillo grape. Fermented by modern methods, these reveal a large amount of fruit and delicate acidity. After being totally dismissed in earlier years as oxidated, broad wines, these have recently experienced a quiet renaissance. Progress has also been made with red wines, and beside fresh Tintos we also find premium wines from the Tempranillo grape that should certainly be taken seriously.

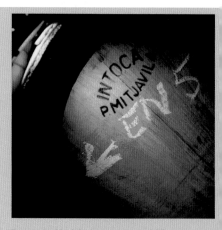

Even in Madrid the best reds are aged from Tempranillo in *barriques*.

arrels, mostly of American wood, in which to
ature the region's *crianzas*, *reservas*, and *gran
eservas*.

These account for the region's comeback in
wine production, for despite not insignificant
white-wine production in Airén and Macabeo,
oday Valdepeñas is again known for reds.
encibel grapes mature marvelously under the
merciless sun of the southern Mancha and slide
moothly into oak casks. Thanks to the climate,
ll vintages achieve more or less consistent
uality, and result in harmonious reds which
re the ideal accompaniment to food. Often

Left
Near the town of
Valdepeñas windmills
indicate that the climate
here is good for wine
growing.

Right
Valdepeñas not only gave
this wine region its name
but also contains most of the
well-known *bodegas*.

dismissed as cask-wine for the non-connoisseur,
these rather light wines reveal a wealth of
harmony, and are among Spain's export hits.

SELECT PRODUCERS IN CASTILE-LA MANCHA II

ODEGAS LOS LLANOS***
ALDEPEÑAS (D.O. VALDEPEÑAS)
*65 acres (360 ha); bought-in grapes; 15,000,000
ottles • Wines: Armonioso Blanco; Loma de la Gloria,
eñorío de los Llanos: Crianza, Reserva, Gran Reserva,
ata Negra Gran Reserva*
large-scale *bodega*, with a stock of 30,000 barrels,
hich produces an enormous quantity of good quality
ed wines aged in wood. Famous reds include the Señorío
e los Llanos Reservas and Gran Reservas. These often
eveal a mild, almost sweetish, fruit, in general superbly
vocative of wood. A good record for winning prizes.

ODEGAS REAL***
ALDEPEÑAS (D.O. VALDEPEÑAS)
*65 acres (350 ha); 1,000,000 bottles • Wines include:
iñaluz Blanco; Bonal Tinto, Vega Ibor Varietal,
alacío de Ibor Crianza*
he owner Sergio Barroso swears by classic red wines
ot aged in wood, which he produces in a modern way,
ithout oxidation. His *crianzas*, however, are
oticeably underscored with wood.

ODEGAS ORUSCO**−***
ALDILECHA (D.O. MADRID)
*o acres (12 ha); bought-in grapes; 150,000 bottles
Wines: Viña Main: Rosado; Tinto, Crianza*
his young family winery cultivates old vineyards. The
ell pure varietal Tempranillo-Crianza Viña Main could
ell be a classic, more subtle than ostentatious, more
otund than rigid, and is a pleasure to drink.

BODEGAS RICARDO BENITO***
NAVALCARNERO (D.O. MADRID)
*198 acres (80 ha); bought-in grapes; 850,000 bottles
• Wines include: Tapón de Oro: Maceración Carbonica,
Crianza; Señorío de Medina Sindonia, Divo*
The wine style of this old wine cellar is unexpectedly
modern, especially regarding the reds. With young
wines, the company has specialized in Beaujolais-like
carbonic maceration. They have freshness, but also body.
The Crianza Tapón de Oro offers a lot for a little money.

CASA DE LA VIÑA***
LA SOLANA (D.O. VALDEPEÑAS)
*741 acres (300 ha); 1,000,000 bottles • Wines include:
Casa de la Viña: Rosado; Crianza, Señorío del Val*
Quite early on, the region's premier winery developed a
gentle but well-structured style, which is regarded as
setting the standard for present-day Valdepeñas wines.
It belongs to the still-wine colossus, Bodegas y Bebidas,
which invests enough money to ensure high quality.

MIGUEL CALATAYUD***
VALDEPEÑAS (D.O. VALDEPEÑAS)
*124 acres (50 ha); 2,500,000 bottles; • Wines include:
Vegaval Plata: Blanco; Tinto Crianza, Vegaval Tinto
Reserva*
Wines from this *bodega* have everything needed in a
Valdepeñas: delicacy, maturity, a discreet note of wood,
drinkability, and rounded fruit. The Vegaval Plata-
Reserva offers the best quality that a varietal Cabernet
or Cencibel can give.

WINE REGIONS OF THE LEVANT

VALENCIA

Valencia, the wine-growing region of Spain's third largest city, must unfortunately still be considered a headache for Spanish wine growing. By far the largest part of over 41,990 acres (17,000 ha) of vineyards produce white wine, at a time when the world demands red. For quality wine, the staples are classic liqueur wines from the Moscatel grape, while the bulk of production is sold en masse. The main varieties are white Merseguera, with 18,525 acres (7,500 ha), and Moscatel, with 5,434 acres (1,200 ha). Cleanly produced, the Merseguera wines have fruit appropriately suggestive of lemon and apple. These need to be drunk quickly. The same applies to the reds, which are

generally made from different blends of Boba[l], Monastrell, Tempranillo, and Garnacha. Sever[al] *crianzas*, with Bobals usually setting the ton[e,] offer a slightly higher quality. To balance t[he] shortage of red wines in Valencia, some fronti[er] districts in the neighboring region of Utie[l-] Requena are allowed to market their reds und[er] the D.O. Valencia.

UTIEL-REQUENA

Due west of the sub-zone Moscatel de Valenc[ia] lies the red wine reservoir of the autonomo[us] region of Valencia. The 98,800 acres (40,0[00] ha) of vines in the D.O. Utiel-Requena are dom[i-] nated by one variety, the Bobal, which alo[ne] covers 79,040 acres (32,000 ha). The regio[n]

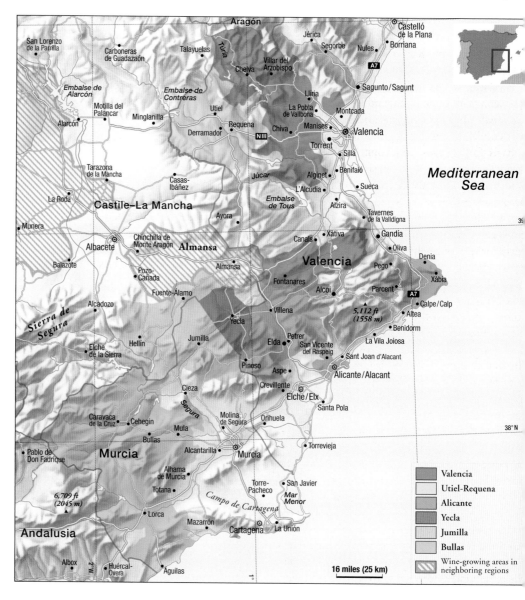

ame comes from the cities of Utiel and Requena. Located only about nine miles (15 km) apart on a slightly hilly high plain, these cities form the D.O.'s center.

Half of all the vines are planted around Requena. Alongside Bobal and other reds, there are small quantities of Macabeo. Sadly Bobal was condemned to being either a table wine or a basis for *rosados* and young reds, and the variety's potential was never fully explored. Another factor, as always, was paramount: the highlands of Valencia can fall prey to autumn frosts, so that winegrowers, who generally consider quantity before quality, harvest very early for fear of nature's depredations. As these early picked grapes have few sustaining tannins, it should surprise no one that Bobal wines do not survive long in barrels. Today, some pioneers let the harvest hang longer and blend the grapes with Tempranillo or Cabernet Sauvignon. This produces first-class results, for the Bobal develops delicate aromas of black berries such as elderberry. Many Spanish experts believe that Utiel-Requena bodes well for the future—pointing to the production of excellent *crianza* qualities. In the past the D.O. produced masses of table wines or simple red cask-wine. This reached its customers via the nearby harbor of Valencia, through which most of Spain's exported cask-wine used to pass. Furthermore, Utiel-Requena was home of *doble pasta* table wines. The process is as follows: After the red grapes have been macerated a few hours, the must for *rosados* is removed; then the remaining macerated grapes are mixed with

Utiel-Requena is one of the up and coming regions of Valencia.

those from other tanks, to ferment together in a so-called "double maceration." The resulting press wine is appropriately concentrated, and reveals magnificent color. This explains why formerly Utiel-Requena was known only for its *rosados*.

ALICANTE

Most tourists visiting the Costa Brava are completely unaware of the D.O. Alicante's existence. Yet one is struck by the vineyards in the sub-zone, La Marina, about 47 miles (75 km) north of the region's capital city, also called Alicante. Here the main crop is Moscatel grapes, grown on a broad spit of land between Denia and Calpe, extending far out into the sea. The very hot temperatures virtually rule out the cultivation of any quality red grapes. By far the largest section of vineyards is sited inland at a height of 1,640–1,969 feet (500–600 m). Here, in January and February, the vineyards are sometimes exposed to frost, for even inland the Mediterranean countryside often encounters cold. The heartland of wine growing in Alicante lies in the cities of Villena and Pinoso. This southwestern sub-region, also simply called Alicante, which represents four-fifths of the D.O.'s total area of 35,000 acres (14,000 ha), is dominated by the red, Monastrell—as are the neighboring wine areas of Jumilla and Yecla. The difference from the extremely bleak neighboring areas lies in deeper, more fertile soil, which would facilitate wine growing if only rain fell more regularly. Monastrell is mostly converted into *rosado* or fresh young wine. However, the region's few top producers have also started pressing wines from Tempranillo, Pinot Noir, Cabernet Sauvignon, or Merlot grapes. Their maturity and spiciness have taken some of these wines to the forefront of Spanish *tintos*.

Traditionally, Alicante is famous for its Moscatel wines, which still play a certain role recently. One notable wine that still exists is the Mistela de Moscatel, or Vino Licor Moscatel. Strictly speaking, this is not a wine, as the sweet must is not fermented but raised to the desired strength by adding wine alcohol—generally a blend of about 85 percent must and 15 percent alcohol. To this end, the vine-leaves are stripped before harvesting, to allow maximum penetration of sunshine. Thus, Moscatel Romano, as the Muscat of Alexandria is known here, is harvested highly ripe. The added alcohol helps preserve this Moscatel type superbly.

The present-day version of Moscatel is macerated cold and fermented down to a residual sugar content of 2.8–3.5 oz (80–100 g), and only then muted with ethyl alcohol. This is significantly more "winey" and differently structured, especially as star performers have recently started to be aged in oak barrels. Furthermore—as in Valencia—dry or semi-dry white Moscatels are fermented from ear[ly] gathered grapes, which produce from 0.04[–] 0.18 oz (1–5 g) of residual sugar. Well chille[d] these light wines are appealingly refreshi[ng] and straightforward.

Another chapter is the Fondillón, a true rel[ic] of Alicante's wine-growing past. To the delig[ht] of all friends of real, unadulterated wine, th[is] wine-monument is again gaining groun[d.] Fondillón, which is comparable to the superla[-] tive Pedro-Ximénez wines from Montill[a] Moriles, is a naturally sweet wine, which [is] produced from late-picked Monastrell grapes—and some Garnacha grapes—and contai[n] 16–18 percent alcohol. The minimum of eig[ht] years aging in oak barrels makes the win[e] develop colossal complexity, thereby making [it] an ideal dessert wine.

SELECT PRODUCERS FROM THE LEVANT

BODEGAS CASTAÑO**−****
YECLA (D.O. YECLA)
790 acres (320 ha); 850,000 bottles • Wines include:
Castillo de Barón, Castaño: Cabernet, Monastrell, Merlot, Tempranillo; Pozuelo: Crianza, Reserva, →Hécula, Castaño Colección Crianza; Método Tradicional, →Casa Cisca (no D.O., the bodega's new top wine)
Without the Castaño family the D.O. Yecla would have sunk without trace, continuing to concentrate on commercial cask wine. The Castaños have proved impressively versatile wine producers and show a great aptitude for creating *cuvées*. Naturally, an important role is played by Monastrell, which appears in almost every wine, and is achieving better and better success with aging in wood. In style, the vintages are very aromatic and never heavy or clumsy. A beguiling red sparkling wine.

ENRIQUE MENDOZA***−****
ALFÁS DEL PÍ (D.O. ALICANTE)
210 acres (85 ha); 250,000 bottles • Wines include:
Enrique Mendoza Moscatel, Enrique Mendoza Merlot, Enrique Mendoza Shiraz, Enrique Mendoza Santa Rosa Reserva
Enrique Mendoza's fame rests on both crystal-clear Moscatel wines and robust, modern-style reds. The secret of the house *tintos* is that they come from high-altitude vineyards in the hinterland of Alicante and therefore, in spite of ripeness and volume, never seem overripe or heavy. Santa Rosa, the top wine, is produced from Cabernet Sauvignon, Merlot and Syrah, and in every vintage it is powerful and concentrated.

ENRIQUE·MENDOZA
L'Alfàs del Pí
ALICANTE
Denominación de origen
Producido y embotellado en la propiedad
75cl.E 15%vol.
L.30/2002-MU ELV 7030-A
2002

MOSCATEL de la MARINA

JULIA ROCH E HIJOS****
JUMILLA (D.O. JUMILLA)
469 acres (190 ha); 300,000 bottles • Wines:
Casa Castillo Monastrell, Casa Castillo Crianza, →Pie Franco, Las Gravas
The *bodega* has old Monastrell vineyards at its disposal—a solid basis for the wines produced here. However, the Vicente family also produces a pure Tempranillo following the Beaujolais method. It is amazing that the top vineyards manage without irrigation in the hot Jumilla region. The result is the bes[t] quality wine from minimal yields. The wines are fruity and have superb juice. His new wine, Pie Franco, has brought the son of the family, winemaker José María, to the top of Levant wine producers. Also powerful an[d] very juicy is the second selection wine Las Gravas with a *cuvée* of Monastrell and Cabernet Sauvignon.

VIÑEDOS AGAPITO RICO***−****
JUMILLA (D.O. JUMILLA)
247 acres (100 ha); 700,000 bottles • Wines: Carchelo: Crianza, Reserva, →Merlot Crianza, Syrah
With its modern style, this *bodega*, established by Agapito Rico in 1990, has quickly achieved fame. The wine producer was the first in this D.O. to venture planting French varieties on a grand scale. His wines ar[e] stylish and well structured.

Naturally sweet dessert wine specialty of the D.O. Alicante: Gran Reserva de Fondillón by Salvador Póveda

Murcia and its Appellations

The wine regions of the autonomous region of Murcia could be called the hinterland of the Levant region. The three D.O.s: Bullas, Yecla, and Jumilla have not yet become very famous either abroad or in Spain. A lot of money was made here in the second half of the 19th century, when the French market looked about for robust wines of good color to fill the gaps that phylloxera had made in French vineyards. This prompted the winegrowers to plant red Monastrell grapes—and these served the purpose. Accordingly, this grape came to dominate vineyards in the Levant heartlands, and the region is therefore called the kingdom of the Monastrell. Overall, Spain must have some 247,000 acres (100,000 ha) of this supposedly indigenous grape. It is, however, also fermented outside the area, especially in southern France, where it is called Mourvèdre. The variety is popular among connoisseurs. With its small, thick-skinned berries, high tannin content, and—when young—rather earthy taste, it is considered a neglected quality wine.

In Spain, too, until recently it was common practice for Levant wines to give the paler wines from central Spain more color, and, incidentally, a higher alcohol content. Even today the cooperatives, which in no way produce solely D.O. wines, sell some products to the large table-wine consortia in Spain and the E.U.

Murcia is one of the hottest places in Europe, with very dry, sometimes desert-like landscapes. The sun burns down for 2,900 hours a year, with

West of the town of Murcia, in the D.O. Bullas, the dominant grape is Monastrell, which generally produces fruity reds, and are best drunk when young.

The cooperative Bodega San Isidro in Jumilla, established in 1935 and covering 19,760 acres (8,000 ha), ages some of its Monastrell wines in older casks.

rain generally falling only in spring and autumn. The landscapes are almost always ocher or brown. When no village is visible, it is easy to imagine being in a classic John Ford western. Furthermore, Murcia comes up against the Catalan coast for the honor of which region produced the Peninsula's first wine. Archeological finds seem to suggest that in Murcia must was fermented into wine at the end of the Early Stone Age. For the Carthaginians, the Phoenicians' successors, Cartagena, the province's harbor, was a most important strongpoint on the Iberian Peninsula.

Bullas

The similarities between the three D.O. regions are restricted to Monastrell and the climate. They are all in different stages of development. The D.O. Bullas was created as recently as 1994. Stretching from the center of Murcia toward the coast, and containing some 6,175 acres (2,500 ha) of vineyards, the D.O. is still in its infancy. Licensed grape varieties include red Monastrell and Tempranillo, and also the whites: Airén and Macabeo. Only a few wine producers are registered, of whom only half bottle D.O. wines. Typical of this region, which produces some 700,925 gallons (30,000 hl) of which only a tenth is sold as quality wine, are the fruity aged red wines made from red Monastrell. However interesting the bouquet of typical Monastrell is, even when young, it is sadly often not suited to aging

in oak, as it tends to oxidate rapidly. Only top quality grapes allow pure Monastrell wines to age in barrels. Nowadays, the monopoly of this main varietal is limited primarily to the region's most important sub-zone, around Bullas and Caravaca de la Cruz, although more Tempranillo is being planted. Nevertheless, one cooperative ventured to mature a pure Monastrell 95-vintage Crianza in American oak. This example was soon followed, for other producers are starting to explore the potential of the many old Monastrell vines still available. Now as ever, this grape comprises 94 percent of all vines.

JUMILLA

With almost 99,000 acres (40,000 ha), extending more thinly across the New Castilian province of Albacete and parts of Murcia, Jumilla is now one of the country's leading *appellations*, not merely quantatively. Even though the underestimated Monastrell is also paramount here, some expert winemakers have joined the ranks of Spain's top producers. As in the Old Castilian Toro, the area's potential is rated very highly. As early as the late 1980s a group of famous French wine producers settled here, to entice superlative wines from the dry, chalky soil. Sure enough, notable successes were achieved with Monastrell, by bringing forward the harvest and producing more stylish, lighter reds with greater definition in their fruit—for the intense sunshine removes any concern about ripening.

However picturesquely the castles stand guard over Murcia and its wine regions, dryness and heat make conditions for wine growing very hard.

The red Syrah, which achieved fame mainly in the Rhône valley, develops its magnificently fruity, spicy character here on the slightly undulating high plateau, totally surrounded by precipitous, bare mountain chains. It is exploited by the small but enterprising avant-garde of the local *bodegueros* with remarkable success.

Cabernet and Merlot also produce small but qualitatively significant yields. Some of the finest *crianza* reds from the country's southern half are produced in Jumilla. Blended with Monastrell and those foreign varieties already mentioned, these show the region's immense potential.

Also worth specifying are those naturally sweet wines usually produced from Monastrell. After oxidating fermentation, these combine complex aromas like cocoa, coffee, and quasi oriental spices in their intensive bouquet.

YECLA

Yecla is the only wine region in the whole of Spain comprising one single district. Overall about 49,400 acres (20,000 ha) of vineyard surround the city, some of them planted with old grape varieties. Here, also, are ancient vineyards untouched by phylloxera. The very dry climate, the extremely bare soil, and the mountains that divide the region from the coast and the north, have halted the pest's advance. Even today, nearly half of all the vines have the original roots, which yield the characteristics of specific grapes better than grafted plants.

Upon its foundation, the D.O. Yecla decided to devote only 8,645 acres (3,500 ha) to quality wines, probably to remain competitive toward commerce in cask-wine. Logically, large areas of the vineyards were set aside for table-wine varieties like Garnacha-Tintorera or Forcallat. As in other inland areas of the Levant, the main varietal—with over 60 percent of the whole area—is Monastrell. There are also modest plantings of Cabernet Sauvignon, Merlot, and Tempranillo. The whites, Macabeo and Airén, are also found.

To produce reds that can also be drunk young, the Monastrell is often macerated carbonically—a process that eminently suits it. This method relies on the traditional regional cellar technique, whereby the grapes are fermented unpressed and without being hulled. Nonetheless, the leading local producer—only three companies bottle wines—produces excellent *crianza* reds from his harvests of old, tannin-rich Monastrell grapes. To increase complexity, blends of Cabernet Sauvignon, Tempranillo, and Monastrell are often prepared. These remain stable and, thanks to their proportion of Monastrell, are opulent and richly aromatic.

The men of the Castaño family can feel justly proud—their wines have become a byword for the quality of the D.O. Yecla.

The new vineyard planted by the Bodegas Castaño on a particularly stony slope is tended with loving care.

WINE IN ANDALUSIA

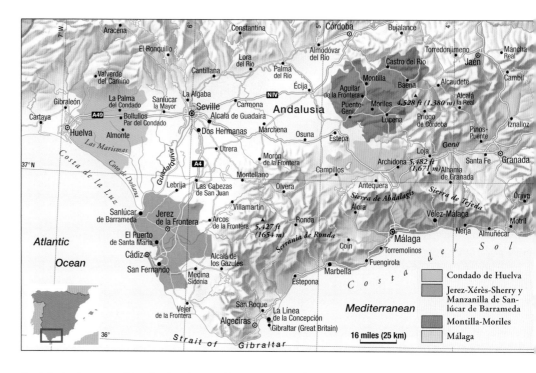

Andalusia is a world of wine in itself. Even within Spain it is known only superficially. Paradoxically, traditional wines from Jerez, Málaga, Huelva, and Córdoba are very unfamiliar. Nevertheless, they are unique in the world, and thus represent Spain's sole authentic contribution to the international history of wine. In Spain's most southerly autonomous region, wine growing is concentrated geographically in the area's western and central areas. Here, 3,000 years ago, the Phoenicians founded today's Cádiz, and planted the first vines. Presumably the Greeks, who introduced pruning, were the first to produce wine professionally. Each of the four *appellations* can look back on its own distinguished history. Only in the crisis years of the 20th century did the classic wines experience marketing problems, and these have persisted until today.

To contradict assumptions about sunny Spain, in winter and spring the coastal wine regions get heavy rain. Indeed, the Grazalema Mountains in Cádiz Province, which jut out near the sea, contain Spain's wettest area. Nonetheless, at 3,000 hours annually, the total hours of sunshine in Jerez and Sanlúcar de Barrameda are among the highest worldwide. Although the classic wine varieties in the four D.O. regions are not identical, they belong in the same category. They are all robust wines, which acquire a high alcohol content either by natural means or by having it added; for this reason they are often classified as aperitif or digestive wines. Yet several of these wines (the FINOS or Manzanillas, for instance) are agreeable accompaniments to food, ideal for Andalusian specialties such as air-dried ham, roast and fried seafood, or *tapas*.

The Bodega del Toro near Barbadillo in Sanlúcar de Barrameda.

Full-bodied Wines from the South

By the High Middle Ages, at the latest, wines in Andalusia were systematically mixed with alcohol—the difference being that brandy, not pure ethyl alcohol was used. The industrialization of distillation had still not happened. Furthermore, the Arabs' advanced knowledge of this area (they used alcohol for medicinal purposes) had, like so much else, been forgotten. Adding alcohol helped make wines last longer. This way they could oxidate for longer in barrels and be transported halfway around the world without turning into vinegar. Most classic wine varieties from Jerez, Huelva, and Córdoba are prepared like this.

The famous sweet wines of Málaga, whose range and subtlety can give unique experiences to both tongue and nose, are also prepared in this particular way. In Andalusia—and more especially Huelva—in the last two decades of the 20th century, there was a switch toward producing table wines, as the market for fortified wines continued to shrink from year to year. Accordingly, the most western of Andalusia's quality wine D.O.s first obtained a license to register a non-fortified white wine in the D.O. The large cooperatives quickly adopted this new trend, and began pressing light, fresh whites, whose grapes were harvested very early to keep the alcohol content low. Nearly half the region's production is now devoted to this kind of wine. Unfortified wines are now also produced in the other D.O.

No work in the vineyards without protection from the sun.

regions, although compared to Huelva the quantity is negligible and the wines may not be accorded D.O. quality.

The recent boom in Spanish wine has led more than one winemaker from central Spain to look around in Andalusia, and seek out new sites for red-wine production. For some time now, the German Prinz von Hohenlohe has been cultivating vineyards he planted near Ronda, in the highlands of Málaga. Every year his *bodega* amply proves that it is perfectly possible to produce superior red vintages from Andalusian vineyards.

The Wine Regions of Andalusia

D.O. Montilla-Moriles

This region's 24,700 acres (10,000 ha) of vineyards, sited in the south of Córdoba Province, are dominated by the variety Pedro Ximénez, which is well-suited to the heat. From their grapes it is largely aromatic, full-bodied Finos that are produced by the SOLERA method, though Amontillados, Olorosos, and Palo Cortados are also fermented. These grapes develop so much potential alcohol content on the stem that the wines do not need to be fortified. For the heavy, sweet, very complex dessert wines the grapes are left to dry in the sun before being pressed and muted by additional ethyl alcohol.

D.O. Málaga y Sierras de Málaga

The D.O. Málaga was already famous in the 13th century for its sweet wines, and sometimes outclassed wines from Jerez. The worldwide image problem for sweet wines in the second half of the 20th century led to a loss of interest in Málaga wines, with devastating results for the vineyards. Today 2,430 acres (950 ha) of vines are still designated a D.O. region, and the number of companies has dwindled to twelve. The main variety is Pero Ximén, as the Pedro Ximénez is called hereabouts, accompanied by Moscatel. The D.O. also covers red wines originating from the mountainous interior around Ronda.

D.O. Jerez-Xérès-Sherry y Manzanilla de Sanlúcar de Barrameda

Between the cities of Jerez de la Frontera, Puerto de Santa María, and Sanlúcar de Barrameda lie this famous region's 24,700 or more acres (10,000 ha), highly praised by the Moorish geographer, Ibn Adbd al-Mun'im, 1,000 years ago. The white wine, Palomino Fino, which initially only yields neutral wines, comprises 96 percent of output. Remaining sweet wines are Ximénez and Moscatel. These are fermented by the *solera* method. A recent specialty is to offer old-vintage sherries. Some *bodegas* also produce fresh whites from Palomino grapes.

D.O. Condado de Huelva

Separated from the city of Seville and the Jerez wine region by the massive Gualadquivir Delta lies the D.O. region of Condado de Huelva. Here, the variety Zalema holds sway. Also matured by the *solera* method, this produces outstanding old Condados, which are similar to Olorosos. Recently most companies have switched to bottling dry, refreshing whites, although these are hardly known outside the region. After drastic cutbacks 18,525 acres (7,500 ha) are still cultivated.

MÁLAGA AND MONTILLA-MORILES

Gabriel Gómez Nevado, an outstanding Fino producer in Villaviciosa de Córdoba, is a master at managing Venencia, a cask sample of which he is pouring into a glass.

Unfortunately, the marvelous sweet wines from Málaga, and the sherry-like wines from Montilla-Moriles in central Córdoba Province are not as popular as they should be. Once, alongside wines from Marsala, Sicily, and Madeira, they were among the world's most sought-after dessert wines, and around the middle of the 19th century—with a growing area of 247,000 acres (100,000 ha)—the province was Spain's second largest wine region. Three factors have depressed production below 659,907 gallons (3,000,000 liters), namely decreasing sweet-wine consumption in our calorie-conscious age, the unsystematic selling-off of sweet wines in supermarkets at knockdown prices, and a steadily shrinking acreage, triggered by the land speculation that came with mass tourism. Three-quarters comprise sweet wines, of which huge quantities are still sold as cask-wine. Even so, this small D.O.'s top quality wines are still among the most astonishing enological treasures Europe has to offer!

Two kinds of Málaga are made. The first is the natural sweet wine, called *dulce natural* or simply Málaga, which must have at least 11 oz (300 g) residual sugar, and it contains at least 13 percent alcohol by volume without any additions. It consists mainly of Pero Ximén, Pedro Ximénez as is called hereabouts, though it may also contain a small shot of Moscatel.

Pedro Ximénez grows in the *zona norte*, and comprises a little over half the 2,470 acres (1,000 ha) registered in the D.O. The second type is the liqueur wine made from Moscatel grapes; when produced, this is like the *licor de Valencia*. The D.O.'s new statute now protects another Moscatel variety, which does not need to be ripe, and to which no sugar, must, or alcohol are added. This *Mosacatel natural* represents a fruity, highly successful updating of classic Moscatel.

The quality of such a wine depends on old vines. Given minimum yields, in the *zona norte* these produce excellent Pedro Ximénez and in the sub-region of Axarquía—on alkaline slate soil—Moscatel, whose grapes produce thick, highly concentrated musts with a strong aroma. Once wine alcohol has been added, to raise the minimum alcohol content to the required 15 percent, they are OXIDATED to maturity in oak barrels—a process which, depending on the wine's age, gives them either an amber or blackish tone. That said, a classic Málaga does not consist merely of standard must. The proportion of thickened sweet must (*arrope*) and wine from sun-dried grapes (*vino tierno*) is a secret that every wine producer jealously guards.

Since interest in high-quality dessert wines has been rekindled, four of the nine bottling companies have turned increasingly to old Málaga stocks, and offer more and more Tras-Añejo quality varieties. For this quality, threshold wines must be more than five years old, although most of them are much older. López Hermanos is a key figure in the *bodegas*; he is well-known for the Málagas he produces: Virgen, Gomara, López García, and for Suárez Villalba, with the brand name Guita Penas.

The wide variety of descriptions on labels is mainly due to German dealers, who have long dominated the Málaga wine business, even owned some *bodegas*, and precisely prescribed the type of wine they wanted: dry (*seco*), sweet (*dulce*), pale (*pálido*), dark (*oscuro*), old (*añejo*), cream (semi-dry), and *lágrima*. *Lágrima* stands for must that runs freely without being pressed; accordingly, the highest quality wine would be a Lágrima Tras Añejo!

Even if sales figures are low, the northern neighbor, the region of Montilla-Moriles, is in a happier situation than Málaga. A D.O. since 1945, it can look back on a history as glorious

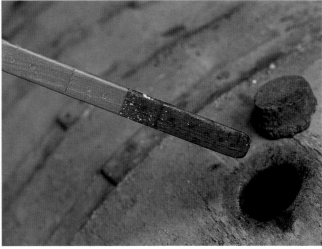

is that of Jerez or Málaga. Possibly the roots of the Andalusian liqueur wine tradition lie here rather than in Jerez, even though their wines are often dismissed as cheap Sherries. In the 1920s connoisseurs still agreed that wines from Montilla and Moriles were among the best five in the world.

The variety most commonly grown on the remaining 25,935 acres (10,500 ha) of vineyards is Pedro Ximénez. It stands the heat far better than Palomino, and, in the highlands' extremely dry climate, easily yields 15 percent alcohol. As in Jerez, a film of yeast (the *flor*) forms on the Finos produced here; the difference being that most Finos do not need any additions. Otherwise, the *criadera* or *solera* systems of maturing in casks are identical to those in Jerez, El Puerto, and Sanlúcar. Today, almost 70 percent of Finos are fermented.

Left
A *flor* has formed on the young wine.

Right
Checking how full the cask is with a wooden rod.

Traditionally, also, Olorosos are made from the second pressing. The Montilla-Moriles Finos tend to have herbal notes, such as thyme or oregano, and with a firmer, more oily body they seem less dry and more rustic.

Increasingly, the region has been acquiring a reputation through its P.X. (P.X. stands for Pedro Ximénez) sweet wines, for which the harvest is sun-dried on slightly inclined nets or woven mats. The work involved in spreading out, turning, and finally selecting the fruit by hand is considerable, though the prices for these exceedingly concentrated, aromatic wines are very favorable. Some companies still have oak casks with high quality oxidated, mature P.X. from the 1920s–1930s. As in Condado de Huelva, some producers have also recently begun pressing dry, extremely light, uncomplicated table wines.

SELECT PRODUCERS IN MÁLAGA AND MONTILLA-MORILES

LÓPEZ HERMANOS***–****
MÁLAGA (D.O. MÁLAGA)
618 acres (250 ha); bought-in grapes; 2,220,000 bottles
• *Wines include: Oloroso Trajinero, Pale Cream Cartojal, →Málaga Virgen, P.X. Don Juan*
Along with their *bodega*, the family, Burgos López, is a byword for quality and quantity in the D.O. Nearly 90 percent of the D.O.'s total production comes from this *bodega* in Málaga's industrial sector. For some time it has offered a line of very old Málaga wines, such as Pedro Ximénez Don Juan.

LARIOS***
MÁLAGA (D.O. MÁLAGA)
Bought-in grapes; 225,000 bottles • *Wines: Oloroso Benefique, Málaga Larios*
This *bodega*, which belongs to Pracsa, presses traditional, very clean quality wines. The Larios Málaga is a classic. The *bodega* also offers a dry, mature, stylish Oloroso Benefique. The company is about to put its wine cellar on the newest technological footing. Now, as ever, a considerable part of production is sold as cask-wine.

TORO ALBALÁ****
AGUILAR DE LA FRONTERA
(D.O. MONTILLA-MORILES)
86 acres (35 ha); bought-in grapes; 500,000 bottles
• *Wines include: Fino Electrico, Amontillado Convento, Dulce Don P.X., →Don P.X. Gran Reserva*
The family *bodega* of the enologist, Antonio Sánchez. With his branded products, such as Fino Electrico, he has brought fresh impetus to the declining D.O. Recently he achieved spectacular success with his vintage-P.X., and unique instalments of very old P.X. and Amontillado wines.

ALVEAR, MONTILLA****
(D.O. MONTILLA-MORILES)
741 acres (300 ha); bought-in grapes; 8,000,000 bottles
• *Wines include: Fino C.B. Amontillado Carlos VII, Oloroso Pelayo, -Pedro Ximénez 1927, →Pedro Ximénez 1830, →Solera Fundación*
One of Spain's oldest *bodegas*—still owned by the Alvear family—which has pioneered very old P.X. varieties at reasonable prices. Alvear is a groundbreaking producer of young wines in the region.

SHERRY AND MANZANILLA

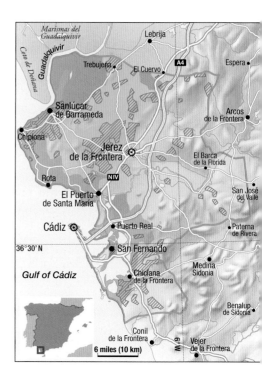

Xeris was the Arabic name for the city of Jerez. As the English could not pronounce this, they simply said sherry. Today the names: Jerez, Xérèz, or sherry are synonymous with the wines from the region of the west Andalusian city of Jerez de la Frontera. In practice, this means the so-called Golden Triangle between the three main districts: Jerez, El Puerto de Santa María, and Sanlúcar de Barrameda. However, the double D.O. of Jerez y Manzilla de Sanlúcar de Barrameda also owns land south of El Puerto, and north of Sanlúcar.

The *albarizas* produce the best-quality grapes, grown on dazzlingly white chalky soils within the triangle and also called Jerez Superior. These soils can absorb water up to 33 percent of their own weight, and, during hot months, form an unbroken crust that prevents high evaporation-loss. Over 80 percent of the D.O.'s 25,688 acres (10,400 ha) of vineyards have this privileged soil.

Jerez is the uncontested kingdom of the Palomino grape, which thrives particularly well here. Additionally, there are 494 acres (200 ha) of Moscatel, and 247 acres (100 ha) of Pedro, primarily for sweetening wine. However, the secret of Jerez wines lies less in their location or in the vines and more in the unique climate, the venerable, extremely intelligently designed *bodegas*, and above all in the old casks in which

☐	Jerez-Xérès-Sherry y Manzanilla de San-lúcar de Barrameda
▨	Areas of vineyard
☐	*Albarizas*
▨	Loamy and sandy soil
▨	Marshland

The dazzlingly white *albariza*-soil in Jerez.

they are prepared. The first step toward eventual sherry involves fermenting Palomino grapes into a dry white wine. Then the chief cellarman decides which sherry variety should result from the delivered harvest. For Finos and Manzanilla wines only grapes from the best strips, growing Jerez Superior, are used. Once the finished wine has been poured into old casks of American oak, it is reclassified. After tasting, the *botas*, as the 132-gallon (500-liter) wooden casks are called, are marked as listed on the following page.

Clearly recognizable in the glass: the yeast *flor* has formed a protective layer.

The best Amontillados and Olorosos age in casks for decades.

Fino, Amontillado, and Oloroso—the three most important sherry varieties.

The Barbadillo chief cellar man evaluating an old wine in Sanlúcar de Barrameda.

MARKS ON THE BOTAS

• One stroke: The finest, most stylish wines with an aroma suitable for maturing into Finos, Manzanillas, and Amontillados.
• One stroke and a dot: More full-bodied wines to be used to mature Olorosos.
• Two strokes: Wine that is destined for varieties other than Fino and must be reclassified as it develops.
• Three strokes: Wines of lesser quality that are destined for distillation.

Once the casks have been marked according to the sherry variety applicable, the wine will be variably fortified with wine-alcohol: 15–15.5 percent for future Finos and Manzanillas; about 17.5 percent for Olorosos. The casks of young wine then go into the vintage-cellar, where they stay for different periods of time, according to variety, and are fed into the famous *solera* system.

Who does not know him?

At a 15 percent by volume alcohol level, the wine-surface in the cask develops a film of yeast called *flor*. As this yeast-film needs oxygen as well as alcohol, the casks are never completely filled. The *flor*, a foam-like, dirty white film, protects the wine from contact with the air, and over the years provides its distinctive aroma. This covering of *flor* yeast arises only in southwest Andalusia's special climate, with the humidity of the sea air playing a decisive role.

The average age of the casks (over 1.1 million of them) used in the D.O. Jerez is about 40 years. The fungus feels at home in these casks and needs no human stimulus. However, to guarantee the *flor* nourishment, fresh wine must constantly be added, and this is one reason behind the *solera* system. Below the *flor*, only Finos and Manzanillas mature. In both cases the result is the same pale, fresh wine tasting of yeast.

That said, the Finos that mature in the *bodegas* of Jerez de la Frontera and El Puerto de

Santa María are a touch darker and more robust. This is because in the east of the D.O. Jerez y Manzanilla de Sanlúcar de Barrameda the *flor* finds less favorable climatic conditions, and can therefore form no complete covering to the wine—though one side-effect is that a subtle scent of almonds can sometimes develop.

Manzanillas, however, only originate from Sanlúcar de Barrameda, the D.O.'s western region, near the Guadalquivir estuary. Here, a distinctly higher humidity level guarantees a constant yeast-covering, which protects the wine fully. Accordingly, the Manzanillas are paler, lighter, and harsher, often developing a uniquely distinctive note of iodine.

In the February after the grape-harvest, once a film of the all-important *flor* yeast has developed, the wines selected to mature into Olorosos are given two percent by volume of alcohol more than Finos. This kills the fungus. Subsequent maturing takes place solely by oxidation, without the help of the *flor*.

At the foot of the Alcázar of Jerez de la Frontera and near its cathedral, the cellar-halls of González Byass, the city's largest sherry *bodega*, stand side by side.

Varieties of Sherry

Almacenista-Sherry: Rarities from small, private producers

Amontillado: Aged, oxidated, and matured Finos of an exquisite amber color; dry top-range varieties are robust, multifaceted, with nutty aromas

Cream Sherry: Oloroso; a sherry to which sweet wine from Pedro Ximénez or Moscatel has been added; very full-bodied and round

Fino: Very dry, pale sherry, matured below *flor*, best drunk in the six months after being bottled; has aromas of yeast and almonds; consume well-chilled as an aperitif, with *tapas* or fish dishes; once opened will not last long

Manzanilla: An especially light, pale Fino from Sanlúcar de Barrameda, which has a subtle note of iodine

Manzanilla Pasada: Rare, exceptional Amontillado-variant from Sanlúcar; highly multifaceted and stylish

Oloroso: Fermented without any *flor*; slowly oxidated, full-bodied, complex wines with aromas of dried fruit and nuts

Palo Cortado: A very rare, dry, subtle and complex sherry, also aged without any *flor*; lying between Amontillado and Oloroso, its aroma tends more toward Amontillado, whereas taste and nose incline more toward an Oloroso

Pedro Ximénez: Rarely appears as a pure varietal; extremely sweet dessert wine, blended with Oloroso

THE SOLERA SYSTEM

From the 13th or 14th century at the latest, Jerez wines have been fortified, ensuring that they last a very long time. However, the *Solera* system dates from only the second half of the 19th century, when the English importers of sherry demanded that wine cellars in Jerez supply homogeneous wines of unvarying taste. Until then Jerez had been aged by a vintage-system, called *añada*. Nowadays old-vintage sherries are extremely rare.

We must imagine the *solera* system in principle as long rows of 110-gallon (500-liter) casks stacked one above the other. The chief cellarman draws out for bottling a certain quantity of sherry—never more than a third—from the lowest cask, called the *solera* (in Spanish *suelo* means floor). Then, from the cask above, the first *criadera*, he draws out the same

Left and right
With the help of a metal can the *capataz* fills the casks of a *solera*. Once he has drawn off wine from the lowest row, he fills the can from the next-youngest row of casks, to replace the drawn-off wine. He continues like this until he has reached the youngest *criadera*, to which he adds young wine.

Utensils like funnels, sieves, tubing, brushes, and spatulas are in constant use in *bodegas*.

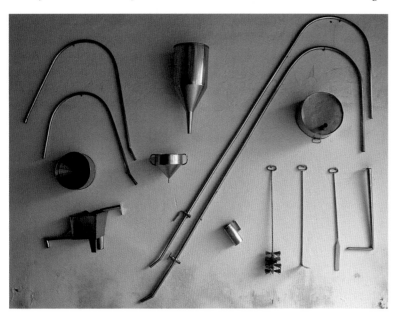

quantity to top up the cask below. He continues like this until he reaches the top row of casks, where the missing quantity is replaced by wine from the vintage cellar. In this way, older wines add their character to the younger ones used to top them up. Through this step-by-step aging process, the *solera*, which retains the wines' specific character, imparts this to all the wines in the system. Thus, in time, all vintage-distinctions are erased, and the wine, which is still called *solera*, has a consistency that delights sherry-lovers.

The number of *criaderas* varies between sherries; with the higher-percentage (figuratively speaking) Olorosos and Amontillados, this total is less significant than with Finos or Manzanillas. Even after years of maturing, these latter two have a certain freshness and a subtle, slightly peppery note of yeast, which, sadly, disappears soon after bottling.

For practical reasons, *criaderas*—the different levels of a *solera* system—are no longer stacked one above the other, but lie separated, often even in different *bodegas*. After a topping-up operation, the missing quantity to come in from the next-youngest *criadera* is simply pumped in. Varying wine styles between one *bodega* and another also apply to Finos, which take longer to mature, and for which another row of *solera* casks is attached. If, after years of aging, a Fino's *flor* dies, the result is an Amontillado, which will be further fortified and matured in a separate *solera* system. Before bottling, many sherries undergo six or seven stages, while a complex *solera* system can pass through 12 to 14 stages.

SELECT SHERRY PRODUCERS

A.R. VALDESPINO****
JEREZ DE LA FRONTERA
741 acres (300 ha); bought-in grapes; 3,500,000 bottles
• Wines include: Fino Innocente, →Amontillado Tío
Diego, →Oloroso Solera 1842, →P.X. Solera Superior
Valdespino is the oldest purely family firm in the city of
Jerez. The company's sherries are among the D.O.'s best
wines. Here you can still find wines immune to fashion.

ANTONIO BARBADILLO****–*****
SANLÚCAR DE BARRAMEDA
*1,759 acres (712 ha); bought-in grapes; 10,000,000
bottles* • Wines: Manzanilla Eva, →Oloroso seco Cuco,
→Manzanilla Solear, →Amontillado Principe, Oloroso
Dulce San Rafael
Sanlúcar's largest *bodega* has over 60,000 *botas* and
produces legendary varieties such as the Oloroso seco
Cuco. Best known is the Manzanilla Solear.

CROFT***–****
JEREZ DE LA FRONTERA
741 acres (300 ha); bought-in grapes; 6,750,000 bottles
• Wines: Fino Delicado, Amontillado Croft Classic,
Dulce Croft Original, →Palo Cortado Croft
This Spanish company dates from only 1970, after
merging with a port wine producer. Yet still has a
sufficient stock of old *soleras* with about 50,000 *botas*
in total. The Fino Delicado is famous and extravagant in
style; the Palo Cortado solid and subtle.

GARVEY****
JEREZ DE LA FRONTERA
124 acres (50 ha); bought-in grapes; 2,500,000 bottles
• Wines: Fino San Patricio, Oloroso Ochavico,
→Amontillado Oñana, Oloroso Puerta Real, →Palo
Cortado Jauna, →P.X. Gran Orden
Garvey was among the first Irishmen to settle in the area
(in 1756). Finos, like the superb San Patricio, comprise
nearly three-quarters of production, but the exceptional
Amontillados, Oñana and Palo Cortado Jauna, or the
P.X. Gran Orden are top quality.

GONZÁLEZ BYASS***–*****
JEREZ DE LA FRONTERA
1,976 acres (800 ha); 14,500,000 bottles • Wines: Fino
Tio Pepe, Manzanilla El Rocio, Solera 1847 →Amon-
tillado del Duque, Oloroso Matusalem, Dulce Noé
The largest *bodega* in Jerez (founded in 1835), with
100,000 *botas*. The Fino, Tío Pepe, is named after an
uncle of the founder: Manuel María González Ángel,
and is the world's best-selling Fino and one of the most
immaculate and reliable sherries ever. Sought-after
rarities include Oloroso Matusalem, P.X. Noé, and
Oloroso Vintage.

HEREDEROS DE ARGÜESO***–****
SANLÚCAR DE BARRAMEDA
445 acres (180 ha); bought-in grapes; 2,000,000
• Wines: Manzanilla: Las Medallas, →San Léon
This wine cellar (founded in 1822) has specialized in
high-quality Manzanillas. Supposedly, some of the
company's *soleras* are 250 years old. Manzanilla San
León is one of the D.O.'s best products.

HIJOS DE RAINERA PÉREZ MARÍN****
SANLÚCAR DE BARRAMEDA
445 acres (180 ha); bought-in grapes; 3,800,000 bottles
• Wines: Manzanilla La Guita
This company, founded in 1865, produces only one
wine, but this is the best-known Manzanilla worldwide,
and one of the best quality.

OSBORNE*** *****
EL PUERTO DE SANTA MARÍA
543 acres (220 ha); 8,000,000 bottles • Wines include:
Fino Quinta, Amontillado La Honda, Oloroso Bailén,
Solera India, →Amontillado Coquinero Dry, Palo
Cortado P Triangulo P; P.X. 1827
Thomas Osborne built his first *bodega* in Jerez in 1772.
Until 1890 all wines were sold abroad under the name
Duff Gordon. Their trademark is the bull, which still
stands on 97 hills in Spain, though now without a
signature. The best-known wines are the Fino Quinta
and Coquinero. The series of Rare Sherries deserve
special attention.

**EMILIO LUSTAU AND EMILIO
LUSTAU ALMACENISTA******–*****
JEREZ DE LA FRONTERA
94 acres (200 ha); bought-in grapes; 2,750,000 bottles
• Wines include: Puerto Fino, Oloroso Don Nuño
→Manzanilla Papirusa, Amontillado Escuadrilla, P.X.
San Emilio
This *bodega*, owned by Luis Caballero, exports nearly
all its products. The firm was founded in 1886, and also
functions as an *almacenista* outlet. From small
producers, like Manuel Cuevas or Viuda de Antonio
Borrego, Lustau buys a few sherries, and markets them
as rarities. His own varieties are also famous.

PEDRO DOMECQ***–*****
JEREZ DE LA FRONTERA
*1,976 acres (800 ha); bought-in grapes; 9,000,000
bottles* • Wines: Fino La Ina, Amontillado Río Viejo,
Dulce Venerable, →Amontillado 51-1ª, Oloroso
Sibarita, Palo Cortado Capuchino
A firm rich in tradition which owns one of finest
bodegas anywhere—the Mezquita. It also has wine
cellars in La Rioja and South America. Domecq
produces one of the region's most popular, stylish, and
lively Finos in La Ina. Furthermore, real pearls are also
bottled from ancient *soleras*.

SANCHEZ ROMATE****
JEREZ DE LA FRONTERA
247 acres (100 ha); bought-in grapes; 1,250,000 bottles
• Wines: Fino Marismeño, Manzanilla Viva la Pepa,
Amontillado Don José, Dulce Iberia, →Amontillado
N.P.U.
This winery has been producing *bodega*-classics in the
heart of the city since 1871, and owns vineyards in the
top sites, at San Julián and Espartina. The Amontillado
N.P.U. and Fino Macharnudo offer superb value.

SANDEMAN**–****
JEREZ DE LA FRONTERA
889 acres (360 ha); bought-in grapes • Wines include:
Don Fino; Oloroso: Armada, →Royal Ambrosante
An innovative company, strong on exports, with highly
valuable old specialties.

VINICOLA HIDALGO***–****
SANLÚCAR DE BARRAMEDA
494 acres (200 ha); bought-in grapes; • Wines:
Manzanilla La Gitana, Amontillado Viejo, Oloroso
Napoleon and Viejo
This very skillful, traditional, family-owned *bodega*,
founded in 1792, produces one of the best-loved
Manzanillas and stocks several outstanding old wines.

CANARY ISLANDS

Wine growing in the Canaries is a complex matter. The yields are even smaller than on the mainland, the planting-systems are generally unusual, and classic aging in *barriques* is not traditional here. Common to all wine growing on these islands is its volcanic origin, and these volcanoes are still active. The last eruption was in 1971, on La Palma. Bizarre landscapes, such as the island of Lanzarote which is covered in volcanic ash, form part of the archipelago's tourist attractions, but they also make great technical demands on wine growing. Today, the islands have eight D.O. regions. These arose from the different soil-characteristics, which are obvious even to the naked eye. The "fortunate islands" are some 4,660 sq miles (7,500 sq km) in area, though only about 22,230 acres (9,000 ha) grow vines. Not until the late 1990s could the downward trend in wine growing be halted.

The seven islands' wine tradition did not begin until the late 15th century, after the Spanish had conquered the archipelago. The new overlords brought most wine varieties to the Canaries, but Portuguese seafarers also contributed. The taste of the time, dictated by England, accorded with the sweet, heavy wines from Malmsey and Moscatel grapes. They were extremely popular all over the old Continent, even at European royal courts. As "Canary Sack" they were shipped all over the world, which vastly sped up their maturing process. In William Shakespeare's famous play, "Henry IV," Sir John Falstaff has the nickname "Sir John Canaries" because he consumes vast quantities of Canary wine.

From the mid-18th century onward the islands yielded importance to Oporto, Madeira, Jerez and Málaga. Furthermore, a century later mildew attacked the vineyards, after which the wine was virtually forgotten. In the 1980s, tourism brought renewed and growing demand. Between 1992 and 1996, to counter cheap wine imports from the Spanish mainland, the D.O. regions were established. These produce highly expensive wines, for which a secure local market has developed, thanks to their personality and special quality as island wine.

There are 33 protected varieties of vine on the islands—19 white and 14 red. Generally, the whites reveal far more character than the reds, while *rosados* are very unpopular. Traditional sweet and liqueur wines offer the most secure quality. For one thing, the islands still have very

Right
Tenerife has three-quarters of all the Canaries' wine growing areas. In the region's northwest, wine terraces on its mountain slopes reach 4,593 ft (1,400 m).

With its 865 acres (350 ha) of vineyards, Gomera has to be content with a *vin de pays* classification. On its highly fertile soils the Forastera Blanca, which produces richly alcoholic, robust whites, predominates.

old Moscatel and Malmsey plantations; for another, the old *bodegas* and cooperatives have relevant experience in preparing these specialties. A traditional liqueur wine is given extra alcohol, then undergoes several years' of oxidation in wood. The modern version of these wines, called *vino natural dulce*, is pressed from extremely ripe grapes. A naturally sweet wine with at least 1.4 oz (40 g) residual sugar, it is spectacular.

The best sweet wines are found on La Palma and Lanzarote. They reveal a subtle balance between clear fruit and sweetness. They also possess delicate salt and mineral notes, thanks to the island location and volcanic soil. Furthermore, because phylloxera spared the archipelago, all the vines still have their original roots. Otherwise, the islands primarily produce fresh young whites and reds that are not aged in

wood. White and red Listán grapes dominate the vineyards; high yields and good alcohol potential have ensured numerous plantings. The white Listán Floreal reveals aromas of exotic fruit and a gentle glow. Sadly, many wines of this variety turn out slack and tired. Listán Negro produces excellent results if blended with another popular *tinto* grape: the Negramoll, which can supply the necessary acidity for successful aging in wood. Among many fresh whites, the most convincing wines are from such exotic-sounding places as Gual or Sabro. Alongside good fruit, these often also offer aromas like smoke, toast, or even discreetly dry, bitter notes redolent of the special volcanic *terroir*.

WINE REGIONS OF THE CANARY ISLANDS

La Palma: The island is covered partly with pure volcanic sand and partly with shingle. Vines are planted in ditches or holes, but also on low espaliers made of branches. Thanks to their long growing cycle, Malvasía (Malmsey) grapes produce highly complex wines here. In the north, wines are still produced by old methods and aged in Canary pine. The resinous nature of Tea wines is a matter of taste, but they are part of the enological local color.

El Hierro: Primarily white wines are produced here, 60 percent of which are from the Verjadiego grape. Whether dry or sweet they always seem soft and velvety, accompanied by floral aromas. The wines are commonly sold unbottled and served as young wines in the taverns.

Taroconte-Acentejo: The most traditional and the largest of the Canary wine-growing regions, it lies on Tenerife. The first part of the name comes from the town of Taroconte. A vast variety of vines grow in innumerable micro-climates up to 3,280 feet (1,000 m). The vines grow close to the ground, always facing the sea, and the twigs are supported by handmade trellises. The focus here is on young red wines.

Valle de Güimar: On eastern Tenerife, the valley slopes gently to the sea. Primarily white grapes grow here on some 1,480 acres (600 ha). The wines are striking for their exotic fruit and good acidity. Alongside Listán Blanco, the area grows Moscatel, Vijariego, and Gual.

Valle de la Orotava: On gentle slopes below Mount Teide, Tenerife, this region produces uncomplicated, subtly fruited whites and reds derived from Listán Blanco and Negro. Numerous winegrowers share the 1,235 acres (500 ha).

In the hot climate of the Canaries the grapes develop a high sugar content. They are especially suitable for sweet wines, which were once a sought-after export.

Ycoden-Daute-Isora: This region, named after the three kingdoms of the original population, lies in the northwest of Tenerife, where we find primarily white vines, trained on trellises, growing at heights of up to 4,600 feet (1,400 m). The micro-climates mean that grapes ripen at very different times. Harvesting takes place from June to October.

Abona: This D.O., in southern Tenerife, has the highest vineyards in Europe. In the Vilaflor district they grow at heights of up to 5,900 feet (1,800 m). Thanks to the height, the vines are very healthy and suitable for organic wine production. The young wines produced here are among the most structured in the archipelago.

Gran Canaria: At 618 acres (250 ha), the D.O. covers almost the whole island. 30 *bodegas* produce straightforward young wines, but also *barrique* quality, from the red varieties Negramoll, Listán Negro, and Tintilla.

Monte Lentiscal: Small D.O. on Gran Canaria, mainly covering the volcanic soils below the Pico de Bandama crater.

Lanzarote: The soil of Lanzarote is covered with a thick layer of volcanic sand. This sand, called *picón*, consists of minute pumice stones. It is able to absorb the infrequent rainfall and the ground dew and then transfer it to the fertile soil underneath, so that it acts as a water reservoir. The vines grow separately in wide holes and are protected from the wind by walls. The yield is often no more than 132 gallons (500 liters) per hectare. This archaic, labor-intensive method of cultivation is unique in Europe. It produces superbly sweet Moscatel and Malmsey wines. The El Grifo *bodega* is famous for the quality of its Malmsey wines.

JOACHIM KRIEGER, WOLFGANG FASSBENDER

PORTUGAL

Portugal:
Land of Explorers

Today, the direct descendants of Portugal's great seafarers and explorers are beginning to discover the value of their wine estates (QUINTAS), which date from Portugal's golden age. Thus they are closing the circle which began when Portugal's wine wealth created Europe's first nation and laid the foundations for a world power. With an amazing dynamism, and fueled by European development programs, the historically minded Portuguese are exploiting the potential of their vineyards, their grape varieties, and their long winemaking traditions to the full.

Toward the end of the millennium there was an explosion of new wines and new *quintas* coming onto the market which has exceeded anything imagined during the bloodless Carnation Revolution of April 25, 1974, with the subsequent dissolution of Salazar's long dictatorship and the opening up of the country to the community of European states.

No new estates were founded, but instead there was a return to the country's own wine-making tradition, a thoroughly reliable base to support a modern fairy tale of success.

Some winemakers, who in the past had been forced to produce old-fashioned and overpriced branded wines, found the courage and spirit of enterprise to demonstrate their almost forgotten skills and to put them to work. The wine

The imposing Quinta da Sanguinhal in Estremadura is an example of the adaptation of the estates to modern times.

The Casa de Sezim near Guimarães produces one of the finest Vinho Verdes. The interior of the house reflects the extraordinarily rich history of many of the wine families.

lover can visit their *quintas* and relive a little wine history with their wines.

Portuguese pride in their nation, and their wines, has often helped to revive the old, the great, and the traditional. This pride has a melancholy aspect, expressed in the Portuguese characteristic *saudade*, which means regret for the fading glory, the lost might and splendor of a great world empire which has declined, leaving Portugal an unimportant nation on the edge of Europe. This melancholy character finds its expression in *fado* music, the plaintive, emotional, and intense songs, which make their listeners weep and feel their own sorrow and pain.

Underdevelopment:
A Blessing in Disguise

The time of Portugal's opening up and moving on was undoubtedly serendipitous; it occurred just as winemakers in other countries were looking to their traditions, and the cult of technology was no longer an end in itself. Well into the 1970s, the market for higher quality and standard wine was dominated by the large and medium-sized wineries, with the cooperatives serving only the cheaper sector, and only a handful of almost unknown *quintas* producing quality wine.

The production of port was still completely in the hands of the large and medium dealers in Vila Nova de Gaia, its story that of a monopoly which only allowed winemakers the role of

suppliers, not of marketers and exporters. To the outside world, the image of Portuguese wine was formed by the most successful and innovative branded wine in the world, the medium-dry, slightly sparkling Mateus Rosé, and its great rival, Lancers Rosé, which was even more successful in America.

Some successful Vinho Verde brands had also arisen, copies, some sneered, of German Liebfraumilch. In fact, the slight fizz of the natural and traditional Verdes, their freshness, was the model for Lancers and Mateus, which were born in the 1940s. Verde, the true original, merely followed.

Vinho Verde which, up to that time, had been 90 percent red wine, was converted into the fashionable, slightly sparkling, white drink by continuous new plantings of white varieties in the 1960s and 1970s, driven by the hunger of those dealing in brand names.

These light wines are still on the market, and they are still successful, selling in millions. The Mateus Rosé bottle, very similar in shape to the German Bocksbeutel, is a permanent feature on the supermarket shelves in many European countries. But for some years now the other Portuguese wines have been attracting attention inside Portugal and on international markets. With evidently around 500 varieties of grape, numerous old stock, and highly committed vintners Portugal has a big future in the modern wine world. Since wine drinkers all over the world are increasingly looking for alternatives to the ever constant Chardonnays and Cabernets, Portugal's wines are certainly in tune with the times.

MICROCOSM OF THE WINE WORLD

Portugal is a microcosm of the wine world, uniting almost everything you could imagine. The diversity of viticultural tradition, nursed over centuries, may not run all the way back to the aboriginal Iberians, but it is certain that the Phoenicians, arriving in the first millennium BC, began the cultivation of vines in the Iberian Peninsula and that the Greeks and later the Romans further encouraged viticulture.

During the 19th century there was a flourishing of middle-class wine culture and the heyday of the great bottled wines. Portuguese wine writers described and analyzed the different characteristics of individual wine regions, and with their knowledge of wine areas and vineyard sites set out in old books, laid the foundations for a great wine culture, mastered in an unparalleled manner by the Portuguese wine producers.

In the standard work, *Memoria sobre os Processos de vinificação* (memories about the

Portugal is a land of contrasts. Ox carts and sports cars use the same roads, and even in viticulture you can see both ancient hand skills and the most modern technology.

Portuguese wine is becoming ever more up-to-date, both in equipment and content. The light, lively Vinho Verde was a forerunner of this development.

process of vinification), dating from 1867, details are researched and described down to the last village, always clearly differentiating between *vinhos de embarque* and *vinho do consumo*, the better wine suitable for export (bad wine could never be exported) and plain wine. Statistics are given about how much wine is consumed within the individual areas and how much is worthy of export.

This was somewhat different to Spain or Italy, where wineries had a stronger regional profile and sophisticated export houses such as those in Portugal (modelled on the early power of the port wine lodges) often simply did not exist.

Today Portugal offers a fascinating range from more than 40 wine-growing districts. Thirty-two are new, but many had already made a name among experts in the 19th century. A growing number of Portuguese reds can stand comparison with the best of Bordeaux or Burgundy—but they are certainly developing their own individuality in fruit, maturity, acidity and aging potential. The wines from the Douro, Bairrada, Alentejo or Dão regions are well set to become famous. But with all due praise for the reds, one should not forget the white wines. Really top growths are rare, but there are some.

INTO THE MODERN AGE

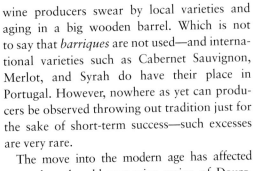

In Portugal, tradition and modernity are not opposed to each other. Quite the contrary—the old traditional methods of wine production are more popular than ever. One of the pioneers of modern Portuguese wine has laid good foundations for the current respect in which ancestral methods of vinification are held. "Pick ripe grapes with ripe stalks," was the principle formulated by Ruis Alves, the great master of Barraida wine. And he went on to emphasize, "Fermented in the *lagar*, with natural stabilization and no artificial aids." The new young winemakers are also attracted by such consistent adherence to old traditions. And even if the more creative of Portuguese winemakers, or the big cooperatives looking for new markets, or foreign investors don't always follow Alves' ideas, tradition is definitely in fashion in Portuguese wine production.

After a long period of stagnation, more and more Portuguese producers have recognized the treasures they possess—unique *terroirs* and old vines with native grape varieties. Even many of the rapidly increasing number of innovative

In earlier times in the Douro valley, round masonry containers were built outside the cellars. Wine was stored in them until it was collected.

wine producers swear by local varieties and aging in a big wooden barrel. Which is not to say that *barriques* are not used—and international varieties such as Cabernet Sauvignon, Merlot, and Syrah do have their place in Portugal. However, nowhere as yet can producers be observed throwing out tradition just for the sake of short-term success—such excesses are very rare.

The move into the modern age has affected more than the old port wine region of Douro. Suddenly, from all corners of the country, exciting wines are appearing at prices that are still surprisingly low. Dão and Bairrada, Minho and Alentejo, Ribatejo and Palmela have become fashionable. If you want to mention a great Portuguese wine today, you are no longer limited to Vintage Port, Moscatel de Sétubal, or the great classic red wine Barca Velha. The competition among the *quintas*, wine estates which produce and market their own wines, is increasingly giving the large cooperatives and wine companies new ideas about wine. Wine dealerships are suddenly discovering such terms as "*terroir*" or "individuality," buying up *quintas* and bottling their wines as a separate line. Even the big companies, oriented more toward short-term success for balance sheet reasons, are following an amazing policy of quality, which is by no means a matter of course in other parts of the world. Even leading companies such as S.O.G.R.A.P.E. are managing exemplary wine estates in many parts of the country, supporting local varieties, and seeing no contradiction in having top quality wines in their range alongside mass produced ones.

For the consumer, the name of the wine producer is today more important than the traditional terms of maturity in the wine laws. Terms such as *Reserva* or *Garrafeira* have by no means disappeared from labels, but these definitions—referring to longer periods of aging in the barrel—have lost much of their original meaning. The "new winemakers" of Portugal often show little interest in the traditional legal terms.

Portugal's entry into the E.U. in 1986, the new markets, the subsidies—all of this has certainly contributed to the Portuguese wine miracle. However, the remarkable and exciting developments of the last few years were by no means a matter of course.

Today, the country has about 642,000 acres (260,000 ha) under vine, producing an average

annual harvest of around 185 million gallons (7 million hl). That isn't much—the old vines and traditional Portuguese cultivation methods don't produce massive yields. This means that there are hardly any mass-produced wines. Apart from the not exactly sophisticated wines of the Mateus or Lancers brands, even standard Portuguese wines are often of remarkable quality. The marked differences between vintages in quantity and quality, along with the numerous unknown grape varieties, may not encourage the marketing of Portuguese wines abroad—but the considerable size of most estates, at 124 acres (50 ha) or more, can make up for these failings. The traditional dealership structures of the port business also have their advantages in making the new red and white wines of Portugal internationally known. Portugal could, at least in this regard, move "old world" European wines back into the foreground. True innovation in wine production is probably no longer limited to the New World (to the U.S.A., Chile, Australia, or South Africa). Given the developments in Alentejo or in the Douro valley, there is no reason to cast envious glances at the excellent New World wines and winegrowers. At some future time, Portugal could serve as an example of old traditions also being suitable—and perhaps particularly appropriate—for modern marketing.

For Vintage Port, the best results are achieved if the grapes are trodden by foot. As this is a very exhausting method, Peter Symington has devised a mechanical system which was used for the first time in 1998.

Conditions that elsewhere in Europe apply only to a few areas—Priorat in Spain, for example, or Languedoc-Roussillon in the south of France—are valid for the whole of Portugal. This vinicultural nation in the far west of Europe is a treasure trove for wine experts searching for the unusual. However, to be successful you do need to have detailed knowledge of what is on offer. Portugal is not really the place for impulse buying.

The *garrafão* culture

Wine containers like the Portuguese *garrafão*, bottles wrapped in straw or plastic containing 1½ gallons (5 liters), are to be found in many southern European countries, but nowhere are they such a country-wide feature as in Portugal, where they are used for wine and for mineral or table water. The Portuguese take them everywhere, originally mainly into the fields. Now, in today's more leisured society, they dominate every beach, picnic site, and natural beauty spot, for the Portuguese like eating in the open air. They take a piece of *presunto* (raw ham), a piece of *pão* (bread) and the unavoidable *vinho*, the people's drink, spoken more tenderly in this language than in any other. Only the young are increasingly doing without wine in the *garrafão*.

Portugal has long since lost its former first place among the wine-drinking countries for consumption per head, at over 34 gallons (130 liters). Now, at around 13 gallons (50 liters), the country has slipped below France and Italy, but is still well ahead of its neighbor Spain, which consumes less than 10.5 gallons (40 liters). However, the consumption of home-produced wine is unrecorded and this probably obscures the actual situation. The *garrafão*, which even today is still popular in

The 1.3 gallon (5 l) bottle: training for wine drinkers.

Portugal's former colonies, is an unloved object for many a serious winery, shamefully concealed behind the better-quality bottled wines. But it cannot be dispensed with, because that would amount to an insult to the people and their most enthusiastic representatives, the small and larger-scale dealers who would never give up selling wine by the *garrafão*, however small the profits.

Whether the *garrafão* is valued or despised, one factor has been completely overlooked; its secret contribution to the Portuguese taste

in wine, to the surprisingly stable forces of tradition, which defend harsh, difficult, original wines, and despise the superficially more pleasant ones. It is, so to speak, a popular education, especially by the *garrafão* from Dão, which has always been available to the most ordinary worker as well as to the revolutionary intellectual.

Portuguese wines and regions, taken as a whole, are world leaders in wine styles, though this fact is not well enough known for the country to become a leader of world opinion. There is one reason for this. The former students and soldiers of the Revolution, that is to say the present day opinion leaders in the area of sought-after quality wines, schooled their palates with good *garrafão* or Alentejo liter wines, at home or in the bars. Someone used to such fare develops a distaste for pleasing, smooth, and polished wines and prefers the genuine, uncompromising drink, such as is common in Portugal today, popular with all people and not only in high society.

The old *garrafão* may, with a bit of luck, contain very good quality wine, perhaps not the most refined, but rarely thin. In certain circumstances, over the years, it can develop into a very fine wine indeed.

THE WINE REGIONS

Paradoxically, Portugal was the first country in the world to give wine-growing regions exact geographical boundaries and to classify the vineyards: the first in Porto e Douro in 1756 and the second in Vinho Verde in 1906 to 1911. Portugal also has perhaps the greatest tradition in Europe for anonymous wines, of which no more is known than that they originate in Portugal.

This game of hide and seek has long affected Mateus Rosé, for many years the most successful brand wine in the world, just as it did the famous Garrafeira wines or the legendary Barca Velha, which has only recently taken to printing its origins as a Douro wine on the label. Preparatory drafts of wine legislation lay for years in the files of the Salazar and other regimes. These bureaucracies favored monopolies and therefore had little interest in innovation. With the 1974 revolution, the opening out toward Europe, the entry into the E.C., everything was set in motion. Finally, regional wines were allowed onto the market with their names of origin.

Since the removal of restrictions, the Portuguese wine industry has undergone stormy developments, for example, in the case of Bairrada, which was demarcated as a region in 1979, swiftly followed by a partial withdrawal and redefinition of the region. However, there are now signs of consolidation. The Alentejo was one case in point, in which first of all individual regions acquired I.P.R. status (*Indicação de Proveniência Regulamentada*), then later D.O.C. (DENOMINAÇÃO DE ORIGEM CONTROLADA). Eight former regions have now been turned into sub-regions and the highly attractive wine, Alentejo, previously only permitted to be known as a Vinho Regional, has been designated D.O.C.

The upper course of the Douro, with its terraced vineyards, is one of the most spectacular wine-growing landscapes in the world. However, more profitable new sites are threatening this great heritage.

The same happened with D.O.C. Ribatejo in May 2000. Many of the wines on the market still carry the old terms, such as D.O.C. Borba. The six former I.P.R. regions became a new D.O.C. region at a stroke, and the wine-growing areas which had for some years acted as regions may now only appear as mere sub-regions.

As statistics show, the classic D.O.C. regions of Porto (1756) and Vinho Verde (1908) are still leaders of quality wine production, which is also in part due to their size. The third great classic region, Dão (1907), has over recent years dropped behind the highly dynamic Alentejo. Even the really extraordinary eagerness for innovation in the Douro region has come up with little that can really be compared to the classic Dão. The monopoly of port dominated this region for far too long and, apart

Vinho regional

Vinho regional (the Portuguese equivalent of *vin de pays*, often used in other countries only as a term for very plain wines), has an important part to play in Portugal.

First, many top-quality wine estates have been created on a TERROIR where wine growing has never been the center of attention, or has faded so far into the background that a wine region never properly developed. Second, for many Portuguese wineries, *vinho regional* is, to a certain extent, a substitute for their putting even their best brands onto the market with no indication of origin, and focusing on the house's

guarantee. While this is useful both to the consumer and the winery, it is a hindrance to the distinctive development of the regions. Even today there are still areas where you can buy excellent wines but the region itself knows little or nothing of its potential.

Vinho regional is linked to the tradition of freedom from the indication of origin. The brand name is considered more important than the more confining region. If a VINTAGE in a region turns out to be less good than usual, it is possible to use wine from a neighboring region instead. *Vinho regional* is also

important for the description of blended wines or CUVÉES which do not fit into the scheme of quality wine regions. The term is used only in a few regions by individual cooperatives and wine estates as a particular label for second- or third-class wines, i.e. to indicate a lower level of quality than the best D.O.C. wines. However, the opposite is also possible: *vinho regional* for the top quality, and D.O.C. for the plainer wines. There is therefore less of a golden rule here than in any other country—apart from one: respect the bottles containing *vinho regional*!

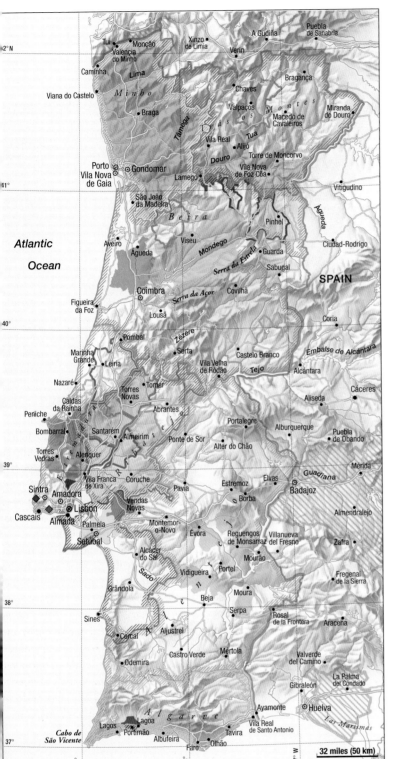

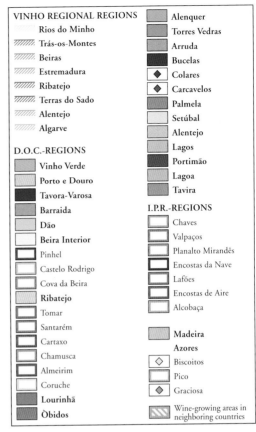

VINHO REGIONAL REGIONS

- Rios do Minho
- Trás-os-Montes
- Beiras
- Estremadura
- Ribatejo
- Terras do Sado
- Alentejo
- Algarve

D.O.C.-REGIONS

- Vinho Verde
- Porto e Douro
- Tavora-Varosa
- Barraida
- Dão
- Beira Interior
- Pinhel
- Castelo Rodrigo
- Cova da Beira
- Ribatejo
- Tomar
- Santarém
- Cartaxo
- Chamusca
- Almeirim
- Coruche
- Lourinhã
- Òbidos
- Alenquer
- Torres Vedras
- Arruda
- Bucelas
- Colares
- Carcavelos
- Palmela
- Setúbal
- Alentejo
- Lagos
- Portimão
- Lagoa
- Tavira

I.P.R.-REGIONS

- Chaves
- Valpaços
- Planalto Mirandês
- Encostas da Nave
- Lafões
- Encostas de Aire
- Alcobaça
- Madeira

Azores

- Biscoitos
- Pico
- Graciosa
- Wine-growing areas in neighboring countries

from legends such as Barca Velha, prevented the development of what is undoubtedly one of the best red wine regions in the world. Even some of the regional wine descriptions are now more important than Dão which, as far as exports are concerned, is still in third place behind Porto and Verde.

Of the other classics, Bucelas (1911) is experiencing a cracking revival at present, Carcavelos (1907) is struggling to survive, as is Colares (also 1907), which for many wine drinkers was long considered the best and most interesting red wine in Portugal. Both are in areas near the capital where building land is worth much more than the last few vineyards.

Some regions have not yet brought any quality wines onto the market because the companies concerned are not yet in a position to fulfill the required legal conditions, especially as regards the grape varieties, which in many ancient vineyards can hardly be determined with any accuracy.

PORTUGUESE WINE STYLES

There is a great deal to be said about styles of Portuguese wine, in particular about the white wines. Vinho Verde may be a highly individual wine because of its regional origin and its fresh, crisply accented acidity and lightness, but it is increasingly being produced by international methods. Things are no different for the other white wines of Portugal, which in many regions have extraordinary potential and which can, in their fruitiness, acidity, and refined quality, stand alongside the wines of other cooler European regions such as Burgundy, the Loire, and Germany. Cool FERMENTATION, careful processing of the grapes, and stainless steel tanks often bring out qualities in the wines unimaginable only a few years ago—clean and at the same time demonstrating the *terroir* and grape variety in their delicacy and expressiveness. All modern and traditional methods of white wine preparation are being used, such as stirring the YEASTS, and maturation in new wood barrels. However, the new wood is often used as a short-term additional procedure instead of a noble instrument of aging. Traditional wines from old wooden barrels are sadly becoming ever more rare, as they have brought too few good results.

New barrels are a contentious issue in Portugal, as for generations it has been the practice to use old ones. However, there are already some groundbreaking examples of their successful use.

Portugal is at present searching for the best grape varieties and the best styles for its wine, and a clear structure and hierarchy can be seen in only a few companies. Producers with international experience seem, at the moment, to have an advantage. One could mention a number of examples: top of the list would be Esporão, partly managed by the Australian David Baverstock; J. P. Wines, previously developed by Australian Peter Bright, who now matures wines on his own behalf; and J. M. Fonseca, with their Californian-trained boss. Among the new famous names in the Alentejo are Cortes de Cima with the Dane Hans Kristian Jorgensen, and on the Douro the German wine producers Bernhard Breuer, Bernd Philippi, and Werner Näkel at the Quinta do Carvalhosa have attracted attention. And we mustn't forget Dirk van der Niepoort, whose ambition is big enough to tackle white and rosé wines.

However, apart from the great dessert wine specialties of port, Madeira, and Muscat from Setúbal, true originality is offered by red wine. Here a simply inexhaustible potential of good regions, vineyard sites, and grape varieties is pouring onto the market, dividing journalists and consumers into supporters of *estilo moderno* or *estilo classico*, sometimes also known as *estilo tradicional*. There is probably no other country in which this subject of style is so frequently, so passionately, and so systematically debated in periodicals and books, at the table, or during wine drinking and wine tasting. Basically, no journalist in Portugal can discuss wine without

The Portuguese wine label

Colheita de 1984

Reserva Especial

VINHO TINTO 4
CASA FERREIRINHA
A. A. FERREIRA S.A. – V. N. GAIA – PORTUGAL
PRODUTO DE PORTUGAL
11,5% vol. e 75 cl.

1. Vintage wine
2. Vintage year
3. Quality of the *cuvée*
4. Type of wine, here red wine
5. Name of estate or wine dealer
6. Bottler
7. Place
8. Nominal volume
9. Alcohol percentage by volume
10. Country of origin

Innovative energy on the banks of the Douro

"What varieties are my wines produced from?" Dirk van der Niepoort laughs mischievously and looks thoughtfully up at the sky. "Not such an easy question to answer." The name "Niepoort" crops up at some point whenever there is any discussion of the new style of Portuguese viticulture. Portuguese by choice, of Netherlandic ancestry, Dirk van der Niepoort promotes his cause most articulately in several languages. He is the founder of modern Douro wine and brought dry Portuguese wines to the world's attention.

The house of Niepoort has been famous for high quality port wine for a century and a half. But in the late 1980s Niepoort began to create wines without residual sugar or added alcohol, which became known outside the country in the 1990s. Sturdy independent products made from native varieties, the range of varieties used to make them differed from vintage to vintage. Together with his enologist, Jorge Serôdio Borges, Niepoort first created Redoma, a cask-aged red wine with class and elegance. The Douro valley wine producer is also interested in white and rosé wines. His Redoma Branca is considered one of the new classic whites, and the rare Redoma Rosé is far more than a by-product of red wine production.

Further projects are Niepoort's estate Quinta do Napoles and his new top red Batuta, but these are by no means the only

Portugal is a land with many different styles of wine—from plain everyday wines to full-bodied products, and truly royal Vintage Ports.

ones. Even classic port wines are benefiting from Niepoort's delight in experimentation. In Quinta do Passadouro, he has created a Single Quinta Port full of character, by no means to be considered a lesser variant of Vintage Ports. The new definition Single Quinta Vintage has also been shaped by Dirk van der Niepoort. This is a Vintage Port of very individual character, not just a secondary vintage from a big port house in poorer years. What could be more interesting than, in top

years, to taste the classic Niepoort Vintage alongside Passadouro?

And now there is yet a third Vintage Port on the market: Niepoort Secundum Vintage is intended to establish a different style, but not to form the "secondary, therefore lesser quality" port. More accessible, more favorably priced, uncomplicated: Vintage Port for beginners. This is no frivolity of Niepoort's, but an attempt to interest a younger public in the occasionally seemingly rather antiquated Vintage Ports. The high prices, unquestionably often justified by quality, do sometimes get in the way of this most noble of port wines, however.

Van der Niepoort was also one of the first producers in the Douro region to understand the important function of marketing. Wines of such a special nature as ports, or to an even greater extent dry reds, do not sell themselves. For this reason (and also because he enjoys it) you will often see Niepoort at trade fairs and wine events all over the world. He is then happy to explain on what occasions port wines are particularly enjoyable: not just with a cigar or chocolates, as most of the wine books insist "Try port wine with steak *au poivre*," is Niepoort's suggestion.

mentioning the subject of wine style. On the one hand are the wines with primary fruit aromas, with or without wood aroma (José Neva is a master of this area), on the other uncompromising wines aged in the old manner.

A focal point of these discussions is the *lagar*, the open basin of granite, slate, concrete, or even marble, in which the vineyard workers, singing, dancing, playing around, or stamping in military order, carry out the millennia-old work of treading the grapes. This is the only method in which not one pip or stalk is damaged and therefore the green, aggressive, bitter, and tannic ACID flavors, which can be tasted in countless wines, are avoided. Apart from *pisar a pé*, another topic of conversation, at all levels and not only for a few top wines, is the question of whether wine should be filtered, and made without any kind of prettification. Tradition is popular among the Portuguese, but even more decisive are the enticing density and rounded character of the tannins and the fruit you can taste in traditionally made wines. Despite the trends toward fruity wines for drinking while young, red wine in Portugal is still more of a stronghold of tradition than in any other country.

Vinho Verde is one of the most successful types of wine in Portugal, and has even been imitated abroad. This applies particularly to the Vinho Verde based on the Alvarinho variety.

At the moment there is a traditionalist movement, almost amounting to a dismissal of technology, as can be read on the back labels of wine bottles; *feito em lagares, pisar a pé*, or *estabiliazicão natural, esta sujeito a criar depósito com o envelhecimento* (natural stabilization, intended to form a deposit with age), or *não foi tratado pelo frio* (not cold stabilized).

VINHO VERDE

The Vinho Verde region, in the extreme northwest of Portugal between Porto and the Spanish border, covers the same area as the Minho, the *vin de pays* named after the region. It is the largest D.O.C. region in Portugal and one of the biggest in the world. At around 86,450 acres (35,000 ha), the Vinho Verde region is the largest quality wine region in the country. Unofficial estimates assume even higher figures. On average, 21,000,000 gallons (800,000 hl) of wine and sparkling wine are produced—however, there are considerable variations from vintage to vintage. The proportion of wine exported is constantly rising.

In Minho, the former county of Portucale and the heartland of Portugal, Afonso Henriques of Guimarres once proclaimed the first Portuguese nation. The Minho contains only nine percent of the land area of Portugal, but 20 percent of the population. This has led to the creation of an intensive landscape of small farms in which the rampant growth of the vines is proof of the

Modern viticultural methods are advancing even into the north of Portugal. The vines in the new plantings near Cruzeta are growing on low trellises.

Opposite
The Quinta da Cerejeiras is decorated with magnificent blue tiles, the famous *azuelos*.

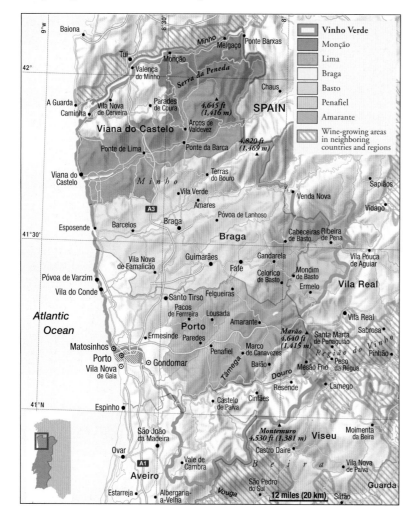

fertility of this area. It is the greenest region of Portugal, receiving 38 to 51 inches (150 to 200 cm) of rainfall a year. The vines shoot up the trees on the sides of the roads for 30 feet (9 m) or more, and this is not by accident, but to make harvesting easier. In meadows and pastureland where cattle graze, they are grown, intentionally, up trees, on poles, on wires strung on granite posts, or along wooden trellises. The pergola, already known to the Romans, is present everywhere and provides shade for small paths, tracks, and avenues, with grapes thriving at the top.

Despite the mainly unprolific sandy granite soils (only a few slate enclaves offer better conditions), often with only a few inches of topsoil, the Minho is one single green garden, which is probably the reason for the name of the wine. This miracle, in the Atlantic north of Portugal, has been created by the people of Minho in the smallest possible space, with their very own form of intensive cultivation, often based on an archaic system of self-sufficiency, which has only decreased in recent years due to the rise of numerous small textile and shoe factories. Once there was a great wine tradition here: wine from Monção is believed to be the first export wine of the Middle Ages, and many wealthy *quintas* all over the Minho are evidence of the profits to be made then. It was above all the strict legislation of Salazar which in 1930 interrupted this tradition by prohibiting the planting of vineyards and allowing vines only as hedging. While this encouraged the improvisation skills of the inhabitants, it also led to the division and break-up of their lands.

In a region where 100,000 farmers are registered, of which 90,000 consider themselves to be wine producers, it is a waste of time counting vineyards or even surveying them; some of the vineyards are simply borders to two or three

pieces of land and fill the occasional cask of wine. Here there is a unique mixture of intensive use of land with extensive growing of grapes. There are old vines with stems as thick as tree trunks and arm-thick twisted cords, which may spread for 240 or more square yards (200 sq.m) with the aid of supporting posts and wires. They may yield 22 to 44 pounds (10 to 20 kg) of little ripe grapes. These are made into the typical Verde which, unlike any other wine in Portugal or even in the world, often has difficulty in reaching the minimum alcohol content of 8.5 percent by volume. And yet this weakness is at the same time its strength. The acid red Verde, with its dry taste and its lightness, is the only proper red wine for summer; it even tastes good chilled. Unfortunately it is drunk almost exclusively within the country, because no one understands it as a red wine. In one of the typical little bars of the region, where the acid blackish-purplish red Vinho Verde, topped with white froth, is drunk from white porcelain bowls to quench the thirst, there is a lovingly framed piece of parchment. On it is a quote from the great professor of chemistry and wine expert António Augusto de Aguiar, dating from 1876, and it is a perfect description of Vinho Verde and its effects: "Vinho Verde is one of the most unusual of wines. It is original, young, refreshing, good for diets. It does not inebriate. That is the only reason I love it. It knows how to respect intelligence."

This judgment may have applied to red Vinho Verde, which at the time, and indeed up until a few years ago, dominated 90 percent of the country; it has since shrunk to around 50 percent. However, it does also apply to the core of the white Vinho Verde which, since the prohibition on planting vineyards was lifted, has had an unparalleled successful career as a lightly

Grape vines as natural boundaries between small fields are a typical sight in the Vinho Verde region.

Opposite
In the Vinho Verde area, the vines are trained on tall pergolas. This makes harvesting into a balancing act on ladders.

Spring pruning in the Vinho Verde region.

sparkling fashionable wine. It was the model for Mateus Rosé, for Verde sparkles naturally from the second fermentation which spontaneously occurs with rising temperatures in spring and in summer. This was perfected by the great brand-name wineries and bottled in quantity, today mostly with a little help from added carbon dioxide and some RESIDUAL SUGAR. Casal Garcia from Quinta da Aveleda, Gatão from Birges, and Gazela from S.O.G.R.A.P.E. are world brands today and sell several million bottles. Twenty-five other wineries are fighting for a market share of the highly drinkable light wine sector, ensuring that the last and smallest wine producer will have his *vinho* sold either by contract grape delivery or via a cooperative, in rounded, narrow-necked flagons, in Bordeaux-style or drumstick-shaped bottles, or in some other special form. The technical production standard of the bigger brands is quite high, the taste acceptable, if you are looking for an uncomplicated summer drink and not a sophisticated wine. Even in the cheap wine sector there are drinkable clean wines, though there are also coarse, thin, and over-frothy versions.

Some of the great wineries have concerned themselves with excellent dry Verdes as well as their mass-market brand names. Companies such as S.O.G.R.A.P.E., Quinta da Aveleda, and Solouro even bottle the rare and expensive specialty wine Alvarinho. However, the real revolution, in Vinho Verde as well, and earlier here than elsewhere in Portugal, consists in the rise of the *produtores-engarrafadores*—estates which bottle and sell their own wine. These prefer to produce a classic dry wine which contains less (and increasingly only natural) carbon dioxide. However, the picture is not a uniform one; there are also producers who make sweet and very fizzy carbon dioxide wines. In the late 1970s there were at most five of these *quintas*; a few years ago there were almost 200, with roots that can often be traced back to the Middle Ages. As *casas antigas*, they offer top-quality rooms to stay, and thus make an attractive stopover on a journey through this region, which is full of culture in every sense.

The driving force behind the increasing trend toward wine estates, higher quality and better marketing, was the A.P.E.V.V., the association of *produtores-engarrafadores*, founded in 1985. This association also contained the seeds of today's national marketing organization F.E.N.A.V.I. Many of the top *quintas* are members. There are at present 150 estates and these are constantly being joined by more. Many also give up, however, because sales are a problem for small unknown estates in a country dominated by large distributors; and marketing, following on the heels of the infant wine tourism industry, is still at an early stage. Too much optimism after planting, and certainly also the variable quality, have led many a producer to go back to vine growing.

The true Vinho Verde, a uniquely dry, steely wine which, like dry Saar or Mosel Rieslings, runs counter to popular taste, can still be found in the *quintas*, and it cannot be stressed often enough that those who like acidity should leave it well alone. Even the best, well made, ripe Verdes with alcohol volumes close to the upper limit of 11.5 percent by volume have an after-taste that is more or less restrained in acidity. For lovers of seafood who want to quench their thirst, this is a positive, not a negative quality. Verde is not a wine to taste, sip and contemplate. It is a wine which definitely encourages the appetite.

Lovers of Portuguese wines are impressed not only by Vinho Verde, but also by the architectural treasures of many estates such as the Quinta de Côtto in Mesão Frio.

All the sub-regions produce wines with similar characteristics: the finely aromatic Loureiro, which was the first to make a sensation, particularly in the Lima region, because of its fine expressiveness; or the recently discovered refinement of Azal, from the Basto or Amarante region. A higher alcohol content is not necessarily considered an advantage for the Verde connoisseur, but rather a weakness in style which deforms the otherwise very straight spine of the acidity.

However, there are two exceptions, and these regions should really be independent and not known as Verde, as some maintain. One of these is the area around Baião, down by the Douro, which is much warmer. Its wines should be placed between the very ripe Douro white wines and Verde. The other is Alvarinho, the king of Portuguese wines, a position held long before

Trás-os-Montes

The regional wine term for D.O.C. Douro is also the name for the barren, wild, deserted landscape north of the Douro, the isolated area toward the Spanish border.

It contains the I.P.R. Valpaços, from which, in the past, many a famous Garrafeira wine has drawn its red grapes. The I.P.R. Chaves, famous for its ham, is cooler and produces somewhat less full-bodied white and red wines. However, there are only a few producers.

The huge remaining areas of Trás-os-Montes offer scattered vineyards with one center,

among others, in the Macedo de Cavaleiros region, which is able to produce high-quality classic red wines.

The wine estate of Valle Pradinhos (with a large area planted with Cabernet Sauvignon vines) has frequently come to prominence with one of the best Portuguese red wines.

The opening up of the region by the new Porto–Bragança highway may make its vinological discovery possible. The geological conditions, with the finest eroded slate soils in many places, offer excellent opportunities for

further development of modern viticulture. There could soon be some interesting bottled wines starting to appear from this region apart from the good peasant wines to be found in bars and pubs. Besides red wines from the rougher highlands, some white wines with attractive acidity should now be possible.

the Spanish Albariño, beyond the Minho river, became fashionable and began its own brilliant career under the D.O.C. label Rías Baixas. In Portugal, wine from this thick-skinned, aromatic grape variety, whose alcohol content according to statute begins where Verde leaves off, is booming. The wine starts at 11.5 percent by volume and may rise to 13 percent.

Alvarinho does not taste like Verde. It is a specialty from the Monção region with opposing characteristics from the sub-zones of Monção and Melgaço. But the dryness and freshness—caused by the combination of unprolific granite soils (mixed in Monção with typical river gravels), a high volume of precipitation (here around 5¹/₂ inches/140 mm), together with high summer temperatures and cold September nights that encourage aroma —are combined in Alvarinho with elegant ripeness and an aroma with peach, lychee, pear, and citrus notes. Alvarinho—or medium-dry Verde—is the wine for lobster with a sweetish sauce, while the classic Verde Seco is the ideal wine for fish.

Alvarinho vines cover 1,730 acres (700 ha) in Monção, and nowadays the variety is even spreading as a minority vine beyond the borders of its home sub-region into other regions. There are 20 producers, including the market-dominating cooperatives of Monção. It is a pity that, as with almost all Verdes, it is difficult to recommend estates: the quality of the vintages is so variable, depending on the weather, that it is almost impossible to make a judgment and praise an estate without systematically following up all its vintages. "Once it's drunk, it's drunk, once it's sold, it's sold" is a comment regularly made on Verde. And yet Alvarinhos cannot really bloom until they are five or six years old, and other Verdes also develop very fine notes in their maturity. Reliable selection, tasting, and evaluation of estates can therefore be made only in a few cases. The dominant wineries, which represent only two percent of the wine estates but sell 70 percent of the wines, have got a better grip on the variations between vintages. They do not name the vintage for brand name wines, even on their quality products, or, like Quinta da Aveleda, they simply leave out the vintage for their better grape variety wines if the year was not a success. This historic wine, which is only beginning to be discovered as an individual and not as a brand, has a long way to go before the consumer and the dealers have learned that a good Verde is really only able to demonstrate all its qualities when it's no longer quite young or fresh.

SELECT PRODUCERS FROM THE VINHO VERDE REGION

CASA DE SEZIM*¯***
NESPEIRA, GUMARÃES
49 acres (20 ha); 100,000 bottles • Wines include: Colbeita Seleccionada Branco, Casa de Sezim Branco
One of the finest Verdes of the region.

CASA DO VALLE***
CABECEIRAS DO BASTO
74 acres (30 ha); 150,000 bottles • Wines include: Branco, Azal, Casa do Valle Tinto
Colonel Sousa Botelho's historic *quinta* produces one of the most brilliant Verdes of the region.

PALACIO DE BREJOEIRA**¯***
PINHEIROS, MONÇÃO
42 acres (17 ha) • Wines: Alvarinho, Aguardente Vínica, Aguardente Bagaceira
Dona Maria Herminia d'Oliveira Pães devised the first great modern Alvarinho estate, and has often demonstrated the richness of aroma that Alvarinho is capable of.

PROVAM, CABO-BARBEITA***
MONÇÃO
300,000 bottles • Wines: Alvarinho/Trajadura Varanda do Conde, Alvarinho Portal do Fidalgo, Alvarinho Vinha Antiga
The *Produtores de Vinho Alvarinho de Monção* formed a company in 1992 and produce brilliant wine with great expertise in a modern winery.

QUINTA DA AVELEDA*¯****
PENAFIEL
296 acres (120 ha); some bought-in grapes; 13,000,000 bottles • Wines include: Vinho Verde: Casal Garcia,

Quinta da Aveleda, Grinalda, Alvarinho; Beiras: Quinta d'Aguiera Chardonnay, Touriga Nacional/Cabernet Sauvingon; Estremadura; Tinto
A beautiful estate with standard brands and red wine ambitions in other regions of Portugal.

QUINTA DA S. CLAUDIO***
CURVOS, ESPOSENDE
16 acres (6.5 ha); 15,000 bottles • Wine: Branco
One of the few traditional quintas in Portugal which began bottling its own wines as early as 1960.

QUINTA DE COVELA**¯***
S. TOMÉ DE COVELAS, BAIÃO
44.5 acres (18 ha); 60,000 bottles • Wines include: Covela, Quinta de Covela
Nuno Cunha Araújo's ambitious *quinta* is an experimental area with many different grape varieties.

QUINTA DA LIXA**¯***
LIXA
74 acres (30 ha); 100,000 bottles • Wines include: Quinta da Lixa, Trajadura, Terras do Minho Branco, Terras do Minho Tinto; Espumante Branco, Tinto
Still a tip for those in the know. The Vinho Verdes, from various *terroirs*, have strong character. The sparkling wines, red or white, are more than just a curiosity.

SOALHEIRO (ANTONIO ESTEVES FERREIRA)***¯****
MELGAÇO
25 acres (10 ha); 50, 000 bottles • Wines: Alvarinho, Soalheiro Espumante Brut Alvarinho
João Antonio Cerdeira pioneered Alvarinho planting in 1974. His sparkling wine is masterful.

Port Wine and Douro

Port wine, otherwise simply known as port, *o vinho do Porto*, is a wine named not after its place of origin but after Porto, the harbor from which it is shipped (sometimes called Oporto). The Douro, its region of origin, begins some 60 miles (100 km) inland up the river of the same name, and stretches from around Régua, the first town worthy of the name, for about the same distance further into the interior, as far as the Spanish border.

It is the most imposing, the most intensive, and the wildest vine-growing landscape in the world; an isolated area, where donkeys and mules still provide the most valuable help and grapes still have to be carried on someone's back for a couple of miles until they reach a track suitable for wheeled transport. Even today, you can get an idea of the pioneering efforts of the first wine producers of the Douro and the first dealers.

If you look at the evidence of prehistoric times—preserved grape pips from the Bronze Age and charred vines in burial sites—you will get some idea of the great extent of viticulture even in these early times. During the Roman occupation, wine must have been produced in the Douro for export. It certainly cannot have been profitable to make wine for home consumption alone, given

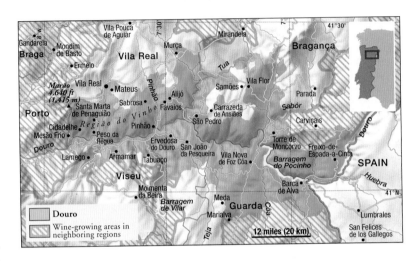

the intensive labor needed to grow vines in this rough, wild, steep, and difficult country of slate and granite.

The twin towns of Porto (the harbor) and Vila Nova de Gaia, on the opposite side of the river, where the majority of port wines still lie today, maturing in the cellars on the cooler northern slopes, were always the dominant economic pulse of the region, due to the dynamism of the wine trade and the people who worked here.

To trace the origin of the name of this famous wine, we need to go back to the Middle Ages. Alfonso Henrique, Count of Portucale, first called himself king of Portugal in 1139 and thereby founded the first European nation, in the modern sense. This would have been unthinkable without the economic power and importance of his county and its outstanding harbor and trading place. This was the first great economic golden age for Portugal, thanks to the dynamism of the monastic orders (the Cistercian monks alone founded more than 100 monasteries in Portugal during the 12th century). Viticulture was the absolute summit of all profitable—and profitably exportable—cultivation. Since 1096, the Burgundian dynasty had ruled in Portugal, providing its kings from 1139 to 1385. This dynasty knew the finest wines of its time.

Perhaps the most important ruler was King Diniz I (1279–1325), who was, among other achievements, successful in implementing a national language throughout Portugal, which remains almost unchanged today. It was derived from the former Latin dialect of Porto.

Diniz had the nickname *rei lavrador* (the farmer king). He strongly encouraged land clearance and agriculture and, with the profits

The Quinta do Noval has an unusually high proportion of stone terraces.

from agricultural production such as wine and olive oil, he built up an unequaled trading fleet —professional management by today's standards. He founded the University of Lisbon in 1290, which he moved a few years later to Coimbra, a city nearer to Porto and firmer in its faith. He also founded the Order of Christ in 1318, for which he bought up most of the resources of the Templars. In doing this he laid the foundations for Portugal's rise to become a world power, the nation of great explorers. Trade, export, and import were Portugal's great strengths which it used to secure its influence and its wealth. Only when you know this history does it become clear why port wine became the most widespread exported wine in the world and why, even today, export is still the identifying characteristic of Porto.

Today, it is not only the port wine trade that is flourishing. The demand for dry wines has dramatically increased. In two decades, the area under vine has almost doubled and now covers more than 98,800 acres (40,000 ha). Almost 40,000 winegrowers each cultivate plots of about two and a half acres (1 ha) each. The foundation for this renaissance, contrary to the development in most European regions, is not only to be found in successful sales, but also in the regulated, disciplined policies of the Instituto do Vinho do Porto, which annually forges agreement between the powerful export association and the equally powerful wine producers' organization Casa do Douro. It does this by determining exactly the amount of port wine that may be harvested on each vineyard plot, always basing it on the previous year's sales.

The character of the region is based on its infrastructure. It was the first and possibly most precisely recorded and classified region in the world. The creation of the *Companhia Goral da Agricultura das Vinhas do Alto Douro* (General Association of Viticulture on the Upper Douro) in 1756, pushed through by the absolutist prime

Once, the vine terraces above the Douro were laid out by hand and supported by dry-stone walls. Now bulldozers level the slopes for new plantings and the terrace walls are often too much work and too expensive for even the best producers.

Left
Work on the steep slopes is still largely carried out by hand.

Right
Picking grapes is hard work for those carrying the harvest. In order to provide top quality, the small modern grape boxes often have to be carried long distances on someone's shoulders.

minister later known as the Marquis de Pombal, may even today be seen as a model, in its consistency, of the protection of the reputation, market, and exports of a region. The project, known as the "Demarcation of the Hills," was probably undertaken by a Dominican monk named Father João de Mansilha. In its first articles of association, the organization stated that "the cultivation of wine is supported by the reputation of this wine, so that trade may profit by it, agriculture may be rewarded, and this all to be thus cleverly balanced that consumption should not be made impossible by high prices, nor yet cultivation by lowering of prices."

THE CAREER OF A REGION

Following the Marquis de Pombal's delimitation of the Douro region in 1756, the area was immediately extensively surveyed and divided into different price ranges. At a stroke, all imports of wine into the region were prohibited and the practice of blending wines to produce lower-priced products was stopped. Typically, the economic fate of a wine region is that, following a period of success, the wine producers, driven by the desire for profit, move toward bankruptcy because of unlimited increases in the quantity of wine produced, whether by extending the area under vine, or by blending or adulterating the wines. In the Douro, this process was reversed. Within 20 years, due to Pombal's authoritarian regime, not only was the protection of the wine area established, but prices even tripled. New port wine houses were founded, and the region flourished again, this time with organized and regulated quantities.

Demand was strong but cultivation was extended only in small stages, to prevent negative consequences. Only after increasing liberalization did the market become more unstable and crisis-prone. The final step toward stabilizing the market and securing the region which had contributed so much to Portuguese economic power and history was carried out during the Salazar dictatorship between the years 1930 through 1974.

More than 40,000 wine producers want a part in today's port wine boom.

The treasure-house of port wine begins near Regma.

Since the over-generous demarcation of borders of 1907 (corrected and made stricter in 1921), a policy of intensive brand protection for Porto had been implemented, but the prices were not high enough. In 1933, the organizations were formed which still protect the industry today: the Casa do Douro (Association of Wine Producers), the Grémio dos Exportadores do Vinho do Porto (Association of Port Wine Exporters) and the Instituto do Vinho do Porto (Port Wine Institute), an official institution responsible for the overall interests of the port wine industry. Among other bodies, the Câmara dos Provadores was set up to test port wine in the glass. However, the Casa do Douro's most important service was the provision of a new viticultural register of all wine producers and vineyard plots. This continues to the present day and has collected a wealth of data. Within the register, the most important information is the classification of all plots into six classes from A to F, devised by the agricultural engineer A. Moreira da Fonseca in 1947–8. Each vineyard is evaluated according to a points system to take account of all the factors affecting quality. This is still important today for the annual issue of *beneficio* (the right to produce a certain quantity of port wine). It also helps to decide the price when purchasing port.

If you also take into consideration the *Lei do Terço*, the rule that producers can sell only a third of their store of port wine a year, and that the port lodges are therefore forced every year to buy more wine if they want to keep selling, you

get an idea of the extent to which this cost-intensive business and this region are protected by a complicated system of rules. There was only one change as a result of Portugal's joining the E.C. in 1986: the monopoly of the port wine lodges in Vila Nova de Gaia to export port was broken. The Douro, a region previously protected but at the same time restricted, became free.

The development of the Douro and its vineyard sites marks a turning away from the exclusive production of fortified port wine. In 1982, the Douro was also officially declared a region for red and white wines (D.O.C.).

Sensational red wines come from the vineyards of the lower Corgo. In contrast, the Douro Superior often has temperatures over 130°F (45°C) and rainfall of 12 inches or less (30 cm). There are now test projects for root irrigation in progress. Barca Velha, and some of the other new top-quality red wines from Ferreira and Ramos Pinto, exploit this reservoir of the ripest grapes and tannins imaginable, although they mostly work with a blend which brings in acidity and freshness from grapes grown at a height of 1,600 to 2,000 feet (500 to 600 m). The upper Corgo, the region responsible for most of the better quality ports, lies in the heart of the Douro, not quite as dry and hot as the Douro Superior. Here you will also find the greatest number of high-quality port wine *quintas*.

Many families have been working for generations on the *quintas* in the Douro valley.

It is impossible, in the Douro region, to ignore the trend toward dry red wines—and the range on offer is vast. Compared to port wines, the unfortified wines previously amounted to no more than five percent. Now, apart from ambitious newcomers (for example, Quinta do Fojo), established producers (such as Niepoort's Quinta do Napoles) are also becoming more and more interested in this new branch of the wine trade. Traditional *quintas*, in earlier years interested only in sweet wines, are increasingly reacting to world-wide interest in Portuguese wine growing and in particular in dry reds. Modern technology, after all, has made possible what was in previous centuries hardly practicable: reductive production of non-fortified wines. There is as yet no distinctive style; native varieties are competing with international ones, and there is some enthusiastic experimenting with *barriques*. Traditionalists who will have pressing done only in *lagares* are competing with out-and-out modernists who are gathering experience from Spain and France. Red wine no longer plays a secondary role—indeed, the most far-reaching innovations are being made in this area.

PORTUGAL: LAND OF 500 GRAPE VARIETIES?

Portugal is often described as the country with the greatest variety of grapes in the world—according to frequently quoted estimates, there are supposed to be around 500 of them. But because no one has ever counted them all and distinguished genuine varieties from regional synonyms, there has to be some doubt about this figure. Wine experts assume, though, that there are 250 to 300 genuine grape varieties. Many have their origins in the early Middle Ages, and some may even be older. Over the centuries, they have often adapted perfectly to their individual *terroir*.

The climatic, geological, and topographical wealth on offer in Portugal is the principal reason for the development of such a great variety of grapes. The large wineries' tradition of blending wines, and taking no notice of the character of individual varieties, led to a situation which had lasted right up to the early 1980s, when research and registration was carried out for the purposes of joining the E.C. Before then, research into grape varieties and wines from single varieties was mainly a matter of accident, limited to a few initiatives such as that of the house of Ramos Pinto in the Douro region. Suddenly, decisions were needed as to which varieties were to be recom-

Pisar a pé (treading with the feet): this is the least damaging method of crushing grapes. However, it requires hours of rhythmical steady trampling. Not until the late evening does the bottle go round and people begin to enjoy themselves.

mended and authorized, to formalize the requirements for the quality wine regions. Single variety plantings are rare, except for a few regions which rely mainly on one variety, such as Baga in the Bairrada, or Periquita in Palmela. These decisions did not begin in any significant extent before the 1980s and continued into the 1990s.

Since these new plantations have started to bring in sufficient grapes, a positively meteoric fashion has arisen over the last few years of the last millennium for *vinhos varietais* or *vinhos estremes*, as the single-varietal wines are known. From a mixture of curiosity on the part of the wine producers and consumers, and hard work and good business sense on the part of the producers (who can thus sell specialty wines at higher prices), the range of these new wine varieties has increased enormously. Any sort of summing up is almost impossible. Some wine connoisseurs may be dubious that the aristocratic grape of the extreme north, the Alvarinho, has suddenly turned up in the south, and that there have been attempts to plant the Touriga Nacional, generally considered the noblest grape in Portugal (and possibly in the world), all over the place, wherever a producer's image needed a

boost. But the fact that there are now many wines of all kinds coming onto the market is certainly more democratic and consumer-friendly than decisions taken in scientific experiments as to what grows best where. The overall picture of what varieties are to be recommended is changing with every new exciting wine that appears on the scene.

The danger exists, however, that if producers short-sightedly limit the varieties they grow to just a few, the diversity will soon become noticeably less. But given their love of the peculiar, the typical Portuguese *bairrismo*, it is extremely likely that the unusual content of certain local specialties will continue.

It is important for the consumer to know that most of the single-VARIETAL wines come from new plantings. They cannot, therefore, ever have the concentrated expressiveness of older grape varieties. Some wines, though, do provide spec-

The traditional grape baskets in Portugal are tall woven baskets which may hold more than 100 lb (45 kg) of grapes.

tacular fruit and refinement. The *varietais* offer memorable, and often exciting, individual new wine experiences. Given the high prices, however, it is worth asking whether, in some cases, cheaper wine from a blend of mixed-variety old vines would not have offered better value for money. The majority of leading dealers, such as the biggest Portuguese company S.O.G.R.A.P.E., are convinced that they should not invest everything in native or international grape varieties, and believe that blending varieties provides better, more complete wines. Many producers admit that the *vinhos estremes* are, at least for the moment, experimental, and they may perhaps go back completely or almost completely to *cuvée* wines. And for those who dismiss *cuvées* of varieties because they cannot provide the traditional complexity of Portuguese wines, especially of port, we should point to the old traditional mixed blend of 10 or 20 varieties.

White grape varieties

- *Alvarinho*: A thick-skinned grape with only around 50 percent juice which combines body with a lot of freshness. It is the basis for Vinho Verde in the Monção sub-region. Often it is too smooth, and matured from vines which are too young; at the moment it is still searching for a style.
- *Arinto*: This variety from Bucelas, praised by Shakespeare, is widespread in Portugal; it has unique piquancy and fine acidity and, though not related to Riesling, has a surprisingly similar flavor; it is traditionally also famed for fine sweet wines.
- *Azal*: A variety, underrated until now, from the Vinho Verde. In the Basto and Amarante sub-regions it can produce deliciously fresh, acid-accentuated, piquant aromatic wines.
- *Encruzado*: The best variety in Dão, with a low yield. Complex in aroma, it may, if aged in a *barrique*, approach the style of a good Burgundy.
- *Esgana Cão Sercial of Madeira*: Perhaps the finest and most stylish of all the varieties on Madeira. In Portugal itself it has impressively fine acidity, making it a rival of Arinto.
- *Loureiro*: The first grape variety developed in Verde after Alvarinho, this is extraordinarily fine and aromatic and reminiscent of Muscat; a slender delicate variety.

Red grape varieties

- *Aragonez (Tinta Roriz)*: The equivalent of the Spanish Tempranillo, with its deep blackish-red color, this is full of wild but fine fruit and intensive tannins. In the Douro, Dão, and other places it is also one of the top varieties if the yield is not too high.
- *Baga*: Small, thick-skinned grape which ripens late and has high acidity. It is vulnerable

Portugal's extraordinary wealth of native grape varieties is a treasure for the future.

to not ripening, and to rotting due to rain. In Bairrada it represents 90 percent of all vines and is mainly responsible for splendid wines with elegant fruit (blackcurrant) and tannin structure, and also for characteristic table wines.
- *Bastardo*: Known in the French Jura as Trousseau, this is very rich in sugars and low in acidity, with a solid firmness but little refinement.
- *Castelão Nacional (Camarate)*: Because of its generous harvests, this is a popular variety in Estremadura, Ribatejo, and Bairrada. The first single-varietal wines have displayed complex fruit, class, and elegant, firm tannins.
- *Castelão Francês (Periquita)*: Probably the main variety in Portugal, particularly in the south and west. It has a very characteristic berry fruit; together with firm tannins, this can make great, maturable red wines in *terroirs* with low yield.
- *Tinta Barroca*: One of the five main port varieties, produces dark sweet grapes and a good yield. In northern sites the bite is missing.

- *Tinto Cão*: One of the top varieties in Douro, now also discovered in Dão. Low yields, herby flavors and sinewy acids; could rise to become a top wine.
- *Touriga Francês*: At 26.5 percent, this is the most frequently planted, stable-yield, late-ripening variety in the Douro region. Typically, it has fine fruit with plenty of blackberry and black cherry, and a herby note; very attractive red wines now also produced in the south, for example in Alequer.
- *Touriga Nacional*: The praises of this thick-skinned, small-berried, low-yield variety have been sung since the 13th century. In Dão, this grape is supposed to have provided 90 percent of all grapes until the phylloxera catastrophe in the 19th century. In Douro, it has always been praised as the Touriga Fina. Deep blackish-red opaque wines with complex aromas and no superficiality. The wine may vary from blackish to yellowish-red and contain flowery accents and herby notes. It is a miracle of complexity, ripeness, and tannins, but always astonishingly well balanced, and this applies to almost all Touriga Nacional wines that come onto the market. It is currently being discovered in Spain and could soon become one of the absolute top grape varieties in the world. Undoubtedly, it is one of the secrets of the greatness of Vintage Port.
- *Trincadeira (Douro: Tinta Amarela)*: One of the leading Portuguese grape varieties, this produces herby, spicy wine with plummy, chocolate fullness; in Ribatejo it often has excessive, sickly fruitiness. It can, however, depending on the vineyard site, produce good wines.
- *Vinhao (Douro: Sousao)*: This is the characteristic variety for the blackish-purplish-red Vinho Verde, but in the Douro it has produced spectacular wines for laying down.

THE CULT OF VINTAGE PORT

Vintage Port, the most interesting object of speculation among connoisseurs and collectors all over the world, was a cult wine long before the fine, fashionable wines of Italy, France, Spain, or the New World attracted the attention of wine enthusiasts. Port, in the past the standard drink in upper-class English society, was promoted to a popular status symbol for a new generation of American wine connoisseurs who liked particularly full-bodied wines. The development of port wine has been closely linked with British firms of shippers for several centuries, and the style of the wine has been formed by the demand from this export market. Many of today's port shipping firms, who still play a central role in the trade, show this legacy in their British names.

Vintage Port is not a liqueur, it is a wine. Only grapes, grown on a particular *terroir*, can produce such a wealth of aromatic substance, such an incomparable concentration of fruity sweetness, balanced by a restrained acidity and unrelentingly full, firm tannins. Anyone who has experienced the way in which slate soils can influence the elegance of many great white and red wines throughout the world will be able to discover the same inimitable delicacy and

The lines of the network of port production all meet up opposite Porto, in Vila Nova de Gaia. Here, nearly all the port houses keep their wineries, known as "Lodges."

subtlety in port wine, thanks to this type of rock, so common in Portugal and raised to exclusive status in the Douro valley (since 1756, grapes for port may be grown only on slate soils). No one would even think of producing port from grapes grown on granite soils. Granite can produce splendid dry red wines, as has been demonstrated in other regions, but never that degree of refinement in the sweetness of the fruit. Port wines from other regions, for example South Africa, Australia, or California, may be worthy of respect, but when it comes to the refinement and complexity of expression that distinguish a great Vintage Port,

The hour before midday

Eleven o'clock in the morning is the time for the daily wine tasting in Vila Nova de Gaia—the time for important decisions. With the greatest possible concentration, purchasing decisions are reached on samples from the Douro, or blends of wines in the cellars are devised and tasted. Such blends are necessary to keep up the stylistic continuity of a brand, but also to make delicate attempts at improvement, or to try out innovations.

Producing port wine is considered the most difficult task in any winery. All the classic improved wine-based drinks such as champagne, cognac, or sherry obtain their character from the master winemaker's work, and are creations made by experts, as different as they are difficult. But port, in all its diversity, its intensity, its delicacy, requires more than just a good master winemaker. The harmonious cooperation of sweetness, tannins, alcohol, and innumerable fruit notes in young port demands a genius. The port winemaker must always make the right decision among the many different sub-regions and vineyard sites, decide what should go in which corner of the cellar, whether the TAWNIES go into barrels for further maturing or

into the tank to support the character of the young fruit. He or she must subtly approach the desired nuance of color, find the balance between round, ripened and young, aggressive tannins, between the quiet maturity of age and energetic youthfulness. It is not an easy task. In many port lodges this gift, for it is a gift, has been handed down through the generations.

Probably the greatest of all port winemakers was the almost legendary Fernando Nicolai de Almeida, who not only formed a completely individual style of tawny for Ferreira, but also created, in Barca Velha, the most famous red wine in Portugal, and thereby began a development which today is being introduced to more and more port lodges.

In an age of technology, of academically qualified enologists with sober intellectual ideas about wine, in an age when marketing strategists and vintner-managers look on the grapes and wines of individual regions as the stuff of which entrepreneurial success is made, the respect shown in Gaia to styles of taste, as well as the serious discussion between modernism and tradition, may seem surprising. However, despite all the routine, in many lodges tasting is

a real process, and analysis is still decisive. It is interesting to note the way the taster, who is also in charge of the cellar, is able to express or convey his point of view to all the modern technicians and engineers, marketing experts, owners, and business managers, while in many other places it is the other way around. Long years of practical experience meet technical, chemical, and business knowledge, and all parties are bound to profit by it. Wine experts and business people create something together. Newly fashionable wine theories, such as those which dominate many regions today, making intrusive changes and influencing winemakers, thankfully do not yet have the last word in Gaia.

In the confrontation between wine theory and complex intuitive experience, gathered and increased over the years, the wines themselves are still the most convincing argument. How can such wines be produced in all their individuality and diversity according to a schedule based on dry facts? The last great port wine tasters, of whom only a few are left, are greatly superior to the wine experts, but the wine experts can learn about tasting from port wine—and they soon see that technology isn't everything.

The Douro river, which made wine history, is the lifeline of Porto.

the imitations cannot compete. Fortified sweet wines or "Port Wines" from other countries seldom achieve the complexity of a real Vintage Port. This guarantee is founded on the fact that the region was the first in the world to be demarcated, and then divided into levels of quality. As long as port wine was the monopoly of the port lodges and the estates were unable to export on their own behalf, Vintage Port was almost always made from A-sites, at worst from B-sites. The decisive factor for the unusually high standard, however, was the fierce competition in the narrow streets of the port of Vila Nova de Gaia, from which port wine was exclusively distributed until 1986. In addition, consumers could rely on the exporters' association, the Instituto do Vinho do Porto (I.V.P.), which would never have acknowledged a weak vintage in its sample testing. These quality-conscious guardians of a unique wine would never have tolerated any damage to the reputation of the most reliable economic power of the north, *vinho do Porto*, at least not in the top class. A certain readiness to compromise probably existed in the other categories.

This traditional system has started to change, due to the admission of the "Douro people," the estates and cooperatives in the region. With rather less in the way of experience and knowledge of winery techniques, but balanced by more confidence in producing good wines even from C-sites, some of them manage to do just that. Even if the reliability of the guarantee has suffered from these changes, it is still higher than for other wine categories, due to the tasting committee of the I.V.P., with their long experience and high standards. In the end, however, the strict selection of vintages decides the quality. Many houses produce Vintage Port only in really good years. In less favorable years the wine is sold as Single Quinta Vintage. But alongside these "second rank" Single Quinta Vintages, there are now a number of "first class" Single Quinta Ports, bottled both by new estates and the great port houses. Symington, for example, sells Quinta dos Malvedos as a so-called "off" port, but Quinta do Vesuvio is declared a Single Quinta Port even in top quality years.

SELECT PRODUCERS OF PORT WINE AND DOURO

The range offered by the port wine lodges comprises Ruby, Tawny, 10 Years, 20 Years, Vintage, Vintage Character, L.B.V. (Late Bottled Vintage). Colheita, 30 and 40 Years are rarities. There are also Single Quinta Vintages (S.Q.V.). To avoid repetition, the following section will refer only to dry, mainly red wines. Unless otherwise mentioned, the companies are based in Vila Nova de Gaia.

J. W. BURMESTER & CA***–*****
The new owners, the Amorims, have undertaken to keep up the high-quality stock of old Colheitas and Tawnies. The traditional Vintages and L.B.V.s display great structure, even in less good years.

FERREIRA***–*****
• *Wines: Douro Tinto: includes Barca Velha, Reserva Especial, Callabriga, Quinta da Leda and Touriga Nacional, Vinha Grande*
The company, founded in 1751 and now taken over by S.O.G.R.A.P.E., is the market leader and synonymous with good port in Portugal. Excellent older Tawnies. Outstanding position in the red wine world with Barca Velha, the legendary and most expensive red wine in the country.

NIEPOORT S.A.***–*****
• *Wines include: Redoma Tinto, Batuta, Quinta do Passadouro, Secundum*
More than almost any other winemaker, Dirk van der Niepoort has created a furor in recent years with his excellent ports and complex dry wines. His Quinta do Napoles has become synonymous with a new generation of Douro wines.

QUINTA DAL CAVALHOSA****
SANTA ADRIÃO
• *Wine: Campo Ardosa*
The German wine-producing trio Werner Näkel, Bernhard Breuer and Bernd Philippi brought their first wine onto the market in 2002. The Campo Ardos red, from their 20 acre (8 ha) estate, is produced solely from local grapes: Roriz, Touriga Francese, Touriga Nacional and Tinta Barocca.

QUINTA DE COVELOS**–****
PESO DU RÉGUA
• *Wines: Tinto and Reserva, Calheiros Cruz Grande Escolha*
Until 1994, José Carlos Calheiros sold his wine to the big port houses. Together with the enologist Anselmo Mendes, he then began to produce Douro wines. His top quality wine thrives at a height of 1,500 feet (450 m).

QUINTA DO CÔTTO***–*****
CIDADELHE
• *Wines: Douro: Branco, Tinto, Grande Escolha Tinto, Vinho Regional Minho, Paço de Teixeiró*
As early as the 1970s, Miguel Champalimaud was one of the first to work on devising top quality red wines.

1 A.A. Cálem & Filho Lda
2 A.A. Ferreira S.A.
3 Adriano Ramos Pinto-Vinhos S.A.
4 Barros, Almeida & Cª Vinhos S.A.
5 C.N. Kopke & Cª VINHOS S.A.
6 C. da Silva (Vinhos) S.A.
7 Churchill Graham Lda
8 Cockburn Smithes & Cª S.A.
9 Croft & Cª Lda
10 Delaforce Sons & Cª Vinhos S.A.
11 Fonseca Guimaraens-Vinhos S.A.
12 Forrester & Cª S.A.
13 Gran Cruz Porto-Soc. Comercial de Vinhos Lda
14 Hunt Constantino-Vinhos S.A.
15 J. Carvalho Macedo Lda
16 J.H. Andresen, Sucrs. Lda
17 J.W. Burmester & Cª Lda
18 Manoel D. Poças Júnior-Vinhos S.A.
19 Martinez Gassiot & Co. Ltd
20 Niepoort (Vinhos) S.A.
21 Osborne (Vinhos de Portugal) & Cª Lda
22 Quarles Harris & Cª Lda
23 Quinta do Noval-Vinhos S.A.
24 Romariz-Vinhos S.A.
25 Rozés Lda
26 Sandeman & Cª S.A.
27 Silva & Cosens Lda
28 Smith Woodhouse & Cª Lda
29 Sociedade Agrícola e Comercial dos Vinhos Messias S.A.
30 Sociedade dos Vinhos Borges S.A.
31 Taylor, Fladgate & Yeatman-Vinhos S.A.
32 W. & J. Graham & Co.
33 Warre & Cª S.A.
34 Wiese & Krohn, Sucrs. Lda
35 Associação das Empresas de Vinho do Porto

rofiting from a mixed blend from many old vines, his plain Douro is often magnificent, while Grande Escolha, made only in top quality years, is a unique wine with a wild but fine expressiveness.

QUINTA DO FÓJO****
SABROSA
• *Wines: Fójo Tinto, Vinha do Fójo*
After supplying the most select Vintage brands for many years, Margarida Serôdio amazed the Portuguese wine world in 1996 with her first red wines.

QUINTA DA GAIVOSA***−****
SANTA MARTA DE PENAGUIÃO
Wines include: Branco, Tinto, Quinta das Caldas, Quinta do Vale da Raposa, Grande Escolha
Domingos Alves e Sousa claimed their place as top Douro producers in 1992 with Gaivosa. An outstanding range of classic and red Douros.

QUINTA DO NOVAL***−*****
PINHÃO
This house produces excellent Vintages and fully fruited old Colheitas. The Nacional Vintage, from ungrafted vines, is legendary.

QUINTA DE LA ROSA**−****
PINHÃO
• *Wines: Tinto, Reserva, Vale da Clara Tinto*
One of the pioneers of port marketing. Even in weaker years, the Vintages are of a very high standard.

QUINTO DO VALE DE DONA MARIA***−****
PORTO
• *Wines: Tinto, Vintage*
This quinta on the Rio Torto has vines which are over 40 years old. Christiano van Zeller, previously the owner of the Quinta do Noval, produces both remarkable port and concentrated dry red wines.

For the latter, pressing in the *lagar* and aging in French *barriques* is a matter of course.

RAMOS PINTO***−****
• *Wines: Duas Quintas Tinto, Reserva*
A pioneer in the 1970s and 1980s of research on new types of cultivation and varieties, this company, still run by João Nicola de Almeida, now belongs to the champagne house of Louis Roederer. The red wines are among the best in the Duoro region.

REAL COMPANHIA VELHA**−****
• *Wines include: Douro Branco: Quinta do Sidrô Chardonnay; Douro Tinto: Porca de Murca Reserva, Evel Grande Escolha, Quinta dos Arciprestes*
The most important vineyard owner in the Douro can look back on a great past. The director of this family business, Pedro Silva Reis, is now bringing the house back to its origins in the Douro.

SYMINGTON GROUP: DOW's**−*****/
W. & J. GRAHAM & CO.**−*****/
WARRE & CA. S.A. QUINTO DO VESUVIO****−*****
The fourth generation of the family is in charge of this company, which consists of seven houses (30 percent share of the market) and is mainly active in the higher quality sector. The Symingtons also own the *quintas* do Bomfin, da Cavadinha and dos Malvedos.

TAYLOR, FLADGATE & YEATMAN
VINHOS S.A.***−***** / FONSECA ***−*****
Taylor, founded in 1692, was the first port house in 1744 to own vineyards, and has remained one of the most innovative today. One only needs to call to mind dry white port, S.Q.V., L.B.V., or the First Estate, a higher quality Ruby. With its sister house of Fonseca, it has become synonymous for top Vintages. Quinta de Vargellas is Taylor's most famous S.Q.V.

Port wine categories

• *Ruby*: The sweet, fruity and full-bodied wines are deep ruby red, usually aged without wood and two to three years old. Small houses often offer a better choice than the big brand producers.
• *Tawny*: This light-colored wine, about three years old, is today the standard aperitif in France. It is soft, harmonious, and uncomplicated. A noticeable maturity of wood, from aging in the barrel, and fine nut and caramel notes are displayed mainly by older Fine Tawnies.
• *New-Type Port*: This category, as yet without an official name, describes higher-quality port wines from the better vineyards, with a maturing period of four to six years. These are classified between the fruity Ruby type and Tawny.
• *Vintage Character*: These are concentrated, fruity, deep red port wines, rich in tannins, separated from Vintage only by the very last bit of finish and concentration.
• *L.B.V./Late Bottled Vintage*: A less expensive variation on Vintage Port, which does not need to be decanted as the wine has already spent four to six years in the barrel and/or in the tank. As with Vintage Character, it is a deep,

almost blackish red, full-bodied and fruity, with an individual expression according to the vintage year, just as with the true Vintage. It also often possesses a specific refinement.
• *Port Wine with Age*: The age information refers to the average age of the blended wines. A reddish tone in the Tawny color indicates a share of younger wines, but it may provide attractive fruitiness. The increase in demand for truly old Tawnies has led to prices shooting upwards in recent years.
• *Colheita Port*: A port with a vintage year matured entirely in wooden casks, which has kept and concentrated its density of aroma and even its fruit notes. The argument as to whether Colheita is preferable to Vintage Port continues: it should be noted that the great Vintages of the 20th century were often in essence Colheita types, only being bottled after ten years or longer. Today, Colheita will be aged in the cask for at least eight years, but will not come onto (or back onto) the market for 50 or more years.
• *Vintage Port*: This is bottled after only two years. It is a reductively aged wine, which will keep its entire youthful fruit for the whole of its long bottled life. For good Vintage Ports,

this may last many decades, whereas somewhat weaker Vintages reach their optimum level after 10 or 20 years. The most famous port wine lodges declare a vintage only in truly great years, at best three times in a decade. Over the last ten years Single Quinta Vintage Port has been produced. For these, the wine comes from a single *quinta* in the so-called off years, when quality and quantity are not worthy of a Vintage declaration, but the wine of the individual *quintas* has still been aged and bottled in the Vintage manner. Many new wine estates are bottling a Vintage every year, convinced that they can produce Vintage quality regularly. They are not wrong in this, as the great port houses are mainly concerned with sophistication and their exclusive reputation.
• *White Port*: A sweet alternative to red port, the white version is usually very plain and somewhat superficial by comparison, although there are a few very convincing examples which have been aged for longer periods in the cask. The dry (or *seco*) and extra dry (*extra-seco*) varieties are better known. Most are rather neutral, though some display a more intensive, nutty, finely matured style.

BAIRRADA

In the wine world it would be virtually impossible to find another region with such an unmistakably original and striking style, liable to split critics equally and irreconcilably into devotees and opponents. The Baga grape produces 90 to 100 percent of Bairrada red wine. This variety has a tendency to bear high yields and ripen late, which means that problems with the rain that slowly creeps up in October are often unavoidable. This wine is often accused of being too sour, too heavy in tannins, and sometimes also not intensive enough in color, that is to say that its deep red is not dark enough. All this may be true. Bairrada wine is not good in every year, and it is therefore unpopular among those who want to rely on as consistent a taste as possible for their marketing (or drinking) strategies, and who are not prepared to take on special qualities. The wine can change its character from a harsh, yet often amazingly hearty and drinkable wine to a highly concentrated, firm classic with many years of maturing potential. (The wines from the many old vines with low yields excel themselves particularly here.) Anyone who takes the trouble to judge the lesser wines together with the cuisine of the region, for instance in combination with *chanfana*, goat's meat marinated for a week in Bairrada and then slowly braised, will realize that no other wine suits it so well.

The weaknesses and the strengths of the Bairrada wines are reminiscent of Barolo, the Italian wine most highly estimated by connoisseurs. In bad years Barolo is not known by this name, but is leveled down to Nebbiolo d'Alba. Only the best producers in Bairrada do the same—bottling wine only in good or great years, and sometimes putting only *reservas* or

Coimbra, once the seat of the kings of Portugal, is better known as the oldest Portuguese university city than for its wine. But the quality of the surrounding red wine areas of Bairrada and Dão have made Coimbra into a popular place for wine connoisseurs.

garrafeiras (which means Private Reserve) onto the market. In general, however, this is not the case. "Little" Bairradas can be obtained from one of the six cooperatives, which produce quite worthy and occasionally even excellent wines, or you can go to one of the 30 or so wineries within the region (or to one of the 20 wineries outside—they mostly purchase their wine from cooperatives).

The "great" Bairradas are also reminiscent of the best traditional Barolos in their purity, but they are perhaps even more unwilling to compromise. Ruis Alves, who grew up in the Bairrada and has been a wine expert with practical experience for 35 years, runs a small laboratory although he is no chemist. He represents the anachronistic fundamentalism of the region. Do not take the grapes off the stalks (or at most de-stem only part of them), ferment them all in cool *lagares*, which traditionally hold about 530 gallons (2,000 liters), do not improve, filter, or stabilize anything, age the wine in large wooden barrels holding many hundreds of gallons (as is done in Barolo) and allow it to clarify naturally over many years by RACKING.

On many estates today, wine is still made in exactly this manner. Some of these estates, led by those advised by Ruis Alves, are so consistent in following this line and their wines are so highly selected (late harvesting of grapes with ripe stalks is Alves' main tenet of belief), that a connoisseur of great wines would fall silent in awe at the effect on nose and tastebuds of such a 10-, 20-, or 30-year-old *garrafeira* or *reserva*. These wines are more drinkable, more elegant than a Barolo, sometimes close to Bordeaux and yet purer and wilder.

Acidity, tannin, and fruit, the three elements which characterize a great wine, are always

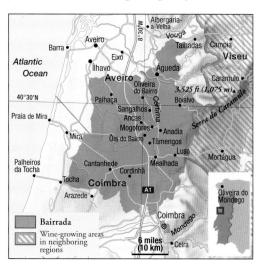

present. Sugar comes from the late ripening process. This striking authentic style probably has its origins in history. Bairrada has been cultivated at least since antiquity, and it is believed that vines may have been grown here in prehistoric times. The region is close to the sea, there is sufficient rainfall (40 inches/100 cm), and the best vineyards, with their clay, marl, and chalk soils on rocks from the middle and upper Jurassic, lie along main roads. There has always been intensive trade, both within and outside the region, and successful exports can be made only with good quality, stable wines. Natural acidity, added to ripeness, originally made Bairrada an ideal blending partner for Douro wines.

In the Middle Ages, the powerful monasteries of Lorvão and Vacariça encouraged cultural development in the region, as, to an even greater extent, did the church in Coimbra, promoting this third largest city in Portugal to be the religious center of the country, which it remained for centuries. The concentration of sacred knowledge was extended by the more profane variety (a small part of which may even have been viticultural knowledge) in 1307, when the University of Lisbon, founded in 1290, moved to Coimbra. In the 14th and 15th centuries, in the golden age of seafaring and trade, around 28 percent of the total area of the region is said to have been stocked with vines. Today, the wine-growing area is a modest 32,100 acres (13,000 ha), of which more than 80 percent is stocked with red varieties (primarily Baga). A few winegrowers are beginning to pay more attention to white varieties.

SELECT PRODUCERS IN BAIRRADA

CASA DO CANTO (ALEXANDRA TRINIDADE)−****
ACAS, ANADIA
25 acres (10 ha) • *Wines: Tinto and Tinto Garrafeira*
This estate, dating from the 17th century, was in 1856 the largest *adega* in the entire region. Extraordinarily stern, classic, very pure red wines from the best *barrinhos* (mineral-rich clay) soils and old vines.

CASA DE SAIMA***−*****
SANGALHOS, ANADIA
49 acres (20 ha); 80,000 bottles • *Wines: Colheita Tinto, Tinto Reserva, Tinto Garrafeira, Branco*
The star of the region ever since the great Garrafeiras of 1985, 1987 and 1990. Even straightforward Colheita, the estate's only wine in weaker years, provides a classic red Barraida for not much money.

CAVES ALIANCA*−****
SANGALHOS, ANADIA
753.5 acres (305 ha); some bought-in grapes; 10,000,000 bottles • *Wines: Barraida: Geleria Bical, Tinto Reserva, Tinto Garrafeira; Dão: Reserva Tinto, Tinto Particular; Douro: Foral Reserva Tinto, Foral Grande Escolha Tinto; Alentejo: Alabastro Tinto, Quinta da Terrugem; Vinho Verde: Casal Mendes; Alenquer: Quinta da Cortezia Tinta Roriz*
The biggest winery in the Barraida is the third biggest name in the country after S.O.G.R.A.P.E. and J. Fonseca. Its range runs from simple branded products to some of the best wines. Alongside their outstanding in-house enologist, Franciso Antunes, the company has recently appointed the world-famous Michel Rolland as consultant.

CAVES SÃO JOÃO, AVELÃES DE CAMINHO**−****
ANADIA
62 acres (25 ha); some bought-in grapes; 1,300,000 bottles • *Wines include: Barraida: Frei João Tinto, Frei João Reserva Tinto, Reserva Tinto V.R. Poco do Lobo: Tinto, Arinto, Cabernet-Sauvingon; Dão: Porta dos Cavaleiros Branco, Tinto, Reserva Tinto, Espumante Branco Bruto, Espumante Tinto Bruto*
Luiz Costa and the Caves São João, which he manages with his brother Alberto, are an institution in the Barraida. Among the winery brands, the wines are the most reliable in the traditional style.

LUIS PATO*−****
ÓIS DE BAIRRO, ANADIA
173 acres (70 ha); 300,000 bottles • *Wines include: Quinta do Ribeirinho, João Pato Cabernet Sauvignon, Vinhas Velhas Branco, Tinto, Vinha Fromal Branco, Quinta do Moinho Tinto, Vinha Pan Tinto, Vinha Barrosa Tinto, Vinha Barrio Tinto, Baga pé Franco, Espumante Rosé Bruto, Baga Bruto*
As a protest against political in-fighting, the chemist Luis Pato, the best and most internationally renowned winemaker of the region, sells his wines as Vinho Regional Beiras. The wines are modeled on the style of Bordeaux.

QUINTA DAS BÁGHEIRAS
59 acres (24 ha); 90,000 bottles • *Wines: Tinto, Reserva, Garrafeira, Espumante Super Reserva Bruto Branca, Rosé Bruto, Tinto Bruto, Velha Reserva Bruto*
The young Mário Sérgio Alves Nuno, a wine and sparkling wine enthusiast, produces some of the best sparkling wines in the region.

QUINTA DE BAIXO ****
CORDINHÃ, CASTANHEDE
25 acres (10 ha); 25,000 bottles • *Wines: Reserva Tinto, Garrafeira Tinto*
Traditional *lagar* winery with many old vines on excellent clay and limestone soils. The 1991 Garrafeira was the first great wine, and it has demonstrated consistency and class ever since.

QUINTA DA RIGODEIRA***−****
FOGUEIRA, ANADIA
37 acres (15 ha); 65,000 bottles • *Wines: Branco; Tinto: →Quinta da Dona Tinto, Espumante Branco Bruto*
Ataide Demedo produces the most classic and finest wines of all the "modern" winemakers. This is due to the best *terroir* and careful production.

SIDONIO DE SOUSA****−*****
LARGO DA VILA, SANGALHOS
25 acres (10 ha) • *Wines: Reserva and Garrafeira Tinto*
These wines have enjoyed cult status since the 1985 Garrafeira. The best are characterized by high tannin concentration but also by deep red fruit and elegance.

Dão

Old Dão wines are often still a pleasure today. Without new wood, indeed almost without wood at all, they display everything—apart from that final finishing touch of elegance—that makes a great wine, and is often missing in would-be great and high-priced ones: substance, character, hidden fruit, acidity, tense and delicate tannins, and an aging capacity of more than 10 or 20 years, together with a life span that can exceed this term considerably.

The secret of this quality is none other than the Dão region itself, which is still dominated by vineyards 50 years old and more. These are scattered and hidden among the hilly landscape between thick forests of eucalyptus and pines, partly on terraces of granite which often have to be broken up or dynamited for new plantings. Few yields here exceed 530 gallons (20 hl). Of the 100,000 wine producers in Dão, nine-tenths produce less than 1,320 gallons (5,000 liters) a year, and their production makes up 55 percent of the total for the region. A quarter of the 49,000 acres (20,000 ha) under vine is set out as hedging for other cultivation. Of the remaining three quarters, 19,026 plots are smaller than a half acre (0.25 ha), and 27,785 are even smaller than a quarter acre (0.1 ha).

In the summer heat, the grapes tend to be extraordinarily thick-skinned and thereby achieve a high concentration of color and tannins. High annual rainfall of over 40 inches

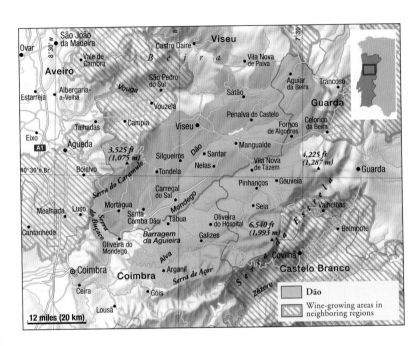

(100 cm), in places even over 47 inches (120 cm), also creates enough reserves of moisture somewhere in the granite and slate soils to do the old vines good. Other advantages of the region are the vineyard sites at a height of 2,600 feet (800 m), where the grapes are subject to distinct variations in temperature which help to conserve, in the best possible way, acidity, aromas, substance, and class. This means that natural qualities are developed in the grapes which in other places can be achieved only by the most cunning winemaking technology and aging in new oak casks. Dão vintners still have to learn that a *barrique* does not add anything new, but merely intensifies what is there already. The exceptions are Senhores Costa and Alves, who have always maintained a healthy skepticism when it comes to the use of new wood.

One of the Dão region's great disadvantages is, paradoxically, also a decided advantage and has secured it a reliable following. Its prices are in a class in which such compromise-free, solid, and even delicate wines are usually no longer to be found. In comparative tastings, it may show up worse in a class of wines costing less than 5–8 euros (US $6–10) than in a tasting of international quality wine costing 15, 20 or 25 euros (US $18, 25 or 31), according to how many true connoisseurs are present in each group. This has unfortunately led to many Dão wines being made more pleasant, more rounded, and more stable, so that discovering their quality is not such hard work and they fit better into the

Apart from the numerous small producers, the hilly lands of the Dão region also boast some larger estates, which plant and cultivate vines in a modern manner on the crumbly granite soils.

under 5 euros (US $6) category. To save Dão wine's honor, it should be stressed that many wineries offer very reliable wines and most Dãos are well worth the money. At present, probably the most reputable and classic range is that offered by Maia Encosta from Borges, among the big brands (about a million bottles).

A good Dão, therefore, forms the taste of all levels of society, and Porta dos Cavaleiros is the evidence. It is a top-quality wine served in numerous small and simple *tascas* and bars. Often excellent Portuguese home cooking can be enjoyed together with this good, almost too great wine, and the landlord will enthuse about his wine because he treats himself to it on his few days off in the year. It is also the wine served every day at lunch, both in the works canteen and in the restaurant for the knowledgeable and experienced management of many famous port lodges. More's the pity that we can't get enough of it.

The wine has just the right strengths that characterize Dão as a whole, and have made it the greatest, most recognized, and first origin-demarcated red wine in the country. Luíz Costa, above all, is the man who has always tended these very strengths. He has never narrowly confined himself to his home ground—the Bairrada—but has considered the superior class of Dão and knows how to make use of it. All new developments in the Dão region, whether by the estates or the cooperatives, should always keep his long-term and consistent model in mind. The goal should be an improvement, a refinement of Costa's Porta dos Cavaleiros. Any divergence into aggressive new wood, to single-

In the Dão region, people are used to all too frequent rainfall, which even allows grass to spring up between the rows of vines. Quite surprisingly, the yields still remain minimal, but they produce wines of notable intensity.

Following page
Dão *garrafão*—the everyday wine of the inhabitants—is a basic commodity for the Portuguese population.

varietal wines, or toward young vines could take more class out of Dão than Porta already has. Its *reserva*, with the labelled cork, should long hold its place among the top wines of Dão. To better this wine in elegance and depth is a challenge which some have now risen to successfully.

Luíz Costa and Ruis Alves

It may seem surprising that Luíz Costa, the driving force behind Caves São João, the Bairrada, and indeed the whole Portuguese wine economy, should receive his well-deserved honors in this, the section on Dão. He is one of those responsible for the renaissance in the Bairrada and also the initiator and a co-founder of the Bairrada wine association, the Academy of Bairrada Wine, which has provided so many services after only two years. The list of Luíz Costa's great and remarkable services is a long one. He has inspired the whole wine world, devised a cork label and had it printed, opened the Portuguese market for the regular magnum bottle, supported the numbering of bottles, just as he does the regular indication of the vintage year even for his plain wines, not just for *reservas* and *garrafeiras*. At a time when Dão region is once more receiving praise from the critics, it is right and proper that we should honor the man who has been a constant advocate and champion of

Dão wine, even in times when (with a few exceptions) its reliability and continuity have been missing, and with them, the proof that Dão is always a vastly underrated wine, especially in the lower price categories.

In the 1960s, with his Dão brand Porta dos Cavaleiros, Luíz Costa created and nurtured a brand which perfectly expresses the greatest traditional strengths of the Portuguese wine trade up to the present day. These are the tracing and purchasing of good wines, in particular from good cooperatives, the care of these wines in his own winery, and their presentation to the market at the best possible time for the wine to have its full effect.

To be sure, Costa's Dão, from cultivation to aging, is not as finely formed as many of the Bordeaux wines which Costa considers as his models. Working within the established tradition of the great port wine houses, he demonstrates that a determined purchasing policy toward the raw material of the wine and its

origin from good vineyard sites can be used to create a quality standard, a brand which certainly approaches the great wines in purity and in character.

Wines nurtured since the 1970s by the Bairrada fundamentalist Ruis Alves display a style of aging which is otherwise only seen in top-quality grapes. These combine the classic Dão quality—a wine which may show greatness even as a peasant wine—with the greatest luxury and the eloquence of the wines of some cult wine producers. These are completely unsweetened, unimproved, unfiltered, unstabilized. They become ready for bottling and drinking only by repeated racking of the wine from barrel to barrel, or in this case mainly from tank to tank. While his João brand from the Bairrada is an excellent example of the success of this philosophy, an even better one is his plain Dão Porta dos Cavaleiros. (It goes without saying that the *reserva* is also an excellent wine.)

The undiscovered Beiras

As a Vinho Regional term, the Beiras extend across a great part of central Portugal and are divided into the sub-regions of Beira Litoral, to which the Bairrada and the areas extending beyond it belong, and the Beira Alta, the regional wine term for Dão. In the north, an additional part of the Beiras is the Lafoes I.P.R., producing its acidic fresh wine, both white and red, which is similar to Vinho Verde. In the interior of the country, just bordering on the Douro, is the D.O.C. region Tavora-Varosa which, until quite recently, consisted of the two separate I.P.R. regions of Varosa and Encosas da Nave.

Traditionally this region is the well-kept secret of wineries throughout Portugal, who see it as the source of base wines for their better-class sparkling and white wines. It was a deliberate move for the Sociedade Agrícola e Comercial do Varosa, also known as *Caves Murganheira*, to settle in delightful Tarouca with its famous monastery. It is one of the oldest and biggest Portuguese sparkling wine producers, using the traditional method, and it is now also involved in producing red, white and rosé wine, although success has to date been variable.

The red wine potential of this region—of which 116,250 gallons (4,400 hl) have already been registered as D.O.C. in 1998—is excellent, as has been shown again and again by individual bottles. Slate soils like those in the Douro region, but combined with a higher altitude climate leading to more acidity and less alcohol, are guarantees of success.

Right in the east of Portugal, with a climate that is already clearly continental, the new D.O.C. Beira Interior has been formed from the I.P.R.s Castelo Rodrigo, Pinhel, and Cova da Beira. As in the rest of the region, the white wines here are interesting, while the red wine potential has not yet been sufficiently exploited or is still hidden away and dormant.

The Quinta do Cardo in Figuera do Castelo Rodrigo is undoubtedly the most active company in the region at present. The exceptionally fruit-accented red wines, some of them single-varietal wines, are unfortunately aged for drinking young and do not make the most of their resources. The white wines, in their elegance and refinement, are already among the best that Portugal can offer, and demonstrate the potential excellence of the region.

If you look at the former greatness and fame of the Cistercian and Benedictine monasteries which existed in all the wine centers of the Beiras, and if in the vineyards you sample any of the grapes, which are outstanding even for Portugal, you can foresee a great future for interesting wines. However, for mass-produced wine, the region is much too barren, dry, and stony.

SELECT PRODUCERS IN DÃO

CASA DE SANTAR***–****
NELAS
296.5 acres (120 ha); 600,000 bottles • Wines: Tinto, Branco, Reserva Tinto, Castas de Santar Branco, Tinto, Touriga Nacional, Encruzado, Alfrocheiro Preto, Tinta Roriz
Casa de Santar is the oldest and biggest wine estate in the Dão area, but its rise to the top did not begin until 1991 with large-scale investment in its own production. Under the management of Pedro de Vasconcelos de Sousa, who studied enology in Montpellier, the wines have, over the last few years, increasingly shown the potential of the outstanding vineyard sites, which have granite soils partly mixed with slate.

MARIA DE FÁTIMA TEIXEIRA RIBEIRO SILVA***
22 acres (9 ha); 60,000 bottles • Wines: Tinto Reserva, Branco, Reserva, Tinto Garrafeira
On the south-facing granite soils, Maria de Fátima Teixeira Ribeiro Silva cultivates a classic mix of varieties. After fermentation in the traditional *lagar*, the wine is aged for two years in stainless steel and used French wood. Supple, relatively soft, and yet long-lasting Dão type.

QUINTA DA FONTE DE OURO***–****
MORTÁGUA
25 acres (10 ha); 70,000 bottles • Wines: Tinto, Touriga Nacional Vinho Regional: Quinta da Giesta Tinto, Branco
In 1991 Nuno Cancella Abreu, winemaker on the Quinta da Romeira in Bucelas, together with colleagues, decided to build up a new style of Dão wine *quinta* in his home region in Mortágua. With vineyards in Nelas and Mortágua (50 percent with the top-quality variety Touriga Nacional, the rest other classic Dão varieties), the aim is to create a premium Dão, to be sold only in good years, with careful aging. In other years, the Vinho Regional, to be drunk earlier, will be produced.

QUINTA DA PELLADA/QUINTA DE SÃES***–*****
PINHANCOS, SEIA
99 acres (40 ha); 100,000 bottles • Wines: Quinta de Sães: Branco, Tinto, Reserva Tinta Roriz, Quinta da

Pellada: Branco, Tinto, Tinta Roriz, Jaen, Jaen/Touriga Nacional, Tinta Roriz e Touriga Nacional. Touriga Nacional/Alfrocheiro, Touriga Nacional
Even if none of the new Dão *quintas* have yet come out of the stormy experimental phase, Alvaro de Castro has impressively demonstrated in recent years the great density and complexity, and the supple beguiling opulence that a great Dão can reveal.

QUINTA DOS ROQUES***–****
QUINTA DAS MAIAS
173 acres (70 ha); 150,000 bottles • Wines: Quinta dos Roques: Branco, Tinto, Reserva, Branco Encruzado, Alfrocheiro Preto, Tinta Roriz, Tinto Cão, Touriga Nacional; Quinta das Maias: Branco, Tinto, Malvasia Fina, Jaen
Manuel Lopes de Oliviera is a newcomer to the business with ideas. His recently planted vineyards are now coming into their "prime"; concentrated, spicy reds and surprising whites.

S.O.G.R.A.P.E.*–****
AVINTES
889 acres (360 ha); bought-in grapes; 35,000,000 bottles • Wines: Mateus Rosé, Branco, Vinho Verde Branco: Quinta de Azevedo, Morgadio da Torre, Gazela; Bairrada: Reserva Tinto, Branco; Dão: Grão Vasco Tinto, Branco, Sogrape Reserva Tinto, Quinta das Carvalhais →Tinto Reserva, →Touriga Nacional, Tinta Roriz, Alfrocheiro Preto, Duque de Viseu →Branco, →Tinto, Encruzado
The world's first great brand specialist today makes half its turnover with a diversified, in part very high-class, range. Gazela and Grão Vasco have been built up to sell millions. The most surprising thing about the company is that there are hardly any wines that are not worth the money; some, such as the Douro Reserva Tinto or the Duque de Viseu Branco and Tinto, are, especially in good years, excellent wines at an acceptable price. The Quinta da Carvalhais wines, especially the *reserva (cuvée)*, and the Touriga Nacional in some years come close to the very peak of excellence of Portuguese wines.

ESTREMADURA

Estremadura, in the past known simply as "Oeste" (the West), today means the wine region formed by the 19-mile (30-km) wide coastal area from Lisbon to north of the town of Leira. Here an Atlantic-influenced climate provides freshness. In the past, Oeste was seen as a provider of cheap, light, mainly white wines. Hybrids, lower-quality grape varieties and mass yields were widespread. There were only a few quality products, such as the red wine from Obidos, one of the eight D.O.C. regions of today's Estremadura.

The old Oeste region, never precisely demarcated, was joined with the D.O.C. regions of Carcavelos, Colares, and Bucelas, making this region today the most complex creation of the new regional wine divisions. The classic Bucelas goes from strength to strength, and its Arinto, with its unbelievably attractive acidity, provides what is perhaps the most elegant and refined white wine in Portugal. Wines from the unfortunately almost moribund Colares region, with soils so sandy that PHYLLOXERA never had a chance there, can be magnificent and almost as capable of development as the legendary Colares red from Ramisco grapes, a wine of pure dune sand with powerful tannins and a distinct hint of salt.

Until recently no Syrah was grown in Portugal, but the new generation of wine producers are cosmopolitan.

It is a long time since red wine from the Ramisco grape has flowed as steadily as water from the fountain in Colares. Cultivation of this ungrafted variety in the dune sands is such hard work that it has been given up almost completely.

Carcavelos is an interesting nutty dessert an aperitif wine, not as sweet as port or Musca from Setúbal. Together with port and Madeir these form the quartet of famous Portugues *appellations* and specialties in the fortified wir sector. Unfortunately the spread of villas an hotels in the environs of Lisbon has almo destroyed Carcavelos.

The greatest potential, apart from Bucelas, held by the Alenquer region with more than 16 historic, often palatial *quintas*, some wit medieval roots. In some, modern wine estate have been set up, using both native and interna tional varieties to produce fruity red wines wit great individuality which may, once the vine increase in age, compete with the best Portugues wines. Chardonnay and Arinto also provide fir fruit aromas such as are hardly known i southern areas. In the Arruda and Torres Vedra regions there are also indications of better re and white wines.

The form of the young *appellations* and thei producers is at present not yet decided, but it progressing as dynamically as elsewhere. Div sions within the wine commission are hinderin exchange and pollination of vines in this larg region (150,000 acres/60,000 ha under vine which is marked by a shortage of companies.

THE ORCHARD OF PORTUGAL

Ribatejo is the name of the region along the Tagu (Tejo) between the Atlantic-influenced Estrema dura and the drier, hotter, less fertile norther Alentejo. In Ribatejo there are numerous hug estates covering many hundreds or even thou sands of acres, with only a small part under vine The region is not too dry, with 28 inches (70 cm of rain a year, and all sorts of grain, fruit, an vegetables, from orchard fruit to rice, thrive here For wine, however, the fertility of the region something of a drawback, as far too much mass produced wine has been cultivated in the floo plain along the Tagus. Nowadays the vineyard are retreating to the poorer soils in the hinterland which are better for vines.

In recent years a comprehensive restructurin has taken place. As in Alentejo, six I.P.R. region have been set up and in March 2000 they wer turned into sub-regions. The whole region is nov the D.O.C. Ribatejo, while the same area ca also produce a *vinho regional*, Ribateja, which i more significant than the old I.P.R.

Vine varieties from abroad may be freely used here. It is no accident that the most famous and best Pinot Noirs and Syrahs in Portugal come from Ribatejo, which previously had no reputation as a wine region except for *vinho carrascão*. This is bottled in 1¹/₃-gallon (5-liter) flagons or sold directly from the cask in simple bars, especially in Lisbon. It can taste quite good as an accompaniment to typical dishes such as fried sardines, liver, or other meats cooked with lots of onions and garlic.

These traditional wines have occasionally created quite a stir, even among wine connoisseurs, as famous but anonymous *garrafeiras*. However, it is now well-known in Portugal that Ribatejo red wines, which are coming onto the market from seven cooperatives and more than 20 *quintas* (some of them huge), have now, after a rather weak start in the early 1990s, reached a remarkably good standard in some wine estates.

Almeirim and Cartaxo, previously I.P.R.s and now sub-regions, produce the most bottled wine by a large margin—a sector that is rapidly growing. Tomar, Santarém and Chamusca are

"Oeste," the West, was the earlier name of the wine-growing country in the coastal area of Lisbon.

lagging behind as regards wines and development. Coruche, right in the southeast on the borders with Alentejo, comprises only 8,650 acres (3,500 ha), but at the moment its light sandy soils show the best potential for finer red wines. The Ribatejo wine region cannot magically call up marble, slate, or the other geological advantages of the Alentejo vineyards, so it will remain interesting mainly for the relationship between price and quality.

SELECT PRODUCERS IN ESTREMADURA

COMPANHIA DAS VINHAS DE SÃO DOMINGOS**‒***
QUINTA DA BOAVISTA
MERCEANAN
321 acres (130 ha) • Wines: *Espiga Branco, Tinto, Setencostas Branco, Tinto, Palha-Canas Branco, Tinto, Touriz, Varietais Casa Santos Lima, Camarate Touriga Nacional, Touriga Franca, Tinta Minda, Tinta Roriz, Preto Martinho, Chardonnay*
José Luis Oliveira da Silva, formerly a baker, has made this historic estate into one of the model operations in the region, with passion and the help of wine expert José Neiva. He uses the various hill sites to produce what is perhaps the most exemplary range of grape varieties in Portugal. They are not classically aged, but matured for fruit, allowing the drinker the pleasure of getting to know the typical character of the varieties.

QUINTA DA ABRIGADA***
ALENQUER
• Wines include: *Tinto, Branco, Vinha Nobre Tinto, V.R. Raizertinto*
This *quinta* at the foot of the Serra de Monganto today belongs to the ceramics manufacturer João Machada, who has been producing a respectable, classic red wine for decades. The Vinho Nobre, available only in great years, is a top-quality product with the length and firmness of a great red wine.

QUINTA DE PANCAS**‒***
ALENQUER
198 acres (80 ha); 500,000 bottles • Wines: *Cabernet Sauvignon, C-S Spec. Selection, Touriga Nacional Spec. Selection, Quinta de Parrotes, Quinta D. Carlos Arinto, Chardonnay, Cabernet Sauvignon/Tinta Roriz*
With Pancas in the early 1990s, the Guimarães family was the first to show the great potential of Alenquer.

Pancas is the most ambitious of the three fellow *quintas*. However, the race to rise to the top group of red wines became too aggressive in the end with the investment in new vines. At present, the white wines appear to show the soil's class better than the red.

QUINTA DA PONTE PEDRINHA***‒****
LAGARINHOS, TAZÉM
123 acres (50 ha); 50,000 bottles • Wines: *Tinto, Touriga Nacional*
This 618-acre (250-ha) estate has 74 acres (30 ha) of young and 49 acres (20 ha) of old vines, with an extension planned to 247 acres (100 ha). It is an absolute newcomer which, with the help of João Portugal Ramos, has been providing the market with very good, elegant, deep-red fruity wines from the beginning. The majority of this wine is sold in *garrafãos* and from the barrel. A marked development in a modern style, oriented more toward Bordeaux than toward traditional Dão, is becoming apparent.

QUINTA DA ROMEIRA (ALCANTARA AGRICOLA)**‒***
BUCELAS
190 acres (77 ha); bought-in grapes • Wines: *Arinto, Morgado de Santa Catherina, Calhandriz, Prova Regio Branco, Tinto, Perfumes da Romeira: Arinto, Chardonnay, Gewürztraminer, Rabo de Ovelha, Riesling, Sauvignon, Sercial, Espumante, Tradição; Beiras, Douro, Palmela, all Tinto*
Famous for centuries, this *quinta* was the starting point for the energetic revival of the white wines of Portugal. The unique delicate fruit of the Arinto grapes growing on the *caeiras* (a particular limestone) of Bucelas is very good when made in stainless steel and now also harmonizes with *barriques*. The respected wine expert Nuno Cancella Abreu is also involved with various reds from other regions and whites of single varieties.

Terras do Sado:
The Wealth of Setúbal and Palmela

The two D.O.C. regions of Palmela and Setúbal, together with a few other regions, are linked together as the Peninsula de Setúbal, after the peninsula which directly adjoins the capital city of Lisbon. The term for the regional wine is the more harmonious Terras do Sado, which is widely used for dry whites, for some medium-dry white wines, and even for a few sweet specialties, as well as some of the best red wines in Portugal. The great historic name of this region was defined as early as 1907 as a

This is where the successful history of the Fonseca family empire was made.

Opposite
Cheerful wine festival in Palmela, directly west of Lisbon on the Setúbal peninsula. Here, the Periquita variety is made into long-lived and full-bodied red wines.

quality wine-growing area and protected accordingly. The name Setúbal may be used on the labels for Muscat from Setúbal only, which acquires its fine aroma on the light, stony, lime-stone soils of the Serra da Arrabida, with their definite maritime influence. It is indisputably one of the great classics of the wine world, but because of the relatively low quantities produced (which have, however, now risen to about 264,000 gallons/more than a million liters), and because of the very slow revival of popular taste for sweet dessert wines, it is nowhere near as well known as it deserves to be today. In addition, the second largest wine-dealing and production company in Portugal, José Maria de Fonseca, a very traditional company, always—though surely unintention-ally—seems to draw attention away from Muscat by its very extraordinary successes throughout the broad range of all its wines, both red and white.

However, it was the house of Fonseca who, in the middle of the 19th century, further per-fected the production and aging of Muscat, which was famous as long ago as the 17th century. They soon acquired an increasing number of regular customers in three continents and the reputation that goes with such a customer list. João Ignacio Ferreira Lapa, in one of the great standard works on Portuguese wine published in 1867, describes the wine company's founder, who developed this style, not only as an experienced practitioner, but as a

A piece of Portuguese wine history

Ownership of more than 2,470 acres (1,000 ha) of vineyards, its traditions and innovative skills, and its numerous contacts to almost all the great wine producers, have combined to give the great house of J. M. da Fonseca a kind of monopoly, that has lasted for a long time, at least in the production of better-quality bottled wines. The enologist and vice-president of the company, Domingos Suares Franco, who trained at the Department of Viticulture and Enology of the University of California at Davis, is carrying on the family tradition, together with his brother António.

In the early 1980s, there was furious competition in the Setúbal peninsula, when António d'Avillez left the J. M. da Fonseca management and took his creative ideas to the João Pires winery. In the mid-1980s, the João Pires wine, medium-dry and at the time

displaying the finest fruit, was a sensational success. With the aid of the Australian enolo-gist Peter Bright, d'Avillez demonstrated to the world the delicacy of the native Muscat grape in fresh white wines. From skillfully produced cheaper brands of a high standard, through to top wines from foreign grape varieties; from a Late Harvest Sauternes type to classics made from native varieties, the company, now re-named simply J. P., pro-duced wines which showed how the Setúbal peninsula, with its mainly unprolific soils and maritime-influenced climate, is suitable for the most diverse styles of wine.

Nowadays other cooperatives and wine estates which previously sold to Fonseca and other dealers, are looking for their own niches to produce better-quality wines themselves. The first successes look very promising. How-

ever, for Moscatel de Setúbal, none of them is yet in the Fonseca class. The red wines of Palmela are among the most interesting, made from the Periquita grape, introduced to the region by José Maria da Fonseca about 160 years ago. Today this variety dominates the area at around 95 percent. But white wines, fresh, clean and in part finely adjusted with Muscat, are also on the increase. The Palmela area, at 32,000 acres (13,000 ha), contains about 70 percent of all the vines growing in the Terras do Sado, while Setúbal itself covers no more than around 2,800 acres (1,130 ha).

The sandy to clay soils of the Palmela bring out the characteristic fruit spectrum of the Castelão Frances grape (Periquita), in con-trast to the grape's very individual soft and yet firm tannin, which gives the wine its excellent potential for laying down.

nan familiar with the whole of contemporary wine literature who exchanged information with many wine experts of this time.

This dessert wine is fortified more lightly than port to only 17.5 percent by volume. A 20-year-old Moscatel de Setúbal (a blend in which the youngest wine included is 20 years old) contains RESIDUAL SUGARS of about seven ounces (200 g) and has almost double the sweetness of port. The very top-quality, even older, vintage wines are even more concentrated in their density of sugars and flavors. The secrets of producing the perfect Muscat wine are stopping fermentation at a residual sugar content of just over three ounces (90 g), and evaporation. As they age, the wines become thicker and sweeter. Wooden barrels, not completely filled, relatively warm storage (the old wines, of which a few still exist, were, like Madeira, shipped to India to be exposed to high temperatures), very clever OXIDIZATION, and evaporation turn the fresh and fruity, almost citrus-like Muscat grapes into dense, unforgettable wines, exotic and full of dried fruit aromas.

SELECT PRODUCERS OF TERRAS DO SADO

Co-op. Agricola de Santo Isidro de Pegões**−***
Pegões Velhos
2,223 acres (900 ha); 4,000,000 bottles • Wines: Fontinario de Pegões Branco, →Tinto, Fontanario de Pegões Garrafeira, Vale de Judia →Branco, Tinto
An exemplary cooperative, advised today by João Portugal Ramos. Fruity reds with a fine *barrique* note can be recommended, as can the delightful dry Muscat (Vale de Judia).

José Maria da Fonseca*−*****
Azeitão
• Wines: Lancers Rosé, V.R. Albis Branco, Pasmados Branco, Tinto, Periquita Tinto, Tinto Classico; Quinta de Camarate Branco Seco, Branco Doce, Tinto; Primum Branco, Rosé, Tinto; Garrafeira C.O., R.A., T.E.; Alentejo: José de Sousa Tinto, D'Avillez Tinto, Tinto Garrafeira; Moscatel de Setúbal: Alambre Vintage, Alambre 20 Years, Superior 1962, and others, Trilogia
The top wine bottler in Portugal (excluding the port trade). This is a highly traditional family business which has had a decisive effect on viticulture in Setúbal, in Alentejo, and even in the Dão. Apart from its unique old Muscats, the house offers impressive wines in all price ranges, with constant and delightful new developments or new versions of traditional wines. A remarkable feature is their pioneering role in planting unusual grape varieties on the Setúbal peninsula: in earlier years, these tended to be more international, today they are national varieties, even Alvarinho.

Soc. Agr. de Pegos Claros***
Palmela
198 acres (80 ha); 100,000 bottles • Wines: →Palmela Tinto, →Palmela Reserva Tinto

From the Periquita grape came the most notable red wine Periquita around 1850.

This country estate, founded in 1920, today owns 123.5 acres (50 ha) of old and 74 acres (30 ha) of new vineyards, exclusively planted with the Periquita grape. In the past, these were partly de-stalked and trodden by foot in *lagares*, and they are still treated in this very delicate way today. Consistent, classic, firm Periquita reds are produced here under the direction of João Portugal Ramos.

Soc. Vinicola da Palmela (S.I.V.I.P.A.)**−***
Palmela
988 acres (400 ha); bought-in grapes; 1,200,000 bottles • Wines: V.R.: Branco, Tinto, Veritas Palmela Tinto, Moscatel de Setúbal, Moscatel Roxo
A society founded in 1964 which over the last few years has produced ever improving wines at prices that are sometimes surprising, ranging from the characterful Veritas to the Muscat series, which are traditionally produced.

J. P. Vinhos*−****
Pinhal Novo
1,111 acres (450 ha); bought-in grapes; 12,000,000 bottles • Wines include: J. P. Branco, Tinto, Loridos Espumante Bruto, Moscatel de Setúbal, Chardonnay Cova da Ursa, →Quinta da Bacalhoa Cabernet Sauvignon, →Má Partilha Merlot, Catarina Branco; Alentejo: →Tinto do Anfora
You could call J. P. Vinhos a wine factory in which mass-produced wines are skillfully created, as are better-quality wine brands from the company's own estates, and a few highly individual "hand-made" wines which are among the best wines in Portugal. In the range here you can find quite consciously undogmatic wines for everyone, even the elite. António d'Avillez has recently sold J. P. Vinhos after 20 years. However, thankfully for wine lovers everywhere, the good wine experts have stayed.

ALENTEJO

The Alentejo region is sometimes termed the California of Portugal. This is explained by the wine estates covering up to 1,500 acres (600 ha)—the biggest of all of them being the Herdade do Esporão—and the broad plains or only slightly rising slopes which are in marked contrast to the otherwise rather small-scale Portuguese agricultural and viticultural scene. Very efficient, sometimes even first-class cooperatives produce the bulk of the wine, but more and more committed wine estates are attracting attention with top class wines. Cortes de Cima is one of the most prominent companies. More than 40 wine estates and efficient regional organizations have succeeded in giving Alentejo an image of modernity and of generosity, which seems to suggest that success will result simply from the enjoyment of the right wine.

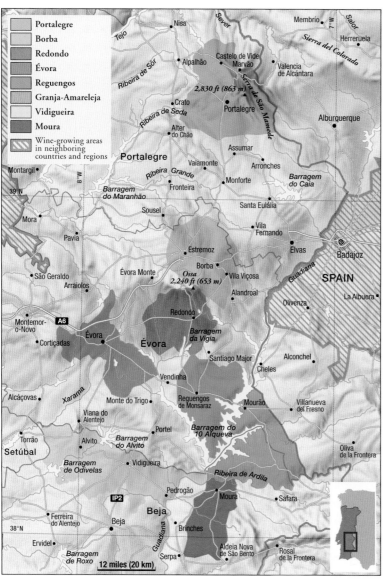

However, looking more closely, it is clear that history and tradition have played their part here too. It is still possible to find viticultural practices dating from Roman times in this otherwise very modern region: in some *lagares* grapes are still trodden by foot and in some estates great earthenware jars stand ready to age the wine. The principle of cooling by evaporation in earthenware amphorae is, after all, the oldest method of cooling fermentation in hot regions. The only place in Portugal that may possibly get hotter than Alentejo, where temperatures of 104°F (40°C) are often the rule in summer, is the Douro valley, the second great region for fashionable Portuguese wines. The heat—which often leads to picking taking place as early as August—has demanded considerable technical winery investment, which today makes it possible for some companies to produce elegant, fine, and structured white wines, even in a region generally estimated, and to an extent even celebrated, as a red wine area. Today, the Alentejo area once more has 47,000 acres (19,000 ha) under vine, about as much land as in the 19th century, before the region was turned into a grain-growing area. This is complemented by the biggest and best-quality cork oak plantations in the world, and by countless olive trees whose oil is sold by some estates and cooperatives as single-variety specialties.

Of the 2,640,000 to 8,000,000 gallons (100,000 to 300,000 hl) of red wine produced in an average year (only years with frost can drastically reduce production), about half are classified as Vinho Regional Alentejano and D.O.C

Alentejo. Alentejo red wine is very fashionable today in Portugal and especially in Lisbon, and is the wine of which there is most awareness in other countries, apart from Douro. This is probably due to its taste as well as its history.

The taste is immediately decisive, for a number of reasons, that affect both the vines and the cork oaks. One factor is the dry climate which here, in contrast to many other Portuguese regions, almost guarantees no rain at harvest time. Rotten grapes or corks damaged by damp are almost unheard of. Healthy, thick-skinned, blue-black grapes, however, guarantee a fruity wine with warm, ripe aromas.

The soils, the second factor, are equally positive in their effect on cork and wine. They tend to be unprolific and not suited to mass production. They often consist of slate, granite, and quartzite, with a proportion of other types of rock, among them the finest marble which, especially in the Estremoz and Borba areas, is quarried in great blocks. In addition, discipline and tradition, encouraged by an effective viticultural commission and technical advice, only permit vines on less fertile soil. The discipline for aging wine varieties

Alentejo has for centuries been the granary of Portugal. The number of old windmills are evidence of its past.

Opposite
Alentejo is a modern wine region with many newly created wine estates.

is also higher in Alentejo than elsewhere, which may be a result of the large-scale structures. Among the red varieties, Aragonês, known in the Douro as Tinta Roriz, and in Spain as Tinto Fino or Tempranillo, clearly excels in elegance and structure. Here it reaches its full ripeness.

The Trincadeira is valued equally highly, but is not necessarily better than Alfrocheiro or

Select Producers in Alentejo

Co-op. Agr. Reguengos de Monsaraz*⁻***
Reguengos de Monsaraz
8,398 acres (3,400 ha); bought-in grapes; 10,000,000 bottles • Wines include: Reserva Tinto, Garrafeira dos Sócios, Aragonez, Trincadeira, Monsaraz Tinto
The biggest cooperative in the Alentejo, with 576 members, advised by João Portugal Ramos, has made the leap from simple, average Alentejo wine to classic top-quality wine, the Garrafeira dos Sócios; also high-class red wines.

Cortes de Cima**⁻*****
Vidigueira
86.5 acres (35 ha) • Wines include: Courela, Cortes de Cima, Aragonez, Syrah, Incógnito, Reserva
The rising star among wine estates in the Alentejo region. The Dane Hans Kristian Jørgensen and his Australian consultant Richard Smart produce wines of character from local grapes (Aragonez) or international varieties (Syrah).

Herdade do Esporão**⁻***
Reguengos de Monsaraz
1,383 acres (560 ha); 1,800,000 bottles • Wines: Alandra Tinto, Branco; Vinha da Defesa Tinto, →Branco; Esperão →Reserva, Tinto, Branco, Garrafeira Tinto; →Aragonês, Trincadeira, Touriga Nacional, Cabernet Sauvignon, →Arinto, →Roupeiro
This is the largest wine-bottling estate in Alentejo. The Australian David Baverstock is the director of enology. Especially at the simple or medium price level, the quality is very high.

Herdade do Mouchão***⁻****
Sousel
57 acres (23 ha) • Wines: Mouchão Tinto, Tonel No 3–4, Dom Rafael

The red wines of Ann Reynolds and Emily Richardson are grown outside the demarcated region and are only *vinho regional*, but are sought-after classics. They are prepared in *lagares*, matured for three years in oak and chestnut casks, bottled with no improvement or FILTRATION.

Quinta do Carmo***⁻****
Estremoz
235 acres (95 ha) • Wines: Quinta do Carmo Branco, Tinto, Tinto Reserva Dom Martinho Tinto V.R.
The Rothschilds acquired 50 percent of a "dream château" for a joint venture with the previous owner Julio Bastos.

João Portugal Ramos**⁻****
Estremoz
Bought-in grapes; 500,000 bottles • Wines: Marquês de Borba Branco, Tinto, Tinto Reserva, Antão Vaz, Tinta Caida, Trincadeira, Aragonês, Vila Santa, Roupeiro, Syrah
Portugal's best-known wine expert superbly displays the potential of some varieties (using grapes from his own vineyards and from contracted growers). With the 1997 Marquês de Borba Reserva, Portugal Ramos brought out a new classic from Alentejo.

Tapada de Coelheiros***⁻****
Igrejinha, Arraiolos
49 acres (20 ha) • Wines: Tapada de Coelheira Branco, →Tinto, →Tinto Garrafeira
With the aid of António Saramago, J. M. Fonseca's second enologist, Joaquim and Leonilde Silveira built up an exemplary wine estate in the 1980s, with red wines that are among the most structured and polished in Alentejo. The blend of Cabernet Sauvignon, Trincadeira, and Aragonês, aged in French oak, is unusual.

Periquita, which are also recommended. Some of the best wines are produced from the southern French mass variety Alicante Bouschet, and recently fashionable varieties such as Syrah or Cabernet Sauvignon have been introduced. Always fascinating in Alentejo wines is the combination of a high degree of pleasantness and character. Even the plainer wines possess, as well as charming ripe fruit, a certain tannin structure and a fineness determined by the soil, so clearly different from the jam-like fruitiness of the moister regions nearer to the coast. Despite early harvesting and the lack of harder acidity and tannins which may be so distinctive in Dão or Bairrada, despite the softness and character reminiscent of great Rhône wines, the wines are mostly well balanced, which is why the best wines are distinguished by great firmness and longevity. It is only a pity that this last

Today, both young and old have reason to be cheerful in Alentejo. The hard times under the dictator Salazar and the blind mass production which followed on the Carnation Revolution are almost forgotten. With quality-oriented wine and cork production, the future of the region is looking good.

Opposite
From their 25th year on, cork oaks are peeled every ninth year.

Quercus suber—the cork oak—has a major part to play in the Portuguese economy.

quality is rarely fully exploited and too rapid and reductive an aging process is used to maintain the strong emphasis on the charm of the young fruit. The danger of even high quality Alentejo wines being tailored to fast consumption in the near future probably cannot be entirely dismissed at the moment. With regard to complexity, however, a slower aging of the wine, and also the use of old vines, more closely planted, are important. The sub-regions of Portalegre and Granja-Amareleja, with their cooperatives of many small farmers, produce some quite outstanding classic wines in their more continental climate.

Another reason for the fashionable part played by the Alentejo, which has made it the most expensive wine, and the one most in demand, from the barrel, may have a historical explanation. After the end of Salazar's dictatorship, the communist party was the ruling party in Alentejo—as it is today in many towns and cities. Young people and students were enthusiastic about the wine of Alentejo and learned to treasure and love it. The cooperatives were already producing to quite a high standard in the 1970s, and Alentejo found popularity because it was the wine with the best symbolic red color, and was also nearly always the best and most reliable wine at an affordable price. The new *crus* don't have that much in common with these standard wines, which of course still exist. The new wines are most often produced using old native varieties but new methods of aging, and at peak quality will fetch prices of 30 euros (US $37) or more. Some of the new Alentejo reds are already on their way to cult status. But we shouldn't forget the white varieties because of the popularity of the red wines. White grapes may only cover ten percent of the cultivated vineyards, but they do have a very independent character, and the discovery is well worthwhile.

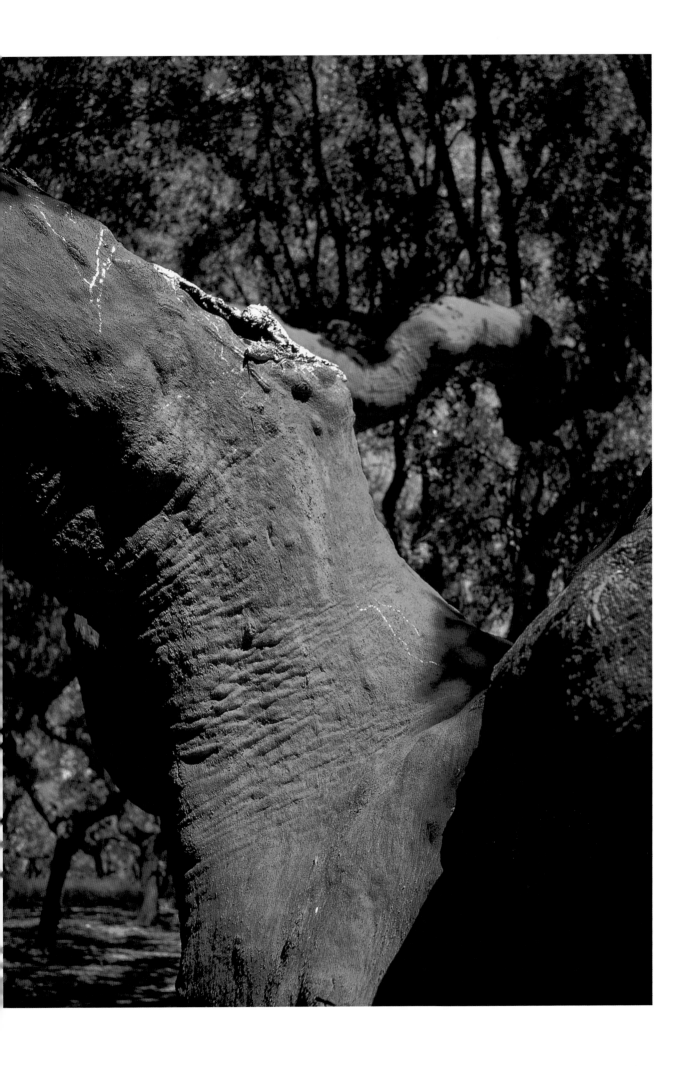

CORK MANUFACTURE

The traditional bottle cork is cut from the bark of the cork oak (*Quercus suber*), a tree which grows mainly in Mediterranean countries. It grows very slowly and takes about 45 years to produce a cork layer thick enough to cut bottle corks. The harvest, also described as lifting or peeling, consists of removing the bark as carefully as possible from the tree. The cork layer should be as undamaged as possible to make it easy to work the material. Serious injury to the tree should also be avoided, as this will damage cork formation in the next growth cycle.

Cork oaks can first be peeled around their 25th year, and the bark is then lifted at regular nine-year intervals. The first harvests are used in construction, especially for soundproofing. The mats of bark are usually left in the forests for several months so that the tannins oxidize and the layer of tissue in direct contact with the trunk can dry out. Once the sheets have been delivered to the factory, they are first of all immersed for one or two hours in boiling water to kill off microorganisms and insects, to dissolve tannins, and to increase the thickness and elasticity of the material in order to make the subsequent work easier.

After resting for one or two weeks, the cork may be boiled a second time. Afterwards the sheets are sorted according to quality and thickness and cut into strips, and then the corks are punched out, following the direction of the grain. This may be done by machine, but the results are not as good as with hand-operated or semi-automatic tools. Only a person working the machine can select the best place to punch.

The waste material is made into agglomerate from which pressed corks are manufactured.

After this, the corks are processed mechanically. The ends are cut to the desired size and the

The tree must not be damaged when the cork is peeled off.

Left
After drying in the forest, the bark mats are transported to the factory.

Right
Selecting the best place to punch out the cork comes with lots of experience.

body is smoothed. Any cork dust produced is also used in the manufacture of pressed corks.

Next, machines sort the bottle corks according to the number of bark pores visible on the surface. The corks are then disinfected in bleach. Few cork producers now use chlorine, because it may bring out an unpleasant taste in the wine. It is being replaced by peroxide. The dosage used and the time left to take effect depend partly on the color desired by the customer. Some countries prefer natural tones, others want very pale corks. Drying the corks once or twice gives a moisture content of six to nine percent. They are sorted one more time. The machines check the body of each cork, but not its ends.

The corks are then marked by branding or with ink; this may be a personalized mark with the name of the wine producer, the estate and/or

The outer surface of a piece of cork bark.

The structure of the inside of the bark.

The punching out is done by machines that are in part hand-operated.

Corks from Portugal

Portugal occupies first place among cork producers. With 1,655,000 acres (670,000 ha) of cork oak forest, it contains 31 percent of the cork-growing area in the world, more than Spain (24 percent), Algeria (19 percent), and Morocco (17 percent). At 190,000 tons a year, Portugal produces 51 percent of the corks used world-wide. In addition to its home productions, the country imports raw cork for further processing. Well behind Portugal is Spain in second place, with 26 percent of world production, in front of Italy at seven and Morocco at six percent. Corks are also manufactured in small quantities in northern countries, yet the best reputation for cork processing remains with Portugal. It is estimated that exported cork, in particular bottle corks, accounts for a turnover of about 610 million US dollars (500 million euros).

the *appellation*, and sometimes also the vintage, or it may be more general—it is left to the instructions from the customer. The higher the quality of the wine, the more precise is the marking of the cork. It should be possible to identify the wine by the information on the cork, which usually survives the label.

The final step is the treatment of the cork surface with silicon or paraffin. This allows the consumer to remove the cork without too much difficulty.

German top vintners reveal their cork secrets: the quality is good to very good all the way through, but length is deliberately limited.

Corking

Just like wine, cork is a natural living product. As a result, a certain quota of errors have to be reckoned with, and this can lead to your being confronted—despite all the cork manufacturer's efforts—with a corked bottle of wine. The wine smells very intensely of cork, a smell which usually increases on contact with the air. This has many causes, of which the two most common are improper storage of the corks or insufficient disinfection.

It may also happen that the wine, without displaying a definitely "CORKED" flavor, does not reach its usual standard or has an unpleasant note, reminiscent of wet dishcloths, mold, or something similar. In such cases it is not always easy to find the culprit, because the explanation may lie with the cork, with the adjustment of the corking machine, with hygiene problems in the winery, with storage conditions of the corks, or many other causes. Often one person will blame another, and the understandably disappointed consumer will usually blame the wine.

This is why some wine producers have decided to use non-cork stoppers for their bottles. In the face of this threat, European cork manufacturers have drawn up an international charter of cork manufacture. More and more of them voluntarily undergo quality controls which guarantee the quality of cork manufacture.

Natural wine cork
Quality: low
approx. 1 × 1 in (24 × 28 mm)

Pressed cork
Colored, in two sections
Quality: average
approx. 1 × 1¹/₂ in (23 × 44 mm)

Pressed cork
Colored, in two sections
Quality: low
approx. 1 × 1¹/₂ in (23 × 40 mm)

Natural wine cork
Quality: average
approx. 1 × 1 in (24 × 28 mm)

Natural wine cork
Quality: lower range
approx. 1 × 1¹/₂ in (24 × 45 mm)

Pressed cork
approx. 1 × 1¹/₂ in (22.5 × 38 mm)

Synthetic cork

Sparkling wine
cork
Quality: very good
approx. 1 × 2 in (30 × 48 mm)

Sparkling wine
cork
Quality: average
approx. 1 × 2 in (30.5 × 48 mm)

Natural wine cork
Quality: average
approx. 1 × 1½ in (24 × 45 mm)

Natural wine cork
Quality: very good
approx. 1 × 2 in (24 × 54 mm)

Cork from
Château d'Yquem,
1945

Bottle stoppers

The first bottles used in the 17th century were stoppered with a hemp-wrapped, tallow-drenched wooden bung. Corks were first used to close bottles securely by Dom Pérignon in Champagne. Since this time, cork has been the favored stopper for quality wines, and as a consequence several types of bottle cork have been devised.

There are many categories of natural corks, according to the number of pores in the bark, and their various lengths. The longer they are and the higher their quality is, the more expensive they become. The cheapest bottle corks, which are most often used for cheaper wines, are pressed corks, made of small particles of cork agglomerate glued together. An intermediate quality cork is made from cork dust and glue. This improves the appearance, but not the actual quality of the cork. Some producers resist using these corks because the wine will come into contact with the glue, and so cork manufacturers have devised a pressed cork with a slice of natural cork glued to each end.

For sparkling wines, the closures are made from glued and pressed cork. One or two thin discs of natural cork are glued onto one of the two ends of the cork. Natural corks with a plastic head are used for spirits such as cognac.

The range of products for closing bottles has been much expanded in recent years. For instance, a cork producer has developed a cork made of finest cork particles, less than 0.03 of an inch (1 mm) in size, held together by a synthetic tissue based on polyurethane. This product looks like a cork on the surface, but has, so it is claimed, none of its disadvantages.

The screw-top closure is at present undergoing surprising expansion in Swiss white wines, as it completely protects the wines from oxidization, which is particularly useful for the Chasselas variety. This system also has the advantage of allowing the bottle to be simply and effectively re-closed. However, many wine producers hesitate to introduce this form of closure, as it is claimed that consumers prefer the traditional cork. However, some experience has now been gained with wines under screw fastenings—and the results in regard to aging are positive.

The latest invention which is now spreading into continental Europe from California, Australia, and the big British wine companies, is the synthetic cork. These look just like natural corks; they can be used in bottling lines just as natural corks, and are removed from the bottle in the same way. These types of stoppers mean that the "corked" flavor is a thing of the past. They do not claim to replace natural cork but have been introduced as an alternative for lower priced wines in which otherwise only lower-quality corks would be used.

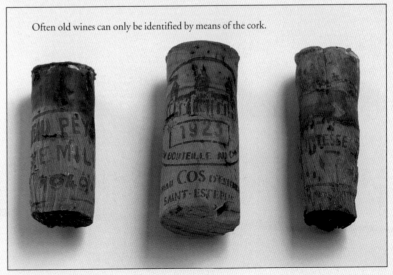

Often old wines can only be identified by means of the cork.

Madeira

In 1420, the Portuguese captain, João Gonçalves Zarco, in the service of Prince Henry the Navigator, landed on the legendary and cloud-surrounded shores of an island 370 miles (600 km) off the Moroccan coast. This mid-Atlantic mountain range rises to 6,100 feet (1,861 m) above sea-level, and was then thickly forested and uninhabited. Having cleared the island, Zarco planted sugar cane and Malvasia, the sweet grape variety known as Malmsey. After the discovery of America, Madeira gained in importance as a supply stop on the Atlantic route, as well as to Africa, and Asia. It was the only place that English ships were allowed to take on supplies.

Madeira wine began to be fortified with brandy, to allow it to survive these sea voyages without deteriorating. It was soon discovered that the wine improved astonishingly in the tropical climate. After 1750, British dealers, who took over the wine trade, began sending barrels of the fortified wine to India and the Far East to mature it. The last eight of 70 wine companies now recreate the tropical effect with

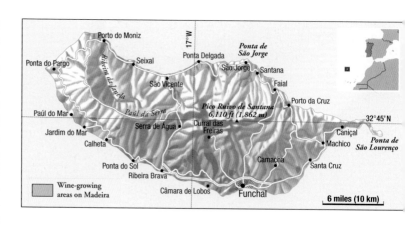

the original technology. They keep the wine in *estufas*, tanks warmed by heaters, for three to five months at a temperature of 112°F (45°C). There are two more elegant methods—they have now become rare, but are still practiced. In the luxury version of the *estufa*, the wine is put in pipes, typical barrels holding 160 gallons (600 liters), and developed in a room heated by steam. The second method is to store the pipes in a *canteiro* (attic) and thus expose them to extremes of temperature. The best wines are given 20, 30, or more years of aging in barrels. Only these are bottled with a vintage year, and often only in small quantities.

Of the 5,200 acres (2,100 ha) of vineyards on the island, which produce about 38 million gallons (10 million liters) per year, only a tenth are planted with the four noble varieties—Sercial, Verdelho, Boal, and Malmsey. Cultivation seems rather archaic. The vines of Madeira are mostly grown in low pergolas on terraces to allow the 4,000 wine producers to make the best possible use of the precious land. Picking is carried out crouching or kneeling. The harvest often has to be carried by hand 660–980 feet (220–300 m) uphill from the nearest road. The grapes are then crushed in simple continuous presses. Careful grape preparation is not necessary—the long aging process is all that matters.

Madeiras aged from the four noble varieties are unique specialties in the wine world. They have an incredible quality: they can age forever and seem steadily to improve, as some vintages still available from the 19th and early 20th centuries demonstrate. Unfortunately, the dominant grape grown on the island today is the Negra Mole, which growers and producers treat in a cavalier fashion, producing cheap Madeira for all sorts of tastes, and which now makes up 40 percent of the total production.

The vine terraces rise up the steep slopes beyond the fishing village of Câmara de Lobos. The most extensive wine-growing area on the island is located here on the south coast.

A Rarity from the Atlantic

Wine from the Azores? If the wines from the island group far out in the Atlantic are virtually unknown even in Portugal, this may be due to their remote location—but the reason is probably rather that viticulture on the Azores, which can look back on a tradition of 500 years, has failed to keep up with modern developments. Even now red wine on the Azores—mainly made from American varieties—is sometimes fermented in amphoras that are dug into the ground. The wine lies there for two or three years and develops into a light, fruity variety with a low alcohol content of rarely more than ten percent proof. Viticulture is now pursued to any notable extent on only four of the islands, with one single cooperative and a few private producers continuing the tradition. Most of these wines are drunk locally.

Excellent Madeiras

• *Boal* or *Bual*: Medium-sweet Madeira is produced from this rare variety with small, astonishingly hairy leaves. It is planted on the south side of the island, as it needs more warmth, but does not produce more sugar. The wines develop, relatively early, with interesting aromas of dried apricots, raisins, nuts, caramel, and RANCIO, the typical Madeira note.

• *Malmsey*: Malvasia grapes, less often met with than Verdelho, need even more warmth than Boal, but they also develop a higher sugar content, making Malmsey the sweetest of the Madeira wines. The greater acidity of this variety, however, balances it out. It is very popular in Anglo-Saxon countries as a liqueur wine. It has great fullness and length and in age

Two birds with one stone: vegetables can be grown under the trellises where the vines are cultivated. This is a necessity of life for the farmers, who often only cultivate very small areas.

Madeiras seem to have the ability to age forever, and the very oldest vintages are among the rarest delicacies in the world.

it displays fine notes of cocoa and chocolate.

• *Sercial*: This variety prefers the north side of the island and cooler vineyards. It produces the driest and rarest Madeira which, after ten years, develops its exceedingly full and elegant BOUQUET, increasing in subtlety and refinement over further decades.

• *Terrantez*: There are a few very rare old wines of unbelievable refinement and longevity left from this legendary variety, almost exterminated by the phylloxera outbreak. The Barbeito Terrantez of 1795 became very famous.

• *Verdelho*: This widespread, early-ripening variety also likes the north side of the island. It produces a medium-dry Madeira with a restrained sweetness and fine acidity, which after long aging develops a highly individual smoky aroma with a tang of iodine.

Not all Madeira is the same

Not even the island in the Atlantic was safe from phylloxera, the vine louse. Here, too, the greedy pests did their work and destroyed the stock of high-quality vines. In replanting, many of the wine producers on the island took the cheaper option for economic reasons, and that meant either hybrids or Negra Mole. This is why there are only a few areas left today planted with high-quality varieties and producing high-quality wine. It is also why most Madeira is destined to be used for cooking, and is made by the *estufa* procedure in tanks.

Finest is the lowest level of drinkable Madeira and is three years old. Reserve is five years old, partly aged in the barrel. Special Reserve or 10 Years Old is mainly based on the top-quality grape varieties and is aged for at least 10 years in the barrel. After 15 years of aging, the label is marked 15 Years Old or, more rarely, Extra Reserve. Vintage Madeiras are the peak of quality, aged for at least 20 years in pipes and matured for a further two years in the bottle.

Patrick Fiévez

EASTERN EUROPE

EASTERN EUROPE

Following the collapse of the former communist bloc in 1989, eastern Europe's wine-growing countries have now started to reorganize. The greatest challenge many of them faced, and indeed still face, is the need for a complete change of outlook. When the wine industry and prices were regulated by the state, the emphasis was on the size of yields, with quality very much a peripheral concern. Today, the wines have to be exported to the West, as the export markets in the East are no longer available to the same extent that they were before the political changes. This means that the managers of cooperatives and growers have to adapt to a completely new state of affairs. The need for reorientation will be even greater after these countries join the E.U.—in 2004 for Hungary and the Czech and Slovak Republics; Romania and Bulgaria should follow in 2007. Once they join, these countries will also be subject to E.U. regulations on wine

production, not those of their own country. Competition with other countries is fierce, and wines from eastern Europe must measure up against products from everywhere in the world in order to win customers. Suddenly, the focus is on the quality of the wines, while the quantities produced have to be drastically reduced. Although great progress has been made the reorientation process is not yet complete.

Until 1990 there was a clear *status quo* in the European wine industry. On the one hand, there were the twelve member states of the European Community, as it was then, of which seven were wine producers (representing almost 50 percent of the world's wine-growing area, with 10 million acres or 4 million ha), and on the other hand the ten C.O.M.E.C.O.N. states with five wine-producing countries, Bulgaria, Romania, Hungary, Czechoslovakia, and the U.S.S.R. (representing around 20 percent of the world's

wine-growing area with 5 million acres or 2 million ha). But while this second economic community no longer exists, many of the old structures persist, in terms both of people's attitudes and their everyday circumstances. Despite privatization, the vineyards of numerous cooperatives and estates in Hungary and Bulgaria remain in the hands of the state. In some coun-

tries, however, a new generation of wine producers is developing who have recognized how important a change of outlook is. They are open to advice from colleagues in other countries on matters such as cultivation, grape picking, and winemaking techniques, and their first efforts are already bearing fruit. In Slovenia and Hungary some excellent examples have been in existence for a few years now. These wines are well able to stand comparison with those produced by their international competitors. Croatia, too, is on the path to producing some genuinely good wines.

In order to attract consumers in the West, products from the past, such as basic branded wines, must be replaced with quality products. There is great ambition, a lot of potential in terms of soil types and climate, and a solid basis in the form of both indigenous and foreign grape varieties. Growers from the western wine-producing countries who have recognized this are investing a great deal of commitment into their attempts to exploit the change of circumstances in the East. Primarily in Hungary, but also in the other countries, first-class producers from Tuscany, major growers from Bordeaux, and German merchants and wine companies are joining forces with local growers to produce wines to international standards. In many cases, this is being done with grape varieties that have a worldwide reputation, such as Cabernet Sauvignon, and the remarkable results have already been unveiled at various trade fairs. Journalists traveling through the region have reported high levels of investment and great effort on the part of local figures in the wine business.

A number of producers are also now putting their faith in the quality of regional grapes such as Furmint, Rebola, and Plavac Mali in an attempt to capture the West's specialty wine market. When made using modern techniques, these wines are perfectly capable of taking up the position they deserve in the world of wine.

Left
Along with international varieties that have now become very widespread, native red wines can also be heartily recommended.

Right
In the case of white wines, these lesser-known regional grape varieties are a constant source of surprise.

Not only do Hungary's wine-growing regions have a glorious past, they also have a lot of potential for the future.

Hungary

Of all the countries of eastern Europe, it is probably only Hungary that can boast a truly world-famous wine of exceptional quality. Tokaji Aszú has been a source of self-indulgent pleasure for lovers of rare wines for centuries.

Volcanic Subsoil

At one time the area we know today as Hungary was covered by the Pannonian Sea, and surrounded by the foothills of the Alps, the Carpathians, and the Dinaric Alps. The country's unique landscape is dominated by numerous small and long-extinct volcanoes, which created ideal soils for the cultivation of vines. The wine-growing area of Tokaj in the north of Hungary lies on the same degree of latitude as Colmar, in Alsace, while Hungary's most southern wine region, Villány, shares its latitude with that of Cognac, in southwest France.

In all likelihood it was the Romans who introduced wine and winemaking expertise to the area around the Danube, which at that time was part of their province of Pannonia. When the Magyars conquered the territory in the 9th

Wine from the previous year's harvest is poured at the wine festival in Badacsony, named after its box-shaped mountain.

Opposite
At the winegrowers' procession in Szigliget, in the Balaton region, grapes of the popular Szürkebarát variety, a type of Pinot Gris, are arranged into the shape of the traditional "wine bell."

century, they discovered thriving vineyards there. The Mongol invasion of 1241 caused such devastation to the vineyards that King Béla IV deemed it necessary to promote the replanting of vines, as Hungary's climate is so ideally suited to vine growing and a wide spectrum of grape varieties. These provide the basis for a range of wines, from dry and very aromatic whites to the famous Aszú, the sweet wine from the Tokaj region. In addition to these are many powerful reds made from both indigenous and international grape varieties.

The Hungarian wine industry faced enormous problems when the state put a stop to all subsidies in 1989. The area under vine cultivation shrank from 618,000 acres (250,000 ha) in the 1960s to 242,155 acres (98,000 ha) today. The areas that were closed down and cleared were, however, chiefly vineyards without *appellation*. Up to the time of the Soviet Union's collapse, Hungarian wine producers exported 50 percent of their production to the U.S.S.R. After its disintegration, export to countries in western Europe was made difficult by the high levels of competition. By the end of the 20th century, only 25 percent of production was being exported.

Hungarian Wine Laws

In July 1990 the old wine legislation, which dated back to 1970, was replaced by a stricter set of laws that took its cue from the regulations of the European Community, as it was known then. The classification system comprises five new grades of quality: table wines (*Asztali Bor*), regional wines or *vins de pays* (*Tajjelegü Asztali*), quality wines (*Minösegi Bor*), special quality wines (*Különleges Minösegi*), and finally wines made from overripe grapes and grapes affected by NOBLE ROT (*Aszú*), and VINTAGE wines (at least five years old).

Wine-growing Regions and Grape Varieties

Hungary has three large wine-growing areas, all of which are governed by a continental climate with hot, dry summers and very cold winters. Stretching down from Budapest to the south, between Hungary's two great rivers, the Danube and the Tisza, lies the Great Hungarian Plain, the Puszta, with its sandy soil. Growers in this region, also known as the Alföld, produce roughly half the output of the entire country, predominantly light red wines and medium-dry or sweet whites. The wines from Transdanubia, the area surrounding Lake Balaton, are primarily medium-dry and sweet whites. In north and northeastern Hungary are the Eger and Tokaj regions (Tokajhegyalja). The soil in Eger is dominated by black loam of volcanic origin. Mainly red varieties thrive here, although there are also some white wines worth mentioning. Tokaj is almost certainly the

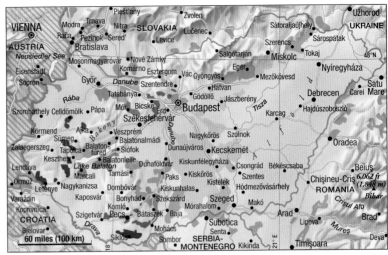

Tokajhegyalja
Bükkalja
Eger
Mátraalja
Ászár-Neszmély
Pannonhalma-Sokoróalja
Sopron
Mór
Etyek-Buda
Somló
Balatonmelléke
Balatonfelvidék
Badacsony
Balatonfüred-Csopak
Dél-Balaton
Tolna
Kunság
Csongrád
Hajós-Baja
Szekszárd
Mecsekalja
Villány
Wine-growing areas in neighboring countries

country's oldest wine region. Its world-famous dry and sweet white wines are made from grapes grown on volcanic soil and loess-rich subsoil.

These main wine-producing areas are subdivided into a total of 22 smaller distinct regions, each with its own stock of grape varieties. Along with the popular varieties such as Cabernet Sauvignon, Cabernet Franc, Merlot, Pinot Noir, Sauvignon Blanc, Chardonnay, Riesling, Muscat Ottonel, and others, there are also indigenous varieties. These are Ezerjó, Furmint, Mézesfehér, Hárslevelü, Cirfandli, Leányka, and Szürkebarát for white wines and Kadarka and Kékfrankos for red.

Along with Tokaji, Hungary's best-known wine, light, dry and fruity whites, such as the Alföld wines with their frequently pronounced acidity, are also made almost exclusively by cooperatives. The wines made from the Chardonnay grape are often very well structured and light. In the Etyek-Buda region to the

Each individual bunch of grapes is carefully cut from the vine.

The grapes are emptied into tubs ready for transporting.

In the winery, the stalks are removed before PRESSING.

The grapes are pushed down into the pressing vat.

Even today, traditional wooden winepresses are used.

The fresh MUST flows out of the press.

west and southwest of the capital Budapest, the international grape varieties Chardonnay, Pinot Noir, Pinot Blanc, and Sauvignon Blanc are grown. Furmint, the grape from which Tokaji Aszú is made, is grown in the Somló region northwest of Lake Balaton, likewise in volcanic soil. In northern Transdanubia, north of Lake Balaton, central Europe's great white grapes, such as Riesling, Pinot Gris (Szürkebarát, meaning the "gray monk," after the Cistercians who brought it with them to these parts), Traminer, Muscat, and Müller-Thurgau are widespread. They make a fruity white wine with peach and apricot aromas. To the south of the lake, predominantly the Dél-Balaton region, Cabernet Sauvignon, and Pinot Noir (Nagyburgundi) grapes are also encountered; they sometimes turn out slightly sweet due to a certain amount of RESIDUAL SUGAR. The renowned and once sought-after indigenous Kadarka variety is still grown in the southern Transdanubia region of Szekszárd, on the eastern bank of the Danube, albeit in small quantities. It is virtually non-existent in the north, however, and is grown only on one well-known vineyard on the road leading from Budapest to the Tokaj region, where it was once widespread. In the Eger region, named after one of the most visited cities in Hungary, at the foot of the Bükk mountains, the soil is also volcanic.

This area is where Bull's Blood, the famous Hungarian red wine, is made, as well as Egri Bikaver, today a blend of Cabernet, Merlot, Kékoporto (Blauer Portugieser), and Kékfrankos (Blaufränkish or Lemberger) grapes.

ALFÖLD (THE GREAT PLAIN)

The largest single wine-growing area south of Budapest is also one of Hungary's youngest. The vines here were planted mainly after the PHYLLOXERA catastrophe, as the vine pests do not survive terribly well on sandy soil. This part of the country is characterized by hot summers and cold winters. In the spring there are frequent late frosts, which pose a danger to the young shoots, but in the summer the sandy subsoil heats up to such an extent that, on occasions, ground temperatures as high as 140°F (60°C) have been recorded.

In the remaining regions, mainly Olaszrizling (Welschriesling or Riesling Italico) and certain indigenous grape varieties are grown, as well as international grape varieties such as Cabernet Sauvignon, Merlot, and Pinot Noir. The wine producers make light red wines and whites that are low in acidity. The best red wines of this area originate in the Hajós-Baja region. Hungarovin, a Budapest-based wine company, is one of the major large producers here.

The end of grape-picking is celebrated with a large festival at which some lively dancing takes place.

The Wine Regions Around Lake Balaton

Sheltered vineyards and steep slopes with a sandy basalt base, assisted by a climate regulator in the form of Lake Balaton, provide perfect conditions for the cultivation of vines. This fact was recognized by the Romans, who planted more vineyards here than in any other part of their province of Pannonia.

The large wine-growing area of Transdanubia is split into two parts by Lake Balaton, each of which embraces a number of different regions, and stretches from Sopron in the northwest to Villány, the region around Siklós, in the south. The elongated shape of this large lake harmonizes the temperatures and provides the soils with a balanced source of water. In summer it lowers the heat and in winter it acts as a natural store of warmth. The northern part of Transdanubia stretches down to the lake from the Austrian and Slovak borders. This side of the lake, in particular, has been of special significance to wine production in Hungary for centuries. A high proportion of the vineyards are on slopes made of volcanic loam soils. Predominantly white wines are made from the grapes grown here. The most widely grown grape is Olaszrisling, which produces a fresh, spicy wine.

In the northwesterly region of Sopron, on the other hand, exclusively red wines are made. In Somló, a small wine-growing area to the northwest of the lake, around 1,483 acres (600 ha) of vines grow on the slopes of the

extinct volcano Mount Somló. The white wines from this region were once as highly prized as the famous Tokaji, and there was a very good reason for this: for centuries the wine was supplied to the Habsburg court. It was drunk on rulers' wedding nights in the belief that it would help them father male offspring. Presumably it was enjoyed on other occasions as well.

The area south of the lake, reaching down to the Croatian border, was planted with vineyards only a few years ago. Both red and white varieties thrive in the sandy, loess-rich subsoil. The other important areas are Villány, Szekszárd, and Mecsekalja. While mainly red grapes are grown in the mountains of Villány, growers around Siklós concentrate on making white wines. Some of this region's most ambitious and promising growers are Attila Gere, József Bock, and Kúria Malatinszky from Villány.

The most famous grape variety in Szekszárd is the Kadarka, which, given its long vegetation

phase, is able to ripen fully here before being harvested. Among the best local producers are Ferenc and Csaba Vesztergombi. Powerful, spicy wines are made in Hungary's warmest region, the Mecsek mountains (also known as Mecsekalja). This is possible in spite of the long periods of very dry weather.

SELECT PRODUCER

BALATONBOGLÁRI R.T.✶✶✶
BALATONBOGLÁR
8,648 acres (3,500 ha); 24,000,000 bottles
• Wines: Riesling, Chardonnay, Muscat, red wines
This formerly state-owned enterprise, founded in 1952, is today one of the largest in the country and is now owned by a German firm, Henkell & Söhnlein. Most of the wines made here originate in the Lake Balaton region.

Extensive vineyards stretch back all the way around Lake Balaton, Europe's largest lake.

EGER

The old town of Eger is without doubt one of Hungary's most beautiful towns and is also one of the country's most important centers of wine trading. The most famous wine from the area of the same name is the red wine Egri Bikavér, or Bull's Blood. It has gone on to become the region's main brand-name wine and has made the region famous abroad too. The Kadarka grape, which was once the predominant variety in this blend, has now been replaced by Kékfrankos. The other grapes that go into Bull's Blood are Cabernet Sauvignon, Kékoporto, and Merlot. The name is taken from a legend that describes how, in the 16th century, the Eger fortress had to be defended against Turkish attackers. When the Magyars' strength abandoned them after five weeks of siege, the castle commander ordered the men to be given wine. After drinking it, their fighting spirit returned and their beards, dripping with wine, glistened red. At the sight of this, the Turks, who were superior in number, took flight, in the belief that their opponents had been drinking the blood of bulls.

Hungary's winegrowers are showing an impressive dynamic with these new plantings near Eger.

Opposite
The scenery around the old wine town of Eger is dominated by a patchwork of small vineyards.

Eger's "Bull's Blood" has a modern profile thanks to Cabernet and Merlot.

In its early years, Bull's Blood is a dark red, powerful wine and has very dominant TANNINS immediately after bottling. It is a legendary wine that recalls a time when wines were allowed to mature properly in the cellar. Today, western European palates demand wines with softer tannins that can be drunk young. When buying a bottle of Egri Bikáver, you should make sure it is sealed with an official state serial number. This guarantees that the wine really is from Eger, and protects the producers from counterfeiting.

The climate around the town of Eger is dry and very warm during the summer, although due to its long winters, the vegetation phase starts particularly late. In addition to the renowned Bull's Blood, interesting white wines are made from the Olaszrisling and Leányka varieties, with the latter producing the better examples. This grape is grown exclusively in the Eger region and, as a general rule, matures very early. The grapes have a high sugar content and the wines possess an intense honey AROMA.

Just as famous as its wines are the town's enormous wine cellars. With branches extending out from beneath the castle under large parts of the town, visitors are repeatedly fascinated by this extensive underground system. In earlier centuries, these cellars not only provided winemakers with storage space for their wines, they were also used as a place of refuge during times of war.

The wine industry in Eger remains in a state of transition. There is a new emphasis on quality and the wineries have started to modernize. Visiting the Egervin cooperative, it is difficult not to make a comparison with the cooperative wineries of southern France of around 25 to 30 years ago, with their large wooden barrels and old concrete vats. This winery, privatized in June 1993, was updated in 1997 to meet today's standards through the introduction of modern technology and equipment.

SELECT PRODUCERS IN EGER

G.I.A.***
EGER
Wine was first produced by this cooperative enterprise, formed by the Hungarian Tibor Gál (G), the Tuscan Marchese Incisa (I), and the German merchant Burkard Bovensiepen with his firm Alpina (A), in 1993. Since then, this winery has been responsible for some of Hungary's best wines, among them Chardonnay, Cabernet Sauvignon, and Kékfrankos.

HUNGAROVIN**
BUDAPEST
This enormous company makes wines from grapes grown throughout the whole of Hungary, but its Eger wine is worth mentioning in its own right. The enterprise has been owned by the German wine company Henkell & Söhnlein since the beginning of the 1990s and has switched since then from concentrating exclusively on quantity to placing a firm emphasis on quality.

Tokaji

This famous wine, and the region it comes from, Tokajhegyalja, take their names from the town in the north of the country. The name of the wine has nothing to do with Tokay d'Alsace (the Alsace synonym for Pinot Gris), however, nor with Tocai Friulano, which is widespread in northern Italy. Tokaji, meaning "from (the town of) Tokaj"—has been a wine of renown since the 17th century, although it was hardly ever seen in western Europe following the collapse of the Austro-Hungarian Empire in 1918, and even less so after the communists came to power in 1949. The vineyards are situated just a few miles from the borders with Slovakia and the Ukraine, and cover 12,350 acres (5,000 ha) of mostly south-facing slopes. The Bodrog and Tisza rivers dominate the plain and create the specific climatic conditions which allow the indigenous grape varieties (Furmint and Hárslevelü) to concentrate their sugar content in the fall, either as a result of BOTRYTIS CINEREA (noble rot) or by allowing the grapes to dry out on the vine. These are the same conditions that are found in the Sauternes region. But the climatic conditions alone do not explain the exceptional properties of the best-

The exquisite sweet Eszencias and Aszús are once again delighting wine lovers. But extremely good dry Furmints as well as Hárslevelüs, benefiting from modern winemaking techniques, are also achieving considerable success.

Thanks to international joint ventures, the area around Tokaj is currently undergoing change on a large scale.

known of Tokaji wines produced from the overripe grapes known as *aszú*. The grape varieties, the volcanic soil, the classic VINIFICA-TION, and excellent storage conditions in tuf (volcanic detritus) caves with their rich micro-flora and walls thickly coated with mold—a these factors help make Tokaji what it is. The yield naturally depends on the crop and number of vines per acre. As a rule, the vine yards are planted with up to 10,000 vines allowing the required quality to be achieved But vineyards dating back to the communis era, with little more than 800 vines per acre

(2,000 per ha) produce outstanding results. Thanks to foreign investment from France, Spain and Britain, the vineyards in the northeast of the country are today experiencing a genuine renaissance. In the last few decades obsolete winemaking methods have affected quality and the producers could not keep pace with international developments. In addition to the high-quality sweet wines, dry white wines are also made in the Tokaj region, among them the well-known Tokaji Szamorodni Száraz.

OLDER THAN THE WINES OF SAUTERNES

Wine has been made in this region since before the invasion of the Magyars, who gave their name to the present-day inhabitants of the country. In the Middle Ages, winegrowers moved into the area around Tokaj from Italy, and also from Wallonia in the south of what is now Belgium. The wine's breakthrough did not come until the end of the 15th century, however, when the first Aszú sweet wines were made, predating the wines of Sauternes by about 200 years, and the first great wines from the Rhine valley by a century. Supposedly from the 16th century onwards, large quantities of the legendary Magyar wine were exported. Pope Pius IV was given some Tokaji Aszú as a gift by the Hungarian archbishop Draskovich at the Council of Trent in 1562. This could have marked the beginning of the wine's ascent. It should come as no surprise, therefore, that the world's prominent figures were initially astonished and then delighted by the unusual taste and character of Tokaji Aszú. It rapidly became the wine of kings and Czars, and for several centuries was a regular feature at the banquets of all the courts of Europe. "*vinum regorum, rex vinorum*" (the wine of kings and the king of wines) declared King Louis XIV of France, who prized the wine beyond measure. Writers such as Voltaire, Rabelais, and Goethe looked to this Hungarian wine for inspiration, valuing as they did its creative powers. During the course of the following centuries, numerous heads of European countries sang the wine's praises and helped it acquire its reputation. It is even extolled in the Hungarian national anthem.

Like countless others, the vineyards of Hungary were attacked and largely destroyed by phylloxera at the end of the 19th century. While they were being built up again, the country experienced major political upheavals, from the announcement of the republic at the end of the First World War to the agricultural reforms of 1945 and the end of the communist era in 1989.

These were decades that unfortunately did not serve Hungarian wine well in terms of quality. Since the fall of the Iron Curtain, however, the situation has started to change for the better, thanks to foreign investment and the long-overdue modernization of the wineries. Following some turbulent times, the great Tokaji Aszú has woken up again from its Sleeping Beauty-like slumber, as has the very aromatic and dry white wine made from the Furmint grape.

INTERNATIONAL INVESTMENT ENCOURAGES A NEW START

Following recovery from the phylloxera catastrophe, which was responsible for destroying a large part of the vineyards, and the replanting of vines, the wines of Tokaj became difficult to obtain in the west as a result of the isolationist policy of the communist bloc. The vineyards were nationalized in their entirety during the communist era and run by agricultural combines that were set up from 1949 onwards. Quality began to sink steadily: systematic pasteurization and OXIDIZATION, or even the

The wine of kings, the king of wines—but also now a treat for democrats.

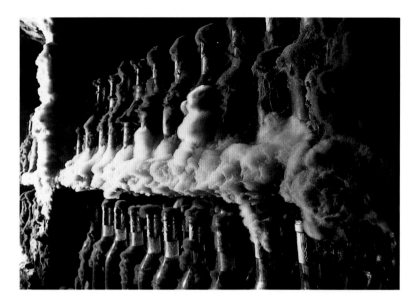

Tokaji Aszú matures in cellars, some of which date from the 18th century. In the Tokaj wine museum the bottles filled with this nectar are stored with thick layers of mold growing on them, which heightens the impression that this place is truly ancient.

addition of alcohol to stop the FERMENTATION process, brought it to an all-time low. This mass-produced wine with its oxidized taste was exported (mainly in exchange for natural gas) primarily to the Soviet Union, its largest market in the period following the Second World War. From 1991, western European investors from France, Spain, and Britain took advantage of the Hungarian government's decision to dispose of 12,360 acres (5,000 ha) of vineyards. This resulted in the formation of a number of jointly owned companies, many of them involving the investment of French insurance companies. The management of Château Pajzos was entrusted to two Bordeaux enologists, Arcaute and Rolland. Today Jean-Louis Labarde owns the majority of the estate. The company that makes the most famous of all Spanish wines, Vega Sicilia (the Oremus winery), Cana (a cooperative from the Nantes region), G.M.F. (the Etzele estate), and

many others also produce wine in the Tokaj region. All these operations are striving to revive the original quality of the product.

VINIFICATION OF ASZÚ

Tokaji Aszú is made using a unique method. The overripe Furmint, Hárslevelü, and Muscat Lunel grapes, affected by the *Botrytis cinerea* mold, are individually picked and collected in small, 55-pound (25-kg) tubs (*puttonyos*) throughout October and November, according to strict selection criteria. Careful mashing of the grapes produces Aszú (meaning "dried") paste. Next, the desired number of *puttonyos* (between three and six) is added to 36 gallons (136 liters—the volume of the local barrel or *gönc* used) of fresh, white grape must. In contrast to previous methods, today's ambitious Tokaji vintners make sure this base wine is also of very good quality and has a certain amount of residual sugar. The number of *puttonyos* used determines the grade of sweetness under which the wine is later classified: the more *puttonyos* used, the sweeter the wine. The labels on the bottles indicate this level of sweetness. After mashing and pressing, the wine is matured in small wooden barrels for five to seven years and later bottled in the characteristic white, 17-fl oz (50-cl) bottles. Tasting a great Tokaji vintage is an unforgettable experience. The more *puttonyos* one uses, the more concentrated, rich, intense, and complex the wine becomes. As the high degree of sweetness fades it is met by a gentle acidity, providing balance and perfect harmony. The wines display an amazingly wide-ranging raisin, honey, plum, and apricot aroma. Sweet wine rarities such as this taste wonderful with warm apricot tart,

SELECT PRODUCERS OF TOKAJI

THE OLDEST A.O.C. IN THE WORLD?
As long ago as 1700, many years before the geographical limits were set for the fine Portuguese wines of the Douro valley, a list was drawn up of the best Tokaji vineyards, classifying the wines (in Latin) into three grades. The wines were placed in the first, second, or third categories according to characteristics that would still win A.O.C. plaudits today. Such a system was not introduced in France until 1935.

GRÓF DEGENFELD***
TARCEL
173 acres (70 ha) • Wines: Furmint, Hárslevelü, Sárga Muskotály
The former enologist with the Royal Tokaj Wine Company, Sarolta Bárdos, has already vinified her first top vintage with this estate that was newly established in 1996. The family of Count Degenfeld formerly owned two castles in the Tokaj region.

ISTVÁN SZEPSY***
MÁD
49 acres (20 ha)
István Szepsy is one of the great reformers of Tokaj. He has introduced a strict reduction in yields and gentle processing in the winery, which make his wines the very best of the region. With the backing of an American investor, he has also succeeded in resurrecting the Királyudvar winery. Since 1998 he's been president of the Tokaj Renaissance organization.

BODROG VÁRHEGY**
BODROG-KERESZÚR
37 acres + 370 acres (15 ha + 150 ha); bought-in grapes; 250,000 bottles • Wines: Furmint, Hárslevelü, Muscat Lunel
This enterprise buys in grapes from various contract growers and produces dry and white Szamorodni, both well worth trying, and an excellent Aszú, all of which are also exported to the West.

Behind the simple facades of the fermentation buildings in Tokajhegyalja extensive cellars stretch far back into the hill.

Tokaji enjoys its excellent reputation because it ages so well.

The Tokaj wine museum has typical cellar storage and a collection of legendary vintages.

Tokaji is still an exceptional wine today, although it is now available to a wider public.

hazelnut cake, duck with plums or orange, or endive leaves with Roquefort and green walnuts.

In very good years there is an even sweeter variety of Aszú, which is known as Eszencia. A particular type of YEAST is required for this. The wine can have residual sugar of up to 92 ounces per gallon (650 grams per liter) and matures for ten years in the barrel before being bottled. This Eszencia variety is really a viscous Tokaji with low levels of alcohol, which is made from the run-off must of the Aszú. Because of the high sugar content (up to 60 percent), fermentation requires several years.

Szamorodni (meaning "as grown") is also produced in Tokaj and is a simpler variety of the wine, made from common grapes widely grown in the region. The grapes used are only partly affected by botrytis, and are not selected individually. This wine displays varying levels of sweetness, depending on the quality of the harvest and the proportion of Aszú grapes it contains. In addition to sweet varieties of Szamorodni, there are also medium-dry and dry varieties. The grapes not affected by noble rot yield a pleasant-tasting white wine with a pronounced light fruit and a delicate aroma. To distinguish between the two types, Szamorodni is known as *száras* when it is dry, and *edes* when it is sweet.

THE CZECH REPUBLIC AND SLOVAKIA

At the beginning of the 1990s, the former Czechoslovakia was split into the Czech Republic and Slovakia. At this time the two countries had a total of 116,000 acres (47,000 ha) of vineyards, of which 89,000 acres (36,000 ha) were in production. Today the area is smaller. Most of the vineyards are in Slovakia, mainly in the south and southwest of the country, while in the Czech Republic, grapes are grown only in the southeast, in Moravia, and around the town of Melnik in Bohemia. Other than these Bohemian vineyards, the vine-growing areas border Austria directly, and those in Slovakian territory extend as far as the Hungarian Tokaji-producing region.

The vineyards of Slovakia cover around 49,419 acres (20,000 ha) of gentle slopes, a maximum of 800 feet (250 m) above sea level, and extend as far as the plain of the Danube basin. They are protected from cold northerly winds by high elevations. The climate is continental, with hot summers, cool winters, and moderate precipitation. The range of grapes grown is similar to that of Austria. The main white varieties are a tangy Riesling, Pinot Blanc, Ryzlink Vlassky (Welschriesling or Riesling Italico), a fresh Müller-Thurgau, peppery Grüner Veltliner (Veltlinské Zelené), a pleasant Sylvaner, and a spicy Irsay Oliver, a native variety resembling Muscadelle. Among the best reds are the full-bodied and fruity Blaufränkisch (Frankovka) and Saint Laurent (Vavrinecké or Svatovavrinecké), representing around 35 percent of the total. The best wines of Slovakia come from the area around the capital, Bratislava, and the extreme east of the country,

the Slovakian part of Tokaj. The estates of Milan Pavelka and the Matysák family in Pezinok, 12½ miles (20 km) from Bratislava, are currently two of the country's best-known wineries. Pavelka has been running the area's largest estate himself since 1995. The Matysák family is developing the estate to entice an increasing number of visitors interested in wine from Bratislava. They have built a restaurant on their estate and sell their best wines on the spot. The Ostrozovic estate, in Kosice in Slovakian Tokaj, has 17 acres (7 ha) of vineyards and concentrates on the production of superb Aszú wines. Very good dry varieties are produced here too.

As in the Czech and Slovak Republics, the number of privately-owned vineyards is also rapidly increasing in Slovenia, and they are producing more and more pleasing wines.

SLOVENIA

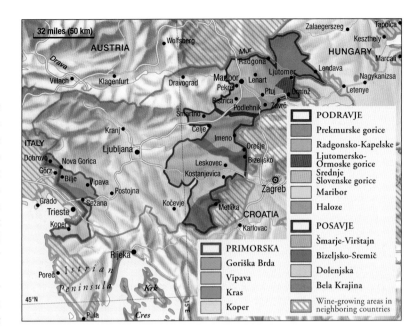

Slovenia, in 1991, was one of Yugoslavia's first republics to demand independence. Its wine-growing areas can be divided into three: Primorski, Podravski, and Posavski, with the first two of these having the largest share of the growing area (about 40 percent each). When Slovenia was part of the Austro-Hungarian Empire, its wines were much sought after. At that time, the vineyards covered around 124,000 acres (50,000 ha) of land; today they cover about 59,303 acres (24,000 ha).

Primorski lies on the country's eastern border with Italy, and the Italian wine-growing region of Collio was part of what is now Slovenia right up to the First World War. The soils are dominated by limestone and red clay. Podravski runs along the border with the Austrian region of southern Styria. Its vineyards are often situated on steep, sometimes terraced slopes with chalky or clay subsoil. The wines produced here are predominantly aromatic, fruity whites.

Among the grape varieties now offered by the Slovenian growers are Laski Riesling (Welschriesling), Gewürztraminer, Pinot Blanc, Riesling (Renski Rizling), Sauvignon Blanc, and the native Sipon variety (comparable to the Hungarian Furmint). A high plateau in the Primorski wine-growing area supports mainly red varieties, such as Refosco (Teran), Barbera, and Cabernet Sauvignon.

A large proportion of the wine is still produced by cooperative wineries, although the number of private estates is growing steadily. Techniques used in the cooperatives do not yet match the latest modern standards, as a rule. Indeed, many wines are still being sweetened and can be relatively characterless, but there are praiseworthy exceptions. More and more committed winemakers are recognizing the potential of their vineyards and are on the way to producing wines that will soon stand up well to comparison with those of neighboring Collio in Italy and Styria in Austria. A small number of producers also now enjoy international recognition.

SELECT SLOVENIAN PRODUCERS

MOVIA****
DOBROVO
44 acres (18 ha) • *Wines: Tokay, Rebula, Pinot Gris, Pinot Blanc, Chardonnay, Sauvignon Blanc, Merlot*
This winery is currently being run by the seventh generation of Ales Kristancic's family. He was the first winemaker in Yugoslavia, as it was then, to experiment with red wine matured in *barriques*—and with great success too, his aim being to preserve the characteristics of the grape without overloading the wine with wood. By increasing the density of the vines and radically reducing the quantities produced, he has managed to produce concentrated, characterful wines.

RADGONSKE GORICE***
GORNJA RADGONA
741 acres (300 ha); bought-in grapes; 2,500,000 bottles • *Wines: Welschriesling, Sipon, Riesling, Sauvignon Blanc, Traminer, Müller-Thurgau, Chardonnay, Ranina*
This combine and winery are backed up by 150 years of winemaking tradition. They are well-known for their sparkling wines, which have received numerous awards and won a degree of international recognition.

UNIVERZA V MARIBORU***
MARIBOR
44 acres (18 ha); 20,000 bottles
The wine estate belonging to the university of Maribor, founded in 1820, can look back on nearly 200 years of history.

VIPAVA***
VIPAVA
4,201 acres (1,700 ha) • *Wines: Zelen, Pinela, Rebula, Malvasia, Sauvignon Blanc, Chardonnay, Pinot Blanc, Welschriesling, Merlot, Cabernet Sauvignon, Barbera*
This winery, founded in 1894, is one of the most innovative cooperative associations in the country. It has its origins in the oldest peasants' cooperative winery in Slovenia, which had branches in Vienna, Prague, Graz, and Trier. Its wines, which are typical of the region, are popular abroad, and have won a number of awards. Those made from the local Zelen and Pinela grapes are an unusual feature.

Bulgaria

Vineyards in the Land of Roses

Of all the countries belonging to the former eastern bloc, Bulgaria, which borders Romania to the north, Serbia and Macedonia to the west, the Black Sea to the east, and Turkey and Greece to the south, has benefited most from the new political and economic conditions. New export markets in many west European countries (notably Great Britain, Germany, and the Benelux countries) have been discovered for its red and white wines. Both the state-run and newly privatized wineries have thus been able to prepare for the future with new investment and, thanks to their exceptionally good value for money—a strong argument for buying Bulgarian wines—win a good market position for themselves.

The history of the kingdom of Bulgaria began in 680. Two hundred years later the nation experienced a golden age that brought important innovations to a wide area. The brothers St. Cyril and St. Methodius developed the Cyrillic alphabet which was to have a decisive influence on the whole of Slavic literature and culture. Numerous buildings, still standing or in ruins, bear witness today to the flourishing architectural activity and prosperity of this period and the centuries that followed. Until the end of the Second World War, which brought communist

Melnik, south of Sofia, has its own variety of grape, also known as Melnik. Another name for this is Bulgarian Syrah.

rule to the country, Bulgaria's wine industry had been almost exclusively in the hands of small growers who pressed their own wines. In 1944 the government took the decision to introduce a system of collectivization, which had been virtually unknown hitherto. New specialists were trained in winemaking schools, and numerous foreign grape varieties, for example Cabernet Sauvignon, Merlot, and Riesling were planted in addition to indigenous varieties such as Gamza and Mavrud.

Bulgaria's main wine exporter today has around 365,700 acres (148,000 ha) of vineyards, a smaller area than it had in the past. In fact, according to experts only around 247,100 acres (100,000 ha) are under cultivation. Bulgaria used to export a large amount of wine to the U.S.S.R. but, in the 1980s, as a result of a campaign against alcoholism in the Soviet Union, many Bulgarian vineyards were closed. Since the opening-up of western European markets, new vineyards are being planted again, mostly on sloping sites.

The climate is similar to that of Bulgaria's neighboring countries: hot summers and cold winters. Temperatures can climb to over 104°F (40°C) in the summer months and drop below –13°F (–25°C) in winter. The Black Sea in the north and the two big rivers, the Danube and the Maritsa, generally soften the effect of these extreme differences in temperature. Annual precipitation ranges roughly from 18^1/$_2$ inches (47 cm) to 37^1/$_2$ inches (95 cm).

The Main Wine-growing Areas

There are seven main wine-growing areas in Bulgaria, of which five have very well-defined borders: Dunavska Ravnina in the northwest, Thrakien in the south, Tsjernomorski Raion in the east, Dolinata na Struma in the southwest and Podbalkanski Raion in central Bulgaria.

In the north, in the Danube valley, and in the plains between the Danube and the Balkan Mountains, grapes grow both in the plains and in the mountains (up to 1,300 feet/400 m). The main varieties grown in the alluvial and loess plains are Cabernet Sauvignon, Merlot, Aligoté, Muscat Ottonel, Gamza (a Bulgarian grape with distinctive aromas, spicy and full-bodied while relatively young), and the white Misket grape, which is indigenous to the famous Valley of the Roses in central Bulgaria, and produces a flowery wine with overtones of Muscat.

Soil conditions in the south of the country are ideally suited to the Mavrud grape, from which a powerful wine is made, full-bodied in its early years and sometimes reminiscent of Mourvèdre.

The characterful white wines from the regions close to the Black Sea attain a real finesse: Riesling, Sauvignon, Chardonnay (aged in barrels made from young American oak), and some Gewürztraminer are the main ones. The coast in this area has a predominantly Mediterranean climate.

Another indigenous grape variety, Melnik, thrives in the warm climate of the Struma valley, to the south of the capital, Sofia. This grape, from the region that has given it its name, yields powerful wines with an intense BOUQUET and pronounced tannins. To a certain extent it can be seen as the Syrah of Bulgarian wines.

BULGARIAN WINE CLASSIFICATION

In 1978 regulations were introduced to classify Bulgarian wines. The standard-quality wines are known as *vins de table* and *vins de pays*. Wines with a geographical designation of origin (D.G.O., Declared Geographical Origin) carry the name of the *appellation*, region, district, and town or village. The top-quality wines are marketed under the name *controliran*, corresponding to the French A.O.C. designation (specific region of production, specific grape variety, prescribed quality), which has so far been awarded to 30 areas. In addition to these, there is a further category for fortified wines. The *kolektzione* quality designation is used for wines aged in wooden barrels, made of either native Bulgarian or American wood.

Yield levels—frequently too high—are a delicate subject, but Bulgarian growers deliver reasonable quality, in their export wines at least.

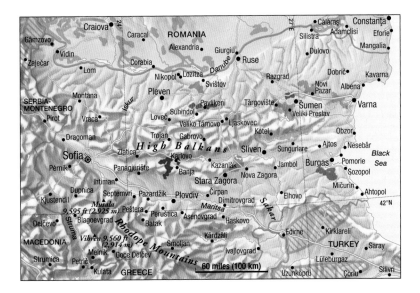

Average yields are 428 to 535 gallons per acre (40 to 50 hl/ha) for the D.G.O. wines and between 267 and 428 gallons per acre (25 and 40 hl/ha) for *controliran* wines.

PREPARING FOR THE FUTURE

Of all the countries of eastern Europe, Bulgaria is making the most determined efforts to ensure that the quality of its wines is directed toward the standards of its overseas sales markets. The fact that receipts are being invested in the re-equipping of the wineries is also having a positive effect. Around 70 percent of profits are reputedly flowing into the acquisition of new fermentation vats, presses, refrigeration plants, and *barriques*. The enologist Atanas Babaev is of the opinion that "the overall quality of Bulgarian wine has risen over the last few years thanks to this investment." He cites further reasons, for example the switch from large barrels made of Bulgarian oak to *barriques*, the mandatory de-stalking, and picking

DUNAVSKA RAVNINA
- Novo Selo
- Lozitza
- Svishtov
- Pavlikeni
- Suhindol
- Lyaskovetz

TSJERNOMORSKI RAION
- Preslav
- Chan Krum
- Varna
- Jujen Briag

PODBALKANSKI RAION
- Sungurlare
- Rozova Dolina

THRAKIEN
- Oriachovitza
- Asenovgrad
- Stambolovo
- Sakar

DOLINATA NA STRUMA
- Harsovo

Wine-growing areas in neighboring countries

Left
The areas bordering Macedonia and Greece offers an ideal climate for good red wines.

Next double page
Although Bulgaria is now exporting modern consumer wines, many of its producers are still dependent on old implements and methods.

at higher levels of ripeness than before. CHAP-TALIZATION (enriching with sugar) is hardly necessary, he claims, but nevertheless allowed, depending on the sugar levels of the grapes that have been picked. Californian Chardonnay and Sauvignon Blanc clones are currently being tested at a special site, as the use of these two grape varieties is going to become increasingly widespread over the next few years.

Although many vineyards remain in the hands of the state, the privatization of a number of wineries has brought some beneficial changes to Bulgarian wine production. Once Bulgaria is a member of the E.U. the attitude of the wine-growers will certainly gradually change. The Suhindol winery, founded in 1909, one of the oldest in the country, is Bulgaria's showpiece winery and has been displaying a remarkable dynamism over recent years. So far 400,000 U.S. dollars have been invested in its modernization, and each year sees the creation of new top-class wines, some of which are aged in barrels made of French oak. In 1998 American investors also put money into the former state-owned producer Vinprom Russe. In 2001 it merged with the Boyar Domain to make the new Boyar Estate, which is now the biggest wine producer in Bulgaria.

BULGARIA'S FIRST PRIVATE WINE PRODUCER

BOYAR ESTATE**−***
65,000,000 bottles • Wines: Sauvignon, Chardonnay, Riesling, Cabernet, Merlot, Gamza, Varietals, Reserve
This organization (Bulgaria's first private wine-producing enterprise) is known throughout the country as a producer that can be relied upon for its quality. For a while now Domaine Boyar has been concentrating on the production of first-class wines, with the aim of creating a new style of Bulgarian wine by combining the best features of the old and new worlds. Examples are:
• Cabernet Sauvignon Premium Oak, Iambol Winery (wine production in an ultra-modern winery, aging in new oak barrels).
• Merlot Premium Cuvée, Shumen Winery (one of Europe's most modern wineries).
• Cabernet Sauvignon Premium Reserve, Iambol Winery.
In addition to these wines, which represent the new Bulgarian wine industry, the following wine deserves a special mention:
• Royal Reserve***, 20,000–30,000 bottles per year; this Cabernet Sauvignon special reserve wine is made by one of the best wineries in the country, that of Lovico Suhindol for Boyar Estate, and is matured for 36 months in barrels of American oak.

Romania

After 6,000 years of vine growing, Romania is now undergoing a fresh start with an emphasis on quality.

Romania, the result of the unification of Walachia and Moldavia in 1862, is one of eastern Europe's major wine-producing nations and one of the ten largest wine exporters in the world. Wine production in the area of present-day Romania has an ancient tradition going back over 6,000 years. The vineyards currently cover around 617,500 acres (250,000 ha), and 20 percent of these are given over to the production of table grapes. The climate is mainly continental.

The Major Wine-producing Regions

Of the total vineyard area, 79 percent is to be found in the Moldavia, Muntenia (Greater Walachia), and Oltenia (Little Walachia) regions. Moldavia, where winter temperatures can fall to –22°F (–30°C), is famous for Romania's best-known wine, Cotnari, which has been produced here for 600 years. This sweet, aromatic wine is made from the region's traditional grape varieties (Grasa, Feteasca Alba, Francusa, and Tamaioasa Romaneasca). Within the Muntenia and Oltenia regions are other areas similarly famous for their wines, for example Dealul Mare ("the big hill"). International red wine varieties such as Cabernet Sauvignon, Merlot, and Pinot Noir are grown here alongside the indigenous Feteasca Neagra. The white varieties are Welschriesling (Riesling Italico), Pinot Gris, Sauvignon Blanc, Muscat Ottonel, and Feteasca Alba.

The remaining wine-producing regions are centered around Transylvania, where the vineyards climb up the slopes to heights of 1,300 feet (400 m). In Tarnave, Alba, Sebes Apold, and Lechinia, mainly dry white wines, but also some pleasant sweet (some of them liqueur-like) white wines, are made from the Traminer, Sauvignon

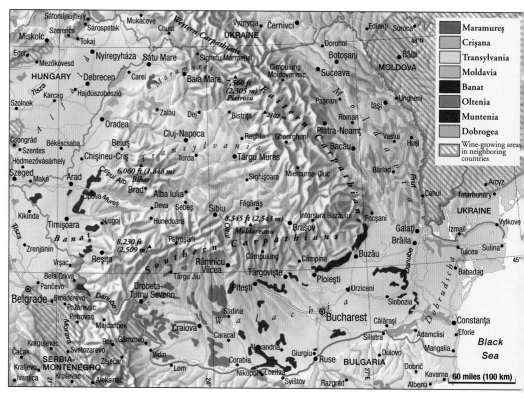

In Buzau, in Greater Walachia, vintners are achieving success with international varieties like Cabernet Sauvignon.

Blanc, Muscat Ottonel, Pinot Gris, Feteasca Alba, and Welschriesling grapes.

Between 1991 and 1996, 76 percent of Romanian producers and properties passed into private ownership, which mainly took the form of joint ventures with foreign investors.

GRAPE VARIETIES AND APPELLATIONS

Romania possesses a wide range of imported grape varieties (for example Pinot Noir, which is very common in Dealul Mare) as well as numerous native grape varieties. The proportion of vineyards planted with local varieties is relatively large. Feteasca Regala is grown over an area of 42,500 acres (17,200 ha), mainly in Transylvania and on the slopes of Moldavia. It produces dry and sparkling wines. Feteasca Alba (57,000 acres/23,000 ha) is also found predominantly in these two regions. In good years this grape makes a substantial contribution to the success of sweet Cotnari wines. In terms of red varieties, Babeasca Neagra, 17,800 acres (7,200 ha) of which are planted in Moldavia, and Teteasca Neagra (over 2,800 acres/1,120 ha), a very old Romanian variety that has been indigenous to Muntenia for 1,500 to 2,000 years, are both widespread.

Romania introduced *appellations* in 1998 based on the models of other European wine-growing countries. Its wine laws created the following classification: everyday wines, superior quality wines (V.S.), superior quality wines with designation of origin (V.S.O.), and special quality wines with designation of origin (V.S.O.C.). This last category includes wines made with botrytized grapes (C.I.B.), two late-picked wines (C.M.D.), and two specialty wines (a liqueur wine and a sparkling wine). These legally binding regulations are set by the national wine authority.

MAJOR WINE PRODUCERS

Romanian producers can be divided into two groups: the private producers, who have no funds for the necessary investment and simply sell their wine in canisters, and the state wineries. The privatization of a small number of state wineries has been made possible with the injection of foreign investment.

The Vinvico winery is today Danish-owned. A majority share in producer Vinalcool Prahova, now trading as Prahova Winecellars, has been taken by a British company. Vinarte also now finds itself under foreign management. This firm, founded in 1998, is owned by Italians and is currently investing large sums of money in new winemaking technology. All these wineries have managed to raise the quality of their wines within a short space of time, albeit using international grape varieties. The indigenous varieties do not yet have a significant role to play in all of this, but at least a start has been made in establishing much-needed international relationships.

CROATIA AND THE WESTERN BALKANS

Veliki Tabor—monumental guardian of the vineyards.

Opposite
The wine village of Buje in western Istria.

CROATIA
- Istra
- Hrvatsko Primorje
- Sjeverna Dalmacija
- Dalmatinska Zagora
- Srednja i Južna Dalmacija
- Zagorje-Medimurje
- Prigorje-Bilogora
- Plešivica
- Pokuplje
- Moslavina
- Slavonija
- Podunavlje

BOSNIA HERZEGOVINA
- Hercegovina

SERBIA-MONTENEGRO
- Slibotičko-Horgoška Peščara
- Banat
- Sremski Karlovki/Fruška Gora
- Belgrade
- Pocerina
- Sumadijsko-Velikomoravski
- Timočki
- Zahodnomoravski
- Nišavsko-Juznomoravski
- Crna Gora
- Kosovo

MACEDONIA
- Pčinsko Osogovski
- Povardarski
- Pelagonijsko-Pološki
- Wine-growing areas in neighboring countries

Not only in terms of wine growing, but also in a more general sense, Croatia can be divided into two main geographical regions: on the one hand there are the interior regions such as Slavonia and Krajina, and on the other there is the long, narrow strip of Adriatic coastline, comprising Istria and Dalmatia. The Greeks started to establish colonies on the Adriatic 700 years before Christ, and this narrow strip of coast later experienced an unprecedented golden age under the Romans. Not only were magnificent buildings erected, such as the palace of Emperor Diocletian in Split, but the large-scale cultivation of wine and olives was also established. In the 11th century AD, the coastal region was conquered by Venice, which managed to maintain its influence despite the occupation of the whole of the Balkans by the Turks. The Yugoslav kingdom was created after the Balkan wars and the end of the First World War, and this became a people's republic in 1945. Under the communists the emphasis was less on the quality of the wines than on the quantities produced. Since the independence of Croatia in 1991, an increasing number of both private and cooperative winemakers have been concentrating on improving the quality of their products and modernizing their wineries.

Croatia's climate is varied, with both continental and Mediterranean influences. The wine-growing areas are divided into two regions, each in turn subdivided into different areas: Kontinentalna Hrvatska, inland, and Primorska Hrvatska, on the coast. The country has around

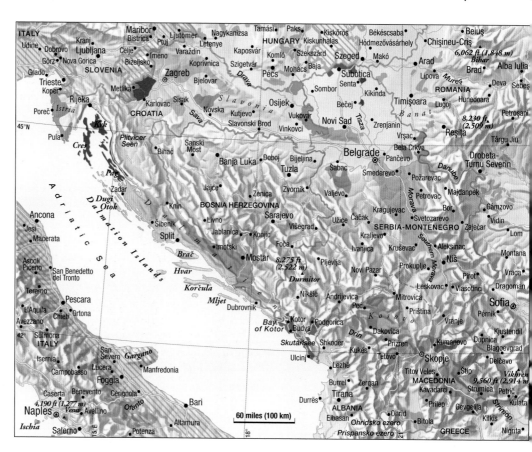

148,000 acres (60,000 ha) of vineyards, many of which are planted mainly with indigenous varieties. The local grape, Plavac Mali Crni, forms the basis for some of the country's best reds, and also for some of its mass-produced wine. Among the best wines are those made by Mike Grgich, the top grower who emigrated to California in 1958 and travels back specially from the U.S.A. for the harvesting and bottling of his Plavac Mali. Other producers, such as Frano Milos, Ivo Skaramuca and the Domaine Zlatan Otok, also make top-flight wines with this strong-willed grape.

Croatia's winemakers have also concentrated on the Pinot Noir, Frankovka (Blaufränkisch), Merlot, Teran (Refosco), Blatina, Vranac, and Zweigelt varieties. Among the best-known white wines are Grasevina (Welschriesling), Zlahtina, Bogdanusa, Malvasija, Vugava, Posip, and international varieties such as Chardonnay, Pinot Blanc, Riesling, and Pinot Gris. One of the country's specialties is the sweet wine Prosek, which is made from a combination of white and red grapes. The best Grasevina wines come from the area around Kutjevo in northeast Croatia. They are graded from KABINETT through to

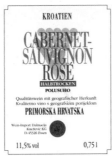

Trockenbeerenauslese in a classification system similar to the one that is used in Germany. Vlado Krauthaker and Ivan Enjingi are two of the major producers. Viticulture in Slovenia, which was also a part of the former Republic of Yugoslavia and became independent in 1991, was described at length previously.

RUMP STATE WITH A FUTURE IN WINE?

The Greeks and Romans also busied themselves with winemaking in the former Yugoslavia's other territories, i.e. the present-day state of Serbia-Montenegro, Kosovo, and Macedonia, which has been independent since 1991. The wines they produced enjoyed centuries of popularity, but under Turkish rule many vineyards were destroyed or fell victim to phylloxera. Today the larger part of the approximately 237,000 acres (96,000 ha) of vineyards is run by state-owned cooperatives.

The best red wines are made in the Kosovo region, along Montenegro's Adriatic coast, and in Macedonia. The other areas produce grapes that are mainly suited to making basic red and white wines.

Confederation of Independent States (C.I.S.)

The West as Primary Sales Market

The former Soviet Union was one of the biggest wine producers in the world. In 1985 it occupied third place behind Italy and France, even ahead of Spain. Large quantities of wine are still produced by the new southern republics of what was previously the world's largest state, around the Black Sea and Caspian Sea. What they lack is international recognition.

Before the collapse of the Soviet Union, most of the wine production of the present-day republics of Moldova, the Ukraine, Georgia, and Armenia was exported to Russia, usually in exchange for oil or natural gas, a system still in use in many areas today. In 1984 Mikhail Gorbachev, president of the Soviet Union at the time, declared war on alcoholism. Numerous vineyards were abandoned or closed down, a measure also carried through in friendly countries like Bulgaria. Today, attempts are being made, under a new set of conditions, to step up exports again, this time mainly to countries in western Europe.

Wine growing has a very long tradition in the southern republics of the former Soviet Union. But it was not until after the Second World War that anything resembling a proper wine industry developed, for two principal reasons: first, because countries such as the Republic of Moldova (Moldavia) became part of the Soviet Union; and second, because of attempts made by the authorities to replace consumption of vodka with wine drinking.

Moldova—Land of the Czars

The Republic of Moldova is one of the smallest member states of the Confederation of Independent States (C.I.S.), but has the largest acreage of vineyards, which are favored by a continental climate. In this emphatically agricultural country, around ten percent of the total area, or over 444,774 acres (180,000 ha), is planted with vines. The vineyards extend south toward the coast and also around the capital, Chisinau, which lies on the same latitude as Beaune in Burgundy. Archeological discoveries have revealed that wine production in this area of land, bordered by the Danube, the Dniester and the Black Sea, and once known as Bessarabia, has a history stretching back approximately 4,000 years.

Old wine cellars in the East are a treasure trove for wine globetrotters.

Until its annexation by the U.S.S.R. in August 1944, Moldova was officially part of Romania. Since gaining its independence in 1991, the Russian language and Cyrillic alphabet have no longer been stipulated by law. Moldavian, a Romance language that is also widespread in Romania, is spoken once again. The Republic of Moldavia used to be the largest wine producer in the Soviet Union, and its red and white wines were both extremely popular in Moscow.

The consequences of the collapse of the Soviet wine market are not as strongly felt here as in the other eastern bloc countries. Moldova's wines remain in demand. Since the political changes, various wine producers from abroad have either invested in or are advising Moldovan enterprises. But in spite of this support from western Europe (for example, by companies such as Wines of Moldova, an export company founded by the Dutchman Joop van de Kant), and the activities of well-known French enologists (such as Jacques Lurton), numerous problems still need to be overcome before the European market is opened up for Moldovan wine.

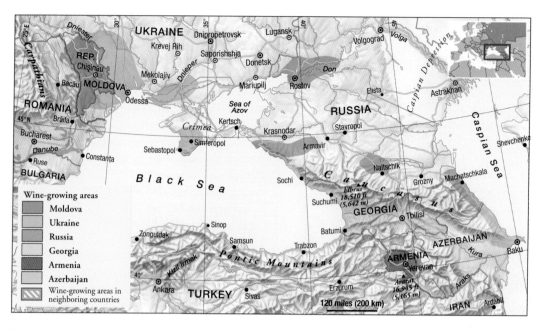

THE UNIQUE ROMANESTI

Following Moldova's entry into the Soviet Union after the end of the Second World War, Stalin created the first *sovchos*, after the Soviet model, on the estate of the Romanov family, the former Czars. Today, the estate's vineyards cover over 1,480 acres (600 ha) and are planted with Rkatsiteli, a local white variety, and the mainly French, Swiss, and German grape varieties introduced at the request of the Czars. But, as elsewhere throughout the country, international varieties such as Aligoté, Traminer, Pinot Noir (known here as Pinot Franc), Malbec, Merlot, and Cabernet Sauvignon are also grown. These last three join forces to make Romanesti de Moldova, Moldova's best-known, and without doubt also its best wine. This wine will certainly make a name for itself again, once its quality has been improved through the use of modern presses, better vinification, and good oak casks.

Before the outbreak of phylloxera, almost exclusively hybrid varieties grew on the Moldovon mountainsides. Following the reorganization of the vineyards, this was no longer the case, as it was considered desirable to replant with modern varieties. It was decided, however, that indigenous grapes such as Rkatsiteli and Feteasca (for white wine—the Dream of Maidens), and Saperavi (for reds) should be retained. A large number of sparkling wines are made in Moldova using traditional techniques, mostly with Riesling, Chardonnay, Aligoté, and Pinot Noir grapes. Wines with added alcohol are also produced with the SOLERA method, used in the production of fortified wines.

The old Soviet wine laws still apply, but Moldova has now also introduced an A.O.C. classification for some of its wines.

UKRAINE

The former "granary of the Soviet Union" has approximately 371,000 acres (150,000 ha) of vineyards, almost a tenth of the total growing area of the former Soviet Union. In ancient times the Greek colonists used to make wine on the Crimean Peninsula and along the whole of the southern coastal area. Ukraine's climate is predominantly continental, with hot summers and severe winters when temperatures can drop

Moldova has enormous potential, a fact that has already been recognized by several foreign investors. Hand-picking using the small crates shown here is reserved, however, for a very small number of top-quality wines.

and held in storage on the Crimean Peninsula ever since, were sold at a wine auction. The winery, founded at the end of the 19th century, was one of the most modern operations of its time. Its wines were destined exclusively for the Czars' summer residence. The company still makes excellent dessert wines today.

The most famous enological teaching and testing institution in the C.I.S. was founded in 1828 and is also located on the Crimean Peninsula, in Yalta.

RUSSIA

Wine has been made in the south of the country, between the Black Sea and the Caspian Sea, for over 2,000 years. Following a period of decline under the Czars, the Russian wine economy experienced an upturn, in particular during the Napoleonic wars. But inevitably, Russian president Mikhail Gorbachev's campaign against alcohol in the 1980s had a serious effect on wine production here too.

The most important wine-growing regions are in the valleys and on the slopes of the northern Caucasus and, to a lesser extent, on steeper ground as well. They can be divided into five main areas: Rostov, in the estuary of the river Don surrounding the city of Rostov, Krasnodar, on the Black Sea south of the city of Krasnodar, Stavropol, Checheno-Ingush, and Dagestan at the eastern end of the Caucasus, on the Caspian Sea.

Many grape varieties are found among the 272,000 acres (110,000 ha) of vineyards, with Rkatsiteli among the most widespread. The climate is continental, and during the icy winter the vineyards in the least favorable positions need to be protected from the cold. Nearly 90 percent of the wine is still produced by the state cooperatives.

to −22°F (−30°C). The loess-rich soils are very fertile. Among the country's major grape varieties are Rkatsiteli, Aligoté, Cabernet Sauvignon, Saperavi, Riesling, Gewürztraminer, and indigenous varieties. Along with its production of still and sweet wines there is also a long tradition in Ukraine of making sparkling wine. Major producers have always appreciated the potential of these vineyards, and today around 50 million bottles a year are produced.

The wine world was amazed when, in 1990, some dessert wines made by the Massandra winery, once owned by the Russian royal family

Galina and Valentin proudly displaying some of their competitive products.

Opposite
The extensive vineyards are harvested by machine.

Left
Sparkling wines are among the best-known and most popular exports.

Right
Massandra, in the Crimea, has a reputation for producing outstanding dessert wines.

Patrick Fiévez, Sabine Rumrich, Klaus Feiten, Michael Ben-Joseph

THE MEDITERRANEAN COUNTRIES

The Mediterranean Countries

Vineyards in the Mediterranean countries often look archaic.

In ancient times grapes were cultivated in almost all of the lands bordering the Mediterranean. The wine produced from them was sealed into amphorae and distributed by an extensive network of trading routes, mostly by sea, to virtually every region of the known world.

Wine production is thought to have originated in the region of present-day Georgia or Armenia, between the Caspian Sea and the Black Sea. From there it spread westward as far as Egypt and the Aegean. Archeological finds of grapes show that vines must have been grown in Egypt as early as about 3000 BC. The plants used are thought to have come from the region of the ancient land of Canaan, which was probably originally only the Phoenician and Palestinian coastal strip, where Egyptian influence had made itself felt from the earliest times. The oldest evidence for the existence of wine in Egypt dates back to around 1000 BC, when it was used as a libation in the context of religious ritual—many tomb paintings depict details of wine production. Vine growing was based chiefly in the Nile delta; only in the 4th century BC did it extend further up-river.

It was the Greeks, whose ancestors settled in the Aegean region at some time before 2000 BC, who revolutionized wine production in Europe in the course of the following centuries. It is thought that wine was already being consumed on the island of Crete during the 2nd millennium BC. Excavations have revealed traces of grapes, and paintings on ceramics show that wine was used in religious ceremonies. Given that the Minoans on Crete were in close contact with the Egyptians, it is quite possible that viticulture was among the skills learned from them. There is definite proof of wine being part of the Mycenaean culture that succeeded the Minoan culture in the Aegean. Discoveries made in the Mycenaean palace complexes include grape pips and storage vessels containing vestiges of wine, as well as a seal with a vine-leaf design and clay tablets with inscriptions including words such as "wine" and "vineyard." From the 8th century BC onwards, as the Greeks colonized other parts of the Mediterranean, they introduced vines first to Sicily and Italy, and then southern France and Spain. Soon wine production and a wine trade flourished in these regions too. In southern France, amphorae from the seaport of Massilia (Marseille) have been found, documenting the vigorous commercial activity of that town, founded around 600 BC, which was the first Greek settlement on present-day French soil.

For the Greeks, wine was a central part of their daily life and culture, and so it was natural for settlers to take vines with them to other lands where olives and figs grew. Recent research suggests, however, that the Greek settlers did not use only the cuttings that they had brought with them, but very probably hybridized them with wild vines they found growing in Italy and the other regions that they colonized. They did not consider that grapes might also do well in more northerly parts.

It was left to the Romans to spread the art of viticulture more widely across Europe, starting in the 1st century BC. With the conquest of Gaul and Spain, new vine-growing areas developed along the trade routes that opened up between Rome and those lands. This period saw all manner of experiments and developments in wine production, since both wine for mass consumption and products of the highest quality were in great demand. The collapse of the Roman Empire brought the development of viticulture to a standstill all around the Mediterranean, but winemaking and drinking continued to be an essential part of daily life.

Following the Islamic conquest of most of the southern and eastern Mediterranean region across to Spain, from the 7th century AD

onwards, the consumption of wine was banned in the conquered territories, the majority of which have remained Muslim to this day. Vines continued to be grown, but chiefly for the purpose of producing table grapes or, as in Spain under the Moors, for medicinal use.

In many countries during the Christian Middle Ages it was chiefly the monasteries that were concerned with viticulture, partly in order to produce the wine needed for the celebration of the Eucharist. Thanks to a warming of the climate, wine growing spread northwards. The disastrous PHYLLOXERA infestation, which afflicted more and more regions from the late 19th century onwards, did not leave the

Left
Testimonies to ancient viticulture on Crete: the grapes were trodden underfoot on the flat stone and the juice ran down into the hollow in the rock beneath the stone, where it fermented.

Right
"I am the vine, ye are the branches" (John, 15:5). This icon illustrates the symbolic significance of wine in the Christian faith.

On the difficult terrain of these Mediterranean islands the harvest is often brought in on mules and donkeys.

Mediterranean countries unscathed. They too had to wrestle with its devastating consequences, and their wine producers made only a slow recovery.

Over the course of a few thousand years there has been a shift in the relative standing, in terms of wine, of the regions around the Mediterranean. At one time the Greeks led the field in the production and trading of wine, but now the western Mediterranean countries have moved ahead. While Greek wine is once again carving out a place for itself in the export market, France and Italy are among the foremost wine-producing countries in the world.

GREECE

Ancient Greece, on which our Western civilization and culture are founded, led the way in winemaking too. Evidence of this can be found in written accounts of techniques of viticulture and wine production which sound quite modern. Today, in the Greek wine-growing districts—where half of the total of 370,500 acres (150,000 ha) is devoted to growing table grapes—great emphasis is still laid on maintaining the huge diversity of varieties. Even here, however, international grape varieties are gaining ground and threatening to oust the native varieties.

The history of Greece is inextricably linked with the history of its wine production, to which we owe a great deal. The Greeks saw wine as an invention given to them by the god Dionysus, whose cult was celebrated with rituals that were sometimes orgiastic in nature. Poets, philosophers, and artists sang the praises of wine, among them Homer in his *Iliad* and *Odyssey*, and Plato in many of his philosophical writings. During the period of the Ottoman Empire, Greek winemaking collapsed completely. Only when Greece gained independence in 1830 was wine once more considered to be an economic factor. It was not until 1937 that the Institute of

Greece's vine-growing regions extend from rugged mountains in the north to the coastal areas.

Roditis is one of the main grape varieties grown for white wine.

Wines was founded in Athens, and right up to their accession to the European Community in 1981 no laws were in force to regulate Greek wine production. This put Greece at a great disadvantage compared to other European wine producers, namely France, Portugal, Spain, and Italy. These countries had recognized at an earlier stage the need to guarantee the quality of wines (not least by rigorously limiting the yield) and to protect the *appellations*. For some 3,500 years the Greeks knew how to apply a range of pruning and training techniques appropriate to different soils and grape varieties, but they still had much to learn about wine laws. After joining the European Community (now the European Union), Greece rapidly set about introducing a legal framework for wine production in accordance with European regulations.

CULTIVATION AND CLIMATE

When viticulture began in Greece, most of the vineyards were in the coastal regions. From here they gradually spread into the interior, where the terrain, particularly on the border with Bulgaria to the north, becomes steeply mountainous. In some places vines are grown at altitudes of over 3,280 feet (1,000 m). Even in these locations the Mediterranean climate, with its hot summers and mild winters, and the limestone and volcanic soils provide ideal growing conditions. There are, however, great differences of climate between the various regions. While it is sometimes so cool in the mountains that the grapes cannot become fully ripe, down on the plains and on the islands the summers are so hot that harvesting has to begin very early. A majority of these vineyards, though, are situated close to the sea, where the constant wind provides some cooling. A major problem every year is the long dry period. Irrigation of the vine rows is prohibited except in newly planted vineyards, so that many of the vines suffer from an extreme shortage of water during the spring and summer months.

The Roman poet Virgil wrote of Greek wines that it was easier "to count all the grains of sand on the seashore than to name every variety of vine." By and large this still holds true today. About 300 different varieties are to be found in the vineyards. They are the sign of an ancient native tradition of winemaking, and the vintners take great pride in them. Of all this diversity,

MACEDONIA· THRACE
- Amynteon
- Goumenissa
- Naoussa
- Côtes de Meliton

THESSALY
- Anchialos
- Rapsani

EPIRUS
- Zitsa

PELOPONNESE
- Mantinia
- Nemea
- Patras, Mavrodaphne of Patras, Muscat of Patras, Muscat de Rio of Patras

IONIAN ISLANDS
- Robola of Kefalonia, Mavrodaphne of Kefalonia, Muscat of Kefalonia

CRETE
- Archanes
- Daphnes
- Peza
- Sitia

CYCLADES
- Paros
- Santorini

EASTERN AEGEAN ISLANDS
- Limnos, Muscat of Limnos
- Samos

DODECANESE
- Rhodes, Muscat of Rhodes

CENTRAL GREECE
- Kantza

Wine-growing areas in neighboring countries

The Cretans take minor problems in their stride.

THE APPELLATIONS

It was not until 1971 that a system of controlled *appellations* was introduced in Greece, and since the country's accession to the European Community (now the European Union) Greece has had laws regulating wine that comply with the European directive defining a "quality wine from a designated region." To this category belong 22 quality wines (O.P.A.P.) and 13 quality liqueur-wines (O.P.E.), including all the Muscat wines (Muscat of Samos, Patras, Rhodes, Lemnos, and Kefalonia). Besides these very aromatic wines, the most widely known ones are the *appellation* wines produced in Macedonia and Thrace (Naoussa, Côtes de Meliton) and the wines from the Peloponnese (Nemea), Crete (Peza), and the Cyclades (Paros, Santorini). The bottled wines are given a numbered label as proof of their origin. Some of the Greek quality wines are designated *réserve* and *grande réserve*. These terms indicate that the wines have been matured in wood for a certain minimum period. *Réserve* denotes maturation for at least two years (for white wines) or three years (for red wines). For *grande réserve*, a maturation period of at least three years is required for white wines and four for red.

Alongside the designation "quality wine," two other categories have been introduced: *vin de pays* (*topikos oinos*) and table wine (*epitrapezios oinos*). The designation *cava* is permitted for table wines that have been laid down to mature. They must mature, in the producer's own cellar, for a minimum of two years (for white wines) and three years (for red wines). As in France, the term *vin de pays* signifies a wine with a specified local origin and a limited yield.

most wine lovers are familiar only with retsina and with Muscat of Samos, the great aperitif and dessert wine that is prized as highly by the Greeks themselves as by visitors to their country.

THE PRINCIPAL WINES

About two dozen varieties of grape are of interest to the wine market, but even these are still relatively unknown internationally.

• Among the most important white wines are Assyrtiko (Santorini, Athos), Vilana (Crete), Robóla (Kefalonia), Roditis (Macedonia, Thrace, Peloponnese), and retsina wines, Muscat and Savatianó (Retsina).

• The most significant red wines are Xynómavro (chiefly in Macedonia and Thrace: Goumenissa, Naoussa), Agiorgitiko (in the Peloponnese, *appellations* from Nemea bear the name "Blood of Hercules"), Mavrodaphne (sweet wines: Patras, Kefalonia, Achaia), Mandelaria (Paros, Crete, Rhodes), and Limnio (a very ancient grape variety).

In addition, a large number of international grape varieties play a major part in the Greek wine industry. The red wines include Cabernet Sauvignon, Cabernet Franc (under the *appellation* Côtes de Meliton), as well as Grenache and Syrah. Of the white wines the most popular with growers is Chardonnay. All these varieties are used either to create one-grape wines or for blending with native grapes.

For the Greeks, wine is a gift from God and is the pride of even the smallest producer.

Opposite
Every year the harvest in Naoussa starts with a symbolic picking for which traditional costumes are worn.

Top of the range among red wines is Xynómavro.

Retsina and Muscat

Greece's best-known wine is without a doubt retsina. Its origins can be traced back to antiquity, when it was found that the addition of pine resin during FERMENTATION not only improved the wine's keeping qualities but also gave it an agreeable tangy flavor. Retsina currently accounts for ten percent of the country's entire production of wine. The European Union has recognized it as a "traditional designation." Retsina is produced from dry white wine (table wine) made from Savatianó and Roditis grapes, flavored with Aleppo pine resin, most of which comes from the Attican Peninsula. Attica, Boetia, and Euboea (Evvoia) are the principal growing areas for this wine, which is as popular as it is characteristic. In cafés and restaurants it is enjoyed as an aperitif or as an accompaniment to the famous *meze*—starter courses with stuffed vine-leaves, *tarama*, *calamari*, and various salads. In recent years, an effort has been made to improve the image of this wine abroad by offering retsinas of higher quality. The wines are aged reductively and have a lower alcohol content than in the past, and the added resin is limited to 13.3 ounces per 375 gallons (100 g/hl).

The dry tang of retsina goes well with the local cuisine.

The soils of the Cycladic island of Santorini were produced by a volcano that is now extinct.

Apart from retsina, which every visitor to Greece ought to try, the best-known Greek wine is Muscat from the Aegean island of Samos. The vines grow on steep terraces, using a special method of production dating back to ancient times, and nowadays Samos is available in several styles. These include the Samos Doux liqueur-wine, Samos Doux Naturel (the fermentation of which is cut short), and Samos Nectar, which is prepared from sun-dried grapes and has an alcohol content of 15 percent by volume.

THE GREAT WINE-GROWING REGIONS OF GREECE

THE PELOPONNESE

Separated from the Greek mainland by the Corinth Canal, the islands of the Peloponnese have from time immemorial been the location of great vineyards producing both grapes for wine-making and grapes (for instance Sultanina and Korinthiaki) for the production of raisins.

There is great variation in the soils and the climate of the islands to the west of Athens. The lowland is at sea level and reaches to the very foot of the high mountains in the interior. The weather also differs markedly from one set of islands to another. In the west there is plentiful rain, while the east experiences dry conditions for most of the year. The great vineyards of this region—with the exception of Nemea and Mantinia—are located along the coast of the Gulf of Corinth and the Ionian Sea at altitudes rising to 1,476 feet (450 m).

The young Nemea wine called "Blood of Hercules" is produced from the Agiorgitiko (St. George) variety, which is found here between 820 and 2,600 feet (250–800 m) above sea level. The wines have a very strong color and keep well. The dry, light, and fruity Moschofílero variety is used for the white Mantinia wines and grows in hilly terrain up to 2,132 feet (650 m). The well-known Mavrodaphne from Patras, a wine with a good deal of RESIDUAL SUGAR, is a potent, oily wine with added alcohol. From the same locations close to Patras comes the white Muscat, another wine with high residual sugar and one that brings out this grape's extraordinarily aromatic quality. In the immediate vicinity of Patras, a dry and very light white wine is produced from the ancient and once very widespread Roditis grape.

CRETE

Historians believe that this southern Greek island was the location of the first vineyards in the Mediterranean region. For five months of the year the oppressive summer heat bears down on the island. One unusual aspect of growing vines here is that in the Cretan vineyards none of the vines are grafted onto American rootstock. Like Chile and Cyprus, Crete 215 miles long and 37 miles wide (350 km × 60 km) has up to now escaped the scourge of phylloxera, so that there has been no need for phylloxera-resistant rootstock. Of the local *appellations*, mention must be made of Sitia, a vigorous red wine made from the Liatico variety, which thrives up to heights of 1,968 feet (600 m), and Daphnes. The latter is a liqueur wine containing a proportion of the Liatico variety, and it embodies the history of the legendary and mythic Malvasia, the "nectar of the gods" once produced in great butts in the palace of King Minos. The wines produced under the *appellations* Archanes and Peza are red wines blended from Kotsiphali grapes (with a strong BOUQUET) and Mandelaria (which is ruby-red when young). In Peza, the traditional Cretan grape variety Vilana is also used for producing white wines.

CENTRAL GREECE AND EUBOEA

Attica, Boetia, and the Aegean island Euboea constitute a unified wine region based on a single grape variety, Savatianó. In addition, these areas supply fresh MUST to inns and restaurants in Athens, which produce their own retsina from it. Light white, red, and rosé wines are also to be found in this part of Greece.

Some of the best Greek red wines are produced in the Côtes de Meliton, on one of the three peninsulas of Halkidiki, near Porto-Carras.

In Greece, as in many Mediterranean countries, an ancient tradition of winemaking by small growers still flourishes, using the simplest of methods.

MACEDONIA AND THRACE

The red wines of these two regions in northeastern Greece have long been known for their outstanding quality, and include important *appellations* such as Naoussa and Côtes de Meliton. The climate in northern Greece is quite different from that of the rest of the country and the warmth of the sun on the south-facing slopes enables the large red grape variety of this area, the Xynómavro, to ripen superbly.

The Naoussa vineyards, situated at a height of about 1,148 feet (350 m), provide a good example of this celebrated red grape's potential for quality. The young wine has an intense color, and after a few years' aging in bottles it achieves an expressive bouquet with overtones of herbs, spices, and balsam, while the flavor contains restrained hints of TANNINS. Together with Negoska, the Xynómavro grape is used in the country's two most northerly *appellations*, Goumenissa and Amyndeo. However, these two reds do not have the body of the Naoussa wines.

Above the picturesque harbor of Porto-Carras on the Sithonian Peninsula, the middle one of the three fingers of Halkidiki, the Côtes de Meliton vineyards produce Cabernet Sauvignon and Cabernet Franc as A.O.C. wines. The Limnio grape is also found here. The white varieties Athiri, Assyrtiko, and Roditis give wines that are light and fresh.

EPIRUS

The vineyards of Metsovo in northwestern Greece, near the Albanian border, are situated in a mountainous region with very cold winters, and are often covered with snow for months at a time. After the phylloxera infestation the slopes were replanted with Cabernet Sauvignon (still rare in Greece), from which very vigorous red wines are produced. In the same area, the Debina variety, which is only found here—it grows in the Zitsa vineyards at around 1,968 feet (600 m)—gives a light, dry, semi-sparkling white wine with a delicate sweetness.

THE IONIAN ISLANDS

The western Greek islands, especially Corfu, are well known to tourists. The mild climate is ideally suited to wine growing, especially as there is adequate rainfall. The traditional *appellation* of these islands bears the name Verdea and is a white wine with a flavor reminiscent of RANCIO. The largest of the islands, Kefalonia, produces the light white wine made from the famous Robola grape, which thrives in the dry, mountainous terrain. Here, too, the Mavrodaphne and Muscat varieties give liqueur wines and wines with high residual sugar. Around Lafkáda on the island of Lefkas, Vertzami grapes grow on terraces reaching up to 2,624 feet (800 m) and give a red wine of individual character called Santa Mavra ("healthy black").

THESSALY

In Thessaly great quantities of grapes for table wines are grown. But here, as in many parts of Greece, there are also little-known and unique varieties, for instance the Noir de Messenikola and the white Batiki grape, which produce wines that are greatly prized in the region. On the coast of the central mainland, much frequented by tourists, the Savatianó and Roditis varieties are grown to produce Nea Anchalios and a range of good dry whites which are best drunk young. In the foothills of Mount Olympus, amid some of Greece's most striking scenery, are the vineyards of Rapsani. Here the Xynómavro, Krassato, and Stavroto varieties give a wine which, while young, has a deep red color.

THE ISLANDS OF THE EASTERN AEGEAN

The legendary islands of Samos, Limnos, Lesbos, and Chios are very well known. Samos has one of Greece's most renowned vineyard sites. Its

5,680 acres (2,300 ha) produce one of the best Muscat wines in the world. The vineyards stretch from the plains up to almost 985 feet (300 m) and so give grapes of greatly varying degrees of ripeness. The *appellation* Muscat of Samos may not be produced from anything other than Muscat Blanc à Petits Grains, to which 98 percent of the growing area is given over. The vineyards are often terraced, mostly planted with only two rows on each level.

The volcanic island of Limnos is less mountainous than Samos. According to legend, this was the home of Hephaistos, the god of fire and of blacksmiths, who was known to the Romans as Vulcan. The grape variety Limnio, also widely grown on the Greek mainland (Côtes de Meliton), was highly spoken of by Aristotle in his day and gives a very agreeable red wine. As on Samos, an outstanding Muscat is also produced, though on Limnos it is made from the Muscat of Alexandria variety; this is available both as a dry wine and a liqueur wine.

The Cyclades

On the islands of Paros and Santorini (site of the ancient city of Thera), the frequently strong winds oblige the growers to keep their vines very low in height. On Santorini the vine is trained into a kind of basket shape, an ingenious and unique way of protecting the grapes from violent gusts of wind. The soil of this wild volcanic island consists of slate and limestone. The vineyards defy the baking sun by storing the moisture that accumulates during the night. The island's characteristic microclimate enables excellent white wines to be made from the Greek

Assyrtiko grape. The white Santorini wine, which used to have a very high alcohol content, is nowadays produced to suit a "modern" palate and has a good balance of fruit, alcohol, and acid. The island also produces a VIN DE PAILLE known as Liastos, a name derived from *helios*, the ancient Greek word for the sun. On Paros the Mandelaria variety is used to make a Mistelle from must fortified with alcohol. This variety is also highly prized by many vermouth producers around the world.

The Dodecanese

On Rhodes, in the extreme southeast of this group of islands, the ancient traditions of winemaking have been faithfully preserved. It is thought that labeling of wine with its place of origin began here: amphorae of wine exported from Rhodes were always marked accordingly.

The island has two different types of terrain. One comprises mainly sandy soils, has little in the way of hills, and is exposed to the hot winds from North Africa; the other has high ground rising to more than 3,940 feet (1,200 m) and is the home of the white Athiri grape and the red Amorgiano, as the Mandelaria variety is known locally. It is to these grapes and this region that the *appellation* "Rhodes" refers. The white wines are generally fresh and dry, while the reds are slightly dry and supple. This is also where the celebrated sweet Muscat of Rhodes is produced.

Following page
The improving quality of present-day wines naturally does not go unnoticed among seasoned wine-drinkers.

The other face of wine production in Greece: large-scale modern vineyards growing international grape varieties.

Select Wine Producers in Greece

BOUTARI**−***
THESSALONIKI

803 acres (325 ha); 1.2 million cases per year • Wines: white and red country wines, Nemea, Paros, Cava, Goumenissa, Naoussa; varietal selections of French and Greek grape varieties

The wine house of the Greek producer and merchant Boutari, with a history stretching back more than 100 years and beginning in Naoussa in Macedonia, offers both classic and more modern wines, and interesting one-grape wines or blends of two varieties ("varietal selections"). Also worthy of note are the Agiorgitiko, Greece's other great red wine grape (from the *appellation* Nemea), the Moschofílero (a white grape from the *appellation* Mantania on the Peloponnese), and blends of Roditis and Xynómavro (the white and red grape together give an interesting white wine) and of Merlot and Xynómavro, which are made in an ultra-modern fermenting tank on the island of Santorini.

DOMAINE CARRAS****
THESSALONIKI

1,110 acres (450 ha) • Wines: →Château Carras. Red and white quality wines from the Côtes de Meliton region (Vin de qualité produit dans une région déterminée); Athiri, Assyrtiko, Roditis, Sauvignon, Limnio, Cabernet Sauvignon, Cabernet Franc

Domaine Carras was created in 1960 by John Carras and has 1,110 acres (450 ha) of vines, grown on terraces, on an estate of 4,446 acres (1,800 ha) bordering the Aegean. On this huge estate several native varieties are grown (Limnio, Assyrtiko, Athiri, and Roditis), together with French varieties, chiefly ones that are common in the Rhône valley such as Syrah and Cinsault. On the terraces facing the sea the yields rarely exceed 425 gallons per acre (40hl/ha). Picking is done entirely by hand. The wine matures for 18–20 months in barrels of French oak and is nowadays blended with the three great Bordeaux varieties (Cabernet Sauvignon, Cabernet Franc, and Merlot) and with Limnio. Of the white wines, the estate's premium wine, the Melissanthi, is produced from Assyrtiko and Athiri grapes. This wine, introduced in 1990, is matured in barrels of French oak. So too is the red Limnio wine (for 6–12 months), which contains a small admixture of Cabernet Sauvignon. Domaine Carras has led the way in the development of modern Greek quality wines and still represents an undisputed standard of reference.

DOMAINE GEROVASSILIOU****
THESSALONIKI

99 acres (40 ha) • Wines: →red wine made from the varieties Grenache and Petite Sirah, Assyrtiko, Malagouzia, Chardonnay

This outstanding estate is owned by the agronomist and enologist Evangelos Gerovassiliou. His vineyards, located right next to the sea, are allowed to carry the label "Vin de Pays from Epanomi." He uses both Greek and French grape varieties and has established a modern winery, producing noteworthy red wine, which is among the best in Greece.

DOMAINE HATZIMICHALIS**−****
ATHENS

247 acres (100 ha) • Wines: →Cabernet Sauvignon. Exclusive table wines: white wines (Roditis, Robóla, Sauvignon, Chardonnay) and red wines (Cabernet Sauvignon, Xynómavro, Limnio)

On his estate close to Parnassus, Dimitris Hatzimichalis has planted traditional Greek and French varieties. The first Cabernet Hatzimichalis was launched in 1982 and was extremely successful. The grower is convinced of

the Greek origin of this variety, now grown worldwide and once known in Greece as *kapnias*. Excellent wines are also produced here from the major traditional Greek grape varieties.

DOMAINE COSTA LAZARIDI***
ADRIANI

494 acres (200 ha) • Wines: →Château Julia, red wine (Merlot) and white wine (Chardonnay); Vin de Pays from Dráma (white, rosé, and red wines); Sauvignon, Semillon, Assyrtiko, Cabernet

The Macedonian estate, with a growing area of about 494 acres (200 ha), offers two distinct lines. One bears the name Amethystos (white, rosé, and red wines) and comprises wines produced from native and French varieties; the other is called Château Julia and consists of one-grape wines—whites (Chardonnay, Sémillon, Assyrtiko) and reds (Merlot).

DOMAINE MERKOURI***
PELOPONNESE

123.5 acres (50 ha) • Wines: Vin de Pays from Letrinon (Refosco, Mavrodaphne)

Situated on the west coast of the Peloponnese, this estate produces an unusual red wine made from the Italian Refosco variety (85 percent). One year's aging in barrels.

DOMAINE SPIROPOULOS*−***
PELOPONNESE

124 acres (50 ha); 400,000 bottles • Wines include: Orino, Mantinia: Réserve, Fumé; Meliasto; Porfyros; Ode Panos (quality sparkling wine)

In 1993 this extensive estate on the eastern Peloponnese adopted organic principles, and planted—as well as the native varieties Moshofilero, Agiorgitiko, and Lagorthi—Cabernet, Merlot, Chardonnay, and Sauvignon. From these varieties it produces modern, clean-tasting, aromatic wines such as the white Orino or the fruity and spicy *barrique* red wine Porfyros.

SEMELI***
ATTICA

19 acres (7.5 ha) • Wines: →Château Semeli, Nemea, table wines in the form of white, rosé, and red wine (Agiorgitiko, Cabernet Sauvignon, Savatianó)

Anne and Georges Kokotos run this small family winery in Attica. Supreme among the wines they produce is the Château Semeli, usually a blend of 90 percent Cabernet Sauvignon with 10 percent Merlot. Two years' aging in new French oak barrels.

TSANTALIS**−***
CHALKIDIKE

617.5 acres (250 ha) • Wines: →Rapsani epilegmenos; a wide range of white and red quality wines and Vins de Pays; Assyrtiko, Sauvignon, Chardonnay, Athiri, Xynómavro, Syrah, Agiorgitiko, Merlot

As Greece's largest wine exporter, this firm deals in wines from almost all of the country's winemaking regions. Alongside its basic range, Tsantalis has also developed a premium selection which includes an interesting Rapsani epilegmenos *réserve*, which is matured for 12 months in French barrels and is produced using only native grape varieties.

CYPRUS AND THE WINES OF THE CRUSADERS

The wine-growing tradition of this island is among the oldest in the world. Mosaic floors at Paphos on the southwestern coast of Cyprus show that wine was already being made here in ancient times. The period of the Crusades saw a new blossoming of viticulture. The English king Richard the Lionheart, who took the island in 1191, was the first to promote the spread of wine-making, followed by the Knights Hospitallers of St. John of Jerusalem. *Commandarias*—estates with vineyards—formed part of the Hospitallers' organization, and the most famous wine still bears their name. Under Turkish rule, between the middle of the 16th and the end of the 19th century, wine production came close to dying out completely; it was revived only after England assumed control of Cyprus in 1878.

Recently Cyprus has around 74,000 acres (30,000 ha)—approximately 10 percent of its agricultural land—planted with vines. The island's wine industry represents an important economic sector, directly or indirectly employing almost 25 percent of the population. Vine growing is concentrated mostly on the slopes of the Troodos Mountains, 750–3,650 feet (250–1,300 m) above sea level. Of the total grape production, 90 percent is destined for the wineries, and the remainder for eating.

The island's vines are not grown on American rootstock, unlike those of most wine-growing

On the southwestern coastal strip—as for example here at Paphos—mixed farming is practiced. This includes the growing of table grapes and the production of *vin de pays*.

First preparations for a new vintage: pruning near Tsada.

regions of the world, since Cyprus has never fallen prey to phylloxera. The varieties grown here are mainly native grapes such as Mavro and Ophthalmo (red), Xynisteri (white), and Muscat of Alexandria. In the last few years international varieties have been gaining ground on what, since the Turkish invasion of 1974, has been a divided island. The restoration of the Cypriot vineyards has led to the introduction of Cabernet Sauvignon, Syrah, Carignan, Mourvèdre, and Grenache. These grapes are to be found on no more than seven percent of the area given over to vine growing. It is to be hoped that the introduction of these varieties will not detract from the great originality of the island's wine production.

The soils on Cyprus are chiefly limestone. In this Mediterranean climate, with its long and very dry summers, only the mild winters bring long-awaited rain. Then the whole island is transformed into a sea of green vegetation. However, from the flowering of the vines through to the ripening of the grapes there is almost no rain at all, and the sun shines for about 330 days of the year. The wine harvest extends over more than two and a half months, with the picking starting as early as the second half of August and finishing, in the higher locations, early in November.

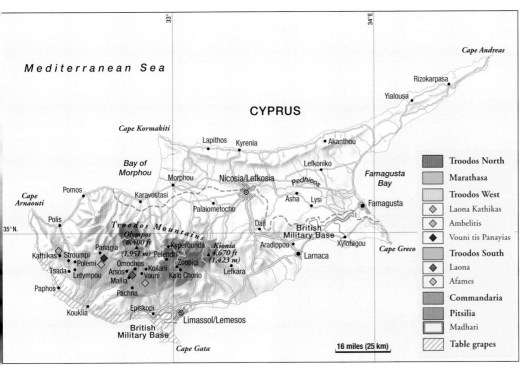

CYPRUS

Mediterranean Sea

Cape Andreas

Cape Kormakiti

Cape Arnaouti

Bay of Morphou

	Troodos North
	Marathasa
	Troodos West
◇	Laona Kathikas
◇	Ambelitis
◆	Vouni tis Panayias
	Troodos South
◆	Laona
◇	Afames
	Commandaria
	Pitsilia
	Madhari
▨	Table grapes

16 miles (25 km)

The Most Important Wineries

The island's major wineries are all based in the region surrounding Limassol (Lemesos). This is close to the main wine-producing areas and has a port with modern facilities. The four biggest wine concerns, Etko, Keo, Loel, and Sodap, together process around 95 percent of all the island's grapes.

Etko, the oldest of Cyprus's wineries, has been producing wine since 1844. Of its annual turnover of some 3 million gallons (11 million liters), 3 million are bottled and the remainder sold in barrels. The Keo winery, established in 1927, is best known for its Commandaria. Keo processes mainly native varieties. Loel, founded in 1943, is experimenting on its 163 acres (66 ha) of vines with varieties that include international grapes such as Cabernet Sauvignon or Riesling. Sodap, the last of the four to be founded, was set up in 1947 and now has a contractual relationship with growers from 144 villages. It was one of the first concerns to introduce the pressurized fermentation tank method, which allows very precise observation and control of the fermentation process.

In recent years a number of smaller wineries have made their mark by producing, in very small quantities, wines of excellent quality. One of the best of these enterprises is the Fikardos Winery, which since its establishment in 1990 has managed to increase its annual production volume to 250,000 bottles. The fruit is obtained from the same vineyards every year, and some of the contract growers specialize in organic production.

Commandaria: A Legend Among Wines

Is this really the oldest wine in the world, still made by the original method? At all events it was already here for Richard I of England to taste and enjoy during his stay in Cyprus. It is said to be the descendant of the straw wine (*vin de paille*) which in ancient times was called "*nama*." After picking, the grapes were sun-dried on straw. The Turkish Sultan Suleiman II is supposed to have conquered the island of Crete purely because of his fondness for this wine.

Today, the celebrated St. John Commandaria is still produced in the same villages as in the days of the Crusaders, in the region around Limassol in the southwest of the island. The Mavro (red) and Xynisteri (white) grapes are sun-dried for about ten days, just as they always have been. After fermenting very slowly, for two to three months, like the Italian Vino Santo, the wine is matured for at least two years in wooden barrels. This thousand-year-old method, known as *mana*, requires that the barrels always contain a small remnant of older wine; this is a variant of the SOLERA method used in the production of fortified wines, especially sherry. Like sherry, Commandaria is served as an aperitif or a dessert wine. The 5,000 acres (2,000 ha) of vineyard are distributed among 14 villages. Since March 2, 1990, the protected designation *Appellation Contrôlée* (A.C.) has been in force, limiting the production of Commandaria to specified districts. Exact provisions are laid down for the timing of the picking and processing of the wine in the winery.

Turkey

Vines—in this case the Emir variety—grow even among the strange rock formations of Cappadocia.

California in the volume of raisins it produces. Around 75 percent of the crop is sold as table grapes, making Turkey the biggest producer of this commodity.

The earliest statistical evaluations of Turkish wine production date from 1928, when official figures record the production of 708,610 gallons (2,682,090 liters) of wine. Today the average figure is around 15 million gallons (60 million liters) of wine, about a quarter of which is used in the distillation of alcohol and the production of *rakı*, a brandy made with aniseed.

Alongside Tekel, the state alcohol and tobacco monopoly, which produces some 45 percent of all Turkish wine and which is about to be privatized, Turkey has a large number of private wineries, though only a small number of these are of real economic significance.

Regions and Varieties

Turkey is one of the few agriculturally self-sufficient countries in the world. What is particularly striking is the difference in climate between the wet peripheral regions, which provide favorable conditions for farming, and the dry hinterland. In the north, the plateau is bounded by the

That wine growing originated in what is now Turkey is a matter of surmise. But scholars are fairly certain of a strong link between parts of Turkey and the earliest growing of the cultivated vine *Vitis vinifera*. Archeological finds from the time of the Hittites show that vines were cultivated in Anatolia as early as 4000 BC. Pictorial representations discovered during excavations of the city of Çatal Höyük, which was built in the 7th century BC, suggest that even at this early date wine was being made from berries, most probably from the Mediterranean nettle tree (*Celtis australis*). The tradition of winemaking, continued by the Greeks and Byzantines, was not developed further during the Seljuk and Ottoman Empires because of the Islamic prohibition on alcohol, but ethnic minorities continued to produce wine. Modern Turkish wine growing began in 1925 when, under the modernizing rule of Kemal Atatürk, the first technically advanced winery was established.

Nowadays Turkey's vineyards, at around 1,435,630 acres (581,000 ha), are the fourth largest in the world. However, only two to two-and-a-half percent of the average annual crop of 3.7 million tons/tonnes of grapes is made into wine. About three percent of the remainder is used for making Pekmez, a grape must thickened into a syrup, and some 20 percent for producing raisins—Turkey is second only to

Pontic Mountains, on the northern slopes of which high rainfall and mild temperatures have led to the development of a zone of lush, damp deciduous forest. In the south are the Taurus mountain ranges, where mild sea breezes reach into the valleys and the vegetation on the slopes facing the Mediterranean has a subtropical character. Thrace, the region around the Sea of Marmara, and the Aegean coast enjoy a mild Mediterranean climate.

It has been estimated that recently between 500 and 1,000 different grape varieties are grown in Turkey; according to the Turkish wine expert Altay Yavuzeser 130 of these are properly described. About 60 varieties are cultivated and made into wine or sold as table grapes or raisins. For the production of wine no more than three dozen varieties are economically significant.

It is mainly in Thrace, in the Marmara region, and on the Aegean coast that international varieties are grown, though they still occupy only a very small part of the total growing area. The local varieties continue to be those that sustain the Turkish wine industry by providing a range of wines of original character.

• Thrace and the Marmara region: Traditionally it is chiefly Cinsault, Gamay, and the native Papazkarası grape that are grown here for red wines, and mainly Semillon for whites. Thrace and the Marmara region lead the way with 40 percent of Turkey's wine production, closely followed by central Anatolia and the

Doluca is a hill close to Mürefte on the Sea of Marmara, which gives its name to the region's traditional wine producer.

Aegean region. Of the 70 wine-producing concerns, six are under state control.

• The Aegean region: The predominant varieties here are those that are used as table grapes and for drying. Only 20 percent of Turkey's wine production is based in this region around Izmir. The white varieties cultivated are Semillon, Colombard, and to a very limited extent Chardonnay, as well as the native Bornova Misketi (a Muscatel grape) and Sultanye. The red varieties include the native Çalkaras as well as Cabernet Sauvignon, Carignan, Grenache, Merlot, and Alicante Bouchet. Of the 20 wine-producing firms three are state-controlled.

• Mediterranean coast: In the regions close to the Mediterranean coast the wine industry plays only a minor role. Among the varieties widely grown are Dökülgen (white), and Sergi

Karası and Burdur Dimrit (red). A large proportion of the crop sold from this region consists of very early ripening table grapes which are available as early as mid-June.

• Black Sea region: Here the climatic conditions impose strict limits on wine production. The Narince grape, commonly cultivated in the Tokat, Çorum, and Amasya provinces, crops well and forms the basis of CUVÉES of white wines; other local varieties, for example Öküzgözü and Boğazkere, are also grown in very small quantities.

• Central Anatolia: It is mainly native varieties that grow here. Among the white grapes, the Hasnadede variety is found in Ankara province, whilst in the Nevşehir, Kayseri, and Nigde areas, set among the imposing scenery of Cappadocia, the Emir grape is cultivated; the red varieties are Papazkarası and Dimrit.

• Eastern Anatolia: A small amount of wine is made here because of the chilly mountain climate. Even so, far eastern Anatolia is the main growing region for the significant local varieties Öküzgözü and Boğazkere.

• Southeastern Anatolia: Although this region has Turkey's largest area of vineyards and produces the highest volume of grapes, it holds only fourth place in the production of wine. Here, too, red varieties such as Öküzgözü and Boğazkere are used (in the provinces of Gaziantep and Kilis), as well as Horzkarası and Sergi Karası, and for white wine Dökülgen, Rumi, and Kabarçık.

Over centuries perhaps only the carrying-baskets have changed.

WINE PRODUCERS AND WINES

The dominant alcoholic drink in Turkey is *rakı*, a double-distilled brandy made from fermented dried grapes, with aniseed added during the second distillation. While for many Turks *rakı* diluted with water is the essential accompaniment to *mezeler*, or starter courses, wine is gradually gaining in popularity.

The production of *rakı* is still firmly in the hands of the monopoly company Tekel. In the case of wines, those available from the private producers are now generally of higher quality. Turkey's oldest private winery is Doluca, established in 1926 by Nihat Kutman at Mürefte on the Sea of Marmara. Doluca nowadays produces around 3,086,000 gallons (12 million liters) of wine annually, about 20 percent of which is exported to other European countries and to Japan and the U.S.A. The firm Kavaklıdere ("Poplar Valley"), founded by Cenap And in Ankara in 1929, produces 3,698,000 gallons (14 million liters) per year, and the proportion sent for export is again about 20 percent. In third and fourth positions are the Sevilen winery in Izmir, with 1,056,800 gallons (4 million liters) of wine, and Kutman in Istanbul, with half that amount.

Connoisseurs throughout the world generally rate Turkey's red wines above its whites, whereas in Turkey itself white wine is preferred. Kavaklıdere's Çankaya, a *cuvée* of the Emir, Narince, Semillon, and Sultanye grapes, is now the top-selling wine in Turkey. Another white wine for everyday consumption is Villa Doluca, blended from Sultanye and Semillon. Tekel's Trakya, a one-grape Semillon, is less expensive still, but markedly more rustic in flavor.

Wines worthy of note are the Muscats from Kavaklıdere and Sevilen, Doluca's Nevşah from the Emir grape, Kavaklıdere's fruity Kimiz (with $^1/_4$ oz residual sugar per pint/18 g per liter), and a *cuvée* of Narince and Sultanye, which together with Muscat and Emir are regarded as the best local white wine varieties. Kavaklıdere uses especially ripe Sultanye grapes for a sweet variant (sultanye with $^1/_2$ oz residual sugar per pint/34 g per liter) as well as for a delicately dry wine named Efsane.

Turkish white wines are not generally intended to be aged for any substantial length of time, but in the higher quality ranges there are *cuvées* made from the best grapes of Anatolia, Thrace, and the Aegean region, which have potential. More complex wines of this kind usually bear the supplementary designation *özel* (special).

Since 1990, the Doluca winery has been experimenting with adapting French varieties. On the

The total area of vineyards in Turkey is among the world's largest, but most of the grapes—like those being transported by this procession of tractors—are destined for eating or for the production of raisins. However, there is increasing interest in wine both for the tourist trade and for export.

Gallipoli Peninsula Chardonnay, Sauvignon Blanc, Cabernet Sauvignon, and Merlot have been planted and used to make single-grape wines under the brand name Sarafin. Sevilen markets a Chardonnay from the Çeşme Peninsula.

Among the most popular Turkish red wines is Kavaklıdere's Yakut, a full, dry, almost tannin-free *cuvée* of Boğazkere, Öküzgözü, Carignan, and Alicante Bouchet, which is one of the firm's great export successes.

Other red wines for everyday use include Villa Doluca, Kavaklıdere's Dikmen, Kutman's Kırmızı Şarap, or Sevilen's Majestik, a one-grape Carignan. Tekel's Buzbağ, which is known outside Turkey, is a *cuvée* of Boğazkere and Öküzgözü. A slightly more expensive wine than these is Sevilen's *cuvée* Şihrazat, a full-bodied blend of Carignan and Merlot.

There is a significantly better quality, higher priced category of red wines that are marked out from the rest by the special care with which the grapes are selected and the wines produced. Doluca's *cuvées* Özel Kav and Antik Red, for instance, are aged in oak barrels to enable them to achieve full maturity. Two other top quality wines are Kavaklıdere's Özel Kırmızı, an Aegean wine made from Alicante Bouchet and Carignan grapes, and the same producer's Selection. This latter wine, made from eastern Anatolian Boğazkere and Öküzgözü grapes, reaches peak maturity (and price) only after about seven to ten years' aging in the bottle. Another of Kavaklıdere's top wines is Kalecik Karası, a one-grape wine from central Anatolia, which is produced only in very limited quantities.

Rosé wines are made by various producers. Kavaklıdere, for example, markets the dry Lal wine, prepared from Çalkarası grapes that are grown in the region around the Aegean, and the

semi-dry Rosato (with ¼ oz residual sugar per pint/18 g per liter).

Apart from these wines, Turkey also produces very good red and white *vins de primeur*. Other popular wines are sparkling Altın Köpük, semi-sparkling Pembe Köpük (a rosé), and Inci Damlası from Kavaklıdere. Many Turkish wine-drinkers prefer sweet wines, which can be recognized by the description *tatlı* on the label. Among the high quality sweet wines, the most noteworthy include Kavaklıdere's Tatlı Sert (red and white) and Sevilen's Harmandalı (from the Muscat grape), which are equally suitable for drinking as aperitifs or as dessert wines.

FUTURE PROSPECTS

At present the annual per capita consumption of wine in Turkey is less than 32 fl oz (1 liter). The reasons for this low figure are twofold: on the one hand wine is relatively expensive (at the end of 1999 the duty on wine stood at 69 percent), and on the other the drinking of wine is mainly the preserve of the Western-oriented—non Muslim—sections of the population. Nevertheless, wine consumption is gradually rising, with improving quality going hand in hand with increasing public interest. In recent years the large firms have invested heavily in modern winemaking methods: many of the old concrete tanks are being replaced by stainless steel ones, and modern processing procedures are being introduced.

Turkey's wine industry is in a phase of optimism and change—this is apparent, for instance, in current experiments for adapting foreign grape varieties, from which as yet only small quantities of wine are produced. If the country can continue to forge ahead rapidly and purposefully to make up for so many years of technological backward-ness, Turkish wine has a very promising future.

Lebanon

Lebanon is one of the oldest wine-producing regions in the world. Excavations of the ancient city of Byblos have shown that wine must have been made here more than 5,000 years ago. The first vines used for wine production were probably brought into the country as part of the trading activities of the Phoenicians, who controlled the region from 1200 to c. 330 BC.

The center of the modern wine industry is located near Baalbek. This city was especially prosperous during the classical Roman era, and a temple to Bacchus dating from the 2nd century AD reflects the importance of wine and wine-making during that period. In the Middle Ages, too, Lebanese wines were extremely popular, and not only in Lebanon itself. Wines from Tyre and Sidon were drunk in all countries of Europe, exported there by Venetian merchants, since the territory that is now Lebanon was for some time a Venetian possession.

The Bekaa valley, with the city of Baalbek as its focal point, forms the present-day center of Lebanese wine cultivation; grapes intended for eating are also grown in the plain. The slopes of the Bekaa valley are planted with vines up to a height of 3,280 feet (1,000 m), and the climatic conditions are ideal: the sun shines for about 300 days of the year, while temperatures are moderated by the proximity of the Mediterranean. In the higher locations the nights are chilly and there is ample rainfall, so that the grapes can ripen fully before being harvested. Training on

■ 1	Château Musar
■ 2	Fakra
■ 3	Massaya
■ 4	Domaine wardy
■ 5	Ksar
■ 6	Château Kefraya
■ 7	Clos St. Thomas

Opposite left
Cabernet Sauvignon is without doubt the best grape grown in the Lebanon.

Opposite right
The great pioneer of modern Lebanese wine growing: Serge Hochar of Château Musar.

Ksara, the oldest wine-growing estate in the Bekaa Valley, originally founded by monks, offers a broad palette of wines, with the reds attaining the highest standard.

wire frames is still rare: for the most part the vines are grown as low bushes and require only a little attention.

Up to the beginning of the 1980s wine was in great demand in Lebanon itself. However, with the start of the war in Lebanon this demand suddenly collapsed and for the duration of the hostilities most estates were unable to harvest their crops. The exception was Château Musar, the only estate in the country that managed to bring in a crop every year, except for 1984. Most vines grown during the war were used for the production either of table grapes or of the national drink, *arak*, a brandy flavored with aniseed, which continued to achieve huge sales even during the war.

The total area of vineyards is nowadays about 66,690 acres (27,000 ha). Of the annual crop yield around 8 million gallons (300,000 hl) are used for wine production, while the rest are sold as table grapes.

The range of principal varieties mainly follows the pattern of the French wine growing regions, because from 1920 to 1946 Lebanon was under French mandate. During that period many vines were planted that still give good yields today. The predominant varieties are reds such as Cinsault, Carignan, Mourvèdre, Grenache, and Alicante, together with Cabernet Sauvignon and Syrah. *Cuvées* with Cabernet Sauvignon are the specialty of the celebrated Château Musar estate in Ghazir, where since the 1950s these wines have been aged in barrels of French oak. The wines are heavy and full-bodied, with a most attractive fruity and spicy flavor. Often they are described as a mixture of Bordeaux and Rhône wines with a slight hint of the exotic. An indication of their high standing is that they are regularly compared with great wines such as the premier quality Australian wine, Penfolds Grange.

Among the white varieties the most popular are Sauvignon Blanc, Ugni Blanc, Semillon, and Chardonnay. There are also a large number of local varieties, such as Merweh or Meroué (both whites).

The Principal Lebanese Estates

Château Musar, the 296-acre (120-ha) estate north of Beirut, was founded in 1930 by Gaston Hochar, and after a sensational tasting event in 1979 it became the star of the country's wine industry. Currently the wines produced by Gaston's son Serge represent the epitome of winemaking in Lebanon.

In the main, Serge Hochar processes the traditional varieties Cabernet Sauvignon and Cinsault, as well as white varieties such as Obaideh (Chardonnay) and Merweh, in the French manner (he received his training as an enologist in Bordeaux) without clarifying the juice or using filters. The estate's first experiments with MATURING wine in wooden barrels were undertaken in the mid-1950s with the assistance of the Barton family of Bordeaux. In recent years this pre-eminent firm has added further luster to its name with its opulent, oak-aged white wines. Around 80 percent of all the wine produced by Château Musar goes for export. Serge Hochar recommends most strongly that his wines should be laid down in a cellar for several years—preferably as long as 15 years—before being opened. Then the wine lover will enjoy them at the peak of perfection.

Château Kefraya began to catch up to Château Musar in the 1990s, and its wines are now regarded as almost equal to its rival's, especially the outstanding Cuvée Comte de M. It has 740 acres (300 ha) 3,280 feet (1,000 m) up on the slopes of Barouk, a mountain in the Bekaa valley, growing Cabernet Sauvignon, Cinsault, Carignan, Syrah, Grenache, Mourvèdre, Clairette, Bourboulenc, Chardonnay, and Viognier. After picking, the grapes go straight

The slopes rise above the Bekaa Valley. Here, due to the moderate climate, the growing conditions are ideal for red varieties in particular, giving balanced wines with remarkable keeping qualities.

to the nearby winery, unlike those of Château Musar which have to be taken by truck across the mountains to the winery north of Beirut where they are processed.

Near Kefraya, the first district in Lebanon to focus entirely on viticulture, the ultra-modern Cave Kouroum de Kefraya was established in 2000. It is producing convincing reds, mostly using Cinsault grapes, but the range also includes rosés and a delightful Blanc de Noir.

The traditional Ksara estate, near the town of Chtauradas, has existed in its present form since 1857. It has 790 acres (320 ha) of vineyards in very varied locations in the Bekaa region and produces wines of an excellent standard. It has won major awards at a range of international competitions, particularly with wines based on the Sauvignon Blanc, Chardonnay, Grenache, and Cabernet Sauvignon varieties. Beside these three big Lebanese estates Clos St. Thomas, Domaine Wardy, Château du Grand Seigneur (Fakra), and Tanail (Massaya) are well on the way to establishing themselves in the international wine world.

ISRAEL

The Israel of Biblical times is regarded by historians and archeologists alike as the "cradle of vineyards and wines," the home of a wine industry that was also much admired by the Greeks and Romans. The word "wine" occurs in the Bible 207 times, "vine" 62 times, "vineyard" 92 times, and "winepress" 15 times, with images of grape growing and harvesting constantly being introduced to illustrate religious ideas. From time immemorial wine has been used by Jews for religious rituals, from celebrating a birth, bar mitzvah, marriage, the Sabbath and Pesach, the festivals of Purim and the New Year, to the mourning ritual following a burial, where the consolation cup consists of ten glasses of wine.

The first documented winery in modern times was established by Rabbi Shore in Jerusalem in 1848, and in 1870 the first Jewish agricultural college on the European model was founded at Miqve Israel to ease the way for the development of modern wine production. The decisive step, however, was taken in 1882 by "Hanadiv" (the benefactor) Baron Edmond de Rothschild, owner of the famous Château Lafitte estate in Bordeaux, France.

The history of the Carmel estate, which currently has an annual output in excess of 20 million bottles, is also the history of the Rothschild family's commitment to the land of Israel. The story begins in 1882 at Rishon-le-Zion, one of the early Jewish settlements in Palestine supported financially by Baron Edmond. Plans were drawn up for a winery and work began at once on its construction. There was not another building in the country of a similar scale. When it came to the ears of the Turkish Sultan that Rothschild was building a

Excavations constantly produce evidence of the ancient history of winemaking in this country.

Left and right
In 1882, with the help of Baron Rothschild a model winery was established.

"fortress" with the aim of liberating Palestine from the Turks, the work was immediately stopped. To this day it is not entirely clear what it was—a lavish bribe, or Rothschild's solemn promise not to attempt to conquer Palestine—that finally convinced the Sultan that the Baron's project was harmless.

Since the 1980s Israel's wine industry has moved from merely supplying simple, sweet wines for ritual use (Kiddush wines) to being a respected competitor on the international wine market. Growing and picking are nowadays carried out in accordance with the latest scientific knowledge. Stainless steel vats have replaced concrete tanks, and computer-controlled fermentation procedures have become the norm. The use of French and American oak barrels is steadily increasing. Finally, automated bottling allows more bottles to be filled more quickly.

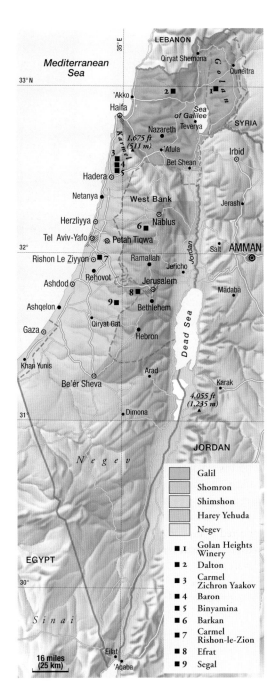

Galil
Shomron
Shimshon
Harey Yehuda
Negev

■ I Golan Heights Winery
■ 2 Dalton
■ 3 Carmel Zichron Yaakov
■ 4 Baron
■ 5 Binyamina
■ 6 Barkan
■ 7 Carmel Rishon-le-Zion
■ 8 Efrat
■ 9 Segal

The citadel of Arad and the new plantings at Carmel well illustrate the coexistence of ancient and modern, the past and the future in the everyday life of Israel.

An ancient winemaking site: there are thousands like this all over present-day Israel, showing that wine has been produced between the Golan Heights and the Negev Desert since 3000 BC.

HISTORY AND GEOGRAPHY

In ancient times, Israel lay on the "historic grape route" which later became the wine route from Mesopotamia to Egypt. A long navigable stretch of coast with easily accessible harbors enabled the wine trade to flourish. In addition to this, the region's relatively mild climate and unimpeded access to the sea both played a decisive role.

The Jews at first confined themselves to growing and producing wine, but later took to trading in it too. The areas suited to vine growing extend from the Golan Heights and the mountain ranges of Galilee in the north to Beersheba and Arad in the south. As an experiment, vineyards were planted some time ago

even further south, on the Mizpe Ramon plateau. In addition, vines are grown at Neot Samadar, a kibbutz located out in the desert, about 31 miles (50 km) north of Eilat.

Israel is blessed with a relatively mild climate with only two seasons: a long dry summer without a drop of rain, and a short wet winter with an average rainfall of about 20 inches (50 cm). Most of the rain falls in the northern half of the country. Ramot Naftaly, one of the best vineyards for Cabernet Sauvignon, receives as much as 35 inches (90 cm) of rain annually. Wine producers in the south have been able to exploit the special characteristics of the desert climate. The wide variation in temperature between day and night helps to maintain the acidity level in the grapes, while the dry conditions prevent the development of many diseases that might attack the vines and grapes in a damper climate. All the vineyards are equipped with the most up-to-date irrigation technology.

Israel's vine-growing areas vary in situation, topography, and soil type. The basis of the soil is limestone laid down in lakes, marl, or other sediments such as hard dolomites. These range in color from red to gray, and are found in the mountains of Judaea around Massua, in Galilee on Mount Tabor, and in the mountain range stretching from Mount Carmel to Zichron Jaakov. Basalt eruptions and flows of lava have led to the formation of a wide variety of soils, composed of basalt clays and tuff, which are characteristic of large areas in Lower and Upper Galilee and most of the Golan Heights. Marine sedimentation and erosion by water have formed the loam in the coastal plain, at the base of elevated ground (Latroun, Gezer Saidun, Givat Ada), and in the valleys among the foothills of the mountain ranges, while wind-blown deposits have determined the character of the loess soil, mingled with alluvial sand, in the Negev around Ramat Arad. The soils that are characteristic of the valleys in the mountains of Judaea, from Samaria to Galilee, and those between Mount Carmel and Zichron Jaakov are on the one hand clay and marl and on the other heavy loam formed by flooding and erosion, which in some cases lack drainage.

Israel's Most Popular Grapes

"Two years ago I tasted Israeli wine, and I was impressed." Robert Mondavi, a legendary wine-maker in his own lifetime, went still further in his praise of Israel's wines when he asked at the Golan Heights Wine Seminar: "However is it possible to produce such an extraordinary wine in this hot climate?" The idea that good grape varieties cannot thrive in warm climates is mere

Israel's climate offers ideal conditions for both excellent table grapes and well matured wines

Left
Professor Roy Spiegel with the new hybrid, Argaman.

Right
Ely Ben Zaken of Domaine du Castel.

prejudice. Israel, with its Mediterranean climate, proves that the reverse is true.

Of the classic red varieties, Israel grows chiefly Cabernet Sauvignon and Merlot, and of the whites mainly Chardonnay and Sauvignon Blanc. The white Emerald Riesling is of local significance only. Cabernet Sauvignon is the undisputed favorite among the reds, because it ages and matures better than any other. The Merlot vine is relatively new to this country, and Merlot wines are all the rage, being produced and sold in great quantities. Their smooth texture and mild flavor make them extremely desirable. Israeli Chardonnay has what the French call *couleur locale*, a distinctively local character with a quite individual taste that is not only characteristic of the particular region but can be identified as coming from a specific vineyard. Unlike other grape varieties, Chardonnay does not give wines of a uniform style. The variations are due to soil, climate, the origin of the vines, and the vintner. The Chardonnay grape is also the basis of Blanc des Blancs. The Golan Heights and Baron wineries produce a number of extremely creditable sparkling wines made by the French MÉTHODE CHAMPENOISE, the traditional method of fermenting the wine in the bottle.

Emerald Riesling is the country's most popular wine. It is included on every restaurant wine list, to accompany any meal at any time of day. The grape is a cross of Muscadelle and Riesling and is a relatively new variety, developed in the 1950s by Professor Harold Olmo at the University of California. His aim was to create a grape that would give light, distinctly acidic wines for regions with a warm inland climate. Israel was one of the few countries, together with South Africa and some parts of the U.S.A, to adopt this grape. Generally the wines from this variety are classed as semi-dry to semi-sweet.

The Principal Wineries

Israel's wineries have an annual production of around 30 million bottles of white, rosé, red, and sparkling wines. The range is truly remarkable, extending from the most unpretentious *vin ordinaire*, which has to be consumed within six months of picking, to the most sophisticated *cuvée*, capable of maturing, and gaining in quality for years or even decades in the cellar. The eight most important wineries, in terms of the volume of their production, are: Carmel, Barkan, Golan Heights, Efrat, Binyamina, Baron, Segal, and Dalton.

As efforts have been made to raise standards of wine production, a lesser branch of the industry, consisting of the so-called boutique

wineries, has grown up alongside the major wineries. Small-scale winemaking is very much in vogue: it is a hobby practiced by many but mastered by few. The latest statistics record no fewer than 52 boutique winemakers. The proprietors not only harvest the grapes but also make the wine themselves, for sale both in their own shops and on the wider market. Some are still at a relatively early stage in production development, but others, with greater experience and improved technique, are already marketing wines that are good to very good, and in some cases outstanding. Most produce a few thousand bottles per year, but those with more experience produce up to 20,000.

The principal boutique winemakers in Israel are Ben-Haym, Castel, Caesaria, Chateau Golan, Diko, Flam, Har-Meron, Kfira, Kibbuz Nachshon, Kibbuz Tzor'a, Latroun Monastery, Lavie, Margalit, Mirage, Mishar, Neot Smadar, Racanati, Saslove, Sde-Boker, Sea Horse, Soreq, Teqoa, and Tavor.

Select Wine Producers in Israel

Barkan*−***
Barkan and Hulda
1,483 acres (600 ha); 6,000,000 bottles • Wines include: Cabernet Sauvignon, Merlot and Chardonnay; Superior: Cabernet and Syrah
In the mid-1980s the parent winery and distillery Stock-West was hit by the great wine crisis. It bounced back with the foundation of the Barkan winery and distillery under new ownership and new management. With its sophisticated technology, Barkan is now the second largest modern winery in the country.

Binyamina Winery***
Binyamina
395 acres (160 ha); 2,200,000 bottles • Wines: Special Reserve: Cabernet, Merlot, Chardonnay
This winery passed through many hands after it was established in 1952 until finally two Hollywood producers acquired it and became its new and serious owners. They have invested huge sums in new cellar equipment and have signed long-term contracts with local producers. A new and gifted wine maker, Sasson Ben-Aharon, heads production and he has taken Binyamina into the league of very good wine producers.

Carmel*−***
Rishon le-Tsion, Zichron-Yaacov and Arad
5,436 acres (2,200 ha); 22,000,000 bottles • Wines include: Private Collection: Cabernet Sauvignon, Merlot, Chardonnay and Emerald Riesling; Ramat Arad
Carmel has made the greatest contribution to the development of Israel's viticulture and wine production. With 1,200 active members, it is the biggest wine cooperative in the country. Though the buildings date

back to the original foundation in 1882, they now contain modern computer-based technology. There is something here for every budget.

Château Golan Winery*−***
Ely-Ad
67 acres (27 ha); 100,000 bottles • Wines: Cabernet Sauvignon, Merlot, Cabernet-Merlot
It is the aim of the winery run by Shuky Shai and Itzhak Riebak to combine wine and art; a wine school is part of the plan. The basaltic slopes above the Yarmuk river are planted with Cabernet Sauvignon and Franc, Merlot, Petit Verdot, Syrah and Petit Syrah, Grenache and Pinot Noir.

Domaine du Castel Winery*−***
Ramat-Raziel
32 acres (13 ha); 100,000 bottles • Wines: Castel Grand Vin, Petit Castel, Chardonnay 'C'.
Ben-Zaken is a francophile, and he and his family began to plant their first vines in 1989, although they had no knowledge of viticulture at all. They were soon one of the first *boutique wineries* in Israel and since then Castel wines have won many international awards.

Golan Heights**−***
Katzrin
1,235 acres (500 ha); 5,000,000 bottles • Wines include: Katzrin Chardonnay; Katzrin Red; Yarden: Chardonnay, →Cabernet Sauvignon, Merlot, →Syrah
The Golan Heights winery, a partnership comprising seven settlements on the Golan Heights and one in Upper Galilee, has as yet only a short history. The first vineyards in this region were laid out in 1976 and further planting took place in 1983. In the following year they produced their first Sauvignon Blanc.

Malta

This small island republic with an area of 121 square miles (316 sq km) and population of 400,000 is situated 62 miles (91 km) to the south of Sicily, and in the course of its history, until it achieved independence in 1961, a succession of different cultures left their mark on it. It still possesses extraordinarily impressive megalithic monuments as well as both underground burial chambers and above-ground cult structures dating from the Neolithic and Bronze Ages.

Exposure to Diverse Influences

It is known that winemaking here goes back to the days of the Phoenicians, who settled on the island from about 800 BC. The Roman occupation began in 218 BC, and the development of vine growing and winemaking was sustained without interruption until the 9th century AD. Then followed centuries of unrest, during which the importance of wine declined. It was the Knights of St. John (Knights of Malta), in whose possession the island remained from the 16th to the 18th century, who resumed the cultivation of vines, mainly in order to produce their Eucharist

Marsovin obtains a large proportion of its grapes from other Maltese producers or from Italy.

Meridiana owns Malta's largest vineyard of 47 acres (19 ha) and uses only its own grapes.

wine. Finally, until its independence in 1961 Malta was under British rule.

Winemaking has been an integral part of the history of this multicultural island over the centuries, but the impetus for expansion of the industry always came from outside, since the islanders were not sufficiently interested in wine to initiate winemaking themselves. Currently vines are grown on some 791 acres (320 ha) distributed across the north and northwest of the two main islands, Malta and Gozo. In the spring the vineyards are often assailed by deluges of

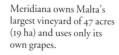

ain and in the summer they are exposed to extreme heat. Only two estates cultivate areas of any real size—Meridiana has 47 acres (19 ha) and Marsovin 21 acres (8.5 ha). The other wine-making firms use only extremely small areas, but precise figures are not known. Nor is there any precise record of the multiplicity of varieties grown. In recent years international varieties have been appearing more and more, but the small-scale growers still prefer the local varieties. These include Girgentina and Gennarua (both white grapes) and Gellewza (a red), and wine is also made from some table-grape varieties. Although the red and white wines rarely rise above the quality of table wine, Malta is known for its very sweet Muscat.

On average 2,642,000 gallons (100,000 hl) of wine are produced annually. Some growers have their own wineries and take the wine that they have bottled themselves to markets to sell, keeping back a proportion for their own consumption. Others sell all or part of the wine they produce to merchants.

Not all of the wine that is bottled in Malta comes from the island's own vineyards. The land available for wine growing is nowhere near sufficient to satisfy local demand. It is estimated that about 70 percent of wine is imported from Italy. The two biggest Maltese producers, Marsovin and Delicata, each achieve a volume of around 3.5 million bottles per year.

Marsovin harvests about 65 tons/tonnes of its own grapes each year, all of which are international varieties (Chardonnay, Merlot, Cabernet Sauvignon, and others). Some 400 tons/tonnes of grapes are bought in from local growers and about 4,000 tons/tonnes are imported from Italy. The Delicata firm has opted for a different solution. The winery does not have any vineyards of its own, but works with local producers: 53 local growers, whose area of vineyards amounts to about 62 acres (25 ha) in all, supply their grapes to Delicata, which imports the remainder from Italy.

Both companies generally try to process the Maltese and the Italian grapes separately, to ensure that the product of the Maltese grapes can be exported into the European Union as "Wine of Malta." Wines made from Italian grapes, on the other hand, are only allowed into the European internal market so long as they bear no information about origin, variety, VINTAGE, or producer. The label may only specify red or white wine. Under European regulations the "origin" of a wine denotes where the grapes are grown, not where the wine is made. On estimate, 90 percent of the wine produced in Malta is drunk on the island itself or is bought

by tourists to take home with them. In most wineries, therefore, only a small proportion of the wine produced is intended for export. But Malta is an E.U. membership candidate for 2004 and sooner or later will have to come into line with European regulations. Marsovin and Delicata intend to increase the proportion of local grapes they use so that the wines produced can be identified with Malta. In addition, the cost of transporting grapes from Italy would be avoided. However, the island is very small and because of urban growth agricultural land is at a premium. The wine merchants need to persuade the farmers to concentrate more effort on growing vines, and financial subsidies will need to be provided to ensure that only high-quality grapes are grown.

POSSIBLE WAYS FORWARD

An exceptional case in Malta's wine sector is the Meridiana estate, founded in the early 1990s. It uses production methods which, although untypical of Malta, are the norm in other wine-producing countries. Its aim is to grow grapes for top-quality wines in its own vineyards, so avoiding the need to buy in either grapes or wine. In 1994 and 1995, on the former British air force base near the ancient city of Medina, a total of 47 acres (19 ha) of vines were planted, giving Meridiana the largest single-site vineyard on the island. However, its annual production of 100,000 bottles still lags far behind that of its two big rivals.

When Meridiana embarked on its new planting program, the owners opted for the traditional international varieties (Chardonnay, Cabernet Sauvignon, Merlot, Syrah, and Petit Verdot), because they judged the local varieties unsuitable for top-quality wines. Other growers, however, believe that the native grapes are a part of the country's cultural identity and should continue to be grown. But these varieties, grown in the customary way without stakes or frames, need expensive, labor-intensive care if they are to reach the minimum must weight required for table wines in this region. It remains to be seen how Maltese wine production will develop from the present situation.

Tunisia, Algeria, and Morocco

winemaking took an unexpected turn. Very rich wines with a high alcohol content were produced and were designed to improve the colorless and diluted high-volume wines from the Languedoc. After the declaration of independence by the French protectorate of Tunisia in 1956, followed only a few years later by Algerian independence, exports of these blending wines declined dramatically.

A further reason for the stagnation of the wine industry here was the later decision of the European Community to prohibit the admixture to table wines of any wine that did not originate in a member state. As a result, huge numbers of vines were destroyed (there are now only 100,000 compared to 355,000 in 1962), and the future of winemaking in these countries, where the drinking of alcohol is banned on religious grounds, remains uncertain.

In the three North African countries of Tunisia, Algeria, and Morocco, the history of winemaking can be traced back to the Phoenicians. Vital contributions to the development of viticulture were made by the Romans and the Arabs, long before the arrival of French colonists in the late 19th century. The French in particular were keen to make wine on the spot, producing wines that were highly alcoholic and strongly colored. These were blended with wines from the southern French Languedoc region to give the famous *gros rouges*, which were sold in the equally famous liter bottles with stars on them.

The importance of these three countries is underlined by the fact that in the 1950s they accounted for two-thirds of the volume of wine on the world market. Though large numbers of vineyards ceased to exist following the final departure of the French, the wine industry of the Maghreb—significantly boosted by capital from European investors—is now once again committed to the production of quality wines.

As a melting-pot of cultures and civilizations, the three countries profited from the introduction of many Phoenician, Carthaginian, and Roman grape varieties, and the French, Spanish, and Italian ones that followed later. After the arrival of the Arabs at the end of the 7th century, viticulture was dedicated to the growing of table grapes, since the Koran forbids the drinking of alcohol. But with the entry of French colonists into Algeria in 1830, and Tunisia in 1881,

In the countries of the Maghreb the history of winemaking goes back to the Phoenicians. Nowadays these former citadels of very alcoholic blending wines are seeking a new direction.

Tunisia

Since ancient times vines have been grown in Tunisia, probably since the Phoenicians founded the city of Carthage on the coast. However, after the conquest by the Turks in 1574, wine production came to a standstill; only under French rule in the last century was it resumed on a commercial basis.

Nowadays about 10,526,000 gallons (400,000 hl) of wine are produced on a total area of 43,225 acres (17,500 ha). The vineyards are concentrated in the regions around Nabeul, Bizerte, Tunis, Béja, and Jendouba. Three factors will fundamentally alter the profile of Tunisian wines in the next few years: the cultivation of traditional varieties as well as Carignan, Alicante Bouchet, Cinsault, or Pedro Ximénez; an active policy of planting superior grape varieties (Chardonnay, Cabernet Sauvignon, Merlot, Syrah); and the modernization of winemaking technology, such as pneumatic presses and refrigeration.

Tunisia is building up its wine industry. It now produces eight times more wine than Algeria on half the area of land. Seventy percent of Tunisian wine carries the French A.O.C. mark of quality (*Appellation d'Origine Contrôlée*). The wines concerned are the seven *appellations* of Mornag, Coteaux de Tébourba, Thibar, Kélibia, Coteaux d'Utique, Grand Cru Hornag, and Sidi Salem. The Tunisian Office du Vin is concerned to meet the wishes of customers, who include large numbers of European tourists, and is currently promoting the development of one-grape wines. For this purpose, at least 80 percent of the grapes used must be of the variety named on the label.

ALGERIA

Only a few decades ago, this huge North African country had more land under vines than almost any other country in the world. In 1962 Algeria gained its independence and imposed a ban on exports to France, which at that time was by far its greatest market for wine. Until its independence Algeria had been subject to French wine laws, and some wines were classified as V.D.Q.S. (*Vin Délimité de Qualité Supérieure*). Nowadays, this former French *département* has its own laws on wine and its own national wine institute regulating production and marketing—Office National de Commercialisation des Produits Viticoles.

Some of the vineyards around Algiers and Oran carry the A.O.G. mark of quality (*Appellation d'Origine Garantie*) instituted on the French model, among them the Coteaux de Zaccar, Médéa, Aïn-Bessem-Bouira, Coteaux de Tlemcen, Dahra, Monts de Thessalah, and the famous Coteaux de Mascara. However, the unclassified Cuvée du Président is also rated as one of Algeria's best wines. All of these wines are produced from grape varieties brought in by French settlers, and Cinsault, Alicante, Alicante Bouchet, Grenache, Mourvèdre, and Cabernet Sauvignon are found. As well as the introduced varieties, native grapes are grown, namely Farhana (in the region around Tlemcen) and Tizourine, both white varieties. Algeria's present political situation makes export conditions difficult and the outlook for wine in this vast country is bleak.

MOROCCO

Algeria's neighbor, Morocco, also has a very ancient tradition of winemaking, probably going back to the period before the Phoenicians arrived. The Romans followed them and later the Arabs, who introduced the grape varieties widely grown around the Mediterranean coasts. But because of the Koran's prohibition on alcohol consumption, wine production rapidly switched to the production of table grapes. Shortly before the First World War, large numbers of French colonists entered the country and established vineyards on some 197,600 acres (80,000 ha). In Morocco, as in Algeria, there were heavy losses following the halting of exports to France, and many vineyards were

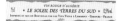

Traditional methods of cultivation are still used in the Cap Bon region.

closed down. Currently the area of land under cultivation for wine is a mere 29,640 acres (12,000 ha). The Moroccan wines, some of which carry the A.O.G. mark, are often sold under arbitrarily chosen names such as Chante Bled, Chaudsoleil, or Spécial Coquillage. The best known is undoubtedly *vin gris*, a wine made with red grapes, from Boulaouane, a site between Casablanca and Marrakech. The best vineyards are for the most part situated around Fez and Meknes, and produce mainly (85 percent) red wines. Moroccan wines are made by about 40 wineries, three-quarters of them cooperatives with state participation. In the last few years, however, French investors have returned to the country. Among them are important groups such as Castel, William Pitters, and Taillan in conjunction with Domaines Delorme. These three new concerns alone now grow some 7,400 acres (3,000 ha) of vines. The most dominant varieties are the classic reds Carignan and Cinsault, as well as such great varieties as Cabernet Sauvignon, Grenache, Syrah, and Merlot. The commitment of winegrowers and the financial resources provided by the new investors may well usher in a new period of prosperity for Morocco's wine industry, with some interesting products.

André Dominé

SOUTH AFRICA

THE WINE LAND ON THE CAPE

For Europeans and North Americans wishing to escape their northern winter for at least a few days, South Africa—and especially the Cape of Good Hope—is an attractive destination. Fascinated by the dramatic landscape, where steep mountains sweep down almost to the sea, travelers coming here for the first time discover to their surprise that the country is actually quite European in character, and its climate Mediterranean.

A long, mostly sunny, summer with great intensity of light, and a mild but damp winter lasting from May to September, promise favorable conditions for wine growing. Where the oceans make their presence felt—and that can often be more than 60 miles (100 km) inland—thick banks of clouds build up with almost daily regularity, keeping the temperature down to reasonable limits, providing for relatively cool nights and adequately long ripening periods. Sometimes the so-called Cape Doctor puts in an appearance: a storm coming in from the southeast, which can cause great damage to the vineyards. But the climate of the best wine-growing regions, those near the coast, is changeable, and conditions are not always so ideal as winegrowers would wish. One consequence is that VINTAGES of South African wines are just as important as they are for those of Europe.

In 1652 a group of Dutch mercenaries went ashore at the Cape of Good Hope to establish a

Cape Town harbor is the starting point for South African wines on their journey to the world's export markets, where they are gaining steadily in importance.

provisioning base along the Spice Route on behalf of the Dutch East India Company. As the conditions for producing wine seemed good, Commander Jan van Riebeck, the Company's former ship's doctor, quickly had vines delivered from Europe—after all, wine was considered an effective antidote to scurvy. On February 2, 1659, the grapes from the first three vines were pressed. They are thought to have been Muscat de Frontignan (Muscat Blanc à Petits Grains) and Palomino; the Hanepoot (Muscat of Alexandria) was not yet ripe. The result was sufficiently encouraging for further vines to be planted, especially since new settlers were given the opportunity to set up their own farmsteads on allocated lands, as the growing demand on company ships could not be satisfied otherwise.

Produced without adequate experience, the wines of these "Boers" may well have left considerable room for improvement. This was to change with the new commander, Simon van der Stel. Very shortly after his arrival in 1679, he issued decrees which imposed heavy penalties on the winegrowers if they harvested their grapes before they were properly ripe, or fermented the juice in dirty barrels or cellars. He also advised them to plant six acres of grain for every acre of vines.

Although regulations forbade company employees to acquire colonial possessions or engage in trade on their own account, van der Stel succeeded in having an exception made for himself. Accordingly, in 1685 he was able to acquire, to the southeast of Cape Town, extensive estates which he named "Constantia." His well-managed vineyards were largely stocked with Muscat de Frontignan, since it produces decidedly finer wines than the Hanepoot. As early as 1692, a year after his appointment as first governor of the aspiring new colony, van der Stel succeeded in having his wines mentioned in the same breath as the most highly regarded European wines.

While Constantia underwent various divisions in the following years, and saw different owners come and go, the wines produced there rose to become an expensive and highly sought-after specialty in the courts of Europe. It was Napoleon's favorite wine—the largest quantity of Vin de Constance was supplied to him during the final years of his life while in exile on St. Helena —and right up to the middle of the 19th century it remained South Africa's enological showpiece.

A further decisive impulse for viticulture on the Cape came from the arrival, between 1688

and 1690, of some 200 French Huguenots, who were mostly settled in what is now called the Franschhoek Valley. Some of them already possessed wine-growing skills, and they established estates which soon developed a considerable reputation. Their descendants continue to play an important role in South African viticulture to this day.

During the 17th century, the colony supplied Great Britain for the most part with brandy and fortified wines in the port and sherry styles. Later, Cape wines profited from the Continental System, the blockade of the British Isles imposed by Napoleon in 1806, especially as it was in that same year that the British occupied the Cape for the second time. But this advantage turned out to be short-lived. Having neglected the quality of their wines, the Boers were hit by an ongoing sales crisis when France and Britain settled their differences once more. In the late 19th century, the mildew and phylloxera epidemics reached the Cape region too, forcing numerous winegrowers out of business. The start of the 20th century was a bad time for viticulture worldwide, and the export trade dried up almost completely. It was hoped that the establishment of the Kooperatieve Wijnbouwers Vereniging, a cooperative to which 95 percent of South Africa's winegrowers soon belonged, would improve matters. But it was not until 1924, when the government gave the K.W.V. powers to fix the price of the wine used for making brandy, that it was able to exercise any authority. But even this measure did not have the desired salutary effect on the market for fortified and dry table wines. As a result, in 1940 the government transferred the entire supervision of the wine sector to the K.W.V. From then on the organization determined not only prices but also permissible yields, varieties, planting rights, and production methods; it also controlled the disposal of surplus production, and the entire trade in wine and wine products. Not until 1992, when the quota system was abandoned, was new life injected into South African viticulture. As a result, old estates and merchants were able to develop and new ones were founded, while the K.W.V. and other cooperatives reoriented their activities.

For years, the boycott of South African produce by other countries in protest at the apartheid policy had meant that the South African wines were difficult to export, and with domestic consumption at only 2.37 gallons (9 liters) per person per year, there was little demand for quality wine. There was, however, a home market for brandy, where average consumption was 16 fl. oz (0.5 liters) per person. This situation was reflected in the small proportion of internationally popular varieties grown on the country's vineyards. For example, in 1981 only 3.3 percent of the area was devoted to Cabernet, Merlot, and Shiraz (the grape known in France as Syrah), while Chardonnay and Sauvignon accounted for just 0.4 percent of the total area. During the 1980s, however, interest in these varieties revived. In 1990 the red varieties had reached a share of more than 5.4 percent by area, and the whites 5.1 percent. In 2002 the three reds had reached more than 24 percent, while the two whites had almost 12 percent. The total area devoted to wine production had risen to about 266,860 acres (108,000 ha). The abolition of apartheid in 1991 resulted in a huge and sudden increase in demand from abroad, especially for inexpensive wines of good quality. Thus the winemakers also used naturalized varieties, in particular the dominant Steen (Chenin Blanc) and the Colombard, in order to supply internationally convincing wines. At the same time, the Pinotage, a variety obtained in 1925 by crossing Pinot Noir with Cinsault, also enjoyed a renaissance as an original red variety, and is being planted on a large scale. Today, about 4,350 winegrowers deliver their harvests to 66 winemaking cooperatives; 88 estates, 266 private cellars and 13 wholesalers bottle their wine themselves. Wine has become one of the Republic of South Africa's most important exports.

Top
Groot Constantia is where South African wine growing began.

Above
Cool humid breezes from False Bay outside Cape Town keep down the temperatures of the best-known wine regions: Constantia, Stellenbosch, and Paarl.

WINE GROWING IN SOUTH AFRICA

As in this vineyard near Stellenbosch, most South African winegrowers try to use eco-friendly methods of cultivation.

WINE OF ORIGIN

In 1973 the Wine and Spirit Board set up a scheme under which, following the European example, wines were classified by origin. If the Wine of Origin description is awarded, it guarantees that the location indicated on the label is indeed the origin of all the grapes used in making the wine in question. If, in addition, the grape variety and vintage are indicated on the label, this certifies that at least 75 percent of the grapes used to make the wine are of that variety and that year. For export wines at least 85 percent must come from the stated variety. Each individual wine must undergo exemplarily thorough analytical and organoleptic examination. However, it is up to producers whether or not they have a wine recognized as a Wine of Origin and submitted to this rigorous examination. So far, only a small proportion have decided to do so. But with rising export figures the value of this quality mark is also increasing, and more and more domestic producers are seeking to achieve the necessary standards.

Under the general term "origin," the South African description scheme recognizes five subdivisions:

• *Estate* stands for an estate consisting of one or more farms; it must use grapes exclusively of its own production and VINIFICATION must take place on its own premises.

• *Ward* signifies a small, precisely defined growing area. The best-known wards are Constantia and Franschhoek.

• *District* means a large contiguous growing area, for example Stellenbosch or Paarl.

• *Region* refers to an extensive growing zone consisting of a number of districts or sub-districts, for example Breede River Valley or Boberg. It is only used for dessert wines from Paarl and Tulbagh.

• *Wineland* is not an official description, but takes account only of the importance of the wines, irrespective of whether they are classified as ward, district, or region.

Geographical Unit does not designate an *appellation*, but only, since 1993, the Western Cape, the only supra-regional wine-growing area to date.

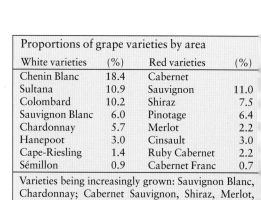

Label for back of bottle

1. Producer's logo
2. Name of the estate
3. Estate bottled
4. Variety of grape or blend
5. Vintage
6. Bottler
7. Place of origin
8. Country of origin
9. Alcoholic strength
10. Nominal volume

Increasingly wine producers in South Africa are adding a label on the back of the bottle as well as the attractively designed main label on the front. The back label gives the consumer additional information about the wine. It also provides enough space for compulsory information, such as the alcohol content and the nominal volume.

Proportions of grape varieties by area			
White varieties	(%)	Red varieties	(%)
Chenin Blanc	18.4	Cabernet	
Sultana	10.9	Sauvignon	11.0
Colombard	10.2	Shiraz	7.5
Sauvignon Blanc	6.0	Pinotage	6.4
Chardonnay	5.7	Merlot	2.2
Hanepoot	3.0	Cinsault	3.0
Cape-Riesling	1.4	Ruby Cabernet	2.2
Sémillon	0.9	Cabernet Franc	0.7
Varieties being increasingly grown: Sauvignon Blanc, Chardonnay; Cabernet Sauvignon, Shiraz, Merlot, Ruby Cabernet, Cabernet Franc			

Healthy, clean wines

The motto "South African wines are healthy, clean and environmentally friendly," addresses wine lovers all over the world. Since 2000, the entire wine production of South Africa has been converted to integrated production (I.P.). This system came into force with the publication of a notice in the *Government Gazette* on November 6, 1998, which defined Integrated Production as "the use of methods, techniques and practices that:

• are in harmony with the environment;

• are based on the non-use or minimal use of artificial fertilizers, agricultural methods, and other harmful substances in the growing of such grapes and the production of such wines;

• ensure that the wines in question contain no more than the permitted maximum levels of substances that are regarded as detrimental to human health."

At the same time, detailed specifications were published covering all operations from the preparation of the soil to the recycling of glass and packaging materials. With these regulations, South Africa has gone significantly further than other countries in this respect, all the more so since it required all producers to register their operation as adopting I.P.

This revolutionary step was the result of years of work by the well-known Nietvoorbij Enological Institute in Stellenbosch where the most important research into viticulture and enology is carried out, and it has been geared to I.P. for years.

The I.P. system enjoys the support not only of the powerful Wine and Spirit Board and all other domestic wine organizations and relevant industrial associations, but also of the O.I.V., the international wine office in Paris.

The initial criteria are relatively broadly defined and make it possible for virtually all South African operations to produce I.P. wines. However, the framework has been laid out in principle in such a way that further training and codes of practice will allow the wine production of an entire country to be raised to an increasingly eco-friendly level. In Stellenbosch they dream of the whole world following this example.

Wine region	Number of vines	Share of total volume (%)	Area under cultivation acres (ha)		Share of total area under cultivation (%)
Worcester	61,144,147	19.3	44,807	(18,133)	16.8
Paarl	55,021,730	17.8	43,383	(17,557)	16.2
Stellenbosch	54,298,810	17.1	42,469	(17,187)	15.9
Orange River	29,005,328	9.1	38,130	(15,431)	14.3
Malmesbury	37,522,437	11.7	36,531	(14,784)	13.7
Robertson	43,101,169	13.6	30,648	(12,403)	11.5
Olifants River	27,189,825	8.5	23,544	(9,528)	8.8
Klein Karoo	9,385,171	2.9	7,356	(2,977)	2.8
Total	316,668,617	100.0	266,868	(108,000)	100.0

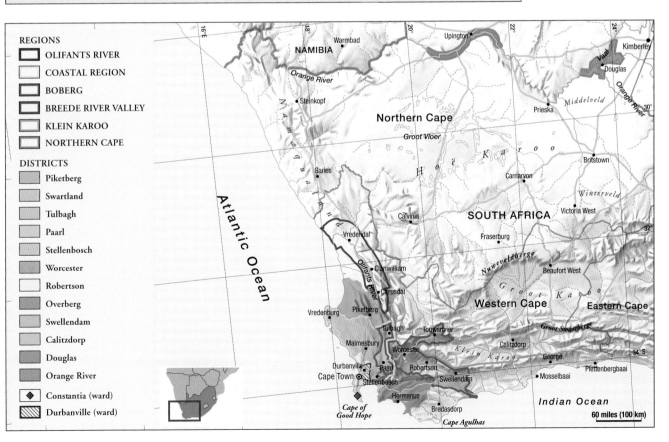

DYNAMISM AND FRESH THINKING

If one traveled through the wine-growing regions of South Africa at the end of the 1990s one would have been assured by all the vintners and winemakers that their region was predestined for white wines. But since then there has been a change. In 1997 four-fifths of the vineyards were planted with white varieties, but today it is around three-fifths. A large proportion of the harvest is still used either for spirits or sweet wines, but with exports taking off in recent years the production of dry wines has increased. As with dry wines, the demand for red wines is far greater, which in South Africa has led to substantially more widespread planting of Cabernet, Merlot, Shiraz, and Pinotage. Careful observation of the various wine regions shows that where quality wines are concerned, red wines are now clearly ahead. The preference for white wine—which can still be found among Afrikaans-speaking winemakers—may be due to the fact that, not least for linguistic reasons, many received their training in Germany. Nowadays South African winegrowers and winemakers can be found in all of Europe's wine-growing regions, where they take advantage of the northern autumn to gather experience in the field of vinification for a second time in the year.

The modern cellar building at Rustenberg in Stellensbosch symbolizes South Africa's emergence. In the *barriques* high-quality whites are aged in new oak.

There is no overlooking the fact that, as a wine-producing country, South Africa is in a state of upheaval. Vines are being planted everywhere with great energy. The increased demand is only one of many reasons for this phenomenon. The actual cause is probably due to a more fundamental problem. The years of boycott, which the country suffered as a result of its apartheid policy, not only substantially restricted wine exports, but also, and more importantly, affected the vine stocks.

While in other wine-growing countries great progress had been made in respect of the resistance of clones to viruses and disease, and planting had been improved accordingly, the South Africans had to continue using and propagating their virus-infected material year after year. On infected vines the leaves rolled up so that the grapes rarely ripened evenly and well. The consequence, which can still be seen in red wines in particular, takes the form of vegetal tastes and unpleasantly green and dry TANNINS. Many reds from the 1990s still have that fault, but the situation has changed. First, the vine nurseries, particularly those in Wellington, have succeeded in supplying new and healthy plants by utilizing all their capacities, and second, new plants have also been imported. Major new plantings are now already yielding crops.

EASY DRINKING WINES

There are already enough wines from healthy vines to show the extraordinary potential which South Africa enjoys as a wine-producing country. Whether this potential is exploited lies entirely in the hands of the producers. While the climatic conditions in general can be classified as Mediterranean, there is in reality a very broad spectrum, ranging from cooler locations such as Walker Bay to desert-like areas in Klein Karoo.

Although most of the regions in the vicinity of the coast receive sufficient rainfall, taking each year as a whole, providing a regular and adequate supply of water is a problem for all regions. Most vineyards have to be artificially irrigated, since in the often very hot and dry months from January to March the grapes would simply vegetate rather than ripen. And so the winegrowers' ponds form a characteristic element of the landscape, especially in Stellenbosch and Paarl. On some estates the water requirements of the vines are already

The wine-growing estates provide thousands of South Africans with employment.

constantly monitored and supply is managed electronically via a drip mechanism. This means the vines are subjected to less stress and produce higher yields. Until recently farmers, estate-owners, and winemakers saw themselves as an industry primarily oriented toward producing "easy-drinking wines." They are doing this with considerable success, producing good wines at surprisingly low prices. This industrial way of thinking is due not least to the structure of the operations. A typical estate consists of 370 acres (150 ha) or more. Fewer than 247 acres (100 ha) counts as small. In recent years, however, this has begun to change. On average, a new business is being set up every week. They include a growing number of small holdings aiming to produce high-quality wines. Many of the existing estates and private wineries have also added premium and super-premium wines to their range in recent years, and they certainly do not need to fear international comparison. The more moderate climate zones, in particular, are showing an astonishing potential for high-quality wines, and this development, which started rather hesitantly in the 1980s, is by no means complete.

GETTING THE CELLARS INTO TOP SHAPE

While the problems we have mentioned in relation to the vineyards can only be solved in the longer term, the South African winemakers are taking every opportunity to modernize by investing in efficient equipment. As long ago as the late 1920s the first experiments with temperature-controlled FERMENTATION began, with

Georgio Dalla Cia, the Friulian enologist at Meerlust, is quite an individual.

the result that this method had come to be generally used by the 1950s. This allowed the hot temperatures of the harvest months and the resulting OXIDATION of the must to be countered, which unleashed a veritable revolution in white wine production in particular.

As a rule, white wines are vinified between 53°F and 59°F (12°C and 15°C), but the yeast that occurs naturally on the skin is not capable of multiplying in such low temperatures. As a result, winemakers were forced to develop purebred yeast which could work at these temperatures. The enological research department of the Nietvoorbij Wine Institute has achieved noteworthy progress in this area. The downside can be seen in the clear standardization of all wines, because low temperatures and the corresponding YEAST have a decisive influence on the aromatic spectrum. In addition, as it is entirely up to individual winemakers whether or not they acidify or de-acidify their must (the addition of sugar is prohibited), they have the enological means in their hands to produce clean, fresh, modern wines. At the same time, though, the character of the individual varieties, determined as it is by the TERROIR, is largely suppressed.

Leading winemakers realized this long ago, and are trying to do something about it. Noteworthy results have been achieved in particular by the red-wine specialists, who continue to use walled fermentation tanks that correspond to the *lagares* of the Douro Valley. The best port wines continue to be vinified in these to this day.

The Legendary Constantias

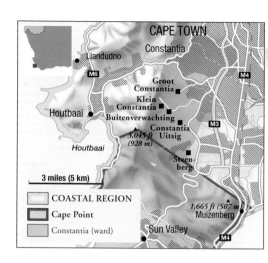

The road to Constantia runs past the foot of famous Table Mountain. Like all the celebrities who honored the Cape with their presence in the past, modern-day tourists from home and abroad now make the pilgrimage to the peninsula, which juts out southwards into the Atlantic Ocean. And the object of all their veneration is the Groot Constantia estate. This is the cradle of South African wine: a neat-and-tidy château in the Cape Dutch style, a cellar that makes wines for every wallet, with a museum in the former cellar building. It is the most regularly visited attraction in Cape Town. Today, this former property of the first governor has become a desirable residential suburb, where real estate agents and winegrowers fight over every piece of ground. Sub-divided into five wine estates, this most renowned of all South African viticultural locations is currently enjoying a remarkable renaissance.

It owes its advantages primarily to the Atlantic Ocean. Toward the southeast, it faces False Bay, which is overlooked from the vineyards. But the Atlantic also stretches away to the west, behind the red hills. From there, gentle breezes waft over the vineyards, substantially reducing the temper-

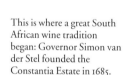

This is where a great South African wine tradition began: Governor Simon van der Stel founded the Constantia Estate in 1685.

ature during the ripening period. The average temperature here during the South African summer is only 66°F (19°C). In winter it rains a great deal. Average rainfall is more than 39 inches (100 cm) a year, making irrigation unnecessary, especially as the red loam soil retains the water well. Depending on the location, the dominant rock in the fertile earth is either weathered granite or powdered sandstone from Table Mountain. Since some of the lower-lying vineyards have had to make way for elegant residential estates, new ones have been scrambling up the hillside, which may well result in better-quality wines.

Governor Simon van der Stel managed to make the sweet wine from Constantia well known. His

son, Wilhelm Adriaen, who succeeded his father both as governor and as owner of the estate, was altogether too selfish and too arrogant in the way he used his power, which led to his falling out of favor with the Dutch East India Company. As a result, he was banished from South Africa. Constantia was divided up into Buitenverwachting, Groot Constantia, and Klein Constantia, and the estates were sold off separately. The following 70 years saw a succession of owners, which had a negative effect on the wine. Finally, in 1778, the estates were bought by Hendrik Cloete, a descendant of German settlers and an experienced winegrower. In Stellenbosch and on his lands at Weltevrede and Zandvliet in Robertson, he was already growing vines successfully. The first thing he did was to put some order into the vineyards, and then he turned his attention to making wine. He allowed the small grapes of the Muscat de Frontignan variety to overripen, so that their natural sugar content may well have lain between 5–6 oz per pint (300–350 g per liter) or more. And so the wine fermented until its alcohol content reached 13 percent by volume, often retaining 2½ oz of residual sugar per pint (150 g per liter). Under Cloete's management, Groot Constantia and its Muscat wine reached the zenith of their fame, becoming—alongside Tokaji—one of the favorites of the royal and imperial courts of Europe and the first cult New World wine.

The newly erected cellars at Buitenverwachting blend harmoniously with the landscape.

It was the Dutch East India Company and the colonial government which profited most from this development, because each had a right to buy one-third of all the wine produced at a minimal price. In other words, only one-third could be traded on the free market. When the British took over the colony in 1795, Hendrik Cloete junior, who had meanwhile inherited the estates, hoped for an end to this restrictive imposition. His hopes were in vain: the new masters found the old agreements altogether in their interest. Even so, Hendrik Cloete junior managed to maintain the high quality of his wine. His son, Jacob Pieter Cloete, inherited the estates upon his father's death in 1818, but was granted little more than a decade in which to enjoy his inheritance. Wine growing in South Africa fell on hard times. In Europe, the Continental System (Napoleon's blockade of the British Isles) had been lifted and the British, having regained access to their old favorites, the wines of Bordeaux, lost interest in those of South Africa. And if that was not enough, the winegrowers on the Cape, like their counterparts in Europe, had to contend with the devastations of pests and disease. First, the vines were attacked by powdery mildew, which decimated the vineyards. Cloete died in poverty in 1875. Ten years later, when phylloxera reached South Africa, Groot Constantia was taken over by the government as an experimental and teaching estate. When it was forced to replace all the rootstocks with resistant American species, exclusively, dry wine varieties were selected marking the end of a great chapter in South African viticultural history.

In the early 1980s Constantia slowly roused itself from its long slumber. At this time, not only Klein Constantia but also Buitenverwachting were acquired by owners who realized the great potential of their estates. They began to renew and extend the vineyards and

invested in new winemaking facilities. They also carefully restored the old stately homes and built model housing estates for their workers. This example by private growers was followed on the neighboring estate of Groot Constantia too. Today, the estate is independent and under the management of a trust.

The leading white varieties are Chardonnay and Sauvignon. The latter in particular develops a well-balanced and fresh expressivity in this temperate climate. The predominant AROMAS are reminiscent of fruits such as gooseberries and grapefruit, but in warmer years, stronger, exotic accents are present. Winemakers often prefer a vegetal character, with very green notes, reminiscent of grass and asparagus. A mineral quality is seen as especially characteristic. As a rule, winemakers go in for reductive low-temperature vinification, avoiding contact with the air, and for this reason the wines need either several months to mature in the bottle or else good ventilation, if they are to develop their BOUQUET. In the case of Chardonnay, there are unwooded versions, fermented in stainless steel tanks, and also wines fermented in barrels. In the case of Semillon, too, which is becoming increasingly popular with winemakers, fermentation in the wood is frequently employed. In addition, Groot Constantia also grows fresh Rieslings, as well as a certain amount of Pinot Gris, and of course Steen, as the almost ubiquitous Chenin Blanc is known here. White varieties considerably outnumber reds: the higher, south-facing slopes are particularly suited to them.

The example of Klein Constantia is especially noteworthy. Here, the Muscat de Frontignan has been replanted, and in 1986 the first new Vin de Constance was harvested and vinified in

THE FIVE CONSTANTIA ESTATES

BUITENVERWACHTING***−****
270 acres (110 ha); 900,000 bottles • Wines: Sauvignon, Chardonnay, Riesling, Buiten Blanc, Méthode Cap Classique, Christine, Cabernet Sauvignon
Lars Maack runs this exemplary family estate, which is known not just for wine but also for its gourmet restaurant. He grows well proven whites and more recently has achieved a marked rise in quality with his reds.

CONSTANTIA UITSIG***
79 acres (32 ha); 200,000 bottles • Wines: Chardonnay, →Chardonnay Reserve, Semillon, Sauvignon, Merlot, →Cabernet-Sauvignon-Merlot
An estate with a country lodge and two restaurants. Remarkable quality in the Chardonnay Reserve and the Cabernet-Merlot-Cuvée.

GROOT CONSTANTIA**−***
247 acres (100 ha); 560,000 bottles • Wines include: Sauvignon, Chardonnay, Riesling, Gourneurs Reserve, Cabernet Sauvignon, Shiraz, Pinotage, Port
The cradle of South African viticulture is constantly improving its quality. The Bordeaux-Cuvée (Cabernets and Merlot) is outstanding; the Pinotage is very good.

KLEIN CONSTANTIA**−****
182 acres (74 ha); 540,000 bottles • Wines include: Sauvignon, Chardonnay, Riesling, Semillon, Marlbrook, Cabernet Sauvignon, Shiraz, Vin de Constance
Under the Joostes and their winemaker Ross Gower, the estate is harking back to its legendary roots, in particular with its non-fortified Vin de Constance, made from Muscat de Frontignan. The dry wines don't reach the same level.

STEENBERG**
161 acres (65 ha); 400,000 bottles • Wines: Sauvignon, Chardonnay, Semillon, Cabernet Sauvignon, →Merlot; second label Motif, →Sauvignon Reserve
Complex investment project on Constantia's oldest farm, with a golf course, luxury hotel, restaurant, and wine-growing estate with hi-tech cellar; outstanding Sauvignon Reserve.

total accord with the old method. It is sold, after five years' maturation in the bottle, in bottles that are copies of those used in the 18th century. The 1997 vintage is amber-gold, a convincing wine with an intensive and complex bouquet, in which hints of orange and mandarin combine with honey and gingerbread. These aromas appear once more on the palate, enriched with toasted almonds. The oily texture and the sweetness are balanced by an elegant acidity. The example of Klein Constantia has inspired Groot Constantia to follow suit and plant its own Muscat grapes.

As there is so much to be said in favor of Constantia as a *terroir* for white wines, the quality of its reds is all the more surprising. Evidently Cabernet, Merlot, and Shiraz also like the red loam, and on the lower-lying locations they can produce outstanding results. Although many vines are still too young to deliver the required concentration, there are already some great *cuvées*. Groot Constantia bottles a wine known as Governor's Reserve, in which—as a rule—four-fifths Cabernet Sauvignon combines with one-fifth Cabernet Franc to produce a spicy, deep-red wine of medium structure with clear hints of eucalyptus.

Marlbrook, the top red wine from Klein Constantia, with its hints of toast and leather, is aged for a maximum of two years in French oak barrels. Klein Constantia's Shiraz Reserve is currently the subject of much discussion among the winemakers of Constantia. The dark wine, violet when young, has a very powerful bouquet in which the aromas of eucalyptus,

coffee, and smoke combine. Very rounded on the palate, with ripe fruit and a marked, albeit harmoniously integrated, spiciness derived from aging in American oak. It is the prime example of a modern red wine, which should set a precedent in South Africa too.

By contrast, Buitenverwachting's Cuvée Christine, which is aged in French *barriques*, is a classic. The clear emphasis of Cabernet Sauvignon, supported by a little Merlot and Cabernet Franc, leads to a dense wine characterized by black berries, damsons, undergrowth, eucalyptus, and spices. It achieves great harmony after several years in the bottle.

The wines from Buitenverwachting have made a decisive contribution to South Africa's image as a wine-producing country.

Opposite
Klein Constantia, one of the world's most attractive wine-making estates, also produces the highest quality wines of the five Constantia estates.

Constantia's vineyards seen from the air. The individual plots can easily be made out; recently they have been laid out on the slopes, too.

STELLENBOSCH

Stellenbosch, only 40 kilometers from Cape Town, is today the best-known wine region in South Africa. The town of the same name, with its famous university (founded in 1918), has succeeded in preserving much of its charm. This includes the numerous shade-giving oak trees, planted at the instigation of Simon van der Stel, who founded the township as the second European settlement on the Cape in 1679. The settlers built neat and tidy homes in the Cape-Dutch style, surrounded by gardens. These were joined later, in the immediate vicinity, by stately mansions built by the English in the Georgian and then Victorian styles.

In addition to the university, where most South African winemakers receive their viticultural and enological training, there is the highly regarded Elsenburg Agricultural College, and just outside the town, the Nietvoorbij Enological Institute. With its experimental vineyard and laboratory, Nietvoorbij is the center of South African wine research. This is also where control tastings take place for the recognition of a wine as a Wine of Origin.

Originally Stellenbosch was regarded as the stronghold of grain growing and cattle farming. The fertile flood meadows on the banks of the Eerste River produced much of the food needed by the ships of the Dutch East India Company. Even though wine, by dint of its non-perishable nature, was on the list of provisions at an early date, viticulture was of no great importance for the company, in spite of the decrees, mentioned above, which had been issued by its governor. The company's interests were not in the Cape, but in the huge profits to be made in India and

Like many of South Africa's estates, Meerlust looks after its Cape Dutch architecture. Its effect is enhanced further by the contrast with the spectacular Stellenbosch landscape.

the East Indies. For this reason it did nothing to market and publicize any wines other than Constantia. Nevertheless, viticulture developed spontaneously among the first, generally poor settlers who were allocated land in Stellenbosch. There was neither demand for, nor recognition of their wines, however, until the region came under British rule. In order to satisfy the demand for wine in England from 1812 to 1823, large quantities were exported. But this was the only period during the 19th century when farmers could make a living from wine. Not until the 20th century could Stellenbosch and Paarl create an image for themselves as viticultural centers.

From the point of view of landscape, Stellenbosch is one of the most beautiful wine regions in the world. In recent years, it has enjoyed a substantial boom, and now has the largest concentration of interesting winegrowers. Boland, with its well-equipped slopes and high-yield valleys, but especially its impressive hills, provides a wide variety of conditions, both in respect of climate and soil. This is reflected in the broad spectrum of wines produced here, ranging from the Cap Classique—

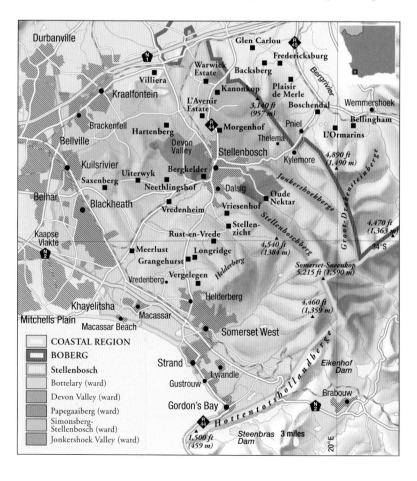

the South African version of champagne—to fruity, peppery Pinotages and noble, sweet Rieslings and fortified wines.

For red wine, the best *terroirs* are the hillside locations of weathered granite with acid soils. Some vineyards in the mountains lie at an altitude of nearly 2,000 feet (600 m) or more, and are characterized by a much sought-after temperate climate. To the west, the character of the soil is determined by the sandstone of Table Mountain, and produces convincing white wines. Altogether, Stellenbosch accounts for one-eighth of the country's total wine-producing area. Here, more often than elsewhere, there are dry farmed, in other words non-irrigated, vineyards. The yields are smaller, but the wines are well concentrated. Even so, the reservoirs are still a characteristic feature of the landscape.

Alongside various *cuvées* that are based on Cabernet Sauvignon, Merlot, and Cabernet

Left
Formerly an arable and cattle-farming region, Stellenbosch is now a stronghold of viticulture.

Right
Grape picking at Neethlingshof, one of the oldest and most important South African estates. In the background is the imposing Heldersberg.

Franc, impressive Shiraz wines are being produced on an ever-increasing scale. More and more winemakers are aging the wine in American oak, an unfamiliar taste for European palates at first, but with time a convincing combination with a typical hint of cinnamon. Stellenbosch is also the home of the best-quality Pinotages. Where white wines are concerned, the region produces not only good Sauvignons but also balanced (or in some cases very fruity) barrel-fermented Chardonnays with a hint of caramel. The Semillon, rich in finesse, is enjoying increasing popularity. And if these were not enough, the Noble Late Harvest Riesling from Neethlingshof, with its strong BOTRYTIS character, remains one of the region's most attractive wines.

Pinotage

Pinotage is without doubt an attractive red variety, with marked aromas of red berries, cherries, wild herbs, and often a discreet hint of banana peel. Its delights are quite different from those of the international standard varieties. Sometimes its fruit is reminiscent of stewed fruit, and its spiciness of pines and cinnamon. Occasionally it can smell of nail-varnish. While some producers praise this acetone note as typical, it points to grapes harvested too early and fermented at too low a temperature.

Pinotage is a variety first produced by Abraham Perold at Stellenbosch University in 1925. He crossed Pinot Noir with Cinsault, a widespread variety that thrives in a Mediterranean climate. Cinsault was known in South Africa at the time as Hermitage—quite unjustifiably, but that is how the new variety got its name. It was planted on the Kanonkop estate, for example, in 1941, and enjoyed its greatest historic success in 1959,

when it received first prize as a young wine from the Bellevue estate. There were few winemakers who treated it as a major variety, producing such great wines as the 1973 Kanonkop, which turned out, after a quarter of a century, to be a highly complex red wine, by no means too old, and reminiscent of an old Pinot. However, badly vinified and over-produced, the Pinotage gave rise to unpleasant, coarse red wines, and its acceptance increased only slowly. When it was exposed to the criticism of British wine experts in 1976, it finally fell into disfavor, and it was planted less and less. Fortunately, however, winegrowers such as the Kriges at Kanonkop and their then winemaker Jan Boland Coetzee were not dismayed by the negative propaganda. While he later continued to make outstanding Pinotages on his own Vriesenhof estate, which he bottled as Paradyskloof, his successor at Kanonkop, Beyers Truter, succeeded in attracting attention once more to this idiosyncratic variety.

With a greater understanding of the natural preconditions which it requires, Pinotage has now embarked on a new career. At precisely the moment (1990) when it accounted for its smallest-ever proportion of South Africa's vines (1.9 percent), it started to attract interest again. It now accounts for 6.4 percent and is beginning to stabilize on that level.

Although the growers have now discovered how to make very pleasing, fruity wines from young Pinotage vines, the best results are from old, non-irrigated bush vines trained in the traditional Gobelet system. They yield some extraordinarily concentrated, highly individual wines. Recently Pinotage has been the focus of discussion as the essential component of the Cape Blend and a growing number of estates are blending it with Cabernet Sauvignon and Merlot. The results are often very convincing, and an unmistakeable and highly individual character has been achieved.

Distill

The restructuring of South Africa's wine industry has brought a merger between the old big names Distillers Corporation, the country's major brandy distributor, and Stellenbosch Farmers' Winery, with their associated estates, trading and sales companies to create a new giant, Distill. It now dominates nearly 30 percent of South Africa's total wine output; however, a wide range of well-known names have survived the merger and continue to live their own lives as before. Nevertheless, Distill has brightened up its product philosophy and is now giving preference to fruity, lively, modern wines.

Bergkelder is still one of the big attractions of the corporation, which is now operating internationally. Private customers can deposit bottles to age in the cellars of its Papegaai Mountain. Fleur du Cap, the best known of Bergkelder's brands, has acquired new prestige with its Unfiltered Collection. Among the company's sparkling wines Pongrácz, from J.C. le Roux's cellar, is now rivalling the company's own Cap Classique, made from Pinot Noir. A new marketing company, *Lusan Premium Wines*, has been set up for the well known estates Alto, Le Bonheur, and Uitkyk; it also handles the production of Neethlingshof and Stellzicht.

Established in 1970, Distillers Corporation was the life work of Anton Rupert.

Stellenbosch Farmers' Winery, on the other hand, is the work of one of the most lively personalities in South Africa's wine history, William Charles Winshaw, who was born in Kentucky in 1871. After spending years as gold digger, Texas ranger, and gambler he studied medicine and came to South Africa in charge of a mule transport. After serving as a doctor in a military hospital during the Boer War he began to specialize in wine production, and in 1924 bought the Oude Libertas Farm. Then he established his winery. The Farm is now a visitors center with a tasting area, restaurant, and an amphitheatre.

SELECT PRODUCERS IN STELLENBOSCH

L'AVENIR ESTATE***
STELLENBOSCH
133 acres (54 ha); 260,000 bottles • Wines include: Chardonnay, Sauvignon, Chenin, →Pinotage, Cabernet Sauvignon
Excellent Pinotage, Chenin with slight residual sugar, and original Vin de Meurveur Noble Late Harvest made from Colombard.

BEYERSKLOOF***−****
STELLENBOSCH
17 acres (7 ha); bought-in grapes; 800,000 bottles • Wines: Cabernet Sauvignon, Pinotage, →Synergie
"Winemaker of the Year" in 1991. Mature reds from Pinotage and Cabernet Sauvignon, excellent Cape Blend.

J.P. BREDELL***
HELDERBERG
235 acres (95 ha); 80,000 bottles • Wines: Pinotage, Shiraz, Merlot, →Cape Vintage Reserve, Late Bottled Vintage
Specialist in fortified wines; owner Anton Bredell makes more red wine and fills his own bottles.

CLOS MALVERNE***
STELLENBOSCH, DEVON VALLEY
62 acres (25 ha); 300,000 bottles • Wines include: Auret, →Pinotage, Cabernet Sauvignon, Cabernet Sauvignon/Shiraz
The Pritchards' flagship is the Auret, a full-bodied red wine made from Pinotage, Cabernet Sauvignon, and Merlot, a Pinotage Reserve intended for aging.

DELHEIM**−****
STELLENBOSCH, KOELENHOF
371 acres (150 ha); 600,000 bottles • Wines include: Sauvignon, Chardonnay, Rhine Riesling, Cabernet Sauvignon, Merlot, Pinotage, →Grand Reserve, →Vera Cruz Shiraz
"Spatz" Sperling, has been a champion of dry wines since 1951. Now his son Victor and daughter Nora run the vineyards, distribution, and the summer restaurant. Delheim produces an excellent Vera Cruz Shiraz.

NEIL ELLIS WINES***−****
STELLENBOSCH, JONKERSHOEK
259 acres (105 ha); 420,000 bottles • Wines: Sauvignon, Chardonnay, Riesling, Cabernet Sauvignon, Cabernet/Merlot, Pinotage, Pinot Noir, Shiraz

This highly regarded winemaker has set up an outstanding, waterfall-cooled winery on Hans-Peter Schröder's Japanese-styled Oude Nectar estate. Excellent Zwalu Cuvée with winegrower Werner Näkel since 1998.

KEN FORRESTER**−****
HELDERBERG
Bought-in grapes; 360,000 bottles • Wines include: →Forrester Meinert Chenin, →Noble Late Harvest, Gipsy, Grenache-Syrah
With the winemaker Martin Meinert, Ken Forrester is conjuring excellent white wines from Chenin Blanc and producing reds with a highly individual character on the historical Scholzen estate.

GRANGEHURST****
HELDERBERG
Bought-in grapes; 100,000 bottles • Wines: Pinotage, Cabernet Sauvignon-Merlot, Nikela
Jeremy Walker bought grapes from four selected locations. Now better equipped, he produces top quality red wines.

JACOBSDAL ESTATE***
STELLENBOSCH
247 acres (100 ha); 120,000 bottles • Wine: Pinotage
Cornelis Dumas ferments Pinotage in open concrete tanks with natural yeast and ages it in French *barriques*.

JORDAN**−****
STELLENBOSCH
272 acres (110 ha); 600,000 bottles • Wines include: →Chardonnay, Fumé Blanc, Merlot, →Cabernet Sauvignon, →Cobblers Hill
Gary and Kathy Jordan have been producing wines on their family estate since 1993. Cobblers Hill, a Bordeaux blend of Cabernet Souvignon, Merlot, and Cabernet Franc, is a great success.

KANONKOP****−*****
STELLENBOSCH
345 acres (140 ha); 360,000 bottles • Wines: Pinotage, Cabernet Sauvignon, Paul Sauer, Kadette
The Krige brothers have made great South African red wines since 1973; they ferment them in stone basins, and age them in French *barriques*. They only showed their great class after ten years. Beyers Truter is the winemaker.

MEERLUST***
STELLENBOSCH
370 acres (150 ha); 500,000 bottles • Wines include:
→*Chardonnay; Rubicon, Merlot, Pinot Noir*
The Myburgh family has lived on this entrancing vineyard since 1756 and since 1978 Giorgio Dall Cia has been making outstanding wines in the classical French style; they are put on the market after maturing in the bottle for four to five years.

MORGENHOF**−****
STELLENBOSCH, SIMONSBERG
161 acres (65 ha); 250,000 bottles • Wines include:
Chardonnay, Chenin, Brut Reserve, →*Merlot Reserve,*
Première Séléction
Anne Cointreau, a scion of the famous liqueur dynasty, and her husband Alain Huchon have transformed the historic property into a must-see attraction. The reserve wine and *cuvée* quality is high.

MULDERBOSCH***
STELLENBOSCH
67 acres (27 ha); bought-in grapes; 230,000 bottles
• Wines: Steen-op-Hont, Chardonnay, →*Sauvignon,*
Faithful Hound
Winemaker Mike Dobrovic produces very good white wines with his highly motivated crew.

MURATIE***
STELLENBOSCH, KOELENHOF
86 acres (35 ha); 120,000 bottles • Wines include: Ansela,
Cabernet Sauvignon, Merlot, Pinot Noir, →*Shiraz, Port*
Young Charla Melck is now running this family estate, which is 300 years old. It is now producing a very full-bodied Shiraz with a dense fruity flavor and a spicy sweetness.

NEETHLINGSHOF**−****
STELLENBOSCH
519 acres (210 ha); 500,000 bottles • Wines include:
Chardonnay, Gewürztraminer, →*Riesling Noble Late*
Harvest, Shiraz, Lord Neethling: →*Pinotage,* →*Laurentius*
An estate founded in 1682, with a renovated manor house (a protected heritage site) dating from 1814. Since 2001 a new team has been running the estate, producing a very convincing Lord Neethling range; it includes Cuvée Laurentius, with Shiraz as the dominant element.

RAATS FAMILY WINES****
STELLENBOSCH
15 acres (6 ha); bought-in grapes • Wines: Chenin
Blanc, →*Original Chenin,* →*Cabernet Franc*
Bruwer Raats, formerly with Delaire and now wine-maker with his brother Jasper at Zorgvliet, makes excellent Chenins and probably the best Cabernet Franc in South Africa.

RUST-EN-VREDE****
HELDERBERG
104 acres (42 ha); 240,000 bottles • Wines: Rust-en-
Vrede Estate Wine, Tinta Barocca
In the future high flyer Jean Engelbrecht intends to bottle only the outstanding estate wine. With golf star Ernie Els he created a joint venture with a convincing Bordeaux blend at top price.

RUSTENBERG**−****
STELLENBOSCH
198 acres (80 ha); 680,000 bottles • Wines include:
Chardonnay, Sauvignon, Q.F.1, Cabernet Sauvignon,
Rustenberg
A versatile 2,470-acre (1,000-ha) estate consisting of three historic farmsteads. Top wines: Cabernet Sauvignon Peter Barlow (who built up the estate after 1940), Chardonnay Five Soldiers. The second label, Brampton, is rather disappointing.

SAXENBURG****
STELLENBOSCH
222 acres (90 ha); 300,000 bottles • Wines include:
Sauvignon, Chardonnay, Cabernet Sauvignon, Merlot,
Shiraz, Pinotage, Saxenburg Shiraz Select
The estate has enjoyed a rapid rise under Nico van der Merwe since 1991 with five single-variety Private-Collection wines from the best-quality grapes. He also owns the Château Capion in Languedoc.

SIMONSIG *−***
STELLENBOSCH
506 acres (205 ha); 2,000,000 bottles • Wines include:
Méthode Cap Classique, Chardonnay, Sauvignon,
Riesling, Cabernet Sauvignon, Pinotage, →*Tiara,*
Syrah Merindol
19 different grape varieties. Three quality series. Produced the first South African sparkling wine, Kaapse Vonkel, in 1971. →Bordeaux-*cuvée* Tiara; fruity Pinotage; full, spicy Syrah.

STELLENZICHT**−****
HELDERBERG
563 acres (228 ha); 600,000 bottles • Wines include:
Chardonnay, →*Semillon Reserve, Shiraz, Pinotage,*
Malbec, Merlot, Stellenzicht, →*Syrah*
Sister estate of Neethlingshof with first-class vineyards. Apart from the complex Semillon, the estate's best products are its reds, especially those from Syrah grapes, like its "Syrah," which has won many awards.

THELEMA MOUNTAIN VINEYARDS****
STELLENBOSCH
124 acres (50 ha); 300,000 bottles • Wines include:
Sauvignon, Chardonnay; Shiraz, →*Merlot Reserve,*
→*Cabernet Sauvignon*
Gyles Webb has planted his vines high up on the Simonsberg, and makes some of the most celebrated South African wines.

DE TRAFFORD***
STELLENBOSCH
7.5 acres (3 ha); bought-in grapes; 36,000 bottles • Wines:
Chenin Blanc, Cabernet Sauvignon, Merlot, Pinot Noir,
Vin de Paille
The increasingly good Cabernet Sauvignon and Merlot have now been joined by an amazing *vin de paille* made from Chenin.

VERGELEGEN****
HELDERBERG
254 acres (103 ha); 440,000 bottles • Wines include:
Chardonnay Reserve, Sauvignon, Shiraz, Merlot,
→*Cabernet Sauvignon,* →*Vergelegen*
The super-estate of the Anglo-American concern with the octagonal gravity winery, now run by winemaker André van Rensburg. Superb blend of the Cabernets and Merlot.

VRIESENHOF AND PARADYSKLOOF***−****
STELLENBOSCH
86 acres (35 ha); bought-in grapes; 330,000 bottles
• Wines: Vriesenhof: Pinotage, Pinot Noir, Cabernet
Sauvignon, Kallista, →*Talana Hill Chardonney*
After Kanonkop, Jan Coetzee took over Vriesenhof and the nearby Talana Hill Winery on his own account; he makes highly individual wines, some bottled as Paradyskloof. Many experiments in the vineyard and cellar; exquisite Pinot Noir Winemaker's Guild.

WARWICK ESTATE***−****
STELLENBOSCH
173 acres (70 ha); 250,000 bottles • Wines: Chardonnay;
Pinotage, Cabernet Franc, Three Cape Ladies, →*Trilogy*
Under Mike Radcliffe even more stress is laid on quality and precision in the vineyard and cellars of this family estate. Merlot and Cabernet Sauvignon are now only for the blends.

Paarl

In Paarl, which with its 90,000 or so inhabitants is the second-largest town in the Cape region, you can still admire the numerous witnesses to Boer and British building styles, and stroll along the 7 miles (11 km) of the jacaranda-lined main street. The town, which dates from 1717, takes its name from the granite mountain at the foot of which it was established. When the sun shines on the mountain after a shower, it glitters like a pearl, or in Afrikaans, *paarl*. On the southeast slope is the Taal Monument, with its dazzling white columns of different heights, which is dedicated to Afrikaans, the language of the majority of the community in South Africa. Paarl Rock affords a magnificent view stretching to the Atlantic Ocean and even to Cape Town, 37 miles (60 km) away. From the summit you can also look down into the valley of Berg River, which makes possible the irrigation of the sandy soils on which the extensive vineyards are laid out. The Paarl region produces one-fifth of all the wine grown in South Africa.

On the slope above the town of Paarl is the Taal Monument, erected in 1875 in honor of the Afrikaans language.

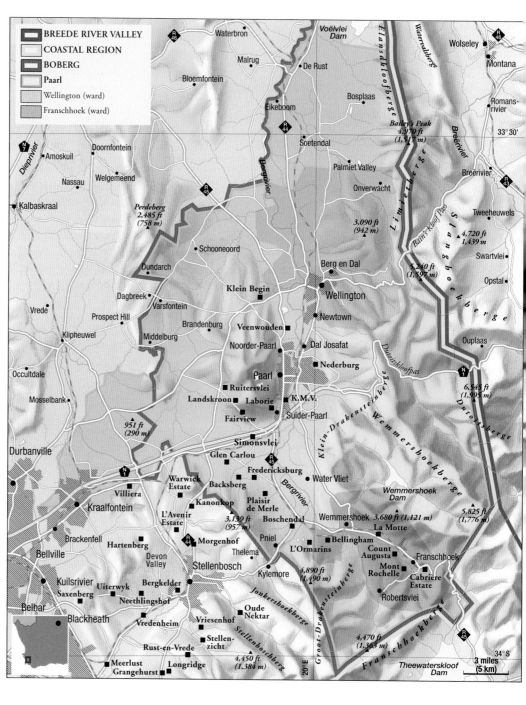

BREEDE RIVER VALLEY
COASTAL REGION
BOBERG
Paarl
Wellington (ward)
Franschhoek (ward)

In the past, the broad, flat vineyards were used almost exclusively for growing Chenin Blanc, Colombard, and Palomino (known as White French), which supplied the must for sherry production. After all, Paarl lies at the same latitude in the southern hemisphere as Jerez de la Frontera in the northern, and enjoys comparably favorable conditions for the SOLERA system of aging sherry. From about 1940, sherry and port dominated wine production in the region for a long time. But demand for fortified wines has declined dramatically in the meantime, while there has been a marked increase in the demand for dry white wines. Chardonnay and Sauvignon are gaining in popularity, but Chenin Blanc is now also used to produce attractive white wines.

The Paarl wine district is characterized by a decidedly Mediterranean climate, with hot, dry summers alternating with damp winters. The average temperature in the months from December to March (the decisive growing

Veenwouden—the red-wine refuge of a wine-obsessed opera singer.

period) is 72.5°F (22.5°C), two degrees higher than in Stellenbosch.

Maritime influences are of no great importance here. These natural conditions are reflected in the character of the wines, which often evince more volume and strength, and less frequently the elegance and delicate natural acidity of more temperate zones. The winemakers can be glad of South African legislation, which allows them to acidulate their wines. This is done at the pressing stage, and when done properly it provides for good balance; in other respects the wines always have a harmonious finish.

These days a broad spectrum of noteworthy white grape varieties can be found in Paarl. Besides those already mentioned, these include the White Riesling and Cape Riesling, Gewürztraminer and Bouquet, Hanepoot and Muscat de Frontignan (known here as Muscadel), Semillon, and Pinot Gris. The higher locations, including the neighborhood of the town where granite predominates (in contrast to the area

The Nederburg Auction

To the east of Paarl lies Nederburg, the best-known South African estate worldwide. It vinifies not only the produce of its own 247 acres (100 ha) of vineyards, but also the grapes from a further 1,358 acres (550 ha) belonging to three other estates. It maintains its own plantation to ensure the best clones and rootstocks.

The old-established property with its historic mansion enjoyed its first success under the German brewery director, Johann Georg Graue, who emigrated to South Africa in 1937 to get away from the Nazis. Graue planted first-class vines and was the first to conduct temperature-controlled vinification. After the death of his son Arnold, the winemaking was taken over by another German, Günther

Brözel, who created South Africa's first botrytis wine, Edelkeur.

In 1966 Nederburg was taken over by the Stellenbosch Farmers' Winery, and 1975 saw the first auction to be staged here. Every year since, in the spring, 120 to 150 different wines come under the hammer. Nederburg produces special wines for these occasions, but there is also a jury to select outstanding rare wines from other producers.

At this, which must surely be one of the most important enological and social events on the South African calendar, to which 1,600 guests are generally invited, the country demonstrates its top products to an amazed international public. Part of the proceeds goes to charity.

collapse in times of crisis. The most powerful weapon of the K.W.V. was a quota system which allowed it to fix, even for non-members, the quantity of surplus to be handed over to the organization free of charge for the purposes of distillation. At this time brandy and alcohol production—which still comprises two-thirds of its business—was very much at the focus of its interest. The repeal of this law and the sudden increase in demand from abroad not only transformed the situation of the independent producers but also forced the K.W.V. to re-orient itself.

A major restructuring took place in 1995 when K.W.V. International was set up as an independent trading company. It now maintains branches in Great Britain, the Netherlands, Germany, and the United States, as well as the historical Laborie Estate in Paarl. Since January 1, 2003 it has been an independent joint stock company, with shares traded on the stock market. K.W.V. Limited and Wijngaard Ko-operative is an entirely separate entity, and it handles production. The conversion of K.W.V. into a group of companies, which was completed in 1997, can truly be described as revolutionary, for the wine division has been separately structured since that date. Investments in the millions, state-of-the-art vinification technology, and a barrel park of 14,000 units are the outward signs of this new orientation.

In terms of range, K.W.V. lays particular emphasis on slim lines, and it concentrates on a limited portfolio of well established brands. The most famous is Cathedral Cellar, named after the great cellar in Paarl, and it guarantees good to very good quality in whites and reds. At least as convincing are the other series like K.W.V., Roodeberg, Robert's Rock, and Perly Bay, if one considers that each name covers several million bottles. They are all cleanly made, very fruity and balanced wines. With Perold K.W.V. acquired a wine that achieved cult status. It was godfathered by Abraham Perold, the famous wine professor and grower of Pinotage. Made from the produce of a single vineyard near Paarl, this impressively intensive and complex Shiraz has only been made in great vintage years since 1996. K.W.V.'s own Laborie Estate, well known for its Cap Classique, has outstanding full-bodied reds and also offers the delicious Pineau de Laborie liqueur wine, made from Pinotage.

northeast of Malmesbury, which is characterized by a crumbly slate), are eminently suited to red wines. In general, the Bordeaux varieties are preferred, with Cabernet Sauvignon and Merlot often used for single-variety wines, or as a blend with or without Cabernet Franc. But here, too, there is increasing interest in Pinotage, which in line with tradition has hitherto been used for making port, often in combination with Tinta Barocca. Shiraz is also finding more and more devotees. The hot climate produces adequate ripeness and gentle tannins. Increasingly, ultramodern, electronically regulated irrigation techniques are being deployed. The DOSAGE is regulated by measuring stations, so that the vines get the right amount of moisture at the proper time.

The town of Paarl is the headquarters of the umbrella organization of wine-growing cooperatives, the Kooperatieve Wijnbouwers Vereniging founded in 1918. The cellars of the largest cooperative in the world cover an area of more than 47 acres (19 ha). The umbrella organization, with its various subsidiaries, is owned by the 4,000 wine-growing members. Beside the attractive facade of the head office building, La Concorde in Main Street, which was designed by the Spanish sculptor Florencio Quiran and provides K.W.V.'s logo, the Cathedral Cellar has become the company's trademark. Set up in 1930, the cellar contains huge oak vats with carved fronts illustrating the history of South African wine production.

The K.W.V. determined the course of history for all South Africa's wine industry for decades. From 1940 to 1992 the K.W.V. held unrestricted sway over it, and was able to prevent its

Cathedral Cellar in Paarl is the showpiece of the K.W.V., the winemaking cooperatives' umbrella organization. It serves as a cellar hall and gives its name to a series of wines. The carved ends of the barrels tell the story of South African viticulture.

CATHEDRAL
—CELLAR—
2002
CHARDONNAY
WINE OF ORIGIN · COASTAL REGION
PRODUCE OF SOUTH AFRICA
14.0% VOL 750ml A100

Franschhoek

The name means "French Corner," and it is developing into an autonomous growing region thanks to the cohesion of its 20 or so estates and the high quality of their products. Classed as a ward, it is officially part of the Paarl wine district. Located to the south of Paarl and the east of Stellenbosch, the area, however, has a character all of its own. From its source in the Franschhoek Mountains, the Berg River has found its way through the narrow valley, which is just 8 miles (14 km) long. This valley is not only closed off to the south by the mountains; but it is also sealed off to the east by a steep chain of cliffs. From this gorge, the only exit is by means of a road leading over a single pass, formerly the elephant trail. To the north, the valley is framed by the Drakenstein Mountains. Compared with Paarl, Franschhoek has a somewhat cooler, wetter climate, with annual rainfall of 46 inches (120 cm).

At the entrance to the valley lies the historic Boschendal Estate of almost 1,236 acres (500 ha) of vineyard; it now belongs to the Anglo-American Farms group. In 1685 Boschendal was transferred by Simon van der Stel to the Huguenot Jean de Long. Between 1688 and 1690 the Governor encouraged the immigration of around 200 Huguenots forced to flee France after the Revocation of the Edict of Nantes. However, van der Stel forbade them to set up a village of their own and settled them among immigrants of Dutch and German origin. The allocation of land took place largely between

Well-tended wine estates are the symbol of Franschhoek.

Huguenots settled in Franschhoek in about 1690, and set up villages and well-tended estates, most of which bear French names to this day.

1693 and 1695 and is reflected in the dates of foundation of estates such as La Motte, La Provence, Haute-Provence, Cabrières, and Bellinchamp (now Bellingham). The Huguenots brought their experience of wine growing and winemaking with them. Jacques de Villiers was the first to plant grapes in the green valley, and together with his brothers, Pierre and Abraham, founded a wine dynasty whose eighth generation is once more growing wine in Franschhoek—the only Huguenot family still doing so. Beyond the boundaries of the little valley, Huguenots exerted their influence on wine growing in the whole of the Cape region. This makes it all the more peculiar when the French state calls for a change in the names of estates that have been producing wine for three centuries.

The types of soil vary considerably, ranging from fertile, loamy alluvial land near the river to red, stony locations with some clay, or broken granite on the higher slopes. The mountains that frame the valley on three sides provide sloping locations facing in almost every direction. These influences are modified by the differences in the altitude of the vineyards: from little more than 328 feet (100 m) near the river in the lower part of the valley, to about 1,640 feet (500 m) on the highest usable slopes.

At first, the winegrowers and winemakers of Franschhoek made a name for themselves with Sauvignon Blanc, Semillon, Chardonnay, and Cap Classique, the bottle-fermented sparkling wine for which Boschendal and Pierre Jourdan of Cabrières were particularly well-known. In the case of Chardonnay and Sauvignon there are definite differences in expression depending on the altitude of the vineyard. The grapes that ripen in the valleys lead to rounded, full-bodied wines, sometimes on the heavy side. Those grown above 985 feet (300 m) are definitely fresher and more elegant, and are marked by delicate, fruity aromas. But with red wine too, the

Left
Boschendal, the ward's oldest and largest estate, is known for the high quality of its wine, for splendid picnics, and an excellent restaurant.

Right
The potential of the *terroir* is given priority in Mont Rochelle.

Franschhoek is a small but beautiful valley, surrounded by high mountains on three sides.

domains in this attractive valley are very successful. The Bordeaux varieties and blends still account for most of the wines produced, but for a long time the Shiraz has shown that it can often ripen excellently here, and one of the best Pinotages in the whole Cape region comes from Bellingham.

Apart from the natural charms of the countryside and its remarkable wines, the pleasant little town of Franschhoek has one more attraction: gastronomy. Alongside its hotels and the often extremely comfortable guest houses, it has more than 20 restaurants, some of which are among the best in South Africa.

Select Producers in Paarl & Franschhoek

PAARL

BRAHMS****
62 acres (25 ha); • *Wine: Shiraz*
With their very first product, their 1999 Shiraz, Gesie and Braam Lategan showed that they were going for top quality.

FAIRVIEW**−****
494 acres (200 ha); 1,500,000 bottles • *Wines include: Sauvignon, →Viognier, Goats do Roam, Zinfandel, →Primo Pinotage, Pegleg Carignan, →Cyril Back Shiraz*
Charles Back is never lost for ideas, but he is devoted to Rhône varieties; deep dark concentrated reds from Shiraz and Pinotage, a very palatable Goats Cuvée—to go with the farm's own goats cheese—and an exemplary Viognier.

GLEN CARLOU***
161 acres (65 ha); 440,000 bottles • *Wines: Chardonnay Reserve, Pinot Noir, Zinfandel, Shiraz, Grand Classique*
A project by David Hess from Switzerland (Napas Hess Collection) and Walter Finlayson. Mainly solid reds and top Chardonnay.

PLAISIR DE MERLE***
988 acres (400 ha); 500,000 bottles • *Wines include: Chardonnay, Sauvignon; Cabernet Sauvignon, Merlot, Shiraz*
The show estate of Distill (see page 764) only bottles its best wines under its own label, while the rest goes to Nederburg. Good Chardonnay and Cabernet Sauvignon Reserve.

RUITERSVLEI*−***
865 acres (350 ha); 800,000 bottles • *Wines include: Shiraz, Merlot, Cabernet Sauvignon*
The estate, belonging to the Faure family, produces a wide variety, headed by the powerful Reserve Cabernets and Merlots.

RUPERT & ROTHSCHILD***−****
494 acres (200 ha); c. 250,000 bottles • *Wines: →Baroness Nadine, Classique →Baron Edmond*
Even after the death of Anthonij Rupert the joint venture is being successfully continued with S.-W. Joubert as master of the cellar and Michel Rolland as consultant.

SEIDELBERG ESTATE**−***
247 acres (100 ha); 400,000 bottles • *Wines include: Chenin Blanc, Chardonnay, Viognier, Merlot, Shiraz, Cabernet Sauvignon, Un Deux Trois, Red Muscadel*
Roland Seidel took over this very advantageously located estate in 1997 and has devoted much energy to building it up and expanding it. He offers a big range of wines under the "Seidelberg" and "De Leuwen Jagd" labels. The estate's best wines are Roland's Reserve Syrah and its Cabernet Sauvignon.

VEENWOUDEN****
36 acres (14.5 ha); 70,000 bottles • *Wines: Veenwouden Classic, Vivat Bacchus, Merlot, Thornhill Shiraz*
Operatic tenor and wine fanatic Deon van der Walt and his brother Marcel produce three magnificent red wines from Merlot, Cabernet, and Malbec. New young Shiraz.

VILLIERA***
740 acres (300 ha); 1,200,000 bottles • *Wines include: Méthode Cap Classique; Sauvignon, Chardonnay, Chenin, Riesling, Cru Monro, Shiraz, Merlot, →Pinotage*
Jeff Grier favors an accessible wine style with a lot of fruit. He offers a complex Bush Wine Sauvignon Blanc and a spicy Shiraz with good length.

FRANSCHHOEK

AGUSTA**
Haute Provence, Franschhoek
99 acres (40 ha); bought-in grapes; 700,000 bottles.
Wines include: Chardonnay, Sauvignon, Chenin, Cabernet Sauvignon
Graf Agusta took over this historic Huguenot farm in 1998. His Chardonnay and Cabernet Sauvignon are very promising.

BELLINGHAM**−***
296 acres (120 ha); bought-in grapes; 4,000,000 bottles • *Wines include: Chardonnay, Sauvignon; Cabernet Franc and Sauvignon, Pinotage, Merlot, Shiraz*
In its premium "Spitz" (=Top) range this big enterprise offers a very convincing Pinotage and Cabernet Franc; the Chenin Maverick is also very good.

BOSCHENDAL***
741 acres (300 ha); 3,000,000 bottles • *Wines include: Sauvignon, Chardonnay, Brut, →Shiraz, Cabernet Sauvignou, Merlot, →Grand Reserve*
This very beautiful historic estate has greatly increased its share of reds in recent years, and also notably raised the quality of the wines.

CABRIÈRE ESTATE***
74 acres (30 ha); 300,000 bottles • *Wines: various Méthode Cap Classique Pierre Jourdan; Chardonnay, Pinot Noir*
To gain the right impression, try the Cap Classique or the Pinot Noirs in the Haute Cabrière restaurant.

MONT ROCHELLE**
114 acres (46 ha); 120,000 bottles • *Wines: Chardonnay, Sauvignon; Cabernet Sauvignon, Merlot, Pinotage*
Now owned by Miko Rwayitare from the Congo, this pretty estate is developing a new dynamic and looking for a new identity.

LA MOTTE**−***
267 acres (108 ha) • *Wines: Sauvignon, →Chardonnay, Cabernet Sauvignon, Shiraz, →Millenium*
Cellar master Jacques Borman has been running this old Huguenot estate and its vineyards since 1984. He is putting his intensive experience in France into classical red wines, with his Bordeaux blend Millenium at the very top.

L'ORMARINS***
420 acres (170 ha); 500,000 bottles • *Wines include: Chardonnay, Sauvignon, Optima, Shiraz, Cabernet Sauvignon*
A historic, beautifully restored farmstead owned by the Rupert Family Trust. Particularly successful are the Cuvée Optima made from Merlot, and the single-variety Cabernet Sauvignon.

ROBERTSON

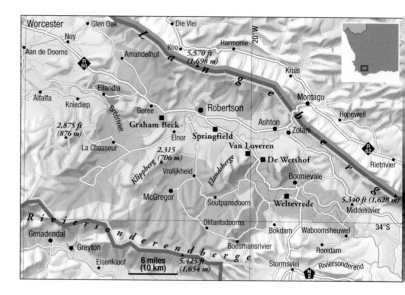

Since the reservoirs of the Du Toitskloof mountains have provided enough water even in the dry summer months, the character of the Robertson region has been transformed. Where settlers only began to start breeding sheep and ostrich on the steppe-like terrain at the start of the 19th century, the valleys are now lush green and vineyards extend right up the lower slopes of the mountains.

Wine growing here is only possible because of the assured water supply—most of the estates lie along the river. But two further phenomena have a positive effect. The summer heat is regularly tempered in the afternoons by the clouds which blow in from the ocean, 50 miles (80 km) distant, which push against the mountain tops and cause temperatures to fall. The comparatively cool nights bring about a lengthening of the ripening season, and preserve the grapes' aromas. The second factor gives the district a position all of its own: everywhere else in the Cape region, the soils are mainly acid, but in Robertson they are rich in lime. This is also the reason why horses are bred here: the calcium strengthens their bones. As for the wines, it helps to give them a very special finesse.

In the past Chenin and Colombard, used for the production of spirits, were the predominant varieties here, and they are still the most widely grown. The local producers have learned how to produce very pleasant, aromatic, and balanced white wines. Chardonnay and Sauvignon, in particular, gain a final polish from the calcium, but chiefly they are used to make easy drinking wines without much in the way of structure or character.

▭	KLEIN KAROO
▭	BREEDE RIVER VY.
▭	**Robertson**
▭	Vinkrivier (ward)
▭	Eilandia (ward)
▭	La Chasseur (ward)
▭	Agterkliphoogte (ward)
▭	Hoopsrivier (ward)
▭	Klaasvoogds (ward)
▭	McGregor (ward)
▭	Boesmansrivier (ward)
▭	Bonnievale (ward)

Left
Young springboks on the barren steppe that surrounds fertile Robertson valley.

Right
While roses bloom in other wine-growing regions, the winegrowers of Robertson are proud of their flame-red *cañas.*

The realization that you have a special *terroir* at your disposal has obviously had an inspiring effect. Certainly, the white wines above all have benefited, but more and more estates are proving that they can also achieve Shiraz and Cabernet of extraordinary quality on this soil. As a result, the proportion of red wine is steadily rising; while previously it accounted for just ten percent of the total, some operations are now aiming at a figure of 40 or even 50 percent in the future. One specialty of Robertson is its sweet, seductive Muscadel wines, which come in both gold- and copper-colored versions.

Lime soils in combination with humidity also attract snails, however. In Robertson this pest is being countered by a thoroughly ecological method. Weltevrede, for example, has 200 badgers on the payroll. The animals regard snails as a delicacy, and every morning they are driven to their workplace, where they make short shrift of the vermin. Having performed their day's work, they are so tired and bloated that they jump back on to the trucks quite voluntarily, in order to be driven back to their sleeping quarters.

Other Wine Regions

Wellington

Wellington belongs to Paarl District and used to supply mainly white grapes for sherry production. Now, however, the vineyards are being comprehensively restocked and supplemented with red varieties. The three cooperatives and the few estates are in a privileged position here, because the area surrounding the small town is South Africa's largest nursery area for vines.
Recommended: Mont du Toit, Linton Park, Wellington Wijnkelder, Bovlei Winery, Wamakersvallei.

Klein Karoo

The Hottentot name of this wine region, which extends for more than 155 miles (250 km) to the east, means something like "land of thirst." In these extreme dry and barren conditions, vines can only thrive where irrigation is possible. In the west, near Montagu and Barrydale, where the cooperatives are used mainly to produce wines for distilling, they are now changing over to dry white wines such as Chenin and Colombard, as well as newly planted international varieties. Calitzdorp in the east, with its district, is the stronghold of port production, and Muscat wines have a tradition there too. Alongside the convincing whites, there will also be red wines made from Cabernet, Pinotage, and Merlot in the future.
Recommended: Die Krans, Boplaas, Grundheim, Calitzdorp Winery, Mons Ruber.

Worcester

From Paarl, a tunnel leads east through the Du Toitskloof mountains, providing easy access to the wine-growing region. The very broad valley is home to extensive vineyards, which provide almost a quarter of all South African wine, in spite of the hot dry climate, but thanks to irrigation from the Brandvlei reservoir and the River Breede. The 16 cooperatives produce easy-drinking wines at reasonable prices, almost all of it sold in tanks. Now all effort goes into bottling their own.
Recommended: Botha, Slanghoek, Du Toitskloof, Nuy, Romansrivier, Bergsig, Deetlefs, Goudini, De Wet Co-op.

Durbanville

Situated to the north of Cape Town, and enjoying a cooler climate, this ward is one of the oldest wine-growing areas: some of the few estates are 300 years old and are today threatened by encroaching suburbia. Although well-suited to white wines, highly convincing Pinotages also grow here, along with Shiraz, Merlots, and Cabernets.
Recommended: Altydgedacht, Bloemendal, Meerendal.

Swartland

To the northwest of Paarl, extending up along the Atlantic coast, is the wine district known as Swartland. The name means "black country" and its soil is indeed black and fertile. This is South Africa's granary. Further inland, with its hot, dry climate and just-about-adequate water supply, vines are grown on the gobelet system, and rarely irrigated. Yields are low, but the grapes are healthy and concentrated. The four progressive cooperatives together supply one-eighth of the country's wine. Cabernet and Pinotage are particularly successful here, but the Shiraz is also good. Piketberg is an adjacent region, albeit of little importance. The up-and-coming area around Darling, nearer the Atlantic, produces a good Sauvignon, among other wines.
Recommended: Allesverloren, Spice Route, Swartland Wine Cellar.

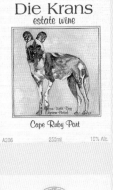

Tulbagh

The smaller area bordering on Swartland to the east, around the little town of the same name, has been lovingly restored since the 1969 earthquake. It is mainly known for its sherries, but is now making a name for itself with aromatic white wines, and not least, with Rieslings.
Recommended: Twee Jonge Gezellen, Theuniskraal, Tulbagh Co-op, Drostdy-Hof, Kloofzicht, Paddagang.

Olifants River

This region adjoins Swartland to the north. Vredendal, alongside Citrusdal its most important center, is about 276 miles (450 km) away from Cape Town. In spite of the very dry climate, even here the Atlantic exerts a temperate influence, although wine growing is only possible with artificial irrigation. The cooperative in Vredendal is proud of its 50,000-barrel harvest, which exceeds that of many wine-producing countries.
Recommended: Lutzville, Klawer, Cederberg, Vredendal, Citrusdal Cellars.

Douglas and Orange River

More than 490 miles (800 km) to the north of Cape Town is the hottest of all South African wine-growing districts. It supplies one-tenth of all the country's production, but only by dint of its very high yields: around 29,000 gallons per acre (450 hl/ha) on irrigated—and in winter, flooded—alluvial soil. Most of the harvest is used for distilling.
Recommended: Douglas Winery.

Graham Beck has created a model modern estate in Robertson, which has become known for its excellent sparkling wine.

ELGIN AND WALKER BAY

Overberg is the name of the region, which comprises two up-and-coming wards. Elgin is a plateau to the east of False Bay, whose conditions make it a natural growing area for fruit. As can be seen from the newly laid out vineyards, more and more farmers are turning to grape production, and the first attempts are being made at bottling their own wine.

While Elgin still has to acquire a reputation in wine circles, Walker Bay is already a secret tip among *cognoscenti*. It is Africa's southernmost wine-growing area, and at the same time its coolest, lying as it does directly on the Atlantic, the water temperature of which rarely exceeds 59°F (15°C), because of strong Antarctic currents even in the summer.

Behind the hills which frame the charming little seaside resort of Hermanus, the former advertising manager Tim Hamilton Russell found excellent conditions for wine growing in Hemel-en-Aarde Tal ("Heaven and Earth

Hermanus is surely the most popular seaside resort in the Cape region and is always booked out at Christmas. Burgundy grape varieties thrive in its hinterland.

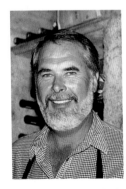

Peter Finlayson, director of the Bouchard-Finlayson joint venture.

Valley"). The climate is moderated by strong, humid Atlantic winds. The clay soil requires a hefty addition of lime, but the dominant slate promises great character and elegance. The first vines were planted in 1976. Three years later Peter Finlayson joined the operation, bringing with him substantial enological expertise gained in Burgundy. From the very first vintage, the pair aroused attention, and soon it was obvious that the future of the valley would be inseparable from Pinot Noir, Chardonnay, and Sauvignon.

In the 1980s Hamilton Russell's wines attracted international attention. They received numerous awards, and price-wise climbed to the top of the South African charts. While Tim Hamilton Russell sought to imitate Burgundy, his son, Anthony, has gone a step further. Everything is being done on the 160-acre (65-ha) estate to bring out the special flavor of the *terroir* and develop an individual style.

The first step was to subdivide the vineyards according to their natural character and different rootstocks. Separate harvesting and vinification then led, under the present winemaker Kevin Grant, to an internal classification of the various plots. Strenuous efforts were made to replace virus-infected stock. At the same time, the density of planting was substantially increased. Since 1993, the proportion of grapes from healthy vines has been steadily increased. In the great wine year of 1997, Hamilton Russell was finally able to vinify his Pinot Noir exclusively from totally healthy vines, enabling him to produce the best red wine made on the estate up until then. The Chardonnay is also top quality.

After 11 years of intensive work with Hamilton Russell, in 1990 Peter Finlayson finally succeeded in making his dream, of an estate of his own, come true. Together with Paul Bouchard from the Burgundy wine dynasty of that name, he acquired the neighboring estate of Hemel-en-Aarde. From the outset he stocked the vineyards with virus-free clones, planting 7,000 vines per hectare.

In the extensive, gently curving valley, which does not look at all African, irrigation ponds point to the fact that in this region you must still be prepared for periods of drought. Bouchard Finlayson grow Pinot Noir and Chardonnay in particular, with a small proportion of Pinot Blanc and Sauvignon. They have selected two locations: Galpin Peak for the reds, and Missionvale for the white varieties; they treat these as separate CRUS. From the outset they have produced—with the necessary investment in technology and winery equip-

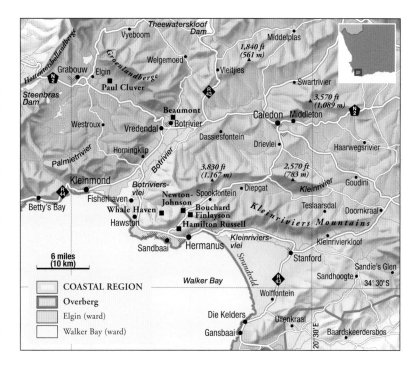

ment—top wines at top prices. They also succeeded in making outstanding wines, both Chardonnay and Pinot Noir, in 1997. If that vintage is still unsurpassed for Walker Bay Pinot Noir, the wines in the following good and great vintage years have gained in depth and richness as the vines have aged. The *terroir* is also gaining in character.

Walker Bay also includes Bot River, which lies a good bit closer to Cape Town than Hermanus. Raoul and Jayne Beaumont acquired the historic Compagnes Drift Farm in 1973. As it turned out, this former outpost of the Dutch East India Company also included about 123 acres (50 ha)

Hamilton-Russell is doing pioneering work with Pinot and Chardonnay.

of vineyard which had already been planted during the colonial period. It was not until 1993 that the Beaumonts started to make their own wine, at first in the surviving concrete basins using old Pinotage stock. In their very first year, the noteworthy 1994 vintage gave them the breakthrough they needed into the quality league. Son Sebastian Beaumont and Niels Verburg work together as winemakers. Alongside Pinotage, the estate concentrates on Chenin, with the delicious Goutte d'Or Late Harvest, and the high-quality, dry Hope Marguerite. The range is rounded off by highly aromatic Sauvignons, Shiraz, and now also Mourvèdre.

The owners of the vineyards in Hemel-en-Aarde valley are justifiably proud of their properties.

SELECT PRODUCERS IN ELGIN, WALKER BAY, AND OTHER REGIONS

ALTYDGEDACHT*
DURBANVILLE
346 acres (140 ha); 80,000 bottles • Wines include: Chardonnay, Sauvignon, Gewürztraminer, Barbera, Cabernet Sauvignon, →Merlot
Old farm cultivated in a variety of ways, with a wine-cellar dating from 1705. Remarkable Merlot and South Africa's only Barbera.

BEAUMONT*—****
BOT RIVER (WALKER BAY)
123 acres (50 ha); 100,000 bottles • Wines: Chenin, Hope Marguerite, Goutte d'Or, Chardonnay, Sauvignon, Pinotage, Shiraz, port
Raoul and Jayne Beaumont have brought about a renaissance at Compagnes Drift Farm. Winemaker Niels Verburg and now also son Sebastian Beaumont have further improved the quality. Irresistible Pinotages, Chenins, and ports with rarity value, and now also delightful Shiraz and Mourvèdres.

GRAHAM BECK WINERY*—****
ROBERTSON
507 acres (205 ha); 1,200,000 bottles • Wines include: Chardonnay, various Cap Classique, Pinno, →Old Road Pinotage, →The Ridge Shiraz, →William Wine
Under cellar master Pieter Ferreira this huge farm is now producing increasingly interesting red wines as well as its convincing sparkling wines.

BON CAP ORGANIC WINERY**
EILANDIA (ROBERTSON)
111 acres (45 ha); 100,000 bottles • Wines: Viognier, Pinotage, Syrah, →Cabernet Sauvignon, →Cabernet-Shiraz, Cabernet-Merlot
The De Preez family has been making wine in Ward Eilandia for six generations and they have been working biologically for 15 years now. But it was not until 2002 that Roelf and Michelle landed an immediate huge success with their first own acknowledged biological Pinotage. Now their modern cellars are also producing convincing reds from the other varieties as well, and a Viognier and a Cape Vintage.

BOPLAAS*—****
CALITZDORP (KLEIN KAROO)
160 acres (65 ha); 300,000 bottles • Wines include: Pinotage, Shiraz, Cabernet Sauvignon, →Vintage, Tawny, Muscadel
Port champion Carel Nel supplements his magnificent Vintage Reserves, including a single-variety Touriga Nacional, with demanding Cabernets.

BOUCHARD FINLAYSON**
HERMANUS (WALKER BAY)
40 acres (16 ha); bought-in grapes; 160,000 bottles • Wines: Chardonnay, Sauvignon, Blanc de Mer; Pinot Noir
Big Pinot Noir wines and Chardonnays. The produce of the top Galpin Peak and Missionvale vineyards is vinified plot by plot. Amusing Blanc de Mer made from five varieties.

CEDERBERG KELDERS*
CEDERBERG (OLIFANTS RIVER)
104 acres (42 ha); 100,000 bottles • Wines include: Sauvignon, Chenin, Bukett, →Cabernet Sauvignon, Pinotage, Cederberger
A family estate situated high in the Cederberg mountains, where David Nieuwoudt has brought a fresh breeze and fruity, increasingly characterful wines.

PAUL CLUVER ESTATE*—**
ELGIN
148 acres (60 ha); 180,000 bottles • Wines: Chardonnay, Sauvignon, Riesling, Cabernet Sauvignon, →Pinot Noir
Since 1997 the De Rust farm has been working as an estate marketing its own wines. At the same time the Cluver family has been sponsoring a self-help project for 60 black families.

VAN LOVEREN*—**
ROBERTSON
618 acres (250 ha); 2,400,000 bottles • Wines include: Méthode Cap Classique, Chardonnay, Sauvignon, Pinot Gris, Gewürztraminer, River Red, Cabernet Sauvignon, Shiraz
The Retief family produces River Red, an easy-drinking red wine from Pinotage, Merlot, and Ruby Cabernet.

The assured Burgundy style from Hamilton Russell.

Walker Bay is still a secret tip as "wine country."

Mont du Toit****
Wellington
69 acres (28 ha); 90,000 bottles • Wines: Hawequas, →Mont du Toit, →Le Sommet
Lawyer Stephan du Toit had the right instinct when he chose the top German vintners Bernd Philippi and Bernhard Breuer as consultants. Le Sommet is one of South Africa's best reds.

Newton-Johnson***−****
Hermanus (Walker Bay)
Bought-in grapes; 600,000 bottles • Wines include: Sauvignon, Chardonnay, →Pinot Noir, Cabernet Sauvignon
The Johnsons are developing their own vineyards near Hermanus and producing first-class Pinot Noirs and Sauvignons. They are also very successful with *vins de plaisir* under the Cape Bay and Sandown Bay labels; now the range also includes First Cape.

Romansrivier Winery*−**
Wolseley (Worcester)
1,556 acres (630 ha); 200,000 bottles • Wines include: Chardonnay, Chenin, Colombard, Pinotage, Merlot, Cabernet Sauvignon, Vino Rood, →De Kijker Pinotage
One of the most dynamic cooperatives on the Cape, supplying good, full-bodied reds, a fine Chardonnay, and easy-drinking Chenins and Colombards.

Hamilton Russell***−****
Hermanus (Walker Bay)
158 acres (64 ha); 350,000 bottles • Wines: Chardonnay, Sauvignon; Pinot Noir
This pioneering estate continues to set standards with its Pinot Noir and Chardonnay, while its subsidiary Southern Right Cellars concentrates on Pinotage and Sauvignon.

Spice Route***
Suider-Paarl (Swartland)
494 acres (150 ha); bought-in grapes • Wines include: Sauvignon, →Chenin; Viognier, Shiraz, →Pinotage, →Merlot, →Syrah
The first private winery in the hot Malmesbury district, set up by Charles Back in 1997, is a fascinating and revolutionary project. In the meantime Barbera and Sangiovese, and Zinfandel and Tannot have been planted.

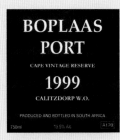

Springfield****
Robertson
494 acres (200 ha); 1,500,000 bottles • Wines include: →Sauvignon Life from Stone, →Chardonnay Méthode Ancienne, Pinot Noir, Cabernet Sauvignon: Whole Berry, →Méthode Ancienne
Abrie Bruwer is putting a lot of energy into this estate. With new plantings and a cellar for whole fruit fermentation the wines' style and sophistication are on the rise.

Twee Jonge Gezellen**
Tulbagh
676 acres (274 ha) • Wines include: Méthode Cap Classique; Chardonnay, Sauvignon, "39," Light, Schanderl, Night Nectar, Pinot Noir, Shiraz, →Engeltjiepipi
Three hundred year old family estate with excellent sparkling wine, Krone Borealis Brut, popular white *cuvées*, now red wines too; sweet Engeltjiepipi.

Weltevrede*−***
Robertson
235 acres (95 ha); 360,000 bottles • Wines include: Méthode Cap Classique, Chardonnay, Sauvignon, Privé du Bois, Riesling; Merlot-Cabernet Sauvignon; dessert wines, Oma se Wyn, Oupa se Wyn, →Muscat de Hamburg
Founded 1912. Convincing white wines, now three different Chardonnays, the Gewürztraminer, and the very good Cap Classique Philip Jonker, as well as Merlot and Cabernet.

De Wetshof**
Robertson
395 acres (160 ha); 480,000 bottles • Wines: Chardonnay, Sauvignon, Riesling, Gewürztraminer, Muscat de Frontignan
Danie de Wet learned the art of winemaking in Germany. The high point is a Riesling *Trockenbeerenauslese* known as Edeloes; now also Pinot Noir and Cabernet. Exemplary social facilities!

WhaleHaven***−****
Hermanus (Walker Bay)
Bought-in grapes; 70,000 bottles • Wines: Chardonnay, Sauvignon; Pinot Noir, Cabernet Sauvignon, Merlot, Baleine Noire
Winemaker Storm Kreusch has acquired a reputation for stylish Pinot Noir wines and Chardonnays. Now the business is moving in a new direction, as is WhaleHaven.

ANTHONY ROSE

ASIA

WINE GROWING IN CHINA AND INDIA

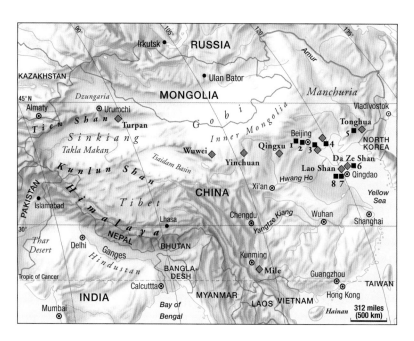

Asia has some vine varieties of its own, including *Vitis amurensis*, the grape from the Amur Valley that flourishes furthest north and whose winter hardiness is often used for crossing to improve the relevant characteristics of other species of vine. In terms of the wine industry, however, the countries of the Far East are important mainly for their potential sales markets. In the five years that preceded the serious economic crisis of 1998, interest in high-quality wines in Japan, Taiwan, and South Korea and subsequently also China, Hong Kong, and Singapore rose by leaps and bounds. Though the demand for prestigious wines initially came predominantly from the commanding heights of management and high finance, it soon spread to other parts of the population with astonishing rapidity. The 1998 crisis led to a drop in the consumption of top wines in many countries, in Thailand virtually collapsing completely. In contrast, demand in Japan was not to be contained. Indeed, scientific reports about the positive effects of the regular enjoyment of red wine brought considerable growth in consumption and with it a more diverse range of products, so that per capita consumption rose to 10 pints (2.5 liters). In other countries, especially India, drinking wine is a privilege still reserved for the better-off, and is often restricted on religious grounds.

Yet market strategists think that Asia has extraordinarily high potential, particularly China. This relates both to imports and to the

	Wine-growing area
■ I	Great Wall Winery
■ 2	Dragon Seal Winery
■ 3	Sino-French Joint Venture Winery
■ 4	Huaxia Winery
■ 5	Tonghua Winery
■ 6	Changyu Winery
■ 7	Huadong Winery
■ 8	Gungdao Winery

development of a domestic Chinese wine industry increasingly involving foreign drinks groups. For the present, however, we cannot expect Asia to add to the world's list of outstanding CRUS and its importance remains as a sales market with growth potential.

CHINA

The vine was first introduced to China following the mission of General Chan K'ien to Iran in around 128 BC during the reign of the Emperor Wu of the Han. Seeds of the *vinifera* vine were sent from Uzbekistan to the Emperor and planted in Xinjiang and Shaanxi (now Xian). After the Chinese conquest of Turpan in the 7th century AD vines with the improbable names of snake, dragon pearl and mare's nipple were imported and successfully cultivated.

Wines made of rice, wheat, and millet—looks more like a pharmacy.

Viticulture prospered thereafter with Shansu wine being especially popular. Many of the early references to the vine however are to grapes grown for eating or for raisins. Moreover, a tradition of making "wine" from rice or wheat was also already well established from early on.

At the end of the 19th century, a Chinese officer, Xang Bi Shi returned to China in 1892 to establish the Chang Yu winery in Yantai, introducing, among 150 assorted *vinifera* vines from Europe, Welschriesling. In 1910, French Catholics set up the Shang Yi winery (today the Beijing Winery) and in 1914 Germans established the Melco winery at Tsingtao (now Quingdao), while the Tung Hua winery at Jilini was managed by the Japanese. As the foreign involvement suggests, the aim in each case was to make wine for the foreign communities resident in China.

Today, although China has extensive vineyard plantings of 407,700 acres (165,000 ha), most of the grapes are table grapes and raisins. The most suitable area for wine grapes is the Shandong Peninsula north of Shanghai and south of Beijing. This is on the same latitude as California with south-facing slopes and a maritime climate which would be almost Mediterranean if it weren't for monsoon winds and storms which come from the direction of the South China Sea. Since China opened its doors to the outside world in 1978, a number of overseas companies have commenced joint ventures. Rémy Martin developed the muscat-influenced blend, Dynasty, with the Tianjin Winery; Pernod-Ricard established the Dragon Seal brand with the Beijing Friendship Winery. Other joint ventures include the Huadong Winery, set up in 1986 and run by Allied Domecq, an Italian venture set up by the Marco Polo Winery in 1990 at Yantai, the Summer Palace and Great Wall.

Most vineyards are state or collectively owned and subdivided into individual units of less than half a hectare. Vines are largely ungrafted with no apparent major PHYLLOXERA problems. Viticulture however is a hit-and-miss affair with high yields, inappropriately dense canopies, hefty irrigation, early picking to avoid rot and

Karnataka, and Andhra Pradesh. There are also plantings in the north in Kashmir and Punjab, and in the south in Tamil Nadu. A monsoon climate creates hot and humid summers. Indigenous grapes include Arkawati, Arka Shyam and Anab e Shahi, while Bangalore Purple is pressed with imported varieties to produce sweet wines.

The best known cellar was set up by Sham Chougule in 1982 in Narayangaon, 93 miles (150 km) from Poona, with the help of the Piper Heidsieck champagne experts to produce sparkling wines. The Omar Khayyam sparkling wine, which was the result, is more than respectable. Made using the Champagne method it was originally made from Thompson Seedless grapes but increasing amounts of Chardonnay and a small admixture of Pinot Noir are now being added.

manifold diseases of the vine. To a certain extent, western investment and Australian expertise have mitigated the worst excesses of Chinese viticulture and winemaking with the introduction of modern equipment and viticultural expertise. The Chinese themselves drink little wine compared to beer, but a gradual increase in consumption along with the return of Hong Kong to the fold could change all that.

A Chinese oddity— Tsingtao white wine in round bottles

INDIA

Historically, wine has played only a minor role in India mainly because of the ambivalence surrounding its consumption in Hindu, Buddhist, and Muslim laws. Despite this ambivalence, it seems that wine was consumed at least by the aristocratic Ksatriya caste, although the masses stuck to stronger drink made from wheat and barley. There have been pockets of wine production limited to local areas as a result of colonial influence, notably through the Portuguese in Goa in the 16th century and the British in the 19th, who esablished vineyards in Kashmir and Baramati. In the 1890s however, such vineyards as there were succumbed to phylloxera, like their European counterparts.

Today approximately 123,550 acres (50,000 ha) are planted with vines. The vast majority are devoted to table grapes, with only ten percent used for wine. This is in spite of the fact that wine production has gradually increased under the auspices of the Indian government, since Indian independence in 1947, although production remains private for the most part. More than two-thirds of India's vines, are in the three southwestern states of Maharashtra,

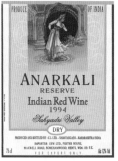

Opposite
India is famous for sunsets against a picturesque backdrop but not for its wine. However, Château Indage offers qualities to be taken seriously.

Wine in Bali

Despite the tropical climate, wine can be grown in Bali. The Australian-founded winery processes grapes of the American Isabella hybrid as this requires no cold period to initiate blossoming. The consistently warm climate on Bali permits five harvests every two years. Of course the blue grapes develop few pigments thereby, so that the wine remains light in color. Once the must reaches the required rosé color, it is pressed, pre-settled under chilled conditions and subsequently fermented. During the two-week cold stabilization, sugar is added during the second filtering (medium dry) before the wine is sterile-filtered and bottled. It is ready to drink after 5–6 weeks. A sparkling wine is also made from the same grapes; like the still wine it is mainly sold locally.

CHINA

HUADONG, QINGDAO
SHANDONG-HALBINSEL

*1,750 acres (700 ha); 3,600,000 bottles • Wines:
Chardonnay, Riesling, Sauvignon, Gewürtztraminer;
Cabernet and Cabernet Franc, Merlot, Pinot*
Huadong winery, which became part of Allied Domecq
in 1990, was the first wine enterprise in China to
introduce French grape varieties. Five years earlier
42,000 vine stocks had been imported from France.
They were planted out on the Laoshan and Dazeshan
slopes in the Qingdao region, and took well. In the
prevailing maritime climate, Huadong produces a series
of single-variety wines and *assemblages*.

INDIA

CHÂTEAU INDAGE**
MAHARASHTRA

*3,710 acres increasing to 16,100 (1,500 ha to 6,500);
1,330,000 (increasing to 10 million) bottles; bought-in
grapes • Wines: Chardonnay, Ugni Blanc, Pinot Noir,
Cabernet Sauvignon, Bangalore Purple, Arkavti,
Anabeshi, Perlet, →Omar Khayyám sparkling wine,
Riviera and Chantilli brands*
Best known in the west for its well-made sparkling wine,
Omar Khayyám, the Indage group, established by
Indian businessman Sham Chougule in 1984, owns two
modern wineries based at Narayangaon producing
wines supervised by Californian winemaker John Locke
from vineyards on the slopes of the Sahyadri Mountains.

Kazakhstan

There is evidence of viticulture going back to
the 7th century AD in Kazakhstan with the
development of a modern industry beginning
in the 1930s. There are upwards of 49,420
acres (20,000 ha) of vines planted in the
central Asian republic of Kazakhstan in the
foothills of the Dzhambul, Chimkent, and
Almaty regions, producing 24.5 million
gallons (350,000 hl) of wine. The climate here
is continental with mild summers and
extremely cold winters, necessitating winter
protection for the vines. 43 grape varieties are
allowed, 24 for table grapes, and the main
wine grapes are Riesling, Rkatsiteli, Aligoté,
Saperavi, and the Bordeaux varieties,
Cabernet Sauvignon and Cabernet Franc.
Table wine, sparkling wine, and dessert wine
styles are all produced here.

Tajikistan

Tajikistan's mountainous terrain lies between
Uzbekistan and China and it has a continental
climate. There are three major wine-producing
regions, the Leninabad region and the Vakhsh
valley and Kuliab regions of the south.
Viticulture was developed here in ancient times
but the arrival of Islam meant that grapes suitable for a wine were largely replaced by eating
and dried grapes. Commercial wine production
started up in earnest in the 1920s with the
establishment of state farms for the purpose
and there are now 20 wineries. There are some
96,370 acres (39,000 ha) under vine with ten
wine grapes which include the Russian
Rkatsiteli (widespread in eastern Europe and
central Asia), Riesling, Muscat, Saperavi, and
Cabernet Sauvignon.

Uzbekistan and Kyrgyzstan

Uzbekistan had long produced wine in the
Fergana Valley and continued to do so until
Islam changed the varieties, as in Tajikistan,
from wine to table grapes. The major zones
are now in Bukhara, Samarkand, and Tashkent
where table grapes still dominate production
from this central Asian republic's 309,000-odd
acres (125,000 ha) of vines. Of the 36 grape
varieties officially sanctioned for viticulture,
wine grape varieties include Riesling, Aleatico,
Muscat, Rkatsiteli, Saperavi, and Morrastel.

Kyrgyzstan, like Uzbekistan, has a continental climate. With some 22,240 acres
(9,000 ha) of vineyard and 45 permitted
grape varieties (including 23 wine grapes), its
two main wine regions are the Chuia Valley
and the Osh region, producing some strong
and sweet wines too.

JAPAN

In the decade of the 1990s, and in particular during the last five years of the millennium, wine drinking became quite a phenomenon in Japan. In this health-conscious country this is partly due to the belief—taken to extremes in *French Paradox*—that red wine is good for you and for one's health. Most of the wine drunk today in Japan is either fine wine from the classic regions of Europe, France in particular, or everyday wines imported from the New World. Fine wine drinkers are more interested in older VINTAGES since cellars are virtually impossible to insure because of earthquakes. Investment itself in fine wines stopped after the financial bubble burst in the late 1990s.

The culture of wine as it's known in Europe is a relatively recent phenomenon in Japan, nevertheless cultivation of the vine goes back to the 8th century AD. According to legend, vines first started to appear in the country in AD 718 thanks to Buddhist missionaries who planted vines at Katsunuma with the medicinal value of the grape in mind. The first documented wines appeared with the arrival of Portuguese missionaries in the 16th century. St. Francis Xavier, introduced Portuguese red, or *tinta*, which became known as *tintashu*, a word which combines the Portuguese *tinto* and the Japanese *shu*, meaning sake. Wine did not find favor, however, with the Tokugawa shogunate of the 17th century, and Japan's early attempts at wine production were not allowed to develop.

It wasn't until 1875 that attempts were once again made to produce wine on a commercial scale. This was at Yamanashi, near Mount Fuji, east of Tokyo, where a local merchant established a vineyard to make wine from local grapes. On the basis of his efforts, the local authorities began to permit the importation of *vinifera* and American vines for plantation. The Muscat of Alexandria and the Delaware, respectively, became the most popular wine varieties. Today, Yamanashi, along with Yamagata and Nagano north of Tokyo, account for 40 percent of grape production, with Kofu, the hilly area in Yamanashi, probably the best known name for wine production in Japan. In a country which takes its cue from the West in many aspects of day-to-day living, Japanese wine from its own indigenous grapes is not as highly regarded as wine imported from overseas. Nevertheless, a small industry exists where about a tenth of grape production is used for making wine.

The traditional method of growing allows the grapes a lot of air.

Japan's climate is not ideally suited for viticulture. While, Honshu, the Japanese archipelago's main island, is on the same latitude as the Mediterranean, the climate is much more extreme, with biting Siberian winds in the winter and heavy monsoon rainfall in summer from the Sea of Japan and the Pacific. As a result of excess humidity, wines are traditionally trained high onto overhead wires with bunches hanging down, allowing maximum ventilation to circulate throughout the canopy to prevent rot. This traditional method is known as *tanazukuri*, but new vineyards are also being planted using European trellising such as the Lyre CULTIVATION SYSTEM, and in central Hokkaido, Japan's most northerly island, which is extremely cold, plantings are on conventional horizontal wires.

With Delaware the most popular grape, along with Kyoho, the majority of Japan's grapes are hybrids based on *Vitis labrusca*, following their introduction from the United States. Perhaps the best-known Japanese *vinifera* grape variety is the Koshu, a pink-tinged berry which can be used for table grapes as well as wine. Neo-muscat and Ryugan are related to the Koshu and are generally used to make a light, sweetish style of wine. At the Tokachi winery in Ikeda on the island of Hokkaido, a red wine is made from

MERCIAN KATSUNUMA WINERY
YAMANASHI
• *Wines: Chardonnay, Cabernet, Merlot, →Château*
Mercian Jyonohira Cabernet
The Mercian Katsunuma Winery, which has also
owned Markham in the Napa Valley in California
since 1987, and since 1988 Château Reysson in the
Haut-Medoc, has grown to be one of the leading wine
producers in Japan. It actually has its own museum
of art. The celebrated Jyonohira vineyard with its 25
acres (10 ha) under vines was set up on steep slopes
west of Tokyo in 1984. It supplies the grapes for the
firm's top red wines in the Bordeaux style aged in new
French oak barrels.

the wild *yamabudo* (mountain grape) vine,
which is from the cold-resistant *Vitis amurensis*.
A crossing has been made with *yamabudo* and a
Seibel hybrid to produce a grape named Kiyomi,
which makes another light style of red wine
which has been compared with Pinot Noir.
More recently European varieties have been
planted such as Cabernet Sauvignon and
Cabernet Franc in the west of Yamanashi,
Chardonnay and Merlot in Nagano and the
earlier-ripening Müller-Thurgau and Zweigelt in
Hokkaido.

Wine production is dominated by the industry
giants, Suntory, and Sanraku (Mercian) with
Manns Wine, Sapporo (Polaire), and Kyowa
Hakko Kogyo (Ste. Neige) also major players in
the domestic market. In addition, the Tokachi
winery in Hokkaido is significant, with a
number of smaller, family-owned wineries such
as Marufuji (Rubaiyat), Shirayuri, and Toshihiko
Tsukamoto's Château Lumière. Most of the
grapes are bought in from a large number of
grape growers whose average vineyard size
varies between half to one acre (quarter to half a
hectare). In the 1990s new vineyard management techniques and modern cellar equipment
have been introduced along with European
vinifera varieties to produce wines aimed at
matching imported styles. And yet without a
strong indigenous wine culture, it is hard to say
that Japanese wines will ever compete on equal
terms in price or taste.

After lax labeling laws allowed imported
produce to be labeled "produce of Japan,"
the industry has adopted a voluntary labeling
code aimed at regulating industry practices.
Wine bottled under domestic labels must be
declared either as *kokunai san* (domestic wine)
or as *yunyu san* (imported bulk wine). In the
Katsunuma area, as evidence of a commitment to quality wine production, there is
even a Certificate of Origin seal for the region's
top wines.

A picnic in Marufuji
Winery's own vineyard.

SAKE

Sake, Japan's national drink, is of course, not
really wine in the strict sense at all, but the
fermented product of rice. Sake comes in a
variety of shapes and sizes, from a young, easy-
drinking style to a delicate aged style. There are
some 2,000 Japanese brewers making sake all
over Japan, the most traditional areas being
Nada in Hyogo, as well as Fushimi in Kyoto,
Itami in Hyogo, Ikeda in Osaka and Hiroshima.
Sake can be sweet or dry, drunk as an aperitif or
with food, variable in its alcohol content and
served warm or chilled, depending on your
taste. It is served in china decanters and drunk
from small porcelain cups.

Three factors are crucial to sake: the raw materials used, the method of brewing and the processing after brewing. The extent to which the rice has been "polished" is the first important factor. Basically, the more highly polished the rice, usually to between 50 and 55 percent of its original size, the finer the quality of the sake. Next the question arises whether it is a "pure rice" sake or whether it has had alcohol added. In a "pure rice" sake, the starch in the rice is first turned to sugar by obtaining a *koji*, or rice mold, which is added to rice, YEAST, and water, and FERMENTATION then takes place. This "pure rice" sake is known as *junmaishu*. A second type of sake, known as *honjozo*, has a limited amount of brewer's alcohol added, and tends to be lighter than a *junmaishu*, if not quite as delicate.

Above
Suntory is Japan's leading producer and distributor of alcoholic products.

Right
Grape harvest in Suntory's Yamanashi Winery, Japan's largest.

André Dominé

NORTH AMERICA

WINE IN NORTH AMERICA

Many of the European settlers who landed in the New World to seek their fortunes soon realized that there was something missing from their lives that had previously had a very firm place there: wine. However, as wild vines grow well in many areas of America, this did not appear to be an insuperable problem. The first wine was fermented from native grapes in 1607 in Jamestown, Virginia. Even so, it was to be another 200 years before reasonably drinkable wines began to be made on the East Coast, and only after 1960 was *Vitis vinifera*, the European vine species, cultivated successfully there. It was impossible to make acceptable wine from the wild American grape varieties, so innumerable experiments were undertaken with vines introduced from Europe, but none were successful. The European plants were unable to withstand the unsuitable climate or the unfamiliar diseases and pests.

It was not until the early-19th century that new hope dawned, when a white hybrid created by the spontaneous crossing of an American *Vitis labrusca* variety and a European *Vitis vinifera* variety was discovered. This grape was called Alexander, and it made wine that was, indeed, drinkable, though its rather foxy AROMA could hardly be described as attractive. Nevertheless, winemaking now spread in the eastern states as Alexander and other specially bred hybrids were planted.

After the Second World War there was an increasing concentration on French hybrids, which produced more palatable wines. Thanks

Buena Vista, one of the oldest wineries in California, in Sonoma Valley.

Sonoma City is a small town that has developed into a much visited wine center. Even the gas stations there sell "vintage" fuel.

to the development of chemical pesticides and insecticides, it also became possible to acclimatize European quality vines.

THE CALIFORNIAN MISSION

The conditions for winemaking were quite different in the south and west of the area that is now the United States. Thanks to the favorable climate, it was possible to cultivate vines imported from Europe in the Spanish colonies right from the beginning. Hernán Cortés had the first vines planted in Mexico in 1521, and the Spanish laid out vineyards in New Mexico and Texas about 100 years later. In 1769 the Spanish Crown began to send Franciscan monks to California in order to maintain Spanish claims in the region. The *padres* could not imagine life or work without wine, so they took the techniques of viticulture to California with them, introducing the appropriately named Mission grape variety.

Slowly the Franciscans moved up the *Camino Real* (Royal Road) to the north, establishing 21 mission stations, of which Sonoma (founded 1823) was the most northerly. Los Angeles was then an unimportant settlement, but it has now swallowed up San Gabriel, where the most extensive vineyards were planted, producing yields that went far beyond the missionaries' own requirements. Jean-Louis Vignes, who came from the Bordeaux area, founded his winery not far away in 1833, stocking it with French vines. Apart from this, ever more people were coming from the east to settle in Sonoma.

THE GOLD RUSH AND WINE FEVER

In 1848 an event took place that was to be decisive for Californian winemaking in general, and the wine-growing areas of the North Coast region in particular: gold was found at Sacramento. Hundreds of thousands of people were attracted to California, hoping to find riches overnight. Among them were many former winemakers from Europe, some of whom quickly saw their future in satisfying the gold diggers' thirst rather than digging for themselves. In consequence, viticulture experienced a completely unexpected boom in Sonoma, while in the neighboring Napa Valley cattle were still being grazed. However, wine fever soon spread there too, as well as to Livermore Valley and

Santa Clara Valley just south of San Francisco. The driving force behind this development was the Hungarian aristocrat and adventurer Agoston Haraszthy, who founded the Buena Vista vineyard in the Sonoma Valley. He went on a state-funded journey through the European winemaking countries, gathering information about cultivation methods and collecting cuttings of 300 vine varieties. America was beginning to take wine seriously.

Scientific research began to be conducted at Berkeley in 1880, and the results were put directly into practice. Viticulture had also been developing in the Central Valley from 1830, and the evident suitability of this area for the production of wine on a large scale was soon being exploited. The opening of the transcontinental railroad at about this time also caused demand to rise further.

The wine business was controlled by a small group of bottlers, who purchased wine by the barrel from about 800 wineries, and then mixed it to make blends with a wide range of different flavors to meet the requirements of the retail trade.

Business was flourishing when a catastrophic disaster struck the industry: the PHYLLOXERA (vine louse) epidemic. This rapacious insect originally came from the eastern United States, but around 1880 it began systematically to destroy all the crops planted on the West Coast. Almost all of California's vineyards fell victim in the two decades that followed. The winegrowers had hardly finished replanting their land with resistant rootstocks when the next blow hit them. Prohibition was introduced on January 17, 1920 and was not lifted until 1933. Though winegrowers and producers in Napa, Sonoma, Central Valley, and elsewhere managed to get round the restrictions by various ruses, such as producing communion wine or grapes for home

The Finnish captain Gustave Niebaum built this winery and château in 1887 with the aim of outdoing the wines of Bordeaux. Today the entire estate belongs to Francis Ford Coppola, the famous Hollywood director. He has restored the Niebaum-Coppola Estate to its former glory and made it a magnet for tourists.

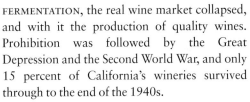

The German Walter Schug built his winery in Carneros in the traditional style of his home, Assmannshausen am Rhein. His wines are equally European in style.

FERMENTATION, the real wine market collapsed, and with it the production of quality wines. Prohibition was followed by the Great Depression and the Second World War, and only 15 percent of California's wineries survived through to the end of the 1940s.

A NEW BEGINNING, NEW PROBLEMS

The remaining winemakers were confronted with the problem of having to maintain their position in the face of rising imports from Europe, so they marketed their own wines under foreign names. The most famous example was "Chablis," which denoted a relatively dry white wine, regardless of the kind of grape from which it was made. In Napa and Sonoma, wineries such as Beaulieu Vineyards, Inglenook, and Charles Krug re-established their former fame and quality, but it was only in the 1960s that greater investment became possible. Since 1970 there has been a growth of interest in wine among the American population, and this has been accompanied by an expansion of the areas under cultivation with vines and an increase in the number of wineries being launched (there are now well over 800).

In the 1990s, however, disaster struck yet again as the vine louse made a comeback. It became apparent that the rootstocks used when the vineyards were expanded in the 1980s were not actually resistant to phylloxera, and thousands of acres of vines were ravaged by a mutation of the insect. Farmers and wineries had to replant their vineyards, but in doing so they applied the latest techniques of quality wine production, establishing the foundations for an extremely promising future.

AMERICAN VITICULTURAL AREAS

In the United States the development of modern viticulture was associated from the very beginning with a serious interest in the natural conditions from which vines benefit. Indeed, this topic has probably been studied more systematically there than in any other country. In the last three decades of the 20th century the winemaking areas of all the American states were examined very carefully, and their geographical characteristics and boundaries defined. Of course, this work led to the identification of grape varieties that were particularly suitable for certain regions, but, by contrast with the European *appellation* systems, these findings have not been incorporated into the regulatory framework, and no maximum yields have been set.

Some geographical areas were defined as early as 1978, thereby creating the preconditions for the establishment of the American Viticultural Areas (A.V.A.s), the American *appellation* system. In 1983 the government agency responsible, the Bureau of Alcohol, Tobacco and Firearms (B.A.T.F.), a division of the U.S. Treasury Department, declared them generally binding.

Other than the delimitation of the wine-growing areas, the only restrictions are as follows:

- If a grape variety is given, it must make up three-quarters of the wine in question.
- At least 85 percent of the grapes must come from the A.V.A. designated on the label.
- If a vineyard is named, 95 percent of the grapes must have been cultivated there (but only if a regional A.V.A. is given).
- If a vintage is given, at least 95 percent of the grapes must date from the year in question.

There are now more than 70 recognized A.V.A.s in California alone, and there are more than 55 in the other states.

The A.V.A. system has a hierarchical structure. At the top we find the state, California, for example, which encompasses a number of smaller regions, such as Central Valley, Central Coast, and North Coast. In turn, these regions are divided into counties, such as—to take the example of North Coast—Napa, Sonoma, and Mendocino. Wine-producing counties are automatically regarded as *appellations* of origin. Sonoma County itself possesses a large number of smaller A.V.A.s, such as Sonoma Valley, Russian River Valley, Chalk Hill, Green Valley, and Dry Creek Valley. In turn, these areas may be divided into smaller units, so we find Sonoma Mountain as a separate sub-A.V.A., though it is also part of Sonoma Valley. By contrast with European conventions, A.V.A. is not printed on the label.

If California, North Coast, or some other generic region is given on the label, the wine is usually a blend made with grapes from different growing areas. The more precisely a wine's origins are defined—the more precise the *appellation*—the smaller is the area from which the grapes are allowed to come, and the more strongly the wine will reflect the characteristics of a particular TERROIR. This is particularly the case, of course, where the grapes have been cultivated in a single vineyard.

Appellations in Canada

The Vintners' Quality Alliance (V.Q.A.), the Canadian *appellation* system, was introduced in 1989 in Ontario and 1990 in British Columbia. Under the V.Q.A., wines can only be made from grapes cultivated in the province designated on the label and also have to be bottled there. At the same time, the system involves a ban on *labrusca* varieties, so only hybrids and *vinifera* varieties are permitted. Although minimum sugar levels have been set, no limits have been placed on output.

The following rules apply and are enforced under the V.Q.A. system in Ontario and British Columbia:

- If a province is named on the label, at least 75 percent of the grape variety declared must come from this region.
- If an *appellation* of origin is given, 85 percent of the grape variety declared must have come from this area.
- Only specified hybrids and *vinifera* varieties are permitted.
- If two grape varieties are given on the label, the second variety must make up at least 10 percent of the wine.
- If a VINTAGE is given, at least 95 percent of the grapes must date from the year in question.
- The information on the label must be given in English and French.
- Furthermore, all V.Q.A. wines have to be approved by a tasting panel. Only once they have passed this test are they entitled to bear

the black V.Q.A. seal. Wines that are scored with marks between 15 and 20 are awarded a gold seal.

ICE WINE, or *vin de glace*, is subject to strict control and is a registered trademark.

Commercial wineries are allowed to mix 25 percent Canadian wine with a maximum of 75 percent imported wine and still market the resulting blend as Produit du Canada/Produce of Canada. In recent years most of these imported wines have come from Chile and South Africa.

Grape varieties that are not permitted under the V.Q.A. scheme are either used to make imitation port wine or sherry, or processed into light wines that have an alcohol content of 7 percent.

American label

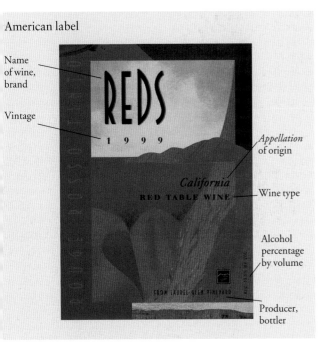

Name of wine, brand

Vintage

Appellation of origin

California
RED TABLE WINE — Wine type

Alcohol percentage by volume

Producer, bottler

Canadian label

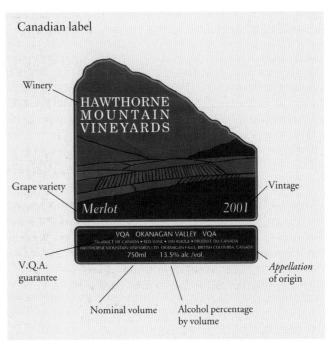

Winery

HAWTHORNE
MOUNTAIN
VINEYARDS

Grape variety

Merlot   2001

Vintage

VQA OKANAGAN VALLEY VQA
PRODUCT OF CANADA • RED WINE • VIN ROUGE • PRODUIT DU CANADA
HAWTHORNE MOUNTAIN VINEYARDS LTD. OKANAGAN FALLS, BRITISH COLUMBIA, CANADA
750ml   13.5% alc./vol.

V.Q.A. guarantee

Appellation of origin

Nominal volume   Alcohol percentage by volume

CT   Connecticut
MA   Massachusetts
MD   Maryland
NH   New Hampshire
RI   Rhode Island
VT   Vermont

300 miles (500 km)

CANADA
British Columbia
Ontario

UNITED STATES
Washington
Oregon
California
New York
Connecticut

Massachusetts
Pennsylvania
Maryland
Virginia
West Virginia
Ohio
Kentucky
Indiana
Other wine-growing areas

Canada

Wine growing in Canada has a relatively short history. The first cautious steps in this field were taken in 1811 by Johann Schiller, a German officer who took part in several North American wars. After leaving the army, he retired to a plot of land near Toronto and undertook some very successful experiments with domesticated wild vines. After 35 years he sold his vineyard to a French aristocrat.

Canada is not the most ideal land for cultivating vines. Indeed, its winters are notorious for their harshness, and even in the most southerly regions that border the United States temperatures can easily drop to below 5°F (−15°C). But Canadian winemakers know how to make a virtue of necessity. Each year the Riesling and Vidal grapes freeze in the two most important wine-growing areas, Ontario and British Columbia, making this raw land the largest and most reliable producer of ice wines in the world. And the Vidal grape, which was bred by crossing Ugni Blanc and Seibel, is exceptional in being a hybrid with a touch of class.

The fact that ice wine has become one of the typical national specialties gives a clear indication of Canada's key characteristic as a wine-producing country: its cold climate. Although the main producing area, Ontario, where six sevenths of the roughly 20,300 acres (8,200 ha) of vines planted in the country are concentrated, is on the same latitude as the Midi region of France and also profits from the moderating influence of the Great Lakes, the outbreaks of cold weather in the spring and autumn restrict the period during which grapes can ripen. There are only a few wine-growing areas in Nova Scotia and Quebec, where each autumn the vines are protected from the frost with a covering of piled-up earth and then dug out again in the spring.

In view of the extremely difficult conditions prevalent in Canada, wine growing relied at

The Oakanagan Valley is the most promising area in British Columbia.

first on resistant *labrusca* varieties, and subsequently on hybrids. The light red grapes of the indestructible Concord vine are still used for the production of sweet-sherry and port-wine imitations, while the Niagara variety is a popular choice for dry white wine. Nearly three-fifths of the vines grown in Canada are hybrids. Concord is the most common, followed by Elvira, De Chaunac, then—some way behind—Niagara, Seyval Blanc, Maréchal Foch, and Baco Noir. Vidal is the variety most often used for ice wine.

The modernization of the winemaking industry began in Canada after Inniskillin (not far from the Niagara Falls) was granted a license in 1975. It was the first private winery founded in Ontario. Since then, many winegrowers have succeeded in demonstrating that *Vitis*

vinifera can flourish in Canada. At first they experimented mainly with German varieties, but Chardonnay and red French grapes are gaining more and more ground.

The increased awareness of quality issues led to the adoption of a wine-growing philosophy which resulted in the establishment of the Vintners Quality Alliance, an *appellation* system first introduced in Ontario in 1989, then, a year later, in British Columbia. Under this system, wines are defined by either the province or the wine-growing area where they originate (see page 792).

The Province of Ontario has three areas of *appellation*: Pelee Island, Lake Erie North Shore, and Niagara Peninsula.

On the whole, the Ontario climate is similar to that of Burgundy, and conditions are practically the same as in the nearby Finger Lakes region of New York State. With the exception of the ice wines, the area's most reliably successful products are Riesling and Chardonnay, which is often very reminiscent of Chablis. In warm years the region produces excellent, rounded Gamays and Pinot Noirs, and pleasant Cabernet Francs and Cabernet Sauvignons, while Merlot has recently begun to reach high standards as well. There are 45 wineries in Ontario, the best known being Cave Spring, Château des Charmes, Henry of Pelham, Hillebrand, Inniskillin, Konzelmann Winery, Pelee Island Winery, Reif Estate, Southbrook Farm, Stoney Ridge, and Vineland Estates.

Four geographical *appellations* are recognized in the Province of British Columbia: Vancouver Island, Fraser Valley, Similkameen Valley, and Okanagan Valley.

The most important region is the Okanagan Valley, a semi-arid area where there are extreme variations between night and day temperatures. As in the nearby Columbia Valley, heavy irrigation is needed to grow vines, though Okanagan Lake softens the climate. No hybrids are planted

The wine and souvenir shop of the Château des Charmes in Ontario: In a climate very similar to Burgundy the growers here produce very interesting Chardonnays.

The first real winery on Pelee Island in Lake Erie was founded in 1866. Pelee Island Vineyards continue the tradition.

in the Okanagan Valley, and most of the growers have chosen to cultivate German grape varieties, such as Bacchus and Ehrenfelser, as well as planting Chardonnay, while trials are being conducted with Pinot and Merlot. Mention should be made, above all, of Blue Mountain Vineyard, Calona Wines, Cedar Creek Estate, Gehringer Brothers, Gray Monk, Hainle Vineyards, Mission Hill, Quail's Gate, Sumac Ridge, and Summerhill.

There are two other wine-growing regions in Canada that do not meet the V.Q.A. requirements. Three producers are active in Nova Scotia, working 160 acres (65 ha) of vineyards where they cultivate hybrids and old Russian black grape varieties. And, whereas wine-growers in all of Canada's winemaking areas also offer guest rooms, in Quebec, where nine-tenths of the small yield is white wine, primarily Seyval Blanc, the industry is completely dependent on tourism.

United States of America: New York and the East

The first wine-growing experiments on the East Coast were undertaken in the early-17th century, but the native VITIS species did not produce good wines. Not until 200 years later, when it was discovered that an American *Vitis labrusca* variety had crossed spontaneously with a European *Vitis vinifera* variety, was the breakthrough made with deliberately bred hybrids, of which Concord became the best known.

The resistance of American vines, especially *Vitis riparia* and *Vitis rupestris*, has been invaluable to the wine industry, providing it with rootstocks that are not susceptible to phylloxera. Most of the vines used to produce fine wines around the world are now grown on American rootstocks.

The winegrowers on the East Coast did not find themselves in a position to improve the quality of their grapes significantly until the 1960s, when the first plantings of French hybrids were successful. Thanks to the optimization of rootstocks, clones, and treatment techniques, European varieties were eventually acclimatized. The Farm Winery Act of 1976 made it possible for small producers to open their own wineries, and today there are more than 125 enterprises producing wine in the region, making Finger Lakes New York's most important wine supplier.

The most easterly of the lakes, Cayuga Lake, is recognized as a separate *appellation*. The other three lakes, Seneca, Keuka, and Canandaigua, where the Canandaigua Wine Company is based, form the Finger Lakes A.V.A. Hybrids still dominate the scene, and are

Vines have been cultivated since 1820 in the Finger Lakes region, which produces 90 percent of the wine made in New York State. The Taylor Wine Company is one of nearly 50 wineries in this area to the southeast of Rochester.

cultivated on some 34,600 acres (14,000 ha) of land, making New York the U.S.A.'s largest wine-producing state by area after California. None of the other wine-growing regions grows a comparable range of grapes. The wineries continue to vinify *labrusca* varieties, such as the white Catawba, Delaware, Diamond, Duchess, Elvira, Isabella, and Niagara, and the black Concord, Ives, and Steuben, while the hybrids include Aurora, Cayuga, Seyval Blanc, Vignoles or Baco Noir, Chambourein, Chancellor, Rosette, and Villard Noir. However, hardly any of these grapes make wines of convincing quality, which is why the businesses here, as throughout the rest of the eastern U.S.A., are beginning to cultivate *Vitis vinifera* varieties, such as Chardonnay, Riesling, Gewürztraminer, Semillon, Sauvignon Blanc, Merlot, Cabernet Sauvignon, Cabernet Franc, Gamay, and Pinot Noir.

Apart from Finger Lakes, there are three other A.V.A.s on the East Coast: Long Island, Hudson River, and Lake Erie.

The influence of the Atlantic ensures that the climate on Long Island is mild, with a rather long growing period. In consequence, Bordeaux varieties are able to ripen there, and the vineyards laid out since 1973 have been planted with European vines. With nearly 1,480 acres (600 ha) of vines, North Fork is the larger of the two *appellations* on the island. The more southerly Hampton consists of just 125 acres (50 ha).

Grapes have been cultivated for 300 years in the Hudson Valley to the north of New York City. Sea air rises up this river valley, moderating the climate. About 25 mostly small wineries produce wine from hybrids, but are increasingly using Cabernet, Chardonnay, and other European varieties.

The most extensive plantings in New York State extend along the banks of Lake Erie, covering more than 19,800 acres (8,000 ha), but these vineyards are mainly used for the production of grape juice.

Well-known producers in the Finger Lakes region include: Canandaigua Wine Company, Four Chimneys Farm, Fox Run, Glenora, Heron Hill, Knapp, Treleaven, and Wagner and Wiemer; on Long Island: Bedell Cellars, Bridgehampton, Gristina, Hargrave, Lenz, Palmer, Peconic Bay, and Pindar Vineyards; on the Hudson River: Benmarl, Brotherhood America's Oldest Winery, Millbrook, and Rivendell.

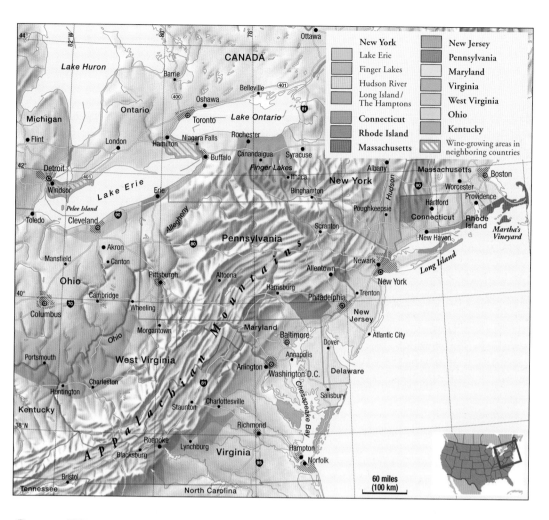

OTHER WINE-GROWING STATES

There is an active wine-growing industry in New England. Wine is produced there by some 40 enterprises, led by the pioneering Haight Vineyards, Chamard, Chicama, and Sakonnet. New Jersey's vineyards are concentrated in the valley of the Delaware River, where the first winery to be established was Renault. It was founded in 1864 and, like Unionville, has now revived its former glory. Some of the vines in the states of Pennsylvania and Ohio extend along the banks of Lake Erie, but there are larger plantings further to the south. Debonné and Firelands are the best-known vineyards in Ohio, where the area under cultivation is approaching the 2,500-acre (1,000-ha) mark. In Pennsylvania there are around 9,400 acres (3,800 ha) planted with vines, three quarters of them with *labrusca* varieties. Good wines are produced there by Allegro and Chadsford. With 370 acres (150 ha) of vines, Maryland offers interesting Cabernets and Chardonnays, particularly from Catoctin, Elk Run, and Montbray, while Boordy concentrates on hybrids. The white wines of the East Coast are fruity and light, though some of the Chardonnays have pleasant roasted and caramel notes thanks to their maturation in oak barrels.

In the Midwest, Michigan's wine industry profits from the insulating influence of Lake Michigan. The Concord vines grown on 12,108 acres (4,900 ha) mainly supply the juice industry, but 34 wineries also do good business. They have concentrated on Chardonnay, Riesling, Pinot Grigio, Cabernet Franc, and Pinot Noir, and some also produce excellent sparkling and fruit wines. The best known operations are Château Chantal, Château Grand Traverse, Fenn Valley, Good Harbour, L. Mawby, St. Julian, and Tabor Hill.

The 46 wineries in Missouri rely on an attractive mixture of beautiful countryside and pleasant wines, which are almost all based on hybrids. Notable producers include Augusta, Hermannshof, Les Bourgeois, Mount Pleasant, St. James, and Stone Hill Winery.

There is also a lively wine scene in the south. There are now more *vinifera* vines than hybrids growing in Virginia, and the most convincing wines being made there are Chardonnay and Bordeaux VARIETALS from Château Morisette, Linden, Meredyth, Montdomaine, Prince Michael, and Tarara. European grapes are also successful in Arkansas, North Carolina, and Georgia, while in Tennessee and Florida the best results are achieved with hybrids.

Sharon Mills Winery is based in a historic grist mill on the banks of the River Raisin in Michigan owned by the Henry Ford Foundation. Sharon Mills uses grapes from the Old Mission Peninsula.

WASHINGTON

No one who stays in Seattle, the capital of Washington State, and visits the lush green landscape around Puget Sound, would suspect that, after California, Washington is the most important American producer of quality wines based on European grapes. Nevertheless, about 79 acres (32 ha) are cultivated on the islands in this inland sea, and varieties like Müller-Thurgau, Madeleine Angevine, Siegerrebe, and Pinot are vinified by the *appellation's* four wineries. On account of its mild climate, only the most northerly varieties, principally white grapes, can be grown in the Puget Sound A.V.A.

The Columbia Winery near Seattle was founded in 1962 by university lecturers and business people.

	Puget Sound
	Columbia Valley
	Yakima Valley
	Walla Walla Valley
	Wine-growing areas in neighboring regions

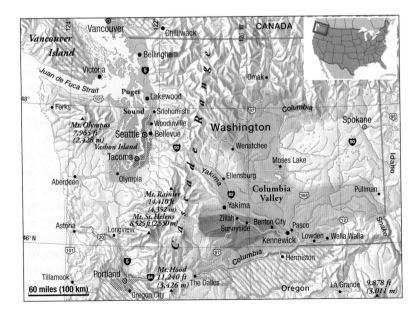

The heart of the wine industry is near the city of Seattle, despite the fact that 99 percent of the grapes actually grow far to the east of the capital, beyond the Cascade Range, which rises to almost 14,500 feet (4,400 m) above sea level in Washington, drawing heavy rainfall from the clouds generated by the Pacific. Woodinville, a few miles outside Seattle, is the center of operations for the state's two most important wineries, Château Ste Michelle and Columbia Winery. Three other large companies, and the exquisite DeLille Cellars, have been there since 1994. Their decisions to locate close to the state capital were based purely on commercial grounds, because Washington's largest *appellation*, the wide desert-like Columbia Valley, lies in the rain shadow to the east of the mountains. It is only the waters of the Columbia River and its tributaries, the Snake River and the Yakima River, that make it possible to grow vines there at all. Columbia Valley also includes the state's two other important *appellations*, Yakima Valley and Walla Walla Valley, as well as the small A.V.A. Red Mountain in Benton County. Another four sub-A.V.A.s have made a name for themselves on account of their particularly favorable conditions: Wahluke Slope, Royal Slope, and Cold Creek for Chardonnay and other varieties; Lower Snake River for Merlot, Sauvignon Blanc, and Semillon; Canoe Ridge for Merlot, Cabernet, and Chardonnay; and Southwest Washington for Pinot Noir and Chardonnay.

WATER RIGHTS AND WINTER KILLERS

Agriculture arrived relatively recently in the Columbia Valley. Only after 1930 did people become aware of the unexplored potential in the region and make efforts to develop the area by building irrigation systems. The first vines were planted in Yakima Valley by the predecessors of Château Ste Michelle in 1951 and Columbia Winery in 1957, and the first official wines then came onto the market in 1967. More businesses were founded in the 1970s, and it was possible to list 19 wineries by 1981. The ensuing decade saw new growth that continued into the 1990s. There are now more than 240 wineries, and the area cultivated with vines has expanded at a spectacular rate. Some 29,150 acres (11,800 ha) are currently under vines, and there are still farmers who hope to make better profits from winemaking. The future development of the region will depend on them, because only long-established landowners enjoy water rights, and the State of Washington will not award new rights. No vines can grow in the area's semi-arid inland climate without artificial irrigation. Apart from the large, established wine companies that have invested in extensive estates, more than 300 farms supply the majority of the grapes. Successful wineries have begun to offer technical and financial support to farmers interested in the business, with the aim of going into partnership with them. This is a way of securing grapes for the future, and also allows the winegrowers to exert an influence on the quality of the product through their participation. Although there are a few BOUTIQUE WINERIES, winemaking here is on an industrial scale and mechanical techniques are applied extensively.

Apart from the most easterly areas, where the temperatures are reduced by marine influences

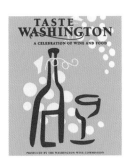

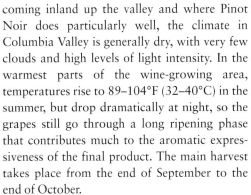

Almost all Washington's vineyards extend along the Columbia River, and vines could not grow here without the water taken from the river. The Cascade Range provides shelter from the rain.

coming inland up the valley and where Pinot Noir does particularly well, the climate in Columbia Valley is generally dry, with very few clouds and high levels of light intensity. In the warmest parts of the wine-growing area, temperatures rise to 89–104°F (32–40°C) in the summer, but drop dramatically at night, so the grapes still go through a long ripening phase that contributes much to the aromatic expressiveness of the final product. The main harvest takes place from the end of September to the end of October.

Although these conditions are highly favorable for winemaking, the region's farmers face an enemy that causes problems for them year after year: the winter killer. Winter killers are sporadic frosts that can reach –13°F (–25°C) or even lower, killing the wood in the vines. This has caused very low yields in some years, such as 1991 and 1996. Happily, there is no danger from phylloxera in Washington, so only producing vines are planted. This means that the farmers can simply cut the frozen vines off above the ground with chain saws. If the vine puts out buds again the following year, all but two are cut back. The next year it will bear a small harvest, and then produce a perfectly normal yield in the third year after the freeze. To protect against frost damage, there is a tendency to plant close to rivers or on south-facing slopes. Some wineries also try to compensate for frost damage by blending the wine from a poor year with that of the previous vintage.

MERLOT, MERITAGES, AND FINE WHITE WINES

Blends are very popular in Washington, where combinations of Bordeaux varieties are particularly successful. This is true of the large number of blends sold as varietal Cabernets and Merlots, but containing up to 25 percent wine from other grapes, as well as the MERITAGES many wineries

Idaho

The mountainous state of Idaho borders Oregon and Washington to the east. Its most important vineyards are located east of the state capital Boise in the warmest part of Idaho, Sunny Slope. The Sainte Chapelle Vineyards winery was established there in 1976, and has remained by far the most important producer in the area ever since. With its cold nights and raw winters, the state's high altitude is particularly suitable for Riesling, which is made into wines with an interesting balance of sweetness and acidity. Apart from Chardonnay, sparkling wines also play a major role in the region.

make by blending Merlot and Cabernet in various proportions (see page 819). Merlot enjoys great popularity and is the leading black grape variety in Washington, ahead of Cabernet Sauvignon. Unfortunately, the Merlot harvest is sometimes poor, resulting in harsh, thin wines with vegetable notes. By contrast, the area's good Merlots are very full, silky, and ripe with berryish fruit and pleasant spices. The really convincing Cabernet Sauvignons in Washington have an intensive, juicy fruit, not infrequently reminiscent of black cherries and blackberries, but tend to taste of plums and stewed fruit when overripe. Newcomers to the trade often mature their wines with balance and finesse in barrels, but the notable winemakers of the pioneer generation are inclined to give their red wines excessively strong wood flavors.

In recent years Syrah and Sangiovese have received attention, though the fruity, rather light Lemberger remains something of a curiosity. Chardonnay is the leader among white varieties, but the best white wines are made from Semillon and Sauvignon Blanc. With their intense, fresh aromas of lemon, guava, and balm, highly nervous character, and elegant spiciness, the wines made with these grapes can be very exciting. Apart from this, the local Riesling, which is still the second most important grape variety, is sometimes highly vivacious.

SELECT PRODUCERS IN WASHINGTON

APEX—WASHINGTON HILL CELLARS**–***
SUNNYSIDE
Bought-in grapes; 1,200,000 bottles • Wines include: Chardonnay, Sauvignon Blanc, Semillon/Chardonnay; Lemberger, Merlot, Cabernet; →Apex Merlot
Apex is the prestige label of this winery, which produces good-value, often excellent wines in a former dairy.

CHÂTEAU STE MICHELLE*–****
WOODINVILLE
3,398 acres (1,375 ha) • Wines include: Columbia Valley Wines; 11 Sorten; Single Vineyard Wines, Reserve Wines; →Eroica, →Col Solare
A visitor center and white winery near Seattle; a red winery on the Canoe Ridge Estate on the Columbia River; three more grape farms. Like Columbia Crest, Ste Michelle belongs to Stimson Lane, the biggest wine enterprise in Washington. Eroica, a dry Riesling, is a highly successful joint venture with Dr. Ernst Loosen from the Mosel.

DELILLE CELLARS****
WOODINVILLE
Bought-in grapes; 40,000 bottles • Wines: one white wine, three red wines, all blends; →Chaleur Estate white and red, →Harrisson Hill
A boutique winery founded in 1992 by the DeLille family, who originally came from Karlovy Vary in the Czech Republic. Winemaker Chris Upchurch vinifies superb Bordeaux blends. Top of the range are the Chaleur Estate and the Harrisson Hill. The D2 is the second wine.

HEDGES CELLARS**–****
BENTON CITY
74 acres (30 ha); bought-in grapes; 700,000 bottles • Wines: Fumé-Chardonnay; Cabernet-Merlot; →Red Mountain Reserve Cabernet, →Three Vineyards
Tom and Anne-Marie Hedges began to plant red varieties on Red Mountain in 1987; the vineyard now has its own A.V.A. They also set up a château. They only produce four wines, and one, the rare Reserve, is top quality.

LEONETTI CELLAR**
WALLA WALLA
25 acres (10 ha); bought-in grapes; 55,000 bottles • Wines: Merlot, Cabernet, Sangiovese
Walla Walla's first winery, founded in 1978. Gary Figgins concentrates on the red wines matured in new barrels that have made him famous. Too much wood for some palates.

MATTHEW CELLARS***–****
WOODINVILLE
Bought-in grapes; 36,000 bottles • Wines: →Red, Yakima Valley
Matthew Loso is one of the most interesting young winemakers in Washington. This former restaurant manager certainly has a way with red wine, in which he specializes, composing blends of Cabernet Sauvignon, Cabernet Franc, and Merlot.

McCREA CELLARS***–****
LAKE STEVENS
Bought-in grapes; 36,000 bottles • Wines: Chardonnay, Viognier; Syrah, Grenache, →Tierra del Sol
Apart from his Chardonnays, Doug McCrea loves Rhône varieties. His Tierra del Sol is made of Syrah and Grenache, and tastes pleasantly fruity and herby. The Viognier is good, and the excellent Syrahs have a unique texture and fruit.

COLUMBIA*–****
BELLEVUE
Bought-in grapes; 1,500,000 bottles • Wines include: Gewürztraminer, Riesling, Pinot Gris, Semillon, Chardonnay; Sangiovese, Merlot, Cabernet Sauvignon, Cabernet Franc, Syrah; →Red Willow Merlot, Otis Cabernet
This enterprise was founded in 1962 by ten university lecturers and has been managed since 1979 by David Lake, a Master of Wine from Britain. The Otis and Red Willow lead his wide range.

COLUMBIA CREST*–***
PATERSON
2,471 acres (1,000 ha); bought-in grapes; approx. 14,000,000 bottles • Wines: Reihen: Columbia Valley, Grand Estates, Reserve: →Syrah
This winery opened in 1982 and it has grown to be the biggest wine producer in Washington. Under winemaker Doug Gore it has not only produced popular starter's wines but also several outstanding top quality wines, from Merlot and Syrah, for instance.

COVEY RUN*–***
ZILLAH
193 acres (78 ha); bought-in grapes; 840,000 bottles • Wines include: Riesling, Chardonnay, Sauvignon Blanc, Semillon; Merlot, Cabernet, Lemberger; →Riesling Icewine, Chardonnay Celilo, Chardonnay Reserve

The cozy tasting room of Woodward Canyon at Lowden in the Walla Walla area.

Formerly known as Quail Run, this winery is known for its pleasant, good-value white wines made by Dave Crippen.

KIONA**−****
BENTON CITY
32 acres (13 ha); bought-in grapes; 180,000 bottles • Wines include: Chardonnay, Chenin, Riesling; Cabernet Sauvignon, Merlot, Lemberger; →Red Mountain Reserve Cabernet, Late Harvest Riesling, Chenin Icewine
Two couples, the Holms and the Willimans, have been running this vineyard and winery together since 1979, selling some of their grapes to well-known vineyards. Kiona pioneered Lemberger in Washington.

L'ECOLE NO.41***−****
LOWDEN
More than 125 acres (50 ha); bought-in grapes; 240,000 bottles • Wines: Chardonnay, →Semillon; Merlot, Cabernet →Seven Hills Barrel Select Merlot, →Pepper Bridge Apogée
Marty Clubb, who is a partner in several important vineyards, has set standards for Merlot in Washington, but his barrel-fermented white wines are considered to be just as good. Apogée is a blend of Merlot and Cabernet Sauvignon.

NORTHSTAR****
WALLA WALLA
Bought-in grapes; 30,000 bottles • Wine: Merlot
This luxury brand, which was started in 1994 and also belongs to Stimson Lane, only markets a single wine, selecting the best Merlot and Cabernet grapes from the company's 8,649 acres (3,500 ha) of vines spread among 14 different plots of land. After five days in open fermentation vats the wine completes its fermentation in new *barriques*, where it lies for 19 months. Then follows the *assemblage* from 18 separate lots; the result is a grandiose wine, consisting of 80 percent Merlot and 20 percent Cabernet Sauvignon.

QUILCEDA CREEK*****
SNOHOMISH
Bought-in grapes; 30,000 bottles • Wine: →Cabernet Sauvignon
For many years Alex Golitzen only made one wine, Cabernet Sauvignon, which he and his son Paul compose with grapes from various areas, adding a hint of Merlot. Matured slowly in the finest oak, this wine is a monument. They now produce a second wine of the same quality.

SOOS CREEK****
RENTON
Bought-in grapes; approx. 6,000 bottles • Wine: Cabernet
Many producers in Washington began like Dave Larson and started making wine with bought grapes in their garage or a shed. Larson only makes Cabernet Sauvignon, which he matures for four years in the barrel. It is very voluminous, juicy, and silky: quite unique.

WALLA WALLA VINTNERS***−****
WALLA WALLA
Bought-in grapes; 50,000 bottles • Wines: →Merlot, →Cabernet Franc, Washington State Cuvée, Sangiovese
This winery is run by three wine lovers with fine palettes and a great deal of dedication. They make superb, finely crafted red wines, the best being their Cabernet Sauvignon.

ANDREW WILL****−*****
VASHON ISLAND
Bought-in grapes; 48,000 bottles • Wines: Chenin; →Merlot, Cabernet Sauvignon; Sangiovese Sorella
Chris Camarda only buys the best fruit from well-known vineyards, such as Ciel du Cheval, Pepper Bridge, Seven Hills, and Klipsun. The amazing texture he unlocks from these grapes is perfectly matched by the new French *barriques* he uses. His Sorella is astonishing.

WILRIDGE****
SEATTLE
Bought-in grapes; approx. 6,000 bottles • Wines: →Cabernet Franc, Cabernet Sauvignon, →Merlot
A lawyer making amazing wines with wild fruit, incredible structure, and real passion right in the middle of Seattle.

WOODWARD CANYON**−****
LOWDEN
27 acres (11 ha); bought-in grapes; 150,000 bottles • Wines: Chardonnay; Cabernet Sauvignon, Merlot; →Old Vine Cabernet Sauvignon
Rick Small founded the region's second winery in 1981 and is now planting vineyards above his vinification shed with Barbera, Nebbiolo, and Syrah. Well known for butterscotchy Chardonnay and powerful reds.

OREGON

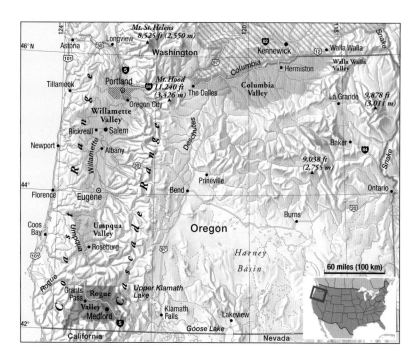

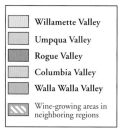

Willamette Valley

Umpqua Valley

Rogue Valley

Columbia Valley

Walla Walla Valley

Wine-growing areas in neighboring regions

Cristom Vineyards in Salem are passionate defenders of a traditional approach to Pinot Noir.

The Coast Range runs along the 300 or so miles (500 km) of the Oregon seaboard, softening the influence of the Pacific on the winemaking areas of the Willamette, Umpqua, and Rogue Valleys that shelter behind the hills. In the east the Cascade Range, which rises to 11,240 feet (3,426 m) above sea level in Oregon, acts as a barrier that holds back the rain clouds from the Pacific. The few vineyards on the other side of

the mountains therefore rely on intensive irrigation to cultivate their vines. The areas along the Columbia River, which forms the border with the state of Washington for more than 250 miles (400 km), are much better developed to the north of the river, but the section of the Walla Walla Valley that extends into Oregon is also seeing a boom now.

Oregon lies on the same latitude as the south of France, but the west of the state has a rather cool, damp climate. By contrast with California, where the winemaking regions that produce the best-quality wines are those in which the top temperatures are reduced by the influence of the Pacific during the summer and autumn, it is necessary to use the warmest, sunniest locations in Oregon's main wine-growing areas, as otherwise the grapes do not ripen sufficiently. Nature therefore presents the winemakers of Oregon with a unique set of difficulties. They cannot plant on the off chance or expand their vineyards on demand, but have to research their area very carefully in order to identify the few really suitable locations. Successful results are only achieved by committed winegrowers who bring prudence, a feel for the lie of the land, and real stamina to their work.

Wine growing in Oregon is a challenge. The region has none of the nonchalance, light-hearted entrepreneurial spirit, fashionable flair,

or lively business sense common in California. Rather, the visitor will find friendly, open, but rugged individualists and philosopher winemakers. These are not people who have diversified into winemaking from show business. Nor is it the large wine companies or drinks multinationals that have made Oregon well known among wine lovers, but rather its Pinot Noir. The International Pinot Noir Convention draws passionate fans and producers of this grape from all over the world to the small town of McMinnville every year to exchange experiences and taste wines together.

THE RISE OF THE INDIVIDUALISTS

The first pioneers in Oregon began to produce wine in the second half of the 19th century. Winemaking also experienced a considerable boom in the state after Prohibition was repealed, but companies like the Honeywood Winery in Salem, which was founded in 1934, mainly produced fruit wines at this time. To the present day the favorable climate and fertile soils of Oregon ensure that there are rich harvests of berries, apples, pears, and stonefruit.

The pioneer of modern winemaking in the state was Richard Sommer. After studying at the University of California at Davis, he planted Riesling and other varieties in the Umpqua Valley, and launched the Hillcrest Winery there in 1963. The climate is comparatively dry and

The famous Burgundy wine house, Drouhin, have planted their own estate in Dundee, specializing exclusively in Pinot Noir and Chardonnay.

warm in the wine-growing area around Roseburg, with its low hills and wide valleys, so it is even possible to plant Cabernet Sauvignon, though varieties that are more resistant to low temperatures predominate, such as Riesling, Pinot, and Chardonnay. Pinot Noir and Pinot Gris dominate the scene closer to the Pacific in the Illinois Valley, while Oregon's best Cabernets and Merlots flourish in the warmer sub-A.V.A.s Applegate Valley and Rogue Valley, where vines are grown at higher altitudes.

Vineyards were being planted in the northern Willamette Valley as early as the 1960s, and 17 wineries had been founded there by the end of the 1970s. The majority concentrated on Pinot Noir and Chardonnay, varieties that were believed to be particularly promising on account of the area's climatic similarities with Burgundy. This confidence proved to be justified: the 1975 Pinot Noir from Eyrie Vineyards outclassed many a noted Burgundy at BLIND TASTING sessions. As a result, in about 1980 a succession of winemakers began to stream into the region, the majority of whom already had experience in California. There are now more than 220 wineries, mainly in the Willamette Valley. Most have their own vineyards, but still purchase grapes from specialized farms. The majority of these producers are small businesses that can be classed as boutique wineries. They concentrate on quality and seek to develop the individual character of their wines. Prices are correspondingly high.

Left
The Beaux Frères Winery at Newberg belongs to Michael Etzel and his brother-in-law, the world-famous wine critic Robert Parker.

Opposite
The red soils of the Dundee Hills are regarded as one of the best *terroirs* for Pinot Noir, as is confirmed by the red wines produced there by Domaine Drouhin.

A Local Specialty: Pinot Noir

Pinot Noir has become a local specialty, and almost 50 percent of the approximately 12,100 acres (4,900 ha) of vineyard in the state are now planted with this demanding vine. After sunny, ripe vintages during the 1980s, the weather was more changeable and rainy in the 1990s, causing problems for the winegrowers as they had to harvest their grapes before they were fully ripe. Many of the new vineyards were planted without sufficient specialist input and have proved to be disappointing. They produce wines that have fresh aromas of red berries, but not infrequently need to be sweetened and de-acidified due to a lack of body and vegetable notes.

Most of the vineyards have been planted on slopes that face away from the sea wind and are cultivated without irrigation. The red earth of the Dundee Hills is famous, but aspect is more important than soil in this region. The higher locations are generally regarded as the best *terroirs* and do better in good years, but in poor years the grapes do not ripen there. Medium altitudes are the safest, while grapes that are planted in low situations often ripen too early. Winegrowers have to be as flexible as possible in reacting to weather conditions in a particular year, but most believe in "getting things right by doing them slowly," as Steve Doerner, the winemaker at Cristom, puts it.

Quality-conscious producers currently plant between 2,200 and 3,000 vines per acre (5,400–7,400 vines/ha) at new plantings, but 1,900 per acre (4,700/ha) is the norm at high locations, which is about twice as many as previously. Thanks to these higher vine densities, the grapes have a third less volume, which gives the wines a better texture and makes their flavors more concentrated. In general, Pinot Noir produces yields of 425 gallons per acre (40 hl/ha) or less. Picked grapes that have been affected by rot and would cause bad tones in the flavor are discarded before they leave the vineyard. Many winemakers rely on natural YEASTS, which work slowly but give the wine greater expressiveness. The VINIFICATION time of wines fermented in this way is about 15 to 21 days, after which the wine is usually matured for 12 to 15 months in small oak barrels.

July and August are usually very hot and dry in Oregon. The harvest then begins at the end of August and often goes on until well into October, with most of the picking being done by hand. The second most important grape is Chardonnay. In the Oregon climate it often develops a noticeable acidity and sour fruity aromas of lemon, gooseberry, and apple, which may be rounded off with buttery, nutty, and roasted notes, depending on its maturity and the vinification techniques used. Pinot Gris is now the third most popular grape and makes pleasing, pale, refreshing, fruity white wines. Riesling still has its supporters, but the interest in Gewürztraminer has faded. Bordeaux varieties ripen best in the south. If Cabernet Sauvignon is printed on the label, 75 percent of the wine must consist of the named variety, but all other varietal wines made in Oregon have to contain a prescribed minimum of 90 percent of the named variety.

WILLAMETTE VALLEY

David Adelsheim, one of the pioneers in the Willamette Valley, sells his best Pinots as vineyard bottlings.

The broad, green valley of the Willamette River stretches some 155 miles (250 km) south from Portland and is Oregon's main wine-producing area. Many winegrowers have been attracted to the north of the valley, especially its sheltered western slopes. Apart from the first outstanding *terroir* to be identified, the Red Hills of Dundee, with their red, volcanic soil, the Eola Hills to the northwest, the Salem Hills to the south of Salem, and the Forest Grove district to the west

of Portland have proved to be remarkable wine-growing areas. At the moment, interest is concentrated mainly on the Chehalem Mountains. The plentiful precipitation of about 60 inches (152 cm) a year falls mainly during the mild winter months. By contrast, the summer weather is relatively dry for the most part, and the temperatures that make the valley a cool Region I area (see page 812) result in an extended ripening phase, which helps to give the grapes their intense flavor.

"Contains sulfites"

Producers are obliged by U.S. law to include the declaration "Contains sulfites" in the information on their bottles. This is intended to warn asthma and allergy sufferers of the sulfur added to wine. In reality, the sulfur-dioxide content of wine is so low that there is only cause for concern in very rare cases. Sulfur dioxide, which is commonly known in the European Union as E220, is used as a preservative during vinification, which is why it is obligatory to label bottles with "Preservative (220)" in Australia.

SELECT PRODUCERS IN OREGON

ADELSHEIM**−****
NEWBERG
161 acres (65 ha); bought-in grapes; 260,000 bottles
• *Wines: Chardonnay, Pinot Blanc, →Pinot Gris, Riesling; Pinot Noir, Merlot; →Elizabeth's Reserve*
This winery's first Pinot Noir was planted in 1972. Adelsheim went into partnership with the Loackers in 1993, and produces very convincing single-vineyard Pinots.

AMITY**−***
AMITY
16 acres (6.5 ha); bought-in grapes; 150,000 bottles
• *Wines: Gewürztraminer, Pinot Blanc, Riesling; Pinot, Gamay*
The first winery in Oregon to bring out a Gamay. Their Gewürztraminer is one of the best.

ARCHERY SUMMIT*****
DAYTON
84 acres (34 ha); 180,000 bottles • *Wines: →white cuvée; Pinot; →Archery Summit Estate Pinot*
Gary Andrus specializes in single-vineyard Pinot Noirs.

ARGYLE**−****
DUNDEE
494 acres (200 ha); 300,000 bottles • *Wines: sparkling wines; Chardonnay, Pinot Gris, Riesling; Pinot Noir*

This joint venture between Carl Knudsen and Brian Croser is the most important sparkling wine producer in Oregon. They also make interesting still wines.

BEAUX FRÈRES*****
NEWBERG
27 acres (11 ha); 36,000 bottles • *Wines: →Pinot Noir Beaux Frères; second wine: Belles Soeurs*
Robert Parker and Michael Etzel began planting their vineyard in 1988, following all the rules of the art as it is practiced in Burgundy. Outstanding wines.

BETHEL HEIGHTS**−****
SALEM
55 acres (22 ha); 140,000 bottles • *Wines: Chardonnay, Pinot Blanc, Pinot Gris, Gewürztraminer; Pinot Noir; →Wadenswil Block Reserve*
Former grape farmers Ted and Terry Casteel have been making clearly differentiated, block-designated wines since 1984.

BRICK HOUSE***−****
NEWBERG
27 acres (11 ha); 29,000 bottles • *Wines: Chardonnay; Gamay, →Pinot*
Ex-journalist Doug Tunnell grows high-quality grapes using organic and biodynamic methods and makes them into very convincing wines.

CHEHALEM***–****
NEWBERG
138 acres (56 ha); 120,000 bottles • Wines: Chardonnay, →Pinot Gris, Riesling; Pinot Noir; →Ridgecrest
The two couples that own this winery use grapes from four vineyards and have taken advice from Burgundy. The results are the fine Rion Reserve, concentrated Pinots, and delightful whites.

CRISTOM**–***
SALEM
37 acres (15 ha); bought-in grapes; 130,000 bottles • Wines: Chardonnay, Pinot Gris, Viognier; Pinot; →Marjorie
Winemaker Steve Doerner (formerly of Calera) insists on fermenting Pinot Noir with wood chips, which often give the wine vegetable notes. Good white wines.

DOMAINE DROUHIN****–*****
DUNDEE
89 acres (36 ha); 160,000 bottles • Wines: →Chardonnay; →Pinot
Robert Drouhin from Beaune began visiting Oregon in 1961. In 1987 he finally bought land there, planted vineyards, and built a futuristic four-story, 8.5-level winery. His daughter Véronique has produced some splendid Pinot Noirs.

ERATH*–***
DUNDEE
110 acres (45 ha); bought-in grapes; 600,000 bottles • Wines include: Chardonnay, Pinot Gris, Pinot Blanc, Riesling; Pinot, Dolcetto
Dick Erath is one of the pioneers of wine growing in Oregon and founded this vineyard and winery in the Red Hills in 1968. The broad range is dominated by Pinots.

EVESHAM WOOD****
SALEM
10 acres (4 ha); 24,000 bottles • Wines: Chardonnay, Pinot Gris; Pinot; →Chardonnay Tête de Cuvée
Russell and Mary Raney have been making outstanding wines on their estate since 1986. They only use their own grapes.

EYRIE**–****
McMINNVILLE
55 acres (22 ha); 120,000 bottles • Wines: Chardonnay, Pinot Gris, Muscat Ottonel; Pinot Noir
In 1966 David Lett became the first grower to plant *vinifera* stocks in Oregon after Prohibition. This winery was also the first to introduce Pinot Gris, which is now so popular in the region.

FORIS*–***
CAVE JUNCTION
74 acres (30 ha); bought-in grapes; 400,000 bottles • Wines include: Chardonnay, Pinot Gris, Pinot Blanc, Pinot, Merlot, Cabernet; →Maple Ranch Pinot
The Berards and Gerbers have demonstrated Rogue Valley's potential for Pinot Noir and Merlot.

PONZI**–****
BEAVERTON
110 acres (45 ha); bought-in-grapes; 150,000 bottles • Wines include: Chardonnay, Pinot Gris, Riesling (Vino Gelato), →Arneis; Pinot, Dolcetto
The Ponzis were among the wine pioneers of Oregon and began planting vines in 1970. They have built up a reputation with their full-bodied, fruitily spicy Pinot Noirs and their Pinot Gris.

REX HILL**–****
NEWBERG
250 acres (100 ha); 480,000 bottles • Wines: Chardonnay, Pinot Gris, Riesling, Gewürztraminer; Pinot; →Pinot Reserve, →Adams Vineyard

Paul Hart and Jan Jacobson only make wine with grapes that come from vineyards they own or manage themselves.

ST. INNOCENT***–****
SALEM
Bought-in grapes; 66,000 bottles • Wines: Chardonnay, Pinot Gris, Pinot Blanc, S.F.G.; Pinot
This winery was founded by wine fans and makes outstanding single-vineyard Pinot Noirs.

SOKOL BLOSSER*–***
DUNDEE
150 acres (60 ha); bought-in grapes; 360,000 bottles • Wines: Müller-Thurgau, Riesling, Chardonnay, Pinot Gris, Gewürztraminer; Pinot
Susan Sokol and Bill Blosser first planted vines in 1971. Today they are associated with two other farmer-winemakers and make several often good Pinot Noirs.

TORI MOR**–****
McMINNVILLE
32 acres (13 ha); bought-in grapes; 40,000 bottles • Wines: Chardonnay, Pinot Gris; Pinot; White Rose Pinot
Patty Green makes balanced wines with a strong structure and real finesse.

TUALATIN**
146 acres (59 ha); 300,000 bottles • Wines include: Pinot Blanc, Chardonnay, Muscat, Sauvignon, Pinot Noir
Bill Fuller and Bill Malkmus produce a wide range of white wines and a very spicy Pinot Noir on the estate, which was established in 1973.

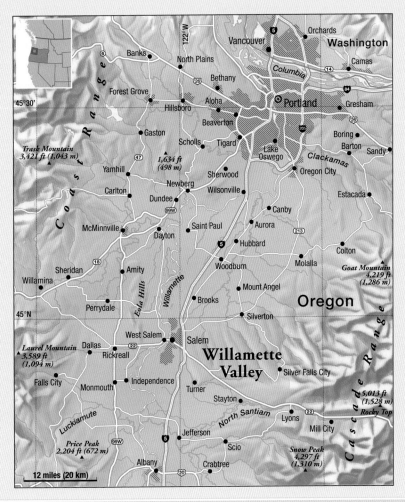

CALIFORNIA: LIFESTYLE, OPEN-MINDEDNESS, KNOW-HOW

CREATIVITY, OPEN-MINDEDNESS, KNOW-HOW

California radiates a unique flair and has an enduring appeal. The magnificent landscape, the extraordinarily fertile valleys, and a kind, sunny climate have rubbed off on the inhabitants, and they find expression in the natural cheerfulness that pervades this tolerant, multicultural society, with its openness to innovations of all kinds. For all their wealth of invention, all their business sense and all their productivity, Californians have not forgotten how to enjoy life—one of the things that most delights visitors. It is certainly no accident that both the hippy movement and the electronic revolution of Silicon Valley began here.

This open-mindedness and willingness to experiment, and the fusion of the most varied influences, are reflected in Californian cuisine, which draws inspiration from all hemispheres,

Top
San Francisco is just a stone's throw from Napa and Sonoma.

Opposite, top
The imaginative cuisine of Napa Valley makes use of culinary ideas from all round the world.

Opposite, bottom
Wine has been essential to the Californian lifestyle for many years, from refined dinners to informal garden parties.

combining very different sorts of food fearlessly and ingeniously in a surprising, but delightful fashion to create completely new flavors. The Mediterranean vines introduced by the Spanish *padres* found ideal conditions in California, and wine has become an essential part of the state's unconstrained, communicative, creative way of life. The Californian lifestyle began to develop in a completely new way after 1970, and the state's wine growing also gained a wholly new dimension at the same time. It suddenly became an expression of the art of living, and the Californians learned to see wine as something malleable, something that could be shaped artistically. The creativity of the newcomers to the business was unhindered by traditional wine-growing ideology. They traveled to the European wine-growing centers, helping out in vineyards and wineries, and gathering all the experience and information they could. Their pioneering work in the area of viticulture, as well as their willingness to share it, helped spread knowledge around the whole globe and fostered a completely new generation of cosmopolitan wine producers. Once they were back in Napa, Sonoma, Benito, and Santa Barbara, they put the knowledge they had gained into practice as soon as possible, but adapted it to local conditions and thinking. If something didn't work, they were quick to change and adapt it and they soon found out what really promoted quality.

In an atmosphere unbound by traditional customs and rigid regulations, there is nothing to hold back American winegrowers and winemakers. This situation, like that in the other wine-producing countries of the New World, is viewed with envy by their European colleagues from the classic, heavily-regulated wine-growing countries, and many have been inspired to look for lucrative opportunities in one of the New World wine-producing centers.

CALIFORNIAN WINEMAKING

Nine-tenths of all American wine is now produced in California, which has over 553,500 acres (224,000 ha) of vineyards. In the state with the largest population in the U.S.A., wine has been integrated more completely into the lifestyle than anywhere else in the country, except possibly New York. California is also the main purchaser of its own wines. By contrast with the wine industry on the East Coast, winegrowers in California consciously aimed to make wines with premium European grapes from the very beginning, and products from the Napa Valley were already being showered with high honors at European wine competitions at the end of the 19th century.

California's image—like that of the famous European wine regions—is based on the quality of a manageable number of excellent wines. The buying habits of American wine drinkers are also like those of their European counterparts, that is, they all want pleasing wines at the lowest possible prices. For seven out of ten bottles they spend less than eight dollars a bottle. Recently, wines selling for only two dollars have been a raging success. Two out of ten bottles cost up to twelve dollars, and only every tenth bottle may be more expensive. Mass-produced wines dominate the market. They are called "jug wines" and are often filled in boxes ("bag in a box" wines) and sold by the glass. "Blush wines," which are slightly sweet white or rosé wines made from dark grapes like White Zinfandel, are particularly popular. But although there are plenty of cheap blended table wines, varietal wines do predominate, and

It once used to be rare for Californian vineyards to be laid out as well as this planting on the Kunde Estate in Sonoma, but Californian winemaking went through a radical transformation during the 1990s.

Bien Nacido in Southern California's Santa Maria Valley is one of the most famous grape farms in the U.S.A. The special form of espalier cultivation used there gives the vines plenty of air.

in these at least 75 percent has to come from the variety of grape named on the label.

GRAPE FARMERS AND WINEMAKERS

In most Old World wine countries winemakers manage their own vineyards and vinify what they harvest or combine to set up wine-producing cooperatives. By contrast, in California, the majority of the grapes come from specialized farms. Wineries with their own vineyards are something of an exception. But the dynamism of the Californian wine world is not least a result of the fact that just about anyone can set up a winery, even if he or she does not own a single vine. All that's necessary is to find or construct a suitable building in which to make wine, and then try to purchase good grapes. This requires hardly any capital and makes it easy to get into the trade. Many winemakers first demonstrate their ability with large companies before taking the risk of going independent, while grape farmers can build strong reputations if talented winemakers make convincing wines with their fruit.

This has often resulted in cooperative arrangements, under which farmers have even been prepared to cultivate the varieties their winemaking clients requested. "In order to get good grapes, you first have to have good contacts, and they can only be built up over the years," says William Knuttler of Tria Winery. And a firm handshake still means a great deal more in this trade than meticulously negotiated contracts.

The "landless" wineries are now using their economic success and investing in vineyards so as to secure top-quality grapes for the future. Often, however, it is the other way round: winemakers with their own vineyards produce exciting wines, creating levels of demand that soon exceed their capacity, then buy in grapes in order to meet customers' requirements. Well-known producers have built up extensive ranges of wines in this way.

The division of labor between grape farming and winemaking allows the winemakers a great deal of scope for experimentation. Some of the most creative among them no longer use standard grapes like Cabernet Sauvignon, Pinot Noir, Chardonnay, and Sauvignon Blanc. Many have discovered a preference for Rhône varieties, such as Syrah, Mourvèdre, Viognier, and Roussanne, and now Italian varieties have come to their attention—not just Sangiovese, but Barbera, and even Teroldego as well. Borders and distances are no barrier, and the grapes can be transported for hundreds of miles in refrigerated trucks. As a result, it is possible to buy Pinot Noir from Oregon that has been fermented in Santa Barbara.

A Bright Future Ahead

The number of excellent quality wines has risen markedly in recent years, although California has only just begun to exploit the huge potential of its terrain, for apart from a few exceptions in other growing regions, only in the Napa and Sonoma valleys have the best positions been recognized and carefully planted. The phylloxera disaster of the 1990s gave the growers the opportunity to put an end to the old method of planting, in which the fertile plains were covered with only a few vines per hectare, which were then amply fed with artificial fertiliser and irrigated until they grew into huge plants. This form of vine training, in which the individual canes put forth dozens of buds, is known as the TRUNK SYSTEM and made it possible to attain yields of up to 4,250 gallons per acre (400 hl/ha)! More serious producers worked with much lower yields, but even now people in California talk about 850 to 1,100 gallons per acre (80–100 hl/ha) as low yields, and maximum yields of 2,100 to 2,600 gallons per acre (200–240 hl/ha) are not uncommon in places that produce pleasant, average wines. By contrast, David Abreu, a winery consultant and top winemaker who lives in the Napa Valley and specializes in modern, natural winemaking, believes that just under 640 gallons per acre (60 hl/ha) is ideal. In this respect, some of the most outstanding wines hardly differ from their European counterparts, producing yields of less than 315, and certainly no more than 535 gallons per acre (30–50 hl/ha).

Phylloxera: A Blessing in Disguise?

A great many new vineyards were planted in the 1970s when the renaissance of Californian wine was beginning to gain momentum. At this time the University of California at Davis was recommending the use of the high-yielding AxR 1 rootstock (a *rupestris-vinifera* hybrid). Only obstinate winegrowers insisted on the Saint George rootstock, which had proved itself to be resistant to phylloxera in practice. The majority chose AxR 1, so that eventually about three-quarters of all the vineyards in Sonoma and Napa were planted with it. However, it soon became apparent that this rootstock was susceptible to a mutation of the vine louse. In the meantime, the rapacious insect had destroyed almost all these vinestocks, wiping out vineyards that failed to meet the standards established by the latest research. Farmers, winemakers, and wineries have taken the opportunity to plant new vineyards, consciously taking steps to produce grapes of the highest quality. To this end, vine density has been increased decisively, and many vineyards have converted to natural-cultivation techniques.

It is possible to detect another new trend. In the past, winegrowers planted on the most convenient sites, such as valley bottoms and flat plains, where the subsequent costs of processing could be kept down, but a new generation of winemakers and wineries is consciously choosing to work on hillside *terroirs*, placing emphasis on the importance of aspect. Now that it has been established which types of vine do best in certain climates, scientists are also beginning to develop a better understanding of which soils are likely to achieve the most satisfactory result with particular grapes. As many of the Californian wines are already of high quality, there is every reason to expect great things in future.

The irony of fate: America supplied the world with resistant rootstocks, only to suffer its own phylloxera epidemic. More than three-quarters of the Californian vineyards were devastated by this rapacious insect during the last few decades of the 20th century.

THE BLESSINGS OF THE PACIFIC

California is a strip of land almost 1,250 miles (2,000 km) long on the western coast of North America. After Texas, it is the largest of the American states by area. Its most easterly part, which is dominated by the Sierra Nevada and the Mojave Desert, is hot, dry, and inhospitable. Between this area and the coastal region, we find the Central Valley, which is 55 miles (90 km) wide in some places. This is one of the most fertile regions in the world, and also one of the most intensively cultivated by fruit and vegetable growers. Thanks to highly refined irrigation systems, a great many agricultural products flourish here at high temperatures, under skies that are rarely overcast. Visitors to the area will understand why the Spanish called California *caliente fornalla*, or "hot oven," when they first arrived.

Thousands of acres are planted with vines, but most are the Thompson Seedless variety,

The hot climate in Napa and Sonoma would be far less favorable if it were not for the banks of fog that roll inland from the Pacific, moderating temperatures in the area.

and the grapes are sold as table grapes or made into raisins. Thanks to modern technology, appealing dry wines are now produced in Central Valley, but the high temperatures do not permit very high quality standards in this part of California.

The climate only becomes milder in the coastal areas, where ranges of hills run from north to south parallel to the sea. The water of the Pacific Ocean is comparatively cold, which is why banks of fog form along the coast during the summer and early autumn, extremely important times of the year for wine growing. Away from the coast, the air heats up and rises during the day, drawing moist air inland from the ocean. This helps the fog and cool sea winds to find their way into the interior wherever there is a gap in the mountains or they fall below a height of 2,000 feet (600 m) above sea level. The fog hides the sunshine, which has the direct consequence of reducing temperatures and, over the longer term, delays the ripening of the grapes. This is one of the basic conditions for the formation of intense, complex AROMAS, as long as it takes place within limits.

In places where the Pacific is able to exert its influence unhindered, including almost half of the Californian coast, the climate is too cold and wet for wine growing, though it is ideal for the redwood and other types of tree. The amount of protection from the Pacific afforded by the mountain ranges varies, and the temperature-reducing fogs and winds find their way inland at different speeds in different places, creating a large number of diverse microclimates. It is these variations that have ultimately been decisive in the delimitation of the region's A.V.A.s.

Climatic regions

The significance of climate for winemaking—temperature in particular—prompted Maynard Amerine and Albert Julius Winkler, two enologists at the University of California at Davis, to develop, in 1944, a regional classification method based on average daily temperatures during the growth period of the vine between April 1 and October 31.

According to the heat summation system they created for California, winemaking areas are defined and classified into five regions. The best dry wines come from Region I and Region II, which have the lowest heat sums, such as Sonoma and Napa Valley. Region III is

particularly suitable for red varieties that benefit from heat, but the hottest areas, Region IV and Region V, which include the Central Valley and the warmest parts of the San Joaquin Valley, usually produce wines of less convincing quality. The university also used this system as the basis for recommendations regarding the planting of particular grape varieties, but it proved not to be sufficiently sophisticated for this purpose. And that is not the only point of criticism: as the system is based on specifically Californian climatic conditions, it is transferable only to a limited extent.

Amerine and WINKLER calculated the number of "degree days" in various locations by taking the mean daily temperatures for all days during the chosen period on which the temperature exceeded 50°F (10°C) and adding up the sum of degrees Fahrenheit above this baseline.

Region	I	less than 2,500
Region	II	2,500 to 3,000
Region	III	3,001 to 3,500
Region	IV	3,501 to 4,000
Region	V	greater than 4,000

(To convert Fahrenheit to Celsius, subtract 32 and divide by 1.8.)

Medford
Upper Klamath Lake
Oregon
Idaho

Klamath Mountains
Mt. Shasta
▲14,162 ft
(4,317 m)

Eureka

Redding

Mt. Linn
8,094 ft
(2,466 m)

40°

Pyramid Lake

Elko

Humboldt

Utah

Great

Mendocino

Ukiah

Reno

Lake Tahoe
Carson City

Nevada

North Coast

Napa

Sacramento

Sierra Foothills

Basin

Novato

San Francisco

Central

Modesto

Mono Lake

San Jose

Valley

Santa Cruz

Salinas

Monterey

Fresno

Mt. Whitney
▲14,494 ft
(4,418 m)

Las Vegas

San Simeon

Visalia

Lake Mead

Central Coast

California

Arizona

Pacific

Bakersfield

Mojave

Ocean

35°N

San Luis Obispo

Barstow

Mt. Pinos
8,831 ft
(2,692 m)

Desert

Colorado

Santa Barbara

San Bernardino

Blythe

Santa Cruz

Los Angeles

Palm Springs

Salton Sea

Santa Rosa

South Coast

Santa Catalina

Imperial Valley

San Clemente

San Diego

120°W

60 miles (100 km)

Tijuana

MEXICO

North Coast
Sierra Foothills
Central Valley
Central Coast
South Coast
Wine-growing areas in neighboring regions

Mendocino is a pretty fishing village popular with artists drawn by the rugged beauty of the Mendocino County coastline.

NORTH COAST

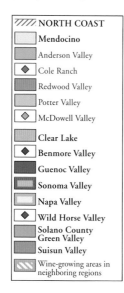

Carneros rises to the north of San Francisco Bay and enjoys a very mild climate that has proved to be ideal for Chardonnay and Pinot Noir.

Mountains rise covered in vineyards from the San Pablo Bay, the northern inlet of the San Francisco Bay. Apart from the fog coming off the Bay, these hills are also exposed to cool winds from the northwest. At the end of the 1960s the winemaking pioneers realized that, in combination with the area's generally poor soils, this mild, but dry climate was ideal for Chardonnay and Pinot Noir. Ten years later the area saw a second wave of wineries being established, including Saintsbury. During the 1980s it became ever more obvious what high-quality wines Carneros could produce, and a number of major wine companies drew the obvious conclusions and began to invest there, including Robert Mondavi. The winemakers of Carneros have cooperated with scientists from the University of California on a series of experiments, which first clearly defined the character of their Pinot Noir, and then of their Chardonnay, underpinning the area's status as an A.V.A. Its extraordinary Chardonnays and Pinot Noirs have also attracted the CAVA producers Freixenet (Gloria Ferrer) and Codorníu, as well as Taittinger, who built a Champagne château at their Domaine Carneros estate.

If you leave San Francisco over the Golden Gate Bridge, you come first to Carneros, which is divided administratively between the counties of Sonoma and Napa, and forms what might be described as the gateway to the most famous wine-growing areas in the United States. The gently rolling foothills of the Macayamas

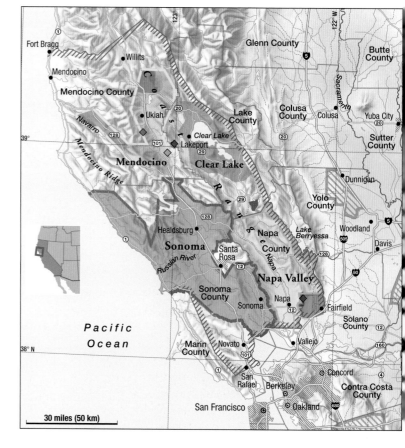

NORTH COAST
Mendocino
Anderson Valley
Cole Ranch
Redwood Valley
Potter Valley
McDowell Valley
Clear Lake
Benmore Valley
Guenoc Valley
Sonoma Valley
Napa Valley
Wild Horse Valley
Solano County Green Valley
Suisun Valley
Wine-growing areas in neighboring regions

There can be no question that the Napa Valley is the best-known wine-growing region in America. By far the majority of the great wines of the United States come from the Napa, and, with more than 220 wineries, the county also has the greatest concentration of producers in one place.

Sonoma extends from San Pablo Bay to Mendocino, and there are now ten different A.V.A.s in the county. Sonoma Valley is the place where Californian winemaking first began, and it is still the state's most important wine-growing area, as well as being the base for many outstanding wineries.

Anyone who drives from Sonoma to visit the attractive coastal town of Mendocino—where whales can occasionally be seen from the coast in spring—will probably take Highway 128, which runs directly through the Anderson Valley along the Navarro River. This route gives a vivid impression of one of the extremes of winemaking in Mendocino: the climate in this narrow valley, surrounded as it is by ranges of hills, is dominated by fog and moisture from the ocean, and its Chardonnay and Pinot Noir develop clearly northern characteristics. Anderson Valley grapes are made into high-quality sparkling wines by the Champagne houses Pommery, which has bought up the local wine company Scharffenberger, and Roederer. The smaller wineries in the valley mainly make white wines, including remarkable Gewürztraminer, as well as fruity Zinfandel. Further inland, about 35 miles (60 km) from the coast at Ukiah in the Redwood Valley, we find a growing area with extensive flat vineyards that

Codorníu Napa, the winery owned by the great Spanish cava producer, blends perfectly into the Carneros landscape. Nowadays, it concentrates mainly on the production of still wines.

exemplifies another remarkable extreme: here the climate is warm and dry—according to Amerine and Winkler's heat-summation system (see page 812), the area is classed as Region III. The old Carignane grape can still be found here and there, but today most of the harvest is Cabernet Sauvignon, Petite Sirah, Zinfandel, Sauvignon Blanc, and Chardonnay. The largest wine company in the region is Fetzer, which now grows a proportion of its grapes by organic methods. Potter Valley to the north of Ukiah has become famous for white varieties and Pinot Noir, while the more southerly McDowell Valley is best known for its Syrah.

To the east of McDowell Valley is Lake County, which surrounds Clear Lake and has a mainly warm climate. The first estates were developed in the 1980s, and Kendall-Jackson is regarded as the best of the area's producers. The vineyards have expanded rapidly and now provide many companies with Cabernet Sauvignon, Zinfandel, Merlot, Chardonnay, and Sauvignon Blanc.

The Sierra Foothills, where the gold diggers once sought their fortunes—most of them in vain—lie to the east of Sacramento at the foot of the Sierra Nevada. The area's once defunct winemaking industry has been revived since 1970, principally in the districts of Amador and El Dorado. Depending on the altitude, which varies between 800 and 3,250 feet (250–1,000 m) above sea level, various varieties are cultivated there, but, as in the past, the Sierra Foothills' reputation is based on Zinfandel from the Shenandoah Valley and Fiddletown.

Sonoma

Visitors to the small town of Sonoma City can still admire the cradle of North Californian winemaking, the Mission Station, which was built in 1823 and carefully restored recently. Although winemaking spread from here to the rest of California in the middle of the 19th century, Sonoma Valley soon fell into the shadow of its neighbor Napa. On account of its dramatic topography, there are significantly fewer areas suitable for wine growing in this valley, and as a result, far fewer wineries were established here. To the present day there are still only about 30 of them cultivating approximately 6,900 acres (2,800 ha) of vineyards.

Cattle continue to be farmed in this attractive valley, parts of which are richly wooded. In general, it makes a more modest, more rural impression than its famous neighbor. Only in a few exceptional cases will you find magnificent buildings like the ones in Napa Valley at these wineries. The people of Sonoma are more modest, they build more conservatively, and, rather than professional bustle, the visitor is often met with hearty, unaffected hospitality.

Some wineries had made a good name for themselves before Prohibition, such as the pioneering Buena Vista estate or the company founded by Jakob Gundlach from Aschaffenburg in Germany that began selling wine in 1858. Even so, there was a dearth of outstanding winemaking personalities who might have been able to consolidate Sonoma Valley's reputation during the years of crisis.

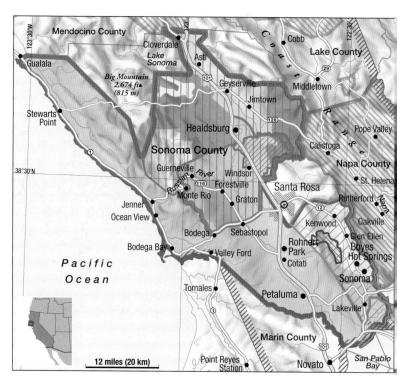

	NORTH COAST
	Sonoma
	Sonoma Coast
	Alexander Valley
	Dry Creek Valley
	Knights Valley
	Northern Sonoma
	Russian River Valley
	Chalk Hill
	Green Valley
	Sonoma Valley
	Sonoma Mountain
	Los Carneros
	Wine-growing areas in neighboring regions

The man who started the renaissance in Sonoma was former ambassador James D. Zellerbach, a lover and connoisseur of great Burgundies. In 1953 he started planting Chardonnay and Pinot Noir at Hanzell, his 200-acre (80-ha) farm north of Sonoma City, eventually devoting one-sixth of his land to grapes. He vinified his rich Chardonnay in small oak barrels, which he also used to slowly mature his Pinot Noir, demonstrating how Burgundy-style wines could be created with Californian grapes. It was not until the 1970s that more companies began to be founded and the quality of Sonoma's wine started to attract increasing attention in the world of wine.

Gallo

Anyone who happens to go to Modesto, a town of 30,000 in the Central Valley, will find that even on Yosemite Boulevard there is no indication that this is the headquarters of the largest wine company in the world, the E. & J. Gallo Winery. There is absolutely nothing about the imposing administrative building or its surrounding gardens to suggest wine production. But it is here that decisions are taken concerning the production of an estimated 720 million bottles of wine, and probably not much less than a million bottles of wine-based beverages and spirits. Effectively shielded from the gaze of visitors and passers-by, great rows of gigantic tanks stand ready to vinify grapes transported over long distances using the latest precision technology.

Despite its scale, Gallo remains a family firm. Ernest and Julio Gallo, who were born in the United States to a family of Italian immigrants from Piedmont, founded their winery in 1933, after Prohibition was repealed. Their presses, fermentation vats, and even their grapes were "borrowed," because the two self-taught winemakers had practically no capital and had to make their first 185,000 gallons (7,000 hl) of sweet wine on credit. But they had no problems selling it, and this wine remained their most important

Boxes full of Chardonnay grapes and a classy vehicle on the Frei Ranch.

product until 1967, when it was overtaken by standard American jug wines, before the varietal wines began to dominate the market in the 1980s. All this time, the brothers kept enlarging their empire, working constantly to keep their cultivation methods and winery technology at the cutting edge.

The brothers began purchasing grapes from the Frei Ranch at Sonoma in 1934 and eventually bought the farm in 1977 together with Laguna Ranch. Their first oak-matured Chardonnay came onto the market four years later. Since 1989 Gallo has pursued a careful policy of expansion, buying up another seven wine farms in Sonoma County so that the company now has over 3,954 acres (1,600 ha) of vines at its disposal there. A conscious decision was made in favor of Sonoma, with its diversity of distinctive growing zones, and they built an exquisite winery on the Frei Ranch in Dry Creek Valley, equipped with 2,000 barrels for MATURING the company's wines. Julio Gallo's granddaughter Gina is responsible for vinification there and produces some excellent premium wines. These are only sold under their estate names in the U.S.A., because the family has been associated with cheap wines for so long, but Gallo is conquering the European markets with Sonoma wines under its own brand. The good-value Turning Leaf is the most important product in terms of quantity, followed at some distance by Gallo Sonoma and the already excellent single-vineyard wines, while the Gallo estate wines form a rare, expensive group of select bottlings produced in quantities of 700 to 2,000 cases per wine.

SONOMA COUNTY

The situation in Napa is quite easy to survey, because the vineyards there have conquered the entire valley floor, but only extend to a few nearby hillside *terroirs* and small mountain valleys that are included in the Napa Valley *appellation*. Matters are quite different in Sonoma. Sonoma Valley, which includes the Sonoma Mountain sub-A.V.A., is only about 15 miles (25 km) long, but is the most famous growing area of this large county, which extends from San Pablo Bay to Mendocino and boasts a long, wild coastline and impressive redwoods. It now has a bigger wine-growing area than Napa—in all 48,926 acres (19,800 ha)—but it is divided into eleven clearly demarcated *appellations*. The area is divided into a number of clearly defined A.V.A.s, which differ very markedly from one another in their situations and climatic conditions. However, many producers prefer to market their wines using the better-known Sonoma County A.V.A.

The Russian River Valley extends to the west of Santa Rosa. It is surrounded by deep forests, and most of its soils are sandy and gravelly. This wide valley forms a significant gap in the Coastal Range, allowing low cloud to penetrate inland during the afternoon, and the area is well known for Gravensteiner apples, pears, and goat's cheese. Pinot Noir and Chardonnay

Opposite
Beginning in 1956, the Hanzell Winery created a Chardonnay style that has inspired countless Californian winemakers.

grow magnificently here, but its Sauvignon Blancs and Gewürztraminers are also satisfying, and the district's Zinfandel and Syrah produce particularly aromatic wines. More than 12,350 acres (5,000 ha) of land are now planted with vines, which makes this valley the largest growing area in Sonoma County.

Dry Creek Valley lies to the northwest of Healdsburg. It is 15 miles (25 km) from end to end and nearly two miles (3 km) across at its widest point. The winegrowers in the valley bottom concentrate mainly on white varieties and have a particular liking for Sauvignon Blanc, but the stony hillside *terroirs*, with their clayey, gravelly soils, also produce interesting red wines.

The wide, fertile Alexander Valley runs almost parallel with the Russian River Valley, but further to the east, and extends as far as the border with Mendocino County. It is significantly warmer and therefore perfectly suited for Cabernet Sauvignon and other red varieties. As a result, there has been feverish planting activity among the area's grape farmers in the last ten years. The Zinfandel grown in Geyserville has become especially famous.

To the south, bordering on the northern edges of the Napa Valley, the small Knights Valley A.V.A. offers conditions that particularly favor Cabernet Sauvignon. The quality of the grapes there has encouraged further planting.

Select Producers in Sonoma County

There are a great many wineries that make superb wines in Sonoma County. We can only give a small, highly subjective selection.

Château St. Jean**–****
Kenwood
128 acres (52 ha); bought-in grapes; • Wines include: Chardonnay, Sauvignon; Merlot, Pinot Noir, →Meritage Cinq Cépages
Set up in 1973, this was the first fully technological winery in Sonoma. It first gained respect for its white wines but now its reds are among the best produced in California. Like the very good Château Souverain it is now part of the Beringer Estates.

De Loach*–***
Santa Rosa
395 acres (160 ha); bought-in grapes; 1,200,000 bottles • Wines include: →Chardonnay, Gewürztraminer; Pinot Noir, →Zinfandel
Cecil de Loach, a former fireman, bought his first old Zinfandel patch of land in 1970. Adding more plantings he became one of the pioneers of the Russian River Valley. In 1975 he began to make wine himself, acquiring a name for white wines and seven different Zinfandels.

Dehlinger****
Forestville
59 acres (24 ha); 110,000 bottles • Wines: Chardonnay; Pinot, Cabernet, Syrah; →Octagon Pinot
Tom Dehlinger's range includes up to five different well-structured, juicy Pinot Noirs of the highest quality. His Syrahs are now superb.

Dry Creek***
Healdsburg
200 acres (81 ha); bought-in grapes; 1,500,000 bottles • Wines include: Sauvignon, Chardonnay, Chenin; Cabernet, Merlot, →Zinfandel
As one of the pioneer winemakers in Sonoma County and Dry Creek Valley, Dave Stare decided early in his career to concentrate on what is now his top variety, Fumé Blanc. His Old Vines Zinfandel is very good.

Duxoup Wine Works***
Healdsburg
Bought-in grapes; 24,000 bottles • Wines: Syrah, Zinfandel, Gamay, Charbono
Music fans Andy and Deborah Cutter run a winery where everything really is done by hand. Their wines are as inspiring as the great operas they love.

Fetzer Vineyards*–****
Hopland
450 acres (182 ha); bought-in grapes; 10,000,000 bottles. Wines include: brands: Dual Varietals, Bonterra, Fetzer Vineyards; Premium Varietals, Barrel Select, Private Collection; Eagle Peak, Sundial, Echo Ridge
Bonterra has made Fetzer, which has been owned by Brown-Forman since 1992, into the biggest producer of organic wine in the world. Altogether the enterprise buys grapes from 9,998 acres (4,046 ha), of which 911 are organically farmed. The estate has its own cooperage, bio garden and restaurant with cookery courses.

Gallo Sonoma*–***
Healdsburg
3,954 acres (1,600 ha) • Wines include: Series: Sorioma Selection (five varieties), Single Vineyard (four wines), Estate Wines: Chardonnay, Cabernet Sauvignon (see box on page 817)

Gina and Matt: the third generation of the Gallo dynasty.

Gundlach-Bundschu Winery**–***
Sonoma
232 acres (94 ha); 600,000 bottles • Wines: 13 wines, 9 grape varieties, including Kleinberger, Riesling, →Gewürztraminer, Chardonnay; Gamay, Cabernet, →Cabernet Franc, Merlot, Zinfandel; →Reserve Cabernet
Grapes have been harvested at the Rhinefarm Vineyard since 1858. Its renaissance was initiated by Jim Bundschu in 1973. Reliably high standards.

Hanzell****
Sonoma
42 acres (17 ha); 35,000 bottles • Wines: Chardonnay; Pinot
Beginning in 1956, Ambassador James Zellerbach showed what strong, unique wines Sonoma can produce with the bottlings from his estate. Powerful, concentrated Chardonnays and Pinot Noirs.

Kistler Vineyards*****
Sebastopol
32 acres (13 ha); bought-in grapes; 150,000 bottles • Wines: Chardonnay; Cabernet, Pinot
Steve Kistler and Marx Bixler certainly know what they are doing with Chardonnay. Fermented separately by the vineyard in French *barriques*, their Chardonnays combine fruit and spices, power and finesse.

Laurel Glen*****
Glen Ellen
37 acres (15 ha); 60,000 bottles • Wines: →Laurel Glen Cabernet, →second wine: Counterpoint
Patrick Campbell planted his vines high in the Sonoma Mountains and has worked with Ray Kaufman since 1981, producing red wines that owe their outstanding quality to the painstaking approach taken in the vineyard and winery. The partners are now making a number of very successful wines from grapes they buy in. The range extends from simple table reds to the recently created Zazin.

Limerick Lane***
Healdsburg
32 acres (13 ha); 54,000 bottles • Wines include: Late Harvest Furmint; Rosé Sec, Syrah, Old Vine Zinfandel
Beside their specialty, a beery, spicy Zinfandel, these producers are now offering Syrah, a blend, and the original sweet Furmint. They use only home-grown grapes.

MARCASSIN★★★★★
CALISTOGA
11 acres (4.5 ha); bought-in grapes; 15,000 bottles
• Wines: Chardonnay, Pinot
Helen Turley, California's most famous woman winemaker, makes wines with grapes from her own vineyard on the Sonoma Coast and occasionally uses bought-in grapes of a very high quality.

PETER MICHAEL WINERY★★★★★
CALISTOGA
60 acres (24 ha); bought-in grapes; 240,000 bottles
• Wines: Chardonnay, Sauvignon; Cabernet, →Cabernet Les Pavots
Sir Peter, the inventor of the pop video, has found an outlet for his passionate interest in wine at his estate in Knights Valley, where he has done everything possible to make great wines—and succeeded. Six highly intriguing Chardonnays and the superb Bordeaux blend "Mon Plaisir."

NALLE★★★
HEALDSBURG
Bought-in grapes; 25,000 bottles • Wines: Zinfandel, Pinot Noir
Doug Nalle has created an exquisite Zinfandel, characterized by finesse and complex aromas. Now there's also a fine Pinot Noir.

RAFANELLI★★★–★★★★
HEALDSBURG
54 acres (22 ha); 120,000 bottles • Wines: Cabernet Sauvignon, Zinfandel
The Rafanellis began as grape farmers and still sell Chardonnay and Merlot to other winemakers. Since 1974 they have specialized in Zinfandel and Cabernet Sauvignon, making very ripe, spicy, concentrated red wines.

RAVENSWOOD★★–★★★★
SONOMA
Bought-in grapes; 1,800,000 bottles • Wines: Chardonnay; Zinfandel, Cabernet Sauvignon, Merlot, Petite Sirah, Cabernet Franc
Joel Peterson began making Zinfandel in a garage in 1976 and became famous with wines from old vines that are still wonderful today.

ROCHIOLI WINERY★★★★
HEALDSBURG
131 acres (53 ha); 120,000 bottles • Wines: Chardonnay, Sauvignon Blanc; Pinot Noir, Zinfandel, →Pinot Noir Cellar Select
The Rochiolis have been farmers in Russian River Valley for decades. They began cultivating premium varieties and selling the grapes in 1959, but have been making their own wines since 1983. Their single-vineyard Pinot Noirs are outstanding.

SEGHESIO★★–★★★★
HEALDSBURG
400 acres (162 ha); 800,000 bottles • Wines include: Arneis, Pinot Grigio; Pinot Noir, Sangiovese, Zinfandel

Edoardo and Angela Seghesio planted their first Zinfandel in Alexander Valley in 1895. A hundred years later the family is concentrating on quality; they have reduced their yield by two thirds and created a delightful range with five Zinfandels alone.

STONESTREET★–★★★★
HEALDSBURG
Bought-in grapes; 800,000 bottles • Wines include: Chardonnay; Pinot, Cabernet, Merlot, →Legacy
The former Zellerbach vineyard was bought by Kendall-Jackson in 1989 and has become the flagship of Jesse Jackson's empire, which produces 50 million bottles each year. After initially brilliant wines, the Stonestreet range is now much wider and production is increasing.

TRIA WINERY★★★
SONOMA
Bought-in grapes • Wines include: Syrah, Zinfandel, Pinot Noir, Labyrinth
Phillip Zorn founded Tria with his friend Bill Knuttel. Their wines are always of a good standard, especially the Syrah, Labyrinth Meritage, and Zinfandel.

WILLIAMS & SELYEM★★★–★★★★
HEALDSBURG
Bought-in grapes; 90,000 bottles • Wines: Pinot, Zinfandel
Pinot Noir is the specialty with which Williams and Selyem became famous. Since 1998 this winery has been owned by grape farmer John Dyson. The work continues to be done largely by hand, and kiln-dried barrels are used to make smoky, strongly fruity Pinot Noirs.

Bob Sessions, winemaker and general manager at Hanzell.

Meritage

At one time winemakers who wished to leave the well-trodden paths of varietal wine ran the danger, under the American laws, of seeing their new creations quietly ignored as inferior table wines. Until, that is, the term "Meritage" was coined and registered as a trademark in order to underline the special "merit" and the great "heritage" of quality blended wines. In doing so, the Californian wine world was following the example of Bordeaux and its *cuvées*, which is why only Bordelais varieties were permitted in these blends. Winemakers who wish to advertise a wine as a Meritage also have to make a commitment to offer the blend as their second most expensive wine, at least, and not to sell more than 300,000 bottles. Regardless of the fact that some Meritages are nowhere near as good as varietal wines, which may in any case contain as much as 25 percent of other grape varieties, top producers often decide to market their best *cuvée* as a distinct brand.

Napa Valley

The Napa Valley is not just the flagship of Californian winemaking, but of the whole wine trade in the U.S.A. This was not always the case. At first Sonoma had a better start and left the neighboring county lagging behind. However, in the years after 1860 winemaking also developed here, not least thanks to the Prussian Charles Krug. He established an exemplary winery at St. Helena and trained a group of young men who would later go on to become successful independent winemakers. They included Karl Wente, who was drawn to the Livermore Valley, and Jacob Beringer, who founded an independent winery with his brother Frederick in 1876 and built the famous Rhine House, a traditional German building that has now become a tourist attraction. Three years later Gustave Niebaum established the Inglenook Winery, and another 140 wineries were founded in the decade that followed. They all profited from the rising sales of wine that were a direct consequence of the Gold Rush. By this time, Napa Valley wines already stood comparison with top European products. The increasing pace of development faltered due to the phylloxera epidemic, Prohibition, the Depression, and the Second World War, but companies like Beaulieu Vineyards, Charles Krug, Inglenook, and Louis M. Martini continued to make very good wines and were able to maintain the area's reputation during this period.

The industry in the Napa Valley reached its lowest point in 1960, with only 25 wine producers still in business. However, in 1966 Robert Mondavi, whose family owned the Charles Krug winery, ushered in a new era when he founded his own company and built a winery inspired by the architecture of the Spanish mission stations. Mondavi's building was a dramatic symbol of the renaissance of winemaking throughout the valley, which is now one of the most prestigious and expensive wine-growing areas in the world.

The Valley's Three Zones

The Napa River winds southward through a valley about 25 miles (40 km) long with rugged hills on either side. It should come as no surprise that Napa Valley produces a remarkably large number of outstanding wines, because its natural conditions are ideal. To the

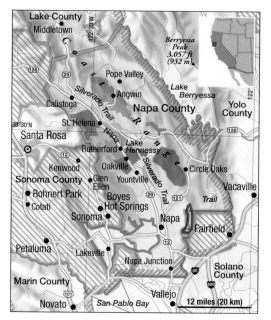

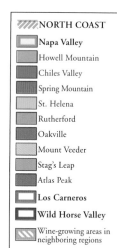

NORTH COAST
- Napa Valley
- Howell Mountain
- Chiles Valley
- Spring Mountain
- St. Helena
- Rutherford
- Oakville
- Mount Veeder
- Stag's Leap
- Atlas Peak
- Los Carneros
- Wild Horse Valley
- Wine-growing areas in neighboring regions

south of Napa City the valley enters Los Carneros, a district that slopes down to the San Pablo Bay. Banks of fog roll across the bay, blocking the sun and reducing temperatures so much that this part of the valley has the coolest possible winemaking climate, making it a Region I area as far as Yountville (see page 812). In the central zone, which extends from Yountville through Rutherford and St. Helena to about Freemark Abbey, the fog only arrives later in the afternoon, so the heat summation method classifies it as Region II. The bay influences the weather less as the valley rises up toward Calistoga, which is classified as a Region III area. There are also a great many

The wild flowers sown at St. Helena illustrate just how seriously Californians take ecology.

exceedingly diverse microclimates within the valley's three broad climatic zones.

The coolest, most southerly zone is particularly suitable for Pinot Noir and white wines, and some of the best Chardonnays come from this area. Even if they grow in Carneros, many wineries further up the valley prefer to label them with the generic Napa Valley A.V.A. A little further up the valley Cabernet Sauvignon finds ideal climatic conditions in Oakville and Rutherford, particularly where it is grown on the lower slopes, and profits from the morning sun. However, Chardonnay also develops depth and a wonderful aftertaste here. Cabernet Sauvignon, Zinfandel, and Petite Sirah gain impressive ripeness and power in the strong sunshine of the upper valley.

DIVERSITY AND QUALITY

It should be obvious that there can never be a uniform Napa style, if only on account of the diversity of climatic conditions. When the amazing variety of soils in the area is taken into consideration, it becomes clear that the topography and weather merely help to underline the individuality of the different producers. As far as Napa's soil is concerned, there is just one—very important—characteristic that is found almost everywhere. It drains very well, which prevents the ground from getting waterlogged, something that can have disastrous consequences for planted vines. In many places this can be attributed to loose, gravelly, meager soil structures. Although the ranges of hills to the east and west are of volcanic origin, there are only isolated patches of volcanic soil in the valley. The ocean that once covered the entire area has had a more noticeable influence, creating the vast range of

Spring frosts often threaten the harvest in some parts of the Napa Valley. Many winemakers seek to protect their vines with wind turbines that keep the air moving (left) or oil stoves (right).

distinct deposits that are responsible for at least 62 important types of soil identified there.

Napa is the word for "plenty" in the language of the Native American tribe that once lived there. The lower valley, where the county town is situated, is more than 4 miles (6 km) wide. Here, the flat, easily cultivated valley floor is densely planted with vineyards and provides the great majority of the Napa grapes. However, the most famous *terroirs* extend along its western edge on the gently sloping terraces originally formed by the river. North of St. Helena the valley narrows dramatically and is less than a mile (1.5 km) across at its narrowest point, before widening out to 2.5 miles (4 km) at Calistoga.

Along with the differences of aspect, altitude, and soil structure in specific parts of the Napa Valley and the surrounding hills, the area's distinctive climate has created clearly marked characteristics in the wines produced there, ultimately providing the basis for about 20 separate sub-A.V.A.s. Their borders have not always met with approval from the wineries involved, which has led to them being treated rather freely.

Varieties in Napa
Although Napa is chiefly renowned for its great Cabernet Sauvignons and also produces some of the best Zinfandels, Chardonnay is still the most-planted variety, covering 15,567 acres (6,300 ha). Cabernet comes second with 11,799 acres (4,775 ha) in Napa County. Around 1970 only 3,707 acres (1,500 ha) were planted with vines but now the figure is 57,653 (23,332 ha). Pinot Noir showed the biggest increase in recent years, moving up to third place with 10,057 acres (4,070 ha). White wine grapes account for just under 19,027 acres (7,700 ha) and reds 38,548 acres (15,600 ha). Merlot covers 7,324 acres (2,964 ha), Zinfandel 5,050 (2,044 ha), followed by Sauvignon Blanc with 2,100 (850 ha) and Syrah with only 1,724 acres (698 ha), although it is greatly on the increase.

The most important sub-A.V.A.s in the Napa Valley are:

• Rutherford: A river terrace with gravelly clay soils on the western edge of the valley. Famous as the Rutherford Bench, it produces balanced, vivacious, delicately spiced, dense, world-class Cabernet Sauvignon.

• Oakville: This A.V.A. encompasses part of the Rutherford Bench, though the climate here is slightly cooler and the soils more complex than in the Rutherford A.V.A. This district makes high-quality Cabernet Sauvignon with a great deal of finesse.

• Stag's Leap District: The red soils of Stag's Leap District lend Cabernet Sauvignon and Merlot particularly soft TANNINS, an attractive roundness, and emphatic, berryish fruit.

Left
Larry Turley works magic with Zinfandel.

Right
Cathy Corison—the Cabernet Queen.

Hordes of tourists flock to the Niebaum-Coppola Estate to taste its wines and see its film museum.

• Mount Veeder: The vineyards on this mountain between Sonoma and Napa rise to 2,500 feet (800 m) above sea level. Its volcanic soils produce low yields of fruity, wildly spicy, well-structured Cabernet Sauvignon and Chardonnay.

• Spring Mountain: Powerful Zinfandels, Petite Sirahs, Cabernet Sauvignons, and Merlots ripen here on the Macayamas Mountains to the west of St. Helena. Also attractive Chardonnays and Rieslings.

• Diamond Mountain: The steep slopes of this elevation in the Macayamas Mountains to the southwest of Calistoga get plenty of sun and produce ripe, full Cabernet Sauvignon with dark, berry fruit flavors and well-developed tannins.

• St. Helena: Chardonnay gains remarkable power on the valley *terroirs* around this charming wine town, while the Cabernet Sauvignon that is planted on the terraces at its western edge makes dense, full-bodied, tannin-rich wines with ripe cassis and raspberry fruit aromas.

• Calistoga: The warm climate of this Region III area is reflected in its powerful, well-rounded Cabernet Sauvignon and Zinfandel, and its very creamy Sauvignon Blanc.

• Howell Mountain: This mountainous, wooded district northeast of St. Helena has traditionally produced highly concentrated Zinfandels. But since the 1980s the district's growers have also enjoyed success with extraordinarily dense, fruity, rich Cabernet Sauvignons, which ripen at altitudes of over 1,400 feet (400 m) above sea level.

Conserving Napa's Future

The most famous wineries in the Napa Valley are found on Highway 29 between Oakville and St. Helena, and by the Silverado Trail that runs along the other side of the valley. The eccentric architecture of many of these wineries makes the pretensions of the confident Napa producers plain for all to see. As visitors are usually received in appropriately equipped tasting rooms with integrated souvenir shops, the valley is now the most visited destination in American wine tourism. Not everything that is served there is of fantastic quality, because most of the wineries buy in grapes from other regions in order to meet demand and offer wines that someone on a normal salary is able, or willing, to afford. Only a small percentage of the annual quarter of a million visitors is prepared to pay 50 dollars or more for a bottle of wine.

Some decades ago fears began to be expressed that this attractive valley, within commuting distance of San Francisco, might be designated a residential area. In response, far-sighted agricultural authorities set a process in motion that was intended to make the Napa Valley an Agricultural Preserve. Although things were hard economically for the farmers

Napa Valley has many sub-A.V.A.s that underline the clear differences between its various wines. The most famous districts are Rutherford and Stag's Leap.

in the valley at that time, the initiative was successful and resulted in the protection of a good 35 square miles (9,000 ha) from urbanization. The area covered by the Preserve has now grown to 47 square miles (12,000 ha).

Select Wineries

A large number of new wineries have been set up in Napa County just in recent years, and now the region has nearly 400. Wine consultants and experienced winemakers either run the wineries themselves or have been directly responsible for their quality. Only a very limited selection can be discussed in more detail here, but it will at least give an indication of the range of the Napa wineries, most of which are making wines of above-average quality. These operations tend to produce just a few hundred bottles, or at best a few thousand, which American collectors go to great lengths to lay their hands on. On the one hand, this has resulted in astronomical prices; on the other, it means that these wines are practically impossible to track down. We do not have space to discuss these star producers in detail here, but their ranks include David Abreu, Bacio Civino Cellars, Bryant, Colgin-Schrader Cellars, Grace Family, La Sirena, Screaming Eagle, Selene, and Vineyard 29.

Select Producers in the Napa Valley

Beringer Vineyards**−****
St. Helena
12,400 acres (5,000 ha) • *Wines include: Beringer Wine Estates: Chardonnay; →Bancroft Ranch Merlot, →Cabernet Sauvignon Private Reserve, Zinfandel; Napa Ridge*
Founded in 1876 by German immigrants. The Private Reserve is one of the most powerful Cabernet Sauvignons in the valley. In 1997 the company acquired the legendary Estrella Vineyards at Paso Robles, now marketed under the Meridian brand.

Cain Vineyard and Winery**−*****
St. Helena
87 acres (35 ha); bought-in grapes; 300,000 bottles • *Wines include: Napa Valley: Cain Musqué; →Cain Five, →Cain Cuvée*
Jim and Nancy Meadlock founded their estate in the hills above St. Helena in 1980 with the aim of producing a great Bordelais blend. Their Cain Five is one of the most elegant Napa wines.

Cakebread Cellars**−****
Rutherford
75 acres (30 ha); bought-in grapes; 780,000 bottles • *Wines include: Napa Valley: Chardonnay, Sauvignon; →Cabernet Sauvignon Rutherford Reserve, Merlot, Zinfandel*
This winery is a very active exporter and owns vineyards right next to the St. Helena Highway. The Cabernet Sauvignon Rutherford Reserve is one of the best.

Caymus Vineyards**−****
Rutherford
75 acres (30 ha); bought-in grapes; 720,000 bottles • *Wines include: Napa Valley: Sauvignon Blanc Barrel Fermented, Conundrum White; Œil de Perdrix Pinot Noir; Cabernet Sauvignon Special Selection; Central Coast: Mer Soleil*
Caymus is one of the icons of Napa and has been celebrated by the magazine *Wine Spectator* for years, but there are also many observers who criticize their wines as crude and extremely overpriced.

Chateau Montelena Winery***−****
Calistoga
220 acres (89 ha); 420,000 bottles • *Wines include: Chateau Montelena; Silverado Cellars; Chardonnay, Riesling; Cabernet Sauvignon, Zinfandel*
The estate became famous in 1976 when its Chardonnay outdid the best Burgundies. Its most important product is the costly Estate Cabernet.

Corison****
St. Helena
8 acres (3.2 ha); bought-in grapes; 36,000 bottles • *Wines: Cabernet Sauvignon: Nappa valley, →Kronos Vineyard*
Cathy Corison was winemaker at Chappellet before she finally started working for herself. Stylistically, her wines are very clear and fine. They also store extremely well.

Dominus Estate***−****
Yountville
104 acres (42 ha); 70,000 bottles • *Wines: →Dominus Estate Napa*
A joint venture led by Christian Moueix from the famous Bordeaux wine dynasty (Pétrus). In good years Dominus is a dense, firmly structured, very elegant wine.

Dunn Vineyards*****
Angwin
10 acres (4 ha); bought-in grapes; 60,000 bottles • *Wines: →Howell Mountain Cabernet Sauvignon*
Randy Dunn has worked on Howell Mountain since 1996. He only makes Cabernet Sauvignon, but has shown the potential power and elegance of Napa wines away from the overcultivated valley floor.

Forman****
St. Helena
124 acres (50 ha); 60,000 bottles • *Wines: Napa Valley: Chardonnay; →Cabernet, →Merlot*
Ric Forman makes low-yield, high-quality wines that he matures in the tunnels of his underground winery.

Franciscan Vineyards**−****
Rutherford
1,090 acres (440 ha); 4,200,000 bottles • *Wines include: Napa Franciscan Oakville Estate: →Chardonnay Cuvée Sauvage; Cabernet, Meritage, Merlot; Pinot Noir Monterey Pinnacles, Estancia Estates, Mount Veeder Winery, Quintessa*
The U.S.-based multinational Canandaigua recently bought Franciscan from the German firm Eckes. It also owns the very good Mount Veeder Winery.

Harlan Estate*****
Oakville
40 acres (16 ha); 18,000 bottles • *Wines: Harlan Estate Red Wine*
Real estate agent H. William Harlan produces one of the most eagerly sought-after cult wines in the United States, with the help of Michel Rolland and Bob Levy. The four Bordeaux varieties are used.

Havens Wine Cellars***−****
Napa
19 acres (7.6 ha); bought-in grapes; 165,000 bottles • *Wines: Napa Valley: Merlot, Syrah, Carneros; Albarino, →Merlot Reserve, →Bourriquot, Hudson Vineyard "T" Syrah*
Michael Havens, a former Professor of Literature, farms his own land and a further 36 acres (14.5 ha) of rented vines; his Merlots and Syrahs are fresh and refined.

The Hess Collection Winery***−*****
Napa
1,122 acres (454 ha) • *Wines include: Collection, Select; Estate Napa Valley Cabernet Sauvignon*
Swiss businessman Donald Hess has transformed the old Christian Brothers winery into a museum of winemaking and art. Its top product is the Cabernet Sauvignon made with the estate's own grapes. Wines from Monterey are also bottled under the Hess Selection label.

Robert Mondavi Winery*−*****
Napa
1,399 acres (566 ha); 3,200,000 bottles • *Wines: Napa Valley, District, Reserve, Spotlight Wines*
The winery now makes wines from its own estates in its state of the art cellars that were completed in 2001. The Cabernet Sauvignon Reserve is still the star (see following double page).

Niebaum–Coppola Estate**−****
Vineyards & Winery; Rutherford
299 acres (121 ha); bought-in grapes; 3,600,000 bottles • *Wines include: Niebaum-Coppola, Rubicon, Francis Coppola Family Wines, Gustave Niebaum Collection, Edizione Pennino*

In the 1970s Francis Ford Coppola purchased a share in the famous Niebaum estate and extended his holding over the years. In Chateau Inglenook, he owns one of the most spectacular winery buildings in the valley. The Cabernet Sauvignon marketed as Rubicon has become excellent under the enologist Scott McCleod.

JOSEPH PHELPS VINEYARDS***−*****
ST. HELENA
183 acres (74 ha); bought-in grapes; 1,200,000 bottles • Wines include: Insignia, Vin du Mistral, Backus
Insignia was the first outstanding non-varietal Bordeaux blend to be made in Napa in the 1970s and has remained consistently excellent. The most interesting wines in recent years have been made from Rhône varieties.

PINE RIDGE WINERY***−****
NAPA
222 acres (90 ha); bought-in grapes 1,000,000 bottles • Wines include: Chardonnay, La Petite Vigne; Merlot, Five Cabernet Sauvignons
This winery makes one of the best Cabernets in Napa in the Stag's Leap District, but the wines from its other estates, in Carneros, Oakville, Howell Mountain, Yountville and Oak Knoll are also of excellent quality.

ST. SUPERY VINEYARDS & WINERY***−****
RUTHERFORD
655 acres (265 ha) • Wines include: Sauvignon, Chardonnay; Cabernet Sauvignon, Merlot; →Meritage; Rutherford
The Skalli Group from the South of France produces very pleasing wines at the Dollarhide Ranch, the Rutherford Estate and the Hardester Ranch.

SAINTSBURY***−****
NAPA
55 acres (22 ha); bought-in grapes; 600,000 bottles • Wines include: Carneros: Chardonnay; Pinot Noir, →Pinot Noir Brown Ranch
David Graves and Dick Ward make fundamentally solid Chardonnays and Pinot Noirs with careful use of French oak and polished vinification. Excellent reserve wines.

SHAFER****−*****
NAPA
200 acres (81 ha); bought -in grapes; 384,000 bottles • Wines include: →Red Shoulder Ranch Chardonnay; Merlot, Firebreak, →Relentless, →Hillside Select Cabernet Sauvignon
John Shafer and his son Doug are two of the top winemakers in Napa and own the best *terroirs* in Stag's Leap, Oak Knoll, and Carneros. Their best wines are the Hillside Select Cabernet Sauvignon and the Chardonnay from Red Shoulder Ranch.

SPOTTSWOODE****
ST. HELENA
37 acres (15 ha); bought-in grapes; 70,000 bottles • Wines: Sauvignon Blanc; Cabernet Sauvignon
The Spottswoode estate was founded in 1882 and the Novaks acquired it in 1972. They renewed all the plantings and finally set up the winery in 1982. They have been working biologically since 1985. Only for their Sauvignon are grapes also bought in. Their wines are on a very high level.

SPRING MOUNTAIN VINEYARD****
ST. HELENA
225 acres (91 ha); 60,000 bottles • Wines: Sauvignon, Sirah, Cabernet Estate, Cabernet Reserve
A combination of three old estates, with impressive terraces on the eastern slopes of Spring Mountain. Their own wines are made from only the best grapes.

STAG'S LEAP WINE CELLARS***−*****
NAPA
371 acres (150 ha) • Wines include: Napa Valley: Chardonnay; Cabernet, →Cask 23, →S.L.V.; Hawk Crest
Warren Winiarski was a protagonist in the rapid rise of Stag's Leap District and has been making some of the best wines in the valley there since 1972. The company's top wines are the Cask 23 and S.L.V. Cabernet Sauvignons.

TURLEY WINE CELLARS****
ST. HELENA
99 acres (40 ha); approx. 80,000 bottles • Wines include: Viognier; various vineyard Zinfandels, →Hayne Vineyard Petite Sirah
Larry Turley and his winemaker Ehren Jordan have caused a sensation with their tremendously concentrated Zinfandels and Petite Sirahs. The Hayne is quite superb.

VIADER VINEYARDS****−*****
DEER PARK
42 acres (17 ha); 53,000 bottles • Wines: →Viader, V, Sirah
Delia Viaders' blend of the two Cabernets has now become a classic of Napa Valley. She also produces a blend in which Petit Verdot predominates, and a Sirah from a rocky site 1,640 ft (500 m) above sea level.

Petite Sirah

For a long time this variety was thought to be Durif, a low-quality grape from the Rhône region, though some believed it was a mutation of the real Syrah, but both theories have proved to be false. With a deep red color, plenty of volume and high tannin content, it came into its own as a blending wine in the 1970s, until it was uprooted or regrafted in the 1990s. Some winemakers use it to make stubborn, inky-black wines. The best places for Petite Sirah are old vineyards in Napa, particularly in Howell Mountain and Spring Mountain (York Creek).

ROBERT MONDAVI

Robert Mondavi (left) presents the first case of Robert Mondavi wine to John Daniels Jr. from the Inglenook Winery, his supporter and friend of many years. Fred Holmes, Mondavi's partner during 1967–68, stands to the right.

In 1966, when Robert Mondavi founded his winery in Oakville with his son Michael, it was the first new wine company in the Napa Valley since the Prohibition era. The prominent buildings at their headquarters and visitor center are built in the style of the Spanish missions and have come to stand for the revival of the Californian wine industry, just as Robert Mondavi himself has become its most famous ambassador around the world. He was born in June 1913 in Virginia, Minnesota three years after his parents left their home in Italy. His father Cesare traded in fruit and grapes and established a business in Lodi in 1923. Cesare made his own wine for the family purely for pleasure, but eventually began to see it as a commercial proposition. After Robert had completed his studies at Stanford University in 1936, his family took over the Sunny St. Helena Winery in the Napa Valley.

The family only became serious about winemaking in 1943, when Cesare took over a vineyard with one of the richest traditions in the Napa, the Krug winery, which had been founded in 1861 by the Prussian emigrant Charles Krug. By the 1950s and 60s the Mondavis were gaining plenty of plaudits for their Cabernet Sauvignon, as well as achieving considerable success on the market with their C.K. brand of jug wines. Soon Robert took sole responsibility for marketing, while his younger brother Peter was in charge of the vineyards and winemaking. The Charles Krug Winery was the first to introduce temperature-controlled fermentation and created a sweetly

fruity Chenin that caused a stir throughout California.

After the death of their father in 1959, the two brothers began to argue with increasing bitterness. Finally, Robert Mondavi—who was deeply convinced of the Napa Valley's great potential—set up his own company in 1966. His first visit to Europe in 1962 had opened his eyes to what could be done by maturing wine in *barriques* (barrels). He diligently researched the method, and used it for his red and white wines. Robert Mondavi created his own style with the fully fermented, dry Sauvignon Blanc matured in oak barrels that he christened Fumé Blanc, a wine that was copied throughout California and helped to build respect for this grape variety. A readiness to experiment, and unceasing efforts to improve the company's vinification technology and raise standards in its vineyards, have been characteristic of the Mondavi Winery, from its foundation to the present. In addition to the harvest from Mondavi's three vineyards, which now cover a total area of 1,410 acres (570 ha) in Oakville, Stag's Leap District, and Carneros, grapes are purchased from various producers, who are rewarded for the quality of their fruit through a bonus system introduced by Robert Mondavi. In addition to the approximately 25 million bottles produced in the Napa Valley and Carneros, Mondavi makes about 60 million bottles of popular varietal wines at the Woodbridge Winery

Robert Mondavi—the grand old man of wine.

in Lodi that the company purchased in 1979. These wines are based on grapes bought in the Lodi, Central Valley, and North Coast areas, and are matured in a high-tech aging cellar accommodating 40,000 barrels. Of his joint ventures, the first, Opus One, which was launched in 1979 with Mouton Rothschild over the road from the main Mondavi winery, is still the most famous. Others include Luce, Lucente, and Caliterra.

All the members of the Mondavi family have taken an active role in the company's development since its foundation. Since 1993 it has been managed by Robert Mondavi's sons, Michael and Tim. The company bottles wines grown in the Oakville, Stag's Leap, and Carneros sub-A.V.A.s, as well as various Italian varieties branded as La Famiglia di Robert Mondavi. Mondavi also runs the Byron Vineyards in Santa Maria Valley, but in the crisis of recent years the company has greatly reduced its activities.

Left
The modern art at the Mondavi Winery is a reminder of the links between wine and culture.

Right
The hacienda-style Mondavi Winery attracts wine pilgrims from all over the world.

Satellite thermal imaging provides information about suitable sites for new plantings.

Natural wine growing

Since the 1970s natural wine growing has become a firm part of the Mondavi philosophy. Tim Mondavi, who graduated from the University of California at Davis in 1974 with a degree in ENOLOGY and winemaking, is responsible for the consistency with which this approach has been implemented.

Numerous research projects and experiments have been undertaken, and about two-thirds of the company's own vineyards are now managed using "natural" methods. These are based on the following principles:
• Use alternatives to chemicals, wherever possible.
• Replace the use of herbicides by mechanical cultivation techniques, such as hoe plowing.
• Counter insect attacks, powdery mildew and bunch rot by removing leaves.
• Use raw materials that are low in pollutants for soil building (e.g. composted pomace).

The motto is "natural." Meantime, vineyards are being planted and maintained on biological viticultural methods, like these new areas in Carneros.

• Use COVER CROPS and added organic matter in order to replenish the soil with nitrogen. Cover crops reduce the need to take action against phylloxera attacks and provide varied, and therefore diverting food for a range of pests.

All the recently laid-out vineyards, such as the plantings in Carneros, are cultivated using organic methods. However, this does not mean that the Mondavis are slow to exploit the latest technology. As an example of this, satellite thermal imaging has been used to examine the heat conditions on the various slopes in Carneros in order to identify those sites where grapes will ripen uniformly and optimally.

Beyond its own vineyards, Mondavi takes part in more broadly based ecological projects that are intended to combat erosion and reduce water usage. As well as this, they promote the expansion of biotopes and woodland on their estates, and have reduced noise levels so as not to disturb nesting birds. Mitchell Klug, the company director responsible for Mondavi's vineyards in the Napa Valley, was chosen as Conservationist of the Year in 1991.

CENTRAL COAST

Monterey Pier, not far from the famous Cannery Row, looks tranquil enough from the waterfront. But appearances are deceiving—the city's streets are crowded with tourists. The best Monterey wines are Chardonnay and Riesling.

This A.V.A. extends from San Francisco to Santa Barbara and includes 25 sub-A.V.A.s in seven main *appellations*. On the whole, temperatures are moderate in the valleys of the Central Coast, where the fog from the Pacific lessens the power of the sun, while the mountain *terroirs* rise into the sunshine above the low cloud and therefore tend to be warmer.

More and more of the traditional vineyards on the outskirts of San José are falling victim to urban sprawl. The Wente family has a 1,240-acre (500-ha) estate to the north of San José that is well known for Chardonnay and Semillon, while good Cabernet and Chardonnay grapes flourish at Gilroy and Hecker Pass in Santa Clara Valley. The most spectacular *terroirs* in the Santa Cruz Mountains, such as the excellent Ridge Winery, rise directly above Silicon Valley. There are another two dozen small wineries on these hills, which extend as far as the coast, where the weather is rather cooler. Hillside vineyards are cultivated by individualists in San Benito, where Josh Jensen's Calera Winery bottles surprising single-vineyard Pinot Noirs and Chardonnays on Mount Harlan, and Chalone has gained A.V.A. status thanks to Richard Graff and Phil Woodward's winery of the same name.

The largest growing area is Monterey, though the only district that actually looks out over the famous bay is Carmel Valley, which is home to some small wineries. Extensive vineyards have been planted in the fertile, but dry Salinas Valley, where heavy irrigation is required and the main grapes are Chardonnay and Riesling. The warmer, upper part of the valley to the south has been awarded the Arroyo Seco A.V.A. and is increasingly being used for the cultivation of Cabernet Sauvignon.

The South-Central Coast begins at Paso Robles, where winemakers are experimenting with Rhône and Italian varieties, and tends to attract greater attention. The western ranges provide very good Zinfandels from old vines. It is cooler in the Edna Valley south of San Luis Obispo, the county town that gives its name to the local *appellation*, so the winemakers there rely on Chardonnay and Pinot Noir. However, astounding Grenache, Syrah, and Viognier grapes will also flourish on well-situated hillside *terroirs* in this area, as Alban Vineyards have demonstrated. Temperatures are higher inland in Arroyo Grande.

There is a concentration of high-quality producers in Santa Barbara County. Thanks to the different direction of the mountain chains, which run from west to east here, cooler sea air can penetrate inland, creating a climate that produces Pinot Noir and Chardonnay of high quality. These valleys became famous thanks to grape farms like Sanford & Benedict and Bien Nacido Vineyards, whose grapes have been made into top wines by highly talented independent winemakers. Some of them have now turned to Rhône varieties, while others are experimenting with Italian grapes.

South Coast

To the south of Los Angeles in Riverside County is the 15-mile (25-km) long Temecula Valley, which has survived as the only noteworthy winemaking area in southern California today. Although the climate is warm, due to the fog that drifts in off the Pacific, it is generally unsettled as well, which usually favors white varieties. Good results are achieved by Callaway and the Culbertson Winery, which specializes in sparkling wines. There are also nearly a dozen smaller producers who make Chardonnay and

Sauvignon Blanc. The area's Riesling is very impressive, but its red wines are usually too light. This is a heavily populated region, and a large proportion of the valley's wine is sold direct from the estates in tasting rooms.

Temecula Valley was involved in the Rancho California Project, which was intended to promote the mixed usage of residential and industrial districts in the Los Angeles area. It appears to have achieved its aims, as can be seen today.

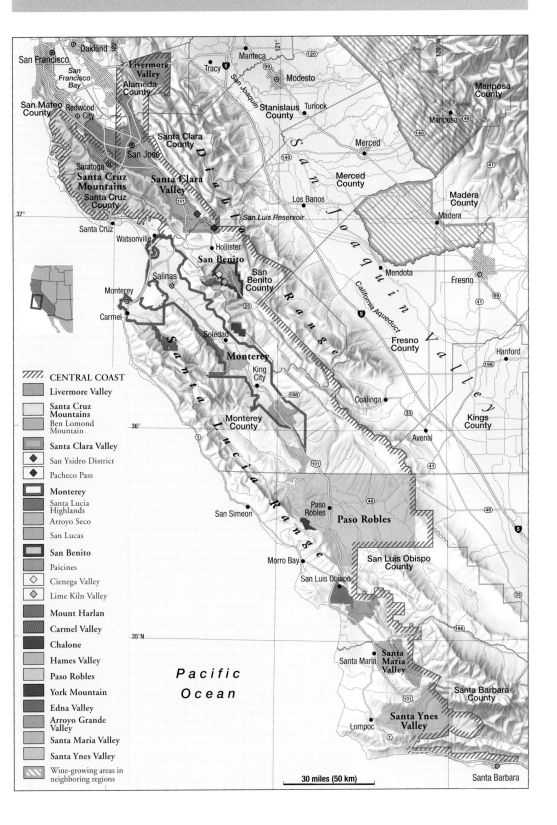

CENTRAL COAST

- Livermore Valley
- **Santa Cruz Mountains**
  Ben Lomond Mountain
- **Santa Clara Valley**
  - ◆ San Ysidro District
  - ◆ Pacheco Pass
- **Monterey**
  Santa Lucia Highlands
  Arroyo Seco
  San Lucas
- **San Benito**
  Paicines
  - ◇ Cienega Valley
  - ◈ Lime Kiln Valley
- **Mount Harlan**
- **Carmel Valley**
- **Chalone**
- **Hames Valley**
- **Paso Robles**
- **York Mountain**
- **Edna Valley**
- **Arroyo Grande Valley**
- **Santa Maria Valley**
- **Santa Ynes Valley**
- Wine-growing areas in neighboring regions

30 miles (50 km)

Select Producers in the Central Coast Region

ALBAN VINEYARDS***−****
ARROYO GRANDE

374 acres (30 ha); 26,000 bottles • Wines: Arroyo Grande: Viognier; Grenache, Syrah
John Alban gained experience on the Rhône, then settled in Arroyo Grande in 1989. He produces excellent wines with the best Rhône varieties, which he grows in the highest vineyards in the area.

AU BON CLIMAT***−*****
SANTA MARIA

45 acres (18 ha); bought-in grapes; 360,000 bottles • Wines include: Chardonnay, Pinot Blanc; Pinot Noir; Il Podere dell'Olivos: Tocai Friulano, Arneis; Teroldego, Barbera, Sangiovese
Jim Clendenen uses the *barrique* with real mastery, and makes Chardonnays and Pinots of world class in a shed next to the Bien Nacido Ranch that he shares with Bob Lindquist of Qupé. His range includes amusing Italian wines and other agreeable bottlings under labels such as Vita Nova. He buys grapes from a wide variety of vineyards, including Alban, Talley, and Bien Nacido.

BABCOCK VINEYARDS***−****
LOMPOC

69 acres (28 ha); bought-in grapes; 180,000 bottles • Wines: Babcock, Riverbreak, Eleven Oaks, Fathom, Grand Cuvée, Cuvée Lestat
This estate is located directly next to the most strategically important air base in the U.S.A. It produces excellent Chardonnay, Pinot Noir, and even Gewürztraminer.

CALERA WINE COMPANY**−****
HOLLISTER

64 acres (26 ha); 300,000 bottles • Wines: Mount Harlan: Chardonnay, Viognier; Pinot Noir; Central Coast: Chardonnay; Pinot
Josh Jensen established one of the most remote wineries in San Benito after he discovered calceous soils suitable for Pinot Noir in the hills near Hollister. The wines from his own grapes are quite excellent.

CHALONE VINEYARD**−****
SOLEDAD

321 acres (130 ha); 420,000 bottles • Wines include: →Estate Chardonnay, Pinot Blanc; Estate Pinot Noir; Acacia; Echelon
The Chalone corporation also owns the small Acacia Winery in Carneros, Edna Valley Vineyard, and Canoe Ridge in Western Australia. Known for its well-structured Chardonnays and Pinots, but standards vary.

CLAIBORNE & CHURCHILL WINERY***
SAN LUIS OBISPO

3 acres (1.2 ha); bought-in grapes; 60,000 bottles • Wines: →California Edelzwicker, →Dry Gewürztraminer Alsatian Style, Edna Valley Chardonnay; San Luis Obispo County Cabernet Sauvignon
There is even an Edelzwicker in the selection produced by this small, friendly winery on the edge of Edna Valley. Almost all its wines are sold direct to the public on the estate.

DURNEY VINEYARDS***−****
CARMEL VALLEY

99 acres (40 ha); 250,000 bottles • Wines: Carmel Valley: Chardonnay, Chenin, Johannisberg Riesling Late Harvest; →Cabernet Sauvignon Private Reserve and Chachagua
Originally this winery was intended to be a cattle ranch, but there was a change of plan after the chance discovery of old vines. The best of just five wineries in this A.V.A.

on the hills above the picturesque Carmel Valley, Durney is now run by the Austrian company Schober.

EBERLE WINERY***−****
PASO ROBLES

38 acres (15.4 ha); bought-in grapes; 300,000 bottles • Wines include: Paso Robles: →Chardonnay; Counoise Rosé; →Cabernet Sauvignon, Cabernet/Syrah, →Côtes du Rôbles, →Syrah Fralich Vineyard, Zinfandel Steinbeck Vineyard
Gary Eberle made the Paso Robles district famous decades ago with his legendary Cabernet Sauvignons from the Estrella Vineyards. He produces very reliable, good-quality wines.

EDNA VALLEY VINEYARD**−***
SAN LUIS OBISPO

605 acres (245 ha); 1,100,000 bottles • Wines include: →Edna Valley Chardonnay, →Viognier Fralich Vineyard; Cellar Master's Selection: Sauvignon Blanc, Semillon, Muscat Canelli; Edna Valley Brut; Pinot Noir Paragon
This joint venture between Chalone and the enormous Paragon Vineyards surprises with fresh, almost light white wines, led by the Chardonnay.

FIRESTONE VINEYARDS***
LOS OLIVOS

593 acres (240 ha); bought-in grapes; 2,400,000 bottles • Wines include: California: Gewürztraminer, →Santa Ynez Valley: Chardonnay Barrel Fermented, Johannisberg Riesling Selected Harvest; Cabernet Franc, Firestone Reserve, Prosperity Red; Santa Ynez Valley Merlot, Carey Cellars
Bruce Firestone's winery was one of the first in this area of California to produce premium-quality wines. The barrel-fermented Chardonnay is the most impressive.

FOXEN**−****
SANTA MARIA

35 acres (14 ha); bought-in grapes; 150,000 bottles • Wines include: Chardonnay: Santa Maria, Bien Nacido, Tinaquaic; Pinot Noir: Santa Maria, Julia, Bien Nacido, Sanford & Benedict; Mourvèdre, Syrah, Cabernet Sauvignon, Cabernet Franc
Bill Wathen and Richard Doré offer a broad and original range of wines, including top-quality Chardonnay, Pinot Noir, Cabernet Sauvignon, and Cabernet Franc.

KATHRYN KENNEDY WINERY***−****
SARATOGA

7 acres (2.8 ha); bought-in grapes; 36,000 bottles • Wines: →Estate Cabernet Sauvignon Santa Cruz Mountains
After a few years of unreliability, this vineyard has found its equilibrium again with its famous Cabernet Sauvignon.

MORGAN WINERY***−****
SARATOGA

44 acres (18 ha); bought-in grapes; 480,000 bottles • Wines include: Classic series with Sauvignon, Chardonnay; Pinot, Cabernet; Single vineyard series: Chardonnay; Syrah, Pinot
Known for excellent Chardonnays and Sauvignons, Dan Lee is now aiming to produce highly complex wines from his own estate, using a big range of clones.

ANDREW MURRAY VINEYARDS***−****
LOS OLIVOS

35 acres (14 ha); 60,000 bottles • Wines: Santa Ynez Valley: Roussane, Viognier; Syrah
This 200-acre (80-ha) estate is located at 1,650 feet (500 m) above sea level. It was founded in 1990 and is

planted with 35 acres (14 ha) of Rhône varieties. After initially uneven results, the winery is now fulfilling its potential in ever more impressive style, especially with its Syrah and the rare Roussane.

OJAI VINEYARD****
OAK VIEW
Bought-in grapes; 80,000 bottles • Wines: Chardonnay, Sauvignon Blanc, Viognier; Pinot Noir, Syrah, Mourvèdre
Adam Tolmach creates very individual, unusual wines with grapes from various contracted vineyards, such as Roll Ranch, Bien Nacido, and Stolpman Vineyard. Outstanding Syrah, silky Pinot Noir, and attractive Sauvignon Blanc.

QUPÉ****
SANTA MARIA
Bought-in grapes; 240,000 bottles • Wines include: Chardonnay/Viognier, →Marsanne; →Syrah, Los Olivos Cuvée
Bob Lindquist works under the same tin roof as Au Bon Climat. He has specialized as one of the leading "Rhône rangers," and his Syrahs are among the best in the U.S.A.

RIDGE VINEYARDS*****
CUPERTINO
242 acres (98 ha); 780,000 bottles • Wines: →Santa Cruz Mountains Chardonnay; Cabernet Sauvignon: →Montebello, Santa Cruz Mountains; California Zinfandel: Lytton Spring, Geyserville; California Mataro Evangelo Vineyard
Vineyards on the Santa Cruz Mountains high above San José provide the grapes for the high-quality Montebello, which was conceived as a Bordeaux-style wine. Paul Draper made the winery famous in the 1970s, and standards have not dropped in the slightest since then. The Zinfandels are outstanding.

SANFORD WINERY**−****
BUELLTON
Bought-in grapes; 600,000 bottles • Wines include: Chardonnay, Sauvignon Blanc; Pinot Noir: Central Coast, Santa Ynez Valley; Santa Barbara County Sanford & Benedict Vineyards
This estate is part of the historic El-Jabali Ranch and was founded by Richard and Thekla Sanford in 1981. The most famous Pinot Noir vineyard in southern California has now changed owners, but continues to be managed by Sanford, who is well known for his stylish Chardonnays and Pinots.

TALLEY VINEYARDS***
ARROYO GRANDE
140 acres (57 ha); 144,000 bottles • Wines: Chardonnay; Pinot Noir
Don, Rosemary, Brian, and Johnine Talley own two of the best vineyards in Arroyo Grande: Rosemary's and the Rincon Vineyard. Their outstanding grapes are made into some of the most sought-after wines in the U.S.A. by other winemakers.

LANE TANNER WINERY***
SANTA MARIA
Bought-in grapes; 27,000 bottles • Wines: San Luis Obispo County Syrah, Pinot Noir: Santa Maria Valley, Bien Nacido Vineyard, →Julia's Valley
Lane Tanner has been making innovative wines since 1989. She shares the storehouse in which her wines are made with other winemakers, who all use their barrels and equipment in common. Her grapes come from leased parcels.

VENTANA VINEYARDS WINERY***
MONTEREY
300 acres (120 ha); 500,000 bottles • Wines include: Chardonnay, Dry Riesling, Orange Muscat, Dry Rosado; Syrah, Sangiovese; J. Douglas

MONTE BELLO VINEYARD: 75% CABERNET SAUVIGNON
23% MERLOT, 2% CABERNET FRANC
SANTA CRUZ MOUNTAINS   ALCOHOL 13.4% BY VOLUME
PRODUCED AND BOTTLED BY RIDGE VINEYARDS   BW 4488
17100 MONTE BELLO ROAD, BOX 1810, CUPERTINO, CA 95015

A Syrah Worth Fighting Over?

You Bet Shiraz!

EBERLE
A Pioneer of California Syrah.
Extremely Limited.
Extremely Good.

HE QUIT HIS JOB! HE SOLD HIS MORTAL SOUL! HE EVEN FORSOOK THE WOMAN HE LOVED!

ALL TO COMMIT A LITTLE...
EBERLE WINERY
MUSCAT LOVE!

I Want My WHAZ!

EBERLE
COUNOISE ROSÉ

The Finest Counoise Rosé in the World! It's the Only Counoise Rosé, too.

Let's Hit the Patio, With...

EBERLE
Zinfandel!

Doug Meador runs a recognized experimental vineyard in Monterey County that complies with the strict criteria of the University of California at Davis. He cultivates many varieties that are still rare in California. The vine density of about 2,000 per acre (5,000 per ha) is unusual, as are the finesse and aromatic richness of some of his wines. Great variations in output during the 1990s.

WENTE VINEYARDS**−***
LIVERMORE
371 acres (150 ha); 4,800,000 bottles • Wines include: Wente, Family Selection, Murrieta's Well, Ivan Tamas, Concannon Vineyard, Vineyard Reserve, Brut Reserve, Ch. Wetmore Reserve, →Herman Wente Reserve, Blanc de Blancs, Johannisberg Riesling
The descendants of the German Karl Wente did good business in the 1960s with sweet Chenin Blanc and Gray Riesling, but also pioneered Chardonnay in California. Apart from Livermore, they own vineyards in Arroyo Seco and Monterey. Technically brilliant wines of impressive quality. The top of the range is the Herman Wente Chardonnay.

WILD HORSE WINERY & VINEYARDS**−****
TEMPLETON
37 acres (15 ha); bought-in grapes; 1,100,000 bottles • Wines include: →Central Coast: Chardonnay Unbridled, Arneis, Malvasia Bianca, →Pinot Blanc, →Cienega, Tocai Friulano, Roussane Late Harvest; Merlot, Pinot Noir, Negrette, Trousseau, Valley Old Vine Field Blend, Cabernet Sauvignon, Mourvèdre, Syrah, Cheval Sauvage, Santa Lucia, Equus
Ken Volk produces just about every grape variety he can find on this former horse farm. His wines are distinguished by their good fruit and firm structure. Many of the more exotic varieties are only sold in his tasting room.

Zinfandel

Although it is really the southern Italian Primitivo, Zinfandel is regarded as a Californian star. Its career has known extreme heights and depths, but it has been consistently successful since the 1990s. Its showpiece role comes in good-quality red wines. Depending on the climate, it can be either cool and elegantly balanced, with fresh fruitiness and fine tannins, or baked, with overpowering fruit, spiciness, fullness, and almost staggering strength. California's best Zinfandels come from Dry Creek Valley, especially Geyserville and Lytton Springs, Howell Mountain, and Paso Robles.

CENTRAL VALLEY

Central Valley is the longest valley in California, running from Sacramento in the north to Bakersfield in the south. It is also one of the most intensively cultivated agricultural landscapes in the world. Not only do most types of fruits, nuts, and vegetables flourish here, but cotton and rice are also grown, and a large proportion of the table grapes and raisins consumed in the United States come from Central Valley vineyards. In the north of the valley, the Sacramento A.V.A., where the renowned University of California is based in Davis, is well-known for its excellent Chenin, and Rhône varieties have been planted there recently.

Well over half the acreage of vineyards in California is found in Central Valley, particularly in the San Joaquin Valley to the south. The region supplies more than two thirds of the state's wine production.

However, the American wine industry's main growing area is the San Joaquin Valley, which is 220 miles (350 km) long and more than 55 miles (90 km) wide in some places. This valley has a total of 120,000 acres (48,000 ha) of land under vines, and produces about 70 percent of Californian wine. The climate is hot and dry, and the growing areas are classified as Region IV and Region V (see page 812). The extensive grape fields require heavy irrigation, and there is always new planting or regrafting going on here so as to meet changing expectations and consumer tastes as flexibly as possible. Even cheap wines are having to meet higher quality standards, which is leading to considerable improvements in grape handling.

The wineries in this area are truly gigantic. They apply electronically controlled wine-making processes, using the latest technology to produce "easy drinking wines." Modesto is the headquarters of E. & J. Gallo, the biggest winery in the world, while Mondavi and Sebastiani own large plants at Lodi, and many famous wineries purchase the grapes for their basic brands from Central Valley. The local Colombard and Chenin were once prized for their acidity, but are increasingly being replaced by more popular varieties. At one time a large proportion of the Thompson Seedless harvest was fermented, but this leading table grape and raisin variety is hardly used for winemaking any more.

To the north of Stockton is Lodi A.V.A., which has a mild climate and rich soil, making it ideal for Zinfandel, Ruby Cabernet, and even Cabernet Sauvignon. The Clarksburg area to the south of Sacramento on the Sacramento River now produces various grape varieties, though its real strength, individual-

Texas

Texas is regarded as the cradle of U.S. wine-making, because the conquering Spanish planted the first vines there in the early-17th century. Of 25 wineries operating in the state in 1900, only one managed to survive until the repeal of Prohibition—the Val Verde Winery founded in 1883.

The 1970s saw a renaissance in Texan wine-making. The decisive stimuli were given by the 990-acre (400-ha) Sainte Genevieve Vineyard in Escondido Valley, a joint venture between the University of Texas and the famous Bordeaux wine merchants Cordier that has achieved very satisfactory results over the years.

Interest in Texas has been growing of late, because its high *terroirs* offer very good, healthy conditions for wine growing, and there are now more wineries here than ever before. The six American Viticultural Areas (A.V.A.s) recognized so far in the state are the cool Texas High Plains, Escondido Valley to the north, Texas Hill County, with its sub-*appellations* Bell Mountain and Fredericksburg, and the westerly Melissa Valley, the state's most recent

A.V.A. A wide range of European varieties enjoy the conditions here, where the climate is dry and sunny with cool nights. Apart from Chardonnay, Sauvignon Blanc, and Cabernet Sauvignon, Merlot, Trebbiano, and Zinfandel are now being planted, while Chenin and Riesling are on the retreat. However, the first wines to demonstrate Texas's remarkable potential were a Carnelian—a cross based on Carignan, Cabernet Sauvignon, and Grenache —and a Colombard from Fall Creek Vineyards in Texas Hill County.

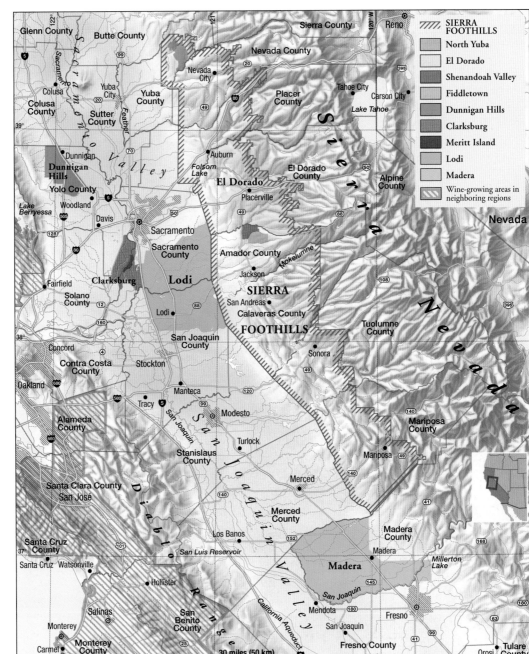

SIERRA FOOTHILLS
- North Yuba
- El Dorado
- Shenandoah Valley
- Fiddletown
- Dunnigan Hills
- Clarksburg
- Meritt Island
- Lodi
- Madera
- Wine-growing areas in neighboring regions

30 miles (50 km)

WOODBRIDGE
California
CABERNET SAUVIGNON

DUETTO
RED ASSEMBLAGE
SANTO TOMAS & LIVERMORE VALLEYS
MEXICO & USA
1997

13.9% ALC/VOL.   PRODUCT OF MEXICO   750 ML

istic Chenin, is increasingly neglected. In the middle of the San Joaquin Valley the Madera A.V.A. produces popular mass-market wines and the dessert wines reminiscent of port wine or Muscat that used to be so common in California.

Mexico and Cuba

The first vines were cultivated in Mexico as early as 1522, making it the oldest winemaking country in the Americas, and 100,000 acres (40,000 ha) of vineyards were planted in the 1990s. However, although it can successfully claim to be the fourth-largest wine producer in Latin America after Argentina, Chile, and Brazil, only a small proportion of its grapes is used for wine. Most of the country's vineyards are found on the sandy soil in the north of the country in the state of Sonora, but their fruit is primarily used for brandy, table grapes, and raisin produc-

tion. Quality wine is mainly produced in the heavily irrigated vineyards of Baja California, where some excellent Petite Sirah and Cabernet Sauvignon grapes are now being grown.

There are also vineyards further south on the high plains of Aguascalientes and Zacatecas, and in the new winemaking area of Querétaro. The historic Mission grape, which was probably introduced by the first Spanish settlers, continues to predominate, though modern vineyards are increasingly being planted with French varieties, such as Cabernet Sauvignon,

Syrah, Merlot, and Malbec, together with varieties that are mainly cultivated in California, including Petite Sirah, Zinfandel, and Ruby Cabernet. Apart from Californian grape varieties, U.S. expertise is also reaching Mexico via the University of California at Davis.

Though it is more famous for cigars and rum, Cuba produces small quantities of wine. Thanks to a joint venture with an Italian producer, Chardonnay, Pinot Grigio, Tempranillo, and Cabernet Sauvignon have been planted in the region of Pinar del Río.

Anthony Rose

SOUTH AMERICA

WINE GROWING IN SOUTH AMERICA

The development of wine production in South America is one of the most fascinating of wine stories. It is the Spanish and their great 16th-century voyages of discovery and conquest that we have to thank for the early dissemination of the vine and wine culture on the South American continent. As successive waves of settlers came to appreciate, South America's position, south of the Tropic of Capricorn, is well suited to viticulture. In particular, the slopes of the Andes provide the ideal terrain, complemented by ample sunshine, dry heat, cooling breezes, and irrigation waters from melted snow which feeds the many rivers flowing down the Andes to east and west. As a result, South America today is the second most important wine-producing continent after Europe. Argentina is the biggest producer by some way, followed by Chile and Brazil. Wine is also produced in Uruguay, Peru, and Bolivia, and even in Ecuador and Venezuela.

Mexico is the oldest wine producer on the American continent. In fact, records show Mexico to be the first New World country in which *vinifera* vines from Europe were planted. It was of the utmost importance to the conquistadors in the 16th century that there was an abundant supply of sacramental wine for religious purposes. Ships from Spain carried wine but supplies were limited. Hernán Cortés first sent for vine cuttings from Spain in 1522. He made *repartimiento* grants (of land and Indian slaves)

Like many other wine-growing estates, the Undurraga estate with its old barrel cellars was created in Chile's Maipo Valley in the 1880s.

Viña Santa Mónica in the Rapel Valley south of Santiago was created in 1976, partly by the acquisition of older vineyards. It has since become increasingly export-focused.

conditional on the planting of a quota of 1,000 of the best vines obtainable, for every hundred Indians. Criolla vines were most likely grafted onto native vines, and it seems quite possible that it was this measure that spared Mexico the disasters that befell those growers in North America who tried unsuccessfully to establish *Vitis vinifera* in the ubiquitous presence of PHYLLOXERA.

FROM INCA GOLD TO GOLD MEDALS FOR WINE

Viticulture spread throughout South America, following the Jesuit missions, in the first phase of the conquest of the Incan empire of Tahuantinsuyu—Chile, Peru, Bolivia, Ecuador, and small parts of some other South American countries as they are now—which was completed in 1533. Peru and Chile were the first to be planted, simply because these were the most important parts of the Incan empire and rich in the right kind of mountain terraces, complete with irrigation channels, for the cultivation of the vine. The earliest record of the cultivation of the vine in Peru is 1550, based on the records of a Spanish settler, Bartolomé de Terrazas, who had received a *repartimiento* near Cuzco. Within 20 years, vineyards were flourishing in Chile.

Although it was the Jesuit missions which were initially responsible for the spread of viticulture, it seems likely that a gathering trend toward commercial production was fostered by secular and non-religious estates. The rate of viticultural expansion was considerable, despite the fact that the native Indians, who then grew grapes, regarded the vine as the very symbol of the white conquerors' power.

The first wide distribution of the vine throughout Peru, Chile, and Argentina was due mainly to Hernán de Montenegro, early in the 17th century. As the market for wine in South America grew, so did supply. From Chile, enthusiasm for wine spread to Argentina, but Madrid still had greater influence there and could, at first, keep production under control. Since the Spanish and Portuguese wanted to export their own wine in exchange for silver and gold, their governments soon became alarmed at the rapid rate of viticultural expansion in South America, and, in an echo of the Roman Emperor Domitian's ban on viticulture at the end of the 1st century AD, the king of Spain imposed a ban on vine planting and wine production in Peru and Chile. Later, a ban was laid on Argentina, with somewhat greater success. It appears, however, that the ban was generally ignored, and planting continued steadily. In 1767, Madrid again attempted to put a stop to it, but again it failed to keep expansion in check.

With the establishment of better transport links and trading opportunities with Europe, the foundations for the modern industries of South America were laid in the 19th century, when a number of pioneering enthusiasts started importing French vines and changing the fabric of the vineyards as well as modernising the wineries.

In Chile, the range of *vinifera* vines increased with the establishment of a nursery for the purpose in the early 1800s by a Frenchman, Claude Gay. With a direct shipping service between Valparaiso and Liverpool, and the fashion for all things French, in 1851 Bertrand Don Silvestre Ochagavía Echazareta began importing classic Bordeaux varieties from great French vineyards, a move which inspired a number of gentlemen farmers to follow suit. The new French vines made an invaluable contribution to the improvement of Chilean wines.

Argentina's viticultural revolution, based in Mendoza, did not really get under way until around 1870. The "grandfather" of the first new era of the Argentinian wine industry was Don Tiburcio Benegas, who was born in Rosario de Santa Fé in July 1844, and moved to Mendoza in 1865 following the devastating earthquake of 1861. He founded a bank and in 1870 he married Lubina Blanco, whose father published a pamphlet, *Viñas y vino en Mendoza*, in 1872. In 1883 he bought El Trapiche, and extended the existing 618 acres (250 ha) by planting French vines imported first from Chile and later from Europe. In 1886 he was elected governor of Mendoza. By 1910 many vineyards were planted with French varieties, known as *francescas*. Viticulture in Argentina was given a fresh boost by Leopoldo Suárez, who imported 600 varieties from every major viticultural region in Europe.

Left
One of the great Chilean wines on the international market—Santa Rita.

Right
Concha y Toro, founded in 1883, now exports to more than 75 countries worldwide.

Opposite
In Chile, vineyard workers habitually use horses to get around the huge vine plantations.

Criolla was the first grape variety introduced into South America. This ancient Argentine specimen has in the meantime grown into a tree.

With the maturation and bottling of the wines on the estate, the export trade flourished, aided by the fact that Chile managed to escape the scourge of phylloxera which devastated most of the world's vineyards in the latter part of the 19th century. In 1889 Chilean wine-growers were awarded a First Class Award at the Paris Exhibition and took six gold medals.

In contrast with North America, the avoidance of phylloxera damage ensured that the blueprint created by successive settlers over three centuries remained intact right up until the second half of the 20th century. By 1965 there were 272,000 acres (110,000 ha) under vine in Chile, most of it in smallholdings of less than 2$^1/_2$ acres (1 ha) and with only 250 growers owning more than 618 acres (250 ha). As domestic demand dried up, however, the industry went into decline and half of Chile's vineyards had to be pulled up. Only since the late 1970s and early 1980s has the industry reversed the decline and started to flourish.

Sadly, as late as the 1960s, a large part of the heritage of the main wine-producing countries was destroyed by systematic uprooting of vines in the wake of falling consumption and prices. Only with the arrival of the millennium have South America's two most important wine producers, Argentina and Chile, really started to regain the confidence, prosperity, and prestige that they once enjoyed.

ARGENTINA

Argentina can lay claim to a wine culture stretching back to the early Spanish settlers in the 16th century, who found the foothills of the Andes ideal for the cultivation of the vine. *Vinifera* vines are believed to have entered Argentina via at least three different sources, namely from Spain in 1541, from Peru a year later, and from Chile in 1556. The first record of a vineyard was at Santiago del Estero in 1557, planted by the priest Juan Cidró a year or two earlier. Soon after, the city of Mendoza was founded. At the time, the important variety cultivated was a version of the Mission vine, or *criolla chica*, which itself laid the foundations of a vast wine industry based on Criolla, and Argentina's other workhorse variety, the Cereza.

Given Argentina's hot, dry climate, the early settlers established the beginnings of the modern industry by creating a series of dams and irrigation channels. A wave of European immigrants in the early part of the 18th century was followed by a second wave of settlers, mainly from Italy, Spain, and France, toward the end of the century, and the establishment of important railway networks from Mendoza and Patagonia to Buenos Aires. Bringing their European vines with them along with their winemaking expertise, these later settlers established a blueprint for the great diversity of wine styles to be found in Argentina today. At the same time, at the behest of the Governor of Cuyo, Domingo Faustino Sarmiento, the French

In old vineyards, the vines are trained on tall trellises, which are notoriously laborious to trim.

Spectacular landscape in Cafayate Valley.

agronomist, Miguel Aimé Pouget, brought the first Malbec vines to Argentina.

The upshot was that table wine consumption increased rapidly, becoming a significant part of Argentinian culture. Early prosperity under General Juan Domingo Perón came to an abrupt end in the mid 1950s, and for the next 30 years the fortunes of the Argentine wine industry, under a succession of corrupt military governments, declined. Wine consumption was extremely heavy at around 24 gallons (90 liters) per head in 1970, but it was for the most part large volumes of rotgut red and white made from the ubiquitous Criolla and Cereza grapes. A dramatic fall in domestic consumption combined with a period of prosperity under the new, democratic regime of President Menem has resulted in major changes in the Argentine wine industry in the 1990s. Investment in new plantings of premium varieties and wineries has brought a resurgence of natural confidence and a positive, outward-looking approach to winemaking which is now making itself felt in both the domestic and overseas markets.

The ten wine regions of Argentina are almost entirely concentrated in the narrow strip in the west of the country ranging from latitude 25° south in the Cafayate Valley down to 40° south in Patagonia. It is a unique environment of high, semi-desert ranging from between 980 and 5,250 feet (300 and 1,600 m) above sea level, traditionally irrigated by the waters that run off the Andes in a sophisticated system of man-made irrigation channels. Annual rainfall is low, at between 6 and 12 inches (15 and 30 cm), and so is humidity, while the air is clean and pollution-free. Sunlight is intense, and in most regions there are considerable differences between day and night-time temperatures. Although summers are for the most part hot, altitude and/or proximity to the Andes moderate the temperature in cooler regions such as Cafayate, upper Mendoza (Luján de Cuyo), Uco Valley (Tupungato), and Río Negro.

Irrigation is the lifeblood of Argentina's vineyards, which are mostly sandy and clay/loam soils over gravel, limestone, and clay. Traditionally, the system was based on flood and furrow irrigation, using a series of channels to bring water to the vineyard and flood it. This system is recognized as encouraging high yields and hence, in most modern vineyards, it has been replaced by drip irrigation, allowing the

grower more control over the vine's vigorous growth. While flood irrigation is almost certainly responsible, along with Argentina's sandy soils, for keeping the destructive root louse, phylloxera, at bay, there are fears that drip irrigation may not be so effective in this regard. For this reason, most vineyards which have introduced drip irrigation have also introduced resistant American rootstocks.

With its summer heat and sunshine and plentiful water supply from irrigation, Argentina's vineyards have tended toward very high yields. In the 1970s, in particular, the trend was exacerbated by concentration on high-yielding grape varieties grown using the *parral cuyano* trellis system in place of the more traditional, lower-yielding *espaldera* system. Since producers began to take a renewed interest in producing quality wines, however, with the replacement of workhorse by noble grape varieties, there has also been a sea change in attitudes toward viticulture. Today, rigorous control of yields is the chief concern of the quality-conscious producer. It is achieved by plantings at higher densities, using noble vines, careful pruning, drip irrigation instead of flood irrigation, and generally looking for a better balance between fruit and foliage in the vineyard.

One of the most fascinating features of the Argentinian wine industry is the diversity of grape varieties planted, compared to many other countries of the New World. While the high-yielding Criolla and Cereza still account for the lion's share of the crop, their importance is rapidly diminishing as the consumer's increasing appetite for fine wines puts the focus on premium varieties. It is a paradox that Argentina's greatest red grape variety, the Malbec, is one that has failed to shine in its southwestern French homeland of Cahors. This is simply because it flourishes better in Argentina's semi-desert and warm, dry climate, where it produces a soft, mouth-filling, perfumed style of red.

Unfortunately, most of the old Malbec vines were pulled out in the white wine boom of the 1970s, but today there is upwards of 39,500 acres (16,000 ha) of Malbec and more is being planted. It is second only to Bonarda, a north Italian variety, which until recently has been regarded as suitable only for blending in Argentina's domestic product. Bonarda is a soft luscious variety, which, along with Tempranillo and, to a certain extent, Barbera and Sangiovese, has the potential to make good-value, everyday reds. Among new French premium varieties introduced, Cabernet Sauvignon shows good potential, along with Syrah and Merlot, but it

Michel Torino in Mendoza has a wide range of wines.

has yet to show that it can reach the peaks of good, old vine Malbec.

Argentina's most distinctive white wine style is made from the Torrontés grape, which is said to have come originally either from Galicia in Spain or from Muscat seeds brought to Argentina. There are three types, Torrontés Riojano (from La Rioja), Torrontés Mendocino (from Mendoza), and Torrontés Sanjuanino (from San Juan). It produces a uniquely perfumed, Muscat-like, dry white and does particularly well in the northern province of Salta. Argentina also has large quantities of Pedro Ximénez and Muscat of Alexandria, but it is, not surprisingly, Chardonnay, as yet for the most part undistinguished, which gives Argentinian white wine its best shot at achieving a respectable international range.

Traditionally, winemaking has been geared to volume production for an undiscriminating, brand-conscious domestic market. With demand for its wines overseas, however, winemaking is being adapted in order to produce superior quality wines from premium varieties. Temperature-controlled stainless steel FERMENTATION for whites, along with barrel fermentation for Chardonnay, is becoming the norm for export-orientated wineries. The aim with reds is to improve extraction by picking at optimum maturity, fermenting in smaller tanks, managing the cap of TANNINS with frequently longer macerations of up to three or four weeks, and better use of oak-cask maturation.

Argentina's Wine Regions

Mendoza

With its dramatic backdrop of the snow-capped Andes, Mendoza sits at the heart of the Argentine wine industry and is far and away the biggest and most significant of Argentina's wine areas, with its five distinct regions generating some two-thirds of the country's wines. Covering 356,000 acres (144,000 ha), they are: North Mendoza, the High Area of the Mendoza River, East Mendoza, Valle de Uco, and South Mendoza. The next biggest chunk is San Juan, immediately north of Mendoza, which accounts for upwards of 25 percent of Argentinian wine, depending on the vintage, followed by La Rioja, north of San Juan. Compared to these three regions, Salta, or Cafayate Valley, in the far north, and Río Negro in Patagonia, are comparatively minor producers, but because they both produce distinctively different, quality wines, the importance of these two regions outweighs the comparatively small area of their vineyards.

Mendoza is an attractive provincial city, low-rise due to the San Andreas fault, which creates a small earthquake every week or so. Plane and poplar trees line the long avenues, testimony to an era when growers had the foresight to protect weary laborers and animals from the glare of the midday sun. Along the tree-lined roads, monster

Tupungato and Uco valleys are developing rapidly. Lying at over 3,000 feet (900 m) above sea level, aromatic, balanced wines are guaranteed.

Mendoza is by far the most important area of cultivation in Argentina. The huge vine plantations stretch out along the foot of the Andes, which supply the region with the necessary water.

olive trees producing large Arauco olives run parallel to the vineyards, a vivid demonstration of the twin effects of solar energy and irrigation water. Looking at their oak-like trunks, it's easy to see how the vines are similarly affected. Three and a half percent of the surface area of Mendoza is cultivated. The rest is desert.

Irrigated by the Mendoza River, North Mendoza varies between 1,970 and 2,300 feet (600 and 700 m) in altitude and contains the sub-zones of Lavelle, Las Heras, Guaymallén, San Martín, and part of Maipú. Southwest of North Mendoza, the High Area of the River Mendoza ranges in altitude from 2,300 to 3,600 feet (700 to 1,100 m) and includes the important

viticultural sub-zones of Luján de Cuyo and most of Maipú. The backdrop of the snow-capped peaks of the Cordón del Plata and the rounded peak of Tupungato makes these vineyards among the most picturesque in the world. This is Malbec country, with some of the best vineyard sites of old vine Malbec in Luján at Carrodillas, Las Compuertas, Vistalba, Perdriel, and Agrelo, and in Maipú, which is also well-known for quality Cabernet Sauvignon, at Cruz de Piedra, Barrancas, and Lunlunta. Many of Mendoza's most important wineries are here, among them Catena, Trapiche, and Norton.

The Valle de Uco, close to Tupungato, is becoming an increasingly important viticultural area due to its altitude of between 2,950 and 4,100 feet (900 and 1,250 m) and cool climate. Typically, it is a good area for aromatic white varieties and elegant Chardonnay as well as Semillon. The French winemaker, Jacques Lurton, has built a new winery at Vista Flores in this up-and-coming area close to the town of Tunuyan.

East of the Valle de Uco, East Mendoza is one of the biggest volume-producing areas and includes the sub-zones of Junin, Rivadavia, San Martín, and Santa Rosa. From the latter come many of La Agricola's best wines. South Mendoza includes General Alvear and San Rafael, where the family firm of Valentín Bianchi has its vineyards.

SAN JUAN AND LA RIOJA

North of Mendoza, San Juan is Argentina's second biggest wine region with 88,000 acres (35,600 ha). The climate is hotter than in Mendoza and, like Australia's Riverland, the region is best known for large quantities of cheap wine from undefined grape varieties. It has its moments, however, particularly in the sub-zones of Ullum, Calingasta, and Valle del Tullum, and, as wineries like Peñaflor and Santiago Graffigna have demonstrated, it is capable of producing good, robust, everyday red wines.

Further north still, La Rioja is much smaller, with 17,300 acres (7,000 ha). It is the oldest of the wine-producing provinces and produces attractive Torrontés.

CAFAYATE

Faraway Cafayate is best known in Argentina for its white wines. At 5,446 feet (1,660 m) above sea level, the vineyards of Cafayate are high, remote, and sunny. The Cafayate Valley sits in a delta formed by the Río Calchaquí and

Humberto Canale began producing wine in the extreme south of Argentina in 1913. The estate's museum preserves mementoes of those pioneering days.

The beaming faces of the harvesters cannot conceal the fact that the greater part of the output still fails to meet export standards.

Río Santa Maria, varying to as much as 12½ miles (20 km) from east to west and flanked on both sides by mountains. The föhn effect, as it is known, traps the clouds in the mountains, leaving the sunny, dry valley protected from cloud and rain. Its sandy, stony topsoils are covered in scrub and cactus. In summer the temperature rises to 100°F (38°C), dropping to between 54°F and 57°F (12°C and 14°C) at night. In winter the temperature can plummet as low as 21°F (−6°C). Irrigation, even more so than usual in Argentina, is the *sine qua non* of vine growth.

Representing a mere 1.5 percent of Argentina's production, with only 4,450 acres (1,800 ha) under vine, it makes a noise out of all proportion to its size. First, because of Torrontés, which produces a delicate, perfumed style here, and

second, because of a gradual shift from white wines to reds, notably Cabernet Sauvignon, Tannat, and Malbec. Vines are grown on a combination of vertical trellises and pergola trellises, with new vineyards using vertical trellises. The big two wineries here are Etchart and Michel Torino, but there is also a handful of smaller operations, including Colomé, probably the highest vineyard in the world at 7,900 feet (2,400 m), and an experimental vineyard by Michel Rolland and Arnaldo Etchart with grapes at high altitude at San Pedro de Yacochuya.

RÍO NEGRO

Río Negro is named after the "black river" whose waters are the lifeblood of southern Argentina's fruit and wine industries. 5,440 acres (2,200 ha) of vines produce just three percent of Argentinian production, while 111,200 acres (45,000 ha) of orchards, producing mostly apples and pears, are the mainstay of the region's agricultural industry. Thanks to its dry heat and lack of rainfall, wide variations in temperature between day and night, and the remarkable topography, Río Negro is one of Argentina's most natural and potentially exciting regions.

Soils here are composed of alluvial sand and

Grower Vollmer almost at the peak of Mount Cabernet.

gravel, becoming lighter and sandier the closer the vineyards are to the river, and vice versa. The region was unaffected by the trend toward volume production in the 1960s and the widescale conversion of vineyards to the pergola trellising system. As a result, the traditional vertical cordon training system still holds sway.

The British pioneered Río Negro's irrigation system at the start of the 20th century by damming the Río Neuquén upriver from the Río Negro to create a fertile valley some 75 miles (120 km) long by five miles (8 km) wide. The first to plant vines on a commercial basis was Humberto Canale, who brought vines from Bordeaux. Today, Humberto Canale is Río Negro's major winery, with Merlot, Malbec, Cabernet Sauvignon, and Pinot Noir the principal red varieties, the main whites being Semillon, Sauvignon, Torrontés, Chardonnay, and Riesling. Canale has been joined by a number of Mendoza-based companies, notably Fabre Montmayou, with its Infinitus range, and the giant Catena group, which has purchased 740 acres (300 ha) of land south of the Río Negro. For some time, in the Patagonian province of Chubut further south, Weinert has been planting Pinot Noir, Merlot, Chardonnay, Riesling, and Gewürztraminer.

Select Producers in Argentina

Achával Ferrer*****
Luján de Cuyo, Mendoza
59 acres (24 ha); 60,000 bottles • Wines: Malbec-Cabernet Sauvignon-Merlot, Malbec-Merlot, →Finca Altamira Grand Malbec
Achával Ferrer is the creation of four friends, one of whom is the Italian enologist Roberto Cipresso. Old genuine-rooted vineyards set high on the hills, and with low yields provide the grapes from which the magnificent single terroir Malbecs and Malbec blends are made.

La Agricola**—***
Maipú, Mendoza
1,483 acres (600 ha); 10,000,000 bottles • Wines: various varieties; brands Santa Julia, Santa Rosa, →"Q"
José Alberto Zuccardi, a tireless innovator, is one of the most enthusiastic and most respected ambassadors for Argentinian wine. A true practitioner, he introduced biological methods and is experimenting with a range of new varieties on 37 acres (15 ha).

Alta Vista***—****
Luján de Cuyo, Mendoza
764 acres (309 ha) • Wines include: Cosecha, →Premium Torronte, Chardonnay; Malbec Grande Réserve, →Alto
The Aulan family from Bordeaux has restored the Bodega restaurant dating from 1890, and they own vineyards in famous locations on different heights. With advice from Michel Rollands they are succeeding in making quality wines that earn the respect this *terroir* deserves.

Altos Las Hormingas***—****
Luján de Cuyo, Mendoza
99 acres (40 ha); bought-in grapes; 350,000 bottles • Wines: Altos la Hormigas Malbec, →Malbec Vina Hormigas
Six Italian friends and the Argentinian Carlos Vazquez started in 1995 with the aim of producing the best Argentinian Malbec from their excellent *terroir*. New cellar amidst the vineyards.

Bodega Lurton**—***
Alto Valle del Uco, Tunuyán
371 acres (150 ha); 2,000,000 bottles • Wines include: →Pinot Gris, Chardonnay; Bonarda, →Malbec, Gran Lurton, Piedra Negra
The Lurton brothers were the first to plant in Vista Flores and they set up their *bodega* in 1997. Initially they produced low-cost brand name wines, but now they are also making high-quality reds.

Bodega Norton***
Luján de Cuyo, Mendoza
1,680 acres (680 ha); bought-in grapes; 7,500,000 bottles • Wines include: Torrontés; Barbera, Tannat, →Privada, Perdriel, →Lo Tengo Malbec
Norton is a winery in the Napa style and under its winemaker Jorge Riccitelli it is making white and red wines that are very good value. Its Malbec is particularly convincing thanks to the hard work put into the vineyard.

Bodegas Esmeralda**—****
Mendoza
4,942 acres (2,000 ha); 20,000,000 bottles • Wines: wide variety of grapes and diverse brands
Nicolas Catena is one of the architects of the modern Argentinian wine industry. As well as the family winery Esmeralda, the Bodega Catena Zapata, built in the Inca-Maya style, produces 3,600,000 bottles of Alamos, Catena, →Catena Alta and →Nicolas Catena Zapata

from 1,050 acres (425 ha). The range also includes La Rural and Bodegas Escorihuela.

Bodegas Salentein***
Alto Valle de Uco, Tunuyán
862 acres (349 ha); 1,200,000 bottles • Wines include: Chardonnay, Sauvignon, Cabernet, Malbec, Tempranillo, Pinot Noir
In the Uco Valley vines are grown on the highest slopes of the Fincas of Salentein. Winemaker Laureano Gomez combines traditional craftsmanship with progressive technology in his cruciform cellars.

Bodegas Terrazas de los Andos**—***
Luján de Cuyo, Mendoza
988 acres (400 ha) • Wines include: Chardonnay, Malbec Reserva, Gran Malbec, →Gran Cabernet
The premium winery of the Chandon Group owns vineyards in the best locations. Director Roberto de la Mota has developed a convincing range here.

Bodegas y Cavas de Weinert***—****
Mendoza
99 acres (40 ha); bought-in grapes; 1,600,000 bottles • Wines include: Chardonnay, Chenin; Malbec, Cabernet, →Carrascal, →Gran Vino
Founded in 1893, this traditional winery, with its spectacular brick-vaulted cellars, was renovated by Bernardo Weinert after his purchase in 1975. The reds age in big old vats but retain a remarkably clear fruit. New and promising investment in the cool Chubut in Southern Patagonia.

Humberto Canale***
Río Negro, Patagonia
371 acres (150 ha) • Wines include: brands Canale Black River, Diego Murillo
Father Guillermo Barzi, and son Humberto Canale run the first winery to be set up in Patagonia. It was established by the family in 1913 and is still Patagonia's foremost winery, exploiting the region's potential for wines of impressive concentration in color, aroma, and taste.

Domaine Vistalba***
Mendoza/Río Negro
581 acres (235 ha); 700,000 bottles • Wines: Chardonnay, Sémillon; Cabernet, Merlot, Malbec, Syrah
The Frenchman Hervé Joyaux-Fabre founded Fabre Montmayou near Mendoza and the Bodega Infinitus in Rio Negro. While the former makes fine Malbecs and a Bordeaux blend, the latter produces elegant white and red *cuvées* with a clear, fruity aroma.

Finca La Anita****
Agrelo, Mendoza
297 acres (120 ha) • Wines include: →Semillon, Syrah, →Malbec
The brothers Antonio and Manuel Mas tend their vineyards using natural methods and they follow their own ideas in their cellars as well. The result is highly individual white and red wines with a growing range of *cuvées* as well.

Peñaflor**—***
Mendoza
3,212 acres (1,300 ha); bought-in grapes; 150,000,000 bottles • Wines: various brands
This enterprise sells most of its wines in Argentina under the brand names Termidor, Tomba, and Finca La Escondida, and in Great Britain as Bright Brothers. The estate belongs to the DLJ, Donaldson, Luftkin, & Jenrette investment fund, which also owns Trapiche, Finca La Moras, Michel Torino, and Santa Ana.

CHILE

When, in the 1970s, the Spanish producer Miguel Torres declared Chile "a viticultural paradise," his words provided inspiration to a new generation of winemakers and producers in a country whose wine industry had, until that turning point, been in decline.

In fact, Chile's wine industry has a long and often illustrious history, dating back over four centuries to the time when the Spanish conquistadors brought vines to make wine for sacramental purposes. It is not clear whether the first vines came via Peru, Mexico, or Spain itself, but it seems that the vine was first planted by Don Francisco de Aguirre at La Serena in 1551, and arrived in the Central Valley in 1554 with his son-in-law, Juan Jufré. While the early settlers brought not just the País, or Mission grape, but also Muscatel, Torontel, and Albilho, a wide range of *vinifera* cuttings was not brought to Chile until the early 1800s. Bertrand, Don Silvestre Ochagavía Echazareta started importing the vines of Bordeaux in 1851. Chile's geographic isolation helped it keep out the destructive phylloxera louse and so achieve a continuity not vouchsafed to wine industries in other countries.

After the glut and decline of the late 1960s, a law was passed in 1974 repealing the ban on establishing new vineyards and, gradually, more liberal legislation eased the industry forward. Attracted by low production costs and Chile's climate, with its long growing season and the big differences between day and night-time

The Viña Santa Amelia estate (founded in 1850) in Requinoa south of Santiago has been in Alsatian hands since 1990. They plow the 620 acres (250 ha) of vine plantations and run it ecologically. The wines are exported as Château Los Boldos.

Red wines from the Chilean market leader, Concha y Toro.

temperatures, Spain's Miguel Torres acquired a winery in Curicó in 1978. It was his investment, with temperature-controlled stainless steel tanks and small French oak BARRIQUES, which helped kick-start the modern industry. Since then, massive investment has gone into new plantings, with premium grape varieties and a real consciousness, for the first time, of making wines to international standards. Exports have indeed given the industry the incentive to focus on quality and character.

As a result, a number of smaller, boutique wineries have sprung up alongside the giants, with passionate Chilean winemakers such as Ignácio Recabarren, María del Pilar González, and Álvaro Espinoza determined in their resolve to express the character and complexity of their country's wine. At the same time, the quest for suitable vineyard locations for individual varieties has led to the discovery of new quality areas such as the Casablanca Valley, as well as cooler regions in the far south.

Chile's 264,000 acres (107,000 ha) of vineyard lie between the latitudes 27° and 39° south, a marginally smaller band than that of Argentina, with a hot climate mitigated by the influence of the Pacific's cold Humboldt current to the west, and by cool downdrafts off the Andes on its eastern border. While the Aconcagua and Casablanca Valleys are two important viticultural sub-regions north of Santiago, most of Chile's premium wines come from the sub-regions of the vast Central Valley, south of the capital. This consists of a series of transverse river valleys, Maipo, Rapel, Curicó, and Maule, in which the rivers run from the eastern slopes of the Andes to the Pacific Ocean. Further south still is Chile's Southern Region, consisting of the Itata and Bío Bío Valleys. The climate here is for the most part Mediterranean, with hot summers, relatively low humidity, and rainfall confined to winter. Generally, vines grow on flat, fertile land in which alluvial soils and clay/limestone predominate. Vineyards rise to around 1,970 feet (600 m) above sea level on the western slopes of the Central Valley, and up to 3,300 feet (1,000 m) on the sunny, eastern slopes of the Andes.

Historically, yields have tended to be high, thanks to a combination of irrigation, high-yielding grape varieties, and the high pergola system of trellising. In the 1990s there was greater awareness of yield reduction and the relationship between trellising, canopy manage-

ment, and optimum yield. The result is that, increasingly, premium vineyards are being planted according to TERROIR and climate, with better clones and greater vine density, partly with a view to mechanisation in the vineyard, and partly with quality in mind. Inspired by the enologist Alvaro Espinoza the growers are now also showing more interest in biological and biodynamic viticulture.

The most commonly planted grape variety in Chile is the País, also known as Mission in California and Criolla in Argentina, planted for the most part in unirrigated areas, a legacy from the Spanish conquistadors. The irrigated zone of the Central Valley, however, is host to a number of premium grape varieties descended from those brought back by pioneering Chileans in the 19th century. They remain ungrafted because of the lack of phylloxera.

The main premium red varieties are the Bordeaux varieties, Cabernet Sauvignon, Merlot, Cabernet Franc, and Malbec. Cabernet Sauvignon has an established record in the Maipo Valley where it can take on minty, herbal undertones. Merlot produces an especially appealing, soft, supple, easy-drinking style in Chile. Carmenère, or Grande Vidure, is an ancient Bordeaux variety, which has also been found to suit Chilean conditions well. Pinot Noir is used mostly for sparkling wine production but it can, in certain capable hands, make a surprisingly good-quality, and good-value, red table wine.

Viticulture would be impossible in Chile without water from the Andes. Irrigation has hitherto been by means of ditches created alongside the rows of vines. Modern plantations use drip irrigation.

Chile's rise to international fame as a wine producer began with the top Catalan grower Miguel Torres.

Chile's ability to produce good-value everyday whites from Chardonnay and Sauvignon has made it a natural focus for avid overseas importers. Chardonnay in Chile is often best cool-fermented in stainless steel to produce a richly flavored but not overly tropical style, while barrel fermentation can often add a degree of complexity, especially when the Chardonnay comes from cooler areas. A cooler climate is even more important for Sauvignon. Much of Chile's Sauvignon is not in fact Sauvignon Blanc at all, but Sauvignon Vert, or Tocai Friulano. Chile also produces smaller quantities of attractive Gewürztraminer, as well as decent Riesling, Semillon, and Chenin Blanc.

Investment in the modern industry has brought not just modern winemaking equipment to Chile's wineries, but also a fundamental shift in attitude, including an awareness of the difference that hygiene can make at all stages of the winemaking process. This was initially thanks, in large part, to the expertise of overseas winemakers, and because Chile's own winemakers went abroad to experience, at first hand, winemaking in other countries. The old-fashioned oxidized styles have been replaced by fresher, fruitier wines, thanks to new equipment, better selection of grapes, and the need to bring grapes into the winery in the healthiest possible state. The old chestnut-wood casks have mostly been removed and replaced by French and American oak, and much-needed cooling and bottling facilities have been provided.

CHILE'S WINE REGIONS

NORTH
☐ Atacama
☐ Coquimbo
ACONCAGUA
☐ Aconcagua
☐ Casablanca
CENTRAL VALLEY
☐ Maipo
☐ Rapel
☐ Curicó
☐ Maule
SOUTH
☐ Itata
☐ Bío Bío
☐ Wine-growing areas in neighboring countries

North of Santiago, the Aconcagua region contains the two sub-regions of the Casablanca Valley and the Aconcagua Valley itself. Cooled by Pacific morning fogs and breezes, the Casablanca Valley, which lies on the coastal plain about 18½ miles (30 km) southeast of Valparaíso, has become, in a short space of time, one of Chile's top regions for crisp, elegant whites made from Sauvignon and Chardonnay, at the same time producing flavorsome, minty reds from Merlot and Cabernet Sauvignon. With upwards of 7,400 acres (3,000 ha), this temperate sub-region was pioneered by Pablo Morande in 1982 and is now planted with vineyards owned by, among others, Concha y Toro, Santa Carolina, Viña Casablanca, Franciscan, Villard, and Santa Rita. The much higher Aconcagua Valley is also much smaller, with around 990 acres (400 ha), but in Errázuriz Estate's Don Maximiano, it includes one of Chile's top premium wines.

If any region can lay claim to the word "classic," it is the Maipo Valley to the west and south of Santiago. The Maipo Valley, which is sub-divided into six districts, comprises nearly 19,800 acres (8,000 ha) of vineyards, some of which overlook the city of Santiago, split evenly between red and white. The climate of Maipo, which is bisected by the river of the same name, is warm and temperate. Because of its proximity to Santiago, Maipo contains the head-

Cousiño Macul is well-known for red wines with aging ability.

Although San Pedro is one of the wine giants of Chile and has a highly modern winery, the grapes continue to be picked and brought in by hand.

quarters of many of Chile's oldest and biggest wineries, among them Concha y Toro, Santa Carolina, Santa Rita, and Valdivieso, and some of its most traditional in Cousiño Macul and Undurraga. Concha y Toro's Don Melchor, Santa Rita's Medalla Real, and Cousiño Macul's Antiguas Reservas are among Chile's best Bordeaux-style red wines, while Carmen is a modern winery to watch.

Further south, the Rapel Valley contains the two main sub-regions of the Cachapoal Valley and the Colchagua Valley, and comprises some 48,430 acres (19,600 ha) of vineyards planted on mainly alluvial soils at between 1,970 and 3,280 feet (600 and 1,000 m) above sea level. With Rancagua at the heart of the region, the Mediterranean climate is marginally wetter and windier than that of Maipo. It is a predominantly red wine region, with traditional wineries such as Bisquertt, Porta, Santa Emiliana, Santa Mónica, Torreón de Paredes, and Château Lafite's Los Vascos at Peralillo. There are a number of up-and-coming stars here, notably Viña Gracia, Luis Felipe Edwards, Casa Lapostolle, and MontGras, while Cono Sur is noted for its Cabernet Sauvignon and Pinot Noir.

There are approximately 36,000 acres (14,600 ha) planted in the Curicó Valley, which is subdivided into two smaller regions of the Teno and Lontue Valleys. Important wineries here include Viña Montes, San Pedro, and Torres. It is best known for the quality of its Chardonnay, although Valdivieso makes excellent value-for-money reds from Pinot Noir, Cabernet Sauvignon, Cabernet Franc, and Merlot.

With the coastal mountain range to the west and the Andes to the east, the Maule Valley contains three major sub-zones in the Claro, Loncomilla, and Tutuven Valleys, and comprises more than 56,830 acres (23,000 ha) of vineyard. With its volcanic soils and rolling hills, the climate here is Mediterranean, with relatively

Harvest workers having a break in the shadow of the vines. The wine-growing estates of Chile are among the country's biggest employers.

heavy winter rainfall, while its Pacific-influenced vineyards are often cooler than those of the regions immediately to the north. Notable producers here are Viña Calina, Carta Vieja, Bouchon, and Terra Noble, and reds are generally better than whites.

The southern region is subdivided into the Itata and Bío-Bío Valleys. Unlike regions further north, it is not sheltered by the coastal mountain range, so rainfall is much higher here, while average temperatures and sunshine hours are lower. Most of the wine from this unirrigated region is derived from the prolific País, or Mission vine, although there is also a significant amount of Muscat of Alexandria. Following research into this area's potential, new locations for premium-quality wines are sprouting up, notably Mulchen, which is well-suited to aromatic varieties such as Riesling and Gewürztraminer.

Pisco

The name of pisco, the national spirit of Chile, is derived from *piscu*, meaning "flying bird" in the language of the Incas, Quechua. It is made in the Pisco region of northern Chile around La Serena and Coquimbo, by distilling wine made mostly from Moscatel (Muscat) grapes. On May 16, 1931 it became the first alcoholic beverage to be protected by its own *denominación de origen*. There are some 14,800 acres (6,000 ha) of vineyard planted for the production of pisco, the main ones located in the Elqui and Limari Valleys. After fermentation and distillation in copper stills, the spirit is aged in large chestnut or oak casks for between four months and a year. The spirit is then diluted to one of four grades, varying between 30 percent (*selección*), 35 percent (*especial*), 40 percent (*reservado*), and 43 percent (*gran pisco*). It is a highly aromatic spirit, with characteristic aromas of prune, plum, bitter almond, and vanilla.

Pisco Sour

4 *measures pisco*
1 *measure fresh lemon or lime juice*
ice cubes
1 *teaspoon egg white (optional)*
sugar to taste

Combine in a cocktail shaker, shake vigorously and strain into glasses. The egg white gives the drink a foaming head.

Made with fresh lemon (or lime) juice, this is one of the great summer drinks.

A typical pisco bar in Chile.

Select Producers in Chile

Antiyal****
Maipo Valley
7 acres (3 ha); 55,000 bottles • Wine: Antiyal
The enologist Alvaro Espinoza cultivates his own vineyard of two and a half acres (1 ha), plus another 5 acres (2 ha) belonging to his parents in the Isla de Maipo. Antiyal, introduced in 1998, is a blend of Cabernet, Syrah, and Carmenère. One of Chile's authentic red wines, it is very balanced, with clean fruit and a mineral quality.

Carmen***
Maipo Valley
1,186 acres (480 ha); 6,000,000 bottles • Wines: various varietals; brands: Classic, Reserve, Nativa, →Gold Reserve
Vineyards in Maipo, Casablanca, Rapel, and Curicó. After the departure of Alvaro Espizo, who developed the organic Nativa range, the chief winemaker María del Pilar González has given the wine more distinct fruit since the spring of 2000. She carefully watches for the precise harvesting point which will achieve an optimum balance between ripeness, alcohol, tannins, and acidity.

Casa Lapostolle***–****
Santa Cruz, Colchagua Valley
790 acres (320 ha); some bought-in grapes; 1,800,000 bottles • Wines: Chardonnay, Sauvignon; Cabernet Sauvignon, Merlot; Series: Tanao, →Cuvée Alexandre, →Clos Apalta
Thanks to the talented French winemaker Michel Friou and the advice, exclusive within Chile, of Michel Rolland, Marnier-Lapostolle, owners of the Grand Marnier liqueur, succeed in producing some of Chile's best red wines. Vineyards in Apalta, Requinoa, and Casablanca.

Concha y Toro**–****
Santiago
9,243 acres (3,742 ha); some bought-in grapes; 73,200,000 bottles • Wines: various varietals and blends under several labels, including Concha y Toro, Casillero del Diablo, Trio, Explorer, Marques de Casa Concha brands; Amelia Chardonnay, →Don Melchor Cabernet Sauvignon, →Almaviva
Chile's biggest wine company, with extensive vineyards and wineries in Maipo, Rapel, Casablanca, and Lontue. Chief winemakers are Marcello Papa for Casillero del Diablo and Marques, Ignácio Recabarren for Trio, Terrunyo, and Amelia, and Enrique Tirado for Don Melchor and Almaviva, a joint venture with Baron Philippe de Rothschild in Puento Alto in the Maipo Valley.

Cono Sur**–***
Chimbarongo, Rapel Valley
741 acres (300 ha); some bought-in grapes; 3,600,000 bottles • Wines: Chardonnay, Riesling, Gewürztraminer, Viognier, Pinot Noir, Cabernet, Merlot, Carmenère, Syrah; brands: Tocornal, Isla Negra
Owned by Concha y Toro, this winery was put on the map by Ed Flaherty. In 1997, Adolfe Hurtado became principal winemaker. Since then, Cono Sur has been able to consolidate its position as one of Chile's most reliable brands.

Cousiño Macul***
Maipo Valley
956 acres (387 ha) • Wines include: Sauvignon, Riesling, Cabernet, Merlot, Antiguas Reservas, →Finis Terrae
Chile's most traditional winery, set in beautiful grounds just outside Santiago, produces classic reds which age well in good vintages. The winery has purchased a second modern estate plus a high quality winery in Buin. The wines now mature for a shorter period in new *barriques*.

Errázuriz**–****
Aconcagua
4,800,000 bottles • Wines: various varietals. Series: Max Reserva, Don Maximiano, →Seña, →Chadwick
Based at Panquehue, and owned by the Chadwick family since 1983, this is one of Chile's top estates. The Californian winemaker Ed Flaherty produces fine, elegant whites using grapes from the Casablanca valley, and good reds, in particular a ripe, fruity Merlot, a berry-rich Syrah and a rich, minty Don Maximiano using Cabernet grapes from the eponymous vineyard. The ultra-premium wine Seña is produced together with Robert Mondavi. Caliterra, the sister company, has a range of standard wines with six varietals, three *reservas*, and the premium series Arboleda.

Montes***–****
Apalta, Colchagua Valley
1,235 acres (500 ha); some bought-in grapes; 3,600,000 bottles • Wines include: Chardonnay, Sauvignon; Cabernet, Merlot, Malbec, Syrah, Pinot Noir, Montes Alpha, →Montes "M," →Montes Folly
In 1988, four partners, including winemaker Aurelio Montes, started this premium winery with its own estates in Curicó and Colchagua. Quality rapidly increased, with substantial Chardonnay, aromatic Sauvignon, and interesting Malbec; selected grapes go to make Montes Alpha, and there are also the premium wines Montes "M" and the Syrah Montes Folly from the new vineyards in the Apalta Valley.

Santa Carolina**–***
Santiago
4,076 acres (1,650 ha); 15,000,000 bottles • Wines (export) include: Chardonnay, Sauvignon, Gewürztraminer; Cabernet, Merlot, Carmenère, Syrah, Pinot Noir, Malbec, VSC
Chile's fourth largest wine company, with five wineries in different wine regions. Among the brands is Viña Casablanca, whose Casablanca Valley Isabel Estate produces intense whites and reds.

Santa Rita**–****
Maipo Valley
5,385 acres (2,180 ha); 15,500,000 bottles • Wines (export) include a broad range of varietals and blends; series: Reserva, Medalla Real, Floresta, Triple "C," →Casa Real
Purchased by the businessman Ricardo Claro in 1980, Santa Rita is today the second biggest wine group in Chile. It produces a competent range of varietals and blends with some high quality wines under the new Floresta and Triple "C" labels. Carmen and Sur Andino also belong to Santa Rita.

Torréon de Paredes**–***
Rapel Valley
371 acres (150 ha); 1,200,000 bottles • Wines include: Chardonnay, Sauvignon, →Semillon; Cabernet, Merlot, →Don Amado. Series: Collecíon Privada, Reserva
On this family estate, cultivated using natural methods, the brothers Javier and Alvaro Paredes bottle wines made exclusively from their own grapes. Their winemaker Yves Pouzot succeeds in producing very stylish wines, including what is probably the best Sémillon in Chile.

Torres**–***
Curicó
1,840 acres (745 ha); 3,000,000 bottles • Wines include: Chardonnay, Riesling; Cabernet, Merlot, Carmenère; brand: Santa Digna
After declaring Chile to be a viticultural paradise, Miguel Torres from Spain invested here in 1979. He

pioneered fruitier wines using modern fermentation methods. In the 1990s he was overtaken by others, but is now back on form with a crisp Sauvignon, a juicy Cabernet, and a full, cassis-centred red, Manso de Velasco.

VALDIVIESO**−***
CURICÓ
494 acres (200 ha); some bought-in grapes; 4,800,000 bottles • Wines: Chardonnay, Sauvignon, Merlot, Cabernet, Malbec, Pinot Noir; →Caballo Loco; series: Barrel Selection, Reserve
This wine company is owned by the Mitjans family, formerly known for their sparkling wine. Since the late 1980s it has been producing serious still wines, now made by the New Zealander Brett Jackson.

VIÑA MONTGRAS**−***
COLCHAGUA VALLEY
1,235 acres (500 ha); 3,800,000 bottles • Wines: various varietals; series: estate series, Reserva, Special Reserva Limited Edition, →Quattro, →Ninquén
The MontGras estate was the first to plant hillside sites, investing five million US dollars in Ninquén. With the American Paul Hibbs as consultant, and winemaker Hernan Gras, MontGras also pioneered Carmenère and single vineyard varietal bottlings such as Viognier, Syrah, and Malbec.

VIÑA LA ROSA**−***
RAPEL VALLEY
1,828 acres (740 ha); 6,000,000 bottles • Wines: various varietals; brands include: Viña La Rosa, La Pamería, →Casa Leona
Owned by the Ossa family since 1824, this estate in Puemo makes a good, commercial range of varietal wines under winemaker José Ignacio Cancino and consultant Goetz von Gersdorff.

VIÑA MORANDÉ**−***
RAPEL VALLEY
988 acres (400 ha); 6,000,000 bottles • Wines: various varietals; series include: Pionero, Premium House of Morandé, →Vitistera Gran Reserva, Terrarum Reserva, →Dueto
Pablo Morandé was the first to cultivate vines in the cool Casablanca Valley. This innovative project comprises several premium wines from the Casablanca, Rapel, and Maipo valleys, with an unusual range of varietals made from Cabernet Franc, Pinot Noir, Carmenère, Malbec, Carignan, Sangiovese, or Gewürztraminer.

VIÑA SAN PEDRO**−***
CURICÓ
6,175 acres (2,500 ha); some bought-in grapes; 36,000,000 bottles • Wines include: Chardonnay, Sauvignon; Cabernet, Merlot, Malbec, →Cabo de Hornos
Thanks to a new vinification plant, Frenchman Jacques Lurton and winemaker Irene Paiva have helped to turn this Molina-based giant into one of Chile's most successful commercial enterprises. The Sauvignon 35 Sur is a model of Chilean wine, with an outstanding price-performance ratio.

VIÑA SANTA INÉS DE MARTINO***
MAIPO VALLEY
741 acres (330 ha); some bought-in grapes; 3,600,000 bottles • Wines include: Chardonnay, Sauvignon; Merlot, Cabernet, →Malbec, Pinot Noir, Syrah, →Gran Familia; series: Santa Inés, De Martino
After successfully researching the best suited grape varieties for the best situated vineyards, this family winery, with the help of winemaker Marcelo Retamal and consultant Aurelio Montes, has achieved a marked improvement in the quality of its wines. Their first organic wine, under the Nuevo Mondo label, was bottled in 2001.

The Casablanca Valley in the north of the country was only discovered as a wine region in the 1980s by the enologist Pablo Morandé. With a climate tempered by a wind from the Pacific, the main varieties to flourish are convincing Chardonnay and Sauvignon.

Other Wine-growing Countries in South America

Brazil

Brazil comes next in importance to Argentina and Chile, with an average production of some 79 million gallons (3 million hectoliters). The vine was first introduced into the country by the Portuguese in 1532 and disseminated, as in the case of other parts of South America, by the Jesuits. Unlike Chile and Argentina, however, a major wine industry was not established until the 20th century and, even then, Brazil has no strong indigenous wine culture. Despite the relatively high level of production, consumption is at only around a half gallon (2 liters) per head.

Vines from cuttings in Madeira and the Azores were brought to Brazil by 18th-century settlers, but they struggled in Brazil's humid, warm climate. The hybrid *labrusca* vine, Isabella, was the first to be able to withstand Brazil's climate, while in the late-19th century, Italian settlers brought their own Barbera, Bonarda, Moscato, and Trebbiano to the high Serra Gaucha region, in the northeast of the Río Grande.

The modern industry began in the 1970s with the arrival of international wine companies Moët et Chandon and Martini & Rossi. Premium grape varieties were imported, notably Chardonnay, Semillon, Gewürztraminer, Cabernet Sauvignon, Merlot, and Cabernet Franc. The main viticultural area is the Rio Grande do Sul, in the far south, with vineyards concentrated in the hilly Serra

French grape varieties dominate Uruguay's vineyards.

Gaucha region. Rainfall is high, with high humidity which brings with it problems of ripening and rot. More recently, vineyards have been planted in the flatter Frontera region bordering Uruguay and Argentina with its well-drained sandy soils. This looks to be the region with the greatest potential for quality wine.

Uruguay

In contrast to Brazil, in Uruguay wine consumption is as high as 8½ gallons (32 liters) per head in a country with a tiny population of only 3.2 million, and consequently Uruguayans drink 98 percent of production.

The first commercial vineyard was established near Salto by a Basque, Pascal Harriague. A wave of Italian settlers brought Italian varieties with them, but French varieties, as in Chile, still predominate, with Ugni Blanc, Semillon and smaller quantities of Chardonnay, Gewürztraminer, and Sauvignon Blanc for whites, and for reds, Cabernet Sauvignon, Cabernet Franc, Syrah, and Merlot. Vineyards are concentrated close to the capital in the departments of Canelones, San José, and Montevideo, although there are vines planted also in Colonia, across the River Plate from Buenos Aires, and in the hotter zone north of the River Negro in Salto, Paysandú, and Rivera.

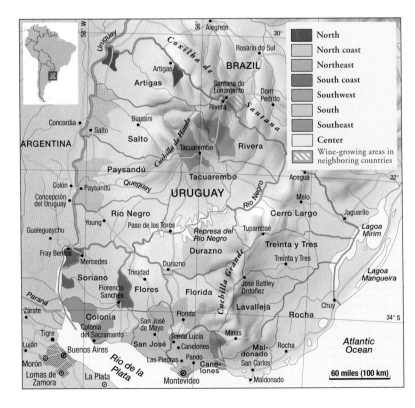

SELECT PRODUCERS IN BRAZIL AND URUGUAY

BRAZIL

CHANDON BRAZIL**
SÃO PAULO
74 acres (30 ha); bought-in grapes; 2,300,000 bottles
• *Wines: sparkling brands: Chandon Brut, Chandon Demi-sec, Chandon Passion, Chandon Excellence, Chandon Cuvée du Millénaire, Chandon Cuvée Brazil 500 years*
Established as one of Moët et Chandon's outposts in the face of the limits to growth within the Champagne region, Chandon Brazil has now become so successful on the domestic market that it is Moët's only overseas set-up not to export under the Chandon brand name. Vineyards are at Garibaldi in the Serra Gaucha region, where it also buys in grapes.

URUGUAY

PISANO FAMILY VINEYARDS**
PROGRESO COASTAL REGION
74 acres (30 ha); bought-in grapes; 300,000 bottles
• *Wines include: Torrontés, Viognier-Chardonnay;*
→ *1st Vineyard Collection Tannat, Merlot-Tannat, Syrah-Tannat, RPF Tannat, Pinot Noir, Petit Verdot,*
→ *Pisano-Arretxea*
This family enterprise was founded in 1924 and it has its own vineyards on clay and chalky soil in the cool, maritime climate of the Rio de la Plata, 15½ miles (25 km) north of the capital, Montevideo. Pisano began to buy in more grapes in 1998, when demand for exports rose. Now that the new vineyards are yielding full crops he can supply almost all his need from his own estate. The winery is particularly well known for its Tannat.

Tannat has been grown in Uruguay for more than a century, since its introduction by Basque settlers in the 19th century. Today 7,166 acres (2,900 ha) of the country's total of 22,240 acres (9,000 ha) of vineyards grow Tannat. It is also known as Harriague after the famous wine pioneer. Tannat is a dark, thick-skinned variety, rich in tannin and with a rich fruity aroma that recalls blackberries. It well suits Uruguay's relatively moist climate. The wines range in style from the traditional dark rosé to the modern reds matured in *barriques*, like Casa Lunto by Jacques Lurton, Juanico, Stagnari, and Pisano; it is also often blended with Bordeaux varieties.

PERU AND OTHER COUNTRIES

Peru was the first country in South America in which vines were systematically cultivated, with an estimated 99,000 acres (40,000 ha) of vineyard as early as the 16th century. But whereas Chile and Argentina escaped the ravages of phylloxera, Peru's vineyards were extensively damaged in the late 19th century by the pest. Only since the 1970s has a modern wine industry really started up again, and today there are some 29,652 acres (12,000 ha) of vines mostly on the central coast near Pisco and in the south around Inca. Given its northerly location, winters are warm, which makes vine dormancy impossible and two crops a year obtainable. A mixture of French, Italian, and Spanish grape varieties has been planted, but most grapes are used for the production of pisco.

Ecuador, Bolivia, Colombia, and Venezuela all produce small amounts of wine. Bolivia's climate is both tropical and continental and most vineyards here are planted at over 6,600 feet (2,000 m) above sea level. There are some 4,200 acres (1,700 ha) of vineyard based in the southern zone of Canargo and Tarija. Muscat of Alexandria accounts for three-quarters of Bolivia's *vinifera* grapes.

Ecuador's tropical climate can produce up to three crops a year, although the best wine comes from the cooler mountain provinces. Colombia is also tropical, with some 3,700 acres (1,500 ha) of vines. Most of its wines are produced from hybrid vines in the northern zone of Santa Marta, although there are experimental plantings of premium French varieties, notably Cabernet Sauvignon and Chardonnay. Venezuela is a minor player in South America, with mostly hybrid grapes grown, plus small quantities of Grillo, Barbera, and Malvasia.

In Uruguay, wine is bottled in traditional demijohns.

ANTHONY ROSE

AUSTRALIA AND
NEW ZEALAND

FROM THE FIRST VINES TO AN INDUSTRY

On a condescending note, not untypical of the British toward the colonies, the English wine merchant T.G. Shaw wrote of Australia in the 1864 edition of *Wine, the Vine and the Cellar*: "So far as I can learn, Australia is not well adapted, either by soil or climate, for growing wine, and this opinion seems confirmed by the unsuccessful efforts of many years." Perhaps you cannot blame the man for being skeptical. The composition of Australia's climate and soil is so different from European standards that a man raised on claret, port, and champagne might well take a dim view of Australia's potential as a wine producer.

The first vines in Australia had already been planted back in 1788 on the site of the Intercontinental Hotel in Macquarie Street, Sydney, soon after Captain Arthur Phillip established Port Jackson as a convict settlement on January 26. From a few vines, an industry grew. It was the sheep-breeder, Captain John Macarthur, who laid the early foundations for Australia's 19th-century wine industry, bringing a wealth of vines back from France after investigating the French industry with his sons William and James. The explorer Gregory Blaxland, together with a young immigrant from

The imposing Yalumba Winery in the Barossa Valley was built at the end of the 19th century. The best-known wine of the family-owned firm is Angas sparkling wine.

At Penfolds, the pioneer George Fife Angas is commemorated on a barrel. From 1838, Angas brought refugee Lutheran Protestants to the Barossa Valley, and their role in developing viticulture was vital.

Edinburgh, James Busby, were major pioneering figures. Busby in particular, "the father of the Australian wine industry," brought a host of vines to Australia which he had collected on his travels in France and Spain, among them the Pineau Chardonnay (*sic*) and Pineau Noir (*sic*) from Clos Vougeot. In Western Australia, botanist Thomas Waters planted vines in 1829.

By the 1850s, Victoria's vineyards were spreading as the rush to the goldmines of Ballarat, Rutherglen, and Bendigo gathered pace. South Australia received a boost from the influx of Lutheran dissenters from Silesia, who were brought to Australia in the mid-1850s by, among others, the Smiths of Yalumba and the philanthropic Scotsman George Angas. By 1870, the author Anthony Trollope was able to report: "In all the Australian colonies, except Tasmania, wine is made plentifully." In that year, about 2.3 million gallons (8.7 million liters) were produced, and Australian wines started to win medals. At the 1873 Vienna Exhibition, a Victorian "Hermitage" was judged best of its type by an international jury, causing the French to walk out in disgust (they had assumed one of their wines would be picked).

Soon after, in 1877, the PHYLLOXERA louse struck. Discovered near Geelong in Victoria, it caused extensive damage in Victoria, but South Australia and New South Wales escaped. Nevertheless, the early promise faded, partly due to phylloxera but also because of changes in export markets and a developing local taste for stronger, sweeter wine.

Victoria was the pre-eminent wine state in the latter half of the 19th century, earning itself the nickname "John Bull's vineyard" for its exports to the United Kingdom. Then, in the first half of the 20th century, South Australia usurped the crown. Lutherans from Silesia had already established the Barossa Valley as a wine-growing center, and by 1930 South Australia, with the Barossa Valley at the hub, was producing three-quarters of all Australian wine. Many grapes were grown in the warm, irrigated area known as Riverland, and processed by the Teutonic winemaking families of the Barossa Valley. Between 1927 and 1939, when Australian trade benefited from the British imperial preference system, Australia exported a huge amount of wine to the United Kingdom, some with a high alcohol content, designed to strengthen thinner French wines, and some FORTIFIED WINES.

Delusions of Grandeur and Paradox

In the post-war era, immigrants who had a tradition of drinking wine with meals came to Australia. Technology brought stainless steel and with it the ability to make dry wines in volume. At the same time, big companies started to expand plantings in existing locations such as Riverina, Loxton, Berri, and Renmark, and plant new regions such as Padthaway and Drumborg. Regions with a developing reputation for fine wines continued to grow, among them Coonawarra, Clare Valley, McLaren Vale, and the Hunter Valley.

It was in 1951, following a visit to France, that Max Schubert of Penfolds created Grange Hermitage, based on the Shiraz grape. Now the most famous of all Australia's wines, Penfolds Grange was trashed by critics when it first appeared, being described as a dry port and worse. Schubert was ordered to cease production, but fortunately for Penfolds and Australian wine he had the foresight to disobey his master's orders and carry on. When the 1955 vintage was entered in the open claret class in the 1962 Royal Sydney Show, it duly struck gold and went on to win a total of 51 gold medals and 12 trophies.

In the 1960s, eating and drinking societies and wine clubs proliferated throughout Australia. Along with this movement, the demand for red wine accelerated so rapidly that Len Evans, one of Australia's most outspoken and influential proponents, wrote at the time: "The rapid acceleration in interest and consumption has caught the wine companies with their production pants down." He also pointed out that Shiraz was the variety best suited to Australia's soils and climate, a prescient point, which has been confirmed by the passage of time.

The red-wine boom coincided with plantings on unsuitable soils, overcropping in some instances and, as has so often happened in other countries in response to demand, a downturn in quality. Then, in the mid-1970s, the red-wine boom suddenly ended and there was a glut. For a while, demand switched from red to white wines, but now the wheel has turned full circle, with premium reds made from Shiraz and Cabernet Sauvignon once again in demand.

The Wine Barons

The robustness of Australia's reds has been matched by a number of equally forthright characters who, either in their winemaking or through their communication skills, have been influential in the development of Australian

Cyril Henschke made his Shiraz Hill of Grace one of Australia's most sought-after red wines. His son Stephen has succeeded in maintaining the quality.

Left
Grower and writer James Halliday.

Right
Peter Lehmann, the legendary Baron Barossa, a pioneer of German descent.

wines. Len Evans, who has been mentioned already, left England in 1958 for Sydney, where he began a lifelong mission to preach the joys of Australian wine as well as produce it. James Halliday, an equally forthright character, gave up a lucrative legal practice to make wine at Coldstream Hills in the Yarra Valley and communicate his enthusiasm for the grape in countless books and newspaper articles.

Each region in Australia has had its share of winemakers who have innovated, set standards, and articulated the pleasures of Australian wine with a quality and style that equals the wines they have produced. Along with Len Evans, both Max Lake and Murray Tyrrell were instrumental in putting the Hunter Valley on the map in the late 1960s. In Victoria, Mick Morris and the Campbells of Rutherglen honed the rich aromatic fortified Muscats and Tokays of northeast Victoria, while in Western Australia Jack Mann created Houghton's White Burgundy, which became one of Australia's best-selling white wines.

Among those who have been highly influential in the South Australian wine industry are Max Schubert at Penfolds, and Cyril Henschke with Hill of Grace, who set standards for Shiraz that others still strive to emulate. With his immaculate blending and barrel-aging of reds, Wolf Blass dominated the wine shows in the mid-1970s, winning three consecutive, coveted Jimmy Watson trophies for Wolf Blass Black Label in 1974, 1975, and 1976. In 1977, when the big companies stopped buying grapes from their growers because of the red wine glut, Peter Lehmann, the legendary "Bear of the Barossa," kept the flame alight by purchasing grapes and making wine himself. His robust attitude contributed in no small measure to the subsequent revival of Barossa Valley wines.

THE EMANCIPATION OF AUSTRALIAN WINES

Before varietal wines established themselves and Australia's growers pursued an individual path, attempts were made to sell wines imitating famous labels such as Chablis, Moselle, and even Lambrusco.

Australia's wine regions have established images of their own, and the number of premium wines on offer is rising sharply. This is very evident from the range of wines available in Australian wine stores.

"The traditional market in the U.K. will not grow greatly, and our top-quality wines will always suffer from the inborn, carefully perpetuated, and slightly supercilious snobbery that exists there." A generation after writing this fortuitously ill-fated pronouncement, the celebrated author and winemaker Len Evans is no doubt as delighted as anyone to have been forced to eat (and drink) his own words. For Australia is the success story of the modern era, coming from nowhere to become a significant player on the world stage.

While the modern Australian wine industry is founded on a diversity of styles, broadly based on the classic styles of Europe, the legacy of a century-old industry has given Australia a wealth of original wine styles. These range from the toasty Semillons of the Hunter Valley, the big, bold reds made from Barossa Valley Shiraz, to the sticky fortified Muscats and Tokays of northeast Victoria.

While many European countries have been busy uprooting unwanted vines, Australia has planted them. Where European countries have been casting around for importers, Australia has embarked on an aggressive export plan for the new millennium. It is a success story based on the confident will to succeed, together with an awareness of quality and appreciation of consumer tastes, whether for aromatic or dry table wines, sparkling or fortified. Today, Australia has about 1,500 wineries, from big concerns like Southcorp, Orlando, and Constellation Brands Thomas Hardy to committed one-man enterprises that are often run by a doctor or lawyer determined to give the Australian wine industry a little individuality.

Australia has gone through major changes since the late 1950s, when the modern wine industry was born. In that period, not much more than 98,400 tons/tonnes of basic grape varieties were crushed. Less than 10 percent of the total harvest was of premium varieties. By the mid-1980s, roughly 80 percent of Australian wine was sold in BAG IN A BOX or bulk with some five percent premium bottled wine. Since then, there has been a dramatic shift to premium varieties, notably Chardonnay, Semillon, and Riesling among the white varieties, and Shiraz and Cabernet Sauvignon among the reds. At the start of the new millennium, the total amount of grapes crushed was nearly one million tons, of which premium varieties represented well over 60 percent, and was increasing.

ENERGY FROM THE SUN AND COOLING TECHNOLOGY

As Australian wine producers have adopted and adapted the styles of the producers they most admire, they have come to realize that they can produce wines in a style that is uniquely Australian and, as such, much in demand. What is that style? In a nutshell, Australian wine is about intense fruitiness, abundance of flavor, and softness of texture, molded by exceptional sunshine and warmth. With fruit and flavor come cleanness of taste and the less appreciated, but no less discernible, texture. Typically, Australian wines have a lovely softness and rounded texture that makes them instantly accessible. These are not wines that have to be laid down forever in dark, damp cellars. Their appeal is not their longevity but their drinkability.

Technology (in particular, refrigeration), and subsequently night-harvesting and care in handling the grape juice, have played a crucial role in the modern evolution of Australian wine. The modern industry is founded on cold FERMENTATION, which enabled producers to move away from fortified wines to lighter table wines. The necessity for this is brought home by the author Oliver Mayo, who points out that while "in Europe grapes are grown on the warm fringes of a cold continent, in Australia they are grown on the cold margins of a hot continent." This means that, for the most part, Australia's viticultural regions are not in the hottest parts of the country and, with only a handful of exceptions, are never far from the ocean.

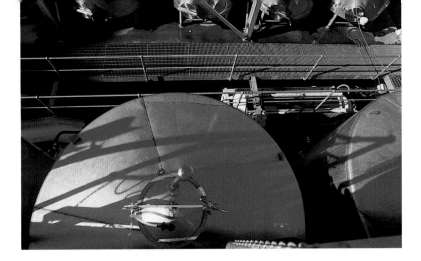

The Australian wine-show system has been instrumental in honing style and maintaining the quality of Australian wines. Australian wine producers submit their wines, almost without exception, to the local, regional or national show to be judged, like cows or sheep, for bronze, silver or gold medals, and trophies. Not only does this system have its marketing and promotional uses, but it also acts as a benchmark for winemakers.

Perhaps the most obvious difference between Australian and European wines is that the choice of Australian vineyards is not influenced by TERROIR in the way that traditional European vineyards are. In a hot country such as Australia, climate is considered to be of greater importance to producers than the composition of the soil, the slope of the hillside, and the altitude. Grapes are grown where it is most convenient to plant vines and so market the wines. It is no coincidence that the concentration of Australia's wine industry is around such major conurbations as Sydney, Melbourne, Adelaide, and Perth.

Thanks to this tradition, Australian wines are also blends that cut across regional or even state boundaries. The master winemaker in Australia is the master blender, the person who knows exactly what properties each region contributes to the final blend. Even Australia's greatest wine, Penfolds Grange Hermitage, is a regional blend of wines from various different vineyards within South Australia, blended to the proportion desired by the winemaker. For this reason, the winemaker has always been an important character on the Australian scene.

THE RISE OF REGIONAL IDENTITY?

Traditional attitudes are changing, however, as the focus turns towards the vineyard. Not content to settle for fruit and flavor, Australian producers have gone in search of some more elusive qualities, namely subtlety, structure, elegance, and complexity. Regional differences are becoming increasingly important as producers who previously supplied grapes to the big companies have set up on their own and started to win back some regional identity. At one time, the map of Australian vineyards

The breakdown of Australian wines (in %) of world-wide production, consumption, export, and import				
Year	Production	Consumption	Exports	Imports
1966–1970	0.8	0.7	0.3	0.0
1986–1990	1.4	1.4	0.7	0.2
1997	2.4	1.5	2.5	0.3
2000	3.1	1.6	4.5	0.2
2001	3.3	1.6	5.2	0.2

showed little more than state boundaries. Today, vineyards such as McLaren Vale, Clare Valley, Mudgee, Mornington, and Eden Valley are staking their claim, while newer names, including Pemberton, Kuitpo, Robe, and Orange, are adding detail.

Australian producers have realized that to obtain elegance and structure they need to go in search of cooler locations, either up hillsides or in regions further south. And so Victoria, which lost out to South Australia in terms of importance, is now very much back on the map, with a host of small districts and regions under development. Tasmania is becoming more important, along with the southernmost parts of Western Australia. And in South Australia itself, huge vineyard sites have been planted on the Limestone Coast at Cuppacup, Robe, and Wrattonbully. Even New South Wales is coming up with cool climate areas such as Orange, and, for sparkling wines, the dramatically named Tumbarumba. The vineyards of the future have laid down the gauntlet to the vineyards of the present. The result is that by adapting to change, both can survive and prosper to increase the range of wine styles and improve the quality of Australian wines.

Australia has become a pioneer of modern enology and winery technology. Temperature-controlled, stainless steel fermentation tanks are standard equipment here.

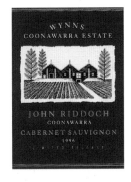

Australian wine statistics	1997–1998	1998–1999	1999–2000	2000–2001	2001–2002
Wine producers	1,104	1,115	1,197	1,318	1,465
Area planted to vines in acres	243,571	303,719	345,592	366,383	391,880
Grape output in tons/tonnes	1,075,675	1,108,268	1,126,969	1,401,575	1,580,709
Wine output in million gallons	180	210	213	274	n.a.
Wine consumption in million gallons	96	99	105	105	n.a.
Wine exports in million gallons	51	57	76	90	110

For hectares × by 0.4
For liters × by 3.8

CLIMATE, SOIL, AND WINE GROWING

Australia does not have the luxury of tried and tested *terroir à la française*. Its history shows us that it started out in the early part of the last century with all the noble grape varieties introduced by winemakers such as James Busby and William Macarthur. For reasons of identification of style, as much as in deference to the Old World, descriptions of wines were based on Old-World *terroir*—for example hock, chablis, burgundy, and sherry. Nowadays, varietal labeling has become the norm, primarily due to pressure from the European Union. It is the grape variety, and not the *terroir*, which has become the important descriptive term.

Much of Australian viticulture is based on what the bigger companies have found expedient. The use of the most cost-effective mechanization and trellising to get the highest yield from the vineyard is one example of this. In order to fulfill commercial goals, the bigger producers have deliberately sought out regions where the summers are dry and the rainfall minimal, using irrigation where necessary to correct any deficit. It is not entirely surprising that Australians treat the importance of soil and climate with less reverence than Europeans.

In Australia, vineyards are often located conveniently close to urban centers: the Hunter Valley to Sydney, the Barossa Valley to Adelaide,

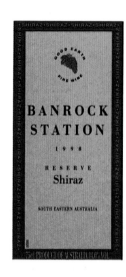

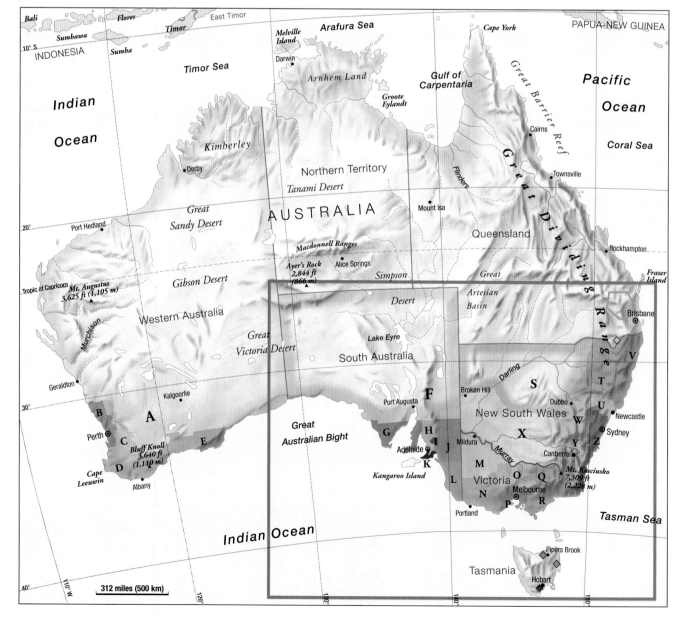

Australia's system of geographic indications

Since October 1994, Australia has given a legal framework to the labeling of its wine. At the same time, it has been grappling with the process of defining the boundaries of its wine regions, with a view to giving consumers the same guarantee of origin as is given under the French laws of *Appellation Contrôlée* (A.C.).

As far as labeling is concerned, where a wine claims a single vintage, a single region and/or a single grape variety, at least 85 percent of the wine must be from that vintage, region and/or grape variety. If more than one region or variety is specified, they must be listed in descending order of importance. Although these three defining features are normally found on a wine label, the decision whether or not to use them is voluntary.

As far as geographic indication is concerned, a hierarchy of regional descriptions now exists. The system is not based on climatic or geographic features, but rather it represents a practical and convenient approach to dividing up terri-

1. Producer's logo and name
2. Vintage and designation of origin
3. Type of grape
4. Producer's name, location, and wine locality
5. Alcohol percentage by volume
6. International designation of origin, production country
7. Volume of the bottle

states, followed by wine zones, of which there are 26, appropriately with letters A–Z. Each zone is sub-divided into regions and then into sub-regions. A sub-region must contain at least five vineyards of at least 12 acres (5 ha) each, producing a minimum of 490 tons/tonnes of grapes a year.

While many regions have now been formally declared, there have been a number of spectacular arguments over boundaries, specifically at Coonawarra, and at neighboring Koppamurra, which has been renamed Wrattonbully because of a disagreement over the name.

tory. The broadest category is southeastern Australia, Victoria, and Tasmania and the areas of Queensland and South Australia in which grapes are grown. Next there are individual

▭	South Eastern Australia
A	Eastern Plains, Inland and North of Western Australia
B	Greater Perth
C	Central Western Australia
D	South West Australia
E	Western Australia South East Coastal
F	Far North
G	The Peninsulas
H	Mount Lofty Ranges and Adelaide
I	Barossa
J	Lower Murray
K	Fleurieu
L	Limestone Coast
M	North West Victoria
N	Western Victoria
O	Central Victoria
P	Port Philip
Q	North East Victoria
R	Gippsland
S	Western Plains
T	Northern Slopes
U	Hunter Valley
V	Northern Rivers
W	Central Ranges
X	Big Rivers
Y	Southern New South Wales
Z	South Coast
▭	Burnett Valley
◇	Granite Belt
◆	Launceston
◆	Hobart

the Swan Valley to Perth, and the Yarra Valley to Melbourne. Equally, for commercial reasons, much of Australia's bulk production centered on the hot, irrigated wine regions bordering the Murray and Murrumbidgee Rivers.

CLIMATE AS THE PRINCIPAL FACTOR

On the other hand, within Australia, climate is considered of great importance as an influence on wine quality and style. In particular, the temperature during the growing season plays a crucial role in the ripening process. Optimum conditions include ample sunshine, a degree of humidity, minimal temperature variability, and the right

average temperature for the grape variety. The system of measurement, which broadly defines regional climate, is the classification system introduced by Amerine and WINKLER, based on Heat Degree Days (H.D.D.s).

In this system, the irrigated "riverland" regions of Australia—from South Australia through Victoria to New South Wales—are the hottest, in excess of H.D.D. 3,500°F (2,000°C) and, Swan Valley and Cowra apart, relatively low rainfall. The Swan Valley in Western Australia is an equally hot region.

Warm regions with continental-type climates account for the majority of quality wine. Here, given variations in grape varieties and the vaga-

Barossa Valley: international vine varieties in a distinctive landscape.

Clare Valley north of Adelaide is a wine region with one of the longest histories in Australia. It was formerly known for its Rieslings, but nowadays Cabernet Sauvignon and other more fashionable varieties are planted on trellises and watered by drip irrigation.

Left
The lush vegetation indicates that it often rains on the Margaret River.

Right
In cold Tasmania, vines are trained on tall trellises to get maximum benefit from sunshine.

ries of the weather, the tendency to budburst and moderate temperatures during the final ripening months contributes to overall quality. There are few cold regions in Australia. Those considered to be cool are the Macedon Ranges, Ballarat, far southwest Victoria, and northern Tasmania, while southern Tasmania is positively chilly, with about the same H.D.D.s as Champagne in France.

Soil Characteristics

Generally speaking, Australia's soil varies so widely that it is impossible to characterize regions by specific soil type. The main soil types are so-called duplex soils, the most common of which have a red-brown subsoil overlain by a sandy loam surface. However, Coonawarra has become Australia's most famous region, not solely by virtue of the quality wines it produces, but because its boundaries are defined by the chocolate-brown (*terra rossa*) soils that sit on a limestone bedrock.

The emphasis of wine producing has shifted from the winemaker to the vineyard itself, in terms of density of vines, trellising systems and canopy management, and irrigation. In Australia, traditional density of between 1,500 and 3,000 vines per 2$\frac{1}{2}$ acres (1 ha), to allow for mechanization, is considerably lower than the norm (between 4,000 and 8,000) in Europe. However, attention to yield and achieving a better balance between fruit and foliage has meant that many of the newer vineyards in cooler areas have been established with greater vine densities and more complex trellising systems. There has also been a move toward sustainable viticulture, which utilizes environmentally friendly ways of dealing with pests and diseases.

GRAPE VARIETIES ON DEMAND

Historically, premium grape varieties were brought in by pioneering growers in the first half of the last century. As tastes and commercial demands changed, the industry veered away from table wines toward sweeter, fortified wines. The kind of grape varieties best suited to Australia's so-called TAWNY ruby and vintage ports, are principally the Rhône grapes Shiraz, Grenache, and Mourvèdre (called Mataro in Australia). Shiraz was considered Australia's finest red grape for a long time, but as the more fashionable premium varieties, notably Cabernet Sauvignon, came into the frame, Shiraz became a "poor relation," along with its Rhône counterparts. Fortunately, visionary winemakers such as Max Schubert—and more recently small wineries such as Rockford and St. Hallett in the Barossa Valley—have kept the faith and tirelessly promoted Shiraz as Australia's best red variety.

SHIRAZ, CABERNET SAUVIGNON, AND MERLOT

Today, Shiraz is once again Australia's supreme red grape variety, its "trump card," which aligns it with the pedigree of France's great classic regions, yet differentiates its top premium reds from those of all other countries. With nearly 91,425 acres (37,000 ha), it is also Australia's most widely planted premium red variety. Stylistically, it changes considerably from region to region. So while its reputation is founded on the Barossa, where it produces richly concentrated, full-bodied reds, it becomes a more elegant creature in Victoria with wines of subtle fruitiness combined with mint, ginger, and spicy undertones. The Hunter Valley still produces traditional Shiraz, while Western Australia has examples that align themselves with the northern Rhône style.

Cabernet Sauvignon is a modern variety that barely existed in the 1950s. As a late-ripening, thick-skinned variety, it suited Australia's warm climate well, surging to prominence at the expense of Shiraz and staying there until the mid-1980s. Today there are nearly 72,900 acres (29,500 ha) of Cabernet Sauvignon, which is particularly suited for the soils in Coonawarra. Often blended with Shiraz, it is also mixed in perhaps the more classical style with the other Bordeaux varieties Merlot and Cabernet Franc. Thanks to its fashionable status in California, Merlot quickly became the most frequently planted premium grape in

High-quality varieties are not exactly a novelty in Australia. This Shiraz vine stock is a century old.

Down under, Shiraz turns out some very individual red wines that arouse much interest internationally.

Australia, and now covers 24,700 acres (10,000 ha). Mainly used in blends with Cabernet Sauvignon its future as an independent variety is already in view. Cabernet Franc only accounts for ten percent and is mostly used in Bordeaux blends.

GRENACHE, MOURVÈDRE, PINOT NOIR

Clinging to the coat-tails of Shiraz, Grenache and Mourvèdre have undergone a revival of sorts, particularly in areas of South Australia where old vines, typically bush-pruned in vineyards that have not been irrigated, are capable of producing concentrated, distinctive fruit. Although much Grenache and Mourvèdre was removed in the Vine Pull Scheme of the 1970s, fresh demand for these Mediterranean varieties has resulted in a modest increase in plantings, so that now they amount to some 9,266 acres (3,750 ha) in total. They do particularly well in the Barossa Valley and McLaren Vale and, as you might expect, blend well with Shiraz.

Pinot Noir, the grape of red Burgundy, is still the pimply adolescent of the Australian wine scene. Its recent successes, more than any other variety, reflect not only considerable dedication on the winemaker's part, but also a general move toward cool-climate viticulture. Tyrrells pioneered Pinot Noir in the warm Hunter Valley, but because it is acknowledged to grow best in a marginal climate, producers have actively sought out cooler areas like the Yarra Valley and other southern regions of Victoria, Adelaide Hills, Tasmania, and the cooler areas of Western Australia. As a result Pinot Noir, which covers more than 10,870 acres (4,400 ha), quickly yielded a wine of structure and complexity, pleasing to the senses.

CHARDONNAY & CO.

You might not guess it, but Australia is in fact more of a white- than a red-wine country. If this comes as a surprise, it is because much of Australia's white-wine production comes from bulk white varieties such as Sultana, Doradillo, Muscat Blanc, Palomino, and Trebbiano. Between bulk and premium, there is a significant amount of Chenin Blanc and Colombard, while Muscat Gordo Blanco is the variety that puts the flavor into cask wine. The four top premium varieties—Chardonnay, Semillon, Sauvignon Blanc, and Riesling—account for just over a quarter of Australian wine production, but their value to the industry and the consumer is much more important.

If Australia is the success story of the final two decades of the last millennium, Chardonnay takes the starring role in that story. It is far and away the most widely planted premium white variety, with in excess of 53,620 acres

LEEUWIN ESTATE

1996
Margaret River
Chardonnay
14.5% vol.   PRODUCE OF AUSTRALIA   750 m

(21,700 ha). When it first arrived on the scene in the mid to late 1980s, Chardonnay offered excitingly new, tropical fruit flavors along with the tremendously appealing taste of oak. Many of these early Chardonnays were one-glass wonders, which palled after the second or third glass. Australian winemakers responded rapidly by increasing the range of styles, and adding greater elegance and structure by taking grapes from cooler areas, using more sophisticated fermentation techniques and less heavy-handed oak treatment. More than any other grape, Chardonnay is the making of the modern Australian wine industry, because it has given the consumer exactly what he and she wants at an affordable price. Its versatility in the vineyard and cellar allows it to be grown in a style that not only reflects the climate but can also be molded to the particular style of the winemaker. It can be made as an affordable mass-market variety, such as Lindemans' hugely successful Bin 65, or, often using barrel-fermentation, turned into something more elegant, concentrated, and complex, such as Leeuwin Estate's world-class Art Series.

RIESLING AND SEMILLON

By adding a new string to its bow, Chardonnay has done for Australian white wine what Cabernet Sauvignon has done for its reds. Yet there are existing varieties, which, although less popular than Chardonnay, have nevertheless given Australian white wine an extra dimension. Thanks to its introduction by the Silesian settlers in the 19th century, Riesling has come into its own in the South Australian regions of Clare Valley, Eden Valley, and, of course, the Barossa Valley, along with parts of

Only nets are any use in keeping birds off, but of course they have to be removed before harvesting. They are then rolled up into large balls for re-use the following year, as here on the Margaret River.

Victoria and the lower part of Great Southern Region of Western Australia. Riesling produces full-flavored, lime-zesty, full-bodied dry wines of distinction and character, as well as some of Australia's best botrytized sweet wines.

The Semillon grape is another variety that produces wines of unique character in Australia, particularly in the Barossa Valley and parts of Margaret River, but most famously in the traditional region of the Hunter Valley, where, as an unoaked white, it develops haunting flavors of buttered toast and grilled nuts. It is often barrel-fermented in the Barossa Valley and also in Western Australia, where it is sometimes blended with Sauvignon Blanc in the Graves style. Sauvignon itself, rather like Pinot Noir, first began to gain recognition after being planted in cooler areas such as the Adelaide Hills, Frankland River, and Tasmania.

Grape Varieties as Brand Names

It is strange to think that a generation ago it was considered forthright to label an Australian wine by its grape variety. Varietal labeling began in California, but has become synonymous with wines from the New World. In Australia it is the key to a wine style and, once linked to the name of the producer and the region, becomes an integral part of the brand. As already mentioned, this is partly because Australia does not hold to the concept of *terroir* in the way that the French do. The Australian tradition is much more geared to blends of wine across district and regional boundaries.

Nets are particularly essential for varieties that need longer ripening, as here in Tasmania.

AUSTRALIAN WINEMAKING

Rotation tanks and computer/temperature-controlled fermentation tanks at Haselgrove in McLaren Vale, where—as everywhere in Australia—the latest technology is the norm.

Cheap aging technique: oak shavings instead of a barrel.

The remarkable progress of Australian wine on the world stage has as much to do with the expertise of winemakers trained to deal with the continent's specific growing conditions as with the huge investment in winemaking equipment. In the well-equipped Australian winery, efficient overall quality control is the key, using up-to-date, hygienic equipment, in particular stainless steel for crushers, tanks, and presses, and caustic soda and citric acid solutions to keep equipment spotless. Cellars are also equipped with a laboratory for the analysis of sulfur, pH, acidity, sugar, and alcohol levels.

One of the keys to wine quality has been greater control over the maturity and soundness of the fruit as it arrives at the winery. Hence the importance of the liaison between winemaker and viticulturalist. With a tendency to pick on flavor rather than just sugar levels, the composition and soundness of the grapes is of vital importance, since this dictates the quality of the resulting wines. The yield, degree of TANNINS, and ripeness of the grapes at harvest depend on the style of wine to be made.

Above all, stylistic improvements have come about thanks to a gradual, systematic change in planting policy, from workhorse, wine-cask varieties such as Muscat Gordo Blanco, Sultana, and the unusually named Doradillo, to premium white grape varieties. This is especially the case in cooler parts of Australia, where the spread of Chardonnay, Sauvignon Blanc, Rhine Riesling,

and Semillon has resulted in more elegant wines. The same goes for red grapes, in particular the increase in plantings of Shiraz, Cabernet Sauvignon, Merlot, and Pinot Noir, at the expense of Grenache and Mourvèdre.

NO AIR FOR WHITE WINE

From the moment the grapes are harvested, the general modern approach is to employ reductive rather than oxidative winemaking. Reductive enology is centered on preventing air from oxidizing the MUST and wine by carrying out operations under inert gas, in clean conditions, and with effective temperature control. Keeping the grapes cool, preferably in the range of 45–60°F (8–16°C), is often best achieved by harvesting at night or the coolest part of the day. Another major factor in the process is the use of cooling during winemaking operations to conserve AROMA and flavor.

At harvest it used to be considered wise to add sulfur to prevent OXIDATION, although winemakers are increasingly conscious of reducing the levels of chemicals. The general aim is to limit sulfur dioxide levels to 50 parts per million (ppm) and free sulfur dioxide to 20 ppm. For careful control of pH, tartaric acid is usually added at the fermentation stage, while CHAPTALIZATION, or enrichment of the must, is not permitted. Closely monitoring the appearance of hydrogen sulfide by adding diammonium phosphate is important, and so is reductive treatment after fermentation by using inert gas and cooling to avoid unwanted YEASTS and bacteria.

Generally speaking, white winemaking avoids skin contact and aims for better-quality, free-run juice, and cooling during settling to allow wines to be clean with minimal PHENOLIC character. The use of enzymes and selected pure yeasts for white is widespread. Fermentation temperatures are normally relatively low, in the 54–60°F (12–16°C) range. MALOLACTIC FERMENTATION—the conversion of malic to lactic acid—is normally avoided in aromatic varieties to retain the natural crispness of the grape.

Although Australian winemakers normally aim for minimum handling of the must and wine, not all Australian winemaking follows the enology formula. A small percentage of premium wines, mainly Chardonnays, are produced by so-called "dirty winemaking" techniques, in which whole bunches are pressed, followed by barrel fermentation with LEES contact and stirring. Premium red wines, although normally fermented in stainless steel, may be run off before the fruit sugars are fermented out, and left to finish fermenting in small oak casks.

RED WINE ROTATED

Red wines are normally fermented in stainless steel tanks or, in the case of Pinot Noir, open-top fermenters, using selected yeast and tannins with control of pH. There is plenty of pumping over and widespread use of vinimatics, or rotofermenters, to achieve good color extraction and temperature control. Australian winemakers normally press off the skins as soon as they achieve the required color and tannin. In some instances, however, extended MACERATION may be used after fermentation, but this is done infrequently because it extracts tannins which then need to be softened by polymerization, a process that runs counter to standard Australian practice.

Malolactic fermentation immediately after fermentation is encouraged to achieve a more stable wine during winter. Racking the wine from barrels is handled in such a way as to avoid excessive oxygen. French oak is used for premium wines, both white and red, and particularly for Pinot Noir and Cabernet Sauvignon. American oak is widely used for Shiraz and Shiraz-Cabernet blends, although there is a move toward French or part-French oak for Shiraz, too. Oak chips, which Australian winemakers refer to as "microcasks," may be used for cheaper wines during or after fermentation to give some semblance of the effect of oak-cask maturation at a fraction of the cost. Inner staves are preferred because oak chips tend to have a coarse, almost resinous character.

To clarify the wines, many large wineries use centrifuges to reduce the chance of stripping flavor immediately after fermentation. After this, they employ diatomaceous earth FILTRATION, which doesn't take too much out of the wine. Pad filtration is used prior to bottling so that all yeast and bacteria are removed, avoiding any problems of spoilage in the bottle. Whites, particularly those containing RESIDUAL SUGAR, also go through a membrane filtration.

For sparkling wines, the links between Australian companies and Champagne houses have been vital to progress. Moët et Chandon's Green Point in the Yarra Valley has a direct input from its parent house in Épernay, and Croser in Adelaide Hills draws on the experience of Bollinger. The switch to champagne grape varieties and cooler areas for sourcing the raw material has had a tremendous impact on sparkling wine quality. And instead of picking the grapes for their acidity levels, winemakers are increasingly picking for flavor. Sparkling wines used to be made almost entirely by bulk fermentation or carbonation, but the transfer and champagne methods are on the increase.

The preliminary stage of making the wine is successfully completed.

Flying winemakers

The flying winemaker is essentially an Antipodean phenomenon. The term is credited to Tony Laithwaite, founder of Direct Wines in the U.K., who hired Australian Martin Shaw to work with a team of winemakers in French cooperatives in 1987. The aim was to tailor wines to the requirements of his customers by applying Australian technology and expertise to a relatively cheap source of grapes.

The practice works because Australian-trained winemakers can adapt to almost any situation. It is also possible because once vintage has finished in the southern hemisphere, Australians and New Zealanders are free to fly to Europe, where there is a demand for well-trained winemakers. This enables them to do two vintages in a year and gives them valuable experience to take back home.

The practice started in the south of France, a vast region full of cooperatives and outdated working methods. Flying winemakers were able to bring about instant improvements in other countries, too, through hard work and the application of standard hygiene and scientific practices. In the vineyard, the role of the flying winemaker has been to influence fruit quality by concentrating on flavor and picking riper fruit of the best quality.

Flying winemakers usually work in countries where the grape source is cheap and the potential for improvement considerable. The south of France, eastern Europe especially Hungary, southern Italy, parts of Spain and Portugal, Greece, South Africa, Chile, and Argentina have all seen improvements, thanks to the wholesale importation of Australian expertise and technology.

Some of the most successful flying winemakers have gone on to establish their own wineries. Others have gone on to employ teams of winemakers in various countries, with whom they communicate by telephone, fax, and e-mail.

New South Wales:
An Excess of Sun

The first vines in Australia were planted in New South Wales. With Sydney as its capital, the state has always had a captive market for wine in its discriminating residents and numerous tourists. The early industry was based in the Hunter Valley, but in the absence of a gold rush, as in Victoria, or the influx of hard-working Lutheran immigrants to South Australia, New South Wales never experienced the rate of expansion of neighboring states. Nevertheless, through the Murrumbidgee Irrigation Scheme, established in 1914, a prolific state wine industry grew up around mass-market, mainly white-wine grapes, as well as some high-quality, BOTRYTIS-affected, sweet whites made from Semillon. More recently, Cowra, Mudgee, and Orange are gaining increasing recognition as quality regions in their own right.

Diversity in the Hunter Valley

At very first glance the viticulture landscape in the Hunter Valley region is remarkable for the large number of wineries, 64 on the relatively small area of around 10,870 acres (4,400 ha).

Although the climate in New South Wales is wet, irrigation is still necessary during the hot weather. At Lindeman's Winery in the Hunter Valley, water tanks take care of this.

Hunter has one of the hottest and wettest climates in Australia, with most of the rainfall coming in the summer months. With the varied soil, the difficult climate, and the big number of fiercely competing producers, it is not surprising that the region has produced a wide range of individual styles, especially in Shiraz and

S	**Western Plains**
T	**Northern Slopes**
U	**Hunter Valley**
	Hunter
V	**Northern Rivers**
	Hastings River
W	**Central Ranges**
	Mudgee
	Orange
	Cowra
X	**Big Rivers**
	Murray Darling
	Swan Hill
	Riverina
	Pericoota
Y	**Southern New South Wales**
	Hilltops
	Canberra District
	Tumbarumba
Z	**South Coast**
	Shoalhaven
	Wine-growing areas in neighboring regions

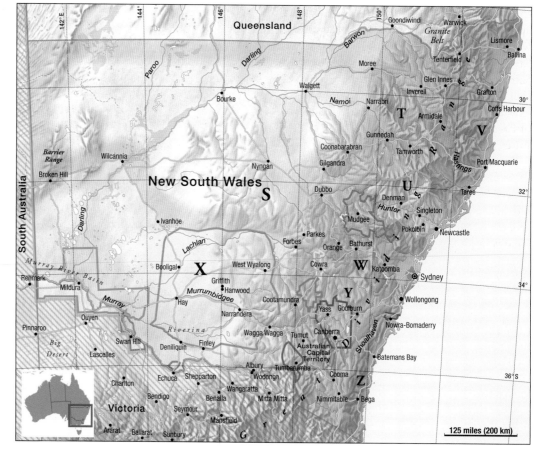

Semillon. Shiraz often provides a warm, heavy red wine that can age very well. Hunter Semillon (the grape variety behind the early Hunter River Chablis), is responsible for a unique style that develops a buttered-toast-and-lime-marmalade character with age. The Hunter Valley is the early home of Chardonnay too, introduced in 1971 by Murray Tyrrell, whose Pinot Noir was no less pioneering but not so successful. Meanwhile, Cabernet Sauvignon was reintroduced to the Hunter at Lake's Folly in 1963, by Dr. Max Lake, another of the region's great egos.

ACTIVE NEIGHBORS

With far fewer producers, the Upper Hunter Valley has almost as many acres/hectares of vines planted as the Lower Hunter, over half given over to Chardonnay and more than a quarter to Semillon. This is the home of Rosemount, one of Australia's richer, more complex styles of Chardonnay, produced at the Roxburgh vineyard. Cowra has long been a source of quality grapes for the Hunter's wineries, and in the 1990s it increased in both size and importance, with some 1,850 acres (750 ha) of vineyards, all producing grapes processed elsewhere. By contrast, Orange is a much smaller region, less than half the size of the Hunter Valley. Yet this fast-developing cool-climate region, which is best-known for its apples and pears, already has a number of wineries producing elegant Chardonnay, Sauvignon Blanc, Cabernet Sauvignon, and Shiraz. The small area of Hastings River is significant for its warm climate, its unirrigated vineyards and the fact that the relatively obscure Chambourcin is its main red grape variety.

On the other side (the inland western slopes) of the Great Dividing Range, Mudgee is a region which, despite a history stretching back to 1858, has had comparatively little recognition until recently. This is perhaps because, like other regions such as Langhorne Creek in South

Queensland's Granite Belt

Lying to the west of the Great Dividing Range, the distinguishing features of the Granite Belt are its relatively northerly latitude (28°S), its high altitude—2,650 feet (810 m) above sea level—and its lunar landscape of massive granite outcrops and boulders. The first vines were planted in Queensland's only quality wine-producing district in 1878, and it was only after 1965 that a modern industry of sorts was developed, with the city of Brisbane a natural captive market for wine. There are some 20-odd small wineries in the Granite Belt, but just over 1,458 acres (590 ha) of vines. Queensland's best wine is made from Shiraz, which produces a strong, spicy red. The aptly named Bald Mountain is the Granite Belt's most prominent winery.

Australia, it was traditionally a supplier of grapes, in this case to the Hunter Valley's bigger companies. Nevertheless, it has more than 22 small wineries of its own, mainly producing the typical New South Wales quartet of Shiraz and Cabernet Sauvignon, Chardonnay and Semillon. Mudgee was one of the first regions to introduce a rigidly controlled *appellation* scheme.

The unromantically named Murrumbidgee Irrigation Area, or Riverina, is New South Wales' answer to the irrigated Riverland of South Australia and Sunraysia of Victoria. Centered on Griffith, its hot dry climate produces nearly two-thirds of the state's entire wine crop, mainly from high-yielding, white grape varieties, the principal of which is Semillon. Reds are generally well made and based principally on Shiraz. Some 17,790 acres (7,200 ha) of Murray River vineyards, most of which fall on the Victorian side of the border, are situated in New South Wales. The Canberra district is home to 15 small wineries, many of which were established by academics or civil servants.

Despite the extreme continental heat they often succeed in producing interesting wines on their 618 acres (250 ha). Hastings River is an outsider, and with less than 494 acres (200 ha) under cultivation it is also one of Australia's small wine-growing regions. Close to the Pacific Ocean, far north of Sydney, it has a climate of high temperatures and high rainfall, actually anything but ideal conditions for wine. The first attempts to produce wine here were in the first half of the 19th century, but it is only since 1980 that viticulture has enjoyed a renaissance, thanks to the commitment of the Cassegrain family. The French hybrid Chambourcin has been the key factor. Resistant to downy mildew, this vine produces pleasant, fruity, very dark but lightly structured reds.

Tyrrell pioneered Pinot in the Hunter Valley.

VICTORIA:
GOLD RUSH AND WINE

The distinctive "witch's hat" tower at Mitchelton Winery attracts many visitors to Goulburn Valley in Central Victoria.

De Bortoli, a family business with Italian roots, has established itself in the Yarra Valley.

If New South Wales is Australia's most historic wine region and South Australia the hub of the industry, Victoria, thanks to its diversity of styles and off-the-beaten-track districts, is in many ways the most fascinating. In sheer production terms, the vast, irrigated hinterland of Sunraysia produces the lion's share of Victorian wine. But it is the hundreds of small premium wineries north and south of Melbourne, which have sprouted up in a generation, that are setting the quality pace. The trend toward cool-climate viticulture in the last decade of the 20th century put the focus back on a state which, until the arrival of phylloxera and the shift to fortified wines a century ago, was Australia's most important wine producer.

Established by the Swiss in the mid-19th century, the picturesque Yarra Valley is one of Victoria's most historic wine regions and, thanks to the success of its Pinot Noir, probably its best-known today. As evidence of the Yarra Valley's claim to historic fame, there were already some 45 separate vineyards in the Yarra Valley by the end of the last century, including Yeringberg and St. Huberts. Today, there are some 44 wineries, but because of investments in new wineries by companies such as Moët et Chandon (Domaine Chandon), and acquisitions such as Mildara Blass (Yarra Ridge and St.Huberts), B.R.L. Hardy (Hoddles Creek), and Southcorp (Coldstream Hills), the area under vine has more than doubled the 2,470-odd acres (about 1,000 ha)

since the 1990s. Its relatively cool climate has been responsible for producing some of Australia's best Pinot Noir. Chardonnay in the elegant, melon-and-tropical-citrus-fruit style also does well here.

South of Melbourne, the Mornington Peninsula is a cool region with a maritime climate, strongly influenced by northerly winds and ocean breezes blowing across the Bass Strait. The region is a kaleidoscope of small, lifestyle wineries, many started up by city professionals with money to burn. Here you will find elegant, often complex, cool-climate Chardonnay, as well as some delicate Pinot Noir from producers such as Stoniers. In contrast to Mornington, Geelong, on Corio Bay, has never really recovered from its devastation by phylloxera, although Bannockburn, Scotchman's Hill, and Prince Albert all make creditable Pinot Noir.

The high altitude of the cool Macedon Ranges has made this one of the major new areas for the planting of Pinot Noir and Chardonnay grapes, destined for sparkling wines. Given the relatively small area under vine, there is also a surprising number—around 26—of small wineries, the best-known of which are Hanging Rock and Virgin Hills, the latter producing sulfur-free wines.

As a result of the gold rush, the mining towns of Ballarat and Bendigo gave rise to a significant wine industry in the 19th century. However, as in the case of Geelong, phylloxera put paid to the golden era, and it was not until 1969 in the case of Bendigo and 1971 in Ballarat that vines reappeared. Ballarat is the cooler of the two, more suited to sparkling wine production, while Bendigo has a number of wineries, among them Jasper Hill and Balgownie, making quality Shiraz. To the east, in central Victoria, lies the Goulburn Valley, where the ultra-traditional winery Château Tahbilk has set a trend, followed by Mitchelton, for the production of an unusual white made from Marsanne. It is also a good region for Riesling, Chardonnay, and powerful Shiraz. The Central Victorian High Country, formerly the Strathbogie Ranges, is well-suited to Riesling, a specialty of Delatite, elegant Bordeaux blends at Mount Helen, and the production of sparkling wine.

SWEET WINES AND DRY REDS

While much of the development of Victoria's wine reflects the trend toward cool-climate viticulture, there are two staunchly traditional districts, namely Rutherglen and Glenrowan in northeast Victoria, which resolutely stand out against the modern search for elegance. Steeped in history, this is an area that was established on the back of the 1850s gold rush. In terms of production, table wines account for about 2,300 acres (930 ha) of plantings, as opposed to only 170 acres (70 ha) of Muscat Blanc à Petits Grains and Muscadelle. They produce the fortified Muscats and Tokays that are known as "stickies." The grapes that make these rich and rare wines are allowed to shrivel on the vine. They are fortified during the winemaking process before being aged for years in small oak barrels to produce rich, sweet wines of intense aromatic power and concentration of fruit. The older the wine, the more complex it becomes, with flavors of rose petal and raisin (Muscat) as well as toffee, malt, and tea (Tokay).

The King Valley in northeast Victoria is perhaps best known as the home of Brown Brothers, a family company that has worked tirelessly to produce good-value table wines, particularly from Chardonnay, Riesling, and Cabernet Sauvignon. Next to it is the high Ovens Valley where Giaconda has established a reputation for exceptional Pinot Noir and Chardonnay. These are the two varieties that form the backbone of Gippsland, too—a sprawling, remote region on the undulating coastal plain of Victoria, capable of producing elegant Burgundian-style red and white wines.

Redefining the West

West of Ballarat in the Western Victoria zone is the Pyrenees. Its soft, undulating landscape is wholly unlike the spectacular European mountain range from which it takes its name. This is mainly red-wine country. Grapes ripen later in the Grampians, formerly the Great Western, which became famous in the gold rush. The sparkling wine production of Seppelt Great Western, the best-known Australian brand, was set up with French technical help in the galleries abandoned by the miners. It is still made there, but the Grampians have in the meantime developed into a table-wine region that produces relatively small quantities of red and white wines.

Mass production is concentrated in an area of 437,360 acres (177,000 ha) in Victoria's river region. Agrarian technology allows a third of Australia's entire wine output to be produced here on flat, clay and sandy soil in a dry climate. A further 5,000 acres (2,000 ha) over the state frontier in New South Wales add their bit. Sultana and the aromatic Muscat Gordo Blanco go into the mass product here, while Chardonnay yields reasonably priced whites. However, this is also the home of Lindemans' very successful Bin 65 Chardonnay.

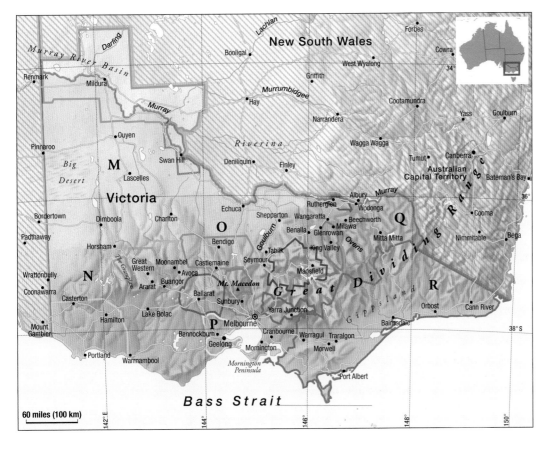

Select Producers in New South Wales and Victoria

New South Wales

Botobolar**
Mudgee, Mudgee

78,000 bottles • Wines include: Low Preservative Chardonnay, Marsanne, Preservative Free Dry Red, Shiraz, Cabernet, → The King

One of the few organic wineries in Australia, this was also one of the first, established by Gil Wahlquist in 1971. It has now been taken over by Kevin Karsyrom, who is continuing where Wahlquist left off, bringing organic practices to the winery with preservative-free wines.

Brokenwood***−****
Pokolbin, Lower Hunter Valley

720,000 bottles • Wines include: → Cricket Pitch Unwooded Chardonnay, Sauvignon Blanc Semillon, → Graveyard Chardonnay; Shiraz, → Graveyard Shiraz

Established in 1970 with wine writer James Halliday as one of the leading lights, Brokenwood is now producing, under winemakers Iain Riggs and Dan Dineen, well-crafted, sought-after Semillon and Shiraz.

Lindemans**−****
Karadoc, Coonawarra, Padthaway, Hunter Valley

Bought-in grapes; 40,000,000 bottles • Wines include: Coonawarra reds, notably Limestone Ridge, → St.George (Cabernet); varietals from Padthaway, from the historic Ben Ean winery in the Hunter Valley, Leo Buring brand, and various bin number varietals at the giant Karadoc facility

Part of the giant Southcorp group, in addition to the above Lindemans produces the fruit-driven, consistent, and inexpensive →Bin 65 Chardonnay, the biggest-selling Chardonnay brand in the world, blended by chief winemaker Philip John.

McWilliams**−****
Hanwood, Riverina

2,051 acres (830 ha); bought-in grapes; 2,000,000 bottles • Wines include: varietal wines from Riverina; Chardonnay, Shiraz, and Cabernet from Barwang at Hilltops, N.S.W., → Lovedale Semillon, → Eden Valley Riesling, and diverse fortified wines

Under winemakers Jim Brayne and Phillip Ryan, McWilliams' reputation for its fine Hunter Valley Semillon and fortified wines continues to grow, while table wines range from decent basic varietals to finer table wines.

Rosemount Estate**−***
Denman, Upper Hunter Valley

6,177 acres (2,500 ha); bought-in grapes; 36,000,000 bottles • Wines: a large range of varietal wines, including premium brands → Orange Chardonnay, → Roxburgh Chardonnay and wines from other regions

One of Australia's pioneering export companies, the rapidly expanding Rosemount, now under the umbrella of Southcorp, makes juicy, easy-drinking wines at the commercial end, appealing McLaren Vale Shiraz, and fine Chardonnay at the top end of the range.

Rothbury**−***
Pokolbin, Lower Hunter Valley

455 acres (184 ha); bought-in grapes; 3,000,000 bottles • Wines: → Brokenback Shiraz, Cowra Chardonnay, → Rothbury Estate Chardonnay, Semillon, and Shiraz

Founded by Len "Mr. Wine Australia" Evans and taken over by the Beringer Blass group in 1996, Rothbury is producing pleasantly commercial wines from vineyards and contract growers in the Hunter Valley, Mudgee, and Cowra, following a major A $2 million investment.

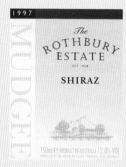

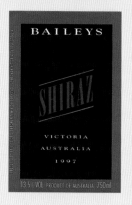

Tyrrell's**−****
Pokolbin, Lower Hunter Valley

803 acres (325 ha); bought-in grapes; 9,600,000 bottles • Wines include: varietal reds and whites; single vineyard wines including → Shee-Oak Chardonnay, → Lost Block Semillon, → Brokenback Shiraz, Vat 47 Chardonnay, → Vat 6 Pinot Noir

Murray Tirrell is celebrated for introducing Chardonnay and Pinot Noir to the Australian wine industry. His Long Flat label was sold to Cheviot Bridge; now this traditional family business concentrates on higher quality production. Vat 1 Hunter Semillon has joined the top wines; it can age for years.

Victoria

Bailey's of Glenrowan***
Glenrowan

343 acres (139 ha); bought-in grapes • Wines include: Tokay, Muscat; Shiraz, Cabernet, Merlot, Touriga; 1904 Block Shiraz, → 1920s Block Shiraz; →Founder Muscat and Tokay

Bailey's continues to make well-structured reds with dark aromas, while the fortified "stickies" are of world class.

Bannockburn Vineyards***−****
Bannockburn, Geelong

Bought-in grapes; 84,000 bottles • Wines: Riesling, Sauvignon Blanc, Chardonnay, Pinot, Noir, Shiraz

The pick of Geelong's small band of wineries, Bannockburn, under Gary Farr, has consistently produced high-quality whites from low-yielding vineyards. The rich, complex Pinot Noir benefits from Farr's experience of winemaking at Domaine Dujac in Burgundy with Jacques Seysses.

Best's****
Great Western, The Grampians

163 acres (66 ha); bought-in grapes; 360,000 bottles • Wines include: Chardonnay, Riesling, Pinot, Shiraz, Cabernet, and fortified wines

Best's is a more traditional winery of the Grampians region, producing wines from varieties which include Ondenc and golden Chasselas, and the northwest Italian red variety Dolcetto. Shiraz is probably its best wine.

Brown Brothers**−***
Milawa, King Valley, Northeast Victoria

1,502 acres (608 ha); bought-in grapes; 10,000,000 bottles • Wines include: Chardonnay, Riesling, Sauvignon, → Orange Muscat & Flora; Tarrango, Barbera, Tempranillo, Sangiovese, Shiraz, Cabernet, Graciano, and sparkling, fortified wines

The fifth generation of this family business are varietal specialists who experiment tirelessly, making good use of their "kindergarten winery," which is dedicated to research and development. But their broad range can be unreliable.

Campbells***
Rutherglen, Rutherglen

Bought-in grapes; 420,000 bottles • Wines include: Riesling, Semillon, → Bobbie Burn Chardonnay, Malbec, Cabernet, Muscat, and Tokay

Impressive, full table wines, notably the ginger and oak notes of Bobbie Burn's Shiraz. The real specialty is the range of aged, fortified Muscats and Tokays.

Coldstream Hills***−*****
Coldstream, Yarra Valley

116 acres (47 ha); bought-in grapes; 420,000 bottles • Wines: Semillon, Sauvignon, Chardonnay, Pinot, Merlot, Cabernet

James Halliday founded this winery in 1985. It is particularly respected for its Chardonnays and Pinot Noir wines, especially the Reserve. Since it was taken over by Southcorp in 1996 production has been increased, but with Andrew Fleming as winemaker and Halliday's name unchanged at the top high standards are still being set.

DALWHINNIE****–*****
MOONAMBEL, PYRENEES
64 acres (26 ha); 54,000 bottles • Wines: Chardonnay and Pinot, Moonambel Shiraz, and Cabernet, Eagle Series
Situated in the Pyrenees, Dalwhinnie, owned by David and Jenny Jones, is making some of the greatest Chardonnay, Cabernet, and Shiraz to come out of Australia.

DE BORTOLI**–****
DIXON'S CREEK, YARRA VALLEY AND RIVERINA
Bought-in grapes; 3,500,000 bottles • Wines: varietal wines, Deen de Bortoli, → Noble Semillon in Riverina, Semillon, Chardonnay, Pinot, Shiraz, Cabernet, Cabernet-Merlot
Traditional family winery producing bread-and-butter varietals in quantity but a good, sweet white in Noble One, and in the Yarra Valley high-quality Pinot Noir.

DOMAINE CHANDON****
YARRA VALLEY
198 acres (80 ha); bought-in grapes; 1,500,000 bottles • Wines include: Marke Green Point, Chardonnay, Sauvignon-Semillon; Pinot Noir, Shiraz; sparkling wines under Green Point and Chandon labels
Founded in 1989 by Moët et Chandon, Green Point has acquired a reputation for its high-quality sparkling wines under the direction of Dr. Tony Jordan. It is also developing a range of equally high-quality still wines. Jordan has also been entrusted with the direction of Cape Mentelle, Cloudy Bay, and Mountadam by Veuve Clicquot.

MITCHELTON WINES***
NAGAMBIE, GOULBURN VALLEY
Bought-in grapes; 1,500,000 bottles • Wines include: brands: Thomas Mitchell; Mitchelton Airstrip with Marsanne, Roussanne, Viognier; Mitchelton Crescent with Shiraz, Mourvèdre, Grenache, → Mitchelton Print Shiraz
Under experienced winemaker Don Lewis, Mitchelton, the winery with the distinctive witch's hat tower, produces tasty wines typical of Central Victoria at reasonable prices.

MORRIS****
RUTHERGLEN, RUTHERGLEN
Bought-in grapes • Wines include: Shiraz, Durif, → Mick Morris Old Tawny Port, → Old Premium Liqueur Tokay and Muscat
Established in 1859, this northeast Victorian fortified wine producer carries on the family tradition of making "stickies" of high quality and style.

MOUNT LANGHI GHIRAN VINEYARDS***–*****
BUANGOR, THE GRAMPIANS
185 acres (75 ha); bought-in grapes; 1,200,000 bottles • Wines: Riesling, Chardonnay, Pinot Grigio, Shiraz, Cabernet, Merlot, → Billi Bill Creek Shiraz Cabernet
Trevor Mast makes distinctive, intense, cool-climate Shiraz with a twist of the pepper mill and plenty of spice, as a result of which Mount Langhi Ghiran Shiraz is in the top flight of Australian reds today.

MOUNT MARY****–*****
LILYDALE, YARRA VALLEY
• Wines: Chardonnay, Triolet (Sauvignon, Semillon, Muscadelle); Pinot, Cabernet, Quintet
Media-shy John Middleton has created a reputation for exclusive, high-quality reds made from Pinot Noir and

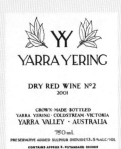

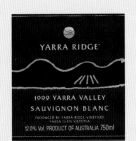

Cabernet, with Quintet in particular the only non-Shiraz blend to achieve "outstanding" status in Langton's classification of Australian wines.

SEPPELT**–****
GREAT WESTERN, THE GRAMPIANS
Bought-in grapes; 7,500,000 bottles • Wines: a wide range of varietal and sparkling wines, → Dorrien Cabernet, → Show Reserve Sparkling Shiraz, → Salinger
Owned by Southcorp, Seppelt is best-known for the sparkling wines it produces and ages in its historic subterranean cellars. It also produces excellent fortified wines from the Barossa Valley.

STONIER***–****
MORNINGTON PENINSULA
Bought-in grapes; 150,000 bottles • Wines: → Pinot Noir, → Chardonnay, and a Reserve range
Lying within sound of the surf beaches of the Bass Strait Stonier is a star of the cool climate of the Mornington Peninsula south of Melbourne. In its 20-year history the estate has earned an international reputation for exemplary Chardonnays and Pinot Noirs.

TAHBILK WINERY***–****
NAGAMBIE LAKES
452 acres (183 ha); 1,400,000 bottles • Wines: → Marsanne, Riesling, Chardonnay, Viognier, Shiraz, Cabernet Sauvignon
Founded in 1860 and still owned by the Prubrick family, Tahbilk produces a striking Marsanne and traditional reds, including small quantities from vines planted in 1860 and known to be the oldest Shiraz vines in the world

TARRAWARRA ESTATE***–****
YARRA GLEN, YARRA VALLEY
180 acres (73 ha); 180,000 bottles • Wines: Chardonnay; Pinot Noir, Shiraz, Merlot
Under winemaker Clare Halloran, this small winery makes easy-drinking styles under the Tunnel Hill label, which allows it to pursue a policy of making long-lived, complex, structured Chardonnay and Pinot Noir under the main winery label.

YARRA BURN***
YARRA JUNCTION, YARRA VALLEY
Wines include: Chardonnay, Sauvignon-Semillon, Cabernet Sauvignon, Shiraz, → Pinot Noir
This small winery also belongs to the big Hardy's Group. Under Steve Flamsteed it makes elegant Chardonnays and Pinot Noirs, mainly from two vineyards in Hoddles Creek and Bastard Hill.

YARRA RIDGE***
YARRA GLEN, YARRA VALLEY
304 acres (123 ha); 1,080,000 bottles • Wines: Semillon, Sauvignon, Chardonnay; Merlot, Shiraz, Pinot Noir, → Yarra Ridge Reserve Pinot Noir
Winemakers Nick Walker, Fiona Purnell, and Daniel Bettio are making increasingly good Burgundy-style whites and reds following the winery's purchase by Beringer Blass.

YARRA YERING****–*****
COLDSTREAM, YARRA VALLEY
49 acres (20 ha); 65,000 bottles • Wines: Dry White No. 1 (Sauvignon/Semillon), Chardonnay, Pinot Noir, Dry Red No. 1, Dry Red No. 2, Merlot, → Underhill Shiraz
Dr. Bailey Carrodus is one of the great eccentrics of the Australian wine industry, making intensely flavored, complex and much sought-after wines from low-yielding vineyards in wooden fermenting vats.

SOUTH AUSTRALIA: MASS PRODUCT AND RARITIES

South Australia

F	**Far North**
G	**The Peninsulas**
	Port Lincoln
H	**Mount Lofty Ranges and Adelaide**
	Clare Valley
	Adelaide Plains
	Adelaide Hills
I	**Barossa**
	Barossa Valley
	Eden Valley
J	**Lower Murray**
	Riverland
K	**Fleurieu**
	McLaren Valley
	Langhorne Creek
L	**Limestone Coast**
	Padthaway
	Wrattonbully
	Coonawarra
	Mount Benson
	Robe
	Mount Gambier
	Wine-growing areas in neighboring regions

South Australia has long been the engine room of Australian wine production, thanks to the large volumes of wine made in the irrigated Murray Valley, which accounts for nearly 30 percent of Australia's total grape production. But the Barossa Valley was originally the heart and soul of South Australia's quality wine industry, largely due to the English who settled there in the first half of the 19th century and German immigrants who brought their wine culture with them. In the latter half of the 19th century, the wineries of Clare Valley, McLaren Vale, and Coonawarra were developed; Padthaway was not established until the 1960s. In addition to the Barossa Valley's revival, from the late 1980s new areas such as Adelaide Hills have come on line, together with the expansion of Langhorne Creek and the development of the Limestone Coast zone either side of Coonawarra and Padthaway.

The rolling green hills and transverse valleys, neat stone buildings, and Lutheran spires of the Barossa Valley make it one of Australia's prettiest wine regions. Its winery composition is varied and interesting, with large and small companies co-existing, for the most part, in peaceful harmony. Alongside industry giants such as Penfolds, Orlando, Beringer Blass, and Seppelt, sit a large number of smaller wineries which, with Peter Lehmann at the helm, have contributed to the Barossa's reputation through a combination of commitment to quality, courage in the face of adversity, and imaginative marketing. Notable among these are St. Hallett, Rockford, Charles Melton, and Grant Burge.

The Barossa's warm climate makes it ideally suited to rich, chocolatey Shiraz, the base for Grange and the most widely planted grape in the district. Full-bodied styles of Riesling and Semillon, which both outnumber plantings of Cabernet Sauvignon, also do well here. In line with the trend toward cool-climate wines, Riesling, largely thanks to Yalumba, with Pewsey Vale and Heggies, is moving away from the warm valley floor to the cooler, hillier slopes of the East Barossa Ranges. The Barossa's revival has come about with the help of clever exploitation of the Valley's heritage of old, gnarled Shiraz BUSH VINES and, to a lesser extent, the old Grenache and Mourvèdre used to produce fortified wines prior to the table-wine boom. To the southeast of Barossa, the high country of Eden Valley is most famous for its elegant styles of Riesling, as well as Henschke's Hill of Grace and Mount Edelstone vineyards.

AN EL DORADO FOR SMALL WINERIES

North of Adelaide, the Clare Valley is one of South Australia's oldest and most traditional regions. Unlike Barossa, this beautiful region, with its stone-clad buildings, is covered with small wineries, many of which—notably Jim Barry, Tim Adams, Jeffrey Grosset, Petaluma, and Tim Knappstein—have gained a reputation for the quality of their perfumed, steely Rieslings, which develop a toastiness with age. Riesling is the dominant grape here, although Cabernet Sauvignon and Shiraz also perform well. A short drive east of Adelaide brings you to the high, wooded Adelaide Hills, a spectacular, cool-climate region which, in areas like Piccadilly and Lenswood, is rapidly gaining a reputation for elegant styles of Chardonnay and Sauvignon Blanc, as well as quality Pinot Noir. Just south of here, Kuitpo is a new sub-region, being developed by, among others, Rosemount Estate.

Until recently, McLaren Vale was one of the less well-known traditional regions of South Australia. To the south of Adelaide, it is an area of rolling hills and interesting small wineries, often called "the spiritual home of the small winery." Among the most notable wineries in this region are Wirra Wirra, Chapel Hill, d'Arenberg, Geoff Merrill, Clarendon Hills, Tatachilla, and Coriole. With its Mediterranean climate, it produces rich, smooth reds, with Shiraz and Cabernet Sauvignon the dominant red varieties, and Chardonnay far and away the major white grape. Still little known, Langhorne Creek is dominated by Cabernet Sauvignon and Shiraz, which supply much of the content of Orlando Jacob's Creek red.

Riverland comprises a series of sub-regions with a hot continental climate along the banks of the Murray River. It was originally developed by George and William Chaffey, who chose Renmark on the west bank of the Murray River as the site for their pioneering irrigation schemes. Not surprisingly, given its warm climate, there are significant plantings of Shiraz, Grenache, and Mourvèdre, used until recently for fortified and cask wines. There are also substantial plantings of Chardonnay, although the biggest category of grape here is generally described as "other," a term that covers the multitude of fruity Gordo, Doradillo, and Sultana varieties that go into the ubiquitous Australian wine cask.

RED EARTH AND RUBBER TREES

Almost certainly one of Australia's most haunting and mystical wine regions is Coonawarra. The reasons are simple. First, Coonawarra is Australia's first region to have its own *terroir*, in particular its famous chocolate-brown *terra rossa* soil, which sits on a bed of soft limestone. Second, the topography itself, the flat land surrounded by gum trees, is quite magical in a strangely peaceful way. And thirdly, Coonawarra has become synonymous with top-quality Cabernet Sauvignon and, perhaps to a lesser extent, Shiraz. Although overshadowed by reds, Chardonnay and Riesling also produce consistently good wines here on Coonawarra's black soils.

Top
Rosemount Estate proudly displays its award of Winemaker of the Year.

Above
The history of the wine giant Penfolds began near Adelaide in 1844. Its modern head office is now in Nuriootpa in the Barossa Valley.

Some of the best Shiraz wines in Australia grow in the Barossa Valley.

This small, cigar-shaped region was first planted by John Riddoch back in 1890, but has only really started to fulfill its potential with the red table-wine boom of the 1960s. It is a relatively cool region, 37 miles (60 km) inland from the ocean, with cloud cover contributing to the length of the growing season. Dominated by big companies such as Wynns, Lindemans, Beringer Blass, and Penfolds, there are nevertheless a significant number of smaller wineries in this region, among them Hollick and Bowen Estate, which produce wines of substance and quality. From Coonawarra, on the road to Adelaide, Padthaway is a giant expanse of vineyard almost entirely planted with premium grape varieties by the big companies: Seppelt, Lindemans, Hardys, and Wynns. Chardonnay is the most notable, but Padthaway Shiraz can be surprisingly good, even great. Along the Limestone Coast, a number of new grape-growing regions are emerging; among the best are Robe, Mount Benson, and Wrattonbully.

Select Producers in South Australia

Tim Adams****
Clare, Clare Valley
40 acres (16 ha); bought-in grapes; 300,000 bottles
• Wines include: →The Aberfeldy Shiraz, →The Fergus Grenache, Riesling, Semillon
Tim and Pam Adams buy in fruit from local growers and have developed a cult following for some of the best, hand-crafted examples of Clare Valley Semillon and Riesling. The wines are made at the Adams' immaculate winery on the outskirts of Clare, along with old vine Shiraz and Grenache, with →the Aberfeldy the pick of a fine crop.

Angove's**
Renmark, Riverland
1,235 acres (500 ha); bought-in grapes; 14,000,000 bottles • Wines: Butterfly Ridge, Stonegate, Bear Crossing, Long Row, Nine Vines
Traditional, family-owned and run winery in the Riverland, whose Nanya Vineyard provides the volume of premium wine production, which is evenly split between red and white wines. Unpretentious, good-value wines.

Jim Barry**−****
Clare, Clare Valley
790 acres (320 ha); 1,800,000 bottles • Wines: Watervale Riesling, Chardonnay, Cabernet, Merlot, Shiraz
Family winery Jim Barry is one of the Clare Valley's top producers of Riesling, but it is probably best known for its expensive, blockbuster, long-lived Shiraz, The Armagh, and the better-value but equally powerful and gutsy McRae Wood Shiraz.

Wolf Blass**−***
Nuriootpa, Barossa Valley
1,170 acres (474 ha), 508 acres (206 ha) under development; bought-in grapes; 8,400,000 bottles
• Wines: varietals and blends under Red, Yellow, Brown, Grey, and Black labels (reds), White, Yellow, Green, and Gold (white), from vineyards in Barossa Valley, Eden Valley, Langhorne Creek, plus McLaren Vale and Padthaway
Now part of the giant Beringer Blass group, this winery, which owes its name to one of Australia's great characters, makes good-value, oaky reds and whites.

Bowen Estate****
Coonawarra, Coonawarra
132,000 bottles • Wines: Chardonnay; Shiraz, Cabernet Sauvignon
In Coonawarra, with its widespread big company plantings, Doug Bowen's small estate is known for its hand-pruned vines and handcrafted wines, particularly his oak-matured reds, which stand out for their quality and finesse.

Chapel Hill***−****
McLaren Vale, McLaren Vale
110 acres (44 ha); bought-in grapes; 800,000 bottles
• Wines include: Chardonnay, Verdelho, Shiraz, Cabernet, The Vicar, Il Vescove
Pam Dunsford, an established, excellent winemaker, is responsible for the attractive whites and muscular, concentrated, oaky reds of Chapel Hill, sourced from Coonawarra and Padthaway and, of course, from McLaren Vale itself.

Clarendon Hills****
Blewitt Springs, McLaren Vale
5 acres (2 ha); bought-in grapes; 216,000 bottles
• Wines: Chardonnay; Pinot, Merlot, →Blewitt Springs Grenache, →Clarendon Vineyard Grenache, →Astralis

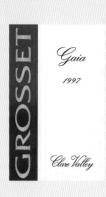

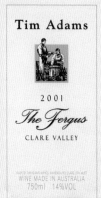

Winemaker Roman Bratasiuk produces 18 densely concentrated single-vineyard wines in small lots from low-yielding, old vines. These have developed a cult following, in particular the sought-after Astralis.

D'Arenberg***−****
McLaren Vale, McLaren Vale
Bought-in grapes; 1,300,000 bottles • Wines: Dry Dam Riesling, Last Ditch Viognier, →Money Spider Roussanne, →Twenty Eight Road Mourvèdre, →Dead Arm Shiraz
Behind amusing names and a confusing number of wines, winemaker Chester Osborn maintains a consistently high quality in his range.

Grosset Wines*****
Auburn, Clare Valley
62 acres (25 ha); 100,000 bottles • Wines: →Watervale Riesling, →Polish Hill Riesling, Piccadilly Chardonnay, →Semillon-Sauvignon; Adelaide Hills Pinot Noir, →Gaia
Jeffrey Grosset established Grosset Wines in the Clare Valley in 1981, since when he has achieved a deserved reputation for one of the longest-lived, most elegant styles of Riesling to come out of Australia, as well as a fine Cabernet blend in Gaia.

Hardys**−****
Reynella, McLaren Vale
Bought-in grapes • Wines: brands: VR, Stamp of Australia, Nottage Hill, →Tintara, →Eileen Hardy, Thomas Hardy, Château Reynella
The winemakers Peter Dawson, Stephen Pannell, Paul Lapsley, and Ed Carr head this big concern which is part of Constellation Wines. Hardy's buys premium grapes from more than 33,000 acres (2,500 ha) of vineyard in the best regions.

Henschke*****
Keyneton, Eden Valley
Bought-in grapes; 480,000 bottles • Wines include: Eden Valley Riesling, Gewürztraminer, Semillon, plus Riesling and Semillon from Adelaide Hills; →Mount Edelstone Shiraz, →Hill of Grace Shiraz, →Cyril Henschke Cabernet; Abbotts Prayer Cabernet Merlot
Stephen and Prue Henschke's precision winemaking has made this Eden Valley winery the best of its size in Australia, and, in →Hill of Grace, it makes a premium, old-vine Shiraz to rival Penfolds Grange.

Knappstein***
Clare Valley
600,000 bottles • Wines include: Riesling, Fumé Blanc; →Enterprise Reserve Shiraz, Cabernet Sauvignon, Sparkling Chainsaw Shiraz
In the capable hands of winemaker Andrew Hardy since 1995, Knappstein has increasingly concentrated on hand-picking and varieties that best suit this picturesque valley. Owned by Allied.

Knappstein Lenswood Vineyards***−****
Lenswood, Adelaide Hills
62 acres (25 ha); only Merlot grapes bought in; 102,000 bottles • Wines: Chardonnay, Sauvignon, Semillon, Gewürztraminer, →Pinot Noir, The Palatine
Tim and Annie Knappstein have a densely-planted vineyard in the cool Adelaide Hills. Tim makes intense and elegant white premium varietal wines and concentrated Pinot Noirs.

Leasingham***−****
Clare Valley
247 acres (100 ha); 1,200,000 bottles • Wines include: Bin 7 Riesling; Bin 56 Cabernet Malbec, Shiraz, Cabernet Sauvignon; Range →Classic Clare

On this estate, which belongs to Hardy's, Kerri Thompson makes excellent Rieslings and concentrated, powerful reds in the Classic Clare range.

Peter Lehmann**–****
Tanunda, Barossa Valley
Bought-in grapes; 2,400,000 bottles • Wines include: varietal whites and reds; premium wines under the Cellar Collection label; →Stonewell Shiraz, →Mentor Cabernet, Eight Songs Shiraz
Peter Lehmann, the Baron of Barossa, held out when Barossa went through the red wine flood crisis of the 1970s. Today the company is producing low-cost commercial wines and strong, hearty Shiraz from old vines.

Charles Melton Wines****
Tanunda, Barossa Valley
121 acres (49 ha); bought-in grapes; 180,000 bottles • Wines: Cabernet Franc, Shiraz, Grenache, Cabernet, →Rose of Virginia, Nine Popes, Shiraz-Sekt
Graeme "Charlie" Melton specializes in southern Rhône-style reds, notably Nine Popes, whose style and name (Charlie's French being as eccentric as the man) was created in homage to Châteauneuf-du-Pape.

Mount Horrocks Wines***–****
Auburn, Clare Valley
25 acres (10 ha); 54,000 bottles • Wines: Watervale Riesling, Cordon Cut Riesling, →Chardonnay, Semillon, Cabernet Merlot
This estate was founded in 1982 and purchased by Stephanie Toole in 1993. The yields are being reduced to achieve quality and character from the individual *terroirs*. Mainly hand-made, dry wines.

Nepenthe***
Lenswood, Adelaide Hills
198 acres (80 ha); 250,000 bottles • Wines: Semillon, Sauvignon, Chardonnay; Pinot, Zinfandel, Cabernet, Merlot
Established in 1984 by the Tweddell family, Nepenthe, under winemaker Peter Leske, is producing handcrafted whites and reds of increasingly good quality and varietal intensity.

Orlando**–***
Rowland Flat, Barossa Valley
4,940 acres (2,000 ha); bought-in grapes; 96,000,000 bottles • Wines: →Jacob's Creek, plus a number of brands including →Gramps, →St.Hilary Chardonnay, →St.Hugo Cabernet, →Jacaranda Ridge Cabernet and →Lawson's Padthaway Shiraz
The highly successful Jacob's Creek brand is the engine which drives this traditional Barossa Valley giant winery, now owned by Pernod-Ricard.

Penfolds**–*****
Nuriootpa, Barossa Valley
Bought-in grapes; 12,000,000 bottles • Wines include: →Yattarana Chardonnay, Eden Valley Riesling; →Grange, →Bin 707 Cabernet Sauvignon, Kalimna Bin 28 Shiraz; numerous brands of Shiraz, Cabernet Sauvignon, Chardonnay, Riesling
Penfolds' stable range goes from low-cost blends like Rawson' Retreat and Bin 2 through high-quality, medium-priced reds like Bin 389 Cabernet Shiraz to the flagship Grange. Peter Gago, the new winemaker, is carrying on where John Duval and the legendary Max Schubert stopped. Penfolds is part of the Southcorp Group.

Petaluma***–*****
Adelaide Hills, Coonawarra, Clare Valley
495 acres (200 ha); 800,000 bottles • Wines include: Chardonnay, Riesling, Viognier; Merlot, Shiraz; labels Petaluna, Bridgewater Mill

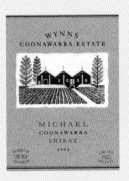

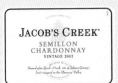

Despite the departure of the former owner Brian Croser to take over the directorship of the Allieds Premium winery, Petaluma is still making one of Australia's most refined Chardonnays from grapes grown on the Adelaide Hills. There are also fine Rieslings from the Clare Valley and an elegant blend of Cabernet Merlot in Coonawarra, as well as its sparkling wine Croser.

St. Hallett***–****
Tanunda, Barossa Valley
Bought-in grapes; 1,800, 000 bottles • Wines include: Poachers Blend, →Faith Shiraz, →Blackwell Shiraz, →Old Block Shiraz, Barossa Valley Cabernet Sauvignon Franc Merlot, Tawny
With Stuart Blackwell (2003 Barossa Winemaker of the Year) at its head St. Hallett became one of Australia's cult wineries. That is largely thanks to the concept developed by the Old Block, which is based on up to 60 small plots of old Shiraz vines in the Barossa Valley. It remains to be seen whether the level can be maintained under the Allied roof.

Shaw & Smith***–****
Balhannah, Adelaide Hills
69 acres (28 ha); bought-in grapes; 360,000 bottles • Wines: Sauvignon, Unoaked Chardonnay, →M3 Vineyard Chardonnay; Merlot
Cousins Martin Shaw and Michael Hill-Smith are close to their goal of producing high-quality, contemporary wines that are among the best of their kind. In 2000 they built new cellars in Balhannah.

Tatachilla***
McLaren Vale, McLaren Vale
Bought-in grapes; 2,500 bottles • Wines include: Breakneck Creek Chardonnay; →Foundation Shiraz, →Keystone, Partners, McLaren Vale Cabernet; Tawny
After its purchase in 1993, followed by renovation, this traditional winery has undergone a significant revival since 1995 and now produces reds—in particular—of exuberant fruit quality.

Wirra Wirra***–****
McLaren Vale, McLaren Vale
Bought-in grapes; 500,000 bottles • Wines: →hand-picked Riesling, Sauvignon, Chardonnay, →The Angelus Cabernet, Church Block (Cabernet, Shiraz, Merlot), →R.S.W. Shiraz, fortified wines
This medium-sized winery is continuing to hone the quality of its wines, particularly its top Cabernet and Shiraz.

Wynns**–****
Coonawarra, Coonawarra
Bought-in grapes; 4,000,000 bottles • Wines: mainly Riesling, Chardonnay; Cabernet, Shiraz, →Michael Shiraz, →John Riddoch Cabernet Sauvignon
Wynns, now part of the Southcorp empire, is the largest land holder of established vineyards in the Coonawarra region, making good-value varietal Shiraz, Cabernet, and Riesling under experienced winemaker Sue Hodder.

Yalumba**–****
Angaston, Barossa Valley
1,132 acres (458 ha); bought-in grapes; 10,800,000 bottles • Wines include: →Angas Brut, →Oxford Landing, →The Menzies Cabernet, →The Octavius Shiraz, varietals and brands
The oldest family winery in Australia has built up a good reputation for its high-quality premium wines, The Reserve, The Octavius, The Menzies, and The Signature. Under winemakers Brian Walsh and Louisa Rosa the winery is acknowledged as Australia's pioneer in Viognier, with wines like The Virgilius. Other well-known labels include Oxford Landing, Yalumba Barossa, and the Y range.

Western Australia:
A Dream Country for Elegant Wines

While Western Australia is the country's biggest state, its wine regions are tucked away in the remote southwestern corner. Partly for that reason, and partly because there is no region like Riverland to drive volumes, the wine industry is on a smaller scale here than in Australia's three main wine-producing states—New South Wales, Victoria, and South Australia. Nevertheless, mirroring the trend towards the cool-climate viticulture of the other states—Victoria, in particular—Western Australia has become synonymous with premium-quality wines made in styles that are markedly different from their counterparts in the east of the country. In the Margaret River region, Cabernet Sauvignon produces one of the more European styles, and, around Mount Barker, Shiraz can have the elegant spicy and peppery quality of Syrah from the northern Rhône. Riesling, too, develops delicate flavors not encountered in many other parts of Australia.

Far Away in the Heat

The foundations of the Western Australian wine industry were laid in the first half of the 19th century, when both Thomas Waters and John Septimus Roe planted vineyards in the hot Swan Valley. It was, for a long time, the focus of Western Australian production. Subsequently, it was Yugoslav immigrants who turned the region into a significant wine-producing area. In the early days of the modern era, Swan Valley became known for Houghton's White Burgundy. Released in 1937 and made by the legendary Jack Mann, it was a wine of considerable rich-

Left
Morning mist is a common phenomenon in the Margaret River wine region.

Right
The direct vicinity of the Indian Ocean is the key factor tempering the climate of Margaret River.

Below
Nature looks its colorful best in the Margaret River region.

ness, thanks to the Swan Valley's hot climate—the hottest in Australia—and the fact that just about anything but Chardonnay (mainly Semillon with Muscadelle and Chenin Blanc) went into the blend. A short drive from Perth, there are a handful of wineries in the criss-cross valleys of the Perth Hills and spread out along the coast south of Perth. Geographe is a newly created region, with Bunbury at its center, which encompasses the coastal area around the Capel River, the Donnybrook area, and the Bunbury Hills. Chardonnay and Shiraz are the principal varieties here.

Margaret River

A stone's throw from the Indian Ocean, and 150 miles (240 km) south of Perth, Margaret River is a beautiful region of creeks and valleys, native trees, and wild flowers. It is characterized by surfing beaches, motels and restaurants, hardwood and pottery craft shops, and wineries, of which there are more than fifty. In its early inception, it was pioneered by doctors-turned-winemakers, but more recently it has been taken over by big companies. Southcorp Wines took over Devil's Lair and Brookland Valley, part of which now belongs to Thomas Hardy and so to Constellation Wines. The region is particularly good for Cabernet Sauvignon and Bordeaux blends, with Merlot producing ripe but elegant reds in the blackcurrant and redcurrant spectrum of fruit. Bordeaux blends apply to whites too, producing Sauvignon Blanc with Semillon in some highly successful wines; Chardonnay is also made into consistently excellent whites.

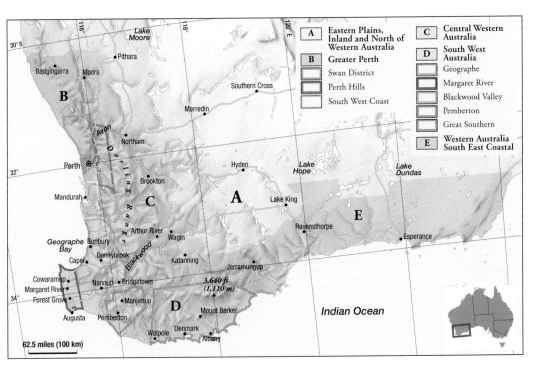

Leeuwin Estate has been credited with producing Australia's finest and perhaps longest-lived Chardonnay.

Also influenced by a maritime climate, the rambling Great Southern Region, with its spectacular jarrah, marri, and karri gum forests, is, for the most part, cooler than Margaret River, with a more continental climate inland. Its development is relatively recent, only beginning a decade or so after the Californian viticulturalist Harold Olmo reported its potential for good-quality wine to the Western Australian government in 1955. Riesling is as successful in Frankland River as in the Clare and Eden Valleys of South Australia, aging well with citrus undertones. Good Chardonnay is produced in the region, along with elegant styles of Cabernet Sauvignon and Shiraz. There appears to be considerable potential, too, for Pinot Noir in the cool-climate vineyards around Mount Barker and Albany. Climatically, Manjimup and Pemberton are respectively the Bordeaux and Burgundy of the region, with Chardonnay, Cabernet Sauvignon, and Pinot Noir the predominant varieties.

Left
The Voyager estate has some stunningly unusual architecture and full, spicy white wines.

Right
Vanya Cullen turns out high-class, stylish but individual wines on the family estate.

Select Producers in Western Australia

Alkoomi Wines***–****
Frankland River

198 acres (80 ha); bought-in grapes; 1,000,000 bottles • Wines include: Riesling, Chardonnay, →Sauvignon, Shiraz, Cabernet Sauvignon, Blackbutt, →Jarrah Shiraz, Wandoo; Southlands range

Alkoomi, established by Merv and Judy Lange, is a family-run business that always produces fine wines. Apart from a small amount used in the Southlands range all the grapes are home-grown.

Cape Mentelle***–*****
Margaret River, Margaret River

321 acres (130 ha); bought-in grapes; 1,300,000 bottles • Wines: Semillon Sauvignon, Chardonnay, Cabernet Merlot, Shiraz, →Zinfandel

Cape Mentelle, now owned by Veuve Clicquot, has developed into one of Western Australia's best quality wineries since it was set up under David Hohnen in 1970. Its winemaker John Durham is producing excellent whites and outstanding Cabernets and Shiraz wines, as well as Australia's best Zinfandel.

Capel Vale**–***
Capel, Geographe

395 acres (160 ha); bought-in grapes; 1,800,000 bottles • Wines include: Chenin, Chardonnay, Verdelho; Merlot, Cabernet Sauvignon, Shiraz, Pinot Noir, Tawny, sparkling

This family-run winery owned by Dr. Peter and Elizabeth Pratten offers three series of wines: the CV range for day-to-day drinking, a white-labelled range for celebration meals, and a limited Reserve range of wines from individual plots, sold with a black label.

Cullen's*****
Cowaramup, Margaret River

79 acres (32 ha); 150,000 bottles • Wines: Chardonnay, Sauvignon, Semillon, →Cabernet Merlot, Pinot Noir

Established in 1971, Cullen was one of the pioneers of the Margaret River region. Now run by Vanya Cullen, Cullen's wines are made in an individual, full-flavored and intense style. Excellent blends.

Devil's Lair**–****
Forest Grove, Margaret River

110 acres (45 ha); bought-in grapes; 300,000 bottles • Wines: Chardonnay, Pinot Noir, Cabernet Merlot; second label Fifth Leg

Bought by the giant Southcorp group in 1996, Devil's Lair continues to carve out a reputation for high-quality Chardonnay, in addition to good Burgundy and Bordeaux-style reds. A winery to watch.

Evans & Tate***
Margaret River

Bought-in grapes; 1,200,000 bottles • Wines: Semillon, Sauvignon, Chardonnay; Merlot, Shiraz, Cabernet, Gnangara Shiraz Cabernet, Barrique 61 Cabernet Merlot

Having moved its quality varietal wine operations to the Margaret River from Swan Valley, this winery continues to make easy-going whites and reds, although it does not scale the heights of the best that Margaret River can do.

Ferngrove Vineyards Estate**–***
Frankland River

704 acres (285 ha) • Wines include: Premium Orchid range with →Cossack Riesling; Chardonnay, Semillon-Sauvignon; Malbec, Cabernet-Merlot, Shiraz

Ferngrove's prize-winning wines are made from its own grapes, which ripen in a cool climate. The winery is run for the tourist market and affords magnificent views of the Stirnling Range.

Houghton**–****
Middle Swan, Perth

593 acres (240 ha); bought-in grapes; 3,600,000 bottles • Wines: a broad range of varietals and blends, including Chardonnay, →Verdelho, Sauvignon, Merlot, Shiraz, Cabernet Sauvignon

In Hardy's Western Australia outpost Larry Cherubino creates a range of good, low-cost varietals and blends, and increasingly interesting wines from the Frankland Valley and Mount Barker. He also makes Hardy's Brookland Valley wines and the second label Verse I in Nannup.

Howard Park***–****
Denmark, Great Southern

74 acres (30 ha); bought-in grapes; 400,000 bottles • Wines include: Riesling, Chardonnay, →Cabernet Merlot and second label Madfish Bay

Chief winemaker Michael Kerrigan is regarded as one of the best in Western Australia. His wines are made from carefully grown grapes from Margaret River and Great Southern. He also has a pleasing MadFish range.

Leeuwin Estate***–*****
Margaret River, Margaret River

346 acres (140 ha); 530,000 bottles • Wines: →Chardonnay, Riesling, Sauvignon; Pinot, Cabernet, →Art Series Chardonnay

Since 1974 Denis and Tricia Horgan's low-yielding vines from unirrigated vineyards have helped to create what is arguably Australia's most intense, finest Chardonnays in the Burgundian mold. Good Cabernet too from this estate, which has simultaneously developed a reputation for its high-profile, open-air concerts.

Moss Wood****–*****
Wilyabrup, Margaret River

20.6 acres (8.34 ha); 67,000 bottles • Wines: Semillon, Chardonnay; Cabernet, Pinot

Winemaker Keith Mugford has earned a reputation for finely crafted, barrel-fermented Semillon, as well as excellent Cabernet and Pinot Noir with finesse and structure.

Picardy***–****
Pemberton

20 acres (8.1 ha); 60,000 bottles • Wines include: Chardonnay, Pinot Noir, →Shiraz, Merlimont

Picardy is a boutique winery, founded in 1993, but it is one of the leading premium wineries in Western Australia, growing Chardonnay, Pinot Noir, Shiraz, and Bordeaux varieties. It belongs to Bill, Sandra, Dan, and Jodie Pannell, who run it. All the wines are made exclusively from estate-grown grapes.

Plantagenet***–****
Mount Barker, Great Southern

247 acres (100 ha); bought-in grapes; 1,200,000 bottles • Wines: Riesling, Chardonnay; Pinot, Cabernet, Shiraz, →Omrak Chardonnay

Tony Smith's winery makes high-quality wines across the range with fine Cabernet; the Shiraz, in particular, most resembles a wine from northern Rhône.

Vasse Felix***–****
Wilyabrup, Margaret River

395 acres (160 ha); bought-in grapes; 1,000,000 bottles • Wines: Semillon Sauvignon, Riesling, Semillon, Chardonnay; Shiraz, →Cabernet

The wines of Vasse Felix have been revitalized, thanks to a new winery and vineyard, which promises to bring continuing improvements. The winery suffered in the early 1990s, but their Cabernet in particular now appears to be back on form.

TASMANIA

As you might expect for an island some way south of the mainland, Tasmania is not like any other state in Australia. It has its own distinct topography, climate, culture and, not surprisingly, wine styles. Life is lived at a slower pace in Tasmania, one of Australia's natural beauty spots and, from a tourist's point of view, one of its most idyllic. More than half of Tasmania's wine is consumed by visitors to the island.

There was a small-scale wine industry in Tasmania in the 19th century, but it was not until Jean Miguet and Claudio Alcorso planted vineyards near Launceston and Hobart that the modern wine industry grew up. To speak of a wine industry in Tasmania would be an exaggeration, in view of the relatively small area of around 2,965 acres (1,200 ha) under cultivation and yielding grapes. On the other hand there is no lack of quality and individuality among the 50 wineries around Hobart in the south and in the sub-regions of Pipers River and Lamar Valley in the north.

Perhaps the best known is Pipers Brook, which was established by the pioneering Dr. Andrew Pirie, the driving force behind Tasmanian wine. With its closely-planted, European-style vineyards, Pipers Brook produces consummate Chardonnay and long-lived Riesling and, despite being one of the coolest regions in Australia, gets good results from both Cabernet Sauvignon and Pinot Noir—a veritable Bordeaux, Burgundy, and Alsace rolled into one.

With its cool climate, the coolest of all Australia's wine regions, the northern region around Pipers River is particularly suited to the production of sparkling wines, mostly made from the classic champagne grapes, Chardonnay and Pinot Noir. The aromatic Alsace varieties—

St. Matthias Vineyard in the Tamar Valley is known for Riesling and Pinot Noir.

Riesling, Gewürztraminer, and Pinot Gris—do well here, and to a lesser extent so does Pinot Noir. The picturesque Tamar Valley produces richer, fuller-bodied styles.

The southern pioneering winery is Moorilla, on the Derwent River near Hobart, planted by Claudio Alcorso. In addition to the Derwent River wineries, the region comprises the southernmost Huon Valley, the eastern zone with Freycinet Vineyards at Wine Glass Bay of particular note, as well as Domaine A in the Coal River Valley. Pinot Noir is the dominant grape variety in the south, and much of it, along with Chardonnay, is used for premium sparkling wine production.

SELECT PRODUCERS IN TASMANIA

PIPERS BROOK VINEYARD***–****
PIPERS BROOK, NORTHERN TASMANIA
494 acres (200 ha); bought-in grapes; 1,200,000 bottles • Wines: Pipers Brook Pinot Gris, Gewürztraminer, Riesling, Sauvignon Blanc/Chardonnnay; Pinot; reserve range and single-vineyard range, →Summit Chardonnay, →Pellion Pinot, Opimian, second label Ninth Island, →Pirie (sparkling)
This vineyard was set up in 1974 after a study identified the specifically "bio" climate of North Tasmania. The wines have maintained their quality although the founder Andrew Pirie has left, and they still have their intense, unique aromas and finesse.

PIPERS BROOK VINEYARD
1998 PELLION
Pinot Noir
Tasmania

MOORILLA ESTATE***
BERRIEDALE, SOUTHERN TASMANIA
Bought-in grapes; 106,000 bottles • Wines: Riesling, Chardonnay, Gewürztraminer, Pinot Noir, Cabernet, Cabernet Merlot, sparkling vintage brut
Founded by the Alcorso family in 1958, Moorilla pioneered intense, fruity white varietals. The future is less certain since its takeover, but this Derwent-River-based winery should continue to retain a captive market in Hobart, Tasmania's capital.

WINE IN NEW ZEALAND

New Zealand is the most southerly wine-producing country of the southern hemisphere. The gravelly riverbed soils, and the unique, cool, maritime climate which governs North and South Island, make it the ideal spot for the production of wine from premium grape varieties. These grow best in marginal climates, notably the Burgundy grapes Chardonnay and Pinot Noir and the Loire Valley's Sauvignon Blanc. In warmer areas, Merlot, and to a certain extent Cabernet Sauvignon, can ripen well, too. Although vines were first planted in New Zealand back in 1819, the New Zealand wine industry is a modern success story beginning in the late 1960s.

In 1960, only 12 percent of wine sold in New Zealand was table wine, the rest being fortified wine. The main grape variety was the American hybrid Albany Surprise, or Isabella, a hangover from the bad old days of phylloxera and prohibition. Despite a vine pull scheme in 1986, following over-enthusiastic planting and subsequent heavy discounting, subsequent growth has been rapid. The number of wineries has increased from just over 100 to nearly 400, and the vine area has kept pace, jumping from just over 9,800 acres (4,000 ha) in 1989 to about 39,000 acres (15,800 ha). Over three-quarters of the country's vineyards are concentrated in the three principal regions of Marlborough, Gisborne, and Hawke's Bay.

A PARADISE FOR SAUVIGNON

From the mid-1960s, the culture of wine began to take hold and New Zealand experienced a period of unrivaled expansion, interrupted only

According to statistics, the cold climate makes it impossible to grow wine in the mountainous Otago region of southern South Island. Nonetheless, growers produce very convincing wines against a dramatic scenic backdrop.

At Hawke's Bay in the east of North Island, palms testify to the warmth that enables the Cabernets in New Zealand to prosper.

by the vine pull scheme of 1986. In the 1970s the industry was strongly influenced by Professor Helmut Becker of Geisenheim, whose advice to plant the Müller-Thurgau grape led to the production of an easy, fruity style of white wine. It was not until the 1980s, however, that producers started to realize that New Zealand's climate was capable of better things.

Grape varieties from marginal climates, responsible for France's top wines, were planted. As a result of this, New Zealand gained a reputation in little more than 20 years for world-class Sauvignon Blanc to rival the Loire Valley's best, and there is potential to make superb reds and whites from the Burgundy and Bordeaux varieties. Chardonnay and Sauvignon Blanc have now overtaken Müller-Thurgau as the country's most widely planted white varieties; in the case of red wines, Pinot Noir has overtaken Cabernet Sauvignon. The development of quality sparkling wines has added another string to New Zealand's bow. Exports have rocketed, and today New Zealand wines command the highest price per bottle of any country.

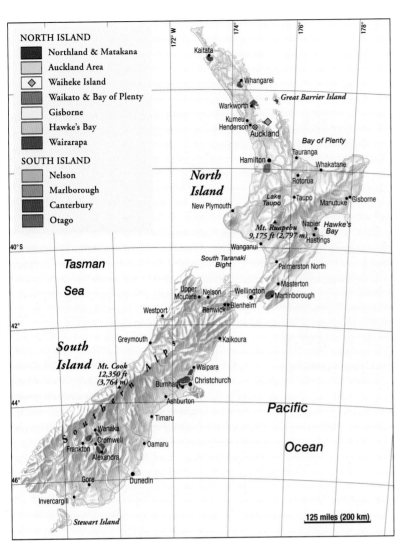

NORTH ISLAND
- Northland & Matakana
- Auckland Area
- Waiheke Island
- Waikato & Bay of Plenty
- Gisborne
- Hawke's Bay
- Wairarapa

SOUTH ISLAND
- Nelson
- Marlborough
- Canterbury
- Otago

Kaitata
Whangarei
Warkworth
Great Barrier Island
Kumeu
Henderson
Auckland
North Island
Bay of Plenty
Tauranga
Hamilton
Whakatane
Rotorua
Lake Taupo
Taupo
Manutuke
Gisborne
New Plymouth
Napier *Hawke's Bay*
Mt. Ruapehu 9,175 ft (2,797 m)
Hastings
Wanganui
South Taranaki Bight
Palmerston North
Masterton
Upper Moutere
Nelson
Wellington
Martinborough
Westport
Renwick
Blenheim
Tasman Sea
Greymouth
Kaikoura
South Island
Mt. Cook 12,350 ft (3,764 m)
Waipara
Christchurch
Burnham
Ashburton
Pacific Ocean
Timaru
Wanaka
Cromwell
Frankton
Oamaru
Alexandra
Gore
Dunedin
Invercargill
Stewart Island

125 miles (200 km)

Statistics and the Weather

New Zealand's seven wine regions span a distance of some 750 miles (1,200 km), roughly the equivalent of the distance from North Africa to Paris. On the scale devised by Amerine and Winkler in California, based on heat degree days (H.D.D.), which is the daily average temperature above 50°F (10°C) during the growing season, New Zealand falls in Region 1, along with Bordeaux and Burgundy. The maritime climate, with its relatively cool summers and mild winters, is a New Zealand wine producer's greatest asset, but there are considerable differences between north and south. There is an almost subtropical, humid climate around Auckland in the north, while the climate of Otago in the south is continental and, according to statistics (but not in fact), too cool for the production of quality wines.

The flip side of the coin is New Zealand's abundant rainfall, which occurs mostly on the western side of the two islands. Nevertheless, heavy winds and torrential rain can and do, on occasion, adversely affect the New Zealand

Sauvignon Blanc attains a quite distinctive character on this stony alluvial soil in Marlborough, arousing interest in New Zealand wines worldwide.

harvest. On poorly drained soils in particular, rainfall can encourage unwanted leaf and shoot growth, creating dense foliage in which fungal disease is rife. Because of this moisture problem, and the fertility of the country's vigorous soils, New Zealand (thanks largely to the pioneering viticultural work of Dr. Richard Smart) has been in the forefront of the development of canopies that give access to sunlight and ventilation. At the same time, the search is on for more free-draining shingle soils of lower fertility.

Traditional Varieties and Modern Technology

Although Sauvignon Blanc was the first to establish a world-class reputation for New Zealand wines, plantings of Chardonnay have outstripped those of any other grape variety. Chardonnay extends throughout the main wine regions, resulting in a range of intensely flavored wines, from refreshing, unwooded dry whites to richer and more complex Burgundy styles. Of the principal regions, Marlborough is the only one in which plantings of Chardonnay are outnumbered by those of Sauvignon Blanc. Plantings of Riesling and Tokay Pinot Gris are on the increase. Both make a delicate, dry, Alsace-style of white and, in the case of Riesling, some delicious sweet, botrytized styles.

Pinot noir is the most exciting and enterprising red grape variety, with fine red Burgundy-style wines being produced at Martinborough, Marlborough, Canterbury, and Otago. Most of the Marlborough crop is made into sparkling wine, although the trend is toward still wines. The late-ripening Cabernet Sauvignon tends toward herbaceousness on South Island, but flourishes on the gravel soils of Hawke's Bay and on Waiheke Island near Auckland. In conjunction with Merlot, it creates a Bordeaux-style blend which, in warmer vintages, can be soft, elegant, and complex.

White wines have greatly benefited from stainless steel technology, inherited from the dairy industry. Cool fermentation in temperature-controlled stainless steel is the normal method for Sauvignon Blanc, for instance. While Chardonnay is made in this way in order to preserve the primary fruit, more complex styles have been developed, employing traditional French techniques such as whole bunch pressing in new oak casks, lees stirring, and partial or full malolactic fermentation. With a better understanding of tannin management, reds have gained complexity. For instance, Pinot Noir can benefit from cold soaking on occasion, and maturation in new and part-used French oak casks.

North Island

The early growth of Auckland as a wine-growing area owed much to the migration of Dalmatian settlers to work in the Kauri gum fields in the late 19th century. Auckland is still the headquarters of many of New Zealand's best-known wineries, including industry giant Montana and wineries whose names—Babich, Delegat, Selaks, Nobilo—testify to their European origins. However, Auckland's star has waned as regions further south have grown in importance. There has been a revival of sorts, with some excellent Chardonnay coming from both Kumeu River and Collards, while Stonyridge and Goldwater on Waiheke Island have the potential to produce spectacular reds in the Bordeaux style. Despite their humid summers, the far northern regions of Northland and Matakana also show potential for big, hearty reds. Immediately southeast of Auckland, the small region of Waikato and the Bay of Plenty is home to a handful of well-established wineries. Most of their grape sources come from Hawke's Bay and further south.

Red wines of the island—Goldwater Estate on Waiheke.

The Poor and the Classy Bays

On the east coast and at the northern tip of Poverty Bay, Gisborne has rather suffered by comparison with the more prestigious Hawke's Bay and Marlborough. In a decade, plantings here, along with production, have marginally declined. It's a rather remote region, with only a handful of wineries, of which Matawhero and the organic Millton stand out. Gisborne is white-wine country, with Chardonnay easily the most widely planted variety. Perhaps for

As everywhere in New Zealand, the presentation of wine in Auckland is a very straightforward, uncomplicated matter.

that reason, producers like to call it "the Chardonnay capital of New Zealand," but it has the dubious distinction of being best known for producing large volumes for the big companies, most of which goes into wine casks. Some premium Chardonnay is made here at Montana and Corbans.

South west of Gisborne on the east coast, Hawke's Bay is New Zealand's finest wine region for reds in the Bordeaux style and, arguably, for Chardonnay too. Plantings here have risen by a third in a decade, with Cabernet Sauvignon, Merlot, and Cabernet Franc together outstripping Chardonnay in vineyard area, even though Chardonnay is the most widely planted variety. It is a sunny region, but it is also prone to severe autumn rainfall, as occurred in 1988 and 1995. The terrain in the hinterland behind the town of Napier is diverse, with a mixture of fertile, coastal alluvial, and gravelly soils, and less productive, well-drained gravel soils not unlike the Médoc region of southwest France in parts. Hawke's Bay is home to more than 50 wineries, including Te Mata, C.J. Pask, Montana's McDonald Winery, Esk Valley, Te Awa Farm, Stonecroft, and Sacred Hill. Many of these produce notable Chardonnay and red wines of distinction.

Wairarapa and Pinot Noir

This cool, dry, small region to the east of Wellington, which includes the district of Martinborough, has emerged in the last decade as one of New Zealand's most exciting new wine areas. It is remote sheep-grazing country, in which a handful of small but highly determined growers have made their mark. Whether the gravelly Martinborough terraces are better suited to Pinot Noir or Cabernet Sauvignon is a moot point, but there is little doubt that many of New Zealand's top Pinot Noirs are from this region, notably those of Dry River, Ata Rangi, Martinborough Vineyard, and Palliser Estate. Pinot Noir is the most widely planted variety here. At the same time, the region produces fine Chardonnay and highly aromatic dry whites from Sauvignon Blanc, and in the Alsace mold from Riesling and Tokay Pinot Gris. With over 40 small wineries and plenty of restaurants, cafés, and hotels, it is one of the most attractive wine regions to visit.

South Island

Of all New Zealand's wine regions, Marlborough has established the strongest reputation for itself, based on the quality and unique flavors of its Sauvignon Blanc. This is so much the case that it seems extraordinary that the region was not developed (by Montana) until 1973. Among the Sauvignon Blancs of the world, Marlborough Sauvignon stands out for its pungent aromas, ranging from asparagus and green bean to the more tropical flavors of citrus, mango, and passionfruit. Two-thirds of New Zealand's Sauvignon Blanc are planted in Marlborough, on the diverse, stony alluvial flats of the Wairau Valley. It is a cool region with a strong maritime influence, characterized by sunny days and cold nights, which keep acidity levels high.

In New Zealand's largest wine region, two wineries—Cloudy Bay and Montana—have blazed a trail for Sauvignon Blanc. Today, there are around 70 wineries producing consummate examples of the style, notably Hunter's, Jackson Estate, Wairau River, Vavasour, Villa Maria, and Seresin Estate. Marlborough also produces excellent Chardonnay and fine Riesling, as well as sparkling wines made from the champagne grapes Chardonnay and Pinot Noir. Fromm Estate is leading the way with table wines made from Pinot Noir, but Montana, Corbans, and Cloudy Bay, among others, are also producing good examples of the style.

Despite Wet and Cold

Closest of New Zealand's wine regions to the rainy west coast, Nelson is 46 miles (75 km) to the west of Marlborough. It is a small but rapidly expanding region of mainly white wines with a predominance of Chardonnay and Sauvignon Blanc produced at its 20 wineries. On soils not unlike Marlborough's alluvial flats, production has more than trebled in a decade here. Seifried is easily the biggest of Nelson's wineries, while Neudorf is not only its best, but one of New Zealand's best, particularly for its exceptional Chardonnay, which can be as sumptuous and complex as *premier cru* white Burgundy.

New Zealand's fourth-largest wine region, Canterbury, has vineyards concentrated in three zones: the flat plains surrounding the pretty city of Christchurch, the hills around Waipara, and the Banks Peninsula. Considered by many to be too cold for viticulture, the region was given a new lease of life when research carried out by

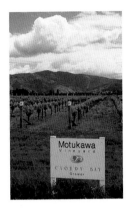

Thanks to its outstanding Sauvignon, Cloudy Bay in Marlborough has become the best-known New Zealand estate worldwide.

Rippon Vineyards by Lake Wanaka own one of the finest Pinot Noir vineyards in the world. It extends along the lake against a backdrop of New Zealand's Southern Alps and is run on biological principles.

Dr. David Jackson demonstrated its true potential. It is an extremely cool region, exposed to the ocean and consequently well suited to white grape varieties, in particular Chardonnay, Riesling, and Sauvignon Blanc. However, Pinot Noir is perhaps the best variety, creating wines of intense flavors in the elegant, red-berry spectrum. There are around 40 small wineries in the region, of which Giesen is the leader. There are also good wines from the Donaldson family's Pegasus Bay.

Dramatic Vineyard Scenery

If you want to see the most wildly beautiful vineyards in the world, you must travel to Central Otago and its capital Queenstown. Here, in the natural lakeland setting of southern New Zealand, you will find extremes of altitude, latitude (45° south), temperature, remoteness, and also dramatic beauty. The area is a tourist's paradise and a focus for exciting sports. Central Otago is the fastest growing wine region in New Zealand, with plantings of Chardonnay and Pinot Noir in more that 40 wineries now rivaling those of Canterbury. Although the Otago region defies conventional norms of suitable climate for viticulture, its long summer sunshine hours and relatively low rainfall suggest that grape-growing is not only possible here but, for certain styles, highly desirable. Chardonnay produces good, melon-and-citrus-style wines, while the potential of Pinot Noir's varietal character, from wineries such as Mount Edward, Mount Difficulty, Quartz Reef, Felton Road, and Rippon Vineyards, is starting to manifest itself.

Select Producers in New Zealand

NORTH ISLAND

ATA RANGI★★★★
MARTINBOROUGH, MARTINBOROUGH
*62 acres (25 ha); 66,000 bottles • Wines: Pinot Gris,
→Craighall Chardonnay, Sauvignon; →Ata Rangi Pinot
Noir, Célèbre, →Summer Rose*
With low-yielding vines and meticulous attention to
detail, Clive Paton and Oliver Masters make some of
New Zealand's most intense Pinot Noir along with a
concentrated, flagship Bordeaux blend in Célèbre.

BABICH★★★
HENDERSON, AUCKLAND
*Bought-in grapes; 1,400,000 bottles • Wines include:
Sauvignon, Chardonnay, Pinot Gris, Riesling; Syrah,
Pinot; international renommee: Marlborough
Sauvignon, Irongate Chardonnay, Cabernet Merlot*
The winery is owned by Peter and Joe Babich, the two
sons of pioneer Josip Babich, who founded the company
in 1916. They produce consistent quality, premium
varietal wines from the Hawke's Bay, Gisborne, and
Marlborough regions.

C.J. PASK★★★−★★★★
HASTINGS, HAWKE'S BAY
*222 acres (90 ha); 600,000 bottles • Wines: Chardonnay,
Sauvignon, Cabernet Merlot, Syrah, Merlot*
High-profile winemaker Kate Radburnd makes equally
high-profile wines, in particular fine Bordeaux-style
reds, sourced from Pask's gravelly vineyard site at
Gimblett Road, which many—including owner Chris
Pask himself—claim to be New Zealand's best site for
Cabernet-Merlot-based reds, and where Syrah is now
gaining importance.

CRAGGY RANGE WINERY★★★
HAWKE'S BAY AND MARTINBOROUGH
*49 acres (20 ha); bought-in grapes; 300,000 bottles
• Wines include: Sauvignon, Riesling, →Chardonnay,
Merlot, →Syrah, Pinot Noir*
Wines of great character from individual vineyards in
Gimblett Gravels, Martinborough, and Marlborough.
Very successful Sauvignon and highly-praised Prestige
Collection, especially Les Beaux Cailloux Chardonnay,
Sophie on a Merlot base and the Syrah Le sol.

DRY RIVER★★★★★
MARTINBOROUGH, MARTINBOROUGH
*23 acres (9.5 ha); 30,000 bottles • Wines: Riesling,
Pinot Gris, Chardonnay, Gewürztraminer, Sauvignon;
Pinot Noir, Syrah*
Neil McCallum's Dry River is one of the most
extraordinary vineyards in the world, producing
arguably the best Pinot Noir in the southern hemisphere.

ESCARPEMENT VINEYARD★★★
MARTINBOROUGH
*59 acres (24 ha) • Wines include: Chardonnay, Pinot
Blanc, Pinot Gris, Riesling, →Pinot Noir*
Vineyards and winery, partnership between the
McKennas—Larry took Martinborough Pinot Noir to
international fame—and the Kirbys at the foot of the
Aorangi Chain. The aim is clear—New World wines of
complexity, texture, and structure.

GOLDWATER ESTATE★★★−★★★★
PUTIKI BAY, WAIHEKE ISLAND
*35 acres (14 ha); bought-in grapes; 312,000 bottles
• Wines: Chardonnay; Cabernet and Merlot from
Waiheke Island, →Waiheke Island Esslin Merlot,
Sauvignon and Chardonnay from Marlborough*

The Goldwaters have turned a lifestyle choice into a
thriving business, expanding production from picturesque
Waiheke Island into Marlborough, where 86 acres (35 ha)
under contract produce quality whites for them.

KUMEU RIVER★★★★
KUMEU, AUCKLAND
*64 acres (26 ha); bought-in grapes; 250,000 bottles
• Wines: Chardonnay, →Mate's Vineyard Chardonnay,
Pinot Gris, Melba, Pinot Noir*
Michael Brajkovich makes finely honed, intense,
Burgundian-style Chardonnay, which is a major
achievement in Auckland's subtropical, humid climate.

MARTINBOROUGH VINEYARD★★★★
MARTINBOROUGH
*90,000 bottles • Wines: Riesling, Pinot Gris, Sauvignon,
Chardonnay; Pinot*
Since Larry McKenna left in 1999 the estate has ceased
to grow, and under Claire Mulholland it has devoted
itself to a constant range of classical wines. The vines
are now fully grown and their yields are reduced. They
are pruned and trained by hand and the grapes are
hand-picked. The winery is well known for classical,
complex Pinot Noirs and elegant Chardonnays.

THE MILLTON VINEYARD★★★
MANUTUKE, GISBORNE
*49 acres (20 ha); 144,000 bottles • Wines: Chardonnay,
Chenin, Riesling, Viognier, Malbec, Merlot Cabernet
from Te Arai, Riverpoint and Opou vineyards,
→Naboth's Chardonnay and Pinot*
In 1984 James and Annie Millton, New Zealand's first
commercial, fully certified organic winegrowers,
established the Millton Vineyard, which rapidly gained a
reputation for sweet, late-harvested Rieslings and Chenin.
The distinctive wines are produced from estate-grown
grapes employing biodynamic cultivation techniques.

PALLISER ESTATE★★★−★★★★
MARTINBOROUGH, MARTINBOROUGH
*210 acres (85 ha); bought-in grapes; 480,000 bottles
• Wines: Chardonnay, Riesling, Sauvignon, Pinot Gris,
Noble Riesling, S.F.G.; Pinot*
Winemaker Allan Johnson makes very intensive wines and
a Sauvignon that puts many others from Marlborough in
the shade.

TE MATA★★★−★★★★
HAVELOCK NORTH, HAWKE'S BAY
*321 acres (130 ha); 420,000 bottles • Wines include:
Woodthorpe: Viognier, Chardonnay, Gamay;
→Colerain Cabernet-Merlot, →Awatea Cabernet-
Merlot, Bullnose Syrah*
Under the stewardship of John Buck and winemaker
Peter Cowley, Te Mata has become one of New
Zealand's foremost premium New Zealand red
wineries. It's noted in particular for fine Chardonnay
and the Bordeaux-style finesse of its red blends.

TRINITY HILL★★★−★★★★
HASTINGS, HAWKE'S BAY
*99 acres (40 ha); bought-in grapes; 420,000 bottles
• Wines: Chardonnay, Sauvignon, Riesling, Pinot Gris;
Cabernet/Cabernet Franc, Merlot/Syrah, Pinot*
John Hancock produces two ranges under the Gimblett
Road and Shepherds Croft labels. Warren Gibson is the
winemaker at Trinity Hill, where Hancock's joint venture
with London and Auckland partners is bearing fruit in the
form of excellent Chardonnay and improving reds. He is
also experimenting with Viognier and Montepulciano.

Villa Maria Estate**–****
Mangere, Auckland

494 acres (200 ha); bought-in grapes; 6,000,000 bottles
• Wines include: Chardonnay, Sauvignon, Riesling,
Pinot Gris; Pinot, Cabernet/Merlot
Founded in 1961, with the dynamic George Fistonich at
the helm and Michelle Richardson the winemaker, Villa
Maria has become New Zealand's third largest company
and consistently one of the best. It shines with excellent
Marlborough Sauvignons →Wairau Valley and
→Clifford Bay wines, with Botrytis Riesling, a fine reserve
Chardonnay, prize-winning Cabernet-Merlot blends
from Hawke's Bay, and Pinot Noirs from Marlborough.

SOUTH ISLAND
Cloudy Bay***–****
Blenheim, Marlborough

247 acres (100 ha); bought-in grapes; 800,000 bottles
• Wines: →Sauvignon, Te Koko, →Chardonnay, Pelorus
N.V. and Vintage Brut, Late Harvest Riesling,
Gewürztraminer; Bay Pinot Noir
Chief winemaker and star photographer Kevin Judd
produces the best Sauvignon in the New World, but it
was recently outshone. However, his Chardonnay is also
good, and the Pinot Noir from this Veuve Clicquot Cape
Mentelle enterprise is very promising.

Felton Road Wines****
Bannockburn, Central Otago

74 acres (30 ha); 120,000 bottles • Wines include:
Riesling, Chardonnay, Pinot Noir; →special bottlings
from individual blocks
Since its first vintage in 1997 the winery on Felton
Road, near the little town of Bannockburn, which
tends its vines most carefully, has been giving the fruitiness and complexity of the vineyards of this region
full expression. The Pinot Noirs of Blocks 3 and 5 are
among the best in the southern hemisphere.

Fromm****
Blenheim, Marlborough

10 acres (4 ha); bought-in grapes; 54,000 bottles
• Wines: Chardonnay; Pinot, Merlot
Despite tiny production, Swiss George Fromm has made
an impact, thanks to his highly concentrated, complex
Pinot Noir from very low-yielding vines.

Giesen**–***
Burnham, Canterbury

86 acres (35 ha) (Canterbury), 165 acres (67 ha)
(Marlborough); bought-in grapes; 650,000 bottles
• Wines: Sauvignon, Chardonnay, Riesling, Late
Harvest and Botrytized Riesling, Reserves; Pinot
Bringing German expertise with them, the three Giesen
brothers, together with winemaker Andrew Blake, have
worked assiduously to carve out a reputation for fine
Canterbury whites as well as a refined Pinot Noir.

Hunter's****
Blenheim, Marlborough

222 acres (90 ha); bought-in grapes; 660,000 bottles
• Wines: Chardonnay, Sauvignon, Chardonnay Reserve,
Riesling, Gewürztraminer, Breidecker; Pinot, Merlot,
Estate Red; →Miru Miru
With experienced winemaker Gary Duke, Jane Hunter
is responsible for making Hunter's one of
Marlborough's best estates, with fine Sauvignon and a
Graves-style, oak-aged blend as well as a finely crafted,
champagne-method fizz in Miru Miru.

Isabel Estate****
Renwick, Marlborough

128 acres (52 ha); 180,000 bottles • Wines: Sauvignon,
Chardonnay, Riesling, Pinot Gris; Pinot Noir
Winemaker Jeff Sinnott seems to make better wines
every year.

Purism in demand—a
tasting at Cloudy Bay.

New Zealand's wine giant
Montana maintains various
estates. The O from
Ormond Estate is an elegant
Chardonnay.

Montana**–****
Blenheim, Marlborough

5,187 acres (2,100 ha); bought-in grapes; 27,000,000
bottles • Wines include: Sauvignon, Chardonnay,
Riesling, Gewürztraminer, Semillon, Müller-Thurgau;
Pinot, Merlot, Cabernet, Cabernet Franc
In 1973 Montana decided to plant in Marlborough, and
today the region is world-famous for its Sauvignon.
Following substantial investment, Montana, under
senior winemaker Jeff Clarke, is now New Zealand's
largest producer.

Mount Edward****
Gibbston, Central Otago

2.5 acres (1 ha); bought-in grapes; 20,400 bottles
• Wines: Riesling, →Pinot Noir
Alan Brady was the first to plant vines in Gibbston in
1981. He set up Gibbston Valley Wines and ran the
company during the pioneer years from Central Otago.
In 1998 he built Mount Edward in order to specialize on
Pinot, signing exclusive contracts for three young Pinot
Noir plots of 17 acres (7 ha). The small winery
concentrates on quality and now exports 70 percent of
its hand-made wines to Europe.

Neudorf Vineyards***–****
Upper Moutere, Nelson

60 acres (24 ha); bought-in grapes; 120,000 bottles
• Wines: →Moutere Chardonnay, Riesling; Pinot; plus
Nelson label varietals, Brightwater Riesling and
Sauvignon
Tim and Judy Finn make some of New Zealand's finest
wines, in particular the Moutere Chardonnay, whose
occasional botrytis adds complexity to the power and
textural richness of the wines.

Pegasus Bay***–****
Waipara, Canterbury

69 acres (28 ha); bought-in grapes; 150,000–200,000
bottles • Wines: Chardonnay, Riesling, Sauvignon; Pinot
Noir, →Prima Donna, Cabernet Merlot, →Maestro
(Cabernet), second label called Main Divide
Founded by Professor Ivan Donaldson Pegasus Bay is
now making most attractive wines under winemakers
Matthew Donaldson and Lynnette Hudson in its cellars
that are reminiscent of cathedrals.

Quartz Reef****
Quartz Reef, Central Otago

37 acres (15 ha); bought-in grapes; 90,000 bottles
• Wines: Pinot Gris, →Chauvet Sparkling Wine,
→Pinot Noir
Rudi Bauer, formerly winemaker with Rippon, has
specialized on sparkling wine and Pinot Noir. He is
arousing much attention with this small, quality-conscious winery.

Rippon Vineyards****
Wanaka, Otago

31 acres (12.6 ha); 72,000 bottles • Wines: Riesling,
Chardonnay, Sauvignon, Gewürztraminer, Osteiner,
→Emma Rippon; Pinot Noir, Merlot/Syrah
Founded by Rolfe and Lois Mills, the tradition of
making elegant Pinot Noir at this wonderfully located
lakeside winery continues with winemaker Russell
Lake. They also produce varietals with exceptional
intensity of flavor.

Seresin Estate***–****
Renwick, Marlborough

279 acres (113 ha); 180,000 bottles • Wines: Pinot
Noir, Pinot Gris, Sauvignon, Chardonnay, Riesling,
Noble Sauvignon, Noble Riesling, Moana (sparkling)
Cinematographer Michael Seresin has had the vision
and energy to start Seresin Estate from scratch and turn
it into one of the top producers in Marlborough.

APPENDIX

GLOSSARY

A.C.
Stands for *Appellation Contrôlée*. See also *Appellation d'Origine Contrôlée*.

ACID
A key component of wine, acid is present in all grapes, mainly in the form of tartaric acid. It gives wine freshness and long life, provided the acidity is in balance.

ADEGA (COOPERATIVA) (Portuguese)
Term for a grower's cooperative. Lit. "winery."

AMARONE
Dry Italian wine made from the must of air-dried berries.

AMONTILLADO
Designation for a mature dry Fino sherry aged naturally. Also a term for blended sweet sherries.

APPELLATION D'ORIGINE CONTRÔLÉE (A.O.C.)
The French system of defining wine by region, which has become the prototype in the wine world. Also prescribes yields and other viticultural practices.

AROMA
The scent of a wine that lends it its distinctive "nose" or "bouquet."

ASSEMBLAGE
Blending of high-value wines (*cuvée*), in contrast to *coupage*.

ASTRINGENT
Furry feeling on the tongue, often resulting from high tannin content.

AUSBRUCH
The famous wine style of Austria, a specialty of the town of Rust on the Neusiedler See.

AUSLESE
One of the *Prädikate* of the Q.m.P. category as defined by the German Wine Law, literally meaning "selected harvest." Sweet wines with a high must weight.

A.V.A. (American Viticultural Area)
The American version of France's *Appellation Contrôlée* system. It defines a wine by its geographic and climatic region but does not prescribe yields or grape varieties.

AZIENDA AGRICOLA
Italian term for an estate that makes wine exclusively from its own grapes, in contrast to an *azienda vinicola*.

BAG IN A BOX
Wine retailed in quantities of a liter or more. The box is furnished with a tap and often with a soda siphon that slows down the oxidation of the remaining wine.

BALLING
System used in South Africa to determine the concentration of the must. Roughly the same as the Brix scale used in the U.S.A.

BARRIQUE
Originally referred to the barrel type used in Bordeaux but now refers to the internationally used standard barrel in the wine trade containing 60 gallons (225 liters), used to age red wines and ferment and age white wines.

BASE STOCK
The base stock or root onto which another variety of vine is grafted.

BÂTONNAGE
The lees (deposit left after fermentation) are stirred periodically to ensure that the oxygen in the barrel is carried right to the bottom, preventing the development of any faults in the aroma of the finished wine.

BEERENAUSLESE
One of the *Prädikate* of the Q.m.P. category as defined by the German Wine Law, literally "selected berries." It should be made with botrytized grapes for an intense, sweet wine.

BENTONITE
A porous clay, rich in mineral and derived from volcanic rock. It is used to improve white wines.

BIODYNAMIC CULTIVATION (France)
An organic approach to viticulture, heavily influenced by the theories of Rudolf Steiner. It is the most ideological of the organic systems and includes elements of astronomy.

BIOLOGICAL ACID CONVERSION
See Malolactic acid conversion.

BLIND TASTING
A wine tasting term that means that wines are tasted with the labels hidden.

BLUSH WINE
American term for mostly light, sweetish white or rosé wines from dark grapes. The most popular is White Zinfandel.

BOCKSBEUTEL
Wide, rounded bottle used only by growers from Franconia and Portugal.

BÖCKSER
Sulfurous smell reminiscent of bad eggs arising during fermentation due to faulty processing.

BODEGA
Spanish term for a winery.

BODEGA COOPERATIVA
Spanish winegrowers' organization.

BOTRYTIS CINEREA
Noble rot, a fungus that attacks grapes and causes them to shrivel, thereby concentrating the flavors, sugar, and acid. It produces a complex and sweet wine, commonly referred to as "botrytized" wines: the most famous examples are Chateau d'Yquem from Sauternes, Sekt from Germany, and Tokaji from Hungary.

BOTTLE FERMENTATION
A method used in the production of sparkling wine, when the second fermentation takes place in the bottle. See also *Méthode champenoise*.

BOTTLE-MATURATION (also called Bottle-aging)
Maturing a wine in the bottle rather than a tank or barrel.

BOTTLE-READY
A term to describe a wine that has aged enough to be ready for bottling.

BOTTLING LIQUOR
In champagne production, the induction of the all-important second fermentation is achieved by the addition of a mixture called *liqueur d'expédition* or *liqueur de triage*. This bottling liquor consists of reserve wine, into which a small amount of cane sugar has been dissolved.

BOUQUET (NOSE)
The totality of aromas given off by a wine.

BOUTIQUE WINERY
Small winemaker producing wines with great care in small quantities, mostly at high prices. Contrasts with industrial-scale wineries.

BRIX
A system, used mainly in the U.S.A. and adapted from the sugar industry, to measure densities and by extension the density of must concentrates. See also Balling.

BRUT
Term for dry sparkling wines with less than $^1/_4$ oz/pint (15 g/l) residual sugar. Often used to denote a very dry sparkling wine.

BULK
Wine by the barrel.

BUSCHENSCHANK
Austrian term for → *Straußwirtschaft*, where home-grown wine is sold by the glass.

BUSH VINES
Bush-type vines found in some areas of Australia and South Africa that are not cultivated on wire frames (see also Cultivation systems), but have a short trunk on which the shoots are arranged in circles. Also called Gobelet-trained vines.

CARBON DIOXIDE
CO_2, carbonic acid; a natural gas, produced as a by-product during fermentation.

CARBONIC MACERATION
Process to soften and ferment grapes by means of carbonic acid. Used in the production of lighter, fruitier red wines that are to be drunk young. Uncrushed, undamaged berries are fermented in a container by adding carbonic acid. A small quantity of grape sugar (dextrose) is added to start fermentation.

CAVA
Term for a Spanish sparkling wine made by traditional fermentation procedure in the bottle. Literally "cellar."

CAVE
French term for "cellar."

CHAI
A term used in Southwest France for cellars, some of which are above ground.

CHAMBRER
French term meaning "allow to breathe," i.e. open a bottle of wine and leave in contact with the air to reach room temperature.

CHAMPAGNE METHOD
See *Méthode champenoise.*

CHAPTALIZATION
To add sugar before fermentation, to increase the alcohol content. Not permitted with every kind of wine.

CHARMAT METHOD
Tank fermentation process in the production of sparkling wine, where the second fermentation takes place in a pressure tank, not in the bottle.

CHÂTEAU-BOTTLED/ESTATE-BOTTLED
Term used on labels to show that a wine was grown, made and bottled in the same place. Also applies to cooperative-made wines but not to winery bottlings or bottlings of →bulk wines.

CLARET (CLAIRET)
Originally a medieval Norman English term for light red wines from the Haut Pays shipped through Bordeaux. In England the term later came to mean Bordeaux wines or wines in the Bordeaux style rather than Haut Pays (Bergerac or Gaillac). *Clairet* is now used in France again to designate light-colored Bordeaux wines.

CLARIFICATION
Clarification of wine, helping to stabilize it. A clarification agent is added to the wine that binds with cloudy substances and other unwanted particles and settles on the bottom with them as sediment.

CLASSICO
Precisely defined geographical zones in Italy from which the grapes of a *classico* wine must come.

CLIMAT
A term used in France, particularly in Burgundy, to describe a vineyard site by its climatic and geographical characteristics.

CLONE
Vine reproduced from a genetically identical parent plant.

CLOS
Term used in France to describe a vineyard enclosed by a wall or hedge.

COLD SOAK
Cold maceration, especially with Pinot Noir, when the grapes are left for some days in the tank at a cool temperature so that the pigment and aroma molecules are released in the juice before fermentation begins.

COOPERAGE
The place where coopers, those who make and repair barrels, work.

COPITA
A type of glass commonly used for sherry in Spain, but also used by wine tasters.

CORKED
Wine affected by a faulty cork, generally with an infiltration of 2.4.6 Trichloranisole, which is formed by mildew.

COSECHA
Spanish for "vintage," i.e. year of production.

COSECHERO
Spanish for "winegrower."

COUPAGE
Blending of simple wines, in contrast to →*assemblage.* (Hides bad qualities rather than bringing out good qualities.)

COVER CROPS
A crop other than vines planted in the vineyard to benefit the soil.

CRÉMANT
French sparkling wine produced according to traditional fermentation in the bottle but not from Champagne (→*Méthode champenoise*).

CRIANZA
Spanish wine that can only be sold after a certain period of aging in →*barriques.*

CRU
Literally, a "growth." By extension, an outstanding vineyard site or the wine from it.

CRYOEXTRACTION
The practice of artificially replicating the natural conditions necessary to produce sweet white Ice Wine.

CULTIVAR
Botanical term for cultivated varieties not widely used in the wine world except in South Africa.

CULTIVATION SYSTEMS
There are various methods of training and pruning vines, the choice depending on the variety, the location and how strongly the vine grows. Formerly the free standing bush varieties, or *Gobelets*, were widespread, but now most vines are trained on wire frames or stakes. The aim is to prevent the shoots and leaves from hanging down to the ground and give the plant enough air, to make it less vulnerable to disease. Vines yielding a full harvest have to be trained on wire frames. Beside Single Gobelet and Double Guyot the most important systems are Lenz-Moser, Cordon, Tendone, Lyr, and Scott-Henry.

CUVÉE
Blend of high-value wines →*assemblage*; in sparkling wine production, a term for the initial pressings from the wine press.

DECANT
To transfer wine slowly from a bottle into a carafe, either to add oxygen to it or to separate it from the → sediment.

DECANTING METHOD (TRANSVASER)
Method of producing sparkling wines, with the second fermentation taking place in the bottle, as with the *méthode champenoise*. In order to avoid the lengthy and expensive process of "degorging," the bottles are emptied into a pressure container, the wine is filtered and

subsequently bottled with the required *dosage* and the aid of a back-pressure bottling apparatus. In the shorter or longer term, more practical methods with yeast balls could well replace this technically expensive process.

DÉGORGER, DÉGORGEMENT
To remove the sediment from a sparkling wine, also called "disgorgement."

DÉGUSTATION
Wine-tasting.

DENOMINACÃO DE ORIGEM CONTROLADA (D.O.C.)
Guarantee of origin for Portuguese quality wines.

DENOMINACIÓN DE ORIGEN (D.O.)
Guarantee of origin for Spanish quality wines.

DENOMINAZIONE DI ORIGINE CONTROLLATA (D.O.C.)
Guarantee of origin for Italian quality wines.

DENOMINAZIONE DI ORIGINE CONTROLLATA E GARANTITA (D.O.C.G.)
Top guarantee of origin for Italian quality wines.

DISGORGEMENT
See *Dégorger.*

DOMAINE
French word for a wine-growing estate.

DOMÄNE
Term for a German estate that belongs to the state.

DOSAGE (DOSING)
French term for a mixture of wine and sugar or must that is added to sparkling wines. A distinction is made between full dosing (added before the second fermentation, by way of inducing it) and the final dosage given after the removal of the sediment, to add the right degree of sweetness.

DRINKING TEMPERATURE
The ideal temperature to serve a wine.

DRY
An adjective that refers to the lack of sweetness of a wine.

EISWEIN
A German and Austrian specialty with high sweetness and acidity. Produced with grapes that are picked and pressed at a temperature of 18°F/−7 °C or less.

ÉLEVAGE
A term used in France that has no direct English translation but refers to what a winemaker might do to his wines in the processes between fermentation and bottling.

EN VRAC
French term meaning "in bulk." Term for unbottled wine bought in volume, mainly by large shippers.

ENOLOGY
The science of wine production.

ENRICHMENT
The process of increasing the alcoholic strength of a wine, originally and still usually by chaptalization, i.e. adding sugar.

ESPUMANTE
Portuguese term for sparkling wine. Wines made by the traditional method (*metodo classico*) that have had 12 months maturing in the bottle are called *reserva*, from 24 months *super reserva* and from 36 months *velha* or *grande reserva*.

ESTATE-BOTTLED
See Château-bottled.

ETHANOL
Scientific name for ethyl alcohol, the intoxicating constituent of wine.

EXTRACT(ION)S
The totality of all non-volatile substances in the wine such as acidity, minerals, sugars, phenols, and glycerine.

FEDERSPIEL
Category introduced in the Wachau region of Austria to describe elegant wines of medium weight. See also *Steinfeder* and *Smaragd.*

FERMENTATION
Process in winemaking in which the sugar in the grape is turned into alcohol and carbonic acid, and must is turned into wine.

FILTRATION
The technique of quickly separating solids from the wine using filters. Its use for wines of high quality or high value is controversial, as it may lead to loss of color tone and remove valuable substances from the wine. A distinction is made between "membrane filtration" and "layer filtration" using a diatomite filter or other powder. See also Settlement, Deposit.

FINING
The process of removing unwanted particles from the wine. See also Clarification.

FINISH
The aftertaste of the wine retained on the tongue after you take a sip. It should last as long as possible.

FINO
Light, less alcoholic, and dry sherry.

FLOR YEAST
This is a naturally forming yeast called *flor*, which is derived from wild yeasts that are present in the atmosphere of the cellars. The *flor* protects the developing wine from the influence of too much oxygen, while imparting a characteristic nutty taste to classic Fino. Sometimes the *flor* breaks up and sinks to the bottom of the cask, thus allowing the wine more direct exposure to oxygen and causing it to darken. This style of sherry is known as Amontillado.

FLURBEREINIGUNG
A reorganization of the West German wine industry in the mid-20th century, affecting over half the total planted area. The vineyards were reparceled in order to make them easier to run.

FORTIFIED WINES
Port, sherry, madeira, malaga, marsala, Banyuls, Rivesaltes, etc.

FORTIFY
To add alcohol to the must to stop fermentation and increase the alcohol content of wines, especially with port, sherry, and madeira.

FOXY
Marked aroma reminiscent of the smell of wet fur that characterizes wines made from American hybrid vines. Most noticeable in the Concord grape cultivated in New York State.

FRIZZANTE
Italian sparkling wine.

GARRAFEIRA
Legendary term (lit. "bottle cellar") for Portuguese wines that are aged longer, i.e. at least two years in the barrel (red wines) or one year in the barrel and one in the bottle (white wines).

GOBELET
A method of training vines without using a wire construction frequently used in France. (→Cultivation systems); the vines remain low and their shape resembles a goblet.

GRAFT ROOTSTOCK/PROPFUNTERLAGE
Vine rootstock that is grafted with another variety in order to improve (refine) it.

GRAND CRU
Means "great growths" in French. Used generally for outstanding wines in Burgundy and Alsace, it refers to a specific group of superior vineyards.

GRAN RESERVA
Spanish classification. *Gran reserva* red wines have to be aged at least two years in small wooden barrels and then a further three in the tank or bottle before they are sold. Whites remain at least six months in the bottle and then four years in the tank or bottle.

GROWTH
A term for a particular wine or type of wine. A translation of →*cru.*

HEAT DEGREE DAYS
A system introduced by Amerine and Winkler in California to classify climate. Important in California and Australia. The system shows heat degree days for each month during the growing season, with the sum of daily average temperatures over 50°F/10°C being added up.

HECTARE
Metric unit of area, equivalent to 10,000 m² or 2.47 acres.

HECTOLITER
Metric unit of volume meaning 100 liters or 26 U.S. liquid gallons.

HERDADE
Portuguese term for a very large estate or vineyard, especially in the Ribatejo or Alentejo regions.

HEURIGER
The Austrian equivalent of the French *Nouveau*, which can be retailed from November 11 of the year in question to the end of the following year, mostly on a →*Straußwirtschaft* basis. *Heuriger* bars are called →*Buschenschänke* in Austria. See also *Nouveau, Novello,* and *Primeur.*

HOCK
Term for Rhine wine or German wines in general. Short for "hockamore," an anglicization of Hochheimer in a 17th-century English play (referring to wines from Hochheim in the Rheingau).

HYBRID VINES
The issues of two varieties of vine that do not belong to the same species. Also called "interspecies cross." The aim of hybridization (crossing) is to unite the positive qualities of various species in one variety.

ICE WINE
Made in exactly the same way as the German and Austrian *Eiswein*, from grapes that are left to overripen on the vine and then freeze as night-time temperatures start to fall with the onset of winter. Used particularly by Canadian producers making luscious, spicily exotic wines from the frozen grapes of varieties like Vidal.

INDICAZIONE GEOGRAFICA TIPICA (I.G.T.)
A category of Italian country wine. The designation was created in 1992, largely to give legal status to the good quality *Vino da Tavola* wines (table wines).

INTEGRATED WINE GROWING
The aim of this is to largely do without pesticides in order to protect beneficial insects and the environment.

JEROBOAM
Wine bottle with the capacity of four normal bottles, i.e. 112 fl oz (3 liters). Two →magnums.

JUG WINE
Wine sold over the counter by the jug in the U.S.A., i.e. open rather than bottled. Often sold in glass carafes.

KABINETT
The most basic of the *Prädikate* of the Q.m.P. category as defined by the German Wine Law.

KLOSTERNEUBURG MUST GAUGE
Unit of measurement for the specific density of a wine. 1°KMW = 10 g of natural sugar per kg of must.

LEES
Dead yeast cells or sediment remaining in tank after fermentation.

LIBRARY WINES
Older vintages offered for sale in small quantities.

LIQUOREUX
Literally, like liqueur. A term used for sweet wines, often made from grapes with *botrytis cinerea.*

LYRE (TRELLIS) SYSTEM
See Cultivation systems.

MACERATION
The steeping of the grape skins, seeds and stems in the fermentation process in order to increase the take-up of the phenolics.

MACÉRATION CARBONIQUE
Use of carbon dioxyde in the mash to produce light, fruity red wines that are drunk young.

Perfectly whole, unpressed grapes are fermented in a vat to which carbon dioxide is added. This forces the grapes to ferment inside their skins, which release particularly strong aromas.

MADEIRIZATION
Term derived from Madeira wine and applied to greatly aged, or even too old wine.

MAGNUM
Wine bottle equal to two standard bottles, i.e. 56 fl oz (1.5 liters).

MALOLACTIC ACID CONVERSION
Conversion of malic acid into softer lactic acid by using lactobacilli, with the aim of reducing the (perceived) acid content of the wine. Also called biological acid reduction.

MARC
Solid residue left in the winepress after pressing (white wines) or fermentation (of red wines). Can also be distilled into brandy. See also Pomace.

MARC CAP/CAP OF SKINS
The layer of grape skins and other solid substances that collects at the top of a container during the fermentation of red wines. It has to be immersed and stirred up with the must. See also Punchdown.

MASH
The lightly pressed grapes that are put into the fermentation vats with the must; red wines are fermented on mash.

MASH HEATING
To soften and break up/ferment the grapes by steeping them in a liquid, possibly by heating. The mash is heated to around 158°F/70°C before fermentation, to release pigments from the skins. Rarely used with high-value wines.

MATURING (AFFINAGE)
Additional ripening in the bottle before a wine goes on sale.

MERITAGE
An invented term in the U.S.A. for a *cuvée* made from several varieties of grape, usually of the Bordeaux range (combines "merit" and "heritage").

MÉTHODE CHAMPENOISE
Method of producing sparkling wine (evolved in Champagne) whereby the second fermentation takes place in the bottle. See also Bottle-fermentation.

MÉTHODE TRADITIONELLE
Alternative term for *méthode champenoise*.

MICRO-ORGANISMS
A minute but continuous dose of oxygen introduced to wines in tanks even before the conversion of biological acidity, which is intended to replace part of the aging in wood. Widely used in many wine-growing estates in France.

MICRO-OXYGENATION
A method of wine-making developed by Patrick Ducourneau, an enologist and Madiran vintner. Very small and very carefully measured quantities of oxygen are blown into the tank or the vats.

MISCHSATZ
Austrian wine made from various grape varieties that all grow in the same vineyard, and are harvested and processed together.

MOELLEUX
French term for mellow wines (medium-sweet).

MOUTHFEEL
U.S. term to describe the overall impression of the wine on the palate.

MUST
Unfermented grape juice. (The raw material of wine after the first stage of processing.)

MUTAGE (MUTE)
The action of muting a must, i.e. stopping the fermentation by adding alcohol or sulfur dioxide.

NÉGOCIANT
A French wine merchant.

NOBLE ROT
See *Botrytis cinerea*.

NOSE
The general smell of a wine. Four noses can be distinguished.

NOUVEAU
Term for French wines that may be retailed soon after the harvest. See also *Heuriger, Novello*, and *Primeur*.

NOVELLO
Term for Italian wines that can be retailed soon after the harvest. See also *Heuriger, Nouveau*, and *Primeur*.

OECHSLE
A unit of measurement based on the specific weight of the must. The name comes from that of the physicist Ferdinand Oechsle. A must with a specific weight of 1.09 has 90° Oechsle. The term is used in Germany and Switzerland.

OENOLOGY
Alternative spelling of Enology.

OINOTRIA
When the Greeks popularized wine growing around the Mediterranean, this was the word for Italy, literally the "land of vine stocks attached to posts," more generally a wine paradise.

OLOROSO
A strong dry sherry with full body. A second basic type along with →*Fino*. Often used for sweet blends of simple sherry.

ORGANOLEPTIC
Refers to the process of tasting (wine).

OXIDATION
Chemical reaction when the wine comes into contact with excess oxygen. The wine loses freshness and changes color. The process can take place in the bottle, or even in the barrel or when still must.

PALO CORTADO
Rare dry sherry. In taste, it lies between Oloroso and Amontillado.

PARTHENOCARPY
In botany, parthenocarpy is the production of fruits without fertilization or seeds. Grapes can sometimes develop without pollination taking place; they are small, seedless and have a high sugar content when ripe.

PASSERILLÉ
(Grapes) left on the vine to dry out. (A feature of Béarnais winemaking.)

PASSITO
Italian method of making wine from dried grapes (raisins).

pH VALUE
Unit of measurement of a wine's acidity. The lower the pH value, the more acidic the wine tastes, pH7 is a neutral value (e.g. plain water).

PHENOLICS
Substances extracted from the skins of grapes that provide the coloring and texture for red wine.

PHYLLOXERA
The vine louse, the most dangerous enemy of the vine. It attacks the vine's roots and kills it. Imported from America to Europe in 1860. Most of the American varieties were resistant, the European ones were not and therefore succumbed, with devastating effects on European wine growing. Only by grafting European vines onto phylloxera-resistant American rootstocks could a remedy be provided. In the 1980s there was an epidemic in the U.S. due to non-resistant rootstocks being used.

PIGEAGE (PUNCHDOWN)
Breaking up and re-immersion of the cap of skins (marc) during the fermentation of red wine. Traditional with Pinot Noir and now many top wines.

POLYPHENOL
Chemical component of wine contained in pigments, tannins, and taste substances. Has a beneficial effect on the human body.

POMACE
The pulpy residue left in the press after the grapes are pressed. Originally a term reserved for apple pulp.

PREMIUM
A mark of top quality for grape varieties and the wines made from them in English-speaking and other wine-growing countries. The premium varieties include Chardonnay and Sauvignon, Cabernet Sauvignon, Merlot and Shiraz (Syrah).

PRESSING
Pressing takes place at different points in the winemaking process. There are a number of different techniques such as the horizontal press (which most producers use) where a press head forces the juice or wine through the perforated wall of a revolving cylinder. The latest stage in the development of horizontal presses is the pneumatic press. In the latter, an airbag inside the cylinder is inflated, squeezing the must against the walls.

PRIMEUR
Term for French wines that can be retailed soon after the harvest. See also *Heuriger, Nouveau*, and *Novello*.

PRÜFNUMMER

German term for the control number on the label of a *Qualitätswein* (= V.d.Q.) in Germany and Austria. Bestowed after the quality of a wine is checked.

PUNCHDOWN

American term for →*pigeage*.

PURE-YEASTING

Using cultured yeast for fermentation to convert the must in the wine. Its reactions are more predictable than the yeast in the grapes, whose fermentation can be difficult to control.

QUALITÄTSWEIN

General word for a higher-quality wine with a designation of origin, in contrast to a simple table wine. Roughly equivalent to *vin de qualité* in French and "fine wine" in English.

QUINTA

Portuguese estate or vineyard, comparable with *château* in viticultural French.

RACKING

Process by which the clear wine is pumped into an empty container to get rid of unwanted sediment.

RANCIO

Term for the aroma of very old fortified wines and brandies. It is reminiscent of walnut shells and is a sign of supreme quality.

REDUCTION (DEOXIDATION)

The opposite of oxidation. A chemical reaction in airtight conditions. Wines produced reductively are particularly fresh and aromatic.

REFRACTOMETER

Optical precision instrument used to measure the specific gravity of a wine so that its maturity can be assessed.

REMONTAGE

In the production of red wines, the grape juice is pumped over the cap of skins in order to keep the marc in the must so that as much pigment and aroma as possible is released from the skins. (In Australia, a system of rotating fermenters is used.)

RESERVA

A Spanish and Portuguese quality grade for the wines of a particular vintage that have to meet specific requirements—for Spanish reds, minimum aging of 36 months (12 of them in oak barrels), for whites 24 months (including 6 in the barrel). In Portugal, the alcohol content for these wines must be 0.5% above the prescribed minimum levels.

RESIDUAL SUGAR

The sugar not converted to alcohol during fermentation. Produces the natural sweetness of a wine.

REVERSE OSMOSIS

Reverse osmosis is the process of purifying water or other liquids such as fruit juices by passing them through a semi-permeable membrane that filters out unwanted substances. In winemaking, this is a filtering process whereby the must circulates along the filtration membrane, but does not penetrate it. A pressure differential allows only water to get through.

RIDDLING

Called *remuage* in French, it is the process in the →*méthode champenoise* whereby the sediment is shaken to the neck of the bottle for disgorgement.

RISERVA

An Italian quality grade comparable with Spanish →*reserva*.

SEDIMENT

Deposits of tannin and pigments in the bottle that can be separated from the wine by decanting. See also lees.

SEKT

German classified sparkling →*Qualitätswein* that carries an official control number (*Prüfnummer*). In Austria, applies to any sparkling wine. A sparkling *Qualitätswein* in Austria is called *Qualitätssekt*.

SÉLECTION MASSALE

The best vines of a vineyard are selected, in contrast to the cloned selection, where a single seedling is reproduced with genetically identical structure.

SETTLEMENT/DEPOSIT

Natural process that allows undesired solids present in the wine or must to settle slowly on the bottom of the container. See also Filtration.

SILICA (KIESELGUR)

Crystalline form of silicon dioxide [SiO2] that is used to clarify the wine.

SKIN CONTACT

Macération pelliculaire or *macération préfermentaire*. A process of leaving the pressed grape juice in contact with the skins in the must in order to extract taste elements from the skin. This term is used more for white wines, while for reds the term *cold soak* is used.

SMARAGD (EMERALD)

A category introduced in the Wachau in Austria to designate mature, strong wines. See also *Steinfeder* and *Federspiel*.

SOLERA

System for making fortified wines, especially sherry and madeira, in order to obtain the same quality year after year. The basis is blending wines aged in the barrel. *Solera* is the lowest of a multi-grade series of barrels. The next up is *criadera*, the top one *sobretabla*. For every new sherry the *solera* is taken out and bottled, the bottles being topped up with *criadera* and finished with wines from the *sobretabla*, which are refilled with young wine.

SOMMELIER

French term for wine waiter.

SPARKLING WINE

General term for all carbonated wines, whether natural sparkling or not.

SPÄTLESE

One of the *Prädikate* of German Wine Law, literally "late picked."

SPECIFIC GRAVITY

Expresses the degree of ripeness of the berries. In Germany and Switzerland, it is measured on the Oechsle scale, in Austria on the Klosterneuburg Must Gauge (K.M.W.). In many countries the quality grade of a wine is calculated in terms of the prescribed minimum specific gravity of the must.

SPUMANTE

Italian term for sparkling wine.

STABILIZATION

A condition achieved when a wine has had all the undesired particles, suspension matter and cloudinesses removed, so that it looks clear in the bottle and no gas forms.

STALK SEPARATOR

The machine for plucking the stalks from the grapes before fermentation.

STEEN

South African term for Chenin Blanc, the most widespread grape variety. It serves as the basis for brandy and sherry production.

STEINFEDER

Category of wine in the Wachau region of Austria, designating light, tangy wines. See also *Federspiel* and *Smaragd*.

STRAUSSWIRTSCHAFT

A bar in Baden, Franconia, Württemberg and Austria that sells home-grown wine during a defined period each year. A broom is displayed at the entrance to the estate to show when it is available. Light food can be served with the wine. See also *Heuriger*.

SULFUR

Used in winemaking in a variety of ways, e.g. to protect the vines, sterilize wooden barrels, or as a preservative.

SUR LIE (ON THE LEES)

French term used in connection with Muscadet and Gros Plant wines of the Loire. Refers to the practice of leaving the wine on the lees in the barrel over the winter and then bottling it without filtering. The process adds a touch of zest.

TANNIN

A vegetable element in wine that gives it its astringent effect. Important for the aging of red wines. It is especially prominent in young reds, but becomes less marked as the wine ages.

TARTRATES

Crystals deposited on the bottom of a wine bottle, created by the degeneration of the acid in the wine. Not a cause for complaint, as they do not affect the quality of the wine.

TAWNY

For port wines the word 'tawny' indicates that the wine has been aged in wood for several years. Simple tawny ports must spend an average of 7 years in pipes (long wooden vessels). Other categories of tawny include 10-, 20- and 30-year-old tawny port.

TENUTA

Italian term for a wine-growing estate.

TERROIR

In France, an agricultural region or area

whose soil and microclimatic characteristics give its produce its unique features.

TOASTING
A process in barrel-making which gives wine a "toasty" flavor.

TRANSVASIER METHOD
Method of producing sparkling wine in which, as in the traditional Champagne method (→ *Méthode champenoise*) the second fermentation takes place inside the bottle. To avoid the ensuing costly and lengthy process to remove the sediment, the bottles are emptied into a pressurised container where the wine is filtered. It is then bottled with the desired dosage and with the help of a counter pressure plant.

TROCKENBEERENAUSLESE (T.B.A.)
One of the *Prädikate* of German Wine Law, literally "selected dried berries." This is the premium German and Austrian sweet wine.

TRUNK SYSTEM
Form of vine training whereby individual canes put forth dozens of buds. Vines are trained into enormous trunks. See also Cultivation systems.

TYPICITÉ (TYPICITY)
A wine tasting term that implies that a wine is typical of its type and *terroir*. It is the character given to it by the site in which it grows.

VARIETAL
Term used for a wine named after the dominant grape variety from which it is made.

V.D.Q.S.
In the French *appellation* system an interim classification between *vin de pays* and *appellation contrôlée*.

VEGETATIVE
A term for wines with unripe, green vegetable overtones, due to inadequate maturation.

VERAISON
A term applied to the intermediate stage of the ripening process where the grapes begin to change from their green state to their colored form.

VERBAND DEUTSCHER PRÄDIKATSWEINGÜTER (V.D.P.)
Registered and abbreviated name for the association of around 200 vintners in Germany known for the high quality of their produce.

VIN DE CALITATE SUPERIOARA CU DENUMIRE DE ORIGINE (V.S.O.)
Romanian designation for superior quality wines, also denoting origin.

VIN DE CALITATE SUPERIOARA CU DENUMIRE DE ORIGINE SI TREPTE DE CALITATE (V.S.O.C.)
Romanian designation for superior quality wines, their origin and degree of quality.

VIN DE GARAGE
A wine produced in only very small quantities but of supreme quality and often sold at top price. The first and most famous Vin de Garage is Château de Valandraud in Saint-Émilion.

VIN DE LIQUEUR
Official name for beverages made from grape must with the fermentation entirely prevented by adding sufficient amounts of ethyl alcohol.

VIN DE MASA/REGIUNE SUPERIOARA (V.S.)
Romanian designation for high quality wines.

VIN DE PAILLE
A strong, sweet white wine whose grapes are dried on straw mats.

VIN DE QUALITÉ PRODUIT DANS DES RÉGIONS DÉTERMINÉES (V.Q.P.R.D.)
General European name for *appellation* wines. In France it includes *Appellation d'Origine Contrôlée* (A.O.C.) and *Vin Délimité de Qualité Supérieure* (V.D.Q.S.).

VIN DE TABLE (V.D.T.)
The simplest category of French wine.

VIN DOUX NATUREL (V.D.N.)
Fortified wine from southern France.

VINE PRUNING
Drastically cutting back the shoots on the vine in order to promote growth and improve the quality.

VINIFICATION
The production of wine from the delivery of the grapes to the winery to the bottling.

VINO DE CALIDAD PRODUCIDO EN UNA REGIÓN DETERMINADA (V.C.P.R.D.)
Spanish term for wines of guaranteed origin (see also *Vin de Qualité Produit dans des Régions Déterminées*, V.Q.P.R.D.); includes *Denominación de Origen* (D.O.) and *Denominación de Origen Calificada* (D.O.Ca.).

VIN SANTO (HOLY WINE)
The classic dessert wine of Tuscany, made of dried grapes, aged oxidatively, dry or with various sugar residues.

VINS DE PLAISIR
Well-made, accessible, easy-drinking wines that do not claim to be high-value.

VINTAGE (MILLÉSIME)
Term for the year in which the grapes for a wine were grown, or more generally the qualities of a particular year relating to the weather and growth cycle of the grapes. Even more generally, as an adjective (millésimé) either refers to a wine for an exceptionally fine year (a vintage wine), or (in the case of champagne) old wine, though not necessarily from a particular year (vintage champagne).

VITIS
Vitis is the name of one of the 50 genera in the botanical family Vitaceae. The genus *Vitis* contains 22 species, including the vine *Vitis vinifera* from which around 8,000 cultivated varieties have been derived.

WATER SHOOT
A vigorous but unproductive shoot growing directly from the trunk.

WEISSHERBST (WHITE AUTUMN)
A rosé made from single grape variety in Germany. This is noted on the label.

WINERY
Used to mean both the winemaking facility and the wine-growing business or estate as a whole.

WINKLER SCALE
A system of viticultural climate classification for California, based on the average temperature. Growing zones are graded into five regions.

YEAST
Micro-organisms. Some of them are capable of making grape juice ferment. See also Pure-yeasting.

YIELD
The amount of wine produced from a grape harvest.

Vintages

Assessments of vintages are always only an approximation to the reality. The influence of climate on the varying grape varieties is too diverse, and the influence of microclimates in individual districts or sites too important.

The quality of the vintage is rated by means of stars.

*	poor vintage
**	moderate to good vintage
***	very good vintage
****	outstanding vintage

Vintages in Australia

2000**−***
High volumes (especially Cabernet Sauvignon and Shiraz), difficult weather conditions for Pinot Noir and white varieties).

1999***
Record volumes, very good quality (e.g. in Coonawarra).

1998***−****
Excellent Cabernet Sauvignons and Shiraz, but Chardonnays not always inspiring.

1997**−****
Varying from very good (Coonawarra, Barossa) to good (New South Wales).

1996***
Turned out very well particularly in the hotter areas of cultivation.

1995**−***
Low volumes but, with some exceptions, good quality.

1994**−****

1993**−***

1992*−***

1991****

1990***
Earlier very good and outstanding vintages: 1989, 1988, 1987, 1986, 1984, 1983, 1982, 1981, 1979, 1976, 1975, 1971, 1966, 1963, 1962.

Vintages in California

1999**−****
Low yield and very diverse qualities. The best Cabernets and Zinfandels have outstanding class.

1998**−***
Uneven vintage. Many Chardonnays and Pinot Noirs have potential.

1997**−****
High volumes, in part outstanding reds (Cabernet Sauvignon, Zinfandel).

1996**−***
Elegant red wines and noteworthy whites.

1995***
Remarkable whites and often very good red wines.

1994****
A great red wine year.

1993**

1992***

1991***−****

1990***−****

Earlier very good or outstanding vintages: 1987, 1986, 1985, 1984, 1981, 1979, 1978, 1975, 1974, 1971, 1970, 1968, 1966, 1958, 1951, 1946.

Vintages in France

Bordeaux

1999**−***
A good vintage (especially for Merlot), with some upwardly mobiles.

1998**−***
Successful especially in Saint-Émilion and Pomerol-another good Merlot vintage.

1997**
Tends toward early-ripening red wines.

1996***−****
Excellent particularly in the Médoc and for white wines.

1995***−****
In Saint-Émilion and Pomerol, but particularly good reds also in Pauillac or Graves; notable whites.

1994**−***
Good mainly on the right bank (Merlot), with the dry whites tending to the very good.

1993*−**
Almost a total write-off for sweet wines, while the red varieties are often only so-so.

1992*
Light wines with no great aging potential.

1991**
Very few interesting wines.

1990****
Great, long-lived wines and fabulous, concentrated Sauternes.

1989****

1988***−****

1987*−**

1986***−****

1985***−****

1984*

1983***−****

1982****

Earlier very good or outstanding vintages: 1979, 1978, 1975, 1971, 1970, 1967 (Sauternes) 1966, 1964, 1961 (!), 1959, 1955, 1953, 1952, 1949, 1947, 1945, 1937 (Sauternes) 1929, 1928, 1921 (Sauternes), 1900.

Burgundy

1999***
High volumes, generally considered very good, also in Beaujolais.

1998***
Consistently good wines.

1997**−***
Very good ripe Chardonnays, notable Beaujolais. The other reds tend to be early ripening.

1996****
A great year in every respect for red and white varieties.

1995**−****
Numerous very good white wines and mature reds.

1994**
High volumes, but rarely of impressive quality.

1993**−****
Slow-maturing, elegant reds. Whites at best good.

1992**−***
Early-ripening reds, some very good Chardonnays.

1991*−***
Good for Pinot Noirs of the Côte de Nuits, very good for Beaujolais, passable for white wines.

1990****
A great vintage in every respect.

1989***

1988**−***

1987*−***

1986**

1985***−****

1984*

1983 *−***

1982**

Earlier very good or outstanding vintages: 1978, 1971, 1969, 1964, 1962, 1961, 1959, 1955, 1953, 1952, 1949, 1948, 1947, 1945.

Rhône and Languedoc-Roussillon

1999***
Good growers produced elegant wines to lay down. The vintage turned out particularly well in the southern Rhône.

1998***
Potentially great vintage, especially in the southern Rhône and Languedoc-Roussillon, but sometimes wines with excessive tannins.

1997**
A sometimes underrated vintage with some elegant reds and whites, especially of the early-ripening varieties.

1996**−***
Generally better in the northern Rhône than the south.

1995****
A warm wine year with very good, long-lived wines.

1994**−***
Rain during the harvest, but even so generally successful.

1993**−***
Very successful in the southern Rhône, and often very good in Languedoc-Roussillon. Not much luck for the northern Rhône.

1992*−**
Decent wines at best, and only in the northern Rhône.

1991*–*

Very good mainly in the northern Rhône, also in Languedoc-Roussillon, less so in the southern Rhône.

1990*–****

A great vintage on the Rhône, but not so impressive in Languedoc-Roussillon.

Earlier very good or outstanding vintages: 1989, 1988, 1985, 1983, 1982, 1981, 1979, 1978, 1970, 1967, 1966, 1961, 1959, 1953, 1949, 1945.

Vintages in Germany

1999–***

Not the long-awaited vintage of the century, but a plentiful harvest and very successful in some regions (e.g. Saar, Ahr, Franconia).

1998–***

Very good wines in the Palatinate, but only so-so elsewhere (Baden, Württemberg, Franconia). Variable in Mosel-Saar-Ruwer.

1997*–****

A sunny wine year with many Spätlese wines and selections. Particularly successful in the Moselle region, on the Nahe and in the Palatinate, also the Ahr reds.

1996*

Fruity wines worth laying down, without exception.

1995–***

Many Spätlese and selections. Particularly successful in Rheingau and Mosel-Saar-Ruwer.

1994–***

Very good in many areas (Rheingau and Moselle), numerous botrytized wines.

1993*–****

1992–***

1991**

1990**

Earlier very good and outstanding vintages whose best representatives (mainly Riesling) may still be in good condition: 1989, 1988, 1986, 1985, 1983, 1981, 1979, 1976, 1975, 1971, 1964, 1959, 1953, 1949, 1945.

Vintages in Italy

Piedmont

1999*

Generally considered very good, especially for the late-ripening varieties (e.g. Nebbiolo).

1998**

Excellent particularly for red wines.

1997**

Fabulous, concentrated red wines, with very convincing Barolos and Barbarescos.

1996*–****

An excellent red wine vintage.

1995*–****

The first in a series of remarkable red wine vintages, with great Barberas and Nebbiolos.

1994*–*

A disappointing vintage.

1993–***

1992*

1991**

1990**

Earlier very good and outstanding vintages: 1989, 1988, 1985, 1982, 1980, 1979, 1978, 1974, 1971, 1970, 1964, 1961, 1958, 1947.

Tuscany

1999*–****

Very good, elegant red wines.

1998**

Good to very good red wines.

1997**

Outstanding, dense red wines in the top labels.

1996–***

Mostly successful, but few great Chiantis or Brunellos.

1995–****

Very variable quality due to autumn rain.

1994**

Brunello and Vino Nobile turned out better than Chianti.

1993*

1992**

1991**

1990**

Earlier very good to outstanding vintages: 1988, 1986, 1985, 1983, 1982, 1980, 1979, 1978, 1975, 1971, 1970, 1967, 1964, 1961, 1958, 1955, 1945.

Vintages in Portugal

1999–***

Generally considered good to very good.

1998–***

Some good red wines, but not an outstanding year for port.

1997**

The vintage ports look outstanding.

1996–***

Varying quality, with Dão reds turning out best.

1995**

Very good red wines in the Douro region.

1994*

Outstanding port and Madeira vintage.

1993*–*

1992*

1991–***

1990

Earlier very good or outstanding vintages for port: 1985, 1983, 1980, 1977 (!), 1970, 1966, 1963 (!), 1960, 1955, 1950, 1948, 1947, 1945, 1935, 1934, 1931, 1927, 1924, 1922, 1920, 1912, 1908, 1904, 1900.

Vintages in Spain

Rioja

1999–***

Varying qualities, but generally good to very good.

1998–***

Good yields and mostly equally good qualities.

1997

Very variable, but rarely truly inspiring.

1996*–****

Late-harvesting growers produced great wines.

1995**

Relatively low yields, but excellent, long-lived wines.

1994**

A hot year produced superb wines.

1993–***

1992*

1991*

1990*

Earlier very good or outstanding vintages: 1989, 1988, 1987, 1985, 1982, 1981, 1978, 1976, 1975, 1973, 1970, 1968, 1964 (!), 1959, 1952.

Ribera del Duero

1999*

High volumes, very good quality.

1998*

Low volumes because of hail damage, but many good red wines.

1997

Rarely inspiring, but notable wines do occur.

1996**

The third top-quality vintage in a row, producing mature, long-lived wines.

1995**

Great red wines from perhaps the best vintage of the century.

1994**

Many remarkable wines, and for many producers as good a year as 1995, presumably long-lived.

1993

1992

1991*–****

1990–***

Earlier very good or outstanding vintages: 1989, 1987, 1986, 1985, 1983, 1982, 1981, 1978, 1974, 1970, 1964.

Vintages in South Africa

2000*

Despite the very dry weather, successful white and red wines.

1999*–*

A warm vintage with mature wines.

1998*–****

Excellent, long-maturing red wines.

1997–****

Fabulous red wines, but also less successful varieties. A vintage for the courageous grower.

1996

A cool year with heterogeneous quality.

1995**

Mature red wines to lay down.

1994*

1993*

1992*

1991**

1990–***

Earlier very good or outstanding vintages: 1989, 1988, 1987, 1986, 1984.

BIBLIOGRAPHY

ADAMS, L.
The Wines of America. New York 1990

AINSWORTH, JIM
The Mitchell Beazley Red Wine Guide. London 1999

ALLEN, MAX
Crush—The New Australian Wine Book. London 2000

ALLEN, MAX
New World of Wine. London 1999

AMERICAN EXPRESS TRAVEL GUIDES
San Francisco and the Wine Regions. London and New York 1992

ANDERSON, BURTON
The Wine Atlas of Italy. London and New York 1990

ASHLEY, MAUREEN
Touring in Wine Country: Tuscany;Touring in Wine Country: Northwest Italy. 1996

BECKETT, FIONA
Wine Uncorked. London 1999

BELFRAGE, N.
Barolo to Valpolicella-The Wines of Northern Italy. London and New York 1999

BERRY, E.
The Wine of Alsace: A Buyer's Guide. London 1989

BERRY, E.
The Wines of Languedoc-Roussillon. London 1992

BROADBENT, MICHAEL
Michael Broadbent's Wine Notes. London 1994

BROADBENT, MICHAEL
My Favourite Wines. London 1994

BROOK, STEPHEN
A Century of Wine: The Story of a Wine Revolution. London 2000

BROOK, STEPHEN
Sauternes and Other Sweet Wines of Bordeaux. London 1995

BROOK, STEPHEN
Sauvignon Blanc and Sémillon. London 1992

BROOK, STEPHEN
The Wines of Germany. London 2003

BURROUGHS, DAVID
Wine Regions of the World. London 1988; *The New Wine Companion.* London 1988

CASS, BRUCE/JANCIS ROBINSON (EDS.)
Oxford Companion to the Wines of North America. Oxford and New York 2000

CATHIE, KYLE
The Wine Experience. London 2000

CERNELLI, DANIELE/MARCO SABELLICO
A Complete Guide to Italian Wine. London 2000

CLARKE, OZ
Introducing Wine. Little Brown. New York 2000

CLARKE, OZ
Oz Clarke's Pocket Wine Guide 2004. London 2003

CLARKE, OZ
Oz Clarke's Wine Atlas. London 2002

CLARKE, OZ/RAND, MARGARET
Grapes & Wines. London 2001

COATES, CLIVE
An Encyclopedia of The Wines and Domaines of France. Berkeley and Los Angeles 2000

COATES, CLIVE
Cote d'Or: A Celebration of the Greatest Wines of Burgundy. Berkeley and Los Angeles 1997

COATES, CLIVE
Grands Vins. London 1994

COUVREUR, DOMINIQUE/A. GERBELLE
Vins et Vignobles en France. Paris 1998

COX, JILL
Australian Wine with Food. Ashbourne 1990

DUIJKER, H./M. BROADBENT
The Bordeaux Atlas. London 1997

DUIJKER, HUBRECHT
Touring in Wine Country: Alsace. London 1996; *Touring in Wine Country: Bordeaux.* London 1996; *Touring in Wine Country: Burgundy.* London 1996; *Touring in Wine Country: The Loire.* London 1997; *Touring in Wine Country: Provence.* London 1998

DUIJKER, HUBRECHT
The Wines of Rioja. London 1987

DUIJKER, HUBRECHT
The Wine Atlas of Spain. London 1992

FAITH, N.
The Winemasters. London 1998

FAITH, NICHOLAS
Australia's Liquid Gold. London 2002

FIELDEN, CHRISTOPHER
The Wines of Argentina, Chile and Latin America. London 2001

FLOWER, RAYMOND
Chianti: The Land, the People and the Wine. London 1988

FOULKES, CHRISTOPHER (HG.)
Larousse Encyclopedia of Wine. Paris 2001

FRIEDRICH, J.A.
Wine and Food Guide to the Loire. London and New York 1997

GAYOTT, A.
Guide to the Best Wineries of North America. New York 1993

GEORGE, ROSEMARY
*Chianti and the Wines of Tuscany.London 1990

GEORGE, ROSEMARY
French Country Wines. London 1990

GLUCK, MALCOLM
The Sensational Liquid: A Guide to Wine Tasting. London 1999

GLUCKSTERN, WILLIE
The Wine Avenger. New York 1998

GOOLDEN, JILL
The Taste of Wine. London 1990

HALLIDAY, JAMES
Australian Wine Companion. London 2004

HALLIDAY, JAMES
An Introduction to Australian Wine. Pymble 1992

HALLIDAY, JAMES
Atlas of Australian and New Zealand Wine. Sydney 1998

HALLIDAY, JAMES
Classic Wines of Australia and New Zealand. Sydney 2002

HANSON, ANTHONY
Burgundy. London 2003

HUGHES, D./P. HANDS
Complete Book of South African Wine. Cape Town 1988

ILAND, PATRICK/GAGO, PETER
Australian Wine. Adelaide 2002

IRVINE, R./W. CLORE
The Wine Project. Vashon, Washington 1997

JAMIESON, IAN
German Wines. London 1991

JEFFS, JULIAN
Sherry. London 1992

JOHNSON, HUGH
Hugh Johnson's Modern Encyclopedia of Wine. Simon & Schuster Books, U.S.A. 1998

JOHNSON, HUGH
Hugh Johnson's Pocket Winebook 2004. London 2003

JOHNSON, HUGH
Hugh Johnson's Wine Companion. London 2003

JOHNSON, HUGH
The Story of Wine. London and
New York 1989

JOHNSON, HUGH
Wine. London 1997

JOHNSON, HUGH
How to Enjoy Wine. London 1999

JOHNSON, HUGH
Tuscany and its Wines. London 2000

JOHNSON, HUGH/HALLIDAY, JAMES
The Art and Science of Wine. London and
New York 1994

JOHNSON, HUGH/ROBINSON, JANCIS
The World Atlas of Wine. 5th edition,
London 2001

JOSEPH, ROBERT
Sunday Telegraph Good Wine Guide.
London 1999

JOSEPH, ROBERT
The Essential Guide to Good Wine.
London 1990

JUKES, MATTHEW
*Wine: Everything You Ever Wanted to Know
About Wine But Were Afraid to Ask.*
London 1999

KING, ALICE
Atlas of Wine. London 1990; *Enjoying Wine.*
London 1990

LAMBERT-GOCS, MILES
The Wines of Greece. London 1990

LAPSLEY, JAMES T.
*Bottled Poetry: Napa Winemaking from Prohi-
bition to the Modern Era.*
Berkeley, California 1996

LAROUSSE WINE
Dictionary of Vine and Wine. Paris 1999

LAUBE, JAMES
California Wine. Wine Spectator Press,
New York 2000

LEITH, PRUE
Leith's Guide to Wine. London 1995

LIVINGSTONE-LEARMOUTH, J.
The Wines of the Rhône. London 1992

MATTHEWS, PATRICK
Real Wine. London 2000

MAYSON, R.
Portugal's Wines and Winemakers.
San Francisco 1998

McWHIRTER, KATHRYN/METCALFE, CHARLES
The Wine of Spain and Portugal. London 1988

MEREDITH, T.J.
Northwest Wine. Kirkland, Washington 1990

MO, YAN
The Republic of Wine. London 2000

MUSCATINE, D./M.A. AMERINE/
B. THOMPSON (EDS.)
*The University of California/Sotheby Book of
California Wine.* Berkeley, California 1984

NORMAN, REMINGTON
The Great Domaines of Burgundy.
London 1996

NORMAN, REMINGTON
Rhône Renaissance. London 1995

PARKER, ROBERT M. JR.
*Bordeaux: A Comprehensive Guide to the Wines
Produced from 1961–1997.* New York 1998

PARKER, ROBERT M. JR.
A Consumer's Guide to the World's Finest Wines.
New York 2003

PARKER, ROBERT M. JR.
Wines of Burgundy. New York 1990

PARKER, ROBERT M. JR.
Wines of the Rhone Valley. New York 1997

PARKER, ROBERT M. JR.
Parker's Wine Buyer's Guide. 6th edition,
New York 2002

PENNING-ROWSELL, EDMUND C.
The Wines of Bordeaux. London 1989

PEPPERCORN, DAVID
Bordeaux. London 1991

PEYNAUD, ÉMILE
*The Taste of Wine: The Art and Science of
Wine Appreciation.* New York 1996

PHILLIPS, ROD
A Short History of Wine. London 2000

PHILPOTT, DON
The Wine and Food of Bulgaria. London 1989

PIGOTT, STUART
*The Mosel and Rheingau: Including the Ahr,
Nahe and Pfalz.* London 1997

PIGOTT, STUART
Riesling. London and New York 1991

PINNEY, THOMAS
*A History of Wine in America from Beginnings
to Prohibition.* Berkeley, California 1989

PLATTER, JOHN
South African Wine Guide 1996. Antique Collectors Club, U.S.A. 1996

RADFORD, JOHN/STEPHEN BROOK
Aperitif and Dessert Wine. London 2000

READ, JAN
The Wine and Food of Spain. London 1987

RIBEREAU-GAYON, P. (ED.)
*The Wines and Vineyards of France: A Complete
Atlas and Guide.* London and New York 1990

ROBINSON, JANCIS
Jancis Robinson's Guide to Wine Grapes. Oxford and New York 1996

ROBINSON, JANCIS
The Oxford Companion to Wine. Oxford 1999

ROBINSON, JANCIS
Vines, Grapes and Wines. London 1997

ROBINSON, JANCIS
Jancis Robinson's Wine Course. London 1999

ROSSO, GAMBERO
Guide to Italian Wine. London 2000

SCHOONMAKER, FRANK
Frank Schoonmaker's Encyclopedia of Wine.
London 1979

SCHUSTER, MICHAEL
Understanding Wine. London 1989

SCHUSTER, MICHAEL
*Essential Winetasting: The Complete Wine
Tasting Course.* London 2000

SKELTON, STEPHEN
The Wines of Britain and Ireland.
London 2001

SLOAN, JOHN C.
*The Surprising Wines of Switzerland: A Practi-
cal Guide to Switzerland's Best Kept Secret.*
London 1995

SPURRIER, STEVEN
Académie du Vin Wine Course. London 1994

STEIMAN, HARVEY
Essentials of Wine. Wine Spectator Press,
New York 2000

STEVENSON, TOM
The New Sotheby's World Wine Encyclopedia.
1997

STEVENSON, TOM
*Millennium Champagne and Sparkling
Wine Guide 2000.* London 1999

STEVENSON, TOM
The Wines of Alsace. London 1993

THOMPSON, BOB
Wine Atlas of California. London and
New York 1993

VOSS, ROGER
Food and Wine of France. London 1993

WALDIN, MONTY
Wines of South America. London 2003

WALTON, STUART/ BRIAN GLOVER
*The Ultimate Encyclopedia of Wine, Beer, Spi-
rits and Liquers.* London 1998

WATSON, JEREMY
The New & Classical Wines of Spain. Barcelona 2002

WHICH? WINE GUIDE
London 1981–

WILLIAMS, V.
The Penguin Good New Zealand Wine Guide.
London, Auckland, New York 2000

WINE SPECTATOR
Wine Spectator's Pocket Guide to Wine.
Wine Spectator Press, New York 2000

WINE SPECTATOR
*Wine Spectator's Ultimate Guide to Buying
Wine.* 7th edition, New York 2000

WRIGHT, HILARY
*Water into Wine: A Wine Lover's Cruise
Through the Vineyards.* London 1996

Subject Index

PLACE INDEX

Index of People

Index of Producers and Estates

PICTURE CREDITS

ILLUSTRATIONS
All photos by Armin Faber and Thomas
Pothmann, Düsseldorf except those listed below.

MAPS
Studio für Landkartentechnik, Detlef Maiwald,
Norderstedt

GRAPHICS
Elisabeth Galas, Cologne

© AKG, Berlin: 23 top, 24 top / Photo: Werner
Forman: 16 top / Photo: Erich Lessing: 16
bottom
© Ben-Joseph, Michael, Herzelia: 742 top, 743,
744,
© Beer, Günter, Barcelona: 300, 302 bottom,
303 bottom, 311 top, 313, 591
© Bildarchiv Preußischer Kulturbesitz, Berlin:
18 left
© Bodegas Castaño: 631
© Bodegas Pirineos: 603
© Bouchard-Finlayson: 774 bottom
© Budd, Jim, London: 794, 795
© Carmel: 742 bottom
© Celliers des Templiers: 14
© Chateau Ste. Michelle: 799 bottom
© C.I.V.S., Chambéry: 299
© Dieth + Schröder Fotografie, St. Johann:
716 bottom / Photo: 717–719
© Dominé, André, Trilla: 80, 82, 88, 89 top
right, bottom left, 90 left, 93 top left, center
right, 94 top right, bottom left, 96 top, 111
center right, bottom left, 115 except box, 184,
186, 187, 189, 192, 198 bottom, 199, 205, 212
bottom, 220 top, 238 top, 251 bottom right,
285 top left, bottom, 295, 302 top, 304, 305
top, 306 bottom, 308, 316, 324 bottom, 325
top, 329, 571 top, 572 top, 578, 596 bottom
center, bottom left, 606, 607, 610 bottom,
614–618, 632, 636, 637 bottom, 638, 639,
640 bottom, 648, 688, 689 top, 759 top, 789,
791 top, 798, 801–806, 810 bottom, 813–816,
819, 820, 821 left, 822 top, 827 top right, 828
© Doluca: 736, 737
© dpa, Frankfurt a. M.: 26, 27
© Enate: 602 bottom
© Fédération Française des Syndicats de Liège:
684
© Forschungsanstalt Geisenheim / Photo: Dr.
B. Berkelmann: 101 bottom, 103 bottom left /
Photo: Prof. H. Holst: 99 top, 100 right, 102
top right, bottom, 103 top left, bottom right,

104–106 / Photo: Lehmann: 102 top left,
bottom / Photo: Lorenz: 103 top right / Photo:
B. Loskill: 100 left / Figure: B. Loskill 107
© Germanisches Nationalmuseum, Nürnberg: 20
© Gallo: 817
© Graham: 664, 665 top
© Gütkind, C. S., Wolfskehl, K., "Das Buch
vom Wein," 1927, München: Hyperion-Ver-
lag, (pp. 32, 34, 35): 21
© Hamilton-Russell: 777 top left
© Hartmann, Ulli, Bielefeld: 624, 625
© Hulton Getty, London: 454 top
© I.C.E.X., Madrid / Photo: C. Navajas: 87 bot-
tom right, 579 bottom / Photo: I. Muñoz-
Seca: 84 top left, 579 center / Photo:
C. Tejero: 85 bottom right
© Image Company, Thessaloniki / Photo: Heinz
Troll: 721–732,
© Kavaklidere: 738, 739
© Könemann Verlagsgesellschaft mbH, Cologne /
Photo: G. Beer: 51, 130 bottom, 131 bottom,
132, 133, 165, 221, 303 top, 310, 311 bottom, 315,
330, 331, 396, 602 top, 620–622, 627–630,
702, 703, 748, 780, 781 / Photo: H. Claus:
150, 200, 201, 204, 206, 212 top, 213, 275–279,
283, 286 right, 290, 318, 319 top, 321, 323 / Food
Foto Cologne: 716 top / Photo: R. Halbe:
576–577 / Photo: R. Stempell: 97, 347, 370,
388, 392 box, 429, 439, 634, 635,693 top right,
694–699 / Photo: J. Zimmermann: 783
© Krieger, Joachim, Neuwied: 645, 649 bottom,
654, 657, 660, 661 bottom, 662 top, 663, 665
bottom, 672–674, 681
© Ksara: 740, 741 bottom left
© K.W.V. Cellars: 768
© laif, Cologne / Photo: Zanettini: 435
© Martin-von-Wagner-Museum der Universität
Würzburg / Photo: K. Öhrlein: 17
© Marufuji Winery: 785
© Mercian Winery: 784 bottom
© Michigan Wine Institute / Photo: Steve Sad-
ler: 797

© Robert Mondavi: 826 top, 827 center, bottom
© Napa Valley Wine Commission: 822
© Neethlingshof: 763 top right
© Rose, Anthony, London: 836 top, 838 bottom,
840, 841, 842 top, 843 top, 849 bottom, 851,
882 top, 883, 885 bottom
© Saint-Gobain, Courbevoie: 140
© Sandeman: 640 top left
© Scala S.p.A., Florenz: 18 right, 19
© Scope, Paris / Photo: Jacques Guillard: 128,
129
© Seguin Moreau, Cognac: 131 top
© Stermann, Thorsten, Cologne: 642, 643
© South American Pictures, Woodbridge /
Photo: Tony Morrison: 852, 853
© StockFood, München / Photo: J. Lehmann: 11
/ Photo: M. Skultety: 782 / Photo: Gandara:
357
© StockFood / C.E.P.H.A.S.: Photo: N. Blythe:
779, 784 top, 786, 787 / Photo: N. Carding:
714, 715 / Photo: Christodolo: 842 bottom /
Photo: A. Jefford: 741 top, bottom right/
Photo: K. Judd: 85 top left / Photo: R. and
K. Muschenetz: 825, 843 bottom / Photo:
Mick Rock: 85 top right, center left, bottom
left, 86 top right, center, bottom left, 87 top
left, center, 243, 346, 367, 420, 423 bottom,
443 bottom, 567, 5668 top, 569, 574 top, 656,
691,701, 712, 713, 734, 796, 832 / Photo: M.
Taylor: 749
© Südtiroler Weinwerbung: 84 bottom left
© Supp, Eckhard, Offenbach: 162, 168 bottom,
172 bottom, 351, 352, 356, 358, 359, 362, 368,
369, 371–373, 382 bottom, 397, 398, 400,
401 bottom, 419, 427 top left, 430 top,
431–433, 435, 438, 445, 541 bottom, 551 top,
592, 593 bottom
© Ullstein Bilderdienst, Berlin: 119 bottom
© Vannini, Sandro / CORBIS: 347
© Vignobles D'Alsace, Coll. Civa Colmar /
Photo: Zvardon: 170, 171
© Washington Wine Commission: 799 top, center

ACKNOWLEDGEMENTS

This book could never have been produced without the understanding and cooperation of growers, wine shippers and viticultural organizations in every wine-growing country. Our sincere gratitude is due to all of them.

We should also like to thank the following people, who have given advice and practical assistance in the production of the book: Erich Andrey, Lingerz; Javier Ausás, Penafiel; Marie-Pierre Bories, Villeneuve-de-la-Rivière; Jim Budd, London; Ray and Emiko Kaufman, Sonoma; Heinz Hebeisen, Madrid; Andreas Keller, Zürich; Martin Kössler, Nuremberg; Perta Mayer, Karlsruhe; Andreas März, Lamporecchio; Victor Rodríguez, Madrid; Alejandra Schmedes, Haro; Christina Tierno, Roa de Duero; Alexandre Wagner, Paris

Also Anne Marbot, C.I.V.C.; Hazel Murphy, Wine of Australia; Katharine O'Callaghan, New Zealand Wine; Françoise Peretti, Wine of Argentina; Sue Pike, Wines of Chile; Jean-Charles Servant, B.I.V.B.; Riette Steyn, Swasea; Julia Trustram-Eve, English Wine Producers; Laurent Overmans, our food stylists and Pamela Bober, Mareile Busse, Ina Kalvelage, Stefanie Rödiger and Claudia Voges for tireless commitment.